SEXUAL LIVES

A Reader on the Theories and Realities of Human Sexualities

EDITORS

Robert Heasley
Indiana University of Pennsylvania

Betsy Crane
Indiana University of Pennsylvania

Boston   Burr Ridge, IL   Dubuque, IA   Madison, WI   New York   San Francisco   St. Louis
Bangkok   Bogotá   Caracas   Kuala Lumpur   Lisbon   London   Madrid   Mexico City
Milan   Montreal   New Delhi   Santiago   Seoul   Singapore   Sydney   Taipei   Toronto

McGraw-Hill Higher Education

A Division of The **McGraw-Hill** Companies

SEXUAL LIVES: A READER ON THE THEORIES AND REALITIES OF HUMAN SEXUALITIES

This book is printed on acid-free paper.

4 5 6 7 8 9 0 FGR/FGR 0 9 8 7

ISBN 978-0-07-249364-1
MHID 0-07-249364-X

Publisher: *Phillip A. Butcher*
Sponsoring editor: *Sally Constable*
Developmental editor: *Jill S. Gordon*
Senior marketing manager: *Daniel M. Loch*
Project manager: *Karen Nelson*
Production supervisor: *Carol A. Bielski*
Senior designer: *Jenny El-Shamy*
Supplement associate: *Kate Boylan*
Cover Images: *Getty Images*
Typeface: *10/12 Times Roman*
Compositor: *GAC Indianapolis*
Printer: *Quebecor World Fairfield, Inc.*

Library of Congress Cataloging-in-Publication Data

Sexual lives : a reader on the theories and realities of human sexuality / editors, Robert Heasley, Betsy Crane.
    p. cm.
    "Intended for use in social science courses on sexuality"—Pref.
    "Internet resources" : p. .
    ISBN 0-07-249364-X (softcover : alk. paper)
    1. Sex. 2. Sex (Psychology) 3. Sex customs. 4. Sex crimes. 5. Sex—Cross-cultural studies. I. Heasley, Robert. II. Crane, Betsy, 1949–
HQ21 .S47373 2003
306.7—dc21

                                               2002075355

www.mhhe.com

To the young people in our lives—especially our children, Rachel-Storm Heasley, Nathanael Heasley, and Jesse Crane-Seeber—and so many students and friends who have shared their lives with us. For putting up with us always discussing sex at the dinner table. For finding your own ways. And for teaching us.

ABOUT THE EDITORS

ROBERT HEASLEY is currently at Indiana University of Pennsylvania in the Department of Sociology, where he teaches courses on sexuality and on men and masculinity. Previously on the faculty at Ithaca College and at University of Alaska, Anchorage, Robert received his Ph.D. from Cornell University. He has lectured, led workshops, and worked with school systems for over 20 years on issues related to men's lives, raising boys, and confronting homophobia. Having previously worked as a health and human services administrator, his teaching and research interests, in addition to sexuality, include gender-related problems and interventions, clinical sociological practice, human service theory, program development, and mental health/life issues. Robert has taught courses in sexuality at Cornell University and SUNY Upstate Medical School. He was selected to give the 1998 lecture on sexuality for the Dorothy Everett Martin Lecture Series at the University of Pennsylvania School of Social Work.

Contact information: *heasley@iup.edu* or 724-357-3939; Department of Sociology, McElhaney Hall, Indiana University of Pennsylvania (IUP), Indiana, PA 15705

BETSY CRANE is currently in the Department of Sociology at Indiana University of Pennsylvania, teaching and coordinating an Administrative and Leadership Studies/Human Services doctoral program. Betsy received her Ph.D. from Cornell University, where, as a member of the extension faculty, she co-developed the *Empowerment Skills for Family Workers* curriculum now used in Family Development Credential training programs across the country. She brings nearly

30 years of experience as a sexuality and family-life educator and has published on topics related to sexuality education and homophobia. As director of a women's health agency, Betsy worked to ensure reproductive rights and access. In addition to courses in human sexuality, Betsy has taught courses on women and health and human service practice. Betsy served on the board of the National Campaign to End Homophobia and founded a community-based organization providing HIV/AIDS services. Her extensive work with community-based groups has included leading workshops for children, teens, parents, teachers, and youth workers, as well as writing and developing elementary school curricula on family life and sexuality.

Contact information: *bcrane@iup.edu* or 724-357-3814; Department of Sociology, McElhaney Hall, Indiana University of Pennsylvania (IUP), Indiana, PA 15705

CONTENTS

PREFACE

About This Book

This book of readings is intended to be both accessible and challenging. Based on our own life experiences—personally, professionally, and in the classroom—we have sought to include what we believe students really want and need to know about sexuality and what they want to talk about. Taking a social constructionist approach, this reader is intended for use in social science courses on sexuality. It provides an anthology of articles that mix social theory and critical analysis with narratives and images of sexuality in people's lives. These narratives, viewed through the lens of theory, help us understand the construction of sexuality and its influence in our lives.

The articles provide contemporary critiques on sexuality and social norms as well as addressing practices and institutions that contribute to people's experience of sex. Personal narratives and descriptions of "sexual journeys" are included as a way to help the reader understand the connection between theories and abstract concepts, and the lived experience of others' sexual journeys. The anthology gives voice to new authors as well as established ones.

What We Believe

As editors of this book and educators in the field of sexuality, both of us hold onto a tremendous faith that the United States, and other countries, can do better than we've been doing when it comes to sex. We can do better in thinking about sexuality, about gender, and about relationships. We can do better as men and women in teaching children, in supporting young people, adults, and the elderly, in thinking well about sex, and in living better informed and positive sexual lives.

It may be bold to be so optimistic and to hold onto this belief. But we have both worked in the field of sexuality for years, have led numerous workshops for parents, teens, and human-service workers, written school curricula to improve sexuality education, and taught college courses on gender and sexuality. Betsy has worked with women who have been raped, counseled women and men on reproductive and birth control choices and concerns, lobbied legislators on women's issues, and directed a women's health agency. Robert has worked with men who batter women and men who have raped. He has lectured extensively on changing men's roles, reducing violence in schools, and improving the quality of the relationships in men's lives. We have both also experienced the confusion of sexuality in our own lives, the mixed messages, the shame, guilt, and anxiety that comes when young people aren't informed or prepared well for being sexual. And we have tried to create a better world for our children.

Sexuality is a critical and vibrant part of human life. It is what the ancient traditions of Tantric sexual practices held up as life-enriching, energizing, and powerful. However, instead of honoring the range of sexual expressions possible between consenting adults, society has for too long imposed pressures that create a sense of shame and guilt. Young people are likely to have sex before marriage, and most have been sexual with another person to the point of orgasm by the time they complete high school. Yet too few ever talk with their parents about their experience, ask questions, or pursue professional assistance in getting appropriate birth control or guidance. For many people, feelings of shame and guilt about the use of pornography, past hurts from being victimized, or guilt about sexual aggression will stay with them throughout their lives. And most of us continue to witness an ever-elaborate ritualization of heterosexuality that places more emphasis on social status than on having meaningful relationships between authentic people.

Breaking through these limiting ways of experiencing sexuality is a process—one that takes time and attention, not just to our individual journeys but to the societal values, beliefs, attitudes, and behaviors that prevent the United States from doing better, as Surgeon General David Satcher suggested and as studies on sexuality continue to confirm.

At the same time, it is clear that change will come only when we are willing to listen to others' voices and be open to the analysis needed to understand the complexities of sexuality and sexual relationships. Ira and Harriet Reiss, sexuality educators and writers, argue that we need to move from the sex-negative culture we've inherited to one that enjoys a pluralistic approach to sexuality. It is our hope that this volume will invite its readers into the kind of critical reflection that is self-empowering and leads to increased appreciation of the other.

SUPPLEMENTS

Instructor's Manual/Test Bank

We have prepared an Instructor's Manual/Test Bank to accompany this text. For each Part, it contains a variety of useful tools such as: suggestions for teaching Sexual Lives, assignments, interactive activities, discussion and reflection questions, multiple choice and true-false questions, essay questions, and many suggestions for videos and Internet sources.

Race/Class/Gender/Sexuality SuperSite

This companion website provides information about the book, including an overview, summaries of key features, information about the authors, and Practice Test Questions. Non-text-specific content on this site includes an annotated list of Weblinks to useful sites; a list of professional resources (e.g., professional journals); links to Websites offering Census 2000 information; a glossary; flashcards; and a comprehensive list (annotated and listed by category) of films and videos in the areas of race, class, gender, ethnicity, and sexuality.

Visit the SuperSite by going to www.mhhe.com/raceclassgender

Acknowledgements

There is no end to the list of people who have influenced our work, and this book. To be brief, however, we want to appreciate Judith Barker at Ithaca College, who was involved in conceptualizing the original proposal and whose insights have been important throughout the process.

Next, of course, we want to thank the many colleagues and friends who responded to our requests for articles, whether by recommending pieces they have used and/or by creating original work. Colleagues from various colleges who reviewed our proposal and the initial draft of the book provided us with tremendously helpful feedback. We also appreciate the students who gave permission to use their writings in this book, providing a tremendous gift to this project. When given the opportunity, students write to speak their truth, to tell about their journeys, and when doing so, they contribute to creating a more honest social discourse on sexuality. This is where students become the teachers of the teachers.

Our editorial assistant, Regina Rivers has dedicated nearly a year of her life and time to this project. She has reviewed articles, written one herself for this book, managed the incredible details that go into a project such as this, and has been consistently encouraging about the project. Like many of us working in this field, Regina keeps saying—

this stuff is important, just think how it would be if we all had good information and ways of thinking about sexuality. How much better life would be!

We particularly thank Sharon Abbott who provided extensive feedback and early in the process, along with Liahna Gordon, agreed to write an article that framed the book's theoretical perspective. Graduate assistants, Joleen Loucks and Melanie Grant assisted with literature reviews and internet searches. They were both able to "get it" immediately when we introduced the concept of the book, and then provided valuable support in the process of its development.

Finally, our sincere thanks to the folks at McGraw-Hill. Sally Constable has provided tremendous encouragement from the time of our very first contact. Jill Gordon has been a valuable resource, guiding us through the details in developing this project. Karen Nelson, the project manager, and her staff have kept things going on a very tight deadline. Clair James who did the initial copyediting, and Jenny El-Shamy who did the cover design, have both been a pleasure to work with. All of these people have helped make doing this project a fun and exciting adventure.

This book has been a three-year process—one that has led us to appreciate the effort of compiling a book, and led us to interactions with students, colleagues, reviewers, and editors that have enriched our lives. It's been a blessing. Thank you.

LEARNING TO THINK CRITICALLY ABOUT SEXUALITY: AN INTRODUCTION

This book is about sex. But not just sex. It is about theories of sexuality and about people's sexual journeys. Both the theories and journeys reflect the ways in which the human experience of sexuality is connected to virtually all other aspects of our lives. It influences our actions and interactions beyond what we might normally see as being related to sexuality.

Why Analyze Sex?

Making informed decisions about sexuality—whether personal choices or judgments we make about other people's sexuality—requires that we be open to thinking critically. Social theory is a resource for helping us think abstractly about the human experience, providing a framework or lens for viewing events through varying perspectives. When it comes to sex, rather than saying, "I think this or that is wrong," or "I don't want to hear about other people's sexuality or other values," theory invites us to reflect on our perspectives. Without critical thinking, humans would still think the earth was flat, or that women were inferior to men, or that slavery could be justified. It is all too easy to hang onto narrow viewpoints when such beliefs are reinforced through family, religion, education, medicine, public policy, economics, and the media—the major institutions influencing our socialization.

As social scientists whose focus is on human sexuality, our interest is in raising questions and presenting stories other than just the ones that are "comfortable" or conform to what is non-controversial. We want to encourage critical exploration of ideas and sexual narratives that can help us understand the human sexual experience in the context of the social world. Let's begin with a shared definition of sexuality.

An Expansive Definition of Sexuality

There is a difference between sex, as in doing it, and sexuality, which encompasses many parts of our lives. Our sexuality is one of the core ways we know ourselves and think about our relationships with others. We are sexual from birth through old age—we are sexual until we die. Mary Steichen Calderone (1981), a pioneer advocate in the field of sexuality education, promoted an expansive definition of sexuality that includes both biological and social aspects. Using this perspective we can define sexuality as *all that we are as women and men including the ways that we relate with other women and men in our lives*. This definition encompasses the connection sexuality has to our bodies, emotions, spiritual nature, and intellect; how we see ourselves as sexual beings; and how we handle our sexual lives.

"All that we are" takes us to:

- *Self-esteem*—feelings of basic worthiness.
- *Body-image*—how we perceive our bodies.
- *Emotions*—feelings about sexuality; our own and others'.
- *Spirituality*—our connectedness with others, with community, including past and future generations, and the spiritual nature of life itself.
- *Intellectual strength*—knowledge and security about our own sexuality and also that of others.

"As women and men" takes us to:

- *Sex*—defined at birth as male or female; for intersexed individuals, this is complex.
- *Gender roles*—"scripts" or expectations of what it means to be masculine or feminine as if these were opposites.

"How we relate with other women and men in our lives" takes us to:

- *Sexual orientation*—how we to relate sexually with other women and men; who we have crushes on and fall in love with.

- *Relationships*—our skills in being in intimate and social relationships with men and women, our hopes and dreams, what we want and don't want in relationships.
- *Sexual choices*—decisions we make about our sexuality; values about our own sexual behavior and that of others, and how we act on those values; what kind of "sex" we choose to have, with whom, and under what circumstances.
- *Reproductive choices*—when and whether we get pregnant or impregnate; the meaning of fertility and the effects of fertility or infertility on our lives, which can affect our self-esteem, taking us back to the beginning of the definition.

Sociological Perspective on Sexuality

A sociological perspective on sexuality focuses on how social systems at the micro or personal level, as well as the broader macro or societal level, influence our sexuality. Sociologists and social psychologists consider the individual in the context of society. How we come to know ourselves, George Herbert Mead suggests, is a product of what Charles Cooley called the "looking glass self." This "self" is the reflection of how others see us. We become a product of the norms, values, beliefs, and role expectations we see around us.

This process, when applied to sexuality, can be particularly profound. In order to understand what individuals come to believe and experience, we need to question the social forces shaping sexual norms. Family, religion, education, media, government policy, and even economics have an effect on sexuality and sexual arrangements. The influence of these social institutions is a product of the distribution of power in the culture. Who gets to say what are, and what are not, acceptable sexual feelings, thoughts, or behaviors? Whose voices get heard and validated? Who are the "authorities" and what are their values?

Conflict theory considers the effect of the distribution of power in society. Some people are able to influence social norms and practices, while others are relatively powerless. Stephen Lukes (1974) suggests that to understand how those in power influence us, we consider three dimensions of power:

1. Ability to control resources—those who control material wealth or the ability to extend status or safety to members in society will have greater influence than others in setting the norms.

2. Ability to "set the agenda"—those who control resources can determine not only what issues or policies get raised and acted on, but who in society has access to making their views and experiences known.

3. Ability to limit knowledge and awareness—those who set agendas can limit those who are less powerful from knowing there are options.

As an example, most women in the early part of the 20th century in the United States were not aware that women in Europe had access to birth control devices and could therefore control pregnancy. Religious leaders and politicians had worked together in the late 1800s to pass the Comstock Laws, which prohibited dissemination of information about and access to contraceptives. This had a particularly harsh effect on poor families who lacked resources to support large numbers of children. Today, even though birth control is legal in every state, after a Supreme Court ruling in 1964, access varies by income levels, depending on health insurance coverage.

Another example relates to parents and schools restricting children's access to positive information about gay or lesbian sexuality. This sets the stage for the high rate of homophobia in the United States compared, for instance, to Scandinavian countries, where positive information about homosexuality is the norm. Young people in the United States grow up not knowing about the range of sexualities and live in fear and ignorance of sexual differences. The "norms" go unquestioned, while youth who are gay become the target of oppression. These are examples of the ways that power and social control affect our sexuality.

Feminist perspectives can contribute to a critical analysis of the effect of such power relations on sexuality. *Feminist* is a loaded term to some, but it refers simply to those working to end sexism and sexist oppression. A feminist analysis questions the effects of gendered social relations. Feminist theory, like other conflict theories, explores ways that structured social inequality is supported by ideologies accepted by both the privileged and oppressed. This has implications for sexuality given the polarization of sexual expectations for males and females that is evident in hegemonic heterosexuality. Heterosexuality is seen as the norm around which all societal institutions are organized.

Postmodern theory challenges us to deconstruct social paradigms such as hegemonic heterosexuality by calling into question the categories of gender and sexual orientation. Such categories are, after all, social constructions, not reality. Social constructionist theory contests the assumption that biology can adequately explain the human experience of sexuality. Rather, as articles in this book illustrate, it is through the social environment that we learn how to be sexual.

Socialization

In sociological terms, we learn how to be sexual as a process of socialization. Our sexual socialization begins at birth and continues throughout life, as we take in and respond to messages from parents, peers, media, school, and other social institutions. By modeling what we see in social interactions, and by responding to sanctions against some behaviors and reinforcements for others, we learn how to be a sexual person within the context of our culture.

The messages we receive about sex are often confusing, contradictory, oppressive, and maladaptive. Sex can be seen as a tool of oppression when we realize that the beauty of our bodies, our ability to experience pleasure, and our capacity for reproduction have historically been used as a form of social control by religious and political systems. Resulting societal norms and expectations, including rigid gender roles and assumptions about sexual orientation, present us with an alienated and distorted sense of sexuality. Having been pornographized and commodified, images of bodies and sexuality are sold back to us in a form that often does not fit. Do we look the part? Do we act the "right way"? Who gets to decide? And we are not encouraged to critically analyze the package we have been sold. This alienation starts from a very young age.

Conspiracy of Silence In the United States, sex is often kept a secret from children. Earlier in our history, and in some other cultures today, birth and death were familiar parts of life. Now, parents ponder when and what to tell their children about "the birds and the bees." In many families there is little, if any, discussion about sexuality, even as the children approach adolescence. But children do learn, long before their parents decide to talk about it. What they learn is often coded inside other messages and images. Sex itself goes unnamed, alluded to but never discussed openly.

There seems to be a conspiracy of silence between adults and children about sex, even though sex is everywhere. Children watch birds build nests, hear sexy songs on the radio, and reports about AIDS or rape on the news. They see sexualized bodies in cartoons on Saturday morning television—large breasts, mouths open just so, legs positioned to attract attention to the groin. The media is a major source of sexual socialization, as are peers. School playgrounds are filled with the language of sex, teasing and homophobic put-downs for having "girlfriends" or "boyfriends," as well as sexual jokes and slang. What children learn about sex is limited and distorted, with little opportunity to ask questions or talk about it with adults who are knowledgeable and comfortable.

This way of being introduced to sexuality teaches children that sex is secretive, mysterious, dangerous, and to be hidden from public view. Talk about sex happens, if at all, within generations but not between them. While it soon becomes obvious to most young people that sex is a powerful and potentially enjoyable force in people's lives, they don't hear many intelligent, analytical discussions that help them move from thinking *of* sex to thinking *about* sexuality. In any aspect of our lives, if we can't think critically, we are vulnerable to becoming victims of others' perceptions, policies, and practices.

Ironic isn't it? Compared to other countries, including many European and all of the Scandinavian countries, we provide little information about sexuality to young people, in part due to fears about young people becoming "sexually active." In fact, the majority of teens in the United States have sex at about the same rates as teens in Europe (Reiss, 1997). The major difference is that in the United States there are higher rates of teenage pregnancy, sexually transmitted diseases, rape, sexual abuse, and fear or hatred of people who are gay, lesbian, or bisexual (Kelly & McGee, 1998/1999). Not a pretty picture, but one that reflects the difference between societies and the influence of culture and social institutions on attitudes, beliefs, and behaviors when it comes to sexuality.

Limited and distorted information is not just a factor of socialization in childhood and adolescence but, sadly, continues throughout life. The resulting litany of problems is familiar: sexual dysfunction, unintended pregnancies, sexually transmitted diseases, homophobic attacks, and rape. Even as adults, we lack sexual information and find it difficult to talk about sex, which affects our ability to make healthy decisions and find sexual pleasure.

The ongoing socialization we experience as adults draws from the societal messages we experience over time. The language used for sex is one reflection of those messages.

Language: Symbols Through Which We Image Sex   Symbolic interactionist theory suggests that we respond to the symbols that are encoded in our social environment, without necessarily being aware of the meaning or influence of these symbols. The language we use tells us something about the sex we have. For instance, the words males use for the penis. Two examples are *cock* and *dick,* both terms commonly used to intimidate or demean others or as a joking put-down to conjure up an image of stupidity, as in calling someone a "dickhead" or "cocksucker." Dickhead? Cocksucker? These words, however odd, are powerful when used in social interactions. They reveal perceptions of male sexuality and sexual relationships.

The symbolic representation of the sexual body influences the way we think about the penis. The terms we use, the images presented in art and media, even the medical community's varying practices regarding circumcision, are a result of socially constructed images that inform actions at the individual and societal level. If a culture sees the penis as a source of disease, it is likely to be circumcised. If it is perceived as an expression of male strength, attempts are made to enlarge it by artificial extension devices that are used in some cultures, or adorn it with attachments that make it appear longer. In Western culture, popular pornographic images depict very large penises. By comparison, early Greeks and Romans saw the smaller penis as more desirable, and its representation were more likely to emphasize the beauty of the more intricate, smaller size. Michelangelo's statue of David is not known for its large penis (Laqueur, 1990).

What about the language ascribed to acts involving the penis? Self-pleasuring by males is referred to by terms that don't exactly reflect gentle or soothing touch—jacking off, choking the chicken, beating the meat, and spanking the monkey—all portray aggressive images. Ironically, the slower, less violent the act, the greater the pleasure is likely to be. Yet young men are not encouraged in this direction by the words they hear.

Such language reflects the distance males can feel from their own sensuality. In Western culture, images of masculinity have represented the antithesis of sensuality and the antithesis of gentleness. The penis is often seen as having a mind of its own, being a source of ridicule and teasing, and then is pornographized as a tool for aggression and power. After all the jacking, jerking, choking, beating, and shaking, males take this abused body part to their lover, offering it as something to be cared for and valued. Or something they use to exercise dominance and control. This isn't the only way, or a very useful way to experience or think about male genitals. It is, however, a common experience within our cultural context. Such symbolic representation of genitals is a product of the gendered aspects of sexuality.

Gender and Sexuality

Gender infuses every article of this book, so it is helpful to think consciously about gender and its relation to sexuality. There is a difference between *sex*, as in biological female and male, and *gender*, the social, cultural, and psychological characteristics we associate with being female or male. Both sex and gender are core identities and can be complex, as well as evolving. A designation of male or female is assigned to us at birth, and then we are socialized into the gender roles associated with that sex. For some intersexed individuals, the sex assigned at birth may feel wrong or too narrow. Transsexuals are people, who for a wide variety of reasons, do not feel right in their sex and have chosen to change their biological sex. *Transgender* is an umbrella term referring to people who modify their gender by changing how they look and behave, and yet may not have not medically or legally changed their sex.

Many people find gender roles—or scripts—to be confining, and so they develop differing ways to be masculine or feminine, even as the scripts themselves are changing due to feminism, industrialism, media, and other social influences. Psychologists refer to people who exhibit characteristics traditionally associated with both femininity and masculinity as androgynous (Bem, 1976).

The identity of female or male is associated with ascribed power and influence, in ways similar to that of social class and race. Who has power, access to voting, jobs, money, political office, safety, and the like is based on how society interprets gender. Feminist theory helps us see that gender and the distribution of power, both within and between genders, is critical to consider in any area of human interaction. In societies in which power is distributed differentially based on sex, competition for status affects the relationships between women and men, among women, and among men. Both sexes compete for resources and status within the social system. In the United States and other societies organized around patriarchal values, this means vying for male acceptance.

Gender affects even our everyday associations with sexual behaviors. For example, when asked to define *intercourse*, most people say it is when a man puts his penis into the woman's vagina, a classic health textbook description. But think about the gendered power relations. What if we said intercourse is when a woman takes a man's penis into her vagina? This definition presents a very different picture of who is the actor and who is acted on.

Like gender, sexual identities and classifications lead to differential treatment depending on the distribution of power in society. Who determines what sexual expressions are considered normal or deviant? Who decides whether sex itself is good or evil, for pleasure or for reproduction? Who decides whether women who have a range of sexual partners are adventuresome or "sluts"?

Gender and Sexual Orientation

Homophobia, which is usually defined as fear of, or discomfort with same-sex intimacy or homosexuals, is also about gender. Homophobia can be seen as a weapon of sexism in which males are targeted if they appear "too feminine," as are women if they appear "too masculine" or don't conform to heterosexual male expectations for attractiveness or behavior. Thus, homophobia serves to keep males and females stuck in rigid gender roles. Young boys hear taunts of "sissy" and "fag," from other boys if they deviate even slightly from traditional ways of being male. Young girls learn early on to adopt qualities that boys will find attractive.

There is no right or wrong way to act in terms of gender, but rather only a socially constructed way that reflects cultural perceptions about sexuality that too often go unquestioned. Homophobia is an insidious influence, since parents and teachers may treat children in certain ways, even unconsciously, for fear of turning their children "gay," or making them less successful as heterosexuals. Males don't get touched gently as much as girls, even as little boys, which is a tremendous loss, given the importance of touch for all of us. Girls are often reinforced to be sexy and cute instead of assertive and bold, which is also a tremendous loss, given the importance of having a sense of efficacy or control over our lives. So the way we construct heterosexuality in American culture, and its ties to homophobia, often leads to the diminution of human potential.

In the United States, cultural norms are such that a male walking through a community wearing a dress may become a victim of abuse by other males, or at least cold stares. In many cases, physical attacks on people suspected of being gay or lesbian have led to death. Two women holding hands while walking down the halls of their high school who look unconventional—meaning they aren't buying into traditional ways of trying to be attractive to males—may be called "lezzies" or even attacked, by boys and by girls as well.

Similarly, if two college-age males go to a movie together, they may sit one seat apart. It isn't that they need leg room. More likely, these males don't want to be perceived as being gay, even if they are gay. Although the two may not talk about the reason, they assume it is safer to sit apart so that neither of them will get the "wrong" idea about the other, and also, to reduce the chance of being harassed or teased by other guys.

Heterosexism is the assumption that everyone is heterosexual, or if they are not, they should be. This assumption, along with the extreme homophobia in some families and communities, is what keeps people who are gay, lesbian, and bisexual "in the closet." It's not that they're hiding—all the time. People miss the cues that their lives are constructed differently, or ignore the cues out of discomfort or disapproval. Heterosexism and homophobia also prevent "straights" from exploring the range of their own sexual feelings, and from noticing how their lives are restricted by pressure to adapt to what is perceived to be heterosexual.

Hegemonic heterosexuality is such a strong social construction that it often goes unnoticed and unchallenged. A central thesis of queer theory—a framework for critical analysis like other theoretical perspectives—is that sexuality influences every area of our lives. The way we arrange behaviors associated with being masculine and feminine cannot be understood without address-ing sexuality and the associations of the culture with the sexual. Just as feminism has taught us to think critically about gender when analyzing any aspect of social arrangements and interac-tions, queer theorists ask us to understand the sexual element in all human relations.

Sexualities

Much of the recent thinking about sexuality in Western civiliza-tion has been monolithic and singular. In this paradigm there is one kind of sexuality that we all inherit in some biological way—heterosexuality. Then there are "deviations" from hetero-sexuality or "deficits" that contribute to problems people have. This position takes a narrow view of sexuality. An essentialist position maintains that we know absolutely what sexuality is and that there is an ideal sexuality based on the need for repro-duction. In reality, there are many sexualities or ways of being sexual. Sexualities vary widely in orientation, desire, feelings, and experience. A person may be heterosexual, but his or her heterosexuality is not the same as a roommate's or neighbor's heterosexuality. Each may have different desires for sensual connection, companionship, emotional intimacy, and sex, and even widely different levels of attraction for a person of the other sex. Similarly, it is folly to assume that if someone identi-fies as bi-sexual, she or he is attracted to all people of all gen-ders. As you will see in reading the articles in this book, even the classification of sexuality into hetero, homo, and bi is too narrow and misleading.

Culture, personality, personal experience, and environment all have a great deal of influence on our attractions and desires. Some of us are homo-emotional or homo-social, that is, we prefer emotional closeness or sociability with people of the same gen-der, even though our primarily sexual attractions are to those of the other gender.

While we may like the convenience associated with creating categories, fitting people into the straight-bisexual-gay/lesbian schema, it is not likely that everyone will "fit," nor that we can assume a whole lot about what people do sexually, what experi-ences they've had, or what feelings they carry with them by such a label.

Transgender: Challenging Our Concepts of Gender and Sexuality

It's one thing for society to try to get males and females to stay in the sexual, relational roles we want them in as practicing heterosexuals, what about people who won't even stay in the gender they have been assigned? It is obvious, if only because of the number of sociologists and psychologists studying the transgender experience, and more important, the number of transgendered people speaking out (and stepping out!), that this phenomenon challenges many of our most deeply held notions of human nature.

The transgender phenomenon calls for us to confront our feelings, values and norms about not only what it means to be a male or a female, but also how changing our perception of gender challenges other aspects of life. If a woman in a lesbian relationship with another woman changes her gender legally to be a male, can he legally marry his partner? And is this person, who was homosexual, now straight?

"Gender pioneers" are challenging their own and society's notions of the male and female body. Some men who feel they are women, and want to be in the world as women, don't necessarily want to have genital surgery (or can't afford to). They may take hormones and feminize their body, but still have a penis. There are women who similarly do not change their genitals but appear as male and may change portions of their body, such as removing their breasts, as you will read in this book, or wrapping them to flatten their appearance.

As with issues of sexual orientation, we could respond to transgendered people in a judgmental way, saying, "Should they do this?" A more useful response, however, is one that says, "Given that people are identifying as transgender, how can we respond in the most supportive way, that will accommodate to this increasing awareness of people's sexual and gender reality?" The film "Boys Don't Cry," based on the true story of Teena Brandon/Brandon Teena, is about a person born female who in her late teens assumed the identity of a male, resulting ultimately in her/his death at the hands of two "straight" males. Such stories raise awareness not only of the struggle for acceptance and respect by the transgendered community, but also for awareness and respect by society as a whole.

Creating a Vision of Sexuality Without Oppression

The many articles, stories and reports in this book will at times bring a smile to your face, while at other times you may react with dismay, confusion, or disgust. Regardless of your initial response, what we hope you will do next is think. Think about your reactions, where they come from, and what they mean. How did you learn the values and feelings you are having? What are some other ways to see the issues involved? As you develop your own analysis of the social construction of sexuality, through critical thinking, and raising questions about your own socialization, you can move toward a deeper understanding of sexuality. Such analysis can help us move from reactions into thoughtful response and decisions, about how we want to conduct our own sexual lives, and how to make things work better for others as well.

The final section of this book explores "possible sexualities," as a spur for readers to envision sexuality without oppression. The way we experience our sexuality, as defined and constrained by social systems, leaves much to be desired. Gender roles, relationships, and the pace of modern life often inhibit sexual desire itself. While it is helpful to be aware of the problems, having a vision of how it could be different enhances the possibility of change. Enjoy your fantasies!

REFERENCES

Best, A. (2000). *Prom nights: Youth, schools, and popular culture*. New York: Routledge.

Bem, S. L. (1976). Probing the promise of androgyny. In A. G. Kaplan and J. P. Bean (Eds.). *Beyond sex-role stereotypes: Readings toward a psychology of androgyny* (pp. 48–62). Boston: Little Brown.

Calderone, M.S., and Johnson, E.W. (1981). *The family book about sexuality*. New York: Harper & Row.

Cooley, C. H. (1964, orig. 1902). *Human nature and the social order*. New York: Schocken Books.

Kelly, M., and McGee, M. (Dec. 1998 / Jan. 1999). Report from a study tour: Teen sexuality education in the Netherlands, France, and Germany. *SIECUS Report*, 11–14.

Laqueur, T. (1992). *Making sex: Body and gender from the Greeks to Freud*. Cambridge: Harvard University Press.

Lukes, S. (1974). *Power: A radical view*. London: Macmillan Press.

Mead, G. H. (1934). *Mind, self and society*. Chicago: University of Chicago Press.

Reiss, I. L., and Reiss, H. M. (1997). *Solving America's sexual crisis*. Amherst, NY: Prometheus.

Rich, A. (1980, Summer). Compulsory heterosexuality and lesbian existence. *Signs, 5*, 631–660.

PART ONE

SEXUALITY IN HISTORICAL, RELIGIOUS, AND CULTURAL PERSPECTIVE

The influence of culture on sexuality is clear. Sexual norms become institutionalized based on historical and social conditions. These norms are communicated and reinforced by family, religion, education, medicine, media, government, and economic systems. Our lives are constructed around and constantly affected by these social norms, regardless of whether they are harmful (such as racist policies) or helpful (such as equal rights across race and ethnicity). Thus, when we look at sexuality as a social construction, we can see how sex itself presents a picture of complexity and is vulnerable to distortion.

Women in most cultures around the world today do not have access to sexual expression at the same level as men. Such limits are not the result of natural differences between women and men. Rather, they reflect historically and socially constructed differences that result from social attitudes, beliefs, and values. Think about the practices in Afghanistan under the Taliban, where women could only go outside if accompanied by a husband or male relative, and girls could not go to school. Closer to home, women in the United States only gained full citizenship rights, such as the right to vote, just a little more than 80 years ago. Thus, women's ability to gain access to birth control, to keep their own names after marriage, or to be sexual outside the institution of marriage without being condemned as immoral is a product of relatively recent social and political changes in the United States. The historical perspective is important. Things were not always as they are now, nor do they need to be in the future.

The articles in Part One provide a backdrop for learning to think critically about our sexual lives. Many of us have heard parents, teachers, politicians, and religious leaders announce prophetically what "good" and "bad" sex is, when we should be sexual, and the conditions under which sex will be allowed. This advice may be well intended, somewhat useful, and important, yet it may not be well informed. Too few people have ever studied sexuality, its history, cultural variations, or the theories and research that help us understand sexual norms and practices. Without this information, educators, moralizers, and policymakers are presenting their ideas in something of a vacuum, leaving many young people, parents, and other adults confused and misinformed. As sexuality analyst Ira Reiss (1997) has said, "Growing up sexually in America is like walking through a minefield." Our bodies, emotions, and experiences of sexuality don't mesh with the information and directions we receive. It is now your opportunity to make your way across the minefield with at least some field-maps as guides.

The first articles, "sexual journeys" by two undergraduate students, provide illustrations of lives lived within the gendered-sexual norms of our culture and some of the effects of confusing messages and assumptions people have about sexuality. You may find similarities as well as differences between their stories and yours. The purpose of sexual narratives such as these and others that appear in this book is to encourage reflection, not agreement or disagreement. It is to bring to light real stories of real lives, for discussion and analysis. As you read the other articles in this section, which are more theory-based, use the insights you gain to reflect back on the experiences of "Patricia" and "Josh" and how societal influences may have affected their lives.

Liahna E. Gordon and Sharon A. Abbott's article, "The Social Constructionist's 'Essential' Guide to Sex," presents a guide to thinking about essentialist as contrasted with social constructionist theories of sexuality. This article lays the foundation for many of the readings in this book. It invites us to think about sex as something much more than a biological "drive" used to justify all sorts of social norms when it comes to sex, including rape. It also invites you to ask yourself to what extent your own sexuality is influenced by social forces, even if they feel like biological drives. In what ways do societal messages around what is sexy influence our idea of what a sexually attractive person looks like? How do the feelings and ideas we have about our bodies and sexual organs reflect societal messages about women's and men's sexuality? In what ways have the notion of what is right and what is wrong in terms of sexuality been presented to you as natural versus unnatural?

Jeffrey Weeks' article, "The Invention of Sexuality," offers a historical approach to sexuality, drawing on a social constructivist perspective. He asks, how and why has the domain of sexuality achieved such a critical and symbolic significance in Western culture? Why is there so much concern about people's sexual behaviors? Why do we have categories for those who are sexually active, such as "slut" and "whore," or "gay" and "straight"? He asks about how sexuality came to be important as a factor in power relations in contemporary society, looking at issues of class, gender, and race. Reading Weeks can help you to understand how sexuality can be (and has been) used as a tool to oppress groups of people in society. The norms and customs society has around sex vary over time, become interpreted depending on who has power, and can be used to punish and demean members of society who don't conform, regardless of whether the norms and customs are reasonable or designed to imposed stigma and fear. In what way has the invention of heterosexuality—the norms and customs—influenced your life? What are the inventions within your own family, community, and culture that are different from those in other families, communities, and cultures?

In "The Role of Religion in our Sexual Lives," Ira and Harriet Reiss trace views of sexuality in early Christianity and then discuss the unique mixture of religion and secularism in America. They consider the ways in which sexuality is viewed within conservative and liberal Christian traditions and denominations, making a case for religious pluralism as a way to release sexual pleasure from the confinement imposed by early theologians. As you read this article, we encourage you to think about how the history and analysis provided by the authors relates to your own religious tradition, if any. In what way does this analysis relate to Jeffrey Weeks' notion of heterosexuality being a social invention?

Oliva M. Espìn provides a cultural and historical analysis focusing on the development of sexuality in Latin women in the United States. Her article, "Cultural and Historical Influences on Sexuality in Hispanic/Latin Women," spotlights the way cultural norms influence sexuality for one cultural group, and one gender within that culture. Her article can help us see the ways in which our heritage, regardless of our cultural background or our gender, continues to affect us today, as do issues of immigration, language, and oppression. In reading this piece, reflect on your own ethnicity and social class background. In what ways do your assumptions around gender and sexual norms grow out of these traditions? Have they ever been questioned by others in your family or community? What reasons are given for the norms and expectations? What sanctions (rewards or punishments) are associated with the norms and customs?

Diane di Mauro's article, "Sexuality Research in the United States," finishes this section by providing a context for sexuality research, both historically and through a political lens. Sex is political. And so is sexuality research. Since research offers a critically important resource for exploring an area as complex as sexuality, it is important to note the many barriers that have prevented investigations because the controversial nature of sex. This helps us to realize that much of what is assumed to be true about sex has never been systematically studied. As you read di Mauro's article, consider the implications of not doing research on sexuality. Can the resistance to research itself be a way of reinforcing myths and beliefs based on information that may be misleading or wrong? What aspects of sexuality are appropriate for research? Are there areas that should not be investigated? Who should decide?

Sexual Journeys: *Two Essays*

These essays were written by undergraduate students about their experiences of becoming aware of their sexuality. We begin the book with their stories as a way to set the stage for the theories and personal essays that follow.

BECOMING A WOMAN

"Patricia"

When I think of a woman, the image of my mother comes to mind. I relate nurturing, caring, giving, and compassion to the necessary characteristics of a real woman. A woman is a bounty of knowledge who sees, hears, and feels things in a very unique way. The mere presence of a woman is comforting to me, and I would assume for many others too. However, the powerful aura of a woman has been coined as threatening in our phallocentric society, and she has been forced, since the beginning, to be the silent mentor.

When I was very young, I can remember thinking that a "real woman" had blond hair, blue eyes, big breasts, long legs, and small hands and feet. I in no way viewed her mind or personality to be more important than her physical self. I grew up with the idea that a woman's major asset was her body. She could capture a room with her looks and never say a word. I do not remember if there was a specific person or event that made me think this way; it was just the way it was, almost as if I had been born with this idea in my head.

I now look back upon this very narrow view of womanhood, and I am left confused and upset. Upset because I want to know why I thought this way, if this is really how it is supposed to be. I want someone or something to blame. I can't blame my mother, because I look up to her. Granted, I'm sure she made

some serious impressions on me when I was a child, which I will describe later. Yet, society as a whole has created my images of a woman. Through magazines, television, politics, and interpersonal relationships, my views of woman and woman's sexuality were shaped. As I grew older I consciously but more subconsciously defined a woman as purely sexual, thus interrelating women and women's sexuality. I believed a woman's goal was to obtain a man, and men wanted sexy, good-looking women. However, this woman could not be out of control in anyway. She could never let on that she was trying to be sexy or desired sex. She had to be innocent about everything she did, because wanting sex or being sexy was viewed as promiscuous and sinful. This was and still is an unachievable ideal, because real people have real emotions and real desires. By denying a person, a woman, these rights, it takes away from the experience of living.

Since I've been in college, I've questioned my values, attitudes, and beliefs for the first time in my life. Why do I think and act the way that I do? Was I born this way, programmed to think and act in a certain way? I don't think so. I am a strong believer that society is an enormous factor in human development, both mind and body. It amazes me that I spend so much time psychoanalyzing people around me but never really look at myself. I am sure that part of the reason I never tried to analyze myself is because I was afraid to find out what I was all about. That would require me to question the very values and beliefs that made me feel in control. For example, did my childhood full of Barbies and My Little Pony contribute to my low self-esteem and lack of control, and did that eventually lead me to anorexia? Why can I never be comfortable when I am naked? Why am I never happy with my body? I realize that I cannot answer all of these questions; I can only learn how to come to peace with my self-doubts and move on.

When I was a young girl, I was in love with Barbie. My girlfriends and I would spend hours upon hours in my basement with Barbies. We would dress Barbie up for her date with Ken, and after the date was over we could make Ken and Barbie have sex. That was the ultimate, making Ken and Barbie have sex. However, we always had to be careful not to let any of the adults know what we were doing, because they might take the dolls away. We never did get caught, but we assumed that the parents would be mad because sex was naughty and something we were not supposed to know about. As a young girl, I assumed that when I got older I would have a body just like Barbie. She always looked so nice in her clothes, and I wanted to be just like her. Barbie had purple eyes and pink eyeshadow on at all times; she never looked bad. She was beautiful, sexy, mysterious, and innocent, everything a man wanted. This idolization of Barbie created an internal challenge in me to look like her in any way possible. Be it through colored contacts, hair dye, or self-starvation, I strived to resemble this unachievable ideal.

My whole life my mother has been on my case about my weight. When I was younger I was chubby, and when I was older I was too thin. I wanted to please my mother, and controlling my weight made her happy. She took me to Weight Watchers when I was in seventh grade, and I hated every minute of it. Every time I went to one of these meetings, I felt like I was going because I had failed. I failed my mother, my friends, and the rest of the world because I was too fat and unattractive. I went to the meetings for about a year and then quit and gained all the weight back. I was always trying to diet, but it never worked and I was not committed to it.

As the four years between seventh and tenth grade went past, my weight was always fluctuating and I had no control over my eating. I was unable to solve my family problems,

and I was struggling to find something that I could control. At the end of my sophomore year, I decided to lose about ten or fifteen pounds over the summer. It started off healthy. I ate right and exercised. However, as time went on I began to feed off of others' comments about my weight loss and realized the kind of control that I had. The more weight I lost, the more attention I got from others. My family was happy with me, and I was gaining a lot of new friends. Yet, no one knew the obsession with food that was going on in my head. I ate under five hundred calories a day and compulsively exercised. Naomi Wolf in *Promiscuities*, her book about her sexual coming of age, says, "You want to be a full woman, don't you? Then get down to business" (Wolf, 116). That is exactly what I did. I got off on the feeling of an empty stomach because I could control it.

At this time in my life I began to bleach my hair blond, wear colored contacts, and dress in short, revealing clothes. I was finally getting the attention from boys that I wanted and needed so much. I figured the thinner I got the prettier I was, because you could never be too skinny. As Wolf says, adolescence is a time of fascination and obsession, each girl chose her own path. Some girls chose sports, boys, or schoolwork; I chose anorexia. I thought that being skinny was a guaranteed ticket to being a woman and getting a man. Eventually, all this self-deprivation caught up with me and I was hospitalized. After leaving the hospital, I slowly began to realize that I was going to go nowhere in life if I constantly defined my self-worth by my body weight. This is something I still struggle with everyday because these expectations are so deeply ingrained in society and my self.

My sexual self has been greatly affected by this experience. I have never really been able to feel comfortable around someone if I am naked. Even my boyfriend of 10 months constantly questions why I have such a poor self-image. He constantly tells me how beautiful I am inside out. Yet, I find it so hard to believe him, because there is still this voice that tells me that he really wants a skinny Barbielike girlfriend, and that is something I cannot be. Having a serious sexual relationship with someone is very hard for me when I am still dealing with these insecurities. However, I cannot help but notice how I spend less time every day focusing on my faults and spend more time enjoying myself and our relationship. I am beginning to realize that by starving myself and obsessing over my physical presentation I am allowing others to determine my self worth and not myself. As Mariana Valverde states, the battle for self control takes place in the kitchen and not under the sheets. I honestly believed that if I could control my weight, the rest would follow. This distorted view has been the root of many of my personal and sexual problems. I feared sex because it involved me exposing the one thing I was always trying to hide, my body. When I started having sex, my mother encouraged me to go on the birth control pill. To me this idea was crazy, because girls gain weight when they are on the pill, and who wants to have sex with a fat girl. My obsession with thinness was affecting every part of my life. I would rather stress every month about getting my period than take a pill and risk gaining a few pounds.

I now realize that I need to define my sexuality by what makes me happy and comfortable, not by what society says is right or wrong. There is a serious power imbalance between the thin people and fat people, and that is what our society needs to address. Since I have been attending college, I have spent most of my time figuring out who I am and what I need to do in order to achieve happiness and a healthy sexual relationship.

I am a victim of sexual oppression like so many other girls who have allowed their bodies to be their only redemption. The woman that I once strived to be is part of the "dream world" that society has created. I now realize that the most powerful thing about women is their individuality. There is no room for creativity and imagination if one strives to achieve the Barbie doll image. It is impossible for a woman to be silent, seductive, and sexy and still be truly happy with herself. Each woman creates her own sexuality through trial and error, eventually coming to a balance between sexuality and womanhood.

I am not sure if I will ever be truly comfortable with myself and my sexuality. I have a lot more living and learning to do before I get to that point. This is a very difficult time for a woman to grow up. She is stuck between the beliefs of the past and the changing attitudes of today's society. Society's ideal woman is both powerful and painful, because for most women, she is an unrealistic goal. I have spent the last three years developing a more positive outlook on my body, eating, and attractiveness. I honestly believe that I have overcome my disease through my relationship with my boyfriend. I have a more realistic and satisfying view toward sex and my body because of him. Poor self-esteem and distorted body images will always be part of my personality, yet I have come to peace with this part of my life and I will continue on my journey to womanhood.

REFERENCES

Wolf, N. (1997). *Promiscuities*. New York: Random House.

Valverde, M. (1985). *Sex, Power, and Pleasure*. Toronto: Women's Press.

MY AWAKENING

Josh

Like people my age, say, 18–22, learning about my sexuality was not an overnight phenomenon. In fact, this process is still going on. There is no clean cut, black-and-white answer to any of the questions about sex, only many speculations, nor is there any way of finding the answers. I've learned about my sexuality through a maze of girlfriends, guy friends, gay friends, and opinions from a variety of sources. There have been magazines, movies, pictures, articles, music, games, toys, sex shops, conversations, experiments, feelings, fights, love, hate, jealous rages, drunken binges, depression, anxiety, drugs, and lots of confusion, all geared toward molding me into the man that is typing this narrative. As I journeyed through this maze, I learned that there were people who had a lot fewer and many who had a lot more problems discovering their sexuality than I did. I also learned that, though it may not seem so, we are all in the same boat, floating around aimlessly, looking for our sexual destination. When did it start? I don't know. My guess is birth, but of course, I don't remember.

My earliest memories of being a boy all include some sort of "manly" paraphernalia. Whether it was my little work belt with the plastic tools and work boots or the baseball glove that was placed in my crib when I was born, there was always some sign of a future, stereotypical, heterosexual man. Because of my sister Sharon's particular handicap, my parents always had more unisex toys, like big bright rubber balls or blocks, for her educational purposes. This meant that there really weren't female-oriented toys, like dolls, tea sets, or play kitchens, lying around our house. It was always a ball or cars or blocks, mostly male-dominant toys. I never really had any ac-

quaintances with female-oriented toys until I was in nursery school. Even then, I stuck with the blocks and the balls.

My mother didn't help the fact either. She was not your typical mother who would baby her kids and grant every wish. She was an athlete, a very good athlete. She was brought up as a tough young woman, with strong morals. It's funny, but I remember conversations between my mother and me from years ago in which she stated that "she was the son that my grandfather never had." Don't get me wrong. My grandfather is my idol today. He was a typical male. He was an amazing man. As a survivor of World War II, he taught my mother to stand up for herself and what she believed in. He loved sports, fishing, and working with his hands. My memories of him always having dirty fingernails and scrapes and bruises remain with me, just like the smell of his Budweiser or the Christian Brothers Brandy he always enjoyed.

I was brought up the same way my mother was, by both my parents and my grandfather. There was never any early teaching of nurturing, but the appreciation of hard work and working with your hands. Sports were a must from the day that I was able to walk. Wrestling with my parents and uncles, baseball in the backyard, archery when I was old enough and strong enough, camping trips and fishing, and any means of taking care of myself and my family, despite any situation. I was a man before I was old enough to realize that there is more than one sex. I never had a chance to think about becoming anything other than a heterosexual male by the standards set by my mentors. To be honest, I don't think my mother ever wanted anything but a strong-willed male, for she instilled the same values into me that had been instilled in her years before. I'm not saying that this caused my sexual orientation, but the foundation had been laid.

My first remembered sexual experience was a kiss from a sweet little redhead in my second grade class. We had been moving books from one classroom to another. I was assigned to help move the science books with a couple of girls. We were standing on line waiting for our teacher to hand us the books when this girl, Joanna Berk, grabbed my hand and planted a kiss smack on my lips. Now, believe me, it was more embarrassing than enjoyable, as was most interaction with girls in the second grade. Right away, the boys and girls started singing:

> Josh and Joanna
> Sitting in the tree,
> K-I-S-S-I-N-G.
> First comes love,
> Then comes marriage,
> Then comes Josh
> with a baby carriage . . .

This was utterly the most humiliating way to tease somebody in the second grade. It was the type of thing that we can look at now and say, "How cute." But then, I would have rather had the diarrhea songs sung about me.

I did have one friend from that time until we graduated high school who was always with the girls. All his closest friends were girls. His sleepovers always included girls. He was the first to have a boy/girl birthday party, and he was the one boy in our class that apparently everybody but me always knew was a homosexual. From the second grade until our senior prom, nobody except his close friends knew the truth. He was legendary to all the guys in our grade, and he was the perfect man to all the girls. Matt started the whole craze of "fooling around" at our eighth grade graduation parties. He was the first one of all the guys in our class to lose his virginity, and he was the first person in our grade to confront his parents about being sexually active and survive without physical or emotional pain. He was smooth, suave, handsome, smart, and best yet, he was a guy. All the details came out in the locker room. He never held back. He showed

us how to "win the girls," while actually being a sensitive guy whom all the parents never feared. Mothers beamed when their daughters told them they had a date with Matt Vaughn. Fathers commended their daughters for their choice of the young man. We waited for the details and held all the most intimate secrets. We called it "carnal knowledge," a reference from the Tom Cruise movie, *Top Gun*. We knew the truth. Or so we thought. But the truth comes later.

Now that I think back, Matt held all the keys to my friends and my sexuality. In the sixth grade, an underground was whispered and notes were passed from guy to guy informing us of a special opportunity being offered for the guys only. We knew what it was. *Playboy* magazine. We knew where it was. The first-floor bathroom, across from the wood shop. We knew what we were to do with it. If you were part of the "in" crowd, you had a chance to "rent" the magazine for the night. Records were kept by the owner, Matt. He had taken them from his dad's closet when his father was away on a business trip. The rebellion had begun.

We had three different magazines to choose from. One per customer for one night only. The embarrassment lasted only momentarily, because we knew that the guys who were laughing were not laughing at us. We were laughing at the fact that we were trying to become men. We were joining a club, a rite of passage, that our fathers all talked about in private. We were part of it now.

Pornography came not only in the form of magazines but in movies too. *The Happy Hooker in Hollywood, The Happy Hooker in Washington,* and *Debbie Does Dallas* were just a few of the pornos we were able to get our hands on. I think they definitely warped our imaginations with the images of women just jumping on anything that moved. We even got hold of a porno that involved bestiality. I thought I had seen everything till that point, but the sight of a woman giving a blow job to a horse just blew my mind. Nor did it do anything for me. But we didn't care what the women were doing. They were women, they were naked, and they were moaning. Good enough for us.

These pornographic movies became a staple any time somebody slept over at my house, or anybody else's house for that matter. Matt even went as far as to take the scrambler that his brother bought, tape pornos off the television, and sell them to guys who weren't lucky enough to "rent" the magazines before we got caught with them. Soon enough, every guy in our class had his own collection of pornography, thanks to Matt.

Pornography was our life up until high school. This is where all the major lessons began. I think mine began with a sport. When I was in eighth grade, I began to physically grow. I was an early bloomer as compared to some of the guys I knew in school. I grew eight inches and gained fifty pounds in a year. This newfound size enabled me to get involved in sports other than baseball. I decided that football and wrestling were my callings. It was understood that if you played football, you got the girls. So, in eighth grade, I was ready to get the girls. I decided that I was going to join the football team. Though we had a miserable season, my first year was successful. I was the biggest, quickest, and strongest defensive end in the junior league. I set league records for sacks in a game and a season, most tackles in a season, and even scored a few touchdowns from fumble recoveries. I was a beast. I was named defensive player of the year for our team. That was when the girls started to notice me. It's too bad that was when the high school football and wrestling coaches noticed me also.

I began working out with the high school wrestlers every day. I was toning and shaping my already muscular frame. Girls really started to notice me then. In eighth grade, I was meeting high school junior and senior

girls that nobody else could meet. These girls were the cream of the high school crop. I didn't notice them. You see, my coach filled my head with visions of greatness, visions that would only be a reality if I ate, slept, and breathed football and wrestling. So I did.

The eighth grade craze of fooling around during the graduation parties came and went, and I was not a part of it. The summer was equally uneventful in the realms of my sexuality. In fact, experimenting with sex was the least of my worries or interests. I had totally neglected my friends that year because I wanted to walk into high school a varsity football player and a productive member of the varsity wrestling team. I achieved both goals, becoming the only person in my high school history to be a four-year letterman in both football and wrestling. In doing this, I missed out on some pretty wild times. As I was practicing or lifting weights, my friends were experimenting with drugs and alcohol, and experimenting with sex, which of course was good and bad. The quiet whispers of the weekend activities in our Monday morning homeroom just floated in and out of my ears, as all I could think about was getting through that day of school and getting to practice.

By now, more and more of my friends were losing their virginity and joining Matt in the world of locker-room gossips. While my health teachers were teaching one thing, my friends were learning another. And even though I listened intently and stored away the knowledge, I had no desire to get involved. I had more important things to worry about. That was when all the jokes began.

Wrestlers are not only well-oiled machines physically, but they are also the most mentally unbalanced people you can think of. The amount of concentration it takes to step on a wrestling mat in a skin-tight suit and roll around touching another male for six minutes while as many as 10,000 people watch is overwhelming. To be secure with your sexuality and perform this is another step. But the largest step to overcome is being able to look people in the eye and say, "Yes, I roll around with men in my underwear. If you think you are a bigger man than I am, why don't you try it?" I once heard an insult on the mat that strikes every wrestler right in the heart. I heard somebody call one of my teammates a "homo." He turned around and said, "Homo? I pinned you like I pinned your girlfriend last night, and she put up more of a fight than you did." To be able to put up with the mental abuse from the outsiders of a wrestling team was one of the toughest things I had to deal with. Those jokes were meant to be funny or to piss me off, but deep down I began to wonder if I did like to touch guys and was always self-conscious if a little bit of an erection was forming when I stepped on the wrestling mat in my singlet.

Sophomore year came and went much the same as freshman year. It wasn't until my junior year that I had my first girlfriend. By this time, my grandfather had died and the fighting between my parents became increasingly closer to the final straw, divorce. At this point I was open to anything, just as long as it would get my parents to stop fighting. Then one night, on a varsity club trip to the Meadowlands to see a Nets basketball game, my sexuality began to take a turn.

It was just a month into school when Sarah and I met. We knew each other in passing. She was a head cheerleader, I was the quarterback. A perfect match. She was good friends with none other than Matt. And better yet, she had just broken up with her boyfriend. Sarah and I happened to sit together on the bus ride there. We struck up a conversation and before we knew it, although it seemed like everybody else knew it, sparks were flying and there was nobody else on the bus but us. She asked me if I wanted to sit next to her at the game. At that point I was head over heels and already falling.

To make a long story short, Sarah was my first everything. My first real kiss, my first love, my first girlfriend, and my first heartbreak. I had never cared for anybody as deeply as her until I met my present girlfriend.

Sarah and I had nothing but love and respect for each other. Our love was the innocent, storybook first love. Sarah would fit in between the strong-willed, freedom loving typed of girl and Mother Theresa. Sarah was a saint who was very free-spirited and strong-willed, yet had a deep belief in the Catholic religion and a strong sense of family instilled in her. I don't think she could have been a better mix. In my eyes, as well as numerous others, Sarah was perfect. And nobody ever let me forget that.

I think that is part of the reason why we did break up. I believed that she was perfect and knew that I wasn't, so I tried to treat her as if she were perfect. She wanted to be treated as a regular person. I also think that is why the breakup was easy for her but incredibly hard for me. I wouldn't kick and scream to keep her from leaving. I simply said, "I love you." I wasn't willing to fight for what I loved, but gave in to what she wanted. And that's not what she wanted. She wanted me to kick and scream. She wanted me to fight back. She wanted to know that I wanted her in my life. Instead, I did as I always did and gave her what I thought she wanted and didn't listen to what she really wanted.

Sex with Sarah was not sex. It was love making. It was two kids having fun, exploring their bodies with somebody they cared about. There was no trying to impress anybody or an overachieving attitude for the perfect orgasm. There was no one perfect orgasm for us. They all were. We didn't have to try and live up to expectations because there were nobody else's to live up to. We didn't know what we were doing. We were learning, experimenting, and growing together. Sex and love making was fun. Again, until my present girlfriend, Ali,

Sarah was the only girl I never had to live up to any expectations with.

After my relationship with Sarah ended, I dated a few girls, but nothing too serious. Just lots of good times. No sex. Occasionally, there was an intimate moment or two, but no sex.

By March of my senior year, I had girls lining up to ask me to the senior prom. There were freshman girls who would giggle every time I said hi and, of course, the girls who would travel all over the state to watch me roll around on a rubber mat with another guy. There were notes in my locker and there were phone calls and messages, but finally, I decided I was going to go with my friend Joni. Joni was a good friend but very flirtatious. I actually thought I was going to get some action that weekend. To be frank, I just wanted to fuck her. Little did I know that there were going to be some big surprises the night of the prom.

The after-prom parties were all busted this year. There were too many drugs and too much alcohol for the parents to handle. So instead of bothering with these, Matt, his date Trish, Joni, and I decided to go to a bar. It was more of a club that Matt knew of. It was an 18 to party, 21 to drink deal, so I figured more dancing and hanging out. I was already drunk, but what I saw that night sobered me up. As we proceeded to "The Yacht Club," Joni asked me if I knew about this place. No. Her face kind of went white. I asked what was wrong and she said just to stay close to her and Trish. I said ok. As I walked into the bar, I saw a sign that said "The Gay Spirit is here." I took one look at this sign and all the rumors that had circulated throughout our town during the last 10 years or so had come true. Matt was gay. Joni said something like, "We all thought you knew." Knew what? It turned out that I wouldn't be fucking anybody that weekend. Joni and Trish were budding lesbians, and Matt was a gay male. I can't even explain the emotions that ran through my body. Shock. Anger. Shame. Fear. These words don't do it

justice. Yet, I was with my friends; I didn't care what people thought about me. Nobody knew me. All they knew was that four people had just walked into the bar. This will sound horrible, so please forgive me, but I did get hit on and it was kind of fun to reject him. I told him my partner was going to meet me here in a few minutes. After a few minutes, it wasn't a gay bar, it was a bar. The people there were just dancing and drinking and having a good time. Even myself, probably the only person in that bar who had never experimented with a member of the same sex.

The part that I am ashamed to admit is that I was afraid to face my friends the next day. Not just Joni, Matt, and Trish, but all my friends. I was afraid I would act differently around all of them. I was afraid the guys on the wrestling and football teams would find out what happened. I was afraid of my own sexuality because I was scared. Even now that I'm a college senior, my relationship with Joni, Trish, and Matt has not changed one bit. I can't remember the last time I talked to one of the guys from the football or wrestling teams. Senior prom night was one of the single most gratifying, as well as educational, experiences of my life.

College is a whole different story. Girls have walked in and out of my life. They have walked over me; I have walked over them. Sex? Yes, lots. Making love? Only with Ali. Love? There have been many different kinds, each one new and exciting, each one disappointing in a way, each one completely worth my time.

Experiences? Let just say that homosexual sex is not just for homosexuals. I have seen "straight" males kiss. I have seen "straight" females kiss. I have seen "straight" females do a lot more than kiss. I even had a girlfriend suggest a threesome, but never engaged in the act (damn).

I think that the biggest thing I have learned about my sexuality is that it is OK for me to love a man, hug a man, even kiss a man, and be in love with a woman. A question was asked at the beginning of the semester. Are you heterosexual? Somebody answered yes. My answer is, I don't know. I act heterosexual. I have heterosexual tendencies. The role I play is a white heterosexual male. I have never had any homosexual experiences other than being hit on and rejecting him. I don't know if I am. I do know that I love to make love to my girl friend. I know I love my friends, my house-mates, my brothers.

I live in the most liberated city in America. I see people everyday who are gay, yet I don't know it. I see men dressed as women and vice versa. But the way I see it, they are the same as me, doing the same thing as me. They are just doing what makes them happy. If that's not what it is all about, then I'm completely lost.

The Social Constructionist's "Essential" Guide to Sex

Liahna E. Gordon

Sharon A. Abbott

Think about this scenario for a moment:

> A man is married to a woman he truly loves. They have had a long, relatively happy mar-riage. He would describe their sex life as ade-quate, but not great. A few times over the years he has had sex with prostitutes—both female and male. He has never had an actual affair, but has had casual or anonymous sex three times: once he had intercourse with a woman he met while at a conference for work, once he let a man perform oral sex on him in a park, and once, back in college, he got drunk at a party and let a woman perform oral sex on him in the bath-room. When he fantasizes, it is usually about men.

What is this man's sexual orientation? Some might say he is bisexual, while others would say he's a heterosexual man who is just "curi-ous." Some might argue that his lack of enthu-siasm for his sex life with his wife, combined with his fantasies, mean he's really gay but closeted, and that though he may love his wife, it's not a *sexual* love. There are many dif-ferent ways of interpreting this scenario, and some of us make one interpretation more eas-ily than another. Our background, past experi-ences, context, and prior knowledge all affect what interpretations we make of this scenario. But is one of those interpretations any more right than another? Can't we just as easily say he is bisexual as heterosexual? Could someone really *prove* that one of those labels is more ac-curate than another?

ESSENTIALISM

Most of us assume there is a right answer in the scenario above. We think that even if we do not know what that answer is, it exists, and it's valid: the man is "really" gay, but does not want to admit it, or he's "really" straight but just curious, or maybe he's "really" bisexual. In all of these cases, we believe that this reality is independent of ourselves—it is an objective fact. This belief in a reality separate from ourselves—an Ultimate Truth—is a basic framework that many of us walk around with and use in our daily lives. This type of thought is the basis for what some call *essentialist* thinking.

Source: Original work © 2002. Printed by permission of the authors.

Essentialism is the notion that there is a Truth that exists independent of the observer and that ultimately we can know that Truth.[1] The truth might not be immediately available to us, because we do not have advanced enough equipment or have been deluded by cultural myths. Eventually, however, like people who thought the earth was flat, when we just become advanced enough, we will be able to know this Truth. In the case of our example, we might do genetic, hormonal, or psychological testing, or have him undergo psychotherapy to "work out" his sexual orientation. In all of these cases, we would be looking for something that would verify the Truth about his sexual orientation for us.

Essentialism also maintains that a given truth is a necessary and natural part of the individual or object in question. For example, essentialists believe that sexual orientation does not change across cultures—all people have a sexual orientation, and everyone is either gay, straight, or bisexual. Essentialists do recognize that sometimes people haven't been able to express their true orientation (such was the situation in Afghanistan under the Taliban government, where any man accused of being gay would be stoned to death). In an essentialist's mind, however, this does not actually change the person's sexual orientation; it just shows that their orientation is suppressed.

Sometimes essentialism is expressed by talking about biological givens. For example, some people may say that sexual orientation is biologically determined, whether by genetics, brain structure, or hormones. However, essentialism isn't always about biology. Many other types of statements can be essentialist, such as "premarital sex is wrong." This is an essentialist statement not because it has anything to do with biology, but because it assumes that there is something inherent and integral to sex before marriage that is always wrong, regardless of context. It also assumes that sex before marriage is somehow categorically different in na-ture than sex within marriage. Finally, it assumes that people who disagree are simply denying or are not aware of the Truth about premarital sex. This Truth (that premarital sex is wrong) is unchanging.

SOCIAL CONSTRUCTIONISM

In contrast to essentialism, social constructionism is a theoretical framework that says that "objective reality" doesn't really exist. Rather, we make *subjective interpretations* of what we experience, and therefore, by interpreting the world around us, we come to construct our own reality. In other words, what is important is not what *IS*, but *what we interpret something to MEAN.* Going back to the scenario at the beginning of this chapter, we could assign different meanings (gay, bisexual, or straight) to the "facts" about the man's sexual behavior and fantasies, depending on the context in which they occur. For example, when Kate Bornstein, an author and actor, had a sex change, her continuing attractions for women meant that she went from being a straight man to a lesbian woman. Several years later, when her female partner decided to have her own female-to-male sex change, Bornstein might then have been classified as a heterosexual woman. Note that "the facts" (her desires, thoughts, feelings, attractions, and behaviors regarding women) never changed, and yet, her sexual orientation category changed from straight to gay and back again. Her category changed because the meanings we attached to those facts changed. We, together as a society, construct different definitions of the situation.

Let's take another example: drinking urine for sexual gratification. The essentialist might say that not only does this have nothing to do with sex, but the practice is gross. People who agree with this statement see it as universally true—drinking urine at any time for any reason is disgusting, and anyone who does it as a turn-on must be sick. Its assertion of universality—

that there is something unsavory about the very nature of drinking urine that is inherent in the act itself—makes it essentialist. A social constructionist would look at cases in which people have engaged in this act as part of a sexual repertoire (sometimes called "playing watersports") and find that participants often define the act to be sexually arousing or gratifying. In addition, constructionists would argue that many of the same people who think drinking urine is gross also swallow semen or vaginal fluid during the course of sexual activities— both bodily fluids associated with the same area of the body—and think that's perfectly natural and even arousing. The real difference, the social constructionist would say, is not that these fluids are really all that different or that semen is somehow more clean or pure than urine (indeed, urine is sterile, while semen is not), but rather that we think about, or construct, these fluids differently.[2]

Social constructionism usually has to do with categorizing. When we put things into categories, we define reality. For example, when we define sexual orientation based on who someone has sex with, we are creating a definition, and therefore an experience and understanding of, sexual orientation. This experience and understanding of it would change if we defined sexual orientation based on sexual attraction or fantasy. The essentialist maintains that there are distinct differences between categories. In this case, gay, straight, and bi are separate categories, and we can determine which one a person is really in. The social constructionists, however, argue that regardless of whatever categories we create, and whatever criteria we choose to determine membership, this is just one way of characterizing orientation. There are others, and one does not represent reality any more accurately than another. In regard to sexual orientation, we could define it by the content of one's fantasies rather than by whom one has sex with. (After all, people may conform to society's expectation of heterosexuality by ap-

pearing to be straight, but have strictly homosexual fantasies.) We could also categorize people based on which gender they are attracted to, regardless of whether they act on it or not. Or, we could categorize people based on what they themselves consider their orientation to be (self-identity). Social constructionists would say that the very fact that we can come up with different categories for the same individual based on how a category is defined illustrates that sexual orientation is socially constructed and that using one set of criteria is no more accurate than using another set.

Social constructionists maintain that categories and their definitions can vary and that none are more accurate than others. For instance, they might imagine completely different ways to categorize sexual orientation other than by the sex of our partners (real and fantasized). For example, we could divide sexuality based on when people like to have sex. Some people prefer having sex in the morning, while others like to have sex at night. A difference in time preference can adversely affect a couple's sex life. So, important as it is, we *could* divide sexuality based not on *who* you prefer to have sex with, but *when.* Or we could divide sexuality into those who prefer monogamy and those who prefer to have sexual relationships with more than one person at a time. It might save a lot of relationships if we defined ourselves based on *those* categories! We could divide people based on whether they like their partners to be older or younger than themselves, the sex acts in which they like to engage, whether they tend to be sexually assertive or passive, sexually conservative or kinky, experimental or not…The possibilities are endless. To the social constructionist, any of these ways of defining and dividing sexuality would be just as logical, just as meaningful, and just as "right" as the way we currently do it.

Despite the fact that there may be many cultural definitions we could assign to something like sexual orientation, cultural definitions and meanings are not random or arbitrary. Rather, social constructionists argue that meanings reflect social, political, and economic conditions of the historical period and culture in which they were created. The categories "homosexual" and "heterosexual" were born in Germany and the United States in the mid 1800s.[3] Social constructionists have argued that, although the circumstances leading to these categories are complex, reactions to the first wave of feminism, the increasingly prominent role of the psychology, and industrialization all contributed to the creation of these categories.[4]

The primary "proof" for the validity of social constructionist theory is that cultural categories and definitions change across time (history) and place (culture). The fact that there is not a universally constant definition of homosexuality or sexual orientation signifies to the social constructionists that there is no ultimate Truth to know about it. If such a Truth existed, the categories or definitions would divide themselves naturally (i.e., there would be no difficult cases to determine), and there would be no variation in these categories across time or cultures.

Thus, social constructionists spend much time "deconstructing" things: demonstrating that a group of categories have no Truth and showing how they are socially accomplished. They do this by breaking down the categories. Specifically, they try to show examples where the categories do not hold up, where the categories have been different, how the categories have changed, and how the categories have varied in order to show that the categories are not natural, or Truth. We find it easiest to see this when we can look at a contradictory set of definitions and find that we have been focused on one way of thinking about and defining something, but that the same set of circumstances might mean something entirely different to people in other places or other times. So, in order to deconstruct, or break down, the categories, social constructionists often point

out different definitions and alternate constructions across cultures, time, subpopulations, etc. This, in fact, is the test to determine whether something is socially constructed: *The meanings, at a cultural level, change not only in different circumstances, but across cultures and throughout history.*

ESSENTIALISM AND SOCIAL CONSTRUCTION IN PRACTICE: EXAMINING CONTEMPORARY RESEARCH

Theory is often easier to understand when applied to empirical research. As we have already argued, essentialists use taken-for-granted categories, while social constructionists work to deconstruct these categories.

There is a great deal of essentialist research from a variety of disciplines that studies sexual orientation. The most obvious of these examples are the biological theories of homosexuality. In recent years, scientists have attempted to use biological differences among individuals to categorize them as lesbian, bisexual, or gay. Hormones, genetics, and brain structure have been used to explain sexual orientation.[5] This research is essentialist because the researchers do not question the categories of sexual orientation themselves. Psychologists have also used these categories of sexual orientation to examine such things as childhood development,[6] gender nonconformity,[7] substance abuse,[8] and the consequences of living with a stigmatized identity.[9] Sociologists take an essentialist framework when they use these unexamined categories to study such things as differences between "heterosexuals" and "homosexuals" in relationship styles[10] and preferences for sexual partners.[11]

In contrast, social constructionist research examines cross-cultural differences and historical contexts to show how these categories have changed. This research has tried to broaden our understanding of sexuality beyond the narrow nature versus nurture debate by examining the constructed nature of the categories homosexual, heterosexual, and bisexual. Jonathan Katz's research deconstructs these categories by showing other ways in which sexuality has been divided.[12] In colonial America, for instance, people did not distinguish between heterosexual sex and homosexual sex as we do today, but rather between procreative (or fruitful) sex and nonprocreative (barren) sex. Thus, men having sex with men was not considered any different from any other type of sex that did not lead to procreation, including oral sex between married people, masturbation, or coitus interruptus (withdrawal). Because opposite-sex attraction was not considered the norm, same-sex attraction was not considered deviant. Instead, the colonists gave a deviant label to any sexual activity that didn't lead to reproduction.

Katz further deconstructs the categories by giving us the fascinating history of the term *heterosexuality*. According to his research, the term *heterosexuality* was first used in 1892 to mean a perversion, since it was defined as the desire for both males and females, rather than an attraction for the "opposite" sex. This definition was used until the 1920s. A second definition of the term *heterosexual* emerged at this time, and it focused on the nonprocreative (and therefore deviant) aspects of opposite-sex desire. A 1923 entry in Webster's *New International Dictionary* defines *heterosexuality* as "a medical term meaning morbid sexual passions for one of the opposite sex." Another decade would pass before the term would lose its deviant status, and nearly forty years would go by before *heterosexuality* would be completely separated from reproduction.

Social constructionists are also interested in our understandings of sexual categories at the individual level. For example, Paula Rust compares the ways that lesbian and bisexual women identify and understand their sexual orientations, and the differences between them.[13] She argues that the lesbians and bisexuals disagree over whether it is sexual feeling or whether it is sexual behavior that determines a person's sexual orientation. The self-identified lesbians in her study reported that as long as they do not act upon their heterosexual feelings, they are lesbian, even if they have occasional attractions to men. In contrast, the self-identified bisexuals reported that if they have both homosexual and heterosexual feelings, even if they don't act on them, their identity should be bisexual. Lesbians and bisexual women use these different understandings of the categories to identify themselves and to classify others. As a result, they identify their sexual orientations differently, despite similarities in their sexual histories.

When deconstructing, social constructionists highlight both the cultural constructions and the historical periods in which discussions about sexuality occur. A topic that shows this clearly is masturbation. Throughout the history of sexuality research, many key theorists have discussed masturbation as a common activity, although they have varied widely in their endorsement of it.[14] For example, in the late 1800s Richard von Krafft-Ebing published *Psychopathia Sexualis,* in which he argued that masturbation presented an obstacle to normal sexual development and could lead to such "perversions" as fetishism and sadomasochism. He claimed that the dangers of masturbation were even more extreme in early adolescence and could change a budding teenager into an insatiable sexual animal. Later, Alfred Kinsey disputed these claims, suggesting that masturbation was harmless no matter how often one did it. Sex therapists Virginia Johnson and William Masters elaborated on Kinsey's ideas, arguing that masturbation has many benefits, including increasing enjoyment of sex, improving sexual fitness in older age, and relieving menstrual cramps. The researchers further claimed that female masturbation produces orgasms that are physiologically superior to those attained through heterosexual intercourse. Although significantly more sex-positive than Krafft-Ebing, Kinsey and Masters and Johnson made the same type of essentialist claims Krafft-Ebing did by suggesting that there is a Truth about the very nature of masturbation (that is, it is either good or bad).

A constructionist would ignore the question of "good" versus "bad" (as well as "born" versus "choice") in favor of exploring the discussions (or discourse) surrounding a practice, concept, or attitude during a particular historical period in a specific culture. One excellent example of this is Alan Hunt's[15] research on the "moral panic" surrounding masturbation in the early 1900s. Sociologists define moral panics as periods in which a substantial number of people in a community have intense feelings of concern about a perceived threat that is later shown to pose very little, if any, harm. As Hunt and others have illustrated, masturbation certainly spurred a large-scale moral panic.

According to Hunt, the "Masturbation Panic" arose as part of the purity movement of the time, which stressed self-control and was fueled by social imperialist fears about the state of the British empire. Hunt demonstrates that many of the messages were aimed specifically at middle-class and upper-class boys, particularly those at boarding school. Social purists were also worried about the sexual permissiveness allowed boys compared to the strict regulations placed on female sexuality. Part of the campaign, therefore, focused on increasing control over the sexual norms of boys to make them more similar to the restrictions on female sexuality. Doctors and headmasters became the gatekeepers of decency, freely mixing medical and moral reasoning to scare young men away from lives of sin and corruption.

Not only did social purists try to control public sexual norms, but they also turned their attention to a behavior that was ironically private and thus very difficult to control. Masturbation was reported to cause negative consequences at both the individual and community level. Warned against masturbation through the use of such colorful euphemisms as "solitary vice," "self-abuse," "temptations of the flesh," and "pampered passions," young men and women were told that engaging in this dangerous behavior carried some visible public signs. Male masturbators could be detected by their pale skin, flabby flesh, weak lungs, pimples, poor eyesight, and persistent sore throats. Female masturbators gave themselves away by their dull eyes, soft and clammy hands, and smelly feet.

As evidenced by Hunt's work, social constructionist research examines the discussions surrounding sexuality to highlight the beliefs of the time, but resists labeling those beliefs as right or wrong. For the social constructionist, it is far too simplistic to think that the social purists of the 1900s and theorists like Krafft-Ebing were misguided, but that Kinsey and Masters and Johnson got it right. Instead, they aim for a deeper understanding of sexuality by paying attention to how sexuality is discussed and controlled at various points in history and how this may have affected people living during that period. Social constructionists feel that examining, or deconstructing, these attitudes and beliefs leads to a better understanding of the social and economic conditions that produced these particular constructions.

Deconstruction can also mean examining the language people use to participate in and examine the social world. Essentialist research often assumes that all people share definitions of words and that the meanings behind words do not affect how people understand behavior and categories. A well-known example of this is a large study conducted by Philip Blumstein and Pepper Schwartz.[16] The researchers interviewed 120 heterosexual couples, 90 lesbian couples, and 90 gay male couples. The respondents were asked a variety of questions about how often they have sex, which partner initiates sex, and how satisfied they are with the sex they have. They found that lesbians had less sex than the other types of couples, and they suggest that this may be the result of female socialization. According to the authors, because women do not learn to initiate sex, lesbian women are reluctant to assume the assertive role even with a female partner, and thus the couple remains at a sexual standstill.

Other theorists, such as Marilyn Frye, were quick to critique this research.[17] In particular, they questioned whether lesbians would read the question "how often do you have sex?" in the same way as the other couples. In a culture that typically defines sex as penile-vaginal penetration, some women responding to this survey may not have thought the question applied to them, and thus underreported the frequency with which they were sexually intimate. The complex possibilities of meaning surrounding the word sex became even more apparent with Special Prosecutor Kenneth Starr's investigation of Bill Clinton's affair.

Deconstruction also involves uncovering the ideological biases (gender, racial, economic, cultural, political) and taken-for-granted assumptions that give rise to essentialist "truths." Since the constructions we buy into are politically important, deconstructing them can shift balances of power and promote social change. A recent example of research on this focuses on how one community purposely changed language in order to promote acceptance. Kleinfeld and Warner used interview data with hearing interpreters and deaf students at Gallaudet University to show words such as how sign language for *gay, lesbian, bisexual* ,and *coming out* reflect politics and attitudes.[18] For example, respondents reported that the sign for bisexual used to be the same

as the sign for *slut*. That sign is now considered inappropriate, and a new sign has been constructed for it (finger spelling *bisexual*). Similarly, it used to be that the sign for *coming out* was a combination of the sign *admit* and the sign *gay* or *lesbian*. The researchers say that these signs were altered intentionally so that the meanings behind them would change, and thus, people would change the way they felt about gay, lesbian, and bisexual people. Now, *admit* has been replaced by *announce* in the sign. This research exemplifies the tenets of constructionism because it demonstrates how shared cultural meanings can be changed by altering the language we use.

POTENTIAL PITFALLS

In reading work by both students and sex researchers, we have seen many mistaken assertions and conclusions made about social constructionism and essentialism and about the differences between them. Here are some to avoid:

1. Myth: *Since everything is socially constructed, everyone should just believe what they want, because it doesn't matter anyway.* Just because something is a social construction does not mean it is unimportant. Indeed, social constructionists argue that it is the *meaning* and *not* the "objective facts" that are the most important in constructing people's realities. No one would say that just because sexual orientation is a social construction, it doesn't have a real impact on people's lives. Homophobia, gay bashing, discrimination, families that reject or accept their gay children, pride parades, the bonding of the gay community—all of these are very real, and it would be foolish to think they don't affect people's lives. As W. I. Thomas said, "What is real to people will be real in its consequences." Things that are socially constructed *are* important. They underlie not

only what we do, but also what we perceive, feel, and think. The meanings we assign to behaviors and to circumstances shape our realities.

2. Myth: *Because we all construct our own reality, whatever I believe will be true for me.* Just because you believe that having sex with blow-up dolls is exactly the same as having sex with a live person, it does not mean you are socially constructing the category "sex partner." Social constructionism is *not* about what an individual believes to be true, but about how we come to construct *shared* meanings at the *cultural* level. The members of a society implicitly agree on the definition of what is going on, and then cooperate to maintain that definition. Often, those who do not cooperate in maintaining these definitions get labeled as deviant or crazy. For a sociologist, society consists of our shared definitions and our interaction based on them. Defining reality is therefore a *social* process, accomplished by teamwork (hence the name *social* constructionism). This process is occasionally overt, but, like physical growth, we often do not realize it is happening or that we are participating as we go along. You probably do not realize, for example, that every time you talk about gay rights, or define yourself as gay or straight, or use those terms to describe someone else, you are participating in maintaining those definitions, meanings, and categories. Sometimes social constructionists do examine the process of construction at the level of the individual, but then they are concerned with the ways that individuals interpret the definitions of *socially agreed-upon categories,* and the patterns and variations in how individuals assign things to these categories.

3. Myth: *Essentialism and social constructionism are just fancy ways of talking about the classic nature versus nurture debate.* Essentialists can and often do talk about learned behavior. It

is just as essentialist to say that being gay is a "choice" as it is to say that it is "inborn." In both cases, the categories themselves are not being questioned, and therefore, these are essentialist, not social constructionist, statements. In addition, social constructionists would go beyond assigning a nurture-based explanation to challenge the categories themselves.

4. Myth: *Essentialists believe in fixed categories, and therefore they think sexuality never changes.* It is true that essentialists assume that sexuality is something within the individual, whose nature remains virtually the same at all times and places. It is the *categories* that they see as fixed, however, not necessarily how an individual fits into those categories. For example, some (certainly not all) essentialists believe that certain circumstances or events can "make" someone gay; a person may not be born homosexual, but some believe that being sexually abused, having an unloving father, experiencing an overprotective mother or being seduced by a gay person can cause someone to change their sexual orientation from straight to gay or bisexual. Although a person may change categories, for the essentialist this does not throw into question the validity of the categories themselves. Essentialists would argue, for example, that all people have a sexual orientation, and even though that orientation could possibly change at some point, nobody is *without* a sexual orientation. We can also use the example of a sex drive. Essentialists believe that everyone, everywhere, in all cultures, has a sex drive. They readily admit that this drive changes over the lifetime and varies by circumstances: pregnancy, the death of a parent, illness, stress at work, having the same sex partner for a long time, or getting older can all lower one's sex drive, at least temporarily. Similarly, falling in love, having a mid-life crisis, or taking Viagra might similarly

increase one's libido. Despite these changes, however, essentialists maintain that how we define the sex drive stays fixed, and the nature of it remains the same for everyone, everywhere, regardless of how strong an individual's drive is at any particular time.

5. Myth: *It's bad to believe in, use, or create constructions, so we just shouldn't categorize anything at all.* Social constructionists are *not* making the point that there is anything wrong with constructing or categorizing. In fact, we cannot avoid categorizing—we do it every time we use language to put a word to an object, person, or idea. Categorizing is important because categories help us to process information and to interact with one another. What social constructionists *are* saying is that we should be aware that these categories don't represent the Truth any better than a different set of categories would and that distinctions between the categories depend not on the nature of the thing or person but on our definitions of the category. If it is no more (or less) truthful to categorize sexual orientation based on what time of day you like to have sex instead of with whom you have sex, then it doesn't make sense to discriminate against people based on their partner choice.

6. Myth: *Social constructionists are liberal and essentialists are conservative.* Politically, essentialists can be both liberal and conservative. It is equally essentialist to say that because sexual orientation is genetic, we should grant equal rights to gay people and to say that because sexual orientation is a choice, we should not reward the choice to be homosexual with such rights. In addition, it is just as constructionist to say that sexual orientation is a socially agreed upon category that does not accurately represent a Truth, as it is to say that incest is not always "bad" because it is a socially agreed upon category that does not accurately represent a

Truth. Both essentialist and constructionist assertions can be used to support either politically liberal or conservative policies.

7. Myth: *If we believe the social constructionists' claim that categories are culturally and historically specific, we cannot make any generalizations about sexual behavior. This makes social constructionist research useless.* Because social reality is shared, we can make some general statements about shared beliefs, although these generalizations are limited to a specific population in question. A researcher's task is to uncover these shared categories. Furthermore, it is possible to talk about shared beliefs, typical attitudes, and common behaviors within defined parameters even though we recognize that there may be individual variations to these patterns. Although we cannot apply these general statements to different populations, we can offer comparisons between them once these patterns are identified, described, and analyzed. In the example of the "masturbation panics" discussed previously, Hunt suggests that the discussions about masturbation in the 1900s share a number of similarities with discussions about child sexual abuse in the 21st century, particularly in regard to their focus on childhood sexual innocence. Similarly, research on sex workers (e.g., strippers, prostitutes, and porn actors) has found a number of similarities between sex work and other types of service work, such as waiting tables.[19] Although there are unique aspects to every job, identifying these similarities gives us a better understanding of sexualized work both within and outside the sex industry.

8. Myth: *Social constructionist research is free from flaws.* Social constructionism offers a critique of all social science research, including research from a social constructionist perspective. For example, researchers are always confined to the categories, concepts, and research topics available to them. Al-

though they may deconstruct these categories in the course of their research, they must rely on the accepted categories to disseminate their findings. Ironically, then, social constructionists may unwittingly reinforce the very categories they are deconstructing. For example, to demonstrate the socially constructed nature of a gay identity, some theorists have drawn attention to the social construction of heterosexuality. In doing this, they may have inadvertently reinforced the categories heterosexual and homosexual. In addition, researchers must rely on the research methods considered valid in their disciplines. Social constructionists have pointed out that these methodological decisions, however, are affected more by politics and popularity than by actual questions of validity. Social constructionists do offer some safeguards against biases and errors common in research. For example, social constructionists do not attempt to make definitive statements of Truth. Instead, their research offers the most likely interpretations based on the data they have. They also advocate using a variety of research methods, and they limit their conclusions to the shared reality of a particular culture or time period.

CONCLUSION

If we return to the scenario at the introduction of this article, we find another illustration of the difference between essentialism and social constructionism. The essentialist might feel frustrated that the question—Is he or isn't he gay?—has yet to be answered. She or he would argue that this is a valid question and that we can determine a meaningful answer to it. The social constructionists, on the other hand, might pose a different set of questions altogether. For example, they might try to uncover why we as a culture place such importance on "knowing" a person's sexual orientation. They

might ask what the particular question "Is he or isn't he?" tells us about this moment in our cultural history. They might question the implications of assuming only a few mutually exclusive, and static, categories of sexual orientation. What would happen, they might ask, if we got rid of these categories? A constructionist would also be attuned to how people attempt to answer the "Is he or isn't he?" quandary. For example, as a culture, do we place more importance on sexual behaviors or sexual fantasies in assessing sexual orientation? Is sexual orientation better determined by how a person self-identifies, or by how that individual is viewed by others? As argued previously, how we talk about sex and sexuality provides an understanding of the context in which these constructions are made.

For the constructionists, the "Is he or isn't he?" question is valid not because it can be answered definitively, but because the mere asking provides us with information about sexuality. The goal of social constructionism is not solely to find an answer to any particular question, but to deconstruct the question itself. This is not to say the questions posed by constructionists cannot be answered (they can), but to suggest that the questions themselves are informative. Rather than attempting to discern the nature of an act, individual, or attitude, the constructionist focuses on meanings, interpretations, and understandings as exhibited in a particular setting. Because of this focus, we argue that the constructionist approach leads to a richer investigation of sex, sexuality, and sexual identity.

NOTES

The authors share equally in the authorship of this paper. We would like to thank Pennie Baxter and Joanna Swyers for their thoughtful comments on earlier drafts.

1. We are indebted to a number of influential works that have shaped, challenged, and

refined our understanding of essentialism and social constructionism. Although not an exhaustive list, some of these works include Arnold Davidson, (1987), "Sex and the Emergence of Sexuality," *Critical Inquiry, 14* (Autumn), 16–48; John D'Emilio, (1989), "Capitalism and Gay Identity," in Laurel Richardson and Verta Taylor (Eds.), *Feminist Frontiers II: Rethinking Sex, Gender, and Society,* (pp. 83–190), New York: Random House; Michel Foucault, (1978), *The History of Sexuality, Vol. I,* New York: Random House; Gail Hawkes, (1996), *A Sociology of Sex and Sexuality,* Bristol, PA: Open University Press; Celia Kitzinger (1987), *The Social Construction of Lesbianism,* Newbury Park, CA: Sage Publications Inc.; Mary McIntosh (1968), "The Homosexual Role," *Social Problems, 16,* 182–192; Robert Padgug, (1979), "Sexual Matters: On Conceptualizing Sexuality in History," *Radical History Review, 20* (Spring/Summer), 3–23; Edward Stein, (1992*), Forms of Desire: Sexual Orientation and the Social Constructionist Controversy,* New York: Routledge; Leonore Tiefer (1995), *Sex is Not a Natural Act and Other Essays,* Boulder, CO: Westview Press; Vera Whisman, (1996), *Queer by Choice: Lesbians, Gay Man, and the Politics of Identity,* New York: Routledge.

2. A constructionist might also point out nonsexual contexts in which drinking urine is practiced. For example, among the Hindu, this practice is known as *shivambu* or *amaroi,* and is believed to have restorative powers. In the United States and elsewhere, some holistic healers have claimed that "auto-urotherapy" can cure many illnesses, including cancer. Those who support drinking urine for health or religious purposes may have different attitudes toward those who engage in watersports, and vice versa, as the context influences how the behavior is interpreted.

3. Jonathan Ned Katz, (1995), *The Invention of Heterosexuality,* New York: Dutton.

4. For discussions of these factors, see Katz (1995), Davidson (1987), D'Emilio (1989), and Padgug (1979).

5. Simon LeVay and Dean H. Hamer, (1994, May), "Evidence for a Biological Influence in Male Homosexuality," *Scientific American, 270,* 44–49.

6. Richard A. Isay, (1999), "Gender and Homosexual Boys: Some Developmental and Clinical Considerations," *Psychiatry: Interpersonal and Biological Processes, 62* (2), 187–194.

7. Matthew Rottnek (Ed.), (1999), *Sissies and Tomboys: Gender Nonconformity and Homosexual Childhood,* New York: New York University Press.

8. Jeffrey R. Guss and Jack Drescher (Eds.), (2000), *Addictions in the Gay and Lesbian Community,* Binghamton, NY: Haworth Medical Press.

9. Bentram J. Cohler and Robert M. Levy-Galatzer, (2000), *The Course of Gay and Lesbian Lives: Social and Psychological Perspectives,* Chicago, IL: The University of Chicago Press.

10. Richard A. Mackey, Matthew A. Diemer, and Bernard A. O'Brien, (2000), "Psychological Intimacy in the Lasting Relationships of Heterosexual and Same-Gender Couples." *Sex Roles, 43* (3–4), 201–227.

11. Zubulon A. Silverthorne and Vernon L. Quinsey, (2000), "Sexual Partner Age Preferences of Homosexual and Heterosexual Men and Women," *Archives of Sexual Behavior, 29* (1), 67–76.

12. Jonathan Ned Katz, (1995), *The Invention of Heterosexuality,* New York: Dutton.

13. Paula C. Rusts,(1992), "The Politics of Sexual Identity: Sexual Attraction and Behavior among Lesbian and Bisexual Women," *Social Problems, 39* (4), 366–385.

14. A discussion of these theorists and their historical works can be found in Paul Robinson (1998), *The Modernization of Sex: Havelock Ellis, Alfred Kinsey, Williams Masters, and Virginia Johnson,* Ithaca, NY: Cornell University Press.

15. Alan Hunt, (1998) "The Great Masturbation Panic and the Discourses of Moral Regulation in Nineteenth- and Early Twentieth-Century Britain," *Journal of the History of Sexuality, 8* (4), 575–615.

16. Philip Blumstein and Pepper Schwartz, (1983), *American Couples: Money, Work, and Sex,* New York: Pocket Books.

17. Marilyn Frye, (1988), "Lesbian Sex," *Sinister Wisdom, 35,* 46–54.

18. Mala S. Kleinfeld and Noni Warner, (1997), "Lexical Variations in the Deaf Community Relating to Gay, Lesbian, and Bisexual Signs," in Anna Livia and Kira Hall (Eds.), *Queerly Phrased: Language, Gender, and Sexuality*, New York: Oxford University Press."

19. Wendy Chapkis, (1997), *Live Sex Acts: Women Performing Erotic Labor.* New York: Routledge Press; Amy Flowers, (1998), *The Fantasy Factory: An Insider's View of the Phone Sex Industry*, Philadelphia: University of Pennsylvania Press.

READING 3

The Invention of Sexuality

Jeffrey Weeks

> *. . . sexuality may be thought about, experienced, and acted on differently according to age, class, ethnicity, physical ability, sexual orientation and preference, religion, and region.*
>
> —Carole S. Vance[1]

A BRIEF HISTORY OF THE HISTORY OF SEXUALITY

When I first began writing about the history of sexuality I was fond of using a phrase from the American historian, Vern Bullough: that sex in history was a "virgin field."[2] This may have been a dubious pun but it was useful in underlining an important, if often overlooked, reality. "Sexuality" was much talked about and written about but our historical knowledge about it remained pretty negligible. Those would-be colonizers who ventured into the field tended either to offer transcultural generalizations ("the history of a long warfare between the dangerous and powerful drives and the systems of taboos and inhibitions which man has erected to control them")[3] or to subsume the subject under more neutral and acceptable labels ("marriage" and "morals" especially). Sex seemed marginal to the broad acres of orthodox history.

Over the past decade or so much has changed, sometimes dramatically. There has been a minor explosion of historical writings about sex. We now know a great deal about such topics as marriage and the family, prostitution and homosexuality, the forms of legal and medical regulation, pre-Christian and non-Christian moral codes, women's bodies and health, illegitimacy and birth control, rape and sexual violence, the evolution of sexual identities and the importance of social networks and oppositional sexualities. Historians have deployed sophisticated methods of family reconstitution and demographic history, have intensively searched for new, or interrogated old, documentary sources and made fuller use of oral history interviews to reconstruct the subjective or the tabooed experience. Encouraged by a vigorous grass roots history, fed particularly by the impact of modern feminism and gay and lesbian politics, there is now an impressive library of articles, pamphlets and books. The history of sexuality may not yet be a respectable field of enquiry: sex research, as the sociologist Ken Plummer has noted, still makes you "morally suspect."[4] But it now at least has a degree of professional recognition and an interested, sometimes passionate, audience. It no longer seems quite such a bizarre and marginal activity as it once did. There is even a dawning recognition that it just might throw light on our confusing and confused present.

But having said this, we are still left with a dilemma—as to what exactly our object of study is. I can list, as I did above, a number of activities that we conventionally designate as sexual; but what is it that connects them? What is the magic element that defines some things as sexual and others not? At the heart of our concern, clearly, is an interest in the relations between men and women. One particular form of their interaction is the process of biological and social reproduction. No historian of sex would dare to ignore that. But a history of reproduction is not a history of sex. As Alfred Kinsey bitingly observed:

> Biologists and psychologists who have accepted the doctrine that the only natural function of sex is reproduction have simply ignored the existence of sexual activity which is not reproductive. They have assumed that heterosexual responses are a part of an animal's innate, "instinctive" equipment, and that all other types of sexual activity represent "perversions" of the "normal instincts." Such interpretations are, however, mystical.[5]

Most erotic interaction, even between those we easily call "heterosexual," does not lead to procreation. And there are many forms of non-hetero-sexual sex, amongst women, and amongst men. Some of these patterns involve intercourse of one sort or another. Others do not. Most have at least the potentiality of leading to orgasm. Yet some activities which are clearly sex related (for example transvestism) may lead to only chance "sexual release" or none at all. Not even intimacy seems a clear enough criterion for judging what is sexual. Some activities we quite properly describe as sexual (masturbation) do not, on the surface at least, involve any other person at all; some aspects of intimacy have nothing to do with sex (and some sex is not intimate). Modern sociobiologists who wish to explain every manifestation of social life by reference to the "timeless energy of the selfish genes" may see some biological logic in all of these activities.

The rest of us, wisely in my opinion, are probably a little more sceptical. We are rather more than the "survival machines—robots blindly programmed to preserve the molecule" that the sociobiologist Richard Dawkins describes.[6]

So what is a history of sexuality a history of? My rather disappointing answer would be that it is a history without a proper subject; or rather as Robert Padgug has suggested, a history of a subject in constant flux.[7] It is often as much a history of *our* changing preoccupations about how we should live, how we should enjoy or deny our bodies, as about the past. The way we write about our sexuality tells us as much about the present and its concerns as about this past.

We are not, of course, the first generation to speculate about the history of sexuality, nor the first to be so revealing about our preoccupations in doing so. Some sense of the past has always been an important element for those that have been thinking about the meaning and implications of erotic life. In her book *Patriarchal Precedents*, Rosalind Coward has described the complex and heated debates in the last half of the nineteenth century about the nature of contemporary family and sexual forms.[8] Pioneering social scientists saw in sexuality a privileged site for speculations on the very origins of human society. From this flowed conflicting theories about the evolution and development of the various patterns of sexual life. Had the modern family evolved from the primitive clan, or was it already there, "naturally," at the birth of history? Did our ancestors live in a state of primitive promiscuity, or was monogamy a biological necessity and fact? Was there once an Eden of sexual egalitarianism before the "world historical defeat of the female sex," or was patriarchal domination present from the dawn of culture? On the resolution of such debates depended attitudes not only to existing social forms (marriage, sexual inequality, the double standard of morality) but also to other, "primitive" cultures that existed contemporaneously with the Western. Could we find clues to our own evolutionary history in the rites and behaviours of the aborigines, stunted on the ladder of progress? Or did these people tell us something else about the variability of cultures?

We have still not fully escaped the effects of these evolutionist controversies. For much of this century racist practices have been legitimized by reference to the primitive condition of other races. Even those who extol the virtues of the sexual freedom of non-industrial societies rely on a belief that their peoples are somehow "closer to nature." Similarly, many of the contemporary feminist debates about the permanence of patriarchal male domination re-till the ground so feverishly worked over a century ago. Yet from the 1920s the older questions about the evolution of human culture were being displaced by a new anthropological approach, which asked different questions about sexuality.

This was associated in the first place with writers such as Bronislaw Malinowski and Margaret Mead. They recognized the danger of trying to understand our own pre-history by looking at existing societies. As a result, there was a new effort to try to understand each particular society in its own terms. This gave rise to a kind of cultural relativism in looking at other sexual mores, and a recognition of the validity of different sexual systems; however exotic they may have looked by the standards of twentieth-century industrial societies. This new approach was highly influential in helping to put Western culture, with all its discontents, into some sort of context. Moreover, by recognizing the diversity of sexual patterns all over the world, it contributed to a more sympathetic understanding of the diversity of sexual forms within our own culture. Social anthropology helped to provide a critical standard by which we could begin to judge the historical nature of our own society.

The most famous example of this genre, Margaret Mead's romantic picture of "coming of age" in Samoa, was enormously influential in the 1930s in large part because it demonstrated that the (repressive) American way of dealing with the problem of adolescence was neither desirable, inevitable, nor necessary.[9]

There were, however, difficulties. On the one hand, there was the danger of attempting to understand all sexual acts by their function, as finely tuned responses to the claims of society. For Malinowski a grasp of the laws of society needed to be matched by a scientific understanding of the laws of nature, and he paid homage to Ellis and gave critical respect to Freud for helping him to grasp "the universally human and fundamental."[10] Malinowski saw cultures as delicate mechanisms designed to satisfy a basic human nature; in the process, the status of "the natural" was not so much questioned as reaffirmed, though now it was less a product of evolution and more of basic instinctual needs. On the other hand, the endorsement of an "infinite plasticity" of human needs by Ruth Benedict, Margaret Mead and their followers led not to a more historical account of sexual patterns but to a purely descriptive anthropology in which readers were offered wonderful, shimmering, evocations of the sexual lives of other peoples, but little sense of why these patterns were as they were. In the absence of any theory of determinative structures, again essentialist assumptions surreptitiously reasserted themselves.

The originality of contemporary attempts to develop a historical approach to sexuality lies in their willingness to question the naturalness and inevitability of the sexual categories and assumptions we have inherited. The sociologists Gagnon and Simon have talked of the need which may have existed at some unspecified time in the past to *invent* an importance for sexuality—perhaps because of underpopulation and threats of cultural submergence.[11] The French philosopher Michel Foucault has gone further by attempting to query the very category of "sexuality" itself:

> Sexuality must not be thought of as a kind of natural given which power tries to hold in check, or as an obscure domain which knowledge tries gradually to uncover. It is the name that can be given to a historical construct.[12]

Foucault's work has made a vital contribution to recent discussions on the history of sexuality precisely because it burst onto and grew out of work that was creatively developing in sociology and in radical social history. It helped to give a focus for questions already being formed. To questions about what shaped sexual beliefs and behaviours, a new one was added, concerning the history of the idea of sexuality itself. For Foucault, sexuality was a relationship of elements, a series of meaning giving practices and activities, a social apparatus which had a history—with complex roots in the pre-Christian and Christian past, but achieving a modern conceptual unity, with diverse effects, only within the modern world.

The most important result of this historical approach to sexuality is that it opens the whole field to critical analysis and assessment. It becomes possible to relate sexuality to other social phenomena. Three types of questions then become critically important. First: how is sexuality shaped, how is it articulated with economic, social and political structures, in a phrase, how, is it "socially constructed"? Second: how and why has the domain of sexuality achieved such a critical organizing and symbolic significance in Western culture; why do we think it is so important? Third: what is the relationship between sex and power; what role should we assign class divisions, patterns of male domination and racism? Coursing through each of these questions is a recurrent preoccupation: If sexuality is constructed by human agency, to what extent can it be changed?

THE IMPORTANCE OF SEX

All societies have to make arrangements for the organization of erotic life. Not all, however, do it with the same obsessive concern as the West. Throughout the history of the West, since the time of the Ancient Greeks, what we call sexuality has been an object of moral concern, but the concept of sexual life has not been the same. For the Ancient Greeks concern with the pleasures of the body—*aphrodisia*—was only one, and not necessarily the most important of the preoccupations of life to be set alongside dietary regulations and the organization of household relations. And the object of debate was quite different, too. Freud, with his usual perceptiveness, was able to sum up one aspect of this difference:

> The most striking distinction between the erotic life of antiquity and our own no doubt lies in the fact that the ancients laid the stress upon the instinct itself, whereas we emphasise its object.[13]

We are preoccupied *with whom* we have sex, the ancients with the question of excess or over-indulgence, activity and passivity. Plato would have banned pederasty from his city not because it was against nature, but because it was in excess of what nature demands. Sodomy was excessively licentious, and the moral question was not whether you had sex with a man if you were a man, but whether you were active or passive. Passive homosexual practices and the people who practised them were rejected not for homosexuality but for passivity.[14] We, on the other hand, have been obsessively concerned whether a person is normal or abnormal, defined in terms of whether we are heterosexual or homosexual. We seek the truth of our natures in our sexual desires. This represents a major shift in the organizing significance given to sexuality.

This is the product of a long and complicated history. But there seem to be three key moments in its evolution. The first came with innovations of the first century A.D., before the generalized advent of a Christianized West. It was represented by a new austerity and by a growing disapproval of *mollities*, that is, sex indulged in purely for pleasure. The Church accepted and refined the view that husbands should not behave incontinently with wives in marriage. The purpose of sex was reproduction, so sex outside marriage was obviously for pleasure and hence a sin. As Flandrin has said, "marriage was a kind of preventive medicine given by God to save man from immorality."[15] The sins of the flesh were a constant temptation from the divine path.

The second crucial moment came in the twelfth and thirteenth centuries after a series of intense critical and religious struggles with the triumph of the Christian tradition of sex and marriage. This did not necessarily affect everyone's behaviour in society. What it did do was to establish a new norm which was enforced by both the religious and the secular arm. Marriage was a matter of family arrangement for the good of families. So for two people thrown together often as strangers, a tight set of rules had to be elaborated. As a result, "the couple were not alone in their marriage bed: the shadow of the confessor loomed over their frolics."[16] Theologians and canonists discussed the sex lives of married couples to the last detail, not simply as an intellectual game but to provide detailed answers to practical moral questions.

The third crucial, and decisive, moment occurred in the eighteenth and nineteenth centuries with the increasing definition of sexual normality in terms of relations with the opposite sex, and the consequent categorization of other forms as deviant. This last change is the one of which we are immediate heirs.

It was represented by a shift from religious organization of moral life to increasingly secular regulation embodied in the emergence of new medical, psychological and educational norms. Alongside this, new typologies of degeneracy and perversion emerged and there was a decisive growth of new sexual indentities. Homosexuality moved from being a category of sin to become a psychosocial disposition. Sexology began to speculate about the laws of sex and "sexuality" finally emerged as a separate continent of knowledge with its own distinct effects.

The emergence of the category of homosexuality and "the homosexual" illustrates what was taking place. Homosexual activities are of course widespread in all cultures and there is a sustained history of homosexuality in the West. But the idea that there is such a thing as *the* homosexual person is a relatively new one. All the evidence suggests that before the eighteenth century homosexuality, interpreted in its broadest sense as involving erotic activities between people of the same gender, certainly existed, "homosexuals" did not. Certain acts such as sodomy were severely condemned: In Britain they carried the death penalty, formally at least, until 1861, but there seems to have been little idea of a distinct type of homosexual personage. Sodomy was not a specifically homosexual crime; the law applied indifferently to relations between men and women, men and beasts, as well as men and men. And while by the eighteenth century the persistent sodomite was clearly perceived as a special type of person, he was still defined by the nature of his act rather than the character of his personality. From the mid-nineteenth century, however, "the homosexual" (the term *homosexuality* was invented in the 1860s) was increasingly seen as belonging to a particular species of being, characterized by feelings, latency and a psychosexual condition. This view was elaborated by pioneering sexologists who produced ever more complex explanations and descriptions. Was homosexuality a product of corruption or degeneration, congenital or the result of childhood trauma? Was it a natural variation or a perverse deformation? Should it be tolerated or subjected to cure? Havelock Ellis distinguished the invert from the pervert, Freud the "absolute invert" the "amphigenic" and the "contingent." Rather later, Clifford Allen distinguished twelve types, ranging from the compulsive, the nervous, the neurotic and the psychotic to the psychopathic and the alcoholic. Kinsey invented a seven-point rating for the spectrum of heterosexual/homosexual behaviour, which allowed his successors to distinguish a "Kinsey one" from a "five" or "six" as if real life depended upon it.[17]

This labelling and pigeonholing energy and zeal has led a number of historians to argue that the emergence of distinct categories of sexual beings over the past century is the consequence of a sustained effort at social control. Writers on the history of lesbianism have suggested that the development of a sexualized lesbian identity at the end of the nineteenth century and early twentieth century was an imposition by sexologists designed precisely to split women from women, breaking the ties of emotionality and affection which bind all women together against men.[18] There is clearly an element of truth in this. Nevertheless I think it much more credible to see the emergence of distinct identities during this period as the product of struggle against prevailing norms, which had necessarily different effects for men and women. Sexologists did not so much invent the homosexual or the lesbian as attempt to put into their own characteristic pathologizing language changes that were taking place before their eyes. Pioneering sexologists like Krafft-Ebing were confronted by people appearing in the courts or coming to them for help largely as a result of a new politically motivated zeal to control all manifestations of sexual desire. The definition of homosexuality as a distinct perversion was one attempt to come to terms with this new reality. It produced an inevitable response in the urge to self-definition.

Sexual activity was increasingly coming to define a particular type of person. In return people were beginning to define themselves as different and their difference was constituted around their sexuality. One Thomas Newton was arrested in London in 1726, entrapped by a police informant in a homosexual act. Confronted by the police he said: "I did it because I thought I knew him, and I think there is no crime in making what use I please of my own body."[19] Here we can see, embryonically, the urge to self-definition that was to flourish in the proliferation of homosexual identities in the twentieth century. In turn, the growth of the category of the homosexual at the end of the nineteenth century presaged a profusion of new sexual types and identities in the twentieth century: the transvestite, the transsexual, the bisexual, the paedophile, the sadomasochist and so on. Increasingly in the twentieth century people have defined themselves by defining their sex. The question we have to ask is why sexuality has become so central to our definition of self and of normality.

Sexuality is shaped at the juncture of two major axes of concern: with our subjectivity—who and what we are; and with society—with the future growth, well-being, health and prosperity of the population as a whole. The two are intimately connected because at the heart of both is the body and its potentialities. "As the human body becomes autonomous and self-conscious," Lowe has written, that is, as it becomes the object of a fully secular attention:

> as emotion recoiled from the world and became more cooped up, sexuality in bourgeois society emerged as an explicit phenomenon.[20]

And as society has become more and more concerned with the lives of its members, for the sake of moral uniformity, economic well-being, national security or hygiene and health, so it has become more and more preoccupied with the sex lives of its individuals, giving rise to intricate methods of administration and management, to a flowering of moral anxieties, medical, hygienic, legal and welfarist interventions, or scientific delving, all designed to understand the self by understanding sex.

Sexuality as a result has become an increasingly important social and political as well as moral issue. If we look at all the major crises in Britain since the beginning of the nineteenth century we see that in one way or another a preoccupation with sex has been integral to them. In the crisis of the French revolutionary wars in the early nineteenth century one of the central preoccupations of ideologists was with the moral decline which it was believed had set off the train of events leading to the collapse of the French monarchy. In the 1830s and 1840s, with the first crisis of the new industrial society, there was an obsessive concern with the sexuality of women and the threat to children who worked in the factories and mines. By the mid-nineteenth century, attempts to re-order society focused on the question of moral hygiene and health. From the 1860s to the 1890s prostitution, the moral standards of society and moral reform were at the heart of public debate, many seeing in moral decay a sign of impending imperial decline. In the early decades of the twentieth century these concerns were re-ordered in a new concern with the quality of the British population. The vogue for eugenics, the planned breeding of the best in society, though never dominant, had a significant influence in shaping both welfare policies and the attempt to re-order national priorities in the face of international competition. Inevitably it fed into a burgeoning racism during this century. During the

inter-war years and into the 1940s, the decline of the birth-rate engendered fevered debates about the merits of birth control, selective encouragement of family planning policies, and the country falling into the hands of the once subject races. By the 1950s, in the period of the Cold War, there was a new searching out of sexual degenerates, especially homosexuals, because they were apparently curiously susceptible to treachery. This was to become a major aspect of the McCarthyite witch hunt in the USA which had echoes in Britain and elsewhere. By the 1980s in the wake of several decades of so-called permissiveness, minority forms of sexuality, especially homosexuality, were being blamed for the decline of the family and gave new energy to a revival of right wing political forces.

A series of concerns are crystallized in these crises: with the norms of family life, the relations between men and women, the nature of female sexuality, the question of sexual deviance, the relations between adults and children, and so on. These are critical issues in any society. The debates about them in Britain over the last few decades have been heated precisely because debates about sexuality are debates about the nature of society; as sex goes, so goes society.

SEXUALITY AND POWER

This is another way of saying that issues of sexuality are increasingly important in the whole working of power in contemporary society. I mentioned earlier that one of the effects of a historical approach to sexuality was to see power over sexuality as productive rather than negative or repressive. The metaphor of repression comes from hydraulics: it offers the image of a gushing energy that must be held in check. The historical approach to sexuality would stress rather the impact of various social practices that construct sexual regulations, give meaning to bodily activities, shape definitions and limit and control human behaviour.

The rejection of a repression model (what Foucault called the "repressive hypothesis") does not of course mean that all regimes of sexual regulation are of equal force or effectiveness. Some are clearly more harsh, authoritarian and oppressive than others. One of the important results of the new historical investigation of sexuality has been a reassessment of the whole Victorian period. Classically this has been seen as a period of unique moral hypocrisy and sexual denial. It is now increasingly apparent that this is highly misleading. Far from witnessing an avoidance of sex, the nineteenth century was not far from being obsessed with sexual issues. Rather than being the subject that was hidden away, it was a topic that was increasingly discussed in relation to diverse aspects of social life. This does not mean, however, that the Victorian period can now be seen as peculiarly liberal. In England the death penalty for sodomy was still on the statute book until 1861. Restrictions on female sexual autonomy were severe and the distinction between respectable women and the unregenerates (the virgin and the whore, the madonna and the magdalen) reached their apogee during this period. Although the present may not have produced a perfect resolution of all conflict, for many of us who live in it it is infinitely preferable to what existed a hundred years ago.

The usefulness of abandoning the repressive model, in its crude form, however, is that it does direct us towards an attempt to understand the actual mechanisms of power at work in any particular period. Power no longer appears a single entity which is held or controlled by a particular group, the state or the ruling class. It is, in Schur's phrase, "more like a process than an object,"[21] a malleable and mobile force which takes many different forms and is exercised through a variety of different social practices and relationships. If this approach to power is adopted then we need to abandon any theoretical approach which sees sexuality moulded by a dominant, determining will—whether it be of "society," as functionalist sociology tended to suggest, or "capitalism" as Marxists might argue, or "patriarchy," as some feminists would propose. Power does not operate through single mechanisms of control. It operates through complex and overlapping—and often contradictory—mechanisms which produce domination *and* oppositions, subordination *and* resistances.

There are many structures of domination and subordination in the world of sexuality but three major axes seem peculiarly important today: those of class, of gender, and of race.

(1) Class

Class differences in sexual regulation are not unique to the modern world. In the slave-owning society of pre-Christian Rome, moral standards varied with social status. "To be *impudicus* (that is, passive) is disgraceful for a free man" wrote the elder Seneca, "but it is the slave's absolute obligation towards his master, and the freed man owes a moral duty of compliance."[22] What was true in the ancient world has become more sharply apparent in the modern. It has in fact been argued (by Foucault) that the very idea of "sexuality" is an essentially bourgeois one, which developed as an aspect of the self-definition of a class, both against the decadent aristocracy and the rampant immorality of the lower orders in the course of the eighteenth and nineteenth centuries. It was a colonizing system of beliefs which sought to remould the polity in its own image. The respectable standards of family and domestic life, with the increased demarcations between male and female roles, a growing ideological distinction between private and public life, and a marked concern with moral and hygienic policing of non-marital, non-heterosexual sexuality, was increasingly the norm by which all behaviour was judged. This does not, of course, mean that all or even most behaviour conformed to the norm. There is plentiful evidence that the behaviour of the working classes remained extremely resilient to middle-class manners. Nevertheless, the complex sexual patterns that exist in the twentieth century are a product of a social struggle in which class was a vital element. This has resulted, not surprisingly, in distinct class patterns of sexual life. Kinsey's American sample of 18,000 in the 1940s suggested that whether it be on masturbation, homosexuality, the incidence of oral sex, petting, concourse with prostitutes, pre-marital or extra-marital sex, or "total sexual outlet," there were significantly different class patterns amongst men. For women, on the other hand, class differences played a relatively minor part: their age and gender ideologies were much more critical factors in shaping behaviour. Later surveys, while taking note of the gradual erosion of class boundaries, have confirmed the continuing existence of class sexualities. It is hardly surprising, then, that the literature abounds with images of relations between men and women (and indeed between men and men) where class, power and sexual desire are intricately interwoven.

(2) Gender

Class, as we have seen, is not an undifferentiated category. Classes consist of men and women, and class and status differences may not have the same significance for women as for men. Gender is a crucial divide.

A number of feminist writers have seen the elaboration of sexual difference as crucial to the oppression of women, with sexuality not merely reflecting but being fundamental to the construction and maintenance of the power relations between women and men.[23] As a general statement this is clearly apt. The patterns of female sexuality are inescapably a product of the historically rooted power of men to define and categorize what is necessary and desirable. "To be a woman," Rosalind Coward has said:

is to be constantly addressed, to be constantly scrutinized . . . Female desire is crucial to our whole social structure. Small wonder it is so closely obscured, so endlessly pursued, so frequently recast and reformulated.[24]

And it is, of course, still pursued, recast and reformulated by men. As Richard Dyer has put it, male sexuality is a bit like air—"you breathe it in all the time, but you aren't aware of it much."[25] We look at the world through our concepts of male sexuality so that even when we are not looking at male sexuality as such we are looking at the world within its framework of reference.

It would be wrong, however, to see this power of definition as either monolithic or unchallenged. The law, medicine, even popular opinion is highly contradictory and changes over time. Before the eighteenth century female sexuality was regarded as voracious and all-consuming. In the nineteenth century there was a sustained effort to inform the population that female sexuality amongst respectable women just did not exist. In the twentieth century there has been a general incitement to female sexuality as an aid to all forms of consumerism. The sexuality of women has at various times been seen as dangerous, as a source of disease, as the means of transmitting national values in the age of eugenics, as the guardian of moral purity in debates over sex education, and as the main focus of attention in the debates over permissiveness and sexual liberation in the 1960s. Female sexuality has been limited by economic and social dependence, by the power of men to define sexuality, by the limitations of marriage, by the burdens of reproduction and by the endemic fact of male violence against women. At the same time, these contradictory definitions have as often provided the opportunity for women to define their own needs and desires. Since the late nineteenth century the acceptable spaces for self-definition have expanded rapidly to include not only pleasure in marriage but also relatively respectable forms of unmarried and non-procreative heterosexual activity. Yet, as Vance observes, gross and public departures from "'good' woman status"—such as lesbianism, promiscuity or non-traditional heterosexuality—still invite, and are used to justify, violation.[26] The patterns of male privilege have not been broken. At the same time, the real changes of this century and the continued vitality of feminism testify that these patterns are neither inevitable nor immutable.

(3) Race

Categorizations by class or gender intersect with those of ethnicity and race. Historians of sex have not actually ignored race in the past, but they have fitted it into their pre-existing framework. So the evolutionary model of sexuality put forward by the theorists of the late nineteenth century inevitably presented the black person—the savage—as lower down the evolutionary scale than the white, as closer to nature. This view survived even in the culturally relativist and apparently liberal writings of Margaret Mead. One of the attractions of her portrayal of Samoan life was precisely the idea that Samoans were in some indefinable sense freer of constraints and closer to nature than contemporary Americans. The most abiding myth is that of the insatiability of the sexual needs of non-European peoples and the threat they consequently pose for the purity of the white race. A fear of black male priapism, and the converse exploitation of black women to service their masters, was integral to slave society in the American South in the nineteenth century and has survived in a series of stereotypes in the twentieth century. In apartheid South Africa the prohibitions of the Mixed Marriages Act and section 16 of the Immorality Act designed to prevent miscegenation were among the first pieces of apartheid legislation to be introduced after the National Party came to power on a policy of racial segregation in 1948. As the regime attempted to deal with the crisis of apartheid in the 1980s by reshaping its forms, one of the first pillars of apartheid it attempted to remove was precisely these acts. As a result the regime came under heavy criticism from extreme right wing groups which argued that the whole edifice of apartheid would be undermined if the laws were repealed. On a global scale, the belief in the superiority of European norms is perhaps most clearly revealed in the obsessive Western concern with the population explosion of the Third World, which has led to various efforts on the part of development agencies as well as local authorities to impose Western patterns of artificial birth control, sometimes with disastrous results as the delicate ecology of social life has been unbalanced. It should serve to remind us that modern attitudes to birth control are rooted both in women's desire to limit their own fertility and also in a eugenic and "family planning" policy whose aim was the survival and fitness of the European races. Elements of this eugenicist past are common in current practices. In Israel Jewish families receive higher child allowances than Arab ones, while in Britain the dangerous contraceptive injection, Depo Provera, has been given virtually exclusively to black and very poor women. One study has even found more birth control leaflets in family planning clinics in Asian languages than in English. Behind all such examples is the assumption that there is an appropriate civilized norm of sexual behaviour to which all people have to bend a knee. This belief in turn is encoded in a series of practices, from immigration laws to birth control propaganda, from medical attitudes to the pathologizing in psychology and sociology of different patterns of family life.[27]

It is not surprising, then, that many black and ethnic minority peoples in both Western countries and the Third World reject the analyses of contemporary feminist and radical sexual politics as being irretrievably shaped by more or less unconscious racist beliefs. This has led to the exposition and development of forms of sexual politics which are particular to the experience of black people and simultaneously engaged with anti-racist politics.

The boundaries of race, gender and class inevitably overlap. Black people in Britain who are most subject to racist practices tend to be working class, while the definition of membership within the ethnic group can often depend on performing gender attributes successfully. Power operates subtly through a complex series of interlocking practices. As a result political challenges to oppressive forms are complex and sometimes contradictory. Sexual politics therefore can never be a single form of activity. They are enmeshed in the whole network of social contradictions and antagonisms that make up the modern world. There is, however, an important point that we can draw from this discussion. Instead of seeing sexuality as a unified whole, we have to recognize that there are various forms of sexuality: There are in fact many sexualities. There are class sexualities, and gender-specific sexualities, there are racial sexualities and there are sexualities of struggle and choice. The "invention of sexuality" was not a single event, now lost in a distant past. It is a continuing process in which we are simultaneously acted upon and actors, objects of change, and its subjects.

REFERENCES

1. Carole S. Vance (ed.), *Pleasure and Danger: Exploring Female Sexuality*, Routledge & Kegan Paul, Boston and London (1984), p. 17.
2. Vern L. Bullough, *Sex, Society and History*, Science History Publications, New York (1976; the particular essay, "Sex in history: a virgin field," was first published in 1972).
3. Gordon, Rattray Taylor, *Sex in History*, Thames & Hudson, London (1953), p. 13.
4. Kenneth Plummer, *Sexual Stigma: An Interactionist Account*, Routledge & Kegan Paul, London (1975), p. 4.
5. Alfred C. Kinsey, Wardell B. Pomeroy, Clyde E. Martin, and Paul H. Gebhard, *Sexual Behavior in the Human Female,* W. B. Saunders Company, Philadelphia and London (1953), p. 448.
6. Richard Dawkins, *The Selfish Gene*, Granada, St Albans (1978), p. x. I discuss sociobiology in Chapter 3 below.
7. Robert A Padgug, "Sexual matters: On conceptualizing sexuality in history," *Radical History Review*, no. 20, Spring/Summer 1979: special issue on "Sexuality in History."
8. Rosalind Coward, *Patriarchal Precedents: Sexuality and Social Relations*, Routledge & Kegan Paul, London (1983).
9. Margaret Mead, *Coming of Age in Samoa: A Study of Adolescence and Sex in Primitive Societies*, Penguin, Harmondsworth (1977; first published 1928). For a highly critical dissection of this work, see Derek Freeman, *Margaret Mead and Samoa: The Making and Unmaking of an Anthropological Myth*, Harvard University Press, Cambridge, Mass., and London (1983).
10. The phrase is used in Bronislaw Malinowski, "Culture as a determinant of behavior," reprinted in his *Sex, Culture and Myth*, Rupert Hart Davis, London (1963), p. 167.
11. J. H. Gagnon and William Simon, *Sexual Conduct: The Social Sources of Human Sexuality*, Hutchinson, London (1973).
12. Michel Foucault, *The History of Sexuality*, Vol. 1, *An Introduction*, trans. Robert Hurley, Allen Lane, London (1979), p. 105.
13. Sigmund Freud, "Three essays on the theory of sexuality," in James Strachey (ed.), *The Standard Edition of the Complete Psychological Works of Sigmund Freud*, Vol. 7, Hogarth Press and The Institute of Psychoanalysis, London (1953–1974).
14. Paul Veyne, "Homosexuality in ancient Rome," in Philippe Ariès and André Bejin (eds.), *Western Sexuality: Practice and Precept in Past and Present Times*, Blackwell, Oxford (1985), p. 27.
15. Jean-Louis Flandrin, "Sex in married life in the early Middle Ages: The Church's teaching and behavioural reality," in Ariès and Bejin, op. cit., p. 115.
16. Ibid., p.126.
17. See the discussion in Jeffrey Weeks, *Sexuality and Its Discontents: Meanings, Myths and Modern Sexualities*, Routledge & Kegan Paul, Lon-

don (1985), pp. 89–91, and Chapter 8.

18. Lillian Faderman, *Surpassing the Love of Men,* Junction Books, London (1981).

19. Alan Bray, *Homosexuality in Renaissance England,* Gay Men's Press, London (1982), p. 114.

20. Donald M. Lowe, *History of Bourgeois Perception,* University of Chicago Press, Chicago (1982), p. 100.

21. Edwin Schur, *The Politics of Deviance: Stigma Contests and the Uses of Power,* Prentice-Hall, Englewood Cliffs, N.J. (1980), p. 7.

22. Veyne, op. cit., p. 31.

23. See for example the arguments of L. Coveney et al., *The Sexuality Papers: Male Sexuality and the Social Control of Women,* Hutchinson, London (1984).

24. Rosalind Coward, *Female Desire: Women's Sexuality Today,* Paladin, London (1984), p. 13.

25. Richard Dyer, "Male sexuality in the media," in Andy Metcalf and Martin Humphries, *The Sexuality of Men,* Pluto Press, London (1985), p. 28.

26. Carole Vance, *Pleasure and Danger,* p. 4.

27. See the summary of evidence in Valerie Amos and Pratibha Parmar, "Challenging imperial feminism," *Feminist Review,* no. 17, "Black feminist perspectives," July 1984; and Floya Anthias and Nira Yuval-Davis, "Contextualizing feminism—gender, ethnic and class divisions," *Feminist Review,* no. 15, Winter 1983.

<hr>

READING 4

The Role of Religion in Our Sexual Lives

Ira L. Reiss and Harriet M. Reiss

FATAL ATTRACTION: SEX AND SIN

In the year 313 C.E. Emperor Constantine converted to Christianity. The persecuted Christian sect had become the religion of the Roman Empire and Christian beliefs began to change and adjust to this newfound legitimization. By the end of that century one of the most famous saints of all time, Augustine (354–430), began to convert people to his innovative interpretation of the biblical story of Adam and Eve. Augustine tied the Gordian knot that links sexuality to sin and thereby influenced the Catholic Church right down to the present day. His conception of the story of Adam

and Eve became a key part of the orthodox Church's approach to sexuality.

St. Augustine's view of original sin was strongly opposed by many powerful contemporary figures in the church, such as St. John Chrysostom, the bishop of Constantinople, Pelagius, a Catholic ascetic from Britain, and Julian, a bishop from southern Italy. To understand the newness of Augustine's idea, it is necessary to realize that prior to the fourth century, most Christians read the message of Adam and Eve in Genesis quite differently from the way Augustine did.

Early Christians read the story of Adam and Eve as symbolizing the importance of human freedom and the power of human choice. They felt Christ had said the same thing in his Sermon on the Mount by demanding that his followers exercise their will and learn to master anger and to control sexual desire. The exercise of one's free will to achieve moral ends was seen as the fundamental message of the story of Adam and Eve for the first four hundred years of Christianity. Most Christians today are not aware of this.

Princeton University historian Elaine Pagels, who carefully studied this time period, comments on this early Christian perspective:

Source: Solving America's Sexual Crises © 1997. Prometheus Books, Amherst, N.Y.

Adam's sin was not sexual indulgence but disobedience: thus . . . the real theme of the story of Adam and Eve is moral freedom and moral responsibility. Its point is to show that we are responsible for the choices we freely make—good or evil—just as Adam was . . . . [F]or nearly the first four hundred years of our era, Christians regarded freedom as the primary message of Genesis 1–3—freedom in its many forms, including free will, freedom from demonic powers, freedom from social and sexual obligations, freedom from tyrannical government and from fate; and self-mastery as the source of such freedom.[1]

Early Christians believed God had created human beings in His image and thus all humans were equal and responsible for their actions. Parts of this early belief have survived and have formed one key basis for our Western ideas today of human freedom and democracy. But St. Augustine promoted a radically different interpretation of the story of Adam and Eve. Before his conversion to Christianity, Augustine had been a member of the Manichaean sect. This group espoused a religious philosophy that denied the goodness of creation and the freedom of the will which Christians believed in. Although in 386 he converted to Christianity, traces of his past convictions were to remain.

What others saw in the story of Adam and Eve as human freedom, Augustine saw as human bondage. Augustine's message was that the human will was impotent against sexual desire. To control such desire humans needed external government consisting of a Christian state and an imperially supported church. He challenged the view held for four hundred years that slaves and freemen, men and women, even children were equal and all had the right and the ability freely to choose what they believed in and what they did. Thousands of Christians during those early centuries had risked their lives and many had died for those beliefs.

It is true that the ascetic idea of renouncing the world and its temptations and choosing a life of celibacy was appealing to many early Christians. But that was a choice that one made and not something imposed. To Augustine all humanity was "fallen" and human will corrupt and even the ascetic person was incapable of self-mastery. Augustine believed that we were all damned by the original sin of Adam and Eve. When they ate from the tree of knowledge, they had freed their uncontrollable sexual desires and marked all humankind with that original sin. From then on, Augustine believed, all humans would carry that original sin from the very moment of conception. Augustine had joined sexuality with sin in a way that up to the present influences our thinking and feelings about sexuality.

Many churchmen argued with Augustine against this new doctrine, for they saw the nature of human beings as good. Since God had created mankind, He would not visit "original sin" upon all humanity just because of the actions of Adam and Eve. Julian, an influential bishop from Eclanum in the south of Italy, argued most strongly against Augustine. For over twelve years Augustine and Julian debated and argued their very different views.

Julian saw the story of Adam and Eve as symbolizing the subjective experience of sin through Adam and Eve's disobedience to God when they ate from the tree of knowledge. Julian read this message not as one of resignation to original sexual sin but as saying that we are capable by an act of will to commit or to avoid sin, and since we have this power of choice, we must strive to make the right moral choices in our lives.

Augustine saw the disobedience by Adam and Eve, when they ate of the tree of knowledge, as releasing forever the power of sexual disobedience in all human beings. In Genesis, he thought, God was telling us that human sexuality would now be uncontrollable.

Because of Adam and Eve's sin, we all would be cursed with "original sin"—it would be present in the sexual conception of every human being. As a result sex was too dangerous and uncontrollable for men and women to engage in except under very special circumstances. Augustine therefore believed sex should be allowed only for procreation and never for pleasure—never, not even in marriage.

The late Yale University historian John Boswell, in his award-winning book on Christianity, explains that erotic love even between husband and wife was rejected by Augustine and his followers due to their radical antierotic doctrines.[2] As I noted above, every sexual act had to be a marital act aimed at reproduction or it was evil. Saint Jerome went so far as to say that "A man who loves his wife very much is an adulterer . . . The upright man should love his wife with his judgment, not his affections."[3]

Augustine had suffered during his life from his own inability to control his sexual desires and he felt that the same must be true for all people. He was a man with two very powerful passions—one for religion and the other for sexuality—and they conflicted and tormented him for much of his life. In his *Confessions* Augustine notes the immense conflict he felt between these two passions.

> But I in my great worthlessness . . . had begged You for chastity, saying: "Grant me chastity and continence, *but not yet.*" For I was afraid that You would hear my prayer too soon, and too soon would heal me from the disease of lust which I wanted satisfied rather than extinguished.[4]

Augustine feared sexual desire so much that he felt it should be severely restricted, for if one ignited the flame of sexual desire, one would never be able to extinguish it. The Victorian view of sexuality . . . clearly is a recent version of this very same fearful view of sexuality.

Bishop Julian argued vehemently with Augustine saying that God has given us free will to choose the good and that we have no "original sin" from Adam. Julian did not see all people as having the same problems of sexual control that plagued Augustine. Pagels sums up the different perspectives of Augustine and Julian:

> Augustine was, by his own admission, insatiable, a man who never married and whose experience of sexual pleasure was illicit and guilt-provoking. Augustine assumes that frustrated desire is universal, infinite, and all-consuming. Julian, who had once . . . been married to the daughter of a bishop . . . obviously wrote from a different kind of experience. For Julian, sexual desire is innocent, divinely blessed, and, once satisfied, entirely finite. Sexual desire, as Julian sees it, offers us the opportunity to exercise our capacity for moral choice.[5]

Augustine's views asserting that human beings cannot govern themselves justified the power of the church and of the state. His notion of the corruptedness of all humanity and the need for control fit perfectly with the new alliance of the Christian Church and the imperial power of Rome. It was a way of uniting the church with the state and it therefore had strong backing and appeal. After all, Christians were now the emperor's coreligionists. The original sin of Adam and Eve was now seen as a sexual sin that illustrated the human inability to control one's own nature. Pagels affirms the political appeal of Augustine's doctrines:

> . . . what Augustine says, in simplest terms, is this: human beings cannot be trusted to govern themselves, because our very nature—indeed all of nature—has become corrupt as the result of Adam's sin. In the late fourth century and the fifth century, Christianity was no longer a suspect and persecuted movement; now it was the religion of emperors obligated to govern a vast and diffuse population. Under these circumstances . . . Augustine's theory of human depravity and correspondingly, the political means to control it—replaced the previous ideology of human freedom.[6]

Nevertheless, Pagels believes that there was another powerful reason why Augustine's views triumphed. Original sin justified why we suffer in life. If some unexplainable bad event occurred, such as the death of an infant, we could blame it on the fact that all of us, even infants, are cursed with the original sexual sin in which each of us is conceived. Therefore, the death of an infant is more understandable. That belief might induce some guilt in us for our own sexuality, but guilt was preferable to admitting that we have no explanation for the bad things that happen to us. The view of Julian and his followers, on the other hand, made human mishaps simply a natural part of living and was therefore not as satisfying to a people who knew so little about controlling the physical world. Julian's views were rejected and he was eventually denounced by the Church as a heretic.

Augustine's view of sexuality has had an extraordinary impact on Western civilization. The foundation of a negative, fearful view of sexuality is clearly visible in Augustine's perspective. The impact of these views on us even today is born out by Pagels:

> From the fifth century on, Augustine's pessimistic views of sexuality, politics, and human nature would become the dominant influence on western Christianity, both Catholic and Protestant, and color all western culture, Christian or not, ever since.[7]

. . . Many people are still very much bothered by problems of sexual control. Many of these individuals have been raised with the strict doctrines of sexual control that emanate from Augustine's perspective. The notion of original sin makes sex something that is to be feared and so it informs one that there is great difficulty in controlling this dangerous force. The advice of Augustine that sex for pleasure must be avoided sounds very much like the advice of Patrick Carnes and other sex-addiction therapists. This danger-soaked view of sex, in my opinion, helps produce the very outcome it fears. With so much forbidden, so little tolerated, and a philosophy of helplessness promoted, is it any wonder then that even today many people are unable to think clearly and plan rationally for their sexual behaviors?

The Western world was not always so antierotic in its views of sexuality. The Greeks and Romans had a far more ambivalent but acceptant view of sexuality for a thousand years before Augustine. John Boswell points out that these civilizations accepted, and in many ways, valued homosexual relationships. Greeks and Romans had in fact no special name for persons who engaged in sex with someone of the same gender. It was simply thought to be a natural part of the sexual repertoire of human beings and so no special name was given to those who practiced same gender sexuality. But by the time of Augustine, as the Roman empire was collapsing, intolerance had developed and homosexuals were disparaged.

By the end of the sixth century this sexual intolerance subsided. But it was to reappear at the end of the twelfth century. Here is how Boswell describes that rejuvenation of this antieroticism:

> Beginning roughly in the latter half of the twelfth century, however, a more virulent hostility appeared in popular literature and eventually spread to theological and legal writings as well. The causes of this change cannot be adequately explained, but they were probably closely related to the general increase in intolerance of minority groups apparent in the ecclesiastical and secular institutions throughout the thirteenth and fourteenth centuries. Crusades against non-Christians and heretics, the expulsion of Jews from many areas of Europe, the rise of the Inquisition, efforts to stamp out sorcery and witchcraft, all testify to increasing intolerance of deviation from the standards of the majority, enforceable for the first time in the newly emerging corporate states of the High Middle Ages.[8]

During this time of growing intolerance in the thirteenth century, St. Thomas Aquinas (1225–1274) expanded upon the antierotic views put forth centuries earlier by St. Augustine. St. Thomas's views, too, have prevailed until the present day in the Catholic Church. Aquinas emphasized a "natural" view of sexuality which stressed that sex was to be engaged in only for purposes of producing children.

Semen, he believed, was intended by "nature" to produce children and any other use of it was "contrary to nature" and therefore against the will of God. This meant that any acts that "impeded the natural propagation of the human species" must be condemned as "unnatural." Masturbation, oral sex, anal sex, homosexual relations, and nonprocreative heterosexual intercourse all failed to produce progeny and thus were "unnatural" and evil. In this perspective, rape became more acceptable than masturbation or sodomy because rape could cause pregnancy! To modern ears that ranking sounds unbelievable, but it was incorporated into Christian codes of the Middle Ages.[9] Thomas's thinking was not accepted without controversy, but like Augustine his perspective eventually became Church dogma. Undoubtedly one major reason for the eventual victory of Thomas's ideas was their conformity with the growing sexual and religious intolerance in thirteenth and fourteenth century Europe.

Augustine's view of original sin and Thomas Aquinas's conception of "unnatural" sexuality have both contributed greatly to the sex-negative dogmas that still impede our ability to cope with today's sexual crisis. With our increased egalitarian ideas and our ability to control the consequences of sexuality, our view of sexuality has become more positive. Many modern-day theologians have challenged and rejected the views of Thomas and Augustine, but consciously or not, those views still influence our emotions about human sexuality.

THE UNIQUE MIXTURE OF RELIGION AND SECULARISM IN AMERICA

When the French historian Alexis de Tocqueville came to America in the 1830s, he was amazed by what he saw. He found a country composed of people far more religious and yet also far more secular and pragmatic than any in Europe. Our very unusual blending of religiosity and worldliness has remained to this day.

Americans have been able to produce this unusual cultural mixture because we have viewed our religion in a very individualistic fashion. We never had only one established church as so many European countries have. Rather, we have been the haven for refugees fleeing the persecution of established churches. Because of that, America has developed its own unique form of religious organizations. We have literally hundreds of different denominations and we stress the right of the individual to choose which church or synagogue, if any, he or she wishes to identify with.

In short, we take a pluralistic approach to religion. We are taught to accept all types of freely chosen religion. Even though we may prefer our own, we are taught not to deny or to restrain the acceptability of the religious preferences of others. That is precisely the same kind of pluralistic attitude that I am promoting . . . as the way to remedy our sexual crisis. An essential part of any pluralistic approach is an affirmation of the individual's right and ability to make a free choice. Democracy encourages such freedom of choice. Pollster George Gallup and reporter Jim Castelli arrived at this same point in their conclusions about religion in America:

> Americans do . . . take a very independent approach to religion. Their faith must make sense to them, and it must reflect the values of freedom that they assume in their daily social and political lives.[10]

But despite this individualism, we Americans share an unusually powerful set of religious beliefs. We often don't realize it, but we are far more devout in our religious beliefs than most other modern Western nations. We would have to look at countries like Ireland or perhaps Spain to find a nation with as devoutly held beliefs.

The Gallup people have been asking questions on religion to representative samples of Americans for over sixty years. They note that in response to the question "Are your religious beliefs very import to you?" 58 percent of the adult American population said they are very important. In Western Europe the percent saying religion is very important averaged only about 25 percent. The Gallup surveys also found that over 95 percent of Americans believe in God and almost three in every four pray to God at least once a day. About two-thirds of our population belong to churches or synagogues and over 40 percent attended services in the past week. These figures are very high compared to Western European countries. In addition, over 40 percent of our adult population say they have had a "born again" religious experience.[11]

Still, even in America, the "highly spiritually committed" amount to only about 10 percent of the adult population.[12] But to be called highly spiritually committed in Gallup's reckoning, you had to answer "completely true" to statements about the divinity of Christ, belief in the Bible, religion as of first importance in your life, seeking God's will in your prayers, and several more questions about your religious faith. Women and people with less than a college education were more likely to be in this "highly spiritually committed" group. About 13 percent of Protestants fit that label, but only 8 percent of Catholics did. Taking all these indices together, religious beliefs are very widespread and common in America despite our many modern social changes.

Nonetheless, since the mid-1960s there have been secular trends showing some weakening of parts of this powerful emphasis upon religion. Ironically, the baby boomers who were destined to break so many of the conservative religious norms about sexuality were born during the high point of religious growth in this century. From the late 1940s until the early 1960s—exactly the time when our seventy-six million baby boomers were born—church attendance, prayer, and the general importance of religion was cresting.

This religious emphasis and the baby boom were both part of the post–World War II prosperity and the renewed emphasis on the family and religion that accompanied that prosperity. Divorce rates were low—not much higher than they were in the 1920s, young people were marrying at earlier ages than at any time in this century, and there was a strong emphasis upon traditional religion and the family. But all this was to change. The long-range twentieth-century trends in this country were away from stability and in the direction of less traditionalism in the family and religion. Those long-range trends were to reassert themselves starting in the mid-1960s.

Elaine May, a Professor of American Studies at the University of Minnesota, argues that this postwar emphasis on the family and religion in the baby-boom years occurred because Americans emerged from the stresses and uncertainties of World War II yearning for peace and prosperity and temporarily sought security in family and religion.

> With depression and war behind them, and with political and economic institutions fostering the upward mobility of men, the domesticity of women, and suburban home ownership, they were homeward bound. But as the years went by, they also found themselves bound to the home. This ambiguous legacy of domestic containment was not lost on their children. When the baby boom children came of age, they would

have different priorities and make different choices.[13]

In the 1950s the percentage of Americans who felt religion was very important in their lives was 75 percent![14] By the early 1960s, as the first wave of the baby boomers entered their late teens, things began to change dramatically. I noted above that only 58 percent of Americans in the mid-1990s said that religion was very important in their lives. The percentage of people who saw religion as capable of "answering today's problems" also dropped sharply from the 1950s to the 1980s (81 percent to 61 percent). In those same years church membership also decreased, and among Catholics, church attendance dropped from about three in four attending church weekly to only one in two attending church weekly.[15]

THE SOUNDS OF RELIGIOUS CONFLICT

Surprisingly, Catholics today practice abortion and birth control in about the same proportion as Protestants.[16] In fact, one study found that Catholics had a higher abortion rate than Protestants or Jews. The Guttmacher Institute conducted that study and they felt that Catholics may not be using birth control as effectively as other groups because they are ambivalent about it and so their abortion rates are higher.[17] I fully expect that Catholics will become less ambivalent about birth control and their abortion rates should decline accordingly.

A major change in Catholic sexual and gender-role attitudes occurred right after the 1968 encyclical *Humanae Vitae* which maintained the Vatican's ban against birth control by insisting that "every conjugal act must be open to the transmission of life." Since the Commission of the Second Vatican Council in 1963 had supported removing the ban on birth control, many Catholics had expected that the 1968 decree would take the same stand. But a

new Pope was reigning and in his 1968 edict he saw sexuality in accordance with St. Thomas Aquinas's views—solely as a reproductive act. The great majority of Catholics in America have rejected that stance. The Second Vatican Council had shown American Catholics that the church could be more pluralistic and Catholics liked that position too much to retreat from it even after the 1968 encyclical. Recent surveys indicate only about 15 percent of Catholics accept the official church doctrine on birth control.

There are other debates about sexual and family values within the Catholic faith.[18] Catholics today support the following changes in considerable numbers: women as priests (65 percent); priests being allowed to marry (72 percent); acceptance of birth control (84 percent); Catholics being allowed to remarry (78 percent); and the ability of homosexuals to be good Catholics (47 percent).[19]

The issue about condoms was one of the most contentious. A position was put forth in December of 1987 by a fifty-member administrative board of the U.S. Catholic Conference that represents the nation's three hundred Catholic bishops. The board was formulating a Catholic AIDS program and felt that discussion of condoms would have to be included in order to make sexuality safer for those who did not abide by the official teaching of abstinence. The conference board explained their stance:

> We are saying that we don't like [condom use] at all, but we know that ignorance about this matter could cause death. Our position is a toleration of a lesser evil to prevent a greater evil.[20]

When the matter was taken up by the full complement of bishops in November of 1989, this position was rejected and the discussion of condoms was removed from the educational recommendations. The ancient dogmas of Augustine and Aquinas still prevail—at least in the church hierarchy.

Catholic theologians around the world have questioned the official stance of their church. Some of them, like Stephen Pfürtner in Switzerland, Ambrogio Valsecchi in Italy, and Anthony Kosnick and Charles Curran in the United States, have been dismissed from their teaching positions because of their writings on sexuality.[21] Charles Curran, the former theology professor at Catholic University of America, is perhaps best known. In 1987 he was fired for his unorthodox views and in 1989 he sued his university for violating his rights of academic freedom. The judge in the case ruled that the university, being a religious institution, had the right to show its loyalty to Pope John Paul II instead of to academic freedom. Curran had criticized his church for its patriarchal nature, its stance against homosexuality and abortion, and other matters of sexual ethics. He predicts much more dissent from many other Catholic theologians in the future.

The clashes within the Catholic Church are not unique. Protestants and Jews find similar divisiveness within their denominations. Sociologist Wade Roof and Seminarian William McKinney examined value differences among and within religious groups. They compared responses to questions on sex, race, women's rights, and civil rights to see if there was any difference between those who were very active in a particular church and those who were not. Those who were the most active members of a church were significantly *less* tolerant on all questions regarding values. Then they compared the different religious denominations on these same value questions. There were very large differences among the religions. For example, on almost all the issues Jews came out as more tolerant than Catholics and Catholics came out as more tolerant than Protestants.

Within the Protestant group the Religious Right represented by conservative Protestant denominations like Southern Baptists, Church of Christ, Assemblies of God, Mormons, and other Evangelical groups had by far the least tolerant values. The most tolerant attitudes among Protestants were found among Episcopalians, United Church of Christ members, and Presbyterians—the old mainline Protestant religions. In between the liberals and conservatives were the Methodists, Northern Baptists, and Lutherans.

To make what I am saying more concrete, let's look at the attitudes toward homosexuality examined by Roof and McKinney. Their question asked whether homosexuality was or was not "always wrong." The percentage of people affirming that "homosexuality was *not* always wrong" was 60–94 percent for Jews and for Unitarian-Universalists, 31 percent for Catholics, 36 percent for liberal Protestants, and 11 percent for conservative Protestants.[22] The range of differences, then, was vast and reflected the degree of pluralism or tolerance of each particular religious group.

Liberal and conservative religious groups can be distinguished by many social characteristics. One of the most important is educational level. The higher the education of the congregants, the more liberal the congregation on most value questions. For example, only 11 percent of college graduates believe that the Bible is the actual word of God, whereas 34 percent of high school graduates and 45 percent of those with less than a high school education believe that.[23] As one's education and income change, there may be a tendency to switch denominational affiliation. A great deal of such switching does occur in America. About 40 percent of Protestant adults say they are no longer in the denomination in which they were raised.[24]

Most of our major denominations have a liberal/conservative or what is often called a moderate/fundamentalist split within their congregation that causes a great deal of strife. These two religious subdivisions do not think highly of each other. Princeton sociologist Robert Wuthnow sums up their impressions of each other:

People who identified themselves as religious liberals were prone to stereotype their conservative brethren as intolerant, morally rigid, fanatical, unsophisticated, closed-minded, and simplistic. The animosity recorded from the other side was equally blatant. Self-identified religious conservatives thought religious liberals were morally loose, were too hung up on social concerns rather than truly knowing what Christianity was all about, had only a shallow knowledge of the Bible, and were deeply compromised by secular humanism.[25]

Religious liberals and conservatives have been battling each other for a long time. I wouldn't look for a final victory for either side in the near future. Rather, I would predict an intensification of the battle as pluralism increases in all areas of social life. One of the major reasons that fundamentalist groups became so well organized was their feeling that religion had become too pluralistic, too secular, and too individualistic. Those trends will continue and therefore so will the battle. After the Scopes trial on evolution in 1925, people thought fundamentalism was finished, but by the 1970s it had returned to take up the fight once more.

Analysis of the membership trends of the last forty years indicates that mainline religions like Episcopalians, United Church of Christ, and Presbyterians have lost ground. The Evangelical religions such as Southern Baptists did not lose ground. Catholics, despite the rejection of official beliefs among parishioners, did not decline in membership—in fact they grew due to the immigration of Hispanics and somewhat higher birthrates. Overall, however, there has been a rise in the percentage of people who do not belong to any church. That now stands at about 33 percent. Many Americans are expressing their religion in their own personal ways rather than by joining or believing in organized religion. But among those who do belong, the largest gains have been in Evangelical/fundamentalist denominations.

In terms of the religion people identify with *(whether they join a church or not)*, Protestantism is named by just 58 percent of our population—the lowest percentage ever. Catholics have grown to 25 percent and Jews have fallen to just over 2 percent of the population. Of the remaining people, a record 8 percent have no religious preference and a few percent identify with a wide variety of other small and/or Eastern religious groups.

What all this indicates is that both ends of the religious continuum are now more fully occupied. We have a sizable minority who are conservative or Evangelical/fundamentalist and another sizable minority who have no preferences or who do not join the denomination of their preference.[26] In between are the majority in the mainline religions, but they seem to be losing members to both ends of the religious continuum. The gains by the Religious Right in the last twenty years have important implications concerning how Americans think about sexuality, and so we should take a closer look at that segment of our religious spectrum.

THE AGENDA OF THE RELIGIOUS RIGHT: TELEVANGELISM AND THE FAMILY

Although televangelists are but one segment of the Religious Right, they are worth some attention because of their views on sexuality. One of the most discussed televangelists was Jim Bakker. He is of some interest to us because it was his sexual activities that got him into trouble with the Assemblies of God Church. Bakker was a personal friend of Oral Roberts and had worked for several years for 1988 presidential candidate Pat Robertson at his Christian Broadcasting Network. He had become a top star of the televangelists when the sex scandal broke in 1987. Bakker espoused a kind of "prosperity theology."[27] He felt that those who believed in the Bible should be materially rewarded. The trouble began when sex became part of the reward system.

The Bakker scandal was triggered in 1987 by the revelation of his 1980 sexual encounter with Jessica Hahn, a Pentecostal Church secretary. The resulting investigation also revealed a great deal of questionable handling of many millions of dollars of his church's money by Bakker and an eventual conviction and sentence of forty-five years.* But most relevant to our interests in this book, that investigation showed the ways in which a fearful, dangerous, sex-negative view flourishes in the Evangelical Christian tradition. In 1983, after his encounter with Jessica Hahn but before that had become public, Bakker made some revealing comments about sexuality. See if you recognize the Victorian and Augustinian thinking in these comments by Bakker:

> And in the heat of lust, who thinks of the awful price being paid for a moment of passion? No one expects to feel so guilty, so dirty, so ashamed . . . so dirty. No one intends for those he really loves to be hurt. No one expects to end up diseased—permanently marked with an insidious infection like herpes for which medical science can find no cure.[28]

Note the stress on the inability to control this dangerous force and his horror of a sexually transmitted disease. Of course, there are problems in handling any strong feeling, but why picture sexuality as so unique? Herpes is no fun, but over one quarter of the adult population in America has the genital herpes virus and most of manage to live a normal life. It is the association with sex that makes what otherwise would most often be seen as a tolerable disease seem so disastrous. The stress is on anxiety and fear and not on preparation and decision making. When sex does occur, it is handled very badly. No one illustrated that better than Jim Bakker.

---

*Bakker is now out of prison and is seeking to rebuild his life.

The Bakker scandal greatly raised the visibility of Evangelicals. It made Americans more aware of the immensity of the Evangelical communication network in America. There are over sixteen hundred televangelist ministers who operate over three major religious networks, with about two hundred television stations and over a thousand radio stations carrying their message. During Reagan's eight years in the White House, this conservative religious grouping was able to develop strong ties with the Republican party.[29] One indication of this was the fact that in 1988, Pat Robertson, a former televangelist minister and a founder of one of the three religious networks, was able to get enough support to run for the Republican nomination for President.

As I have indicated, the Religious Right takes a conservative stance on abortion, sex outside of marriage, homosexuality, gender roles, and husband/wife family roles. Their views are often based on a conception of America as a religious nation with a divine destiny.[30] In 1989 the Republican Party in Arizona even passed a resolution, with support from Pat Robertson's backers, stating that "the United States is a Christian nation" and that the U.S. Constitution created "a republic based upon the absolute laws of the Bible, not a democracy."[31]

The passage of that resolution in Arizona is not a major threat in itself, but it does demonstrate the reason for our constitutional principle of separation of church and state. Without that principle, one church, or a coalition of churches, could seek to dominate our government and promote a theocracy instead of a democracy. Our earliest settlers were fleeing from just such a tyrannical rule by religious organizations. The principle of separation of church and state was our founding fathers' attempt to make certain that would never happen here.

That separation principle has been increasingly violated by religious conservatives over the past twenty-five years. Religious conservatives were incensed by the liberal changes in abortion, premarital sexuality, divorce, and other areas of social life. As a consequence, many of the Evangelical/fundamentalist religious groups in America have striven, particularly since Reagan's presidency, to gain increased influence in our political system. Back in 1987, Bill Moyers, the Public Broadcasting System's well-known special reporter and himself a Southern Baptist, commented upon the political action taken by fundamentalist Southern Baptists against political candidates with "anti-Biblical" views. In a reference to the fact that Baptists in the nineteenth century had fought for their own freedom from oppression by dominant religious groups, Moyers commented: "Of all people, Baptists must know that making biblical doctrine the test of political opinion is democratic heresy."

Baptists are surely not the only religious group moving into politically aimed activities. For example, some bishops of the Catholic Church have denied communion to Catholic politicians who come out on the "wrong" side of issues such as abortion. This "punishment" was meted out to Lucy Killea who in 1989 ran for a California State Senate seat in San Diego. The tactic boomeranged. Killea won the election and credited her victory to the public's negative reaction to the communion ban.[32]

In 1990 Mario Cuomo, the governor of New York, was criticized by Cardinal John O'Connor of New York and by one of his auxiliary bishops, Austin Vaughan. They speculated that Cuomo might be spending eternal life in Hell because of his abortion stance. Governor Cuomo responded by asking:

> Must I, having heard the Pope renew the Church's ban on birth-control devices, veto the funding of contraceptive programs for non-Catholics or dissenting Catholics in my state? I accept the Church's teaching on abortion. Must I insist you do? By law? By denying you Medicaid funding? By a constitutional amendment.[33]

Many of these battles between religious liberals and conservatives center on family and gender role conceptions. . . . Conservatives often criticize today's family and cite the family of the 1950s and earlier generations as the model to pursue. But remember what those "good old days" were like—married women denied equal access to jobs, contraceptive information legally banned, abortion illegal, male dominance much greater than today in all walks of life. Women were viewed as gullible and in need of male protection, preparation for sex was almost totally absent, and very high *rates* of disease and pregnancy existed for those who did venture forth into "Satan's playground."

Perhaps what is really being proposed by the Evangelical fundamentalists is a return not to the 1950s family but to the family of biblical days. What sort of family was that? The Old Testament is clear that this was a strong patriarchal family. Men were permitted wives and concubines. Children were legitimately conceived by these concubines outside of marriage. In fact, four of the twelve sons of Jacob were born to two women, Bilhah and Zilpah, who were the maids of Jacob's two wives, Leah and Rachel.[34] Is this the Evangelical's idea of an ideal family?

If we look at the traditional relationship of husband and wife as pictured in the New Testament, we also find severe restriction on the rights of women:

> Wives, submit yourselves unto your own husbands, as unto the Lord. For the husband is the head of the wife, even as Christ is the head of the church; and he is the savior of the body. Therefore, as the church is subject unto Christ, so let the wives be to their own husbands in everything. Husbands, love your wives, even as Christ also loved the church, and gave himself for it.[35]

The Victorian family of a hundred years ago does not fare much better in terms of gender equality when you examine it. It was simply a nineteenth century innovation on male-dominant family forms. It was in fact common mostly on the East Coast and not elsewhere in the country. In part the Victorian family form was a result of the desire of nineteenth-century middle-class men to show that they could earn enough so that their wives did not need to work. Middle-class men in the nineteenth century took great pride in providing a private home for their wives and their children.

The increased emphasis upon care of children was another nineteenth-century innovation. Prior to that time children were not the center of attention they were to become. The Victorian bourgeois family was popular in England and parts of Europe as well as in America.[36] In time the working classes, too, came to strive to achieve that new type of family. As a result, the remnants of opposition to a wife working outside the home is most noticeable today among the working classes.

The trends of the last thirty years are toward a more pluralistic view of married and family life. We have older ages at first marriage, longer delays in having children, fewer children per family, and more people who choose not to marry.[37] All of these trends indicate that although marriage and the family are still very important institutions, increased choices are being allowed. People can with greater ease design a lifestyle inside or outside of marriage to fit their personal needs. One can choose a traditional family lifestyle or a nontraditional one. We no longer have one Procrustean family bed that all people must be stretched or cut to fit into. These modern changes make it easier for women to choose, if they wish, to work outside the home and to gain equal status with men in our society.

All such changes have costs as well as benefits. But if there were a magic button that would return one to the family of the 1950s, or the biblical family, or the Victorian family, not very many people would press that button.

Still it is anyone's right to choose to live in a traditional family form. Pluralism simply rejects the position that this is the *only* acceptable form that everyone must strive to live up to.

Nevertheless, some of my fellow sociologists do believe we are underestimating the power of the Religious Right. They think we are moving back to those "good old days" in more ways than we realize.[38] Let's take a closer look at changes today in the Religious Right so we can learn more about these possible future trends.

COMING DOWN TO EARTH

Just how unified is the Religious Right in its beliefs and what trends are visible? In reality the Religious Right is quite a diverse group. "Evangelicals" is a general term used by some to include fundamentalist, Charismatic, and Holiness groups even though these groups are by no means identical. Professor James Hunter, a sociologist at the University of Virginia, studied the Religious Right to find out just what they do believe and what trends have been occurring.[39] He uses the term "Evangelical" to include the full range of those in the Religious Right. In the 1980s Professor Hunter surveyed a few thousand Evangelical college students, Evangelical seminary students, and faculty at sixteen institutions committed to the Evangelical worldview.

Evangelical leaders claim that they want to maintain "the purity and integrity of theology." They profess that the Bible is faultless and inerrant and that it is to be literally interpreted as the precise word of God. Despite this official policy, only 40 percent of Hunter's Evangelical collegians and seminarians maintained this traditional orthodox position on the Bible. Another 50 percent qualified this official position by saying that "The Bible is the inspired Word of God, not mistaken in its teachings, *but* is not always to be taken literally in its statements concerning matters of science, historical reporting, etc."[40] In addition, the Evangelical students said they felt that spiritual concerns take precedence over social and political justice. In that sense they were distinct from most mainline religions where social justice takes first place. So purity of belief is more important to the Religious Right than are efforts to correct social problems. This is an old distinction between conservative and liberal religions and it still makes some sense today.

Nevertheless, over the last decades there has been a tendency for Evangelicals to become less orthodox in their religious beliefs. The social changes in the broader society have had an impact on them, too. For example, Hunter compared findings from previous studies on Evangelical students in 1951 and 1961 with his data from the 1980s. He found a clear trend toward greater acceptance of activities like card playing, social dancing, movies, and drinking.

But does this mean that Evangelical students are no different than any other group of students? Hardly—they are quite distinct. Hunter compared his Evangelical students with students taking classes in religion at a public university in California in order to get a rough measure of difference. The differences found were vast. About 90 percent of the Evangelical students believed that premarital intercourse was always wrong, whereas only 15 percent of the public university students believed that. Over 95 percent of the Evangelical students believed that homosexual relations were always wrong compared to only 30 percent at the public university. Sixty-five percent of the Evangelical students felt that watching X-rated movies was always wrong compared to 13 percent at the public university. So, despite the trend toward more permissive attitudes, large differences remain between Evangelical and public university students.

Hunter came up with some interesting findings in the area of beliefs about the family. As we've discussed, religion and the family have always been intimately related. As Hunter puts it:

> It is difficult . . . to exaggerate the significance of the "traditional family" to Evangelicals. It is viewed as the bedrock of the American way of life—its social, cultural, and political institutions . . . its defense has become an Evangelical passion. It is its cause célèbre.[41]

Evangelicals picture the nineteenth-century middle-class Victorian family as the ideal traditional family. The husband is responsible for providing materially and spiritually for the family. He must see that his children are raised in traditional religion and that they will follow the Lord. A wife is expected to devote herself to her husband and her children. Children are to be shaped and directed. They are never to talk back to their parents. But social pressures against this family type are increasing today and changes can be seen even among Evangelicals.

Hunter asked the Evangelical students about their degree of acceptance of this nineteenth-century version of the family. He found that about two-thirds supported the view that the husband had the final say in the family's decision making and that he should be primarily responsible for the spiritual well-being of the family. Just 12 percent of the public university students agreed with that statement. However, my key point here is not that difference but the fact that over a third of the Evangelical students did *not* endorse that traditional view of husbands. Furthermore, women at these Evangelical schools were even less likely to endorse this dominant husband view. There seems to be a "liberal" minority even within the Evangelical group of students.

Even more variance from tradition is found in the case of child rearing: only about a third of the Evangelical students say that strict, old-fashioned upbringing is the best way to raise children, and less than half of them think it is best if a wife stays home and the husband supports the family. Other research on Evangelicals by the National Opinion Research Center (NORC) indicates that Evangelicals under age thirty-five are far more likely to reject traditional views of the family than are those over age thirty-five.[42] So the younger Evangelicals do seem to be moving away from the traditional family view promoted by their religious leaders. In answer to the question as to what proportion of the Evangelical students endorse the nineteenth-century model of the middle-class family, Hunter states:

> On average only about one in ten of the collegians and seminarians would be likely to endorse, enthusiastically, the model of the family advocated by Evangelical spokesmen. Another one-fourth to one-third would be sympathetic with that model, but this still leaves less than half of the coming generation holding to the ideal of traditional bourgeois familism.[43]

This divergence from the traditional family model is even more striking when one asks about the female role rather than the male role. Both men and women are even less likely to accept the traditional female role than they are to accept the traditional male role. So there is a faint echo of feminist influence here, too.

The faculty at Evangelical colleges rejects even more so the older dogmatic views of religion and the family. Here are the words of one faculty member:

> Who wants to preserve [religious] dogmatism and [moral] parochialism? Not me—and not most of my colleagues. We want salient evangelical faith, but since when must this type of religious commitment also include a firm commitment to male-centered households and all the rest of that nasty stuff? What [some] may call "contamination" or "erosion" I call a "success." Maybe Jerry Falwell thinks what we're doing is "counterproductive" but most of us who teach here . . . do not.[44]

Hunter also reports that the majority of Evangelicals have serious reservations about some of the extreme rhetoric of their more abrasive and radical leaders. Among Evangel-ical members there is a tradition of civility plus a hesitancy to be confrontive that keeps Evangelicals from joining political movements. Fundamentalists like Falwell are commonly viewed as too abrasive and combative. When one adds to this the modernizing changes that are occurring in the beliefs of many of the Evangelicals, the prediction that America will be increasingly dominated by a Christian theocracy professing fundamentalist religious beliefs is rather difficult to sustain. It is much more likely that the fundamentalists will change with America rather than the other way around.

A fascinating insight into the liberalization of Evangelical views comes from the work of two sociologists, Lionel Lewis and Dennis Brissett,[45] on Evangelical attitudes toward marital sexuality. They studied thirteen sex manuals written by Evangelical clergy, published by sectarian publishers, and sold in stores selling religious materials. (Many readers may well be surprised to find that there were thirteen sex manuals written by Evangelical clergy! It shows an openness toward sexual discussion that you might not expect from Evangelicals.) Lewis and Brissett found that while sex outside of marriage was condemned, sex within marriage was celebrated as a spiritual act in these manuals. For married couples, sexual play was encouraged. In addition, the authors of these sex manuals seemed to be saying that good Christians are better lovers. Lewis and Brissett comment on this point by quoting from one manual:

> A Christian's relationship with God produces a greater capacity for expressing and receiving love than is possible for a non-Christian. The fruit of the Spirit (love, joy, peace, kindness, etc. . . .) removes the specter of resentment and bitterness that devastates an exciting bedroom life.[46]

The theme often presented in these manuals is of marital sex as a confirmation of God and as an act that can and should be pursued for its own pleasure. Traditional views of male dominance are present in these manuals but so is marital sex as fun and pleasure. The old uncontrollable view of sexuality has clearly been abandoned by these Evangelical sex manuals. This is a significant change, for if sexual pleasure is seen as manageable and good in marriage, then the children of these people may well raise the question as to whether they can also learn to control the unwanted outcomes of premarital sexuality.

I expect that many of the younger Evangelicals are in increasingly serious conflict over these modernizing changes. There is little support for such new ways of thinking from their older leadership. So the burden falls upon the younger generation. Some of the loud complaints about the evils of society from the leaders of the Religious Right may be in part an anxiety response to their increasing awareness that the old ways are "a-changin'" and new more moderate traditions are being formed.

THE NEW RELIGIOUS LEFT AND SEXUALITY

The religious emphasis in America on the importance of a personal relationship with God is a major support for a liberal interpretation of religion. Most Americans believe in what the Baptists call the "priesthood of the individual." Each person interprets God's meaning through his or her own conscience. In several recent Gallup Polls, about 80 percent of all Americans agreed that "one should arrive at his or her religious beliefs independent of any church or synagogue." In addition, 76 percent said that they believe that a person can be a good Christian or Jew without attending church or synagogue.[47] These beliefs prevail despite the fact that about 84 percent of Americans believe in Christ and two-thirds have made a "commitment" to Christ.

Thus, while we do indeed have a very religious nation, the style of religion reflects the pluralism and individualism upon which this country was founded. Most Americans take a rather private view of their relationship to God. There is thus resistance to bend to any dogma that demands that one believe there is only one way to honor God. This means that if your conscience is so inclined, even if you are a member of an Evangelical group, you can personally accept liberal notions of sexuality, family, and gender. As Hunter's research shows, some Evangelicals have done precisely that. *The doctrine of freedom of conscience opens the door to a more pluralistic view of sexuality even for members of orthodox religions.*

There is a liberal element in all three major religious groups about which I should at least briefly comment. The Reform and Conservative Jewish groups, but not the Orthodox, score very high on liberal beliefs on sexuality, gender equality, and family roles. As Catholics have risen to a position of equality in economic and educational areas, they too have become more liberal religiously. As I have noted, on the average, Catholics are more liberal than Protestants on most issues. However, that difference would disappear if only mainline Protestant denominations were compared to Catholics because 40 percent of the Protestant group is composed of Evangelical/fundamentalist churches.

Bishop John Shelby Spong of the Episcopal Church in New Jersey is one representative of the liberal religious thinking. Bishop Spong's views concern new ways of conceptualizing human sexuality. He accepts homosexuality as a part of life, not a curse, and he does not accept any biblical condemnation of homosexuality. He notes that the same Bible that condemns homosexuality says many other things that even members of orthodox religions would never support today:

I have yet to meet a conservative Christian who would advocate execution for cursing (Lev. 24:14), blasphemy (Lev. 24:16), being a false prophet (Deut. 13:5), worshipping a false god (Deut. 17:1-8), or cursing or dishonoring one's parents (Lev. 20:9). Though we have discarded these Torah injunctions, some still continue to presume that the Torah's condemnation of homosexuality is valid, that it is not based upon ignorance, and that it is still binding on the church today. That point of view simply will not hold.[48]

Bishop Spong argues further for the acceptance by the Church of the full range of caring, loving relationships whether they be homosexual or heterosexual: "My assumption is that sexual activity is designed by the Creator not just for procreation but also for the enhancement of human life.[49]

At the heart of the liberal religious view of sexuality is the rejection of the orthodox Augustinian notion that pleasure leads inevitably to loss of control. Fear of loss of control is a key part of the sex-is-dangerous view that came to dominate Victorianism and is still influential in so much of Christianity.

Another liberal theologian is James B. Nelson, professor of Christian ethics at the United Theological Seminary of the Twin Cities in Minnesota. Professor Nelson belongs to the United Church of Christ and he believes that we can teach restraint and responsibility even in areas of pleasurable sexual acts. We can make moral judgments on the basis of whether a sexual act promotes love. He believes that what we need:

> . . . is an ethics that finds its center and direction in love rather than in a series of specific, absolute injunctions . . . love is the central (albeit not the only) norm for Christian ethics, it is the central meaning of human sexuality and the measuring standard and justification for any particular sex act. . . . An ethics centered in . . . love . . . will not guarantee freedom from mistakes in the sexual life. It will place considerable responsibility upon the individual. . . . It will be more concerned about the authentic fulfillment of persons than the stringencies of unyielding laws or the neat cataloguing of types of sexual acts.[50]

There are even televangelists ministers with similar liberal views. Dr. Robert H. Schuller

from the Crystal Cathedral in California has said:

> We have not given human beings the teaching that they should be leaders—and a leader is a person who is aware of his personhood, meaning his freedom to make choices. But basically, the dominant influence of Christianity, that is, Roman Catholicism and Protestantism, resulted in a tendency which was not to train believers to be persons or leaders or individual thinkers—hence truly moral creatures—but rather to be followers. The church would make the decisions as to what ought to be done, and the believers would be expected to learn what ought to be done, and then they were supposed to obey.[51]

So there have been for the past few decades new ideas coming out of conservative as well as liberal groups and they may ultimately change sexuality in the conservative as well as the mainline churches in America. Favoring greater freedom of choice for everyone implies support for pluralism and acceptance of those who choose sexual standards other than abstinence, and backing for gender conceptions other than male dominance.

Those who leave the liberal churches most often become the nonaffiliated people, and that group is growing at a rapid pace. The disenchanted member of a liberal church does not usually become a member of a conservative religion. The liberal church is searching, with the leadership of people like Spong and Nelson, to add new vigor and boldness to their religions and thereby increase the commitment of their congregants. The Catholic and Jewish groups have their own liberal leaders too. What they all are constructing is a more pluralistic ethical view. Here, for example, is a statement of hope by James Nelson that the church will recognize a far broader range of sexual events:

> Is it too bold to suggest that we consider ways of naming and celebrating the onset of a girl's menstruation? Or a boy's coming of age—in the face of the currently destructive secular rituals of

naming and achieving "manhood"? Or the affirming of one's sexual orientation? Or the commitment to a new relationship of intimacy other than marriage? Or rites of abortion which convey faith's healing resources after agonized choice? The church is losing countless teenagers and young adults, not to mention older persons, because it continues to be silent, timid and negative about sexuality.[52]

I know that some readers will feel that Professor Nelson's suggestions are pretty far out. But brace yourself, I want to go a step further. I praise what the Religious Left is doing, but I do feel it is not pluralistic enough. They have released sexual pleasure from the solitary confinement imposed by St. Augustine and St. Thomas, but they have released it only in the custody of love. If we examine ourselves, we are aware that sexual pleasure has a value to each of us—without being joined to love or anything else. Most of us masturbate for reasons other than love and many people have had sexual relations with people they were not in love with.

A pluralistic approach has to recognize that there are circumstances in which people can benefit from freely chosen sexual relations that are pleasure- and friendship-centered. As long as the basic pluralistic values of honesty, equality, and responsibility are present, then the respectful treatment of each person is present, even though lasting affection and love may not be there. Sometimes love may develop, but more often than not, it won't. Most Americans view love relationships as ideal, but we are not always in ideal circumstances in our lives. My point here is that we ought not to back away from endorsing pleasure- and friendship-centered sexual choices as legitimate options for single people at some times in their lives. The key check should be: Is the sexual relationship HER-oriented? If it is, then it meets the ethical test of pluralism.

ENHANCING RELIGIOUS PLURALISM

All generations transform religion to make it meaningful for themselves. Rodney Stark and William Bainbridge, two university sociologists, have presented strong evidence that when an established religion does not fulfill the needs of its members, new religious sects are formed which, over time, will become new established denominations.[53] Some of the new Evangelical religions were formed because some people found the mainline religions lacking. Religion is an essential and a dynamic element in society. No one religious view—whether it be mainline or Evangelical—can fulfill the needs of everyone. From a pluralistic perspective all the religious views of sexuality are acceptable as long as they do not claim to be the one right way. There are those who would say that God is behind their position and so they must condemn all others. I would simply reply that the God of a democratic society would surely be seen as a pluralist.

We need the flexibility afforded by our traditional pluralistic approach to religion. Our country was founded on a belief in religious pluralism. We cannot allow any one specific religious view—liberal or conservative—to monopolize our country, our conception of sexuality, or our understanding of God. Pluralism permits persons to choose for themselves among a wide variety of perspectives; that freedom to search is vital. Religion can supply the motivation for us to help one another resolve the multiple sexual crises we face. It is the place of religion to make us believe in a better world. And it is the responsibility of those who believe in a better world to use religion in ways that make it an ally rather than an enemy in our search for how to restructure our society so as to make it a more honest, equal, and responsible place in which to live.

NOTES

1. Elaine Pagels, *Adam, Eve, and the Serpent* (New York: Random House, 1988), pp. xxiii–xxv.
2. John Boswell, *Christianity, Social Tolerance, and Homosexuality: Gay People in Western Europe from the Beginning of the Christian Era to the Fourteenth Century* (Chicago: University of Chicago Press, 1980), p. 165.
3. Ibid., p. 164.
4. St. Augustine, *The Confessions of St. Augustine: Books I to X,* trans. F. J. Sheed (New York: Sheed and Ward, 1942), p. 139 (italics added). For another fine scholarly coverage of early Christianity see Vern Bullough, *Sexual Variance in Society and History* (New York: John Wiley and Sons, 1976).
5. Pagels, *Adam, Eve, and the Serpent,* p. 141.
6. Ibid., p. 145.
7. Ibid., p. 150.
8. Boswell, *Christianity, Social Tolerance, and Homosexuality,* p. 334.
9. Jeffrey Weeks, *Sexuality* (London: Routledge, 1986), p. 82. See also Vern Bullough, *Sexual Variance,* p. 380, and Boswell, *Christianity, Social Tolerance, and Homosexuality,* pp. 318–32.
10. George Gallup and Jim Castelli, *The People's Religion: America Faith in the 90s* (New York: Macmillan Publishing Company, 1989), p. 90.
11. George H. Gallup Jr., *Religion in America, 1996* (Princeton N.J.: Princeton Religion Research Center, 1996).
12. The Gallup Report, *Religion in America: 50 Years: 1935–1985,* Report no. 236 (May 1985): 24–25.
13. Elaine Tyler May, *Homeward Bound: American Families in the Cold War Era* (New York: Basic Books, Inc., 1988), p. 207.
14. The Gallup Report, *Religion in America: 50 Years: 1935–1985,* pp. 4–5.
15. Ibid., p. 42.
16. For national data on attitudes toward birth control and abortion in different religious groups see *General Social Surveys, 1972–1996: Cumulative Codebook* (National Opinion Research Center, University of Chicago, 1996); William F. Pratt, W. D. Moshen, C. A. Bachrach, and M. C. Horn, "Understanding U.S. Fertility: Findings from the National Survey of Family Growth, Cycle 111," *Population Bulletin* 39, no. 5 (1984).
17. Stanley K. Henshaw and Jane Silverman, "The Characteristics and Prior Contraceptive Use of U.S. Abortion Patients," *Family Planning Perspectives* 20 (July/August 1988): 158–68.
18. For a few introductory comments on some of these controversies see Kendell Cronstrom, ed., *Tradition and Transition: Religion in the Twin Cities* (Minneapolis, Minn.: March, 1987); Daniel C. Maguire, "Catholic Sexual and Reproductive Ethics: A Historical Perspective," *SIECUS Report* 15 (May/June 1987); Wilson Yates, "The Church and Its Holistic Paradigm of Sexuality," *SIECUS Report* 16 (May/June 1988); Ruth A. Wallace, "Catholic Women and the Creation of a New Social Reality," *Gender and Society* 2 (March 1988): 24–38; Pagels, *Adam, Eve and the Serpent;* and Lawrence Lader, *Politics, Power and the Church: The Catholic Crisis and Its Challenge to American Pluralism* (New York: Macmillan Publishing, 1987).
19. Gallup, *Religion in America, 1996,* pp. 39–44.
20. *Minneapolis Star Tribune,* December 11, 1987.
21. *Minneapolis Star Tribune,* March 1, 1989. See also Charles E. Curran, "Roman Catholic Sexual Ethics: A Dissenting View," pp.49–56 in James B. Nelson, ed., *Sexual Ethics and the Church: A Christian Century Symposium* (Chicago: The Christian Century Foundation, 1989); and James Davison Hunter, *Evangelicalism: The Coming Generation* (Chicago: University of Chicago Press, 1987), p. 219.
22. Wade Clark Roof and William McKinney, *American Mainline Religion: Its Changing Shape and Future* (New Brunswick, N.J.: Rutgers University Press, 1988), pp. 211–12.
23. The Princeton Religion Research Center, *The Unchurched American: 10 Years Later* (Princeton, N.J.: Princeton University Press, 1989), p. 7.
24. Roof and McKinney, *American Mainline Religion,* p. 165.
25. Robert Wuthnow, *The Restructuring of American Religion: Society and Faith since World War II*

(Princeton, NJ.: Princeton University Press, 1988), p. 132.

26. Tom W. Smith, "America's Religious Mosaic," *American Demographics* 12 (June 1984): 18–23.

27. A simple but interesting account of the Bakkers can be found in Joe E. Barnhart, *Jim and Tammy: Charismatic Intrigue inside PTL* (Amherst, N.Y.: Prometheus Books, 1988). See also parts of Jeffrey K. Hadden and Anson Shupe, *Televangelism: Power and Politics on God's Frontier* (New York: Henry Holt and Co., 1988).

28. Barnhart, *Jim and Tammy*, p. 140.

29. Frances FitzGerald, *Cities on A Hill: A Journey through Contemporary American Cultures* (New York: Simon and Schuster, 1986), pp. 121–201 ("Liberty Baptist"). See also Lader, *Politics, Power and the Church*, and Hadden and Shupe, *Televangelism*.

30. Arthur Schlesinger Jr., the noted Harvard historian, has commented on the long-standing clash in American society between a view of America as an experiment with risks that requires a realistic approach to succeed, and a messianic view of America as a country of destiny, a redeemer nation that can save the world. See Arthur Schlesinger Jr., *The Cycles of American History* (Boston: Houghton Mifflin, 1986).

31. *Minneapolis Star Tribune*, March 15, 1989.

32. *Newsweek*, December 18, 1989, p. 28.

33. *Minneapolis Star Tribune*, February 11, 1990, column by Colman McCarthy. For an excellent account of authoritarianism and its relation to religion see Bob Altemeyer, *Enemies of Freedom: Understanding Right-wing Authoritarianism* (San Francisco: Jossey-Bass, 1988). Altemeyer found that fundamentalist religious training tends to foster authoritarianism.

34. Genesis 35:22–26.

35. Ephesians 5:22–28.

36. For an excellent brief summary of historical change in the family see David Popenoe, *Disturbing the Nest: Family Change and Decline in Modern Societies* (New York: Aldine D. Gruyter, 1988), ch. 4.

37. Bert Adams, *The Family: A Sociological Interpretation*, 5th ed. (New York: Harcourt Brace, 1995); and Arlene Skolnick, *The Intimate Environment: Explaining Marriage and the Family* (New York: Harper Collins, 1996).

38. Hadden and Shupe, *Televangelism*, p. 297.

39. Hunter, *Evangelicalism: The Coming Generation.*

40. Ibid., p. 24.

41. Ibid., p. 77.

42. Ibid., p. 100.

43. Ibid., pp. 111–12.

44. Ibid., p. 176.

45. Lionel S. Lewis and Dennis D. Brissett, "Sex as God's Work," *Society* 23 (March/April 1986): 67–75.

46. Ibid., p. 70.

47. The Princeton Religion Research Center, *The Unchurched American*, p. 3; also Gallup, *Religion in America, 1996.*

48. John Shelby Spong, *Living in Sin: A Bishop Rethinks Human Sexuality* (New York: Harper and Row, 1988), p. 147.

49. Ibid., p. 226.

50. James B. Nelson, *Between Two Gardens: Reflections on Sexuality and Religious Experience* (New York: Pilgrim Press, 1983), pp. 81–85.

51. Quoted from a personal conversation in Ruth Westheimer and Louis Lieberman, *Sex and Morality: Who Is Teaching Our Sex Standards?* (Boston: Harcourt, Brace, Jovanovich, 1988), p. 192.

52. Nelson, *Sexual Ethics and the Church: A Christian Century Symposium*, p. 69.

53. Rodney Stark and William Sims Bainbridge, *The Future of Religion: Secularization, Revival, and Cult Formation* (Berkeley and Los Angeles: University of California Press, 1985). For a short, updated, one-chapter presentation of this perspective see Rodney Stark, *Sociology* 6th ed. (Belmont, Calif.: Wadsworth Publishers, 1996), ch. 14.

READING 5

Cultural and Historical Influences on Sexuality in Hispanic/Latin Women

Oliva M. Espín

This paper will examine four major factors which affect the development of sexuality in Latin women in the United States: historical influences, immigration, language, and the psychological effects of oppression.

Despite shared features of history and culture, attitudes toward sex-roles are extremely diverse among Hispanic women. For instance, some Latin women are willing to endorse "modern" and "liberated" sex-roles concerning education and employment, while maintaining very "traditional," "conservative" positions concerning sexual behaviors or personal relationships. Others are traditional in all respects and still others reject all traditional beliefs concerning the roles of women. Consequently, it is very difficult to discuss the sexuality or sexual behavior of Latin women without the danger of making some sweeping generalizations. The experiential and emotional distance between an immigrant worker of peasant extraction who barely knows how to write her name in Spanish and a "Latin princess" who comes to the United States to study at a private educational institution with all expenses paid by her parents is enormous. If these two women met each other, they probably would not acknowledge any commonalities between them. And yet, as their therapist, I can recognize a common thread and a historical background to their lives, a thread shared with daughters of immigrants born and raised

in the streets of New York and in the rural areas of the Southwest.

What are the commonalities among Hispanic women in the United States that manifest themselves in spite of the enormous differences among them? *Historical influences* have left their mark in cultural processes and in class and race differentiation. Other commonalities have to do with the experience of separation implied in *immigration;* with the cognitive and affective effects of sharing a common *language;* and with the experience of *oppression.*

The enormous differences between the Spanish and British conquest of Latin America and North America set these two cultures apart.[1] On the one hand, the British came with their families, escaping persecution; North America became a dumping ground for religious dissidents. The Puritans and many of those who followed turned away from England with no desire to return to the homeland, seeking a place where they could remain separated and independent from all those who were different or held different beliefs. The Spaniards, on the other hand, came to America as a male army for the specific purpose of conquering new land for their king. They landed anticipating territory full of gold, silver, and abundance where land was fertile all year long. These resources, plus the centralization of power already achieved by the native Indian empires, provided an environment profoundly different from that encountered by the Pilgrims.

Most "conquistadores" were men without fortune, nobility, or other resources. The majority of them did not come with their wives or with any female relatives; marrying women of Spanish descent was practically impossible. They initially intended to return to Spain full of honors and riches in order to marry Spanish women of a higher class. Difficult communications and the hardships of an enterprise that did not produce "gold at first sight" as they had expected delayed their return to Spain indefinitely. Many of them never returned and, instead, stayed in the Americas for the rest of their lives.

Thus, the conquerors' temporary sexual use of Indian women developed into more enduring relationships. They set up homes with the native women who were originally taken only as concubines. These relationships—some temporary, some stable—created the Mestizo population of Latin America. In spite of their known cruelties, many of the Spanish conquerors were willing to legally marry Indian or black women and to recognize, support, and pass their inheritance on to their children by those marriages. A similar behavior would have been unthinkable not only to the Puritans, but to most white gentlemen in the United States to this day. It is well known that even Thomas Jefferson had children by a black woman. However, those children were never called Jefferson and that slave woman was never freed by him.

While Calvinist theology, with its emphasis on predestination, encouraged the separation of the races in North America, the Spanish Catholic clergy battled in Europe and America for the human rights of the Amerindians, following Catholic theological tenets which give the right to salvation to anyone who is baptized and fulfills appropriate duties as a Christian. Once the Indians were declared to be human by the pope, they had the right to be Catholic and, thus, children of God.[2]

The Catholic church's proclamation of the importance of virginity for all women, regardless of their race or social status, became a challenge to a social system that otherwise could have been even more oppressive to non-white women. By emphasizing that all women, regardless of race and social class, hold the duty and the right to remain virgins until marriage, and that all men were responsible to women whose honor they had "stained," the church discouraged consensual union and illegitimacy.[3] However, by upholding the standard of virginity as the proof of a woman's honorability, the church, and later the culture in general, further lowered the status of women who cannot or will not maintain virginity. This also fostered the perspective that once an unmarried woman is not a virgin, she is automatically promiscuous. These standards fell in a disproportionately harsh way on native and Mestizo women, who were less likely to be virgins because of the social and economic conditions in which they lived.

Historical circumstances combined to shape gender and race relations in Latin America in a very distinctive way. This is not to say that racial inequality or prejudice do not exist in Latin America, but that it differs from the forms found In North America. There is a fluidity in racial relationships among Latins that is difficult to understand in the United States. In Latin America, social status is affected more profoundly by factors other than race. Social class and income prevail over color.[4] Different shades of color among members of the same family are not denied. The number of political figures and upper-class Latin Americans who are "non-white" by North American standards attests to the difference in perspective. On the other hand, European ancestry and "whiteness" are highly respected. "Color" makes doors harder to open. People of color are over-represented in the lower socio-economic classes, and many a descendant of an interracial marriage would carefully avoid such a marriage now. The non-white woman may still be seen as not deserving the same respect as the white woman. And, if a white man fathers her children, she may not find the same protection as her white counterpart. Moreover, precisely because many of the conqueror's wives were not white, the lower status of all women was further compounded by racial factors.

Trends created centuries ago in the relationships between men and women of different races, cultures and political status persist to-day in Hispanic cultures. Historical influences have been modified, amplified to give a certain character and tone to the lives of Hispanic women. In addition to their shared cultural, historical and religious heritage described above, Hispanic women living in the United States today share many characteristics as a function of immigration, language, and the shared experience of oppression.

Although some Hispanic women are not immigrants, many of them come from immigrant families. A discussion of the psychological implications of *immigration* is relevant even if not applicable to all Hispanic women. Immigration or any other form of separation from cultural roots involves a process of grieving. Women seem to be affected by this process in a manner that is different from that of men. Successful adaptation after immigration involves resolution of feelings of loss, the development of decision-making skills, ego strength and the ability to tolerate ambiguities, including sex-role ambiguities. Factors pertaining to the psychological make-up of the individual woman as well as specifics of the home culture and class interplay in unique ways with the characteristics of the host culture. Newly-encountered patterns of sex-roles combine with greater access to paid employment for women and may create an imbalance in the traditional power structure of the family.

One of the most prevalent myths encountered by immigrant Hispanic women is that all American women are very free with sex. For the parents and the young women alike, "to become Americanized" is equated with becoming sexually promiscuous. Thus, in some cases, sexuality may become the focus of the parents' fears and the girl's desires during the acculturation process.

Language is another important factor in the experience of Hispanic women. To discuss the affective and cognitive implications of bilingualism and language use will take us beyond the scope of this paper. However, it is important to keep in mind that even for those Hispanic women who are fluent in English, Spanish may remain as the language of emotions because the first language heard and learned and thus it was usually it is full of deep affective meaning.[5]

The preference of one language over another, or the shift from one language to another might be an indication of more subtle processes than even the choice of words.[6] For example, in a recent study of Cuban women in Miami,[7] fluency in English appears as the single most important determinant of attitudes towards the role of women in society. Shifts between languages and the preference for one language or the other may be a means to achieve either distancing or intimacy. When the topic at hand is sexuality, the second language might be an effective tool to express what one does not dare to verbalize in the first language. Conversely, certain emotions and experiences will never be addressed appropriately unless they are discussed in the first language.[8] The emotional significance of a specific word for a particular individual generally depends on the individual personal values and his [sic] developmental history.[9]

The emotional arousal evoked by saying taboo words decreases when they are pronounced in a foreign language.[10] Presumably, erotic language is experienced differently when uttered or heard in either English or Spanish.

The condition of *oppression* under which most Hispanics live in the United States creates certain psychological effects for both men and women, although Latin women, oppressed both as women and as Hispanics, suffer from physical and psychological consequences of oppression in a profound way. The conditions of oppression originating in the economic, political and social structures of the world become psychological as the effects of these external circumstances become internalized.[11] The external oppression of Hispanic women is expressed in political, educational, economic and social discrimination. Psychologically, the oppression of Hispanic women develops through internalized attitudes that designate women as inferior to men, including Hispanic men, while designating all Hispanics as inferior, to the white mainstream of North American society. Oppressive beliefs that affect all women and all Hispanics influence the lives and the sexuality of Hispanic women.

There are specific forms in which the psychology of oppression affects women from all ethnic minority groups. One involves the importance placed on physical beauty for women and, particularly, on standards of beauty inappropriate for non-white women. Women, regardless of ethnic group, are taught to derive their primary validation from their looks and physical attractiveness. The inability of most non-white women to achieve prescribed standards of beauty may be devastating for self-esteem.

Another psychological effect of oppression for Hispanic women is to further increase their subordination to men. As a reaction towards the oppression suffered by minority men in the larger society, minority women may subordinate their needs even further to those of men. Women and children may be suitable recipients for the displaced anger of an oppressed man. Violence takes many forms: incest, rape, wife-beating. Violence against women is produced and sustained by societal messages about women. The prevalent virgin/whore dichotomy in images of women fosters and condones the violence. It is not unusual to hear supposedly "enlightened" persons defending the violent behavior of men in oppressed groups on the grounds that their only outlet is to get drunk and beat their wives. Even if the displacement can be understood in the case of accept and justify it is to condone

injustice and another form of violence against women under the guise of understanding.

In addition, women from oppressed groups may be seen as "easy prey" for white men or as "sexier" than their white counterparts. Their sexual behavior is supposed to be freer and less restrained when, in fact, the opposite might be true. On the other hand, a young woman's sexuality might be the only asset she has in her efforts to break away from oppressive conditions.

CONTEMPORARY SEXUALITY AND THE HISPANIC WOMAN

If the role of women is currently beset with contradictions in the mainstream of American society,[12] this is probably still more true for women in Hispanic groups. The honor of Latin families is strongly tied to the sexual purity of women. And the concept of honor and dignity is one of the essential distinctive marks of Hispanic culture. For example, classical Hispanic literature gives us a clue to the importance attributed to honor and to female sexual purity in the culture. La Celestina, the protagonist of an early Spanish medieval novel, illustrates the value attached to virginity and its preservation. Celestina was an old woman who earned her living in two ways: by putting young men in touch with young maidens so they could have the sexual contact that parents would never allow, and by "sewing up" ex-virgins, so that they would be considered virgins at marriage. Celestina thus made her living out of making and unmaking virgins. The fact that she ends by being punished with death further emphasizes the gravity of what she does. In the words of a famous Spanish playwright of the seventeenth century, "al Rey la hacienda y la vida se han de dar, mas no el honor; porque el honor es patrimonio del alma y el alma solo es de Dios."[13] This quotation translates literally, "To the king you give money and life, but not your honor, because honor is part of the soul, and your soul belongs only to God."

Different penalties and sanctions for the violation of cultural norms related to female sexuality are very much associated with social class. The upper classes or those seeking an improved social status tend to be more rigid about sexuality. This of course is related to the transmission of property. In the upper classes, a man needs to know that his children are in fact his before they inherit his property. The only guarantee of his paternity is that his wife does not have sexual contact with any other man. Virginity is tremendously important in that context. However, even when property is not an issue, the only thing left to a family may be the honor of its women and as such it may be guarded jealously by both males and females. Although Hispanics in the twentieth century may not hold the same strict values—and many of them certainly cannot afford the luxury to do so—women's sexual behavior is still the expression of the family's honor. The tradition of maintaining virginity until marriage that had been emphasized among women continues to be a cultural imperative. The Virgin Mary—who was a virgin and a mother, but never a sexual being—is presented as an important role model for all Hispanic women, although Hispanic unwed mothers, who have clearly overstepped the boundaries of culturally-prescribed virginity for women, usually are accepted by their families. Married women or those living in common-law marriages are supposed to accept a double standard for sexual behavior, by which their husbands may have affairs with other women, while they themselves are expected to remain faithful to one man all of their lives. However, it is not uncommon for a Hispanic woman to have the power to decide whether or not a man is going to live with her, and she

may also choose to put him out if he drinks too much or is not a good provider.[14]

In fact, Latin women experience a unique combination of power and powerlessness which is characteristic of the culture. The idea that personal problems are best discussed with women is very much part of the Hispanic culture. Women in Hispanic neighborhoods and families tend to rely on other women for their important personal and practical needs. There is a widespread belief among Latin women of all social classes that most men are undependable and are not to be trusted. At the same time, many of these women will put up with a man's abuses because having a man around is an important source of a woman's sense of self-worth. Middle-aged and elderly Hispanic women retain important roles in their families even after their sons and daughters are married. Grandmothers are ever present and highly vocal in family affairs. Older women have much more status and power than their white American counterparts, who at this age may be suffering from depression due to what has been called the "empty-nest syndrome." Many Hispanic women are providers of mental health services (which sometimes include advice about sexual problems) in an unofficial way as "curanderas," "espiritistas," or "santeras," for those people who believe in these alternative approaches to health care.[15] Some of these women play a powerful role in their communities, thanks to their reputation for being able to heal mind and body.

However, at the same time that Latin women have the opportunity to exercise their power in the areas mentioned above, they also receive constant cultural messages that they should be submissive and subservient to males in order to be seen as "good women." To suffer and be a martyr is also a characteristic of a "good woman." This emphasis on self-renunciation, combined with the importance given to sexual purity for women, has a direct bearing on the development of sexuality in Latin women. To enjoy sexual pleasure, even in marriage, may indicate lack of virtue. To shun sexual pleasure and to regard sexual behavior exclusively as an unwelcome obligation toward her husband and a necessary evil in order to have children may be seen as a manifestation of virtue. In fact, some women even express pride at their own lack of sexual pleasure or desire. Their negative attitudes toward sex are frequently reinforced by the inconsiderate behavior and demands of men.

Body image and related issues are deeply connected with sexuality for all women. Even when body-related problems may not have direct implications for sexuality, the body remains for women the main vehicle for expressing their needs. The high incidence of somatic complaints presented by low-income Hispanic women in psychotherapy might be a consequence of the emphasis on "martyrdom" and self-sacrifice, or it might be a somatic expression of needs and anxieties. More directly related to sexuality are issues of birth control, pregnancy, abortion, menopause, hysterectomy and other gynecological problems. Many of these have traditionally been discussed among women only. To be brought to the attention of a male doctor may be enormously embarrassing and distressing for some of these women. Younger Hispanic women may find themselves challenging traditional sexual mores while struggling with their own conflicts about beauty and their own embarrassment about visiting male doctors.

One of the most common and pervasive stereotypes held about Hispanics is the image of the "macho" man—an image which generally conjures up the rough, tough, swaggering men who are abusive and oppressive towards women, who in turn are seen as being exclusively submissive and long-suffering.[16]

Some authors[17] recognize that "machismo"—which is nothing but the Hispanic version of the myth of male superiority supported by most cultures—is still in existence in the Latin culture, especially among those individuals who subscribe more strongly to traditional Hispanic values. Following this tradition, Latin females are expected to be subordinated to males and to the family. Males are expected to show their manhood by behaving in a strong fashion, by demonstrating sexual prowess and by asserting their authority over women. In many cases, these traditional values may not be enacted behaviorally, but are still supported as valued assumptions concerning male and female "good" behavior. According to Aramoni,[18] himself a Mexican psychologist, "machismo" may be a reaction of Latin males to a series of social conditions, including the effort to exercise control over their ever-present, powerfully demanding, and suffering mothers and to identify with their absent fathers. Adult males continue to respect and revere their mothers, even when they may not show much respect for their wives or other women. As adolescents they may have protected their mothers from fathers' abuse or indifference. As adults they accord their mothers a respect that no other woman deserves, thus following their fathers' steps. The mother herself teaches her sons to be dominant and independent in relations with other women. Other psychological and social factors may be influential in the development of "machismo." It is important to remember that not all Latin males exhibit the negative behaviors implied in the "macho" stereotype, and that even when certain individuals do, these behaviors might be a reaction to oppressive social conditions by which Hispanic men too are victimized.

Sexually, "machismo" is expressed through an emphasis on multiple, uncommitted sexual contacts which start in adolescence. In a study of adolescent rituals in Latin America, Espìn[19] found that many males celebrated their adolescence by visiting prostitutes. The money to pay for this sexual initiation was usually provided by fathers, uncles or older brothers.

Adolescent females, on the other hand, were offered coming-out parties, the rituals of which emphasize their virginal qualities. Somehow, a man is more "macho" if he manages to have sexual relations with a virgin; thus, fathers and brothers watch over young women for fear that other men may make them their sexual prey. These same men, however, will not hesitate to take advantage of the young women in other families. Women, in turn, are seen as capable of surrendering to men's advances, without much awareness of their own decisions on the matter. "Good women" should always say no to a sexual advance. Those who say yes are automatically assumed to be less virtuous by everyone, including the same man with whom they consent to have sex.

Needless to say, sexual understanding and communication between the sexes is practically rendered impossible by these attitudes generated by "machismo." However, not all Hispanics subscribe to this perspective and some reject it outright. In a review of the literature on studies of decision-making patterns in Mexican and Chicano families the authors concluded that "Hispanic males may behave differently from non-Hispanic men in their family and marital lives, but not in the inappropriate fashion suggested by the myth with its strong connotations of social deviance."[20] This article reviews only research on the decision-making process in married couples and, thus, other aspects of male-female relationships in the Hispanic culture are not discussed.

In the context of culturally appropriate sex-roles, mothers train their daughters to remain virgins at all cost, to cater to men's sexual needs and to play "little wives" to their fathers and brothers from a very early age. If a mother is sick or working outside the home and there are no adult females around, the oldest daughter, no matter how young, will be in charge of caring not only for the younger siblings, but also for the father, who would continue to ex-

pect his meals to be cooked and his clothes to be washed.

Training for appropriate heterosexuality, however, is not always assimilated by all Latin women. A seldom-mentioned fact is that, as in all cultures, there are lesbians among Hispanic women. Although emotional and physical closeness among women is encouraged by the culture, overt acknowledgment of lesbianism is even more restricted than in mainstream American society. In a study about lesbians in the Puerto Rican community, Hidalgo and Hidalgo-Christensen found that "rejection of homosexuals appears to be the dominant attitude in the Puerto Rican community."[21] Although this attitude may not seem different from that of the dominant culture, there are some important differences experienced by Latin lesbian women which are directly related to Hispanic cultural patterns. Frequent contact and a strong interdependence among family members, even in adulthood, are essential features of Hispanic family life. Leading a double life becomes more of a strain in this context. "Coming out" may jeopardize not only these strong family ties, but also the possibility of serving the Hispanic community in which the talents of all members are such an important asset. Because most lesbian women are single and self-supporting, and not encumbered by the demands of husbands and children, it can be assumed that the professional experience and educational level of Hispanic lesbians will tend to be relatively high. If this is true, professional experience and education will frequently place Hispanic lesbian women in positions of leadership or advocacy in their community. Their status and prestige, and, thus, the ability to serve their community, are threatened by the possibility of being "found out."

Most "politically aware" Latins show a remarkable lack of understanding of gay-related-issues. In a recent meeting of Hispanic women in a major U.S. city, one participant expressed the opinion that "lesbianism is a sickness we get from American women and American culture." This is, obviously, another version of the myth about the free sexuality of American women so prevalent among Hispanics. But it is also an expression of the common belief that homosexuality is chosen behavior, acquired through the bad influence of others, like drug addiction. Socialist attitudes in this respect are extremely traditional, as the attitudes of the Cuban revolution towards homosexuality clearly manifest. Thus, Hispanics who consider themselves radical and committed to civil rights remain extremely traditional when it comes to gay rights. These attitudes clearly add further stress to the lives of Latin women who have a homosexual orientation and who are invested in enhancing the lives of members of their communities.

They experience oppression in three ways: as women, as Hispanics and as lesbians. This last form of oppression is in fact experienced most powerfully from inside their own culture. Most Latin women who are lesbians have to remain "closeted" among their families, their colleagues and society at large. To be "out of the closet" only in an Anglo context deprives them of essential supports from their communities and families, and, in turn, increases their invisibility in the Hispanic culture, where only the openly "butch" types are recognized as lesbians.

NOTES

1. For further information about this period, see C. A. Beard and M. R. Beard, *The Beards' New Basic History of the United States*, New York, Doubleday, 1968; and W. H. Prescott, *History of the Conquest of Mexico* and *History of the Conquest of Peru*, New York, Modern Library, no date (originally published in 1843 and 1847).
2. D. V. Kurtz, "The Virgin of Guadalupe and the Politics of Becoming Human," *Journal of Anthropological Research*, vol. 38, no. 2, 1982, pp. 194–210.
3. V. Martínez-Alier, *Marriage, Class and Colour in Nineteenth Century Cuba*, London, Cambridge University Press, 1974.
4. Ibid.
5. O. M. Espín, "Issues of Psychotherapy with fluently Bilingual Clients," unpublished paper presented at the Stone Center for Developmental Studies, Wellesley College, Wellesley, Mass. 1982.
6. L. R. Marcos and L. Urcuyo, "Dynamic Psychotherapy with the Bilingual Patient," *American Journal of Psychotherapy*, vol. 33, no. 3, 1979, pp. 331–8.
7. O. M. Espín and B. Warner, "Attitudes towards the Role of Woman in Cuban Women Attending a Community College," *International Journal of Social Psychiatry*, vol. 28, no. 3, 1982, pp. 233–9.
8. Espín, "Issues of Psychotherapy with Fluently Bilingual Clients," op. cit.
9. F. Gonzalez-Reigosa, "The Anxiety-Arousing Effect of Taboo Words in Bilinguals," in C. D. Spielberger and R. Díaz-Guerrero (eds), *Cross-Cultural Anxiety*, Washington, D.C., Hemisphere, 1976, p. 325.
10. Ibid.
11. P. Freire, *Pedagogy of the Oppressed*, New York, Salisbury, 1970.
12. J. B. Miller, *Toward a New Psychology of Women*, Boston, Beacon, 1976.
13. Calderón de la Barca, *El Alcalde de Zalamea*.
14. S. Brown, "Love Unites Them and Hunger Separates Them: Poor Women in the Dominican Republic," in Rayna Reiter (ed.), *Toward an Anthropology of Women*, New York, Monthly Review Press, 1975, p. 322.
15. O. M. Espín, "Hispanic Female Healers in Urban Centers in the United States," unpublished manuscript, 1983.
16. V. Abad, J. Ramos, and E. Boyce, "A Model for Delivery of Mental Health Services to Spanish-Speaking Minorities," *American Journal of Orthopsychiatry*, vol. 44, no. 4, 1974, pp. 584–95.
17. E. S. Le Vine and A. M. Padilla, *Crossing Cultures in Therapy: Pluralistic Counseling for the Hispanic*, Monterey, Calif., Brooks/Cole, 1980.

18. A. Aramoní, "Machismo," *Psychology Today,* vol. 5, no. 8, 1982, pp. 69–72.

19. O. M. Espín, "The 'Quinceañeras': A Latin American Expression of Women's Roles," unpublished paper presented at the national meeting of the Latin American Studies Association, Atlanta, 1975.

20. R. E. Cromwell and R. A. Ruiz, "The Myth of 'Macho' Dominance in Decision Making within Mexican and Chicano Families," *Hispanic Journal of Behavioral Sciences,* vol. 1, no. 4, 1979, p. 371.

21. H. Hidalgo and E. Hidalgo-Christensen, "The Puerto Rican Cultural Response to Female Homosexuality," in E. Acosta-Belén (ed.), *The Puerto Rican Woman,* New York, Praeger, 1979, p. 118.

READING 6

Sexuality Research in the United States

Diane di Mauro

A. THE HISTORY OF SEXUALITY RESEARCH IN THE UNITED STATES

1) Research Origins

It can be said that modern behavioral research in sexuality in the United States began 40 years ago with the work of Alfred Kinsey, to whom the professional title of "sex researcher" was first given. Since then, sexuality research has been conducted in numerous fields and disciplines, and its history is entwined with many political, social, and educational movements. A brief overview of its varied origins follows, highlighting some of the significant historical markers. As will be shown, the contributions of important sexuality researchers provided legitimacy to the scientific study of sexuality, but did not establish a tradition of systematic and cumulative research in this country.

Early research in sexuality in the United States began in 1892 and was conducted in the form of the sex survey.[1] These early studies were conducted by social scientists and physicians concerned with implementing a "social-minded" preventive health agenda. Especially during the years 1892 to 1930, the explicit rationale behind such surveys was to support sexuality education and to "control" sexuality, particularly masturbation and venereal disease. Also during this period, there emerged what soon became a long tradition of small scale, qualitative research in the form of anthropological cross-cultural comparisons and ethnographic studies on sexuality. While these studies concentrated primarily on the behaviors and practices of communities in other countries (Mead, 1949), they provided some insights into U.S. populations.

In 1921, the paucity of scientific research on human sexual behavior led the National Research Council to form the Committee for Research in Problems in Sex, with funding from the Bureau of Social Hygiene, the research arm of the American Social Hygiene Association, supported by the Rockefeller Foundation. Acknowledging that the need for social education and medical information in this area "was greater than current science could supply," the Committee first determined its agenda by outlining rationales for sexual research. These included: a need to address public concerns about the social and moral problems of sex behavior in the community; a need to prevent certain social conditions, crimes, and diseases which were adversely affecting the well-being of society; and the understanding

Source: *Sexuality Research in the United States,* Prometheus Books © 1997. Reprinted with permission from Prometheus Books.

that problems of human conduct depend upon biological and psychological factors that require scientific study, especially basic research, in order to be illuminated (Aberle and Corner, 1953). Between 1922 and 1947, the Committee received approximately one-and-a-half million dollars in funding to support the fields of endocrinology and biology for the "scientific study of sexuality as a biological phenomenon distinct from the limited study of human social problems of a sexual nature."[2] More than one million dollars was also provided in direct financing to five universities for sex research projects approved by the committee (Bullough, 1985).

Efforts supported during this period ranged from studies of hormones and the biology of sex to Terman and Miles' "Sex and Personality" (1936) to the pioneering social research of Alfred Kinsey and his collaborators (Kinsey et al., 1948, 1953). Of all the research supported, Kinsey's work was clearly the most extensive and also the most controversial. Notably, his was the first work supported by the Committee that focused on human sexual behavior rather than animal sexual behavior. Accumulating data from personal interviews of more than 17,000 individuals, Kinsey documented what he assumed to be a universal sex drive, his primary unit of analysis was the sexual orgasm expressed via masturbation, dreams, bestiality, and homosexual or heterosexual activities. In 1947, the Kinsey Institute was established in Bloomington, Indiana, affiliated with Indiana University. Upon Kinsey's death in 1956, Paul Gebhard, a member of the Kinsey research team, assumed the directorship.

Following the controversy that erupted after the publication of the Kinsey studies in the late 1940s and early 1950s, funding of research that utilized national samples and focused directly on sexuality decreased steadily over the next twenty years. It was not until the 1960s that research support was consistently provided again for studies that focused on sex,

youth, and premarital relations, and in the 1970s, on sex and fertility issues. In 1970, under the auspices of the Kinsey Institute for Sex Research and the National Opinion Research Center, a national sample of 3,000 adults was interviewed regarding "patterned sexual experiences, norms, and moral judgments about sexual activities." Due to legal complications, the study was not published until 1990 (Klassen et al., 1990). During this period, the work of Masters and Johnson (1966, 1970) initiated a new arena of sexuality research, one that addressed the quantifiable and physiological components of sexual behavior within a laboratory setting. This work, grounded in the body, provided the basis for the clinical treatment of identifiable sexual dysfunction.

Some important insights about sexuality were also gleaned from research supported by the federal government during the 1970s, particularly national social survey research funded by the National Institute of Child Health and Human Development (NICHD), focusing on population, adolescent, and fertility issues (Zelnik and Kantner, 1980). Later, both NICHD and the National Institute of Mental Health (NIMH) funded surveys for HIV/AIDS prevention that included sexuality components (Billy et al., 1993; Catania et al., 1992a; and Sonenstein et al., 1989a). Surveys such as the National Survey of Family Growth and the General Social Survey have and continue to be primarily focused on reproduction and fertility choices, yet do include some questions about sexuality. Methodologically strong, these datasets have identified some important trends that would yield important data through secondary analysis.

A proliferation of "popular" and less rigorous research about sexual relationships and personal satisfaction/dissatisfaction occurred during this same period in the 1970s. This research was conducted by surveys and published primarily in national magazines, such as *Cosmopolitan* and *Redbook*. Designed for the magazine market, research in this category focused primarily on women's sexuality. During this period, *The Hite Report* (Hite, 1976) was also published, representing the written responses of more than 1,800 women to open-ended questions about their sexual experiences and relationships. More contemporary forms of less methodologically sound research include national questionnaires conducted through the mail. One of the most recent is the *Janus Report*, which looked at sexual behavior in the context of marriage, divorce, and the family (Janus and Janus, 1993).

Since the advent of the HIV/AIDS pandemic in the 1980s, most of the information about sexuality has been extrapolated from research on the transmission and prevention of the HIV virus. Much of the research during the first five years of the epidemic focused on identifying the behavioral risk factors and epidemiological trends within known risk group samples, such as gay men and intravenous drug users. For the past eight to ten years, a changing epidemiology of AIDS in the United States has been charted (Miller et al., 1990). In turn, the research has expanded to include more diverse populations, such as adolescents, heterosexual and homosexual women, and heterosexual men. Increased attention has been paid to identifying diverse effective behavioral interventions in order to increase the likelihood that safer sex practices will be used. More recently, the need for greater support for social and behavioral sciences to identify and promote these prevention efforts has been widely discussed. In 1987, the National Research Council of the National Academy of Sciences made an important contribution in promoting behavioral research by establishing the Committee on AIDS Research in the Social, Behavioral and Statistical Sciences. The objective of the committee was to:

> describe what is known about the spread of HIV and AIDS in the United States; identify critical populations; describe existing research findings

in the behavioral and social sciences and in intervention research; and to identify new research to be undertaken for more effective interventions to control the spread of HIV.[3]

The National Commission on AIDS, established to promote a consistent national policy on HIV/AIDS, has more recently contributed to the promotion of behavioral research in sexuality. In 1993, the Commission published an important document entitled "Behavioral and Social Sciences and the HIV/AIDS Epidemic," which outlines the priorities of behavioral research in HIV/AIDS, discusses the application of research findings, and addresses crucial issues such as the recruitment and training of behavioral and social scientists to investigate HIV/AIDS prevention measures (National Commission on AIDS, 1993). A third important government endeavor is a recently completed review of HIV/AIDS research programs of the National Institute of Mental Health, the National Institute of Alcohol Abuse and Alcoholism, and the National Institute of Drug Abuse. This Congressionally mandated study, completed by the National Academy of Science's Institute of Medicine, calls for a greater understanding of psychological, social, and biological factors influencing risk-taking behaviors and emphasizes the importance of research designed to explore behavioral change (Auerbach et al., 1994). The National Commission on AIDS (1993) and the National Academy of Science's Institute of Medicine (1991; Auerbach et al., 1994) have each endorsed increasing federal funding for behavioral and social science research to complement biomedical efforts aimed at curbing the epidemic.

2) The Political History of Sexuality Research

A historical account of behavioral research in sexuality would not be complete without exploring its political and controversial history.

Difficulties in supporting sexuality research were recognized as early as 1921 by the National Research Council's Committee for Research in Problems of Sex:

> The founders of the committee hoped that by their concerted effort and with the prestige of the National Research Council they could raise to scientific favor in the United States, a subject which up to that time had remained in relative disrepute, and that they could stimulate and coordinate research in all the related sciences that bear upon human behavior. . . . [For those researchers] who ventured to study human sex problems were seriously hampered by traditional attitudes that placed taboos on mere discussion of the topic, to say nothing of actual investigation. . . . [T]he study of sex as a natural phenomenon was long retarded by disapproval resulting from attitudes of puritanical nature deeply rooted in tradition and religion. This reluctance was eventually broken down by the trend toward applying the scientific method to wider and wider areas in human thought and conduct.[4]

This optimistic account was written before the Committee abruptly cut off support for the Kinsey research in the face of controversy in the 1950s. The public uproar that greeted the publication of the Kinsey research—especially his findings about masturbation, extra-marital relations, and the prevalence of homosexual feelings and activities—was a signal that something "greater than a scientific event had occurred." Kinsey's research on female and male sexuality was attacked for contributing to a wave of sex hysteria, to the depravity of a whole generation, and to the spread of juvenile delinquency (Fausto-Sterling, 1992; Gardner and Wilcox, 1993; Laumann et al., 1994b; and Turner et al., 1989).[5] The controversy that followed the publication of Kinsey's data—accompanied by the refusal of many in the publishing world to review or advertise his books—frightened both researchers and funders from government and private sectors.

The Rockefeller Foundation, Kinsey's primary funder, was warned by the House Committee to Investigate Tax-Exempt Foundations that its non-profit 401C status was being "re-evaluated."[6] As a result of such controversy and the subsequent severance of support, Kinsey's work was not replicated, and in turn, only limited scientific refinement, extension, or correction of his original findings followed.

Forty years later, political opposition effectively abolished two cutting-edge and methodologically sophisticated behavioral studies on sexuality that would have provided the first comprehensive data of sexual behavior in this country since Kinsey's. One of the studies was the American Teenage Study (ATS), which was to be conducted by researchers at the Carolina Population Center at the University of North Carolina. The study would have been longitudinal, focusing on the range of teenage sexual behaviors and the relationship between such behaviors and education, religion, family and peer-group interactions. The second study, known as the Survey of Health and AIDS Risk Prevalence (SHARP), was to be conducted by a research team at the University of Chicago. Designated as a national survey of adults, the SHARP study utilized a social network framework that viewed sexuality as a social transaction between individuals, in order to generate data on sexual practices, contraception, fertility, and disease prevention. Following a successful proposal and peer review process by the National Institute of Child Health and Human Development (NICHD) and, in the case of the ATS, first year funding, both studies were abruptly canceled due to conservative Congressional pressure directed at the Office of Management and Budget (OMB), the House Appropriations Committee, and the then-Secretary of Health and Human Services, Louis Sullivan. The common theme of opposition to both studies was the view that they were "the purview of liberal researchers and would encourage, as an inevitable by-product of sexuality research, a sexually permissive environment."[7]

On other grounds, the opposition to each study was quite distinct. In the case of the SHARP study, critics first and foremost opposed federal funding of sexuality research. Further, they claimed that the content of the research invaded individual privacy and the sanctity of adult sexual relations. Opponents, well organized and effectively mobilized at the grassroots level, launched a major media campaign accusing researchers of promoting an "anti-family, sexually decadent, gay lifestyle" and distributed misrepresentations about the research instruments and design. In the face of these accusations, the research team was forbidden by the Department of Health and Human Services to respond or participate in the public debate over the survey. This prohibition effectively "undermined whatever Congressional and public support had been available and left all public initiatives in the hands of those opposed to the survey. The result was hesitant support in Congress and the public at large of the study's importance in addressing urgent public health issues."[8]

In the case of the adolescent study, opponents claimed that the very act of asking adolescents questions about sexuality would be harmful in that it would breach family privacy and promote sexual activity among this population. In fact, the study was designed so that:

> children's participation would have occurred only with informed parental consent. Children would be asked questions referring to explicit sexual acts only if answers to prior questions indicated that they were sexually experienced. . . . [In any event] there is no evidence that participation in sexual research encourages subsequent sexual behavior.[9]

Moreover, according to longitudinal studies in which children are interviewed once or even many times, no consistent relationship exists between the number of times a child is interviewed about sex and the child's subsequent sexual behavior (Halpern et al., 1992.)[10]

In the end, a significant effort was made to legislate the opposition to these and other behavioral research projects on sexuality. In 1993, when the National Institutes of Health (NIH) funds were re-authorized in Congress, an amendment was introduced to the appropriations bill mandating that all money earmarked for sexuality surveys be removed from the budget and added to the portion of the Adolescent Family Life Act that encouraged premarital celibacy. "The amendment passed in the Senate, failed in the House, and a House-Senate Conference committee later dropped it from the final bill."[11] However, the 1993 bill permanently banned Congressional money for the two discontinued studies, although it did allow the NIH to fund behavioral research on sexuality as long as it is directly linked to disease prevention.

With regard to the SHARP study, its researchers were subsequently able to obtain sufficient support from a group of foundations for a down-scaled version of the project, entitled, "The National Health and Social Life Survey" (NHSLS). The new study presented data from a national sample of 3,432 individuals, ranging in age from 18–59 years, who completed both in-person interviews and self-administered questionnaires (Laumann et al., 1994a). It provided a "social perspective" analysis of a range of sexual activities over the life course, including: sexual partnerships and practices, partner choice, the quality and character of sexuality relationships, sexual preferences, attitudes, knowledge, and auto-eroticism.

With regard to research on adolescents, a large endeavor will be conducted by researchers at the University of North Carolina, in accordance with the provision that any supported research be linked to disease prevention. This broad, national study, entitled, "ADD Health: A National Longitudinal Study of Adolescent Health" has been funded by the National Institute of Child Health and Human Development in the amount of $20 million over a five-year period. While it does include topics on adolescent sexuality, questions in this new study will focus primarily on the range of adolescent risk behaviors and those referring directly to sexual behaviors are limited both in quantity and scope.

3) The Impact of Controversy

The protracted battle of the two "sex surveys" was conducted in the national press, in Congress, and in the government agencies that fund behavioral research. Its most obvious impact was the subsequent reluctance on the part of the federal government to fund large-scale research on sexuality, although support was "quietly" provided for survey research on the subjects of HIV/AIDS, fertility and adolescents, and risk behavior studies which included sexuality components. Additionally, "the cancellation of these studies called into question previously assumed guarantees regarding federal support for this research. . . . that the government will not seek to determine the outcome of public policy discussions by channeling the course of scientific research, and decisions about research funding will not be made on a political basis.[12] Indeed, if funding decisions are made on political rather than scientific grounds, "the quality of science will be degraded, and by defining certain topics as unacceptable for scientific research, the government can keep those topics un-researched and at the margin of public discussion.[13]

On a larger scale, controversies surrounding research on sexuality have historically had significant and chilling effects. The primary outcome of such controversy has been the inconsistent and modest financial support for this work on the part of both the government and the private sector, as well as a hesitancy to publicly promote sexuality research. A number of researchers, however, have been able to ob-

tain funding by incorporating minor sexuality components into larger research projects, especially when the work focuses on HIV/AIDS or adolescent health and is linked to intervention planning, targeted risk behaviors, or a public health context. Having a domino-like effect, this strong research emphasis on risk behavior has had two results. First, little information currently exists about the broad range of sexual behaviors in the general population, and second, most research has used individuals or groups labeled as deviant, victimized, dysfunctional, abnormal, or problematic as study subjects. Subsequently, baseline data is often not available for comparison purposes, or to interpret the results, formulate effective intervention projects, and design future studies.

The impact of controversy within the disciplines that conduct research on sexuality is significant as well. It is often assumed that it is not professionally legitimate to promote or conduct sexuality research for the sole or primary purpose of contributing to existing *knowledge* about human sexual behaviors in the social science disciplines. Consequently, researchers either remain isolated within their respective disciplines, or, if they choose to join the ranks of the sexologists and devote their work to sexuality research, are often seen— and often see themselves—as refugees from the social sciences. Many researchers characterize this state of affairs as a continual search for a professional identity because their work is often invisible, only coming to public attention during periods of controversy. And in the face of opposition, both researchers and their research institutes have been required to divert scarce resources to defend their work. A case in point is the significant legal cost incurred by the Rand Corporation to confront the opposition to its evaluation research of condom availability programs in Santa Monica schools.

Moreover, there exists no coordinating mechanism to provide financial, logistical, or political support to professionals conducting sexuality research. Thus, as a cohesive field of inquiry and investigation, behavioral research in sexuality is largely underdeveloped and under-supported. For future generations of researchers, this situation creates enormous disincentives for entering the field. The fact that sexuality research "is relevant to a variety of disciplines but prominent in none"[14] is evidenced by the lack of specialized training, peer support, and professional recognition for those conducting research on sexual behavior (Abramson, 1990).

It is helpful to address the "origin" of controversy in order to more adequately understand why it has had such a significant impact. Beliefs about and depiction of sexuality in general have historically been paradoxical within American culture. On the one hand, there occurs a saturation and sensationalism of sexual images and words in the public media—a fascination with any sexual subject—and on the other, sexuality remains an extremely private and uniquely complex sphere of human behavior, about which it is difficult to talk openly and comfortably. For some individuals then, research on sexuality may be objectionable for some of the same reasons that sexual behavior is among the most difficult subjects on which to collect reliable data. Reflective of traditional attitudes, opposition to research in this area can represent very deeply felt emotional fears and doubts about the role and significance of sexuality in personal and public life. This analysis perhaps more appropriately characterizes a minor component of the American public and more aptly describes one oppositional faction to Kinsey's work forty years ago, which tapped into widespread ambivalence about sexuality. However, current opposition to sexuality research—and opposition to the two studies in particular—represented an effective mobilization effort by a highly organized minority with a conservative social and political agenda. Utilizing its opposition to

sexuality research and sexuality education as convenient entry points to establish a broader political agenda, this effort made significant use of fear-provoking arguments about sexuality topics, arguments that are not supported by facts or data. Recognizing such a distinction demonstrates the need for well-informed and constructive public/policy discussions about sexuality and the importance of sexuality research.

Given this history of controversy and the current state of social and behavioral research in sexuality, it seems an opportune time to consider how a new research focus on this issue can be initiated. A research assessment should be conducted concerning controversy and opposition to sexuality research with an emphasis on the impact of each. The question of sexuality research and its influence on subjects and the communities studied is an area in need of further investigation. Such data can build a stronger informational base that will be useful in debates about sexuality, as they emerge.

The historical overview of sexuality research and controversy demonstrates that controversy is not unique to any issue that has social and political significance. In this regard, sexuality research is no different. In fact, even in the face of opposition, research in sexuality continued to be conducted and supported, albeit to a lesser degree, and individuals continue to be willing to participate as research subjects. It is only because controversy has in the past been "risked" that sexuality research continues to be a viable and critical area of behavioral research.

B. THE CURRENT STATUS OF SEXUALITY RESEARCH

1) Spheres of Research

Crossing diverse fields, sexuality research in the social sciences requires a multifaceted definition and can include:

- behavioral studies identifying the range of sexual behaviors within different populations;
- cultural and ethnographic studies on the context in which sexual behaviors occur and on the broader social and cultural issues that influence them;
- developmental studies on the evolution of sexual behaviors and practices, and their relationship to sexual values, attitudes, and beliefs within and across specific sample populations;
- clinical studies on the physiology of sexual response and its relationship to sexual behavior and practices;
- reproductive health studies on how reproductive behaviors and decisions impact on sexual behaviors and practices and vice-versa;
- psychological studies on the cognitive and affective processes that affect sexual behaviors and practices, and motivate and effect behavioral change; and
- intervention research on strategies to "motivate individuals to reduce their risks, teach the skills for effective prevention . . . and modify the social and cultural context in order to reduce risk-taking on a societal level."[15] In this report, the phrase "social and behavioral research on sexuality" refers to any and all of these areas.

Sexuality research today represents the continuation of a long tradition of primarily individual scholarship on the topic. Occurring most often within a clinical or academic setting, what is typically identified as sexuality research is that which focuses on sexual physiology, anatomy, and therapeutic issues, rather than research that addresses the social, cultural, or behavioral topics of sexuality. Social and behavioral research on sexuality is often embedded within larger research questions in the range of social science disciplines, including sociology, psychology, anthropology, and

history. Sexuality topics are also being addressed by researchers in education, biology, medicine, and public health, again integrated within larger issues researched by each discipline. Very little of this research has sexuality as its primary focus, and that which does is mostly limited to small population samples with a very narrow focus on specific behaviors, within the framework of the discipline.

Regarding the specific approach to sexuality research by different disciplines, they can be characterized as follows. Researchers in psychology have been concerned with the relationship between mental processes and sexual behavior and with identifying and analyzing the developmental, motivational, affective, and psycho-physiological aspects of sexuality. In sociology, research on sexuality is placed within the context of society and its institutions, social relations, and social networks. Of particular importance is how patterns of behavior are influenced by normative and societal structures. Anthropologists have focused on sexual behavior within cultural contexts and on sexuality as reflected in the values, beliefs, social relations, rituals, and symbolism of cultural groups and their individual members. Of particular importance in history is the analysis of sexuality as influenced by the historical events and normative dictates of specific time periods, including the significance of the "zeitgeist" on sexual behavior.

In the population field, the relationship and impact of sexual practices has only recently been addressed in relation to reproductive issues, events, and processes such as fertility, birth, abortion, and contraceptive use and choice. This increased awareness was represented at The United Nations International Conference on Population and Development (ICPD) held in Cairo in November 1994. The Conference issued a Programme of Action for population programs of the United Nations and individual countries for the next twenty years. This "blueprint" explicitly outlined the role of sexuality, sexual health, and gender issues in reproductive health and development and promoted their consideration in government programs, research, and policies.

Finally, an important sphere of sexuality research with a long history both in the U.S. and in Europe is known as "sexology," or the interdisciplinary science of sex. Originating from a European tradition that focused on the philosophical and clinical issues of sexuality (as represented by the work of Havelock Ellis [1906], Mangus Hirschfield [1941], R. Krafft-Ebing [1886], Wilhelm Stekel [1926] and others), sexology has more recently advocated an integrated view that focuses on the "physiological, psychological, medical, sociological, anthropological, historical, legal, religious, literary, and artistic aspects of sexuality."[16] However, because the sexuality research fields are so fragmented, few efforts exist to bridge the work of individual researchers within or between different social science disciplines and outward to researchers in sexology.

2) Research Institutes and Organizations

While sexuality research has largely been conducted by professionals working within academic or medical arenas, several locales do exist that provide a more institutionalized commitment to the field. In the U.S. there are two research centers whose primary focus has historically been research in sexuality: the Kinsey Institute and the Masters and Johnson Institute. During the 60s and 70s the work of the Kinsey Institute for Research in Sex, Gender, and Reproduction focused on original, small scale research on: sex offenders (Gebhard et al., 1965); homosexuality and the gay community (Bell and Weinberg, 1978; Gagnon and Simon, 1967); and a national survey of college students (Simon et al., 1972). Since that time activities of the Institute have centered on reorganizing the extensive archive collection, converting the original Kinsey database to computer tape for public access, and sponsoring a symposia series of scholars, from which a number of important publications have resulted on the topics of adolescence and puberty, sexual orientation, and AIDS and sexuality. More recent research has included a national survey of sexuality knowledge conducted in 1989 by The Kinsey Institute and the Roper Organization (Reinisch and Beasley, 1990). In the past two years, the Kinsey Institute has undergone significant reorganization stemming from an internal controversy about its direction and focus; curtailed funding from Indiana University has seriously hampered its research productivity. Currently, it has undertaken the process of an international search for a new director.

The Masters and Johnson Clinic had traditionally pursued a clinical research focus on the physiology of sexual response and on the resolution of sexual dysfunction. Following major publications on these topics (1966, 1970), Drs. Masters and Johnson focused their clinical research on the sexual behavior patterns of homosexual and heterosexual samples (Masters and Johnson, 1979), and on refining therapeutic techniques for treating sexual dysfunction. [. . .]

Other institutes which conduct behavioral research in sexuality on specific areas of inquiry are the Alan Guttmacher Institute, which focuses on reproductive health, and the Center for AIDS Prevention Studies (CAPS) and the HIV Center for Clinical and Behavioral Studies, both of which focus on HIV/AIDS research. A number of research centers in social and behavioral studies approach sexuality from a broader perspective and also focus on the methodological issues relevant to sexuality research. These include the Ogburn-Stauffer Center and National Opinion Research Center at the University of Chicago and the Rand Corporation.

Some universities host a combination of efforts relating to sexuality, including post-doctoral fellowships in advanced clinical/

research training and undergraduate and graduate programs in sexuality in the social sciences. Some research wings of medical schools conduct clinical and behavioral sexuality studies in the areas of HIV/AIDS, adolescent sexuality, and urology/sexual dysfunction. Also, private pharmaceutical companies host experimental departments that conduct large-scale drug and product trials, primarily in the area of male sexual dysfunction. Finally, generic public opinion research centers, such as Louis Harris Associates and Roper Starch Worldwide, conduct surveys in affiliation with larger organizations, such as Planned Parenthood, the American Association of University Women, and the Sexuality Information and Education Council of the United States. This research is typically conducted by phone and has included: public attitudes about sex education, family planning, and abortion in the United States (Planned Parenthood, 1985); public attitudes toward teenage pregnancy, sex education and birth control (Planned Parenthood, 1988); American teens' attitudes about sex, myths, TV, and birth control (Planned Parenthood, 1986); and adolescents' personal comfort with sexual activity (SIECUS, 1994).

Professional meetings of social science discipline organizations provide important opportunities for information exchange and networking. At these meetings—such as the annual conferences held by the American Psychological Association, the American Sociological Association, or the American Anthropological Association—research presentations on sexuality are typically integrated into the program agendas on other related topics. Occasionally, a discipline will highlight sexuality topics and issues at an annual meeting, as did the American Psychological Association in 1993 with a presidential mini-conference on "Sex, Love, and Psychology."

There are a limited number of associations whose mandates reflect a specific research interest in sexuality. Most prominent are the International Academy of Sex Research (IASR) and the Society for the Scientific Study of Sex (SSSS). Annual meeting agendas range from scholarly presentations on such diverse topics as gender role socialization, HIV/AIDS prevention, pharmacological influences in sexual behavior, and the nature and evolution of sex and love to more sociopolitical critiques and debates on the origins of sexual orientation, the validity of repressed memory in childhood sexual abuse, and the legitimacy of observational fieldwork pertaining to the sexual behaviors of those observed. The disciplinary diversity of the members of these organizations accurately reflects the varied traditions and approaches represented in the fields of sexuality research.

NOTES

1. See Ericksen, Forthcoming.
2. See Aberle and Corner, 1953. This publication provides a fascinating description of the work of this committee.
3. Turner et al., 1989, p. vi.
4. Aberle and Corner, 1953, p. 13.
5. Personal communications with researcher John Gagnon, 1994, have also served as an important source for the information to this discussion.
6. Fausto-Sterling, 1992, p. 29. Shortly thereafter, the foundation initiated and funded the Population Council to conduct research on contraception as the focus of its support in this area (Bullough, 1985, p. 123).
7. This characterization was made of the political opposition to these surveys at a SRAP brainstorming session on controversy by participants who were referring to the Congressional hearings about the surveys.
8. Laumann et al., 1994b, p. 35.
9. Gardner and Wilcox, 1993, p. 973.
10. Controversy regarding the use of youth samples in sexuality surveys were taking place on the local level as well. In the Santa Monica, CA school system, opponents waged a similar argument against the Rand Corporation's 1992 evaluative study of condom availability programs.

11. Fausto-Sterling, 1992, p. 30.
12. Gardner and Wilcox, 1993, p. 972.
13. Gardner and Wilcox, 1993, p. 978.
14. Paul Abramson 1990, p. 161.
15. National Commission on AIDS, 1993, p. 16–17.
16. Francoeur, et al., 1991, p. 588. Moreover, two important works that provide a critique of sexuality research as conceptualized by the anthropological discipline and by the sexology field include: Vance, 1991 and Irvine, 1990a.

REFERENCES

Aberle, S. D., & Corner, G. (1953). *Twenty-Five Years of Sex Research: History of the National Research Council Committee for Research in Problems of Sex, 1922–1947.* Philadelphia: W.B. Saunders Co.

Abramson, P. (1990). Sexual science: Emerging discipline or oxymoron? *The Journal of Sex Research, 27,* 147–165.

Auerbach, J. D., Wypijewska, C., & Brodie, H. K. H. (1994). *AIDS and Behavior: An Integrated Approach.* Washington: National Academy Press.

Bell, A. P., & Weinberg, M. S. (1978). *Homosexualities: A Study of Diversity Among Men and Women.* An Official Publication of The Institute for Sex Research. New York: Simon and Schuster.

Billy, J. O., Tanfer, K., Grady, W. R., & Klepinger, D. H. (1993, March/April). The sexual behavior of men in the United States. *Family Planning Perspectives,* 52–86.

Bullough, V. L. (1985, May). The Rockefellers and sex research. *The Journal of Sex Research,* 113–125.

Catania, J. A., Coates, T. J., Stall, R., Turner, H., Peterson, J., Hearst, N., et al. (1992, 13 November). Prevalence of AIDS-related risk factors and condom use in the United States. *Science,* 1101–1106.

Ericksen, J. (forthcoming). *Kiss and Tell: The Revelations of Sexual Behavior Surveys,* Cambridge: Harvard University Press.

Fausto-Sterling, A. (1992, June). Why do we know so little about human sex? *Discover,* 28–30.

Francoeur, R., Perper, T., & Scherzer, N. (1991). *A Descriptive Dictionary and Atlas of Sexology,* New York: Greenwood Press.

Gagnon, J., & Simon, W. (1967). *Sexual Deviance.* New York: Harper & Row.

Gardner, W., & Wilcox, B. L. (1993, September). Political intervention in scientific peer review: Research on adolescent sexual behavior. *American Psychologist,* 972–983.

Gebhard, P., Gagnon, J., Pomeroy, W., & Christensen, C. (1965). *Sex Offenders: An Analysis of Types.* New York: Harper and Row.

Halpern, C., Udry, J., & Suchindran, C. (1992). *Effects of Repeated Questionnaire Administration in Longitudinal Studies of Adolescent Males' Sexual Behavior.* Unpublished manuscript. University of North Carolina.

Hirschfield, M. (1940). *Sexual Pathology,* New York: Emerson Books.

Hite, S. (1976). *The Hite Report: A Nationwide Study of Female Sexuality,* New York: Macmillan.

Irvine, J. M. (1990a). *Disorders of Desire: Sex and Gender in Modern American Sexology,* Philadelphia: Temple University Press.

Janus, S. S., & Janus, C. L. (1993). *The Janus Report on Sexual Behavior,* New York: John Wiley & Sons, Inc.

Kinsey, A., Pomeroy, W., & Martin, C. (1948). *Sexual Behavior in the Human Male,* Philadelphia: WB Saunders Co.

Kinsey, A., Pomeroy, W., & Martin, C. (1953). *Sexual Behavior in the Human Female,* Philadelphia: WB Saunders Co.

Klassen, A. D., Williams, C. J., & Levitt, E. E. (1990). *Sex and Morality in the U.S. An Empirical Enquiry Under the Auspices of the Kinsey Institute,* Middletown: Wesleyan University Press.

Kraft-Ebing, R. (1886). *Psychopathia Sexualis,* New York: Medical Art Agency.

Laumann, E. O., Gagnon, J. H., Michael, R. T., & Michaels, S. (1994a). *The Social Organization of Sexuality,* Chicago: University of Chicago Press.

Laumann, E. O., Michael, R. T., & Gagnon, J. H. (1994b, January/February). A political history of the national sex survey of adults. *Family Planning Perspectives,* 34–38.

Masters, W. H., & Johnson V. E. (1966). *Human Sexual Response,* Boston: Little, Brown.

Masters, W. H., & Johnson V. E. (1970). *Human Sexual Inadequacy,* Boston: Little, Brown.

Masters, W. H., & Johnson V. E. (1979). *Homosexuality in Perspective,* Boston: Little, Brown.

Mead, M. (1949). *Male and Female: A Study of the Sexes in a Changing World,* New York: Morrow.

Miller, H. G., Turner, C. F., & Moses, L. E. (1990). *AIDS: The Second Decade,* Washington, D.C.: National Academy Press.

National Commission on AIDS. (1993). *Behavioral and Social Sciences and the HIV/AIDS Epidemic,* Washington, D.C.: National Commission on AIDS.

Planned Parenthood. (1985, August-September). *Public Attitudes about Sex Education, Family Planning, and Abortion in the United States,* Conducted by Louis Harris and Associates, [Study No. 854005]. New York: Planned Parenthood Federation of America, Inc.

Planned Parenthood. (1986, September-October). *American Teens Speak: Sex, Myths, TV, and Birth Control,* Conducted by Louis Harris and Associates, [Project No. 864012]. New York: Planned Parenthood Federation of America, Inc.

Planned Parenthood. (1988, May). *Public Attitudes toward Teenage Pregnancy, Sex Education and Birth Control,* Conducted by Louis Harris and Associates, [Study No. 884004]. New York: Planned Parenthood Federation of America, Inc.

Reinisch, J. M., & Beasley, R. (1990). *The Kinsey Institute New Report on Sex.* New York: St. Martin's Press.

SIECUS. (1994). *National telephone survey of high school students (Grades 9–12) on the topics of sexual attitudes and sexual behavior,* Conducted by Roper Starch Worldwide Inc. New York: Sexuality Information and Education Council of the U.S.

Simon, W., Gagnon, J., & Berger, A. (1972). Beyond fantasy and anxiety: The coital experiences of college youth. *Journal of Youth and Adolescence, 1*(3), 203–222.

Sonenstein, F. L., Pleck, J. H., & Ku, L. C. (1989a, July/August). Sexual activity, condom use and AIDS awareness among adolescent males. *Family Planning Perspectives,* 152–158.

Stekel, W. (1926). *Frigidity in Woman: Vols. I and II,* New York: Grove Press.

Terman, L., & Miles, C. (1936). *Sex and Personality: Studies in Masculinity and Femininity.* New York: McGraw-Hill.

Turner, C. F., Miller, H. G., & Moses, L. E. (1989). *AIDS: Sexual Behavior and Intravenous Drug Use.* Washington: National Academy Press.

Vance, C. S. (1991). Anthropology rediscovers sexuality: A theoretical comment. *Social Science and Medicine, 38*(8), 875–884.

Zelnik, M., & Kantner, J. (1980). Sexual activity, contraceptive use and pregnancy among metropolitan teenagers: 1971–1979. *Family Planning Perspectives, 12*(5), 230–238.

PART TWO

BECOMING SEXUAL: HOW WE LEARN ABOUT SEX (OR DON'T)

For many people, sexual knowledge and awareness come as bits and pieces of a complicated puzzle we are supposed to assemble for ourselves, even as our bodies go through various stages of sexual awakening. We "become sexual" throughout life—it doesn't start and stop with puberty. Sexual changes come and go throughout childhood and adulthood. The newborn infant feels the pleasant sensations of nursing. A little girl senses moistness in her vulva. A preteen boy wakes up to find semen on his sheets. A young woman has her first orgasm. The adult, who once thought of herself as heterosexual, discovers that she is sexually attracted to a woman. A man in his 60s notices that his erections are not as firm or easily attained as they were; he and his wife adapt what they do sexually so their mutual enjoyment of sex continues. As our bodies, emotions, and knowledge change, aspects of our sexuality undergo changes, in part as a result of societal influences.

How we become sexual has both a biological and societal component. What we know and how we think about our sexual feelings and experiences affects how we interpret or respond to them. For instance, boys have erections throughout their childhoods, whether they "feel sexual" or not. Little girls may like touching their vulva, even before they "know" they have a clitoris. One three-year-old told her mother, "Mommy, my bottom has a button!"

Social constructionist theory predicts that the social response children receive as they have these experiences will determine the meaning they give to it.

Let's pursue the example of children a bit further. Many children of both sexes masturbate once they discover the sweet sensation that can come from touching their genitals. In some cultures, and in some families, such behavior is frowned upon, even punished. In others it is treated as a normal part of childhood. If children touching themselves are left alone, or just counseled to do it in private, their experience of their sexuality will be different from children who are reprimanded. The social context influences the meaning the child attaches to the experience of arousal, the language the child associates with the experience, and feelings the child has about his or her sexual organs, and about sex itself. These, and other responses to sexual feelings and behaviors, will influence how the child perceives and experiences sexuality as a teen and later, as an adult. Their perception of their personal experience will be socially constructed.

Although we are sexual from the time we are born until we die, most of us are only aware of "becoming sexual" at the time we enter puberty. Many parents avoid talking with children about sex until they feel the child is about to come of age. For some parents, however, this time never comes, and for many, the parents themselves are not well informed or comfortable with the topic. Parents who don't take the time to read about sexuality from reliable sources and to think critically about the topic will pass on the fears, misinformation, and biases with which they were raised. By the time they reach puberty, children have already received thousands of often confusing and contradictory messages about sexuality from a combination of parents, peers, religion, and the media, though seldom based on informed, open discussion that can help to dispel fears and inaccuracies.

Schools have been at the center of many of the controversies around sexuality, resulting in a "no-talk" rule around some aspects of sex, such as masturbation and homosexuality. In 1994 Surgeon General Joycelyn Elders, the chief medical officer for the United States, lost her job because, in response to a question about AIDS prevention, she said school-based sexuality education programs should affirm that masturbation is normal and won't hurt you, a position taken by mainstream medical and psychological associations. The strength of such responses to controversy leads principals and teachers to take the path of least resistance, to teach only what is not likely to arouse parental or religious ire.

School sex education programs, therefore, tend to focus on the "plumbing, problems, and percentages" of sex, such as anatomy of reproduction (yet seldom are girls or boys told about the clitoris); problems like diseases, teenage pregnancy, and sexual molestation; and numbers, such as how many people are gay or lesbian or at what age people first have sexual intercourse. Sexuality deserves a much broader discourse. For the past decade, the influence of the religious right has led to restrictions on comprehensive sexuality education. This varies by local school board and state, but recent federal legislation restricts funding to "abstinence-only" sex education programs that do not include information about birth control methods.

Yet what is abstinence? For many teens a decision not to have intercourse means they do lots of petting and, for many, have oral sex. Yet the couple, especially the female, maintains a standard of "virginity." Is cunnilingus or fellatio sex? Is virginity, medically interpreted in the female as an unbroken hymen, evidence of "purity?" What is male virginity? Is a female without virginity impure? Is a male? Is a woman who has sex with another woman still a virgin? Whose standards get applied?

Let's get back to the earlier example of the adult woman who thought she was heterosexual, then finds herself attracted to another woman. The way she thinks, feels, or acts on this attraction will be influenced by societal messages and knowledge she has about sexuality, gender, and relationships, both from her earlier life experience and her current situation. If she was raised in a family and community that was highly accepting of the notion that sexual orientation is fluid and can change over time, then her response is likely to be different from someone raised in an environment where same-sex attractions were demonized.

Adrienne Rich (1980) in her classic article on compulsory heterosexuality and lesbian existence, challenges the assumption that women are innately sexually oriented toward men. Rich argues that heterosexuality is a political institution based on men's need to assure sexual access to women. In this analysis the ideology of heterosexual romance, as transmitted in fairy tales, television, proms, and weddings, is a way to indoctrinate females into believing in the socially constructed emotion of "love."

That lesbians, who have an emotional and sensual inclination toward women, are seen as deviant and emotionally deprived is a result of societal attitudes and beliefs. The questions Adrienne Rich raises about the inequality of social conceptions of male and female sexuality, and as she says, the courage it takes to grasp the political and economic implications, are important ones to consider as we explore articles in this section on "becoming sexual."

The readings begin with Laurel Black's "The Kotex Diaries," about her story of coming of age and her confusion surrounding women's menstruation. While she grew up in an earlier time, there are still ways in which the fact that women bleed each and every month is kept very much a secret. If talked about it all, it is only in euphemisms like "having one's period" or needing to buy "sanitary products," as if other items we buy are not sanitary and menstrual blood is unclean. What are the effects on girls and women, and boys and men, that women "being on the rag" is so stigmatized? Are there other ways that such a natural function could be handled that would be healthier and happier? Is there a connection between the secrecy and perception of women's menstrual cycles and how women come to think about their bodies, their sexuality? In what way does male socialization around sexuality lead to men not wanting to know about women's experiences? Could men benefit from knowing more?

Fred Rothman, Avery Grauer, and David J. Rubin examine the often confusing nature of childhood sexuality in their article, "Becoming Sexual: Differences between Child and Adult Sexuality." Children's normal sexual behaviors range over a broad spectrum from curiosity and play, to sensuality and excitement. However, there are ways that childhood and adult sexuality differ. As you read this article, reflect on the ways that culture plays a role in determining "appropriate" sexual expression for children and ways that this may vary by culture.

How women come to be interested in men is the subject of research by Sophia Demasi, who explored women's recollections of heterosexual dating. Her article, "I Just Want to Be Normal: Initiation into Heterosexual Dating," turns the question often asked of lesbians and gay men—How did you turn out gay?—on its head by interrogating initiation into heterosexuality. She found that women's motivation toward dating was driven more by a desire to be normal, as defined by peers and community, than by any specific sexual desire for men.

In "Where'd You Learn That?" Ron Stodghill suggests that although teens have been relatively sexually active before marriage over past generations, there are some differences now. These changes are in part a result of the access to sexual information that is available on television, the Internet, and from peers. As Stodghill reports, the average age for intercourse is now 17 for girls and 16 for boys, down only one year from 1970, yet more teens engage in fellatio and cunnilingus. And the double standard persists. Stodghill quotes a young woman who said, "If you turn him down, you're a bitch. If you do it, you're a ho." It's as if girls are supposed to *appear* sexual but not actually *be* sexual. What are the implications for "becoming sexual" of the conflicting messages between those of the "official" adult world—church, school, and parents—and the kind of sex broadcast on radio and television and encouraged by peers?

Susannah Indigo continues this theme as she discusses the experience of teenage girls who give "blow jobs" even though they find it boring and boys who reciprocate the next night by "going down" on their girlfriends. Is this the new reality of teenage sex? Is the nature of heterosexual relations changing, leaving old notions of virginity and abstinence out of date? Were previous generations really so different, or were such behaviors simply not discussed? Should Americans accept teenage sexual relations, providing open and accessible sexual health services, as an article in Part Eight shows is the case in some European countries?

A research study by Harilyn Rousso, "Daughters with Disabilities," complicates the picture of teenage girls' movement into heterosexuality by presenting the experience of young women with disabilities. Nondisabled teens often have enough independence to be sexual without parents knowing. It is more difficult for the disabled teen whose access to social activities with peers, including sexual encounters, is strongly circumscribed by parents who need to make arrangements for them. Besides limiting opportunities for sex, such restrictions affect the likelihood for "social success" for disabled teens, since having a boyfriend remains a signal of successful initiation into the heterosexual feminine role. Consider the implications for sexual self-image, especially given media and popular images of the attractive female. If you have a disability, how does this experience affect your sexuality? If you are nondisabled, what assumptions do you make, consciously or unconsciously, about the sexuality of people who are disabled?

In her article "Do Women Choose Their Sexual Identity?" Carla Golden reports that for some women, sexual identity feels like a choice or a preference. This is less common in men, who often report that being straight or gay is just "who they are"—that it is biologically determined. This difference may be explained to some extent by the degree of rigid socialization males receive to be heterosexual—a topic discussed later in Part Five. In her interviews with college-age and adult women, Golden found that there is no simple relation between sexual desire, experience, orientation, and identity. Some women described themselves as deciding to become sexually attracted to and involved with other women, for reasons including desire for emotional closeness, and in the process overcoming years of heterosexual socialization. What are the implications of seeing sexuality as fluid, flexible, and open to intentional decision? Does this fit with established norms and common beliefs about sexuality?

Eric Leadbetter, in his story of being "honestly gay," presents a different picture. For him at least, if not for his friend Eppy, his first passionate kisses with a man were the beginning of his celebration of his sexual identity. For Eppy, at least at that time, it was "really good practice for what we do with girls." Why might Eric and Eppy's experience of that night be different?

Rachel-Storm Heasley's experience of coming out was difficult for her, even though she was in a liberal high school where her teacher was out as being lesbian and Rachel's parents were accepting and supportive. What would make coming out so difficult even when there is so much support? Notice how coming to terms with being gay or lesbian requires a person to make a public statement about their sexuality in a way most heterosexual young people can avoid. At the same time, the coming out process itself isn't always going to result in acceptance, as Rachel learned when she went to college. While she might have been comfortable with her own sexuality, she found her roommates to be less than comfortable. What would prevent students attending college from being aware of the diversity of sexual orientations?

Melinda S. Miceli, in "GLB Students: The Impact of School on Sexual Identity, Development," challenges the idea that sexual identity labels are needed or even a good thing. Rather, she sees labels as scientifically and socially produced meanings that function as social controls of individual behaviors and as structured enforcement of the normative dominance of heterosexuality.

Based on observations of a community support group for gay, lesbian, and bisexual teens, she found that teens did not see their acceptance of homosexuality as a critical issue in their being comfortable with themselves, but rather, how other individuals and institutions responded to them. Their decisions about whether to reveal same-sex attractions were based on an assessment of the costs and benefits, punishments and rewards, and danger and safety in their environment.

Looking at all the articles in this section, we can see implications for the importance of adult acceptance and recognition of the realities of childhood and teenage sexuality. Comparing just the Miceli article with the Rousso article on disability, what are the similarities, in terms of effects of social norms and prejudices? Are the teens in the Stodghill and Indigo articles victims of related limitations of societal constructions of teen sexuality? While the articles in this section focus on our early years of "becoming sexual," sexual norms persist, for example, affecting even whether women and men in nursing homes can have access to sexual encounters with each other. Imagine the teens in the Indigo article as old people, if you wonder whether it matters. As you read more articles in this book, consider how societal denial and discomfort with sex, or your own, continues to have an impact throughout our lives.

REFERENCE

Rich, A. (1980). Compulsory heterosexuality and lesbian existence. *Signs*, 5, 631–660.

The Kotex Diaries

Laurel Black

I didn't know what a Kotex pad was until I was 12. Hell, I didn't even know what a period was. I thought maybe a Kotex was part of a first-aid kit, for in the first grade I had ear surgery and again in the sixth, and both times, I came home with a Kotex pad over my ear and lots of gauze holding it on. I knew my mother and father laughed at the headdress in a strange, embarrassed way, but I thought that was because, frankly, it all looked pretty silly. Some little part of me knew that the pad was more than for first-aid, though it remained a mystery not only to me but to my three sisters and my brother for many years.

I realize that not knowing what a Kotex pad was doesn't seem like much. After all, I didn't know what a lot of things were. But recently, a bunch of us women who were aged 30-plus to 60 were eating petit fours and sipping punch after a poetry reading we'd been involved in, and somehow, the subject of Kotex pads and menstrual cycles came up; we discovered that each of us had been traumatized by our ignorance. Some younger students standing near us listened in shock—in only two generations, so many dark spots of our sexuality have been opened up for discussion and so much fear, anger, and mystery has been swept away! Of course, they may also have been shocked that there was a time when tampons were a new invention and when sanitary napkins were called "pads" more frequently and even that they weren't self-adhesive: the user had to "wear" them with a little belt. But I think it

was the intensity of our stories and our need to share them with each other that made them frightened and fascinated. And we knew we were performing, too, because it was important. There are so many things for women to tell bonding stories over—I'm hoping that stories like mine and my similarly aged and older friends' will sound like fairy tales in the not-so-distant future but will continue to be told for the same reasons: to remind us of something fundamental about knowing ourselves.

My mother was incredibly prudish. Part of that was, of course, because of when she grew up: she was born in 1930. But part of it is probably also because of where she grew up—Massachusetts. Many people who aren't native New Englanders think that people in New England are unfriendly, cold, miserly people. My husband and his family are from Kentucky, and they think that way. What you have to understand is that New Englanders just have a really strong concept of respect for personal space. If you're walking down the street and you see someone (and you're both native New Englanders), you nod, and maybe, if you are really good friends, you say, "Nice day." You don't say "Nice day, eh?" because that might force the other person to say something, and they might not want to. If they said it wasn't a nice day, it might start an argument. If they said it was and they didn't really think so but they were trying to be nice, then they'd feel angry inside and at you because you made them lie. And if it really was a nice day, then why say anything at all? No need to comment on the obvious. Conversational gambits just don't work with real New Englanders. Especially in the rural areas. City New Englanders are a bit more like the rest of the United States, I have to admit. But in small towns, you'd never say, "Hi! How are you?" If they wanted you to know, they'd tell you, and they wouldn't do it on the street, either. That thing about being miserly connects to this whole concept of unfriendliness. Talk is not quite so abstract to New Englanders; it's much more material. Words aren't something to be thrown out or away, any more than you'd throw out a chair that only needed a new cushion and some legs. Those summer folk who tossed their stuff in the town dump at the end of the season practically furnished our home and the homes of many others as I was growing up. Damn fools, we thought, but since we all thought the same way, why waste words and say it out loud?

Anyway, back to my mother's prudishness. We didn't talk about sex. She didn't talk about it with us, we didn't talk about it with her, and until the three of us girls who were oldest got pretty desperate to know what the hell was going on, we didn't talk about it with each other. I remember that in the 60s, with the Cold War stuff going on and the Civil Defense teams springing up in every small town just in case Communists invaded, she took a Red Cross emergency medicine course. But she hid the textbooks because they showed body parts. For a long time, I thought that babies somehow came out of women's breasts, because that was where they were always shown. (In an emergency in the 1950s and 60s you'd breast-feed, but otherwise, formula was preferred—part of that "scientific housekeeping/mothering" stuff going on at the time. Plus, if there was nuclear war, your breast milk might be contaminated). A lot of things about my body as a woman were just big mysteries to me, or would have been if I'd even wondered about them. I just "was." It's hard to realize that I once thought that way, but I was truly ignorant. My mother never changed in front of us (there were five children: three girls, a boy, then the last girl—I was girl number three); she was very modest. In fact, though this is really a whole other story, she didn't even sleep in the same room or even the same floor as my father did after the fifth child (and at least three or four miscarriages before that). No farm animals, not even cats or dogs in heat. Nothing.

Our house was the Sahara Desert of sex and sexuality.

In the midst of all this sexual aridity, there was one possible oasis. This was a large cardboard box, maybe 9 × 13, with pastel flowers splashed all over it on every side. It said simply, KOTEX. The box also told us that there were 36 or 48 somethings in there. My mother kept it under the bathroom sink most of the time and told us to leave it alone. Usually, when we were told to leave something alone, we did. Of course, if it was open, we could sneak a peek and close it back up and she wouldn't be the wiser. But what did anyone *do* with all those pads? No one was walking around with head wounds, but still, they kept being used up and more replaced them. Cereal boxes of about the same size told us what was in what we ate and promised some prize. But this told nothing—flowers strewn across the box like a lush spring meadow and no clues.

My oldest sister, Susan, the most rebellious, used to dump out the contents on occasion and use the boxes to make barns for her plastic horses. She cut window and door flaps and lined up her horses inside like they were in stalls. Once she arranged the whole herd, Kotex-barn and all, in the living room. Someone came by—someone not a neighbor—and Susan proudly showed off her setup. I saw my mother's face blanch as Susan picked up the barn and showed the visitor how the flaps worked, KOTEX emblazoned on the side like "Chew Mailpouch Tobacco." I didn't understand that for my mother, this was a horrifying event; I didn't understand what it took for her to laugh off the way her daughter's artistic endeavor had ruptured the private-public wall she worked so hard to maintain. I did know, however, that her anger after the visitor had left was all out of proportion to the act of cutting up a box or even disobeying the order to leave the box alone in the first place. I knew that the box meant something to her that was secret, probably bad and dirty, and that we had to protect that secret for her and not hurt her again with our thoughtlessness.

In the sixth grade—at which point I felt very grown up because I went to school on split sessions and thus from 12:30 to 5:30 every day, coming home at supper time like Dad and hanging out with Mom and finding out what went on at home during the day—we got a slip of paper to bring home and have our parents sign. It was a permission form to see a movie about "menses." First I thought that was some bizarre plural form of "men," but being scholarly, I looked it up in the dictionary. All I remember reading about was some concept of "time" and "cycles" and the "moon." It's possible that the dictionary at school was as conservative then as my mother, but it's also possible that other parts of the definition went right past me. My mother eyed me suspiciously as she held the form in her hand. "Do you know what this is about?" she asked, her eyebrows rising even as her eyes narrowed (a neat trick, try it some time!).

"Oh yeah!" I responded with one of those preadolescent smirks that hide everything from big lies to big truths.

She signed it, and about a week later, all the girls were herded into the library. I don't have a clue what the boys were learning in whatever room they'd been sequestered in. I noticed that the panes of glass on the library doors had been covered with construction paper. I was so dumb about all this that I thought it was to help keep the light down so we could watch the movie better. Duh. All I remember about the movie is some advice to not bathe during "that time" and to take showers that weren't too hot or cold. A cartoon teenager happily scrubbed away at her back. I kept trying to get my friend Jane, a nerd like me but from a family of 11, to make fun of the movie with me, but she kept shushing me and paying careful attention. Of course, my mother never asked me about what I'd learned. (If I'd learned what I needed to, then we both knew

it [refer to the "nice day" example above] and if I hadn't, she didn't want to share it. Ugh.)

So when in seventh grade I spent one week doubled over with cramps, I thought it was something I ate. The next month, the cramps came again, and when I went into the bathroom and saw blood all over my underwear, I put two and two together and decided I was dying from some terrible internal rupture, the symptoms of which I'd ignored the month before. I'd never told anyone about the previous month's agony; after all, why waste money on a doctor? The rule was, if you were conscious and a bone wasn't showing, you didn't go. So it was my own fault that I was dying now. I stuffed toilet paper in my underwear and walked like a stunned ox through the rest of the afternoon, wondering how long I would live with a hemorrhage of this magnitude. I was determined not to cost my family any money, because we didn't have any to spare, especially for me, since I'd had ear surgery twice already in my life and they were still paying off on that. Poor and ignorant, I was going martyrlike to my death.

When I got home from school, my mother was in the kitchen with Pat and Barbara, her friends. They were having coffee and laughing. I waited for Pat and Barbara to leave, but for some reason, the load of housework and cooking seemed light that day and they were lingering. Finally, I went into the bathroom off the kitchen and checked again–yup, still dying. I would have to warn my mother. Maybe this was enough to warrant a visit to the doctor.

"Mom! Can you come in here for a minute?" I yelled from the bathroom There was silence from the kitchen (knowing silence, as I look back on it now). My mother came in, and I showed her my underpants, ashamed, knowing that looking at them would be a violation of her personal space. "I discovered this when I came home from school," I said.

"Oh, you've just started your period," she said. She reached down into THE BOX, pulling out one thick, long Kotex pad. "Pretty soon you'll start growing hair under your arms and between your legs. Some people call it your 'friend,' but I call it a pain in the ass." She matter-of-factly wrapped the long paper tail of the pad in a contraption like a paper clip attached to a little elastic belt. "Damn, I'll have to get you one of these," she said, indicating the belt. "Here, put this on." She shoved the pad at me, dangling by its caught tail like a fish on a line. I must have looked as dumb as I felt. "You put it between your legs and hook this end in here," she said, holding it back up in front of me and showing me. The room was small and close, and it was all too much for both of us, this bodily function/sexuality stuff. She left and I arranged the pad sufficiently. I tried to creep out of the bathroom and bolt up the stairs immediately outside the door, but Pat and Barbara smiled at me like I'd just won an award. They were New Englanders, but had moved out from the city. My personal space was very large at the moment, and they were crowding it. Upstairs, I pondered my future life. I didn't know how long you bled each month and how many years. I picked an average out of the blue—two weeks a month—and decided that if I lived to be 70 (which seemed pretty old to me), then I'd be bleeding for. . . . The math astounded and shocked me, and I began to cry. Half my life I would wear a pad, walk sloped over like an orangutan because of cramps, and not be able to swim—or take a bath. (Thank Heavens I learned something from that movie!)

"You feeling okay?" my mother asked softly when I came downstairs for supper. I nodded, but I felt like everyone was looking at me. I knew I was different. I wasn't dying, I knew that now, but I almost felt like something worse had happened. The Box was mine to use now. If it had shamed my mother all those years to use the pads in that box, I was now a part of that shame. And I realized my two older sisters had known now for a couple

of years and hadn't told me, further proof of the dirtiness of what was happening. I glanced over at my brother, three years younger. He and I were best friends, but now I had to keep the secret from him, too. My days as his tomboyish buddy were over. I felt immeasurably older and sadder.

I didn't realize until later how much my mother didn't tell me. She neglected the part about starting menstruation as sort of, you know, really essential as part of getting pregnant. She didn't even tell me that aspirin would help, until I threw up in the lobby of school in the 9th grade. I learned a lot about periods from Sue G., a friend of mine who'd moved up from Oklahoma and lived in a really dysfunctional home. She even explained tampons for me and talked me through using them for the first time ("Oh, for Christ's sake, you are *not* going to ruin your virginity with a tampon!" she scolded me from outside the bathroom stall). I don't even want to get into how she learned all this, but I keep her in mind as I'm raising my own daughter. The point was, what we talked about took place in bathrooms or in the dark when we talked at sleepovers—it was secret stuff. It made me even more suspicious that there were worse things to come about being a woman, since my mother wouldn't tell me this stuff.

Late in the year that I started my period, my brother, who seemed clueless about female things despite being the only male regularly around, called from behind the bathroom door: "Mom?! What does *K-O-T-E-X* spell?" My mother and the three of us older girls didn't open our mouths in the living room, where his voice was perfectly audible. "MOM!" Eric shouted again. "What does *K-O-T-E-X* spell?" With all four of us using them now, sometimes an extra box sat near the toilet, unremarked upon and still inscrutably packaged. My mother ignored him. After his third call, even louder than the first, she called back, "I can't hear you!" He repeated his question. She repeated her answer. It must have dawned on him that she was lying. After all, if you farted in the bathroom, everyone knew it, so how could she have not heard his yelling? He came out of the bathroom and went upstairs and never asked again. As his footsteps moved up over our heads, not one of us spoke. We were in it together, and I wasn't sure how it felt.

The Kotex pads today, like others, are neither prominently displayed nor hidden away. They occupy a wall at the end of three or four isles in my local Wal-mart, and usually are packaged in plastic. But while the wrapping seems to have a bit more information on it, really, unless you knew what it all referred to, it would be a big mystery. The drawings of "wings" and the charts with lengths and uses ("heavy overnight") seem to offer explanations, but, truly, they don't. What's heavy? Why overnight? What kind of "protection" does this mystery thing offer? Who needs to be protected? It all seems very scientific, these almost blueprint-like drawings and the charts that refer you to only slightly differently designed products depending upon your need. What I needed was information. What I needed was foreknowledge so that when my body began doing what it was created to do, I didn't repackage it in a dark box in a dark place where no one spoke and my guts twisted in fear and loathing. What I needed was a cacophany of voices, dissension, discussion. But from the paper-covered window panes to my mother's and even my sisters' silence, I got one message only. My mother's prudishness was reiterated many times over in household after household—and what was being protected? Young girls and males from the messy, smelly, sometimes painful evidence of womanhood. We continue to do that today, for all

the shock the young students evidenced as I shared my story with friends. Watch any television ad or read any magazine ad carefully. Women wear white slacks and sit on white couches. They hit tennis balls and attend business meetings, and smile slyly at the camera, for they have hidden their secret from their colleagues or that stranger who is viewing them through the camera lens as they sit down with their coffee—you'd never know that woman was having her period because "she's got protection." We don't cover up colds or the flu, we don't hide arthritis. But the evidence of our biological sex is intimately tied to our sexuality through our periods. What those commercials are really saying is, "Why, you'd never know that there is a dark, warm, sometimes bloody and sometimes fertile place inside of this woman that can't be controlled by society!" And when mothers don't talk with daughters about it and *really* talk about it, they teach their daughters to be ashamed of that place, that place that can't really be controlled. (Of course, when we joke about young men getting hard-ons at the drop of a hat, we are celebrating their lack of control.) We are teaching them that their biology and thus they themselves are something to be ashamed of.

I'm not as "modest" (oh, like the pads called "Modess!") as my mother was, and my six-year-old daughter will get answers to her questions, for she does ask. And maybe it's because I've lived away from New England for 20 years now that I can talk about Kotex pads at a public place like a reception after a reading of women's poetry. I have to admit that I'm still reluctant to waste language. I don't "throw out" words lightly, but this is one conversation that has to take place.

Becoming Sexual: Differences between Child and Adult Sexuality

Fred Rothbaum, Avery Grauer, and David J. Rubin

Four-year-old Eric is playing in a sandbox at a park with his father when a couple on a nearby bench begins kissing passionately. Eric asks in a disgusted voice, "Dad, what are they doing?" When his father responds that they are kissing in the way adults sometimes kiss, Eric says, "Oh, gross. I won't ever do that," and returns to playing in the sandbox.

Five-year-old David is enjoying a back rub by his mom as part of their bedtime ritual. Departing from the usual sequence, David turns to face his mom and touches her breast. Slightly startled, his mom asks, "Why did you do that?" David responds matter-of-factly, "I wanted to see what it felt like."

Three-year-old Jennifer and three-and-a-half-year-old Sarah nap next to each other every day at nursery school. Midway through the year, Sarah begins putting her hand down her pants, rubbing vigorously, and making loud panting and moaning noises. The teacher decides to ignore this naptime behavior to see if Sarah will eventually stop. However, Jennifer, on the next mat, begins to copy Sarah, albeit with less vigor. After a few days of observing this joint masturbation, the teachers decides to separate the two girls "so they can get some rest." Napping at her new location across the room, Jennifer stops the sexual behavior; Sarah, however, continues panting and arousing herself on a daily basis.

Parents and teachers sometimes see behaviors in three-to five-year-old children that suggest complete innocence and disinterest regarding sexuality, and at other times they observe behaviors that seem blatantly sexual. Caregivers often wonder how to distinguish normal,[1] healthy behaviors from those that are not. To ascertain the range of children's sexually oriented behaviors with a view toward helping parents and teachers address them, we interviewed and observed parents and teachers of children ages three to five, observed the children at home and in the classroom, and reviewed related studies.

We learned that children's normal sexual behaviors comprise an extraordinarily broad spectrum, which can foster uncertainty and anxiety for caregivers contending with those behaviors.

We believe that parents' and teachers' anxieties about children's sexuality and concerns about its normality stem largely from misunderstanding how it differs from that of adults and attributing to it adult meanings.

Most of the caregivers with whom we talked realize that language, peer play, and other critical aspects of human functioning develop in stages from infancy through adulthood. Yet many of these caregivers seemed surprised to learn that sexuality follows a similar course. Research and anecdotal evidence clearly indicate that children's sexual behavior often does not have the same meaning and is not accompanied by the same thoughts and feelings as manifestly similar adult behavior. We believe that the meaning of children's behavior can be distinguished from that of adults along three dimensions: curiosity and play versus knowing and consequential behavior; spontaneity and openness versus self-consciousness and privacy; and sensuality and excitement versus passion and eroticism. By recognizing and understanding these dimensions, caregivers can learn to defuse their own

Source: Young Children Journal, 52, no. 6. Copyright © 1997. Reprinted with permission from The National Association for the Education of Young Children.

[1]Normality has both a statistical and an evaluative meaning and we are relying more on the latter. In most cases statistical normality alone is insufficient in drawing conclusions about whether a behavior is problematic.

tensions regarding children's sexual behaviors—even those as diverse yet normal as the three described at the opening of the article. (Based on these dimensions, we provide some guidelines at the end of this article for dealing with children's sexual behavior).

We recognize that many adults are deeply concerned about sexual abuse and child behaviors that might indicate abuse. Our decision to focus on normal sexual behaviors stems from the belief that such behaviors have adaptive and educational roles in children's lives. We believe also that a fuller understanding of normal child sexuality is critical to an understanding of that which is abnormal. In the final section we briefly address behaviors that we see as abnormal and problematic.

CHILDREN'S BEHAVIORS THAT APPEAR SEXUAL

Curiosity and play

Just as children are curious about adult roles such as firefighter and teacher, they are also curious and playful about sexuality.[2] Adults, too, are interested in the body, but their knowledge about sexuality and its consequences gives a distinctly different character to their behavior. Children's interest in sexuality centers on the body and its functions and is manifest through direct physical exploration and use of language.

Our interviews and observations yielded abundant examples of children's direct physical exploration. One mother described finding her four-year-old son and five-year-old neighbor (also a boy) in the bathroom playing doctor and inspecting each other's "private

---

DIMENSIONS WHERE IN CHILDHOOD AND ADULT SEXUALITY DIFFER	
Childhood sexuality	**Adult sexuality**
• curiosity and play	• knowing and consequential behavior
• spontaneity and openness	• self-consciousness and privacy
• sensuality and excitement	• passion and eroticism

---

parts." Another mother told of her four-year-old daughter asking her to play the villain while the child played a princess and her father a prince (a classic enactment of Freud's Electra complex). The daughter included in her play the element of jealousy, making her behavior seem even more adultlike. Another child flirtatiously asked his mother to play "cereal girl" while he played "sugar boy."

These examples of exploratory play are consistent with research findings that sex play, such as looking at and touching others' genitals, or games, such as seeing who can urinate farthest, are prevalent prior to adolescence (Gagnon & Simon 1973).

The adultlike quality of some children's comments and behaviors can confuse caregivers into thinking the children's behavior is truly adult. One mother related how her four-year-old son climbed into his parents' bed after his father had left, removed his pants, and said, "I won't be needing these anymore." Yet there are often clues that a child is simply practicing a small part of a much larger adult role. For example, the child who removed his pants seemed to regard this as the culmination rather than the beginning of the act of "seducing" his mother. There was no indication that the child was concerned with any ensuing "sexual" contact.

Similarly, while children's behaviors can be very purposeful, their purposes often differ from those of adults. For example, parents

---

[2]Most of the literature dealing with children's curiosity about sexuality focuses on the development of children's understanding of reproduction. We do not address reproduction here because it is treated extensively elsewhere. For readers interested in this topic, see the list of further readings.

provided considerable evidence of children's attempts to touch a father's penis or a mother's breast. Such acts often involve determined curiosity, attempts at humor, and limit testing—but not erotic fulfillment. Occasionally, such touching may simply be absentminded.

Parents and teachers also reported numerous instances of children experimenting with language related to the body, and particularly to the private parts, going to the bathroom and sexuality. Terms such as *poo poo, pee pee, wee wee, fart, penis, vagina, butt, teat,* and creative combinations of these words, such as *butt-face* and *penis-breath* elicit squeals of delight and hilarity among children. This is eminently normal behavior, deriving in part from children's attraction to the forbidden. Because parts of the body are imbued with special meaning and are generally inaccessible for exploration, children are all the more fascinated with them.[3]

Spontaneity and openness

A second way in which the sexual behavior of children differs from that of adults is that children are much less self-conscious and insistent about privacy. Children enjoy being naked. One mother echoed the sentiments of many parents when recounting how her three-year-old daughter "enjoys running out of the bathroom naked after a bath or after using the potty. I think she feels free."

Most young children are aware that running around naked is generally taboo, but they typically have little understanding of the

rationale behind this prohibition. They know enough to delight in the violation of this rule but not enough to experience adultlike shame. (Fox 1980; Finkelhor 1981).

Parents and teachers also noted children's lack of modesty regarding more blatant sexual behaviors. A father told of his three-year-old son who self-pleasures in the bathtub, when having his diapers changed, and at other "times of opportunity." Parents reported that their three-year-olds are unabashed about self-pleasuring, sometimes calling attention to themselves with such comments as, "Look, Mommy, my penis is getting bigger" and "We are the vagina girls." These comments and behaviors do not always occur in the bathroom or bedroom. For instance, one parent reported that her four-year-old daughter sucks her forefinger and touches her vagina while watching television in the family room.

Teachers noted a clear progression in children's need for privacy regarding self-stimulation behaviors. Such behaviors are more apparent in three-year-olds, who are constantly being watched, than in five-year-olds (Friedrich et al. 1991). For older children, the behaviors seem more likely to occur while playing in groups in "secretive" spaces such as bathrooms and small, enclosed places. One child care setting designed its bathrooms to accommodate children's increasing self-awareness: the five-year-olds' bathroom, as compared to the three-year-olds', is farther from the classroom and more protected from view.

Children are inconsistent in their privacy needs. For example, a young girl using a restaurant bathroom insisted that her mother hold the door open, even though restaurant patrons could see the girl straddling the toilet. Later, when leaving the restaurant, the mother tried to lift her daughter's dress slightly to help her put on her boots, but the little girl protested "because everyone would see my knees."

---

[3]Children have a very limited understanding of the distinction between play and reality. They are sometimes fearful that their curiosity and play will spill over into reality and have dangerous consequences. If adults become alarmed, children are likely to assume that their behavior is indeed serious—without understanding why. Adults need to reassure children that their sexual behavior is playful. In so doing, caregivers can help children separate their curiosity and play from the knowing, consequential sexual behavior of mature adults.

Sensuality and excitement

Most of the behaviors discussed so far lack the passionate, erotic quality that adults tend to associate with sexuality. Even when these qualities seem to be present, closer examination typically indicates otherwise. For example, a six-year-old boy saw a beautiful nurse and commented, "She's a major babe," with all the inflection an adult male might use. In the overwhelming majority of examples of such behavior, the child is engaging in the accoutrements of sexuality and romance (for example, gift giving, declarations of love, sadness at absence) rather than passionate physical displays (such as prolonged kissing, erotic touching, or genital contact). Children go through the motions, but their actions only superficially resemble those of adults; they lack deeper erotic resonance.

Young children's eroticism, when it occurs, is typically a matter of self-stimulation. For example, a father of a four-year-old boy spoke of how, while watching television, his son would lie on top of his stuffed dog and rub his penis against it. A small percentage of children are habitual masturbators, regularly and energetically manipulating their genitals to the point of great excitement and eventual relaxation—not unlike an orgasm (Kinsey, Pomeroy, & Martin 1948). But masturbation with arousal and orgasm is probably the exception (Gunderson, Melias, & Skar 1981). More often, masturbation has a soothing, sedating effect for young children and does not seem to be associated with orgasm. As compared to older children, young children have less awareness of a connection between erotic pleasure and their self-stimulation and thus engage in less purposive efforts to induce the pleasure. Young children have far less understanding of and experience with eroticism than adults. Child behavior that appears erotic to adults is more likely experienced as simple sensuality or excitement by children.

Contributing to simple sensuality and excitement, as opposed to passion and eroticism, are cognitive limitations. Eroticism is more than a physical sensation; it is an awareness and understanding of these sensations. As Dr. Ruth is fond of saying, sexuality is more a matter of what is between the ears that what is between the legs. One eight-year-old boy complained to his mom that his penis was painfully hard. To offer reassurance, the mother said, "When you get older, you will actually enjoy it." The boy responded in disbelief, "What am I going to do, play baseball with it?"

Similarly, most demonstrations of physical affection initiated by children—hugging, kissing, and other sensual touching or stroking—owe more to attachment needs then to Eros. In adulthood, too, physical contact can mix attachment motives and sexual motives; but for young children, attachment needs are primary.

Last, from a biological and evolutionary perspective, it is unlikely that children have the same drive to engage in mating behavior as older, fertile adolescents and adults (Kendrick & Trost 1987). For boys and girls alike, progress in the mating sequence and feelings of eroticism and passion depend in part on testosterone levels, which are low prior to adolescence. Biology limits sexuality for preschoolers, who are not ready to assume the roles and responsibilities accompanying the consummation of relationships.

A MODEL FOR VIEWING CHILDREN'S SEXUALITY

Caregivers too often see only the superficial similarities between the sexual behaviors of children and adults and mistakenly equate them. We believe this confusion is responsible for much of caregivers' anxiety about childhood sexuality.

Children's play involving sexual roles and relationships is universal (Ford & Beach 1951).

In all societies children ages three to five are learning gender-related roles and relationships; they practice "going to work," being a parent, talking on the phone, and other important aspects of adult life. Children's work is to play the roles of adults as a means of learning more about the adoption of those roles. Through play children also develop the larger scripts they will need to experience adult sexuality (Gagnon & Simon 1973). Indeed, cross-cultural studies indicate that practicing coital positions and motions is common in societies that allow it (Money & Lamaze 1989).

Childhood coital practice occurs even in our own society. One mother reported that her four-year-old son asked her to lie down on the couch and to close her eyes. When she asked him why, he responded, "You'll see." He then mounted her, mimicking the behavior of an adult male during intercourse. When later asked about his behavior, he said, "I just wanted to see what is was like to be on you." The parents had no knowledge of their son observing intercourse.

Is this normal behavior? What guidelines should we use to decide? At first glance the behavior seems precocious and worrisome. Based on the three dimensions described above, however, this incident, we believe, falls within the normal realm. First, there are compelling elements of curiosity and play in this child's behavior. He said he wanted to see what it was like to lie on his mother. His demeanor and actions are playful, as opposed to tense, compulsive, or forceful. Second, the behavior is unselfconsciously spontaneous and open, probably because the child had little understanding of the psychological or physical implications of his actions. While there is an element of privacy involved in asking the mother to close her eyes, there is more of a gamelike quality to this request than a sense of self-awareness or secrecy. Even if the child sensed he was engaging in a forbidden activ-

---

Suggestions for Caregivers When Responding to Children's Sexual Behavior

Understanding the ways in which children's sexuality differs from adults' should help in implementing these principles for responding to children's sexual behavior.

- Adopt an attitude that is respectful, matter-of-fact, and lighthearted.
- Be conservative in responding to the children's actions and liberal in responding to their words and requests for information.
- Take your cue from the children: If they don't seem worried or concerned, then in most cases you should not either.

---

ity, his method of obtaining privacy is more typical of younger than older children (for example, he made no demand for secrecy). Finally, there is no indication that his behavior is linked to genital arousal or eroticism, and there is no evidence of his having an awareness of intercourse.

When children say "I hate you," we are prone to read sophisticated adult meanings into their simple statement of anger. The misunderstanding arises because we view the child's behavior through an adult lens. Similarly, when children exhibit behavior the least bit sexual, we tend to assume they have mastered the larger sexual repertoire. In both cases we overlook developmental differences that distinguish children from adults, and we thereby address issues that, for the children, do not exist.

RECOMMENDATIONS FOR DEALING WITH CHILDREN'S DEVELOPING SEXUALITY

We provide here three general guidelines for addressing children's sexual behavior.

Which behaviors are problematic?

If a child's sexual behaviors are frequent, persist despite efforts to redirect them, and become a preoccupation, then they are abnormal and problematic. This rule-of-thumb applies to behaviors ranging from sexual language to masturbation. In instances involving two or more children or the use of force, or if there is several years' age difference between the children or a notable difference in size, then sexual behaviors are abnormal and problematic. Penetration of any bodily orifice with a foreign object constitutes abnormal and problematic behavior. In addition to these "hard" signs, it is useful to know that adaptive sexuality is typically accompanied by pleasure and spontaneity, while maladaptive sexuality is typically accompanied by anger and tension.

When to set limits?

Adults should set limits where clear-cut problematic behaviors, such as those just described, are involved. But there are many sexual behaviors that are not clear-cut: a child repeatedly caressing and kissing a teacher's face; a child saying to another "Suck my dick"; a child passing a note that reads, "I want to sex you"; a seven-year-old boy getting on top of a four-year-old girl and making moves suggestive of intercourse (both children are fully clothed); a child getting under a mother's nightgown "because I love to play house in there"; a child taking a bath and asking his parent, "Would you pour water on my penis? It feels good."

In responding to these and other sexual behaviors, we believe it is best to err on the side of setting limits. Children's positive attitudes about and future enjoyment of sexuality are not likely to be endangered if restraints are placed on their behaviors. For example, it is helpful for a caregiver to say to a child, "I don't want you to touch my breast because that is my private space." As long as caregivers sensitively and thoughtfully redirect the child's activities and adopt a respectful, matter-of-fact, light-hearted attitude, there is little possibility of a downside to the imposition of limits. On the upside, the caregiver is steering the child away from activities that can be problematic in certain situations and behaviors that, over time, can become extreme.

How to talk to children about sexual matters?

There is extensive literature on how to talk to children about adult love, intercourse, and reproduction. Many of the principles identified in that literature pertain to talking with children about their sexually relevant behavior. We have articulated five basic principles.

1. Keep it simple.   An overload of information or emotion is harder to digest than a few well-chosen words. This brings to mind the classic joke about the child who asks, "Where did I come from?" After the parent stumbles through an awkward explanation of the birth process, the confused child says, "Oh, I thought I came from Pittsburgh." Another example involves a mother who works for Planned Parenthood who talks about condoms in her lectures about safe sex. One day her four-year-old daughter asked, "Mommy, what's a condom?" The mother wondered how far she should go in explaining intercourse and, indeed, where she should begin. Remembering to keep it simple, she showed her daughter a condom; the daughter said "Oh" and walked away. The child had gotten the answer she wanted and was satisfied with that level of knowledge.

2. Listen carefully to the child.   The less you say, the more energy you can devote to listening and observing the child—which is how you can be most helpful. Consider carefully the actions of children and their peers before reacting. For instance, a preschooler who says "Suck my dick" has not necessarily been sexually abused; more likely the child has an adolescent sibling. Children's use of sexual words can make it seem as if they know more than they do. Language play is normal and common, and awareness of that type of play makes setting limits and reacting positively that much easier.

3. Give the child basic facts before analyzing her feelings.   Children need to know what is going on before they can figure out how they feel. Adults often make the mistake of probing children's feelings, which young children have great difficulty understanding and articulating, while failing to impart rudimentary information or address the child's misconceptions. When the child asked her mother, "What's a condom?" the mother would have done her child a disservice if she had launched into a discussion about the social and psychological significance of birth control; the child was requesting only basic information about a physical object. As for caregivers concerned that facts will make children less innocent and more knowing, we point out the gulf that exists between children and adults in comprehension and reasoning (Gordon, Schroeder, & Abrams 1990). Children's understanding is limited regardless of how much information they are given.

4. Talk with other adults about your own feelings before talking with the child about his feelings.   The more you clarify your own feelings, desires, and anxieties, the better able you are to separate them from your child's. Coming to terms with your own feelings makes it easier to respond to the child and help him understand this own actions and thoughts.

5. Approach topics when the opportunities naturally occur.   When a child comments about or otherwise responds to nudity, a door closed for privacy, a racy joke, an R-rated movie, a pregnant woman, or the like, parents and teachers should seize the moment and begin a dialogue with the child. Too often we ignore these natural opportunities and arbitrarily create occasions for dialogue. When children's interest is already engaged, they are most likely to share and explore their ideas.

CONCLUSION

Most caregivers have two seemingly conflicting agendas: (a) to foster children's feelings of comfort about sexuality and discussing sexual matters and (b) to facilitate the development of limits regarding sexual expression and preserve children's innocence. The dilemma is that too much comfort may lead to relaxing appropriate limits and jeopardizing innocence, and too many limits may lead to anxiety about sexuality and avoidance of the topic—at least in the parent's presence. We believe that focusing on developmental differences between child and adult sexuality helps resolve this dilemma.

Young children are innocent in that they are curious, playful, open, spontaneous, sensual, and excited. Making children comfortable about childhood sexuality is fully compatible with setting limits regarding sexual behaviors. Innocence is preserved because innocence, as defined above, is the hallmark of child sexuality.

REFERENCES

Finkehor, E. E. 1981. Sex between siblings: Sex play, incest, and aggression. In *Children and sex: New findings, new perspectives*, eds. L. Constantine & F. Martinson. Boston: Little, Brown.

Ford, C. S., & F. A. Beach. 1951. *Patterns of sexual behavior*. New York: Harper.

Fox, R. 1980. *The red lamp of incest*. New York: Dutton.

Friedrich, W., P. Grambsch, D. Broughton, J. Kuiper, & R. Beilke. 1991. Normative sexual behavior in children. *Pediatrics* 88 (3): 456–64.

Gagnon, J., & W. Simon. 1973. *Sexual conduct: The social sources of human sexuality*. Chicago: Aldine.

Gordon, B., C. Schroeder, & J. Abrams. 1990. Age and social class differences in children's knowledge of sexuality. *Journal of Clinical Child Psychology* 19: 33–43.

Gunderson, B., P. Melias, & J. Skar. 1981. Sexual behavior of preschool children: Teacher's observations. In *Children and sex: New findings, new perspectives*, eds. L. Constantine & F. Martinson, 45–61. Boston: Little, Brown.

Kendrick, D., & M. Trost. 1987. A biosocial theory of heterosexual relationships. In *Females, males and sexuality*, ed. K. Kelley, 59–100. Albany: State University of New York Press.

Kinsey, A., W. Pomeroy, & C. Marin. 1948. *Sexual behavior in the human male*, 36–192. Philadelphia & London: Saunders.

Money, J., & M. Lamacz. 1989. *Vandalized lovemaps*. Buffalo, NY: Prometheus.

FOR FURTHER READING

Books for parents and teachers

Bernstein, A. 1994. *Flight of the stork*. Chicago: Perspective.

Brick, P., N. Davis, T. Lupo, A. MacVicar, J. Marshall. 1989. *Bodies, birth, and babies: Sexuality education in early childhood programs*. Hackensack, NJ: Planned Parenthood of Bergen County.

Calderone, M. S., & J. W. Ramey. 1982. *Talking with your child about sex*. New York: Random House.

Gordon, S., & J. Gordon. 1989. *Raising a child conservatively in a sexually permissive world*. New York: Simon & Schuster.

Leight, L. 1990. *Raising sexually healthy children*. New York: Avon.

Lively, V. 1991. *Sexual development of young children*. Albany, NY: Delmar.

Montfort, S., P. Brick, & N. Blume. 1993. *Healthy foundations: Developing positive policies and programs regarding young children's learning and sexu-*

ality. Morristown, NJ: Center for Family Life Education, Planned Parenthood of Greater Northern New Jersey.

Roberts, E. 1980. *Childhood sexual learning: The unwritten curriculum*. Cambridge, MA: Ballinger.

Wilson, P. 1991. *When sex is the subject*. Santa Cruz, CA: ETR Associates.

Books for children

Brooks, R. 1983. *So that's how I was born!* New York: Simon & Schuster.

Gordon, S. 1977. *Did the sun shine before you were born? A sex education primer*. Rev. ed. Fayetteville, NY: Ed-U-Press.

Harris, R. 1994. *It's perfectly normal: Changing bodies, growing up, sex and sexual health*. Cambridge, MA: Candlewick.

Mayle, P. 1990. *Where did I come from?* 2d ed. New York: Carol.

Ratner, M., & S. Chamlin, 1985. *Straight talk: Sexuality for parents and kids 4–7*. West Chester, PA: Planned Parenthood of West Chester.

Schoen, M. 1990. *Belly buttons are navels*. Amherst, NY: Prometheus.

Sheffield, M., & S. Bewley. 1982. *Where do babies come from?* New York: Knopf.

Stinson, C. 1986. *The bare naked book*. Toronto: Annick.

Waxman, S. 1979. *Growing up—feeling good: A child's introduction to sexuality*. Los Angeles: Panjandrum.

READING 9

"I Just Wanted to be Normal": Women's Initiation into Heterosexual Dating

Sophia Demasi

"How did you turn out gay?" is a question heterosexuals frequently ask when they discover someone close to them is lesbian or gay. With this question, inquiring heterosexual minds put nonheterosexuals on the defensive.[1]

Gays and lesbians are compelled to explain their existence and provide an account of where and when their lives deviated from the taken-for-granted, "natural" path of heterosexuality. The responses they provide often take the form of narratives that explain why and

---

Source: Original work. Copyright © 2001. Reprinted with permission of the author.

[1]The term *nonheterosexual* includes people whose sexual practices and desires fall outside the normative boundaries of different gendered relationships. It is meant to include gays, lesbians, and bisexuals. The term *heterosexual* describes people who organize their erotic lives around differently gendered people.

how they came to realize their same-gender desires, when particular feelings revealing an alternative sexuality emerged, and how they confront the daunting task of revealing their sexual selves to parents, friends, and significant others.

Given the widespread assumption that heterosexuality is a natural phenomenon, public inquiries into the origins and development of nonheterosexuals are considered legitimate. Less familiar or frequent is the question, "how did you turn out heterosexual?" The "commonsense" notion that heterosexuality is the result of inevitable biological processes allows heterosexuals to escape this interrogation. Consequently, heterosexuals are rarely asked to think about or account for how and why they became heterosexual.

Scholarly inquiries into the subject of sexuality exhibit a similar pattern. During the last 20 years, sociologists and historians have used the important theoretical insight that sexuality is socially constructed to understand the production of gay, lesbian, bisexual, and transgendered identities.[2] This scholarship demonstrates the profoundly *social* nature of sexual identities and the important role that cultural and historical contexts play in shaping the way individuals interpret and act on their sexual desires. But the focus of most contemporary studies is limited to understanding how people with socially marginal identities create, negotiate, and experience their sexuality. Contemporary scholars have failed to identify heterosexuality—the sex presumably engaged in by most people—as a phenomenon that requires investigation. As a result, heterosexuality remains a largely unexplored and undertheorized practice.[3]

The pervasive academic silence around heterosexuality is troubling for several reasons.

First, it reinforces heterosexuality's taken-for-granted status. The failure to interrogate heterosexuality with the same vigor scholars use to consider lesbian, gay, bisexual, and transgendered sexualities allows heterosexuality to remain the unquestioned and unmarked norm against which less socially valued sexualities are evaluated. Second, scholarly reticence around heterosexuality ignores the logical corollary of the premise that sexuality is socially constructed. If sexuality is indeed a fundamentally social entity rather than a biological given, it is critical that scholars of sexuality examine the social processes that shape both nonheterosexual and heterosexual commitments and desires. Third, the failure to explore heterosexuality has left scholars with an inadequate understanding of how people come to organize their lives heterosexually. Indeed, sociologists have little insight into the experiential and contextual processes that are inevitably involved in shaping commitment to heterosexual roles and relationships.

An analysis of women's initiation into heterosexual dating illustrates the influence of social processes on women's commitment to heterosexuality. Dating is a practice that is integral to the establishment and maintenance of heterosexuality. Recent studies indicate that securing a boyfriend is an urgent goal young heterosexual women seek to attain and that they spend a great deal of time pursuing romantic relationships with boys.[4] Indeed, dating marks

---

[2]See for example Esterberg, 1997; Faderman, 1991; Kennedy and Davis, 1993; Plummer, 1975; Ponse, 1978; Stein, 1997; Warren, 1974.

[3]I do not mean to suggest that researchers have ignored heterosexuality entirely. The literature is replete with studies on heterosexual behaviors, the negative impact of heterosexual relationships on women, and, more recently, cultural representations of heterosexuality (Adams, 1997; Hite, 1976; Katz, 1995; Lottes, 1993; MacKinnon, 1987). However, these studies tend to accept heterosexuality as a taken-for-granted category. They ignore the ways that heterosexuals understand the development of their sexuality and the social forces that encourage men and women to commit to heterosexual roles and relationships.

[4]See for example, Holland, 1996; Thompson, 1995; Holland & Eisenstadt, 1990.

most women's initial contact with organized heterosexuality. Moreover, it is by organizing their lives around boys that women inevitably become personally and socially identified as heterosexual. Given the centrality of dating to the organization of conventional heterosexuality, a close examination of the circumstances that encourage women's initiation into this practice provides a way of identifying the contextual, interactive, and interpretive dynamics that shape their initiation into and subsequent commitment to heterosexuality.

For the women in this study, initial interest in heterosexual dating, and by implication their commitment to heterosexuality, emerged as a result of their interaction with heterocentric social environments that made heterosexuality compulsory. Peer, school, and community environments enforced heterosexual coupling by making social integration and peer solidarity contingent on heterosexual dating. The pressures exacted in these environments were mediated by the symbolic meanings participants attached to dating. The belief that dating secured their social status and integration compelled respondents to seek out boys despite their failure to express an emotional or sexual interest in them.

THEORETICAL APPROACHES TO UNDERSTANDING HETEROSEXUAL COMMITMENT

Since the 1970s, radical feminist theorists have dominated scholarly discussions around the question of heterosexual commitment.[5] There are several variants of radical feminist theories that differ on important particulars, but their overall position on heterosexuality is similar. In their view, women are not free to choose their sexuality. Nor are they innately heterosexual. They are compelled to enter into heterosexual relationships because of the social pressures exacted on them by men and male-dominated cultural and social institutions. In the words of Adrienne Rich, one of the foremost proponents of this view, heterosexuality is "imposed, managed, organized, propagandized, and maintained by force" (1983, p. 191) by patriarchal institutions that seek to ensure the subordination of women.

In her classic essay "Compulsory Heterosexuality and Lesbian Existence" (1983), Rich argues that three central features of male-dominated societies coerce women into organizing their lives around heterosexual relationships. These include the system of hierarchical gender roles that perpetuate male domination over women, the lack of economic and educational opportunities for women, which encourages them to bind themselves to men through marriage, and the social denigration and intentional concealment of lesbian possibilities. In her view, these social conditions exact pressures on women to enter into heterosexual relationships that they would otherwise not freely choose.

Rich forcefully articulates the idea that heterosexual commitment is socially driven. She rejects the conventional wisdom that heterosexuality is an intrinsic property of individuals that emerges absent of external social influences or that it is the predictable outcome of psychological developmental stages. However, she fails to specify exactly how and under what circumstances women might be forced to make heterosexual commitments. The assumption that women are pressured into heterosexual relationships that invariably oppress them is an assertion that requires empirical investigation. Exactly *how* women might be forced into heterosexual relationships is a question in need of a clearer answer.

In order to more clearly specify the dynamics involved in securing heterosexual commitment, it is useful to conceptualize heterosexuality as a product of dynamic social

---

[5]See for example Rich, 1983; Jeffreys, 1985, Dworkin, 1987; MacKinnon, 1987 and Wittig, 1992.

exchange rather than the inevitable result of patriarchal institutional arrangements. That is, in order to gain clearer insight into the critical question of how women come to organize their lives heterosexually, it is vital to consider the social contexts in which heterosexual women negotiate their heterosexual encounters and the particular meanings that they attach to the heterosexual practices and relationships they engage in. Much of the recent literature that explores gay and lesbian sexual identities demonstrates that social, cultural, and temporal environments as well as the symbolic meanings people attach to sexual behaviors and practices play a critical role in shaping sexual commitments.[6] These should also play a role in securing heterosexuality.

RESEARCH DESIGN AND METHODOLOGY

The research findings are based on in-depth life history interviews I conducted in 1999 with 40 white, U.S.-born, middle-class, heterosexual women as part of a larger study on female heterosexual commitment. The 40 married and unmarried respondents who offered to participate were between the ages of 23 and 68 at the time of the interview. Given my interest in understanding the trajectory of "normal" heterosexuality and the fact that most public discussions and representations of conventional female heterosexuality are directed at and reflective of white, middle-class women, I limited the study sample to women from these race and social-class groups.

With the exception of six women who responded to an advertisement I placed in a local monthly publication, I selected participants from personal profiles they placed on various Internet dating and pen pals sites that are intended to facilitate contact between men

and women seeking to establish relationships. Internet sites such as American Singles Network, Love@aol.com, and Friendfinder.com provided a universe of women who were likely to be heterosexual (as expressed in their desire to meet men) as well as willing to meet and talk to a stranger about sexual issues. To ensure confidentiality, I gave all respondents pseudonyms.

I interviewed all participants in a one-time face-to-face meeting of 1½ to 3 hours. In the interviews, I asked women to talk about the history of their interest in men, their motivations for becoming involved in heterosexual dating, and the things they liked and disliked about dating. To get a sense of the degree to which social pressures may have encouraged their involvement with men, I asked participants to discuss the specific circumstances of their initiation into heterosexuality. Respondents' answers to these questions enabled me to identify the contexts that shaped their decision to organize their lives around men as well as the subjective meanings they attached to the relationships they eventually entered (or failed to enter) into.

Throughout the interviews, I encouraged participants to present narrative accounts of situations and critical incidents in their lives that reflected on their dating experiences. Although they might have forgotten some of the factual details of their experiences, they did recall the events and experiences that were meaningful for them. It is the significance of these events and experiences that is the focus of this research. As such, I treated respondents' stories as narratives recognizing that the events participants narrated may not have happened exactly as they recounted them.

I used a thematic coding procedure to uncover the major patterns that emerged from the interviews. I generated initial themes on a case-by-case basis and then cross-checked them across all cases in the study. I developed final

---

[6]See for example, Esterberg, 1997; Stein, 1997, Plummer, 1975.

interpretations from the thematic structure that arose when I compared all cases against each other.

"COMPULSORY HETEROSEXUALITY" WITHIN THE HETEROCENTRIC STRUCTURE OF PEER ENVIRONMENTS

All 40 respondents in this study claimed that their desire to secure a boyfriend emerged sometime during their teen-age years. However, contrary to popular beliefs about the inevitability of heterosexual attraction, their longing to date did not appear to emerge from an intrinsic sexual desire for men. It was the heterocentric structure of participants' peer environments that created their initial desire to seek out boys. Within their peer environments participants found a socio-cultural context in which dating was an expected convention. A number of mechanisms were in place to ensure that they conformed to it.

All of the participants vividly described adolescent peer environments in which securing and maintaining relationships with boys was a normative practice. Dating was a ritualized activity that most felt compelled to participate in. In the words of one 23-year-old respondent: You just had to be interested in boys. Dating was the thing to do. My girlfriends were all interested in boys. It was just like a normal thing." Indeed, when I asked respondents why they wanted a boyfriend, most unequivocally stated that they wanted a boyfriend because their friends had one.

> I wanted a boyfriend because everyone else did. That would be the only reason. It would make me part of the group. (Georgine, 68)

> Because everyone else had one. It was the thing to do. (Lucille, 54)

> Mainly cause all my friends were dating. I wanted the companionship cause all my friends were dating. They would go out with their boyfriends and I wanted the same thing. (Briana, 25)

The peer group structure played an instrumental role in persuading women that getting a boyfriend was a routine activity that all girls engaged in. The fact that dating was an established norm within the peer group incited participants' belief that they too should have a boyfriend.

Participants' female peers rigidly enforced the norm of heterosexual dating by making social integration and solidarity contingent on being heterosexually coupled. Women exacted subtle pressures on other women to date, in part, by excluding those who did not or could not participate in the established convention of heterosexual dating. For example, 54-year-old Lucy, who had difficulty securing a boyfriend, claimed that her uncoupled status kept her from being included in peer activities in which she very much wanted to participate:

> I didn't have a boyfriend until my senior year in high school. Before then there was always this peer pressure from the other kids. If you wanted to hang out with the popular kids, they were always paired up. If you didn't have a boyfriend, you were sort of an oddball.

Similarly, Joan 56, claimed:

> Dating was the thing to do. At that time in life you had to pretty much be matched up with someone. "Who are you dating?" was a frequent question from my girlfriends. I just *had* to have somebody or I would have to stay home.

These women suggest that within the peer environment having a boyfriend was vital to becoming and remaining a valued member of the group. The consequence of not being heterosexually coupled was exclusion from peer activities and social isolation. A boyfriend ensured respondents' social integration within the world of girls and simultaneously allowed them to avoid the social exclusion that rendered them socially marginal.

Precisely because dating was a central feature of peer environments, respondents expressed feeling inadequate if they did not date boys. The failure to secure a boyfriend made women feel "different." For example, 54-year-old Marie stated, "Everybody had a boyfriend. . . . I felt like the odd man out when I didn't." Similarly, 23-year-old Stacey believed that her failure to secure a boyfriend was a signal that something might be "wrong" with her:

> All through high school it was kind of like if you didn't have a boyfriend then what was wrong with you? Everybody put pressure on everybody. I mean that was what you would sit around and talk about at lunch. What you were doing with your boyfriend that weekend? Where were you going?

Twenty-four-year-old Andrea also discussed the inadequacy she felt because she did not have a boyfriend to marry as her peers did:

> In college I had a lot of girlfriends who all had engagement rings. You feel like, "Oh my gosh, why doesn't my boyfriend get me an engagement ring?" It's such an intense pressure. In school all these girls were comparing the size of their diamonds. I kept thinking "Wow, maybe I should be getting one too." I don't know, you just have this pressure. They kind of look at you like, "Why aren't you engaged? Why aren't you planning on getting married?" It's not really said outright, but you feel it. I felt like I could not be a part of the conversation. I felt inadequate in a way.

For these respondents, non-participation in the established convention of heterosexual dating was an indicator of personal deficiency. The feelings of difference that were elicited by the norm of heterosexual coupling could only be erased through active participation in heterosexual dating. In order to avoid being different, these women knew they had to have boyfriends.

HETEROSEXUAL DATING AS A RESPONSE TO COMMUNITY- AND SCHOOL-SPONSORED EVENTS

In addition to pressures exacted by peer environments, there were also institutional forces that inspired some respondents to seek out boys. Several women recalled how school and community events organized around heterosocial activities incited them to get a boyfriend. School-organized dances that required attendees to be heterosexually coupled were especially important in this regard. For example, Joan, 56, said that she "began needing a date for various school activities" when she was 17. She wanted, "a reliable person that would escort me to functions that I had to attend." Similarly, 63-year-old Cynthia claimed that she wanted a boyfriend in the seventh grade "because I wanted someone to go to the sock hop with. I don't think I had any real craving to have a full-time boyfriend, though." Another respondent, 54-year-old Valerie, said she wanted a boyfriend so that she would be able to attend her school prom:

> I wanted a boyfriend primarily for having a date to the prom. It wasn't really a boyfriend as such that I wanted. I wasn't interested in it that much. I just didn't want to be somebody who did not have a date to the prom.

These narratives suggest that social events organized around heterosexual coupling were instrumental in compelling some women to date boys despite their professed lack of desire for them. Joan, for example, spoke of her desire for a boyfriend in terms of a social "need" rather than a desire based on physical or sexual attraction. She did not express an intrinsic interest in a particular man or in establishing a heterosexual relationship. She, like the other participants, engaged in heterosexual dating because she wanted to participate in a social event that happened to mandate heterosexual coupling.

Similar to peer groups, heterosexually structured community events encouraged women to date through their defacto exclusion of women who were not romantically linked to boys. Eligibility for participation in pivotal social events like the prom as well as routine community activities was contingent on having a boyfriend. Thirty-one-year-old Lorraine's experience at the local roller skating rink provides an illustration:

> I didn't want a boyfriend per se. I just wanted to have a boy to hold my hand during the couples skate. It was more to be status quo with everybody else. Everybody else had boyfriends and their boyfriends would call them on the phone, and you would make dates to go to the roller rink. When it was couples skate, they would hold the guy's hand and they would skate around. I would be the girl that nobody would ask to skate. So I always thought it would be nice if I had a boyfriend and didn't have to watch everybody else skate around. Then I would not be so much like an outsider.

By organizing an intrinsically gender-neutral sports activity around heterosexual couples, the local roller rink invariably encouraged Lorraine's desire for a boyfriend. Within the confines of the roller rink, eligibility to participate in the "couples skate" depended on her ability to secure a boyfriend. As such, it provided Lorraine with few alternatives outside of dating boys. Not being heterosexually coupled meant enduring the undesirable consequence of social exclusion. The only possible way that she could avoid feeling like an outsider was to seek out a boyfriend.

The heterocentric conventions of respondents' peer groups were upheld by community and school events that organized social activities around heterosexual couples. By mandating heterosexual coupling, school and community institutions reinforced the peer group value of securing a boyfriend as well as the exclusion of those women who were "different" because they did not date boys.

Community events invariably strengthened respondents' desire to seek out boyfriends and simultaneously limited their sexual options to heterosexuality. Participants may not have particularly wanted a boyfriend, but they understood that they *needed* one in order to secure their social integration.

THE SYMBOLIC SIGNIFICANCE OF BOYFRIENDS

In addition to the pressures exacted by the heterocentric structure of peer environments and community institutions, participants' initiation into heterosexual dating was facilitated by the symbolic meanings they associated with being heterosexually coupled. Within the peer environment, boyfriends were symbols that indicated a woman's status in the group. Girls who had boyfriends were accorded greater social value. It was the desire to increase their social status that motivated women like 37-year-old Gloria to seek out boys:

> Dating was really more of the thing to do to be popular as opposed to [dating because] I really wanted to spend time with a guy. It was just sort of the thing to do. The popular girls had boyfriends, so if you had one you were considered then desirable. It was important if someone showed an interest in you. It was important that you jump on it.

Gloria's attraction to heterosexual coupling was not inspired by a particular interest she had in boys per se. Rather it was elicited by her understanding that a boyfriend would increase her standing among her female peers. Twenty-seven-year-old Heather told a similar story:

> I think the allure was being with the most popular boy at school versus necessarily wanting him to be my boyfriend. Just that association of being with someone who was popular had the whole aura around it. I thought I'd be popular if I had him for a boyfriend. I would be friends with all the girls he was friends with.

Like Gloria, Heather associated having a boyfriend with making a positive and very public social statement about herself. In her view, she would be more highly valued if she was able to get the "most popular boy" to be her boyfriend. A boyfriend definitively confirmed that a girl was popular and "cool." Stacey, 23, explains:

> It was like a lot of my friends were starting to have boyfriends. I would have even wanted to hang out with them just to say that I had a boyfriend. Girls with boyfriends were cool.

These participants suggest that their desire to have a boyfriend was in part shaped by its symbolic value. Boyfriends facilitated respondents' attainment of social popularity and validated their social standing.

Several women in this study also reported that they relished the social approval that was a consequence of having a boyfriend. The attention and public recognition they got from boys and from their peers made them feel special and important. Twenty-three-year-old Stacey explained:

> I liked the fact that I could go to school and we'd walk down the hall together and people would see you. It was more of a thing where I wanted everybody to see that I had a boyfriend. That I was worth it. That somebody liked me.

As well, 28-year-old Kristin claimed she liked the fact that her relationship was publicly acknowledged: "Just the fact that people knew we were together. He was very cute. We were seen as a couple and people acknowledged that." The perception that a boyfriend would provide much wanted attention was shared by 54-year-old Janine.

> I liked when a boy showed me that he wanted me. When he showed me he wanted to be with me. I wanted the attention. I wanted the approval. I want to know that they like me. That they want to be with me.

These respondents sought out boyfriends because they derived pleasure from the public recognition and approval conferred on them when they were involved in heterosexual relationships. Their desire for a heterosexual relationship was a proxy for their need to impress peers and signal their coupled status.

Another critical meaning respondents associated with having a boyfriend was the belief that they were "normal" women because they dated boys. Fifty-four-year-old Marie explained:

> When I had a boyfriend I was like everybody else who was my age. I wasn't different. It made me feel normal. You know all my friends are dating, so I'm dating, too.

By occupying a status similar to her friend's, Marie was able to signal to others that she was not "different" but "normal." Her participation in heterosexual dating erased differences that would otherwise render her socially marginal. It was by demonstrating her "normal" heterosexual status that she ultimately secured her inclusion. The concern with being normal and avoiding the stigmatized status that befell those who were different was also articulated by 54-year-old Lucille. She acknowledged that having a boyfriend eased the social ostracism she felt as a result of her family's working-class status:

> Where I grew up was a mining community, and then there was the town of W. proper. We had a separate elementary school, and then we went to W. High School, where we all kind of migrated. I always felt like the W. proper people were the "in" crowd, and the mining people were like just trying to fit in. Somehow I got into that circle with the W. crowd when I got a boyfriend. It was really neat that I had a boyfriend. It was even more neat that he was from a different school. I liked the sense of belonging.

By participating in heterosexual dating, Lucille demonstrated her similarity to the "W. crowd" and subsequently gained acceptance into a group she coveted. Having a boyfriend confirmed that Lucille, who would ordinarily be perceived as different because of her class status, was in fact the same as the middle-class women in the popular group. Dating was a means of communicating to others that she was not different—she was normal.

The idea that heterosexual coupling confirmed a woman's normal status was further corroborated by participants' answers to the question of whether they felt differently about themselves during the times that they had boyfriends. A majority of the women I interviewed reported that they felt better about themselves when they were someone's girlfriend. They insisted that having a boyfriend made them feel more complete, fulfilled, and content. "I absolutely felt better about myself when I had a boyfriend. I felt wanted and more complete. I felt normal," said 68-year-old Lillian. Thirty-four-year-old Donna suggested the same when she said, "I felt better, more fulfilled and satisfied with my life when I had a boyfriend."

Participants reported very different feelings when they did not have boyfriends. The overwhelming majority commented that without boyfriends they felt unwanted and uncared for, inadequate, and lonely. For example, 53-year-old Delores claimed that the absence of a boyfriend made her feel, "Very upset. Very lonely. I was distraught because I wasn't cared for. In high school. In college. Even now I feel that way." In addition, the failure to be heterosexually coupled made respondents feel socially marginal. Laurie, a 60-year-old participant, explained:

> I was upset when I did not have a boyfriend. I wanted someone to belong to and to belong to me and share things with. I wanted a boyfriend just to be normal, I guess. I thought part of being normal was having a man in my life.

Laurie's lament was shared by 23-year-old Stacey:

> Right before I met my husband, there was a time where I kind of felt out of place. It was a good six

months or so that I didn't have a boyfriend. There would be times when I was hanging out with my friends and they were with their boyfriends, and I'd be kind of like the third wheel. That made me feel odd.

Thirty-two-year-old Anne, who claims that she has never been able to sustain a long-term relationship, also illustrates the anxiety of living outside the boundaries of conventional heterosexuality:

> You wonder. You look around and you think, What is it that everyone else has figured out and I haven't? Or why are all the good ones taken? Why did so and so get him before I got to him? It's very troubling. So I feel sort of like an incomplete person. I feel unsettled. Not quite of this world yet.

The failure to secure a boyfriend rendered these respondents outsiders in a heteronormatively structured world. Thus, they felt excluded, rejected, and different. Only by being heterosexually coupled could they hope to be normal women.

The connections women made between boyfriends, social status, and being normal played an important role in reinforcing their heterosexual commitments. Dating men enabled them to present themselves as normal heterosexual women and avoid the social marginality that ensued when they were "different." When they were someone's girlfriend, they were rewarded with recognition from other girls, inclusion in desirable peer groups, and feelings of confidence, security, and status. In contrast, the failure to date was a signal that they were not normal but different.

WHAT DOES SEX HAVE TO DO WITH IT?

An unexpected but consistent theme in this research was the failure of participants to express a sexual or emotional desire for boys. None of the women I interviewed claimed that sexual desire played a role in motivating their initial interest in securing boyfriends. Indeed, some women like 24-old Barbara explicitly stated that they did not particularly like boys. She said, "I don't think I really ever liked anyone when I first started dating. But all my friends had boyfriends, so I had to have a boyfriend too." Similarly, 31-year-old Lynne claimed that she wanted a boyfriend "because everyone else had one. To be honest with you I never really wanted to have a boyfriend, get married, or have kids. It just wasn't there in the beginning for me."

To gain a clearer understanding of the role that sexual desire played in initiating women's relationships with men, I asked participants whether sex was a reason they sought out heterosexual relationships. All of the women responded with a resounding "No." However, their failure to express a sexual desire for men does not mean that sex played no role in establishing some women's heterosexual relationships. Of the 40 participants, 5 reported that they did engage in sex in order to get or keep a boyfriend. Thirty-eight-year-old Ellen was one of them:

> I had this idea that if I had sex with a guy he'd call me and he'd come back and we'd start this relationship. Sex was a thing I used to get men. I hated sex too. I mean, I hated it almost from the beginning. I lost my virginity when I was 19. I did it cause I knew guys liked it. So I thought, "If I give you something that you like, you'll give me something that I like." Which is that I'd like you to be with me. Hold my hand, and sit and cuddle, and watch T.V.

Thirty-seven-year-old Nancy also claimed that she has used sex to secure a heterosexual relationship: "I've used sex to get a boyfriend. In college it was one way to be a part of the crowd. One way to get a boyfriend was to give up sex." Although these participants did not specifically desire, or enjoy, sexual relations with men, engaging in sex served an important function nonetheless. Sex enabled them to participate in the valued activity of heterosexual dating and secure the valued status of being someone's girlfriend.

Other women reported that they had used sex specifically to maintain an existing heterosexual relationship. They deliberately accommodated their boyfriends sexually because they thought it would enable their relationship to continue. Twenty-seven-year-old Heather illustrates this idea:

> I have definitely used sex to keep a guy. When I separated from my boyfriend eight months ago, I continued a sexual relationship with him for about four or five months after that. I thought by continuing the sex that maybe he would want to come back. We got into more spicier stuff than we did when we were together too. Not crazy stuff but definitely a little bit spicier. Like I went to a strip club with him. I probably would not have done that when I was with him, 'cause I didn't want him to think badly of me as the girl he was going to spend his life with. But since he put a value on doing that, I thought it might work to get us back together.

Justine, 33, also used sex to maintain a relationship. She said, "I have stayed in a relationship because of the sex. I felt that sex was the only reason he was with me, and I was more than willing to give it to him." A similar situation was recalled by 24-year-old Andrea when she discussed her first serious relationship with a boy:

> I felt a lot of pressure to do things sexually that I really did not want to do and probably would not have done. But I also felt like if I didn't have sex with him he'd break up with me. I did it because I felt he might leave.

For virtually all of the participants, sexual desire for men did not figure into their decision to date men. But several did use sex to secure or maintain a heterosexual relationship they valued. Sex, though not always physically pleasurable, was a means through which women derived the pleasure of social recognition and belonging that was the result of being heterosexually coupled.

CONCLUSIONS

Participants' narratives suggest that their desire to date boys emerged in response to their interaction with and interpretation of environments that were structured around normative heterosexuality. They defined being heterosexually coupled as desirable because heterosexual dating was an established norm within peer and community environments. The structure of these environments along with the ensuing symbolic meanings participants associated with dating men were instrumental for securing their initiation into heterosexual dating.

The mechanisms of control established within peer groups effectively limited participants to making heterosexual choices. By making social integration and peer solidarity contingent on having a boyfriend, peers implicitly asserted the normalcy of heterosexual dating and simultaneously engendered participants' desire to be heterosexually coupled. Participants were aware that the failure to secure a boyfriend inevitably led to social ostracism. Thus, they sought out boyfriends because the failure to do so would diminish their social status and the likelihood of integration within their peer group.

Educational and community institutions that organized specifically heterosocial events also played an important role in stimulating participants' interest in heterosexual dating. Several participants reported that they did not consider seeking out boyfriends until school dances or community-sponsored social events made heterosexual coupling a requirement of participation. These events, rather than a specifically articulated sexual desire for boys, compelled participants to secure a boyfriend.

The symbolic meanings women in this study associated with heterosexual dating also facilitated their desire to date. A boyfriend signaled a woman's status and publicly identified her as popular and cool. Moreover, the personal and public recognition that came with being attached to a man ensured the social inclusion participants desired. The feelings of social belonging and recognition women realized when they were someone's girlfriend strengthened their desire to date.

The narratives cited here suggest that the dynamics that shape heterosexual commitment are more complicated than the existing feminist literature suggests. The stories women told about their initiation into heterosexual dating do reveal that their initial relationships with boys were in part coerced by the structural arrangements embedded in heterocentrically organized peer and community environments. Participants "chose" to date boys because these environments defined heterosexual relationships as important and made heterosexuality a condition of social inclusion. But mediating between the external pressures exacted in peer and community environments were the subjective meanings participants associated with heterosexual dating. The accounts women gave of their initiation into heterosexual dating document that they dated largely because they wanted to avoid being outsiders. Respondents' belief that dating boys was the route to social integration and public recognition of their normative status was critical for securing their desire to organize their lives heterosexually.

The findings reported here also raise questions about the "commonsense" understanding that heterosexuality is the outcome of innate "natural" desires. Participants were not compelled toward heterosexuality by a specifically sexual or emotional desire for men. For these women, sex was not the central desire constitutive of heterosexuality. Instead, they reported that they wanted to be heterosexually coupled because they wanted to avoid the social exclusion and ostracism that was the consequence of the failure to date. Their desire to be romantically linked to boys emerged out of the need for social inclusion, the desire to self-present as normal, and the yearning to avoid the stigma of being different. By linking their lives to boys socially, emotionally, and sexually, they made it possible to realize these goals.

Acknowledgement: I am extremely grateful to Julia Ericksen, Rosario Espinal, Margaret Marsh, and Howard Winant for their helpful comments on this work.

REFERENCES

Adams, M. L. (1997). *The Trouble with Normal: Post-War Youth and the Making of Heterosexuality.* Toronto: University of Toronto Press.

Dworkin, A. (1987). *Intercourse.* London: Secker and Warberg.

Esterberg, K. (1997). *Lesbian and BiSexual Identities: Constructing Communities Constructing Selves.* Philadelphia: Temple University Press.

Faderman, L. (1991). *Odd Girls and Twilight Lovers.* New York: Penguin Books.

Hite, S. (1976). *The Hite Report.* New York: Macmillan.

Holland, D. C. & Eisenstadt, M. (1990). *Educated in Romance: Women, Achievement and College Culture.* Chicago: University of Chicago Press.

Holland, J., Ramazonoglu, C., Sharpe., & Thomson, R. (1992). Pleasure, Pressure and Power: Some Contradictions of Gendered Sexuality. *The Sociological Review 40* (4), 645–674.

Holland, J., Ramazonoglu, C., Sharpe., & Thomson, R. (1994). Power and Desire: The Embodiment of Female Sexuality. *Feminist Review 46,* 21–38.

Holland, J., Ramazonoglu, C., & Thomson, R. (1996). In the same boat? The Gendered (In)experience of First Heterosex. In D. Richardson (Ed.), *Theorizing Heterosexuality* (pp. 143–160). Buckingham: Open University Press.

Jeffreys, S. (1985). *The Spinster and Her Enemies.* London: Pandora.

Katz, J. (1995). *The Invention of Heterosexuality.* New York: Dutton Press.

Kennedy, E., & Davis, M. (1993). *Boots of Leather, Slippers of Gold: The History of a Lesbian Community.* New York: Routledge.

Lottes, I. (1993). Nontraditional Gender Roles and the Sexual Experiences of Heterosexual College Students. *Sex Roles 29* (9/10), 645–669.

MacKinnon, C. (1987). *Feminism Unmodified: Discourses on Life and Law.* Cambridge: Harvard University Press.

Plummer, K. (1975). *Sexual Stigma: An Interactionist Account.* London: Routledge & Kegan Paul.

Ponse, B. (1978). *Identities in the Lesbian World: The Social Construction of Self.* Westport, CT: Greenwood Press.

Rich, A. (1983). Compulsory Heterosexuality and Lesbian Existence. In A. Snitow, C. Stansell, & S. Thompson (Eds.), *Powers of Desire: The Politics of Sexuality* (pp. 177–205). New York: Monthly Review Press.

Stein, A. (1997). *Sex and Sensibility: Stories of a Lesbian Generation.* Berkeley: University of California Press.

Thompson, S. (1995). *Going All the Way: Teenage Girls' Tales of Sex, Romance, and Pregnancy.* New York: Hill and Wang.

Warren, C. (1974). *Identity and Community in the Gay World.* New York: Wiley Press.

Wittig, M. (1992). *The Straight Mind.* Boston: Beacon Press.

Where'd You Learn That?

Ron Stodghill II

The cute little couple looked as if they should be sauntering through Great Adventure or waiting in line for tokens at the local arcade. Instead, the 14-year-olds walked purposefully into the Teen Center in suburban Salt Lake City, Utah. They didn't mince words about their reason for stopping in. For quite some time, usually after school and on weekends, the boy and girl had tried to heighten their arousal during sex. Flustered yet determined,

Source: J. Kenneth Davidson Sr. and Nelwyn B. Moore (Eds.). *Speaking of Sexuality: Interdisciplinary Readings.* Copyright © 2001, Roxbury Publishing Co.

the pair wanted advice on the necessary steps that might lead them to a more fulfilling orgasm. His face showing all the desperation of a lost tourist, the boy spoke for both of them when he asked frankly, "How do we get to the G-spot?"

Whoa. Teen Center nurse Patti Towle admits she was taken aback by the inquiry. She couldn't exactly provide a road map. Even more, the destination was a bit scandalous for a couple of ninth-graders in the heart of Mormon country. But these kids had clearly already gone further sexually than many adults, so Towle didn't waste time preaching the gospel of abstinence. She gave her young adventurers some reading material on the subject, including the classic women's health book *Our Bodies, Ourselves,* to help bring them closer in bed. She also brought up the question of whether a G-spot even exists. As her visitors were leaving, Towle offered them more freebies: "I send them out the door with a billion condoms."

G-spots. Orgasms. Condoms. We all know kids say and do the darndest things, but how they have changed! One teacher recalls a 10-year-old raising his hand to ask her to define oral sex. He was quickly followed by an 8-year-old girl behind him who asked, "Oh, yeah, and what's anal sex?" These are the easy questions. Rhonda Sheared, who teaches sex education in Pinellas County, Fla., was asked by middle school students about the sound *kweif,* which the kids say is the noise a vagina makes during or after sex. "And how do you keep it from making this noise?"

There is more troubling behavior in Denver. School officials were forced to institute a sexual-harassment policy owing to a sharp rise in lewd language, groping, pinching and bra-snapping incidents among sixth-, seventh-, and eighth-graders. Sex among kids in Pensacola, Fla., became so pervasive that students of a private Christian junior high school are now asked to sign cards vowing not to have

sex until they marry. But the cards don't mean anything, says a 14-year-old boy at the school. "It's broken promises."

It's easy enough to blame everything on television and entertainment, even the news. At a Denver middle school, boys rationalize their actions this way: "If the President can do it, why can't we?" White House sex scandals are one thing, but how can anyone avoid Viagra and virility? Or public discussions of sexually transmitted diseases like AIDS and herpes? Young girls have lip-synched often enough to Alanis Morissette's big hit of a couple of years ago, *You Oughta Know,* to have found the sex nestled in the lyric. But it's more than just movies and television and news. Adolescent curiosity about sex is fed by a pandemic openness about it—in the schoolyard, on the bus, at home when no adult is watching. Just eavesdrop at the mall one afternoon, and you'll hear enough pubescent sexcapades to pen the next few episodes of *Dawson's Creek,* the most explicit show on teen sexuality, on the *WB* network. Parents, always the last to keep up, are now almost totally pre-empted. Chris (not his real name), 13, says his parents talked to him about sex when he was 12 but he had been indoctrinated earlier by a 17-year-old cousin. In any case, he gets his full share of information from the tube. "You name the show, and I've heard about it. *Jerry Springer, MTV, Dawson's Creek, HBO After Midnight . . .*" Stephanie, 16, of North Lauderdale, Fla., who first had sex when she was 14, claims to have slept with five boyfriends and is considered a sex expert by her friends. She says, "You can learn a lot about sex from cable. It's all mad-sex stuff. If you're feeling steamy and hot, there's only one thing you want to do. As long as you're using a condom, what's wrong with it? Kids have hormones too."

In these steamy times, it is becoming largely irrelevant whether adults approve of kids' sowing their oats—or knowing so much about the technicalities of the dissemination.

American adolescents are in the midst of their own kind of sexual revolution—one that has left many parents feeling confused, frightened and almost powerless. Parents can search all they want for common ground with today's kids, trying to draw parallels between contemporary carnal knowledge and an earlier generation's free-love crusades, but the two movements are quite different. A desire to break out of the old-fashioned strictures fueled the '60s movement, and its participants made sexual freedom a kind of new religion. That sort of reverence has been replaced by a more consumerist attitude. In a 1972 cover story, *Time* declared, "Teenagers generally are woefully ignorant about sex." Ignorance is no longer the rule. As a weary junior high counselor in Salt Lake City puts it, "Teens today are almost nonchalant about sex. It's like we've been to the moon too many times."

The good news about their precocious knowledge of the mechanics of sex is that a growing number of teens know how to protect themselves, at least physically. But what about their emotional health and social behavior? That's a more troublesome picture. Many parents and teachers—as well as some thoughtful teenagers—worry about the desecration of love and the subversion of mature relationships. Says Debra Haffner, President of the Sexuality Information and Education Council of the United States: "We should not confuse kids' pseudo-sophistication about sexuality and their ability to use the language with their understanding of who they are as sexual young people or their ability to make good decisions."

One ugly side effect is a presumption among many adolescent boys that sex is an entitlement—an attitude that fosters a breakdown of respect for oneself and others. Says a seventh-grade girl: "The guy will ask you up front. If you turn him down, you're a bitch. But if you do it, you're a ho. The guys are after us all the time, in the halls, everywhere. You

scream, 'Don't touch me!' but it doesn't do any good." A Rhode Island Rape Center study of 1,700 sixth- and ninth-graders found 65 percent of boys and 57 percent of girls believing it acceptable for a male to force a female to have sex if they've been dating for six months.

Parents who are aware of this cultural revolution seem mostly torn between two approaches: preaching abstinence or suggesting prophylactics—and thus condoning sex. Says Cory Hollis, 37, a father of three in the Salt Lake City area: "I don't want to see my teenage son ruin his life. But if he's going to do it, I told him that I'd go out and get him the condoms myself." Most parents seem too squeamish to get into the subtleties of instilling sexual ethics. Nor are schools up to the job of moralizing. Kids say they accept their teachers' admonitions to have safe sex but tune out other stuff. "The personal-development classes are a joke," says Sarah, 16 of Pensacola. "Even the teacher looks uncomfortable. There is no way anybody is going to ask a serious question." Says Shana, a 13-year-old from Denver. "A lot of it is old and boring. They'll talk about not having sex before marriage, but no one listens."

Shana says she is glad "sex isn't so taboo now, I mean with all the teenage pregnancies." But she also says that "it's creepy and kind of scary that it seems to be happening so early, and all this talk about it." She adds, "Girls are jumping too quickly. They figure if they can fall in love in a month, then they can have sex in a month too." When she tried discouraging a classmate from having sex for the first time, the friend turned to her and said, "My God, Shana. It's just sex."

Three powerful forces have shaped today's child prodigies: a prosperous information age that increasingly promotes products and entertains audiences by titillation; aggressive public-policy initiatives that loudly preach sexual responsibility, further desensitizing kids to the subject; and the decline of two-parent households, which leaves adolescents with little supervision. Thus kids are not only bombarded with messages about sex—many of them contradictory—but also have more private time to engage in it than did previous generations. Today more than half of the females and three-quarters of the males ages 15 to 19 have experienced sexual intercourse, according to the Commission on Adolescent Sexual Health. And while the average age at first intercourse has come down only a year since 1970 (currently it's 17 for girls and 16 for boys), speed is of the essence for the new generation. Says Haffner: "If kids today are going to do more than kiss, they tend to move very quickly toward sexual intercourse."

The remarkable—and in ways lamentable—product of youthful promiscuity and higher sexual IQ is the degree to which kids learn to navigate the complex hypersexual world that reaches out seductively to them at every turn. One of the most positive results: the incidence of sexually transmitted diseases and of teenage pregnancy is declining. Over the past few years, kids have managed to chip away at the teenage birthrate, which in 1991 peaked at 62.1 births per 1,000 females. Since then the birthrate has dropped 12 percent, to 54.7. Surveys suggest that as many as two-thirds of teenagers now use condoms, a proportion that is three times as high as reported in the 1970s. "We're clearly starting to make progress," says Dr. John Santelli, a physician with the Centers for Disease Control and Prevention's Division of Adolescent and School Health. "And they key statistics bear that out." Even if they've had sex, many kids are learning to put off having more till later; they are also making condom use during intercourse nonnegotiable; and, remarkably, the fleeting pleasures of lust may even be wising up some of them to a greater appreciation of love.

For better or worse, sex-filled television helps shape young opinion. In Chicago, Ryan, an 11-year-old girl, intently watches a scene from one of her favorite TV dramas, *Dawson's Creek*. She listens as the character Jen, who lost her virginity at 12 while drunk, confesses to her new love, Dawson, "Sex doesn't equal happiness. I can't apologize for my past." Ryan is quick to defend Jen. "I think she was young, but if I were Dawson, I would believe she had changed. She acts totally different now." But Ryan is shocked by an episode of her other favorite show, *Buffy the Vampire Slayer*, in which Angel, a male vampire, "turned bad" after having sex with the 17-year-old Buffy. "That kinda annoyed me," says Ryan. "What would have happened if she had had a baby? Her whole life would have been thrown out the window." As for the fallen Angel: "I am so mad! I'm going to take all my pictures of him down now."

And then there's real-life television. *MTV's Loveline,* an hour-long Q-and-A show featuring sex guru Drew Pinsky, is drawing raves among teens for its informative sexual content. Pinsky seems to be almost idolized by some youths. "Dr. Drew has some excellent advice," says Keri, an eighth-grader in Denver. "It's not just sex, its real life. Society makes you say you've got to look at shows like *Baywatch,* but I'm sick of blond bimbos."

With so much talk of sex in the air, the extinction of the hapless, sexually naive kid seems an inevitability. Indeed, kids today as young as seven to ten are picking up the first details of sex even in Saturday-morning cartoons. Brett, a 14-year-old in Denver, says it doesn't matter to him whether his parents chat with him about sex or not because he gets so much from TV. Whenever he's curious about something sexual, he channel surfs his way to certainty. "If you watch TV, they've got everything you want to know," he says. "That's how I learned to kiss, when I was eight. And the girl told me, 'Oh, you sure know how to do it.'"

Even if kids don't watch certain television shows, they know the programs exist and are bedazzled by the forbidden. From schoolyard word of mouth, eight-year-old Jeff in Chicago has heard all about the foul-mouthed kids in the raunchily plotted *South Park,* and even though he has never seen the show, he can describe certain episodes in detail. (He is also familiar with the AIDS theme of the musical *Rent* because he's heard the CD over and over.) Argentina, 16, in Detroit, says, "TV makes sex look like this big game." Her friend Michael, 17, adds, "They make sex look like Monopoly or something. You have to do it in order to get to the next level."

Child experts say that by the time many kids hit adolescence, they have reached a point where they aren't particularly obsessed with sex but have grown to accept the notion that solid courtships—or at least strong physical attractions—potentially lead to sexual intercourse. Instead of denying it, they get an early start preparing for it—and playing and perceiving the roles prescribed for them. In Nashville, 10-year-old Brantley whispers about a classmate, "There's this girl I know, she's nine years old, and she already shaves her legs and plucks her eyebrows, and I've heard she's had sex. She even has bigger boobs than my mom!"

The playacting can eventually lead to discipline problems at school. Alan Skriloff, Assistant Superintendent of Personnel and Curriculum for New Jersey's North Brunswick School System, notes that there has been an increase in mock-sexual behavior in buses carrying students to school. He insists there have been no incidents of sexual assault but, he says, "we've dealt with kids simulating sexual intercourse and simulating masturbation. It's very disturbing to the other children and to the parents, obviously." Though Skriloff says that girls are often the initiators of such conduct, in most school districts the aggressors are usually boys.

Nan Stein, a senior researcher at the Wellesley College Center for Research on Women, believes sexual violence and harassment is on the rise in schools, and she says, "It's happening between kids who are dating or want to be dating or used to date." Linda Osmundson, Executive Director of the Center Against Spouse Abuse in St. Petersburg, Fla., notes that "it seems to be coming down to younger and younger girls who feel that if they don't pair up with these guys, they'll have no position in their lives. They are pressured into lots of sexual activity." In this process of socialization, "no" is becoming less and less an option.

In such a world, schools focus on teaching scientific realism rather than virginity. Sex-ed teachers tread lightly on the moral questions of sexual intimacy while going heavy on the risk of pregnancy or a sexually transmitted disease. Indeed, health educators in some school districts complain that teaching abstinence to kids today is getting to be a futile exercise. Using less final terms like "postpone" or "delay" helps draw some kids in, but semantics often isn't the problem. In a Florida survey, the state found that 75 percent of kids had experienced sexual intercourse by the time they reached 12th grade, with some 20 percent of the kids having had six or more sexual partners. Rick Colonno, father of a 16-year-old son and 14-year-old daughter in Arvada, Colo., views sex ed in schools as a necessary evil to fill the void that exists in many homes. Still, he's bothered by what he sees as a subliminal endorsement of sex by authorities. "What they're doing," he says, "is preparing you for sex and then saying, 'But don't have it.'"

With breathtaking pragmatism, kids look for ways to pursue their sex life while avoiding pregnancy or disease. Rhonda Sheared, the Florida sex-ed teacher, says a growing number of kids are asking questions about oral and anal sex because they've discovered that it allows them to be sexually active without risking pregnancy. As part of the Pinellas County program, students in middle and high school write questions anonymously, and, as Sheared says, "they're always looking for the loophole."

A verbatim sampling of some questions:

- "Can you get AIDS from fingering a girl if you have no cuts? Through your fingernails?"

- "Can you get AIDS from '69'?"

- "If you shave your vagina or penis, can that get rid of crabs?"

- "If yellowish stuff comes out of a girl, does it mean you have herpes, or can it just happen if your period is due, along with abdominal pains?"

- "When sperm hits the air, does it die or stay alive for 10 days?"

Ideally, most kids say, they would prefer their parents do the tutoring, but they realize that's unlikely. For years psychologists and sociologists have warned about a new generation gap, one created not so much by different morals and social outlooks as by career-driven parents, the economic necessity of two incomes leaving parents little time for talks with their children. Recent studies indicate that many teens think parents are the most accurate source of information and would like to talk to them more about sex and sexual ethics but can't get their attention long enough. Shana sees the conundrum this way: "Parents haven't set boundaries, but they are expecting them."

Some parents are working harder to counsel their kids on sex. Cathy Wolf, 29, of North Wales, Pa., says she grew up learning about sex largely from her friends and from reading controversial books. Open-minded and proactive, she says she has returned to a book she once sought out for advice, Judy Blume's novel *Are You There God? It's Me, Margaret*, and is reading it to her two boys, 8 and 11. The novel discusses the awkwardness of adolescence, including sexual stirrings. "That book was forbidden to me as a kid," Wolf says. "I'm hoping to give them a different perspective about sex, to expose them to this kind of subject matter before they find out about it themselves." Movies and television are a prod and a challenge to Wolf. In *Grease,* which is rated PG and was recently re-released, the character Rizzo, "says something about 'sloppy seconds,' you know, the fact that a guy wouldn't want to do it with a girl who had just done it with another guy. There's also another point where they talk about condoms."

Most kids, though, lament that their parents aren't much help at all on sexual matters. They either avoid the subject, miss the mark by starting the discussion too long before or after the sexual encounter, or just plain stonewall them. "I was nine when I asked my mother the Big Question," says Michael, in Detroit. "I'll never forget. She took out her driver's license and pointed to the line about male or female. 'That is sex,' she said." Laurel, a 17-year-old in Murfreesboro, Tenn., wishes her parents had taken more time with her to shed light on the subject. When she was six and her sister was nine, "my mom sat us down, and we had the sex talk," Laurel says. "But when I was 10, we moved in with my dad, and he never talked about it. He would leave the room if a commercial for a feminine product came on TV." And when her sister finally had sex, at 16, even her mother's vaunted openness crumbled. "She talked to my mom about it and ended up feeling like a whore because even though my mom always said we could talk to her about anything, she didn't want to hear that her daughter had slept with a boy."

Part of the problem for many adults is that they aren't quite sure how they feel about teenage sex. A third of adults think adolescent sexual activity is wrong, while a majority of adults think it's O.K. and, under certain conditions, normal, healthy behavior, according to the Alan Guttmacher Institute, a nonprofit, reproductive-health research group. In one breath, parents say they perceive it as a public-health issue and want more information about sexual behavior and its consequences, easier access to contraceptives, and more material in the media about responsible human and sexual interaction. And in the next breath, they claim it's a moral issue to be resolved through preaching abstinence and the virtues of virginity and getting the trash off TV. "You start out talking about condoms in this country, and you end up fighting about the future of the American family," says Sarah Brown, Director of the Campaign Against Teen Pregnancy. "Teens just end up frozen like a deer in headlights."

Not all kids are happy with television's usurping the role of village griot. Many say they've become bored by—and even resent—sexual themes that seem pointless and even a distraction from the information or entertainment they're seeking. "It's like everywhere," says Ryan, a 13-year-old seventh-grader in Denver, "even in *Skateboarding* [magazine]. It's become so normal it doesn't even affect you. On TV, out of nowhere, they'll begin talking about masturbation." Another Ryan, 13, in the eighth grade at the same school, agrees: "There's sex in the cartoons and messed-up people on the talk shows—'My lover sleeping with my best friend.' I can remember the jumping condom ads. There's just too much of it all."

Many kids are torn between living up to a moral code espoused by their church and parents and trying to stay true to the swirling laissez-faire. Experience is making many sadder but wiser. The shame, anger or even indifference stirred by early sex can lead to prolonged abstinence. Chandra, a 17-year-old in Detroit, says she had sex with a boyfriend of two years for the first time at 15 despite her mother's constant pleas against it. She says she wishes she had heeded her mother's advice. "One day I just decided to do it," she says. "Afterward, I was kind of mad that I let it happen. And I was sad because I knew my mother wouldn't have approved." Chandra stopped dating the boy more than a year ago and hasn't had sex since. "It would have to be someone I really cared about," she says. "I've had sex before, but I'm not a slut."

With little guidance from grownups, teens have had to discover for themselves that the ubiquitous sexual messages must be tempered with caution and responsibility. It is quite clear, even to the most sexually experienced youngsters, just how dangerous a little information can be. Stephanie in North Lauderdale, who lost her virginity two years ago, watches with concern as her seven-year-old sister moves beyond fuzzy thoughts or romance inspired by *Cinderella* or *Aladdin* into sexual curiosity. "She's always talking about pee-pees, and she sees somebody on TV kissing and hugging or something, and she says, 'Oh, they had sex.' I think she's going to find out about this stuff before I did." She pauses. "We don't tell my sister anything," she says, "but she's not a naive child."

Adapted from Ron Stodghill II. "Where'd You Learn That?" *Time,* 1998, June 15, pp. 52–59. Copyright © 1998, Time Inc. Reprinted by permission.

READING 11

Blow Jobs and Other Boring Stuff

Susannah Indigo

Teens have casually redefined what used to be called sex.

"Jessica and I knelt side by side against the wall of the big cliff behind Red Rocks one night," Lindsay tells me, "and we gave the two boys we'd just met double blow jobs so that they would give us free tickets to the 'Rave on the Rocks' show." Lindsay is pretty and blond and looks like she might sing in a church choir. "It was kind of a dare," she continues. "We raced each other to see who could get her guy off first. Jessica won, but I think her guy's dick was a lot harder to start with. It didn't mean anything to us—it's not like we had real sex."

I am talking with a group of five teenage girls about sex. They are all middle-class kids who attend a large, fairly liberal, highly rated high school. They are all decent students with college plans, and are involved in a variety of school activities and clubs. I will talk later with a similar group of boys. All of the kids have identified themselves as sexually knowledgeable and heterosexual, and they are delighted that I've set up access to an anonymous e-mail account for them to write me afterward about anything they're not comfortable talking about face to face. Tell me a story, I've asked of them—tell me how it is to be a teenager in our sexual world.

I loosen them up by asking about condoms, a word that would have embarrassed me to death as a teenager. But girls are as conversant today about condoms as they are about shoes and belly-button piercings, and proud of their expertise. They all carry a single condom in their purses, just in case. "I've carried one since I was 12," says Amanda, a petite-soft-spoken girl who is on the track team. "Lipstick and a condom, that's about all you need. You can't trust boys." She hasn't actually had intercourse yet, but, she says, "You never know." At 16, she's given blow jobs to five boys. "It was OK, no big deal. A little boring sometimes, because the guys don't say much, and you have to keep sucking until your mouth hurts. I always pretend I'm Drew Barrymore when I do it."

None of the girls swallow. Just the idea of doing so is "gross." They also don't use condoms for blow jobs, because, they reason, they don't swallow. "On my chest, or my face, or his belly, that's the only place it goes," Cara explains. They know all the technical details about safe sex, having been taught in school since third grade that you can die from sex, but they seem to have created their own rules about how it works for them.

Phone sex is very popular with the girls—they're experts, as they demonstrate with their fake oohs and ahs. "I talk to my boyfriend every night from 11 p.m. to 1 in the morning, after my parents are in bed," Katie says. "And in between talking about school and gossiping, we touch ourselves and talk dirty, and then we come together." Her sophistication when she speaks of this rivals any adult woman that I know.

Maintaining virginity means the same to all the girls: You can do anything you want as long as there's no real penetration. "We joke and call it 'outercourse,'" Cara says. She is a straight-A student and plans to be a lawyer some day. "You know, like the opposite of intercourse. It's everything but the penetration—all the making out, the blow jobs, the phone sex, masturbating with each other in person, getting naked and sleeping together. All of it is safe sex." Four of the girls are in the technical "virgin" category, but one is not. She is envied by the other girls a bit, because she seems

Editor's note: Names have been changed to protect identities.
Source: Salon.com. www.salon.com/sex/feature/2000/12/14/teens/index.html. December 14, 2000.

matter-of-fact about having "done it," and not only does she have a good-looking, steady boyfriend of over one year, she also manages to starve herself to stay at size 0.

We get down to the things that matter. Giving acquaintances blow jobs is not a serious concern for the girls. They don't worry much about diseases or pregnancy, and they don't seem to worry about their parents finding out. But they worry a lot about how they look, about being too fat when they get naked, or when their boyfriends go "down there."

"My thighs are flabby," says Amanda, size 2.

"Yeah," agrees Lindsay, perhaps a size 4 at best. "My belly pooches out right below my belly-button ring."

The ideal for every girl in high school, they explain, is to fit into size 0 jeans, a size that didn't even exist 20 years ago.

"Sure," Tyler says, when I ask the boys later about the girls' obsession with their bodies. "It's true, Girls don't eat." The boys all seem to think this is ridiculous, yet they admire the very thin girls. "I don't like when all they can talk about is how they don't eat much or how hungry they are but how they shouldn't eat," Tyler adds. "I like them a little bit athletic, but not fat. They have to be fly to go out with me."

"Fly," the boys explain, means "hot." "Fly," "hottie," "fresh" and "stylin'" have replaced the "babe" of my generation. Even though girls eat only handfuls of dry ramen noodles for lunch to stay fly, this is phat, or a very good thing to be. Boys are pimps, or pimpin', as in extremely successful with the girls. All of the boys are just chillin' with me while we talk, but the language for actual sex tends to focus on good old-fashioned blow jobs, dicks and going down.

"I go down on my girlfriend a lot," Jared says. "But I always ask her first." "Sexual harassment" is a term very loosely defined, but they're conscious of it all the time. Their high school has a policy against it, and everyone knows that although that policy is written gender-free, it only applies to boys. "Girls can say or do anything they want," Jared explains, "but no girl is ever going to be in the dean's office charged with sexual harassment." So they're careful—you can't call a girl a "bitch" on school grounds for fear of retaliation through a sexual harassment complaint; and you never know when your girlfriend might get mad at you and want revenge, so you always ask before you go down on her.

The boys maintain the same definition of virginity as the girls do: actual intercourse, penis to vagina. Three of the boys are not "virgins" and two are, by choice, they say. "Everybody wants to get married someday," Mat, a tall, sensitive basketball player says, "and there's no reason you can't have a fun sexual time until then and still be a virgin. There's lots of ways to get off." This vision of the future surprises me—in this day and age of rampant divorce, every single one of them claims they want to be married and have kids "someday," with that day placed right around the age of 28 to 30.

None of the teenagers know anyone with AIDS, although there is much talk of herpes and other sexually transmitted diseases. All of the boys who are not "virgins" religiously use condoms when having sex, but none of the girls they are with claim to be on the pill. "That marks you as a slut in high school," Jared reports. The word "slut" is not used affectionately or in a sex-positive way; it retains the same slur with these boys as it did before the sexual revolution. Not one of the kids is aware that a teenager can get free medical/sexual checkups and free birth-control pills from the county health department, without their parents being involved.

When I later ask the high school counseling office if this information is available to students, I am shown a book that lists counseling centers, health information, suicide prevention lines and other community information. I ask why they don't make this information available to teenagers via hallway posters or something else more visible, since it is a rare teenager who hangs around the counseling office searching for information, and an even rarer one who wants to ask an adult when they need help. "It's district policy," the counselor tells me. "The district feels that posting information about things like sex or suicide tends to encourage the behavior and that's not our policy."

Fortunately, the teenagers are all comfortable in the online world; they know how to research things, and they are familiar with Web sites like *Go Ask Alice* and *Scarleteen*. "Those sites aren't too bad," Josh says. "A lot of the kids ask really dumb questions, but at least they're honest. I like to read the questions about drugs and alcohol the most." The book *Go Ask Alice,* which is presented as a true story of a young girl writing a diary as she descends into her own personal hell, is a favorite of almost every teenager today. Most of the teens smoke pot and drink beer on weekends, about half have tried ecstasy and one has had at least two bad trips on drugs. They say they don't mix ecstasy with sex, preferring only to dance under the influence instead, because "you can have sex anytime."

I ask them if they think of their sexual activities as a form of recreation. "Sort of. It's just there. It's something we do. We do lots of other things too—go to movies and concerts and stuff. But blow jobs and phone sex are just things everybody has to try before you get too old, like your first beer or cigarette."

Do they think all of this is too much too soon? "No," they say unanimously, with the confidence that teenagers have always owned in thinking they know more than any adult. I understand where they're coming from—all kids want to work at being grown-up, and these kids are layered with sexual images everyplace they go from a very young age. No self-respecting teenager would be caught at anything less than an R-rated movie, and the

Spice Channel is a regular on cable for many of them. None of the kids I talked to spend any serious time looking at pornographic pictures on the Web, because they said it's too "shady."

They all spend hours on Napster instead, downloading the latest music and burning CDs. But they are experienced and jaded recipients of X-rated e-mails via their AOL accounts, and have learned to simply delete all those invitations to see "hot, luscious, horny naked teenagers," a phrase that would have made me deliriously happy just to see it in print when I was a kid.

I am somewhat envious when we are done talking. In my day we went through incredible turmoil just thinking about sex, and knowledge was sketchy at best. The girls seem to be more or less in control of their sexuality, and that's a positive development. But there is something in many of the kids' stories that leaves me a bit sad. Some of it reminds me of the classic frustrated housewife image, deciding what color to paint the ceiling while having sex—"I think girls do blow jobs and stuff just to make us happy," Jared says. "One day I looked up at my girlfriend's face while I going down on her and I caught her staring out the window, looking bored." Some of it makes me worry about them, with their combination of emotional innocence and sexual sophistication—I sense danger lurking around unseen corners.

And some of it just makes me ache for a simpler, more restricted childhood with a lot less information available for all of them. "Sometimes I think the whole world is too focused on sex," Erick, 15 says with a world-weary sigh. "There are nights when I'm locked away in my girlfriend's bedroom while her parents are out, and I know it's her turn to give me a blow job because I went down on her the night before, but sometimes I think, maybe we should really be out doing something else besides sex."

Daughters with Disabilities: Defective Women or Minority Women?

Harilyn Rousso

A noted disability rights activist once stated, "Behind every successful disabled woman is a pushy mother." Although we may rightly be wary of such a simplistic formulation, this article argues that parents, both mothers and fathers, are a powerful influence on the degree of social success, as culturally defined, of adolescent women with disabilities.

The parent-daughter relationship is a complex one, particularly during adolescence. There are the parents' attitudes and expectations, the daughter's perception of those expectations (which may differ from the parents' reality), and the daughter's unique response to those perceived expectations (which may involve agreement, rebellion, struggle, and confusion). The parents, in turn, may be influenced by the daughter's attitudes and behavior.

The intent here is to explore the relation between parental expectations and disabled adolescent women's degrees of involvement and success in the heterosexual arena. The few existing studies suggest that during adolescence, many women with disabilities have less active heterosexual lives than do their non-disabled counterparts; they have their first dates, steady partners, and sexual encounters later, and they engage in most social activities with less frequency. Both the general topic and these particular findings have not stimulated scholarly curiosity or social concern for a variety of reasons, reflecting biases and stereo-

types in the areas of both sexuality and disability. On the one hand, continued societal ambivalence toward the role of sexuality in development results in a major research emphasis being placed on situations in which sexuality seems out of control (for example, out-of-wedlock pregnancies, the spread of venereal disease).[1] Situations that hamper the emergence or expression of sexuality are rarely acknowledged as a problem. On the other hand, there is a myth in our society that disabled people are asexual. It is reflected in our genderless language (paras and quads, the blind, the deaf), in our unsexy associations to disability (sick, helpless, dependent, childlike), and in our pathetic media images (poster children and telethons).

Because so much of female sexuality has focused on physical appearance, disabled women are particularly likely to be misperceived as asexual. Thus, their more limited sexual activities during adolescence may appear to be an inevitable consequence of disability. To the extent that disabled women *are* ever viewed as sexual, they are too often stereotypically assumed to be capable of reproducing only "defective" children or to be unable to nurture any children.[2] From this perspective, their limited heterosexual activities may be perceived as a source of relief, the best form of contraception, not requiring investigation. In addition, civil rights activists frequently state that equal opportunity is hardest to legislate in the social arena. Legal action can require an employer to hire a black or disabled person, but it cannot require a potential partner to date a disabled woman or man. Attitudinal studies suggest that while disability per se is an anxiety-producing topic for many individuals, the prospect of intimate contact with disabled people is far more uncomfortable and distressing than professional or casual interaction.[3]

The intent of this article is to begin to address the research gap, building on existing

Source: Reprinted from Michelle Fine and Adrienne Asch, eds., *Women with Disabilities: Essays in Psychology, Culture, and Politics* (Philadelphia: Temple University Press, 1988).

studies. Presented here are the results of a pilot study on the heterosexual interests and experiences of adolescent women with disabilities and on their relations with parental attitudes and expectations in the heterosexual area. Comparisons are made between disabled and nondisabled women and among disabled women themselves. The focus is on heterosexual activities because we believe these may have particular developmental significance given the biased definitions of womanhood in our culture. By no means is it the intent to devalue other forms of sexual expression; these are expected to become the subject of future research.

THEORETICAL FRAMEWORK

For both women and men, participation in a range of social and sexual activities during adolescence facilitates the completion of a variety of developmental tasks. Peter Blos and others describe how such participation helps the young person begin to break familial ties and form connections with nonfamilial partners in the outside world. It also provides opportunities to explore budding sexuality, to develop social skills, and to establish the capacity for intimacy. In addition, specifically *heterosexual* involvement offers an important avenue for the development of a sense of identity. For adolescent women in particular, dating, kissing, sexual encounters, and going steady may be a significant component of gender-role identity, contributing to feelings of adequacy as women. Whether or not we agree, the traditional and still widely held measure of a woman's success in our culture is her capacity to attract and keep a man, preferably through marriage, and to bear his children. Sharon Thompson acknowledged surprise and distress at the finding of her recent study that for white working-class teenage girls, their ultimate goal was "true, monogamous, permanent, one-man; one-woman couple love," with career as a distant second, only when love fails. Similarly, G. L. Zellman and J. D. Goodchilds reported that more than half the teenagers in their study believed that a woman's most important job remains in the home.[4]

Adolescence is a training ground for adult roles as they are customarily defined. Given these adolescent visions of a woman's role, the flurry of heterosexual activities is assumed by the adolescent woman to be a confirmation of womanhood, whereas the absence of such activities is often experienced by the young woman herself and the world of family, friends, and community around her as a sign of failure. J. M. Bardwick writes, "The sexuality of the adolescent girl fuses with the rewards of dating. Early dating is a testing ground for success in the very new femininity and feminine desirability. As a result, the girl is ready to fall in love again and again and assures herself of her desirability by her collection of broken hearts." C. P. Malmquist adds, "The self-esteem of most girls is more contingent on success in social relationships than on school grades. In a national survey of adolescents, assets for achieving popularity and social acceptance were mentioned three times more often by girls than by boys as one of their worries."[5]

This is not to say that there are no adolescent women who focus instead on school, career, and other areas. Such women exist and do not necessarily suffer from their choices, but they appear to be the exception rather than the rule. The culture and the literature focus on the heterosexual area as the compulsory workplace for young women. The present study maintains this bias in part to consider its impact on the lives of disabled women.

Despite the proclaimed importance of heterosexual activities in adolescence, few research studies focus on what factors help or hinder social success during the teenage years. This is in sharp contrast to the multitude of studies on academic and vocational success and on ways to *reduce* heterosexual contact. Again, this gap may reflect a devaluing of sexuality and, more specifically, "women's work." It may alternatively reflect the fact that social success by adolescent women and men is accepted as the norm. Although many people recall their social lives in adolescence with a certain degree of discomfort and distress, it is generally assumed that most adolescents date, eventually find partners, and lead socially active adult lives. Partnerless people are studied only when they are middle-aged and it is clear that they have not met the norm.

Although direct studies of social achievement in adolescence are lacking, information on this topic is often included or implied in works on gender-role identity. Social success and achievement of gender-role identity are by no means identical and at best complexly related, but gender-role works have something important to offer our present research. They stress that parental attitudes, expectations, and behaviors play a major role in the sexual development of women (and men). Depending on their theoretical orientation, such works note how children imitate or identify with their parents and how parents foster gender-appropriate behavior.[6] Significantly, studies of academic success also have emphasized the importance of parental standards and goals for their children's success. For example, parents who encourage academic performance and set high goals for their children are often rewarded by the child's high achievement, although sometimes children rebel and drop out of the academic arena.[7] These works by no means agree on the nature of the parental influence, nor do they claim that parents are the only important factor. They do, however, lay the ground for an investigation of the heterosexual achievements of adolescent disabled women.

The lack of research on the sexual development of disabled women has already been noted. Existing studies include those by A. Welbourne and colleagues, which compared the psychosexual development of forty-seven women who had become blind before the age of ten with thirty-nine women who were sighted; Yvonne Duffy, which studied the social and sexual experiences of seventy-five orthopedically disabled women, forty-five of whom were disabled before the age of fifteen; and Carnie Landis and Marjorie Bolles, the oldest and most extensive study, which compared the social and sexual history of one hundred women disabled before the age of thirteen with epilepsy, rheumatic heart disease, cerebral palsy, and a range of orthopedic disabilities with one hundred nondisabled women.[8] In all three studies, the disabled women fared less well socially and sexually during adolescence than their nondisabled peers. The studies suggested some of the obstacles that the disabled women faced: transportation problems, architectural barriers, lack of self-confidence, rejecting peers, pessimistic parents and community, and the lack of role models for social success. Some of the disabled women were successful despite the odds. Limited social achievement was never found to be an inevitable consequence of having a disability. Only the Landis and Bolles study attempted to study factors facilitating social success in a systematic way. Family dynamics were studied in depth and found to be an important factor in psychosexual development.

Although the specific formulation of family dynamics that Landis and Bolles provide, described below, may be less relevant today than in the past, their awareness of the importance of environmental factors is impressive and a major contribution. Until relatively recently, developmentalists have taken the position that disability inevitably alters development, causing a host of psychosocial problems, including problems with id, ego, and superego.[9] Only in the past several years have studies confronted this biological determinism, linking environmental factors and particularly parental attitudes to self-esteem and the body image of disabled children.[10] Several studies suggest that disabled children fare better in their development when parents are able to put the disability in perspective, seeing their disabled children as children first, with disability as only one of many characteristics. Problems appear more likely to arise when parents become preoccupied with and unduly pessimistic about the disability. Such parental preoccupation with disability may reflect individual dynamics, but often it also reflects cultural values—the devaluing and stigmatizing of disabled people, and even more so, of disabled women in our society.

The present study builds on these preliminary findings. It also reflects the author's clinical experience as a psychotherapist and personal experience as a woman with cerebral palsy. It hypothesizes that disabled adolescent women fare better in the heterosexual area when parents view them as women first, capable of meeting typical female role expectations. It also assumes that many parents do not have this perspective; for them, "disabled women" translates into "defective woman," which drastically alters their vision of who this daughter could or should become. For this altered vision, disabled women pay a price.

RESEARCH FINDINGS AND DISCUSSION

The present research studied the heterosexual experiences and parental expectations during adolescence of forty-three women with physical and sensory disabilities. The majority of these women were white, heterosexual, and single, in their twenties and thirties, with some degree of college education. The range of disabilities included mobility impairments, brain and neurological disabilities, blindness, and deafness.

Thirty-one of these women were disabled at or before the age of ten, and thus they experienced adolescence with a disability. They are the prime focus of the study. The remaining twelve were disabled after age ten, and most of them after adolescence. Thus, for the most part, this latter group went through adolescence as nondisabled young women; they serve as a comparison group for the original thirty-one, enabling us to compare the disabled and nondisabled experience in adolescence. The two groups are referred to throughout as women disabled before adolescence and women disabled after adolescence.

Building on previous research, this study hypothesized that the women disabled before adolescence would be less socially and heterosexually active during their adolescent years than the group disabled after adolescence. The findings supported this hypothesis. More specifically, when the women in the study were asked at what age they had their first date, kiss, sexual contact, experience with intercourse, and steady relationship, the mean age was later in all areas for the women disabled before adolescence in comparison to those disabled after adolescence (see Table 12-1). It is important to note, however, that the mean age for the first recollection of masturbation was about the same for the two groups. Masturbation is to be distinguished from the other categories listed in that it is a sexual activity that does not require the presence of a partner. The fact that women disabled both before and after adolescence recall beginning to masturbate at about the same age suggests that both groups may have had a similar level of interest in and awareness of sexual feelings, but differences in the opportunity to express those feelings.

In comparing themselves to their peers, almost three-fourths of the women disabled before adolescence felt that they had their first social and sexual experiences later than their peers, and more than three-fifths described themselves as less socially active than their peers. In contrast, among the women disabled

TABLE 12-1

AGE OF FIRST SOCIAL SEXUAL EXPERIENCES

	Age in Years	
Experience	Disabled before Adolescence	Disabled after Adolescence
First date	17.7	14.5
First kiss	17.0	14.2
First sexual contact	18.2	16.1
First experience with intercourse	22.0	18.3
First steady relationship	19.2	17.0
First recollected masturbation	15.9	15.9

after adolescence, only one in four felt that she had her first social and sexual experiences later, and only one in three felt she was less socially active than her peers. Interestingly, although the questionnaire did not specify whether the women should draw comparisons with their disabled or nondisabled peers, most of the women disabled before adolescence indicated that they were drawing comparisons with nondisabled peers or offered answers with regard to each peer group separately. Clearly, the majority of women disabled before adolescence perceived themselves as participating less fully and, by implication, less successfully than their nondisabled counterparts in the social area.

In explaining their less active heterosexual lives during adolescence, almost nine out of ten women disabled before adolescence felt that their disability was an important factor, although there were widely varied perceptions on how the disability impeded their social lives. Some women emphasized their inability to "circulate." One woman said, "Planning to go anywhere was so complex. I was exhausted before I got out the door." Another noted, "Having to have my younger sister tell me what boys were saying on the telephone, since I could not hear myself, was not conducive to romance." Others spoke about their lack of self-confidence and lower self-esteem: "I was so shy—I didn't expect anyone to want to go

out with me." Or: "No one wanted to deal with a blind girl. It makes me tearful to think of it. All of my successes and failures felt connected to my disability." Still others mentioned architectural and transportation barriers. Many described attitudinal barriers, including the prejudices of friends who excluded them from social activities and of potential partners who were reluctant to be seen with them, as well as discouragement from family, professionals, and the community at large. Comments included "Boys treated me like a pal rather than a girlfriend, as though my disability disqualified me from being female" and "People expected so little of me socially; in retrospect, it is shocking to realize that." Many of the women felt that their disability affected their social lives in more than one way. The direction of the effects was predominantly negative.

Those women disabled before adolescence who felt less active in the heterosexual arena than their nondisabled peers reported a variety of consequences, some of them positive. One woman said, "By the time I got involved with someone, my head was in a better place. I did it [had sex] because I wanted to, not because of peer pressure." However, most women reported harsh negative consequences, including lost opportunities and damage to their self-esteem as lovable, complete women. One respondent reported, "All those lost years can never be recaptured, no matter how active I am now." Another wrote, "I felt so abnormal and defective; it was a hard image to shake even when I became happily sexually involved as an adult." Yet another woman added, "I eventually rushed into bed with the first man who asked me." Still another: "I remember one point in my late adolescence painfully asking myself, 'How can I be a *real* woman if I am nineteen years old and have never had a date in my life?'"

All six of the lesbians and bisexual women disabled before adolescence seemed to have had some interest in getting involved in heterosexual activities during adolescence. Most did not become involved with women until well after adolescence. There were no lesbians and only one bisexual woman among those women disabled after adolescence, so cross-group comparisons could not be made. However, we can note that of the six, five felt less heterosexually active and successful than their peers as a result of internal and external barriers rather than choice, and four of the five felt there were negative consequences in terms of both lost opportunities for exploration and lowered self-esteem. One woman stated, "It was difficult enough to be feeling so confused about my sexual identity. Not to be able to experiment with boys only added to any confusion and growing self-doubts." Another noted, "Even though I was beginning to think that boys were not for me, I would have felt better about myself if I had had the opportunity to say no."

These comments suggest that for disabled adolescent women, as for nondisabled women, heterosexual activities may be closely linked to feelings of adequacy as women. In a society that devalues disabled women and questions their womanhood because of their disability, the lack of social success may be one more reason not to feel like "true" women.

The findings from the present research corroborate some of the results of the few studies on the topic. Welbourne and colleagues found that the blind and sighted women they studied followed the same sociosexual patterns. For the blind women, however, there was a longer, later age range for the age of the first date, and the mean age of first experience with sexual intercourse was significantly later. Duffy, in her study of orthopedically disabled women, found that the average age for the first date was substantially later for women disabled before the age of fifteen in comparison to those disabled after age fifteen; her study also indicated that the early-onset group had a more limited range of social and sexual experiences than those disabled later in life.[11]

Landis and Bolles, in comparing the social and sexual histories of one hundred disabled women with those of one hundred nondisabled women, found that more of the disabled women had never dated and had no interest in doing so; those who dated began to do so later; more of the disabled women had never been in love in comparison to the nondisabled women; and as a group, the disabled women had less heterosexual contact, less homosexual involvement, and were less likely to have engaged in masturbatory activities.[12] They also found the disabled women to be less knowledgeable about and less interested in sexual matters. They summarized this set of findings by describing disabled women as "hyposexual."

Landis and Bolles also studied the disabled and nondisabled women's relationships with their families of origin. Their findings on this topic offer introduction to the issue of parental role in sexual development and a considerably different formulation from the present study. In particular, in their sample Landis and Bolles found that disabled women were more closely tied to their parents and less involved with the outside world. Combining information on involvement in the sociosexual arena with information on involvement with family, the authors developed an index of psychosexual immaturity and found that disabled women were "psychosexually immature" in comparison to their nondisabled counterparts.

In explaining their findings, Landis and Bolles suggest that biological and environmental factors surrounding a childhood disability may contribute to psychosexual immaturity, which in turn may lead to "hyposexuality." In particular, their view is that having a disability from childhood may necessitate more parental care and attention, exclusion from childhood activities, and interference with strivings toward independence. A pattern of dependence is established that continues throughout adulthood. Because of young disabled women's close family ties and their failure to move out into the world, sexual development is often delayed. The authors make a clear distinction between delayed development and thwarted development. They do not feel that the disabled women were thwarted in their heterosexual development; if they had been, there would have been higher incidences of masturbatory and homosexual activities, which there were not. Instead, they feel the lack of sexual interest can be explained only in terms of a delay. They note, however, that not all the disabled women developed such dependence patterns, nor were all lacking in social and sexual experience. Some women had a greater separateness from their families, and their sexual development proceeded in a more typical fashion.

The particular family dynamics that Landis and Bolles describe—over-involvement by disabled women with their families and a reluctance to move out into the world—are not documented by the present study, which occurred more than forty years later. When asked to measure their degree of involvement with their families and friends during adolescence, the women disabled before adolescence were no more involved with their families and no less involved with their friends than were the women disabled after adolescence. Despite their more limited direct involvement in social and sexual activities, the early-onset group as a whole was no less *interested* in social life than was the group of women disabled after adolescence. None of the women disabled before adolescence explained their limited involvement in the heterosexual arena in terms of lack of desire and interest—for none of them was it a deliberate choice to abstain. Notably, in the area of masturbation, the early-onset women were on par with the later-onset group, clearly documenting that there was private sexual exploration and sexual interest. What emerges from these findings is a picture, not of complacent dependence on parents and lack of sexual need and interest, but a strong desire on the part of the disabled adolescent women to move into the heterosexual arena and of major difficulty in doing so.

PARENTAL ATTITUDES AND EXPECTATIONS

The present study hypothesized that parents of women disabled before adolescence would have a different set of expectations for their daughters than would parents of daughters disabled afterward. In particular, it was assumed that parents of women disabled before adolescence would have lower heterosexual expectations and higher educational/vocational expectations compared to parents of the other group because they believed that their daughters, because of their disabilities, could not meet typical female role expectations. Many of the findings supported this hypothesis.

In an effort to distinguish the parental expectations of the two groups of disabled women, all the women in the sample were asked to recall their middle adolescence, ages thirteen to seventeen, and to evaluate their parents' future expectations for them in three sociosexual areas and three educational/career areas. In particular, they were asked to what extent they believed their parents expected them to have an active sociosexual life, to get married, and to have children, and to what extent their parents expected them to complete high school, complete college, and get a good job.

While the parental expectations for the two groups were not different to a statistically significant degree, there were some important trends. On all three sociosexual goals, both mothers and fathers of the women disabled before adolescence had lower expectations than did the parents of the comparison group. In contrast, in two of the three educational/career areas (except completing high school) the parents of the early-onset group had higher expectations than those of the later-onset group. In a related question, the women were asked to determine whether during adolescence they thought their parents were more interested in their school life, more interested in their social life, or equally interested in both. Although relatively small percentages of both group felt that their parents were solely interested in their social lives, slightly more than half the women disabled before adolescence felt that their parents were mainly interested in their school lives; only a third of the women in the comparison group felt this way.

There is a possible explanation for the lack of statistically significant differences between the two groups. First, both groups were asked to consider their parents' expectations for them when they were adolescents. The comparison group, consisting of women not disabled until after adolescence, was being asked to recall a time before disability occurred. Their recollections may be colored by the possible change in their parents' expectations of them after they became disabled. Also, many of the women who became disabled before adolescence commented that they did not know what their parents' expectations for them were in the social arena; their parents were noticeably silent about this. When they were adolescents, they interpreted their par-

ents' silence as a confirmation of the societal stereotype according to which they did not have much social potential, but in retrospect they were not sure that this was what the parental silence meant; thus, they were reluctant to acknowledge negative parental expectations in the social arena on their questionnaire, although that is what they felt while they were growing up.

Another measure of parental expectations in the social arena is the extent and nature of parent-daughter communication on sexual and social issues. G. L. Fox reports that mother-daughter communication on sexual matters is important because it raises the daughter's awareness of her own sexuality and enables her to make more responsible choices about her sexual behavior.[13] For nondisabled women this often means taking more contraceptive responsibility. As I have written elsewhere, for disabled women raised in a society that views them as asexual, parent-child communication about sexuality serves to acknowledge and confirm the young woman's social and sexual potential.[14] Such conversations not only encourage contraceptive responsibility in the heterosexual area but also encourage entrance into the arena.

For both groups of women in the sample, mothers were one of three major sources of sex information, friends and literature being the other two; fathers, in contrast, were relatively unimportant. These findings are consistent with other research on the sources of sex information for teenagers in general, as summarized in a recent *ms.* magazine report on teenage sexuality.[15] They also concur with the findings of G. L. Fox and G. L. Inazu, who reported that within the family, mothers, more so than fathers, are the prime sex educators.[16]

When asked whether their parents had talked with them about nine topics on sexuality—menstruation, female anatomy, male anatomy, intercourse, birth control, venereal disease, dating, marriage, and children—the

TABLE 12-2

PERCENTAGE OF PARENTS WHO TALKED ABOUT THE TOPIC

Topic	Disabled before Adolescence (n = 31)		Disabled after Adolescence (n = 12)	
	(%)	(n)	(%)	(n)
Menstruation	77.4	24	83.3	10
Female anatomy	41.9	13	41.7	5
Male anatomy	32.3	10	25.0	3
Intercourse	32.3	10	25.0	3
Birth control	22.6	7	33.3	4
Venereal disease	16.1	5	33.3	4
Dating	51.6	16	83.3	10
Marriage	38.7	12	66.7	8
Children	38.7	12	58.3	7

most striking differences between women in the two groups involved to topics of dating, marriage, and children, for which the early-onset group had considerably lower percentages (see Table 12-2). The women disabled before adolescence also had lower percentages on the topics of venereal disease and birth control. Differences on the remaining four topics were minor.

These findings again suggest differences in parental expectations between the two groups. Parents of women disabled before adolescence might have doubted the need to talk about topics that they felt would be irrelevant to their daughters' future role. They might also have been concerned about stirring up unrequitable longings and feelings of deprivation. Silence may have seemed preferable.[17]

Along related lines of parental communication, the women disabled before adolescence were asked first whether their parents ever spoke with them about the cause and nature of their disability and whether their parents ever spoke with them about the impact of their disability on their social and sexual lives. Although seven out of ten of the women reported that their parents had spoken with them about their disabilities, only about one-fourth of the women reported conversations on the effect of disability on sexuality. Of these women, only one indicated that her parents had given her a positive message about her social potential given her disability.

When those women whose parents did not talk with them about the effect of disability on their sexuality were asked to explain the parental silence, some indicated that their parents did not discuss sex with anyone regardless of disability: "No one in the house ever discussed sex—our Catholic upbringing." Other women interpreted the silence to mean that either they already knew all they needed to know or that they would ask for help when they needed it. "My parents figured in time I'd experience a relationship where I'd confront this and it would be okay to ask or ask for help." However, many of the women interpreted the silence as a pessimistic statement about social possibilities. For example, "They simply did not think that sexuality was going to be part of my repertoire." Also, "By not talking about sexuality and dating with me but by talking to my sister, she implied that it was not for me."

When asked whether their parents had any fears about the emergence of their sexuality, slightly fewer women disabled before adolescence than women disabled after responded affirmatively. There were no differences in the kinds of fears that the parents of the two groups expressed; major fears included pregnancy and being taken advantage of. At the same time, more than half (sixteen) of the early-onset group and only two of the late-onset group described their parents as too protective, not specifically in the sexual arena but in general. These findings suggest that parents of women disabled before adolescence were by no means freer or more trusting of their daughters' capabilities in general but that they might have been somewhat less concerned about sexuality. This may be because they did not perceive their daughters as sexual.

When the women disabled before adolescence were asked what kinds of messages they got about the social and sexual potential of disabled people, almost half of those who answered indicated that they had gotten negative messages, and another quarter indicated that they had gotten mixed messages. Only one woman indicated that she had gotten a positive message. While peers and society were identified as the major sources of messages, parents were also a frequently mentioned source.

A number of women disabled before adolescence expressed appreciation for their parents' emphasis on school and career, noting that had they not been disabled, they probably would not have obtained such a good education or have gone so far in their careers. Indeed, comparing the women disabled before adolescence with those disabled after, the early-onset group did attain higher education levels and were more likely to be working full-time when they filled out the questionnaire. But they may have paid a price. Anna and Paul Ornstein comment on the potentially damaging psychological effects of parents recognizing some of their child's capabilities while disregarding others: "Parents may affirm selectively certain of the child's physical and intellectual attributes. But as far as the

child is concerned, such arbitrary selective affirmation may be experienced as parental failure to validate other aspects of the developing self—that is, outright rejection of his or her total self."[18] Even the appreciative women recognized that emphasis on educational strivings were based on an undermining assumption about their defectiveness as "real" women, that is, their incapacity to marry and have children. As one woman stated, "While I am grateful that my parents recognized my intellectual abilities and applauded me onward to get my Ph.D., it is distressing to think that their applause was partly grounded in their perception of me as a misfit."

Parental difficulty in recognizing and affirming the social and sexual potential of disabled daughters can be understood in terms of the individual dynamics of the parents and family and in terms of broader societal values. For a mother in particular, affirmation of sexual potential and womanhood may require her ability to see herself in her daughter and to be able to identify with her. As a result of their own dynamics and history, for some mothers the daughter's disability may loom too large and make the daughter seem too disparate; these mothers may then have difficulty identifying and may seek to keep their distance. For example, the disability may remind the mother of her own feelings of imperfection, and she may be reluctant to acknowledge that part of herself. Or, having a disabled child may seem like punishment for wrongdoing, a source of guilt safer dealt with from afar.

The father also plays an important role in the confirmation of a female child's heterosexuality. For a father to affirm his daughter's heterosexuality, he must be able to see in his daughter the potential to become the kind of woman he could choose as a mate. Again, as the result of feelings of inadequacy, guilt, or other dynamics, the father may have difficulty seeing his daughter in this light.

In addition, particular family needs may encourage members to keep the disabled daughter or sister an asexual child. This role may serve to give the mother an ongoing mothering function as the children grow older, to avoid conflict between the marital couple, or to address other family problems. Finally, parents may be concerned that should they foster a strong sense of heterosexuality in their disabled adolescent daughters, the daughters may be rejected, hurt, victimized, or abused. It may seem safer to disregard sexuality.

In understanding parental attitudes, however, the larger societal context must be considered. Some of the myths about disabled women have been cited already: that they are viewed as asexual and are seen as incapable of nurturing children and as likely to bear "defective" children. These stereotypes state that disabled women cannot fulfill traditional female role expectations. Parents of disabled daughters are likely to have internalized these myths to some degree. Thus, they may approach their daughters with a different set of standards and expectations.

Ethel Roskies, in her study of parenting children disabled as the result of thalidomide, confirms some of the present findings on parental attitudes and expectations. She notes that parents of disabled children are much less likely to advocate for their children in the social arena in comparison to the educational and vocational areas:

> The area of marriage and parenthood appears to constitute an exception to the mother's usual demands for social equity. More than in any other respect, in their expectations of marriage, the mothers of disabled children were prepared to accept that their children would remain deviant. Perhaps the difference in the mothers' expectations can be explained by the fact that they viewed marriage not only as a social relationship but a personal one. One can demand respect and equal opportunity far more easily from the soci-

ety at large than one can demand love from an individual person. Moreover, to the degree that mothers tended to identify with prospective spouses, the difficulties loomed larger. As one mother expressed it, "How can I expect someone to marry X when I cannot marry someone like him." A mother could learn to love a child with missing arms or legs, but it appeared too difficult for her to imagine that a prospective husband or wife could do this too.[19]

THE RELATION BETWEEN HETEROSEXUAL INVOLVEMENT AND PARENTAL EXPECTATIONS

The findings thus far indicate that women disabled before adolescence had less adolescent involvement in the heterosexual arena than those disabled afterward and that parents of the women in the first group had lower heterosexual expectations than parents of the comparison group. Attention now focuses on the relation between degree of heterosexual involvement and parental expectations.

Because a major goal of the study was to examine why some disabled adolescent women were socially successful while many others were not, the research hypothesis on this topic focused exclusively on the thirty-one women disabled before adolescence. An in-depth study of the women who had disabilities during adolescence seemed likely to produce the most fruitful results.

Nevertheless, some findings on the relation between parental expectations and daughter's degree of heterosexual involvement for the whole sample of forty-three women are briefly considered. An attempt was made to examine this relation by developing an index of parents' heterosexual expectations for their daughters, combining their expectations in three areas: having an active sociosexual life, getting married, having children. The forty-three women then were divided into two groups, depending on whether their parents' expectations were high (optimistic) or low (pessimistic), and the groups were compared on the average age of their first sociosexual encounters (first date, kiss, etc.) and on their own evaluation of their degree of heterosexual involvement in relation to that of their peers (more active, less active, as active). Although the average age for the first events was slightly lower in four out of five event areas (except first steady relationship) for the high-parental-expectations group, the differences were not statistically significant. The women's ratings of themselves compared to peers also were not significantly different for the two groups.

This lack of significant results should not be interpreted to mean that parents are uninfluential; some other findings suggest the parental impact. The women's heterosexual expectations for themselves were found to be positively correlated to their parents' expectations for them, to a statistically significant degree (at less than .05 level). This means that women who during adolescence were optimistic about their ability to have an active social life, marry, and have children when they got older were likely to have parents who were similarly optimistic, whereas women who were pessimistic about their heterosexual future were likely to have pessimistic parents. Although statistically significant correlations do not prove cause and effect, developmental theory and logic suggest that this is likely, that parental attitudes do influence a daughter's attitudes. In turn, the daughter's expectations for herself may influence those of her parents, so the relation may be one of mutual interaction and influence.

As further evidence of parental influence, when the women were asked to identify which factors were most influential in shaping the image of who they would become as adults, mothers were mentioned most frequently, and fathers were in the top five (others included friends, teachers, and other nonfamilial adults). When asked about the direction of their parents' influence, the women responded

in a manner reflecting the complexity of the parent-child relationship. One-fourth of the women said their mothers were a positive influence; another fourth indicated a negative influence; half said their influence was mixed. Findings were similar for fathers: ten women described them as a positive force; thirteen, as negative; and fifteen, mixed.

This complexity may help explain the lack of statistically significant findings in our analysis of the relation between parental expectations and heterosexual involvement. Aside from lack of refinement in the questionnaire and the small sample size, which are definitely problems, there may be difficulties in the formulation. The statistics have attempted to examine whether expectations and degree of heterosexual involvement rise and fall together. The following discussion suggests that the answer may be that this is too simplistic a formulation.

For the thirty-one women disabled before adolescence, the primary research hypothesis was that positive expectations facilitated heterosexual involvement during adolescence, whereas pessimistic expectations hindered such involvement. The findings, however, reveal a more complex relation. Positive expectations did facilitate heterosexual activities, but pessimistic expectations resulted in a range of responses, depending on a variety of factors.

The hypothesis was tested primarily through the clinical analysis of anecdotal material gathered in personal interviews with a small number of women and an even smaller number of their parents; these interviews offered extensive information on expectations, degree of involvement, and a host of factors about the parents, the women, and the environment. The written questionnaires by some of the women who were not interviewed also yielded rich anecdotal information. Secondarily, the questionnaire results were statistically analyzed, keeping in mind the various limitations of this approach.

The statistical findings mirrored those for the sample as a whole. The previously mentioned procedure of developing an index of parents' heterosexual expectations was followed, in which the women were divided into high- and low-expectations groups, and the two groups were compared on two measures of degree of heterosexual involvement: age of first sociosexual activity and degree of heterosexual involvement compared with that of peers. Again, there were no statistically significant findings, although the mean age of the first encounter for the high-expectations group was slightly lower on the same six out of seven activities.

From the anecdotal material it was possible to identify and organize some of the complexity in the relation between parental expectations and degree of heterosexual involvement. In particular, four categories of expectations and heterosexual involvement were identified.

1. *Parents viewed their disabled daughter as an intact woman, and the disabled woman was active in the heterosexual area.* Several women in the sample who were particularly socially and sexually successful during adolescence described themselves as having parents who viewed them as complete, intact women, disability and all. One woman said, "My parents seemed to evaluate me and my sister using the same standard, considering our strengths and our failings; they were aware of my disability, my need to use crutches, and we talked about it; but they didn't seem preoccupied by it." Stated another woman, "In childhood, I was led to believe that the same social performance was expected of me as of my cousins who had no disabilities. I was a social success in part because my mother expected me to succeed. In fact, she gave me no choice."

Interviews with the parents of these women seemed to confirm their perceptions. By and large, these parents tended to set similar expectations for their disabled and nondisabled daughters. To whatever extent these parents had lower social expectations for the disabled daughters, it was a reflection of their awareness of society's prejudices, rather than their own personal statement about their daughters' social capabilities. Some of these parents seemed to feel that their daughters' disabilities would have no impact whatsoever on their social life. Other parents seemed aware of the physical barriers and the prejudices that might result from a disability, but they had faith in their daughters' social capabilities and sought to mediate the environment in order to minimize the barriers. Their strategies included moving the family to geographic locations more likely to be supportive of a disabled young woman—for example, to a location with a small high school, where the other students would interact with the young woman in the natural course of events and thus would eventually see beyond her disability. Another strategy was for the parents to talk directly and effectively with their disabled daughters about social problems as they emerged, such as how you flirt when you cannot see, how you talk with a boy about your disability, or how you handle prejudicial remarks. To a lesser or greater degree, parents who explicitly dealt with disability barriers appeared to be viewing their daughters as intact women, but also *minority* women, in need of advocacy to deal with barriers and have the world affirm their womanhood.

One of the typical characteristics of women and their families in this situation was an ability on the part of the mother to identify with the disabled daughter. One mother said, "When I was growing up, I wanted to complete college, work, marry, and have children. Both of my daughters (a disabled and a nondisabled daughter) were part of me, and I wanted for them the very same good things that I wanted for myself." It is difficult to generalize why some mothers can identify with their disabled daughters and others cannot, but one factor might be the mother's own definition of womanhood. Some of the mothers of women who fell into this first category had broader, nontraditional views of womanhood, definitions that encompassed, for example, a strong emphasis on work and education in one case, or being a lesbian mother in another; a broader definition of womanhood might more readily enable a mother to see the womanliness in a daughter who does not fit the societal (and often unreachable) norm.

Another characteristic of this group was a close relationship between the father and the disabled woman; indeed, a few of the women indicated that they felt closer to their fathers than to their mothers when growing up and that their involvement with their fathers offered the promise of successful involvement with men outside the home. The Landis and Bolles study also found a strong father-daughter tie in socially successful women.

In terms of concerns about the emergence of their daughters' sexuality, parents of the women in this group tended to show many of the concerns typical of parents of nondisabled adolescent women (for example, unwanted pregnancy or being taken advantage of), although their concerns did not seem intense. Several of these parents mentioned an additional concern, that a daughter would settle for a partner who was less attractive, competent, and intellectual than she was because prejudices would keep away men who were on a par with her. This concern seemed to give recognition to both the daughter's social capabilities and the prejudices she faced. One mother stated, "My daughter is an extremely enchanting, amazing young woman with tremendous social potential who may not find her way

to a partner who is her equal, because of people's attitudes."

Other characteristics of this group included the disabled adolescent women's living in a community that offered access to many different social groups, often because the parents made a deliberate choice to move there, and, finally, luck. At least two of the women indicated that they fortuitously fell into good relationships during their early adolescence and that these relationships fostered their self-esteem and helped overcome any doubts their parents might have had about their social potential.

2. *Parents viewed their disabled daughter as a "defective" woman, unable to meet typical social and sexual role expectations, and the disabled woman was active in the heterosexual arena during adolescence.* Disabled women in this group felt that their parents did not expect them to meet typical female role expectations; in particular, their parents did not expect them to marry and have children. One woman said, "My father told me that my disability was a liability when it came to getting married, and he offered to build me a house with the hope that that would perhaps enable me to catch a man; my mother told me, 'Put all your time into school— you'll never get a man.'" Another woman said, "My parents did not expect me to marry—my dad because he'd never marry 'an inferior person' so why would anyone else? My mom thought I'd never marry because I couldn't fulfill the nurturing role and because she was a martyr and felt I should be one too." In direct interviews, the parents of some of these women acknowledged that they had different expectations for their disabled and nondisabled daughters and that they tended to encourage education because they felt that marriage was not an option.

To understand the viewpoint of these parents, one must consider a variety of social, cultural, and psychodynamic factors. Several of these parents agreed with society's stereotypes about the limited potential of disabled people and could not see these as prejudice. This is in sharp contrast to the first group of parents, who acknowledged prejudice, fought against it, but never agreed with it as an accurate assessment of their daughters' potential.

Also, a number of the parents in this second group, particularly mothers, had traditional definitions of womanhood that focused on precisely those concrete skills that the disabled daughter could not perform, at least not in typical ways. For example, one mother emphasized nurturance through housecleaning, ironing, cooking, and feeding as essential for womanhood. She could not understand how her daughter, who was quadriplegic, could find a husband who could tolerate her not accomplishing these tasks and, in fact, would have to nurture her. Another mother, a highly religious Italian woman, felt that it was God's will that she take care of her seriously disabled daughter for as long as she lived, and she felt that it was against her religion and her culture to be fostering independence and encouraging her daughter to move out of the house, with or without a husband. For yet another mother, who had sacrificed her own educational pursuits for marriage, her disabled daughter represented the opportunity to experience career success vicariously.

Despite these discouraging parental attitudes, the women in this group managed to be socially active during their adolescence. What they report was a determination to prove their parents wrong. One woman stated:

When I became about sixteen or seventeen, I pushed myself to have the very things my parents said I could not have. I was determined to prove I was a "normal" woman. I deliberately sought out the most handsome man to parade around. And although I did not consciously intend to do it, I became pregnant out of wedlock at seventeen, which was extremely affirming for me. One of my proud moments was parading around the supermarket with my belly sticking out for all to see that I was indeed a woman and that my body worked like a normal woman's body.

Another woman similarly explained, "I was counterphobic. I had fear that my parents were right, and as soon as I could, I began screwing around like mad to rebel against them and my own fear."

What factors enable some women to rebel rather than internalize expectations? Often a combination of circumstances facilitates the rebellion. Similar to the first group, several of the women described close relationships with their fathers; some of the women who became disabled at age five or six reported strong positive relationships with their fathers predisability, and although the relationship often changed postdisability, the impact of those first few years was sustaining. Other women reported mixed messages from their fathers. While overtly the fathers told them that they could not make it socially in the outside world, these fathers also remained very close to them, sometimes seductively so, providing the young women with the confidence to take on the social scene. Sometimes the presence of a sister, another family member, or a close friend or a group of friends helped a woman to challenge her parents' pessimistic assumptions about her. One woman noted that through her relationships with her girlfriends, she discovered that she had the capacity to give and to nurture, albeit not physically, and that if she could nurture her friends, perhaps she could nurture a husband and children as well.

A third factor appeared to be the nature of the community in which the disabled woman grew up, particularly in terms of architectural and attitudinal accessibility. The presence of curbcuts everywhere was significant for one woman, whereas the availability of a car was crucial for another, allowing both to explore the social arena despite parental prohibitions. The neighborhood's attitudes toward disability—or, more generally, toward difference—could help or hinder the rebellion process. For example, in one community many of the residents were Holocaust survivors who had undergone trauma; they could understand the trauma of polio and receive a young woman with polio into their social environment. Finally, individual personality characteristics were significant. For example, several of the women described themselves as always having been rebellious, spunky risk takers; they were determined not to let their parents' pessimism get them down.

3. *Parents viewed their disabled daughter as a "defective" woman, and the disabled woman had limited heterosexual involvement during adolescence.* Several women typified this situation of low parental expectations and limited involvement by the woman in social activities during adolescence. While the parental view of the daughter as defective was by no means the sole explanation for the limited social activity, or even the major one, it nonetheless was an important influence. Some of these women talked about their lack of self-confidence and low self-expectations as a major reason why they did not become more active in social activities. They held themselves responsible, sometimes describing themselves as "my own worst enemy." We know from clinical theory and research that self-esteem and self-confidence do not develop in a vacuum but that the environment in general and parental attitudes in particular have a major impact.

Even assuming that the parents were not major causes of a daughter's low self-esteem because the parents had serious doubts about her social potential, they were not in a position to challenge her negative assumptions and self-doubts. Stated one parent, "I knew my daughter was depressed because she felt she could not compete with the other girls for boys' attentions, and I felt bad for her, but what could I do? In her situation, I would feel the same; anyone with a disability would." This parent saw feelings of social inadequacy in her daughter as inevitable and biologically constructed rather than as a socially constructed state, and thus did not seek either to help her or to get help for her.

In addition parents who viewed their disabled daughters as defective women often did not recognize and acknowledge the existence of prejudice in the world toward people with disabilities, at least not when it came to the social arena. They were therefore less likely to select environments that would be socially supportive for their daughters, to advocate on their behalf when they were excluded from social activities, and to help them develop coping strategies to understand and deal with prejudice. As one woman stated, "When I would come home crying because I had not been invited to a party or because someone had teased me about my disability, instead of being outraged, my mother would tell me to spend more time practicing in front of the mirror to walk straight and look more 'normal' so that people would accept me; it was like blaming the victim."

What was striking in this group of women was the absence of any positive counterforce in their lives that would affirm their social sexual potential. Either they internalized their parents' and society's negative perceptions of them or they waged an unsuccessful war against a host of barriers without the benefit of backup forces.

4. *Parents not only viewed their disabled daughter as "defective" but felt that sexuality was potentially dangerous for her; and the disabled woman had not only limited social involvement but also a particularly traumatic time in the heterosexual arena during adolescence.* This fourth situation is a variation of the third. Women in the previous category perceived their parents as having relatively few fears about the emergence of their sexuality because they did not perceive them as sexual people. In contrast, women in the present group described their parents as viewing sexuality for them as extremely dangerous; they received strong messages that men would use and abuse them, would take what they wanted sexually and then abandon them, would talk about their sexual conquests with them to the entire community or in other ways humiliate them. These women learned from their parents that they could be sex objects, but unlike nondisabled women, they would not be chosen as permanent partners or potential childbearers; this was another version of the defective woman theme. Most of the women in this group has sensory disabilities (that is, hearing or visual impairments) but otherwise physically intact bodies. Perhaps because they were close to the norm of beauty and attractiveness, parents could see these daughters as capable of giving sexual pleasure but not as intact enough to fulfill feminine roles.

For several of these women, the consequences of such negative messages were devastating. Not only were their social and sexual lives in adolescence restricted by the typical range of barriers, but they actively avoided social situations out of fear of being abused. One deaf woman said, "I learned from my father and others that socializing, getting sexually involved, was a dangerous thing for deaf people to do. As a result, I built a wall around myself based on fear, fear of letting other people in, fear of being intimate." This woman described herself as resorting to drinking and ultimately becoming an alcoholic as a way to deal with her fears. Two women, one bisexual and the other lesbian, reported that they began to explore relationships with women as a preferable alternative to dealing with what they believed would be the inevitably destructive effects of relating to men. Clearly this was not the only factor encouraging their sexual preference for women, but it was one factor. As with the previous group, there was a lack of mitigating forces in these women's environments to counter the powerful negative parental messages.

Given the limited data upon which this study is based, it is difficult to generalize about the relative prevalence of these four kinds of relations between parental expectations and disabled daughters' degree of heterosexual involvement during adolescence. Gross estimates suggest that from two-thirds to three-fourths of the thirty-one women in the sample disabled before adolescence fell into the third category, in which parents viewed their disabled daughters as defective women and the daughters in turn had limited involvement in heterosexual activities; the remaining women were fairly evenly divided among the other three categories. What is most distressing is how few sets of parents—three to four at most—viewed their daughters as intact women clearly capable of meeting female role expectations.

SUMMARY AND CONCLUSIONS

This article has considered the relation between parental expectations and degree of heterosexual success during adolescence for women with physical and sensory disabilities. The research findings suggest that many parents have low heterosexual expectations for their disabled teenage daughters because they view them as unable to fulfill the typical female role of marriage and child rearing. Although they may offer them strong encouragement and support in the educational and career arenas, such support is based on their underlying assumption that these daughters are defective women. In response, some disabled women rebel against their parents' assumptions and have active, satisfying social lives. For many other women, however, pessimistic parental expectations contribute to their limited social and sexual involvement and to their own feelings of inadequacy as women.

In contrast, some parents have positive social and sexual expectations for their disabled daughters; they see them as intact women, with their disability as one of their many characteristics. Such parental attitudes tend to facilitate disabled women's social success in adolescence; they foster high self-esteem and allow a woman to be able to rely on her parents to mediate an often difficult, prejudicial social environment.

These findings add to the growing body of literature that stresses the importance of the environmental influence, and more specifically the parental influence, on the development of women and men with disabilities. They speak against a biological, deterministic viewpoint because there has been no evidence that the fact of disability, type of disability, age of onset during childhood, or any other biological givens (apart from the environmental response) explain degree of heterosexual involvement.

This research raises almost as many questions as it answers. We need to examine more fully the relation between parental expectations and heterosexual involvement using a larger, more diverse sample and more sensitive data-gathering instruments. Some of the questions that need to be considered in further depth are these:

- What factors cause some parents to become overly focused on their daughters' disability and enable others to take a broader view, with disability as only one of their daughters' many features?

- Are certain kinds of disabilities more likely to elicit certain kinds of parental fears and concerns regarding sexuality? If so, why?

- Why and how is the father-daughter relationship an important factor in social success?

- What factors enable some disabled adolescent women to rebel against low parental expectations?

- Can the visible presence of role models (that is, highly socially successful disabled women) serve to alert parental expectations and facilitate the social success of disabled young women?

- Do disabled women have less *homosexual* involvement and interest during adolescence than nondisabled women?

- To what extent does degree of heterosexual success during adolescence have developmental significance for those disabled women aware of being lesbian or bisexual? For these women, how does the extent of parents' heterosexual expectations affect their degree of involvement in heterosexual and homosexual activities?

In addition, although the present research compared disabled and nondisabled adolescent women, it is equally important to compare disabled young women and disabled young men in the heterosexual arena. For example, given that disabled adult men tend to be more socially successful than disabled adult women,[20] are disabled adolescent men any more socially successful than their female counterparts? Also, given that definitions of manhood are much less based on physical appearance and perfection than are definitions of womanhood, are parents of disabled young men any more likely to see their sons as intact rather that defective and hence to set more positive social expectations for them? In addition, for men, sex is more readily recognized as a legitimate physical need than it is for women. Does this view encourage parents of disabled young men to become more active advocates for their sons in the social arena? Finally, it is necessary to consider whether young men are influenced by parental expectations to the same degree as young women. Some preliminary research comparing blind teenage men and women suggests that male youth may be less subject to influence by adult expectations.[21]

Disabled adolescent women have indeed been frustrated in their social and sexual lives. By not actively participating in heterosexual activities, they have too often experienced a sense of difference and have missed out on many of the joys and pleasures, as well as the pains, of budding sexuality. One mother in this study indicated that when the diagnosing doctor told her that her daughter had a disability, he also told her to "raise her like a normal girl." In view of our research findings, this would seem to be good advice, with a significant correction. Disabled girls and young women are not *like* normal girls; they *are* normal girls. Disability does not detract from normalcy. When parents are able to recognize this, they can help their disabled daughters to flourish socially and in other capacities. When they fail to recognize it, they become one more problem for the disabled young women to take on.

NOTES

1. M. A. Carrera, "Some Reflections on Adolescent Sexuality," *SIECUS Report* 11, no. 4 (1983): 1–2.
2. Michelle Fine and Adrienne Asch, "Disabled Women: Sexism Without the Pedestal," *Journal of Sociology and Social Welfare* 8, no. 2 (1981).
3. Adrienne Asch and Harilyn Rousso, "Therapists with Disabilities: Theoretical and Clinical Issues," *Psychiatry* 48, no. 1 (1985): 1–12.
4. Peter Glos, *On Adolescence: A Psychoanalytic Interpretation* (New York: Free Press, 1962); Sharon Thompson, "The Search for Tomorrow: On Feminism and the Reconstruction of Teen Romance," in *Pleasure and Danger: Exploring Female Sexuality*, ed. Carole S. Vance (Boston: Routledge and Kegan Paul, 1984), 355; G. L. Zellman and J. D. Goodchilds, "Becoming Sexual in Adolescence," in *Changing Boundaries:* ed. Elizabeth Allgeier and Naomi McCormick (Palo Alto, Calif.: Mayfield, 1983).
5. J. M. Bardwick, *Psychology of Women: A Study of Biocultural Conflicts* (New York: Harper and Row, 1971), 52; C. P. Malmquist, *Handbook of Adolescence* (New York: Aronson, 1985), 68.
6. P. A. Katz, "The Development of Female Identity," in *Becoming Female: Perspectives on Development*, ed. C. B. Kopp (New York: Plenum Press, 1979).
7. Malmquist, *Handbook of Adolescence.*
8. A. Welbourne, S. Lifschitz, H. Selvin, and R. Green, "A Comparison of the Sexual Learning Experiences of Visually Impaired and Sighted Women," *Journal of Visual Impairment and Blindness* 77, no. 6 (1983): 256–59; Yvonne Duffy, *All Things Are Possible* (Ann Arbor, Mich.: Garvin and Associates, 1981); Carney Landis and M. Marjorie Bolles, *Personality and Sexuality of the Physically Handicapped Woman* (New York: Hoeber, 1942).
9. Asch and Rousso, "Therapists with Disabilities."
10. R. Darling, *Families Against Society: A Study of Reactions to Children with Birth Defects* (Beverly Hills, Calif.: Sage Publications, 1970); Kris Study Group, Beres/Caldor section, "The Influence of Early Childhood Illness and Defect on Analyzability" (Paper presented at the New York Psychoanalytic Institute, 14 September 1971); A. Lussier, "The Physical Handicap and the Body Ego," *International Journal of Psychoanalysis* 39 (1980): 264–72; Harilyn Rousso, "Disabled yet Intact: Guidelines for Work with Congenitally Physically Disabled Youngsters and Their Parents," *Child and Adolescent Social Work Journal* 1, no. 4 (1984): 254–69.

11. Welbourne et al., "A Comparison of the Sexual Learning Experiences"; Duffy, *All Things Are Possible.*

12. Landis and Bolles, *Personality and Sexuality.*

13. G. L. Fox, "The Mother–Adolescent Daughter Relationship as a Sexual Socialization Structure: A Research Review," *Family Relations* 29 (1980): 21–28.

14. Harilyn Rousso, "Disabled People Are Sexual, Too," *Exceptional Parent* (December 1981): 21–25; idem, "Disabled yet Intact."

15. E. Goodman, "The Turmoil of Teenage Sexuality: Parents' Mixed Signals," *Ms.* 12, no. 1 (1983): 37–41.

16. G. L. Fox and G. L. Inazu, "Patterns and Outcomes of Mother-Daughter Communication about Sexuality," *Journal of Social Issues* 36, no. 1 (1980): 7–29.

17. Rousso, "Disabled People Are Sexual, Too."

18. Anna Ornstein and Paul Ornstein, "Parenting as a Function of the Adult Self," in *Parental Influences in Health and Disease,* ed. James E. Anthony and George Pollock (Boston: Little, Brown, 1985), 205.

19. Ethel Roskies, *Abnormality and Normality: The Mothering of Thalidomide Children* (Ithaca, N.Y.: Cornell University Press, 1972), 176.

20. Fine and Asch, "Disabled Women."

21. N. S. Mayadas and W. D. Duehn, "The Impact of Significant Adults' Expectations on the Lifestyle of Visually Impaired Children," *New Outlook* (September 1976): 286–90.

Do Women Choose Their Sexual Identity?

Carla Golden

Rarely is the role of conscious choice taken seriously in scholarly discussions of sexual orientation, an oversight resulting from the failure to include women in much of the research. Listening to the ways in which women talk about their sexuality reveals that, in contrast to men, a significant minority of women experience themselves as having made a choice about the gender of their sexual partners.

Over the last decade, I have conducted in-depth interviews with more than 100 women

actively engaged in the process of sexual self-definition. From an initial study of lesbian college students, I expanded the scope of my research to include nonstudent lesbians in their twenties, thirties, and forties, as well as heterosexual and bisexual women of varying ages. The women were primarily white and from a range of social class backgrounds; interviews were open-ended and involved asking women to tell the story of how they came to know and identify themselves as lesbian, bisexual, or heterosexual. This research led me to believe that the contemporary feminist movement has had a significant influence on how some women make choices about—and reflect upon—their sexuality, highlighting the importance of considering cultural and historical context in discussions of sexual orientation and its causation.

From the interviews, I was able to identify women who experienced their sexuality as a conscious choice, as well as those who felt it was not a matter of choice at all, but something innate and beyond their control. While some women described their sexuality as fixed and unchanging, others experienced it as more changeable, or fluid, over the course of their lives (Cf., Golden 1987, 1994, 1996).

An overview of the growing literature on women's sexual identities confirms that, for some women, choice has been a determining factor in their sexual orientations and/or identifications, and that their sexuality is best described as fluid (Brown, 1995; Esterberg, 1994; Golden, 1996; Rust, 1992; Whisman, 1993, 1996). While many lesbians mention choice only in the context of accepting and embracing a sexuality they believe to be inborn, others describe choosing to be lesbians because they prefer women and because the feminist movement has legitimated that choice. Some women who identify as bisexual speak about how the *idea* of bisexuality appealed to them, and recount that they found it easy to move in that direction after deciding to do so. Some heterosexual feminists also use a language of possibility and preference. Although many have not actively questioned their sexuality, some have considered their options and chosen to pursue the most socially acceptable path. Others leave open the possibility of change in the future, when the situation is right or the appropriate woman comes along. Women's choices around their sexuality are evident not only in the acceptance and adoption of a lesbian or bisexual identity, but also in the conscious rejection of such an identity because it would make life too difficult.

My research reveals that one cannot predict simply on the basis of sexual attractions and involvements whether a woman will consider herself to be lesbian, bisexual, or heterosexual. Among the interviewees, all permutations of attraction, experience, and identity were evident. There were women who had only heterosexual experience, yet reported that they were lesbian, or bisexual; women with bisexual experience who considered themselves to be lesbian, or heterosexual; and women in sexual relationships with women at the time of the interview, who nonetheless reported that they were "really" heterosexual or bisexual. Nor does sexual attraction neatly predict sexual involvement. Some women have experienced same-gender attractions but have never acted on them, while others have made a conscious decision to experience and pursue such attractions. And to complicate the picture further, any part of this system (i.e., attraction, experience, identity) can change over the course of a lifetime.

Are such cases rare exceptions or do they represent common experiences among women exploring their sexuality? The women I interviewed were not randomly sampled from the population, and no claim is made that they represent most or even a majority of lesbians or bisexual women. From a phenomenological perspective, however, numbers are less important than what the interviews reveal about women's subjective experience of their sexuality, and about the variability and diversity among women as they explore their sexuality.

A brief consideration of the ways in which psychologists think about sexual orientation and sexual identity will serve to highlight what is "different," and hence most important, about the interview data. Psychologists define sexual orientation in terms of whether a person's "primary affectional and/or erotic attractions" are to people of the same gender, the other gender, or to both (Gonsiorek & Weinrich, 1991; Greene, 1994). In research on sexual orientation, people are characterized as if they clearly belong to one of four discrete categories: lesbian, gay, bisexual, or heterosexual, even though many psychologists, following Kinsey, Pomeroy, & Martin (1948), acknowledge that human sexuality exists along a continuum and that dichotomous categories represent a distortion of the multiple forms that human sexuality may take.

Sexual orientation is generally considered a stable characteristic that is established by adolescence, often before sexual activity has occurred. People are believed to know their orientation through a subjective awareness of their attractions (Bell, Weinberg, & Hammersmith, 1981; Gonsiorek & Weinrich, 1991). It is assumed that a person's sexual orientation will be consistent with his sexual behavior and sexual identification. Much of this research is based on men and, as with most areas of psychological research and theorizing, may not be generalizable to women's experience. My research suggests that a women's sexual orientation, when defined by attraction and arousal, is not always consistent with her sexual behavior or the sexual identity she adopts. Similarly, the claim that sexual orientation is clearly established by adolescence and stable across the life-course is not consistent with the research conducted with women.

For women, there may be more to sexual orientation than "affectional/erotic attraction." Money (1988) argued that the definitive criterion for sexual orientation is falling in love; a homosexual person is one who falls in love with someone of the same sex. Money also identified other criteria, such as "being sexually attracted to" and "aroused by," assuming that these always occurred in concert. My interviews suggest that they do not. Some bisexual women reported sexual attraction to other females without being in love with them; some heterosexual women described themselves as being in love with their girlfriends without experiencing sexual arousal; and some lesbians reported loving but asexual relationships.

Improving on Kinsey's assessment of sexual orientation according to the two factors of attraction, fantasy and sexual experience, another early model of sexual orientation identified three critical components: the sex of the people one fantasizes about, the sex of the people one has been sexually involved with, and the sex of the people one affectionately prefers (Shively and DeCecco, 1977). While this conceptual scheme allows for multiple defining features of sexual orientation, it fails to take into account that these factors may not always be consistent. For example, *the majority of North American women describe affectional or emotional preferences for women but experience sexual relationships exclusively with men*, a pattern that Nancy Chodorow (1978) characterized as heterosexual asymmetry.

My own discussions with women have identified a range of components as contributing to sexual orientation, including: (1) sexual fantasies; (2) sexual attractions, and how easily they are interpreted as such; (3) falling in love; (4) emotional and affectional preferences; (5) sexual experience and the quality of that sexual experience; and (6) self-identification in the context of social and political affiliations. The interviews revealed striking variability in the criteria women used to define their sexuality. What is apparent is that there is no simple relation between sexual desire, experience, orientation, and identity, and that for some women, choice is seen as influencing their sexual decisions.

Some might argue that the problem here is a failure to distinguish between *sexual orientation* as a biologically-based substrate of desire over which people have no control, and *sexual identification* as a process of labeling by which people choose to identify themselves with one or another social group. The argument here would be that women may choose to call themselves lesbians or bisexuals because they prefer women emotionally or because of political considerations, but that does not mean that they actually choose the objects of their desire. In other words, they may choose their identity, but not their orientation. And yet, women spoke *as if* they chose more than just their self-label; they described themselves as deciding to become sexually attracted to and involved with other women. Without any previous same-gender sexual experience, women *talked about becoming "open" to their attractions to women and overcoming years of heterosexual socialization.* When I asked when and how the possibility had first occurred to them, they mentioned a range of different experiences that kindled their interest: women's studies classes, exposure to lesbians within feminist groups, or more discrete events such as viewing a film or TV program, hearing a lecture, reading an article, or having a discussion with a lesbian friend. These had often prompted ongoing reflection on their part, which sometimes involved their reinterpreting close female friendships and/or attachments to teachers and camp counselors as evidence of the possibility that they *had* been sexually attracted to women all along but had never recognized it until now. This kind of reinterpretation is consistent with the dominant view of sexuality as fixed and unchanging; such reinterpretation of one's history would be unnecessary if sexuality were recognized as fluid.

The argument could still be made that the women described above were "really" bisexual, and that their openness to sexual relationships with women, after a history of sexual attractions and relationships exclusively with men, merely reflects a predetermined (bi)sexuality. This is the view of John Money (1988), who asserts that it is incorrect to use the term "sexual preference," because people cannot choose their sexuality. He argues that sexual orientation "is something that happens . . . like being tall or short, left-handed or right-handed, color-blind or color-seeing." According to him, no one prefers to be homosexual rather than heterosexual, or bisexual rather than monosexual. One wonders whether he has ever listened to women's accounts of their sexual choices.

The growing body of research on women makes clear that some women undeniably experience their sexuality as fluid. Whether this is a result of an underlying bisexual orientation that was always present or a conscious choice cannot be definitively determined. But the case of heterosexual women is illustrative. In my interviews with heterosexually identified women, some indicated that they had sexually "experimented" with other women and found the experiences less than satisfying, concluding that they were "really" heterosexual. In some cases, however, they acknowledged that there were other factors that contributed to the less than fully positive experience, including fear, inexperience, and internalized homophobia. Based on multiple discussions and interviews, my impression is that there are many more women who have considered the lesbian choice and rejected it than have elected to adopt it.

Given the particular tensions around intimacy in heterosexual relationships, with women wanting more emotional openness and intimacy from their male partners (Rubin, 1983; Chodorow 1978; Eichenbaum and Orbach, 1984; Stiver, 1984), one might expect lesbianism to be an obvious choice for women. A relevant question is why so many women avoid it. One answer is that sexual orientation is locked in early and neither changeable nor subject to choice. *Another is that women find it very difficult to overcome the social mandate of compulsory heterosexuality* (Rich, 1980). The latter seems more likely to me, and the current increase in visibility of bisexuality among women on college campuses would support this view.

Taking into account the role of choice allows for a more comprehensive understanding of sexual behavior and self-identification in women. Identities and behaviors that appear puzzling and difficult to explain become clearer within a framework that acknowledges women's fluid sexuality. For example, it helps in understanding those women who have always considered themselves heterosexual but then become aware in adulthood that they are attracted to women as well as men. Some of these women act on their sexual attractions, despite no previous experience, and develop strong identities as lesbians. Other women may consider themselves bisexual, whether or not they ever act on their attractions. If sexuality is fluid, then it is understandable why some women consider themselves "bisexual lesbians," having chosen to be sexually involved with women and to identify as lesbians while acknowledging that they sometimes experience sexual attractions to men. It makes clearer the experience of so-called "transient lesbians," women who for a period of time identify as lesbians and are involved with women, but who subsequently become involved with men. It explains so-called "political lesbians," who decide based on feminist beliefs that it is preferable to be sexually involved with women, and for whom this becomes a distinctly erotic as well as a political choice. And it may explain the increasing visibility and expression of bisexual choices among women who previously assumed but never questioned their heterosexuality. Bisexuality may be the one area of sexual "deviation" in which women not only express more interest than men, but have more experience as well.

From this perspective, bisexuality can be conceptualized as a distinct form of sexual expression, and bisexuals as women who recognize and act according to their sexual fluidity. Some lesbians consider bisexuals to be lesbians who are unwilling to forgo heterosexual privilege; some heterosexuals believe that bisexuals are simply confused and have not made up their minds. But if sexuality is not essential (fixed and unchanging) or dichotomous (focused exclusively on women or on men), then bisexuals are neither confused, nor passing through a stage in the process of coming out, nor unwilling to give up heterosexual privilege.

Conceptualizing sexuality as fluid and as subject to personal choice also helps make

sense of the fear of—and preoccupation with—lesbians and gays in mainstream American culture. Consider the virulent antihomosexual sentiment that characterized recent efforts in Oregon, Colorado, and Georgia to deny civil rights to lesbian and gay people. If sexuality is not fixed and it is possible to choose one's sexual attractions, then exclusive heterosexuality is indeed in danger. As the visibility of lesbian and gay people increases, and as individuals who are "out" and very comfortable with their sexuality are perceived as acceptable, it is more likely that people of all ages could decide that a lesbian, gay, or bisexual lifestyle is as viable a choice as any other. If deviations from the prescribed path of heterosexuality were not a real possibility, people so vigorously committed to the superiority of exclusive heterosexuality would have less to fear from the open integration and inclusion of lesbians, gays, and bisexuals into public life.

For all the current scientific and media emphasis on the biological bases of homosexuality, women's stories suggest that homosexuality may not be as biologically predetermined for women as for men. There is no similar interview research with gay or heterosexual men that explores this issue, but from reading gay male literature, speaking with a small sample of gay men, and exchanging views with therapists who work with them, my impression is that gay men do not experience their sexuality in the fluid manner that some lesbian, bisexual, and heterosexual women do. I suspect that very few gay men could be characterized as having chosen their homosexuality. As for *why* the experience of sexuality might be so different for women and men, psychoanalytic theories of mothering offer some insights. Feminist analyses of British object relations theory provide a framework for understanding how the conditions of early infancy might lead women to have greater bisexual potential than men. To the extent that infants and young children are primarily nurtured by women (and depending on the importance one attaches to this experience as contributing to later sexuality), one might expect boys to be more predisposed toward heterosexuality and girls to be more directed toward lesbianism (Chodorow, 1978; 1994; Dinnerstein, 1976). Adding in the cultural imperative toward heterosexuality, one might expect a greater incidence of bisexuality among women, or at least greater expression of interest in that possibility.

When one incorporates the experiences and words of women into theories of sexual orientation and its development, it is no longer possible to ignore or reject notions of sexual choice and preference. This is not to suggest that sexuality is experienced as a choice by all women, or even by most. That choice is a salient feature of sexuality for a significant minority of women means we must begin to explore its implications.

REFERENCES

Bell, A.P., Weinberg, M.S., & Hammersmith, S.K. *Sexual preference: Its developments in men and women.* Indiana University Press, 1981.

Brown, L, "Lesbian identities: Concepts and issues," in A. D'Augeili and C. Patterson, eds., *Lesbian, gay and bisexual identities through the lifespan: Psychological perspectives.* Oxford University Press, 1995.

Chodorow, N. *The reproduction of mothering: Psychoanalysis and the sociology of gender.* University of California Press (Berkeley); 1978.

Chodorow, N. *Femininities, masculinities, sexualities: Freud and beyond.* University Press of Kentucky, 1994.

Dinnerstein, D. *The mermaid and the minotaur: Sexual arrangements and the human malaise.* Harper and Row, 1976.

Eichenbaum, L., & Orbach, S. *What do women want? Exploring the myth of dependency.* Berkley Books, 1984.

Esterberg, K. "Being a lesbian and being in love: Constructing identities through relationships," in *Journal of Gay and Lesbian Social Services,* 1(2).

Golden, C. "Diversity and variability in women's sexual identities," in *Lesbian Psychologies: Explorations and challenges.* University of Illinois Press, 1987.

Golden, C. "Our politics and choices: The feminist movement and sexual orientation," in B. Greene and G. Herek, eds., *Lesbian and gay psychology: Theory, research, and clinical applications.* Sage, 1994.

Golden, C. "What's in a name? Sexual self-identification among women," in R. Savin-Williams and K. Cohen, eds., *The lives of lesbians, gays, and bisexuals: Children to adults.* Harcourt Brace and Co., 1996.

Gonsiorek, J., & Weinrich, J. "The definition and scope of sexual orientation," in J. Gonsiorek and J. Weinrich, eds., *Homosexuality: Research implications for public policy.* Sage, 1991.

Greene, B. "Lesbian and gay sexual orientations: Implications for clinical training, practice, and research," in B. Greene and G. Herek, eds., *Lesbian and gay psychology.* Sage, 1994.

Kinsey. A., Pomeroy, W., & Martin, C. *Sexual behavior in the human male.* Saunders, 1948.

Money, J. *Gay, straight, and in between: The sexology of erotic orientation.* Oxford University Press; 1988.

Rust, P. "Who are we and where do we go from here? Conceptualizing bisexuality," in E. Weise, ed., *Closer to home: Bisexuality and feminism,* The Seal Press, 1992.

Rich, A. "Compulsory heterosexuality and lesbian existence," in *Signs: Journal of Women in Culture and Society,* 5, 1980.

Rubin, L., *Intimate strangers: Men and women together.* Harper and Row, 1983.

Shively, M., & DeCecco, J. "Components of sexual identity," in *Journal of Homosexuality,* 3, 1977.

Stiver, I. "The meaning of dependency in female-male relationships," in J. Jordan, A. Kaplan, J.B. Miller, I. Stiver, & J. Surrey, eds., *Women's growth in connection. Writings from the Stone Center.* Guilford, 1984.

Whisman, V., "Identity crises: Who is a lesbian, anyway?" in A. Stein, ed., *Sisters, sexperts, queers: Beyond the lesbian nation.* Penguin, 1993.

Whisman, V. *Queer by choice: Lesbians, gay men, and the politics of identity.* Routledge, 1996.

Student Stories

So . . . Honestly Gay

Eric Leadbetter

It consumes your whole life; it's the topic of every good conversation. Your best girlfriend prizes it, and the article on the front page of the arts and leisure section of the paper celebrates it. So what is it, this feeling, this craving, this idea of being gay?

Some days you want to hold it proudly up in the air like a trophy. Other times you want to shove it under your bed with your best dirty magazines, but in reality there is no choice. You are "it."

I knew I was "it" before I could even understand "it." I knew during Sesame Street, during Little League, during the big boy, pin-the-tail on the donkey, "You're four today" birthday parties. Everyone knew, or so I'm told.

It wasn't until I was about 15 that I really decided to understand it, practice it, feel it. I could probably name about a thousand instances and examples, but then I might seem like a trashy porno-addicted pervert. So I'll just keep it R-rated for now.

I guess the first time I really knew, the time that I can really think of as my "coming out" story, would have to be at the age of 15. I had this friend named Eppy. We had so many of the same interests. I can't remember how we met or where we met, but I can tell you every detail of every second after we did. We were the average everyday boys: walks to the 7-11, avid Nintendo champions, long talks about girls. Nothing too crazy, until this one unexpected night. I decided to stay over at his house. His mom was working midnight shift, so we had the house to ourselves. The night

really went on like any other Saturday night sleepover. We decided to sleep out on the porch since it was a great summer night. It was like camping.

We ended up lying next to each other. Now we have done that before, but this night was a little bit different. It was close, cumbersome, but ironically comfortable. I was a nervous wreck, I knew something might happen, but I didn't know what. I had a feeling in the pit of my stomach, like an instinct. Throughout the night, our hands would touch and our feet brush up against one another. It was so quiet that you could hear nothing but my heart beating out from my chest. Both of us had our eyes closed pretending we were sleeping, but we were both waiting to see what was going to happen next, who was going to make the next move. Now I've always been a daring person, but on this particular night I was afraid to budge. Eventually I got up enough courage to touch a kneecap or a wrist. I did make that move. And after I did, it was the most amazing thing ever, because we kissed. Now I don't mean a regular first, kind of boring kiss. This kiss was straight out of a movie, like the kiss from *Gone with the Wind,* just with two boys. It was terrifying and fun. The night went on like this. We would kiss then look away from each other and then brush up against one another so we could have an excuse to kiss each other again. And it was beautiful. I felt complete, whole. My life would be changed forever.

I remember waking up the next morning— after an incredible night—to the birds chirping and the dew on our face from sleeping outside. He looked over at me and he said, "This was really good practice for when we do it with girls." And that was the beginning of the rest of my gay life.

I guess I had a different expectation of that night, a better outcome, a marriage proposal possibly, but for what it is worth I did hold it high like a trophy. I celebrated it. I prized it.

My life has been a roller coaster ride of gay ups and downs, of breakups and breakthroughs, but for the most part I would say it has been an adventure with dating and experiences and hair products. But it is so well worth it.

I'm 24 now and I live in New York, the epicenter of gay life. It's an adventure. I moved here in hopes to live the "Studio 54" life, but instead I'm forced to settle for a *Will and Grace* episode. Someone once asked me, if I could change it, take it back and be straight what would I do. And I answered that I wouldn't change it for the world. It is the one thing that I am most proud of about myself. It is my reality. In truth I am "it," so . . . honestly gay.

Where's Taylor When I Need Him?

Rachel-Storm Heasley

I remember feeling trapped. The thought of anyone finding out, the thought of losing friendships, it was too much for me to speak a word. So I didn't. I was 17 years old when I had my first dating experience. My body was filled with the rush of emotions. I had my first kiss, my first sexual experience, and then the inevitable first breakup. I gather that, for most, these events are shared with friends and family who one chooses to use for support. For those in the heterosexual world, information regarding one's first love can be public knowledge. Being a lesbian can make things a bit on the tricky side, especially when you are young and unsure.

I will have to admit that my coming out was a tad more pleasant than for many. I had a good network of lesbians surrounding me, who helped me realize that it was not shameful to be gay—but on the contrary quite fun. After the experience of my hidden love and heartbreak, I decided that I needed more support than that of just friends. I needed my fam-

ily. My family has to be one of the most liberal, consisting of a father who teaches sociology and a stepmother who, at the time, was the Director at Planned Parenthood. Did that make the coming-out process any easier? Not much.

It took me weeks of preparation. A friend suggested that I wait until dinner, and as I ask for the butter I could simply state, "Could you pass me the butter? I'm gay." Another suggestion was to wait until eating pancakes, and begin to describe how the melting butter reminded me of my girlfriend's soft nipple. I wasn't that bold, so I waited until after dinner and cornered my father on the porch. It was so difficult. There were tears. Luckily, they were tears of joy and support. I realized at that moment that this was just the beginning of the coming-out process. There were so many people to tell, so many uncomfortable conversations to come.

All right, one down and several more to go. It was time for the friends. I wasn't quite sure where to start with this one. Friends are so very important in high school, and I wasn't sure if I was ready to risk losing any of them because of me being a lesbian. I already felt isolated and didn't want to feel any more so. There were a few people at school who already knew, one being a close friend of mine who happened to be a teacher. She was also a lesbian, and I spent a lot of time with her and her five-year-old son, Taylor. Taylor had a key role in my coming out, which was not in the least bit planned. We were on a school trip, far away from the comfort of my own home. I was sitting at a table with a couple of close friends from school, and Taylor was sitting at the table behind us along with some other folks from school. I remember getting up to get some more ketchup for my fries, leaving a conversation about boyfriends. As I pushed down on the ketchup dispenser, I heard Taylor's loud, screechy, five-year-old voice state, "Rachel has a girlfriend." The room went silent.

I could feel the blood rush to my face, and I wasn't sure if I should just run out the door, flinging ketchup behind me, or hold the ketchup for dear life and face the damage. I faced the damage. I will always be thankful for that moment. If Taylor hadn't spoken for me, I'm not sure I could have gained enough courage to have done it on my own. It opened the trail for communication, and thankfully I had friends who were supportive and inquisitive.

The difficulty in being gay is the constant dealing with coming out. It's an everyday venture, and I have discussed and defended my sexuality with more people than I have cared to. I have tried to just be myself and not focus on my sexuality. However, that leaves room for people to make assumptions or judgments.

My first realization of this came in my first semester at college. As a freshman in an overenrolled college, the living arrangements on campus were a bit on the cozy side. I was assigned to a dorm room designed for two, but rearranged for three. It was a tight squeeze, but my two roommates and I tried to make the best of it. We were getting along fairly well at first, but it was evident that we had our differ-

ences. I was feeling more comfortable in my realm of being a lesbian, but not yet ready to disclose this information to them. I quickly found out that I didn't have to. They were sitting in the hallway chatting one day as I headed out of our dorm. I gave them a quick good-bye as I headed down the hall. There was a mirror in front of me, and I could watch them talk as I walked. I was only a few feet away when I saw them turn to look at me, and one of them whispered, "I think she's a lesbian." It wasn't the fact that they knew that made it difficult, it was the tone in which it was said that gave me a strange and unsettling sense in the pit of my stomach. It was then that I realized that not everyone was as tolerant as I had imagined and hoped for.

I'm 25 years old now and still just coming out. Everyday when I meet a new friend, or find a new job, the issue of sexuality arises. The talk is of boyfriends, husbands, and the bars where people gather for cocktails and flirting. Sexuality is everywhere. *Heterosexuality* is everywhere. Where's Taylor when I need him?

Gay, Lesbian and Bisexual Students: The Impact of School on Sexual Identity Development

Melinda S. Miceli

INTRODUCTION

The vast majority of both academic and popular literature describes the lives and experiences of gay, lesbian, and bisexual [g/l/b] adolescents as personal struggles to accept a stigmatized identity. The goal of this article is

to trouble the simplistic understandings of g/l/b students offered by previous research and pop-cultural accounts. The data used here comes from three years of field notes taken at weekly meetings for a community support group for g/l/b youth ages 14-20 as well as 30 in-depth interviews with members of this group. This article focuses on the most frequently discussed topic at these meetings and in these interviews—the experiences of being a g/l/b student in public high school. I establish through an analysis of these data that institutions of public education significantly, negatively, influence g/l/b students' experiences with their sexual identity.

The literature states that sensitization* is closely followed by a period of "identity confusion." This is reported to be a period in which the g/l/b individual struggles to understand what these same-sex attractions mean about who they really are. In other words, their otherwise "normal" identity is shaken by these emerging feelings and they must reassess their identity. I found that this seemingly personal confusion was highly contingent upon the messages the youth received from their social environment. The data revealed that, for the youth in my sample, there was a significant relationship between awareness of their sexual/affectional feelings, identity confusion, and their interaction with the institution of public education. Sometimes such a connection was obvious and immediate in response to my initial question, "When did you first begin to realize that you might be g/l/b?"

> I've always been like . . . When I was younger I had a lot of really close girlfriends and I used to really like them, but never really thought about it because . . . In middle school I had millions of boyfriends, you know, but everyone did. And I guess I didn't really . . . I mean when it first started I was like, "No! No!" you know. But I guess I didn't really say it out loud to myself until like my sophomore year of high school; I've known though.
>
> —Becca, bisexual Jewish female, age 18[1]

Um . . . I guess like junior high. You know? Like the whole puberty thing . . . When girls start talking about boys and stuff and like sexual stuff.

Then, I guess it just seemed like I didn't feel like all those girls did, so something must be wrong with me. So, basically, I just tried to act like them, you know, talk about boys with them and stuff.
> —Chloe, gay biracial female, age 20

In these responses, and many others like them, it is obvious that the students mark their thinking about their sexual identity in relation to what stage they were at in school. This indicates that, in some way, school was significant to their experience of these emerging feelings. In what way it was significant was less immediately clear. To get at a deeper understanding of this relationship, I asked more probing questions of the interviewees.

For instance, after Chloe gave the above response to my initial question about when she began to realize that she was gay, I asked, "When did you know what those feelings you had meant? Did you come out at an early age?" She replied,

> No. I think . . . Like once I realized that, you know, that it was a wrong or like a bad thing to feel I tried to make myself stop. I told myself I didn't really feel that way and never talked to anyone about it. When I was a kid I knew that I really liked girls, friends and teachers, but I didn't think it was a bad thing. So, like I didn't try to hide it or anything, and it wasn't a secret. But once I realized it was like a bad thing, it became this secret I had to keep and like something that I had to fix about myself.

This statement reveals several things about the significance of the relationship between Chloe's "self-realization of sexual orientation" and school. She reports having feelings of affection for other females from an early age, and this was neither something that troubled her nor anything she felt compelled to hide. However, when she entered junior high school, with its environment of normative heterosexuality heightened by "the whole puberty thing," she learned that her feelings for other females could be labeled as homosexual. She was given the message that this was "a

---

*A stage when individuals become consciously aware of their homosexual identities.

[1]All names have been changed to protect the anonymity of the study's participants.

bad thing to feel," that this made her different from her peers, and that she should keep this part of herself a secret and try to be like everyone else. The meaning of the messages she was getting from other students and the school environment was that heterosexuality was the only accepted and reinforced feeling and behavior. The force of these social norms defined her feelings as a discreditable stigma, manipulated her into believing that there was something wrong with her, and coerced her into taking on behaviors that would serve to hide or "closet" that part of herself. They also informed her that these same-sex feelings made her a specific *type* of person, which socially marked her as someone who would be the target of ostracization.

Analyzing Chloe's experience in this manner differs in several respects from the way that this type of situation is usually understood in the literature on homosexual identity development. If we were to apply the analysis used in that literature, we might read her actions as merely personal reactions to the self-hatred caused by her same-sex attractions that she believes are wrong. I argue, however, that the empirical evidence strongly supports an analysis of Chloe's behavior as an active or *reactive* strategy to cope with others' definitions of her feelings and the social forces around her that are hostile to that part of herself. This process, which much of the previous literature describes as an intrapsychic, personal, and staged journey of self-acceptance, is actually a social process—a process constructed by social and structural definitions and categorization of individuals' same-sex feelings and behaviors. Social and cultural definitions of sexual identity, which stigmatize and define homosexuality as unnatural and abnormal, shape and condone negative reactions to g/l/b people. Importantly, these same definitions also serve as the base of information out of which g/l/b people come to understand and define themselves.

Much of the academic and popular literature on g/l/b individuals portrays them as struggling to develop a relatively positive definition of themselves *despite* their "sexual orientation." However, it is more accurate to view them as individuals battling with the social forces that *define* their feelings as an essential and problematic identity. This "developmental" process is not left incomplete by individuals failing to fully accept their stigmatized identity and the limitations it necessarily places on them. It is *made* impossible to complete by a society that continually reinforces both the stigma and the limitations. This is further illustrated by Chloe's statement: "I mean, I'm not upset about it or anything, I'm not unhappy that I'm gay . . . but . . . I don't know. I guess I feel a little left out of the world."

These types of statements were made repeatedly by the youth in my sample. Frequently, the g/l/b students that I talked to expressed a deep understanding that it was not their feelings that were inherently wrong or deviant. It was, instead, the social world that created the difficulties associated with being g/l/b. As Rick stated about realizing that he was bisexual, "It was just like the initial shock of like the first day and then I was over it. But like everybody else had a problem dealing with it. That was the problem, and that fucked me up." In relation to school, Rick stated, "When I was at school I was always on edge. It affected me as far as how I would deal with people, you know, or I didn't deal with people at all. And because I couldn't, nobody could know the truth, otherwise I would die." Rick reported that he perceived his school as a place where harassment of g/l/b students took place often and generally went unpunished by teachers or school administrators. The "truth," that he was not heterosexual, was not a threat to Rick's (and other g/l/b students') self-concept. Rather, this truth was a threat to the normative heterosexuality of the school, and this threat put him in danger of abuse, which, in this context, was often condoned as justifiable punishment.

"Acceptance" and "Identity Synthesis": A Set-up for Failure

The literature on homosexual identity development and g/l/b youth argues that an essential element of this process is a g/l/b individual's struggle for self-acceptance of their stigmatized identity. The concept of "acceptance" in the developmental models is used repeatedly and given great significance; however, it is neither specifically defined nor subjected to critical examination. Instead, it is assumed that homosexual individuals are working to progress along these developmental stages toward a plateau where their "sexual identity" is tolerable or bearable to their self-concept. In this final stage of "identity synthesis," it is assumed that the g/l/b individual integrates their sexual orientation into their identity so that it becomes one feature of rather than their entire identity. These are loaded assumptions. First, they presume that same-sex attractions are inherently unacceptable to the individual—that there is little distinction made between one's perception of oneself and the judgment enforced by one's environment. This deemphasizes the possibility that some individuals might not have to work to accept themselves and yet still find it unacceptable that they are deemed intolerable by society. In fact, according to these models, an essential step in the developmental process is for the g/l/b individual to "accept" the socially defined, structurally ingrained, and institutionally enforced stigma of homosexuality. Secondly, and somewhat of a contradiction in logic, these models take for granted that "self-acceptance" is fully achievable within a society in which homosexuality is so thoroughly defined as unacceptable. Such complexities are not critically addressed in these developmental models or in the research on g/l/b youth that has been informed by them.

My research revealed that the concept of acceptance is an important one in g/l/b students' lives. However, it is important in ways that are distinctly different from those outlined in the previous literature. In group meetings as well as individual interviews, the students spoke of problems with being accepted for who they are in school, at home, and in public, because they were g/l/b. They also spoke of self-acceptance. Acceptance was something that they worried about losing and actively sought out from those they loved as well as from the social world that surrounded them.

The degree to which the members of my sample felt they received acceptance from others ranged from low to high and varied depending on what group of people they were referring to—the general school environment, teachers, peers, family, g/l/b communities, the general public, and so forth. The degree to which the members of my sample accepted their same-sex feelings as a positive part of their own identity also ranged from low to high and seemed largely to vary in relation to their experiences with external social factors. In other words, the factors of self-acceptance and acceptance from others form a reciprocal relationship. The level of tolerance that g/l/b students receive from others and from their environments influences their self-acceptance; and an individual student's level of self-acceptance influences the degree to which she or he seeks out, or worries about, the approval of others. Two major themes emerge from the data in relation to the concept of acceptance. The first is that, for g/l/b students, school is overwhelmingly not a place of acceptance, but rather, it is a place where they feel uncomfortable, fearful or worried, and often hated. The second is that both not receiving acceptance and having to worry about acceptance cause g/l/b students to have feelings of frustration and anger throughout their school experience.

I'm not good at being around kids, you know, people at school. . . . I am really confident outside of school, but once I'm in school I don't feel confident. It's really hard to feel confident at school; I feel uncomfortable.

—Vincent, gay white male, age 16

It's something that is more comforting to know that [my new] high school is not afraid to talk about gay and lesbian issues. It's comforting to know that I can wake up in the morning and not think, Am I going to call in sick or am I just going to lie? you know. I can just go to school and feel comfortable, you know, today is going to be a good day. I can wake up at eight o'clock in the morning and say, I'm gay and feel good about it. I don't have to worry, OK who's going to say what to me today? When I get to school what's my locker going to look like? In gym class—oh god, do I skip or do I go and risk being tortured? So, it's easier for me now to walk around with my head held high. That's something that I can do now.

—Mike, gay biracial male, age 17

These statements illustrate that the way many g/l/b students feel about themselves is conditionally based on their school environment. Vincent reports that his level of self-confidence drops as he enters school walls. Mike's statement illustrates the impact that both a homophobic and an accepting school environment can have on a g/l/b student's life. The majority of g/l/b students in my sample reported that being at school made them feel uncomfortable, unaccepted, isolated, angry, or afraid.

The narrative told by traditional homosexual identity models, and much of the literature on g/l/b youth that is informed by them, positions self-acceptance as a crucial step toward the achievement of a relatively tolerable and contented life for a homosexual individual (relative to that of heterosexuals). On the one hand, this can be read as a positive narrative in opposition to other scientific, medical, and religious discourses that see the future for the g/l/b individual to be one of misery unless they change, cure, or repress their feelings. On the other hand, it can be read as a narrative that inescapably sets the g/l/b individual up for failure. It makes acceptance an accomplishment that the *individual* must work to achieve if they are to be content in a society in which nonacceptance of homosexuality is intertwined with cultural messages, institutions, and structures. This assures that acceptance is, at worst, impossible and, at best, a continuous struggle. By stressing self-acceptance and submitting to the ideology that social stigmatization is justifiable, this view places the onus fully on the individual. It is the individual's failure to accept themselves that is presumed to be the cause of the difficulties they encounter with being g/l/b, and society is absolved.

"Coming Out": A Socially Produced Narrative of Shame and Liberation

The concept of acceptance, both from others and of self, is talked about in the literature as part of the identity development process that builds up to the "coming-out" process. This is basically a procedure through which g/l/b individuals learn self-acceptance of their stigma and the social limitations that this stigma places on them and learn how to make decisions about where and to whom to reveal this discreditable feature of themselves. The terms *coming out* and *the closet*, have become a large part of the cultural discourse about g/l/b people. "Coming-out" stories and narratives of "self-discovery" are now common types of pop-cultural accounts of the lives of g/l/b people. As a result many people feel that in order to understand a g/l/b person they need to know when the person "knew" they were gay, if the person is in or out of the closet, and why they are in or out. The youth in my sample are no exception to this. They often used the language of the coming-out discourse to describe their own and others' experiences. Issues of coming out—to do it or not to do it, how to do it, who to tell and who not to tell, negative and positive results of, the safety or danger of, and so on—were some of the most prevalent themes in the support group meetings I attended and the interviews I conducted.

An important point elucidated by these data is that, for most of the g/l/b students in my sample, the decision to come out or hide in the closet is generally not based on their level of self-acceptance. It is, however, largely based on their perception of the social circumstances in which they find themselves.

> I was out to some of my close friends, and I hinted about it to others and was not at all out to others. Like, it depended on how much I thought that I could trust them or how I thought they would react to it. . . . I'm still afraid to be out in public and be with other gay people, you know, to have people know that I'm gay. I don't want to get hurt or have anyone make judgments about me or anything.
>
> —Ani, gay white female, age 18

> It would be like suicide to come out at my high school. It is worse than the backwoods. It is such a small town and so conservative. In the eighteen years that I've lived there, I've never known anyone who was gay and out there.
>
> —Luke, gay white male, age 18

These g/l/b students discern that it is not their acceptance of homosexuality that is most important to coming out, but rather other individuals', the institution's, or society's level of acceptance of homosexuality that will affect their experiences when and if they decide to come out.

> It was kind of scary in my school because if anybody ever found out that you were gay, everybody would know, like the whole town. There would be no place to hide from people saying stuff about you. . . . I thought that if anybody ever found out then, you better move out because that would be it.
>
> —Kate, gay white female, age 18

> Well, I came out when I was 15 to my family and a few close friends. But I was still in high school

and didn't come out to everybody. I had people come up and ask me after rumors started flying around. I would still say no, you know, I'm straight or whatever. [laughs] I didn't want to get my butt kicked, you know. I live in a small town.
>
> —Rick, bisexual biracial male, age 18

These students' decisions to reveal or not to reveal their same-sex attractions to others are based on an assessment of the costs and benefits, punishments and rewards, and danger and safety associated with such an action.

> I'm out and nobody really bothers me. I have been out since I was fifteen, and it hasn't really been a major thing. Everyone knows who I am and that I am gay, and they don't really bug me much. Then again, I'm the kind of person who thinks that it's better to be who you are. I couldn't stand not being what I am. If people can't deal with it, then fuck 'em—that's their deal not mine. I mean, I don't go around announcing to everyone that I am gay but if they ask me I tell them and I don't censor myself for anyone. . . . If they can't deal with it, then that's their shit not mine. I don't have time for it, and I won't deal with it.
>
> —Warren, gay white male, age 16

> I tried at first to hide that I was gay. I tried really hard to act like everyone else and to just kind of be invisible. It didn't work though, because people could just tell. Like they said by the way I talked and walked and stuff, they could just tell I was gay. And they just made fun of me and threw stuff at me, and hit me in the halls, no matter how much I kept denying it. So finally I just admitted it, because I was so tired of it. But the abuse just got worse.
>
> —Andy, gay white male, age 16

As the preceding statements evidence, there are many social factors involved in this coming-out process for g/l/b students. For example, Ani, Luke, and Rick all perceived their school environments to be risky places to be g/l/b. Based on this evaluation of their surroundings, they felt fearful of others' judgments of them and of the punishment that might accompany these judgments. For Warren, the potential risks of such judgments were outweighed by what he felt to be the cost of "censoring himself." For Andy, neither decision—to hide or to come out—could spare him from the judgment and punishment associated with being outside of the heterosexual norm of his high school. In these assessments, most of the students in my sample conclude that institutions of public education are dangerous places in which to come out as, be found to be, or be suspected of being gay, lesbian, or bisexual. Therefore, some choose to hide this part of themselves at school, while others choose to reveal it. However, regardless of the choice made, all students first assessed the relative safety or danger of their school environment.

Sexual-Identity Labels: The Paradox of "Self-definition"

According to the literature on homosexual identity-development models, an individual's acceptance and situational use of the label gay, lesbian, or bisexual is a sign of successful and mature homosexual identity formation. Therefore, uncomfortableness with these labels is taken to be a sign of a personal difficulty with self-acceptance. The developmental models, and the theoretical perspective of symbolic interactionism that informs them, take the meaning of these labels for granted. They do not discuss or analyze the social construction of these labels, the "natural" binary of heterosexual and homosexual that these labels reinforce, or the compulsion to categorize people within them.

In contrast, poststructuralist, postmodern, and queer theoretical perspectives argue that the terms and conditions on which sexual-identity labels are based, and the very concept of labeling, result from the power of scientifically and socially produced meanings of sexual identity (e.g., Foucault, 1976; Butler, 1993; McIntosh, 1968; Namaste, 1996; Seidman,

1996; Gamson, 1996; Weeks, 1981, 1985). These identity categories are used as social controls of individual behaviors and as structured enforcement of the normative dominance of heterosexuality. Many of the g/l/b students spoke about sexual-identity labels as categories and definitions that they felt were being forced upon them.

The use of sexual-identity labels was, at times, the subject of much debate at the weekly support group meetings. When I interviewed youth individually, they revealed that many found labeling to be personally frustrating, because they felt pressured to define and categorize their "true sexual identity."

> It depends on who I'm talking to. . . . Like, I say that I'm bisexual to people that I think are closed-minded. . . . It seems like a more acceptable term. So I guess I think that people will be more willing to accept that, or like won't get as freaked out if I say that as they would if I said that I was lesbian. . . . I don't think that any term is really an accurate description of who I am. It makes me uncomfortable to use them and, you know, all that it means to people. Like, people make assumptions about it—like it's sexual or disgusting or whatever. . . . But to other people, like my closer friends, I say that I am a lesbian.
>
> —Ani

> I use the term gay, if I use any term at all. . . . I don't like the term *lesbian*. It's like too technical or something. It sounds like a disease or a different species or something.
>
> —Emily, gay white female, age 16

These statements provide examples of how many of the students in my sample make the choice of how and when to label themselves. Many do this not based on their definition, understanding, or tolerance of their attractions, but rather on their perception of the meanings that *others* have attached to these labels of sexual identity. Generally, the students in my sample had little problem with self-acceptance. However, they did have anxiety about coming out and about the pressure they felt to choose a label and define their sexual identity.

> I don't understand why I have to label myself anything. I'm just Adam. If somebody asks me if I'm gay, I'll say yes. But why do I have to go around calling myself anything? Being gay is just a small part of who I am. It happens in my bedroom, not on a big screen in the street. It doesn't affect anyone. I'm just like everybody else; I like to go to the movies and dinner and talk with my boyfriend. I don't want anything radical, and I don't want to talk about it to everyone I meet. I mean, yeah, I want rights like everybody else and the legal right to marry, you know. That stuff's really important. But, it's not radical.
>
> —Adam, gay white male, age 19

The students who respond to labels in this way demonstrate a knowledge that these terms have social meanings beyond being only a simple description of their attractions and that these meanings are, more often than not, beyond their ability to define for themselves. They are generally uncomfortable with using these labels, which they feel do more to take away their ability to fully define and express themselves to others than to assert their identity.

> I don't use any label really. Except like at group where, you know, you kind of are expected to say something. Then I guess I say gay. . . . I mean, I'm not ashamed of it or anything. I just don't like . . . I mean, I don't go around announcing it to everyone. Like, I don't really think that it is anyone's business really.
>
> —Carol, gay white female, age 17

> I don't really label myself that much. . . . I just don't fit one and . . . Well, because my sexual orientation has a bad reputation, you know.
>
> —Becca

Statements like these illustrate social factors, *not* personal problems of acceptance. The discomfort with or reluctance to use a sexual-identity label to refer to themselves does not indicate a lack of acceptance or sense of shame in themselves. It is evidence of their knowl-

edge of and anger at the ways in which others perceive the meaning of these labels and at the way they may be used by others to place limits on who they can be. Some of the g/l/b students I interviewed took an active approach to try to define themselves outside of the definitional boundaries of these sexual-identity categories.

> I use the word *dyke* because I don't like the word *lesbian*. I think when people say it it's like lesss-bee-ann [slow and drawn out]. Like it sounds really like old and . . . I don't know. I'm young and . . . Like ever since I've been out, no one's ever used the word *dyke* against me, like, in a bad way. And so . . . I've been called *lesbo* and I've been called other things having to do with lesbian. So I prefer not to use it, because it has negative meaning to me. . . . *Dyke* is a really powerful word, and it seems like an active word. Because when people say the word *dyke*, people stop and listen. And nobody stops to listen when you say *lesbian*. Ever. It's just like, "OK, whatever. You mean you're gay, right."
>
> —Janice, gay white female, age 19

> Not straight. Because . . . I don't like heterosexuals and I don't like homosexuals, and for me each are incorporated in my thoughts. . . . Just things that I don't like that go along with each trait that I don't like. You know? I don't like extremely flamboyant people . . . homosexuals especially. . . . And I don't like . . . jock-ass heterosexuals . . . like hard-core heteros. Basically they piss me off. . . . Um, but I consider myself bi . . . I can go either way. [Why don't you use that label?] Because I'm not generic. [laughs] Pretty much that's it. I don't like labels.
>
> —Rick, bisexual biracial male, age 18

Statements like these reveal an awareness of the shaping force of sexual-identity categories on these students' lives—setting the definitional terms for who they are and who they can potentially be. They also evidence the possibility of fostering a positive identity and self-acceptance without simultaneously passively accepting the social, structural, and institutional meanings of homosexuality. Many of the students in my sample are actively trying to forge an identity for themselves that rejects the stigma forced on them by society and that moves beyond the definitional limitations of sexual-identity categories.

CONCLUSIONS

I have attempted to present g/l/b students as a population whose lives are often the sites of colliding interests, beliefs, and knowledges—about sexuality, identity, morality, and equality. Despite the rich sociological complexity surrounding this population, social scientists have yet to seriously research them. At this point in time, primary understandings of g/l/b youth have come from psychologists, counselors, and journalists. The general thrust of these depictions is that g/l/b youth universally experience a linear developmental process of "adjusting" to a socially stigmatized identity. I have argued that examining g/l/b youth solely through the lens of developmental models or simple accounts of their sufferings, does not put into question the social factors responsible for constructing the "socially stigmatizing role" or for instigating the anguish this causes. These vantage points also situate g/l/b youth as one-dimensional and impotent subjects, incapable of transcending the limits of the socially inscribed stigma placed on their identity.

Through an analysis of the data of g/l/b youth I collected, I argued that public education is a significant social force influencing g/l/b students' experiences with their sexual identity. Overwhelmingly, the g/l/b students in my sample reported a high degree of self-acceptance of their sexual identity, but at their public schools they felt isolated, rejected, ridiculed, or hated because of this identity. Public schools generally promote a culture of singularly heterosexual behavior, feelings, and language. These cultural norms are enforced through verbal and physical harassment of g/l/b students, the acceptance of this harassment by teachers and administrators, and a lack of accurate information about g/l/b people in the curriculum. All of these aspects of the public schools attended by the g/l/b students in my sample negatively affected these students' school experiences and their experiences with their sexual identity—making them feel invisible; persuading them to lie; compelling them to hide their thoughts, feelings, or beliefs; or forcing them to deal with physical or verbal abuse.

It is important to understand the experiences of g/l/b youth in relation to the social context in which their lives are situated. Not doing this leads to the misguided conclusion that because they are g/l/b they will inevitably have to suffer and the best we can do is counsel them through the inherently difficult process of g/l/b identity development. If we instead understand the social forces that often cause identity development to be a difficult process for g/l/b youth, we can work to change these social forces and prevent many of the problems they cause.

REFERENCES

Anderson, D. A. 1994. Lesbian and gay adolescents: Social and developmental considerations. *High School Journal*, special edition, 13–19.

Bell, A., and Weinberg, M. 1978. *Homosexualities: A Study of Diversity among Men and Women*. New York: Simon and Schuster.

Bell, A., et al. 1981. *Sexual Preference: Its Development in Men and Women*. Bloomington: Indiana University Press.

Butler, J. 1993. *Bodies That Matter*. New York, NY: Routledge.

Cass, V. C. 1979. Homosexual identity formation: A theoretical model. *Journal of Homosexuality, 10,* 77–84.

Cass, V. C. 1984. Homosexual identity: A concept in need of definition. *Journal of Homosexuality, 9,* 105–126.

Chandler, K. 1995. *Passages of Pride*. Los Angeles: Alyson Books.

Cook, J. and Herdt, G. 1990. To tell or not to tell: Patterns of self-disclosure to mothers and fathers reported by gay and lesbian youth. In *Parent and Child Relations across the Lifespan*, edited by Pillemer, K., and K. McCartney. New York: Oxford University Press.

DeCrescenzo, T., ed. 1994. *Helping Gay and Lesbian Youth: New Policies, New Programs, New Practice*. Binghamton, NY: Harrington Park Press.

Dennis, D. I., and Ruth, E. H. 1986. Gay youth and the right to education. *Yale Law and Policy Review*, 4, 445–455.

Due, L. 1995. *Joining the Tribe: Growing Up Gay and Lesbian in the '90s*. New York: Doubleday.

Durby, D. D. 1994. Gay, lesbian, and bisexual youth. In *Helping Gay and Lesbian Youth*, edited by T. DeCrescenzo, 1–37. Binghamton, NY: The Haworth Press, Inc.

Edwards, W. J. 1996. A sociological analysis of an invisible minority group: Male adolescent homosexuals. *Youth and Society*, 27, 334–355.

Epstein, D., ed. 1994. *Challenging Lesbian and Gay Inequalities in Education*. Buckingham: Open University Press.

Foucault, M. [1976] 1990. *The History of Sexuality*, Vol. 1: *An Introduction*. New York: Vintage Books.

Gallois, C., and Cox, S. 1996. Gay and lesbian identity development: A social identity perspective. *Journal of Homosexuality*, 30, 1–30.

Gamson, J. [1995] 1996, "Must Identity Movements Self Destruct? A Queer Dilemma." Pp. 395–420 in *Queer Theory/Sociology*, edited by Steven Seidman. Cambridge, MA: Blackwell.

Gibson, P. 1989. Gay male and lesbian youth suicide. *U.S. Department of Health and Human Services Report of the Secretary's Task Force on Youth Suicide*, vol. 3, pp. 110–142.

Goffman, E. 1963. *Stigma: Notes on the Management of a Spoiled Identity*. New York: Simon and Schuster.

Harbeck, K., ed. 1992. *Out of the Classroom Closet; Gay and Lesbian Students, Teachers, and Curricula*. Binghamton, NY: Harrington Parks Press.

Harbeck, K. 1994. Invisible no more: Addressing the needs of gay, lesbian, and bisexual youth and their advocates. *High School Journal*, special edition, 170–180.

Hayes, W. 1991. "To Be Young and Gay and Living in the '90s." *Utne Reader*, March/April, pp. 94–100.

Herdt, G., ed. 1989a. *Gay and Lesbian Youth*. New York: Harrington Park Press.

Herdt, G. 1989b. Gay and lesbian youth: Emergent identities and cultural scenes at home and abroad. *Journal of Homosexuality*, 17, 1–41.

Herdt, G., and Boxer, A. 1993. *Children of Horizons*. Boston: Beacon Press.

Hetrick, E., and Martin, D. 1987. Developmental issues and their resolution for gay and lesbian adolescents. *Journal of Homosexuality*, 14, 25–43.

Hunter, J., and Schaecher, R. 1987. Stresses on lesbian and gay adolescents in schools. *Social Work in Education*, 9, no. 3, 180–190.

Karp, S. 1995. Trouble over the rainbow. In *Rethinking Schools: An Agenda for Change*, edited by D. Levine, et al., 23–35. New York: New Press.

Kournay, R. F. C. Suicide among homosexual adolescents. *Journal of Homosexuality*, 13, no. 4, 111–117.

Lee, J. A. 1977. "Going Public: A Study in the Sociology of Homosexual Liberation." *Journal of Homosexuality*, 3:49–78.

Margruder, B., and Wider-Haugrud, L. K. 1996. Homosexual identity expression among lesbian and gay adolescents: An analysis of perceived structural associations. *Youth and Society*, 27, 313–333.

Martin, and Hetrick. 1988. The stigmatization of the gay and lesbian adolescent. *Journal of Homosexuality*, 16, 163–183.

Martin, A. D. 1982. Learning to hide: The socialization of the gay adolescent. *Adolescent Psychiatry*, 10, 52–65.

McIntosh, M. [1968] 1996. The homosexual role. In *Queer Theory/Sociology*, edited by Steven Seidman, 33–40. Cambridge, MA: Blackwell.

Miceli, M. 1998. *Recognizing All the Differences: Gay Youth and Public Education in America Today*. Dissertation. State University of New York at Albany.

Namaste, K. [1994] 1996. "The Politics of Inside/Out: Queer Theory, Poststructuralism, and a Sociological Approach to Sexuality." 194–212 in *Queer Theory/Sociology*, edited by Steven Seidman. Cambridge, MA: Blackwell.

Plummer, K. 1975. *Sexual Stigma: An Interactionist Account*. New York: Routledge.

Plummer, K. 1990. Understanding childhood sexualities. *Journal of Homosexuality*, 20, no. 1/2, 231–249.

Ponse, B. 1978. *Identities in the Lesbian World: The Social Construction of Self.* Westport, CO: Greenwood.

Raymond, D. 1994. Homophobia, identity, and the meaning of desire: Reflections on the cultural construction of gay and lesbian adolescent sexuality. In *Sexual Cultures and the Construction of Adolescent Identities,* edited by J. M. Irvine, 115–150. Philadelphia: Temple University Press.

Remafedi, G. 1987. Homosexual youth: A challenge to contemporary society. *JAMA,* July 10, 258.

Rich, A. 1983. Compulsory heterosexuality and lesbian existence. In *Powers of Desire,* edited by A. Snitow et al. New York: Monthly Review Press.

Robertson, R. 1987. Young gays. In *The Theory and Practice of Homosexuality,* edited by J. Hart and D. Richardson. London: Routledge and Kegan Paul.

Rofes, E. 1989. Opening up the classroom closet: Responding to the educational needs of gay and lesbian youth. *Harvard Educational Review, 59,* 444–453.

Savin-Williams, R. C. 1990. *Gay and Lesbian Youth: Expressions of Identity.* New York: Hemisphere.

Schaffer. 1976. "Sexual and Social Problems Among Lesbians" *Journal of Sex Research,* 12:50–79.

Schneider, M. 1989. Sappho was a "right-on" adolescent: Growing up lesbian. *Journal of Homosexuality, 17,* 111–130.

Seidman, S. 1995. Deconstructing queer theory or the under-theorization of the social and the ethical. In *Social Postmodernism: Beyond Identity Politics,* edited by Steven Seidman and Linda Nicholson, 116–140. Cambridge: Cambridge University Press.

Seidman, S. 1996. Introduction to *Queer Theory/Sociology,* edited by Steven Seidman, 1–29. Cambridge, MA: Blackwell.

Sullivan, T., and M. Schneider. 1987. Developmental and identity issues in adolescent homosexuals. *Child and Adolescent Social Work, 4,* 13–23.

Troiden, R. R. 1979. Becoming homosexual: A model of gay identity acquisition. *Psychiatry, 42,* 362–373.

Troiden, R. R. 1988. *Gay and Lesbian Identity: A Sociological Analysis.* New York: General Hall.

Troiden, R. R. 1989. The formation of homosexual identities. *Journal of Homosexuality, 17,* 43–73.

Unks, G. 1993. Thinking about the homosexual adolescent. *High School Journal,* special edition, 1–6.

Unks, G., ed. 1995. *The Gay Teen: Educational Practice and Theory for Lesbian, Gay, and Bisexual Adolescents.* New York: Routledge.

Uribe, V. 1994. Project 10: A school-based outreach to gay and lesbian youth. *High School Journal,* special edition, 109–113.

Walling, D. R., ed. 1996. *Open Lives, Safe Schools: Addressing Gay and Lesbian Issues in Education.* Bloomington, IN: Phi Delta Kappa Educational Foundation.

Weeks, J. [1981] 1996. "The Construction of Homosexuality." Pp. 41–63 in *Queer Theory/Sociology,* edited by Steven Seidman, Cambridge, MA: Blackwell.

Weeks, J. 1985. *Sexuality and its Discontents.* New York: Routledge.

Weinberg. T. 1978, "On 'Doing' and 'Being' Gay: Sexual Behavior and Homosexual Male Self-Identity." *Journal of Homosexuality,* 4:143–156.

Woog, D. 1995. *School's Out: The Impact of Gay and Lesbian Issues on America's Schools.* Boston: Alyson.

Zera, D. 1992. Coming of age in a heterosexist world The development of gay and lesbian adolescents. *Adolescence, 27,* 848–854.

PART THREE

GENDERED SEXUALITY

Sexuality is gendered. A designation of *sex*, male or female, is assigned to us at birth, and then we are socialized into the *gender* roles associated with that sex in the cultural context where we are raised. We learn how to be *sexual* based on a polarized notion of both sex, that males and females are opposites, and gender, that masculinity and femininity must be mirror images of each other. Being masculine thus means not being feminine and vice versa, and we are trained to be attracted to the other, to those representing the largest difference from the way we are. Yet recent developments in social theory, drawing on feminist and queer theory (which asks that we critically examine the relationship between sexuality and social power), as well as research in the biological and natural sciences calls these assumptions into question. We are not all gendered in the same way—we are not all sexual in similar ways even within our categories of hetero-bi-homosexualities.

Constructing gender roles as polar opposites sets us up to deny or constrict those aspects of ourselves that do not fit the traditional idea of being masculine or feminine. As a result of the feminist movement and the introduction of the psychological concept of androgyny, women have reclaimed the right to be seen as healthy females while being decisive, goal-oriented, and strong-minded, characteristics that had been seen as deviant for girls and women. A similar process is taking place for boys and men, so that the full range of male characteristics—which are similar to, rather than opposites of female characteristics—can be encouraged. Let's take a small step by saying "other sex" instead of referring to the "opposite sex." We are more alike than we are different.

Monolithic notions of gender and sexuality (that sexuality and gender have one universal meaning and are absolute) are misleading. And they have profound influences on our concept of self. We attempt to "fit" into categories, based on assigned expectations regarding values, attitudes, beliefs, and behaviors. We do this as if the categories themselves, "male" or "masculine" and "female" or "feminine," each had only one set of possibilities and were absolutely necessary to being a successful heterosexual. Parents become anxious when their children's behaviors stray even a bit from the norm. A little boy refuses to become involved in sports, and his parents fear he will not be masculine, and therefore possibly be gay. A niece refuses to dress "pretty" and her aunt worries that she won't catch a husband.

The way we are taught to be male involves socialization into heterosexuality, and into being heterosexual the way males are supposed to be heterosexual. For some, this implies using pornography, leaving men with pornographized images as mental pictures of how women and sex really should be. It can also mean publicly distancing oneself from anything or anyone who is perceived as gay and not appearing in any way to be emotionally open or femalelike in one's emotional expression. Boys lose their smiles midway through elementary school to avoid looking open or expressive in front of other boys and thus being seen as a sissy and gay (Pollack, 1999; Kindlon and Thompson, 1999).

A similar set of expectations exists for girls. To be female and heterosexual is to learn about the "dos and don'ts" when it comes to getting and keeping a boyfriend. That's what the teen magazines teach. Don't come on too strong, don't be too smart, and don't be too sexual. And don't look like you might be Lesbian—never shave your head and always shave your underarms! Being heterosexual, and gender-appropriate, is encoded in every aspect of our lives. Go ahead. Try it. If you are female and have a boyfriend, tell him (and your parents) that you will no longer be shaving your legs or underarms, and you may shave your head. If you are male, tell your girlfriend (and parents) you will be shaving your underarms and legs. Listen to their concerns and ask them to tell you why. Are they talking about the intersection between sexuality and gender expectations? Maybe.

Jamie Buki's story, "Sisters," leads off this section with her reflections on how her close relationship as a teen with her older brother Timothy may have helped her make the adjustment as Timothy redefined his gender to become Jennifer. To what extent are our sibling relationships a function of shared feelings, even across gender? In an article on black masculinity that appears a little later in this section, bell hooks laments having seen her sweet brother try to reconstruct himself as a male to meet the ideals of patriarchal masculinity. You might reflect on ways your expectations for sibling relationships have been affected by gender stereotypes and roles.

Pepper Schwartz and Virginia Rutter examine gender differences in sexuality and sexual desire. Their article, "Sexual Desire and Gender," offers comparisons between sociobiological and social constructionist explanations of sexuality, including a feminist evolutionary essentialist perspective. An integrative perspective, according to the authors, is one in which biology is neither where sexuality begins nor where it ends. They review the mechanisms of arousal as well as the role of hormones, neither of which are as simple as is popularly understood. For example, they report recent research on testosterone and aggression in men showing low levels of testosterone associated with aggression and higher levels associated with calmness, happiness, and friendliness. If more parents and teachers knew this data, they might stop using "boys will be boys" excuses, based on believing testosterone made them do it! In what ways do you hold onto a biological explanation for gender differences?

In "The Four Boxes of Gendered Sexuality: Good Girl/Bad Girl and Tough Guy/Sweet Guy," Betsy Crane and Jesse Crane-Seeber provide a theoretical perspective on gendered sexuality by presenting a new view of ancient history and its connection with the construction of the gendered roles and sexual expectations we live with today. Their four boxes of gendered sexuality elucidate the sexual oppression faced by both males and females as we encounter the tensions imposed by "tough guy/sweet guy" and "good girl/bad girl" dichotomies. Their categories and analysis can be useful as you think critically about other topics in this book. If you weren't worried about being the "bad girl" or the "sweet guy" how might that influence your sexuality? What is your response to females and to males who don't conform, or don't pretend to conform, to expectations?

In "Reconstructing Black Masculinity," bell hooks discusses the implications for black men, and for women, of not interrogating patriarchal masculinity. By interrogating, hooks means that we need to question the assumptions about men and women in general and how these are related to race and the history of oppression of black men by white men. If we accept that, in European and U.S. culture, to be masculine (and thus heterosexual) means that a man controls others, is influential, and has power, then what are the implications for black males, given the history of slavery and oppression of African Americans? Hooks questions the extent to which black men have internalized this norm. There have been black men who were not at all interested in the white-patriarchal ideal, she says, recalling from her childhood black men who touched her heart, were caring and giving, defied the status quo, and invented themselves. Yet for black men who did absorb white society's notion of manhood, despair and bitterness came as a result of being blocked from achieving the patriarchal ideal of providing for and protecting "their women." With black men given access to few activities that yield masculine status, hooks asserts, the ideal of patriarchal power based on ruling others shifted to a phallocentric model, emphasizing masculine status based on what men did with their penis. A sexually defined masculine ideal, rooted in physical domination and sexual possession of women could be accessible to all men. Hooks discusses the resultant sexism and misogyny and the tensions, often unspoken publicly, this has caused between black men and women. She calls for black people to look at the link between the contemporary plight of black men and their continued allegiance to patriarchy and phallocentrism. As you reflect on this culturally situated exposition, think about what it reveals about power relations within and between marginalized groups. What influence can dominant groups (dominant based on race, but also consider gender, age, and social class) have on the sexual lives of nondominant groups?

Chrys Ingraham theorizes heterosexuality as a highly regulated, ritualized, and organized set of social practices, such as weddings. In "Ritualizing Heterosexuality: Weddings as Performance," she states that heterosexuality can be seen as a social institution, since it is an arrangement involving large numbers of people whose behavior is guided by norms and rules, such as who drives the car, cooks dinner, or initiates sex. Ingraham discusses the theory of compulsory heterosexuality and the normative status of heterosexuality, called heteronormativity. She considers as well queer theorists' denaturalizing of heterosexuality, revealing it as a social and political organizing principle with implications for the definition of committed relationships existing without benefit of marriage. Romanticizing heterosexuality, which Ingraham calls the heterosexual imaginary, is used to "naturalize" rituals like Valentine's Day, proms, and weddings, all of which are major commercial enterprises in the United States.

Judith Barker takes us from the prom and wedding to country music. Her article, "Country Music and Women's Sexuality: What Do Women Want?" uses song lyrics as a lens through which we can hear messages about women's desires. As women gain a voice in the medium of country music, new themes are emerging. And what do women want? The lyrics, Barker finds, carry the message that women want to be loved for being themselves, as real live women, not for a body image, as Barbie dolls or models, or as sex objects. There is also a new sense of willingness to critique male behavior and to encourage other women to face reality, even when it comes to abuse. In their relationships with men—and nearly all country music assumes heterosexuality— women want reciprocity. The popularity of such songs, Barker notes, indicates a willingness to accept them as a legitimate part of country music.

Sandra Lipsitz Bem challenges us to think outside the box and to imagine a complex matrix of gendered/sexual possibilities. A feminist psychologist, Bem is well known for her work in reducing the power of the male/female dichotomy through introducing the concept of androgyny. In "Dismantling Gender Polarization and Compulsory Heterosexuality: Should We Turn the Volume Down or Up?" Bem leads us in a new direction, proposing that rather than trying to shrink gender differences, we add to or proliferate gender categories, all with fluid and permeable configurations. In her utopian vision, she says, this would destabilize the privileged status of the two-and-only-two genders currently treated as normal and natural. She sees a kaleidoscope of potential bio-social-sexual genders that would incorporate variations in biology, emotional makeup, and sexual desire and help break us out of the boxes we've inherited from our history.

Allan Hunter writes from his own experience within what might be seen as one of Bem's many genders, that of a "sissy" heterosexual. Hunter tells his story in "Same Closet, Different Door: A Heterosexual Sissy's Coming-out Party." Although *sissy* derives from the term *sister,* thus connoting the sense of being like a female, Hunter experienced the direct tie to sexuality through homophobic attacks, being called faggot and queer as he was being physically and verbally assaulted. His actual experience as a child was of being more like the girls than the boys primarily in that he behaved like a "good citizen" rather than a "behavior problem." Meanwhile he had strong girl-oriented sexual feelings that have continued, as has his "sissy" identity, making his adult experience of gendered sexuality and relationships both complex and worthy of note.

Leslie Feinberg's "Transgender Warriors: Making History" wraps up this section on gendered sexuality with its presentation of the two-spirit traditions of Native American people. Feinberg's examples provide clear evidence that the dichotomous notion of gender as only male or female is not the reality across cultures. She relates the bloody history of European conquests of North and South America, when soldiers murdered men who were dressed as women, seeing them as hermaphrodites or homosexuals. This stands in stark contrast to the respect such men received within their own culture, where access to both the masculine and feminine spirit was seen as sacred. People with this gift were often shamans and teachers. The two-spirit tradition of sex/gender complexity and fluidity continues among Native Americans today, Feinberg reports, quoting a Navaho who, placing gender on a continuum from male to female, could image 49 different sex/gender identities. Perhaps Bem's idea of proliferating gender categories has already taken place and Western culture is just catching up! What implications does the concept of sex/gender fluidity have for you?

REFERENCES

Kindlon, D., and Thompson, M. 1999. *Raising Cain: Protecting the Emotional Life of Boys.* New York: Ballantine Books.
Pollack, W. 1999. *Real Boys: Rescuing Our Sons From the Myths of Boyhood.* New York: Random House.

Sisters

Jamie Buki

If I could remember the date exactly, then I suppose that I would write it here. It was my first year at high school, and it was my older sibling's first year at college. We were all home for Christmas and happily enjoying each other's company. I could hear laughter filling our rooms downstairs as I was going about my business in my room nearby. There was a knock on the door and my older brother's voice asking if he could come in. Though I thought the question was weird, since he always barged in, I humored him with an answer.

My brother and I had a great relationship, though looking back I suppose it was rather strange. Of the four of us, my brother and I were always the two siblings hanging out. Especially when yearly family vacations came around, we were always pulling practical jokes and getting ourselves into trouble. We loved to make up plays to be put on solely for our own personal entertainment. And to this day, I swear that some of my best friends loved to hang out with Tim more than with me.

But, you know, looking back I don't remember seeing a friend of his in the house. In fact, I don't think that I ever took one phone message for him. I can remember when he was in high school that there would be times when he would come home and lock himself in his room until the next day. Tim was moody if you caught him at the wrong time and was obsessed about writing in a certain little notebook as well as reading books that he tried to keep hidden. The more I think about it, I suppose I was expecting this night my whole life.

So Tim walks in after asking permission to enter and sits on the bed opposite me. I felt the pain in his heart and the uncomfortableness in the air. I was waiting for something, but I really wasn't too sure what it was exactly. Without much delay he says to me, and I will never forget it, "Jamie, I have decided to become a woman." I am not too sure that I even understood what he said, but I remember knowing that it was something so big that I could barely comprehend it. In response and reaction, I fired back, "I love you, Tim." I rushed to his side to hug him, and without much of anything else he walked out of the room and shut the door. I was left alone with my tears and the utter confusion about what had just happened. Even as I tell this story the tears swell up in my eyes as I think of how hard it was for Tim to say what he said. But I suppose I cry more because I know the long struggle that occurred afterward for him.

Let me stop right here for a second and bring the reader up to date with the situation. My older brother Timothy Jarod Allbaugh is now Jennifer Phillips, a 25-year-old exotic dancer at one of the premier clubs in Las Vegas, Nevada. She is now studying psychology and looks to be finished in the next year or so at UNLV. It has been a long road for her, and some days I am not too sure if things are getting better or worse. In October 1997 she had a sex change to redefine her gender and to fulfill her lifetime dream. For years I was unable to talk about it, since it hurt so much that I turned away from the reality.

Being as close as I was to Tim when I was younger, I feel that the topic of transsexuality is something that I should know a lot about. People are confused and ignorant about the whole concept of someone being a transsexual. Transsexuality is a misunderstood topic that has many myths and misconceptions attached to it. The myths about transsexuality make it difficult not only for people who are transgender, but also for families, friends, co-workers, and neighbors. It saddens me, particularly since my sister Jennifer continues to be my best friend.

Sexual Desire and Gender

Pepper Schwartz
Virginia Rutter

The gender of the person you desire is a serious matter seemingly fundamental to the whole business of romance. And it isn't simply a matter of whether someone is male or female; how well the person fulfills a lover's expectations of masculinity or femininity is of great consequence, as two examples from the movies illustrate.

In the movie *The Truth about Cats & Dogs* (1996), a man (Brian, played by Ben Chaplin) falls in love with a woman (Abby, played by Janeane Garofalo) over the phone, and she with him. They find each other warm, clever, charming, and intriguing. But she, thinking herself too plain, asks her beautiful friend (Noelle, played by Uma Thurman) to impersonate her when the man and woman are scheduled to meet. The movie continues as a comedy of errors. Although the man becomes very confused about which woman he really desires, in the end the telephone lovers are united. The match depended on social matters far more than physical matters.

In the British drama *The Crying Game* (1994), Fergus, an Irish Republican Army underling, meets and falls in love with the lover (Dil) of Jody, a British soldier whom Fergus befriended prior to being ordered to execute him. The movie was about passionate love, war, betrayal, and, in the end, loyalty and commitment. Fergus seeks out Jody's girlfriend in London out of guilt and curiosity. But Fergus's guilt over Jody's death turns into love, and the pair become romantically and sexually involved. In the

end, although Fergus is jailed for terrorist activities, Fergus and Dil have solidified their bond and are committed and, it seems, in love. The story of sexual conquest and love is familiar, but this particular story grabbed imaginations because of a single, crucial detail. Jody's girlfriend Dil, Fergus discovers, turns out to be (physically) a man. Although Fergus is horrified when he discovers his lover is biologically different from what he had expected, in the end their relationship survives.

These movies raise an interesting point about sexual desire. Although sex is experienced as one of the most basic and biological of activities, in human beings it is profoundly affected by things other than the body's urges. Who we're attracted to and what we find sexually satisfying is not just a matter of the genital equipment we're born with. This chapter explains why.

Before we delve into the whys and wherefores of sex, we need to come to an understanding about what sex is. This is not as easy a task as it may seem, because sex has a number of dimensions.

On one level, sex can be regarded as having both a biological and a social context. The biological (and physiological) refers to how people use their genital equipment to reproduce. In addition, as simple as it seems, bodies make the experience of sexual pleasure available—whether the pleasure involves other bodies or just one's own body and mind. It should be obvious, however, that people engage in sex even when they do not intend to reproduce. They have sex for fun, as a way to communicate their feelings to each other, as a way to satisfy their ego, and for any number of other reasons relating to the way they see themselves and interact with others.

Another dimension of sex involves both what we do and how we think about it. *Sexual behavior* refers to the sexual acts that people engage in. These acts involve not only petting and intercourse but also seduction and

Source: Pepper Schwartz and Virginia Rutter, *The Gender of Sexuality.* Thousand Oaks, CA: Pine Forge Press. Copyright © 1998.

courtship. Sexual behavior also involves the things people do alone for pleasure and stimulation and the things they do with other people. *Sexual desire,* on the other hand, is the motivation to engage in sexual acts. It relates to what turns people on. A person's *sexuality* consists of both behavior and desire.

The most significant dimension of sexuality is *gender.* Gender relates both to the biological and social contexts of sexual behavior and desire. People tend to believe they know whether someone is a man or a woman not because we do a physical examination and determine that the person is biologically male or biologically female. Instead, we notice whether a person is masculine or feminine. Gender is a social characteristic of individuals in our society that is only sometimes consistent with biological sex. Thus, animals, like people, tend to be identified as male and female in accordance with the reproductive function, but only people are described by their gender, as a man or a woman.

When we say something is *gendered* we mean that social processes have determined what is appropriately masculine and feminine and that gender has thereby become integral to the definition of the phenomenon. For example, marriage is a gendered institution: The definition of marriage involves a masculine part (husband) and a feminine part (wife). Gendered phenomena, like marriage, tend to appear "naturally" so. But, as recent debates about same-sex marriage underscore, the role of gender in marriage is the product of social processes and beliefs about men, women, and marriage. In examining how gender influences sexuality, moreover, you will see that gender rarely operates alone: Class, culture, race, and individual differences also combine to influence sexuality.

This book explores and takes issue with the assumptions that sexuality is naturally gendered and rooted in biology, that men and women are different sexually, and that this difference is consistent and universal across societies. Of course, what appears "natural" in one society may be very different in another. By calling the book *The Gender of Sexuality,* we challenge you to think about how even things that people tend to consider biological, like a woman's producing a baby, are influenced enormously by the social processes that determine what motherhood is all about and how motherhood is different from fatherhood.

As you can see, sexuality is a complex bit of business. The study of sexuality also presents methodological challenges. Sexual thoughts and behavior are typically private. Researchers must rely on what people say they want and do sexually, and these reports, as much as the desire and behavior itself, are influenced by what people believe they are supposed to feel and say. In this book, we will piece together this puzzle of acts, thoughts, and feelings with insights provided by survey research, physiological studies, ethnography, history, philosophy, and even art, cinema, and literature.

DESIRE: ATTRACTION AND AROUSAL

The most salient fact about sex is that nearly everybody is interested in it. Most people like to have sex, and they talk about it, hear about it, and think about it. But some people are obsessed with sex and willing to have sex with anyone or anything. Others are aroused only by particular conditions and hold exacting criteria. For example, some people will have sex only if they are positive that they are in love, that their partner loves them, and that the act is sanctified by marriage. Others view sex as not much different from eating a sandwich. They neither love nor hate the sandwich; they are merely hungry, and they want something to satisfy that hunger. What we are talking about here are differences in desire. As you have undoubtedly noticed, people differ in what they find attractive, and they are also physically aroused by different things.

Many people assume that differences in sexual desire have a lot to do with whether a person is female or male. In large representative surveys about sexual behavior, the men as a group inevitably report more frequent sex, with more partners, and in more diverse ways than the women as a group do.[. . .] First, we should consider the approaches we might use to interpret it. Many observers argue that when it comes to sex, men and women have fundamentally different biological wiring. Others use the evidence to argue that culture has produced marked sexual differences among men and women. We believe, however, that it is hard to tease apart biological differences and social differences. As soon as a baby enters the world, it receives messages about gender and sexuality. In the United States, for example, disposable diapers come adorned in pink for girls and blue for boys. In case people aren't sure whether to treat the baby as masculine or feminine in its first years of life, the diaper signals them. The assumption is that girl babies really are different from boy babies and the difference ought to be displayed. This different treatment continues throughout life, and therefore a sex difference at birth becomes amplified into gender difference as people mature.

Gendered experiences have a great deal of influence on sexual desire. As a boy enters adolescence, he hears jokes about boys' uncontainable desire. Girls are told the same thing and told that their job is to resist. These gender messages have power not only over attitudes and behavior (such as whether a person grows up to prefer sex with a lover rather than a stranger) but also over physical and biological experience. For example, a girl may be discouraged from vigorous competitive activity, which will subsequently influence how she develops physically, how she feels about her body, and even how she relates to the adrenaline rush associated with physical competition. Hypothetically, a person who is accustomed to

adrenaline responses experiences sexual attraction differently from one who is not.

What follows are three "competing" explanations of differences in sexual desire between men and women: a biological explanation, sociobiological and evolutionary psychological explanations, and an explanation that acknowledges the social construction of sexuality. We call these competing approaches because each tends to be presented as a complete explanation in itself, to the exclusion of other explanations. Our goal, however, is to provide a clearer picture of how "nature" and "nurture" are intertwined in the production of sexualities.

THE BIOLOGY OF DESIRE: NATURE'S EXPLANATION

Biology is admittedly a critical factor in sexuality. Few human beings fall in love with fish or sexualize trees. Humans are designed to respond to other humans. And human activity is, to some extent, organized by the physical equipment humans are born with. Imagine if people had fins instead of arms or laid eggs instead of fertilizing them during intercourse. Romance would look quite different.

Although biology seems to be a constant (i.e., a component of sex that is fixed and unchanging), the social world tends to mold biology as much as biology shapes humans' sexuality. Each society has its own rules for sex. Therefore, how people experience their biology varies widely. In some societies, women act intensely aroused and active during sex; in others, they have no concept of orgasm. In fact, women in some settings, when told about orgasm, do not even believe it exists, as anthropologists discovered in some parts of Nepal. Clearly, culture—not biology—is at work, because we know that orgasm is physically possible, barring damage to or destruction of the sex organs. Even ejaculation is culturally dictated. In some countries, it is considered healthy to ejaculate early and often; in others, men are told to conserve semen and ejaculate as rarely as possible. The biological capacity may not be so different, but the way bodies behave during sex varies according to social beliefs.

Sometimes the dictates of culture are so rigid and powerful that the so-called laws of nature can be overridden. Infertility treatment provides an example: For couples who cannot produce children "naturally," a several billion dollar industry has provided technology that can, in a small proportion of cases, overcome this biological problem (Rutter 1996). Recently, in California, a child was born to a 63-year-old woman who had been implanted with fertilized eggs. The cultural emphasis on reproduction and parenthood, in this case, overrode the biological incapacity to produce children. Nevertheless, some researchers have focused on the biological foundations of sexual desire. They have examined the endocrine system and hormones, brain structure, and genetics. Others have observed the mechanisms of arousal. What all biological research on sex has in common is the proposition that many so-called sexual choices are not choices at all but are dictated by the body. A prominent example comes from the study of the biological origins of homosexuality. However, contradictory and debatable findings make conclusions difficult.

The Influence of Hormones

Biological explanations of sexual desire concentrate on the role of hormones. *Testosterone*, sometimes called the male sex hormone, appears to be the most important hormone for sexual function. Numerous research studies identify testosterone as an enabler for male sexual arousal (Bancroft 1978; Masters, Johnson, and Kolodny 1995). But we cannot predict a man's sexual tastes, desires, or behavior by measuring his testosterone. Although a low level of testosterone in men is sometimes associated with lower sexual desire, this is not predictably the case. Furthermore, testosterone level does not always influence sexual performance. Indeed, testosterone is being experimented with as a male contraceptive (Wu et al. 1996), thus demonstrating that desire and the biological goal of reproduction need not be linked to sexual desire.

Testosterone has also been implicated in nonsexual behaviors, such as aggression. Furthermore, male aggression sometimes crosses into male sexuality, generating sexual violence. But recent research on testosterone and aggression in men has turned the testosterone-aggression connection on its head: Low levels of testosterone have been associated with aggression, and higher levels have been associated with calmness, happiness, and friendliness (Angier 1995).

Testosterone is also found in women, although at levels as little as one-fifth those of men. This discrepancy in levels of testosterone has incorrectly been used as evidence for "natural" gender differences in sex drives. However, women's testosterone receptors are simply more sensitive than men's to smaller amounts of testosterone (Kolodny, Masters, and Johnson 1979).

Estrogen, which is associated with the menstrual cycle, is known as the female hormone. Like testosterone, however, estrogen is found in both women and men. Furthermore, estrogen may be the more influential hormone in human aggression. In animal research, male mice whose ability to respond to estrogen had been bred out of them lost much of their natural aggressiveness. Researchers are currently investigating the association between adolescents' moodiness and their levels of estrogen (Angier 1995). Of course, many social factors—such as changes in parental behavior toward their teenagers—help explain moodiness among adolescents (Rutter 1995).

Some biological evidence indicates that a woman's sexual desire may be linked to the impact of hormones as levels change during

TABLE 17.1		
SEXUAL ROLE OF HORMONES		
Hormone	**Influence**	**Weakness to theory**
Testosterone (male hormone)	Triggers sexual arousal	Also present in women and also triggers women's sexual arousal; associated with calmness, not aggression
Estrogen (female hormone)	Triggers menstrual cycle	Also present in men; associated with aggression, not calmness

her reproductive cycle. (No evidence shows men's sexual desire to be cyclical.) Some scientists believe that women's sexual arousal is linked to the fertile portion of their cycle (Stanislaw and Rice 1988). They believe that sexual interest in women is best explained as the product of thousands of years of natural selection. Natural selection would favor for survival those women who are sexually aroused during ovulation (the time women are most likely to become pregnant). These women would be reproductively successful and therefore pass on to their children the propensity for arousal during ovulation. Neat though this theory is, it doesn't fit all the data. Other research (Bancroft et al. 1983; Bancroft 1984) finds no evidence of increased sexual interest among women who are ovulating. Instead, the evidence suggests that women's sexual interest actually tends to peak well before ovulation. Still other evidence finds no variation in sexual desire or sexual activity in connection to the menstrual cycle (Hoon, Bruce, and Kinchloe 1982; Meuwissen and Over 1992).

As Table 17.1 indicates, testosterone and estrogen are not clearly linked to either men's desire or women's. Research shows a complicated relationship between hormones and sexuality. Hormonal fluctuations may not be the central cause of sexual behavior or any social acts; instead, social circumstances may be the cause of hormonal fluctuation. A famous series of experiments makes the point. One animal experiment took a dominant rhesus monkey

out of his environment and measured testosterone level. It was very high, suggesting that he had reached the top of the monkey heap by being hormonally superior. Then the monkey was placed among even bigger, more dominant monkeys than himself. When his testosterone was remeasured, it was much lower. One interpretation is that social hierarchy had influenced the monkey's biological barometer. His testosterone level had adjusted to his social status. In this case, the social environment shaped physiology (Rose, Holaday, and Bernstein 1970).

The Mechanisms of Arousal

Biological explanations of gender differences in sexuality owe a great deal to the work of William Masters and Virginia Johnson, who studied the human sexual arousal system. Unlike other researchers, who had relied on self-reports, these pioneers actually hooked up their participants to machines that could provide information on physiological responses to sexual stimuli. They based their findings on laboratory observation of over 10,000 sexual episodes experienced by 382 women and 312 men (Masters and Johnson 1966). The research team photographed the inside of women's vaginas during arousal and observed circulatory and nipple response, and they observed the rise and fall of men's penises.

Notice that Masters and Johnson focused on bodies rather than the social and relationship contexts in which sex occurs. From the start, the research was limited to information about the mechanisms of sexuality. It's not hard to imagine that the responses of men and women hooked to machines and under observation might well be different from a loving couple's first (or 91st) sexual episode. In addition, the participants were far from "typical" or randomly selected. To the contrary, they were sexual extroverts such as prostitutes, who, as far as we can tell, were not really representative of the population.

Nevertheless, with this information Masters and Johnson created the new field of sex therapy, which sought to understand and modify the mechanisms of human sexual response or, as the case might be, nonresponse. The sexual therapies they developed were based on what they inferred from their data to be differences between male and female patterns of arousal.

One of Masters and Johnson's most important observations was a sexual difference between men and women in the timing of the excitement cycle. The key difference is that male sexual physiology has a quicker trigger. Comparing men's and women's sexual responses is like comparing sprinters (men) to long-distance runners (women). Men are excited sooner, have an orgasm sooner, relatively quickly lose their erection, and require a "refractory" period before sexual excitation and erection can begin again. This refractory period among young or exceptional men could be very brief. But for the majority of men, 20 minutes, an hour, or even a day might be necessary.

The female cycle is, in general, a slower and more sustained proposition. The increase of blood to the genital area that accompanies arousal takes longer and remains longer after orgasm. This slower buildup may in part account for the longer time it typically takes women to be ready for sexual intercourse. Additionally, the longer time women take to reach and stay in the plateau phase theoretically makes orgasm less automatic than it is for men. However, the fact that blood leaves the genital area slowly after orgasm means

that many women require little or no refractory period if restimulated. Consequently, Masters and Johnson described women as potentially "multi-orgasmic." In other words, some women can have more than one orgasm in fairly short succession.

These physiological findings were the basis for a theory about female and male mating styles. Masters and Johnson considered men's more quickly triggered mechanisms to be at odds with the slower mechanisms of women. On the other hand, the ability of women to have more than one orgasm suggested that women might be the superior sexual athletes under certain conditions. Masters and Johnson's followers work within a model that addresses sexual problems by matching male and female sexual strategies more closely than they believe nature has done. In fact, it might be argued that Masters and Johnson's general approach to sexual counseling was to teach men to understand and cope with the slower female sexual response and to modify their own sexual response so that they do not reach orgasm before their partner is fully aroused.

SOCIOBIOLOGY AND EVOLUTIONARY PSYCHOLOGY

The past few decades of research on sexuality have produced a new school of human behavior—*sociobiology* and a related discipline, *evolutionary psychology*—that explains most gender differences as strategies of sexual reproduction. According to evolutionary psychologist David Buss (1995), "Evolutionary psychologists predict that the sexes will differ in precisely those domains in which women and men have faced different sorts of adaptive problems" (p. 164). By "those domains," Buss refers to reproduction, which is the only human function that depends on a biological difference between men and women.

The key assumption of sociobiological/ evolutionary theory is that humans have an innate, genetically triggered impulse to pass on their genetic material through successful reproduction: This impulse is called *reproductive fitness*. The human species, like other species that sociobiologists study, achieves immortality by having children who live to the age of reproductive maturity and produce children themselves. Sociobiologists and evolutionary psychologists seek to demonstrate that almost all male and female behavior, and especially sexuality, is influenced by this one simple but powerful proposition.

Sociobiologists start at the species level. Species are divided into *r* and *K reproductive categories*. Those with *r* strategies obtain immortality by mass production of eggs and sperm. The *r* species is best illustrated by fish. The female manufactures thousands of eggs, the male squirts millions of sperm over them, and that is the extent of parenting. According to this theory, the male and female fish need not pair up to nurture their offspring. Although thousands of fertilized fish eggs are consumed by predators, only a small proportion of the massive quantity of fertilized eggs must survive for the species to continue. In the *r* species, parents need not stay together for the sake of the kids.

In contrast, humans are a *K*-strategy species, which has a greater investment in each fertilized egg. Human females and most female mammals have very few eggs, especially compared to fish. Moreover, offspring take a long time to mature in the mother's womb and are quite helpless after they are born, with no independent survival ability. Human babies need years of supervision before they are independent. Thus, if a woman wants to pass on her genes (or at least the half her child will inherit from her), she must take good care of her dependent child. The baby is a scarce resource. Even if a woman is pregnant from sexual maturation until menopause, the number of children she can produce is quite limited. This limitation was particularly true

thousands of years ago. Before medical advances of the nineteenth and twentieth centuries, women were highly unlikely to live to the age of menopause. Complications from childbirth commonly caused women to die in their 20s or 30s. Where the food supply was scarce, women were less likely to be successful at conceiving, further reducing the possibility of generating offspring.

Sociobiologists and evolutionary psychologists say that men inseminate, women incubate. The human female's reproductive constraints (usually one child at a time, only so many children over a life cycle, and a helpless infant for a long period of time) shape most of women's sexual and emotional approaches to men and mating. According to their theory, women have good reason to be more selective than men about potential mates. They want to find a man who will stick around and continue to provide resources and protection to this child at least until the child has a good chance of survival. Furthermore, because a woman needs to create an incentive for a man to remain with her, females have developed more sophisticated sexual and emotional skills specifically geared toward creating male loyalty and commitment to their mutual offspring.

Sociobiologists and evolutionary psychologists say that differences in reproductive capacity and strategy also shape sexual desire. Buss asserts that reproductive strategies form most of the categories of desire: Older men generally pick younger women because they are more fertile; younger women seek older men who have more status, power, and resources (a cultural practice known as *hypergamy*) because such men can provide for their children. Furthermore, health and reproductive capacity make youth generally sexier, and even certain shapes of women's bodies (such as an "ideal" hip-to-waist ratio epitomized by an hourglass figure, which correlate with ability to readily reproduce), are widely preferred

TABLE 17.2

COMPARISON OF TRADITIONAL AND FEMINIST SOCIOBIOLOGICAL EXPLANATIONS OF GENDER DIFFERENCES IN SEXUALITY

Perspective	Gender difference	Explanation
Traditional	Men seek to maximize number of progeny by changing partners as often as possible. Women seek to maximize well-being of progeny by holding on to their partners as long as possible.	Men have biological capacity to inseminate many women in a short period of time; women's biological job is to incubate and nurture young.
Feminist	Men seek to maximize progeny; women seek to maximize well-being of progeny by exchanging partners when improved options are available.	Men and women both seek to maximize number of partners and quality of partners by exchanging when improved options are available.

(Buss 1994)—despite varying standards of beauty across cultures. Likewise, men who have demonstrated their fertility by producing children are more sought after than men who have not (Buss 1994).

According to evolutionary psychologists, men's tastes for recreational sex, unambivalent lust, and a variety of partners are consistent with maximizing their production of children. Men's sexual interest is also more easily aroused because sex involves fewer costs to them than to women, and the ability for rapid ejaculation has a reproductive payoff. On the other hand, women's taste for relationship-based intimacy and greater investment in each sexual act is congruent with women's reproductive strategies.

In a field that tends to emphasize male's "natural" influence over reproductive strategies, evolutionary anthropologist Helen Fisher (1992) offers a feminist twist. Her study of hundreds of societies shows that divorce, or its informal equivalent, occurs most typically in the third or fourth year of a marriage and then peaks about every four years after that. Fisher hypothesizes that some of the breakups have to do with a woman's attempt to obtain the best genes and best survival chances for her offspring. In both agrarian and hunter-gatherer societies, Fisher explains, women breast-feed their child for three or four years—

a practice that is economical and sometimes helps to prevent further pregnancy. At the end of this period, the woman is ready and able to have another child. She reenters the mating marketplace and assesses her options to see if she can improve on her previous mate. If she can get a better guy, she will leave the previous partner and team up with a new one. In Fisher's vision, unlike the traditional sociobiological view (see Table 17.2), different male and female reproductive strategies do not necessarily imply female sexual passivity and preference for lifelong monogamy.

Sociobiologists and evolutionary psychologists tell a fascinating story of how male and female reproductive differences might shape sexuality. To accept sociobiological arguments, one must accept the premise that most animal and human behavior is driven by the instinct to reproduce and improve the gene pool. Furthermore, a flaw of sociobiology as a theory is that it does not provide a unique account of sexual behavior with the potential to be tested empirically. Furthermore, other social science explanations for the same phenomena are supported by more immediate, close-range evidence.

Consider hypergamy, the practice of women marrying men slightly older and "higher" on the social status ladder than they are. Sociobiologists would say women marry "up" to ensure the most fit provider for their offspring. But hypergamy makes little sense biologically. Younger men have more years of resources to provide, and they have somewhat more sexual resources. Empirically, however, hypergamy is fact. It is also a fact that men, overall and in nearly every subculture, have access to more rewards and status than women do. Furthermore, reams of imagery— in movies, advertising, novels—promote the appeal of older, more resourceful men. Why not, when older, more resourceful men are generating the images? Social practice, in this case, overrides what sociobiologists consider the biological imperative.

THE SOCIAL ORIGINS OF DESIRE

Your own experience should indicate that biology and genetics alone do not shape human sexuality. From the moment you entered the world, cues from the environment were telling you which desires and behaviors were "normal" and which were not. The result is that people who grow up in different circumstances tend to have different sexualities. Who has not had their sexual behavior influenced by their parents' or guardians' explicit or implicit rules? You may break the rules or follow them, but you can't forget them. On a societal level, in Sweden, for example, premarital sex is accepted, and people are expected to be sexually knowledgeable and experienced. Swedes are likely to associate sex with pleasure in this *"sex positive"* society. In Ireland, however, Catholics are supposed to heed the Church's strict prohibitions against sex outside of marriage, birth control, and the expression of lust. In Ireland the experience of sexuality is different from the experience of sexuality in Sweden because the rules are different. Certainly, biology in Sweden is no different from biology in Ireland, nor is the physical capacity to experience pleasure different. But in Ireland, nonmarital sex is clandestine and shameful. Perhaps the taboo adds excitement to the experience. In Sweden, nonmarital sex is acceptable. In the absence of social constraint, it may even feel a bit mundane. These culturally specific sexual rules and experiences arise from different *norms,* the well-known, unwritten rules of society.

Another sign that social influences play a bigger role in shaping sexuality than does biology is the changing notions historically of male and female differences in desire. Throughout history, varied explanations of male and female desire have been popular. At times, woman was portrayed as the stormy temptress and man the reluctant participant, as in the Bible story of Adam and Eve. At other times, women were seen as pure in thought and deed while men were voracious sexual beasts, as the Victorians would have it.

These shifting ideas about gender are the social "clothing" for sexuality. The concept of gender typically relies on a dichotomy of male versus female sexual categories, just as the tradition of women wearing dresses and men wearing pants has in the past made the shape of men and women appear quite different. Consider high heels, an on-again-off-again Western fashion. Shoes have no innate sexual function, but high heels have often been understood to be "sexy" for women, even though (or perhaps because) they render women less physically agile. (Of course, women cope. As Ginger Rogers, the 1940s movie star and dancing partner to Fred Astaire, is said to have quipped, "I did everything Fred did, only backwards and in high heels.") Social norms of femininity have at times rendered high heels fashionable. So feminine are high heels understood to be that a man in high heels, in some sort of visual comedy gag, guarantees a laugh from the audience. Alternatively, high heels are a required emblem of femininity for cross-dressing men.

Such distinctions are an important tool of society; they provide guidance to human beings about how to be a "culturally correct" male or female. Theoretically, society could "clothe" its members with explicit norms of sexuality that de-emphasize difference and emphasize similarity or even multiplicity. Picture unisex hairstyles and men and women both free to wear skirts or pants, norms that prevail from time to time in some subcultures. What is remarkable about dichotomies is that even when distinctions, like male and female norms of fashion, are reduced, new ways to assert an ostensibly essential difference between men and women arise. Societies' rules, like clothes, are changeable. But societies' entrenched taste for constructing differences between men and women persists.

The Social Construction of Sexuality

Social constructionists believe that cues from the environment shape human beings from the moment they enter the world. The sexual customs, values, and expectations of a culture, passed on to the young through teaching and by example, exert a powerful influence over individuals. When Fletcher Christian sailed into Tahiti in Charles Nordhoff's 1932 account, *Mutiny on the Bounty,* he and the rest of his nineteenth-century English crew were surprised at how sexually available, playful, guilt free, and amorous the Tahitian women were. Free from the Judeo-Christian precepts and straitlaced customs that inhibited English society, the women and girls of Tahiti regarded their sexuality joyfully and without shame. The English men were delighted and, small wonder, refused to leave the island. Such women did not exist in their own society. The women back in England had been socialized within their Victorian culture to be modest, scared of sex, protective of their reputation, and threatened by physical pleasure. As a result, they were unavailable before marriage and did not feel free to indulge in a whole lot of fun after it. The source of the difference was not physiological differences between Tahitian and English women; it was sexual *socialization*

or the upbringing that they received within their differing families and cultures.

If we look back at the Victorian, nineteenth-century England that Nordhoff refers to, we can identify *social structures* that influenced the norms of women's and men's sexuality. A burgeoning, new, urban middle class created separate spheres in the division of family labor. Instead of sharing home and farm or small business, the tasks of adults in families became specialized: Men went out to earn money, women stayed home to raise children and take care of the home. Although this division of labor was not the norm in all classes and ethnicities in England at the time, the image of middle-class femininity and masculinity became pervasive. The new division of labor increased women's economic dependence on men, which further curbed women's sexual license but not men's. When gender organizes one aspect of life—such as men's and women's positions in the economy—it also organizes other aspects of life, including sex.

In a heterogeneous and individualistic culture like North America, sexual socialization is complex. A society creates an "ideal" sexuality, but different families and subcultures have their own values. For example, even though contemporary society at large may now accept premarital sexuality, a given family may lay down the law: Sex before marriage is against the family's religion and an offense against God's teaching. A teenager who grows up in such a household may suppress feelings of sexual arousal or channel them into outlets that are more acceptable to the family. Or the teenager may react against her or his background, reject parental and community opinion, and search for what she or he perceives to be a more "authentic" self. Variables like birth order or observations of a sibling's social and sexual expression can also influence a person's development.

As important as family and social background are, so are individual differences in response to that background. In the abstract, people raised to celebrate their sexuality must surely have a different approach to enjoying their bodies than those who are taught that their bodies will betray them and are a venal part of human nature. Yet whether or not a person is raised to be at ease with physicality does not always help predict adult sexual behavior. Sexual sybarites and libertines may have grown up in sexually repressive environments, as did pop culture icon and Catholic-raised Madonna. Sometimes individuals whose families promoted sex education and free personal expression are content with minimal sexual expression.

Even with the nearly infinite variety of sexuality that individual experience produces, social circumstances shape sexual patterns. For example, research shows that people who have had more premarital sexual intercourse are likely to have more extramarital intercourse, or sex with someone other than their spouse (Blumstein and Schwartz 1983). Perhaps early experience creates a desire for sexual variety and makes it harder for a person to be monogamous. On the other hand, higher levels of sexual desire may generate both the premarital and extramarital propensities Or perhaps nonmonogamous, sexually active individuals are "rule breakers" in other areas also, and resist not only the traditional rules of sex but also other social norms they encounter. Sexual history is useful for predicting sexual future, but it does not provide a complete explanation.

To make explanations more useful, sociologists refer to societal-level explanations as the *macro* view and to individual-level explanations as the *micro* view. At the macrolevel, the questions pertain to the patterns among different groups. For example, we may note in our culture that some women wear skirts and all men do not. Why do women and men, generally speaking, differ in this way? *Social conflict*

theory, which examines the way that groups gain and maintain power over resources and other groups, is often used to address macrolevel questions. One might ask: Whose interest does this custom serve, and how did it evolve? What does it constrain or encourage? If the custom changes, what social forces have promoted the change? What social forces resist change? Who has power over customs at any given time, and why?

Symbolic interactionism supplements this macrolevel view by looking at the microlevel: How does a particular custom gain its meaning through social interaction? For example, what is really happening when a man opens a door for a woman? *Symbolic interactionism* proposes that social rules are learned and reinforced through everyday interaction in both small acts, such as a man's paying for a woman's dinner, and larger enactments of male and female roles, such as weddings, manners and advice books, movies, and television. Through such everyday social interaction, norms are confirmed or resisted. When an adult tells a little girl "good girls don't do this," or when boys make fun of her for wanting to be on the football team, or when she observes people scorning or stoning women who venture forth in inappropriate garb (as in countries where women are required to wear a veil), or when she sees women joining a military school getting hazed and harassed, she is learning her society's rules of behavior.

When it comes to sexuality, all these social and behavioral theories hold that biological impulses are subservient to the influence of social systems. Consider high heels again. As anyone who has done so knows, wearing high heels has physical consequences, such as flexed calves while wearing them and aching feet at the end of an evening. But nothing in the physiology of women makes wearing high-heeled shoes necessary, and the propensity to wear high heels is not programmed into women's DNA. A sociobiologist might note that any additional ways a society can invent for women to be sexy accelerate reproductive success. A symbolic interactionist would counter that most rules of sexuality go way beyond what's needed for reproductive success. Footwear has never been shown to be correlated with fertility. Instead, society orchestrates male and female sexuality so that its values are served. A social conflict theorist would go a step further and note that the enactment of gendered fashion norms, individual by individual, serves the political agenda of groups in power (in this case men) at the macrolevel.

An astounding example of gender-based social control of sexuality was the practice of binding the feet of upper-class women in China starting around the tenth century. Each foot was bound so tightly that the last two toes shriveled and fell off. What was left was so deformed that the woman could barely walk and had to be carried. The function was to allow upper-class men to control the mobility of their women. Bound feet, which were thus associated with status and wealth, became erotically charged. Unbound feet were seen as repugnant. By the eighteenth and nineteenth centuries, even poor women participated in this practice. This practice was so associated with sexual acceptability and marriageability that it was difficult to disrupt, even when nineteenth-century missionaries from the West labeled the practice barbaric and unsafe. Only later, in the twentieth century, did foot binding become illegal (Greenhalgh 1977).

Social Control of Sexuality

So powerful are norms as they are transmitted through both social structures and everyday life that it is impossible to imagine the absence of norms that control sexuality. In fact, most images of "liberated" sexuality involve breaking a social norm—say, having sex in public rather than in private. The social norm is always the reference point. Because people are influenced from birth by the social and physical contexts of sexuality, their desires are shaped by those norms. There is no such thing as a truly free sexuality. For the past two centuries in North America, people have sought "true love" through personal choice in dating and mating (D'Emilio and Freedman 1988). Although this form of sexual liberation has generated a small increase in the number of mixed pairs—interracial, interethnic, interfaith pairs—the rule of *homogamy,* or marrying within one's class, religion, and ethnicity, still constitutes one of the robust social facts of romantic life. Freedom to choose the person one loves turns out not to be as free as one might suppose.

Despite the norm of true love currently accepted in our culture, personal choice and indiscriminate sexuality have often been construed across cultures and across history as socially disruptive. Disruptions to the social order include liaisons between poor and rich; between people of different races, ethnicities, or faiths; and between members of the same sex. Traditional norms of marriage and sexuality have maintained social order by keeping people in familiar and "appropriate" categories. Offenders have been punished by ostracism, curtailed civil rights, or in some societies, death. Conformists are rewarded with social approval and material advantages. Although it hardly seems possible today, mixed-race marriage was against the law in the United States until 1967. Committed same-sex couples continue to be denied legal marriages, income tax breaks, and health insurance benefits; heterosexual couples take these social benefits for granted.

Some social theorists observe that societies control sexuality through construction of a dichotomized or gendered (male-female) sexuality (Foucault 1978). Society's rules about pleasure seeking and procreating are enforced by norms about appropriate male and female behavior. For example, saying that masculinity is enhanced by sexual experimentation while femininity is demeaned by it gives men sexual privilege (and pleasure) and denies it to women. Furthermore, according to Foucault, sexual desire is fueled by the experience of privilege and taboo regarding sexual pleasure. That is, the very rules that control sexual desire shape it and even enhance it. The social world could just as plausibly concentrate on how much alike are the ways that men and women experience sex and emphasize how broadly dispersed sexual conduct is across genders. However, social control turns pleasure into a scarce resource and endows leaders who regulate the pleasure of others with power.

Societies control sexuality in part because they have a pragmatic investment in it. Eighteenth-century economic theorist T. R. Malthus ([1798] 1929) highlighted the relationship between reproductive practices and economics in *The Principle of Population.* According to Malthus, excessive fertility would result in the exhaustion of food and other resources. His recommendation to curb the birth rate represents an intervention into the sexual behavior of individuals for the well-being of society. A more recent example is the one-child policy in modern China. Alarmed by the predictions of famine and other disastrous consequences of rapid population growth, Mao Tse-tung and subsequent Chinese leaders instituted a program of enforced fertility control, which included monitoring women's menstrual cycles, requiring involuntary abortions, and delaying the legal age for marriage. To this state, sexual behavior isn't really an intimate, private act at all; it is a social and even economically significant activity. Such policies influence society at large, but they influence private experience as well. In China, raising the legal age for marriage resulted in a shift toward tolerance re-

garding premarital sex, a practice that became more common. How does a society obtain the ideal number of healthy workers to create a thriving nation? How does a society produce enough people to create an army? How does it create a system in which parents control their offspring so that the state will not have to step into an expensive and impractical role? And how do such large-scale policies influence the everyday experiences and definitions of sexuality for individuals?

Society's interest in controlling sexuality is expressed in the debates regarding sex education. Debates about sex education in grade school and high school illustrate the importance to society of both the control of desire and its social construction. The debates raise the question, does formal learning about sex increase or deter early sexual experimentation? The point is, opponents and proponents of sex education all want to know how to control sexuality in young people. Those who favor sex education hold that children benefit from early, comprehensive information about sex, in the belief that people learn about sexuality from birth and are sexual at least from the time of puberty. Providing young people with an appropriate vocabulary and accurate information both discourages early sexual activity and encourages safe sexual practices for those teenagers who, according to the evidence, will not be deterred from sexual activity (Sexuality Information and Education Council of the United States [SIECUS] 1995). On the other hand, opponents of sex education are intensely committed to the belief that information about sex changes teenagers' reactions and values and leads to early, and what they believe are inappropriate, sexual behaviors (Whitehead 1994). Conservative groups hold that sex education, if it occurs at all, should emphasize abstinence as opposed to practical information.

These conflicting points of view about sex education are both concerned with managing adolescent sexual desire. Conservatives fear that education creates desire; liberals feel that information merely enables better decision making. So who is correct? In various studies, a majority of both conservative and liberal sex education programs have demonstrated little effect on behavior. Conservatives believe these results prove the programs' lack of worth. Liberals believe the studies prove that many programs are not good enough, usually because they do not include the most important content. Furthermore, liberals point out that sex education has increased contraceptive (including condom) use, which is crucial to public health goals of reducing sexually transmitted disease and unwanted pregnancy. Other research indicates that comprehensive sex education actually tends to delay the age of first intercourse and does not intensify desire or escalate sexual behavior. There is no evidence that comprehensive sex education promotes or precipitates early teen sexual activity (Kirby et al. 1994).

The passionate debate about sex education is played out with high emotions. Political ideology, parental fears, and the election strategies of politicians all influence this mode of social control. In the final analysis, however, teaching about sex clearly does not have an intense impact on the pupil. Students' response to sex education varies tremendously at the individual level. In terms of trends within groups, however, it appears that sex education tends to delay sexual activity and makes teenage sex safer when it happens.

To summarize, social constructionists believe that a society influences sexual behavior through its norms. Some norms are explicit, such as laws against adult sexual activity with minors. Others are implicit, such as norms of fidelity and parental responsibility. In a stable, homogeneous society, it is relatively easy to understand such rules. But in a changing, complex society like the United States, the rules may be in flux or indistinct. Perhaps this ambiguity is what makes some issues of sexuality so controversial today.

AN INTEGRATIVE PERSPECTIVE ON GENDER AND SEXUALITY

Social constructionist explanations of contemporary sexual patterns are typically pitted against the biology of desire and the evolutionary understanding of biological adaptations. Some social constructionists believe there is no inflexible biological reality; everything we regard as either female or male sexuality is culturally imposed. In contrast, *essentialists*—those who take a biological, sociobiological, or evolutionary point of view—believe people's sexual desires and orientations are innate and hard-wired and that social impact is minimal. Gender differences follow from reproductive differences. Men inseminate, women incubate. People are born with sexual drives, attractions, and natures that simply play themselves out at the appropriate developmental age. Even if social constraints conspire to make men and women more similar to each other (as in the 1990s, when the sensitive and nurturing new man [was] encouraged to get in touch with his so-called feminine, emotional side), people's essential nature is the same: Man is the hunter, warrior, and trailblazer, and woman is the gatherer, nurturer, and reproducer. To an essentialist, social differences, such as the different earning power of men and women, are the consequence of biological difference. In short, essentialists think the innate differences between women and men are the cause of gendered sexuality; social constructionists think the differences between men and women are the result of gendering sexuality through social processes.

Using either the social constructionist or essentialist approach to the exclusion of the other constrains understanding of sexuality. We believe the evidence shows that gender

TABLE 17.3

EXPLANATIONS OF MALE AND FEMALE DIFFERENCES IN SEXUAL DESIRE

Explanations	Causes of desire	Consequences
Essentialist: Desire is biological and evolutionary	Genetically preprogrammed reproductive functions specific to males and females	Male independence in reproduction and female-centered child-rearing practices and passivity are the cause, rather than the result, of gendered social institutions
Social constructionist: Desire is sociological and contextual	Social institutions and social interaction signal and sanction "male" and "female," gendered norms of behavior	Support for or opposition to sex/gender-segregated reproductive and social practices depends on social definitions of men, women, and sexuality
Integrative: Desire is contextual and physical	Bodies, environments, relationships, families, governments shape sexualities	Policies address some biological differences (such as pregnancy and work); emphasize the impact of social forces, interaction, societal programs

differences are more plausibly an outcome of social processes than the other way around. But a social constructionist view is most powerful when it takes the essentialist view into account. In Table 17.3, we describe this view of gender differences in sexual desire as *integrative*. Although people tend to think of sex as primarily a biological function—tab B goes into slot A—biology is only one part of the context of desire. Such sociological factors as family relationships and social structure also influence sex. A complex mix of anatomy, hormones, and the brain provides the basic outline for the range of acts and desires possible, but biology is neither where sexuality begins nor where it ends. Social and biological contexts link to define human sexual possibilities.

The integrative approach follows from a great deal that sexuality researchers have observed. Consider the following example: A research project, conducted over three decades ago, advertised for participants stating that its focus was how physical excitement influences a man's preference for one woman over another (Valins 1966). The researchers connected college men to a monitor that allowed them to hear their heartbeats as they looked at photographs of women models. The men were told that they would be able to hear their

heartbeat when it surged in response to each photograph. A greater surge would suggest greater physical attraction. The participants were then shown a photograph of a dark-haired woman, then a blonde, then a redhead. Afterward, each man was asked to choose the picture that he would prefer to take home. In each case, the man chose the photograph of the woman who, as he believed from listening to his own speeding heartbeat, had most aroused him. Or at least the man thought he was choosing the woman who had aroused him most. In reality, the men had been listening to a faked heartbeat that was speeded up at random. The men thus actually chose the women whom they believed had aroused them most. In this case, the men's invented attraction was more powerful than their gut response. Their mind (a powerful sexual organ) told them their body was responding to a specific picture. The participants' physiological experience of arousal was eclipsed by the social context. When social circumstances influence sexual tastes, are those tastes real or sincere? Absolutely. The social world is as much a fact in people's lives as the biological world.

Now let us look at a case where the body's cues were misinterpreted by the mind. An attractive woman researcher stood at the end of a very stable bridge (Dutton and Aron 1974). She approached men after they had walked across the bridge, engaged them in conversation, and then gave the men her telephone number—in case they had further comments, she said. Then the researcher did the same thing with another group of participants, but at the end of an unstable, swinging bridge. People tend to feel a little nervous, excited, or even exhilarated when they make their way across such a bridge. The pulse rises. Adrenaline pumps. Indeed, the anxiety response of walking across the bridge is much like the arousal response caused by meeting a desirable new person. The question was, would that anxiety response confuse men into thinking that they were attracted to the woman at the end of the bridge, more so than the physiologically calm guys who met her on the stable bridge? Yes, a statistically significant, larger number of men from the swinging bridge called the woman. In this case, participants had interpreted an anxiety response as an attraction response, one compelling enough to warrant inviting a stranger on a date. The physical situation transformed the meaning of a casual meeting from anxiety to attraction, again showing the link between biological and social influences.

A very personal matter that seems to be utterly physical—penile erection, or more specifically a man's inability to get an erection—offers another example. How might an erection be socially constructed? It is more or less understood in the United States that a penis should be hard and ready when a man's sexual opportunity is available. And it is more or less understood that the failure to get or maintain an erection in a sexual situation has two meanings: The guy isn't "man enough," or the other person isn't attractive enough. But there are many other explanations, not the least of which has been poetically explained by Shakespeare (and scientifically documented):

Lechery, sir, (alcohol) provokes and unprovokes: it provokes the desire, but it takes away the performance. Therefore much drink may be said to be an equivocator with lechery: it makes him, and it mars him; it sets him on, and it takes him off; it persuades him, and disheartens him; makes him stand to, and not stand to; in conclusion, equivocates him in a sleep, and, giving him the lie, leaves him. (*Macbeth*, Act II, Scene iii)

The Shakespearean speech refers to the way in which alcohol can undermine robust sexual desire by leaving the penis flaccid. The performance is not the intimate interaction of bodies in pursuit of pleasure; it is strictly focused on the penis, which ought to "stand to." The speech emphasizes the humiliation—the "mar"—for a man who fails to sustain an erection. Though the speech refers to the toll that alcohol takes on the circulatory system that assists penises in becoming erect, the discussion is about the social experience of a man failed by his penis.

Even in the absence of drinking, penises are not nearly so reliable as the mythology of masculinity and attraction would maintain. Erections appear to come and go with odd timing. For example, erections rise and fall on babies and young boys; men often wake up with erections. None of these instances has to do with machismo or sexual desire. Erections are not always evidence of romantic interest, though our culture tends to interpret them as such. But their absence or presence, which is a physical phenomenon, takes on great meaning thanks to Western culture's prevailing beliefs and norms. For example, men required to produce semen for in vitro fertilization who are unable to maintain an erection until orgasm report feeling humiliated; their partners also often report being stunned by this performance failure (Rutter 1996). Growing up in a culture that considers erectile unpredictability a problem influences the way men in that culture feel about themselves and about their sexual partners, and the way sexual partners feel about them.

Even biological research has supported the integrative perspective. A quarter century ago, one team of scientists found that homosexual men had lower testosterone levels than a matched group of heterosexual men (Kreuz, Rose, and Jennings 1972). The traditional interpretation at the time of the study was that homosexual men were less "masculine" than the comparison group and that their lower testosterone levels explained why they were gay. But a group of active military men were also measured and found to be low in testosterone. The researchers were loath to believe that an unusual number of military men were gay or that military men were below average hormonally, so they found an alternative explanation for low testosterone. The researchers speculated that stress, anxiety, and similar negative emotions had temporarily lowered hormone levels in both soldiers and homosexuals. The stressful social context—as either a gay man living in a straight world or as a military man being bossed around constantly—had shaped a biological response, the researchers concluded. Hormones were the cart, not the horse. Biology influences desire, but social context influences biology and gives meaning to bodily sensation.

What do these examples from research illustrate? Sexual desire—in fact, all sexuality—is influenced by the cultural, personal, and situational. But these examples also tell us that people can't escape the biological context of sex and sexuality—nor can they rely on it. Such an *integrative* approach—the intimate relationship between social context and biological experience—is central to understanding sexuality.

What are the implications of using an integrative approach to sexuality? First, an integrationist will raise questions about biology when social context is emphasized as cause, and will raise questions about social context when biological causes are emphasized. The point is, everything sexual and physical occurs and achieves meaning in a social context.

Sexual Identity and Orientation

Nowhere does the essentialist versus social constructionist argument grow more vehement than in the debate over *sexual identity* and *sexual orientation*. These terms are used to mean a variety of things. We use these terms to refer to how people tend to classify themselves sexually—either as *gay, lesbian, bisexual,* or *straight.* Sexual behavior and sexual desire may or may not be consistent with sexual identity. That is, people may identify themselves as heterosexual, but desire people of the same sex—or vice versa.

It is hard to argue with the observation that human desire is, after all, organized. Humans do not generally desire cows or horses (with, perhaps, the exception of Catherine the Great, the Russian czarina who purportedly came to her demise while copulating with a stallion). More to the point, humans are usually quite specific about which sex is desirable to them and even whether the object of their desire is short or tall, dark or light, hairy or sleek.

In the United States, people tend to be identified as either *homosexual* or *heterosexual.* Other cultures (and prior eras in the United States) have not distinguished between these two sexual orientations. However, our culture embraces the perspective that, whether gay or straight, one has an essential, inborn desire, and it cannot change. Many people seem convinced that homosexuality is an essence rather than a sexual act. For essentialists, it is crucial to establish the primacy of one kind of desire or another and to build a world around that identity. People tend to assume that the object of desire is a matter of the gender of the object. That is, they think even homosexual men desire someone who is feminine and that homosexual women desire someone who is masculine. In other words, even among gay men and lesbians, it is assumed that they will desire opposite-gendered people, even if they are of the same sex.

Historians have chronicled in Western culture the evolution of homosexuality from a behavior into an identity (e.g., D'Emilio and Freedman 1988). In the past, people might engage in same-gender sexuality, but only in the twentieth century has it become a well-defined (and diverse) lifestyle and self-definition. Nevertheless, other evidence shows that homosexual identity has existed for a long time. The distinguished historian John Boswell (1994) believes that homosexuals as a group and homosexuality as an identity have existed from the very earliest of recorded history. He used evidence of early Christian same-sex "marriage" to support his thesis. Social scientist Fred Whitman (1983) has looked at homosexuality across cultures and declared that the evidence of a social type, including men who use certain effeminate gestures and have diverse sexual tastes, goes far beyond any one culture. Geneticist Dean Hamer provides evidence that sexual attraction may be genetically programmed, suggesting that it has persisted over time and been passed down through generations.

On the other side of the debate is the idea that sexuality has always been invented and that sexual orientations are socially created. A gay man's or lesbian's sexual orientation has been created by a social context. Although this creation takes place in a society that prefers dichotomous, polarized categories, the social constructionist vision of sexuality at least poses the possibility that sexuality could involve a continuum of behavior that is matched by a continuum of fantasy, ability to love, and sense of self.

The jury is still out on the scientific origins of heterosexuality and homosexuality. One series of studies on the brain (LeVay 1993) identified some differences in the makeup of the brains of heterosexual and homosexual men.

This research has been criticized because the brain samples for the homosexual population were taken from men who had died from AIDS, which may have systematically altered the brain structure of the men. Nevertheless, some researchers believe that sexual orientation is wired into the brain, perhaps even dictating the intensity and specificity of sexual tastes.

Dean Hamer, a researcher at the National Institutes of Health Cancer Research Center, became interested in the genetics of sexual attraction and orientation while he was studying the heritability of Kaposi's sarcoma, a type of skin cancer that some gay men with AIDS develop. Hamer looked further into the possibility that gay men (and, in separate research, lesbians) have a genetic makeup different from that of heterosexuals (Hamer and Copeland 1994). He found a specific gene formation, identified as *Xq28*, that appears to be inherited through the mother's line only in gay males. The lesbian research has not thus far established a genetic link, but the Hamer research is widely believed to be just the first attempt to find a link between genetic inheritance and sexual attraction and arousal.

Hamer himself makes no claim that all attraction or arousal is genetically programmed, but his research lends support to other studies on the genetics of sexuality. For example, genetics researcher Michael Bailey and colleagues looked at identical twins (who have identical genetic material) reared apart. The studies found a likelihood much greater than chance that if one male twin is homosexual, the other will also be homosexual (Bailey et al. 1993). Because the twins in the study did not share the same environment, this finding suggests that the twins' common genes made them similar in their sexual orientation. On the other hand, other recent genetic and twin studies have highlighted the fact that having a certain *genotype* (DNA coded for a particular characteristic, such as heart disease) does not always produce the corresponding *phenotype* (the physical expression of that characteristic, such as actually suffering from heart disease). Researchers speculate that environment and individual history influence the expression or suppression of genetic types (Wright 1995).

These are just a few of the studies that, in some people's opinions, support the idea that homosexuality is not a choice but a naturally occurring phenomenon in a predetermined proportion of births. By extension, they believe, much human sexual desire and behavior must be biologically determined. Of course, social constructionists would disagree. But if biology does not determine whether one is heterosexual or homosexual, is sexual orientation a choice? Not exactly. The notion that sexuality is a preference supposes a person goes to a sexuality bazaar and picks out what to be today. That is not the case either. Physical and social structures and individual biography join together to produce sexual desire and behavior in an individual that may vary over time. Because of powerful social norms regarding sexuality, people are more likely to sustain a single sexual orientation throughout adulthood. The overwhelming evidence supports the idea that biology is a player in the game of sexual orientation but is not the only player or even captain of the team.

The Continuum of Desire

Variation among people has been examined more than changes in sexual orientation within an individual. Alfred Kinsey (see Kinsey, Pomeroy, and Martin 1948), in his pioneering studies on human sexualities in the late 1940s and 1950s, introduced the Kinsey Heterosexual-Homosexual Rating Scale. A person was coded using a zero for "completely heterosexual," a six for "completely homosexual," or a number in between to represent a more ambiguous orientation. Kinsey measured his participants' reports of interest in or attrac-

tion to and explicit past experiences with both same-sex and other-sex people and figured out where his participants fit on the continuum. However, his measurements were more of an art than a science. One cannot weigh or calibrate sexuality so finely. But Kinsey did examine actual behavior, fantasy, intensity of feeling, and other important elements that contribute to a person's sexuality.

Although such a rating scale may be an imperfect way of providing individuals with some sort of sex score, Kinsey made the point that a dichotomous vision of sexual orientation is even more inadequate and inaccurate. The Kinsey scale still defines the polarities of sexuality as heterosexuality and homosexuality, and in that sense it is essentialist. However, it provides alternatives beyond "yes," "no," or "in denial." Kinsey opened the door to thinking in terms of the diversity of sexualities. People may use dichotomous terms in everyday life, but the idea that many people have the capacity to relate sexually to both males and females (at a single point in their life or intermittently over a lifetime) is part of the legacy of Kinsey's sex research.

By using a sexual continuum that blurs the edges of heterosexuality and homosexuality, Kinsey advanced the idea of bisexuality. The mere existence of *bisexuality* (the common term for some history of attraction to or sex with both men and women) is troubling for essentialists, who see sexuality as fixed and linked to procreation. However, biologists can show that bisexuality exists in the animal kingdom. Evolutionary psychologists and anthropologists hypothesize that bisexuality could be useful for a group's bonding and thus have survival value (Fisher 1992). The explanation is that adults who are like aunts and uncles to children—and who are intimate with parents—provide additional support for maintaining a family. But committed essentialists do not usually buy the idea that "true" bisexuality exists. Instead, they code men and women as "true" heterosexuals or homosexuals who have some modest taste in the other direction.

Given the evidence, it is possible to believe that the biological context tends to encourage an individual to acquire one sexual orientation or another but also to believe that society exerts greater influence than biology over behavior. Kinsey's data, as well as controversial data from a small gay and lesbian subsample from the National Health and Social Life Survey (NHSLS; Laumann, Michael, and Gagnon 1994), indicate that many more people report homosexual desire and behavior than those who claim homosexuality or bisexuality as their main sexual orientation or sexual identity. Essentialists might say people who admit to homosexual behavior but deny being homosexuals are kidding themselves. Social constructionists say people are always kidding themselves; in other words, people acquire the desires and behaviors that are available and appealing. These choices will be based on personal history as well as social norms and will emerge in idiosyncratic and diverse ways across the continuum of sexuality. They will also be based on the costs and benefits in a given social system. How many people might code their fantasies differently if it were prestigious to be bisexual? Surely people's impulse to code themselves dichotomously is in part influenced by the social and emotional costs of doing otherwise.

An interesting issue that puzzles essentialists is how different male homosexuality seems to be from female homosexuality. More men than women identify as homosexual, but more women claim homosexual desire and/or behavior than men in those categories. In Lever's (1994) *Advocate* survey, as well, more men than women identify themselves as homosexual. Indeed, much of the sexual attraction and behavior between women is not labeled as sexual. Women hug and kiss each other with impunity, and not necessarily with

specific sexual intent. They can have extended sex play in their youth, or even in adulthood, without being instantly labeled as homosexual, as men who engaged in similar behavior would be. Women are also more likely to report that a same-sex sexual episode had less to do with sexual attraction than with love.

Historically, the waters are even murkier. As Lillian Faderman illustrates in *Surpassing the Love of Men* (1981), eighteenth- and nineteenth-century women were allowed such license to love each other that they could declare truly passionate feelings for one another without labels and identities being bandied about. For example, Faderman quotes Rousseau's eighteenth-century novel La nouvelle Héloïse, in which Julie writes to Clair: "The most important thing of my life has been to love you. From the very beginning my heart has been absorbed in yours" (p. 77). If these women expressed these sentiments today, observers would assume them to be homosexual. Are these the words simply of passionate friends? Essentialists would say these were lesbian lovers who did not have social permission to know who they really were. Historians and sociologists are divided as to whether these women experienced their love as sexual or romantic in the contemporary understanding of those feelings. It is difficult to label people's emotions for them after the fact and from a different historical and psychological vantage point. Just as beliefs and biases influence the way social science is conducted in the present, so such biases influence the views and interpretations of the past. We need to remember that sexual orientation, along with desire and other manifestations of sexuality, is socially constructed and culturally specific.

GENDER AS THE BASIS FOR SEXUAL IDENTITY

Sexual orientation, as nearly everyone in Western culture has come to understand the phrase, signifies the identity one has based on the gender of the sexual partners one tends to pair with—either at a particular time or over a lifetime. In our culture, gender is the focus of sexual identity. But what if instead of discussing sexual identity in terms of one's preference for women or men, we referred to the various tastes one expresses for people who are funny or serious or tall or short or responsive or unresponsive to oral sex? For example, Virginia's sexuality would be "left-handed Jewish intellectual"—for this describes the people whom she tends to pair with. Pepper's sexuality would be "tall, high energy, sociable, and good looking." Instead, our culture zeroes in on which gender is doing what with which gender. Thus, the whole notion of sexual identity requires strict distinctions between male and female. The fact that the gender of sexual partners is of great social interest highlights yet again how gender organizes the definitions of sexuality.

Few can resist gendered distinctions. But a challenge comes from *transsexuals*, men and women who believe they were born in the wrong body. Although anatomically they are one sex, transsexuals experience themselves as the other sex, much the way we described Dil, in *The Crying Game* at the beginning of the chapter, who felt like a woman but was built like a man. Sometimes transsexuals "correct" their bodies with surgery or hormone treatments. And their sexual orientations are diverse. Some male-to-female transsexuals pair with men, some with women. The same is true for female-to-male transsexuals. One male-to-female person, speaking at a sexuality conference in the 1970s, declared, "Personally, I feel it is sexist to love on the basis of gender. You love the person, whatever their sex might be!"

CONCLUSION

There are, it seems, two arguments that help explain the way the genders express sexual desire. On the one hand are the images and statistics showing that men and women have distinct (albeit shifting) patterns of sexual expression, regardless of sexual orientation. On the other hand, the wide range of sexualities among men or among women also calls for an explanation. A continuum of passion, of desire, of sexual acts and feelings is a useful way to reconcile these phenomena. Furthermore, it helps to recognize that sexual phenomena are socially scripted but also highly individualized. Although sexual desire tends to be described in orderly and quantifiable terms, sexual desire is a chaotic playing field on which we, as sociologists, attempt to place some order to understand it better.

Biology or, more simply stated, bodies are the site for passionate experience, even if that experience is in the brain, in the absence of actual sensations in the skin or other sexual organs. In this sense, biology is a prominent context for sexuality. However, interpersonal, biographical, social, and political contexts influence sexuality and interact with biology in surprising ways. Thus, the continuum of sexuality we propose becomes even more diverse.

[. . .] We will remind you that we believe the differences between men and women are not any more important than the wide range of behavior and feelings that exist among men and among women. The social world, and even academic discussions of sexuality, seek to set up distinct categories for understanding sexuality. But individuals rarely fit into distinct categories.

Why do we take this precaution? Because of the inaccurate self-labeling that can happen as a reader sees, or doesn't see, himself or herself in the images we present. The woman who reads that women rarely have over 10 or so partners and has herself had 50 tempestuous love affairs or recreational encounters is not being told she is a man, nor is she being told that she is perverse because she is outside the middle range found in self-report survey data.

Sexuality exists on a continuum. There are people whose experiences reflect either end of the continuum and people whose experiences reflect the middle. It is just as unfair to judge a sexually experienced woman as it is to judge a man who has had one sexual partner his whole life and seeks no more. Such a man is no less masculine than the man with 5 or 10 sexual partners.

Sociologists, who examine overall patterns, are often criticized because people assume that the statistics of the majority are being presented as proper conduct or that other conduct is by definition abnormal. But the social scientist makes no such assumption. In fact, diversity and change in behavior are at the center of social science. Sexuality is one of the most diverse, pervasive, and enigmatic of human experiences. Therefore, far from naming a single sexuality or a dichotomous sexuality (or even a trichotomous sexuality), we may more accurately say that there are as many sexualities as there are people. Yet detecting patterns within the diversity can advance an understanding of gender, sex, and society and show how differences and similarities among groups of men and women came into being and are sustained through social practices. The categorical language of sexuality is difficult to avoid. However, we will try to avoid categorizing people or acts, and we hope you will join us in that effort.

REFERENCES

Angier, N. 1995. "Does Testosterone Equal Aggression? Maybe Not." *New York Times,* June 20, p. A1.

Bailey, J. M., R. C. Pillard, M. C. Neale, and Y. Agyei. 1993. "Heritable Factors Influence Sexual Orientation in Women." *Archives of General Psychiatry* 50:217–23.

Bancroft, J. 1978. "The Relationship between Hormones and Sexual Behavior in Humans." Pp. 493–519 in *Biological Determinants of Sexual Behavior,* edited by J. B. Hutchinson. New York: Wiley.

———. 1984. "Hormones and Human Sexual Behavior." *Journal of Sex and Marital Therapy* 10:3–21.

Bancroft, J., D. Sanders, D. Davidson, and P. Warner. 1983. "Mood, Sexuality, Hormones, and the Menstrual Cycle: III. Sexuality and the Role of Androgens." *Psychosomatic Medicine* 45:508–24.

Blumstein, P., and P. Schwartz. 1983. *American Couples: Money, Work, and Sex.* New York: William Morrow.

Boswell, J. 1994. *Same-Sex Unions in Pre-Modern Europe.* New York: Villard.

Buss, D. 1994. *The Evolution of Desire: Strategies of Human Mating.* New York: Basic Books.

———. 1995. "Psychological Sex Differences: Origins through Sexual Selection." *American Psychologist* 50:164–68.

Coontz, Stephanie. 1992. *The Way We Never Were: American Families and the Nostalgia Trap.* New York: Basic Books.

D'Emilio, J. D., and E. Freedman. 1988. *Intimate Matters: A History of Sexuality in America.* New York: Harper & Row.

Dutton, D., and A. Aron. 1974. "Some Evidence for Heightened Sexual Attraction under Conditions of High Anxiety." *Journal of Personality and Social Psychology* 30:510–17.

Faderman, L. 1981. *Surpassing the Love of Men: Romantic Friendship and Love between Women from the Renaissance to the Present.* New York: William Morrow.

Fisher, H. E. 1992. *Anatomy of Love: The Natural History of Monogamy, Adultery, and Divorce.* New York: Norton.

Foucault, M. 1978. *A History of Sexuality,* Vol. 1: *An Introduction.* New York: Pantheon.

Greenhalgh, S. 1977. "Hobbled Feet, Hobbled Lives: Women in Old China." *Frontiers* 2:7–21.

Hamer, D. H., and P. Copeland. 1994. *The Science of Desire: The Search for the Gay Gene and the Biology of Behavior.* New York: Simon & Schuster.

Hoon, P. W., K. E. Bruce, and B. Kinchloe. 1982. "Does the Menstrual Cycle Play a Role in Sexual Arousal?" *Psychophysiology* 19:21–27.

Kinsey, A. C., W. B. Pomeroy, and C. E. Martin. 1948. *Sexual Behavior in the Human Male.* Philadelphia: W. B. Saunders.

Kirby, D., L. Short, J. Collins, D. Rugg, L. Kolbe, M. Howard, B. Miller, F. Sonenstein, and L. S. Zabin. 1994. "School-Based Programs to Reduce Sexual Risk Behaviors: A Review of Effectiveness." *Public Health Reports* 109:339–60.

Kolodny, R. C., W. H. Masters, and V. E. Johnson. 1979. *Textbook of Sexual Medicine.* Boston: Little, Brown.

Kreuz, L. E., R. M. Rose, and J. R. Jennings. 1972. "Suppression of Plasma Testosterone Levels and Psychological Stress: A Longitudinal Study of Young Men in Officer Candidate School." *Archives of General Psychiatry* 26:479–82.

Laumann, E. O., R. T. Michael, and J. H. Gagnon. 1994. *The Social Organization of Sexuality: Sexual Practices in the United States.* Chicago: University of Chicago Press.

LeVay, S. 1993. *The Sexual Brain.* Cambridge: MIT Press.

Lever, J. 1994. "The 1994 Advocate Survey of Sexuality and Relationships: The Men." *The Advocate: The National Gay & Lesbian Newsmagazine,* August 23, pp. 17–24.

Malthus, T. R. [1798] 1929. *An Essay on the Principle of Population as It Affects the Future Improvement of Society.* New York and London: Macmillan.

Masters, W. H., and V. E. Johnson. 1966. *Human Sexual Response.* Boston: Little, Brown.

Masters, W. H., V. E. Johnson, and R. C. Kolodny. 1995. *Human Sexuality.* 5th ed. New York: Harper-Collins College.

Meuwissen, I., and R. Over. 1992. "Sexual Arousal across Phases of the Human Menstrual Cycle." *Archives of Sexual Behavior* 2:101–19.

Nordhoff, C., and J. N. Hall. 1932. *Mutiny on the Bounty.* Boston: Little, Brown.

Rose, R. M., J. W. Holaday, and I. S. Bernstein. 1970. "Plasma Testosterone, Dominance Rank, and Aggressive Behavior in Male Rhesus Monkeys." *Nature* 231:366–68.

Rutter, V. 1995. "Adolescence: Whose Hell Is It?" *Psychology Today,* January/February, pp. 54–66.

———. 1996. "Who Stole Fertility?" *Psychology Today,* March/April, pp. 44–70.

Seidman, S. 1992. *Embattled Eros: Sexual Politics and Ethics in Contemporary America.* New York: Routledge.

Sexuality Information and Education Council of the United States. 1995. *A Report on Adolescent Sexuality.* New York: SIECUS.

Shakespeare, W. 1983. *Macbeth.* New York: Penguin.

Stanislaw, H., and F. J. Rice. 1988. "The Correlation between Sexual Desire and Menstrual Cycle Changes." *Archives of Sexual Behavior* 17:499–508.

Valins, S. 1966. "Cognitive Effects of False Heart-Rate Feedback." *Journal of Personality and Social Psychology* 4:400–8.

Whitehead, B. D. 1994. "The Failure of Sex Education." *Atlantic Monthly,* October, pp. 55–80.

Whitman, F. 1983. "Culturally Invariable Properties of Male Homosexualities: Tentative Conclusions from Cross-Cultural Research." *Archives of Sexual Behavior* 12:207–26.

Wright, L. 1995. "A Reporter at Large: Double Mystery." *New Yorker* 8/7:44–50.

Wu, F. C., T. M. Farley, A. Peregondon, and G. M. Waites. 1996. "Effects of Testosterone Enanthate in Normal Men: Experience from a Multicenter Contraceptive Efficacy Study." *Fertility and Sterility* 65:626–36.

READING 18

The Four Boxes of Gendered Sexuality: Good Girl/Bad Girl and Tough Guy/Sweet Guy

Betsy Crane and Jesse Crane-Seeber

I have chosen to narrate a history. Closer to myth than argument, it is nonetheless to be distinguished from myth on two levels: first because it is a true story (which myth could, but need not be), and second because my main interest is less a historian's than a moralist's; the present is more important to me than the past.

—T. Todorov, *The Conquest of America*

The Question

"So Mom, why is it that even the coolest girls date the jerks?" This question from Jesse at age 13 prompted an initial response from Betsy about the social construction of gender roles and the effect on sexuality and relationships, and a curiosity about the question that continues for us both.

Why is it that all too often girls and women choose men who "aren't good for them?" Is it, at some level, the promise of status or economic security? In Betsy's generation, it was referred to as the "nice guys finish last" syndrome, as if that were a fact of nature. That was just "the way it is." But it's not. There are social and historical explanations for why we do what we do, feel what we feel, and have the attractions we do. As males and females we carry out our lives within the roles created for us by our cultures, for entirely understandable reasons given our social conditioning and the systems we find ourselves in.

The ways that we "are" men and women, the ways that these identities are "performed" have come under increasing scrutiny over the past 30 years, being studied by observation, cross-cultural analyses, and through examining the development of gender roles through time. It is this latter analysis that Betsy used to explain to 13-year-old Jesse why the relationships he observed in his middle school were so irrational. Why do intelligent, assertive girls overlook sweet, caring guys to date "jerks," the males whose commitment to traditional masculinity makes them popular with other males but who treat girls and women poorly. In order to answer Jesse's question, and to write this piece, we have gone back 30,000 years into history. We will trace notions of gender from the earliest human societies to the dawn of patriarchy[1] in order to understand why women are popular because of how their bodies look, men are valued for their status, power, and aggressiveness, and what all this has to do with sex.

The ways that members of our culture are taught to be men or women have been traditionally dominated by the ideas of good girls versus bad girls, and tough guys or "real men" versus "sweet guys." We describe this historically constructed grid as the four boxes of gendered sexuality. Each of these boxes is a trap providing only limited space for people to be themselves. Each carries certain costs as well as benefits. The cool girls in Jesse's school were, we believe, responding at some level to a feeling that they needed to get a tough guy who could protect and support them in a world dominated by men. While some might say this has a biological basis, we believe that women's perceived need for a "protector/dominator" in order to live well and care for their children, is the legacy of the last 7,000 years of patriarchal social structures.

The power of the boxes has diminished somewhat over the last century. For instance, it is less common today to hear a man say that he won't "allow" his wife to work. Yet we are still very much affected by concepts of what a "real man" or "good girl" is, with very real implications for our personal, romantic, and sexual lives. To understand the force of the boxes, and to provide a complete answer to Jesse's question, requires examining the historical development of our society's notions of 'proper gender roles' that led to the construction of the boxes.

Despite the lingering negative effects of stereotypical roles and pressures, it is important to note that change is possible and, in fact, things are changing. There are many nice, sweet guys who are acting outside of prescribed male dominant ways of being, and doing very well. And there are girls and women who overcome the "good girl/bad girl" dichotomy to move into more authentic ways of living. Males and females who seek to break out of narrowly prescribed gender roles are finding new ways to be in relationships as real partners, who balance who's "on top" in terms of power, nurturance, and sexuality.

[1]A system of social organization in which power is held by and transferred through males.

As we were considering Jesse's question, an important direction for inquiry came from Betsy's need to do some research for a lecture on the history of sexuality. She did not want to start, as such lectures often do, with the Victorians and their pronouncements that women had no sex drive and that men were walking out-of-control penises. She wanted to go further back, to see where those ideas came from. Her search brought her back to the earliest evidence of human religious and communal life.

Since then, Jesse, now 22, and Betsy, now 52, have shared ideas and books and presented the four-boxes analysis to high school and college classes. We come from different generations and different genders, and so our perspectives vary based on what we've seen and felt. We also have different ideological and academic backgrounds, yet we have a remarkable concurrence of ideas about where we think the craziness about sexuality came from and what we can do to get out of it.

The Way That We "Perform" Our Genders is Not "Natural"!

There is an alternative explanation to those offered by evolutionary biologists (e.g., Buss, 1995) who see dominance-oriented male/female relations as the natural order. Biological essentialists claim that women, being physically smaller and weaker, need powerful men to take care of them so they and their children can survive. Such arguments presume the historical naturalness of pair bonding—the "you and me dear, off to conquer the world together" world of marriage and private property. This denies that there were once, and could again be communities where children were supported and protected by matrifocal,[2]

matrilineal,[3] grandmother clans (e.g., Eisler, 1987; Sjoo and Mor, 1991). If we admit that men and women once shared power and responsibilities, the naturalness of man-woman pairs is called into question. If we begin to critically examine the history of gender relations, we can see that what we think of as normal is in fact only one of many ways that men and women have interacted over the 30,000 years of human societies.

What is natural, after all? The roles and relationships we currently live with are the results of social constructions, related to a long heritage of male supremacy that has perverted the lives of both women and men. Taking a social constructionist approach means that we do not see gender or sex as inherent, or as natural, but rather, we see the ways that we human beings experience our bodies and our sexualities as profoundly affected by socialization, social systems, and culture.

What we currently see as the dominant model of gendered sexuality only makes sense if we take into account the past 7,000–10,000 years (depending on the part of the world) of patriarchy. During these relatively recent millennia, by the standards of the long history of human evolution, women's sexuality, spirituality, and independence have been suppressed while men have been socialized into a dominating, aggressive form of sexual and gender performance. We have inherited a poor legacy for gender equality and mutuality. Nevertheless, there is hope. If we can create a new understanding of our past, we can use it to envision a new future.

First we must examine the political, religious, and economic reasons for why the system of patriarchy came about, was maintained,

---

[2]Women-oriented and led by women.

[3]Descent traced through the female line. Matrilineal inheritance, practiced from early Egypt through the coming of Christianity in Europe, meant that property passed from mother to daughter, also typical in property transfers among indigenous peoples around the world.

and continues to cause beautiful, powerful, intelligent women to date "jerks." Patriarchy hurts men too, which is why Jesse and young men all over the United States risk being called "faggot" when they walk with male friends, hug other men, or are emotional.

THE HISTORY: WHEN WE SHARED POWER

There is strong evidence that during prehistoric times,[4] prior to the Neolithic revolution, and in various other cultures in more recent times, women and men shared power and status (Eisler, 1987, 1995; Gimbutas, 1980; Sjoo & Mor, 1991; Stone, 1976; Tannahill, 1992). Women were not dependent on men, or specifically one man, for their economic and physical survival. Yet this does not imply that there was a matriarchy before the patriarchy, or a system of dominance by females before males came into dominance. According to the late archeologist, Marija Gimbutas, who studied early Europe, "a division of labor between the sexes is indicated, but not a superiority of either" (1980, p. 32), what Riane Eisler (1987, 1995) refers to as "partnership societies," an experience of "power with" rather than "power over" (Starhawk, 1990). Such social systems had mutuality and interdependence at their core, rather than domination and submission. The knowledge of existence of such social patterns can inspire us today when we fear that dominance by one gender over another has always been the norm or has to be the way it is.

From what we know about the earliest human groupings, people lived in matrilineal/ grandmother clans. Women were the ones who gathered grains and dug the earth for roots, providing the majority of nourishment as well as healing curatives for the group (Eisler, 1987). Women were the "mothers of invention," creating critical elements of social evolution such as pottery to hold water and grain and weaving to make clothing and fishing nets. The Neolithic era, ca. 10,000–5,000 BCE occurred when groups of women and their children settled, as they became "farmers" through their knowledge of seeds (Sjoo & Mor, 1991). Eventually men came to be the rulers (given events we will explain later), but early in the patriarchy, the power of succession passed through women and the woman's line—a system of checks and balances between men and women, emphasizing interdependence, and allowing resistance to the consolidation of power.

A version of this cultural pattern exists even today in the Haudenosaunee lands, named by the French as the Iroquois. As one historian described the Haudenosaunee political system, the "senior women in the village named the men who represented the clans at village and tribal councils . . . and removed the men from office if they strayed too far from the wishes of the women" (Zinn, 1995, p. 20).

Yet this critically important story of how our European ancestors lived (and many indigenous people live today)—that women were once inventors and leaders, and men and women once shared power—has been minimized or lost. It is not told to our young sons and daughters in school or at home. The story we were raised with teaches us that men have always been dominant, in charge. Not surprisingly, this "his-story," whether based on ancient religious history or interpretations of archaeological findings, was compiled and interpreted by male authors. History is always recorded and told as a story from the perspective of the conquerors. And in the case of gender history, the "winner" of the right to tell the

---

[4]Of course, there is no such thing as pre-history, just pre-his-story. History as recorded through writing is, at the oldest, less than 8,000 years old. But when we use the word prehistory, we would like to remind the reader that history can be (and is) passed on orally through stories, legends, and myths. We do not seek to dismiss these traditions by referring to them as prehistoric, we are simply following convention.

story of the past 7,000–10,000 years has been the men, and more specifically, dominant men, those with money and power.

This is an important distinction because, while it is true that all boys and men benefit to some extent from the "patriarchy"—male control and reproduction of institutions of social and political power such as the church, the state, and the family—it is also true, as we will discuss, that all males suffer from the imposed roles needed to keep this system in place. But first, let's go even further back in time, and then see what happened to get us to where we are today.

The Great Earth Mother Goddess and Her Consort: Earliest Conceptions of the Divine

Who and what we view as divine has a lot to do with who and what we value. The earliest creation stories from around the globe centered on the earth itself, and the female—who gives birth—as the source of all life (Walker, 1983). Hence the concept of the "earth, mother goddess."[5] As Monica Sjoo and Barbara Mor state, "All religion is about the mystery of creation" (1987, p. 71). Earth-based spirituality is the oldest spiritual form, reflecting ancient beliefs that goddesses and gods reflect the material world. "The principle of the immanence of the divine in matter appears to be the underlying religious conviction of the Paleolithic and Neolithic cultures in Europe and the ancient Near East" (Meador, 2000, p. 23). This is hard to imagine for Western people because our heaven-based, male-centered religions claim to have existed since the beginning of time ("In the beginning" . . .").

---

[5]Those of us trained to see "God" as male, and "goddess" as a pampered, self-centered teenage girl, may have trouble conceptualizing an ultimate divinity viewed as female. Yet it is clear from archeological finds as early as 30,000 BCE and poetry, pottery, and ancient texts that this was true throughout the world for most of the time we have been humans.

Influenced by the creation myths that came to us from patriarchal religions, Western science has adopted many of the assumptions of male supremacy and leadership as though they were fact. The founding texts of archeology, anthropology, and other fields of social science were developed by men influenced by Western cultural biases, so history and biology textbooks reflect traditional attitudes toward women and their role in history. The major texts of both religion and science, the leading paradigms for knowledge, tell us versions of our history in which men have always led and women have always been subordinate. These stories have a profound effect on our self-conceptions, both as women and as men, and at their worst they can really mess up our sex lives.

What is the evidence for early peoples' worship of the divine feminine? History textbooks have a tendency to rush from "ape-men" to the Fertile Crescent without pausing to reflect on the 40,000 years of human culture that produced a wealth of religious, technological, and artistic innovations. During this period, the Paleolithic era, anatomically modern humans first appeared and developed what we now call art, ceremony, and music. They created the first paintings, often in caves, the first musical instruments, and small statues of what may have been their primary deity, the earth mother goddess. These statues, carved from ivory and soft stone, and with ample breasts, bulging stomachs, and buttocks, have been found in caves all over Eastern Central Europe, France, Ukraine, and Siberia, preserved from as long ago as nearly 30,000 years BCE (Eisler, 1987; Gimbutas, 1980; Stone, 1976).

Some paintings and statues were found at a far distance from the cave entrance, suggesting that early people had a ceremonial torch-light procession into the earth to view these images. The art works included stick figures of animals, hunters, and people gathering plants and many images of the female. They also

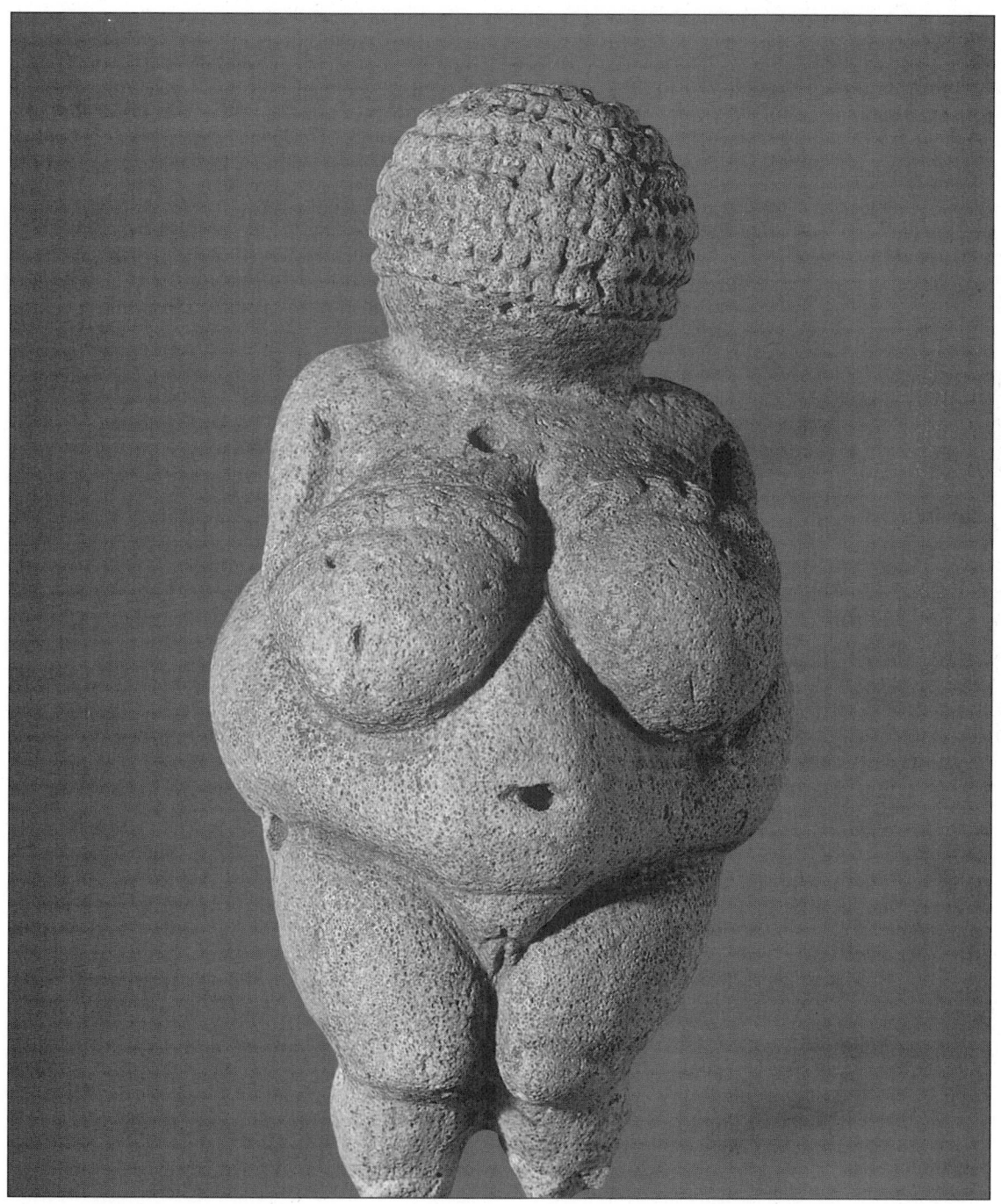

Venus of Willendorf
c. 24,000–22,000 BCE
4¾ inches, oolitic limestone
Copyright Erich Lessing/Art Resource, NY

featured prominent male figures, often horned, that are believed to be the "horned god," the ancestor of the Greek god Pan, and the consort, lover, and son of the supreme mother.

Such images, or "idols" as they are called in the Bible, are mainstays of most human religions. Think of the images of Christ on the cross, the sitting Buddha, and shrines to Shiva in the Hindu tradition. Judaism and Islam may be the only two faiths that do not use any sort of images as devotional triggers to help focus the devotee's thoughts on the divine. In most other traditions, the use of sacred artwork has been continuously used for millennia. The earliest of these images were of the great mother and her lover, the horned one.

While early archeologists saw such art as merely fertility figurines, newer interpretations are offered by authors who look at the connections between earth-based spirituality and sexuality (Eisler, 1987; Walker, 1983), offering us powerful visions of what might have been. People in agrarian cultures depended on the recurring cycles of the seasons, hence their belief in resurrection and rebirth. Bodies of the dead were sometimes placed in caves—which may have been seen as the entrance to the body of the Earth Mother—surrounded by cowry[6] shells shaped like a vulva, the portal through which life comes into the world (Walker, 1983). The vulva-shaped cowry shell may have been used as a symbol of the life-giving power of the female, as was the red ochre used to paint the walls, a surrogate of life-giving or menstrual blood of women. Was this the time remembered as the Garden of Eden, when sexuality and sexual consciousness were viewed as gifts from the Great Ancestress/Mother Nature to women and men? Archeologist G. Rachel Levy (1948) doc-

umented the unbroken continuity of religious images and ideas descending from the Cro-Magnon Peoples of the Upper Paleolithic period down to our own time. Such images include the birth of the sacred child of Christianity in a cavelike shelter, surrounded by magic animals, born to a "virgin mother."

In societies that conceptualized the supreme power in the universe as a goddess, revered as the wise and just source of all our material and spiritual gifts, women would have internalized a very different self-image than they do in cultures that assume a single male god. Girls could see their bodies as images of those who are competent, independent, creative, and inventive (Eisler, 1987). Sexuality would also have had a very different meaning for both men and women. The earliest sacred "communion" may have been imaged as woman, representing the goddess, ritually bringing the penis of the man, as consort of the goddess, into her body. For a male to "enter god" in this way is significantly at odds with the rape imagery of males invading women's bodies. It is important to recognize that the myths we grow up with, whether they be religious, scientific, patriotic, or anything else, have a profound effect on how we see ourselves, our partners, and our sexuality. Indeed anthropologists have found that societies in which women have higher status have lower rates of rape (Grubin, 1993; Sanday, 1981).

The Earliest Families

In cultures that saw the source of all life as a divine mother, both women and men would have had a radically different notion of sexuality, family, and community. The focus on the female among the icons found in the caves reflects the focus on the female in the prehistoric family. Lineage and descent were traced through the mother. Her children were her children—no matter who the biological father was—and were the children of the grandmother's clan, raised and supported by all the

---

[6]Walker (1983, p. 182) says the name of this shell is from "Kauri, or Kali-Cunti, Yoni of the Universe, representing the divine vulva, usually conveying the idea of rebirth." It is still prized in many cultures.

men and women of the clan. In earliest times there may not have been any knowledge of the male role in procreation (Tannahill, 1992), and even when it was known, it may have been seen as equivalent to "planting a seed." In either case it may have been seen as the sacred and even magical fertility of the female that created new life. In some preliterate cultures, "the man's role in procreation is seen as one of opening the womb, but it is believed that children are placed in the mother's womb by spirits, perhaps the returning spirits of dead kin" (Sjoo & Mor, 1991, p. 26)

The evidence shows that neither sex was clearly dominant, nor was there any evidence of an underclass or servants. "Grave goods" appear to be almost universally sparse, and no differences can be seen between genders or classes (Gimbutas, 1980). This can be inferred from the identical gravesites found throughout Eurasia. Unlike later (including modern) graves, there is no clear distinction between various classes of people based on status, gender, or wealth.

These societies were certainly not utopian, but they did manage to organize their economies, ecosystems, and spiritual lives in a way that was sustained for tens of thousands of years and still exists in remote areas of the world where colonization has not yet fully spread. This can be hard to accept if we think that the way things are now must be the way it has always been, and especially if we learned that societies have "progressed" in a linear fashion to get us where we are today. Yet in our own country and around the world, millions of children go without basic needs being met by the modern families and community structures to which we have "evolved."

Patriarchal Social/Religious/Political Order

A major change occurred 6,000–12,000 years ago, varying by region of the world, that affects each one of us, especially our sexual lives. The role of men changed from equal partners in societies that worshiped the life-giving power of women, to one of despots, whose "women" were the property of fathers, husbands, and sons, and lineage began to be traced through the father, rather than the mother. As the traditional hunter-gatherer and small-plot agriculture systems were abandoned in the Neolithic period, two new types of societies emerged.

Agricultural Men's work as a hunter was no more important than women's as a gatherer until men learned to castrate the bull and use it as a draft animal. He, the specialist on animals, became, like women, a cultivator of crops, as he learned to breed animals. Even so, women retained ancestral memories of the worship of the goddess and their own importance and retained their important work as farmers.

Nomadic/Pastoral People depended on flocks and the men who reared them. Men were dominant. As wanderers, women's role in planting and harvesting crops would be gone. They may have come to be seen as chattel, like beasts, used for making and rearing babies, but having little other role or status in the social structure.

One theory used to explain the major change in power relations between men and women says that it occurred after men discovered their role in reproduction (Tannahill, 1992). With livestock domestication, men may have observed what happened if females were kept separate or with males. They also discovered the fantastic power of the seed. One ram could impregnate many, many ewes. Tannahill asserts (p. 47):

Men who emerged from the Neolithic into the period of recorded history had the kind of assurance, arrogance and authority that sprang not just from useful toil… but from a blinding revelation. . . . Was it that, discovering their own crucial role in an area where men's potency had always been denied, they had (very humanly) overreacted? On a more specific level, it was now possible for a man to look at a child and call him "my son," to feel the need to call a woman, "my wife." . . . After it, women's sexual freedom began to be seriously curtailed. A man might have a harem if he chose and he could defend it, but the concept of "my son" required a woman to be monogamous.

According to this theory, the realization of the male role in reproduction led to a desire by men to control women's behavior so they could be sure that the sons born to a woman would be their own. This is known as the patrilineal system (lineage traced through the father), and it required cultural change of a massive order, with severe measures to inhibit female mate selection/sexual assertiveness and prevent other males from having access to a man's woman (or women).

Though in some ways attractive, this theory posits a cultural evolution (mutation might be a better term), that spread as men learned of their own roles in procreation. However, it is far too reliant on the idea that knowledge of the male role in reproduction automatically leads to patriarchy. In fact, there is another theory that has two strong advantages: it doesn't require people to be ignorant of male contributions to reproduction to get along as relative equals, nor does it require men's understanding of their role in reproduction to automatically lead to their domination of women. The second of these points is crucial, for if the fact of men's contribution to the process of procreation *necessarily* causes men to want to dominate women, then there is no way out. We can't unlearn this fact, the knowledge of which (according to the assumptions of the first theory) produces an irrevocable shift in human culture toward the domination and oppression of women. We refuse to accept this conclusion, because it is deeply conservative in its implications for how we can build a more equitable world and because

another version of the story may be more accurate.

The Nomadic Tribes and Invasions

There is another theory that attempts to account for the massive change in power between women and men that relates to politics, the results of invasion and conquest. About 7,000 years ago, 5,000 BCE, nomadic bands from the deserts and steppes of Central Asia began waves of invasion, conquering and destroying agricultural societies in the fertile regions of Eurasia, India, and the Middle East. These people lived in the dry grasslands of Western China, Russia, and the Central Asian republics. On all sides, they were surrounded by people who lived in more hospitable regions, as in the ancient Chinese, Indian, and Iraqi farming communities that grew up along large rivers. Ruled by powerful warrior-priests, they brought with them aggressive and powerful male gods.

Why the gender difference in their conception of divinity? Climatic differences caused a fundamentally different understanding of nature. The small agricultural communities conceived of a world held in balance between mother earth and father sky, reflected in the recurring cycles of death and rebirth of their crops. The Indo-Europeans (people of the steppe, whose language is the root of modern languages as varied as Hindi, Pashto, Persian, German, and Latin) experienced nature as much more hostile. On the dry steppes of Central Asia, these people imaged the divine as a harsh sky god who punished humans through drought, thunder, and lightning.

Unlike the earth mother goddess of the Fertile Crescent, the omnipresent Gaia-like presence of the shamanic and Native American traditions, or the various river goddesses of India and Egypt, the gods of these desert people were thunder beings, angry and not easily appeased. Their god was a partisan who fought with his people against other people and their gods. Skirmishes over pasture were associated with the offering of various types of sacrifice in order to give their god his share in the spoils of war. The herding people were accustomed to fighting with one another for access to rare water and pasture for their herds and were adept at killing both their animals and each other. The Indo-Europeans lived similar lives to those of the Semitic people who came from the deserts of Arabia, and both invaded the Fertile Crescent and Canaan.

The small agricultural communities of China, India, and Mesopotamia (modern day Iraq) were surrounded by less fertile lands, and their nomadic neighbors found them inviting targets. Agriculture had come into being when women moved from the gathering of grains and fruits to growing most of their food in one place, requiring far less roaming and hunting to support their people. Farming communities would have been attractive to those groups who lost a fight over pasturage with other groups, a pattern that would eventually cause the Huns to leave central Asia and conquer most of Europe.

At first the invaders may have just raided their neighbors, taking what they could carry, but some eventually decided to stay, at the expense of the people and cultures they had conquered. The steppe and desert dwellers both brought a fierce god of war, thunder, and the sky (like Jehovah or YHWH of the Old Testament) into the lands they conquered. Their myths and beliefs became integrated into existing religious structures, and the earth-based goddesses and gods, still revered by the people, were co-opted. This can be most clearly seen in the Greek pantheon. Zeus, the sky-thunder-war god had the highest place in a hierarchy of gods and goddesses, most of whom were much more ancient divinities from cultural and religious traditions that had all been absorbed into the Greek mythology from

the various tribes and city-states their empire captured.

After the nomadic herders had conquered their farming neighbors, they claimed authority and dominance over the indigenous populations. The small autonomous farming communities became tribute-paying centers of production, while the nomadic herders became a class of warriors who lived off the tribute paid to them by those that they conquered. A class of warrior-priests used the labor of women and men in the agricultural communities to create food surpluses, to support themselves as full-time soldiers. Armies were created, and because of the pressure to produce ever more food for tribute, communities began fighting over access to water. The first true wars of conquest emerged from this pressure, with wars being fought solely for control of subject-populations and access to irrigation waters.

The Patriarchy Begins

These conditions created both the first class-based societies, and the first true patriarchies, with social institutions based on male domination. This period saw the beginnings of a split between spirituality as a democratic and universal activity of the people, and what became the more modern form, spirituality being the province of a professional ecclesiastical class. It is useful to bear in mind the fact that pagan originally meant "country-person." The victors practiced their brand of religion and mocked that of those they conquered, the pagans, as being simple, satanic, or nonexistent.

Because the conquering culture was one of war and male supremacy, the traditional values of the people were devalued. For example, sexual equality for both women and men was decried by patriarchal religious leaders as "loose moral values," peaceful coexistence came to be seen as weakness, and closeness to the soil was demeaned by labels such as "dirt-scraping peasant." The concept of man as warrior/dominator and woman as virgin/mother emerged from this relationship between the new governing powers and those they conquered, based on male-dominant and female subordinate power relations.

What does all this have to do with Jesse's question about the cool girls and the jerks? This was the beginning of the times, continuing up through the last century and still real in many ways today, when "tough guys win" and "women need protection."

For whatever reasons—males' knowledge of their role in procreation or the spirituality of the nomadic peoples with their "god as male" ideologies—a patrilineal system in which ancestry is traced through the father became instituted through the creation of religious and civic laws. This had major implications for re-imaging female and male sexuality. Severe measures were put into place to inhibit female mate selection and sexual assertiveness and to prevent other males from having access to wives.

With the formation of city-states and greater militarization, men were needed to fight in the wars of control, and people may have begun to value male sons more, since if they were not killed, they would return with pillage and be able to marry as many women as they could afford. It seems probable that the first systems of polygamy emerged after the natural balance of males and females in humans was upset through the constant loss of young men to war.

The new system of male and female relations now called the patriarchy—in which males control access to power and resources—spread to many parts of the world over the millennia leading up to the birth of Christianity. During these years, ca. 7,000 BCE–1 BCE, worship of the goddess as a supreme being was increasingly attacked and diminished, and male gods and male authority gained greater supremacy.

The attitude toward women in the Far East remained more favorable for some of this period. In ancient India, for example, women were not deprived of property rights or individual freedoms by marriage. However, Hinduism, which evolved in India after about 500 BCE, instituted the concept of obedience of women toward men. Women had to walk behind their husbands. Females did not have inheritance rights from their father's land, and widows could not remarry. In both East and West, male children were preferred over female children, a condition that continues today in many cultures.

Because the victorious peoples were able to write the histories and laws—and destroy the art and writing of earlier cultures—what we are able to know about conquered peoples is sparse. But we are able to surmise beliefs and practices of earlier earth-based spirituality societies because they remain evident in folk traditions, such as the solstice traditions of the Yule log and "bringing in the green" at Christmas. Now heretical fertility rites such as Saturnalia—a time of going to the fields and having sex as a way of "praying" for the crops to come once again from the earth—are evident at Easter, the Christian holy day that occurs just as the earth is again giving birth to new life. Witness the association with ancient fertility symbols such as rabbits and eggs. These symbols are holdouts from a time when religion was centered on the cycles of the earth and reproduction and not, as it might first appear, around Near Eastern religious history. Jesus was not born at the end of December; rather, the celebration of his birth was moved to that date, in the third century AD, to coincide with the attempt to co-opt the "pagan" country people's Yule holiday and bring them into the church.

The image of the great earth mother goddess came to be diminished, first by incorporating her into a pantheon of Greek and Roman gods and goddesses, where she was secondary to the gods. Then she was removed from Western culture altogether except in remaining images of Mary, Mother of God. Yet the idea that woman was once imagined as divine is a powerful one. It is important for both females and males today to have images of the female as both sacred and powerful, and as sexual.

Evidence of Women's Leadership and Spiritual/Sexual Potency

What evidence do we have of women's leadership and spiritual and sexual potency? Did you know the earliest known author of written literature was a woman? Enheduanna lived around 2300 BCE in ancient Mesopotamia, now southern Iraq. Holding the most important religious office in Sumer, the high priestess at Ur, Enheduanna had a powerful position, managing agriculture at the temple and overseeing the local fishing industry. Only 300 years after written language had evolved, she wrote with a stylus on wet clay in the earliest cuneiform script. What she wrote were poems of devotion to Inanna, a goddess of unbridled sexuality as exposed in the following lines (Enheduanna, 2000, p. 11).

> peg my vulva
> my star-sketched horn of the dipper
> moor my slender boat of heaven
> my new moon crescent cunt beauty

Inanna has often been described simply as a goddess of love. Yet as Enheduanna's editor, Betty DeShong Meador, states (p. 158):

Her arousal and sexuality is seen as a blessing that engenders growth and prosperity of every kind. In Mesopotamia, the primary focus of religion was to ensure the continuity of life through the fertility of the fields, the animals, and the human beings who tended them. Sexuality became the principle metaphor for the continuity of life, and as such, it was part of ritual in the temple, myths of the gods and the daily life of the populace.

Effects on Roles and Relationships

After about 3,000 BCE, male superiority had become enshrined in law and custom. Rulers treaded a fine line between their political aims and the remaining polytheistic beliefs of the people, who still gave honor to the female, as seen in the poems to Inanna. However, the monotheistic strand of the Near Eastern culture, with the authority of a male god and male rulers, won in the end.

In the Greek, Roman, or Jewish civilizations of the ancient world, the "free woman," as distinct from the slave, was the property of her father during childhood and her husband from adolescence on. Unless love intervened, she was to her husband a mother for his children and a housekeeper. She was a higher level servant to be treated well unless she failed in her duties, such as producing a male heir, for which she could be dismissed or pensioned off. This overall pattern of relationships, established in the Near East over 3,000 years ago, was to persist in Europe, Asia, Africa, and the Americas, with minor variations according to time and place, until the beginning of the feminist revolution in the middle years of the 19th century. It still continues, depending on the part of the world and the attitudes of the people, today.

As social, political, and religious systems and norms evolved to support the patriarchal order—to ensure that all children born into a marriage would be those of the father—certain expectations for males and females developed that came to be seen as "normal." While there have been variations across time and culture, we can see throughout the remainder of history and today patriarchal practices that:

- *Prevent premarital sex by females* For example, moral dictates about virginity, child marriages, and clitorectomies in some cultures, abstinence-only education in U.S. schools.

- *Reduce women's liberty to prevent extramarital sex by wives*   For example, no vote; no education; no job; no owning or inheriting property; "woman's place is in the home"; keep covered with the Burkha in some Islamic countries, threat and practice of rape and battering; keep her terrified of the dark and being alone, as in the United States; subjugation of lesbianism.

- *Allow for extramarital sex for men*   The social role of the harlot, courtesan, and prostitute; in many early cultures, lawful taking of many wives by wealthy men and successful warriors.

- *Brutalize boys*   Make little boys so scared of being victims of bullying, lack of respect, and violence at the hands of other males, that they will become dominators and enforce these codes against their children and wives; denigrate homosexuals.

The bottom line is that men have been taught to "go for it" around sex and power, while women were taught to accept repression. Patriarchal rules and norms required an acceptance of the social order by men, including a rigid set of male roles, dominating personal behavior by males, repression of homosexuality (or institutionalization of it as in ancient Greece, where men had wives for bearing children and young male lovers or female courtesans for sex), and repression of female-like male behavior. There were costs, in the form of male violence against males, to boys and men who did not like brutalizing and repressing the women in their lives, as there still are today.

While women have made large political gains in the past century around citizenship rights such as voting and opportunities for education and making money, the remnants of the previous 7,000–10,000 years of patriarchal social and religious policies are still with us

today. The social institution of marriage, and the roles of wife and husband, still carries symbolically certain expectations for women and men—"boxes"—that we both long for and fear. There is a tug and pull for both men and women, between parts of us that want security and social acceptability and those that represent, in some cases, a more free way of being, free from the limitations imposed by patriarchy.

FOUR BOXES OF GENDER AND SEXUALITY

We face what feel like dichotomies. Either we are the "good girl" who will be a wife and mother, or we are a "bad girl." We are either a "real man," or the "nice guy" who finishes last. There are parts of the second "box" that offer each gender more freedom, but being in that box comes with its costs. Neither box really works for us or represents the full range of our authentic selves. Yet the boxes represent images and labels that can have tremendous power. We have termed this trap, the Four Boxes of Gender and Sexuality. Let's look first at the two boxes for women, based on the good girl/bad girl split.

Good Girl: Wife/Mother

Most of us are familiar with the dichotomy for women of the good girl-bad girl, or the madonna-whore complex. But what is the stereotype of the good girl? She is, of course, the wife/mother, needed to produce children, particularly sons, who will inherit the father's name, money, and class privilege. Given the biological reality that men can never really *know* that they are the "real father" of their children without modern genetic testing, what does this system require? We are talking stereotypes of course, but that is what the boxes are about—pressures to conform.

There are many problems with the good girl, wife and mother role for both women and

Good Girl: Wife/Mother (stereotypes/images)	Bad Girl: Whore/Dyke (stereotypes/images)
• Virgin at marriage. • Monogamous during marriage. • Heterosexual; takes name of husband and produces children/heirs. • Financially dependent on husband. • Nonsexual; low sex interest, doesn't initiate or enjoy sex. • "Feminine"—meets social standards of beauty but isn't too dangerously sexy. • Not too smart, educated, assertive, or goal-oriented. • Middle or upper class or aspires to be. • Doesn't have career (or subordinates own career to husband's).	• Lower class or servant/slave. • Socially and financially independent of men/marriage. • May keep own name if married. • Educated or has mind of her own. • "Welfare queen" or "career girl." • Free in bodily expression, size, and gender expression. May be large. • Sexually free; enjoys sex. • Nonmonogamous. • May have sex with men, women or both; lesbian or bisexual. • May be very sexy or not at all; very feminine or very masculine.

men, as it is a setup. On the one hand, she is supposed to be a partner for life who bears a man's children, looks good, and is an adept social companion and hostess, helping him advance his career so they can both have what they want and need financially. On the other hand, she must not be too sexy, initiate sex too often, or even like "kinky" sex—the kind of sex men must then seek from prostitutes or affairs—so neither she, nor her husband, will worry about her being a "bad girl." She must be smart enough to be interesting socially but not so smart or assertive about her ideas that she threatens or intimidates her husband or business colleagues, or gives the impression she could make it on her own. Above all, she must not make too many demands or be "difficult", or her husband may cast her off once the children are grown and find a new young "trophy" wife to have on his arm.

The wife must be a virgin when married, and not be very interested in sex (or else she might pursue sex with other men). She should be feminine (retiring and demure/not aggressive) and meet current standards of beauty—so she makes *her husband* look good—but not dress or act too sexy and attract other men's interest. These "good girls" are expected to be

ignorant of sex, including their own bodies. In the Bible, "knowing" someone was the code for having sex with them. Women were kept away from information about sex in order to limit their interest in it. This can still be seen today in those who argue that teaching children about sex will cause them to have sex at a younger age.

Socially and politically, the wife and mother depends financially on her husband (so there is less risk of her thinking she could have her own life, have affairs, or leave him and the children) and is not expected to be or act too smart, educated, or goal-oriented. At the same time, it is best if she "has class" so she can manage the household and be a social companion to her husband in such a way as to maximize his chance of financial success. You get the picture. Sound familiar?

Bad Girl: Whore/Dyke

The bad girl represents everything the wife/mother tries not to be and may be accused of being if she steps out of the good-girl role. The bad-girl stereotype is the whore or dyke who is sexually free, likes sex too much, and may even assert her desire to have sex with women. She can be free in her bodily expression, size, and gender expression, looking very sexy or not sexy at all; she may be more masculine in appearance and style. Traditionally such women were seen as lower class and as servants or slaves. Since poor and working-class men had less money and privilege to pass down, poor and working class women had to work to support their children and were thus more socially and financially independent of men and marriage. The image of the welfare queen is that of the bad girl, who cannot get or keep a husband or doesn't care, and wants the government to support her lifestyle. The political pressure for poor women to marry is related to the desire to make these women into good girls. The social pressures to avoid this box are immense and intense.

The Split for Males

There are also two very confining and oppressive boxes for males. Although it is not as readily apparent as the good girl–bad girl split, the split is based on a similar gender–sex dichotomy. For males it comes down to whether you are a boy or a girl, and it is not as simple as blue versus pink. Women know they are women. That is what they are told once they begin menstruating. "You're a woman now." It is generally not contested for most women. But given the social importance of men being "real men" and retaining supremacy in social systems of power and control, males must earn the right to be considered men, at least real men.

If they deviate from a very narrow script, they are threatened, primarily by other males, particularly older males (big brothers, neighborhood bullies) with being seen as girls—sissies, fags, and queers. To young boys raised in a patriarchal society, it can look like you have to be a "tough guy" just to survive. The alternative is the stereotype of the "sweet guy," equated with sissy, and the price paid for being in the wrong box is high. Males, who are supposed to be at the top of the social hierarchy, have a lot to lose if they don't play the game.

Tough Guy: Husband/Father and Dominator/Protector

The corollary to the good girl: wife/mother box is the tough guy: husband/father and dominator/protector box. The stereotype of the male in this box is that of the "real man," ready and able to compete and succeed in the world of men so they can "bring home the bacon" and so their wives won't "wear the pants in the family." The job of the "real man" is to make money, accumulate resources, and pass it all down to their legitimate heirs—males who will carry their name; sons who they are sure are theirs.

They must be willing and able to enforce the rules of virginity and monogamy for females and not let "their women"—their wives and daughters—have lives of freedom and self-defined sexuality. These rules are particularly strong in the most conservative religious traditions, which built patrilineal property exchange into their laws, customs, and dogmas.

Tough guys fear being perceived as a "girl" and thus not making it in the world of men: not getting or keeping the jobs, status, and power that are controlled primarily by men. This fear pushes boys and men toward stereotypical male role behavior such as playing or watching aggressive sports, while devaluing less violent ones, and not studying or reading much but still insisting on winning all arguments, especially with females. The tough guy is likely to be the one who drives the car[7] and controls the television remote. They are in control. They may have male friends but don't share much about their inner lives. Instead they participate in "parallel play"—golfing, fishing, hunting, drinking, and playing or

---

[7]One of the clearest indicators we might have of the "end of the patriarchy" would be if we saw women driving, with men as passengers, as often as men driving when women are in the car. Rationally this would make more sense since statistically, women have fewer accidents, take fewer risks, and are less likely to drive while drunk.

Tough Guy: Husband/Father Dominator/Protector (stereotypes/images)	Sweet Guy: Nice Guy Fag/Sissy (stereotypes/images)
• Needs wife to have his name; displays dominance. • Must "provide" for wife and children, so must succeed in the world of men. • Heterosexual; pursues sex with girls and women whether wife, lover, or prostitute. • Competes with other males for rank and position in hierarcy. • Wants attractive girlfriend/wife as status symbol. • Is a bully or hangs out with bullies. • Only emotion shown is anger. • Dominates; may be abusive to female partner and children. • Restricts lives of wife and children in name of protecting them. • Plays and/or watches aggressive sports. • Doesn't study or read much but likes to win all arguments. • Drives the car and controls TV remote.	• "Finishes last;" is liked by girls as friend but not for marriage. • Got bullied or beat up as boy. • May be artist, musician, or dancer. • Seen as gay or bisexual whether he is or not. • If married, shares housework and parenting. Wife may keep own name. • Not obsessed with sports; may play soccer. • Hugs his friends, male and female. • "Eats quiche"; likes gourmet or health food. • Moves his body in relaxed ways. • Dresses colorfully or fancifully • Reads, studies, thinks; seen as "nerd." • Is sensitive and emotional; can cry. • Is willing to listen; doesn't always have to be right.

watching sports—showing off what they can do and sizing themselves up in comparison to each other.

Being a protector and dominator means that you must protect your wife and children from other males. But being able to protect also requires being able to dominate. And being willing to be the bully means being shut down emotionally. Having been told since they were tiny that big boys don't cry, in fact, tough guys don't cry (Kindlon and Thompson, 1999; Pollack, 1998). Men can struggle emotionally but not know what they are really feeling, because the only emotion they are allowed to feel or express is anger. They may be feeling sad, disappointed, scared, or lost, but all they will show is emptiness or anger.

Sweet Guy: Nice Guy

What's the alternative? The other confining stereotype for males is the nice guy or sweet guy, all too often associated with sissy, queer, fag, or "girl." In a world controlled by males

for the past 7,000–10,000 years, being seen as a girl is the last thing most males want to be, or feel safe being. The sweet guy feels he won't "make it" unless he acts tough enough to compete with the dominator-type males for the high status jobs and positions. Nice guys finish last is what they hear and what they fear. They also worry that no girl will want them, except as a friend, and having friends who are girls ceases to become an option for many boys at a young age, again due to male peer pressure to be a "guy."

The sweet guys are often the boys who got bullied and beat up throughout their childhoods as other males use them to display their tough-guy masculinity to other males. Perhaps they are smaller, or they play the violin, or read books. Perhaps they aren't obsessed with sports, or computers, and perhaps they hold hands with each other, play with dolls, or are close to their mothers or sisters.

As adults many sweet guys are seen as gay or bisexual whether they are or not. If married, they share housework and parenting. Their wives may keep their own names because for these men, being in an equal partnership is more important than the patriarchal symbol of "owning" their wives and children, having their name be the "family name." They hug their friends—male and female. They "eat quiche"—to use a stereotype of the "sensitive guy" from the 1970s. But in fact, men who dare to break out of the dominator/tough guy box may let themselves be a gourmet and eat vegetables or health food, instead of going for the burgers every day; as a result, they may live longer and healthier lives.

Letting go of fears of not being seen as masculine enough lets men dance freely—even outside the male space of mosh-pits—and use their bodies in more relaxed and sensuous ways. They may dress colorfully or fancifully. In Jesse's life this means having male friends who will cuddle on the couch while watching a video, just like their friends who are females do with each other. Perhaps most crucial, in terms of their own health and the safety of others, the "sweet guy" may demonstrate more emotional intelligence, be compassionate, and cry, not just in a crisis but when it could be a helpful way to release distressful feelings or to express joy.

The standard, the pole if you will, that males need to make it over to be able to measure up as male is set pretty high. In fact, it has gotten higher over the last past half century. It used to be that you could be a "gentleman scholar," but that was before girls started going to college and doing well. Now being studious is being nerdy or being a girl. The image of the gentleman scholar or even gentleman soldier has been replaced with a hypermasculinity that plays itself out in extreme sports, extreme drinking, and extreme sex (Faludi, 1999).

The biceps on GI Joe increased in size over the past 34 years, from 12.2 inches in 1964 to 26.8 inches in 1998 (Kimmel and Messner, 2001), almost in proportion to the increasingly excessive curves on the Barbie doll. No real human being could look like either GI Joe or Barbie, and yet millions of people around the world measure themselves up to these symbols of the white, "perfect" body.

THE ANSWER TO THE QUESTION

If it isn't obvious yet, the answer to Jesse's question about why all the "coolest girls" hang out with "the jerks" is that up until just this past century, women had little chance of acquiring the education and income sufficient to support themselves and their children alone. So they needed a "real man" who could "succeed in the world of men," since men controlled power and resources, jobs and money. Perhaps at a conscious or unconscious level, girls and women still believe this is what they need and think it is the tough guys, not the sweet guys, who will be able to take care of them.

Of course, given rates of domestic violence, extramarital affairs, and divorce, it may be a Faustian bargain. Females "sell their soul"—their emotional and possibly physical safety—for what appears to be the promise of financial security for them and their children. This may be true for even the most "liberated" of women, since even though their mothers and fathers may have raised them to be independent, their brothers and boyfriends were still raised to be protector/dominators.

So it is that "cool girls," those who are attractive inside and outside, who are strong, and smart, and loving, and playful (and all of the other ways we can describe the powerful women we all know and love), are still caught in a bind. Their mother's generation fought to create more options for them, more ways to be a woman than the two boxes that 10,000 years of history had left us with. But their male contemporaries are still growing up in an environment in which it is acceptable for men to order the bombing of faraway lands, to ruthlessly slash jobs while making record profits, and to compete with one another at every possible level for advantage.

In this world of hypermasculinity, sweet guys are still very much at a disadvantage. In middle and high school (and even at college), Jesse knew dozens of women who were "liberated," who were strong and had been raised to stick up for themselves. But they still dated men who hit, raped, or abused them emotionally. They would cry on Jesse's shoulder, saying, "I wish more men were like you." But then they would say, "We're friends, we're close; I don't want to ruin that by getting closer." These women were subconsciously looking for men to protect them and were willing to pay the price in violence and domination for the status that dating a "tough guy" brought. They were also trained to believe that a man they could talk to, be emotionally close to, and really relate to was good "as a friend" but not suitable for dating. Until our images and expectations of maleness change, this bind will continue to affect women who want to live fuller lives, causing sweet guys to be measured against GI Joe. Fortunately for Jesse and his sweet-guy friends, increasing numbers of young women are breaking out of the boxes and finding themselves attracted to males who are more box-free as well.

HOW IS THIS SYSTEM REINFORCED?

Betsy: As the mother of a son, I wondered, from a functional perspective, what a society would have to do to raise sweet, innocent, baby boys to grow up to be the dominators that patriarchal societies have historically required. Given my deep belief that we are all really more alike than we are different—hormones vary in both women and men and do not provide the explanation—why would boys agree to a system in which they had to restrict and restrain the women in their lives, whether wives, daughters, or sisters? Current social arrangements in reactionary theocratic

countries show us clear examples of this; women must cover themselves from head to toe and cannot leave their homes without their husband or a male blood relative.

Jesse: It is one question to ask why women would put up with such an arrangement. But given the millennia of male domination, few of us even wonder very long about that; it has been about survival. What is more fascinating to me is why men do. It is too easy to just say that men benefit from the system. While some men benefit, it is also true that most men are afraid. The repercussions for me of not going along are great and real. Men physically and verbally attack, and even kill other men whose way of living defies the normative, heterosexual, patriarchal order. Fathers who turn away from their sons who do not "measure up" help keep the system going.

Men who have looked at patriarchal oppression and its impact on their lives recognize that most men walk around feeling afraid of other men in a different yet similar terror to that which women feel. There is a constant sizing up process going on in which men assess their social standing relative to other men and take action to be in a superior or at least acceptable position. This behavior is both a result of and a cause of bullying. From a very young age, males who are perceived as vulnerable are teased, harassed, and beat up by other boys and men. Teachers and parents come to expect this and allow the "boys will be boys" argument to justify ignoring and masking the reality of this violent social conditioning.

Of course, at some level, men have the most to gain from keeping other men in line. Mocking the sensitive guys who are in egalitarian marriages and who want to stay home with their babies helps keep the tough-guy system functioning. The homophobic insults—sissy, queer, fag—are weapons of sexism that serve to perpetuate a social order in which males are to be "real males" who are superior to women or queers and pass on the oppression of both

Messages females get about sex:	Messages males get about sex:
• Say no to sex (or be swept away). • Pursue love (security, romance). • "Get a man." • Women are to *be*; attractive but passive. • Don't act too knowledgeable about sex or ask for what you want.	• Pursue sex; get as much as you can. • Love is a trap/responsibility. • "Be a man" (get a woman). • Men *do*, plan, accomplish (don't give up; she'll give in). • Act like you know all about sex. Don't ask; just do it.

other males and of females, maintaining the social order.

But it is both women and men who participate in perpetuating the harassment; boys and girls, father and mothers, sisters and brothers, teachers and friends all carry out the socialization process that teaches boys that it's not acceptable to be emotional, to cry, to be seen as weak, or to be anything like girls. Mothers as well as fathers counsel their daughters to become women who will be attractive and acceptable to men; pretty but not too sexy, outgoing but not too pushy, smart but not too accomplished, and so on.

THE FOUR BOXES IN ACTION

The implications of the four boxes are profound. Just look at the messages we get about sexuality. When we've presented this theory in classes and asked students to brainstorm the messages that women and men get about sex, this is what they've created: Let's look at the dynamics behind this. For many males, touching equates with sex. Boys are touched less from the time they are babies, and homophobia keeps them from touching each other, so all their needs for touch must be channeled through the "keyhole" of sex. Males are supposed to "know it all" and be in control. Yet they receive little real information about sexuality from parents or schools; what they know may come from porn. They get pressure from peers to go for it. Some men have sex with females to enhance their status with other males and may bypass learning the sensual, the

sacred beauty of sex as they pursue "it": orgasm. Others, wary of relationships with women, may feel awkward and embarrassed about pursuing sex. Males are "homosocial" (prefer being with males), yet they have higher rates of homophobia, keeping them from having emotionally close male friendships. And males have higher rates of risky behaviors of all types, again in part to impress other males with their toughness and thus their heterosexuality.

Girls are taught not to acknowledge sexual desire or plan for sex, then get caught up in the "swept-away syndrome" (Cassell, 1984), which makes planning for using of birth control and safer sex less likely. The messages are: Don't explore your own "privates," masturbate, or come to orgasm on your own. Don't know or communicate your sexual needs to males (who are supposed to be in control and know what is going on). And don't be angry when he wants more than you feel ready for.

Because females are supposed to say no, and males to pursue sex, neither can easily be honest about what they do and don't want. Neither has a language for talking about sex. Females are socialized to be the relationship builders and may be afraid to put pressure on the relationship for fear of losing it. Males, having been socialized not to have or talk about feelings, may bring less "emotional intelligence" (Goleman, 1997) to relationships, again making honest, intimate communication difficult.

What these historically constructed gender boxes cause is a maze of twisted, strained, and nonexistent communication between men and women. Men are raised to find women attractive for their looks, to desire women sexually, and to open up emotionally only enough to get a woman to have sex with them (or to see female attention as their only outlet for opening up). Women are taught to desire strong men, aggressive and confident men who are born wealthy or will be able to succeed in the male-controlled world of corporate competition. These boxes have often meant that the most attractive women are the "cheerleaders" who are attractive and supportive of male prowess in competition, while the most attractive men are the football quarterbacks, men who are strong, aggressive, respected by other men, and smart enough to "make the play." For everyone else, there is a constant self-criticism that is implanted almost from birth, one that measures our bodies, behaviors, attitudes, and performances against those of the good girls and tough guys.

Yet in everyday life, the sluts/dykes who are strong, self-confident, and independent are often more interesting and dynamic than the nonthreatening good girls, and the fag/sissy is probably better in bed, more caring, and more compassionate a partner than a tough guy.

REEMERGENCE: BREAKING OUT OF THE BOXES

While the picture of traditional gendered sexuality and relationships can be bleak, it is also true that there is not universal participation. There is resistance, now as there has always been. And the resistance may be growing. There is increasing support for change, coming to a large extent from the women's and the gay rights movements of the past 30 years.

There are many men who see themselves as pro-feminist (even if they lack a large visible organization to represent them) and are making changes in their own lives that are liberating, that allow their "sweet self" to emerge

and celebrate itself. And they are finding no shortage of potential partners being interested in them. Such men are willing to risk breaking out of the tough-guy role, the protective and isolating barriers that keep them from truly knowing themselves, other men, women, or their children. But it is also true that there is much less overall societal support for men to change than there is for women. It is more threatening to the patriarchal system for men to claim their "feminine" side than for women to aspire to male values of competition and success (which is, unfortunately, the most concrete way that the feminist movement has made change).

An important ingredient in this emerging change, of imagining and moving into a new partnership-oriented society in which the boxes of gender have much less power, is an understanding and acknowledgement that it hasn't always been this way. The way that men are and women are, and the way we relate with each other. It's been worse, and . . . it's been better. Knowing that can help us now. That is why we spent so much time in this essay telling the story of ancient times.

There is also evidence from other sources. Anthropologist Meredith Small, writing on the evolution of human mating, states (1995, p. 123):

> One cultural strategy to keep women away from other men has been to "castrate" women in the social and psychological sense, and turn them off to sex. Women might be interested in sexual variety, but this kind of behavior is made socially unacceptable in a patriarchal society. . . . Women alone have their reputations ruined when the word gets out they've had sex with many partners.

Small sees strong evidence for a social/cultural explanation (as opposed to an evolutionary biology one) in the narrowing gap between how women and men relate to their sexualities, as women become more liberated. Rates of sexual activity, reports of sexual desire, and enjoyment of sex draw closer and closer in studies as women have more choices in life and face less stigmatization for being sexual.

By paying attention to the history of our ancestors and to evidence from scholars creating new interpretations, we can realize that there is nothing normal or natural about a society that vilifies female sexuality. Then we more fully can believe in the possibility of change.

It means looking as well for models of human society that don't exploit and dominate, models for societies that instead produce for consumption (instead of surplus to support war and conspicuous consumption), allow full partnership and value in various forms of work and play (instead of privileging war, exploitation, and acquisition), and that affirm human connection to the land, the feminine, and to each other. For many young people, challenging the types of gender traps we've been discussing also means challenging the fundamental structures of our society, whether they be capitalist, racist, militarist, or sexist. This has manifested itself in many ways, including the massive antiglobalization movements that have sprung up across the planet in the last 10–200 years. Haitians stood up to colonialism and slavery in the 1790s, and Americans have done so on and off since the days of Tom Paine.

Even some feminists accept the patriarchal notion that humans have always been divided in half by gender, with one half raping and brutalizing the other. They hope that scientific rationalism, based on enlightenment notions of liberty (from 17th- and 18th-century Europe) can create the conditions under which men and women can live as partners. While this hope is certainly valid, by failing to take into account the ways that various tribal societies live today, and that our ancestors once did live, we can easily mistake what is a reality in modern life for what has always been. By remembering the history presented in this article and sharing stories of ancient times, we can see that gender and sexuality are not fixed aspects of our lives. They change over time as the result of religious, political, and military policies.

At a very personal level, it is clear that we need a partnership model for relationships, for families, and for society. We need a way to think about gender that affirms gentleness and nurturance, as well as personal resourcefulness and accomplishment, for both males and females. The "sweet guy" is an integral part of the authentic, conscious male, just as the "bad girl" is a proud, free, sex-affirming part of the authentic, conscious female. A key to this is our ability, as females and males, to accept and affirm all parts of ourselves, instead of denying, running from, or hating (or projecting that hate), the hard, sexual side of women, and the soft, sensual side of men. Denying this leads to depression in women and anger in men. Women implode. Men explode. What we need, if we are to be real with ourselves and with each other, men and women in relationships, is the ability to access our sadness and grieving, as well as healthy expressions of anger when needed for self-protection and defense of our boundaries.

At another level, true partnership will only be possible when we let go of gender dichotomies altogether, or multiply them, as the transgender movement and queer theory suggest. We are neither male nor female as those categories are currently constructed. At some level, we are pure awareness. When we can see spirit in each other and ourselves, we can let go of dominance-oriented "power over" ways of being and cooperate in the ways that "power with" partnerships require. Society will have to change, as will religion and the economy, for the residues of 10,000 years of violence and oppression to be unlearned, but where there has been change, change is possible, and luckily, our history can give us both new memory and hope.

REFERENCES

Buss, D. (1995). *The evolution of desire: Strategies of human mating.* New York: Basic Books.

Cassell, C. (1984). *Swept away: Why women fear their own sexuality.* New York: Simon & Schuster.

Eisler, R. T. (1987). *The chalice and the blade: Our history, our future.* San Francisco: Harper & Row.

Eisler, R. T. (1995). *Sacred pleasure: Sex, myth, and the politics of the body—new paths to power and love.* HarperSan Francisco.

Enheduanna. (2000). *Inanna, lady of largest heart: Poems of the Sumerian high priestess Enheduanna.* B. D. Meader (Ed.). Austin: University of Texas Press.

Faludi, S. (1999). *Stiffed: The betrayal of the American man.* New York: William Morrow.

Goleman, D. (1997). *Emotional intelligence.* New York: Bantam Books.

Gimbutas, M. (1980). *The early civilization of Europe.* (Monograph for Indo-European Studies 131), University of California at Los Angeles.

Gimbutas, M. (1982). *The goddesses and gods of old Europe.* Berkeley: University of California Press.

Grubin, D. (1993). Sexual offending: A cross-cultural comparison. *Annual Review of Sex Research, 3,* pp. 201-217.

Kimmel, M.S., M.A. Messner. (2001). Men's Lives. Boston: Allyn and Bacon.

Kindlon, D. J. and Thompson, M. (1999). *Raising Cain: Protecting the emotional life of boys.* New York: Ballantine.

Levy, R. G. (1948). *The gate of horn: A study of the religious conceptions of the stone age, and their influence upon European thought.* London: Farber & Farber.

Pollack, W. S. (1998). *Real boys: Rescuing our sons from the myths of boyhood.* New York: Random House

Powell, T. G. E. (1966). *Prehistoric art.* London: Thames & Hudson.

Sanday, P. R. (1981). The socio-cultural context of rape: A cross-cultural study. *Journal of Social Issues, 37*(4), pp. 5-27.

Sjoo, M. and Mor, B. (1991). *The great cosmic mother: Rediscovering the religion of the earth.* HarperSan Francisco.

Small, M. F. (1995). *What's love got to do with it? The evolution of human mating.* New York: Anchor.

Starhawk (1990). *Truth or dare: Encounters with power, authority, and mystery.* San Francisco: Harper & Row.

Stone, M. (1976). *When god was a woman.* New York: Harcourt Brace.

Tannahill, R. (1992). *Sex in history.* Rev. Ed. Chelsea, MI: Scarborough House.

Taylor, T. (1996). *The prehistory of sex: Four million years of human sexual culture.* New York: Bantam.

Todorov, T. (1992). *The conquest of America.* New York: Harper Perennial

Walker, B. G. (1983). *Woman's encyclopedia of myths and secrets.* HarperSan Francisco.

Zinn, H. (1995). *A people's history of the United States.* New York: Harper Perennial.

Reconstructing Black Masculinity

bell hooks

Black and white snapshots of my childhood always show me in the company of my brother. Less than a year older than me, we looked like

twins and for a time in life we did everything together. We were inseparable. As young children, we were brother and sister, comrades, in it together. As adolescents, he was forced to become a boy and I was forced to become a girl. In our southern black Baptist patriarchal home, being a boy meant learning to be tough, to mask one's feelings, to stand one's ground and fight—being a girl meant learning to obey, to be quiet, to clean, to recognize that you had no ground to stand on. I was tough, he was not. I was strong willed, he was easygoing. We were both a disappointment. Affectionate, full

Source: bell hooks. *Black Looks: Race Representation.* Copyright © 1992. South End Press, Boston, MA.

of good humor, loving, my brother was not at all interested in becoming a patriarchal boy. This lack of interest generated a fierce anger in our father.

We grew up staring at black and white photos of our father in a boxing ring, playing basketball, with the black infantry he was part of in World War II. He was a man in uniform, a man's man, able to hold his own. Despising his one son for not wanting to become the strong silent type (my brother loved to talk, tell jokes, and make us happy), our father let him know early on that he was no son to him, real sons wanted to be like their fathers. Made to feel inadequate, less than male in his childhood, one boy in a house full of six sisters, he became forever haunted by the idea of patriarchal masculinity. All that he had questioned in his childhood was sought after in his early adult life in order to become a man's man—phallocentric, patriarchal, and masculine. In traditional black communities when one tells a grown male to "be a man," one is urging him to aspire to a masculine identity rooted in the patriarchal ideal. Throughout black male history in the United States there have been black men who were not at all interested in the patriarchal ideal. In the black community of my childhood, there was no monolithic standard of black masculinity. Though the patriarchal ideal was the most esteemed version of manhood, it was not the only version. No one in our house talked about black men being no good, shiftless, trifling. Head of the household, our father was a "much man," a provider, lover, disciplinarian, reader, and thinker. He was introverted, quiet, and slow to anger, yet fierce when aroused. We respected him. We were in awe of him. We were afraid of his power, his physical prowess, his deep voice, and his rare unpredictable but intense rage. We were never allowed to forget that, unlike other black men, our father was the fulfillment of the patriarchal masculine ideal.

Though I admired my father, I was more fascinated and charmed by black men who were not obsessed with being patriarchs: by Felix, a hobo who jumped trains, never worked a regular job, and had a missing thumb; by Kid, who lived out in the country and hunted the rabbits and coons that came to our table; by Daddy Gus, who spoke in hushed tones, sharing his sense of spiritual mysticism. These were the men who touched my heart. The list could go on. I remember them because they loved folks, especially women and children. They were caring and giving. They were black men who chose alternative lifestyles, who questioned the *status quo*, who shunned a ready made patriarchal identity and invented themselves. By knowing them, I have never been tempted to ignore the complexity of black male experience and identity. The generosity of spirit that characterized who they were and how they lived in the world lingers in my memory. I write this piece to honor them, knowing as I do now that it was no simple matter for them to choose against patriarchy, to choose themselves, their lives. And I write this piece for my brother in hopes that he will recover one day, come back to himself, know again the way to love, the peace of an unviolated free spirit. It was this peace that the quest for an unattainable life-threatening patriarchal masculine ideal took from him.

When I left our segregated southern black community and went to a predominately white college, the teachers and students I met knew nothing about the lives of black men. Learning about the matriarchy myth and white culture's notion that black men were emasculated, I was shocked. These theories did not speak to the world I had most intimately known, did not address the complex gender roles that were so familiar to me. Much of the scholarly work on black masculinity that was presented in the classroom then was based on material gleaned from studies of urban black life. This work conveyed the message that black masculinity was homogenous. It suggested that all black men were tormented by their inability to fulfill the phallocentric masculine ideal as it has been articulated in white supremacist capitalist patriarchy. Erasing the realities of black men who have diverse understandings of masculinity, scholarship on the black family (traditionally the framework for academic discussion of black masculinity) puts in place of this lived complexity a flat, one-dimensional representation.

The portrait of black masculinity that emerges in this work perpetually constructs black men as "failures" who are psychologically "fucked up," dangerous, violent, sex maniacs whose insanity is informed by their inability to fulfill their phallocentric masculine destiny in a racist context. Much of this literature is written by white people, and some of it by a few academic black men. It does not interrogate the conventional construction of patriarchal masculinity or question the extent to which black men have historically internalized this norm. It never assumes the existence of black men whose creative agency has enabled them to subvert norms and develop ways of thinking about masculinity that challenge patriarchy. Yet, there has never been a time in the history of the United States when black folks, particularly black men, have not been enraged by the dominant culture's stereotypical, fantastical representations of black masculinity. Unfortunately, black people have not systematically challenged these narrow visions, insisting on a more accurate "reading" of black male reality. Acting in complicity with the *status quo,* many black people have passively absorbed narrow representations of black masculinity, perpetuated stereotypes, myths, and offered one-dimensional accounts. Contemporary black men have been shaped by these representations.

No one has yet endeavored to chart the journey of black men from Africa to the so called "new world" with the intent to reconstruct how they saw themselves. Surely the black men who came to the American continent before Columbus, saw themselves differently from those who were brought on slave ships, or from those few who freely immigrated to a world where the majority of their brethren were enslaved. Given all that we know of the slave context, it is unlikely that enslaved black men spoke the same language, or that they bonded on the basis of shared "male" identity. Even if they had come from cultures where gender difference was clearly articulated in relation to specific roles that was all disrupted in the "new world" context. Transplanted African men, even those who were coming from cultures where sex roles shaped the division of labor, where the status of men was different and most often higher than that of females, had imposed on them the white colonizer's notions of manhood and masculinity. Black men did not respond to this imposition passively. Yet it is evident in black male slave narratives that black men engaged in racial uplift were often most likely to accept the norms of masculinity set by white culture.

Although the gendered politics of slavery denied black men the freedom to act as "men" within the definition set by white norms, this notion of manhood did become a standard used to measure black male progress. Slave narratives document ways black men thought about manhood. The narratives of Henry "Box" Brown, Josiah Henson, Frederick Douglass, and a host of other black men reveal that they saw "freedom" as that change in status that would enable them to fulfill the role of chivalric benevolent patriarch. Free, they would be men able to provide for and take care of their families. Describing how he wept as he watched a white slave overseer beat his mother, William Wells Brown lamented,

"Experience has taught me that nothing can be more heart-rending than for one to see a dear and beloved mother or sister tortured, and to hear their cries and not be able to render them assistance. But such is the position which an American slave occupies." Frederick Douglass did not feel his manhood affirmed by intellectual progress. It was affirmed when he fought man to man with the slave overseer. This struggle was a "turning point" in Douglass' life: "It rekindled in my breast the smoldering embers of liberty. It brought up my Baltimore dreams and revived a sense of my own manhood. I was a changed being after that fight. I was nothing before—I was a man now." The image of black masculinity that emerges from slave narratives is one of hardworking men who longed to assume full patriarchal responsibility for families and kin.

Given this aspiration and the ongoing brute physical labor of black men that was the backbone of slave economy (there were more male slaves than black female slaves, particularly before breeding became a common practice), it is really amazing that stereotypes of black men as lazy and shiftless so quickly became common in public imagination. In these 19th and early 20th-century representations, black men were cartoon-like creatures only interested in drinking and having a good time. Such stereotypes were an effective way for white racists to erase the significance of black male labor from public consciousness. Later on, these same stereotypes were evoked as reasons to deny black men jobs. They are still evoked today.

Male "idleness" did not have the same significance in African and Native American cultures that it had in the white mindset. Many 19th-century Christians saw all forms of idle activity as evil, or at least a breeding ground for wrong-doing. For Native Americans and Africans, idle time was space for reverie and contemplation. When slavery ended, black men could once again experience that sense of space. There are no studies which explore the way Native American cultures altered notions of black masculinity, especially for those black men who lived as Indians or who married Indian wives. Since we know there were many tribes who conceived of masculine roles in ways that were quite different from those of whites, black men may well have found African ideas about gender roles affirmed in Native traditions.

There are also few confessional narratives by black men that chronicle how they felt as a group when freedom did not bring with it the opportunity for them to assume a "patriarchal" role. Those black men who worked as farmers were often better able to assume this role than those who worked as servants or who moved to cities. Certainly, in the mass migration from the rural south to the urban north, black men lost status. In southern black communities there were many avenues for obtaining communal respect. A man was not respected solely because he could work, make money, and provide. The extent to which a given black man absorbed white society's notion of manhood likely determined the extent of his bitterness and despair that white supremacy continually blocked his access to the patriarchal ideal.

Nineteenth century black leaders were concerned about gender roles. While they believed that men should assume leadership positions in the home and public life, they were also concerned about the role of black women in racial uplift. Whether they were merely paying lip-service to the cause of women's rights or were true believers, exceptional individual black men advocated equal rights for black women. In his work, Martin Delaney continually stressed that both genders needed to work in the interest of racial uplift. To him, gender equality was more a way to have greater involvement in racial uplift than away for black women to be autonomous and independent. Black male leaders like Martin Delaney and Frederick

Douglass were patriarchs, but as benevolent dictators they were willing to share power with women, especially if it meant they did not have to surrender any male privilege. As co-editors of the *North Star*, Douglass and Delaney had a masthead in 1847 which read "right is of no sex—truth is of no color. . . ." The 1848 meeting of the National Negro Convention included a proposal by Delaney stating: "Whereas we fully believe in the equality of the sexes, therefore, resolved that we hereby invite females hereafter to take part in our deliberation." In Delaney's 1852 treatise *The Condition, Elevation, Emigration, and Destiny of the Colored People of the United States, Politically Considered*, he argued that black women should have full access to education so that they could be better mothers, asserting:

> The potency and respectability of a nation or people, depends entirely upon the position of their women; therefore, it is essential to our elevation that the female portion of our children be instructed in all the arts and sciences pertaining to the highest civilization.

In Delaney's mind, equal rights for black women in certain public spheres such as education did not mean that he was advocating a change in domestic relations whereby black men and women would have co-equal status in the home.

Most 19th-century black men were not advocating equal rights for women. On one hand, most black men recognized the powerful and necessary role black women had played as freedom fighters in the movement to abolish slavery and other civil rights efforts, yet on the other hand they continued to believe that women should be subordinate to men. They wanted black women to conform to the gender norms set by white society. They wanted to be recognized as "men," as patriarchs, by other men, including white men. Yet they could not assume this position if black women were not willing to conform to prevailing sexist gender norms. Many black women who had endured white supremacist patriarchal domination during slavery did not want to be dominated by black men after manumission. Like black men, they had contradictory positions on gender. On one hand they did not want to be "dominated," but on the other hand they wanted black men to be protectors and providers. After slavery ended, enormous tension and conflict emerged between black women and men as folks struggled to be self-determining. As they worked to create standards for community and family life, gender roles continued to be problematic.

Black men and women who wanted to conform to gender role norms found that this was nearly impossible in a white racist economy that wanted to continue its exploitation of black labor. Much is made, by social critics who want to further the notion that black men are symbolically castrated, of the fact that black women often found work in service jobs while black men were unemployed. The reality, however, was that in some homes it was problematic when a black woman worked and the man did not, or when she earned more than he, yet, in other homes, black men were quite content to construct alternative roles. Critics who look at black life from a sexist standpoint advance the assumption that black men were psychologically devastated because they did not have the opportunity to slave away in low paying jobs for white racist employers when the truth may very well be that those black men who wanted to work but could not find jobs, as well as those who did not want to find jobs, may simply have felt relieved that they did not have to submit to economic exploitation. Concurrently, there were black women who wanted black men to assume patriarchal roles and there were some who were content to be autonomous, independent. And long before contemporary feminist movement sanctioned the idea that men could remain home and rear children while women worked, black women and men had such arrangements and were happy with them.

Without implying that black women and men lived in gender utopia, I am suggesting that black sex roles, and particularly the role of men, have been more complex and problematized in black life than is believed. This was especially the case when all black people lived in segregated neighborhoods. Racial integration has had a profound impact on black gender roles. It has helped to promote a climate wherein most black women and men accept sexist notions of gender roles. Unfortunately, many changes have occurred in the way black people think about gender, yet the shift from one standpoint to another has not been fully documented. For example: To what extent did the civil rights movement, with its definition of freedom as having equal opportunity with whites, sanction looking at white gender roles as a norm black people should imitate? Why has there been so little positive interest shown in the alternative lifestyles of black men? In every segregated black community in the United States there are adult black men married, unmarried, gay, straight, living in households where they do not assert patriarchal domination and yet live fulfilled lives, where they are not sitting around worried about castration. Again it must be emphasized that the black men who are most worried about castration and emasculation are those who have completely absorbed white supremacist patriarchal definitions of masculinity.

Advanced capitalism further changed the nature of gender roles for all men in the United States. The image of the patriarchal head of the household, ruler of this mini-state called the "family," faded in the 20th century. More men than ever before worked for someone else. The state began to interfere more in domestic matters. A man's time was not his own; it belonged to his employer, and the terms of his rule in the family were altered. In the old days, a man who had no money could still assert tyrannic rule over family and kin, by virtue of his patriarchal status, usually affirmed by Christian belief systems. Within a burgeoning capitalist economy, it was wage-earning power that determined the extent to which a man would rule over a household, and even that rule was limited by the power of the state. In *White Hero, Black Beast,* Paul Hoch describes the way in which advanced capitalism altered representations of masculinity:

> The concept of masculinity is dependent at its very root on the concepts of sexual repression and private property. Ironically, it is sexual repression and economic scarcity that give masculinity its main significance as a symbol of economic status and sexual opportunity. The shrinkage of the concept of man into the narrowed and hierarchical conceptions of masculinity of the various work and consumption ethics also goes hand in hand with an increasing social division of labor, and an increasing shrinkage of the body's erogenous potentials culminating in a narrow genital sexuality. As we move from the simpler food-gathering societies to the agricultural society to the urbanized work and warfare society, we notice that it is a narrower and narrower range of activities that yield masculine status.

In feminist terms, this can be described as a shift from emphasis on patriarchal status (determined by one's capacity to assert power over others in a number of spheres based on maleness) to a phallocentric model, where what the male does with his penis becomes a greater and certainly a more accessible way to assert masculine status. It is easy to see how this served the interests of a capitalist state which was indeed depriving men of their rights, exploiting their labor in such a way that they only indirectly received the benefits, to deflect away from a patriarchal power based on ruling others and to emphasize a masculine status that would depend solely on the penis.

With the emergence of a fierce phallocentrism, a man was no longer a man because he provided care for his family, he was a man simply because he had a penis. Furthermore, his ability to use that penis in the arena of sexual conquest could bring him as much status as being a wage earner and provider. A sexually defined masculine ideal rooted in physical domination and sexual possession of women could be accessible to all men. Hence, even unemployed black men could gain status, could be seen as the embodiment of masculinity, within a phallocentric framework. Barbara Ehrenreich's *The Hearts of Men* chronicles white male repudiation of a masculine ideal rooted in a notion of patriarchal rule requiring a man to marry and care for the material well-being of women and children and an increasing embrace of a phallocentric "playboy" ideal. At the end of the chapter "Early Rebels," Ehrenreich describes rites of passage in the 1950s which led white men away from traditional nonconformity into a rethinking of masculine status:

> not every would-be male rebel had the intellectual reserves to gray gracefully with the passage of the decade. They drank beyond excess, titrating gin with coffee in their lunch hours, gin with Alka-Seltzer on the weekends. They had stealthy affairs with secretaries, and tried to feel up their neighbors' wives at parties. They escaped into Mickey Spillane mysteries, where naked blondes were routinely perforated in a hail of bullets, or into Westerns, where there were no women at all and no visible sources of white-collar employment. And some of them began to discover an alternative, or at least an entirely new style of male rebel who hinted, seductively, that there was an alternative. The new rebel was the playboy.

Even in the restricted social relations of slavery black men had found a way to practice the fine art of phallocentric seduction. Long before white men stumbled upon the "playboy" alternative, black vernacular culture told stories about that non-working man with time on his hands who might be seducing somebody else's woman. Blues songs narrate the "play-

boy" role. Ehrenreich's book acknowledges that the presence of black men in segregated black culture and their engagement in varied expressions of masculinity influenced white men:

> The Beat hero, the male rebel who actually walks away from responsibility in any form, was not a product of middle-class angst. The possibility of walking out, without money or guilt, and without ambition other than to see and do everything, was not even imminent in the middle-class culture of the early fifties. . . . The new bohemianism of the Beats came from somewhere else entirely, from an underworld and an underclass invisible from the corporate "crystal palace" or suburban dream houses.

Alternative male lifestyles that opposed the *status quo* were to be found in black culture.

White men seeking alternatives to a patriarchal masculinity turned to black men, particularly black musicians. Norman Podhoretz's 1963 essay "My Negro Problem—And Ours" names white male fascination with blackness, and black masculinity:

> Just as in childhood I envied Negroes for what seemed to me their superior masculinity, so I envy them today for what seems to be their superior physical grace and beauty. I have come to value physical grace very highly and I am now capable of aching with all my being when I watch a Negro couple on the dance floor, or a Negro playing baseball or basketball. They are on the kind of terms with their own bodies that I should like to be on with mine, and for that precious quality they seem blessed to me.

Black masculinity, as fantasized in the. racist white imagination, is the quintessential embodiment of man as "outsider" and "rebel". They were the ultimate "traveling men" drifting from place to place, town to town, job to job.

Within segregated black communities, the "traveling" black man was admired even as he was seen as an indictment of the failure of black men to achieve the patriarchal masculine ideal: Extolling the virtues of traveling black men in her novels, Toni Morrison sees them as "truly masculine in the sense of going out so far where you're not supposed to go and running toward confrontations rather than away from them." This is a man who takes risks, what Morrison calls, a "free man":

> This is a man who is stretching, you know, he's stretching, he's going all the way within his own mind and within whatever his outline might be. Now that's the tremendous possibility for masculinity among black men. And you see it a lot. . . . They may end up in sort of twentieth-century, contemporary terms being also unemployed. They may be in prison. They may be doing all sorts of things. But they are adventuresome in that regard.

Within white supremacist capitalist patriarchy rebel black masculinity has been idolized and punished, romanticized yet vilified. Though the traveling man repudiates being a patriarchal provider, he does not necessarily repudiate male domination.

Collectively, black men have never critiqued the dominant culture's norms of masculine identity, even though they have reworked those norms to suit their social situation. Black male sociologist Robert Staples argues that the black male is "in conflict with the normative definition of masculinity," yet this conflict has never assumed the form of complete rebellion. Assuming that black men are "crippled emotionally" when they cannot fully achieve the patriarchal ideal, Staples asserts: "This is a status which few, if any, black males have been able to achieve. Masculinity, as defined in this culture, has always implied a certain autonomy and mastery of one's environment." Though Staples suggests,. "the black male has always had to confront the contradiction between the normative expectation attached to being male in this society and proscriptions on his behavior and achievement of

goals," implicit in his analysis is the assumption that black men could only internalize this norm and be victimized by it. Like many black men, he assumes that patriarchy and male domination is not a socially constructed social order but a "natural" fact of life. He therefore cannot acknowledge that black men could have asserted meaningful agency by repudiating the norms white culture was imposing.

These norms could not be repudiated by black men who saw nothing problematic or wrong minded about them. Staples, like most black male scholars writing about black masculinity, does not attempt to deconstruct nominative thinking, he laments that black men have not had full access to patriarchal phallocentrism. Embracing the phallocentric ideal, he explains black male rape of women by seeing it as a reaction against their inability to be "real men" (i.e., assert legitimate domination over women). Explaining rape, Staples argues:

> In the case of black men, it is asserted that they grow up feeling emasculated and powerless before reaching manhood. They often encounter women as authority figures and teachers or as the head of their household. These men consequently act out their feelings of powerlessness against black women in the form of sexual aggression. Hence, rape by black men should be viewed as both an aggressive and political act because it occurs in the context of racial discrimination which denies most black men a satisfying manhood.

Staples does not question why black women are the targets of black male aggression if it is white men and a white racist system which prevents them from assuming the "patriarchal" role. Given that many white men who fully achieve normal masculinity rape, his implied argument that black men would not rape if they could be patriarchs seems ludicrous. And his suggestion that they would not rape if they could achieve a "satisfying manhood" is pure fantasy. Given the context of this paragraph, it is safe to assume that the "satisfying manhood" he evokes carries with it the phallocentric right of men to dominate women, however benevolently. Ultimately, he is suggesting that if black men could legitimately dominate women more effectively they would not need to coerce them outside the law. Growing up in a black community where there were individual black men who critiqued normative masculinity, who repudiated patriarchy and its concomitant support of sexism, I fully appreciate that it is a tremendous loss that there is little known of their ideas about black masculinity. Without documentation of their presence, it has been easier for black men who embrace patriarchal masculinity, phallocentrism, and sexism to act as though they speak for all black men. Since their representations of black masculinity are in complete agreement with white culture's assessment, they do not threaten or challenge white domination, they reinscribe it.

Contemporary black power movement made synonymous black liberation and the effort to create a social structure wherein black men could assert themselves as patriarchs, controlling community, family, and kin. On one hand, black men expressed contempt for white men yet they also envied them their access to patriarchal power. Using a "phallocentric" stick to beat white men, Amiri Baraka asserted in his 1960s essay "american sexual reference: black male":

> Most American white men are trained to be fags. For this reason it is no wonder that their faces are weak and blank, left without the hurt that reality makes—anytime. That red flush, those silk blue faggot eyes. . . . They are the 'masters' of the world, and their children are taught this as God's fingerprint, so they can devote most of their energies to the nonrealistic, having no use for the real. They devote their energies to the nonphysical, the nonrealistic, and become estranged from them. Even their wars move to the stage where whole populations can be destroyed

> by pushing a button. . . . can you, for a second imagine the average middle class white man able to do somebody harm? Alone? Without the technology that at this moment still has him rule the world: Do you understand the softness of the white man, the weakness. . . .

This attack on white masculinity, and others like it, did not mean that black men were attacking normative masculinity, they were simply pointing out that white men had not fulfilled the ideal. It was a case of "will the real man please stand up." And when he stood up, he was, in the eyes of black power movement, a black male.

This phallocentric idealization of masculinity is most powerfully expressed in the writings of George Jackson. Throughout *Soledad Brother,* he announces his uncritical acceptance of patriarchal norms, especially the use of violence as a means of social control. Critical of nonviolence as a stance that would un-man black males, he insisted:

> The symbol of the male here in North American has always been the gun, the knife, the club. Violence is extolled at every exchange: the TV, the motion pictures, the best-seller lists. The newspapers that sell best are those that carry the boldest, bloodiest headlines and most sports coverage. To die for king and country is to die a hero.

Jackson felt black males would need to embrace this use of violence if they hoped to defeat white adversaries. And he is particularly critical of black women for not embracing these notions of masculinity:

> I am reasonably certain that I draw from every black male in this country some comments to substantiate that his mother, the black female, attempted to aid his survival by discouraging his violence or by turning it inward. The blacks of slave society, U.S.A., have always been a matriarchal subsociety. The implication is clear, black mama is going to have to put a sword in that brother's hand and stop that "be a good boy" shit.

A frighteningly fierce misogyny informs Jackson's rage at black women, particularly his mother. Even though he was compelled by black women activists and comrades to reconsider his position on gender, particularly by Angela Davis, his later work, *Blood in My Eye*, continues to see black liberation as a "male thing," to see revolution as a task for men:

> At the end of this massive collective struggle, we will uncover a new man, the unpredictable culmination of the revolutionary process. He will be better equipped to wage the real struggle, the permanent struggle after the revolution—the one for new relationships between men.

Although the attitudes expressed by Baraka and Jackson appear dated, they have retained their ideological currency among black men through time. Black female critiques of black male phallocentrism and sexism have had little impact on black male consciousness. Michele Wallace's *Black Macho and the Myth of the SuperWoman* was the first major attempt by a black woman to speak from a feminist standpoint about black male sexism. Her analysis of black masculinity was based primarily on her experience in the urban northern cities, yet she wrote as if she were speaking comprehensively about collective black experience. Even so, her critique was daring and courageous. However, like other critics she evoked a monolithic homogenous representation of black masculinity. Discussing the way black male sexism took precedence over racial solidarity during Shirley Chisolm's presidential campaign, Wallace wrote:

> The black political forces in existence at the time—in other words, the black male political forces—did not support her. In fact, they actively opposed her nomination. The black man in the street seemed either outraged that she dared to run or simply indifferent.
>
> Ever since then it has really baffled me to hear black men say that black women have no time for feminism because being black comes first. For them, when it came to Shirley Chisholm, being black no longer came first at all. It turned out that what they really meant all along was that the black man came before the black woman.

Chisholm documented in her autobiography that sexism stood in her way more than racism. Yet she also talks about the support she received from her father and her husband for her political work. Commenting on the way individuals tried to denigrate this support by hinting that there was something wrong with her husband, Chisholm wrote: "Thoughtless people have suggested that my husband would have to be a weak man who enjoys having me dominate him. They are wrong on both counts." Though fiercely critical of sexism in general and black male sexism in particular, Chisholm acknowledged the support she had received from black men who were not advancing patriarchy. Any critique of "black macho," of black male sexism, that does not acknowledge the actions of black men who subvert and challenge the *status quo* can not be an effective critical intervention. If feminist critics ignore the efforts of individual black men to oppose sexism, our critiques seem to be self-serving, appear to be anti-male rather than anti-sexist. Absolutist portraits that imply that all black men are irredeemably sexist, inherently supportive of male domination, make it appear that there is no way to change this, no alternative, no other way to be. When attention is focused on those black men who oppose sexism, who are disloyal to patriarchy, even if they are exceptions, the possibility for change, for resistance is affirmed. Those representations of black gender relationships that perpetually pit black women and men against one another deny the complexity of our experiences and intensify mutually destructive internecine gender conflict.

More than ten years have passed since Michele Wallace encouraged black folks to take gender conflict as a force that was undermining our solidarity and creating tension. Without biting her tongue, Wallace emphatically stated:

> I am saying, among other things, that for perhaps the last fifty years there has been a growing distrust, even hatred, between black men and black women. It has been nursed along not only by racism on the part of whites but also by an almost deliberate ignorance on the part of blacks about the sexual politics of their experience in this country.

The tensions Wallace describes between black women and men have not abated, if anything they have worsened. In more recent years they have taken the public form of black women an men competing for the attention of a white audience. Whether it be the realm of job hunting or book publishing, there is a prevailing sense within white supremacist capitalist patriarchy that black men and women cannot both be in the dominant culture's limelight. While it obviously serves the interests of white supremacy for black women and men to be divided from one another, perpetually in conflict, there is no overall gain for black men and women. Sadly, black people collectively refuse to take seriously issues of gender that would undermine the support for male domination in black communities.

Since the 1960s black power movement had worked over-time to let sisters know that they should assume a subordinate role to lay the groundwork for an emergent black patriarchy that would elevate the status of black males, women's liberation movement has been seen as a threat. Consequently, black women were and are encouraged to think that any involvement with feminism was/is tantamount to betraying the race. Such thinking has not really altered over time. It has become more entrenched. Black people responded with rage and anger to Wallace's book, charging that she was a puppet of white feminists who were motivated by vengeful hatred of black men,

but they never argued that her assessment of black male sexism was false. They critiqued her harshly because they sincerely believed that sexism was not a problem in black life and that black female support of black patriarchy and phallocentrism might heal the wounds inflicted by racist domination. As long as black people foolishly cling to the rather politically naive and dangerous assumption that it is in the interests of black liberation to support sexism and male domination, all our efforts to decolonize our minds and transform society will fail.

Perhaps black folks cling to the fantasy that phallocentrism and patriarchy will provide a way out of the havoc and wreckage wreaked by racist genocidal assault because it is an analysis of our current political situation that places a large measure of the blame on the black community, the black family, and, most specifically, black women. This way of thinking means that black people do not have to envision creative strategies for confronting and resisting white supremacy and internalized racism. Tragically, internecine gender conflict between black women and men strengthens white supremacist capitalist patriarchy. Politically behind the times where gender is concerned, many black people lack the skills to function in a changed and changing world. They remain unable to grapple with a contemporary reality where male domination is consistently challenged and under siege. Primarily it is white male advocates of feminist politics who do the scholarly work that shows the crippling impact of contemporary patriarchy on men, particularly those groups of men who do not receive maximum benefit from this system. Writing about the way patriarchal masculinity undermines the ability of males to construct self and identity with their well-being in mind, creating a life-threatening masculinist sensibility, these works rarely discuss black men.

Most black men remain in a state of denial, refusing to acknowledge the pain in their lives that is caused by sexist thinking and patriarchal, phallocentric violence that is not only expressed by male domination over women but also by internecine conflict among black men. Black people must question why it is that, as white culture has responded to changing gender roles and feminist movement, they have turned to black culture and particularly to black men for articulations of misogyny, sexism, and phallocentrism. In popular culture, representations of black masculinity equate it with brute phallocentrism, woman hating, a pugilistic "rapist" sexuality, and flagrant disregard for individual rights. Unlike the young George Jackson who, however wrong-minded, cultivated a patriarchal masculinist ethic in the interest of providing black males with a revolutionary political consciousness and a will to resist race and class domination, contemporary young black males espousing a masculinist ethic are not radicalized or insightful about the collective future of black people.

Public figures such as Eddie Murphy, Arsenio Hall, Chuck D., Spike Lee, and a host of other black males blindly exploit the commodification of blackness and the concomitant exotification of phallocentric black masculinity.

When Eddie Murphy's film *Raw* (which remains one of the most graphic spectacles of black male phallocentrism) was first shown in urban cities, young black men in the audience gave black power salutes. This film not only did not address the struggle of black people to resist racism, Murphy's evocation of homosocial bonding with rich white men against "threatening" women who want to take their money conveyed his conservative politics. *Raw* celebrates a pugilistic eroticism, the logic of which tells young men that women do not want to hear declarations of love but want to be "fucked to death." Women are represented strictly in misogynist terms—they are evil; they are all prostitutes who see their sexuality solely as a commodity to be exchanged for hard cash, and after the man has delivered the goods they betray him. Is this the "satisfying masculinity" black men desire or does it expose a warped and limited vision of sexuality, one that could not possibly offer fulfillment or sexual healing? As phallocentric spectacle, *Raw* announces that black men are controlled by their penises ("it's a dick thing") and asserts a sexual politic that is fundamentally anti-body.

If the black male cannot "trust" his body not to be the agent of his victimization, how can he trust a female body? Indeed, the female body, along with the female person, is constructed in *Raw* as threatening to the male who seeks autonomous self-hood since it is her presence that awakens phallocentric response. Hence her personhood must be erased; she must be like the phallus, a "thing." Commenting on the self-deception that takes place when men convince themselves and one another that women are not persons, in her essay on patriarchal phallocentrism "The Problem That Has No Name," Marilyn Frye asserts:

> The rejection of females by phallists is both morally and conceptually profound. The refusal to perceive females as persons is conceptually profound because it excludes females from that community whose conceptions of things one allows to influence one's concepts—it serves as a police lock on a closed mind. Furthermore, the refusal to treat women with the respect due to persons is in itself a violation of a moral principle that seems to many to be the founding principle of all morality. This violation of moral principle is sustained by an active manipulation of circumstances that is systematic and habitual and unacknowledged. The exclusion of women from the conceptual community simultaneously excludes them from the moral community.

Black male phallocentrism constructs a portrait of woman as immoral, simultaneously suggesting that she is irrational and incapable of reason. Therefore, there is no need for black men to listen to women or to assume that women have knowledge to share.

It is this representation of womanhood that is graphically evoked in Murphy's film *Harlem Nights*. A dramatization of black male patriarchal fantasies, this film reinvents the history of Harlem so that black men do not appear as cowards unable to confront racist white males but are reinscribed as tough, violent; they talk shit and take none. Again, the George Jackson revolutionary political paradigm is displaced in the realm of the cultural. In this fantasy, black men are as able and willing to assert power "by any means necessary" as are white men. They are shown as having the same desires as white men; they long for wealth, power to dominate others, freedom to kill with impunity, autonomy, and the right to sexually possess women. They embrace notions of hierarchical rule. The most powerful black man in the film, Quick (played by Murphy), always submits to the will of his father. In this world where homosocial black male bonding is glorified and celebrated, black women are sex objects. The only woman who is not a sex object is the post-menopausal mama/matriarch. She is dethroned so that Quick can assert his power, even though he later (again submitting to the father's will) asks her forgiveness. *Harlem Nights* is a sad fantasy, romanticizing a world of misogynist homosocial bonding where everyone is dysfunctional and no one is truly cared for, loved, or emotionally fulfilled.

Despite all the male bluster, Quick, a quintessential black male hero, longs to be loved. Choosing to seek the affections of an unavailable and unattainable black woman (the mistress of the most powerful white man), Quick does attempt to share himself, to drop the masculine mask and be "real" (symbolized by his willingness to share his real name). Yet the black woman he chooses rejects him, only seeking his favors when she is ordered to by the white man who possesses her. It is a tragic

vision of black heterosexuality. Both black woman and black man are unable to respond fully to one another because they are so preoccupied with the white power structure, with the white man. The most valued black woman "belongs" to a white man who willingly exchanges her sexual favors in the interest of business. Desired by black and white men alike (it is their joint lust that renders her more valuable, black men desire her because white men desire her and *vice versa*), her internalized racism and her longing for material wealth and power drive her to act in complicity with white men against black men. Before she can carry out her mission to kill him, Quick shoots her after they have had sexual intercourse. Not knowing that he has taken the bullets from her gun, she points it, telling him that her attack is not personal but "business." Yet when he kills her he makes a point of saying that it is "personal." This was a very sad moment in the film, in that he destroys her, because she rejects his authentic need for love and care.

Contrary to the phallocentric representation of black masculinity that has been on display throughout the film, the woman-hating black men are really shown to be in need of love from females. Orphaned, Quick, who is "much man" seeking love, demonstrates his willingness to be emotionally vulnerable, to share only to be rejected, humiliated. This drama of internecine conflict between black women and men follows the conventional sexist line that sees black women as betraying black men by acting in complicity with white patriarchy. This notion of black female complicity and betrayal is so fixed in the minds of many black men they are unable to perceive any flaws in its logic. It certainly gives credence to Michele Wallace's assertion that black people do not have a clear understanding of black sexual politics. Black men who advance the notion that black women are complicit with white men make this assessment without ever invoking historical documentation. Indeed, annals of history abound that document the opposite assumption, showing that black women have typically acted in solidarity with black men. While it may be accurate to argue that sexist black women are complicit with white supremacist capitalist patriarchy, so are sexist black men. Yet most black men continue to deny their complicity.

Spike Lee's recent film *Mo' Better Blues* is another tragic vision of contemporary black heterosexuality. Like *Harlem Nights,* it focuses on a world of black male homosocial bonding where black women are seen primarily as sex objects. Even when they have talent, as the black female jazz singer Clarke does, they must still exchange their sexual favors for recognition. Like Quick, Bleek, the black hero, seeks recognition of his value in heterosexual love relations. Yet he is unable to see the "value" of the two black women who care for him. Indeed, scenes where he makes love to Clarke and alternately sees her as Indigo and *vice versa* suggest the dixie cup sexist mentality (i.e., all women are alike). And even after his entire world has fallen apart he never engages in a self-critique that might lead him to understand that phallocentrism (he is constantly explaining himself by saying "it's a dick thing") has blocked his ability to develop a mature adult identity, has rendered him unable to confront pain and move past denial. Spike Lee's use of Murphy's phrase establishes a continuum of homosocial bonding between black men that transcends the cinematic fiction.

Ironically, the film suggests that Bleek's nihilism and despair can only be addressed by a rejection of a playboy, "dick thing" masculinity and the uncritical acceptance of the traditional patriarchal role. His life crisis is resolved by the reinscription of a patriarchal paradigm. Since Clarke is no longer available, he seeks comfort with Indigo, pleads with her to "save his life." Spike Lee, like Murphy to some extent, exposes the essential self-serving narcissism and denial of community that is at the heart of phallocen-

trism. He does not, however, envision a radical alternative. The film suggests Bleek has no choice and can only reproduce the same family narrative from which he has emerged, effectively affirming the appropriateness of a nuclear family paradigm where women as mothers restrict black masculinity, black male creativity, and fathers hint at the possibility of freedom. Domesticity represents a place where one's life is "safe" even though one's creativity is contained. The nightclub represents a world outside the home where creativity flourishes and with it an uninhibited eroticism, only that world is one of risk. It is threatening.

The "love supreme" (Coltrane's music and image is a motif throughout the film) that exists between Indigo and Bleek appears shallow and superficial. No longer sex object to be "boned" whenever Bleek desires, her body becomes the vessel for the reproduction of himself *via* having a son. Self-effacing, Indigo identifies Bleek's phallocentrism by telling him he is a "dog," but ultimately she rescues the "dog." His willingness to marry her makes up for dishonesty, abuse, and betrayal. The redemptive love Bleek seeks cannot really be found in the model Lee offers and as a consequence this film is yet another masculine fantasy denying black male agency and capacity to assume responsibility for their personal growth and salvation. The achievement of this goal would mean they must give up phallocentrism and envision new ways of thinking about black masculinity.

Even though individual black women adamantly critique black male sexism, most black men continue to act as though sexism is not a problem in black life and refuse to see it as the force motivating oppressive exploitation of women and children by black men. If any culprit is identified, it is racism. Like Staples' suggestion that the explanation of why black men rape is best understood in a context where racism is identified as the problem, any explanation that evokes a critique of black male phallocentrism is avoided. Black men and women who espouse cultural nationalism continue to see the struggle for black liberation largely as a struggle to recover black manhood. In her essay "Africa On My Mind: Gender, Counter Discourse and African-American Nationalism," E. Frances White shows that overall black nationalist perspectives on gender are rarely rooted purely in the Afrocentric logic they seek to advance, but rather reveal their ties to white paradigms:

> In making appeals to conservative notions of appropriate gender behavior, African-American nationalists reveal their ideological ties to other nationalist movements, including European and Euro-American bourgeois nationalists over the past 200 years. These parallels exist despite the different class and power base of these movements.

Most black nationalists, men and women, refuse to acknowledge the obvious ways patriarchal phallocentric masculinity is a destructive force in black life, the ways it undermines solidarity between black women and men, or how it is life-threatening to black men. Even though individual black nationalists like Haki Madhubuti speak against sexism, progressive Afrocentric thinking does not have the impact that the old guard message has. Perhaps it provides sexist black men with a sense of power and agency (however illusory) to see black women, and particularly feminist black women, as the enemy that prevents them from fully participating in this society. For such fiction gives them an enemy that can be confronted, attacked, annihilated, an enemy that can be conquered, dominated.

Confronting white supremacist capitalist patriarchy would not provide sexist black men with an immediate sense of agency or victory. Blaming black women, however, makes it possible for black men to negotiate with white people in all areas of their lives without vigilantly interrogating those interactions. A good example of this displacement is evident in Brent Staples' essay "The White Girl Problem." Defending his "politically incorrect taste in women" (i.e., his preference for white female partners), from attacking black women, Staples never interrogates his desire. He does not seek to understand the extent to which white supremacist capitalist patriarchy determines his desire. He does not want desire to be politicized. And of course his article does not address white female racism or discuss the fact that a white person does not have to be anti-racist to desire a black partner. Many interracial relationships have their roots in racist constructions of the Other. By focusing in a stereotypical way on black women's anger, Staples can avoid these issues and depoliticize the politics of black and white female interactions. His essay would have been a needed critical intervention had he endeavored to explore the way individuals maintain racial solidarity even as they bond with folks outside their particular group.

Solidarity between black women and men continues to be undermined by sexism and misogyny. As black women increasingly oppose and challenge male domination, internecine tensions abound. Publicly, many of the gender conflicts between black women and men have been exposed in recent years with the increasingly successful commodification of black women's writing. Indeed, gender conflict between sexist black male writers and those black female writers who are seen as feminists has been particularly brutal. Black male critic Stanley Crouch has been one of the leading voices mocking and ridiculing black women. His recently published collection of essays, *Notes of a Hanging Judge,* includes articles that are particularly scathing in their attacks on black women.

His critique of Wallace's *Black Macho* is mockingly titled "Aunt Jemima Don't Like Uncle Ben" (notice that the emphasis is on black women not liking black men, hence the caption already places accountability for tensions on black women). The title deflects attention away from the concrete critique of sexism in *Black Macho* by making it a question of personal taste. Everyone seems eager to forget that it is possible for black women to love black men and yet unequivocally challenge and oppose sexism, male domination, and phallocentrism. Crouch never speaks to the issues of black male sexism in his piece and works instead to make Wallace appear an "unreliable" narrator. His useful critical comments are thus undermined by the apparent refusal to take seriously the broad political issues Wallace raises. His refusal to acknowledge sexism, expressed as "black macho," is a serious problem. It destroys the possibility of genuine solidarity between black women and men, makes it appear that he is really angry at Wallace and other black women because he is fundamentally anti-feminist and unwilling to challenge male domination. Crouch's stance epitomizes the attitude of contemporary black male writers who are either uncertain about their political response to feminism or are adamantly antifeminist. Much black male anti-feminism is linked to a refusal to acknowledge that the phallocentric power black men wield over black women is "real" power, the assumption being that only the power white men have that black men do not have is real.

If, as Frederick Douglass maintained, "power concedes nothing without a demand," the black women and men who advocate feminism must be ever vigilant, critiquing and resisting all forms of sexism. Some black men may refuse to acknowledge that sexism provides them with forms of male privilege and power, however relative. They do not want to surrender that power in a world where they may feel otherwise quite powerless. Contemporary emergence of a conservative black nationalism which exploits a focus on race to both deny the importance of struggling against sexism and racism simultaneously is both an overt attack on feminism and a force

that actively seeks to reinscribe sexist thinking among black people who have been questioning gender. Commodification of blackness that makes phallocentric black masculinity marketable makes the realm of cultural politics a propagandistic site where black people are rewarded materially for reactionary thinking about gender. Should we not be suspicious of the way in which white culture's fascination with black masculinity manifests itself? The very images of phallocentric black masculinity that are glorified and celebrated in rap music, videos, and movies are the representations that are evoked when white supremacists seek to gain public acceptance and support for genocidal assault on black men, particularly youth.

Progressive Afrocentric ideology makes this critique and interrogates sexism. In his latest book, *Black Men: Obsolete, Single, Dangerous,* Haki Madhubuti courageously deplores all forms of sexism, particularly black male violence against women. Like black male political figures of the past, Madhubuti's support of gender equality and his critique of sexism is not linked to an overall questioning of gender roles and a repudiation of all forms of patriarchal domination, however benevolent. Still, he has taken the important step of questioning sexism and calling on black people to explore the way sexism hurts and wounds us. Madhubuti acknowledges black male misogyny:

> The "fear" of women that exists among many Black men runs deep and often goes unspoken. This fear is cultural. Most men are introduced to members of the opposite sex in a superficial manner, and seldom do we seek a more in depth or informed understanding of them. . . . Women have it rough all over the world. Men must become informed listeners.

Woman-hating will only cease to be a norm in black life when black men collectively dare to oppose sexism. Unfortunately, when all black people should be engaged in a feminist movement that addresses the sexual politics of our communities, many of us are tragically investing in old gender norms. At a time when many black people should be reading Madhubuti's *Black Men, Sister Outsider, The Black Women's Health Book, Feminist Theory: From Margin to Center,* and a host of other books that seek to explore black sexual politics with compassion and care, folks are eagerly consuming a conservative tract, *The Blackman's Guide To Understanding The Blackwoman* by Shahrazad Ali. This work actively promotes black male misogyny, coercive domination of females by males, and, as a consequence, feeds the internecine conflict between black women and men. Though many black people have embraced this work there is no indication that it is having a positive impact on black communities, and there is every indication that it is being used to justify male dominance, homophobic assaults on black gay people, and rejection of black styles that emphasize our diasporic connection to Africa and the Caribbean. Ali's book romanticizes black patriarchy, demanding that black women "submit" to black male domination in lieu of changes in society that would make it possible for black men to be more fulfilled.

Calling for a strengthening of black male phallocentric power (to be imposed by force if need be), Ali's book in no way acknowledges sexism. When writing about black men, her book reads like an infantile caricature of the Tarzan fantasy. Urging black men to assert their rightful position as patriarchs, she tells them: "Rise Blackman, and take your rightful place as ruler of the universe and everything in it. Including the black woman." Like *Harlem Nights,* this is the stuff of pure fantasy. That black people, particularly the underclass, are turning to escapist fantasies that can in no way adequately address the collective need of African Americans for renewed black liberation struggle is symptomatic of the crisis we are facing. Desperately clinging to ways of thinking and being that are detrimental to our collective well-being obstructs progressive efforts for change.

More black men have broken their silence to critique Ali's work than have ever offered public support of feminist writing by black women. Yet it does not help educate black people about the ways feminist analysis could be useful in our lives for black male critics to act as though the success of this book represents a failure on the part of feminism. Ali's sexist, homophobic, self-denigrating tirades strike a familiar chord because so many black people who have not de-colonized their minds think as she does. Though black male critic Nelson George critiques Ali's work, stating that it shows "how little Afrocentrism respects the advances of African-American women," he suggests that it is an indication of how "unsuccessful black feminists have been in forging alliance with this ideologically potent community." Statements like this one advance the notion that the feminist education is the sole task of black women. It also rather neatly places George outside either one of these potent communities. Why does he not seize the critical moment to bring to public awareness the feminist visions of Afrocentric black women? All too often, black men who are indirectly supportive of feminist movement act as though black women have a personal stake in eradicating sexism that men do not have. Black men benefit from feminist thinking and feminist movement too.

Any examination of the contemporary plight of black men reveals the way phallocentrism is at the root of much black-on-black violence, undermines family relations, informs the lack of preventive health care, and even plays a role in promoting drug addiction. Many of the destructive habits of black men are enacted in the name of "manhood." Asserting their ability to be "tough," to be "cool," black men take grave risks with their lives and the lives of others. Acknowledging this in his essay "Cool Pose: The Proud Signature of Black Survival," Richard Majors argues that "cool" has positive dimensions even though it "is also an aggressive assertion of masculinity." Yet, he never overtly critiques sexism. Black men may be reluctant to critique phallocentrism and sexism, precisely because so much black male "style" has its roots in these positions; they may fear that eradicating patriarchy would leave them without the positive expressive styles that have been life-sustaining. Majors is clear, however, that a "cool pose" linked to aggressive phallocentrism is detrimental to both black men and the people they care about:

> Perhaps black men have become so conditioned to keeping up their guard against oppression from the dominant white society that this particular attitude and behavior represents for them their best safeguard against further mental or physical abuse. However, this same behavior makes it very difficult for these males to let their guard down and show affection.

Elsewhere, he suggests "that the same elements of cool that allow for survival in the larger society may hurt black people by contributing to one of the more complex problems facing black people today—black-on-black crime." Clearly, black men need to employ a feminist analysis that will address the issue of how to construct a life-sustaining black masculinity that does not have its roots in patriarchal phallocentrism.

Addressing the way obsessive concern with the phallus causes black men stress in *No Name in the Street*, James Baldwin explains:

> Every black man walking in this country pays a tremendous price for walking: for men are not women, and a man's balance depends on the weight he carries between his legs. All men, however they may face or fail to face it, however they may handle, or be handled by it, know something about each other, which is simply that a man without balls is not a man.

What might black men do for themselves and for black people if they were not socialized by white supremacist capitalist patriarchy to focus their attention on their penises? Should we not suspect the contemporary commodification of blackness orchestrated by whites that once again tells black men not only to focus on their penis but to make this focus their all consuming passion? Such confused men have little time or insight for resistance struggle. Should we not suspect representations of black men like those that appear in a movie like *Heart Condition*, where the black male describes himself as "hung like a horse" as though the size of his penis defines who he is? And what does it say about the future of black liberation struggles if the phrase "it's a dick thing" is transposed and becomes "it's a black thing?" If the "black thing," i.e., black liberation struggle, is really, only a "dick thing" in disguise, a phallocentric play for black male power, then black people are in serious trouble.

Challenging black male phallocentrism would also make a space for critical discussion of homosexuality in black communities. Since so much of the quest for phallocentric manhood as it is expressed in black nationalist circles rests on a demand for compulsory heterosexuality, it has always promoted the persecution and hatred of homosexuals. This is yet another stance that has undermined black solidarity. If black men no longer embraced phallocentric masculinity, they would be empowered to explore their fear and hatred of other men, learning new ways to relate.

How many black men will have to die before black folks are willing to look at the link between the contemporary plight of black men and their continued allegiance to patriarchy and phallocentrism?

Most black men will acknowledge that black men are in crisis and are suffering. Yet they remain reluctant to engage those progressive movements that might serve as meaningful critical interventions, that might allow them to speak their pain. On the terms set by white supremacist patriarchy, black men can name their pain only by talking about themselves in crude ways that reinscribe them in a context of primitivism. Why should black men have to talk about themselves as an "endangered species" in order to gain public recognition of their plight? And why are the voices of colonized black men, many of whom are in the spotlight, drowning out progressive voices? Why do we not listen to Joseph Beam, one such courageous voice? He had no difficulty sharing the insight that "communism, socialism, feminism and homosexuality pose far less of a threat to America than racism, sexism, classism, and ageism." Never losing sight of the need for black men to name their realities, to speak their pain and their resistance, Beam concluded his essay "No Cheek To Turn" with these prophetic words:

> I speak to you as a black gay pro-feminist man moving in a world where nobody wants to know my name, or hear my voice. In prison, I'm just a number, in the army, I'm just a rank; on the job and in the hospital, I'm just a statistic; on the street, I'm just a suspect. My head reels. If I didn't have access to print, I, too, would write on walls. I want my life's passage to be acknowledged for at least the length of time it takes pain to fade from brick. With that said I serve my notice: I have no cheek to turn.

Changing representations of black men must be a collective task. Black people committed to renewed black liberation struggle, the de-colonization of black minds, are fully aware that we must oppose male domination and work to eradicate sexism. There are black women and men who are working together to strengthen our solidarity. Black men like Richard Majors, Calvin Hernton, Cornel West, Greg Tate, Essex Hemphill, and others address the issue of sexism and advocate feminism. If black men and women take seriously Malcolm's charge that we must work for our liberation "by any means necessary," then we must be willing to explore the way feminism as a critique of sexism, as a movement to end sexism and sexist oppression, could aid our struggle to be self-determining. Collectively we can break the life-threatening choke-hold patriarchal masculinity imposes on black men and create life sustaining visions of a reconstructed black masculinity that can provide black men ways to save their lives and the lives of their brothers and sisters in struggle.

READING 20

Ritualizing Heterosexuality: Weddings as Performance

Chrys Ingraham

Since I began teaching courses on gender and sexuality in the early 80s, I've struggled with debates that claim that heterosexuality is both

Source: Originally published as "Heterosexuality! It's Just Not Normal!"

"natural and normal." As a sociologist, I frequently find such positions lacking in that they fail to attend to the social conditions upon which most things depend. In other words, the question is not whether (hetero)sexuality is natural. *All* aspects of our social world—natural or otherwise—are given meaning. The real issue is how we give meaning to heterosexuality and what interests are served by these meanings?

Consider, for example, the case of the child born with the genitalia of both sexes. In some societies to be born a hermaphrodite is revered—the Dine—while in other societies—

the United States, for example—this condition is viewed as a deformity in need of correction. Our society signals to the child (and to their family) that the child is not natural, born wrong, a mistake of nature, in need of correction. Correction, according to the medical science establishment, includes surgically changing the child's genitalia to either male or female, prescribing hormone medication, and providing socialization counseling to assist the child to become "appropriately" gendered. For little girls this means learning how to act feminine, and for little boys it means learning how to act masculine.

What is it about this condition that elicits the need for intervention? The behaviors the child must learn are integral to the gendered division of labor—what girls and boys learn is their place in relation to the institution of heterosexuality. Without a systematic analysis of this institution various questions go unanswered. For instance, is it possible that there are really more than two sexes? What is really "natural" here? Why is it that in this instance we allow society to intrude on "the natural"? What is it about sexual identity that our society is so invested in that it sees this procedure as necessary? But more importantly for the broader question at hand, who decides what counts as appropriate and necessary and under what conditions is their authority legitimate? It is cultural meaning systems that determine (with our agreement, of course) what counts as natural or unnatural. And it is cultural meaning systems that regulate what should be the "proper" treatment or response to anything "inappropriate" or "unnatural."

Historically, we've witnessed the scientific establishment determine which phenomena can be considered normal and natural only to turn around years later and say they were wrong or that their judgment was premature. Consider the instance of women's entry into higher education. At a time when white middle-class women entering higher education was frowned upon, nineteenth-century scientists discovered that women's reproductive organs would be harmed if they were exposed to a college education. And, in a historical moment when the notion of former slaves being equal to whites was not a popular notion, it was scientists who claimed that people of African descent had smaller brains than those of European lineage. In each case, scientists succumbed to the political interests of their time in formulating and interpreting research on such topics. As social conditions shifted, so too did scientific discovery. In each instance, scientists eventually overturned their previous findings in the face of overwhelming evidence to the contrary.

To argue then for a biological or "natural" explanation seems to me to be a dead end. It is much more important and useful to ask: Regardless of whether sexuality (or anything for that matter) is naturally occurring, how does our culture give it meaning? In other words, how do we give meaning to (hetero)sexuality? How have we organized it? The question then becomes *not* whether heterosexuality is natural, and therefore "normal," but, rather how do cultural meaning systems work to normalize and institutionalize heterosexuality? And, more importantly, what interests are served by these processes? In other words, who benefits from the ways we've named, defined, and organized sexuality?

Typically studied as a form of sexuality, heterosexuality is, in reality, a highly regulated, ritualized, and organized set of practices, for example, weddings or proms. Sociologically, then, heterosexuality as an established order made up of rule-bound and standardized behavior patterns qualifies as an institution. Moreover, heterosexuality as an arrangement involving large numbers of people whose behavior is guided by norms and rules is also a *social* institution.

Heterosexuality is much more than a biological given, or whether or not someone is attracted to someone of another sex. Rules on everything from who pays for the date or the wedding rehearsal dinner to who leads while dancing, drives the car, cooks dinner or initiates sex, all serve to regulate heterosexual practice. What circulates as a given in western societies is, in fact, a highly structured arrangement. As is the case with most institutions, people who participate in these practices must be *socialized* to do so. In other words, women were not born with a wedding gown gene or neo-natal craving for a diamond engagement ring! They were taught to want these things. Women didn't enter the world with a desire to practice something called dating or a desire to play with a "My Size Bride Barbie," they were rewarded for desiring these things. Likewise, men did not exit the womb knowing they would one day buy a date a corsage or spend two months income to buy an engagement ring. These are all products that have been sold to consumers interested in taking part in a culturally established ritual that works to organize and institutionalize heterosexuality and reward those who participate.

HETERONORMATIVITY

In the 1970s as second-wave feminists attempted to theorize and understand the source of women's oppression, the notion of heterosexuality as normative emerged. In one of the earliest examples of this effort, The Purple September Staff, a Dutch group, published an article entitled "The Normative Status of Heterosexuality" (1975). They maintain that heterosexuality is really a normalized power arrangement that limits options and privileges men over women and reinforces and naturalizes male dominance.

Ti-Grace Atkinson (1974), the Furies Collective, the Redstockings Collective (1975), Rita Mae Brown (1976), and Charlotte Bunch (1975) all contributed to these debates by challenging dominant notions of heterosexuality as natu-

rally occurring and by arguing that heterosexuality is instead a highly organized, social institution rife with multiple forms of domination and ideological control.

> Heterosexuality—as an ideology and as an institution—upholds all those aspects of female oppression. . . . For example, heterosexuality is basic to our oppression in the workplace. When we look at how women are defined and exploited as secondary, marginal workers, we recognize that this definition assumes that all women are tied to men. . . . It is obvious that heterosexuality upholds the home, housework, the family as both a personal and economic unit. (Bunch 1975, p. 34)

In this excerpt from Charlotte Bunch, the link between heterosexuality and systems of oppression is elaborated.

While many of these arguments were made by heterosexually-identified feminists, some of the more famous works were produced by lesbian feminists, making a link to the interests of both feminism and lesbian and gay rights. Adrienne Rich's essay "Compulsory Heterosexuality and Lesbian Existence" (1980), a frequently reprinted classic, confronts the institution of heterosexuality head on, asserting that heterosexuality is neither natural nor inevitable but is instead a compulsory, contrived, constructed, and taken-for-granted institution which serves the interests of male dominance.

> Historians need to ask at every point how heterosexuality as institution has been organized and maintained through the female wage scale, the enforcement of middle-class women's leisure, the glamorization of so-called sexual liberation, the withholding of education from women, the imagery of high art and popular culture, the mystification of the personal sphere, and much else. We need an economics which comprehends the institution of heterosexuality, with its doubled workload for women and its sexual divisions of labor, as the most idealized of economic relations. (p. 27)

Understanding heterosexuality as compulsory and as a standardized institution with processes and effects is what makes Rich's contribution to these debates pivotal.

Monique Wittig's "The Category of Sex" (1976) takes the argument to a different level, declaring heterosexuality a political regime. The category of sex, she argues, is the political category that founds society as heterosexual.

> As such it does not concern being but relationships. . . . The category of sex is the one that rules as natural the relation that is at the base of (heterosexual) society and through which half of the population, women, are heterosexualized . . . and submitted to a heterosexual economy. . . . The category of sex is the product of a heterosexual society in which men appropriate for themselves the reproduction and production of women and also their physical persons by means of a contract called the marriage contract. (1992, p. 7)

This regime depends upon the belief that women are sexual beings, unable to escape or live outside of male rule.

These positions signal a paradigm shift in how heterosexuality is understood, challenging the very centrality of institutionalized heterosexuality and beginning the work of offering a systematic analysis of heterosexuality. When queer theory emerged in the 1990s, these critical analyses of heterosexuality were revisited and reinvigorated (e.g., Butler 1990; de Lauretis 1987; Fuss 1991; Hennessy 1993; Ingraham 1994; Jackson 1995; Sedgwick 1990; Seidman 1991, 1992, 1995; Warner 1993; Wittig 1992). In his anthology *Fear of a Queer Planet*, Michael Warner rearticulated these debates through his creation of the concept of "heteronormativity." According to Warner,

> So much privilege lies in heterosexual culture's exclusive ability to interpret itself as society. Het culture thinks of itself as the elemental form of human association, as the very model of intergender relations, as the indivisible basis of all community, and as the means of reproduction without which society wouldn't exist. . . . Western political thought has taken the heterosexual couple to represent the principle of social union itself. (1993, p. xxi)

In this same passage Warner relates his notion of heteronormativity to Wittig's idea of the social contract. For Wittig the social contract is heterosexuality. "To live in society is to live in heterosexuality. . . . Heterosexuality is always already there within all mental categories" (1992, p. 40). Like whiteness in a white supremacist society, heterosexuality is not only socially produced as dominant but is also taken for granted and universalizing.

Steven Seidman in his introduction to the ground breaking work *Queer Theory/Sociology* (1996) assesses the role of queer theorists in developing a new critical view of normative heterosexuality. Given the history of sociology as a "de-naturalizing force," he argues that it is time for queer sociologists to de-naturalize heterosexuality as a "social and political organizing principle." Seidman asserts that the contribution of a queer sociology is to analyze normative heterosexuality for the ways it conceals from view particular social processes and inequalities.

Drawing on these early arguments, heteronormativity can be defined as the view that institutionalized heterosexuality constitutes the standard for legitimate and expected social and sexual relations. Heteronormativity insures that the organization of heterosexuality in everything from gender to weddings to marital status is held up as both a model and as "normal." Consider, for instance, the ways many surveys or intake questionnaires ask respondents to check off their marital status as either married, divorced, separated, widowed, single, or, in some cases, never married. Not only are these categories presented as significant indices of social identity, they are offered as the only options, implying that the organization of identity in relation to marriage is universal and not in need of explanation. Questions concerning marital status appear on most surveys *regardless of relevance*. The heteronormative assumption of this practice is rarely, if ever, called into question, and when it is, the response is generally dismissive. (Try putting down "not applicable" the next time you fill out one of these forms in a doctor's office!)

Or try to imagine entering a committed relationship without benefit of legalized marriage. We find it difficult to think that we can share a commitment with someone without a state-sponsored license. People will frequently comment that someone is afraid to "make a commitment" if they choose not to get married even when they have been in a relationship with someone for years! Our ability to imagine possibilities or to understand what counts as commitment is itself impaired by heteronormative assumptions. We even find ourselves challenged to consider how to marry without an elaborate white wedding. Gays and lesbians have participated in long-term committed relationships for years yet find themselves desiring state sanctioning of their union in order to feel legitimate. Heteronormativity works in all of these instances to naturalize the institution of heterosexuality while rendering real people's relationships and commitments irrelevant and illegitimate.

For those who view questions concerning marital status as benign, one need only consider the social and economic consequences for those who do not participate in these arrangements or the cross-cultural variations which are at odds with some of the anglocentric or eurocentric assumptions regarding marriage. All people are required to situate themselves in relation to marriage or heterosexuality, including those who *regardless of sexual (or asexual) affiliation* do not consider themselves "single," heterosexual, or who don't participate in normative heterosexuality and its structures.

To expand the analytical reach of the concept of heteronormativity, it is important to examine how heterosexuality is constructed as normative. A concept that is useful for examining the naturalization of heterosexual relations is "the heterosexual imaginary."[1] The "imaginary" is that illusory relationship we can have to our real conditions of existence. It is that moment when we romanticize things or refuse to see something that makes us uncomfortable. Applied to the study of heterosexuality, it is that way of thinking that conceals the operation of heterosexuality in structuring gender (across race, class, and sexuality) and closes off any critical analysis of heterosexuality as an organizing institution. It is a belief system that relies on romantic and sacred notions in order to create and maintain the illusion of well-being. At the same time this romantic view prevents us from seeing how institutionalized heterosexuality actually works to organize gender while preserving racial, class, and sexual hierarchies as well. The effect of this illusory depiction of reality is that heterosexuality is taken for granted and unquestioned, while gender is understood as something people are socialized into or learn. By leaving heterosexuality unexamined as an institution, we don't explore how it is learned, what it keeps in place, and the interests it serves in the way it's practiced. Through the use of the heterosexual imaginary, we hold up the institution of heterosexuality as timeless, devoid of historical variation, and as "just the way it is," while creating social practices that reinforce the illusion that as long as this is "the way it is" all will be right in the world. Romancing heterosexuality—creating an illusory heterosexuality—is central to the heterosexual imaginary.

---

[1]See "The Heterosexual Imaginary: Feminist Sociology and Theories of Gender," *Sociological Theory,* 12:2 July 1994 for further elaboration of this concept.

Frequently, discussions about the legalization of gay marriage depend on this illusion. Gays and lesbians are seeking equal access to economic resources such as benefits and see marriage as the site for gaining equity with heterosexuals. The central problem with this position is that it constructs the debates in terms of coupling. All those who do not couple for whatever reason are left out of the discussion. Consider some of the other consequences of participating in the heterosexual imaginary, of perpetuating the notion that heterosexuality is naturally a site for tranquility and safety. This standpoint keeps us from seeing and dealing with issues of marital rape, domestic violence, pay inequities, racism, gay bashing, and sexual harassment. Instead, institutionalized heterosexuality organizes those behaviors we ascribe to men and women—gender—while keeping in place or producing a history of contradictory and unequal social relations. The production of a division of labor that results in unpaid domestic work, inequalities of pay and opportunity, or the privileging of married couples in the dissemination of insurance benefits are examples of this.

The heterosexual imaginary naturalizes the regulation of sexuality through the institution of marriage and state domestic relations laws. These laws, among others, set the terms for taxation, health care, and housing benefits on the basis of marital status. Laws and public- and private-sector policies use marriage as the primary requirement for social and economic benefits and access rather than distributing resources on some other basis such as citizenship or ability to breathe, for example. The distribution of economic resources on the basis of marital status remains an exclusionary arrangement even if the law permits gays and lesbians to participate. The heterosexual imaginary works here as well by allowing the illusion of well-being to reside in the privilege heterosexual couples enjoy while keeping others from equal access—quite a contradiction in a democratic social order.

WEDDINGS

To demonstrate how useful these concepts are for analyzing the institution of heterosexuality, consider a practice as pervasive as heterosexual weddings. To study weddings using this theory of heterosexuality is to investigate the ways various practices, arrangements, relations, and rituals work to standardize and conceal the operation of this institution. It means asking how practices such as weddings become naturalized and prevent us from seeing what is at stake, what is kept in place, and what consequences are produced. To employ this approach is to seek out those instances when the illusion of tranquility is created and at what cost.

Weddings, like many other rituals of heterosexual celebration such as anniversaries, showers, and Valentine's Day, become synonymous with heterosexuality and provide illusions of reality which conceal the operation of heterosexuality both historically and materially. When used in professional settings, for example, weddings work as a form of ideological control to signal membership in relations of ruling as well as to signify that the couple are normal, moral, productive, family-centered, upstanding citizens and, most importantly, appropriately gendered. Consider the ways weddings are used by co-workers in line for promotions or to marginalize and exceptionalize single or non married employees. For example, two employees are competing for a promotion. One is single, the other engaged to marry. The engaged worker invites all members of the office, including the hiring committee, to the wedding. Because of the heterosexual imaginary, weddings are viewed as innocuous, fun-loving, and as signaling membership in dominant culture. As such, they give people significant advantage in the workplace and are anything but benign.

To study weddings means to interrupt the ways the heterosexual imaginary naturalizes heterosexuality and prevents us from seeing how its organization depends on the production of the belief or ideology that heterosexuality is normative and the same for everyone—that the fairy tale romance is universal. It's this assumption that allows for the development and growth of a $32 billion per year wedding industry. This multi billion dollar industry includes the sale of a diverse range of products, many of which are produced outside of the United States—wedding gowns, diamonds, honeymoon travel and apparel, and household equipment. Also included in the market are invitations, flowers, receptions, photos, gifts, home furnishings, wedding cakes, catering, alcohol, paper products, calligraphy, jewelry, party supplies, hair styling, makeup, manicures, music, books, and wedding accessories, such as, ring pillows, silver, chauffeurs, and limousines. In the name of normative heterosexuality and its ideology of romance, the presence and size of the sometimes corrupt wedding industry escapes us.

While newlyweds make up only 2.6 percent of all American households, they account for 75 percent of all the fine china, 29 percent of the tableware, and 21 percent of the jewelry and watches sold in this country every year. Even insurers have entered the primary wedding market by offering coverage "if wedding bells don't ring" to cover the cost of any monies already spent on the wedding preparation. Fireman's Fund Insurance Company offers "Weddingsurance" for wedding catastrophes such as flood or fire but not for "change of heart" (Haggerty 1993). In fact, attach the words *wedding* or *bridal* to nearly any item and its price goes up. With June as the leading wedding month, followed by August and July, summer becomes a wedding mar-

keter's dream. According to industry estimates, the average wedding in the United States costs $19,104. Considered in relation to what Americans earn, the cost of the average wedding represents 51 percent of the mean earnings of a white family of four and 89 percent of the median earnings for [similarly sized] black families. The fact that 63.7 percent of Americans earn less than $25,000 per year (U.S. Bureau of the Census 1996) means the average cost of a wedding approximates a year's earnings for many Americans.

The primary wedding market—marketing directed toward prospective newlyweds—depends on numerous production and labor relations issues that underlie the consumption and accumulation involved in weddings. Veiled in the guise of romance and the sacred, the heterosexual imaginary conceals from view the various troublesome conditions underlying the production of the white wedding.

Probably the most significant wedding purchase is the wedding gown. Industry analysts have noted that most brides would do without many things to plan a wedding and stay within budget, but they would not scrimp when it comes to the purchase of the wedding gown. With the national average expenditure at $823 for the gown and $199 for the veil, the bride's apparel becomes the centerpiece of the white wedding. Most of us have heard the various phrases associated with the bride and her gown, the symbolic significance attached to how she looks and how beautiful her gown is. The marketing of everything from weddings to gowns to children's toys to popular wedding films to Disney is laced with messages about fairy-tales and princesses, the fantasy rewards that work to naturalize weddings and heterosexuality. Even couture fashion shows of world-class designers traditionally feature wedding gowns as their grand finale.

One particularly troubling practice widely engaged in by gown sellers is the removal of designer labels and prices from dresses. In many surveys, from *Modern Bride* to Dawn Currie's interview study (1993), brides indicate that they rely upon bridal magazines to give them ideas about what type of gown to choose. They take the ad for the gown they like best to area stores and attempt to try on and purchase that particular dress. What they encounter is a system of deception widely practiced by many bridal shops. First, sellers remove the labels. Brides ask for a Vera Wang or an Alfred Angelo or a Jessica McClintock and are told to get the number off the gown; the clerk will check their book and see which designer it is. The bride has no way of knowing if she actually has the brand she seeks. As I toured various shops and saw how widespread this practice was, I asked store owners why they removed the labels from the dresses. Without exception they told me that it was to maintain the integrity of their business and to prevent women from comparison shopping. The truth is, this practice is *illegal* and provides shop owners with a great deal of flexibility in preserving their customer base and profit margin. In addition to this federal consumer protection law [against removing labels], there are many states which provide similar protections. All in all, bridal gown stores have little to fear: This law is not enforced. And, perhaps more importantly, the romance with the white wedding gown distracts the soon-to-be brides from becoming suspicious of store practices.

If you look at the portion of tags gown-sellers leave in the dresses, you will see that most are sewn outside the United States in countries such as Guatemala, Mexico, Taiwan, and China. Nearly 80 percent of all wedding gowns are produced outside the United States in subcontracted factories where labor standards are nowhere near what they are in the United States and no independent unions or regulators keep watch.

The recruitment of U.S. companies to contract offshore labor benefits manufacturers on many levels: cheap labor, low overhead, fewer regulations, and higher profits. And with the proliferation of free trade agreements such as the North Atlantic Free Trade Agreement (NAFTA) and the General Agreement on Tarriffs and Trade (GATT), labor and environmental abuses abound. In a survey conducted by UNITE in April 1997 of three factories in Guatemala, it was discovered that one American manufacturer's gowns were being made by 13-year-olds in factories with widespread violations of their country's child-labor laws and wage and hour laws, and under life-threatening safety conditions. At two of the firms, 14- and 15-year-olds worked as long as 10 hours a day, earning $20.80 a week.

Another area of the wedding industry dominated by messages about romance is the marketing of diamonds. As part of the fantasy of the ever-romantic marriage proposal, the diamond ring takes center stage. In fact, for 70 percent of all U.S. brides and 75 percent of first-time brides, the first purchase for the impending wedding is the diamond engagement ring. The central marketing strategy of the world's largest diamond mining organization, DeBeers, is to convince consumers that "diamonds are forever." Once you accept this slogan, you also believe that you're making a life long investment, not just purchasing a bauble for your bride! In fact, DeBeers spends about $57 million each year on this advertising campaign and has "committed to spending a large part of [their] budget—some $200 million this year—on the promotion of diamond jewelry around the world" (Oppenheimer 1998, p. 8). DeBeers and its advertisers have developed a new "shadow" campaign to sell to consumers the advice that the "appropriate" diamond engagement ring should cost at least "two-months' salary" for the groom (Jewelers 1996). This advertising strategy signals to newlyweds, grooms in particular, that anything less is not acceptable. In effect, the diamond industry has made use of heteronormativity and the heterosexual imaginary and has convinced us that purchasing a diamond engagement ring is no longer a want but is "natural" and, therefore, a must. Not surprisingly, according to wedding industry estimates, this message is reaching its target. The average annual expenditure for engagement rings is $3,000 (*Modern Bride* 1997). If that constitutes the equivalent of two-months' salary, the groom is expected to earn an annual salary of approximately $26,000 per year, the income bracket many of these ads target. What gets naturalized here is not just heterosexuality and romance but also weddings and commodity consumption.

Hidden behind the romance with diamond rings and wedding jewelry is an industry with a history steeped in intrigue, treachery, and vast wealth. Everyone from global capitalists to governments to political operatives to advertising agencies to jewelry stores is included. The mining, manufacturing, and marketing of diamonds has involved colonial wars, apartheid, racist violence, massive labor abuses, struggles between superpowers, the stability of nations, and the hiring of mercenary armies—hardly the picture of romance each young woman was taught to want. When diamond engagement rings and weddings [are viewed] as "only natural," conditions such as these remain unimaginable and invisible to the average consumer.

This process of naturalization begins with children. By targeting girls and young women, toy manufacturers have seized on the current wedding market and the opportunity to develop future consumers by producing a whole variety of wedding toys featuring the "classic" white wedding and sold during Saturday morning children's television shows. Toy companies, generally part of large conglomerates that also own related commodities such as travel or cosmetics, work to secure future markets for all their products through the selling of wedding toys. Mattel, the world's largest toymaker and a major multinational corpora-

tion, has offices and facilities in 36 countries and sells products in 150 nations. Their major toy brand, accounting for 40 percent of their sales, is the Barbie doll—all 120 different versions of her. Mattel's primary manufacturing facilities are located in China, Indonesia, Italy, Malaysia, and Mexico, employing mostly women of color and at substandard wages. Annually, Mattel makes about 100 million Barbie dolls and earns revenues of $1.9 billion for their El Segundo, California, company. The average young Chinese female worker whose job it is to assemble Barbie dolls lives in dormitories, sometimes works with dangerous chemicals, works long hours, and earns $1.81 a day (Holstein et al. 1996).

The staging of weddings in television shows, weekly reporting on weddings in the press, magazine reports on celebrity weddings, advertising, and popular adult and children's movies with wedding themes or weddings inserted all work together to teach us how to think about weddings, marriage, heterosexuality, race, gender, and labor. Through the application of the heterosexual imaginary, the media cloak most representations of weddings in signifiers of romance, purity, morality, promise, affluence or accumulation, and whiteness. Many newlyweds today experience their weddings as stars of a fairy-tale movie where they are scripted, video-taped, and photographed by paparazzi wedding-goers.

The contemporary white wedding under transnational capitalism is, in effect, a mass-marketed, homogeneous, assembly-line production with little resemblance to the utopian vision many participants hold. The engine driving the wedding market has mostly to do with the romancing of heterosexuality in the interests of capitalism. The social relations at stake—love, community, commitment, and family—become alienated from the production of the wedding spectacle, while practices reinforcing heteronormativity prevail.

The heterosexual imagery circulating throughout the wedding industry masks the ways it secures racial, class, and sexual hierarchies. For instance, in nearly all of the examples offered above, the wedding industry depends on the availability of cheap labor from developing nations with majority populations made up of people of color. The wealth garnered by white transnational corporations both relies on racial hierarchies, exploiting people and resources of communities of color (Africa, China, Haiti, Mexico, South Asia), and perpetuates them in the marketing of the wedding industry.

Women are taught from early childhood to plan for the "happiest day of their lives." Men are taught, by the absence of these socializing mechanisms, that their work is "other" than that. The arguments that second-wave feminists made about institutionalized heterosexuality as the source of male dominance and women's oppression are reinforced by these practices. The possibilities children learn to imagine are only as broad as their culture allows. They are socialized to understand the importance of coupling, appropriate coupling, what counts as beauty, what counts as women's work and men's work, and how to become good consumers by participating in those heterosexual practices which stimulate their interests and emotions and reap the most rewards.

CONCLUSION

Heterosexuality is just not natural! It's socially organized and controlled. To understand how we give meaning to one of our major institutions is to participate as a critical consumer and citizen actively engaged in the production of culture and the social order. Heteronormativity—those practices that construct heterosexuality as the standard for legitimate and expected social and sexual relations—has enormous consequences for all members of a democratic social order, particularly in relation to the distribution of human and economic resources that affect the daily lives of millions of people. When the expectation is that all are equal under the law and that all citizens in a democracy can participate fully in the ruling of that society, rendering one form of sociosexual relations as dominant by constructing it as "natural" is both contradictory and violent. In other words, the heterosexuality we learn to think of as "natural" is anything but.

REFERENCES

Adams, Mary Louise. 1997. *The trouble with normal: Postwar youth and the making of heterosexuality.* Toronto: University of Toronto Press.

Atkinson, Ti-Grace. 1974. *Amazon odyssey.* New York: Links Books.

Best, Amy. 2000. *Prom night: Youth, schools, and popular culture.* New York: Routledge.

Brown, Rita Mae. 1976. *Plain brown rapper.* Baltimore: Diana Press.

Bunch, Charlotte. 1975. Not for lesbians only. *Quest: A Feminist Quarterly.* (Fall).

Butler, Judith. 1990. *Gender trouble.* New York: Routledge.

Currie, D. 1993. Here comes the bride: The making of a "modern traditional" wedding in western culture. *Journal of Comparative Family Studies, 24,* 3, 403–421.

de Laurentis, Teresa. 1987. Queer theory: Lesbian and gay sexualities. *Differences, 3,* iii–xviii.

Field, Nicola. 1995. *Over the rainbow: Money, class, and homophobia.* London: Pluto Press.

Fuss, Diana. 1991. *Inside/Out.* New York: Routledge.

Graff, E. J. 1999. *What is marriage for? The strange social history of our most intimate institution.* Boston: Beacon Press.

Haggerty, Alfred. 1993. Coverage is available if wedding bells don't ring. *National Underwriter* (March 15): 15.

Harman, Moses. 1901. *Institutional marriage.* Chicago: Lucifer.

C. 1883. *Lucifer the lightbearer.* Valley Falls, Kansas.

Helms, Jesse. 1996. The defense of marriage act. Senate. *Congressional Quarterly* September 9. C. 1996. Senate proceedings. *Congressional Record,* September 9.

Hennessy, Rosemary. 1994. Incorporating queer theory on the left. In *Marxism in the postmodern age.* Edited by Antonio Callari, Stephen Cullenberg, and Carole Beweiner. New York: Guilford.

Heywood, Ezra. 1876. *Cupid's yokes.* Princeton, Mass.: Co-operative Publishing Co.

Holstein, William J., Brian Palmer, Shahid Ur-Rehman, and Timothy M. Ito. 1996. Santa's sweatshop. *U.S. News & World Report.* (December 16).

Ingraham, Chrys. 1999. *White weddings: Romancing heterosexuality in popular culture.* New York: Routledge.

———. 1994. The heterosexual imaginary: Feminist sociology and theories of gender, *Sociological theory,* 12, 2 (July), 203–219.

Jackson, Stevi. 1999. *Heterosexuality in question.* London: Sage Publications.

———. 1996. Heterosexuality and feminist theory. In *Theorising heterosexuality.* Edited by Diane Richardson. Buckingham: Open University Press.

Jewelers' Circular-Keystone. 1996. Diamond sales hit record. New York: Chilton.

Katz, Jonathan Ned. 1995. *The invention of heterosexuality.* New York: Plume.

Maynard, Mary, and June Purvis, eds. 1995. *(Hetero)sexual politics.* London: Taylor & Francis.

Modern Bride. 1996. *The bridal market retail spending study: A $35 billion market for the 90's.* New York: Primedia.

Oppenheimer, Nicholas. 1998. Chairman's statement. *Annual Report.* De Beers.

Purple September Staff. 1975. The normative status of heterosexuality. In Myers, Nancy and Charlotte Bunch, eds. Lesbianism and the women's movement. Diana Press.

Redstockings Collective. 1975. *Feminist revolution.* New York: Random House.

Rich, Adrienne. 1980. Compulsory heterosexuality and lesbian existence. *Signs, 5* (Summer), 631–660.

Richardson, Diane, ed. 1996. *Theorising heterosexuality.* Buckingham: Open University Press.

Sears, Hal D. 1977. *The sex radicals: Free love in high victorian America.* Lawrence: Regents Press of Kansas.

Sedgwick, Eve. 1990. *Epistemology of the closet.* Berkeley: University of California Press.

Seidman, Steven. 1991. *Romantic longings.* New York: Routledge.

———. 1992. *Embattled eros.* New York: Routledge.

———. 1993. Identity and politics in a postmodern gay culture: Some conceptual and historical notes. In *Fear of a queer planet,* edited by Michael Warner. Minneapolis: University of Minnesota Press.

———. 1996. *Queer theory/Sociology.* Cambridge, Mass.: Blackwell.

U.S. Bureau of the Census. 1996. *Statistical abstracts of the United States.* Washington, D.C.: Government Printing Office.

Warner, Michael, ed. 1993. *Fear of a queer planet.* Minneapolis: University of Minnesota Press.

Wilkinson, Sue, and Celia Kitzinger, eds. 1993. *Heterosexuality: A feminism and psychology reader.* London: Sage Publications.

Wittig, Monique. 1992. *The straight mind.* Boston: Beacon Press.

READING 21

Country Music and Women's Sexuality: What Do Women Want?

Judith Barker

Men frequently ask, in frustration, "What do women want?" This question tends to be presented as though figuring out what women want is almost impossible. Perhaps it is so difficult simply because men have been taught to not listen to women in everyday life and, until recently, women have been denied public voices in our society. When women are denied voices, both in the public and private areas,

Source: Original work. Copyright © 2002. Reprinted with permission of the author.

then it certainly can be difficult to understand what women want.

The area of sexuality is just one example of what happens when women have no voice, public or private. Whether it is popular culture, medical science, academic scholarship, or a private setting, it has usually been men who have shaped views of women's sexuality. Rarely have men seemed to consider the simple expedient of asking women about women's sexuality: Or asking women, What do women want? Therefore, most heterosexual men attempt to understand what women want sexually by talking to other men or listening to the messages in the male-dominated popular culture.

As with most aspects of our popular culture, country music has been permeated by sexism and has denied women their own voice. A number of authors writing about country music and women have noted that the role of women in country songs has been to be the salvation of men. Some authors have even said that women replace Jesus as a source of salvation. In country music songs, women have existed almost completely to "make life worth living for men." Women's role is an important one, a central one, but still only in the context of serving male needs.

However, beginning in the 1950s women performers began to break the barriers in this industry. By the 1990s new messages, women-positive and woman-centered, began to appear in popular country songs. New female stars began to emerge, stars with as much power and appeal as male stars. By now, one can argue that white working-class women have found a public voice in country music: a voice that allows women to present a woman-centered view of women's sexuality. I'm going to discuss how many of the more recent songs from female country singers present a view of women and women's sexuality that does adequately answer the question of what women want.

I've chosen to focus on what I view as a positive theme emerging in country music. The reader should keep in mind that I'm only discussing those songs that I see as positive. The old themes that allow men sexual freedom and critique women for any "wrongs" still exist side by side with the new themes. For example, a growing number of songs reject the sexual objectification of women; yet at the same time an increasing number of country videos have become explicitly objectifying. So I'm not claiming that all of country has gone feminist, just that a new strong pro-woman aspect of country is emerging. Also, country is completely heterosexual in content. Just last evening I heard a song in which the male singer asserted that it does not matter if we are "gay or straight." I was so shocked that I know my jaw really did literally drop open. I hope that one line in one song means that changes are coming; however, all the songs I discuss assume heterosexuality and are therefore heteronormative in nature.

The attempt on the part of some female country singers to critique a traditional approach to women's sexuality, and offer a more empowering alternative, has actually been a small but consistent theme for many years. In the 1950s two singers, Kitty Wells and Jean Shepard, sang several songs critiquing traditional views of women's sexuality. In "Two Whoops and a Holler," sung by Jean Shepard, the double standard for male and female sexuality is questioned. The singer asks why when a man does something wrong, such as cheating on his wife, it's all right "cause he's just a man," but when a woman does the same: "She's not worth two whoops and a holler. She's lower than a hound." Kitty Wells, in "It Wasn't God Who Made Honkey Tonk Angels," asks why society critiques women for casual sexuality when it's men who "cause a good girl to go wrong." Shepard and Wells do not actually mean that men or sexuality itself are evil; they are just critiquing a double standard that condemns women for sexual activity while applauding the sexual exploits of men.

In the 1970s, as the women's movement gained momentum in our society, some country singers once again reexamined women's sexuality. Loretta Lynn's song "The Pill" (1972) celebrated the sexual liberation the pill would bring women, freeing women from being brooders and incubators. She talks about how lack of access to birth control has kept women "barefoot and pregnant" and therefore powerless. She sees the pill as potentially liberating because women will be able to enjoy sexuality without fearing pregnancy—especially constant pregnancies.

These are just three examples of earlier attempts to assert a positive role for sexually active women. While there have been feminist-type messages in country music as far back as the 1920s, they were few and far between compared to the number of songs with feminist messages that are currently being played on the radio. As far as sexuality is concerned, the more recent country songs continue the earlier themes, the difference being that these messages have become much more common and broader. The message that women can be sexual agents, with drives and desires of their own, is no longer rare or unusual. And these songs are tremendously popular, indicating that they strike a chord with listeners.

Many of the recent songs present a view of female sexuality and male/female relationships that suggests women should have autonomy and freedom, challenging traditional gender roles. A good way to begin discussing these messages is "Man! I Feel Like a Woman!" by Shania Twain. In this song Twain defines what it means to feel like a woman as having fun and being free. She says she's not going to have any inhibitions, she will do what she dares, and above all she's going to be free. There are many songs like this. I call them general celebration songs. What is being celebrated is being a woman and being free.

Any discussion of recent country songs and women's sexuality should begin with the song "Strawberry Wine," by Deanna Carter. This song tells the story of a young woman's first sexual experience. In this song the young woman is "thirstin' for knowledge": knowledge about sexuality. She finds that knowledge and experience with a young man who is working for her father that summer. It's a beautiful and moving song about a woman's first sexual experience that was so popular the DJs and many of the listeners tired of the song after awhile.

This song is also a good place to begin because it illustrates why women need to have their own voice. Bruce Feiler, a writer for the *New York Times,* characterizes this song as "about a teenager who loses her virginity to an older man." The singer is clearly talking about *gaining* sexual experience and knowledge, not about *losing* anything. The so-called older man is actually only two or three years older. The song is an interesting contrast to the prevailing view, accepted by Bruce Feiler, that still tells women we lose something with our first sexual experience. Only when women gain their own voices can views such as "losing virginity" begin to be challenged. Feiler's article also illustrates the reality that the media has often reinterpreted and diminished the new woman-centered messages in some country music.

In "You Will Be Mine," Faith Hill presents a clear view of a female sexuality that is active and passionate. Hill tells the listener that she will have what she wants—to kiss the man, to claim the man, to have the man—he will be hers! Throughout the song, she is the active person and she clearly intends to have what she wants. The unwritten law that says men, not women, initiate sexual activity is dismissed with the following phrase: "But a woman in love, she's above the law." Hill challenges the idea that women should not initiate sexuality, celebrates the idea of a woman pursuing a man, and asserts that women have a sexual drive.

Another song that celebrates women's sexual drive is "Passionate Kisses" by Mary Chapin Carpenter. In this song Mary Chapin Carpenter tells listeners that there are a number of things she wants. She gives several lists of these things (warm bed, clothes, pens that don't run out of ink, etc.). Each list ends with passionate kisses. Thus, the common refrain is that she wants passionate kisses. She keeps asking, "Shouldn't I have this?" At one point she says it's what she deserves, her right. Throughout the song, she asserts that women have sexual needs and desires and that wanting "passionate kisses" is not too much to ask or demand.

In "Guilty as They Come," Suzy Boggus goes much further and talks about "casual sex." She makes it clear that she doesn't see anything wrong with a woman enjoying herself. In this song, the story is about a woman who engages in casual sexual encounters. The singer suggests that women can find positive experiences in casual sex.

A common thread in these songs is the idea that women want, need, and enjoy sex. The immense popularity of these songs suggests that these messages resonate with listeners. In country music the message, or story, is the most important part of the song, and songs with stories that do not resonate with a significant part of the audience do not become popular.

Some songs talk about what women do and do not want from men. In "That Don't Impress Me Much," Shania Twain talks about what doesn't impress her and what does: Being a scientist, looking as good as Brad Pitt, having money, a fancy car, being Elvis; none of this impresses her. What does impress her is if he has "the touch." She is saying that many of the things that men think impress women do not impress her. She also makes it clear that what does impress her is a man who keeps her warm in the middle of the night: I take keeping warm in the night and having the touch as meaning sex. In "Real Man," Bonnie Raitt also says that she isn't impressed by the things that men think impress women. She is not looking for a secret agent, a man with a Cadillac, a million dollars, a diamond ring—just a real man. (She never really defines what a real man is, just what he is not.) Over and over women sing about not being impressed by the things that men think impress women, especially money, and how what they really want is just love and affection. The point is that women don't need men to impress them with various skills or forms of power either; all they need from men is companionship, sex, and love.

Other songs suggest that women do not want aggression or violence. One example is "What Part of No Don't You Understand?" by Lori Morgan. In this song Morgan describes an encounter with a man in a bar. He doesn't seem to be able to hear the word *no:* in response to an invitation to dance, offer of a drink, and so on. Thus, she says, "I'll be glad to explain it, if it's too hard to comprehend. What part of no don't you understand?" In "If You Wanna Touch Her, Ask!," Shania Twain tells a man that if he wants to find a place in a woman's heart, he has to first listen, then understand, then be friends, and then "if you wanna touch her, ask." The message in these and other songs is that women do not want to be sexual prey or passive objects.

There are a growing number of songs that address body image and sexual objectification. The primary theme in these songs is that what women want and need from men is to be loved for ourselves, not for a sexist image of women. In "Any Man of Mine," Shania Twain explains what she wants from a man: "Even when I'm ugly, he still better love me." She makes it clear that she wants to be loved for herself, not for fulfilling some sexist beauty standard. In "My Baby Loves Me Just the Way I Am," Martina McBride explains what women want in a relationship: to be loved for our true selves, not for a male fantasy of what a woman should be. The singer doesn't need to check out *Vogue* magazines, dress like a beauty queen, or wear high heels: Her "baby" loves her for herself, not for some beauty image she fulfills.

In "Take Me As I Am," Faith Hill tells a man that what she really wants from a man is for him to take her as she is. One aspect of wanting to be loved for ourselves is the idea that we are fine the way we are. Mindy McCready in "This Is Me," sings, "This is me. Take it or leave it. Why would I want to be anyone else when it feels so good just bein' myself?" One of the strongest of these songs is "Real Live Woman," by Trisha Yearwood. In this song Yearwood tells us that her man loves her for herself, and she doesn't need to be a beauty queen, or 19 years old, "Or starve myself for some weight I'm told will turn men's heads down that road." Her man prefers a real live woman to the images of sexiness our society offers him. The video for this song demonstrates the theme visually. In the video men are looking at women in rooms with curtains coming down. These rooms are reminiscent of peep shows. However, in these rooms there are real live women, caring for children, working, and so on. The men are clearly fascinated by these real live women, not by fake glossy images.

I've given just a few examples of songs that answer that age-old question, What do women want? These singers tell men clearly that what women want is to be loved for themselves, not for a particular body image. They suggest further that what women want is for men to want real live women, not Barbie dolls or models: That women want men to realize that we are real people not sex objects.

Another related theme in this new music is a new analysis of male/female relationships. In this new analysis, the central point is that women want reciprocal relationships with

men, relationships in which both people do some giving and some taking.

Country music has always had a strong focus on love relationships, so it's not surprising that many of these new songs focus on male/female relationships. While most of the artists producing songs with feminist messages do sing positive songs about male/female relationships, they also strongly state that women need to be more critical of their relationships with men. A song by the Forester Sisters, called "Talkin' 'Bout Men," provides a good overview of the general critique of male/female relationships. This song is meant as a humorous response to the problems women have in relationships with men. The song is a humorous discussion of the trials and tribulations of dealing with men. The singers conclude that women cannot live with men because they are impossible, yet we need them for the survival of the species. This song is a good introduction in the sense that it reflects the general tone, usually friendly and humorous, and the basic level of critique.

In "I Would Be Stronger Than That," Faith Hill tells the story of a woman who isn't critical enough of the problems in her relationship with a man. She forgives him too easily and is afraid to leave. Faith's response is, I would be stronger, I would not stay with him.

In "Shut Up and Drive," by Chely Wright, the singer is talking to a woman friend who doesn't face reality in love relationships. The woman friend keeps leaving her man but then changing her mind and going back to him. In the song, she has left again and her friend is trying to keep her from turning around and going back—hence the title, "Shut Up and Drive." She goes on to say, you'll "only miss the man you wanted him to be."

In "Queen of Denial," Pam Tillis (affectionately entitled the queen of country by DJs) humorously addresses what happens when women are not critical of relationships with men. She sings about the ways in which women sometimes overlook the reality of how some men treat women. She gives several examples of how women deny the reality of bad relationships: denying cheating, selfishness, and inconsiderate behavior. The chorus in the song keeps telling listeners that the singer is the queen of denial. The song is humorous, but the message is clear: the woman is making a mistake when she denies the reality of how this man treats her and, perhaps, that women should not be queens of denial.

Besides suggesting that women need to be more critical of male behavior in male/female relationships, other songs argue that women should insist on reciprocity in relationships with men, with both men and women mutually giving and taking. Some songs assert, quite strongly, that women, like men, have emotional and sexual needs. In "Honey, I'm Home," Shania Twain tells her man that she's had a bad day and needs him to "Pour me a cold one. And oh, by the way, rub my feet, gimme something to eat."

While those songs seem to assume that men will provide support, other songs suggest that men do not generally operate in a reciprocal way in relationships. In "You Say You Will," Trisha Yearwood sings, "It's give and take a little. So I give you everything you choose. And you give me back IOUs." In "He Thinks He'll Keep Her," Mary Chapin Carpenter describes what could be called a gender-traditional relationship in which the woman does all the giving and caring. Mary Chapin Carpenter suggests that this type of relationship is comfortable for the man, who "thinks he'll keep her," but not for the woman, who packs a suitcase to leave after 15 years of doing all the giving.

Other songs attempt to educate men about reciprocity in relationships. Mary Chapin Carpenter, in "It Don't Bring You Love," talks to a man about the general nature of love and relationships. She says, "I can't bring you love if you don't love. And I can't bring you kindness if you ain't kind." The overall point is that love and relationships are, by their very nature, reciprocal.

A very popular version of this theme is Mindy McCready's "Guys Do It All the Time." She asks a man if he likes being treated the way men treat women. This is not a simple role reversal or call for women to treat men the way men treat women. It's an attempt to show the man that life's a two-way street and, therefore, he needs to reciprocate in relationships. What she intends to accomplish by treating him the way he has treated her is obvious in the following lines. "You look like you just took a long look in the mirror. Tell me baby if things don't look a whole lot clearer?"

In "Maybe She's Human," Kathy Mattea argues for reciprocity based on the idea that women are also human. She's "talking" to a man who can't understand why his wife gets upset when he comes home from work and tells her his problems. She points out to him that his wife has problems too and that his wife also needs someone to listen. Her basic point is that this man's wife is also human, and he needs to treat her as another human being with needs and problems, rather than as someone who simply fulfills his needs.

Another aspect of this theme is asking men to be adults within relationships. In order for reciprocity to actually happen, both partners need to be adults. In "Ain't Got Time to Rock No Baby," Lori Morgan makes it clear that she wants to be a partner, not a parent. As Bonnie Raitt sang in an earlier song, "Ain't messin' with no toys. I don't want no boys. . . .I'm a woman not a girl."

Many songs suggest that some men in relationships, far from being supportive, actually attempt to destroy women's self-esteem. The song "Broken Wings," by Martina McBride, is probably the most popular version of this theme. Martina sings about a woman who has been disempowered in a relationship with a man who broke her wings; she leaves him and is able to fly, despite her broken wings. He broke her spirit, shot down her dreams, and told her that she was crazy to believe she would ever fly—"only Angels know how to fly." The song is clearly a metaphor for the ways in which men in relationships disempower women and destroy our dreams. The moral of the story is that relationships that clip our wings are not good for women; we should leave when our wings are being broken or clipped. The chorus is "look how she flies with her broken wings." In many ways this song is a celebration of women's strength to overcome the forces that disempower us, ending with the line "You oughta see her fly."

Even when men are not attempting to clip our wings, women can be disempowered in relationships through a loss of identity. In "Is There Life Out There?" Reba McEntire sings about a woman who married when she was young and doesn't want to leave her family but wonders if there is life beyond her family and home. It seems to me that the message is that women have been taught to live their lives through men, to base their happiness and self-identities on relationships with men. Thus, women may lose a sense of self in these relationships and therefore need to develop a self-identity separate from men.

In "I Can't Do That Anymore," Faith Hill describes a traditional relationship in which a woman has done all the giving. She made herself look the way he wanted, helped him to feel important, quit her job for him, dieted for him, basically lived her life for him. The result: now he's happy and she dreams of washing machines. She concludes, "a woman needs a little something of her own." The point is that living our lives through men, prioritizing what "our" men want, does not lead to happiness. It leads to dreaming about washing machines and a loss of self-identity.

Faith Hill also sings "Someone Else's Dream." The woman in this song has always tried to live up to others' ideals. She was a daddy's girl, a mother's angel, the teacher's pet, and the beauty queen. She has spent her life pleasing everyone but herself, and now she wants to please herself. The overall point is that women lose their identity in the process of trying to please other people. Notice that all the dreams she has been living are sexist ideas about women, suggesting that we have to find ourselves outside of these images and outside of pleasing others.

Where violence within relationships is concerned, the message is very clear. As Shania Twain says, in "Black Eyes, Blue Tears," "Black eyes, I don't need 'em. Blue tears, gimme freedom. I'd rather die standing than live on my knees." The singer is making a strong statement here. She'd rather die than live in fear of a man. In "A Man's Home Is His Castle," Faith Hill tells the story of a woman caught in an abusive relationship. She describes the ideology and social structure that supports domestic abuse, by telling the story of a waitress whose husband physically abuses her. In this story the police and authorities uphold the ideology that a man's home is his castle. The only option the woman has is to run and buy a gun in case he finds her.

In "Independence Day," Martina McBride tells the story of a woman who killed her abusive husband. The song is clearly based on the novel "The Burning Bed." McBride makes it clear that the woman in the song only turned to violence after trying ever other way to end the violence directed at her. What is most interesting about this song is the use of the Fourth of July and the metaphor of freedom. The chorus throughout the song includes the line "Let freedom ring." McBride equates ending domestic violence with independence and freedom.

The message is clear. Women should not be expected to tolerate violence and abuse within relationships with men, and we are better off alone than being abused. These songs also uphold the idea that women have a right to protect themselves and a right to freedom.

How are men responding to these songs? Most of the singers whose songs I've discussed are very popular, including with male fans. So clearly male fans are not so upset about the content that the songs do not sell. The DJs, who are mostly male, express no dislike or concern about these songs. One DJ, after playing a humorous song that made fun of men, said, "That was the Forester Sisters making fun of us guys. Oh well, I guess everyone ought to be able to take a little kidding once in a while." I think his attitude reflects the basic response of men to accept these songs as a legitimate (though not necessarily appreciated) part of country music. There is not much of a male backlash, just a few negative responses. One such response was a male version of Shania Twain's "Any Man of Mine," reasserting a male-dominant view. This song was played a few times on stations, and then listeners complained and the song disappeared. There was controversy over a song by the Dixie Chicks, "Goodbye to Earl." (This song is similar to "Independence Day," discussed above). Many stations talked about refusing to play the song, but in the end the song was played. On the local radio in my town, the male DJ responded to complaints about the song with "I don't know why any man would be upset about this song, unless he was a batterer."

Many male singers are now describing their songs as women-positive.[1] There are also some new themes emerging from male singers, such as instead of "she done me wrong," "she left and it's my fault." In these songs men take responsibility for a woman leaving them because they didn't treat her right or because they did not listen to her. My personal favorite is a song by a man with the following line: "A real man knows the value of a woman." There are other songs by men that suggest that some men would like to challenge traditional views of male gender roles and male sexuality and create some new alternative visions of being a man.

There is an overall message emerging in women's country music that does address the old question from men, "What do women want?" These singers suggest that women are not impressed by the things that men think impress women. Instead they offer the following list of what women actually do want: the same sexual freedoms, desires, pleasures, and expressions that men have; for men to realize that we are real people not sex objects (to be loved and desired for ourselves, not some sexist body image); positive and reciprocal relationships with men; and freedom from violence and aggression. Above all else, as Shania Twain says, women need to "Find your self-esteem and be forever free to follow your dreams."

SONGS

Suzy Boggus, "Guilty as They Come" (Copyright © 1989 Liberty Records).

Mary Chapin Carpenter, "Passionate Kisses" (Copyright © 1989 Lucy Jones Music).

Mary Chapin Carpenter, "It Don't Bring You" (Copyright © 1989 Sony/Columbia).

Mary Chapin Carpenter, "He Thinks He'll Keep Her" (Copyright © 1992 EMI April Music).

Mary Chapin Carpenter, "I Take My Chances" (Copyright © 1992 EMI April Music).

Deanna Carter, "Strawberry Wine" (Copyright © 1996 Longitude Music).

Dixie Chicks, "Goodbye Earl" (Copyright © 1999 EMI Blackwood Music).

Forester Sisters, "Talkin' 'Bout Men" (Copyright © 1991 Warner Bros.).

Faith Hill, "Someone Else's Dream" (Copyright © 1995 Warner Bros.).

Faith Hill, "I Would Be Stronger than That" (Copyright © 1993 Warner Bros. Records).

---

[1]I have included a few songs by men. However, my analysis does not reflect the reality of many songs written or sung by men that redefine masculinity and male/female relationships. This would be important new research, as it is not only women singers who are questioning and challenging the gender structure.

Faith Hill, "I Can't Do That Anymore" (Copyright © 1995 Warner Bros.).

Faith Hill, "A Man's Home Is His Castle (Copyright © 1994 Ariel Caten Sony Tree Pub. Company).

Faith Hill, "You Will Be Mine" (Copyright © 1995 Warner Bros.).

Loretta Lynn, "The Pill" (Copyright © 1972 MCA Records).

Kathy Mattea, "Maybe She's Human" (Copyright © 1994 Mercury Records).

Martina McBride, "My Baby Loves Me" (Copyright © 1993 BMG).

Martina McBride, "Broken Wings" (Copyright © 1997 BMG Music).

Martina McBride, "Independence Day" (Copyright © 1993 BMG).

Mindy McCready, "Guys Do It All the Time" (Copyright © 1996 BMG Music).

Mindy McCready, "This Is Me" (Copyright © 1997 BMG Music).

Reba McEntire, "Is There Life out There?" (Copyright © 1996 MCA Records).

Lori Morgan, "What Part of No Don't You Understand?" (Copyright © 2000 BMG).

Lori Morgan, "Ain't Got Time to Rock No Baby" (Copyright © 1991 CURB Records).

K. T. Oslin, "Money" (Copyright © 1982 Wooden Wonder Music).

K. T. Oslin, "Round the Clock Lovin'" (Copyright © 1982 Tri-Chappell Music).

Bonnie Raitt, "Real Man" (Copyright © 1989 EMD/Capitol).

Jean Shepard, "Two Whoops and a Holler" (Copyright © 1953 Capital Records).

Jean Shepard, "The Root of All Evil Is a Man" (Copyright © 1960 Capital Records).

Pam Tillis, "Queen of Denial" (Copyright © 1992 BMG).

Shania Twain, "Any Man of Mine" (Copyright © 1995 Polygram Records).

Shania Twain, "If You Want to Touch Her" (Copyright © 1997 Mercury).

Shania Twain, "Man! I Feel Like a Woman!" (Copyright © 1997 Mercury).

Shania Twain, "That Don't Impress Me Much" (Copyright © 1997 Mercury).

Shania Twain, "Honey, I'm Home" (Copyright © 1997 Mercury).

Shania Twain, "Black Eyes, Blue Tears" (Copyright © 1997 Mercury).

Kitty Wells, "It Wasn't God Who Made Honkey Tonk Angels" (Copyright © 1952 Peer International Corporation).

Chely Wright, "Shut Up and Drive" (Copyright © 1997 MCA Records).

Trisha Yearwood, "Real Live Woman" (Copyright © 2000 UNI/MCA).

Trisha Yearwood, "Wanna Go Too Far" (Copyright © 1995 UNI/MCA).

Trisha Yearwood, "You Say You Will" (Copyright © 1992 UNI/MCA).

READING 22

Dismantling Gender Polarization and Compulsory Heterosexuality: Should We Turn the Volume Down or Up?

Sandra Lipsitz Bem

At the center of all my previous work on gender and sexuality has been the goal of shrinking both the relevance and the reach of the male-female dichotomy by trying, insofar as possible, to make it as minimal a presence in human social and psychological life as, say, eye color or foot size. Here, however, I argue that a more effective way to undo the privileged status of the two-and-only-two categories of sex/gender/desire that are currently treated in Western culture as normal and natural may be to explode or proliferate such categories (i.e., to turn the volume up) rather than

Source: Journal of Sex Research, vol. 32, issue 4. Copyright © 1995 by Society for the Scientific Study of Sex.

try to eliminate them (i.e., to turn the volume down). In making this argument, I discuss the work of three scholars whose ideas are central: philosopher Judith Butler, anthropologist Mary Douglas, and developmental geneticist Anne Fausto-Sterling.

In the final five pages of *The Lenses of Gender,* I argued that to interrupt the social reproduction of male power, we need to dismantle not only androcentrism and biological essentialism but also gender polarization and compulsory heterosexuality. In other words, we need to sever all the culturally-constructed connections that currently exist in our society between what sex a person is and virtually every other aspect of human experience, including modes of dress, social roles, and even ways of expressing emotion and experiencing sexual desire. Put somewhat differently, we need to cut back the male-female distinction to a narrow—if critically important—relevance having primarily to do with the biology of reproduction.

With complete gender depolarization, the biology of sex would become a minimal presence in human social life. This does not mean that males and females would merely be freer to be masculine, feminine, or androgynous, heterosexual, homosexual, or bisexual than they are now. What it means is that the distinction between male and female would no longer be the dimension around which the culture is organized. Hence, the very concepts of masculinity, femininity, and androgyny, heterosexuality, homosexuality, and bisexuality would be as absent from the cultural consciousness as the concepts of a "hetero-eye-colored" eroticism, a "homo-eye-colored" eroticism, and a "bi-eye-colored" eroticism are now.

Consistent with this argument, I ended *Lenses* by calling not just for a social revolution but also for a psychological revolution:

> Simply put, this psychological revolution would have us all begin to view the biological fact of being male or female in much the same way that we now view the biological fact of being human. Rather than seeing our sex as so authentically who we are that it needs to be elaborated, or so tenuous that it needs to be bolstered, or so limiting that it needs to be traded in for another model, we would instead view our sex as so completely given by nature, so capable of exerting its influence automatically, and so limited in its sphere of influence to those domains where it really does matter biologically that it could be safely tucked away in the backs of our minds and left to its own devices. In other words, biological sex would no longer be at the core of individual identity and sexuality. (Bem, 1993, p. 196)

Shrinking the relevance—or the reach—of sex in both our social and our psychological life is what I here mean by turning its volume way way down.

Anyone familiar with the history of my work on gender and sexuality already knows that the goal of shrinking sex's reach has been at its center for as long as I have been a feminist psychologist, which has now been for some 25 years. I here give only a few examples. In my early work on androgyny, I set forth a genderless model of mental health. In my later work on gender schematicity, I raised the possibility that we humans might not need to look through gender-polarizing lenses to the extent that most of us currently do. In *The Lenses of Gender,* I argued that the allegedly natural links that have long been thought to exist among sex, psyche, and sexuality have been constructed, in part, by more than 100 years of gender-polarizing theorizing in psychology, psychiatry, and sexology. Not only that, I further argued that psychology's 100-year struggle to figure out once and for all what biological sex differences there really are is misguided, in part, because it too much (and too reductionistically) emphasizes sexual difference per se and doesn't enough emphasize sexual difference in context. In other words, it is a distraction from the more urgent question of how our male-centered social world transforms whatever differences currently exist between the sexes (whether biological or not biological) into female disadvantage. Finally, there is even the mantra I recited to my children from the time they were old enough to open their ears: "A boy is someone with a penis and testicles; a girl is someone with a clitoris, vagina, and uterus; and whether you're a girl or a boy, a man or a woman, doesn't need to matter—or shouldn't anyway—until and unless you want to make a baby." [Given Anne Fausto-Sterling's (1993) analysis of intersexuals, which is discussed later in this article, I would clearly have to modify this mantra if I were teaching my children the categories of sexual difference today rather than 20 years ago.]

In my heart of hearts, I am still deeply attached to the principle of dismantling both gender polarization and compulsory heterosexuality by trying to make the male-female distinction as minimal a presence in human social life as, say, eye color or foot size. At the same time, however, I have also come to think that this goal is an unreachable utopian fantasy. After all, not only does the sex of the body (by which I mean the biology of reproduction) matter more than eye color or foot size, from which it follows that there is probably more of a biological limit on how minimal a presence sex could come to have. In addition, history probably imposes a limit as well—unless, of course, we can all manage to come down with amnesia for the many cultural and historical associations between male/female, masculine/feminine, and heterosexual/homosexual.

In an early paper on androgyny, I suggested that "when androgyny becomes a reality, the concept of androgyny will have been transcended" (Bem, 1976, p. 60). I meant by this that when the androgynous message had finally been absorbed by the culture, the concepts of masculinity and femininity would cease to have content, and the distinctions to

which they refer would blur into invisibility. But today I suggest that the content of these male/female associations will be remembered for a very long time; no matter how much we might like to, we thus cannot simply wish them away.

Much as I would still like to wish them away, given what I now see as the realities of biology and history, I have begun to worry that there may be no possible path for getting us from where we are now to where I would like us to be. So I here propose another utopian fantasy, this one based on the reverse strategy of turning the volume up. More specifically, I propose that rather than trying to dismantle the two-and-only-twoness of gender polarization and compulsory heterosexuality by eliminating gender categories, we instead dismantle that two-and-only-twoness by exploding or proliferating gender categories. In other words, I propose that we let a thousand categories of sex/gender/desire begin to bloom in any and all fluid and permeable configurations and, through that very proliferation, that we thereby undo (or, if you prefer, that we de-privilege or de-center or destabilize) the privileged status of the two-and-only-two that are currently treated as normal and natural. If a thousand categories seems too many, then let's begin with at least 18. Why 18? The math is simple: two sexes (male/female) × three genders (masculine/feminine/androgynous) × three desires (heterosexual/homosexual/bisexual). As radical—and outrageous—as this proposal will surely seem to many, it is fully consistent with the ideas of numerous contemporary scholars. I now discuss three of these.

JUDITH BUTLER

Judith Butler is a philosopher, and the book of hers that I know best is entitled *Gender Trouble: Feminism and the Subversion of Identity*, published in 1990. The question Butler set out to answer in this book was how best to make gender trouble, i.e., how best to "trouble the gender categories that support gender hierarchy and compulsory heterosexuality" (p. viii). Her answer was to challenge the conceptual foundations of the sex/gender/desire system. In her words, this means a "genealogical" critique, which is not a search for "origins" or "inner truth" but an investigation of "the political stakes in designating as an origin and cause those identity categories that are in fact the effects of institutions, practices, discourses with multiple and diffuse points of origin" (pp. viii–ix). More simply, her answer was to "trace the way in which gender fables establish and circulate the misnomer of natural facts" (p. xi).

Even in this one-paragraph introduction to Butler's work, we can already see one of its distinguishing hallmarks. Butler is a master of nifty little reversals, three of which I am now going to show you.

The traditional view in both Western culture and Western science is that there are two and only two sexes that are naturally both different from another and attracted to one another. This division of all human beings into two bipolar categories of sex/gender/desire (the one category being male/masculine/attracted to women and the other category being female/feminine/attracted to men) may be differently elaborated in different cultures but, proponents of the traditional system say, it is also the biological foundation upon which culture is built.

Butler's first reversal is as follows. Rather than these two bipolar groups being the cause of exclusive and compulsory heterosexuality, they are instead the effect of exclusive and compulsory heterosexuality. In other words, for there to be a system of exclusive and compulsory heterosexuality, two such bipolar groups had to come into existence and so, voila, the system produces them. That very cultural and historical production is then hidden, according to Butler, by an extraordinarily clever sleight of hand that casts the historical and cultural construction of the two-and-only-two into the realm of the pre-social, the pre-cultural, and pre-discursive. Thus it comes to pass that the two-and-only-two are accepted as a taken-for-granted and natural given of existence.

Another traditional view in Western culture, especially in certain branches of psychoanalysis, is that homosexuality is a pathetic imitation of heterosexuality, which is itself the natural or original form of sexuality. The same assumption holds for both drag and butch/femme roles, at least as enacted by gay men and lesbians.

Butler's second reversal goes like this. First, she argued, all gender is drag. In other words, all gender is an imitation of some phantasmagorical vision of what a man or a woman is supposed to be like. Hence there is nothing more natural, original, or unconstructed about a female dressing up like a woman than a male dressing up like a woman. That, of course, was the subtext of the movie *The Crying Game*. That, of course, is also why all the many dressed-up, made-up, and coiffed-up women walking along New York's Madison Avenue always look, to my eyes at least, not like women, but like people of whatever sex trying to look the way they think women are supposed to look.

Not only, according to Butler, is all gender drag, including that performed by the most conventional of masculine men and feminine women. In addition, heterosexuality can be said to require homosexuality as a foundation at least as much as homosexuality has been said to require heterosexuality. Put somewhat differently, heterosexuality can be seen as having needed to construct an allegedly perverse, unnatural, and imitative homosexuality as the counterpoint against which to define itself as normal, natural, and original.

The same point can be expressed in another way. It is the traditional Western view that people who do not have the so-called normal clustering of sex/gender/desire have something wrong with them. They are anomalies, pathologies, developmental failures; hence they need, in some way, to be corrected, cured, healed, or fixed.

Butler's third reversal is that these so-called anomalies are defined as anomalous not because they really are anomalous but because the system of compulsory heterosexuality requires that they be defined this way. In other words, compulsory heterosexuality requires that there exists only a very narrow range of all possible sex/gender/desire configurations. Hence it excludes all other configurations from the "matrix of intelligibility" (p. 17) and then uses these so-called perverse others as the counterpoint to establish the two-and-only-two that are allowed to exist within the framework of the system. The two-and-only-two is thus created by a historical process in which everything else is either excluded or demonized, and the border between the normal and the perverse is carefully patrolled.

Another way to say all this is that the demonized are as necessary to the system of compulsory heterosexuality as the privileged. This is so because the contrast with the so-called abnormal or perverse is what defines—and thereby brings into conceptual and empirical existence the so-called normal.

MARY DOUGLAS

Mary Douglas is an anthropologist who wrote a book in 1966 entitled *Purity and Danger: An Analysis of the Concepts of Pollution and Taboo*. At first glance, this book seems irrelevant to the current discussion because it was not about gender or sexuality but about comparative religion cross-culturally and especially about why various religions define particular things as polluted, dangerous, impure, or taboo. Nevertheless, Douglas's book has a very important idea to add to this discussion.

Her book begins with a fascinating—and highly contextual—analysis of "dirt" as "disorder" (p. 2) or "matter out of place" (p. 35). So shoes aren't "dirt," but shoes on the table are. Food isn't "dirt" either, but food in the bedroom might be, and so might be food on your sweater.

Douglas analyzed the double edge of these elements out of place. The reason they bother us so much, she suggested, is because they violate and thereby challenge, or threaten, our most cherished classifications. After all, if shoes spend enough time on the table and food spends enough time in the bedroom, pretty soon there won't even be a special place for eating any longer. So we collectively say: "Yuk, this doesn't belong here. It is dirt, pollution, dangerous, disgusting, unholy, taboo." Yet, as much as we may be bothered by these elements out of place, we need them, Douglas argued, because through their very definition as dirt, our category of non-dirt is defined and clarified. Douglas's analysis of dirt obviously shares much in common with Butler's analysis of perversion or abnormality. For both theorists, the very elements defined by a system as anomalies uphold the systematicity—and hence the existence—of the system itself.

But then Douglas added another twist. These elements out of place, she argued, are not only critical to the system; they are also a danger to the system. They must thus be carefully managed, lest their power ends up destroying the very system they are supposed to be upholding. In Douglas's words, "No culture can ignore the anomalies which its scheme produces, except at risk of forfeiting confidence" (p. 39).

Douglas gave many examples of how these dangerous elements are culturally managed. One technique is to incorporate them into public rituals, as a symbol of evil versus good. Another technique is to segregate them—as, for example, when all the Jews are put into a ghetto, and clear-cut rules are established about what kinds of interactions are and are not allowed with them. Still another technique is to eradicate the dangerous elements altogether. Douglas wrote of a culture, for example, that literally wrings the necks of all the night-crowing cocks so their presence cannot contradict the cherished cultural definition of a cock as a bird that crows at dawn.

The applicability of Douglas's analysis to sex, gender, and sexual desire is probably obvious, but I will make the three most important connections explicit. First, all the people who might currently be embraced by the label queer in our society are themselves the "dirt" that both define and threaten the culture's cherished classifications of sex/gender/desire. Second, the culture reduces the threat of all that dirt through a variety of management strategies, including, among others, requiring that lesbians and gay men stay closeted. Finally, there is power in the refusal of queer people to be managed or disciplined, power in their insistence on being unruly bodies.

ANNE FAUSTO-STERLING

The last author I will discuss is Anne Fausto-Sterling, a developmental geneticist who is perhaps best known to psychologists for her 1985 book entitled *Myths of Gender: Biological Theories about Women and Men*. What I want to discuss here, however, is her 1993 article entitled "The Five Sexes: Why Male and Female Are Not Enough."

According to Fausto-Sterling, sex is a continuum that ought to be divided not into just two sexes but into at least five sexes—which she labels women, men, herms, ferms, and merms. According to Fausto-Sterling's definitions, herms are the so-called true hermaphrodites who possess one testis and one ovary; ferms are female pseudohermaphrodites who possess ovaries and some aspect of male genitalia but no testes; and merms are male

pseudohermaphrodites who possess testes and some aspects of female genitalia but no ovaries.

Herms, ferms, and merms are estimated to be at least 4% of all births. So, says Fausto-Sterling, there ought to be as many as 240 such undergraduates on Brown University's 6,000-student campus, where she teaches. But they're not there, she goes on to say, because of our culture's unexamined assumption that they are anomalies in need of surgical and hormonal correction. These absent intersexuals, I suggest, are our culture's counterpart to the night-crowing cocks, discussed by Douglas, whose necks have been wrung. Hence, they are not in existence, either.

Partly for fun, I quote Fausto-Sterling's description of someone named Emma, who was originally described by urologist Hugh Young in a 1937 book entitled *Genital Abnormalities, Hermaphroditism, and Related Adrenal Diseases*. Emma was a hermaphrodite who had grown up as a female. According to Fausto-Sterling (1993, p. 23),

> Emma had both a penis-size clitoris and a vagina, which made it possible for him/her to have "normal" heterosexual sex with both men and women. As a teenager Emma had had sex with a number of girls to whom s/he was deeply attracted; but at the age of nineteen s/he had married a man. Unfortunately, he had given Emma little sexual pleasure (though he had no complaints), and so throughout that marriage and subsequent ones Emma had kept girlfriends on the side. With some frequency s/he had pleasurable sex with them. Young describes his subject as appearing "to be quite content and even happy." In conversation Emma occasionally told him of his/her wish to be a man, a circumstance Young said would be relatively easy to bring about. But Emma's reply strikes a heroic blow for self-interest: "Would you have to remove that vagina? I don't know about that because that's my meal ticket. If you did that, I would have to quit my husband and go to work, so I think I'll keep it and stay as I am. My husband supports

me well, and even though I don't have any sexual pleasure with him, I do have lots with my girlfriends."

Conventional medical wisdom says that, unless surgically and hormonally "corrected," intersexuals are doomed to a life of misery. But that was obviously not the case for Emma, which led Fausto-Sterling to argue for raising all the little Emmas now living in the world as "unabashed intersexuals" (p. 24). Her argument is so provocative that I quote it at some length. According to Fausto-Sterling (p. 24),

> The treatment of intersexuality in this century provides a clear example of what the French historian Michael Foucault has called biopower. The knowledge developed in biochemistry, embryology, endocrinology, psychology and surgery has enabled physicians to control the very sex of the human body. The multiple contradictions in that kind of power call for some scrutiny. On the one hand, the medical "management" of intersexuality certainly developed as part of an attempt to free people from perceived psychological pain (though whether the pain was the patient's, the parents' or the physician's is unclear). And if one accepts the assumption that in a sex-divided culture people can realize their greatest potential for happiness and productivity only if they are sure they belong to one of only two acknowledged sexes, modern medicine has been extremely successful.
>
> On the other hand, the same medical accomplishments can be read not as progress but as a mode of discipline. Hermaphrodites have unruly bodies. They do not fall naturally into a binary classification; only a surgical shoehorn can put them there. But what should we care if a "woman," defined as one who has breasts, a vagina, a uterus and ovaries and who menstruates, also has a clitoris large enough to penetrate the vagina of another woman? Why should we care if there are people whose biological equipment enables them to have sex "naturally" with both men and women? The answers seem to lie in a cultural need to maintain clear distinctions between the sexes. Society mandates the control

of intersexual bodies because they blur and bridge the great divide. Inasmuch as hermaphrodites literally embody both sexes, they possess the irritating ability to live sometimes as one sex and sometimes the other, and they raise the specter of homosexuality.

> But what if things were altogether different? Imagine a world in which the same knowledge that has enabled medicine to intervene in the management of intersexual patients has been placed at the service of multiple sexualities. Imagine that the sexes have multiplied beyond currently imaginable limits. It would have to be a world of shared powers. Patient and physician, parent and child, male and female, heterosexual and homosexual—all these oppositions and others would have to be dissolved as sources of division. A new ethic of medical treatment would arise, one that would permit ambiguity in a culture that had overcome sexual division. The central mission of medical treatment would be to preserve life. Thus hermaphrodites would be concerned primarily not about whether they can conform to society but about whether they might develop potentially life-threatening conditions—hernias, gonadal tumors, salt imbalance caused by adrenal malfunction—that sometimes accompany hermaphroditic development. In my ideal world medical intervention for intersexuals would take place only rarely before the age of reason; subsequent treatments would be a cooperative venture between physician, patient and other advisers trained in issues of gender multiplicity.
>
> I do not pretend that the transition to my utopia would be smooth. Sex, even the supposedly "normal," heterosexual kind, continues to cause untold anxiety in Western society. And certainly a culture that has yet to come to grips—religiously and, in some states, legally—with the ancient and relatively uncomplicated reality of homosexual love will not readily embrace intersexuality. No doubt the most troublesome arena by far would be the rearing of children. Parents, at least since the Victorian era, have fretted, sometimes to the point of outright denial, over the fact that their children are sexual beings.
>
> All that and more amply explains why intersexual children are generally squeezed into one

of the two prevailing sexual categories. But what would be the psychological consequences of taking the alternative road—raising children as unabashed intersexuals? On the surface that tack seems fraught with peril. What, for example, would happen to the intersexual child amid the unrelenting cruelty of the school yard? When the time came to shower in gym class, what horrors and humiliations would await the intersexual as his/her anatomy was displayed in all its nontraditional glory? In whose gym class would s/he register to begin with? What bathroom would s/he use? And how on earth would Mom and Dad help shepherd him/her through the mine field of puberty?

In the past thirty years those questions have been ignored, as the scientific community has, with remarkable unanimity, avoided contemplating the alternative route of unimpeded intersexuality. But modern investigators tend to overlook a substantial body of case histories, most of them compiled between 1930 and 1960, before surgical intervention became rampant. Almost without exception, those reports describe children who grew up knowing they were intersexual (although they did not advertise it) and adjusted to their unusual status. Some of the studies are richly detailed—described at the level of gym-class showering (which most intersexuals avoided without incident); in any event, there is not a psychotic or a suicide in the lot.

Still, the nuances of socialization among intersexuals cry out for more sophisticated analysis. Clearly, before my vision of sexual multiplicity can be realized, the first openly intersexual children and their parents will have to brave pioneers who will bear the brunt of society's growing pains. But in the long view—though it could take generations to achieve—the prize might be a society in which sexuality is something to be celebrated for its subtleties and not something to be feared or ridiculed.

TOWARD A KALEIDOSCOPE OF COLOR

Fausto-Sterling's exuberant call for us to raise little Emmas as unabashed intersexuals brings me all the way back to the proposal I made at the outset of this article, which was that we might more realistically dismantle both gender polarization and compulsory heterosexuality by turning the volume up rather than turning the volume down. In other words, it might be more effective in the long run if all of us sex/gender/desire "anomalies" were henceforth to refuse to be managed, regulated, invisibilized, disciplined, and/or in any other way homogenized into the residual category of dirt that stands in such stark opposition to the two-and-only-two privileged and cherished categories of male/masculine/attracted to women and female/feminine/attracted to men—and that we instead begin madly and exuberantly to proliferate ourselves into as many categories of sex/gender/desire as we seem to need.

Would the creation of these many new categories merely give us 1,000 strait-jackets where before we had two and only two? Not necessarily. At least not if the categories were presumed to be fluid, not if mobility were presumed to be possible from one category to another, and not if the categories acknowledged the 2-, 3-, 4-, 5- (and so on) sidedness in each of us. Who knows? Perhaps these many fluid categories would create such a huge new space of possibility that more and more people who now manage to squeeze themselves, however uncomfortably, into the two-and-only-two would begin, for the first time, to be able to see the shoehorn that is squeezing them, and they would then be motivated to look around for something that fit them better. What interesting gender trouble we would then have made.

For many years, Cornell anthropologist Kathryn March has begun her guest lecture in my undergraduate course on the Social Construction of Gender with the following analogy: Sex is to Gender as Light is to Color. Her idea here is a simple one. Both sex and light are natural physical continua, whereas gender and color are historically and culturally constructed categories that arbitrarily divide sex and light into named clusters invested with cultural meaning. Thus, in neither domain is there anything sacred—or biologically special—about the particular categories constructed by any given culture.

I have always loved this analogy because it allows me to make yet another ironic twist. With respect to color categories, anthropologists have found that some cultures have only two categories and others only three, whereas we in the U.S. have the full 256 of the big Crayola coloring box. Wow, I always say to my class, isn't it wonderful to be so richly blessed with so many possibilities rather that to be so impoverished as to have only light and dark or light and dark and red? But isn't it also ironic, I then say, that in the domain of sex/gender/desire, it's the other cultures who have that Crayola color box of multitudinous possibilities, and we who are impoverished, with two-and-only-two (plus the dirt, of course) from birth to death?

I suggested earlier that I could no longer envision any possible way to dismantle either gender polarization or compulsory heterosexuality by eliminating gender categories, but I could envision a way to do this by proliferating gender categories. Not only can I envision a way to do this; I can already see it happening in the world around me. You can see it, too, if you look under the heading of either identity politics or multiculturalism. Because what is happening there and in many more domains than just sex/gender/desire—is not the silence of turning the volume down on difference and diversity but the cacophony of sound (and also of conflict) that comes from having

finally turned the volume up on the many multidimensional voices that have been silenced far too long—including not just lesbians, gay men, and now bisexuals, but the much more color-full Crayola kaleidoscope of, for example, f-to-m and m-to-f transgendered people, lipstick lesbians, butches, baby butches, stone butches, femmes, butchy femmes, bulldaggers, leather dykes, softball dykes, rugby dykes, dykes on bikes, klesbians, hasbians, dominatrices, fag hags, drag queens, opera queens, size queens, rice queens, bears, bottoms, tops, masters, slaves, leather men, vanilla boys, clones, daddies, friends of Dorothy, and so on and so forth ad (perhaps) infinitum.

REFERENCES

Bem, S. L. (1976) Probing the promise of androgyny. In A. G. Kaplan & J. P. Bean (Eds.), *Beyond sex-role stereotypes: Readings toward a psychology of androgyny* (pp. 48–62). Boston: Little Brown.

Bem, S. L. (1993) *The lenses of gender: Transforming the debate on sexual inequality.* New Haven, CT: Yale University Press.

Butler, J. (1990) *Gender trouble: Feminism and the subversion of identity.* New York: Routledge.

Douglas, M. (1966) *Purity and danger: An Analysis of the concepts of pollution and taboo.* New York: Routledge and Kegan Paul.

Fausto-Sterling, A. (1985). *Myths of gender: Biological theories about women and men.* New York: Basic Books.

Fausto-Sterling, A. (1993) The five sexes: Why male and female are not enough. *The Sciences, 33,* 2, 19–24.

READING 23

Same Closet, Different Door: A Heterosexual Sissy's Coming-Out Party

Allan Hunter

INTRODUCTION

> *It is a universal fact of human existence that what we know best, that which forms part of our everyday mental landscape, is also that which we most take for granted, and question the least. And so some of the strongest jolts to our awareness, the deepest reorientations in our thought, often come from being confronted with the obvious.*
>
> —Miedzian, *Boys Will Be Boys*

There are two types of things that are very difficult for us to understand: the very deviant phenomenon, for which we have no name and no concept; and the very normal one, which we tend to take for granted because we have no concept of any possible contrast. Heterosexuality, for a long time in Western culture, has been of the second category. Until recently, general awareness of nonheterosexual people and their lives was almost totally confined to off-color jokes and murky stereotypes, always looking at them from the outside. Only as gay rights and feminist social movements have drawn more attention to actual non heterosexual people—their actual lives and their political and social concerns—have we started to acquire the beginnings of an understanding of heterosexuality in contrast. Even now, though, we tend to take heterosexuality for granted (and thus are not understanding it) except in

the immediate context of gay, lesbian, or bisexual people and their active communication of their perspective. We have not tended to look at the social forms particular to heterosexuality, or to consider the effects that heterosexuality has on a person, except for the limited times and occasions when they impinge enough on our consciousness to provide a momentary contrasting backdrop.

Consider the following question. My use of the referents "we" and "they" in the preceding paragraph shows that I am consciously writing as a heterosexual person. Can I, a heterosexual person, write about heterosexuality itself if I have only limited secondhand access to the experiences and perspectives of gay, lesbian, and bisexual people? What is the source of my authority to write? Is there any reason to assume that I understand this phenomenon from the inside if I have nothing in my direct experience or awareness to compare it to?

The assumption behind that question is that heterosexuality exists only in contrast to differing erotic practices. Or, to turn an aphorism around, it is as if heterosexuals were interesting and worthy of understanding only for what we do in bed! At the insistence of theorists such as Adrienne Rich, heterosexuals have been challenged to move beyond thinking only of the erotic practices of gay men and lesbians, and to begin to understand the institutional aspects of sexuality. Insofar as heterosexuality is also more than a matter of what individuals with which body parts do to people with which other body parts, there are other possible contrasting positions from which it can be seen from the outside, so as to clarify the meaning of being on the inside. I would like to consider the matter of heterosexuality and what it means from a very deviant position, a phenomenon for which we have no simple name and only rarely even a blurry concept. I assume that you are quite familiar with our culture's commonly shared notions of masculinity, in the sense of prescribed

Source: Feminism and Psychology Special Reader: Heterosexuality, vol. 2(3), pp. 367–385. Copyright © 1993. Reprinted with permission from Sage Publications.

personality and behavioral characteristics associated with heterosexual men. (This would seem to be a reasonable assumption.) Probably you are also aware of stereotyped notions of gay men as nonmasculine—more like women than they are like other (heterosexual) men, or at least less masculine and more feminine than heterosexual men are. What, then, is the proper name for a male who is not masculine in his general personality and behavior if he happens to be sexually oriented toward women? And what are the experiences of such males (and do we call them men?) with heterosexuality—their own (if we still call it that) and that which surrounds them?

This is not a research report. I do not have a nice collection of new, interesting formal data to provide for the expansion of our understanding of heterosexuality. Instead, although I may make reference to various things as examples to illustrate a point I'm trying to make, I intend to work mainly with the large pool of everyday knowledge and shared meanings which we all know so well, and to look at it a bit differently. Feminist theory in general had its origins in that process: it was not as if no one had ever noticed that men dominated women sexually, or got paid more to do the same work until feminists did research to prove it, but rather that people had not looked at these things and questioned them and considered what it all meant.

I will supplement everyday knowledge with some impressions gained from my own life. You see, the unconventional male vantage point I have described is the only position from which I am directly able to consider heterosexuality, since this deviant position is the position of my own experience.

BONDS: HOMOPHOBIA, MASCULINITY, HETEROSEXUALITY

For lack of any adequate pre existent terminology, and since using long strings of words quickly becomes tiring, I will follow the lead of lesbians who call themselves "dykes" and the militant gay rights group Queer Nation, and I will seize a pejorative term that was hurled at me and other such males and I will make it my own: *sissy*. The word is etymologically derived from *sister* and therefore directly connotes the sense of being like a girl or woman. Although this male-centered world tends to emphasize the worst of feminine characteristics, such as dependency and passivity, and the best of masculine ones, such as taking initiative and having courage, femininity is also associated with nurturing, caring, and being sensitive, while masculinity is also associated with violence, vulgarity, and an obsession with winning and dominating. A sissy is a male (regardless of sexual orientation) who is in some way not masculine, who is in some meaningful way more like women than men tend to be, or are "supposed" to be. Maybe he is proud of it. Maybe he has reasons for not wanting to resemble other males in personality and behavior. In my case, I certainly am, and do.

To say "regardless of sexual orientation" is to threaten an assumed connection, a bond which is so rarely challenged that it is rarely recognized as such. When I was being called "sissy," I was also being called "faggot" and "queer" as I was being physically and verbally assaulted. To be a sissy is to be on the inside of homophobia, surrounded by it, experiencing it constantly. You don't even have to be physically attracted to males to get in.

Patriarchal heterosexuality—that is, heterosexuality in a context where male domination is normative and endorsed by the players—is tied to homophobia. The most virulent and commonplace expressions of homophobia are directed toward homosexual males. Since male gay behavior is first and foremost male behavior, it should seem provocatively odd that male domination would constrain male sexual behavior with such fervor. This is a qualitatively different kind of phenomenon from the functional constraints put on male sexual behavior in order to preserve various social institutions. For example, there are social sanctions against men raping women, molesting children, committing infidelities once married, and so on. These sanctions appear to be geared toward the general maintenance of the institutions of marriage and family, but they exist in ambivalence, diluted in large part by men's tendency to permit themselves a wide latitude of sexual behavior as long as it doesn't immediately infringe upon other men. Given that, you would expect that the proscriptions against consensual male homosexual activity would be formal but not necessarily internalized or deeply enforced by strong and (almost) universally shared attitudes. You would expect, perhaps, winks and boasts of homosexual activities as something a man got away with, or intends to get away with. It should be an item of curiosity that an angry man in a bar or an angry boy in the schoolyard will shout "You faggot" but not "You rapist" as a term of abuse.

A closer look reveals that the primary image that heterosexual society has of the homosexual man is an image of a dominated man, one who is taking on the feminine sexual role, or who has had that role forced upon him. The boys in the schoolyard don't just say "You faggot"; they also say "Fuck you." In American prisons, it is widely whispered that there are males (especially young ones) who are utilized as receptacles, who are buggered, sodomized by force—they are considered to be homosexual, but those who rape them or insert into them are not.

All sexual activity tends to require at least one deliberate actor if not necessarily two; but the image that heterosexuals have of the active male who is volitionally causing gay sexual activity to take place is oddly focused on a portrayal of the gay male who actively wants to sexually please other men: to arouse the erec-tion, to provide the mouth or the anus, to be used as women are used. Homosexuality is somehow his doing. Effeminate men make it happen. In an interesting equivocation, even those males who can be put into a position of sexual subserviency through force and intimidation are assigned responsibility, and their identity is blurred with that of males who actively wish to give other males sexual pleasure. More deeply hidden in the shadows of the socially shared concept of gay male behavior is the image of the male who actively lusts after other males for his own sexual pleasure and seeks them out. Our conventional images have no easy word or image of the male who actively seeks his own pleasurable erotic sensations with other men. His existence is denied, ignored almost completely.

The gay liberation movement and the gay cultural motifs of recent years seem to have addressed this, with gay men criticizing the stereotype of the gay male as effeminate and asserting their masculinity as well as their pride in their sexual preference. Fiction author John Rechy strongly implies that it has become almost "politically incorrect" for men in at least some parts of the gay community in America to be effeminate (see, for example, *The Rushes*). This threatens the otherwise absolute bonds between images of masculinity and male heterosexuality and between those of effeminacy and male homosexuality.

The image of the male who is effeminate and whose sexual orientation is toward women threatens that same bond from the heterosexual side. The bond hasn't been threatened from that direction very much yet. People may be somewhat more likely to say or think that not all gay men are necessarily sissies, but they are not likely to assert or actively think that not all sissies are necessarily gay, thus leaving heterosexuality the exclusive province of the masculine male. This is the foreground for an examination of heterosexuality: to recognize that heterosexuality is largely conceptualized, unthinkingly, as a relationship between women and masculine males. It is time to develop a more critical awareness of the effects of that bond and how the pieces fit together.

Gay men sometimes speak of having been "born that way." As a heterosexual sissy, I have a strong tendency to think that the attraction to females was something I was born with—I can recall an intense and erotic fascination with girls' bodies, such as the way that genital differences caused that part of their pants to be shaped differently. It gave me strange naughty-sweet feelings to look at that or think about it. This was happening at an age when I was incredibly naive about sex (all I knew was how babies were made; no one had ever told me that sex was pleasant or that there was an appetite aspect to it), so I didn't know anyone else had ever had such feelings or that they were normal or anything like that. Therefore, when people tell me that sexual preference is all caused by socialization, I'm inclined to doubt them. While it may be true that all people have the capacity to have pleasant erotic experiences with either same-sex or opposite-sex partners, I tend to think that some people may have strong preference tendencies to begin with.

I was not born a sissy, though. My sense of myself as more like the girls that the other boys developed over a period of time during early elementary school, and it had a lot to do with the social status of children. Children were all treated as immature, irresponsible people, not deserving of the respect that adults demanded for themselves. I wanted respect, dignity, and equality with adults, and to my way of thinking at the time, if we demonstrated maturity and responsible control over our actions, we would earn the corresponding autonomy and proper treatment. Furthermore, it was obvious that the girls were doing a very good job of being good citizens and were appreciated for it: teachers and other people's

parents had a strong tendency to trust girls and to praise them for being good, whereas the boys were all treated as discipline problems looking for a place to happen. Therefore, there were many times when I was accused of being like a girl, and I reacted by agreeing and being proud of it.

Meanwhile, although I had strong girl-oriented sexual feelings during these early years, the fact that I didn't know what they were or what the world expected from male sexuality meant that I didn't have a perspective on heterosexuality until later, when being a sissy ran me up against the scripted roles for sexual behavior.

The meaningful processes of heterosexual interaction can be divided into meeting and courtship, which is the first bundle of scripted sexual behaviors, and the structure and dynamics of ongoing sexual relationships, which is a related but separate bundle of roles and scripts.

FLIRTING: THE POLITICS OF GETTING HETEROSEXUALITY STARTED

Stop right there! I gotta know right now
Before we go any further,
Do you love me? Will you love me forever?

Lyrics Source: Paradise By the Dashboard Light. James Steinman. Copyright © 1977. Reprinted with permission from Edward B. Marks Music Company. All rights reserved.

When Kinsey laid to rest the part of the double standard that maintained women got no pleasure at all from sex, everyone cried out that there was a sexual revolution afoot. But such talk, as usual, was deceptive. Morality, outside the marriage bed, remained the same, and children were socialized as though Kinsey had never described what they would be like when they grew up. Boys were taught that they should get their sex where they could find it, "go as far" as they could. On the old assumption that women were asexual creatures, girls were taught that since they needed sex less than boys did, it was up to them to impose sexual restraints . . .

Adolescent boys growing up begging for sexual crumbs from girls frightened for their "reputations"—a situation that remains unchanged to this day—hardly constitutes the vanguard of a sexual revolution.

—Susan Lydon, "The Politics of Orgasm"

These traditional images of heterosexual behavior are well-known, widely shared, and expected to be shared, enough so that virtually all the adolescents and young adults know that this is still more or less the way things are. Sometimes the flirtation stage actually occurs twice, with essentially the same rules but on two different levels. In a context where there is an implied sexual meaning to any male-female encounter, such as a singles bar or a dance, the first level is the occasion of meeting for the first time. Females usually do a great deal to initiate this, but traditionally not in an overt, direct way. They make eye contact and draw attention to themselves, but it is up to the male to make the approach and say the first word. The second level is more universal and revolves more specifically around the question of whether or not to engage in erotic behavior. Some variation on the following stereotyped assumptions tends to operate:

1. The females want to "fall in love" and be loved in return by a cute guy who will be the boyfriend, and, within that context, they want good sex (in earlier times, marriage was necessary first). The males don't really like most females that much, unless they are in love, and they aren't necessarily trying to fall in love at all, and so, in or outside of that context, they want good sex. Therefore . . .

2. Males come on to females, usually because they are physically attracted to them, since their main interest is physical and appear-ance is a physical phenomenon. Sometimes they come on to a female because she has a reputation for being sexually available to males whether they love her or not. Either way, the females can reject the guys they don't have any interest in at all, but the other males have to be kept interested but slowed down so that proximity and time create the possibility that he will really start to like her, perhaps fall in love. Females do not overtly come on to males.

3. Males who are rejected are allowed to keep on trying, since males who think they are not really being rejected, just slowed down a bit, are *supposed* to keep on trying, and sometimes you can't tell which is which anyway. But if a male thinks a female is being too hard to get, so that it isn't fun for him any more, he can quit paying attention to her—he doesn't have to keep on trying. Females are not supposed to pursue the matter. It is up to him to press the issue.

Feminists have made it apparent that the scripted roles for heterosexual behavior are oppressive and humiliating to women—keeping women passive, mutating their own sexual appetite so that it becomes the man's ally and the opposite of their self-determination, making sex a conquering of women by men, and eroticizing male domination itself. They have also indicted masculinity itself, as an identity construct that seems to depend for its existence on being extremely different from females and very glad of it and contemptuous of all things female and feminine. Since the advent of the feminist movement, courting behavior has lost some of its gender-specific rigidity, but for the most part only to a degree. Some individual clauses of the silent "contract" described here may not apply to certain age groups, certain ethnic or cultural subgroups, and so on, but single heterosexual people seldom operate with a blank slate rather than a set of expectations, and those expectations are usually gendered, more or less according to the scripted roles give above.

Interestingly, a concept of women's oppression is actually embedded in the basic sexist courting roles. The assumption woven into the scrip is that casual sex (as opposed to sex in the context of an ongoing, loving relationship) is oppressive to women and that men who seek it are preying upon them. Heterosexuality, then, is a competitive struggle between the male and the female. That men would want to prey upon women is assumed to be part of male nature. A male person with little or no interest in trying to dominate and oppress females might find the male role script distasteful and consider relating sexually to women differently; indeed, from overhearing female conversations, it might seem that women are perpetually on the lookout for such fellows. Unfortunately, as Anaïs Nin once pointed out, women may demand a more sensitive man, but aren't sure of what to do with one when they find one.

The problem actually lies not with the inconsistency of women, nor even directly with an insufficiency of sensitive men, but rather in the structure of the scripted roles themselves. It is a much more serious problem for male sex role nonconformists than for our female equivalents. There is not as strong a conceptual bond between femininity and heterosexuality for females as there is between masculinity and heterosexuality for males. Sex between males and females can and often does result when females do not obey the script—for example, they may take a far more active and overt role in causing sex to happen, or they may act on an interest in casual sex by accepting male overtures without any attempt to play "hard to get" or to slow the man down. This is an important point, even though females who behave in this fashion are subjected to labeling and contempt from both males and females. Nonfeminine females, or masculine females, have a range of images and stereo-

types that include heterosexual activity: the slut, the bitch, the castrating dominating strong woman, and so on. These are negative, of course, but they could be (and sometimes have been) proudly adopted by nonconforming assertive women, and, in theory at least, such women could eventually meet men who like them that way through the operation of the heterosexuality script. When males do not obey their scripted role, there is no provision within the script which calls for heterosexual behavior to take place. If it is to take place at all, it must do so outside, beyond the script and its assumptions about what various behaviors mean.

There is no happy medium. The sissy must behave against a patriarchal backdrop, not in a vacuum. Sexually assertive behaviors which would not be considered oppressive otherwise are open to being interpreted that way precisely because other men, in general, have behaved as they have. Nowhere does this have greater impact than in the matter of the simple, honest declaration of sexual attraction. Surrounded by females complaining of the exploitative, insensitive nature of men's raw sexuality, and often confronted head-on with the generic automatic female response to all male expressions of immediate sexual interest, the sensitive young male who identifies with and respects women is likely to be rapidly polarized. He ends up being driven toward a masculinizing track of ceasing to feel hurt by such interpretations of his sexuality, or else toward complete (or nearly complete) cessation of expressing appetite for women in order to avoid being accused of, to put it tritely, "being only after one thing."

The sissy whose sexual orientation is toward women brings the possibility of very different concepts of heterosexuality, perhaps so much so that a new term would be needed for this as well. But the heterosexual sissy is conceptually homeless. And so was I, until I conceived of myself. Which I did. But that makes it sound easy, and getting to that point was an agonizing, stressful experience. I had to do that alone.

I am a person who has been angrily or sneeringly accused of being gay all my life (usually in uglier terms), and therefore because I always had a strong sexual interest and orientation toward girls (and later, women), I had all the seeds for homophobia planted in my head, too. You see, I was made to be afraid of the idea that homosexuality might be what "happens" to boys like me whether it's what we want or not. Since I didn't particularly like other males, generally speaking, that just made it all the more scary. Constantly being confronted with it, having it shoved in my face as an accusation, I finally reached a point (while still virginally inexperienced with women) when I had to ask myself whether or not they were right—Was I gay? Answer: well, I have the capacity to be, if I want to be. After a lifetime of being accused of it, I give myself permission to enjoy gay sex if I ever want to, and I'll be damned if I'm going to spend the rest of my life worrying about it, but that's not really what I want right now.

The real fear that was revealed by considering it as a possibility was the fear of never having the sexual experiences and close relationships that I had always wanted with women. I saw that I'd have to deliberately search beyond the norm. My sexuality was different.

And in that moment, I came out of *my* own closet, at least to myself (since I was still an invisible identity with no word for it, there was no easy way to express what I understood about myself to anyone else). I stood "acquitted" of having to be anything I didn't want to be. I rejoiced in being a sissy and celebrated the fact that my sexuality is oriented toward women but isn't dependent on or defined by a committed effort to avoid sexual feelings and experiences with men. And suddenly it all seemed really simple. The rest of it was just a matter of coming out to the rest of the world.

EXCITEMENT: A TRANSITION

> Journalist Stephanie Gutmann is an ardent foe of what she calls the date-rape dogmatists. "How can you make sex completely safe?" she asks. "What a horribly bland, unerotic thing that would be! Sex is, by nature, a risky endeavor, emotionally. And Desire is a violent emotion. These people in the date-rape movement have erected so many rules and regulations that I don't know how people can have erotic or desire-driven sex."
> —Nancy Gibbs, "When Is It Rape?"

Stephanie Gutmann is not the only person I've heard say or come close to saying that sex would lose its sexiness if it no longer included the element of the "hunt," the attempt to seduce and the thrill of the chase, any of which blur into coercion and domination if it is not just a game. In the times when I've overheard rare discussions about the heterosexual attractiveness and possibilities of sissy men, it has often been asserted that such men have too much in common with the women for either of them to feel much excitement. There is no gap for the spark to jump. You get two sweet, nice people together, and nobody's going to do anything except with the permission of the other, assuming that anyone has the "balls" to bring the subject up. Nobody getting turned on, chased down, and had by someone who knows how to arouse the traitor body. Nobody feeling the triumph of coming in for the "kill," gleefully and sardonically taking and having the teasing sexy someone they'd been wanting so long. This is the only available image for getting together outside of the scripted sex roles: bringing up the subject verbally and discussing the matter rationally and politely, so that all the cards are face-up on the table. The fun and spontaneity is dead on the cold dry dissecting table of intellectual analysis, and there's no danger, tension, or suspense.

This, they say to me, explains why opposites attract. It explains why heterosexual men must be masculine. Women want real men, and that's all there is to it.

I think they still might find it upsetting to be reminded that some of the women want real women instead. Until the middle of my own feminist-era lifetime, the idea of even one woman actively seeking sexual pleasure on her own initiative was censored out of people's imagery, perhaps because it is so threatening to another one of those bonds, the bond between maleness and the "masculinity" of active sexual lust. As I said before, all sexual activity tends to require at least one deliberate actor if not necessarily two. Lesbians are certainly oppressed, as women and as gay people, but, interestingly, a great deal of their oppression has taken the form of denying their existence or of rendering it "safe," some kind of cuddly, unimportant, not-really-lusty female activity that some women engage in when they can't catch a man. (In contrast, the idea of gay men seems so important for the institution of heterosexuality that I think that if there were no gay men they would have been invented as mythical creatures. There needs to be something that boys are afraid of becoming if they don't embrace the actively dominant, anti woman attitudes of masculinity.) At any rate, the very existence of lesbians and of women's own lusty sexual appetite and tendency to act upon it directly does bring to mind one possible answer to the "opposites attract" argument outlined above for why sissy males would be boring to women because no one would take the initiative—let dynamic, assertive women who are accused of being unfeminine seduce the sweet sissy guys! It would keep the old gendered scripts active, albeit running in reverse order, but at least the women wouldn't have to worry about oppressing the men by expressing and acting upon any sexual desire they felt for them.

But, really, it isn't that simple. For one thing, little boys do not grow up being warned about predatory girls, and for the most part males do not in any other way internalize stuff that would give them the complex of reluctances and ambivalences about sex that makes up that part of classic femininity. There is no sense of danger and suspense because, to paraphrase Mae West, you cannot seduce the willing. To whatever extent we do need a sense of danger and suspense and tension in order to make flirtation sexy, putting the responsibility for sexual initiative on women will not provide it for sissy men, however many other things it might solve. In our society, which eroticizes domination and power conflicts, the most likely location of such an eroticized situation for a sissy male would be with other men—because it is forbidden, because it has been warned against, because it has been so effectively painted as a sexual phenomenon which stalks males and must be feared and fought against. This, really, is the crux of the argument about "opposites attract."

If it is true that all people have the capacity to experience pleasurable erotic sensations in sex with people of the same sex in some situation, and it is also true (at least in the world as we know it) that issues of power, conflict, and vulnerability tend to add the fuel of excitement and suspense to potential erotic situations, then all men in Western society have been set up to respond under the right circumstances with erotic passion by being seduced in some way by other men simply because it is possible and yet forbidden. In a short, tight loop, it becomes possible partly because it is scary, which is why it is so scary! Here, indeed, is the bottom of the valley of homophobia, and from here the links between homophobia, heterosexuality, and masculinity in men start to make sense.

COUPLING: THE POLITICS OF KEEPING HETEROSEXUALITY GOING

If there is any widely shared image of a non-masculine man functioning in an actively heterosexual situation—a "sissy archetype"—then it's Caspar Milquetoast, a mild-mannered ineffectual married man dominated by his wife. He does what she wants him to do. Presumably, she married him in order to use him as a source of money or social status. We still can't visualize him flirting or participating in those brief hedonistic sexual encounters called one-night stands. If the conventional male's sexual interests are constructed first around the fear of being gay and the need to prove otherwise, they are further shaped by a desire to avoid the fate of Caspar Milquetoast, who probably married her because that was the only way he was ever going to have any access to heterosexual erotic experiences. The applicable epithet is "pussy-whipped."

In patriarchal male-dominant society, the logical norm to which one might expect men to aspire would be the opposite of this: a man in an ongoing relationship with a woman in which she does what he wants her to do. And there are such images, head-of-the-family patriarch images, but they aren't the central masculine motif at all. In fact, all images of the male engaged in an ongoing relationship with a female are at least faintly tainted by the Caspar Milquetoast image, and the most masculine images are those in which male-female relationships are the most temporary and superficial, tightly constrained to an impersonal and oppositional erotic contact. These are the forms of male-female contact that are traditionally assumed to be exploitative of women, as discussed previously. In short, it would appear from the imagery that all heterosexual possibilities must involve the domination of someone, either men or women, and that the possibilities for men's domination lies mostly in short-lived, superficial encounters. Since research seems to indicate that marriage is emotionally and psychologically good for men and bad for women, this is another assumption that should seem odd to us without further explanation.

Some forms of exploitation do seem to work best during occasions of short-term contact, such as robbery, whereas others work better over a protracted period of time, such as slavery. Interestingly, the forms involving short-term contact are usually exploitations of people who are not truly weaker in the context where exploitation is taking place: if the thief does not escape quickly, the person whose property has been stolen may gain useful access to systems of law enforcement and the exploitation will not work.

In the case of male domination in a close erotic context, the male is cloaked in shared images of male authority as well as far less ambivalence about the permissibility of his sexual behaviors and, furthermore, is in a much better position to use physical force. These all contribute to male domination, and sometimes suffice to do so over long periods of time.

But not always. Sexual sensations have emotional content in and of themselves and have a tendency to create or strengthen empathic connections and shared identity. Intimacy, in other words, has a tendency to spread. Domination that depends on an ideology of Difference and Superiority, as male supremacy tends to, is incompatible with a sense of connectedness and shared identification. If this is revolution, though, it is confined to the level of individuals. Shulamith Firestone, writing in *The Dialectic of Sex* about how love is the pivot of women's oppression, said that the only thing that makes a man's feeling of connectedness and identification with a woman stand out and look so special is the backdrop of his attitudes toward women in general, within which women are not perceived as equal, interesting, or even as people. And yet, this experience, the "holy grail" of women's sexual existence within patriarchy, merely causes each woman to hope that one man will be led by sexual and related emotional experiences to identify with her and therefore see her as a person while continuing to view other women as subhuman, tangential, unworthy of consideration.

But intimacy has a capacity far more fearful than the mere capacity for undermining ideologies of superiority. When a sense of shared identity and connectedness has been created, and exists strongly, the individual's identity becomes meshed into the relationship itself and with the other person or persons. Like a center of gravity, this shifted sense of identity affects personal orbits. To be in love is to be vulnerable to the opinions, needs, and wants of the other who is now no longer strictly other at all. To be in love is to risk being more deeply in love than the other, to become subsumed in another's life and interests and immediate emotional condition and concerns more deeply than one's own—or, rather, they become one's own.

This is not to say that love is only about power and domination. The person who has the dubious distinction of having someone fall more or less unilaterally in love with her or him must often deal with an emotionally fragile, dependent person who follows about, puppy-eyed and pathetic. For most people, this is not preferable to a more balanced relationship with the richness of needing and feeling needed, enjoying the emotional intoxication of identifying while experiencing the joys of having another become intoxicated with them in turn. But love is not separable from power and the possibility of becoming thoroughly decentered and probably hurt in the process. Love is not safe and cannot be made safe.

Patriarchal custom makes a valiant try, however. When one considers how little the masculine personality construct and the over-

all male experience prepares males for the emotional interplay of interconnection and caring and need, it becomes readily apparent why it has to. The marriage contract and the less formal structures by which ongoing heterosexual relationships are commonly assembled are generally geared toward promises of forever, promises of exclusivity, promises of ever-continuing deep feelings on a mutual basis. In the current era of legal, obtainable divorce and greater individual freedoms in such personal matters, they don't tend to work very well. But to the extent that they do work, creating "safe" situations where leaving the relationship or getting involved with someone else is out of the question for those involved, they result in boring, stagnant, unerotic relationships dragging themselves off into the sunset. Because without the excitement and the fears and the vulnerability that come from risking love with another free person, there is no gap for the spark to jump.

RESOLUTION

Erotic excitement, according to patriarchal ideology, depends on the tension created by setting men against women in a power struggle, setting them at cross purposes, with conflicting interests that create the possibilities of vulnerability and domination. The scene of this conflict is the period of negotiation for sexual experience: if he "scores," he wins and moves on; if he falls in love and sticks around for an ongoing relationship, she wins; if he gives up and moves on without "scoring," it's a draw.

Heterosexuality with sissies involved doesn't include erotic excitement as constructed by that particular system, but if the false patriarchal division between courtship and ongoing relationship is recognized for what it is and discarded, there are other sources of eroticized vulnerability, and I've not found matters boring.

The sissy quite possibly has prided himself all his life for his development of "feminine" strengths. Although contemptuously conceptualized as a dominated Caspar Milquetoast, he has no necessary reason to fear the ongoing relationship that would ordinarily characterize a female win. With no fragile rigid sense of identity dependent on how different he is from women, the possibility of falling in love and identifying deeply with a woman has a less frightening face, and so he is probably more ready to share and care. The hard part, other than figuring out who (or "how") he is in the first place, is finding women who have recognized that there is nothing for them within the boundaries of the heterosexual game script of how boy meets girl and stays with girl, and are therefore looking outside beyond it. Most likely, these are women who are not committed to a sense of themselves as heterosexual feminine women. Fortunately, female identity is less constructed around proving that one is not a lesbian, and feminism has certainly helped. Feminists understand best about discarding the role scripts and starting off from scratch with no sexist assumptions.

It is unclear who holds the advantage at close range. The typical woman available for the sissy to play with is probably more experienced with the specific dynamics of erotic and other intimate emotional connectedness, and could probably get involved with another man much easier than he could get involved with another woman. On the other hand, there are fewer men like him than there are women like her, and they both know it. Furthermore, most strong women are not *used* to playing with men who are their emotional equals in intimate relationships. All in all, it tends to be rather risky and frightening for both, with lots of vulnerability and tenderness and sparks jumping around all over the place.

READING 24

Transgender Warriors: Making History

Leslie Feinberg

I found my first clue that trans people have not always been hated in 1974. I had played hooky from work and spent the day at the Museum of the American Indian in New York City.

The exhibits were devoted to Native history in the Americas. I was drawn to a display of beautiful thumb-sized clay figures. The ones to my right had breasts and cradled bowls. Those on the left were flat chested, holding hunting tools. But when I looked closer, I did a double-take. I saw that several of the figures holding bowls were flat chested; several of the hunters had breasts. You can bet there was no legend next to the display to explain. I left the museum curious.

What I'd seen gnawed at me until I called a member of the curator's staff. He asked, "Why do you want to know?" I panicked. Was the information so classified that it could only be given out on a "need to know" basis? I lied and said I was a graduate student at Columbia University.

Sounding relieved, he immediately let me know that he understood exactly what I'd described. He said he came across references to these berdache* practically every day in his reading. I asked him what the word meant. He said he thought it meant transvestite or transsexual in modern English. He remarked that Native peoples didn't seem to abhor them the way "we" did. In fact, he added, it appeared that such individuals were held in high esteem by Native nations.

Then his voice dropped low. "It's really quite disturbing, isn't it?" he whispered. I hung up the phone and raced to the library. I had found the first key to a vault containing information I'd looked for all my life.

"Strange country this," a white man wrote in 1850 about the Crow nation of North America, "where males assume the dress and perform the duties of females, while women turn men and mate with their own sex!"[1]

I found hundreds and hundreds of similar references, such as those in Jonathan Ned Katz's ground-breaking *Gay American History: Lesbians and Gay Men in the U.S.A.*, published in 1976, which provided me with additional valuable research. The quotes were anything but objective. Some were statements by murderously hostile colonial generals, others by the anthropologists and missionaries who followed in their bloody wake.

Some only referred to what today might be called male-to-female expression. "In nearly every part of the continent," Westermarck concluded in 1917, "there seem to have been, since ancient times, men dressing themselves in the clothes and performing the functions of women. . . . "[2]

But I also found many references to female-to-male expression. Writing about his expedition into northeastern Brazil in 1576, Pedro de Magalhães noted females among the Tupinamba who lived as men and were accepted by other men, and who hunted and went to war. His team of explorers, recalling the Greek Amazons, renamed the river that flowed through that area the *River of the Amazons*.[3]

Female-to-male expression was also found in numerous North American nations. As late as 1930, ethnographer Leslie Spier observed of a nation in the Pacific Northwest: "Transvestites or berdaches . . . are found among the Klamath, as in all probability among all other North American tribes. These are men and women who for reasons that remain obscure take on the dress and habits of the opposite sex."[4]

I found it painful to read these quotes because they were steeped in hatred. "I saw a devilish thing," Spanish colonialist Alvar Núñez Cabeza de Vaca wrote in the sixteenth century.[5] "Sinful, heinous, perverted, nefarious, abominable, unnatural, disgusting, lewd"—the language used by the colonizers to describe the acceptance of sex/gender diversity, and of same-sex love, most accurately described the viewer, not the viewed. And these sensational reports about Two-Spirit people were used to further "justify" genocide, the theft of Native land and resources, and destruction of their cultures and religions.

But occasionally these colonial quotes opened, even if inadvertently, a momentary window into the humanity of the peoples being observed. Describing his first trip down the Mississippi in the seventeenth century, Jesuit Jacques Marquette chronicled the attitudes of the Illinois and Nadouessi to the Two-Spirits.

---

*"Berdache" was a derogatory term European colonizers used to label any Native person who did not fit their narrow notions of woman and man. The blanket use of the word disregarded distinctions of self-expression, social interaction, and complex economic and political realities. Native nations had many respectful words in their own languages to describe such people; Gay American Indians (GAI) has gathered a valuable list of these words. However, cultural genocide has destroyed and altered Native languages and traditions. So Native people ask that the term "Two-Spirit" be used to replace the offensive colonial word—a request I respect.

In a further attempt to avoid analyzing oppressed peoples' cultures, I do not make a distinction between sex and gender expression in this chapter. Instead, I use sex/gender.

"They are summoned to the Councils, and nothing can be decided without their advice. Finally, through their profession of leading an Extraordinary life, they pass for Manitous.— That is to say, for Spirits,—or persons of Consequence."[6]

Although French missionary Joseph François Lafitau condemned Two-Spirit people he found among the nations of the western Great Lakes, Louisiana, and Florida, he revealed that those Native peoples did not share his prejudice. "They believe they are honored . . ." he wrote in 1724, "they participate in all religious ceremonies, and this profession of an extraordinary life causes them to be regarded as people of a higher order. . . ."[7]

But the colonizers' reactions toward Two-Spirit people can be summed up by the words of Antonio de la Calancha, a Spanish official in Lima. Calancha wrote that during Vasco Núñez de Balboa's expedition across Panama, Balboa "saw men dressed like women; Balboa learnt that they were sodomites and threw the kind and forty others to be eaten by his dogs, a fine action of an honorable and Catholic Spaniard."[8]

This was not an isolated attack. When the Spaniards invaded the Antilles and Louisiana, "they found men dressed as women who were respected by their societies. Thinking they were hermaphrodites, or homosexuals, they slew them."[9]

Finding these quotes shook me. I recalled the "cowboys and Indians" movies of my childhood. These racist films didn't succeed in teaching me hate; I had grown up around strong, proud Native adults and children. But I now realized more consciously how every portrayal of Native nations in these movies was aimed at diverting attention from the real-life colonial genocide. The same bloody history was ignored or glossed over in my schools. I only learned the truth about Native cultures later, by re-educating myself—a process I'm continuing.

Discovering the Two-Spirit tradition had deep meaning for me. It wasn't that I thought the range of human expression among Native nations was identical to trans identities today. I knew that a Crow *badé*, Cocopa *warhameh*, Chumash *joya*, and Maricopa *kwiraxame'* would describe themselves in very different ways from an African-American *drag queen* fighting cops at Stonewall or a white *female-to-male transsexual* in the 1990s explaining his life to a college class on gender theory.

What stunned me was that such ancient and diverse cultures allowed people to choose more sex/gender paths, and this diversity of human expression was honored as sacred. I had to chart the complex geography of sex and gender with a compass needle that only pointed to north or south.

You'd think I'd have been elated to find this new information. But I raged that these facts had been kept from me, from all of us. And so many of the Native peoples who were arrogantly scrutinized by military men, missionaries, and anthropologists had been massacred. Had their oral history too been forever lost?

In my anger, I vowed to act more forcefully in defense of the treaty, sovereignty, and self-determination rights of Native nations. As I became more active in these struggles, I began to hear more clearly the voices of Native peoples who not only reclaimed their traditional heritage, but carried the resistance into the present: the takeover of Alcatraz, the occupation of Wounded Knee, the Longest Walk, the Day of Mourning at Plymouth Rock, and the fight to free political prisoners like Leonard Peltier and Norma Jean Croy.

Two historic developments helped me to hear the voices of modern Native warriors who lived the sacred Two-Spirit tradition: the founding of Gay American Indians in 1975 by Randy Burns (Northern Paiute) and Barbara Cameron (Lakota Sioux), and the publication in 1988 of *Living the Spirit: A Gay American Indian Anthology*. Randy Burns noted that the

History Project of Gay American Indians "has documented these alternative gender roles in over 135 North American tribes."[10]

Will Roscoe, who edited *Living the Spirit*, explained that this more complex sex/gender system was found "in every region of the continent, among every type of native culture, from the small bands of hunters in Alaska to the populous, hierarchical city-states in Florida."[11]

Another important milestone was the 1986 publication of *The Spirit and the Flesh*[12] by Walter Williams, because this book included the voices of modern Two-Spirit people.

I knew that Native struggles against colonialization and genocide—both physical and cultural—were tenacious. But I learned that the colonizers' efforts to outlaw, punish, and slaughter the Two-Spirits within those nations had also met with fierce resistance. Conquistador Nuño de Guzmán recorded in 1530 that the last person taken prisoner after a battle, who had "fought most courageously, was a man in the habit of a woman. . . ."[13]

Just trying to maintain a traditional way of life was itself an act of resistance. Williams wrote, "Since in many tribes berdaches were often shamans, the government's attack on traditional healing practices disrupted their lives. Among the Klamaths, the government agent's prohibition of curing ceremonials in the 1870s and 1880s required shamans to operate underground. The berdache shaman White Cindy continued to do traditional healing, curing people for decades despite the danger of arrest."[14]

Native nations resisted the racist demands of U.S. government agents who tried to change Two-Spirit people. This defiance was especially courageous in light of the power these agents exercised over the economic survival of the Native people they tried to control. One such struggle focused on a Crow *badé* (*botè*) named *Osh-Tisch* (Finds Them and Kills Them). An oral history by Joe Medicine Crow

in 1982 recalled the events: "One agent in the late 1890s . . . tried to interfere with Osh-Tisch, who was the most respected *badé*. The agent incarcerated the *badés*, cut off their hair, made them wear men's clothing. He forced them to do manual labor, planting these trees that you see here on the BIA grounds. The people were so upset with this that Chief Pretty Eagle came into Crow Agency, and told [the agent] to leave the reservation. It was a tragedy, trying to change them."[15]

How the *badés* were viewed within their own nation comes across in this report by S. C. Simms in 1903 in *American Anthropologist*: "During a visit last year to the Crow reservation, in the interest of the Field Columbian Museum, I was informed that there were three hermaphrodites in the Crow tribe, one living at Pryor, one in the Big Horn district, and one in Black Lodge district. These persons are usually spoken of as 'she,' and as having the largest and best appointed tipis; they are also generally considered to be experts with the needle and the most efficient cooks in the tribe, and they are highly regarded for their many charitable acts. . . .

"A few years ago an Indian agent endeavored to compel these people, under threat of punishment, to wear men's clothing, but his efforts were unsuccessful."[16]

White-run boarding schools played a similar role in trying to force generations of kidnapped children to abandon their traditional ways. But many Two-Spirit children escaped rather than conform.

Lakota medicine man Lame Deer told an interviewer about the sacred place of the *winkte* ("male-to-female") in his nation's traditions, and how the *winkte* bestowed a special name on an individual. "The secret name a *winkte* gave to a child was believed to be especially powerful and effective," Lame Deer said. "Sitting Bull, Black Elk, even Crazy Horse had secret *winkte* names." Lakota chief Crazy Horse reportedly had one or two *winkte* wives.[17]

Williams quotes a Lakota medicine man who spoke of the pressures on the *winktes* in the 1920s and 1930s. "The missionaries and the government agents said *winktes* were no good, and tried to get them to change their ways. Some did, and put on men's clothing. But others, rather than change, went out and hanged themselves."[18]

Up until 1989, the Two-Spirit voices I heard lived only in the pages of books. But that year I was honored to be invited to Minneapolis for the first gathering of Two-Spirit Native people, their loved ones, and supporters. The bonds of friendship I enjoyed at the first event were strengthened at the third gathering in Manitoba in 1991. There, I found myself sitting around a campfire at the base of tall pines under the rolling colors of the northern lights, drinking strong tea out of a metal cup. I laughed easily, relaxed with old friends and new ones. Some were feminine men or masculine women; all shared same-sex desire. Yet not all of these people were transgendered, and not all of the Two-Spirits I'd read about desired people of the same sex. Then what defined this group?

I turned to Native people for these answers. Even today, in 1995, I read research papers and articles about sex/gender systems in Native nations in which every source cited is a white social scientist. When I began to write this book, I asked Two-Spirit people to talk about their own cultures, in their own words.

Chrystos, a brilliant Two-Spirit poet and writer from the Menominee nation, offered me this understanding: "Life among First Nation people, before first contact, is hard to reconstruct. There's been so much abuse of traditional life by the Christian Church. But certain things have filtered down to us. Most of the nations that I know of traditionally had more than two genders. It varies from tribe to tribe. The concept of Two-Spiritedness is a rather rough translation into English of that idea. I think the English language is rigid, and the thought patterns that form it are rigid, so that gender also becomes rigid.

"The whole concept of gender is more fluid in traditional life. Those paths are not necessarily aligned with your sex, although they may be. People might choose their gender according to their dreams, for example. So even the idea that your gender is something you dream about is not even a concept in Western culture—which posits you are born a certain biological sex and therefore there's a role you must step into and follow pretty rigidly for the rest of your life. That's how we got the concept of queer. Anyone who doesn't follow their assigned gender role is queer; all kinds of people are lumped together under that word."[19]

Does being Two-Spirit determine your sexuality? I asked Chrystos. "In traditional life a Two-Spirit person can be heterosexual or what we would call homosexual," she replied. "You could also be a person who doesn't have sex with anyone and lives with the spirits. The gender fluidity is part of a larger concept, which I guess the most accurate English word for is 'tolerance.' It's a whole different way of conceiving how to be in the world with other people. We think about the world in terms of relationship, so each person is always in a matrix, rather than being seen only as an individual—which is a very different way of looking at things."[20]

Chrystos told me about her Navajo friend Wesley Thomas, who describes himself as *nadleeh*-like. A male nadleeh, she said, "would manifest in the world as a female and take a husband and participate in tribal life as a female person." I e-mailed Wesley, who lives in Seattle, for more information about the nadleeh tradition. He wrote back that "nadleeh was a category for women who were/are masculine and also feminine males."[21]

The concept of nadleeh, he explained, is incorporated into Navajo origin or creation stories. "So, it is a cultural construction," he wrote, "and was part of the normal Navajo culture, from the Navajo point of view, through the nineteenth century. It began changing during the first half of the twentieth century due to the introduction of western education and most of all, Christianity. Nadleeh since then has moved underground."[22]

Wesley, who spent the first thirty years of life on the Eastern Navajo reservation, wrote that in his initial fieldwork research he identified four categories of sex: female/woman, male/man, female/man, and male/woman. "Where I began to identify gender on a continuum—meaning placing female at one end and male on the other end—I placed forty-nine different gender identifications in between. This was derived at one sitting, not from carrying out a full and comprehensive fieldwork research. This number derived from my own understanding of gender within the Navajo cosmology."[23]

I have faced so much persecution because of my gender expression that I also wanted to hear about the experiences of someone who grew up as a "masculine girl" in traditional Native life. I thought of Spotted Eagle, who I had met in Manitoba, and who lives in Georgia. Walking down an urban street, Spotted Eagle's gender expression, as well as her nationality, could make her the target of harassment and violence. But she is White Mountain Apache, and I knew she had grown up with her own traditions on the reservation. How was she treated?

"I was born in 1945," Spotted Eagle told me. "I grew up totally accepted. I knew from birth, and everyone around me knew I was Two-Spirited. I was honored. I was a special creation; I was given certain gifts because of that, teachings to share with my people and healings. But that changed—not in my generation, but in generations to follow."

There were no distinct pronouns in her ancient language, she said. "There were three variations: the way the women spoke, the way

the men spoke, and the ceremonial language." Which way of speaking did she use? "I spoke all three. So did the two older Two-Spirit people on my reservation."[24]

Spotted Eagle explained that the White Mountain Apache nation was small and isolated, and so had been less affected early on by colonial culture. As a result, the U.S. government didn't set up the mission school system on the White Mountain reservation until the late 1930s or early 1940s. Spotted Eagle said she experienced her first taste of bigotry as a Two-Spirit in those schools. "I was taken out of the mission school with the help of my people and sent away to live with an aunt off reservation, so I didn't get totally abused by Christianity. I have some very horrible memories of the short time I was there."[25]

"But as far as my own people," Spotted Eagle continued, "we were a matriarchy, and have been through our history. Women are in a different position in a matriarchy than they are out here. It's not that we have more power or more privilege than anyone else, it's just a more balanced way to be. Being a woman was a plus and being Two-Spirit was even better. I didn't really have any negative thoughts about being Two-Spirit until I left the reservation."[26]

Spotted Eagle told me that as a young adult she married. "My husband was also Two-Spirit and we had children. We lived in a rather peculiar way according to standards out here. Of course it was very normal for us. We faced a lot of violence, but we learned to cope with it and go on."[27]

Spotted Eagle's husband died many years ago. Today her partner is a woman. Her three children are grown. "Two of them are Two-Spirit," she said proudly. "We're all very close."[28]

I asked her where she found her strength and pride. "It was given to me by the people around me to maintain," she explained. "If your whole life is connected spiritually, then you learn that self-pride—the image of self—is connected with everything else. That becomes part of who you are and you carry that wherever you are."[29]

What was responsible for the imposition of the present-day rigid sex/gender system in North America? It is not correct to simply blame patriarchy, Chrystos stressed to me. "The real word is 'colonization' and what it has done to the world. Patriarchy is a tool of colonization and exploitation of people and their lands for wealthy white people."[30]

"The Two-Spirit tradition was suppressed," she explained. "Like all Native spirituality, it underwent a tremendous time of suppression. So there's gaps. But we've continued on with our spiritual traditions. We are still attached to this land and the place of our ancestors and managed to protect our spiritual traditions and our languages. We have always been at war. Despite everything—incredible onslaughts that even continue now—we have continued and we have survived."[31]

Like a gift presented at a traditional give away, Native people have patiently given me a greater understanding of the diverse cultures that existed in the Western hemisphere before colonization.

NOTES

1. Edwin Thompson Denig, *Five Indian Tribes of the Upper Missouri,* ed. John C. Ewers (Norman: University of Oklahoma Press, 1961) 199.
2. Edward Westermarck, "Homosexual Love," *The Origin and Development of Moral Ideas,* 2nd ed., 2 vols. (London: Macmillan, 1917), 2:456.
3. Pedro de Magalhães, *The Histories of Brazil,* trans. John B. Stetson, Jr. (New York: The Cortes Society, 1922) 89–90.
4. Leslie Spier, "Klamath Ethnography," *University of California Publications in American Archaeology and Ethnology* 30 (1930): 51–53.
5. Alvar Núñez Cabeza de Vaca, "Naufragios," *Historiadores primitivos de Indias,* ed. Enrique de Vedia, (Madrid: M. Rivadeneyra, 1852) 538, Vol. 1 of *Biblioteca de autores españoles,* quoted in Jonathan Katz, *Gay American History: Lesbians and Gay Men in the U.S.A.* (New York: Harper & Row, 1976) 285.
6. Jacques Marquette, *Of the First Voyage Made by Father Marquette Toward New Mexico, and How the Idea Thereof Was Conceived,* ed. Reuben Gold Thwaites (Cleveland: Burrows, 1896–1901) 129, Vol. 59 *of The Jesuit and Allied Documents,* quoted in Katz, 287.
7. Joseph François Lafitau, *Moeurs des sauvages ameriquains, comparées aux moeurs des premiers tempts,* 2 vols. (Paris: Saugrain, 1724) 1:52, 603–10, quoted in Katz, 288–89.
8. Francisco Guerra, *The Pre-Columbian Mind* (London: Seminar Press, 1971) 190, cited in Walter Williams, *The Spirit and the Flesh: Sexual Diversity in American Indian Culture* (Boston: Beacon Press, 1986) 137.
9. Cora Dubois, cited in Richard Green, "Historical and Cross-Cultural Survey," *Sexual Identity Conflict in Children and Adults* (New York: Basic Books, 1974) 11.
10. Randy Burns, "Preface," and the Gay American Indian History Project, "North American Tribes with Berdache and Alternative Gender Roles," *Living the Spirit: A Gay American Indian Anthology,* compiled by Gay American Indians, coordinating ed. Will Roscoe (New York: St. Martin's Press, 1988) 1, see language list on 217–22.
11. Will Roscoe, *The Zuni Man-Woman* (Albuquerque: University of New Mexico Press, 1988) 5.
12. Walter Williams, *The Spirit and the Flesh: Sexual Diversity in American Indian Culture* (Boston: Beacon Press, 1986).
13. Ibid., 137.
14. Ibid., 178.
15. Ibid., 179.
16. S.C. Simms, "Crow Indian Hermaphrodites," *American Anthropologist* ns 5 (1903): 580–81.
17. C. Daryll Forde, "Ethnography of the Yuma Indians," *University of California Publications in American Archaeology and Ethnology* 28.4 (1931): 157, quoted in Williams, *Spirit and Flesh,* 38; Lakota informant as cited in Williams, 112.
18. Williams, *Spirit and Flesh,* 182.
19. Chrystos, telephone interview, 14 March 1995.
20. Ibid.

21. Wesley Thomas, e-mail communication, 5 April 1995.
22. Ibid.
23. Ibid.
24. Spotted Eagle, telephone interview, 16 March 1995.
25. Ibid.
26. Ibid.
27. Ibid.
28. Ibid.
29. Ibid.
30. Chrystos, telephone interview, 14 March 1995.
31. Ibid.

PART FOUR

SEX AND THE BODY

Our bodies are sexual long before we become conscious of it, and how we think about our bodies is based on gendered sexuality. Body parts are named and treated differently by gender, such as female breasts and male chests. Both males and females have breasts and nipples. Both also have chests. However, they are coded in very different ways. In the United States, men's breasts can be exposed in public. Women's cannot. Men's nipples are not publicly erotized, at least not to the point where, like women's, they need to be covered to prevent arrest for indecent exposure. Although women's nipples have a clear biological function, that of nursing, they are perceived to be so extremely erotic as to be dangerous when exposed. The danger, of course, is that viewing women's nipples will cause male arousal. At the same time, how males respond depends on how much exposure they have had to women's bodies in a nonsexualized setting. In the United States, women's exposed breasts appear only in sexually oriented materials—films, magazines, video games—all intended to arouse males. In cultures where exposure is much more common and not sexualized, male response is quite different.

A sociological analysis of sex and the body is important to understanding how we respond to our own body and that of others. The body, is after all, a source of social capital—the means through which a person can gain advantage over others. The very slender female body that has recently come into vogue is a social ideal that leads many young women to become anorexic or to suffer from bulimia. However, their thin bodies get attention from males and are presented in the media as the ultimate look. The social ideal of the hypermuscled male body leads young men to take steroids. Both the eating-disordered body and the one on steroids will be likely to have health problems, but the payoff in the moment is considered worth the price.

Bodies can also be a source of stigma. Consider the deformed body or the body that doesn't "fit" with the ideal type. Social status is lost, self-esteem may suffer, and the person is less likely to be perceived as sexual. The pretty, the handsome, and the sexy are likely to be advantaged over those with less of these qualities. Breast implants, removing body hair, piercings, tattoos, and plastic surgery are all forms of overtly adapting the body to gain identity and social status within the peer group or in the larger society. Sexual adaptations of the body are common on some levels and in some form in most societies. It is important, however, to consciously consider what social factors influence our decisions and the effects such adaptations have on our lives.

So why a chapter on sex and the body? Sex *is* the body in many ways. Ask the readers of *Sports Illustrated* or *Penthouse*. Ask women who look at men's buttocks in newspaper ads for designer men's underwear. (The daily newspaper is often the source of subtle, and not so subtle erotica.) To what extent are our bodies the containers for our sexuality? We "feel" our sexuality through the image we have of our own bodies and through experiencing others' bodies, visually or physically.

According to the sociological perspective of Erving Goffman, we "present" our self in everyday life as a response to how we perceive other people's perception of us. We are publicly bombarded by sexual images, which broadcast that our bodies need to be what others would perceive as sexually desirable. These images are used to sell products and, for women particularly, as a basis for determining sexual status. The focus is on bodies that are "clean" and "youthful." Culturally, we have little use for the diseased body, the woman's body with a breast missing, or the male body with symptoms of HIV/AIDS. We don't see a scantily clothed aging woman's body in a monthly men's magazine trying to sell sex to aging men, or any women's magazine, unless it is a claim that a product like eye makeup or breast implants can create an image of youth.

The media and medicine are two major sources of information about our sexual bodies. While the media promote a sexiness that will cost money to achieve (and create wealth for the media industry), medicine has focused on medicalization of the sexual body, sometimes at great expense to individuals and society. "Sexual health," as Leonore Tiefer suggests later in this volume, has become a foundational concept. Yet it is metaphor that presupposes the "dirtiness" of both the body and sexuality. Tiefer is concerned that there has been "a gradual transformation by which medicine, with its distinctive ways of thinking, its models, metaphors and institutions, has come to exercise authority over sexuality" (p. 302). The medical model of sex reflects a biological essentialist view of the body, in that medicine claims to be a morally neutral, objective science, seeing the body and its systems as independent of mind, culture, and spirit. Yet medicine hasn't always had the answer to what the sexual body needs.

Authors in this section invite us to rethink the sexual body, having an awareness of the commercial media portrayals, medical judgments, and other social influences and effects on our sexual lives.

In "The Kindest Un-Cut: Feminism, Judaism, and My Son's Foreskin," Michael S. Kimmel writes about the struggle he and his wife faced in making a decision not to circumcise their newborn son. While his Jewish tradition would have led him to circumcise, medical opinion was mixed. Moreover, they were aware that citizens of few other countries circumcise their male babies at the rate of parents in the United States. Looking into the medical history of circumcision, they learned that routine medical circumcision was quite rare in the United States before the 1870s. Doctors subscribing to Victorian sexual morality, Kimmel reports, saw circumcision as a method for curbing sexual appetite and pleasure and recommended it as a method for reducing masturbation in children. In this way, male circumcision can be seen as linked historically with female genital circumcision, the removal of the clitoris, which is carried out in some cultures in order to reduce sexual urges and make girls more marriageable (less likely to wander). Kimmel's historical inquiry reveals that, as waves of uncircumcised immigrants entered the country, circumcision of newborn males was seen as a way to stake a claim for a truly "American" morality. Circumcision meant social capital.

Kimmel also found there was more of a mixed history in Jewish support for circumcision than he had known. However, the gender politics of the procedure were finally the decisive factor. They chose not to participate in reproducing patriarchy, passing male privilege from one generation to the next, by visiting ritualized violence on their son. The alternative *bris* (the Jewish term for the circumcision ceremony) that welcomed his son into the family and community was nonviolent, leaving the boy, as his father says, "free to feel the pleasures of his body" and ready to participate as a full equal with women in his life. As you read this article, consider ways you have "gone along with" social customs that reify gendered norms, assuming media or the medical community had the best answer for defining what happens to the body. How might Kimmel's historical and religious analysis serve as an example of ways to interrogate other social-sexual practices?

Ironically, the next article, "A Story of Sexuality and Gender in Three Parts" is about body-altering surgery carried out voluntary by an adult and chosen as a means of escaping hegemonic gendered sexuality. L. Maurer and M. Kelly tell the story of a decision by one of them to have breasts removed in order to arrange the sexual body to fit with the gendered identity. They situate the decision within the wider framework of their relationship, the fluid sexual identity of one, and the fluid gender identity of the other. The partner who had surgery chose to be outside of male or female, after a lifetime of "not fitting in." Such actions can be seen as a form of resistance to dominant male–female polarization. They received a great deal of support from family and medical providers. As you read their story, consider how you or your peers might respond to someone announcing they were about to undergo such surgery. To what extent does our physical body reflect our sexuality? Do we have an obligation to our primary sexual partner to maintain a certain type of body? What happens if our partner's sexual body changes, from choice or due to other reasons?

Leonore Tiefer's essay, "Medicine, Morality, and the Public Management of Sexual Matters," uses the example of her work with men who have been referred to a urology department for treatment of sexual problems, to theorize effects of the medicalization of sexuality. As stated earlier in this introduction, the medical model views the body as a biological machine. This mechanistic approach, when applied to sexual "dysfunction," belies the role played by socialization or the current social context. The result, according to Tiefer, is a discourse on erections; the search for the perfectly functioning penis through repair or replacement of parts that don't work. Female partners are considered as "support people" but not as significant players in the diagnosis or treatment. Tiefer asks that we challenge the limited script for heterosexual sexual life. She finds that the contraceptive revolution and the medicalization of sex, with its mind-body dualism and technical focus, are preventing us from doing the emotional, spiritual, and relational work that can resolve many sexual problems. As you consider her analysis, think about the alternatives to medical interventions. What might a broader script include?

Outside of medicine, there is little open public discourse to address sensitive sexual body processes. Girl's periods and boy's ejaculations are two examples of such private experiences. While girls get mixed messages (and often too little information) about menses, boys' first experience of semen is extremely hushed. Few parents or teachers prepare boys for the experience with positive information or use it as a "welcome to manhood" event—as at least is the case with the "You're a woman now!" rhetoric of Kotex pads. Loren Frankel shares his research into cultural attitudes toward boys' first ejaculation. His article, "Hands Off! The Taboo Surrounding Males' First Ejaculation," suggests the coming-of-age experience for boys is, interestingly, both a tabooed act and a universal aspect of male development. He draws on American social history to connect the shroud of anxious silence around first ejaculation and fears and prejudice surrounding masturbation.

Rachel Maines reports another silenced aspect of sexuality in "Socially Camouflaged Technologies: The Case of the Electromechanical Vibrator." Gynecological massage of women by physicians has been a well-documented but seldom noted standard medical treatment for *hysteria*, menstrual disorders, and other female complaints for at least the last 2,000 years. Maines reviews physicians' use in the 19th century of the new electromechanical vibrator, followed by the direct marketing of this device to middle-class women. She discusses this as an example of socially camouflaged technologies, products whose actual design purpose is either illegal or socially unacceptable. As you read this article, written for an electrical engineering magazine, consider how this historical medicalization of a function as natural as orgasm—but one prohibited at the time by social constraints—is an example of how sexual response is socially constructed.

First, women were socially cliterectomized by the good girl–bad girl dualism and related lack of information about their clitoris and the possibility of female orgasm. Then they had to see a doctor to "relieve" them of socially induced anxiety related to constricted gender roles. Vibrators can now be purchased in drug stores, but their sexual purpose is not described on the wrapper. Reflect on the way women (and men) still lack information about the clitoris and women's sexual response and the implications for women's experiences of their bodies.

Sonia Shah's report, "The Orgasm Industry: Drug Companies Search for a Female Viagra," provides an opportunity to relate Tiefer's discussion of male sexual dysfunction and Maines's history of the vibrator. In the wake of the enormous commercial success of Viagra, the pill for erectile dysfunction, pharmaceutical companies are now searching for what Shah calls the next big sex drug, for women this time, an even larger potential market. Consider the meaning of this commodification and medicalization of female orgasm. First, societal norms constrain and prevent female orgasm. Then it is sold back to women in the form of a medication, with related side effects. Biological answers to socially constructed problems may indeed have created more social and biological problems. In what ways, given the stigmatized nature of female sexual response and gendered power relations, might it be easier for a woman to ask a doctor for a pill, rather than talking with her partner about what feels good and what doesn't?

Our sexuality changes when our bodies change because of illness or aging. Helen Gurley Brown, former editor of *Cosmopolitan*, brings her trademark urbane, humorous touch to the discussion of sex after 60. As she says in the title of her article, "Don't Give Up on Sex after 60." Having been a media leader in the creation of the "sexually liberated" female who looks good and buys beauty products, it is interesting to see Gurley Brown's advice to the aging Cosmo girl. Her suggestions for "getting a younger man" presume financial resources. What physical and social adjustments can aging women and men make in order to retain a satisfying sexual life?

In "The Five Sexes, Revisited," a piece adapted from her recent book *Sexing the Body*, Anne Fausto-Sterling brings the concept of multiple genders, and its implications for sexuality and sexual identity, into the arena of the body. She discusses the ways intersexuals test medical values and social norms. The issue is the treatment of infants born with ambiguous genitalia, a mixture of both male and female anatomy, or genitals that appear different from their chromosomal sex. Fausto-Sterling estimates this occurs in 17 out of every 1,000 babies. Can physicians and psychologists accept that people come in bewildering sexual varieties? Will they listen to the voices of their previous consumers, patients whose gender was surgically prescribed, who are now arguing that we should leave intersexed children alone? Can society accept that one's physical genitals may not always match one's presentational gender? This issue problematizes the standard use of *gender* on official documents, in that not everyone can check off *male* or *female*. What other social changes will need to occur if gender proliferation and fluidity become the norm?

The photo "Jack Unveiled," following the Fausto-Sterling article, depicts a gender-ambiguous person in a sexually focused pose. Muscles, breasts, nipple rings, slim waist and hips. What assumptions might viewers make about this person's sex and gender? What about his/her attractions and sexual identity? Why is it anxiety provoking, or even angering for some people, when they "can't tell" someone's gender?

Kai Wright's story, "To Be Poor and Transgender," will challenge any ideas that being transgender is a white, middle-class thing. Wright presents the realities of life for people whose gendered appearance depends on hormone prescriptions and for whom going to a clinic entails confronting judgments of health care workers about their body and gender decisions. Activists trying to build a transgender community and social movement face the same battles gay activists confronted for many years, including divisions among members of a very diverse group, fear of visibility, lack of resources, and the emotional drain of facing prejudice and potential violence every day.

The final article in this section is Kent L. Sandstrom's "Redefining Sex and Intimacy: The Sexual Self-Images, Outlooks, and Relationships of Gay Men Living with HIV/AIDS."

Sandstrom reports findings from his research on the effects of illness on the sexual self-images, outlooks, and relationships of gay men living with HIV/AIDS. Any serious illness affects one's sense of oneself and the response one receives from others. When the illness is sexually related, stigmatized, and sexually transmittable, as Sandstrom's interviewees reflect, the issues are complex. With HIV/AIDS becoming more of a disease that one lives with, rather than immediately dies from, relationships and sexual desires cannot be just put on the shelf. Do you reveal your HIV serostatus (seropositivity indicates the presence of virus in your blood)? When? What kind of sex do you have, in terms of degree of "safety"? Many people face such questions, including those who have herpes or those concerned about becoming infected with HIV. Sandstrom also reports the difficulties and coping strategies used by those with HIV/AIDS as serious disability or death approached. The responses offer insights into the challenges to self and sexuality encountered by people with other diseases affecting one's sexuality, such as breast cancer and genitiourologic cancer. In what ways might it be even more challenging to have a disease that affected your sexuality?

The Kindest Un-Cut: Feminism, Judaism, and My Son's Foreskin

Michael S. Kimmel

Although it was a little late by traditional religious standards, the entire family and many friends gathered in our home three weeks after our son, Zachary, was born. We had gathered for his *bris*, the moment when a young Jewish boy is first brought into the family and the community, the moment of his formal entrance into the world of Judaism. At such symbolic moments, one feels keenly the sinews of connection to family and friends that sustain a life, animate it, give it context and meaning.

The mohel, of course, was running late. When he arrived, everyone gathered in the living room, where we had set up a table on which we had placed the various items we would use in the ceremony. A special chair had been reserved for the "sandek," the honored family male elder, often the baby's grandfather or great-grandfather, who would hold the baby during much of the proceedings. (In our case, a godmother and godfather shared this role.)

As family and friends drew closer together, glasses of wine and champagne in their hands, the ritual began with prayers over the wine and bread. Our first toast to this new creature who had entered all our lives. Then the mohel began the naming ceremony, and some relatives and friends offered their wishes for this young life.

Amy, my wife, and I each offered a thought to the other and to Zachary as we entered this new phase of our lives as parents together. For my part, I quoted Adrienne Rich, who had written that "if I could have one wish for my own sons, it is that they should have the courage of women." I wished nothing more for Zachary than that he would have Amy's courage, her integrity, and her passion.

Then it was the moment for which we had all carefully prepared, about which we had endlessly talked, debated, argued, discussed. We took a pitcher of water and a bowl to the door of the house. Amy and I carried Zachary over to the threshold. With one hand I held his little body and with the other held his tiny legs over the bowl. Amy poured some water over his feet and rubbed it in. They she held him and I did the same. Throughout, the mohel chanted in prayer. And in that way, we welcomed Zachary into our home and into our lives.

By now you are, of course, waiting for the "real" *bris* to begin, for the mohel to stuff a wine-soaked handkerchief into our son's mouth to muffle his cries and slightly anesthetize him, and then circumcise him, cutting off his foreskin in fulfillment of God's commandment to Abraham that he mark his son, Isaac, as a sign of obedience.

Sorry to disappoint, but that's the end of our story. Or at least the end of the story of Zachary's *bris*. There was no circumcision on that day. We had decided not to circumcise our son. Although he enters a world filled with violence, he would enter it without violence done to him. Although he will no doubt suffer many cuts and scrapes during his life, he would not bleed by our hand.

This was not an easy decision, but we had plenty of time to prepare—nine months to be exact. From the moment we saw the sonogram and read the results of the amniocentesis, the debate had been joined. Would we or wouldn't we? How would we decide? The remainder of this essay charts that process.

First, we talked. Constantly. Just when we thought the issue settled, we'd open it again.

Source: Tikkun, 16, no. 3. Copyright 2001. Reprinted with permission of author Michael Kimmel.

Each time one of us would read something, think something, pull something new off the Internet, we would reopen the discussion anew. We talked with friends, family members, religious authorities, doctors, and nurses. We asked our heterosexual women friends whether they had a preference for cut or uncut men. We each sought counsel from the email discussion groups to which we belonged, and we consulted organizations like the American Academy of Pediatrics and the American Medical Association. We ordered and read more than a dozen books and pamphlets.

We contacted advocacy groups like National Organization of Circumcision Information Resource Centers (NOCIRC), National Organization to Halt the Abuse and Routine Mutilation of Males (NOHARMM), and Doctors Opposing Circumcision (DOC). But these organizations, while eager, were too one-sided, and tended to minimize the difficulty of our decision.

And we didn't even bother calling the organizations like Brothers United for Future Foreskins (BUFF), National Organization of Restoring Men (NORM), and RECover a Penis (RECAP) that encourage men who might "feel victimized by the unnecessary loss of their natural anatomical wholeness," as Joseph Zoske writes in *Journal of Men's Studies* (1998), to undergo penile reconstructive surgery to "correct" the circumcised penis. Such procedures (involving either attaching a new flap or pulling the remaining tissue down over the glans to create a pseudo-foreskin) seem as unnecessary as circumcision, and no doubt attend to psychological distress that has only the most tenuous connection to a small flap of penile tissue.

PROS AND CONS

We heard a lot of arguments, for and against. To be sure, there is no shortage of arguments in favor of circumcision. Some are aesthetic, and offer a psychological theory based on that aesthetic. Without circumcision, we heard, our son will look different from his father, and thus develop shame about his body. Our son will look different from other Jewish boys, especially in our heavily Jewish neighborhood, thus be subject to ridicule and teasing, and develop a sense that he does not belong. As one man on an email list to which I posed the question wrote, "I don't want my kid to be an object of interest while taking public showers, such as in gym class or in athletic clubs."

Other arguments are medical. After all, male circumcision is the most common surgical procedure in the United States and medical insurance carriers routinely cover hospital circumcision (which raises the incentives of medical practitioners to advocate the procedure). Our son's risks of penile infection, STD, and especially penile cancer would be significantly lower if he were to be circumcised. The likelihood of uterine cancer in his female sexual partners would be higher if he were not.

In addition, there were conflicting reports on the effects of circumcision on sexual functioning. There is some evidence from sex surveys that circumcised men are more sexually active and more sexually adventurous, especially as regards oral and anal sex. Circumcised men masturbate more often. And because circumcised men have less sexual sensitivity—after all, the foreskin contains about 1,000 nerve endings, fully one-third of the organ's pleasure receptors—there is some evidence that circumcision delays ejaculation somewhat.

And, of course, the weight of family, history, and culture do not rest lightly on the shoulders of the new parent. As Jews we knew full well the several-thousand-year-old tradition of following one of the most fundamental of God's commandments to Abraham—that "every male among you shall be circumcised . . .and that shall be a sign of the covenant between Me and you."

the United States, circumcision of newborns was a way to stake a claim for a truly "American" morality. Rates jumped to 25 percent by 1900. After World War II, when the *Journal of the American Medical Association* reported that rates of STD were higher among blacks and uncircumcised white men, circumcision rates continued to climb, and by 1980, nearly nine of every ten American boys was circumcised.

But it now appears that the rapid spread of circumcision as a routine medical procedure had more to do with Victorian hysteria about sexuality that it did with hygiene. And given the American Academy of Pediatrics' recent backpedaling on the issue—from ritual endorsement to anxious agnosticism to its most recent resigned disapproval—there seems to be no medical argument—historical or hygienic—to compel the procedure.

THE WEIGHTS OF TRADITION

The combined weights of family and religious culture were not so easily negotiated. As predicted, the future grandmothers were somewhat more sanguine about the prospect of non-circumcision than were the future grandfathers. It's ironic that it's always been women—even within Judaism—who have opposed circumcision as a violence done to their babies, and circumcised males who have supported it. Perhaps it is analogous to fraternity or military initiation ceremonies, where the salutary outcome of feeling a sense of belonging to the larger homosocial group is deemed worth any price, including the removal of a third of one's potential sexual pleasure.

In our case, neither Amy nor I felt any strong compulsion towards circumcision, but I was more strongly opposed on moral grounds. Amy's opposition would come later, when she first held Zachary in her arms and she felt a visceral rage that anyone would do anything that would ever hurt this new creature. In very gender stereotyped terms, Amy's opposition grew from her emotional, visceral connection to the baby; mine grew first from a principled opposition grounded in a sense of justice and ethics.

But equally gendered, I suppose, I felt that my Judaism had always given me the ability to stand up against injustice, that the imperative of the post-Holocaust generation of "Never Again!" impelled me to speak out against injustices wherever I saw them.

Ultimately, it came down to Judaism. Jewish law is unequivocal on the subject—it has been a time-honored tradition since the celebrated Covenant with Abraham, the founding moment of monotheism. In Genesis 17, God appears before an aged Abraham—he's ninety-nine!—and commands that Abraham circumcise himself, his son, and all male members of his household (slaves and servants included).

Today circumcision is seen as a mitzvah, linking the family to a 4000-year history of a people. In his masterful, compendium of Jewish law and lore, *Essential Judaism*, George Robinson writes that it is a mitzvah "one performs for its own sake as a subordination of oneself to a larger entity." What's a tiny foreskin compared to 4,000 years of tradition? And so it appears that Jewish tradition might yet extract its pound of flesh—well, more likely about a quarter of an ounce–from yet another innocent baby.

Yet Judaism today is hardly as monolithic as we once thought. Even in biblical times there seems to have been some dissent about the procedure. If one follows the ritual as prescribed by Jewish law, the baby is held during the circumcision on what is called the Chair of Elijah, named after the prophet "who railed against the Jews for forsaking the ritual of circumcision." What that says to me is that not long after circumcision was instituted, there were a lot of people who were already resisting it. Then, too, there is the law that the *brit milah* be performed on the eighth day after the birth of the son, a law so ironclad that it is perhaps the only Jewish ritual that may not be postponed for the Sabbath, or even for Yom Kippur. Those who were interested in enforcing circumcision were determined that there be no excuses—no doubt because a lot of people were trying to wiggle their way out.

In her research, Amy found that even as recently as the mid-nineteenth century, in Eastern Europe and Russia there was a widespread move to stop the practice, ironically, just when it was becoming more widespread in the United States. Led by women—what a surprise!—who thought the practice barbaric and patriarchal, the movement eventually even convinced Theodore Herzl, the founder of modern Zionism, who refused to allow his own son to be circumcised.

It is, after all, quite perplexing: why would God ask Abraham do such a thing to himself and all the males of his household—especially his son? For years, I had a little cartoon in my study that depicted Abraham, standing alone on top of a mountain, looking up at the sky, forlorn and exasperated. The caption read, "Let me see if I have this right: You want us to cut the ends of our dicks off?!?!"

SUBLIMATING PLEASURE FOR TORAH

The circumcision as ritual makes sense, however, in three ways—one sexual, one political, and one symbolic. Throughout history, commentators on circumcision have agreed that the goal was to transform men's (and women's) sexual experience, and thus make men more eager to study Torah. The only thing they disagreed on was how, exactly, circumcision would accomplish this feat of sublimation.

Most observers assumed it would make a man less sexually sensitive, reduce his sexual ardor, and constrain his sexual impulses. In his fascinating study, *Eros and the Jews*, David Biale

finds two contradictory impulses leading towards the same conclusion. Ancient Jews, such as Philo, understood circumcision as "the symbol of the excision of excessive and superfluous pleasure." In *Guide to the Perplexed*, the great medieval philosopher Moses Maimonides prefigured J. H. Kellogg by nearly a millennium when he wrote that the commandment to circumcise was "not prescribed with a view to perfecting what is defective congenitally, but to perfecting what is defective morally." A chief reason for the ritual was "the wish to bring about a decrease in sexual intercourse and a weakening of the organ in question, so that this activity be diminished and the organ be in as quiet a state as possible." After all, he continued, "the fact that circumcision weakens the faculty of sexual excitement and sometimes perhaps diminishes the pleasure is indubitable."

While Maimonides argued that the physiological loss was "the real purpose" of the ritual, others believed that the psychological impact far outweighed the physical. Biale notes that an early medieval Midrash Tadshe suggests that the "covenant of circumcision was therefore placed on the genitals so that the fear of God would restrain them from sin." Later thinkers took the physical to new extremes. The early-nineteenth-century scholar, Nahman of Bratslav, great grandson of the Baal Shem Tov, argued that circumcision symbolizes the complete excision of sexual pleasure so that the "true zaddik" (holy man) experiences pain, not pleasure, during intercourse.

On the one hand, writers were convinced that men would feel less—much less, and therefore their frustration would lead inevitably towards holier devotion to study. On the other hand, some writers were convinced that circumcised men would experience far *more* sexual excitement—so much more, in fact, that it would leave both him and his partner so frustrated that they wouldn't want to have sex again. In an astonishing passage, Isaac ben Yedaiah, a late thirteenth-century French follower of Maimonides described the difference is such overheated prose that it borders on the salacious (which alone makes it worth quoting at length):

> [A beautiful woman] will court a man who is uncircumcised in the flesh and lie against his breast with great passion, for he thrusts inside her a long time because of the foreskin, which is a barrier against ejaculation in intercourse. Thus she feels pleasure and reaches an orgasm first. When an uncircumcised man sleeps with her and then resolves to return to his home, she brazenly grasps him, holding on to his genitals and says to him, 'Come back, make love to me.' This is because of the pleasure that she finds in intercourse with him, from the sinews of his testicles— sinews of iron—and from his ejaculation—that of a horse—which he shoots like an arrow into her womb. They are united without separating and he makes love twice and three times in one night, yet the appetite is not filled. And so he acts with her night after night. The sexual activity emaciates him of his bodily fat and afflicts his flesh and he devotes his brain entirely to women, an evil thing.
>
> But when a circumcised man desires the beauty of a woman . . . he will find himself performing his task quickly, emitting his seed as soon as he inserts the crown. . . . He has an orgasm first; he does not hold back his strength. As soon as he begins intercourse with her, he immediately comes to a climax. She has no pleasure from him when she lies down or when she arises and it would be better for her if he had not known her . . . for he arouses her passion to no avail and she remains in a state of desire . . . (cited in Biale).

So more excitement means less pleasure— for both him and his female partner. Ancient rabbis, like Philo, had argued that not only did circumcision restrain male sexual ardor, but diminished women's pleasure. "It is hard for a woman to separate herself from an uncircum-

cised man with whom she has had intercourse." Everyone now seemed to agree that circumcision reduces the pleasure of the woman, which is precisely why it seems to have been prescribed. And precisely why Amy and I were growing increasingly suspicious.

There were political issues involved as well. It's interesting to observe the expansion of the ritual in terms of the relationship between Jews and their neighbors. Originally, apparently, the ritual consisted of only the *brit milah*—which is the excision of a small part of the foreskin. This enabled some Jewish men to continue to "pass" as gentiles in the ancient edition of those locker room showers that my friends continually discussed. Disgruntled rabbis then added the *brit periah* which removed the entire foreskin, making it impossible to pass as gentile. (It's an ironic twist of history that it is the *brit periah* that was adopted by modern medicine when it still prescribed routine neonatal circumcision.)

But this expansion also raised, for us, the thorniest political and moral dilemma. A close friend, a child of Holocaust survivors, told me the story of his uncle, who was not so lucky. His was the now-classic story of the young man, sneaking his way onto a train leaving Germany, under the watchful eyes of the Nazis. When caught, he was forced to strip in the station, and when it was discovered that he was circumcised, he was shot on the spot.

Here was a political reason *to* circumcise, a slap in the face of anti-Semitism, a way to connect my son to a history of resistance against anti-Semitism, and to recognize the ways in which physical difference (whether congenitally or culturally derived) is grounds for discrimination. In fact, some historians claim that the *brit periah*, the more extensive circumcision, was first used by the Egyptians to mark their Hebrew slaves, so that they would be readily and permanently identifiable. Ironic then, that once free, these same Hebrews made the more dramatic statement a matter of their own *inclusion*.

PENILE PATRIARCHY

But what was ultimately decisive for us was the larger symbolic meaning of circumcision, and particularly the gendered politics of the ritual. After all, it is not circumcision that makes a man Jewish; one can certainly be Jewish without it. Religious membership is passed on through the mother: if the mother is Jewish then the baby is Jewish and nothing that the baby does—or that is done to him or her—can change that basic fact. A rabbi is trained to counsel parents of mixed religious backgrounds (in which the man is Jewish and the woman is not) that circumcision does not make their son Jewish, but that only the mother's conversion will make it so.

No, circumcision means something else: the reproduction of patriarchy. Abraham cements *his* relationship to God by a symbolic genital mutilation of his son. It is on the body of his son that Abraham writes his own beliefs. In a religion marked by the ritual exclusion of women, such a marking not only enables Isaac to be included within the community of men—he can be part of a minyan, can pray in the temple, can study Torah—but he can also lay claim to all the privileges to which being a Jewish male now entitles him. Monotheistic religions invariably worship male Gods, and exhibit patriarchal political arrangements between the sexes. (Looked at this way, since both Judaism and Islam practice circumcision, it is really Christianity that is the deviant case, and it would be worth exploring how Christianity justified its evasion of the practice since it is certain that Jesus was circumcised.)

Circumcision, it became clear, is the single moment of the reproduction of patriarchy. It's when patriarchy happens, the single crystalline moment when the rule of the fathers is reproduced, the moment when male privilege and entitlement is passed from one generation to the next, when the power of the fathers is enacted upon the sons, a power which the sons will someday then enact on the bodies of their own sons. To circumcise our son, then, would be, unwittingly or not, to accept as legitimate 4000 years not of Jewish tradition, but of patriarchal domination of women.

Our choice was clear.

We welcomed Zachary into our family on that morning without a circumcision. We decided that we want him to live in a world without violence, so we welcomed him without violence. We decided that we want him to live in a world in which he is free to experience the fullness of the pleasures of his body, so we welcomed him with all his fleshy nerves intact. And we decided that we want him to live in a world in which male entitlement is a waning memory, and in which women and men are seen—in both ritual and in reality—as full equals and partners. So we welcomed him equally, his mother and I, in the time-honored way that desert cultures have always welcomed strangers to their tents: We washed his feet.

READING 26

A Story of Sexuality and Gender in Three Parts

L. Maurer and M. Kelly

Introduction by the authors: The following passages give a brief and intimate glimpse into our identities, relationship, and some of our deepest desires. Each section examines some aspects of our multifaceted sexual selves. None of these qualities exists in a vacuum—they form the basis for complex interactions, making our relationship more rich and intricate than the sum of its parts. Our intent is to invite you in to share in our thoughts, conversations, and processes as we explore the breadth and depth of sexuality and gender in our lives.

EMERGENCE

It all started over antipasto and zucchini parmesan. The quiet corner table in what would become our first apartment together invited the exchange—something about that night set it apart, upped the ante. Innocently enough, the question was put out for us to devour more eagerly than the meal that sat before us. *"So, what is it about me and bi women?"* It hung there—who would bite first? I was excited and anxious—god forbid I say the wrong thing or the truth, either could hurt a lot.

"Well, you like to move as much as I do . . ." I had defined and evaluated myself so much I had it down to a short and clear understanding—I like to move, take it all in, I'm not too particular about parts. *"What?"* What now? How do you backpedal from that one? What could I really say? How about, *well, simply enough honey, I think you take being a big ole butch dyke to another level, you do more, you experience life from more than one place, but not really two, you've kind of created your own space and it works,*

you don't just pull it off, you do it with grace and style and I love that.

I suddenly had this amusing vision of a blue and red polka dot Little Red Riding Hood doll I had when I was a kid. It was the kind of doll you could turn upside-down, flip the dress over and voila—a new doll emerged. But it was more than your average two-dimensional plaything—you could find Little Red, Grandma, and the Wolf with the proper pulling, flipping, and shifting. I kept this revelation to myself for the time being.

"So, you know how I look out at people and there aren't any gender filters—well, I think you look at yourself and there aren't any either . . . " A wave crossed the table, not a devastating tidal wave but a clarifying one, one that clears away all the rubble so you have an unencumbered view of the shining shell laying below. A short, thoughtful smile surfaced, *"Yeh."*

We've had a knack for creating pictures from the beginning. We're both visual people and sometimes the drawing of a picture gives more clarity when we haven't discovered the words yet. Napkins are a favorite medium—it seems that the nourishment of a shared meal feeds our brains too. The indented floral background of our tissue-thin napkins helps us reveal the unnamed layers we begin to uncover. These pictures have no limits; we draw people and places and sex. We share our past and build our future on paper napkins at home, in restaurants, on road trips. Any scrap will suffice; you'd be surprised at what you can fit on to a small paper square. We even branched out to paper placemats one desperate evening in Washington, D.C. We'd been traveling and talking all day, tired but still wanting to say more; the pictures emerged over soup and bread.

This particular night we start with me. The drawing: a woman looking out toward the sea of possibilities, the desires and potential attractions not limited by the simple distinctions of physical genders. The next napkin further

---

reveals the truth. I watch the drawing emerge: the image is the reverse of mine. The sea of possibility not bound by physical genders exists on the *inside*, not out. It got still. Neither of us wanted to move or speak. What's the protocol? There must be some ritual to signify a beginning, a rebirth. The revelation that sat before us needed a marker.

On the phone with one ex-lover we sought out more of the truth. Funny how we look back to make sense of what's ahead. Shared history sometimes helps make sense of reality. What about that record-breaking batting average of ex-girlfriends marrying men? *"What do you think . . . "* No shocking revelations, but a previously hidden truth was nudging its way onto the table. "It's not like it was that big of a leap, you know what I mean?" After trying so hard to convince everyone it was just coincidence, perhaps it wasn't after all. Perhaps the mobility of gender expression was expressly what attracted them? It was for me. Imagine: A partner whose identity is as mobile, as fluid as my attraction. The limitless possibilities tingle.

It was sad packing up that corner table and leaving that space behind. A couple of places later, we've created new sacred spaces, new revelations that bring us further along. We started keeping the napkins, maybe we'll put together our gender journey coffee-table book some day. Pictures always help. So does the Little Red Riding Hood doll my parents sent us last summer.

RECONCILIATION

When I look back on my history though a gendered lens, there is no mistaking it. My relationship with gender has never been simple. As a citizen of the world, I was an accidental dissident. My mere presence challenged the little upstate New York world I called home. The complexities started when I was very young. An entry in my baby book from my second Christmas says quite matter-of-factly, "wants no part of playing with dolls, so Santa didn't bring any." Santa somehow knew a bat and ball and speeding toy cars were more my style.

My parents' involvement was a strange combination of recognition and respect for the unique person that I was, against the backdrop of a fundamentally dysfunctional household. Nonconventional gender expression was the least of my family's worries. I was basically left to my own devices, free to explore the world and be in it as I chose. Remarkably, there were only minor bumps in the road early on, probably due to that unusual mix of appreciation for difference yet utter chaos that was my home.

Most of the outrage came from older relatives: "Put that girl in a dress!" "Stop roughhousing—what will the neighbors think?" "What would you ever want with a Tonka truck?" were frequent early themes. I filtered out most of these gender skirmishes, not really sure what all the ruckus was about.

When I reached fifth grade, I began to understand a little more. My teacher decided that she would dedicate the year to my much-needed gender re-education. Her plan to hold me back and repeat the fifth grade unless I improved my handwriting stemmed from her strong desire to make me write more like a girl. Somehow the strong slant and tight lettering I was so proud of did not mesh with her idea of how a lady's penmanship should look.

To my parents, both schoolteachers, the threat of their child failing a grade shocked them into a peculiar spiral of action. Their plan was simple. They would bribe me into better handwriting with the promise of a shiny new *boy's* bike. I think they knew exactly what they were doing. This little gender trade meant we would all get what we wanted: my teacher would have the happy illusion that all of her kids fit in just fine; my parents could avoid the utter humiliation of a failing child; and I could simply bask in the glory of my shiny new bike.

In my daily remedial handwriting sessions during recess the teacher encouraged me to write in a more "ladylike" fashion. Sensing that this was more about my whole being rather than just my handwriting, I began accessorizing with more traditionally female items borrowed from my mother's closet—polyester jumpers, flowery skirts, and barrettes. As if by magic, the more I tried to appear feminine, the higher my handwriting grade climbed. Of course, my classmates teased me unmercifully during this short-lived transformation, obviously sensing my gender discord as I dressed in "girl drag." But by the end of the year, soon after I added the rather over-the-top embellishment of dotting my "i"s with flowers, I was waived onto the sixth grade.

That summer was a busy one. Between relearning my own natural style of writing, complete with its distinct slant and tight lettering, I had to reverse all the hard work invested in my unusual fifth grade makeover. There were clothes to be returned to my Mom's closet and barrettes to be given away to girlfriends and my little brother's play dress-up box. And then there were the bike rides. There were plenty of races and daredevil stunts to amaze my friends as I easily slipped back into the role of just being me.

Years after that rigid fifth grade gender-catastrophe, I realized that my true identity is much more flexible than traditionally understood either/or concepts. Like it or not, my life is about defining gender in ways that make other people feel uncomfortable. After years of trying to convince my lovers, friends, a therapist, and myself that I certainly did not want to be a man, I had an intense gender epiphany. My wish to not be a man was only half true— my gender identity simply cannot be neatly wrapped up in a clear-cut pink or blue package. It takes a Crayola 64-pack of colors to truly express my inner sense of gender. Neither male nor female feels accurate or adequate. As a fluid, third-gendered person, I don't fit into any of the pre existing gender camps.

Although not fitting into society's prescribed gender categories comes with a fair amount of challenge, the home I have found in a third-gendered space has opened up a whole new world of genuine self-expression. My relationship with my partner embodies and honors the gender slide with which I live. My partner's bisexual orientation is as fluid as my gender identity, which allows for both our *whole* selves to be actualized.

I am not a woman; I am not a man. Because of these two facts, a "transition" from one to the other doesn't quite make sense. I am, quite simply, me—somewhere in a middle gray space between the two gender poles, or perhaps outside the lines altogether. Essentially, I was not born into a body that truly reflects my multidimensional gender identity.

I chuckle a little when I recount my fifth grade penmanship war to friends—but I also feel a lump in my throat—a lump borne of sadness and regret for the rigid either/or extreme of gender polarization from my fifth grade world. That boy's ten-speed bike is still in my garage today, and I take it out on a spin about once a year—to remember the fifth grade, and the bittersweet beginnings of my gender consciousness . . . and to forget as well. As I pedal into the breeze, I celebrate being me, a grown-up gender rebel with gloriously steady, distinctive, slightly illegible penmanship.

REALIZATION

Fall seemed like the right time. There was something so right about the beauty and death inherent in the season. How different was that from my season? The appointment was made after an initial consultation at a conference in February. The Doctor did and said all the right things. He asked if he could see them, and only then, after being granted sight, did he ask if he could touch. The shame welled from deep. Something about the way touch made them real always took my breath away in a deep sigh that some lovers took as an open door and others learned to respect as a closed one.

It really was time. There was no denying it any longer. Yes, it seemed extreme to some.

Yes, I was scared (mostly about the actual surgery, not the envisioned outcome). Yes, I wanted to have my breasts cut off my body, cast away forever, and have a flat chest reconstructed. The process was jagged. Knowing my partner's mother's struggle with cancer, watching them all mourn the loss of a part of her while I dreamed of gaining a part of myself by losing the exact same things was hard to remedy.

The date was set. November. I cried for hours the day the plans were made final. My tears of disbelief came from a lifetime of wishing my breasts away while knowing that most people who had this surgery really wanted to be men. I thought I'd have to lie. I never thought my partner would stay with me. I worried about being even more of social outcast. I hoped that I would be even more me—even more in the middle of it all where I live my days and nights. This surgery would let me really be what I am: a masculine born female with a multi pack of great dicks, a lovely cunt, and a wispy-haired flat chest. How could this be real—people like me don't often get to realize their dreams—we're set out on the fringes only to look in upon the realized dreams of people who fit. Not anymore.

I was petrified of the actual surgery. I generally prefer consciousness to the alternative. Despite that fear—paralyzing at time—I got everything in order. My support network came through in ways that went beyond my wildest hopes. From phone calls to care packages, I was well cared for. Everyone did have their own process—some wanted all the details, others worried, some gave medical advice, and others just stood strongly by in support of my movement toward a body more aligned with my spirit.

My partner was with me throughout, she was my caregiver before, during, and after. She stood guard, waiting, worrying, wondering what the next days would hold. There are drains, bandages, stitches, bleeding, swelling: this is not a process for the faint hearted. Her mom—the one who weathered the storm of breast cancer—hand-made two small pillows for under each of my arms to cushion the incision points and the drains. People are amazing. The doctor and nurses embodied respect and approval for this massive life-affirming and altering choice. It's all a little fuzzy looking back—a haze of disbelief, relief, and pure joy cloud my memory. Fall has passed, so have winter and spring. My season has just begun.

READING 27

Medicine, Morality, and the Public Management of Sexual Matters

Leonore Tiefer

As many major contemporary theorists in sexology have indicated, we are in a period of paradigm shift in sexology. To understand

Source: New Sexual Agendas, edited by Lynne Segal. NYU Press, 1997. Reprinted by permission of the author.

where we are going, it helps to see where we have been and where we are.

One of the most important of the prevailing sexual ideologies and management forces has to do with the relationship of sexuality and medicine, and I want to devote myself to that subject. Although not a new relationship, I do not need to emphasize that the relationship of sex and medicine is central to the current social construction of sexuality.

How medical authorities currently construct sex—what and who are included and how, as well as what and who are ignored—is fundamental to understanding the current sexual *Weltanschauung*. Medical authorities have an impact far beyond the consulting room in terms of their influence on the mass media, on legislation, on courts of law and on policy-making. In the consulting room, medical 'experts' provide certain kinds of resources and opportunities for certain groups of people, directly influencing the actual sexual lives and experiences of millions upon millions of people in the industrialized world.

MY LOCATION

Let me briefly describe my perspective on these issues. I am employed as a clinical psychologist in the Urology Department of a large New York City hospital. So I am a sexologist, but I could also be described as doing participant-ethnography in sexual medicine. As a sexologist with appropriate credentials and employment, I study the management of sexuality from inside medical practice. This participant-ethnography, I should point out, is done at the frequent peril of losing my job and offending many sexologist friends who don't see their work with a sociopolitico-anthropological lens.

My primary job is to interview men who have been referred to the Urology Department in order to evaluate and treat their sexual problems. Usually, they have been referred by their GPs. My interview is one component of a comprehensive evaluation, which also includes much physical testing. In an interview lasting from 15 minutes to an hour or so, my job is to form an impression of the nature of their problems, the probable cause or causes of their problems, and the type of treatment which might be of most benefit to them. When the patients are accompanied to the interview by a sexual partner, I interview her (only women partners have come) separately.

During the 12 years I have been doing this work, I have interviewed over 2000 men and about 1200 of their sexual partners. I have observed a dozen urologists who do this work and have become familiar with the ever-changing panoply of diagnostic tests and treatments available. I have conducted follow-up research on how men and couples cope with the treatments they undertake, and I have attended dozens and dozens of professional meetings in sexology. I have published the sexological research in scientific journals, and I have published the participant-ethnographic work most recently in a collection of essays.[1]

SOURCES OF POPULAR AND EXPERT INFORMATION

The reality of contemporary society is that there are very few places to go for sexual advice or help, or just to get questions answered. Sex education is practically non-existent, and what there is usually focuses very narrowly on matters of contraception and sexually transmited diseases.

Most people get their sexual information from the mass media, and encounter four different types of message:

1. *Sexual images:* Fictional and celebrity models and images of sexual relationships emphasizing beautiful bodies, drama, passion, transgression and sexual acts. Transsexual tennis stars, lesbian tennis stars, Hugh Grant picks up a prostitute, what Michael Jackson and Lisa Marie do; how many women John Kennedy had sex with in the White House, etc.

2. *Sexual advice for women:* Women's magazine articles and advice columns directed towards heterosexual women, emphasizing sex differences, women's needs for intimacy, the importance of technique, simple rational solutions.

3. *Sexual health news:* Health news and advice, framing sexuality in physiological terms; themes which are duplicated in men's magazines. A typical article, "A Guide to Your Sexual Health—News You Need to Know to Keep Your Body and Mind Primed" (in

Longevity, January 1995, p. 34) begins: "Some of the best news coming out of the lab lately is that good sex and good health often go hand in hand. We're glad to hear it, since we've always felt that a healthy sex life is a cornerstone of longevity."

4. *Current sexual events news:* Sex news—which is always sensational, and focuses either on sex-related crimes (whether the names of paroled child sex offenders should be published in the neighbourhoods they are moving to, sex on the Internet) or marvellous medical breakthroughs (the Italian mother in her sixties, does John Wayne Bobbit's penis work? the gay gene) or political controversies (whether AIDS curricula should emphasize abstinence or condoms, new censorship laws or court cases).

Morals and mechanisms are the dominant themes in all these media categories, and one of the foundational terms is "health." Health *is* morality nowadays (a theme we need to explore further), and calling upon "health" serves as a kind of mantra in popular writing and thinking about sexuality. "Healthy" serves as the modern equivalent to "normal" in terms of endorsing and recommending sexual scripts for what's done, why it's done, when, where and with whom it's done, etc.

I would argue that the language and social value given to health is the most significant underpinning for the dominant ideology of sexuality, the "medicalization of sexuality," which we can define as a gradual social transformation by which medicine, with its distinctive ways of thinking, its models, metaphors and institutions, has come to exercise authority over sexuality.

THE MEDICAL MODEL

The medical model emphasizes that the body has its own empirical laws and processes that work independently of mental or social life.[2]

The body is a morally neutral, self-contained unit which only physicians are fully authorized to evaluate and treat, based on their unique claims to morally neutral, objective science. The body of the medical model is basically a machine, like a piano, with functional purposes which can only be fulfilled if the body and its parts are functioning properly. "Properly" can be determined by objective research and is subject to the natural laws of chemistry and biology.

Modern medicine sees the body as an archipelago of organ systems, with each professional speciality inhabiting an organ system island of its own: the nervous system, the vascular system, the endocrine system, the genitourinary system, etc.

Sexuality, according to the medical model, is a natural property, or set of properties, or individuals expressed in acts which require properly functioning organ systems (although there are ownership contests among the organ system island owners!). Proper sexual functioning can be assessed and studied by laboratory measures according to the medical model (this is a key element) and can be altered and corrected by familiar medical interventions (medicines, devices, surgeries), i.e., by the family of curative, rehabilitative and, less often, prophylactic strategies.

The dominance of this medical specialist evaluation is most visible in urology with regard to men's sexual complaints, as the urologic subspeciality of "impotence" has grown exponentially over the past two decades. I shall return to the urology story below.

THE HUMAN SEXUAL RESPONSE CYCLE (HSRC)

First, however, I want to suggest a contestant for top honours as catalyst for this dominant ideology, the medical way of thinking about sexuality, and that is the physiological research of William Masters and Virginia Johnson published in the 1960s. Masters and Johnson observed hundreds of solo and coupled sex acts in their laboratory, and scrupulously recorded and reported a variety of physiological parameters. In 1966 they described a supposedly universal "Human Sexual Response Cycle" during which various neurological, vascular and muscular events transpired in a predictable and invariant sequence. They argued that this one sexual response cycle characterized men and women, homosexuals and heterosexuals, and that this human sexual response cycle constituted the basic physical bedrock for human sexual expression. Feminists were happy about the gender equality, gays and lesbians were happy for the imprimatur of normality, sex educators were happy about the specificity, and physicians were ecstatic about the medical mandate.

This physical model of sexuality was praised from every quarter, and was immediately enshrined as the centrepiece of sexuality in academic textbooks, research and classification of clinical problems. The American Psychiatric Association has described sexual dysfunctions since 1980 as follows: "The essential feature is inhibition in the psychophysiological changes that characterize the complete sexual response cycle." All of professional sexual treatment is organized around making sure the sexual response cycle works properly.

Specifically, this means that normal, healthy, proper sexuality means that the vagina works properly (opening nicely and getting wet when it's supposed to), the penis works properly (getting hard and ejaculating at the proper time) and the orgasm works properly.

Regularly occurring sexual desire, which Masters and Johnson did not discuss, was later added as an element of the sexual response cycle, and became the only sexual dysfunction defined without reference to proper functioning of the genital organs. But that's been the only change. The physical model has become the medical mandate for proper sexuality—the medicalization of sexuality, the physical bedrock, the physical cycle of genital arousal and orgasm.

CRITIQUE OF THE HSRC

I have written at great length about scientific, clinical and feminist criticisms which can be made of this human sexual response cycle (Tiefer, 1995). Summarizing rapidly, close reading of their work reveals that Masters and Johnson didn't "discover" the HSRC, they (1) selected research participants who were already experienced at coordinating their sexual activity so as to enact a smooth arousal/orgasm performance; (2) they went out of their way to find participants who had a strong interest in effective masturbation and intercourse; (3) participants underwent a training period ("controlled orientation" it was called) to help them perform in the laboratory; and (4) participants whose performance occasionally "failed" were coached on how to avoid recurrences.

There was no investigation of the feelings or motives or fantasies or subjective experiences of the participants. No note was taken of the meaning this kind of sexual activity had for them. No discussion occurred about how these participants had developed this kind of sexual script, or even of how this sexual script operated in their non-laboratory lives.

Because the assumption was that the body has its own empirical laws and processes that work independently of mental or social life, it seemed perfectly appropriate that the only records were of genital changes and nipple changes and respiratory changes on this highly selected group of participants, and that the results be called "the" human sexual response cycle.

So, the outgrowth of this research was perfect for the medical archipelago. Normal sexuality became defined, and remains defined, as specific performance of fragmented body parts. If the parts function normally, you cannot qualify for a sexual dysfunction; if the parts do not function normally, no matter what you say or feel or want, you have a sexual health problem.

A REAL-LIFE EXAMPLE

Let me illustrate how the unquestioning assumptions this approach to sexuality takes segues into modern medical practice.

In June 1989, a conversation took place during the annual meeting of the International Academy of Sex Research in front of a poster titled "Healthy Aging and Sexual Function." One of the figures depicted nocturnal penile tumescence measures for a group of 65–74-year-old male volunteers. A urologist studying the figure said to the poster's author, a psychiatrist, "So, these men did not have rigid nocturnal erections; they may actually have had disease." "No," the psychiatrist replied, "they were healthy, and in fact they were having sex; their wives confirmed that there was no dysfunction." "But," continued the urologist, "their wives may be satisfied, even *they* may be satisfied, but since *some* men in that age group *can* have rigid erections, *these men* must have had some impairment."

This is a rich illustration with many important implications for contemporary sexuality, but I just want to highlight a few:

1. The disagreement about the meaning of the data illustrates the important gap between physical measurements of the body and what they signify. High-technology measurements are subject to multiple interpretations, a fact not well appreciated by the non medical professional. The medical model fosters the illusion that machines reveal the hidden body directly. But actually the body is silent, and many layers of mental (i.e., cultural) decision go into what is chosen to be measured, how it's actually assessed, and how the readout is decoded. Our modern wish to bypass the lies of culture and politics, and get back to the pristine truth of the natural body deludes us here—the body, like God, is a Rorschach, a projection of our ideologies!

2. What's going on in this illustration is the actual establishment of a definition of deviance. In the argument over what is a problem, the specialists are arguing over what is normal and what is healthy. Again, the body doesn't speak; authorities speak and label.

3. The urologist and psychiatrist represent different investments in the machine and the person as sources of authority and definition. This is an ongoing contest within the medicalization movement, and it may be that progressives will find themselves in an unfamiliar coalition with psychiatrists as they contest the biological reductionism of other medical specialists.

THE MEDICALIZATION OF MEN'S SEXUALITY

I could pursue the implications of this illustration, but instead I shall show you how medicalization is playing itself out at the present moment within urology, and perhaps suggest what this portends for the future.

In 1986 I published a paper titled "In Pursuit of the Perfect Penis" in which I described how social interest groups can exert steady pressure and collude to create reality. Very briefly, these groups include:

1. Urologists, highly paid surgical specialists, who, as they are losing some of their surgical opportunities because of technological improvements, are looking for other areas of specialization.

2. Medical industries and pharmaceutical companies who are always on the lookout for new markets, and are especially alert to

opportunities related to changing demographics, i.e., the aging baby boomers of 1946–50.

3. The mass media, which boost sales by capitalizing on the public's interest in health and the perennial attractiveness of sexual topics. Medical sex is "clean sex," and thus appropriate for every kind of show and publication.

4. Various entrepreneurs such as self-help group starters and newsletter promoters who have created markets on many subjects by portraying themselves as something between consumers and professionals, but who, in the area of sexuality, promote an exclusively medical model in terms of language, recommendations, and designated authorities.

5. Insurance companies, who adhere to "objective" measurements and interventions to minimize costs.

6. Men who favour a medical model because it's face-saving, maintains phallic privilege and offers them an "objective" and optimistic world of science to minimize their anxieties over self-disclosure and mental health. Men's socialization and masculine ideology both support a medical model.

7. Some heterosexual women who find it congenial for a variety of reasons to define sexuality in terms of men's erectile and ejaculatory function.

The point is that the overt interests of many groups—economic, psychological, political and ideological—combine to support medicalization. Without an alternative model, itself actively supported and promoted, the need of society to understand the social forces which construct and mediate our understandings of sexuality will be filled by medical language and models.

We might even speculate that covert interests of institutions with a stake in sexual restrictiveness (e.g., conservative political and religious organizations) may indirectly support medicalization because of its potential for sexual social control through specifying norms, eliminating deviance and enforcing conformity.

And what do men get who enter the medical world of men's sexuality at the present time? They get a discourse of reified erections divorced from the body, the person, the couple, the script—erections as universal biophenomena are the focus. Once the patient cooperates in the discourse of erections, it is easy for the physician to move even further down the reductionist ladder, and start talking about how erections merely consist of filling and containing compartments in the penis. This language and construction lead the patient to agree that the next step is to measure these processes and then to repair them or replace them.

Urology currently offers three treatments—penile injections, vacuum devices and permanent penile implants.[3] They all work, i.e., they create secure and functional erections. But this type of evaluation and treatment is a little like a Soviet retail store—you go in, and you get what's there, whether you need it or not, whether you'll use it or not! The patient's sexual unhappiness combined with the usually weeks-long period of evaluation have been exhausting, and he is eager for something, preferably something simple and permanent. Yet follow-up studies generally show a decline in frequency of use and in estimates of satisfaction at the same time as the men say they would take the same path again.

In the urology setting, women's interests are assumed to be central to the evaluation, the prime reason why the man is coming for treatment. Yet, women are usually omitted from the evaluation, and certainly are never invited to speak about their own sexual interests. My work has explicitly invited women to contribute as equal partners to the evaluation, "since sex is a two-person thing." Often, the wife's answer is that she is here merely to be supportive, and that it is clear that her husband feels bad because he can't have an erection, not necessarily because he can't have sex. Of course, she acknowledges, once his erection is restored, he (and she) will be obliged to have intercourse to make it all worthwhile, a prospect she often greets with considerable ambivalence. There are, of course, a million different stories, but the problem with the medical model is that the stories seem far less interesting to the professionals than the penis-archipelago.

CONCLUSION

I have illustrated some of the ways in which medicalization is a major player in the contemporary sexual picture. As an ideology it offers advantages and disadvantages which I can see when I speak, day in and day out, to real couples immersed in renegotiating their sexual lives. The good news is that people of little education who have lots of questions and are troubled with lots of worries about sexuality get to talk to somebody who can listen sympathetically. It's something they are grateful for. Most sites of sexual medicine, however, do not allow much time to help people find a language to talk. Usually there is a medical doctor who "takes a history," "makes a diagnosis" and then it's directly on to the physical fixing.

The gender politics of that medical sexual world seem deeply reactionary and misogynist in terms of the limited space for women to articulate and develop sexual capacities independent of a fixed masculinist pattern focused on genital function and orgasm. This is ironic, given the initial enthusiasm with which feminists embraced the liberatory potential of Masters and Johnson's claims that biological research proved women's sexual capacities (i.e., for arousal and orgasm) were at least equal to men's. Indeed, the point that women's bodies can orgasm is a useful one, and many women have employed this information to raise their expectations and demands of their lovers.

The larger truth, however, seems to be that biological potential has very little to do with sexual scripting for most women around the world, and that aeons of genital research will not create sexual liberation in a world of social inequalities. In fact, biological models seem to constrain options at least as much as they enhance them, especially when the biological information is shunted into a health model of norms and deviances.

Ironically, both the contraceptive revolution and the medicalization of sexuality have only reinforced a limited script for heterosexual sexual life—arousal, intercourse, performance, false universals, technical focus, mind–body dualism. We must look outside medicine if we want more than the rhetoric of sexual health.

NOTES

1. Leonore Tiefer (1995) *Sex Is Not a Natural Act and Other Essays* (Oxford: Westview Press).
2. Will Wright (1982/1994) *The Social Logic of Health* (Hanover, New Hampshire: Wesleyan University Press).
3. It is, of course, only a matter of time before an oral medication is developed which can safely create a temporary erection, whereupon men will be able to treat themselves completely covertly.

Hands Off! The Taboo Surrounding Males' First Ejaculation

Loren Frankel

INTRODUCTION

When I was thirteen I had a very funny sensation, a slight burning sensation in my little willie. I wondered what was the matter, so I went to the lavvie which was out in the backyard and shared by two families. I touched my willie and it started to spit at me. I looked at the gooey result and felt sick as a pig and dirty all over. The door opened and my mother came in. She seemed to know automatically what was happening, gave me a clip on the earhole and said, "Nathan, that'll send thee blind if that does it to thisen too often" (as cited in Miles, 1991, p. 84).

"When I had my first wet dream," seventeen-year-old Chad says, "I had no idea what was going on. I thought I had wet my bed. It was a really strange feeling for me. I remember liking the dream, but I felt very embarrassed. I thought maybe I had some sort of psychological problem. And, who was I going to ask about it—my mother?" (Pollack, 1998, p. 154).

The first testimonial, from a bladegrinder in Sheffield, England, at the turn of the 20th century, is not unimaginable in America at a similar time. In late 19th- and early 29th-century America, masturbation—and by extension, a male's first ejaculation—was often treated as an issue that required direct communication, for fear of physiological harm that would result if the practice continued. Following the advice of many medical professionals, educators, and religious leaders, many parents like the mother cited above must have felt that

Source: Original work. Copyright © 2002 Loren Frankel. Printed by permission of the author.

they were *protecting*, not harming, sons' present and future well-being by admonishing them not to masturbate. Generally, parents and other adults passed these beliefs on to ensure that male youth would develop into healthy, honorable, chaste, reproductive men. Given the cultural context I will describe, it is conceivable that many adolescents and adults in late 19th-century America believed that both masturbation *and* nocturnal emissions caused drastic mental, moral, social, and physical decline. Therefore, for late nineteenth-century American males, first ejaculation occurring as the result of masturbation or nocturnal emission was likely a perilous experience. We need to ask how such a strong anxiety could coalesce around first ejaculation.

The first ejaculation taboo has existed for some time, which provides an understanding of why even today many parents, teachers, sex educators, community leaders, and others feel uncomfortable addressing the topic with early adolescent males. The taboo also may explain why some American boys may feel and have felt in the past century a sense of confusion, shame, and even guilt about their first ejaculation. The second testimonial cited above, from a late 20th-century American male, indicates two important shifts that occurred from the beginning to the end of the 20th century: First, beginning in the 1930s and 1940s, American public discourse shifted from the physical to the psychological harm of masturbation. Second, first ejaculation—especially if by nocturnal emission, also known as "wet dreams"—came to be experienced as something physically pleasurable. Nevertheless, the first ejaculation taboo has endured. Whereas in the 19th and early 20th century there was an explicit first ejaculation taboo, in late 20th- and early 21st-century America there is an implicit taboo. That is, although first ejaculation is often a physically pleasurable event, unlike in 19th-century America there is no public discourse to address this most private of experiences. Boys' first ejaculation experiences are greeted with anxious silence in contemporary America. Despite often feeling a great deal of pleasure, curiosity, and interest, most boys never talk about first ejaculation and never consider its ramifications in their development as sexual beings. The teasing and joking that occurs about masturbation in general, which is so prominent in contemporary American boys' lives, may be the most direct way that boys publicly respond to their first ejaculation.

According to the anthropologist Margaret Mead, taboo is defined as:

> a negative sanction, a prohibition whose infringement results in an automatic penalty without human or superhuman mediation. [Taboo is a prohibition] against participation in any situation of such inherent danger that the very act of participation will recoil upon the violator of the taboo (Mead, 1937, p. 502; as cited in Steiner, 1956, p. 22).

The features unique to first ejaculation—its intimate connections with nocturnal emission, masturbation, sexual desire, and orgasm—have made it and continue to make it highly tabooed. Also, the fact that first ejaculation occurs at a relatively young age strengthens the shroud of mystery and silence around the event. Current data indicate that American boys experience their first ejaculation between 12½ and 13 years of age (Downs & Fuller, 1991; Frankel, 2001; Gaddis & Brooks-Gunn, 1985; Shipman, 1971; Stein, 1990; Stein & Reiser, 1994). Fifty years ago the average age was 13½ years (Kinsey, Pomeroy, & Martin, 1948). In addition, there is a basic contradiction surrounding the first ejaculation taboo: Unlike other tabooed acts in contemporary America (e.g., cannibalism or incest), first ejaculation is simultaneously tabooed and a universal experience of adolescent male development. In other words, like an adolescent female's first menstrual period (menarche), first ejaculation

is a potentially very important event that could signify the end of childhood and the beginning of adult reproductive potential. However, due to social perception and stigmatization, first ejaculation is shrouded in anxious silence—and is therefore markedly different from menarche. The specific features of the first ejaculation taboo are rooted in American social history.

LATE 19TH-CENTURY AMERICA

Far from heralding adult masculinity, first ejaculation in the late 19th and early 20th century could clearly be quite harmful and traumatic. As the 19th century progressed, the overwhelming majority of mainstream medical, religious, educational, popular, and advice writers believed that any form of what were called "seminal losses" indicated that a male was a sinner, destined to be a social outcast, to go insane, to die, to be impotent, and to experience a myriad of other negative physical, mental, moral, and religious outcomes (Barker-Benfield, 1976; Hall, 1904; Haller & Haller, 1974; Kellogg, 1886; Rosenberg, 1973). The first time these emissions occurred signaled danger of *loss* of manhood, not achievement of manhood. There was a religious, moral, and medical evidence for the harm of seminal losses, and as a result drastic preventative measures were prescribed for male youth.

Religious writers and community leaders were a potent force in shaping public opinion about masturbation in 19th-century America. The historian Charles Rosenberg explained that there had been religious condemnations of masturbation in the early 19th century: "Beginning with the 1830s, however, the ritualized prudence of these traditional admonitions became sharpened and applied far more frequently, while for some authors sexuality began to assume an absolutely negative tone" (Rosenberg, 1973, p. 135). Popular religious writers such as Sylvester Graham and John

Kellogg typified the way that Christian doctrines of manhood were utilized to deny any positive connection between masturbation and masculine identity development. In the 1886 edition of his widely read nineteenth-century advice book, *Plain Facts for Old and Young*, Kellogg readily acknowledged that "very few boys are so ignorant or so innocent as to be unacquainted with it [masturbation]," but he labeled masturbation an "awful sin against nature and against God" (Kellogg, 1886, p. 339).

> Those who imagine that this sin is not a transgression of the seventh commandment, may be assured that this most heinous, revolting, and unnatural vice is in every respect more pernicious, more debasing, and more immoral than what is generally considered as violation of the commandment which says, "Thou shalt not commit adultery," and is a most flagrant violation of the same commandment. (Kellogg, 1886, pp. 339–340)

In his widely circulated writings, Kellogg elevated masturbatory ejaculation above coital ejaculation during an adulterous relationship. The prevailing Christian ideology dictated that an adolescent's first ejaculation, especially if by masturbation, was by definition unnatural and immoral.

One of the most likely effects of these condemnations of masturbation was to inspire fear in vulnerable boys. As an adolescent, Theodore Dreiser (born in 1871), author of the widely acclaimed novel *Sister Carrie*, feared that masturbation caused him acne, dizziness, headaches, ringing in his ears, emaciation, brain damage, and could lead him to an early death. He recalled discovering masturbation as an adolescent and indulged every two or three days while fantasizing about the local baker's daughter or other "torrid flames of beauty":

> Sickness! Brain trouble! Total physical collapse, no doubt! The trust was, I was really thinking of

those innumerable advertisements addressed to "Weak Men" or "Victims of Self-Abuse" as the advertisements of those days ran . . . The emaciated, sunken-eyed victims of youthful excess always illustrated by them haunted me. For now was I not one of these? If not as yet, then obviously I was to become one, emaciated, with hair and teeth falling out, eyes sunken, and no hope of any future of any kind save in the particular pills or nostrums advertised or such periods of treatment as could be procured from "Old Dr. Grindle" of Buffalo, New York, or "Old Dr. Grey" of Scranton, Pennsylvania. (as cited in Kiell, 1964, pp. 191–193)

Dreiser eventually overcame his fears of physical harm, but the process was arduous and left him resentful:

> The gradual realization that I was not to die at once gradually led to a modified view of my condition. Perhaps I was only to be crippled sexually for life, as the advertisements I had been reading by the ton invariably asserted. That was bad enough, of course, but after all it was not insanity or death . . .
>
> Poor ignorant humanity! I wish that all of the religious and moral piffle and nonsense from which I suffered in connection with this matter could be undone completely for the rest of the world by merely writing about it . . . Doctors more religionistic than medical, writing endless silly books on hearsay or because of early asinine terrors of their own! (as cited in Kiell, 1964, pp. 191–193)

As an adult, Dreiser identified the medical, religious, and popular forces behind the taboo that deeply affected him as an adolescent and a young man.

It is important to understand that masturbation was not the only form of seminal emission that was seen as harmful during this time. As the 19th century progressed, popular views held that any expenditure of semen outside of—or even including—the marital union was seen as a negative event (Barker-Benfield, 1976; Haller & Haller, 1974; Hare, 1962; Kellogg, 1886). What was called "self-abuse" was only the most prominent way that a man's reserves could be threatened. The historians Haller and Haller explained: "That a healthy man could have vigorous sexual activity in married life without brain damage seemed to matter little to those [nineteenth-century youths] whose minds were filled with the awesome spectacle of destruction following a single wet dream" (Haller & Haller, 1974, p. 225). Purity writers such as John Cowan understood that these tabooed emissions began at puberty. Cowan explained in 1871: "A perfectly healthy, continent man, living a right life socially, morally, and physically, does not and cannot have seminal emissions. Health does not absolutely require that there should ever be an emission of semen from puberty to death, though the individual live a hundred years" (as cited in Haller & Haller, 1974, p. 225). Writers extolled the virtues of "men of intelligence," such as John Locke and William Pitt, who never married and ostensibly "never in any way gratified the sexual desire" (Haller & Haller, 1974, p. 225). Advocates of semen conservation found a statement by Sir Isaac Newton, who claimed that he had never lost a drop of semen (Haller & Haller, 1974, p. 225). These beliefs boded poorly for a young man's first ejaculation experience.

This notion of limited semen was a cornerstone of the physiological evidence for 19th-century beliefs about the harm of ejaculation. The historian Barker-Benfield (1976) identified what he called a "spermatic economy," basing his terminology on the 19th-century belief that sperm was finite, and not something that the body naturally replenished: "Men believed their expenditure of sperm had to be governed according to an economic principle. . . . If the system was economic, then the ejaculation of sperm was equivalent in some sense to the expenditure of money" (Barker-Benfield, 1976, pp. 179–181). Expanding on the economic tenet that there are virtually unlimited ways to spend a limited amount of financial resources,

loss of semen in any form constituted a serious loss of currency.

Although the first ejaculation taboo of 19th-century America was generally strong, it most certainly did not result in complete silence about these matters. Adolescents furtively communicated with medical practitioners (Haller & Haller, 1974; Rosenberg, 1973), as G. Stanley Hall's recollections indicate below. Medical professionals and so-called quacks who specialized in curing seminal losses advertised widely in popular newspapers and magazines during this time (National Police Gazette, 1891), and many youth corresponded and visited these practitioners (Haller & Haller, 1974; Rosenberg, 1973). In addition, another form of discussion probably occurred in some settings, for the common practice of family members sharing beds, bedrooms, and bathing facilities in earlier generations (Brumberg, 1997; Rotundo, 1993) most probably resulted in early adolescent males having a difficult time hiding the evidence of their first ejaculation—or a lack of awareness that such evidence needed to be hidden. However, the conversations that are more commonly recalled, as Hall's testimonial indicates, are ones in which fathers, ministers, and medical professionals conveyed the first ejaculation taboo. Hall (1846–1924), commonly referred to as the "Father of Modern Adolescence," discovered only as an adult that masturbation and nocturnal emission were not signs of disease of dysfunction:

> My father occasionally went in swimming with us and once or twice took occasion to give us crude admonition on sex hygiene. The thing that sunk deepest was his story of a youth who abused himself and sinned with lewd women and as a result had a disease that ate his nose away until there were only two flat holes in his face for nostrils and who also became an idiot. For a long time, if I had any physical excitation or nocturnal experience I was almost petrified lest I was losing my brains and carefully

examined the bridge of my nose to see if it was getting the least bit flat. I understood that any one who swerved in the slightest from the norm of purity was liable to be smitten with some loathsome disease which I associated with leprosy and with the "unpardonable sin" which the minister often dwelt upon.

So great was my dread of natural phenomena that in the earliest teens I rigged an apparatus and applied bandages to prevent erethism [abnormal responsiveness to stimulation] while I slept, which very likely only augmented the trouble. If I yielded to any kind of temptation to experimentation upon myself I suffered intense remorse and fear, and sent up many a secret and most fervent prayer that I might never again break my resolve. At one time I feared I was abnormal and found occasion to consult a physician in a neighboring town who did not know me. He examined me and took my dollar, and laughed at me, but also told me what consequences would ensue if I became unchaste. What an untold anguish of soul would have been saved me if some one had told me that certain experiences while I slept were as normal for boys in their teens as are the monthly phenomena for girls. I did not know that even in college and thought myself secretly and exceptionally corrupt and not quite worthy to associate with girls. This had probably much, if not most, to do with my abstention from them. . . . I should certainly never dare to marry and have children. It was ineffable relief, therefore, to learn, as I did only far too late, that my life in this sphere had, on the whole, been in no sense abnormal or even exceptional. (as cited in Kiell, 1964, pp. 184–185)

As Hall's recollections indicate, there was great fear of the physical and mental degeneration associated with seminal emissions. In medical terminology this was labeled "masturbatory insanity," which was recognized as a category of disease, but the condition was not solely caused by masturbation and the results were not limited to dementia or loss of mental capacity. Medical professionals marshaled physiological evidence to support the common understanding that masturbatory insan-

ity also caused moral, social, and physical decline, including impotence, a physical decimation resembling leprosy, participation in other immoral behaviors, and a loss of self-respect and will power (Barker-Benfield, 1976; Haller & Haller, 1974; Kellogg, 1886; Rosenberg, 1973). For example, in an 1848 report to the Massachusetts state legislature, Samuel B. Woodward, the superintendent of the insane asylum at Worcester, claimed that 32 percent of admissions were due to masturbatory insanity. The allegations of this report were quickly incorporated into almost every pamphlet and book for adolescent males. Across the country, superintendents of asylums were besieged with requests to corroborate the claims of the Massachusetts report (Woodward, as cited in Hare, 1962, pp. 4–7). Also, in 1852, the American medical writer Frederick Hollick posited that a male who masturbated or experienced nocturnal emissions wasted his spine, would suffer from "softening of the brain," and ran the risk of insanity. Seminal emissions would give a male the feeling that "his mind is passing away" or that "his head was really empty" (as cited in Haller & Haller, 1974, pp. 196–197). The theory of masturbatory insanity was upheld by medical writers such as Edward Spitzka, a New York professor of medical jurisprudence, who wrote in 1887 that the typical age of onset of masturbatory insanity was between 13 and 20 and that because of the rarity of female masturbation it was at least five times more prevalent in males than females (Maudsley, 1882, p. 225).

The familial, moral, religious, and medical taboos against seminal losses were supported by the myriad draconian preventative measures. Suggested preventions included tying a boy's hands to bedposts at nighttime, straightjacketing, and fitting the hood of a boy's uncircumcised penis with a ring to keep it from retracting. In the late 19th century a number of inventors patented genital cages for males, including one device that sounded an electrical alarm if an erection occurred (Haller & Haller, 1974). These devices were taken quite seriously. Kellogg reported: "Covering the organs with a cage has been practiced with entire success" in preventing masturbation. Also, he wrote that circumcision without anesthetic "is almost always successful in small boys . . . The brief pain attending the operation will have a salutary effect upon the mind, especially if it be connected with the idea of punishment . . . The soreness which continues for several weeks interrupts the practice" (Kellogg, 1886, p. 295). Given this highly punitive, fear-inducing context, the popular effort was clearly not to assign positive cultural significance to a male's first ejaculation experience. The point of encouraging parents to use very forceful preventative measures was to intervene before masturbatory insanity took hold in vulnerable boys.

EARLY 20TH-CENTURY AMERICA

In 1904, G. Stanley Hall published his two-volume psychological treatise on adolescence, which for the first time identified adolescence as a discrete developmental period. This concept, which is virtually assumed in contemporary America, was quite remarkable at the time. In this book, when discussing adolescent male development, Hall distinguished between masturbatory ejaculation and ejaculation from nocturnal emission. He advocated that adolescent boys should not be reprimanded but instead educated and reassured after experiencing nocturnal emissions. His views changed mainstream conceptions of seminal emissions:

> Self-abuse is often common knowledge among males, but not this involuntary experience . . . Literature that treats any aspect of sex, and often the worst sources of information only are accessible, is devoured with an avidity felt in no other subject. There is a great hunger to know the laws of life and reproduction . . . There is a self-

loathing and loss of respect in the morning, and apprehension at night, that put a heavy strain on the nervous system, and that associate the exercise of this function, which should be the focus of all pleasant states of consciousness, with exquisitely painful emotions. These latter may rise to such strength as to even blight not only the prospects but the fruition of wedlock, and plant misery in the enter of the garden of joy, bringing impotence, temporary and perhaps permanent, to natures that would otherwise be healthful.

> It is in this state of mind that youth most needs father, pastor, mentor, or mature friend. He shrinks from the doctor, for that means fuller revelation, examination or full detection, but he seeks one who understands his trouble from afar, knows his symptoms in advance, has met many such cases, and will give him not generally hygienic, religious or moral advice, but specific and especially material help. (Hall, 1904, pp. 458–459)

Significantly, Hall made the comparison between adolescent males' seminal emissions and adolescent females' menstruation. Furthermore, Hall speculated that many males experienced their first ejaculation by nocturnal emission and that the anxiety produced needed to be addressed:

> Spontaneous emissions are probably as universal for unmarried youth as menstruation for women. Ignorance of this fact, even by the virtuous and normal, causes an amount of mental anguish in young men. . . . Maturity often first announces itself by nightly experiences that rouse the soul to a state of great alarm, that settles to a brooding anxiety. (Hall, 1904, p. 453)

Hall anticipated that there was not physiological evidence to support the prevailing condemnations of first ejaculation by nocturnal emission. However—despite his own experiences as an adolescent—Hall sounded remarkably like his 19th-century colleagues when he discussed masturbation:

> The first orgasm, especially if forced at premature age, consists in a general and diffused glow

and exhilaration of the sense of well-being even before emission is possible. This gives a heightened sense of the value of life, and a flush of ecstasy and joy that tinges the world with a glory that is far more than sensuous. But before this function is well developed the Nemesis of depression follows hard after these exaltations, and both states arouse thought and fancy in new directions and with a vividness unknown before. In bright, nervous children pubescence often dawns with almost fulminating intensity and suddenness, and sweeps the individual into pernicious ways long before moral or even intellectual restraints are operative. Excessive danger here is one of the penalties man pays for that inestimable tool of his development on to the human plane—the hand. (Hall, 1904, p. 438)

Capitalizing on the push for public school sex education in the 1910s and 1920s, new popular guidebooks for adolescents appeared. Reflecting the views of Hall, guidebook authors simultaneously rejected 19th-century beliefs about the harmfulness of nocturnal emission while perpetuating 19th-century beliefs about the harmfulness of masturbation. For example, one team of medical writers, discussing adolescents' "special fluids" in a 1916 educational article for 12 to 16 year olds, explained: "In the boy . . . interference with, or increase of the emissions is most unhealthy. These emissions should occur only involuntarily and not from stimulation or roughness in bathing or from rough, tight clothing" (Armstrong & Armstrong, 1916, p. 335). In light of increasing evidence that masturbation did not directly cause physical damage to male development (as purported in the 19th century), early 20th-century psychologists (Hall, 1904), sex educators (Armstrong & Armstrong, 1916; Exner, 1915), and popular writers in the social hygiene movement (Hughes, 1926; Lowry, 1911) shifted their focus to the *psychologically* negative outcomes of masturbation. After the sexual revolution of the 1920s, many educators and medical writers were willing to consider the universality of the occasional nocturnal emission, but not masturbatory ejaculation. Masturbatory ejaculation was commonly seen as intentional and controllable, whereas nocturnal emission was portrayed as unintentional, uncontrollable, and—most importantly—"normal."

The resulting public school educational efforts were largely aimed at normalizing nocturnal emission and decreasing boys' fears of the experience. For example, in a 1940 educational booklet published by the United States Public Health Service, Surgeon General Thomas Parran and colleagues strongly advocated for universal public school education about the normalcy of nocturnal emissions. The authors wrote that the public school teacher "should emphasize that emissions do not result in lost manhood and are not a disease" (United States Public Health Service, 1940, pp. 66–67). Although efforts to refute 19th-century beliefs about seminal emissions were fairly successful, the effort to normalize nocturnal emissions was not as successful. The overtly sexual nature of nocturnal emissions and the relatively early age at which they first occurred made it difficult for many educators and parents to discuss the topic openly with early adolescent males.

In addition to the limited success of efforts to normalize nocturnal emission, popular beliefs about masturbation clearly contributed to the first ejaculation taboo. Significantly, there was a clear ideological shift about the harm that masturbation caused after the 1920s. Instead of predicting grave physical degeneration like their 19th-century brethren did, mid-20th-century writers held that masturbation resulted in *psychological* harm. For example, in the same 1940 report that refuted 19th-century beliefs about nocturnal emission, Surgeon General Parran admitted that the negative physical outcomes of masturbation had been "greatly overemphasized" but nevertheless maintained that masturbation caused "psychic" losses, including self-respect, self-confidence, self-control, and—most importantly—masculinity:

In the male, from the physical point of view, it makes no difference whether spermatic fluid is lost through emissions, through masturbation, or through sexual intercourse. Further, there is no reason to suppose that the nervous system would suffer if only the loss of spermatic fluid were concerned. Although the physical aspects have been greatly overemphasized, masturbation is destructive because it breaks down self-respect, self-confidence, and self-control . . . It is in its effects on attitudes and self-confidence that masturbation is injurious and the manliness . . . that is lost is not organic, but psychic in its nature. (United States Public Health Service, 1940, pp. 66–67)

These views are simultaneously different from and similar to 19th-century perspectives. The use of the word *loss* in reference both to semen and to manhood echoes 19th-century terminology. On the other hand, the necessity of a man's "self-control" in avoiding masturbation emphasized the 20th-century distinction between the "involuntary" nature of nocturnal emission and the "voluntary" nature of masturbation. Similarly, delineating between "psychic" and "organic" losses distinguished prevailing attitudes of the post-1920s sexual revolution America from the Victorian era. Despite these distinctions, the general perspective that the chief medical officer of the United States conveyed in 1940 was that adolescent males' first ejaculation by masturbation remained a threat to their developing manhood.

THE TABOO'S LINGERING EFFECTS

In mid- and late 19th-century America, there was an explicit taboo on seminal emissions of any kind. This taboo did not bode well for a male youth experiencing his first ejaculation. It was commonly believed that masturbation and nocturnal emission led to physical degeneration, insanity, and even death. It was doubtful that a male youth, his family, his educators, his religious leaders, his doctor, or his peers viewed the event as heralding manhood. After the sex education movement and the sexual revolution of the early 20th century, mainstream medical, governmental, and public school leaders tried with limited success to "normalize" nocturnal emission. However, the first ejaculation taboo remained in place. In light of increasing evidence that masturbation did not directly cause physical damage to male development (as purported in the 19th century), early 20th-century psychologists and sex educators maintained that there were *psychologically* negative outcomes of masturbation. This shift enabled these writers and researchers to maintain agreement with their 19th-century counterparts that masturbation—and, by extension, first ejaculation—harmed a boy's developing manhood.

One turning point to a more modern representation of first ejaculation occurred in 1948, when Kinsey, Pomeroy, and Martin's landmark study of male sexuality was published. The authors were among the first to conceptualize the importance of first ejaculation as a normative developmental event. They proclaimed: "The published studies of younger boys almost completely lack data on the most significant of all adolescent developments, the occurrence of the first ejaculation" (Kinsey, Pomeroy, & Martin, 1948, p. 185). However, given the strength of the existing taboo, their conclusion did not change reality. This taboo is firmly in place today, preventing boys from anticipating first ejaculation and therefore from thinking of the experience as a significant development in their pathway to adulthood. In this sense, adolescent boys' experiences of first ejaculation are markedly different from adolescent girls' experiences of menarche.

In the 50 years that have passed since Kinsey's study appeared, research on this topic has been scant, but results have been telling (Downs & Fuller, 1991; Frankel, 2001; Gaddis & Brooks-Gunn, 1985; Shipman, 1971; Stein,

1990; Stein & Reiser, 1994). Findings indicate that males' responses to first ejaculation are more commonly curiosity, excitement, and pleasure—not shame, fear, or ignorance. Therefore, it would appear that many males would have something to talk about, following their first ejaculation. However, the lack of communication about first ejaculation is the most clear indication of a contemporary taboo. Before experiencing first ejaculation, early adolescent males already know not to discuss it. In addition, few parents, peers, educators, religious leaders, health care professionals, mental health practitioners, or other community leaders discuss first ejaculation with early adolescent males. In a study of parents of 10- to 13-year-old sons, the vast majority of parents reported never having talked with their son about first ejaculation. When asked to explain their reasoning, parents' most common response was that they had never thought about their son's impending first ejaculation (Frankel, 2001). Reflecting the American taboo, there are currently few popular fictional books for boys that mention nocturnal emission, masturbation, or first ejaculation as part of normative development (Blume, 1971). Furthermore, authors of contemporary guidebooks for adolescent boys and for parents are generally content to devote a few paragraphs at most to normalizing and reducing fear about first ejaculation (Gordon & Gordon, 1983; Haffner, 1999; Madaras, 1988). Although findings need to be replicated, across all American studies the vast majority of participants reported having talked with no one about their first ejaculation experiences (Downs & Fuller, 1991; Frankel, 2001; Gaddis & Brooks-Gunn, 1985; Shipman, 1971; Stein, 1990; Stein & Reiser, 1994). One research participant explained:

> I don't remember when it happened or how old I was, but I didn't tell anyone. My friends, we didn't talk about it, but if it came up, you know

> we always played these games—"So have you done this, so have you done this, so have you done this"—I would say I had. But I didn't say, "By the way Mom, my bed is wet." I mean, I knew what an ejaculation was, and I knew that I hadn't wet the bed. (Stein & Reiser, 1994, p. 380)

In the sole study conducted with non-American participants (Adegoke, 1993), there was not clear-cut evidence of cultural silence. In stark contrast to findings of American research, the majority of Nigerian participants reported telling someone after experiencing first ejaculation. The most common confidante was a male peer. These findings, although preliminary, sharply contrast with the experiences of American males and suggest that the first ejaculation taboo may be specific to contemporary American culture.

The existing socio-cultural evidence suggests that a strong taboo has coalesced around American boys' experiences of first ejaculation. In the late 19th and early 20th century, there was much more public discourse about the meaning of seminal emissions—but the overwhelming majority of this discourse promoted the belief that drastically negative physical outcomes would result from a boys' first ejaculation. These negative viewpoints have generally disappeared, but so has the public discussion that examined possible connections between first ejaculation and boys' development. In response to 19th-century hysteria about nocturnal emission, the "normalization" of nocturnal emission has curtailed asking important questions about the meaning of boys' first ejaculation. Discussion of nocturnal emission is rarely found, except for a few reassuring paragraphs in advice manuals or a clinical explanation in sex education classes. In addition, the pervasive fear of masturbation prevents serious cultural consideration of how early adolescent males express themselves as sexual beings. Masturbation is something to joke about anxiously with peers, and it is an act of desperation or comedy when publicly portrayed (alluded to in a *Seinfeld* episode, or represented in contemporary movies). It is in this cultural context that first ejaculation occurs. These scant, limited public representations pale in comparison to what first ejaculation potentially signifies. It is a male's first adult-style sexual experience, and his sense of self might therefore change were it not for the anxious silence surrounding the event.

BIBLIOGRAPHY

Adegoke, A.A. (1993). The experience of spermarche (the age of onset of sperm emission) among selected adolescent boys in Nigeria. *Journal of Youth and Adolescence, 22,* 201–209.

Armstrong, D.B., & Armstrong, E.B. (1916). Sex in life: for boys and girls from twelve to sixteen years. *Social Hygiene,* 2(1): 321–341.

Barker-Benfield, G.J. (1976). *The horrors of a half-known life: Male attitudes toward women and sexuality in nineteenth-century America.* New York: Harper.

Blume, J. (1971). *Then again, maybe I won't.* New York: Dell.

Brumberg, J.J. (1997). *The body project: An intimate history of American girls.* New York: Random House.

Douglas, M. (1966). *Purity and danger: An analysis of concepts of pollution and taboo.* New York: Praeger.

Downs, A.C., & Fuller, M.J. (1991). Recollections of spermarche: An exploratory investigation. *Current Psychology: Research & Reviews,* 10(1–2): 93–102.

Exner, M.J. (1915). *Problems and principles of sex education: A study of 948 college men.* New York: YMCA.

Frankel, L. (2001). *Contradictions and taboos surrounding American adolescent males' experiences of first ejaculation (semenarche).* Unpublished master's thesis. Cornell University, Ithaca, NY.

Gaddis, A., & Brooks-Gunn, J. (1985). The male experience of puberty. *Journal of Youth and Adolescence, 14,* 61–69.

Gordon, S., & Gordon, J. (1983). *Raising a child conservatively in a sexually permissive world.* New York: Simon.

Greif, E.B., & Ulman, K. J. (1982). The psychological impact of menarche on early adolescent females: A review of the literature. *Child Development, 53,* 1413–1430.

Haffner, D.W. (1999). *From diapers to dating: A parent's guide to raising sexually healthy children.* New York: Newmarket.

Hall, G.S. (1904). *Adolescence: Its psychology and its relations to physiology, anthropology, sociology, sex, crime, religion and education.* New York: D. Appleton.

Haller, J.S., & Haller, R.M. (1974). *The physician and sexuality in Victorian America.* New York: Norton.

Hare, E.H. (1962). Masturbatory insanity: The history of an idea. *Journal of Mental Science,* 452(108): 1–25.

Hughes, W.L. (1926). Sex experiences of boyhood. *Journal of Social Hygiene, 12.* Albany, NY: American Social Hygiene Association.

Kellogg, J.H. (1886). *Plain facts for old and young: Embracing the natural history and hygiene of organic life.* Burlington, Iowa: Segner.

Kiell, N. (1964). *The universal experience of adolescence.* Boston: Beacon.

Kinsey, A.C., Pomeroy, W.B., & Martin, C.E. (1948). *Sexual behavior in the human male* (pp. 183–192). Phiadelphia: Saunders.

Lowry, E.B. (1911). *Truths: Talks with a boy concerning himself.* Chicago: Forbes.

MacDonald, R.H. (1967). The frightful consequences of ononism: Notes on the history of a delusion. *Journal of History of Ideas,* 28(3): 423–431.

Madaras, L. (1988). *The What's happening to my body? book for boys.* New York: Newmarket.

Maudsley, H. (1882). *The pathology of mind.* 3rd ed. New York: Appleton.

Miles, R. (1991). *Love, sex, death, and the making of the male.* New York: Summit Books.

National Police Gazette (1891, October 17). Classified advertisements, pp. 14–15. New York: National Police Gazette.

Pollack, W. (1998). *Real boys: Rescuing our sons from the myths of boyhood.* New York: Random House.

Rosenberg, C.E. (1973). Sexuality, class, and role in 19th-century America. *American Quarterly,* 25(2): 131–153.

Rotundo, E.A. (1993). *American manhood: Transformations in masculinity from the revolution to the modern era.* New York: Basic Books.

Shipman, G. (1971). The psychodynamics of sex education. In R.E. Muuss (Ed.), *Adolescent behavior and society: A book of readings* (pp. 326–339). New York: Random House.

Snow, W.F. (1932). White House conference on child health and protection. *Social Hygiene in Schools.* New York: Century.

Stein, J.H. (1990). Attitudes towards pubertal change and first ejaculation in white, middle-class, American males. Unpublished doctoral thesis. New Haven, Connecticut: Yale University.

Stein, J.H., & Reiser, L.W. (1994). A study of white middle-class adolescent boys' responses to "semenarche" (the first ejaculation). *Journal of Youth and Adolescence, 23,* 373–384.

Steiner, F. (1956). *Taboo.* London: Cohen & West.

United States Public Health Service (1940). *High schools and sex education.* Washington, DC: U.S. Government Printing Office.

READING 29

Socially Camouflaged Technologies: The Case of the Electromechanical Vibrator

Rachel Maines

Certain commodities are sold in the legal marketplace for which the expected use is either illegal or socially unacceptable. Marketing of these goods, therefore, requires camouflaging of the design purpose in a verbal and visual rhetoric that conveys to the knowledgeable consumer the item's selling points without actually endorsing its socially prohibited uses. I refer not to goods that are actually illegal in character, such as marijuana, but to their grey-market background technologies, such as cigarette rolling papers. Marketing efforts for goods of this type have similar characteristics over time, despite the dissimilarity of the advertised commodities. I shall discuss here an electromechanical technology that addresses formerly prohibited expressions of women's

sexuality—the vibrator in its earliest incarnation between 1870 and 1930. Comparisons will be drawn between marketing strategies for this electromechanical technology, introduced between 1880 and 1903, and that of emmenagogues, distilling, burglary tools, and computer software copying, as well as the paradigm example of drug paraphernalia.

I shall argue here that electromechanical massage of the female genitalia achieved acceptance during the period in question by both professionals and consumers not only because it was less cumbersome, labor-intensive and costly than predecessor technologies, but because it maintained the social camouflage of sexual massage treatment through its associations with modern professional instrumentation and with prevailing beliefs about electricity as a healing agent.

The case of the electromechanical vibrator, as a technology associated with women's sexuality, involves issues of acceptability rather than legality. The vibrator and its predecessor technologies, including the dildo, are associated with masturbation, a socially prohibited activity until well into the second half of this century.[1] Devices for mechanically-assisted female masturbation, mainly vibrators and dildoes, were marketed in the popular press from the late nineteenth century through the early thirties in similarly camouflaged advertising. Such advertisements temporarily disappeared from popular literature after the vibrator

This research was made possible in part by a grant from the Bakken (Museum and Library of Electricity in Life), August 1985.
Source: IEEE Technology and Society Magazine, June 1989. Copyright © 1989 IEEE. Reprinted with permission from IEEE and the author.

began to appear in stag films, which may have rendered the camouflage inadequate, and did not resurface until social change made it unnecessary to disguise the sexual uses of the device.[2]

For purposes of this discussion, a vibrator is a mechanical or electromechanical appliance imparting rapid and rhythmic pressure through a contoured working surface usually mounted at a right angle to the handle. These points of contact generally take the form of a set of interchangeable vibratodes configured to the anatomical areas they are intended to address. Vibrators are rarely employed internally in masturbation; they thus differ from dildoes, which are generally straight-shafted and may or may not include a vibratory component. Vibrators are here distinguished also from massagers, the working surfaces of which are flat or dished.[3] It should be noted that this is a historian's distinction imposed on the primary sources; medical authors and appliance manufacturers apply a heterogeneous nomenclature to massage technologies. Vibrators and dildoes rarely appeared in household advertising between 1930 and 1955, massagers continued to be marketed, mainly through household magazines.[4]

The electromechanical vibrator, introduced as a medical instrument in the 1880s and as a home appliance between 1900 and 1903, represented the convergence of several older medical massage technologies, including manual, hydriatic, electrotherapeutic and mechanical methods. Internal and external gynecological massage with lubricated fingers had been a standard medical treatment for hysteria, disorders of menstruation and other female complaints at least since the time of Aretaeus Cappadox (circa 150 A.D.), and the evidence suggests that orgasmic response on the part of the patient may have been the intended therapeutic result.[5] Douche therapy, a method of directing a jet of pumped water at the pelvic area and vulva, was employed for a similar purpose after hydrotherapy became popular

in the eighteenth and nineteeth centuries. [6] The camouflage of the apparently sexual character of such therapy was accomplished through its medical respectability and through creative definitions both of the diseases for which massage was indicated and of the effects of treatment. In the case of the electromechanical vibrator, the use of electrical power contributed the cachet of modernity and linked the instrument to older technologies of electrotherapeutics, in which patients received low-voltage electricity through electrodes attached directly to the skin or mucous membranes, and to light-bath therapy, in which electric light was applied to the skin in a closed cabinet. The electrotherapeutic association was explicitly invoked in the original term for the vibrator's interchangeable applicators, which were known as "vibratodes." Electrical treatments were employed in hysteria as soon as they were introduced in the eighteenth century, and remained in use as late as the 1920s.

Hysteria as a disease paradigm, from its origins in the Egyptian medical corpus through its conceptual eradication by American Psychological Association fiat in 1952, was so vaguely and subjectively defined that it might encompass almost any set of ambiguous symptoms that troubled a woman or her family. As its name suggests, hysteria as well as its "sister" complaint chlorosis were until the twentieth century thought to have their etiology in the female reproductive tract generally, and more particularly in the organism's response to sexual deprivation.[7] This physiological condition seems to have achieved epidemic proportions among women and girls, at least in the modern period.[8] Sydenham, writing in the seventeenth century, observed that hysteria was the most common of all diseases except fevers.[9]

In the late nineteenth century, physicians noted with alarm that from half to three-quarters of all women showed signs of hysterical affliction. Among the many symptoms listed in medical descriptions of the syndrome are anxiety, sense of heaviness in the pelvis, edema (swelling) in the lower abdomen and genital areas, wandering of attention and associated tendencies to indulge in sexual fantasy, insomnia, irritability, and "excessive" vaginal lubrication.

The therapeutic objective in such cases was to produce a "crisis" of the disease in the Hippocratic sense of this expression, corresponding to the point in infectious diseases at which the fever breaks. Manual massage of the vulva by physicians or midwives, with fragrant oils as lubricants, formed part of the standard treatment repertoire for hysteria, chlorosis and related disorders from ancient times until the post-Freudian era. The crisis induced by this procedure was usually called the "hysterical paroxysm." Treatment for hysteria might comprise up to three-quarters of a physician's practice in the nineteenth century. Doctors who employed vulvular massage treatment in hysteria thus required fast, efficient and effective means of producing the desired crisis. Portability of the technology was also a desideratum, as physicians treated many patients in their homes, and only manual massage under these conditions was possible until the introduction of the portable battery-powered vibrator for medical use in the late 1880s.

Patients reported experiencing symptomatic relief after such treatments, and such conditions as pelvic congestion and insomnia were noticeably ameliorated, especially if therapy continued on a regular basis. A few physicians, including Nathaniel Highmore in the seventeenth century and Auguste Tripier, a nineteenth century electrotherapist, clearly recognized the hysterical paroxysm as sexual orgasm.[10] That many of their colleagues also perceived the sexual character of hysteria treatments is suggested by the fact that, in the case of married women, one of the therapeutic options was intercourse, and in the case of single women, marriage was routinely recommended.[11] "God-fearing physicians," as Zacuto expressed it in the seventeenth century,

were expected to induce the paroxysm with their own fingers only when absolutely necessary, as in the case of very young single women, widows and nuns.[12]

Many later physicians, however, such as the nineteenth century hydrotherapist John Harvey Kellogg, seem not to have perceived the sexual character of patient response. Kellogg wrote extensively about hydrotherapy and electrotherapeutics in gynecology. In his "Electrotherapeutics in Chronic Maladies," published in *Modern Medicine* in 1904, he describes "strong contractions of the abdominal muscles" in a female patient undergoing treatment, and similar reactions such that "the office table was made to tremble quite violently with the movement." In their analysis of the situation, these physicians may have been handicapped by their failure to recognize that penetration is a successful means of producing orgasm in only a minority of women; thus treatments that did not involve significant vaginal penetration were not morally suspect. In effect, misperceptions of female sexuality formed part of the camouflage of the original manual technique that preceded the electromechanical vibrator. Insertion of the speculum, however, since it travelled the same path as the supposedly irresistible penis during intercourse, was widely criticized in the medical community for its purportedly immoral effect on patients.[13] That some questioned the ethics of the vulvular massage procedure is clear; Thomas Stretch Dowse quotes Graham as observing that "Massage of the pelvic organs should be intrusted to those alone who have 'clean hands and a pure heart'."[14] One physician, however, in an article significantly titled "Signs of Masturbation in the Female," proposed the application of an electrical charge to the clitoris as a test of salacious propensities in women. Sensitivity of the organ to this type of electrical stimulation, in his view, indicated secret indulgence in what was known in the nineteenth century as "a bad habit."[15] Ironically, such women were often treated electrically for hysteria supposedly caused by masturbation.

However they construed the benefits, physicians regarded the genital massage procedure, which could take as long as an hour of skilled therapeutic activity, as something of a chore, and made early attempts to mechanize it. Hydrotherapy, in the form of what was known as the "pelvic douche" (massage of the lower pelvis with a jet of pumped water), provided similar relief to the patient with reduced demands on the therapist. Doctors of the eighteenth and nineteenth centuries frequently recommended douche therapy for their women patients who could afford spa visits. This market was limited, however, as both treatment and travel were costly.[16] A very small minority of patients and doctors could afford to install hydrotherapeutic facilities in convenient locations; both doctor and patient usually had to travel to the spa. Electrically-powered equipment, when it became available, thus had a decentralizing and cost-reducing effect on massage treatment.

In the 1860s, some spas and clinics introduced a coal-fired steam powered device invented by a Dr. George Taylor, called the "Manipulator," which massaged the lower pelvis while the patient either stood or lay on a table.[17] This too required a considerable expenditure either by the physician who purchased the equipment or by the patient who was required to travel to a spa for treatment. Thus, when the electromechanical vibrator was invented two decades later in England by Mortimer Granville and manufactured by Weiss, a ready market already existed in the medical community.[18] Ironically, Mortimer Granville considered the use of his instrument on women, especially hysterics, a morally indefensible act, and recommended the device only for use on the male skeletal muscles.[19] Although his original battery-powered model was heavy and unreliable, it was more portable than water-powered massage and less fatiguing to the operator than manual massage.

Air-pressure models were introduced, but they required cumbersome tanks of compressed air, which needed frequent refilling. When line electricity became widely available, portable plug-in models made vibratory house calls more expeditious and cost effective for the enterprising physician. The difficulty of maintaining batteries in or out of the office was noted by several medical writers of the period predating the introduction of plug-in vibrators.[20] Batteries and small office generators were liable to fail at crucial moments during patient treatment, and required more engineering expertise for their maintenance than most physicians cared to acquire. Portable models using dc or ac line electricity were available with a wide range of vibratodes, such as the twelve-inch rectal probe supplied with one of the Gorman firm's vibrators.

Despite its inventor's reservations, the Weiss instrument and later devices on the same principle were widely used by physicians for pelvic disorders in women and girls. The social camouflage applied to the older manual technology was carefully maintained in connection with the new, at least until the 1920s. The marketing of medical vibrators to physicians and the discussion of them in such works as *Covey's Profitable Office Specialties* addressed two important professional considerations: the respectability of the devices as medical instruments (including their reassuringly clinical appearance) and their utility in the fast and efficient treatment of those chronic disorders, such as pelvic complaints in women, that provided a significant portion of a physician's income.[21] The importance of a prestige image for electromechanical instrumentation, and its role in the pricing of medical vibrators is illustrated by a paragraph in the advertising brochure for the

"Chattanooga," at $200 in 1904 the most costly of the physicians' office models:

> The Physician can give with the "Chattanooga" Vibrator a thorough massage treatment in three minutes that is extremely pleasant and beneficial, but this instrument is neither designed nor sold as a "Massage Machine." It is sold only to Physicians, and constructed for the express purpose of exciting the various organs of the body into activity through their central nervous supply.[22]

I do not mean to suggest that gynecological treatments were the only uses of such devices, or that all physicians who purchased them used them for the production of orgasm in female patients, but the literature suggests that a substantial number were interested in the new technology's utility in the hysteroneurasthenic complaints. The interposition of an official-looking machine must have done much to restore clinical dignity to the massage procedure. The vibrator was introduced in 1899 as a home medical appliance, and was by 1904 advertised in household magazines in suggestive terms we shall examine later on. It was important for physicians to be able to justify to patients the expense of $2–3 per treatment, as home vibrators were available for about $5.

The acceptance of the electromechanical vibrator by physicians at the turn of this century may also have been influenced by their earlier adoption of electrotherapeutics, with which vibratory treatment could be, and often was, combined.[23] Vibratory therapeutics were introduced from London and Paris, especially from the famous Hôspital Salpêtrière, which added to their respectability in the medical community.[24] It is worth noting as well that in this period electrical and other vibrations were a subject of great interest and considerable confusion, not only among doctors and the general public, but even among scientists like Tesla, who is reported to have fallen under their spell. ". . . [T]he Earth," he wrote, "is responsive to electrical vibrations of definite pitch just as a tuning fork to certain waves of sound. These particular electrical vibrations, capable of powerfully exciting the Globe, lend themselves to innumerable uses of great importance . . ."[25] In the same category of mystical reverence for vibration is Samuel Wallian's contemporaneous essay on "The Undulatory Theory in Therapeutics," in which he describes "modalities or manifestations of vibratory impulse" as the guiding principle of the universe. "Each change and gradation is not a transformation, as mollusk into mammal, or monkey into man, but an evidence of a variation in vibratory velocity. A certain rate begets a *vermis*, another and higher rate produces a *viper*, a *vertebrate*, a *vestryman*."[26]

In 1900, according to Monell, more than a dozen medical vibratory devices for physicians had been available for examination at the Paris Exposition. Of these, few were able to compete in the long term with electromechanical models. Mary L. H. Arnold Snow, writing for a medical readership in 1904, discusses in some depth more than twenty types, of which more than half are electromechanical. These models, some priced to the medical trade as low as $15, delivered vibrations from one to 7,000 pulses a minute. Some were floor-standing machines on rollers; others could be suspended from the ceiling like the modern impact wrench. The more expensive models were adapted to either ac or dc currents. A few, such as those of the British firm Schall and Son, could even be ordered with motors custom-wound to a physician's specifications. Portable and battery-powered electromechanical vibrators were generally less expensive than floor models, which both looked more imposing as instruments and were less likely to transmit fatiguing vibrations to the doctor's hands.

Patients were treated in health spa complexes, in doctor's offices or their own homes with portable equipment. Designs consonant with prevailing notions of what a medical instrument should look like inspired consumer confidence in the physician and his apparatus, justified treatment costs, and, in the case of hysteria treatments, camouflaged the sexual character of the therapy. Hand or foot-powered models, however, were tiring to the operator; water-powered ones became too expensive to operate when municipalities began metering water in the early twentieth century. Gasoline engines and batteries were cumbersome and difficult to maintain, as noted above. No fuel or air-tank handling by the user was required for line electricity, in contrast with compressed air, steam and petroleum as power sources. In the years after 1900, as line electricity became the norm in urban communities, the electromechanical vibrator emerged as the dominant technology for medical massage.

Some physicians contributed to this trend by endorsing the vibrator in works like that of Monell, who had studied vibratory massage in medical practice in the United States and Europe at the turn of this century. He praises its usefulness in female complaints:

> . . . pelvic massage (in gynecology) has its brilliant advocates and they report wonderful results, but when practitioners must supply the skilled technic with their own fingers the method has no value to the majority. But special applicators (motor-driven) give practical value and office convenience to what otherwise is impractical.[27]

Other medical writers suggested combining vibratory treatment of the pelvis with hydro- and electrotherapy, a refinement made possible by the ready adaptability of the new electromechanical technology.

At the same period, mechanical and electro-mechanical vibrators were introduced as home medical appliances. One of the earliest was the Vibratile, a battery-operated massage device

advertised in 1899. Like the vibrators sold to doctors, home appliances could be handpow-ered, water-driven, battery or street-current apparatus in a relatively wide range of prices from $1.50 to $28.75. This last named was the price of a Sears, Roebuck model of 1918, which could be purchased as an attachment for a separate electrical motor, drawing current through a lamp socket, which also powered a fan, buffer, grinder, mixer and sewing machine. The complete set was marketed in the catalogue under the headline "Aids that Every Woman Appreciates." Vibrators were mainly marketed to women, although men were sometimes exhorted to purchase the devices as gifts for their wives, or to become door-to-door sales representatives for the manufacturer.[28]

The electromechanical vibrator was preceded in the home market by a variety of electrotherapeutic appliances which continued to be advertised through the twenties, often in the same publications as vibratory massage devices. Montgomery Ward, Sears Roebuck and the Canadian mail order department store T. Eaton and Company all sold medical batteries by direct-mail by the end of the nineteenth century. These were simply batteries with electrodes that administered a mild shock. Some, like Butler's Electro-Massage Machine, produced their own electricity with friction motors. Contemporaneous and later appliances sometimes had special features, such as Dr. H. Sanche's Oxydonor, which produced ozone in addition to the current when one electrode was placed in water. "Electric" massage rollers, combs and brushes with a supposedly permanent charge retailed at this time for prices between one and five dollars. Publications like the *Home Needlework Magazine* and *Men and Women* advertised these devices, as well as related technologies, including correspondence courses in manual massage.

Vibrators with water motors, a popular power source, as noted above, before the introduction of metered water, were advertised in such journals as *Modern Women,* which emphasized the cost savings over treatments by physicians and further emphasized the advantage of privacy offered by home treatment. Such devices were marketed through the teens in *Hearst's* and its successors, and in *Woman's Home Companion.*[29] Electromechanical vibrators were sold in the upper middle class market, in magazines typically retailing for between ten and fifteen cents an issue. As in the case of medical vibrators, models adapted to both ac and dc current were more expensive than those for use with dc only; all were fitted with screw-in plugs through the twenties.

All types of vibrators were advertised as benefiting health and beauty by stimulating the circulation and soothing the nerves. The makers of the electromechanical American vibrator, for example, recommended their product as an ". . . alleviating, curative and beautifying agent . . . It will increase deficient circulation—develop the muscles—remove wrinkles and facial blemishes, and beautify the complexion."[30] Advertisements directed to make purchasers similarly emphasized the machine's advantages for improving a woman's appearance and disposition. An ad in a 1921 issue of *Hearst's* urges the considerate husband to "Give 'her' a Star for Christmas" on the grounds that it would be "A Gift That Will *Keep* Her Young and Pretty." The same device was listed in another advertisement with several other electrical appliances, and labelled "Such Delightful Companions!"[31] A husband, these advertisements seem to suggest, who presented his wife with these progressive and apparently respectable medical aids might leave for work in the morning secure in the knowledge that his spouse's day would be pleasantly and productively invested in self-treatment. Like other electrical appliance advertising of the time, electromechanical vibrator ads emphasized the role

of the device in making a woman's home a veritable Utopia of modern technology, and its utility in reducing the number of occasions, such as visiting her physician, on which she would be required to leave her domestic paradise.[32]

Advertisements for vibrators often shared magazine pages with books on sexual matters, such as Howard's popular *Sex Problems in Worry and Work* and Walling's *Sexology,* handguns, cures for alcoholism and, occasionally, even personals, from both men and women, in which matrimony was the declared objective. Sexuality is never explicit in vibrator advertising; the tone is vague but provocative, as in the Swedish Vibrator advertisement in *Modern Priscilla* of 1913, offering "a machine that gives 30,000 thrilling, invigorating, penetrating, revitalizing vibrations per minute . . . Irresistible desire to own it, once you feel the living pulsing touch of its rhythmic vibratory motion." Illustrations in these layouts typically include voluptuously proportioned women in various states of *déshabillé.* The White Cross vibrator, made by a Chicago firm that manufactured a variety of small electrical appliances, was also advertised in *Modern Priscilla,* where the maker assured readers that "It makes you fairly tingle with the joy of living."[33] It is worth noting that the name "White Cross" was drawn from that of an international organization devoted to what was known in the early twentieth century as "social hygiene," the discovery and eradication of masturbation and prostitution wherever they appeared. The Chicago maker of White Cross appliances, in no known way affiliated with the organization, evidently hoped to trade on the name's association with decency and moral purity.[34] A 1916 advertisement from the White Cross manufacturer in *American Magazine* nevertheless makes the closest approach to explicit sexual claims when it promises that "All the keen relish, the pleasures of youth, will throb within you."[35] The utility of the product for female masturbation was thus consistently camouflaged.

Electromechanical vibrator advertising almost never appeared in magazines selling for less than 5 cents an issue (10 to 20 cents is the median range) or more than 25 cents. Readers of the former were unlikely to have access to electrical current; readers of the latter, including, for example, *Vanity Fair,* were more likely to respond to advertising for spas and private manual massage. While at least a dozen and probably more than twenty U.S. firms manufactured electromechanical vibrators before 1930, sales of these appliances were not reported in the electrical trade press. A listing from the February 1927 *NELA Bulletin* is typical; no massage equipment of any kind appears on an otherwise comprehensive list that includes violet-ray appliances.[36] A 1925 article in *Electrical World,* under the title "How Many Appliances are in Use?", lists only irons, washing machines, cleaners, ranges, water heaters, percolators, toasters, waffle irons, kitchen units and ironers.[37] *Scientific American* listed in 1907 only the corn popper, chafing dish, milk warmer, shaving cup, percolator and iron in a list of domestic electrical appliances.[38] References to vibrators were extremely rare even in popular discussions of electrical appliances.[39] The U.S. Bureau of the Census, which found 66 establishments manufacturing electro-therapeutic apparatus in 1908, does not disaggregate by instrument type either in this category or in "electrical household goods." The 1919 volume, showing the electromedical market at a figure well over $2 million, also omits detailed itemization. Vibrators appear by name in the 1949 *Census of Manufactures,* but it is unclear whether the listing for them, aggregated with statistics for curling irons and hair dryers, includes those sold as medical instruments to physicians.[40] This dearth of data renders sales tracking of the electromechanical vibrator extremely difficult. The omissions from engineering literature

are worth noting, as the electromechanical vibrator was one of the first electrical appliances for personal care, partly because it was seen as a safe method of self-treatment.[41]

The marketing strategy for the early electromechanical vibrator was similar to that employed for contemporaneous and even modern technologies for which social camouflage is considered necessary. Technologically, the devices so marketed differ from modern vibrators sold for explicitly sexual purposes only in their greater overall weight, accounted for by the use of metal housings in the former and plastic in the latter. The basic set of vibratodes is identical, as is the mechanical action. The social context of the machine, however, has undergone profound change. Liberalized attitudes toward masturbation in both sexes and increasing understanding of women's sexuality have made social camouflage superfluous.

In the case of the vibrator, the issue is one of acceptability, but there are many examples of similarly marketed technology of which the expected use was actually illegal. One of these, which shares with the vibrator a focus on women's sexuality, was that of "emmenagogues" or abortifacient drugs sold through the mail and sometimes even off the shelf in the first few decades of this century. Emmenagogues, called in pre-FDA advertising copy "cycle restorers," were intended to bring on the menses in women who were "late." Induced abortion by any means was of course illegal, but late menses are not reliable indicators of pregnancy. Thus, women who purchased and took "cycle restorers" might or might not be in violation of antiabortion laws; they themselves might not be certain without a medical examination. The advertising of these commodities makes free use of this ambiguity in texts like the following from *Good Stories* of 1933:

> Late? End Delay—Worry. American Periodic Relief Compound double strength tablets combine

Safety with Quick Action. Relieve most Stubborn cases. No Pain. New discovery. Easily taken. Solves women's most perplexing problem. RELIEVES WHEN ALL OTHERS FAIL. Don't be discouraged, end worry at once. Send $1.00 for Standard size package and full directions. Mailed same day, special delivery in plain wrapper. American Periodic Relief Compound Tablets, extra strength for stubborn cases. $2.00. Generous Size Package. New Book free.[42]

The rhetoric here does not mention the possibility of pregnancy, but the product's selling points would clearly suggest this to the informed consumer through the mentions of safety, absence of pain, and stubborn cases. The readers of the pulp tabloid *Good Stories* clearly did not require an explanation of "women's most perplexing problem."

Distilling technology raises similar issues of legality. During the Prohibition period, the classified section of a 1920 *Ainslee's* sold one and four gallon copper stills by mail, advising the customer that the apparatus was "Ideal for distilling water for drinking purposes, automobile batteries and industrial uses."[43] Modern advertisements for distilling equipment contain similar camouflage rhetoric, directing attention away from the likelihood that most consumers intend to employ the device in the production of beverages considerably stronger than water.[44]

Although changes in sexual mores have liberated the vibrator, social camouflage remains necessary for stills and many other modern commodities, including drug paraphernalia. The Deering Prep Kit, for example, is advertised at nearly $50 as a superlative device for grinding and preparing fine powders, "such as vitamin pills or spices."[45] Burglary tools are marketed in some popular (if lowbrow) magazines with the admonition that they are to be used only to break into one's own home or automobile, in the event of having locked oneself out. The camouflage rhetoric seems to suggest that all prudent drivers and homeowners carry such tools on their persons at all times. Most recently, we have seen the appearance of computer software for breaking copy protection, advertised in terms that explicitly prohibit its use for piracy, although surely no software publisher is so naive as to believe that all purchasers intend to break copy protection only to make backup copies of legitimately purchased programs and data.[46] As in vibrator advertising, the product's advantages are revealed to knowledgeable consumers in language that disclaims the manufacturers' responsibility for illegal or immoral uses of the product.

The marketing of socially camouflaged technologies is directed to consumers who already understand the design purpose of the product, but whose legally and/or culturally unacceptable intentions in purchasing it cannot be formally recognized by the seller. The marketing rhetoric must extoll the product's advantages for achieving the purchaser's goals—in the case of the vibrator, the production of orgasm—by indirection and innuendo, particularly with reference to the overall results, i.e., relaxation and relief from tension. The same pattern emerges in the advertisement of emmenagogues: according to the manufacturer, it is "Worry and Delay" that are ended, not pregnancy. In the case of software copyright protection programs, drug paraphernalia and distilling equipment, the expected input and/or output are simply misrepresented, so that an expensive finely-calibrated scale with its own fitted carrying case may be pictured in use in the weighing of jelly beans. As social values and legal restrictions shift, the social camouflaging of technologies may be expected to change in response, or to be dispensed with altogether, as in the case of the vibrator.

REFERENCES

[1] Sokolow, Jayme A., *Eros and Modernization: Sylvester Graham, Health Reform and the Origins*

of *Victorian Sexuality in America.* Rutherford, NJ: Fairleigh Dickinson University Press, 1983, pp. 77–99; Haller, John S., and Robin Haller, *The Physician and Sexuality in Victorian America.* Urbana: University of Illinois Press, 1973, pp. 184–216; Greydanus, Donald E., "Masturbation; Historic Perspective," *New York State Journal of Medicine,* November 1980, vol. 80, no. 12, pp. 1892–1896.

[2] On the vibrator in stag films, see Blake, Roger, *Sex Gadgets.* Cleveland: Century, 1968, pp. 33–46.

[3] Vibrators and dildoes are illustrated in Tabori, Paul, *The Humor and Technology of Sex.* New York: Julian Press, 1969; the dildo is discussed in a clinical context in Masters, William H., *Human Sexual Response.* Boston: Little, Brown, 1966.

[4] See, for examples of such advertising, which in fact included a persistent abdominal emphasis, "Amazing New Electric Vibrating Massage Pillow," Niresk Industries (Chicago, IL) advertisement in *Workbasket,* October 1958, p. 95; "Don't be Fat," body massager (Spot Reducer) advertisement in *Workbasket,* September 1958, p. 90; and "Uvral Pneumatic Massage Pulsator," in *Electrical Age for Women,* January 1932, vol. 2, no. 7, pp. 275–276.

[5] For only a few examples of medical discussions of vulvular massage in the hysteroneurasthenic disorders, see Aretaeus Cappadox, *the Extant Works of Aretaeus the Cappadocian,* ed. and transl. by Francis Adams. London: Sydenham Society, 1856, pp. 44–45, 285–287, and 449–451; Forestus, Alemarianus Petrus (Pieter Van Foreest), *Observationem et Curationem Medicinalium ac Chirurgicarum Opera Omnia.* Rothomagi: Bertherlin, 1653, vol. 3, book 28, pp. 277–340; Galen of Perganon, *De Locis Affectis,* transl. by Rudolph Siegel.

[6] Baruch, Simon. *The Principles and Practice of Hydrotherapy: A Guide to the Application of Water in Disease.* New York: William Wood and Company, 1897, pp. 101, 211, 248 and 365; Dieffenbach, William H., *Hydrotherapy.* New York: Rebman, 1909, pp. 238–245; Good Health Publishing Company. *20th Century Therapeutic Appliances.* Battle Creek, MI: Good Health Publishing, 1909, pp. 20–21; Hedley, William Snowdon. *The Hydro-Electric Methods in Medicine.* London: H. K. Lewis, 1892; Hinsdale, Guy, *Hydrotherapy.* Philadelphia and London: W. B. Saunders Company, 1910, p. 224; Kellogg, John Harvey, *Rational Hydrotherapy.* Philadelphia: Davis, 1901; for female masturbation with water, see Aprhodite, J. [pseud.], *To Turn You On: 39 Sex Fantasies for Women.* Secaucus, NJ: Lyle Stuart, Inc., 1975, pp. 83–91; and Halpert, E., "On a Particular Form of Masturbation in Women: Masturbation with Water," *Journal of the American Psychoanalytic Association,* 1973, vol. 21, p. 526.

[7] A bibliography of nineteenth century American works on women and sexuality in relation to hysteria is available in Sahli, Nancy, *Women and Sexuality in America: A Bibliography.* Boston: Hall, 1984. See also Shorter, Edward, : Paralysis: The Rise and Fall of the 'Hysterical' Symptom," *Journal of Social History,* Summer 1986, vol. 19, no. 4, pp. 549–582; Satow, Roberta. "Where Has All the Hysteria Gone?" *Psychoanalytic Review,* 1979–80, vol. 66, pp. 463–473.

[8] Bauer, Carol, "The Little Health of Ladies: An Anatomy of Female Invalidism in the Nineteenth Century," *Journal of the American Medical Woman's Association,* October 1981, vol. 36, no. 10, pp. 300–306; Ehrenreich, Barbara and D. English, *Complaints and Disorders: The Sexual Politics of Sickness.* Old Westbury, NY: Feminist Press, 1973, pp. 15–44; and Trall, Russell Thacher, *The Health and Diseases of Women.* Battle Creek, MI: Health Reformer, 1873, pp. 7–8.

[9] Sydenham, Thomas, "Epistolary Dissertation on Hysteria," in *The Works of Thomas Sydenham,* transl. by R. G. Latham. London: Printed for the Sydenham Society, 1848, vol. 2, pp. 56 and 85; and Payne, Joseph Frank, *Thomas Sydenham.* New York: Longmans, Green and Co., 1900, p. 143.

[10] Gall, Franz Josef, *Anatomie et Physiologie du Système Nerveux en Gènèral.* Paris: F. Schoell, 1810–1819, vol. 3, p. 86; Tripier, Auguste Élisabeth Philogene, *Lecons Cliniques sur les Maladies de Femmes.* Paris: Octave Doin, Editeur, 1883, pp. 347–351; Highmore, Nathaniel, *de Passione Hysterica et Affectione Hypochondriaca.* Oxon.: Excudebat A. Lichfield impensis R. Davis, 1660, pp. 20–35; and Ellis, *Studies in the*

Psychology of Sex, vol. 1, p. 225; see also Briquet, Pierre, *Traitè Clinique et Thérapeutique de l'Hystèrie.* Paris: J. B. Baillière et Fils, 1859, pp. 137–138, 510 and 613.

[11] Cullen, William, *First Lines in the Practice of Physic.* Edinburgh: Bell, Bradfute, etc., 1791, pp. 43–47; Burton, Robert, *The Anatomy of Melancholy,* Floyd Dell and Paul Jordan Smith, eds. New York: Farrar and Rinehart, 1927, pp. 353–355; Horst, Gregor, *Dissertationem . . . inauguralem De Mania . . . Gissae: typis Viduae Friederici Kargeri,* 1677, pp. 9–18.

[12] Zacuto, Abraham. *Praxis Medica Admiranda.* London: Apud Ioannem—Antonium Huguetan, 1637, p. 267.

[13] For an example of conservative views on the speculum, see Griesinger, Wilhelm, *Mental Pathology and Therapeutics,* transl. by C. Lockhart Robinson and James Rutherford. London: New Sydenham Society, 1867, p. 202. On the inefficiency of penetration as a means to female orgasm, the standard modern work is of course Hite, Shere, *The Hite Report on Female Sexuality.* New York: MacMillan Company, 1976.

[14] Dowse, Thomas Stretch, *Lectures on Massage and Electricity in the Treatment of Disease.* Bristol: John Wright and Co., 1903, p. 181.

[15] Smith, E. H., in *Pacific Medical Journal,* February 1903.

[16] For examples of spa expenses in the United States, see Cloyes, Samuel A., *The Healer; the Story of Dr. Samantha S. Nivison and Dryden Springs, 1820–1915.* Ithaca, NY: DeWitt Historical Society of Tompkins County, 1969, p. 24; Karsh, Estrellita, "Taking the Waters at Stafford Springs," *Harvard Library Bulletin,* July 1980, vol. 28, no. 3, pp. 264–281.

[17] See Taylor, George Henry, *Diseases of Women.* Philadelphia and New York: G. McClean, 1871; *Health for Women.* New York: John B. Alden, 1883 and eleven subsequent editions; "Improvements in Medical Rubbing Apparatus,": U.S. Patent 175,202 dated March 21, 1876.

[18] An example of the early Weiss model is available for study at the Bakken (Library and Museum), Minneapolis, MN, accession number 82.100.

[19] Mortimer Granville, Joseph. *Nerve-Vibration and Excitation as Agents in the Treatment of Func-* *tional Disorders and Organic Disease.* London: J.&A. Churchill, 1883, p. 57.

[20] See for example, Smith, A. Lapthorn, "Disorders of Menstruation," in *An International System of Electro-Therapeutics,* Horatio Bigelow, ed. Philadelphia: F. A. Davis, 1894, p. G163.

[21] Covey, Alfred Dale, *Profitable Office Specialities.* Detroit: Physicians Supply Co., 1912, p. 16, 18 and 79–95; Bubier, Edward Trevert, *Electro-Therapeutic Hand Book.* New York: Manhattan Electric Supply Co., 1900; Duck J. J. Co., *Anything Electrical: Catalog No. 6.* Toledo, OH: J. J. Duck, 1916, p. 162.

[22] Vibrator Instrument Company, *Chattanooga Vibrator.* Chattanooga, TN: Vibrator Instrument, 1904, pp. 3 and 26.

[23] Vigouroux, Auguste, *Ètude sur la Rèsistance Èlectrique chez les Melancoliques.* Paris: J. Rueff et Cie, Èditeurs, 1890; Cowen, Richard J., *Electricity in Gynecology.* London: Ballière, Tindall and Cox, 1900; Engelmann, George J., "The Use of Electricity in Gynecological Practice," *Gynecological Transactions,* vol. 11, 1886; Reynolds, David V., "A Brief History of Electrotherapeutics," in *Neuroelectric Research,* D. V. Reynolds and A. Sjoberg, eds. Springfield, IL: Thomas, 1971, pp. 5–12; and Shoemaker, John V., "Electricity in the Treatment of Disease," *Scientific American Supplement,* January 5, 1907, vol. 63, pp. 25923–25924.

[24] "Vibratory Therapeutics," *Scientific American,* vol. 67, October 22, 1892, p. 265.

[25] O'Neill, John J., *Prodigal Genius: The Life of Nikola Tesla.* New York: Ives Washburn, Inc., 1944, p. 210.

[26] *Medical Brief,* May 1905, p. 417.

[27] Monell, *A System of Instrumentation . . . ,* p. 591.

[28] See for example, "Wanted, Agents and Salesman . . ." Swedish Vibrator Company, *Modern Priscilla,* April 1913, p. 60.

[29] "Agents! Drop Dead Ones!" Blackstone Water Power Vacuum Massage Machine, *Hearst's,* April 1916, p. 327; and "Hydro-Massage," Warner Motor Company, *Modern Women,* vol. 11, no. 1, December 1906, p. 190.

[30] "Massage is as old as the hills . . . ," American Vibrator Company, *Woman's Home Companion,* April 1906, p. 42.

[31] "Such Delightful Companions!" Star Electrical Necessities, 1922, reproduced in Jones, Edgar R., *Those were the Good Old Days.* New York: Fireside Books, 1959, unpaged; and "A Gift that will Keep her Young and Pretty," Star Home Electric Massage, *Hearst's International,* December 1921, p. 82.

[32] See for example, the Ediswan advertisement in *Electrical Age for Women,* January 1932, vol. 2, no. 7, p. 274, and review on page 275 of the same publication.

[33] "Vibration is Life," Lindstrom-Smith Co., *Modern Priscilla,* December 1910, p. 27.

[34] Pivar, David J. *Purity Crusade: Sexual Morality and Social Control, 1868–1900.* Westport, CT: Greenwood Press, 1973, pp. 110–117.

[35] See also *American Magazine,* December 1912, vol. 75, no. 2, January 1913; vol. 75, no. 3, May 1913; vol. 75, no. 7, p. 127.

[36] Davidson, J. E., "Electrical Appliance Sales During 1926," *NELA Bulletin,* vol. 14, no. 2, pp. 119–120.

[37] December 5, 1925, vol. 86, p. 1164. See also Hughes, George A., "How the Domestic Electrical Appliances are Serving the Country," *Electrical Review,* June 15, 1918, vol. 72, p. 983.

[38] "Electrical Devices for the Household," *Scientific American,* January 26, 1907, vol. 96, p. 95.

[39] The vibrator is not included in extensive lists of appliances in Lamborn, Helen, "Electricity for Domestic Uses," *Harper's Bazaar,* April 1910, vol. 44, p. 285; and Knowlton, H. S., "Extending the Uses of Electricity," *Cassier's Magazine,* vol. 30, June 1906, pp. 99–105.

[40] U.S. Bureau of the Census. *Census of Manufactures,* 1908, 1919, and 1947, pp. 216–217, 203, and 734 and 748 respectively.

[41] On the early history of appliances, see Lifshey, Earl, *The Housewares Story.* Chicago: Housewares Manufacturers' Association, 1973. For the safety issue, see "Electromedical Apparatus for Domestic Use," *Electrical Review,* October 22, 1926, p. 682.

[42] *Good Stories,* October 1933, p. 2; see also similar advertisement in the same issue for Dr. Roger's Relief Compound, p. 12.

[43] "Water Stills," *Ainslee's Magazine,* October 1920, p. 164.

[44] See for example, Damark International, Inc., *Catalog B-330.* Minneapolis, MN: Damark International, 1988, p. 7, which emphasizes the "Alambiccus Distiller's" usefulness for distilling herbal extracts.

[45] *Mellow Mail Catalogue.* Cooper Station, New York City: 1984, pp. 32–39.

[46] Levy, Steven, *Hackers: Heroes of the Computer Revolution.* Garden City, NY: Anchor Press/Doubleday, 1984, p. 377.

The Orgasm Industry: Drug Companies Search for a Female Viagra

Sonia Shah

Since the launch of Pfizer's tremendously popular erectile-dysfunction drug Viagra in May 1998, pharmaceutical companies have scrambled to find the next big sex drug—for women this time. Start-up pharmaceutical companies and enterprising physicians have jumped into the fray to treat what they see as an underserved market of tens of millions of sexually dysfunctional women.

Feminists tend to bristle at the term "dysfunctional" but acknowledge that many women don't enjoy sex. Some feminists say that women should welcome drug industry products that may provide some relief to those in desperate need of sexual help. Others argue that such products will stigmatize female sexuality and drive women to pop a pill when what they really need are better relationships and more sex education.

Source: The Progressive, October 2001. Copyright © 2001. Reprinted with permission from the author.

"No potion or pill will show you where your clitoris is," says sex writer Susie Bright. "No cream will enlighten you as to your unconscious erotic imagination."

Never mind the ongoing epidemic of sexual violence, spotty access to contraception, and the fact that most women with sexual difficulties say they are too busy and too stressed out to have sex. Pill-pushers with their eyes on the bottom line are eager to gear women up for high-tech sex with new creams, gels, and other products.

While ten million men around the world take Viagra, earning Pfizer $1.3 billion last year, the market for a prescription sex drug for women may be even bigger. According to a much-cited February 1999 article in *JAMA: The Journal of the American Medical Association*, 43 percent of all women suffer from sexual dysfunction, as opposed to just 31 percent of all men.

In April 2000, the Food and Drug Administration approved the first product to treat female sexual dysfunction, which it defines as decreased sexual desire, decreased sexual arousal, pain during intercourse, or inability to climax. The FDA-approved product, called EROS, is manufactured by Urometrics, based in St. Paul, Minnesota. It's a glorified vibrator that applies suction to the clitoris. It costs $359 and is sold by prescription only.

Dozens of other products to alleviate female sexual dysfunction, including body creams and even a remote-control device, are currently in clinical trials. Some of these products may make it to market as early as 2004, say drug company spokespersons.

Nastech, a nasal drug company, recently started the second of three Food and Drug Administration-required phases of clinical trials for its apomorphine hydrochloride product for women, which is designed to improve blood flow and lubricating secretions in female genitals. Apomorphine hydrochloride belongs to the family of morphine-derived drugs that includes codeine. The product would come in a small vial with a nasal spray applicator, which women would spritz into their nostrils about twenty minutes before having sex. The company expects to bring the prescription nasal spray to market within a few years.

BioSante Pharmaceuticals expects results from Phase 2 clinical trials of its female sex drug, LibiGel, by this fall. Women would rub LibiGel onto their shoulders or arms, releasing libido-increasing testosterone into their bodies for up to twenty-four hours. According to BioSante, as women age, their testosterone levels go down, and women who've undergone total hysterectomies have 50 percent lower testosterone levels. Studies show that testosterone-replacement therapy can boost sexual desire, according to a company press release. LibiGel may hit the market in four years, BioSante's CEO Stephen M. Simes says, and would cost about $1,000 a year for daily therapy, a sum BioSante expects insurance companies to cover.

"Just like men who take Viagra who don't have erectile dysfunction, there are individuals who will want to have an orgasm on demand," says North Carolina pain specialist Dr. Stuart Meloy. In January, Meloy was issued a patent for a remote-controlled neural-stimulation device to trigger orgasms. Three years ago, Meloy, like other pain specialists, noticed that a surgically implanted neural stimulation device routinely used to alleviate chronic pain sometimes triggered orgasms instead. He considered it a "funny, unwanted side effect," he says, until he realized that "this unwanted side effect was something that may be quite desirable in another clinical setting." Meloy expects to start clinical trials in the near future.

But who will want to spend $15,000 on a surgical procedure to have push-button orgasms? There are about 23,000 women with orgasmic dysfunction who are not responsive to simpler therapies, Meloy estimates, and CNN pollsters reported that 59 percent of women would want to have Meloy's device implanted in them. "Frankly, for that individual who has the cash in hand, it is kind of on par with cosmetic surgery," he says.

Feminists publicized and politicized women's raw deal in bed decades before drug companies began researching their corporate solutions to the problem. But the women's sexual health movement, with its self-help books, sex-toy shops, sex therapists, and masturbation workshops has never been particularly profitable. The ultimate solution to women's sexual problems, say some, is more time, less stress, better education, and attentive partners—hardly the stuff of glossy brochures for thousand-dollar prescription treatments.

"Women really want a sense of self-empowerment and self-efficacy," says Leonore Tiefer, feminist sex therapist and professor of urology and psychiatry at Albert Einstein College of Medicine. "They don't just want products to choose from." The search for a female Viagra, Tiefer says, exploits for profit "the lack of sex education and sexual freedom we have in this country."

Such products may help a small fraction of women, the National Women's Health Network program director Amy Alma told me, but "in the context of today's health care system structured around profit and patentable products, many women may be sold drugs that they don't need and that can hurt them" with the side effects.

To make it big, drug companies need to mass-market their prescription sex products. Pfizer doesn't market Viagra exclusively to the 5 percent of the U.S. male population that suffers from erectile dysfunction. Pfizer sells Viagra by selling romance.

Urometrics, the maker of EROS, plans to run spots on radio stations and in print media in ten cities around the country, says the company's public relations spokesperson, Saunya Peterson. Both LibiGel and Nastech's nasal spray are also likely to be advertised directly to consumers, the companies say. "Like Viagra, this is something consumers will be hearing about directly," says Matthew Haines, director of corporate communications at Nastech.

"Their marketing implies that you can passively sit back and let the 'chemical' do the work for you," says Bright. "But we already have powerful sexual [chemicals] in our bodies. They're called hormones."

"We are all susceptible to promises that things will be made better," says Carol Ellison, a sex therapist who surveyed 2,632 U.S. women about their sex lives for her book, *Women's Sexualities: Generations of Women Share Intimate Secrets of Sexual Self-Acceptance* (New Harbinger Publications, 2000). She found that women want more free time, less stress, and loving relationships to feel good in bed. But if that's the case, why would women seek medical solutions for nonmedical problems?

"Women are very anxious to improve their sex lives," says Tiefer. "The illusion of sex that is promoted by the entertainment media is that sex is just one big orgasmic scream after another, but that is not what most people's experience is like."

Women who turn to sex drugs may be more than disappointed. Says Ellison: "When a drug doesn't solve your problem of low sexual desire, which is based on your partner not helping out with the kids or taking time to feel close to you before sex, then the woman turns around and says, 'What's wrong with me?'"

"We need to be cautioning the public right now," says Judy Norsigian of the Boston Women's Health Book Collective.

Others, such as Pulitzer Prize-winning writer Natalie Angier, author of *Women: An Intimate Geography* (Anchor Books, 2000), say that women need as much information and support for having orgasmic sex as possible, whether from a friend or a drug-company ad on television. If a product could help even a small fraction of women, she says, it's worth it, given women's widespread trouble with achieving orgasms.

"Most women, if not all women, are capable of learning how to become readily orgasmic," says Angier. When feminists say that women's sexuality is more about intimacy than orgasm, "you end up with a lot of dissatisfied women."

Cultural critic Ellen Willis agrees. "If people are sexually unhappy, anything that helps them is fine," she says. Sex drugs should be seen as "one more resource in dealing with sexual problems. If I have a headache, it may have some larger social cause, but in the meantime I'm going to take aspirin."

The race to find the female Viagra started in 1998, the year Viagra was released. Two telegenic sisters—urologist Jennifer Berman and sex therapist Laura Berman—spearheaded a popular crusade urging women to consider medical solutions to their sexual problems. The two were "convinced that women could benefit from the same medical attention to sexual problems that was given to men," they write on their web site, www.newshe.com.

In the summer of 1998, they founded a women's sexual health clinic at Boston University to combat female sexual dysfunction. With their mentor, erectile dysfunction pioneer Dr. Irwin Goldstein, they organized the first ever conference on female sexual dysfunction a few months later. Their quest transformed them into the darlings of the sex-drug industry, and the Bermans were soon giving a paid lecture about new sex treatments on an industry-sponsored yacht trip. They also appeared on a raft of television and radio programs, including *The Oprah Winfrey Show* and *Good Morning America*, explaining how women could combat the female sexual dysfunction epidemic.

Meanwhile, University of Chicago sociologist Edward O. Laumann, author of a well-respected survey of sexual practices in the United States, reanalyzed data from his influential 1992 survey to look specifically at sexual dysfunction, a topic he previously covered only briefly. In February 1999, Laumann and his coauthor, clinical psychologist Raymond C. Rosen, released their reanalysis in *JAMA*, one of the nation's foremost medical journals. "The

results indicate that sexual dysfunction is an important public health concern," they wrote, coming up with the 43 percent figure for female sexual dysfunction.

Without Laumann's claim, female sexual dysfunction may have become another of hundreds of obscure medical syndromes and conditions. "Because it was published in *JAMA*, was based on a well-known survey, and there's so much interest in women's sexuality and drug treatment, it has attained this status [as] the most accurate figure we have," says the Kinsey Institute's Cynthia Graham.

But critics question whether Laumann's characterization of so many women as dysfunctional is really accurate. "Women may be saying they have these symptoms," says Graham, "but they may not consider it a problem."

Graham's point cuts to the heart of the notoriously murky world of sex research. What is a sexual problem and what isn't? Who decides? Who talks truthfully to researchers about their sexual lives and why?

Most well-known studies of sexual practices—such as those by zoologist Alfred C. Kinsey in 1948 and 1953, Masters and Johnson in 1966, and Shere Hite in 1976—are based on what volunteers chose to tell researchers. But in 1992, Laumann set out to find out what randomly selected ordinary Americans did in bed. The large majority of the 3,159 people his researchers spoke to in ninety minute face-to-face interviews were found to "feel loved, satisfied, and even thrilled by their sex partners," as Laumann and his co-authors wrote in *The Social Organization of Sexuality* (University of Chicago, 1994).

Sometime before 1998, Laumann became a consultant for Pfizer. He teamed up with Rosen, another Pfizer consultant. Rosen urged Laumann to showcase his data on sexual dysfunction in a medical journal where physicians would be more apt to see it, Laumann says. So Laumann reanalyzed his data and came to a different conclusion. In 1994,

Laumann wrote, "comparatively few [men and women] are made to feel sad or afraid or guilty in their sex lives." But in his February 1999 *JAMA* article, he unveiled an epidemic of female sexual dysfunction.

Today, Laumann tries to distance himself from the conclusions in his article. "I've been somewhat annoyed that, because this study was published in a medical journal, it has been spun in a very medical direction," he says.

As Laumann puts it, the article shows that most of the women characterized as having female sexual dysfunction may simply be experiencing "normal responses to the challenges of life." Just more than half of the women characterized as suffering from female sexual dysfunction were those who reported a lack of interest in sex for a period of several months or more over the last twelve months. Another third or so reported arousal problems, that is, they reported having trouble lubricating for a period of several months or more in the past twelve months.

"If you have any kind of life at all," says Laumann, "you are going to have these problems" at some point. Plus, aside from lubrication problems, which many women remedy by using over-the-counter lubricating jellies, most of the other female sexual dysfunction symptoms decrease as women age, Laumann says.

The number of women who truly need medical intervention in their sex lives is probably tiny, Laumann says. "The vast bulk of the 43 percent are probably suffering from social stresses," he says.

Laumann says that corporate interests had nothing to do with the conclusions of his article for *JAMA*. "We were writing for doctors," he says, "so an interpretive spin was simply not possible."

As sex research becomes more beholden to the pharmaceutical industry, Tiefer says, there is a vested interest in painting a picture of sick women in need of new drug treatments. "Profitability motives" are driving research on female sexual dysfunction, she says.

In the past, medical experts condemned women's sexualities as hysterical, nymnphomaniacal, or frigid. Today, according to Laumann's own admission, healthy women in normal life circumstances acquire a medical label of "dysfunctional." Laumann and physicians such as the Bermans consider the classification of normal female sexuality as dysfunctional a step in the right direction. At least now, they say, people are talking openly about women's sex lives.

And that's the irony. Feminists have been whispering, joking, yelling, and agitating about female sexuality for at least three decades. Now that a lucrative market is in view, the experts and entrepreneurs may deign to listen.

Don't Give Up on Sex after 60

Helen Gurley Brown

I had sex last night. I'm 78 and my husband, movie producer David Brown, is 83. Shocking? Shouldn't be. More and more women are continuing to be interested in sex not only in their 40s and 50s, but well into their 60s and 70s. We realize that we don't want to miss out on something. For many years women were brainwashed into thinking that they couldn't have sex after menopause. We now know that's ridiculous, and are more interested in sex than ever, glory hallelujah, although we may need a little help. (We'll get to that in a minute.)

Sex is one of the three best things there are, and I don't know what the other two are. Sex keeps you connected to the human race, prevents you from being a prim, stuffy, puffy, correct, respected, respectable, finished old person! It makes you a functioning female instead of a sexless old crone. After we pass 50 or 60, we've already lost many validations of our femaleness: we don't menstruate, don't have babies and nobody's after us, trying to get us into the broom closet at a party. But having somebody make love to us keeps us one of the girls. So you have to keep reciting to yourself: I'm a sexual person; I want sex in my life; I deserve it, and I'm not gonna let it disappear.

Our libido slows down after 50 because the hormones are no longer raging through our bodies as they did at 18. The thought of piling under a man to make love may hold all the appeal of being thrown into a garbage scow. Marital sex often stops because of boredom, too many fights, too many problems. If you're single (and so many older women are), there's the supply problem. An older woman has to go looking; sex mostly doesn't come looking for her. "Between 50 and 60," says one realistic friend, "sex is out there. If you want it, you can connect. After 60, you have to supply the sled, the snow and the dog team."

Take a tip from the other side. How do older men attract women half their age? By paying for their pleasure with restaurant tabs, tennis lessons, trips to Acapulco, jewelry, furs, even the monthly rent. So if there's a man who might be up for having sex with you, take him to Gucci. Take him to Armani. If that's not your price range, give him a Brooks Brothers shirt!

Give wonderful dinner parties. Pick up some restaurant tabs. I know a woman in Beverly Hills who's quite wealthy. After her husband died, she married somebody considerably younger. He's a wonderful companion and a great host. He helps her with that great Beverly Hills mansion, and I would say that although he was bought and paid for, he delivers, and Mr. Wonderful himself is content.

You appeal to a younger man by being competent, worldly, glamorous, fun, adoring, good in bed and having a little money! (Young women can't or don't offer most of those things.) Some younger men actually prefer older women. Unresolved childhood crush on a teacher? Need for a "mommy" to nurture and protect him? We don't always know why they fall for us.

Here's the biggie: how you can possibly undress in front of a man who's never seen you naked . . . that cellulite, those folds, those pooches! Wear something up to the last minute before getting into bed; turn off the lights if that makes you less nervous and back out of the room when it's over if you think your front is better than your back. If you have been exercising like a good girl, your body will probably look OK—not 16, but maybe 40 (and limber).

Sex to me is the ultimate womanly act—more truly feminine than baking chocolate-chip cookies or doling out money for a grandchild's college tuition. Those things are admirable—but if cookies are the boonies, sex is the big time! Women our age should indulge. Sex is healthy, revitalizing, energizing, nurturing. Be very proud of yourself if you are "of a certain age" and still enjoy sex. Don't feel one hour of guilt. You are exemplary—a role model for other women.

READING 32

The Five Sexes, Revisited

Anne Fausto-Sterling

The emerging recognition that people come in bewildering sexual varieties is testing medical values and social norms.

As Cheryl Chase stepped to the front of the packed meeting room in the Sheraton Boston Hotel, nervous coughs made the tension audible. Chase, an activist for intersexual rights, had been invited to address the May 2000 meeting of the Lawson Wilkins Pediatric Endocrine Society (LWPES), the largest organization in the United States for specialists in children's hormones. Her talk would be the grand finale to a four-hour symposium on the treatment of genital ambiguity in newborns, infants born with a mixture of both male and female anatomy, or genitals that appear to differ from their chromosomal sex. The topic was hardly a novel one to the assembled physicians.

Yet Chase's appearance before the group was remarkable. Three and a half years earlier, the American Academy of Pediatrics had refused her request for a chance to present the patients' viewpoint on the treatment of genital ambiguity, dismissing Chase and her supporters as "zealots." About two dozen intersex people had responded by throwing up a picket line. The Intersex Society of North America (ISNA) even issued a press release: "Hermaphrodites Target Kiddie Docs."

It had done my 1960s street-activist heart good. In the short run, I said to Chase at the time, the picketing would make people angry. But eventually, I assured her, the doors then closed would open. Now, as Chase began to address the physicians at their own conven-

tion, that prediction was coming true. Her talk, titled "Sexual Ambiguity: The Patient-Centered Approach," was a measured critique of the near-universal practice of performing immediate, "corrective" surgery on thousands of infants born each year with ambiguous genitalia. Chase herself lives with the consequences of such surgery. Yet her audience, the very endocrinologists and surgeons Chase was accusing of reacting with "surgery and shame," received her with respect. Even more remarkably, many of the speakers who preceded her at the session had already spoken of the need to scrap current practices in favor of treatments more centered on psychological counseling.

What led to such a dramatic reversal of fortune? Certainly, Chase's talk at the LWPES symposium was a vindication of her persistence in seeking attention for her cause. But her invitation to speak was also a watershed in the evolving discussion about how to treat children with ambiguous genitalia. And that discussion, in turn, is the tip of a biocultural iceberg—the gender iceberg—that continues to rock both medicine and our culture at large.

Chase made her first national appearance in 1993, in these very pages, announcing the formation of ISNA in a letter responding to an essay I had written for *The Sciences*, titled "The Five Sexes" [March/April 1993]. In that article I argued that the two-sex system embedded in our society is not adequate to encompass the full spectrum of human sexuality. In its place, I suggested a five-sex system. In addition to males and females, I included "herms" (named after true hermaphrodites, people born with both a testis and an ovary); "merms" (male pseudohermaphrodites, who are born with testes and some aspect of female genitalia); and "ferms" (female pseudohermaphrodites, who have ovaries combined with some aspect of male genitalia).

I had intended to be provocative, but I had also written with tongue firmly in cheek. So I was surprised by the extent of the controversy the article unleashed. Right-wing Christians were outraged, and connected my idea of five sexes with the United Nations–sponsored Fourth World Conference on Women, held in Beijing in September 1995. At the same time, the article delighted others who felt constrained by the current sex and gender system.

Clearly, I had struck a nerve. The fact that so many people could get riled up by my proposal to revamp our sex and gender system suggested that change—as well as resistance to it—might be in the offing. Indeed, a lot has changed since 1993, and I like to think that my article was an important stimulus. As if from nowhere, intersexuals are materializing before our very eyes. Like Chase, many have become political organizers, who lobby physicians and politicians to change current treatment practices. But more generally, though perhaps no less provocatively, the boundaries separating masculine and feminine seem harder than ever to define.

Some find the changes underway deeply disturbing. Others find them liberating.

Who is an intersexual—and how many intersexuals are there? The concept of intersexuality is rooted in the very ideas of male and female. In the idealized, Platonic, biological world, human beings are divided into two kinds: a perfectly dimorphic species. Males have an X and a Y chromosome, testes, a penis and all of the appropriate internal plumbing for delivering urine and semen to the outside world. They also have well-known secondary sexual characteristics including a muscular build and facial hair. Women have two X chromosomes, ovaries, all of the internal plumbing to transport urine and ova to the outside world, a system to support pregnancy and fetal development, as well as a variety of recognizable secondary sexual characteristics.

That idealized story papers over many obvious caveats: some women have facial hair, some men have none; some women speak with deep voices, some men veritably squeak. Less well known is the fact that, on close inspection, absolute dimorphism disintegrates even at the level of basic biology. Chromosomes, hormones, the internal sex structures, the gonads and the external genitalia all vary more than most people realize. Those born outside of the Platonic dimorphic mold are called intersexuals.

In "The Five Sexes" I reported an estimate by a psychologist expert in the treatment of intersexuals, suggesting that some 4 percent of all live births are intersexual. Then, together with a group of Brown University undergraduates, I set out to conduct the first systematic assessment of the available data on intersexual birthrates. We scoured the medical literature for estimates of the frequency of various categories of intersexuality, from additional chromosomes to mixed gonads, hormones and genitalia. For some conditions we could find only anecdotal evidence; for most, however numbers exist. On the basis of that evidence, we calculated that for every 1,000 children born, seventeen are intersexual in some form. That number—1.7 percent—is a ballpark estimate, not a precise count, though we believe it is more accurate than the 4 percent I reported.

Our figure represents all chromosomal, anatomical and hormonal exceptions to the dimorphic ideal; the number of intersexuals who might, potentially, be subject to surgery as infants is smaller—probably between one in 1,000 and one in 2,000 live births. Furthermore, because some population possess the relevant genes at high frequency, the intersexual birthrate is not uniform throughout the world.

Consider, for instance, the gene for congenital adrenal hyperplasia (CAH). When the CAH gene is inherited from both parents, it leads to a baby with masculinized external genitalia who possesses two X chromosomes and the internal reproductive organs of a potentially fertile woman. The frequency of the gene varies widely around the world: in New Zealand it occurs in only forty-three children per million; among the Yupik Eskimos of southwestern Alaska, its frequency is 3,500 per million.

Intersexuality has always been to some extent a matter of definition. And in the past century physicians have been the ones who defined children as intersexual—and provided the remedies. When only the chromosomes are unusual, but the external genitalia and gonads clearly indicate either a male or a female, physicians do not advocate intervention. Indeed, it is not clear what kind of intervention could be advocated in such cases. But the story is quite different when infants are born with mixed genitalia, or with external genitals that seem at odds with the baby's gonads.

Most clinics now specializing in the treatment of intersex babies rely on case-management principles developed in the 1950s by the psychologist John Money and the psychiatrists Joan G. Hampson and John L. Hampson, all of Johns Hopkins University in Baltimore, Maryland. Money believed that gender identity is completely malleable for about eighteen months after birth. Thus, he argued, when a treatment team is presented with an infant who has ambiguous genitalia, the team could make a gender assignment solely on the basis of what made the best surgical sense. The physicians could then simply encourage the parents to raise the child according to the surgically assigned gender. Following that course, most physicians maintained, would eliminate psychological distress for both the patient and the parents. Indeed, treatment teams were never to use such words as "intersex" or "hermaphrodite"; instead, they were to tell parents that nature intended the baby to be the boy or the girl that the physicians had determined it was. Through surgery, the physicians were merely completing nature's intention.

Although Money and the Hampsons published detailed case studies of intersex children who they said had adjusted well to their gender assignments, Money thought one case in particular proved his theory. It was a dramatic example, inasmuch as it did not involve intersexuality at all: one of a pair of identical twin boys lost his penis as a result of a circumcision accident. Money recommended that "John" (as he came to be known in a later case study) be surgically turned into "Joan" and raised as a girl. In time, Joan grew to love wearing dresses and having her hair done. Money proudly proclaimed the sex reassignment a success.

But as recently chronicled by John Colapinto, in his book *As Nature Made Him*, Joan—now known to be an adult male named David Reimer—eventually rejected his female assignment. Even without a functioning penis and testes (which had been removed as part of the reassignment) John/Joan sought masculinizing medication, and married a woman with children (whom he adopted).

Since the full conclusion to the John/Joan story came to light, other individuals who were reassigned as males or females shortly after birth but who later rejected their early assignments have come forward. So, too, have cases in which the reassignment has worked—at least into the subject's mid-twenties. But even then the aftermath of the surgery can be problematic. Genital surgery often leaves scars that reduce sexual sensitivity. Chase herself had a complete clitoridectomy, a procedure that is less frequently performed on intersexuals today. But the newer surgeries, which reduce the size of the clitoral shaft, still greatly reduce sensitivity.

The revelation of cases of failed reassignments and the emergence of intersex activism have led an increasing number of pediatric endocrinologists, urologists and psychologists to reexamine the wisdom of early genital surgery. For example, in a talk that preceded Chase's at the LWPES meeting, the medical ethicist Laurence B. McCullough of the Center for Medical

Ethics and Health Policy at Baylor College of Medicine in Houston, Texas, introduced an ethical framework for the treatment of children with ambiguous genitalia. Because sex phenotype (the manifestation of genetically and embryologically determined sexual characteristics) and gender presentation (the sex role projected by the individual in society) are highly variable, McCullough argues, the various forms of intersexuality should be defined as normal. All of them fall within the statistically expected variability of sex and gender. Furthermore, though certain disease states may accompany some forms of intersexuality, and may require medical intervention, intersexual conditions are not themselves diseases.

McCullough also contends that in the process of assigning gender, physicians should minimize what he calls irreversible assignments: taking steps such as the surgical removal or modification of gonads or genitalia that the patient may one day want to have reversed. Finally, McCullough urges physicians to abandon their practice of treating the birth of a child with genital ambiguity as a medical or social emergency. Instead, they should take the time to perform a thorough medical workup and should disclose everything to the parents, including the uncertainties about the final outcome. The treatment mantra, in other words, should be therapy, not surgery.

I believe a new treatment protocol for intersex infants, similar to the one outlined by McCullough, is close at hand. Treatment should combine some basic medical and ethical principles with a practical but less drastic approach to the birth of a mixed-sex child. As a first step, surgery on infants should be performed only to save the child's life or to substantially improve the child's physical well-being. Physicians may assign a sex—male or female—to an intersex infant on the basis of the probability that the child's particular condition will lead to the formation of a particular gender identity. At the same time, though, practitioners ought to be humble enough to recognize that as the child grows, he or she may reject the assignment—and they should be wise enough to listen to what the child has to say. Most important, parents should have access to the full range of information and options available to them.

Sex assignments made shortly after birth are only the beginning of a long journey. Consider, for instance, the life of Max Beck: Born intersexual, Max was surgically assigned as a female and consistently raised as such. Had her medical team followed her into her early twenties, they would have deemed her assignment a success because she was married to a man. (It should be noted that success in gender assignment has traditionally been defined as living in that gender as a heterosexual.) Within a few years, however, Beck had come out as a butch lesbian; now in her mid-thirties, Beck has become a man and married his lesbian partner, who (through the miracles of modern reproductive technology) recently gave birth to a girl.

Transsexuals, people who have an emotional gender at odds with their physical sex, once described themselves in terms of dimorphic absolutes—males trapped in female bodies, or vice versa. As such, they sought psychological relief through surgery. Although many still do, some so-called transgendered people today are content to inhabit a more ambiguous zone. A male-to-female transsexual, for instance, may come out as a lesbian. Jane, born a physiological male, is now in her late thirties and living with her wife, whom she married when her name was still John. Jane takes hormones to feminize herself, but they have not yet interfered with her ability to engage in intercourse as a man. In her mind Jane has a lesbian relationship with her wife, though she views their intimate moments as a cross between lesbian and heterosexual sex.

It might seem natural to regard intersexuals and transgendered people as living midway between the poles of male and female. But male and female, masculine and feminine, cannot be parsed as some kind of continuum. Rather, sex and gender are best conceptualized as points in a multidimensional space. For some time, experts on gender development have distinguished between sex at the genetic level and at the cellular level (sex-specific gene expression, X and Y chromosomes); at the hormonal level (in the fetus, during childhood and after puberty); and at the anatomical level (genitals and secondary sexual characteristics). Gender identity presumably emerges from all of those corporeal aspects via some poorly understood interaction with environment and experience. What has become increasingly clear is that one can find levels of masculinity and femininity in almost every possible permutation. A chromosomal, hormonal and genital male (or female) may emerge with a female (or male) gender identity. Or a chromosomal female with male fetal hormones and masculinized genitalia—but with female pubertal hormones—may develop a female gender identity.

The medical and scientific communities have yet to adopt a language that is capable of describing such diversity. In her book *Hermaphrodites and the Medical Invention of Sex,* the historian and medical ethicist Alice Domurat Dreger of Michigan State University in East Lansing documents the emergence of current medical systems for classifying gender ambiguity. The current usage remains rooted in the Victorian approach to sex. The logical structure of the commonly used terms "true hermaphrodite," "male pseudohermaphrodite" a "female pseudohermaphrodite" indicates that only the so-called true hermaphrodite is a genuine mix of male and female. The others, no matter how confusing their body parts, are really hidden males or females. Because true hermaphodites are rare—possibly only one in 100,000—such a classification system supports the idea that human beings are an absolutely dimorphic species.

At the dawn of the twenty-first century, when the variability of gender seems so visible, such a position is hard maintain. And here, too, the old medical consensus has begun to crumble. Last fall the pediatric urologist Ian A. Aaronson of the Medical University of South Carolina in Charleston organized the North American Task Force on Intersexuality (NATFI) to review the clinical responses to genital ambiguity in infants. Key medical associations, such as the American Academy of Pediatrics, have endorsed NATFI. Specialists in surgery, endocrinology, psychology, ethics, psychiatry, genetics and public health, as well as intersex patient-advocate groups, have joined its ranks.

One of the goals of NATFI is to establish a new sex nomenclature. One proposal under consideration replaces the current system with emotionally neutral terminology that emphasizes developmental processes rather than preconceived gender categories. For example, Type I intersexes develop out of anomalous virilizing influences; Type II result from some interruption of virilization; and in Type III intersexes the gonads themselves may not have developed in the expected fashion.

What is clear is that since 1993, modern society has moved beyond five sexes to a recognition that gender variation is normal and, for some people, an arena for playful exploration. Discussing my "five sexes" proposal in her book *Lessons from the Intersexed,* the psychologist Suzanne J. Kessler of the State University of New York at Purchase drives this point home with great effect:

> The limitation with Fausto-Sterling's proposal is that . . . [it] still gives genitals . . . primary signifying status and ignores the fact that in the everyday world gender attributions are made without access to genital inspection. . . . What has primacy in everyday life is the gender that is performed, regardless of the flesh's configuration under the clothes.

I now agree with Kessler's assessment. It would be better for intersexuals and their supporters to turn everyone's focus away from genitals. Instead, as she suggests, one should acknowledge that people come in an even wider assortment of sexual identities and characteristics than mere genitals can distinguish. Some women may have "large clitorises or fused labia," whereas some men may have "small penises or misshapen scrota," as Kessler puts it, "phenotypes with no particular clinical or identity meaning."

As clearheaded as Kessler's program is—and despite the progress made in the 1990s—our society is still far from that ideal. The intersexual or transgendered person who projects a social gender—what Kessler calls "cultural genitals"—that conflicts with his or her physical genitals still may die for the transgression. Hence legal protection for people whose cultural and physical genitals do not match is needed during the current transition to a more gender-diverse world. One easy step would be to eliminate the category of "gender" from official documents, such as driver's licenses and passports. Surely attributes both more visible (such as height, build and eye color) and less visible (fingerprints and genetic profiles) would be more expedient.

A more far-ranging agenda is presented in the International Bill of Gender Rights, adopted in 1995 at the fourth annual International Conference on Transgender Law and Employment Policy in Houston, Texas. It lists ten "gender rights," including the right to define one's own gender, the right to change one's physical gender if one so chooses and the right to marry whomever one wishes. The legal bases for such rights are being hammered out in the courts as I write and, most recently, through the establishment, in the state of Vermont, of legal same-sex domestic partnerships.

No one could have foreseen such changes in 1993. And the idea that I played some role, however small, in reducing the pressure—from the medical community as well as from society at large—to flatten the diversity of human sexes into two diametrically opposed camps gives me pleasure.

Sometimes people suggest to me, with not a little horror, that I am arguing for a pastel world in which androgyny reigns and men and women are boringly the same. In my vision, however, strong colors coexist with pastels. There are and will continue to be highly masculine people out there; it's just that some of them are women. And some of the most feminine people I know happen to be men.

READING 33

To Be Poor and Transgender

Kai Wright

Sharmus has been a sex worker for about five years. She started after breaking up with a boyfriend who was supporting her while she

Source: The Progressive, October 2001. Copyright © 2001. Reprinted with permission from the author.

was out of work. It was quick money, and, as with many of her transgender friends, she didn't believe there were many other jobs out there for her.

"You have your good nights, and your bad nights," says Sharmus, thirty-five. "There are no fringe benefits. Summer time is the best time; the winter is hard," she explains, casually ticking off the pros and cons of being a prostitute. "It's just hard getting a job. Nobody really wants to hire you, and when they do hire you they give you a hard time."

Sex work was not in her plans back when she transitioned from male to female at age twenty-one. "Sometimes I regret it," she sighs. "My lifetime goal was to be a schoolteacher."

Her uncertainty is to be expected. Our culture depicts people whose discomfort with gender norms goes beyond being tomboys or feminine men as mere curiosity items for trash TV ("Your woman is really a man!" episodes of *Jerry Springer).* This collective ignorance leaves people like Sharmus without much guidance. Many go through puberty and into adulthood without meeting people like themselves. The resulting high rates of depression, drug use, violence, and suicidal thoughts are unsurprising.

"One of the greatest agonies one can experience is gender dysphoria," says transgender activist Jessica Xavier. "When your anatomy doesn't match who you are inside, it's the worst feeling in the world."

Sharmus and Xavier are part of a group whose existence challenges normative gender. They include drag performers, heterosexual cross-dressers, and people from all walks of life who live permanently in a gender other than that assigned at birth. They range from individuals who have had thousands of dollars worth of reconstructive surgery to people who simply style themselves in a way that feels comfortable.

Around the nation, a growing cadre of activists is working to build bridges between all of these populations and to encourage the formation of an umbrella community called "transgender." What the members of this latest American identity group share is a far more practical understanding of gender politics than that of the ethereal, academic world to which it is often relegated. From employment to health services, transgender folks, particularly those in low-income environments, face enormous barriers when navigating even the most basic aspects of life—all because of their gender transgressions.

"We continue to be one of the most stigmatized populations on the planet," says Xavier, the former director of a national coalition of transgender political groups called It's Time!—America. Xavier recently cajoled the local health department into financing a survey of around 250 transgender people in D.C. Forty percent of respondents had not finished high school, and another 40 percent were unemployed. Almost half had no health insurance and reported not seeing a physician regularly. A quarter reported being HIV-positive, and another 35 percent reported having seriously considered suicide.

Xavier's was the latest in a series of such studies done in cities where relatively emboldened trans activists have pushed local officials to begin considering public policy solutions to their health care concerns. Across the board, they have found largely the same thing: higher rates of just about every indicator of social and economic distress. "And all because of the stigma," Xavier concludes.

One problem that stands out, Xavier and others say, is the need for accessible counseling and medical supervision for those who are in the process of gender transitioning. Most medical professionals require certain steps, outlined in a set of protocols dubbed the "Benjamin Standards of Care." First, a therapist must diagnose you with "Gender Identity Disorder," which the American Psychiatric Association established in 1979. In adults, the diagnosis essentially confirms that your "gender dysphoria" is profound enough that the drastic step of making physiological alterations to God's plan is an acceptable treatment.

The diagnosis clears you for reconstructive surgery and hormone therapy. Hormone use for gender transitioning is strictly off-label, but select doctors will nevertheless prescribe a particular hormone and simply file paperwork for one of its approved usages. While there is disagreement within the trans community about how this process should be altered, most unite around frustration with the gatekeeping nature of it all—the notion that one must first ask permission, then be declared insane, before being allowed to violate our gender rules.

For Angela (a pseudonym), this means choosing between the career she's spent ten years building and her recent decision to live as a male. Angela, twenty-eight, gained security clearance while serving in the Marines. Despite having climbed to officer rank, she fled the forces when it became clear they were going to throw her out for being a lesbian.

As a civilian, her clearance allowed her to land a well-paying job at an aerospace engineering firm. The position has afforded her partner of four years a comfortable life, and even occasionally helps support her partner's budding acting career. But all of that will be jeopardized once a gender-identity-disorder diagnosis is placed in Angela's medical records. Technically, it's a mental health problem, and that would likely prompt the revocation of her clearance when it next comes up for review. So Angela and her partner are again searching for new ways she can use her skills.

Middle class professionals like Angela have options. The barriers to a legal and safe gender transition are surmountable, if profound. But for people like Sharmus, the whole discussion is absurd.

Sharmus has never had "body work" done, but she's taken some hormones in the past. In her world, spending thousands of dollars on therapy, surgery, and hormone treatments is impossible, but a hyper-feminine appearance is still highly valued—not only for personal aesthetics, but also for professional development. So a thriving black market has developed. In D.C., for $200 to $300, you can have silicone injected into your chest to create breasts. Thirty bucks will get you around 100 hormone pills, though injections are usually cheaper.

"When I was taking the hormone shots, my girlfriend was shooting me," Sharmus explains. "You get a knot in the breasts first, then your skin gets soft. After about two months, my breasts started forming."

With hormones, often someone who has taken them before supplies and mentors a curious friend. Similar arrangements develop with silicone, but just as often there's a dealer in town who also injects clients. The silicone is not encased, as it would be with an implant, but rather injected with large syringes directly into varying body parts. In some cases, the materials injected are not even silicone, but substitutes made from more readily available things such as dishwashing liquid or floor wax. Similarly, some men wanting estrogen will simply take birth-control pills. Testosterone is harder to improvise, but even the real thing can irreparably damage internal organs when taken improperly. All of this can result in fatalities.

"I have known several people that passed," Sharmus sighs. She steers clear of silicone and stopped taking unsupervised hormones. A couple of years ago, she started working with an organization called Helping Individual Prostitutes Survive, or HIPS. She conducts outreach for HIPS, offering information on how to protect against HIV and other sexually transmitted diseases, and encouraging colleagues to leave the silicone alone.

Omar Reyes, whose drag persona is former Miss Gay America, works for La Clinica del Pueblo, a D.C. clinic serving the city's ballooning Latino community. Reyes uses his male birth name and male pronouns but considers himself transgender because of his drag work and his discomfort with male gender "norms." In his monthly transgender support group and in conversations with other *dragas* he meets at his weekly show, Reyes harps on the *malas noticias* about silicone. But he recognizes why it's attractive: It's cheap, and it's fast.

"They put silicone in their face and their bodies and, in just a very short period, they can look like a woman," he says. This is particularly important for drag performers and sex workers, whose income may depend on how exaggeratedly feminine they look. "We have to deal with the fact that they want to look like a woman, and this is the short-term way to do it."

Reyes and Xavier want to see someone in D.C. start a low-cost clinic devoted to counseling and treatment for people who are transitioning. Gay health centers in Boston, Los Angeles, New York City, San Francisco, and Seattle all have such clinics already and are developing their own sets of protocols for how the process should work. Earlier this year, San Francisco became the first jurisdiction in the United States to include sex reassignment surgery and related treatments in its health plan for civil servants. This is the kind of thing Xavier says we need to see more of.

But even if the services were there, getting people into them would take work. Most transgender people tell horrifying stories of the treatment they have experienced in health care settings. In one of the most high-profile cases nationally, a trans woman named Tyra Hunter died in 1995 when D.C. paramedics refused to treat her wounds from a car accident. After removing her clothes at the scene of the accident and discovering her male genitals, a paramedic allegedly ceased treating Hunter and began shouting taunts. She died at the hospital later. Following a lengthy court battle, Hunter's family won a suit against the city.

There are many less prominent examples. From the hospital nurse who gawks when helping a trans woman into her dressing gown to the gynecologist who responds with disbelief when a trans man comes in for a checkup, the small indignities act as perhaps the greatest barriers to health care.

"They feel like when you go for services, people are going to give attitude," Reyes says. "Therefore, you find that they don't even think about going for help when they really need it."

Tanika Walker, who goes by Lucky, is your standard eighteen-year-old hard ass: short-sighted, stubborn-headed, determined to be the toughest guy in the room. Born and raised in rough-and-tumble southeast Washington, D.C., Lucky has a mop of dreadlocks, light mustache, tattoos, and brands—including the name of a deceased sibling spelled out in cigarette burns. These all send one message: I'm the wrong dude to mess with.

Like Angela, Lucky is in the process of transitioning genders to become a young man. It's an emotional journey she began when she was fourteen years old. Along the way, she's been yanked out of school and tossed out of her home. She's also been involved in a lot of disastrous relationships marred by violence, often her own.

"I know that I'm homosexual, that I'm a lesbian," Lucky says, groping to explain her feelings. "But at the same time, it's like, I look so much like a boy. I act so much like a boy. I want to be a boy."

So far, however, Lucky's transition is primarily stylistic. She still uses her birth name and answers to female pronouns, but she describes her gender as "not anything." She uses only the men's bathroom because she's had too many fights with women who thought she was a Peeping Tom in the ladies room. And she'd much rather her friends call her "dawg" than "girlfriend." Among African American lesbians, Lucky fits into a category of women often dubbed "doms," short for dominant.

"I never had chests," Lucky brags. "Never. Around the time you're supposed to start getting chests, I didn't get any. So I was like, am I made to be like this? I was the little girl all of the other little girls couldn't play with 'cause I was too boyish."

The dyke jokes started early, sometime in middle school. She settled on a violent response to the taunting just as early. Her fighting became routine enough that by sophomore year the school suggested counseling for her "identity crisis." She balked and, instead, came out to her mom, who promptly threw her out of the house. "I was like, how am I having an identity crisis? I know what I am," Lucky remembers. "My mom said I had to go."

Lucky enrolled herself in the Job Corps and by the time she was seventeen had her GED. She came back to D.C., moved in with her godsister, and began dating a thirty-two-year-old woman.

But the relationship quickly turned violent, and the godsister put Lucky out as well. She turned to one of her brothers and started dating someone her own age. But it was a stormy relationship, and Lucky battered her partner. After one of their more brutal fights, the young woman called the police and Lucky wound up in jail for a month for aggravated assault. That was this April. In May, she started dating another young woman, and she believes this relationship will work out. She's also started hanging out at the Sexual Minority Youth Assistance League (SMYAL).

One urgent lesson she's trying to learn is that violence isn't her only option when conflict arises. But she dismisses the severity of her problem. "I would be, like, 'Go away and leave me alone,'" she says, describing how the fights started. "And she would just keep hitting me in the arm or something. But it didn't really affect me; it would just be real irritating. She used to do stupid stuff like that to aggravate me. So I just hit her. And when I hit her, I blacked her eye out or something."

She sums up her life in a gigantic understatement, saying, "It's just some things I've been through that a normal eighteen-year-old female wouldn't have been through."

Twenty-year-old Vassar College senior Kiana Moore began transitioning at seventeen. She is articulate and engaging, has never been in trouble, and is studying to become a clinical psychologist. As the only transgender person on her campus, she comes out to the entire first-year class every term during one of the school's diversity programs. She spent this summer interning at SMYAL, counseling Lucky and fifteen to twenty other mainly black transgender youth. What these young folks need, she says, are more role models.

"I am here at SMYAL working as an intern, but where else can you go around this country and see a trans intern? Where can you see a trans person who's in college?" Moore asks. "And so you don't really have anyone to connect to or know about. So if they are at high risk [for social problems], that's why. Because there's nothing there for them at all."

Moore has what Xavier calls "passing privilege." She's a beautiful and confident black woman most people would never assume is transgender. That's something usually achieved only by those with significant resources.

And once trans people have found they can pass—usually middle class whites living in the suburbs—they don't want to ruin it by becoming an activist or a role model.

"You lose something if you help, because then you put yourself in the spotlight. And if you are a pretty, passable female, you don't want to do that," Moore explains. "We don't want to be advocates, because then we're Kiana the transsexual instead of Kiana the new neighbor."

And thus the activists trying to build a transgender community and social movement face much the same battle gay activists confronted for years: Those with the resources to help have too much to lose.

But Moore sees promise in the youth she spent the summer with. "Every time I talk to them I always give them a big hug before, during, and after the session, because that's the only way I can say I'm here and I think you're stronger than me," she says. "They deal with their problems, and they come in here, and they smile, every day. And they take care of each other."

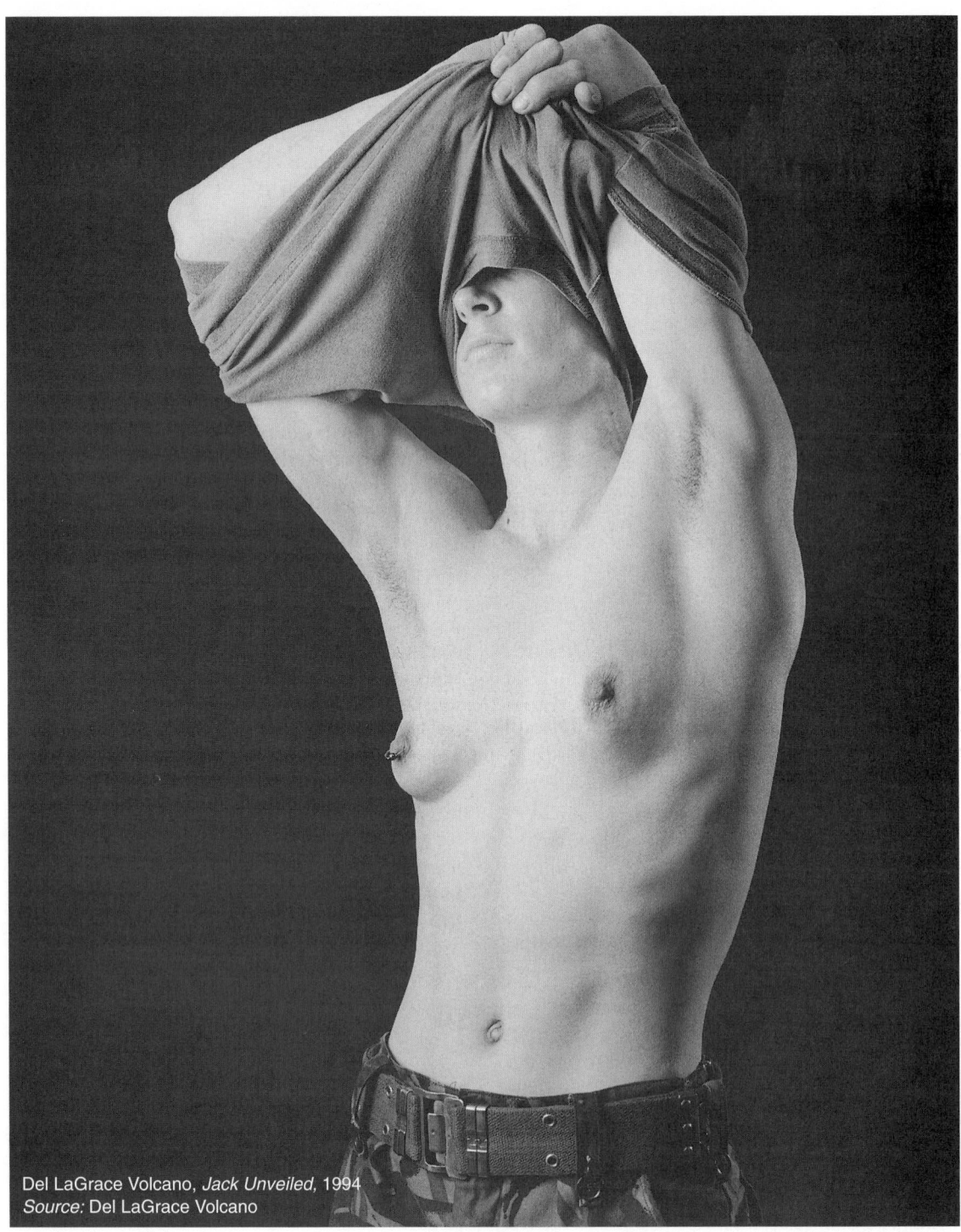

Del LaGrace Volcano, *Jack Unveiled*, 1994
Source: Del LaGrace Volcano

READING 34

Redefining Sex and Intimacy: The Sexual Self-Images, Outlooks, and Relationships of Gay Men Living with HIV/AIDS

Kent L. Sandstrom

DIAGNOSIS WITH HIV: DISRUPTIONS EVOKED IN SEXUAL SELF-IMAGES

When a serious illness comes crashing into a person's life, it provokes a profound sense of disruption, challenging and even shattering cherished images of self (Bury 1982; Corbin and Strauss 1987; Charmaz 1991). The onset of such an illness becomes a "turning point moment" (Strauss 1969) or "epiphany"—a moment of crisis that disrupts and alters the fundamental meaning structures in an affected person's life (Denzin 1989). For persons with HIV disease, an epiphany occurs at the time of initial diagnosis (Sandstrom 1990, 1994; Weltz 1991). When getting diagnosed as seropositive, individuals receive official confirmation that they have a stigmatized, sexually transmittable, and potentially life-threatening illness. They are thereby redefined as social (and sexual) objects; that is, their diagnosis casts them into a new and problematic health status—a status that undermines previously valued self-images and enactments, particularly in the sexual realm.

When telling the story of their initial HIV diagnosis and the disruptions it provoked, the men I interviewed emphasized how it altered their sexual feelings and self-images.[1] For instance, one respondent, Hal,[2] remarked, "My feelings about sex changed at first—they really

did. Yeah, I felt like sex was deadly. And I felt like I was a deadly weapon." In a similar vein, Peter commented, "After I got diagnosed I felt really contaminated. . . . I felt like Typhoid Mary. I even called myself Typhoid Mary."

In light of these feelings, Hal and Peter, like others I interviewed, became more wary of sex and potential sexual involvements. For example, Hal remarked, "I didn't date—I didn't have any sexual contact for a long time [after testing seropositive]. . . . If someone put the hit on me, I didn't respond. I just became kind of asexual." Even the men who had longterm lovers felt anxious and hesitant about being sexual after getting diagnosed, especially if their lovers were seronegative. As one of these men, Dave, explained, "It's because of the guilt—the fear of my ejaculations being contagious and things like that. I mean, let's face it, that's how the disease spreads and it is a fear."

As time passed, these feelings of contamination and anxiety typically declined, particularly for those men whose sexual partner(s) reassured them of their desirability and conveyed little fear of infection. Peter highlighted this theme when describing how his involvement with such a partner had helped him to feel more favorably about himself and sexual activity:

> I dated this one guy who was [sero]negative and that was very good because he taught me that someone could still love me for me no matter what. . . . He was so cool about sex and he handled it so well that it lowered my fears about being sexual . . . and it enabled me to meet Dean, my partner now, and to accept him and have a sexual relationship with him.

Yet, even when having lovers or partners who affirmed their sexual desirability, the men I interviewed continued to grapple at times with a sense of sexual stigma and contamination, especially when engaging in sex. As Neil revealed:

Source: Symbolic Interaction, vol. 19, issue 3, p. 241. University of California Press © 1996. Reprinted with permission from University of California Press.

I feel tainted. I've felt it all along. I don't feel like it's something that I'll ever get rid of. I come to terms with it—I mean, I accept it as a part of the way I am now. But sometimes I feel poisonous—usually when I'm being sexual. I don't usually feel that way when I'm not sexual.

Other men reported similar sentiments, noting how when having sex they had "a kind of leper feeling" and sometimes viewed themselves as having "a killer penis!" Although these feelings could be exacerbated by expressions of anxiety on the part of one's sexual partner(s), they did not seem to hinge on these reactions. Instead, feelings of sexual contamination or stigma derived from a diagnosed individual's realistic appraisal of himself as someone who could potentially transmit HIV through sex—an appraisal reinforced by messages from various social sources, including doctors, educators, friends, family members, partners, and the media.

This sense of sexual pollution became heightened when others, including friends and relatives, conveyed the message that persons with HIV/AIDS ought to no longer have sexual desires or relationships. As Jay observed:

Sometimes I get angry because people expect me not to have any more intimacy needs—you know, intimacy in a physical [sexual] sense. They just feel like "Well, that's finished now, that's done!" Like you can just turn off the switch. . . . Even friends—when I've discussed my feelings about it, and said "You know, maybe I would like to see someone or connect in a sexual way"—they'll kind of look at me and say, "You wouldn't, would you?" You know, as if it was something taboo or, uh, wrong, or something like that. I mean, who more than someone who's been living with AIDS, or HIV, for awhile would have a sense of the boundaries? And who more needs the physical affirmation?

After encountering such reactions, the men I interviewed not only felt stigmatized, but also diminished, vulnerable, and confused. They wondered who they could be or should be as sexual persons. They felt discouraged about the prospect of comfortably pursuing and engaging in sexual involvements. In essence, their sense of sexuality and self became undermined and fragmented. They experienced a "divided self" (Denzin 1984; Athens 1995). In turn, these men struggled to sort out their conflicting self feelings and to reestablish a valued and integrated self, especially in the sexual realm. This meant, however, that they had to place their currently fragile and splintered sexual selves at risk in interaction; that is, only through their interactions and negotiations with others could they find out what kind of sexual selves they might viably realize.

CHALLENGES ENCOUNTERED IN NEGOTIATING SEXUAL RELATIONSHIPS

Despite the sexual stigma and vulnerability provoked by their initial HIV diagnoses, most of the men I interviewed continued to seek and engage in sexual activity. They did not want to end their sexual lives, regardless of the messages others conveyed. As a result, they had to find ways to negotiate desired sexual involvements and, in so doing, to restore valued sexual selves. In pursuing these goals, they encountered a variety of challenges—challenges that differed depending upon whether they were seeking new sexual relationships or negotiating ongoing relationships with lovers.

Challenges Faced in Negotiating New Relationships

Those men who wanted to form new sexual relationships faced the biggest challenges in negotiating sexual activity. They not only had to find ways to connect with prospective sexual partners, but also had to decide whether to disclose their HIV status in sexual negotiations. In making this decision, these men had to decide how to address concerns about the transmission of HIV and how to protect themselves against the prospect of stigma or rejection. When negotiating sexual relationships, they tried to resolve these moral concerns by (a) concealing their serostatus and engaging in only safer sex to minimize the risk of HIV transmission or (b) revealing their serostatus and affirming the right of potential partners to know this information before taking part in any sexual activity with them, regardless of the threats this posed to self.

The men who chose to conceal their serostatus highlighted the sexual norms that had emerged in the gay subculture—norms stressing that people engaging in sex were responsible for protecting themselves against infection and should not rely on their partners to reveal their HIV status (Daly, Hogan, Hildebrandt, Kummer, and Tilleras 1990). Most of the men I interviewed—and especially those without lovers—affirmed this norm of self-protection and believed that people infected with HIV were not obliged to inform partners of their serostatus as long as they engaged in only safer sex. For instance, Dennis remarked, "I don't think that you have to say, 'Hey man, do you want to get together? I'm HIV [positive].' You just need to practice safer sex."

Curtis, who engaged regularly in sex with anonymous partners, not only emphasized how practicing safer sex made it unnecessary to disclose one's health status, but also pointed out that he (and his partners) negotiated sexual exchanges based on the assumption that everyone was seropositive. He explained, "I guess that's something I sort of assume, you know. There's just a certain sort of expectation [that people are seropositive] at public situations or bars. It's really sort of sad. But then again, I would assume that everyone else there would assume that too." Given the salience of this assumption in the contexts where he negotiated sexual liaisons, Curtis concluded that disclosure of his health status would be redundant and unnecessary. Instead, he (as well as others) chose to "steer away from risky stuff,"

and, if a partner showed interest in doing something unsafe, he simply responded by saying, "No, I don't think that would be a good idea."

Although Curtis did not feel obliged to openly disclose his health status to sexual partners, he acknowledged that he was more likely to do so if he thought he might become emotionally involved with them. Another man, Jay, shared similar observations when discussing his sexual negotiations. He mentioned that during the time he had been sexually active, he decided whether or not to disclose his serostatus to partners based primarily on the emotional commitment that characterized his relationship with them:

> I know the one criterion that I used when meeting someone was that I would wait for a trial period and only when I thought there was a serious investment in the relationship would I say something. . . . Of course, that assumed that there was nothing we did that was remotely risky. But, I mean, it seemed really stupid to me to meet someone and then go into that right away—to say, "Well, you should know that I have HIV" and all of that.

In elaborating, Jay explained that if an individual reveals his seropositive status at the beginning of a relationship, he might subtly or unintentionally convey discomfort or rejection to a potential partner:

> In one sense, if you're too "Johnny on the spot" in bringing it up, then the other person may wonder what the hell your agenda is. You know what I mean? What are you saying to someone if you say, "Well, I want you to know right off the bat that I have [HIV]." I mean, the person might think—the person might easily think that it's another way of saying to them, "Well, get lost, I can't deal with this. I can't deal with the intimacy stuff."

In contrast to Curtis and Jay, others I interviewed felt morally obliged to disclose their serostatus to prospective partners before participating in any sexual activity with them. Although these men accepted the legitimacy of the norm of self-protection, they felt compelled to reveal their HIV status to potential sexual partners, even if they abided by safer sex guidelines. As Alan asserted, "If you're going to sleep with someone, you've got to tell him." Like Alan, these men reasoned that they could not have sex with someone unless he knew of their serostatus and the potential risks involved. Because of this, they were more likely to encounter difficulties and anxieties in forming sexual relationships with new partners. Usually, they feared getting rejected when disclosing their health status, particularly if they had already had such an experience. As Greg indicated:

> I kind of dread that whole process of revealing because I've had a couple of very dramatic instances where people were very interested in me and when they found out that I was diagnosed with AIDS, that was the end of it, period! The virus made them feel that I was poisoned and they wanted to stay away.

Of course, disclosure of one's health status did not necessarily result in rejection. The men who chose to disclose their HIV status when negotiating sexual relationships found that at least some prospective partners still remained interested in having sex with them. Yet, the disclosure of one's health status and the arrangement of a sexual liaison did not always mark the end of negotiations regarding either "consent" or HIV-related concerns. For instance, Hal described how he closely monitored the nonverbal expressions of his partners to discern whether they truly felt comfortable engaging in sex with him. If he sensed fear or discomfort in his partner, he would not have sexual relations with him, as revealed below:

> I find myself, when I am sexual and expressing myself that way, I'm really, uh, on guard to pick up anything from the other person about being frightened—like thinking, "What's he gonna give me?" And in one relationship that I had this past winter I sensed that. And, I mean, I, uh, just became impotent right way—there was nothing. And I had to say something. I just said, "Okay, I can sense something's not right here." And we talked about it, and there was a definite fear of infection on his part. And we both decided at that point, "Okay, if that's what you're feeling, let's not do anything."

When negotiating a sexual relationship with a new partner, Hal wanted to feel as certain as possible that his partner felt comfortable with the situation. He sought this assurance by trying to help the partner openly identify and discuss his HIV-related fears or feelings. This strategy, however, was not always appreciated, and it could lead to tense or undesired sexual interactions, as Hal revealed when he said, "That's what I try to do—help the other person identify their fears and talk about it. And sometimes I'm just told to shut up (laughs)! Shut up and enjoy it!"

Other men, such as Bob, noted how their sexual negotiations were not guided simply by concerns about a partner's uncomfortable or negative reactions to their HIV status. They also considered how trustworthy a potential partner would be in preserving the confidentiality of their health status and abiding by the norms of safer sex. For example, Bob commented:

> There are times that I have been downtown [at a bar] with friends and all of a sudden the "lounge lizard from hell" comes up and, you know, he's hell bent on taking you home. And you just say, "No . . . this is not the type of person that I want to divulge this information to before I jump in the rack." And, too, he's not the type of person that would play by the rules [practice safer sex] if you didn't tell him. That puts a cramp in your style. You have to feel pretty safe that someone will play by the rules before you even want to take it any steps further.

As highlighted by Bob, concerns about trust became integral to sexual negotiations with new partners. In most cases, these concerns revolved around whether a partner could be trusted to "stop fucking when asked to" or "to do what it takes" to practice safer sex, such as using a condom and checking its condition periodically during sex. (For a related discussion, see Davies, Hickson, Weatherburn, and Hunt 1993, p. 135.) At times, however, the men who negotiated sex with new partners also expressed concerns about their own trustworthiness, especially if they had engaged in impulsive or unsafe sexual activity in the past. They worried about "losing control" or "using poor judgment" if they "felt horny" and their sexual partners did not care what boundaries were observed. In turn, because they did not trust themselves to always engage in safer sex, these men felt more reluctant to seek and exchange sexual activity with others. As Fred observed when discussing related themes:

> I've said to myself, "Oh yes, I know all there is to know about setting boundaries [on sex] and I feel okay with it." But then, what if you get in a situation where you feel extremely passionate, does it all go out the window? Where's the boundary, you know? And what if someone— what if you meet someone who doesn't give a shit about safe sex? And he tells you, "I don't care, let's do everything! I don't care about it, I'm fine with it." And he doesn't understand why you won't because it's okay with him. Especially if you're doing intercourse and he's on the receiving end. It's almost as if he'd think, "Well, what's wrong with you, you're not the one who is taking the risk? I've decided and that's okay." And maybe he'd convince you in the heat of the moment. But it's not okay, you know. You're putting him at risk. And that's another piece of [why I'm] being hesitant about sex.

To summarize, those men who looked for and negotiated new sexual relationships encountered a variety of dilemmas which made it difficult for them to engage comfortably in sex. Nevertheless, they typically chose to continue being sexually active, albeit in different and "safer" ways than they had in the past.

For some, this meant masturbating more frequently or having more sexual contact with regular partners. For others, it meant sharing more sexual activities with friends, such as watching X-rated videos or taking part in "jack off" parties. Most crucially, regardless of what specific options they chose, these men discovered that they had to adjust or restructure their sexual practices in order to realize erotic satisfaction and viable sexual selves. They also discovered that this reshaping of their sexual activities and interactions became an important aspect of their ongoing identity work and illness experience.

Challenges Faced in Negotiating Ongoing Relationships

In contrast to the men who sought new sexual relationships, the men who had ongoing and exclusive relationships with lovers did not have to worry about disclosing their serostatus during sexual negotiations. They informed their lovers of their seropositive status almost immediately after getting tested. Moreover, half of these men did not have to fear the prospect of infecting their lovers with HIV because their lovers were also seropositive. Yet, as awareness of the problems posed by reinfection increased in both medical and gay circles, these men became more concerned about the specific sexual practices they engaged in with lovers. In fact, one of the challenges faced by men with seropositive lovers was adjusting to the changes that occurred in their sexual practices because of the threat of reinfection. As Lenny observed:

> We've had to change our practices—we'd kind of been exposing each other to the risk of reinfection. And it's been difficult to adjust to the change in some ways. For example, with oral sex it's like, I don't like something about the rubber on his penis—it doesn't taste good. And things like that. Of course, we'd been using condoms for anal intercourse but we had not used them for anything else so that's been an adjustment too.

Lenny additionally noted that in this process of change and adjustment, he and his lover, Ross, "took a little while to sort things out sexually—like finding alternatives—safe and mutually satisfying practices. Like I've been fascinated with leather [but] Ross is absolutely not interested . . . so that hasn't been an option for us."

Overall, the men who had seropositive lovers, like Lenny, felt frustrated by the restrictions that HIV imposed upon their sexual relationships. While these men negotiated some satisfying sexual exchanges with their lovers, they generally resented how the disease precluded them from engaging in the types of sex and sexual self-expression that they most enjoyed.

By comparison, the men who were involved with seronegative lovers shared far fewer complaints about the constraints that HIV imposed upon their sexual practices. Instead, they stressed their commitment to safer sex and their desires to minimize the risk of transmitting HIV to their lovers. They also expressed anxieties about the prospect of infecting their lovers, even if they practiced only safer sex. As Dave revealed, "There's just something about being infected that is a scary thing. You know, what if a condom leaks and my partner turns up infected? God, I'd really go through a guilt thing!"

Given their anxieties about transmitting HIV, the men who were involved with seronegative lovers struggled to feel relaxed and comfortable when having sex with them. For instance, they grappled with concerns about what sexual boundaries they would or should observe with lovers, particularly when these boundaries had become uncertain. Neil addressed these concerns when discussing the tensions he felt in his sexual relationship with his lover:

> There are always those borderlines and those limits that are pressed against. The boundaries that are clear at one time might become a little less clear later on. And, I don't know, I'm just al-ways nervous when I'm having sex and that's not fun. I worry about the boundaries and that diminishes the pleasure. I can't be as playful or adventurous sexually.

In a related vein, the men who had seronegative lovers also struggled with how to address or resolve the sexual anxieties and frustrations evoked by the threat of HIV infection. Paul expressed these feelings when describing a recent interaction with his lover:

> The other night it was obvious, you know, that both of us were interested in having sex. We talked about it and, um, my lover said he wanted to suck my penis. But I noticed that he had just flossed before coming to bed and, um, I knew that flossing causes minor bleeding. Well, that made me worry about letting him suck my penis. I hesitated to say anything but then I mentioned the risk to him and, you know, he agreed that it might be a problem. But he didn't think it would be that risky, especially with a condom on. But I just didn't feel comfortable with that, you know, and I said, "Maybe we should do something else." Well, he got quiet and I knew he was, uh, kind of mad. Then he said, "Maybe we should just go to sleep." And I said, "Maybe so." Well, that's how it ended—we both ended up mad and frustrated. And, um, it was clearly because of HIV.

Because of the anxieties and tensions they felt regarding sex, the men whose lovers were seronegative usually became less interested in having sex. Their lovers' level of interest, however, did not decline as significantly as their own. In turn, this difference in sexual interest could become another source of conflict and resentment in their relationship, as Dave described:

> I'm not as interested in sex as [my lover] is anymore. . . . I'd rather wait a couple of weeks between times (laughs). But with him, it's still at least twice a week. And he's demanding about it. And that just pisses me off—that he can't be patient with me about it. And I start to feel that it's more of a duty.

In addition to feeling concerned about the current sexual conflicts he experienced with his lover, Dave also worried about the tensions they would experience in the future when his health and sexual capacities deteriorated. He remarked, "It's gonna get to the point where I'm not gonna be able to service him. I'm not gonna be able to give him what he wants sexually. So then what am I gonna do?"

In addressing these concerns, Dave and the other men whose lovers were seronegative devised strategies that would allow them to relieve the sexual pressures they felt and enhance their sense of control. For example, they made plans to encourage partners to "take up masturbation on a regular basis" or to seek other sexual relationships. Most importantly, they struggled to find ways to successfully negotiate and deal with the sexual dilemmas and self-challenges they faced. These struggles and negotiations became an integral feature of their unfolding moral experience and identity work. The more effectively they could negotiate sexual exchanges and address sexual dilemmas with their lovers, the more likely they were to realize a valued sexual self and a vitalizing sense of control over their sexuality.

ADVANCED ILLNESS: DECLINES IN SEXUAL ATTRACTIVENESS, DESIRE, AND ABILITY

As their illness advanced, the men in this study found it increasingly difficult to maintain a desired physical appearance and a sense of sexual attractiveness, regardless of whether or not they had lovers. They often developed clearly visible symptoms of sickness, such as a pale complexion, an emaciated appearance, facial or bodily rashes, cancerous (Kaposi's Sarcoma) lesions, or severe physical weakness. This made it difficult or impossible for them to maintain the type of bodily appearance necessary to sustain conceptions of themselves as sexually

desirable persons, as implied by Peter: "Because of it [HIV disease], I'm not as muscular as I used to be. I'm 25 pounds under what I once was. That bothers me because I don't have that body anymore, you know, that turns the eye when you're walking down the street."

Furthermore, those men who became seriously ill faced significant problems in keeping their bodies "in good shape" and, correspondingly, sustaining favorable images of their physical and sexual selves. For example, Rick suffered from severe symptoms of CMV (cytomegalovirus) and he observed:

> I can't really do exercises anymore. For two reasons: one is that I have a port, the other is because of my loss of vision. I have a port because I have a catheter, and you have to be careful so the catheter doesn't separate. So body exercises are pretty much out of the question. And because of my loss of vision, I can't really go running. The only real option is to go swimming and even that is a problem because the needle for the port is in five days a week and I can't swim when it's in. So I really feel out of shape, you know. And that lowers my self-image . . . I mean, I'm not a particularly vain person but I used to have a nice butt and it's gone. I just don't fill out my pants anymore.

In general, the physical changes and deterioration resulting from advanced HIV disease prompted those affected to feel increasingly alienated from or dissatisfied with their bodies. When discussing how his AIDS-related symptoms had affected his body image, Matt commented, "I don't like my body anymore . . . I used to feel good in it—now I don't. I don't really like the way it looks. I mean, all the KS (Kaposi's sarcoma) lesions—they're all over my body now. That doesn't make me feel very attractive—physically or sexually."

In addition to experiencing a reduced sense of sexual attractiveness as their illness advanced, the men I interviewed experienced a diminished desire or ability to have sex, regardless of whether they had lovers or whether their lovers had HIV disease. Although these shifts in sexual desire and functioning became attributed in part to feelings of contamination and anxieties about transmitting the virus, they also became linked to the ongoing physical effects of the disease.

When discussing the decline they experienced in their sexual desire or abilities, those men who had lived with AIDS for at least a couple of years stressed the dampening effects of symptoms such as chronic fatigue and lack of energy. As Neil remarked:

> I'm involved with somebody now and, I don't know, sometimes I'd just rather not be sexual. I do like the touching, you know, but it just seems so hard to do because my energy level is just—it almost seems like not high enough to do it. I mean, of course I can but—it's just like "Ohhh" (groans), you know, it's just not as satisfying.

Like others, Neil also emphasized that it had become more difficult to engage in sex after his symptoms worsened because of the impaired sexual capacity he experienced and the physical "price" he paid after having sex. He stated:

> My sexual functioning has just deteriorated. I don't know if it's only AIDS-related or what, but it ain't easy for me—it takes a lot of energy and a lot of time. And frankly, I end up losing a lot of sleep because of sex so I have to be real careful with that. Because when I lose sleep I'm just dysfunctional—I just can't function. I get like in the state of "fuzzhead."

Along with facing the challenges posed by fatigue, those men who suffered from HIV-induced neuropathy stressed how their symptoms (e.g., severe nerve and limb pain) reduced their sexual desire and constrained their activities. One of these men, Ron, reported that the neurological complications he experienced made it almost impossible for him to sustain an erection and attain an orgasm. When discussing his current sex life, Ron said, "I'm impotent from the neuropathy. They [the doctors] tell me I could still cum but, you know, who has two hours?"

In a somewhat different vein, Vic stressed how his neuropathy-related symptoms made it difficult for him to enjoy sensual touching or erotic activity. He observed:

> Sometimes there can be a lot of discomfort . . . [so] you have to make a lot of adjustments. Even if you do think about, for example, doing something, or sharing an intimate moment with someone, it puts up barriers. For example, it took my lover a long time just to figure out where to touch me. Because things do hurt and he would massage me or something and I'd go "Ahhhh, that's painful!" Well, that certainly puts an excessive damper on how you do things like sensual touching. It certainly puts a damper on getting close or intimate when you're in the middle of things and you say "OUCH!" That's not exactly conducive to any more passion.

Similarly problematic declines in sexual sensitivity and desire could be provoked by the medications taken to alleviate neuropathy or other advanced HIV symptoms. At times, medications directly impaired sexual functioning, and the men who suffered from severe symptoms had to choose between relieving these symptoms or preserving valued sexual capacities. As Jeff described, "My doctor gave me some medication she thought might help [with neuropathy-induced pain] and after I started to take it I found that I couldn't have an orgasm. Well, I figured 'screw this!' I stopped taking it. I thought, 'I'm way too young for that—to stop having orgasms.'"

To summarize, as they made sense of their declining sexual interest and capacity, the men who wrestled with advanced HIV-related symptoms stressed the effects of the pain, fatigue, and devitalization they experienced. When these symptoms flared up, sex became much less appealing and rewarding. In fact, rather than serving as a source of bodily pleasure, sexual activity could provoke or intensify physical pain and exhaustion. In turn, through their efforts to minimize their health problems and sustain a vital self, the men who lived with severe HIV symptoms became less inclined to participate in sex. For them, sexual activity became regarded as something that was likely to diminish rather than enhance their sense of well-being, control, and vivacity. In light of this, these men tried to rely more heavily upon alternative sources and expressions of intimacy, connection, and self-value.

RECONSTRUCTING SEX, INTIMACY, AND INTIMATE IDENTITIES

As their illness unfolded, sex acquired a different sense of importance and meaning for the men I interviewed. As highlighted in previous sections, this was due in part to the changes that took place in their sexual self-feelings, interactions, desires, and functioning. Yet, the differing salience and meaning that they gave to sex also seemed in part attributable to the larger changes that took place in sexual outlooks and practices, particularly within urban gay communities, as the first decade of HIV/AIDS unfolded.

Prior to becoming aware of the threat posed by HIV disease, the men who participated in this study generally had a favorable view of sex and the part it played in their daily lives. Those who were over 30 years old alluded to and reminisced about the sexual climate that had characterized urban gay communities when they "came of age" in the 1970s and early 1980s. They told stories, often fondly, of the open and "party like" sexual atmosphere that surrounded them during the post-Stonewall era—the era when the gay sexual revolution took hold. For example, Bob, who was 39 years old, recounted:

> If you were around in '75—between '75 and I'd say '81—it was a party! (laughs) I mean, all the stoppers were out and you could make friends and sexual connections very easily. . . . We're talking a dozen years ago. We had a pretty live downtown life then—a party life. And a lot of people thought it was just awesome that people were so uninhibited sexually.

During the 1970s and early 1980s, many gay men celebrated and enjoyed the new openness and accessibility of sex. They embraced the libertarian sexual ideology that had emerged in American sexual culture and permeated the gay subculture—an ideology that defined sex as a source of play and pleasure and that promoted a slippage between sex, love, and commitment (Seidman 1992). Oftentimes, they also accepted definitions of "casual" and non-monogamous sex as forms of resistance to the normative practices of mainstream heterosexuals. Those men who had lived in large cities on the East or West Coast during the late 1970s and early 1980s were most likely to become exposed to these sexual outlooks and to have opportunities to participate in a more libertarian or "fast lane" sexual lifestyle. For instance, Dave described the sexual climate and opportunities that existed on the East Coast when he lived there during the early 1980s:

> [My friends and I] used to do the bathhouses and stuff like that when it was available, you know—those were just so fun. We used to all get off of work and go to the baths and, I mean, I remember literally chorus lines of guys in towels doing kick lines, you know, half-naked and exposing themselves. It was such a giant party of sex that you probably would not believe that those things existed, but they did. And it was so fun—it was just a free, fun place to be. . . . We all used to go to the discos, too. I remember one place—it no longer exists today—you'd go in and there would be about 5,000 men in there. And not one of them would have their shirt on! They were just all exposed and showing themselves off. It was very open—there were even sex acts performed on stage. I mean, the bars were out in front of you—you'd go to order a drink and there'd be naked men performing sex right up on stage above you. That's the way it was. It was very [accepted], you know—we just thought that that was just fine, the way to be.

Most importantly, Dave, like a number of men I interviewed, viewed sex as a source of enjoyment, pleasure, and adventure before HIV disease arose and prompted major changes in sexual opportunities, outlooks, and practices within gay male circles. As the disease became more widespread among gay men and its primary routes of transmission became more widely known, the bathhouses closed and the "party like" sexual atmosphere that had characterized some urban gay circles disappeared. In turn, those men who had been involved in a "fast lane" lifestyle usually became more anxious about sex and more conservative in their sexual practices.

In contrast to these men, others I interviewed felt somewhat ambivalent about sex or their sexual involvements even before the threat of HIV disease arose. When describing and explaining his active sexual history, Jay remarked:

> I think a lot of it had to do with . . . cultural expectations and copying other men. I got confused messages and I remember a lot of times having mixed feelings. I would go on these [sexual] rampages and stuff and afterwards I would think, "Why did I do that? I don't think I really enjoyed it that much." I mean, I did for those few brief seconds, you know. It was exciting and you reached that ultimate high. But outside of that, I'd say, "Gee, why did I put myself in those situations?"

In answering this question, Jay stressed how his sexual activity had served as a means to develop relationships with other gay men and to feel connected to the gay community:

> I remember thinking to myself, "It seems kind of sad, but I guess that—having sex—is, uh, the way it's done. I guess that's how you meet people." Sexuality made connections. That's how you bonded . . . in a wider sense. Or so I thought. I thought, "By having sex, that's how I'll feel connected, that's how I'll feel like one of these people."

As HIV disease became more widespread, the men in this study felt more troubled and ambivalent about sex, regardless of their sexual history. Sex became associated with disease and death and thus sexual activity became more threatening and restrained. Moreover, after getting diagnosed with HIV, these men found that it became more difficult to engage in sex and to form or sustain sexual relationships, particularly as their illness progressed. As a result, sex became a less integral source of connection and validation in their everyday lives.

In making sense of the role that sex did and should play in their lives, the men I interviewed were influenced by the interpretations of HIV/AIDS that emerged in urban gay communities. As the HIV epidemic progressed, a number of gay spokespersons proposed that HIV/AIDS revealed the failure of the gay subculture and its libertarian sexual ethos (Bell 1982; Callen et al. 1982; Harvey 1982; Kramer 1983). In their arguments, they implied that the disease was a byproduct of a "sex-obsessed" subculture that promoted "promiscuous" behavior while overlooking or downplaying the virtues of romantic love and monogamy. As Stephen Seidman (1992, pp. 164–165) has documented in his related analyses, these spokespersons also suggested that HIV disease had beneficial and even redemptive implications for the gay community—that is, it could serve as a catalyst for the remaking of gay life and for the development and adoption of more "mature and responsible intimate patterns"— patterns based on the model of heterosexual marriage. According to advocates of this perspective, HIV/AIDS offered gay men an opportunity to reevaluate their sexual outlooks, relationships, and identities and to place greater value upon romantic love and intimacy. For instance, in an editorial in *The Advocate*, David Goodstein (1985, p.3) asserted: "During the last half of the 1970s, it wasn't chic in gay male circles to place a high value on life-companions or close friendships. Now we have another chance for progress: to acknowledge the value of intimate relationships." Most crucially, by the end of the 1980s, this rendering of gay sex and the meaning of HIV/AIDS had gained prominence in many gay circles.

The men that I interviewed, especially those who had engaged more frequently in "casual" or anonymous sex, became influenced by this neoromantic ideology and began to reconsider their understandings of sex and intimacy. Often, they became more critical of the sexual ethos that had prevailed in urban gay communities or they lamented the tendency of gay men, like most American men, to unduly emphasize sex and "mistake it for intimacy."

In some cases, a critical reexamination of the relationship between sex and intimacy became further promoted by participation in support groups based on a "twelve step philosophy" (e.g., Alcoholics Anonymous or Adult Children of Alcoholics). Those men who became involved in such groups and exposed to their guiding philosophies—philosophies that reinforced neoromantic conceptions of sex and intimacy—seemed more likely to reconceptualize the meaning of their sexual behavior for themselves. For instance, Trent, who became highly involved in a support group for "codependents," offered this interpretation of his past sexual behavior:

I think that I confused—I mean, I totally confused what, for example, intimacy was about. I was looking for closeness, support, some kind of kinship and warm—but I confused sex with intimacy. I thought that sex was what intimacy was. I mean, I used to go out and do stuff sexually and then think that was love, you know. But, of course, that wasn't love at all.

Others used the language of "addiction" to describe and explain their past sexual activity. They emphasized how they had "used sex in a dysfunctional way," sometimes in combination with drugs and alcohol, as they tried to avoid painful self-feelings and realize a sense of validation and connection. These themes are conveyed in the following comments offered by Jay:

I'd find myself in a cycle of feeling badly about something and then going off and drinking and doing something sexual in an effort to feel better. It was kind of a constant effort to, you know, feel validated. And the only way it made sense to me, or I knew how to do that, was to, you know, have anonymous sex.

Most significantly, as they struggled to make sense of their illness and to negotiate sexual relationships in light of the constraints it imposed, the men I interviewed began to give different meanings and priorities to sex and intimacy. Those who had lovers typically became more committed to maintaining romantic and monogamous relationships with them. On the other hand, those without lovers often affirmed the romantic ideal of becoming involved in a loving and committed sexual relationship. Also, although they still avowed a "sex positive" outlook, many of these men placed greater emphasis on developing and sustaining intimate, nonsexual relationships, especially as their disease progressed. For example, Greg had lived with advanced symptoms of AIDS for three years and he stated:

I used to be a lot more sexually active and a lot more casual. And I'm not anymore. I'm interested in something that's more intimate, meaningful, and relational. I still think, you know, that sexual play is a good thing. But if I'm looking at myself and making priorities I have a much higher priority on developing intimacy than I do on just playing around. . . . For me, sex is not the important thing anymore at all. It's trying to make sure all my friends know that I love them and care about them. And family, too.

In a related vein, Greg and other participants in this study criticized the priority that gay men accorded to genital-centered sex—a priority rooted in the sexual standards of hegemonic masculinity (Connell 1987). Instead, they stressed the need to rethink and expand masculine notions of sexuality, particularly in light of HIV disease. This tendency is illustrated in the following excerpt:

I think HIV challenges us [gay men] to develop broader notions of what sexuality is. . . . Like most men in this culture, we are far too penis focused. There's not enough interest in touching, kissing, holding—in what comes before and after penetration. It's like, "Where did that disappear to?"

Oftentimes, these men also emphasized that HIV provided gay men with an opportunity to reevaluate their relationships and to reflect more deeply upon their understandings of sex and intimacy. For instance, Kirby remarked:

I think a positive aspect of this disease is that a lot of people who were living with disposable relationships have taken a look at that and found some reasons for staying with those relationships, or for getting more discerning when establishing and continuing sexual relationships. And, also, HIV has gotten them to look more at intimacy issues and to separate out intimacy and sexuality.

A related theme highlighted by the men I interviewed was how living with HIV had enabled them to find new, nonsexual ways to express love and build intimacy. For example, Jay stated:

It seems to me like now I'm pouring out affection and more love in other ways. Like for example, with my friend, Mike, I mean, one hug for me with him can go quite a ways, quite a ways. And I realize that with him, that the affirmation and the hugs and tenderness, that—well, if you want to use the word sexual in any way at all to apply to this—that's what sexualizes the whole thing for me. It's intimate in that sense, and I don't want the other genital stuff. It's just like that's not so important. Because it's like when I hug him, it really feels to me like he's reaching in. I can't quite put it into words but it feels more like he's reaching in and I'm reaching in and there's something left after. It's much more nurturing . . . I never had that before, the ability to get inside someone, and to have that person inside me, in a more nurturing, tender kind of way.

Yet, not all of the men In this study accentuated the "positive" implications of HIV/

AIDS regarding sex and intimacy. For instance, Lee and his lover, Clint, stressed the anger and resentment they felt because of how the disease, and the meanings attached to it, had restricted their sexual activities, relationships, and selves. Lee conveyed his resentment in the following remarks:

I feel robbed of being sexual. . . . I have not had many sexual partners—less than a dozen my whole life—and I feel cheated now of being able to explore sexually. . . . [My lover and I] feel forced into a monogamous relationship and we completely resent that. Because with the few partners we've had, it's been open and honest and delightful. We enjoyed these people and got to know them and they became dear, close friends and all that. And we feel that that is all denied to us now, you know. It would just be a mess, particularly in the small town we're in. So we resent that—that we have to be monogamous.

Thus, from Lee and Clint's viewpoint, HIV impeded, rather than facilitated, the formation of intimate relationships. It also served as an irritating constraint to valued forms of sexual exploration, intimate expression, and self-affirmation.

Of all the men in this study, Lee expressed the most resentment about how his diagnosis had affected his sexual life and self. This could be attributed in part to the restrictive and AIDS-phobic atmosphere characterizing the town where he lived—a small town with a "closeted" gay community. However, Lee's views regarding HIV and sexuality were also influenced by his involvement in national gay networks and political activities. He was highly involved in leftist gay networks and he thus became exposed to critiques of the notion that HIV demonstrated the need for gay men to embrace a more conservative, neoromantic ethic. Instead, he accepted the "liberationist" view that HIV disease did not carry an implicit moral message regarding sex, intimacy, monogamy, or the failure of the gay male sexual culture; it simply meant gay men needed to reconfigure their sexual practices (Patton 1990; Seidman 1992).

Lee also avowed that HIV/AIDS could enhance rather than restrict sexual exploration and alternative sexual practices, especially given the emergence of the norm of safer sex in gay circles. He asserted: "[My partner and I] feel that safe sex could give us more opportunity to explore sexually, particularly if you're not fucking."

Overall, Lee stressed how, on a personal level, HIV disease had provoked as many concerns and questions about sexuality and intimacy as it had resolved. For instance, rather than signalling the virtues of monogamy, it had prompted him to ask questions about the nature and boundaries of monogamy, as reflected in the following comment: "I've wondered, is it really stepping out if you don't fuck? You know, if you have a 'jack-off' party with someone, is that like not being monogamous anymore? What is monogamous these days? You know, what does that mean?"

Lee's views, however, did not reflect the perspective of most of the men who elaborated on the sexual meanings and implications of their HIV diagnoses. They articulated a more conservative, romantic outlook—an outlook that emphasized how HIV/AIDS had prompted them to reevaluate their sexual practices and relationships, to place more value on forming or maintaining a romantic relationship, to rely less heavily upon sex as a way to meet and connect with others, and to find nonsexual ways to develop and sustain intimate identities. This outlook, along with its implicit "rhetoric of self-change" (Frank 1993), was embraced most strongly by those men who had an active sexual history before becoming diagnosed and who currently had serious HIV-related symptoms. Of course, this viewpoint was probably more amenable to men in this situation because it provided them with a framework through which they could give a redemptive meaning to the changes that had

occurred in their sexual functioning, relationships, and identities; that is, by viewing HIV/AIDS as a harbinger of the need to live a more conservative sexual lifestyle rather than as a capricious and oppressive constraint upon sexual expression, they could more easily come to terms with the limitations and shifts they experienced in their sexual lives and selves.

DISCUSSION

This analysis of the sexual self-images, negotiations, and outlooks of gay men with HIV disease is important because it opens up discussion of how sexuality and identity intersect within serious chronic illness. More specifically, it illustrates how a chronic and potentially life-threatening illness—HIV/AIDS—disrupts the sexual lives and identities of diagnosed gay men. It also reveals the ideologies and strategies that these men draw upon to address the disruptions they experience and to construct valued sexual selves.

On a broader, analytic level, this paper offers insight into the challenges to self and sexuality encountered by a number of seriously ill people. For instance, it reveals how diagnosis with an illness such as HIV/AIDS alters the sexual feelings and self-images of affected individuals and undermines their sense of bodily integrity. Furthermore, this paper portrays some of the difficulties that seriously ill people—including not only persons with HIV/AIDS but also those with genitourologic cancer or breast cancer—can experience in forming and sustaining sexual relationships.[3] For example, If these individuals want to form new sexual relationships, they typically grapple with concerns about whether or when to tell prospective partners of their health condition and how to negotiate comfortable sexual exchanges with them. Also, if they fear that their condition (or the radiation from related treatments) can be sexually transmitted, they wrestle with the problem of how to negotiate satisfying sexual practices that minimize these fears (see Anderson and Wolf 1986). On the other hand, if these individuals want to sustain ongoing sexual relationships with spouses or lovers, they must address the tensions that arise because of the declines that take place in their sexual desire, capacity, or sense of attractiveness (Anderson, Anderson, and deProsse 1989). In addition, if they feel concerned that their illness (or the effects of treatments) can be sexually transmitted to a spouse or lover, they have to change the sexual activities they shared with them in the past and find new, safe, and gratifying alternatives (von Eschenbach and Rodriquez 1981; Weitz 1991).

In light of these challenges, people living with illnesses like HIV/AIDS, breast cancer, and genitourologic cancer are likely to become more ambivalent or disheartened about engaging in sexual interactions, especially when their physical health and capacities deteriorate (Anderson and Wolf 1986). In turn, erotic involvements can become a less central feature of their everyday lives and personal identities. Thus, instead of stressing sexuality or sexual activity as important aspects of self, these individuals may place greater emphasis on other, nonsexual activities and involvements. In a related vein, as they reshape their sexual lives, they may draw upon redeeming "ideologies of illness" articulated by colleagues, caregivers, or self-help groups—ideologies which stress the new possibilities for self and intimacy that arise out of serious illness.

NOTES

[1] January of 1993, the Centers for Disease Control (CDC) broadened the classification of AIDS and added tuberculosis and bacterial pneumonia as opportunistic infections. The CDC also proposed that any HIV infected person with a T4-cell count under 200 should be categorized as having AIDS. Under these broadened definitions, 18 of the 25 men I interviewed had AIDS.

[2] All of the names used in this paper are pseudonyms.
[3] While few researchers have considered how serious illness affects sexuality, pertinent studies (Anderson and Wolf 1986; Anderson, Anderson, and deProsse 1989) indicate that men and women with genitourologic cancer and women with breast cancer experience sexual disruptions and dilemmas that resemble those encountered by the men I interviewed. These studies also suggest that the sexual issues and dilemmas provoked by various serious illnesses are not disease specific. For example, men and women suffering from urologic cancers and men suffering from advanced diabetes (Schiavi 1980; Unsain and Goodwin 1982) experience changes in their sexual functioning that evoke similar reactions, including diminished sexual interest, responsiveness, and activity.

REFERENCES

Anderson, Barbara, and Fredric Wolf. 1986. "Chronic Physical Illness and Sexual Behavior: Psychological Issues." *Journal of Consulting and Clinical Psychology* 54:168–175.

Anderson, Barbara, Barrie Anderson, and Charles deProsse. 1989. "Prospective Longitudinal Study of Women with Cancer: Sexual Functioning Outcomes." *Journal of Consulting and Clinical Psychology* 57:683–691.

Asher, Ramona. 1987. *Ambivalence, Moral Career, and Ideology: A Sociological Analysis of Women Married to Alcoholics.* Unpublished Ph.D. thesis, University of Minnesota.

Athens, Lonnie. 1995. "Dramatic Self-Change?" *Sociological Quarterly* 36:571–586.

Bell, A. 1982, June 29. "Where Gays Are Going." *The Village Voice*, p. 1.

Blumer, Herbert. 1969. *Symbolic Interactionism: Perspective and Method.* Englewood Cliffs, NJ: Prentice-Hall.

Bury, Michael. 1982. "Chronic Illness as Biographical Disruption." *Sociology of Health and Illness* 4:167–182.

Bury, Michael. 1991. "The Sociology of Chronic Illness: A Review of Research and Prospects." *Sociology of Health and Illness* 13:451–467.

Callen, Michael, and R. Berkowitz with R. Dworkin. 1982, November 8. "We Know Who We Are." *New York Native*, p. 2.

Charmaz, Kathy. 1983a. "Loss of Self: A Fundamental Form of Suffering in the Chronically Ill." *Sociology of Health and Illness* 5:168–195.

Charmaz, Kathy. 1983b. "The Grounded Theory Method: An Explication and Interpretation." Pp. 109–126 in *Contemporary Field Research,* edited by R.M. Emerson. Boston, MA: Little Brown.

Charmaz, Kathy. 1987. "Struggling for a Self: Identity Levels of the Chronically Ill." pp. 283–321 in *Research in the Sociology of Health Care,* vol. 6., edited by Julius Roth and Peter Conrad. Greenwich, CT: JAI Press.

Charmaz, Kathy. 1990. "'Discovering' Chronic Illness: Using Grounded Theory." *Social Science and Medicine* 30:1161–1172.

Charmaz, Kathy. 1991. *Good Days, Bad Days: The Self in Chronic Illness and Time.* New Brunswick, NJ: Rutgers University Press.

Charmaz, Kathy. 1994. "Identity Dilemmas of Chronically Ill Men." *Sociological Quarterly* 35:269–288.

Charmaz, Kathy. 1995. "The Body, Identity, and Self: Adapting to Impairment." *Sociological Quarterly* 36:657–680.

Connell, Roy W. 1987. *Gender and Power: Society, the Person, and Sexual Politics.* Stanford, CA: Stanford University Press.

Conrad, Peter. 1987. "The Experience of Illness: Recent and New Directions." pp. 1–31 in *Research In the Sociology of Health Care,* vol. 6., edited by Julius Roth and Peter Conrad. Greenwich, CT: JAI Press.

Corbin, Julia, and Anselm Strauss. 1987. "Accompaniments of Chronic Illness: Changes in Body, Self, Biography and Biographical Time." pp. 249–282 in *Research in the Sociology of Health Care,* vol. 6., edited by Julius Roth and Peter Conrad. Greenwich, CT: JAI Press.

Daly, Kevin, Carton Hogan, Darrel Hildebrant, Bill Kummer, and Perry Tilleras. 1990. "After Diagnosis: Sexuality, Intimacy, and Love." *PW Alive* 3(3): 1–2.

Davies, Peter, Ford C. I. Hickson, Peter Weatherburu, and Andrew J. Hunt. 1993. *Sex, Gay Men, and AIDS.* New York: Falmer Press.

Denzin, Norman. 1984. *On Understanding Emotion.* San Francisco, CA: Jossey-Bass.

Denzin, Norman. 1989. *Interpretive Interactionism.* Beverly Hills, CA.: Sage.

Frank, Arthur. 1991. *At the Will of the Body.* New York: Houghton-Mifflin.

Frank, Arthur. 1993. "The Rhetoric of Self-Change: Illness Experience as Narrative." *Sociological Quarterly* 34:39–52.

Glaser, Barney, and Anselm Strauss 1967. *The Discovery of Grounded Theory.* Chicago, IL: Aldine.

Goffman, Erving. 1961. *Asylums.* Garden City, NY: Anchor Books.

Goodstein, David. 1985, August 6. "Editorial." *The Advocate,* p. 3.

Harvey, Steve. 1982, December 21. "Defenseless: Learning to Live with AIDS." *The Village Voice,* p. 121.

Kotarba, Joseph. 1983. *Chronic Pain: Its Social Dimensions.* Beverly Hills, CA: Sage.

Kotarba, Joseph, and Norris Lang. 1986. "Gay Lifestyle Change and AIDS Preventive Health Care." pp. 127–143 in *The Social Dimensions of AIDS: Method and Theory,* edited by D. Feldman and T. Johnson. New York: Praeger.

Kramer, Larry. 1983, March 14. "1,112 and Counting." *The New York Native,* p. 1.

Lefton, Mark. 1984. "Chronic Disease and Applied Sociology: An Essay In Personalized Sociology." *Sociological Inquiry* 54:466–76.

Maines, David. 1983. "Time and Biography in Diabetic Experience." *Mid-American Review of Sociology* 8:103–117.

Patton, Cindy. 1990. *Inventing AIDS.* New York: Routledge Press.

Sandstrom, Kent. 1990. "Confronting Deadly Disease: The Drama of Identity Construction among Gay Men with AIDS." *Journal of Contemporary Ethnography* 19:271–294.

Sandstrom, Kent. 1994. *Confronting Deadly Disease: Challenges to Self Faced by Gay Men Living with HIV Disease.* Unpublished Ph.D. Thesis, University of Minnesota, Minneapolis, MN.

Schiavi, R.C. 1980. "Psychological Treatment of Erectile Disorders in Diabetic Patients." *Annals of Internal Medicine* 82:337–339.

Schneider, Joseph. 1988. "Disability as Moral Experience: Epilepsy and Self in Routine Relationships." *Journal of Social Issues* 44:63–78.

Schneider, Joseph, and Peter Conrad. 1980. "In the Closet with Illness: Epilepsy, Stigma Potential, and Information Control." *Social Problems* 28:32–44.

Schneider, Joseph, and Peter Conrad. 1983. Having Epilepsy: The Experience and Control of Illness. Philadelphia, PA: Temple University Press.

Seidman, Steven. 1992. *Embattled Eros: Sexual Politics and Ethics in Contemporary America.* New York: Routledge Press.

Strauss, Anselm. 1969. *Mirrors and Masks: Transformations of Identity.* New York: Macmillan.

Unsain, I. C., and M. H. Goodwin. 1982. "Effects on Sexual Function." pp. 214–233 in *Nursing Management of Diabetes,* 2nd ed., edited by D. N. Guthrie and R. A. Guthrie. St. Louis, MO: Mosby.

von Eschenbach, A. C., and D. Rodriquez. 1981. *Sexual Rehabilitation of the Urologic Cancer Patient.* Boston, MA: Hall.

Weitz, Rose. 1989. "Uncertainty and the Lives of Persons with AIDS." *Journal of Health and Social Behavior* 30: 270–281.

Weitz, Rose. 1991. *Life with AIDS.* New Brunswick, NJ: Rutgers University Press.

Williams, Gareth. 1984. "The Genesis of Chronic Illness: Narrative Reconstruction." *Sociology of Health and Illness* 6:175–200.

PART FIVE

SEXUALITIES: ORIENTATIONS AND RELATIONSHIPS

Among the most important human characteristics we have is our sexuality. Who we are sexually and how we relate to others of the same sex and the other sex(es) is a major aspect of our lives. At the same time, our understanding of the categories assigned to sexuality may not be deep or clear, nor may we have fully explored their meanings. Do the simple categorizations of straight, bisexual, and gay/lesbian adequately cover the range of human experience, particularly given what we know about the complexity of gender as discussed earlier in this book?

What does it mean to identify as "heterosexual"? Not all heterosexuals find a similar attraction, or have similar levels of attraction to women or to men. A person may identify as "straight" to herself and others around her, implying that she experiences no attraction to women. However, she might find herself romantically and sexually attracted to a woman, but not want to be with that woman in a genitally or orgasmically sexual way. Is this because of her orientation? Or does she censor or deny erotic feelings because she has been socialized "out" of seeing that as possible? Who is to judge?

Classification systems can be dangerous when thinking about sexuality (and other human experiences). Categories limit our ability to see, not the forest for the trees, but rather, the trees for the forest. We make assumptions that we "know" what it means to be heterosexual. As a result, we don't necessarily identify the limits and problems this presents for individuals and society. Heterosexuality, as it is constructed in our culture, relies on homophobia as a central organizing tenet. Homophobia can be described as a fear of those who are not—or are perceived not to be—heterosexual, or of nonheterosexual thoughts or feelings within oneself. Being straight means not being gay, just like being a male is about not being like a female. We have constructed these categories as binary opposites.

There is a variation in the way males and females look at sex-sex behavior. Price and Delecki (1998) found that college men in their study saw gay men as violating conventional gender behavior, or masculinity, whereas men see lesbians as violating conventional sexual behavior. In contrast, women saw both gay men and lesbians as violating conventional sexual behavior. The authors noted that gay men appear to be rejecting masculinity, and thus call into question the naturalness of heterosexuality, masculinity and men's power and privilege.

In the process of demonizing homosexuality, heterosexuality itself goes unquestioned. It is seldom problematized. We don't tend to associate *heterosexuals* with irresponsible sex, yet *those people* do a great deal of sexual "acting out," such as unprotected sexual intercourse (where do all those unintended pregnancies comes from anyway?) and sexual violence in the form of sexual harassment, assault, and rape. Males drinking and fighting to perform masculinity in front of others is part of heterosexualized behavior, as is females competing for males' attention through disordered eating, breast implants, and obsession with physical attractiveness. All of this is about sexual orientation.

As a society, we are more likely to scrutinize the sexual "other," the nonheterosexual or the not so easily classified, such as those who are transgendered. Heterosexuals see problems these *others* experience as due to *their* sexual or gender orientation, and then think they have a right to take a position in response, either affirming or discounting these orientations. Such responses, regardless of type, tend to give meaning to the categories themselves. We shape our position and follow up with actions (or inactions).

Societally, there has been little questioning of the meaning of heterosexuality itself. What are the parameters within which heterosexuality is contained? Does this identity apply only to what we "do" sexually, not what we dream about or feel? Do other feelings, thoughts, and even actions—the ones that don't fit with our sexual identity—just get denied, or reinterpreted, in order to avoid confusion?

For instance, men in prison who have sex with other men—particularly men who are the ones who penetrate their partners orally or anally—are unlikely to think they have had a homosexual experience and certainly don't consider themselves gay or bisexual. They have just had sex with another kind of girl—a sissy or pansy—or through domination have "lowered" another man to that level.

Categories do have a political meaning. People who identify as heterosexual (or who let that be the presumption) have access to sets of privileges and a legitimacy in society that results simply from not being "other." Homophobia is an organizing feature of hegemonic heterosexuality, wherein all institutions are arranged around the assumption, and valuing, of heterosexuality. We are rewarded for our unquestioned loyalty to its demands.

Heterosexuals find themselves in a world that is conveniently arranged for them, where flirting, public displays of affection, dating, and marriage are expected and supported. Heterosexuals' sense of privilege gives them a sense that they should be the ones to determine whether gays and lesbians should be allowed to marry, as if just being heterosexual were the only qualification needed to make a judgment on the topic. Moreover, heterosexuals are unlikely to think they need to be accountable to non-heterosexuals for how they handle their sexual orientation or relationships. Gays don't get to vote on whether straights get privileges.

The readings in this section focus on what it means to be "outside" the box of sexual expectations. Jerome E. Ng leads off the section with "Desire. Love. Sex. Friendship." A young writer from Singapore who is currently a student in the United States, Ng's reflections reveal intersections of identity based on ethnicity, gender, and sexuality. What reactions do the tenderness of his feelings evoke in you? If you are a woman who defines as heterosexual, do any of his experiences mirror yours? If you're male heterosexual, how do his thoughts about men feel to you?

Diane Richardson, in "Heterosexuality and Social Theory," raises questions about the notion of heterosexuality and its meaning, power, and place in society. She discusses ways heterosexuality serves to give order to our lives at the expense of our individuality and the differences in the range of sexual diversity. An example she cites is the linking of parenting to gendered differences constituted in a heterosexual relationship, which leads some people to ask questions such as how a child could have two daddies. Richardson also reviews the work of lesbian feminists who reject definitions of lesbian or gay identity derived from a patriarchal and heterosexual model of society. She notes the ways that queer theory, like earlier feminist theory, challenges the distinction between public and private—the social associated with the public and the sexual with the private. There is an emphasis, she says, on occupying space, both culturally and socially, with increased visibility as a stated goal of queer politics. It is about claiming safe space for public sexualities, challenging the "they're OK as long as they don't flaunt it" attitude, as well as teaching the dangers of gay bashing. She also discusses citizenship and ways that heterosexuality shapes Western social and political thought. What aspects of her thinking are most meaningful to you as you work to make sense for yourself of the ideas in this text?

Michael Messner interrogates the social construction of heterosexuality in sport. He describes his experiences in "Becoming 100 Percent Straight." Having noticed the frequency with which gay and lesbian athletes are studied, he decided to "study up" the social hierarchy, and began by reflecting on his own socialization into sport and its relation to sexuality. Surprising himself, he recalled a basketball teammate, Timmy, whom he had a "crush on" when they were both puberty-aged boys. These feelings later transformed into a direct and overt rejection of Timmy, who had became stigmatized and feminized by other team members. Messner draws on various theories to explicate his actions, including sociologist R. W. Connell's concept of an engagement with hegemonic masculinity, where he took up the male group's task of constructing heterosexual masculine identities in the context of sport. He contrasts his story with that of a long-closeted gay athlete, who portrayed a fiercely heterosexual masculine identity in order to hide what he saw as his true identity and the risks he faced if found out. Messner was not stepping into a closet, but rather, into the entire world of heterosexual privilege. In both cases, they were "doing heterosexuality." It was something they were performing, unrelated to sexual attractions or behaviors. What do you think of the idea of heterosexuality as performance? In what ways do you see examples of this around you?

In "Bi Any Other Name," Loraine Hutchins and Lani Kaahumanu discuss the ways that the very existence of bisexuals challenges the supposed immutability of people's orientations and the bipolar categories of gay and straight. As these authors say, bisexuality challenges other peoples' understanding of *themselves*. The authors critique studies of bisexuals, mostly by non-bisexuals, based on a monosexual framework, that invalidate bisexuals' existence or see them as deviant or just "in a stage." Hutchins and Kaahumanu define biphobia as the irrational fear of bisexuality in oneself or others and the distrust and discrimination practiced against bisexuals because of this fear. They maintain, as they report French writer Elizabeth Badinter argues, that men and women are growing increasingly alike and that the basic bisexuality in all of us will likely be increasingly revealed. Some people have seen sexuality as existing on a bell curve, with a small percentage of people at either end, either exclusively gay or straight, while most people are somewhere within the curve, with openness to same or other-sex attractions depending on their unique social and psychological history and circumstances. What do you think?

Sharon Kelly presents the category of "queer" as a new comprehensive self-definition embracing all sexual dissidents, beyond labels of straight, gay, or bi. Her article, "I Am a Queer Heterosexual," focuses on a political decision she has made about her sexuality. As a political act, Kelly reclaims the oppressive homophobic word and redefines it as an expression of pride. She cites examples of gay men labeled sissy-boys as children who are now questioning whether they accepted the label and trained themselves to deny attractions to women. They are not leaving their gay identity, but instead are seeking a larger range of possible relations. The queer "tent" is also large enough to include heterosexuals. Queer politics, according to a leader of the gay and lesbian group, OutRage, cited by Kelly, is helping create a society in which everyone feels free to relate to anyone else, without guilt or discrimination. To some, queer is a label they feel can follow them throughout whatever changes their fluid definition of self takes them. What does *queer* mean to you? As a tent, is it large enough to encompass lots of forms of sexuality?

Martin Rochlin's "Heterosexual Questionnaire" puts some of the defensive feelings of nonheterosexuals in perspective. It asks a series of questions paralleling those often asked of people who are gay and lesbian. "What do you think caused your heterosexuality?" "To whom have you disclosed your heterosexual tendencies? How did they react?" "Why do you insist on being so obvious . . . ? Can't you just be what you are and keep it quiet?" How does it feel to see such questions?

In "From Holiness to Wholeness: My Sexual Journey," Josiah Gromley describes his personal journey through the social quagmire of sexuality. He paints a picture of the power of the heterosexual expectations he experienced, especially as reinforced by religious institutions and counselors. His journey is not unlike that of many of us, regardless of sexual orientation, who are trying to figure out our sexual paths against the backdrop of misinformation, prejudice, and social pressure. What does his story tell you about the effects of social norms and institutions on young people who are questioning and exploring sexual identity?

Benjamin B. Herold reveals what he sees as his own homophobia. His article, "The *Straight*jacket of My Homophobia," is a chronicle of how homophobia affects him. He wrote this piece as part of a class he took as an undergraduate, where he discovered homophobia doesn't affect just people who define as gay. What does homophobia mean to you? How has it affected your life or those around you? What can you observe about the effects of homophobia in the everyday interactions between males you know? Between females?

The final offering in this section, "Sexualities in Community: Past and Present" takes us beyond how individuals organize their individual lives around sexuality and coupling relationships, to provide examples of how sexualities can be structured in an intentional way within a community, often with a spiritual intent. Lawrence Foster's report on sexuality and relationships in the 1800s in the Shaker, Oneida, and Mormon communities provides a snapshot of intentional communities that have challenged traditional norms in arranging sexuality among their members. Each of these communal religious experiments prescribed a radical restructuring of relations between men and women, varying from celibacy to polygamy to "group marriage." While Foster speaks historically, polygamy continues in some families that have split off from the Mormon church. Last year in a controversial action in Utah, a man was prosecuted for having several wives, and went to jail. Ironically, the women in this relationship were not prosecuted, a statement perhaps about the gendered nature of the law.

Today many intentional communities provide support for interdependent lifestyles involving a range of sexualities. Ivy Bresson describes the special supports that community can provide for people exploring nonmonogamy. The term *polyamorous,* for example, refers to people who are open to loving and being sexual with more than one person. While the Oneida, Mormon, and Shaker communities assumed the norm of heterosexuality, Bresson's experience has been in communities that are open to same-sex as well as heterosexual relationships. As well, Brother Johannes Renatus Zinzendorf reports on a community of gay men in rural Pennsylvania who seek a post-Christian relationship with the divine, wherein sex is seen as part of their spirituality.

In what ways do the ideologies and practices in these communities challenge traditional assumptions about monogamy as well as sexual orientations? What do you think about the role spirituality plays in these communities? As a sociology student, what connections do you see between personal choices and community norms?

REFERENCES

Price, J. & Dalecki, M.G. (1998). The social basis of homophobia: An empirical illustration. *Sociological Spectrum*, 18(2), p. 143.

Desire. Love. Sex. Friendship.

Jerome E. Ng

This is written as a poem of desire that draws on ethnicity, gender, sexuality, and the complexity of the intersections of identity by a young writer from Singapore, currently a university student in the United States.

DESIRE

dancing . . .
Zouk, Singapore, 1997.
My hometown.
I'm in the middle of the dance floor
The lights are flashing, the bass is pounding;
I'm sweating . . .
The melody fills my body.
I close my eyes and raise my hands to the
lights.
Her voice reaches a crescendo
and I pull in my outstretched arm.
I open my eyes and I see him.

Him. This beautiful man!
Trim, tan, athletic, defined, handsome,
oozing manhood . . .
My eyes locked on his every move.
He's dancing on the podium,
grinding his hips, caressing his shirtless body.
He's comfortable with his masculinity.
He knows he's hot. He knows
people are watching him.
But he pretends to move to his own music.

Liar!
Seductive liar. You know I can't have you.
You know that I can't even approach you.
You won't approach me.
I wish you were mine. Yet, can I go up to you?
Should I try? Can I try?

You glance at me.
You know that I won't approach you.
A tease. A cruel tease.

Alas, a girl-friend comes up to him.
They kiss.
They lock in an embrace.
They kiss again.
They leave . . .
an empty spot quickly filled by other hard-
pumping bodies, but none like him.

The Common Ground, a gay dance bar,
Ithaca, New York, USA, 1998.
I'm in the middle of the dance floor
The lights are flashing, the bass is pounding;
I'm sweating . . .
The melody fills my whole body.
I close my eyes and raise my hands to the
lights.
Her voice reaches a crescendo
and I pull in my outstretched arm.

A cool breeze rushes into the room.
I open my eyes and turn to the club entrance
and I see him.
A tall man with blonde hair. Moderately built
with strong sharp facial features.
A hunk. A Caucasian hunk.
Aren't they supposed to be the best lovers?
They know how to treat a boy like me.
I want a Caucasian lover.
I want the new arrival.

Look how he walks—tall and confident;
strong and proud . . .
He leans over the bar counter.
He turns and looks around the room.
Can you see me looking at you?
No, you can't. You don't even notice me.

Another man comes up to him.
This guy is just as big, just as tall.
Tight shirt, tight jeans.
I can't compete.
They shake hands. They talk. They laugh.
They walk away
into a corner where I can't see him anymore.

I don't get to see him for the rest of the night.
My caucasian dream . . .

you and me . . .
Why won't you approach those men?
What are you so afraid of?
You're not going to meet anyone
if you always wait
for someone else to approach you.
Do you think I don't know that?

Fear, I guess. I am afraid.
Of rejection.
Of humiliation.
Of not knowing what to do.
Of being known as gay in Singapore.
Of my parents finding out.

Even in Ithaca, halfway across the globe.
A strange situation, a strange feeling.
Living life in uncertain terms.
Am I going home after graduation?
Am I staying in the U.S.?
Can I fit in if I go home?

Living a possible future in the present.
Living the past into the present,
taking it into the future.

The confrontation still haunts me.
It's in the back of my head and controls my
every action.
It confines me.
It reminds me of home.

Don't ask me to come out to my parents.
Like it or not, believe it or not, we are different.
So, you came out to your parents after much
difficulty,
but you are in America,
I may dress like you, but I'm still an alien in
your nation.
I have to eventually go home.
What happens then?

We still believe that psychotherapy can treat
homosexuality.
A church on Commonwealth Avenue proclaims "Gays Can Change"

but gays cannot legally organize,
not even a forum.
My mum wanted to send me to deportment
class.
Like being gay is in the wrist!
My parents wanted to disown me.
Where do I go?
Are you willing to take responsibility
and face the consequences?

You are in America, in Europe.
You colonized us, you write about us, you
study us,
but you don't know us.
You have the economic and military might,
but you don't know us.
You sell us your culture, your information,
but you don't know us.

I've been in the U.S. for two years.
I've come out.
I've come to terms with myself: I like men!!!
I talk about my sexuality in classes.
But I'm still not like you. I can't be like you.
I am Asian and not American.
I don't know what it means to be gay.

being gay . . .
I asked Scott once, "What does it mean to be
gay?"
He replied, "It's a sexual preference.
It's being attracted to men.
It's who I am."
It was a comforting definition.
I like men.
Then why do I feel that I'm lacking
something?

All around me, I see men—
good-looking men, sexually attractive men.
I sneak a peek, but turn away the moment he
looks in my direction.
I don't lust for him.
I want to feel his arms around me.
I want to live life with him.
Can you imagine yourself growing with an-
other person?

Sharing your experiences . . .
Sharing your life.
Understanding, loving, caring . . .
growing.

What would it take to attract his attention?

It's different here in the U.S. I don't know
whether I'll ever get used to it.
Being gay . . .
being out, loud, and proud.
Going to the clubs, dressing up,
grinding those hips.
Screaming, laughing, talking—loudly
Building up the body, taking off the shirt,
parading in G-strings.
Announcing to the world,
"Yes, I'm here, I'm queer, and proud of it!"
There's an energy, a pulse.
It doesn't have to be this extreme,
but there's a lifestyle.
A way of being gay.
And I'm not used to it.

So, how do I attract him?

Desire.
A powerful force in our lives,
And it manifests itself in multiple ways.
Lustfully, physically, sexually, emotionally,
intellectually, spiritually.
You can desire food.
You can desire a shirt.
You can desire to be on a beach, away from
this Ithaca cold.
But right now, I desire a man.

They're all around—lovely men—but I can't
have them:
Joe, Scott, Dan, Phil, Chris
Jerry, Mark, Matt
Tom . . .
Either straight, attached, or spiritually
incompatible.

I wonder what other men think about me . . .
or if they do.
I have friends, but they're not my lovers
They're just friends.
I desire men,
but the men I desire don't desire me.

So I sit in a corner and watch from afar
The men I can't have and
savor my bittersweet desires
protecting my heart
From what?

Arrogance
Desire. Love. Sex. Friendship.
Each of us has experienced them.
They inform our lives.
They shape our future.
They seem like such a natural part of life.
Yet we are told how to desire,
how to love,
how to have sex,
how to befriend people.
Is there a right way and a wrong way?

These are my experiences.
They are unique to me.
They are who I am
as a man
as a gay man
as a chinese gay man
as a chinese gay man from Singapore.

Different desires.
Different loves.
Different sexual practices.
Different friendships.
One humanity.
One earth.

Desire. Love. Sex. Friendship.
Towards a united world.
Towards a world of peace, understanding,
and respect.

Heterosexuality and Social Theory

Diane Richardson

> . . . an understanding of virtually any as-
> pect of modern Western culture must be,
> not merely incomplete, but damaged in its
> central substance to the degree that it does
> not incorporate a critical analysis of mod-
> ern homo/heterosexual definition.
> —Sedgwick 1990

INTRODUCTION

Within social and political theory little attention has traditionally been given to theorising
heterosexuality. Although it is deeply embedded in accounts of social and political participation, and our understandings of ourselves
and the worlds we inhabit, heterosexuality is
rarely acknowledged or, even less likely, prob-
lematised. Instead, most of the conceptual
frameworks we use to theorise human relations relay implicitly upon a naturalised heterosexuality, where (hetero-)sexuality tends
either to be ignored in the analysis or is hidden
from view, being treated as an unquestioned
paradigm. Where sexuality is acknowledged
as a significant category for social analysis it
has been primarily in the context of theorising
the 'sexual other', defined in relation to a normative heterosexuality. Perhaps more surprisingly is the failure of a great deal of feminist
work, even when writing about the family,
to question a naturalised heterosexuality. Monique Wittig (1981) and Susan Cavin (1985),
for example have criticised feminist theories
which attempt to explain the origins of wom-
en's oppression for assuming the universality
and normality of heterosexuality.

More recently there have been significant
attempts by both feminists and proponents of
queer theory to interrogate the way that heterosexuality encodes and structures everyday
life, and to recognise the impact that ignoring
or excluding heterosexuality has had on the
development of social theory. In this chapter
and in those that follow we shall be exploring
and furthering these debates. Ultimately, this
requires not only a commitment to theorising
heterosexuality, but also a recognition of the
challenge posed by this new theorisation of
heterosexuality in so far as it invites a radical
rethinking of many of the concepts we use to
theorise social relations.

HETERONORMATIVITY

Heterosexuality is institutionalised as a particular form of practice and relationships, of family structure, and identity. It is constructed as a
coherent, natural, fixed and stable category; as
universal and monolithic. Despite being commonly represented in this way, there actually
exists a diversity of meanings and social
arrangements within the category 'heterosexuality', rather than a unitary heterosexual subject and a unified, distinct heterosexual
community. However, whereas there is a growing albeit largely North American literature
documenting how race, class and ethnicity in-
teracts with sexuality in the case of lesbians
and gay men (Moraga and Anzaldua 1981; Torton Beck 1982; Beam 1986; Ramos 1987; Roscoe
1988; Penelope 1994), there is, so far, relatively
little in the case of heterosexuality. Where there
is a substantial literature, it is on the interaction of heterosexuality and gender.

Heterosexuality is a category divided by
gender and which also depends for its meaning on gender divisions. For women it is an
identity defined primarily in relation to desire
for men and/or the social and economic privileges associated with being the partner of a
man, in particular the traditional roles of wife

and mother. How the construction of hetero-sexuality both privileges and disempowers women, and the relationship between hetero-sexuality and feminism, are important [issues]. The meanings of heterosexuality for men, and its interconnections with masculinity, are also [significant questions].

The experience of institutionalised hetero-sexuality is also informed by, and informs, constructions of race and class. Yet, as bell hooks (1989) has pointed out, there has been relatively little public discussion of the con-nections between race and sexuality. This is despite the fact that dominant discourses of sexuality refer primarily to a white, as well as male and heterosexual subject. That is, we tend to assume that '"whiteness" figures the normative center of political and theoretical discussions about sexuality and identity' (Goldsby 1993: 116). When black sexuality is represented in debates about sexuality, it is historically been as a form of hypersexuality. Most commonly, black women and men are portrayed as oversexed—as oversexed hetero-sexuals, that is. It is, moreover, a black espe-cially male heterosexuality that has been perceived as posing a threat to especially white womanhood (Harper 1993). By implica-tion the concepts lesbian and gay are also racialised, as race is (hetero-)sexualised. The image of a gay man and, perhaps to a lesser extent, a lesbian is characteristically white and, increasingly, middle class.

There is also a need to examine further the ways in which class position intersects with sexuality (see, for example, earlier work by d'Emilio 1984; Weeks 1986, 1990). This is true not only in terms of asking how might a per-son's class position affect the formation of sex-ual identities and practices, but also in terms of how notions of class are informed by the as-sumption of heterosexuality and how, conse-quently, our analysis of class may be changed by a questioning of this. Very often, in tradi-tional left discourse, the working class is not

only a masculinised but also, implicitly, a het-erosexualised concept. Thus, lesbian and gay political struggles have often been dismissed as bourgeois.

The privileging of heterosexual relations as the assumed bedrock of social relations with-out which, it is posited, society would no longer function nor exist, reinforces the idea that heterosexuality is the original blueprint for interpersonal relations. According to Michael Warner, following Wittig (1992), 'Western political thought has taken the het-erosexual couple to represent the principle of social union itself' (Warner 1993: xxi). This serves to delimit interpretations of both hetero-sexuality (as stable, necessary, universal) and the social (as naturalised heterosexuality). It also structures and organises understandings of individuals, as well as sexual and familial relationships, that are not included within the construction of the category 'heterosexual'.

In what is often described as the first major study of female homosexuality, Frank Caprio claims that:

> Many lesbian relationships between two women become the equivalent of a husband-wife rela-tionship. The mannish or overt lesbian likes to take on the role of the 'husband' and generally attaches herself to a female partner who is femi-nine in physique and personality. She regards her mate as her 'wife'. (Caprio 1945: 18)

The point is not that butch/femme relation-ships did not exist among lesbians in the 1950s, clearly they did (Nestle 1987), nor that lesbians did not incorporate into their lives meanings drawn from the model of the hetero-sexual married couple: rather, that this view is constituted as scientific truth. Of course a great deal has changed since Caprio wrote this, both in terms of lesbian and heterosexual lifestyles, and such crude characterisations of lesbian re-lationships as copycat 'marriages' are nowa-days relatively rare. However, this is not to say that heterosexuality has relinquished its hegemonic hold on conceptualisations of both the sexual and the intimate. For example recent debates about gay marriages and the right of lesbians and gay men to have legally recognised 'domestic partnerships' have overwhelmingly been framed in a political language of inclusion. In assimilating lesbians and gay men, the dominant discourse of understanding familial forms is hardly undermined. Another example of this is the linking of parenting to gendered difference constituted through a heterosexual relationship. Hence, the tendency to see lesbian and gay parenting as confusing: 'I can't help but wonder what a child would do whose parents are two males; are they both referred to as "Daddy"? Or does the child learn to refer to one of the mean as "Mom?"' (Grover, quotes in Weston 1993: 164). Behind such questions is the belief that if one man is the father, the only identity available to his partner is mother. Similarly, to ask of lesbian parents 'What will a child call the mother's lover?' seems to invoke the idea that there must be two distinct and differentiated parental roles rather than two mothers.

Related to this is the question of identity. As I have already indicated, historically lesbians have been portrayed as virtual men trapped in the space of women's bodies: 'mannish' in appearance and masculine in their thoughts, feelings, and desires, rendering their existence compatible with the logic of gender and heteronormativity. Although she is necessary to this logic, the complementary femme 'type' of lesbian is mentioned much less frequently in representations of lesbians in scientific discourses and popular culture—perhaps not unsurprisingly as she is more problematic.

In the 1970s, both lesbian feminist and gay liberation movements challenged dominant scientific constructions of homosexuals and women as oppressive, claiming the power to name for themselves through the political process of 'coming out'. One might caricature

this as a time of the politics of self-discovery and personal authenticity; a politics of the reformation of the self and an attempt at a new construction of both the female body and the homosexual body. The female body was constituted as no longer sexually passive and 'disciplined'/ordered; the homosexual body as no longer diseased and sexually dis-ordered; the lesbian body as no longer non-reproductive.

Lesbian feminists also critiqued heterosexuality as both an institution oppressive to women, and as practice. In doing so they rejected definitions of lesbian identity, desire and practice that were seen as derived from a patriarchal and heterosexual model of society. The establishment of new lesbian identities, such as lesbian feminist, radicalesbian, political lesbian and woman-identified woman, represented something new: an attempt at the establishment of a definition of lesbianism as a political alternative to, rather than derivative of, heterosexuality.

Viewed from the postmodern 1990s many writers now regard such struggles over lesbian (and gay) identity as just another example of 'identity politics', reinforcing an essentialism which does little to threaten the sexual *status quo* (Wiegman 1994). A new politics of identity, emphasising the fragmentation and fluidity of identity, has arisen in the 1990s, alongside new political movements such as, for example, ACT UP, Outrage, Lesbian Avengers and, in the United States, Queer Nation. In part, this owed something to the shift in the 1980s to a politics of difference, which within feminism was very much prompted by debates about race and class as much as sexuality. Related to this 'the lesbian subject' and 'the gay subject' were increasingly seen as untenable categories, as awareness of diversity and difference increased, aided by a new gay and, to a lesser extent, lesbian commercialism. The postmodern influence on social and political theory was also a key factor in encouraging the deconstruction of sexual and gender categories.

The term most often used to encapsulate this shift in the politics of identity is 'queer', which displaces the categories 'lesbian' and 'gay' *and* heterosexual. According to some writers, queer represents a form of sexual politics which sees 'the labels gay and lesbian as proscriptive, as having become as oppressive as heterosexuality in restrictiveness' (Woods 1995: 31).

The postmodern critique of earlier feminist and lesbian/gay thinking as essentialist and universalist is, I would argue, overly simplistic. The theoretical emphasis within gay liberation and feminism was on understanding sexuality as 'mediated by society, rather than as biologically given' (Segal 1994: 178). The notion of 'choice' featured strongly, especially in feminist accounts which, in many respects, represented a massive shift away from essentialist accounts of sexuality.[1] For example, long before queer theory was ever heard of, concepts such as political lesbianism (Leeds Revolutionary Feminist Group 1981), the woman-identified woman (Radicalesbians 1970) and the lesbian continuum (Rich 1980) challenged the heterosexual/homosexual binary, blurring the boundaries between straight and lesbian. Similarly, Adrienne Rich's (1980) groundbreaking work on 'compulsory heterosexuality', in highlighting the socially and economically constructed nature of heterosexuality, represented an early attempt to denaturalise heterosexual society, an aim which queer theory has more recently claimed.

Judith Butler's work (1990a, 1993a) represents a sophisticated postmodern attempt to theorise heterosexuality and its relationship to lesbian identity. Butler argues, as does Foucault, that we can never escape hegemonic discourses so that even a lesbian feminist identity is produced within hegemonic heterosexual norms. However, she goes on to argue that this is also true of heterosexuality. That is to say, far from being a natural expression of gender and sexuality, heterosexuality is always in the process of being produced. There is, in other words, no original of which homosexuality is an (inferior) copy. Heterosexuality is itself always in the process of being constructed, according to Butler, through repeated performances that imitate its own idealisations and norms and thereby produce the effect of being natural.

If our understandings of the structure of intimate relations is typically mediated through dominant heterosexual and gender norms, it is also the case that conceptualisations of desire and of 'sex' as a specific set of practices are similarly encoded. [. . .] Central to the theorisation of desire in 'sexual' relationships has been the notion of desire as desire for 'the other'. Typically, desire is conceptualised in terms of attraction to difference, where gender is the key marker of difference. Female sexuality has traditionally been defined as different from, yet complementary to, male sexuality. It is this difference, constructed as gendered power difference, that is assumed to be both natural and necessary to sexual arousal and pleasure. This approach suggests that desire is the 'province and the privilege of heterosexuals' (Fuss 1993: 63) or at least that to achieve desire one must identify with and mimic this reading of (heterosexual) desire. Historically, this is evident in theoretical constructions of sex between women as either involving role-playing, with one woman playing the part of the man and the other the part of the woman, or as primarily acts of affection and not really 'sex' at all (see Richardson 1992). Even within the feminist literature, where theorists might have been expected to take a different view, some writers have echoed this model in claiming that unless some kind of tension, difference, power discrepancy is introduced lesbians are unlikely to experience sexual desire. For example, lesbian feminist writer Margaret Nichols suggests that: 'Two women together, each primed to respond sexually only to a request from another, may rarely even experience desire, much less engage in sexual activity' (Nichols 1987: 103).

In this sense, homosexual desire—what Jeffreys (1994) has termed 'eroticised equality'—is not properly desire at all. The eroticisation of sameness is, in short, written out of the picture, as is the possibility of understanding difference, and its relation to desire, in terms other than gender. In this sense heterosexuality inscribes difference; it is a construction of 'otherness' in gendered terms. Clearly, as I have indicated, this has implications for our understanding of the desires of lesbians and gay men; but equally significantly it also shapes the ways in which heterosexual desires are constructed as relations between 'others' or even 'opposites'. [. . .]

Ideas about what is 'normal' and 'acceptable' sexual behaviour, indeed what is regarded as sexual practice, also reflect dominant constructions of sexuality as heterosexual (vaginal) intercourse. If we do not engage in such activity we are not recognised as sexual beings, we are still virgins even after a lifetime of 'foreplay'. Not only does this affect how forms of sexual activity are evaluated as sexually satisfying or arousing or even as counting as 'sex' at all, it also serves to 'discipline' the body (Bartky 1988), marking out the boundaries which represent our private and public zones,[2] and distinguishing the potentially sexual from the non-sexual bodily surfaces and actions.

For instance, both men and women have an anus. Yet the anus as a part of the sexualised body is predominantly encoded as a gay male body. This has led some to ask if the anus is a homologue of the vagina (Bersani 1987), allowing a heterosexualised understanding of penetrative sex between men which, at the same time, denies visibility to female anality and anal intercourse as a heterosexual practice. Indeed the very use of the terms heterosexual—meaning vaginal—intercourse and homosexual—meaning anal—intercourse are

revealing in this respect. Similarly, our understanding of bodies has been bounded within a 'heterosexual matrix', which operates through naturalising a heterosexual morphology (Butler 1993a). That is, heterosexuality depends on a view of differently gendered individuals who complement each other, right down to their bodies and body parts fitting together; like 'a lock and key' the penis and vagina are assumed to be a natural fit. What happens, then, when the lock or the key is missing?

As I have already indicated, lesbians have frequently been portrayed as masculine and feminine types who complement each other. In many accounts the lesbian body too is heterosexualised; for instance through the production of lesbian bodies with spectacular clitorises which can penetrate vaginas or in the characterisation of lesbians as 'boyish' with narrow hips and flat chests. The marking of lesbian bodies as non-procreative is another example of the lesbian body as only rudimentarily female. The conceptualisation of male homosexuals as feminised men with a particular body build and chemistry was also characteristic of early investigations of homosexuality. More recent work has focused on the idea that gay men have 'feminised brains' (see Byne 1995 for a critical review of studies). Another common assumption, which has not altogether disappeared (for a review of studies see Banks and Gartrell 1995), was that male homosexuals had reduced levels of testosterone compared to heterosexual men, resulting in the appearance of 'cross-sexed' physical characteristics such as wider hips, reduced hairiness and small-sized genitalia. In this sense dominant discourses of heterosexuality organise the physical and social space of our bodies.

At an individual level, this may have a significant influence on the way we experience our own bodies and those of others, discouraging us from engaging in certain kinds of bodily activities, whilst at the same time encouraging others. For instance, if a lesbian says 'If I do that I might as well go with a man', what might she mean? Her remark could be interpreted as an example of the depth to which certain conceptions of both the body and the sexual are heterosexualised (and the extent to which heterosexual and lesbian identities are bounded). Thus, certain activities may be seen by some as an imitation of heterosexuality rather than as authentically lesbian. Related to this, an alternative interpretation would be that this statement represents a rejection of heterosexual norms and/or a politicisation of certain activities as patriarchal practices. Sheila Jeffreys, for instance, believes that the emergence of the new lesbian sex industry, with porn videos, sex phone lines, and the marketing of 'sex toys' (but more especially dildos) institutionalises and commodifies the eroticised subordination of women and dominance of men (Jeffreys 1994).

Such inscriptions of the (sexual) body are highly contested. The increasing dominance of deconstructive, postmodern accounts in feminist theory, as well as in social theory more generally, has emphasised the unstable, fragmented nature of categories like heterosexual/homosexual, man/woman, masculine/feminine. In aiming to disrupt and denaturalise such conventional binary divisions, writers have foregrounded parody (as distinct from imitation) and the possibilities of 'playing with gender', in particular through butch, femme and drag.

One form this politics of signification has taken is in relation to the phallus. Traditionally the phallus is understood to symbolise masculine authority and through its assumed absence or lack it is argued that women are constituted as a subjugated class. In accepting this, various writers have argued that instead of rejecting phallic signifiers, as does Jeffreys and others, we should recognise that there is no escape from the phallus because in Western culture it is central to the culturally constructed meanings of gender and sexuality. Thus, it is suggested that 'reclaiming the phallus' is an important strategy for challenging ('displacing') current sexual and gender relations; a way of challenging male authority and thereby empowering women.

What does this mean in practice? Recent cultural productions of lesbian bodies by lesbians themselves have emphasised the postmodern lesbian body as phallic. It is claimed that the effect of appropriating the phallus, through packing/wearing dildos (or 'phallic body prostheses' as some would have it) is to expose the assumed linkage between the phallus and the penis as artificial (Butler 1993a; Griggers 1993). Also, as Judith Butler (1993a) has argued, if the penis is only one phallus and not *the* phallus then it does not 'belong' to men: women can have it too and in their own right, not as copycats. This denaturalisation of the penis as phallus, it is claimed, also undermines heterosexual as well as male power and privilege. Since the phallus as penis symbolises desire—hence lesbians get asked 'What do you do?' as when there is no penis it is assumed there can be no 'real' sex—the lesbian phallus, it is argued, is potentially disruptive and can show how the naturalisation of heterosexuality is imaginary.

Whilst I can follow the above argument, I would question its political significance. I am extremely sceptical of the extent to which 'parodic replication' of heterosexual constructs such as, for instance, understanding the 'lesbian cock', or chicks with dicks, as a parody of the phallus/penis, will challenge heterosexuality as a social institution. For, as Davina Cooper points out, 'not only does hegemony operate through exclusion, but also by making visible failed attempts to attain the status of the real' (Cooper 1995, though I would prefer to use 'real'). In other words, to suggest that we can effect social change through (queer) performances, however transgressive, provocative or challenging, would seem to assume, amongst other things, that such performances will have a revolutionary effect on (straight) audiences, rather than being interpreted as imitating and reproducing heterosexuality. (Paradoxically, the latter would suggest that the norms of heterosexuality are being constituted through such performances, thus confirming the effect of heterosexuality as natural.)

As Colleen Lamos remarks: 'Alas, the dildo-bedecked lesbian may be disappointed that her parody of the phallus is interpreted differently by others, especially by heterosexuals who take the dildo or butch/femme straight, so to speak' (Lamos 1994: 95).

Indeed, the possibilities of a queer reading would seem to be significantly constrained by the fact that historically the dominant (hetero) sexual discourse has positioned lesbians as butch or, to a much lesser extent, femme types who are, albeit in different ways, suffering from penile deprivation, thereby needing to use dildos as a 'penis substitute'.

There are, in any case, other considerations which go beyond the currently fashionable concern with subversive performance as political strategy and social method. Whilst this may indeed by valuable in highlighting some of the contradictory meanings embedded in discourses of gender and sexuality, and the socially constructed and potentially unstable nature of identities and practices, I would argue that we also need to ground this in the context of the material conditions of people's lives at local, national and global levels. If we are to develop social theory which can adequately theorise and challenge the ways in which our everyday lives are structured by heterosexual practices, within a variety of institutional domains such as families, religion, the economy and so forth, we require more than a queerying of the sexual. Much more significantly, we need to rethink the social.

SEXUAL/SOCIAL WORLDS

Having made the above comment, I immediately want to disown it. How can the sexual be separate from the social? What does it mean to attempt, as some have done, to theorise these as separate if related spheres? How, within social theory, are conceptual categories such as, for example, the private/public distinction, mediated through distinguishing the sexual from the social?

Part of the difficulty in discussing concepts such as 'society' and 'sexual', not to mention 'public' and 'private', is the tendency to assume that we each know what these concepts represent. Indeed, we very often use these concepts in a taken-for-granted way, as if their meanings were uncontested. Yet, as we shall see, it is clear that such concepts *are* contested; that there are different discourses which produce different understandings of 'the social' and 'the sexual' and their presumed relationship to each other.

According to some writers, the social realm is a relatively new phenomenon, 'whose origin coincided with the emergence of the modern age and which found its political form in the nation-state' (Arendt 1958: 28, quoted in Warner 1993). Similarly, the emergence of the sexual as a new theoretical object, as a distinct field of knowledge and experience, is also claimed to be a relatively recent historical and cultural production (Foucault 1981; Weeks 1985). As a result, the sexual and the social have been conceptualised as bounded, though interconnected, realms. Thus writers can theorise heterosexuality as sexual practices and as social practices (VanEvery 1995b); work on human identity can treat sexual and social identities as distinct; and theories of social and political change can explore questions of sexuality impacting on social relations or of the possibility of transforming sexual relations through social change (see Cooper 1995).

The problem of separating the sexual and the social, it seems to me, is how can we have a distinct sexual experience which is not interpreted and constructed through social meanings and interactions? The conventional approach sidesteps this by inventing the sexual as something individuals possess more or less independently of their involvement in the social. Nor am I satisfied by the view that, as Connell (1995) suggests, the social is already a part of the sexual domain, and vice versa, as this still seems to imply separate, if dynamically interconnected domains. Much as Butler and others (for example, Nicholson 1994) have argued in relation to the concepts sex and gender, I would argue of a much more sophisticated analysis which examines how the production of the sexual/social is achieved. If we accept that 'the sexual' is always seen through social interpretation, then the sexual is not something that can be separated from the social but is rather that which is produced by it; it is the social organisation of knowledge that establishes meanings for the sexual. However, even this is not enough, for it almost suggests a determinacy of the social as productive of the sexual, when the notion of the social is itself a complex construction. Although I do not have the space here, I intend to develop this analysis further in Richardson (forthcoming).

Most commonly, the relationship between the sexual and the social has been theorised in terms of a distinction between 'the public' and 'the private'. The 'social' realm, at least in Western contexts, is usually equated with 'issues affecting daily life . . . issues like equitable distribution of resources ("poverty"), the environment, and "lifestyle"' (Patton 1993:172). This has the effect of disassociating sexuality, conceptually at least, from many aspects of everyday life and relationships, a belief that it lies outside the sphere of political and economic, and therefore State, influence. [. . .] The sexual, by contrast, is generally associated with the individual, personal aspects of our lives, as well as with the idea of nature, more especially that sexuality is grounded in the body, in our individual, essential natures. Related to this is the belief in sexuality as the basis for human identity, prior to other cultural or social affiliations (Kotz 1993). In this sense, to examine the relationship between the sexual and the social is to raise questions about the relationship between human beings and nature; between the body and social membership; between the social and the natural—what was often referred to in the past as the nature/nurture debate.

What is often presupposed in this connection of the sexual with the natural is that the social sphere acts upon the sexual as a mediating or modifying influence; social institutions having the effect of both liberating and repressing different sexualities at different times. At the same time, the sexual is also conceptualised as outside of the social. It is, in this respect, constitutive of the social, rather than produced by it. Thus, as Diana Fuss comments, 'the natural provides the raw material and determinative starting point for the practices and laws of the social' (Fuss 1990: 3). In so far as this naturalised sexuality is interpreted as heterosexuality, albeit in particular forms of practice, it becomes a central and determining feature of our understanding of social life. The heterosexual couple are the raw material through which society may interpret and imagine itself.

To give a concrete example, in countries such as China, where due to the government's policies on population control there is a policy of one child per family, there is concern that reproductive technologies such as ultrasound and amniocentesis, followed by selective abortion, are currently being used to ensure that the only child is a son. As a result, new laws have been proposed to ban the use of such techniques to determine the sex of the foetus. The main concerns that have prompted this situation are the real and imagined social consequences of demographic change, as more males are being born than females. In particular, there is concern over the state of marriage, with fears that the growing number of single unmarried men within Chinese society will threaten the stability of marriages and lead to rising divorce figures. What this example and most other population control measures elsewhere demonstrate is the assumed natural, heterosexual basis of society. Society must reproduce itself as male and female in more or less equal amounts because heterosexuality, in its institutionalised form as marriage, requires one man for each woman, and vice versa. If we abandon that principle, and the assumption that social stability depends upon it, then there would be no obvious gender basis of society which needs to be regulated in this way by public policy.

If the social is interpreted through heterosexuality, it is also the case that understandings of heterosexuality are informed by definitions of the relationship between the sexual and the social. For example the (naturalised) split between the social and the sexual means that writers can divorce analyses of sexual practices and relations from those about social relations: such as, for instance, analyses of the 'family', the workplace, and domestic living arrangements. [. . .]

The construction of the sexual as relatively autonomous, occupying its own terrain, is also relevant to debates about heterosexuality and social change. One interpretation of this is that the sexual (here, heterosexuality) will not necessarily be transformed by changes in wider social relations. A less essentialist reading of the sexual/social split assumes a sexual which is to a greater or lesser extent modified by the social; thus allowing for the possibility that if society changed, then so might (hetero)sexualities. Campaigners on the 'moral right', for example, have argued for stronger controls over sexuality, such as restrictions on sex education and a ban on access to contraception for young people, as part of an attempt to restore and constrain heterosexuality to married monogamous relationships.

For some, including many on the 'moral right', the sexual/social relationship is also understood to be a two-way process, with a social mediated through the sexual. The latter would seem to assume a direct link between the social and the sexual, with sexual practices presumed capable of generating social change. In the case of the 'moral right' this might be envisaged in terms of sexual immorality in the form of, for example, 'promiscuity', adultery and prostitution leading to moral and social decay. The discourse of sexual liberation, on the other hand, has traditionally seen sexual freedom as a force for social change, as a means for achieving social freedom. More recently, albeit with a different, postmodern conceptualisation of sexuality, queer politics and sex radicalism has also claimed the power to disrupt the dominance of heterosexuality and the hegemony of particular desires and practices through 'transgressive' sexual practices such as butch/femme; S/M; and the (queer) use of dildos (see my earlier comments and Cooper 1995).

Many feminists in the early 1970s also saw a connection between the 'repression' of female sexuality and social powerlessness; believing that 'discovering' one's sexuality, largely conceptualised as heterosexuality, would empower women. With hindsight, many feminists have questioned this association and there has been considerable debate and argument between feminists over the relationship between sexuality and social change. In the context of heterosexuality the tension has primarily been around the extent to which sexual relations are determined by, or are determining of, other social relations. For some, especially radical feminists the main concern is not so much how women's sex lives are affected by gender inequalities but, more generally, how heterosexuality as it is currently institutionalised constrains women in most aspects of their lives. Here, then, the emphasis is primarily upon how the social is constructed and maintained as oppressive to women through the sexual realm, itself a construction, of course. For others, there is a much greater emphasis on how sexual relations are determined through inequalities in the social sphere, limiting personal pleasures (and pains) and desires. For example, Lynne Segal, in her book *Straight Sex: Rethinking the Politics of Pleasure* concluded by saying: 'Straight feminists, like gay men and lesbians, have everything to gain from asserting our non-coercive desire to fuck if, when, how and as we choose' (Segal 1994:318).[3]

The sexual/social distinction is also significant in the construction of boundaries between heterosexual/lesbian/gay. Or, to put it another way, the sexual/social split is also part of the means by which divisions between heterosexuals and sexual 'others' are produced. As I have suggested above, heterosexuality infuses the social realm; it represents the idea of normal behaviour which is central to the concept of the social and the process of socialisation into the social realm. Consequently, heterosexuality is defined primarily in terms of social identification, for instance identities such as 'wife'/'husband'; 'girlfriend'/'boyfriend'; 'mother'/'father' are rooted in heterosexuality. (Although, as feminist writers have pointed out, this is gendered: heterosexuality is more of a principal site of identity construction for women than it is for men; which is not to say that heterosexuality is unimportant in the production of conventional masculinities [. . .].)

Indeed, heterosexuality's naturalisation means that it is rarely acknowledged as a sexuality, as a sexual category or identification. By contrast, historically lesbians and gay men have been defined primarily as sexual beings, placed outside (the underworld) or at the margins (the twilight zone) of the normative boundaries of the social realm. As a result, homosexuality is defined primarily in terms of

sexual identification and very rarely are the social relations within which lesbians and gay men are embedded acknowledged. Once named as lesbians and gays we are at risk of the vast complexity of our lives—even our claim to a certain race, religion, ethnicity, nationality, or even in some cases humanity itself—disappearing under the dominant sexual marker; non-heterosexual. In this sense, the notion of the social/sexual split is a sexualised notion, establishing heterosexuals as a socially inscribed class and lesbians and gay men as a sexually inscribed grouping. It is also a gendered and racialised concept. Thus, for instance, the category 'gay man' is a more sexualised concept than 'lesbian'; as is black heterosexuality compared to white heterosexuality.

DEFINING PUBLIC AND PRIVATE BOUNDARIES

As I mentioned above, the relationship between the social and the sexual has often been understood in terms of the public/private distinction, itself a cultural construction, with the social associated with the public and the sexual with the private. Yet, this division can immediately be questioned: social relations occur in the domestic, increasingly private sphere; and there is public expression of sexual relations, what many refer to as a sexualisation of society. Similarly, feminist theory has critiqued this separation of the public and the private in ways that have illuminated understandings of, for example, women's position in the labour market, the sexual division of labour, as well as violence against women (Walby 1990). The claim that 'the personal is the political', a feminist catchphrase of the 1970s and 80s, also reflects the emphasis placed within feminism on disrupting the public/private binary. In this context, however, I wish to draw attention to the ways in which the private/public distinction serves to influence the process of the production of sexualities.

The association of sexuality with the private as distinct from the public sphere is institutionalised. In the UK, for example, it is part of the current legal constitution and the definition of the role of the State in individuals' lives. The Wolfenden Report (1957), which lead to the liberalisation of laws on prostitution in 1959 and male homosexuality in 1967, concluded that it was not the role of the law to interfere in the private lives of citizens, but rather it was the law's duty to preserve public order and decency. Issues like homosexuality and prostitution (and later pornography) were thus defined as matters of individual conscience, acceptable as private actions of the individual, as long as they did not encroach into the public arena. Thus, whilst homosexuality may have been defined as a matter for individual conscience, the 1967 changes to the law pertaining to sexual acts between men nevertheless maintained legal limitations that did not apply to heterosexuality on the grounds that 'homosexual' acts in public might cause offence to others. By implication, public decency and public order—indeed to the public sphere as it is defined in legal terms—is identified with heterosexuality.[4]

More recently, there has been a shift towards understanding the construction of public space in terms of modes of cultural production, as well as through social institutions such as the law. Once again there is an identification of the public sphere (as cultural space) with heterosexuality. To give a concrete example taken from a letter to the (liberal) British newspaper, the *Guardian*: "Why are homosexual/lesbian issues occupying so many column inches in your publication when these people form a minute sub-culture?" (29 July 1995).

These examples serve to highlight how heterosexuality, more especially within a married relationship, is normally granted both more privacy and more public recognition than other sexualities. In other words, not only can the public be understood as characterised by heterosexual norms, but so too can the private in so far as it is traditionally associated with domestic and (heterosexual) family life. Some have related this to the notion of a 'homosexual diaspora' (Mort 1994), crossing nation-states and linking lesbian and gay communities. However, I wonder whether this term is appropriate for the sense of cultural and spatial exclusion lesbians and gay men frequently experience. Rather than an original 'homeland' from which homosexuals were dispersed, I would argue that any sense of loss/exclusion is largely connected with the heterosexualisation of the private and the public, rather than a loss of country or nation-state. It is from the domestic homeland, their families, that lesbians and gay men are often estranged: 'Citizens who inhabit the same country may live worlds apart. Queer youth often feel homeless in their own homes even before some of them are thrown out onto the streets' (Tucker 1995: 25). Similarly, to become homosexual is to be *en route* from the public as well as the private. It may be that lesbians and gay men do not get told to 'get back from where you came from' on the grounds of their sexuality (although they may in so far as it intersects with their racial and ethnic identifications), but they can be told to get back to the private if they are seen as challenging the boundaries of public 'tolerance'.

The private/public distinction is, then, a sexualised notion: it has a different meaning depending on whether one is applying it to a heterosexual or homosexual context. For lesbians and gays the private has been institutionalised as the border of social tolerance, as the place where you are 'allowed' to live relatively safely as long as one does not attempt to occupy the public. In some instances that might even mean feeling comfortable about talking about lesbian or gay issues in one's own garden or backyard. For heterosexuals not only is the construction of private space likely to be very different, but the public is also likely to be a far less contested or constrained space than for most homosexuals. Although, once again, we need to relate this to race and gender; various forms of oppressive practice most notably racial and/or sexual violence also render the public a contested space and the private/public distinction a gendered and racialised construction.[5]

Much of feminist theory, as I have already mentioned, has focused on how the separation of the public and the private is a patriarchal construction (Nicholson 1984; Walby 1990). Queer theory has also challenged the public/private distinction within its more general critique of the heterosexual/homosexual binary and its resistance to a normalised and naturalised heterosexuality. There is an emphasis on occupying space, both culturally and socially; increased public visibility is one of the stated goals of queer politics. 'Our refusal to live in a closet is one way of "just saying no" to a world, a nation, and a regional culture intent on closing borders to those who are "different"' (Geltmaker 1992: 650).

Being queer is not about seeking the democratic right to privacy, the right to do what one wants in private, it is concerned with establishing safe space for public sexualities that are currently bounded by straight tolerance (for example: lesbians and gays are fine by me, just as long as they don't flaunt themselves)—or not as the case may be (most obviously lesbian and gay bashing). In the United States, for example, one of the stated aims of Queer Nation was to expose the straightness of public spaces and to 'reterritorialise' them (Berlant and Freeman 1993). In this sense queer shares with certain strands of feminism a concern to 'reterritorialise' public space and, in so doing, disrupt the ways in which certain issues as well as subjects (woman/man; heterosexual/homosexual) are constituted in the public or the private sphere.[6]

In the following section I want to relate this discussion to the concept of citizenship, which has often been defined in terms of the right to privacy, the right to private acts and private opinions if not always public identities.

CITIZENSHIP

'Citizenship may be defined as that set of practices (juridical, political, economic and cultural) which define a person as a competent member of society, and which as a consequence shape the flow of resources to persons and social groups' (Turner 1993: 2).

Although we increasingly hear talk about citizenship, whether treating it as a set of civil, political and social rights (Marshall 1977) or, as above, using the concept in the broader sense, as a set of socially and culturally specific practices which define the nature of social membership (Turner 1993), it is important to recognise that it is a contested concept. That is to say that, in addition to its contested meaning, 'all attempts to clarify the concept of citizenship . . . are themselves a part of practical politics' (Shotter 1993: 115).

So far, the tradition of thinking behind the idea of citizenship, which has become a key concept of modern social theory, has given insufficient attention to either gender or sexuality (for a discussion see Lister 1990; Evans 1993; Walby 1994). For example, in *Citizenship and Social Theory*, although passing reference is made to the fact that many of the new issues of citizenship 'appear to centre around gender politics'; and that 'interesting and radical developments appear to be centred around . . . the struggle for homosexual rights' (Turner 1993: 13), none of the contributors elucidate how the study of such social movements might change notions of citizenship and, more significantly, its presumed relation to social theory.[7]

There is therefore a need to broaden the analysis of citizenship to include debates around sexuality and, still, gender. All the more so given that, as David Evans points out in his introduction to *Sexual Citizenship*:

> The history of citizenship is a history of fundamental formal heterosexist patriarchal principles and practices ostensibly progressively 'liberalised' towards and through the rhetoric of 'equality' but in practice to effect unequal differentiation. (Evans 1993: 9)

This is to imply that claims to citizenship status, at least in the West, are closely associated with the institutionalisation of heterosexual as well as male privilege. That this is the case is made abundantly clear when the association of heterosexuality with a certain form of citizenship status is threatened or challenged. If we take citizenship to mean national identity, for example, it would appear that in many if not most nation-states this form of citizenship is equated with naturalised heterosexuality. For example, a representative of the Romanian Ministry of Justice (Cojocaru Octavian) speaking at the CEPES-UNESCO conference in Bucharest on "Homosexuality: A Human Right?' (31 May 1995) declared: 'the nature of the Romanian does not admit this prose of unnatural law [homosexuality], this immorality'.

Although the State may act to construct the nation as heterosexual,[8] this does not necessarily mean that all forms of heterosexuality are regarded equally. It is heterosexuality as marriage and 'the family' which is associated with the nation and, moreover, seen as necessary for ensuring its survival, its strength and well-being. By implication, it would seem that other forms of heterosexuality, for instance young women who are single mothers, imperil the nation. The association of heterosexuality and nation also intersects with race; it is a white heterosexuality which has historically been privileged, with black heterosexual relationships invoked as a supposed threat to the nation (Williams 1989).

Related to this, it would seem that very often nationality is not merely connected to being heterosexual, but also to a heterosexuality that is markedly anti-lesbian and anti-gay.[9] Speaking of nationalisms in the United States, Henry Louis Gates Jr. claims that 'national identity became sexualized in the 1960s, in such a way as to engender a curious subterraneous connection between homophobia and nationalism' (Gates 1993: 234). Similarly, in the UK homosexuality, but more especially homosexual family relationships, has been perceived as a threat to the nation-state (Reinhold 1994). Thus, for example, David Wiltshire (the member of Parliament responsible for introducing the anti-homosexual section 28 of the Local Government Act 1988) justified the need to oppose homosexuality: 'My actions were motivated wholly by the principle of supporting normality. . . . Homosexuality is being promoted at the ratepayers' expense, and the traditional family as we know it is under attack' (*Guardian,* 12 December 1987).

The exclusion of lesbians and gay men from the meaning of 'family', thus reinscribing it as a heterosexualised concept, is evidenced in the government's definition of homosexuality as a 'pretended family relationship' in section 28. The discussion around section 28 also raised other issues of citizenship and its relationship to heterosexuality, where citizenship can be interpreted as social rights expressed through social policy. Although the linking of social rights to welfare policy has been critiqued by feminists and others, it is nevertheless important to recognise the suggestion in what David Wiltshire and others were arguing in support of section 28: not only are lesbians and gay men presumably not ratepayers, but that they are not deserving of social services funded by local authorities. [. . .]

Definitions of citizenship as national identity have been brought into question in recent years as a result of social and political changes which have challenged traditional boundaries of nation-states, in particular the process of 'globalisation'. In part, this has encouraged discussion of whether citizenship might develop within the context of larger forms of social membership than nation-sates, such as humanity itself. If we take citizenship to mean human identity, belonging to what is called the human race, even then it is still possible to argue that citizenship continues to be premised within heterosexuality.

A documentary shown on British television, entitled *Better Dead Than Gay*, described how a young man killed himself because he couldn't reconcile his Christian beliefs with the fact that he was gay. In an interview, his father stated that learning his son was gay was as bad as losing him (*Guardian*, 26 July 1995).

The assumption that heterosexuality and humanity are synonymous, that being human is being straight, is reflected in those who would question the right to life of lesbians and gay men. In some parts of the world such views are institutionalised through laws which recommend the death penalty for homosexuality; in countries where homosexuality is legally 'tolerated', violent attacks on lesbians and gay men have led to killings (for example killings in Plymouth reported in the *Guardian*, 9 November 1995).

More recently, there has been a shift towards defining citizenship in terms of consumerism. It is in this framework that non-heterosexuals seem to be most acceptable as citizens, as consumers with identities and lifestyles which are expressed through purchasing the appropriate products. The awareness of the commercial 'power' of lesbians and gay men is seen by some as important in promoting other forms of citizenship, such as the development of social rights and entitlements. As David Evans states:

> Sexual minorities have progressively become distinct, formal though not necessarily formally

clear, participants within the citizenship of developed capitalism, whilst simultaneously becoming, not surprisingly for of course the two are closely connected, legitimate consumers of sexual and sexualized commodities marketed specifically for their use and enjoyment. (Evans 1993: 2)

For others, however, the impact of the increasing commercialisation and commodification of homosexuality is viewed much more critically, not to say cynically (Woods 1995).

Finally, what if we were to regard citizenship as a set of social practices which 'define social membership in a society which is highly differentiated both in its culture and social institutions, and where social solidarity can only be based upon general and universalistic standards' (Turner 1993: 5)? This raises the question of the power of heterosexuality, conceptualised as universal, natural and normal, as a unifying principle; a means of achieving social solidarity among differentiated groups.

Certainly, implicit in the right to many forms of (public) social membership based on ethnic, religious and racial identifications is a presumed heterosexuality. To give two concrete examples:

> Last month Brian Gordon, a member of the Board of Jewish Deputies, attacked a fellow member for addressing the World Congress of Gay and Lesbian Jewish Organisations in Brussels: 'Their [gays and lesbians] activities have no more legitimacy under a Jewish banner than, say, pork-eating.' (*Guardian*, 8 July 1995: 7)

In 1995 the organisers of the annual Irish Day Parade in Boston successfully sought a court order banning Irish/American lesbians and gay men from marching in the parade. Similarly, writing about the (hetero-)sexualization of black identities Goldsby claims that:

> This ideology [of American slavery] privileged and enforced heterosexuality as authentically 'black' because the regulation of black reproductive rights demanded this definition. . . . No

wonder, then, that black homophobes characteristically malign homosexuality as a 'white thing', as a relationship that, by definition, re-enacts slavery itself. (Goldsby 1993: 122–3)

What these examples and the various forms of citizenship I have examined serve to illustrate is the significance of heterosexuality for shaping Western social and political thought, in ways that dramatically affect all of our lives.

NOTES

1. It is possible, though, to identify a certain essentialism in feminist thinking about sexuality in the early years of the women's liberation movement, in the emphasis on 'discovering' or 'reclaiming' an authentic female sexuality which had been denied women.
2. The use of the term 'privates' to refer to the genitalia is a useful example of such bodily zoning.
3. I do not have the space here to develop the analysis of the ways in which different feminist writers have theorised the sexual/social, but would merely point out that insufficient attention has been given exploring this aspect of feminist thinking on sexuality.
4. There are, of course, parallels and interrelationships with the identification of public space as heterosexualised and feminism's identification and critique of the construction of the public sphere as masculine and the private sphere as feminine.
5. In some cases, the private may also be a site of violence, as is evidenced, for example, by attacks on gay and black people's homes.
6. For example, one might make some interesting comparisons between feminist actions such as Take Back the Night campaigns and, in the United States, Queer Nation's shopping mall 'visibility actions', whose aim is to challenge the heterosexualised family environment of shopping malls through public performances of being 'lesbian' and 'gay'.
7. Ken Plummer (1995b) makes a similar point in discussing the way in which social theorists have ignored and/or marginalised sociological

work on lesbian and gay lives, highlighting 'mainstream texts' on the study of social movements and the study of identities as classic examples. What determines the right, for example, to lesbian citizenship? Are lesbians who have relationships with men 'hasbians', as some have suggested? (see Stein 1993). How does raising questions such as these inform notions of citizenship and social theory?
8. I acknowledge that there are different 'nationalisms', for example, cultural, economic, political, but do not have the space here to elaborate on how these different aspects of nationality may be differently theorised in relation to sexuality.
9. Political contestation of (American) nationality has been apparent within feminism and, more recently, queer politics. Lesbian Nation (Johnson 1973) Bitch Nation (quoted in Berlant and Freeman 1993) and Queer Nation (Berube and Escoffier, and other articles in *Out/Look* 1991) suggested a new nationality.

REFERENCES

Arendt, H. (1958) *The Human Condition.* Chicago: University of Chicago Press.

Banks, A. and Gartrell, N.K. (1995) Hormones and sexual orientation: a questionable link, *Journal of Homosexuality,* 28(3/4): 247–68.

Bartky, S. (1988) Foucault, femininity, and the modernization of patriarchial power, in I. Diamond and L. Quinby (eds) *Feminism and Foucault: Reflections on Resistance.* Boston, MA: Northeastern University Press.

Beam, J. (ed.) (1986) *In the Life: a Black Gay Anthology.* Boston, MA: Alyson Publications.

Berlant, L. and Freeman, E. (1993) Queer nationality, in M. Warner (ed.) *Fear of a Queer Planet: Queer Politics and Social Theory.* Minneapolis: United States of Minnesota Press.

Bersani, L. (1987) Is the rectum a grave? *October,* 43, winter: 217.

Berube, A. and Escoffier, J. (1991) Queer/Nation, *Out/Look: National Lesbian and Gay Quarterly,* 11:13–15.

Butler, J. (1990a) *Gender Trouble: Feminism and the Subversion of Identity.* New York: Routledge.

Butler, J. (1993a) *Bodies that Matter: on the Discursive Limits of 'Sex'*, London: Routledge.

Butler, J. (1993b) Critically queer, *GLQ: a Journal of Lesbian and Gay Studies*, 1(1): 17–32.

Byne, W. (1995) Science and belief: psychobiological research on sexual orientation, *Journal of Homosexuality*, 28(3/4): 303–44.

Caprio, F. (1954) *Female Homosexuality: a Psychodynamic Study of Lesbianism*, New York: Citadel Press.

Cavin, S. (1985) *Lesbian Origins*. San Francisco: ism Press.

Connell, R.W. (1995) *Masculinities: Knowledge, Power and Social Change*. Cambridge: Polity Press.

Cooper, D. (1995) *Power in Struggle: Feminism, Sexuality and the State*. Buckingham: Open University Press.

d'Emilio, J. (1984) Capitalism and gay identity, in A. Snitow, C. Stansell and S. Thompson (eds) *Desire: the Politics of Sexuality*. London: Virago.

Evans, D.T. (1993) *Sexual Citizenship: the Material Construction of Sexualities*. London: Routledge.

Foucault, M. (1981) *The History of Sexuality: Vol. 1*. Harmondsworth: Pelican Books.

Fuss, D. (1990) *Essentially Speaking: Feminism, Nature and Difference*. London: Routledge.

Fuss, D. (1993) Freud's fallen women: identification, desire and 'A case of homosexuality in a woman', in M. Warner (ed.) *Fear of a Queer Planet: Queer Politics and Social Theory*. Minneapolis: University of Minnesota Press.

Gates, H.L. Jr. (1993) The black man's burden, in M. Warner (ed.) *Fear of a Queer Planet: Queer Politics and Social Theory*. Minneapolis: University of Minnesota Press.

Geltmaker, T. (1992) The queer nation acts up: health care, politics, and sexual diversity in the county of angels, *Environment and Planning D: Society and Space*, 10: 609–50.

Goldsby, J. (1993) Queen for 307 days: looking b(l)ack at Vanessa Williams and the sex wars, in A. Stein (ed.) *Sisters, Sexperts, Queers: Beyond the Lesbian Nation*. New York: Plume.

Griggers, C. (1993) Lesbian bodies in the age of (post)mechanical reproduction, in L. Doan (ed.) *The Lesbian Postmodern*. New York: Columbia University Press.

Harper, P.B. (1993) Eloquence and epitaph: black nationalism and the homophobic impulse in responses to the death of Max Robinson, in M. Warner (ed.) *Fear of a Queer Planet: Queer Politics and Social Theory*. Minneapolis: University of Minnesota Press.

hooks, b. (1989) *Talking Back: Thinking Feminist-Thinking Black*. London: Sheba.

Jeffreys, S. (1994) *The Lesbian Heresy: a Feminist Perspective on the Lesbian Sexual Revolution*. London: The Women's Press.

Jeffreys, S. (1996) *Theorizing Heterosexuality*. Buckingham: Open University Press.

Johnson, J. (1973) *Lesbian Nation: The Feminist Solution*. New York: Touchstone.

Kotz, L. (1993) Anything But Idyllic: Lesbian Filmmaking In The 1980s And 1990s, in A. Stein (ed.) *Sisters, Sexperts, Queers: Beyond the Lesbian Nation*. New York: Plume.

Lamos, C. (1994) The postmodern lesbian position: on our backs, in L. Doan (ed.) *The Lesbian Postmodern*. New York: Columbia University Press.

Leeds Revolutionary Feminist Group (1981) Political lesbianism: the case against heterosexuality', reprinted in Onlywomen Press (eds) (1981) *Love Your Enemy? The Debate Between Heterosexual Feminism and Political Lesbianism*. London: Onlywomen Press.

Lister, R. (1990) Women, economic dependency and citizenship, *Journal of Social Policy*, 19(4): 445–68.

Marshall, T. H. (1977) *Class, Citizenship and Social Development*. Chicago: University of Chicago Press.

Moraga, C. and Anzaldua, G. (eds) (1981) *This Bridge Called My Back: Writings By Radical Women of Color*. Watertown, MA: Persephone Press.

Mort, F. (1994) Essentialism revisited? Identity politics and late twentieth-century discourses of homosexuality, in J. Weeks (ed.) *The Lesser Evil and the Greater Good: the Theory and Politics of Social Diversity*. London: Rivers Oram Press.

Nestle, J. (1987) *A Restricted Country*. London: Sheba.

Nichols, M. (1987) Lesbian sexuality: issues and developing theory, in Boston Lesbian Psychologies Collective (eds) *Lesbian Psychologies*. Chicago: University of Illinois Press.

Nicholson, L. J. (1984) Feminist theory: the private and the public, in C.C. Gould (ed.) *Beyond Domination: New Perspectives on Women and Philosophy*. Lanham, MD, USA: Rowman and Littlefield.

Nicholson, L. (1994) Interpreting gender, *Signs: Journal of Women in Culture and Society,* 20(11): 79–105.

Patton, C. (1993) 'Tremble, hetero swine!', in M. Warner (ed.) *Fear of a Queer Planet: Queer Politics and Social Theory.* Minneapolis: University of Minnesota Press.

Penelope, J. (ed.) (1994) *Out of the Class Closet: Lesbians Speak,* Freedom, CA: The Crossing Press.

Plummer, K. (1995a) Sociology under the sign of homosexuality. Paper presented at 'The Future of Lesbian and Gay Studies' conference, Homostudies Department, University of Utrecht, Netherlands, 3–5 July.

Plummer, K. (1995b) *Telling Sexual Stories: Power, Change and Social Worlds.* London: Routledge.

Radicalesbians (1970) The woman-identified woman, in A. Koedt, E. Levine and A. Rapone (eds) *Radical Feminism.* New York: Quadrangle Books.

Ramos, J. (ed.) (1987) *Compañeras: Latina Lesbians: an anthology.* New York: Latina Lesbian History Project.

Reinhold, S. (1994) Through the parliamentary looking glass: 'real' and 'pretend' families in contemporary British politics, *Feminist Review,* 48: 61–79.

Rich, A. (1980) Compulsory heterosexuality and lesbian existence, *Signs,* 5(4): 631–60.

Richardson, D. (1992) Constructing lesbian sexualities, in K. Plummer (ed.) *Modern Homosexualities.* London: Routledge.

Richardson, D. (forthcoming) Social Theory, Social Change and Sexuality. London: Routledge.

Roscoe, W. (ed.) (1988) *Living the Spirit: a Gay American Indian Anthology.* NY, USA: St. Martin's Press.

Segal, L. (1994) *Straight Sex: the Politics of Pleasure.* London: Virago.

Shotter, J. (1993) Psychology and citizenship: identity and belonging, in B.S. Turner (ed.) *Citizenship and Social Theory.* London: Sage.

Stein, A. (ed.) (1993) *Sisters, Sexperts, Queers: Beyond the Lesbian Nation.* New York: Plume.

Torton Beck, E. (ed.) (1982) *Nice Jewish Girls: a Lesbian Anthology.* Boston, MA: Beacon Press.

Tucker S. (1995) *Fighting Words: An Open Letter to Queers and Radicals.* London: Cassell.

Turner, B.S. (1993) *Citizenship and Social Theory.* London: Sage.

VanEvery, J. (1995b) Heterosexuality, heterosex and heterosexual privilege, *Feminism and Psychology,* 5(1): 140–4

Walby, S. (1990) *Theorizing Patriarchy.* Oxford: Blackwell.

Walby, S. (1994) Is Citizenship Gendered?, *Sociology,* 28(2): 379–95.

Warner, M. (ed.) (1993) *Fear of a Queer Planet: Queer Politics and Social Theory.* Minneapolis: University of Minnesota Press.

Weeks, J. (1985) *Sexuality and its Discontents,* London: Routledge and Kegan Paul.

Weeks, J. (1986) *Sexuality.* London: Ellis Horwood/Tavistock Publications.

Weeks, J. (1990) *Sex, Politics and Society* (2nd edition). London: Longman.

Weston, K. (1993) Parenting in the age of AIDS, in A. Stein (ed.) *Sisters, Sexperts, Queers: Beyond the Lesbian Nation.* New York: Plume.

Wiegman, R. (1994) Introduction: mapping the lesbian postmodern, in L. Doan (ed.) *The Lesbian Postmodern.* New York: Columbia University Press.

Williams, F. (1989) *Social Policy: A Critical Introduction.* Cambridge: Polity Press.

Wittig, M. (1981) One is not born woman, *Feminist Issues,* 1(2): 47–54.

Wittig, M. (1992) *The Straight Mind and Other Essays.* Brighton: Harvester Wheatsheaf.

Wolfenden Report (1957) *Report of the Committee on Homosexual Offences and Prostitution.* London: HMSO.

Woods, C. (1995) *State of the Queer Nation: A Critique of Gay and Lesbian Politics in 1990s Britain.* London: Cassell.

Becoming 100 Percent Straight

Michael A. Messner

In 1995, as part of my job as the President of the North American Society for the Sociology of Sport, I needed to prepare an hour-long presidential address for the annual meeting of some 200 people. This presented a challenge to me: how might I say something to my colleagues that was interesting, at least somewhat original, and above all, not boring. Students may think that their professors are especially dull in the classroom but, believe me, we are usually much worse at professional meetings. For some reason, many of us who are able to speak to our classroom students in a relaxed manner, using relatively jargon-free language, seem to become robots, dryly reading our papers—packed with impressively unclear jargon—to our yawning colleagues.

Since I desperately wanted to avoid putting 200 sport studies scholars to sleep, I decided to deliver a talk which I entitled "Studying up on sex." The title, which certainly did get my colleagues' attention, was intended as a play on words, a double entendre. "Studying up" has one generally recognizable colloquial meaning, but in sociology it has another. It refers to studying "up" in the power structure. Sociologists have perhaps most often studied "down"—studying the poor, the blue- or pink-collar workers, the "nuts, sluts and perverts," the incarcerated. The idea of "studying up" rarely occurs to sociologists unless and until we live in a time when those who are "down" have organized movements that challenge the institutional privileges of elites. For example,

in the wake of labor movements, some sociologists like C. Wright Mills studied up on corporate elites. Recently, in the wake of racial and ethnic civil rights movements, some scholars like Ruth Frankenberg have begun to study the social meanings of "whiteness." Much of my research, inspired by feminism, has involved a studying up on the social construction of masculinity in sport. Studying up, in these cases, has raised some fascinating new and important questions about the workings of power in society.

However, I realized that when it comes to understanding the social and interpersonal dynamics of sexual orientation in sport we have barely begun to scratch the surface of a very complex issue. Although sport studies have benefited from the work of scholars such as Helen Lenskyj (1986, 1997), Brian Pronger (1990) and others who have delineated the experiences of lesbians and gay men in sports, there has been very little extension of their insights into a consideration of the social construction of heterosexuality in sport. In sport, just as in the larger society, we seem obsessed with asking "how do people become gay?" Imbedded in this question is the assumption that people who identify as heterosexual, or "straight," require no explanation, since they are simply acting out the "natural" or "normal" sexual orientation. We seem to be saying that the "sexual deviants" require explanation, while the experience of heterosexuals, because we are considered normal, seems to require no critical examination or discussion. But I knew that a closer look at the development of sexual orientation or sexual identity reveals an extremely complex process. I decided to challenge myself and my colleagues by arguing that although we have begun to "study up" on corporate elites in sport, on whiteness, on masculinity, it is now time to extend that by studying up on heterosexuality.

But in the absence of systematic research on this topic, where could I start? How could I explore, raise questions about, and begin to illuminate the social construction of heterosexuality for my colleagues? Fortunately, for the previous two years I had been working with a group of five men (three of whom identified as heterosexual, two as gay) mutually to explore our own biographies in terms of the earlier bodily experiences that helped to shape our gender and sexual identities. We modeled our project after that of a German group of feminist women, led by Frigga Haug, who created a research method which they call "memory work." In short, the women would mutually choose a body part, such as "hair," and each would then write a short story based on a particularly salient memory that related to their hair (for, example, being forced by parents to cut one's hair, deciding to straighten one's curly hair in order to look more like other girls, etc.). Then the group would read all of the stories and discuss them one by one in the hope of gaining a more general understanding of, and raising new questions about, the social construction of "femininity." What resulted from this project was a fascinating book called *Female Sexualization* (Haug 1987), which my men's group used as the inspiration for our project.

As a research method, memory work is anything but conventional. Many sociologists would argue that this is not really a "research method" at all. The information that emerges from the project cannot be used very confidently as a generalizable "truth," and in this sort of project the researcher is simultaneously part of what is being studied. How, my more scientifically oriented colleagues might ask, is the researcher to maintain his or her objectivity? My answer is that in this kind of project objectivity is not the point. In fact, the strength of this sort of research is the depth of understanding that might be gained through a systematic group analysis of one's experience, one's subjective orientation to social processes. A clear understanding of the subjective aspect of social life—one's bodily feelings, emotions, and reactions to others—is an invaluable window that allows us to see and ask new sociological questions about group interaction and social structure. In short, group memory work can provide an important, productive, and fascinating insight on social reality, though not a complete (or completely reliable) picture.

As I pondered the lack of existing research on the social construction of heterosexuality in sport, I decided to draw on one of my own stories from my memory work in the men's group. Some of my most salient memories of embodiment are sports memories. I grew up as the son of a high school coach, and I eventually played point guard on my dad's team. In what follows, I juxtapose my story with that of a gay former Olympic athlete, Tom Waddell, whom I had interviewed several years earlier for a book on the lives of male athletes (Messner and Sabo 1994).

Many years ago I read some psychological studies that argued that even for self-identified heterosexuals it is a natural part of their development to have gone through "bisexual" or even "homosexual" stages of life. When I read this, it seemed theoretically reasonable, but did not ring true in my experience. I have always been, I told myself, 100 percent heterosexual! The group process of analyzing my own autobiographical stories challenged the concept I had developed of myself, and also shed light on the way in which the institutional context of sport provided a context for the development of my definition of myself as "100 percent straight." Here is one of the stories.

When I was in the 9th grade, I played on a "D" basketball team, set up especially for the smallest of high school boys. Indeed, though I was pudgy with baby fat, I was a short 5'2", still pre-pubescent with no facial hair and a high voice that I artificially tried to lower. The first day of practice, I was immediately attracted to a boy I'll call Timmy, because he looked like the boy who played in the *Lassie* TV show. Timmy was short, with a high voice, like me. And like me, he had no facial hair yet. Unlike me, he was very skinny. I liked Timmy right away, and soon we were together a lot. I noticed things about him that I didn't notice about other boys: he said some words a certain way, and it gave me pleasure to try to talk like him.

I remember liking the way the light hit his boyish, nearly hairless body. I thought about him when we weren't together. He was in the school band, and at the football games, I'd squint to see where he was in the mass of uniforms. In short, though I wasn't conscious of it at the time, I was infatuated with Timmy—I had a crush on him. Later that basketball season, I decided—for no reason that I could really articulate then—that I hated Timmy. I aggressively rejected him, began to make fun of him around other boys. He was, we all agreed, a geek. He was a faggot.

Three years later, Timmy and I were both on the varsity basketball team, but had hardly spoken a word to each other since we were freshmen. Both of us now had lower voices, had grown to around 6 feet tall, and we both shaved, at least a bit. But Timmy was a skinny, somewhat stigmatized reserve on the team, while I was the team captain and starting point guard. But I wasn't so happy or secure about this. I'd always dreamed of dominating games, of being the hero. Halfway through my senior season, however, it became clear that I was not a star, and I figured I knew why. I was not aggressive enough.

I had always liked the beauty of the fast break, the perfectly executed pick and roll play between two players, and especially the long twenty-foot shot that touched nothing but the bottom of the net. But I hated and feared the sometimes brutal contact under the basket. In fact, I stayed away from the rough fights for rebounds and was mostly a perimeter player, relying on my long shots or my passes to more aggressive teammates under the basket. But now it became apparent to me that time was running out in my quest for greatness: I needed to change my game, and fast. I decided one day before practice that I was gonna get aggressive. While practicing one of our standard plays, I passed

the ball to a teammate, and then ran to the spot at which I was to set a pick on a defender. I knew that one could sometimes get away with setting a face-up screen on a player, and then as he makes contact with you, roll your back to him and plant your elbow hard in his stomach. The beauty of this move is that your own body "roll" makes the elbow look like an accident. So I decided to try this move. I approached the defensive player, Timmy, rolled, and planted my elbow deeply into his solar plexus. Air exploded audibly from Timmy's mouth, and he crumbled to the floor momentarily.

Play went on as though nothing had happened, but I felt bad about it. Rather than making me feel better, it made me feel guilty and weak. I had to admit to myself why I'd chosen Timmy as the target against whom to test out my new aggression. He was the skinniest and weakest player on the team.

At the time, I hardly thought about these incidents, other than to try to brush them off as incidents that made me feel extremely uncomfortable. Years later, I can now interrogate this as a sexual story, and as a gender story unfolding within the context of the heterosexualized and masculinized institution of sport. Examining my story in light of research conducted by Alfred Kinsey a half-century ago, I can recognize in myself what Kinsey saw as a very common fluidity and changeability of sexual desire over the life-course. Put simply, Kinsey found that large numbers of adult, "heterosexual" men had previously, as adolescents and young adults, experienced sexual desire for males. A surprisingly large number of these men had experienced sexual contact to the point of orgasm with other males during adolescence or early adulthood. Similarly, my story invited me to consider what is commonly called the "Freudian theory of bisexuality." Sigmund Freud shocked the post-Victorian world by suggesting that all people go through a stage, early in life, when they are attracted to people of the same sex.[1] Adult experiences, Freud argued, eventually led most people to shift their sexual desire to what he called an appropriate "love object"—a person of the opposite sex. I also considered my experience in light of what lesbian feminist author Adrienne Rich called the institution of compulsory heterosexuality. Perhaps the extremely high levels of homophobia that are often endemic in boys' and men's organized sports led me to deny and repress my own homoerotic desire through a direct and overt rejection of Timmy, through homophobic banter with male peers, and the resultant stigmatization of the feminized Timmy. Eventually I considered my experience in the light of what radical theorist Herbert Marcuse called the sublimation of homoerotic desire into an aggressive violent act as serving to construct a clear line of demarcation between self and other. Sublimation, according to Marcuse, involved the driving underground, into the unconscious, of sexual desires that might appear dangerous due to their socially stigmatized status. But sublimation involves more than simple repression into the unconscious. It involves a transformation of sexual desire into something else—often into aggressive and violent acting out toward others. These acts clarify the boundaries between oneself and others and therefore lessen any anxieties that might be attached to the repressed homoerotic desire.

Importantly, in our analysis of my story, the memory group went beyond simply discussing the events in psychological terms. The story did perhaps suggest some deep psychological processes at work, but it also revealed the importance of social context—in this case, the context of the athletic team. In short, my rejection of Timmy and the joining with teammates to stigmatize him in ninth grade stands as an example of what sociologist R. W. Connell calls a moment of engagement with hegemonic masculinity, where I actively took up the male group's task of constructing heterosexual/masculine identities in the context of sport. The elbow in Timmy's gut three years

later can be seen as a punctuation mark that occurred precisely because of my fears that I might be failing in this goal.

It is helpful, I think, to compare my story with gay and lesbian "coming out" stories in sport. Though we have a few lesbian and bisexual coming out stories among women athletes, there are very few from gay males. Tom Waddell, who as a closeted gay man finished sixth in the decathlon in the 1968 Olympics, later came out and started the Gay Games, an athletic and cultural festival that draws tens of thousands of people every four years. When I interviewed Tom Waddell over a decade ago about his sexual identity and athletic career, he made it quite clear that for many years sports was his closet:

> When I was a kid, I was tall for my age, and was very thin and very strong. And I was usually faster than most other people. But I discovered rather early that I liked gymnastics and I liked dance. I was very interested in being a ballet dancer . . . [but] something became obvious to me right away—that male ballet dancers were effeminate, that they were what most people would call faggots. And I thought I just couldn't handle that—I was totally closeted and very concerned about being male. This was the fifties, a terrible time to live, and everything was stacked against me. Anyway, I realized that I had to do something to protect my image of myself as a male—because at that time homosexuals were thought of primarily as men who wanted to be women. And so I threw myself into athletics—I played football, gymnastics, track and field . . . I was a jock—that's how I was viewed, and I was comfortable with that.

Tom Waddell was fully conscious of entering sports and constructing a masculine/heterosexual athletic identity precisely because he feared being revealed as gay. It was clear to him, in the context of the 1950s, that being known as gay would undercut his claims to the status of manhood. Thus, though he described the athletic closet as "hot and stifling," he remained there until several years after his athletic retirement. He even knowingly played along with locker room discussions about sex and women as part of his "cover."

> I wanted to be viewed as male, otherwise I would be a dancer today. I wanted the male, macho image of an athlete. So I was protected by a very hard shell. I was clearly aware of what I was doing . . . I often felt compelled to go along with a lot of locker room garbage because I wanted that image—and I know a lot of others who did too.

Like my story, Waddell's points to the importance of the athletic institution as a context in which peers mutually construct and reconstruct narrow definitions of masculinity. Heterosexuality is considered to be a rock-solid foundation of this concept of masculinity. But unlike my story, Waddell's may invoke a dramaturgical analysis.[2] He seemed to be consciously "acting" to control and regulate others' perceptions of him by constructing a public "front stage" persona that differed radically from what he believed to be his "true" inner self. My story, in contrast, suggests a deeper, less consciously strategic repression of my homoerotic attraction. Most likely, I was aware on some level of the dangers of such feelings, and was escaping the risks, disgrace, and rejection that would likely result from being different. For Waddell, the decision to construct his identity largely within sport was to step into a fiercely heterosexual/masculine closet that would hide what he saw as his "true" identity. In contrast, I was not so much stepping into a "closet" that would hide my identity; rather, I was stepping out into an entire world of heterosexual privilege. My story also suggests how a threat to the promised privileges of hegemonic masculinity—my failure as an athlete—might trigger a momentary sexual panic that can lay bare the constructedness, indeed, the instability of the heterosexual/masculine identity.

In either case, Waddell's or mine, we can see how, as young male athletes, heterosexuality and masculinity was not something we "were," but something we were doing. It is significant, I think, that although each of us was "doing heterosexuality," neither of us was actually "having sex" with women (though one of us desperately wanted to). This underscores a point made by some recent theorists that heterosexuality should not be thought of simply as sexual acts between women and men. Rather, heterosexuality is a constructed identity, a performance, and an institution that is not necessarily linked to sexual acts. Though for one of us it was more conscious than for the other, we were both "doing heterosexuality" as an ongoing practice through which we sought to do two things:

- avoid stigma, embarrassment, ostracism, or perhaps worse if we were even suspected of being gay;
- link ourselves into systems of power, status and privilege that appear to be the birthright of "real men" (i.e., males who are able to compete successfully with other males in sport, work, and sexual relations with women).

In other words, each of us actively scripted our own sexual and gender performances, but these scripts were constructed within the constraints of a socially organized (institutionalized) system of power and pleasure.

QUESTIONS FOR FUTURE RESEARCH

As I prepared to tell this sexual story publicly to my colleagues at the sport studies conference, I felt extremely nervous. Part of the nervousness was due to the fact that I knew some of them would object to my claim that telling personal stories can be a source of sociological insights. But a larger part of the reason for my nervousness was due to the fact that I was revealing something very personal about my sexuality in such a public way. Most of us are not accustomed to doing this, especially in the context of a professional conference. But I had learned long ago, especially from feminist women scholars, and from gay and lesbian scholars, that biography is linked to history. Part of "normal" academic discourse has been to hide "the personal" (including the fact that the researchers are themselves people with values, feelings, and yes, biases) behind a carefully constructed facade of "objectivity." Rather than trying to hide or be ashamed of one's subjective experience of the world, I was challenging myself to draw on my experience of the world as a resource. Not that I should trust my experience as the final word on "reality." White, heterosexual males like me have made the mistake for centuries of calling their own experience "objectivity," and then punishing anyone who does not share their worldview by casting them as "deviant." Instead, I hope to use my experience as an example of how those of us who are in dominant sexual/racial/gender/class categories can get a new perspective on the "constructedness" of our identities by juxtaposing our subjective experiences against the recently emerging worldviews of gay men and lesbians, women, and people of color.

Finally, I want to stress that in juxtaposition neither my own nor Tom Waddell's story sheds much light on the question of why some individuals "become gay" while others "become" heterosexual or bisexual. Instead, I should like to suggest that this is a dead-end question, and that there are far more important and interesting questions to be asked:

- How has heterosexuality, as an institution and as an enforced group practice, constrained and limited all of us—gay, straight, and bi?
- How has the institution of sport been an especially salient institution for the social construction of heterosexual masculinity?
- Why is it that when men play sports they are almost always automatically granted

masculine status, and thus assumed to be heterosexual, while when women play sports, questions are raised about their "femininity" and sexual orientation?

These kinds of questions aim us toward an analysis of the working of power within institutions—including the ways that these workings of power shape and constrain our identities and relationships—and point us toward imagining alternative social arrangements that are less constraining for everyone.

NOTES

1. The fluidity and changeability of sexual desire over the life course is now more obvious in evidence from prison and military populations, and single-sex boarding schools. The theory of bisexuality is evident, for example, in childhood crushes on same-sex primary school-teachers.
2. Dramaturgical analysis, associated with Erving Goffman, uses the theater and performance to develop an analogy with everyday life.

REFERENCES

Haug, Frigga (1987) *Female Sexualization: A Collective Work of Memory,* London: Verso.

Lenskyj, Helen (1986) *Out of Bounds: Women, Sport and Sexuality,* Toronto: Women's Press.

——— (1997) "No fear? Lesbians in sport and physical education," *Women in Sport and Physical Activity Journal* 6(2): 7–22.

Messner, Michael A. (1992) *Power at Play: Sports and the Problem of Masculinity,* Boston: Beacon Press.

——— (1994) "Gay athletes and the Gay Games: An interview with Tom Waddell," in M. A. Messner and D. F. Sabo (eds) *Sex, Violence and Power in Sports: Rethinking Masculinity,* Freedom, CA: The Crossing Press, pp. 113–19.

Pronger, Brian (1990) *The Arena of Masculinity: Sports, Homosexuality, and the Meaning of Sex,* New York: St. Martin's Press.

Bi Any Other Name

Loraine Hutchins and Lani Kaahumanu

> *Bisexuals' lives provide new psychological and social understandings of sexuality and closeness, highlighting the mechanics of sexual decision-making as potentially self-determined action. Research is needed about all areas of the bisexual experience, including studies of common qualities of bisexuals, therapeutic case studies, and longitudinal studies of bisexuals' relationships. The bisexual experience calls into question traditional definitions of the nature of sexual identity development. Fluid, ambiguous, subversive, multifarious, bisexuality can no longer be denied.*
> —Rebecca Shuster[1]

DEFINING BISEXUALITY

As Kate Millett once said, "Homosexuality was invented by a straight world dealing with its own bisexuality."[2] So it is not surprising that looking up the word *bisexual* in the dictionary is like blinking into the distorted mirror of Western society's ambivalence over sexuality.

The prefix *bi* means two, or dual. Therefore the word *bisexual* is used to refer to things involving both sexes. However, this can mean an individual who possesses physical organs of both sexes, or it can mean some event or setting that involves both sexes at once. *Bisexual* can also refer to individuals of either sex who are attracted to both sexes. In this essay, we use this last meaning. But our common frame of reference is loaded with the combination of all of these definitions together and how they affect our understanding of what is meant

when one says "bisexual." These multiple and contradictory meanings limit our ability to discuss the subject clearly. For instance, someone who possesses both male and female qualities, either psychologically (as in being androgynous) or physically (as in being an hermaphrodite[3]), is not necessarily attracted to both male and female people. To further complicate matters, the definitions of *androgynous, bisexual, hermaphrodite,* and *homosexual* all overlap in many dictionaries and reference books. For instance, the first definition of *bisexual* in *Webster's Collegiate Dictionary* is "hermaphrodite." Yet the same dictionary defines the actual word *hermaphrodite* as "1 . . . b. homosexual. 2. something that is a combination of diverse elements."[4] Are homosexuals physical hermaphrodites? Not usually. Are they bisexual? Not necessarily. So, what "diverse elements" are combined?

Are we going round in circles? Perhaps what's really got us spinning are the contradictory, confusing definitions of sexual orientation manufactured by this heterosexist, sex-negative society. Unraveling *this* conditioning is the key.

Coming out bisexual, as Shuster's opening quote attests, truly does affect everyone. It breaks the conspiracy of silence, as gay people have also done. But it also challenges current assumptions about the immutability of people's orientations and society's supposed divisions into discrete groups. Bisexuals' coming out challenges other people's understanding of them*selves*. Our bisexuality reflects on society as a whole, threatening the monosexual[5] framework that heterosexism needs to survive.

Since bisexuality threatens how society is organized, bisexuals often become the targets of discrimination, stereotyping and jokes. We are considered more sexual, more confused, more fickle than others,[6] whereas in reality all disempowered groups are sexualized in a hierarchical, sex-phobic society—as a way to divide and maintain fear of The Other.[7]

. . . [W]e have the same hopes, fears, problems, and experiences as monosexuals do in relationships. But we are the target for the projected fear of being "other," from both the gay and the straight sides of humanity.

Bisexuality is much more than, and different from, the sensationalized "third choice," "best-of-both-worlds" phenomena it's made out to be. Bisexuality is an inclusive term that defines immense possibilities available to us, whether we act on them or not. It opens doors and accepts all the in-betweens, including the more conforming "accepted" ways we've identified in the past or will in the future. We have gay and heterosexual experience. We socialize with both, and we go back and forth interpreting each to the other, whether this service is appreciated or not. This will be recognized as more of us come out and take pride in the identity we were told is impossible. But first we must face ourselves. Declaring oneself bisexual means trusting one's own experiences. As Loraine has stated, "Unpredictable is not the same as unreliable. Integrating and balancing opposite parts of oneself is not 'confused' or 'unreal.' It might not be your cup of tea, which is fine, but it's a life-long creation I'm dedicated to and enjoying . . . "[8]

This is difficult, since so many people are confused by and concerned with the (so-called) fluid nature of bisexuality. But think about it. When we examine our lives, they are not neat, well-packaged scenarios. Life is vital and multifaceted, complex. As Adrienne Rich puts it:

> Truthfulness anywhere means a heightened complexity. But it is a movement into evolution. . . . This is why the effort to speak honestly is so important. . . . Does a life 'in the closet'—lying, perhaps of necessity, about ourselves, to bosses, landlords, clients, colleagues, family, because the law and public opinion are founded on a lie— does this, can it, spread into private life, so that lying (discretion) becomes an easy way to avoid conflict or complication? Can it become a strategy so ingrained that it is used even with close friends and lovers?[9]

BISEXUAL WAYS OF BEING

Individual bi identities span many communities. . . . We are bisexuals of all ages and colors. Some of us identify with the gay and lesbian communities, some of us identify with the heterosexual community, some of us identify primarily with other bisexuals. Some of us identify primarily with people of color or with other sexual minority communities such as S/M, cross-dressers, or transsexuals.

Because our society is so polarized between homosexuals and heterosexuals, the bisexual closet has two doors. Both need to be opened. Coming out to the straight world and coming out to the gay world are not the same. Coming out bisexually is also affected by one's gender, one's race and culture, one's class, one's religion, and one's physical abilities or state of health. . . .

In the quote that follows, Jane Litwoman expresses one particularly different and unique view of why she herself does, and does not, identify as bisexual:

> The sexologist Kinsey has created a 0–6 scale in which people are rated as to their homo/heterosexuality. I think of myself as off the scale. To me, the Kinsey scale has as much relevance as if everyone were evaluated on a spectrum of whether they were more attracted to people with brown eyes or green/blue eyes. Gender is just not what I care about or even really notice in a sexual partner. This is not to say that I don't have categories of sexual attraction, that I judge each person as an individual—I have categories, but gender isn't one of them. I'm erotically attracted to intelligent people, to people with dark/colored skin and light eyes and hair, to people with a kind of sleazy, sexy come-on, to eccentrics. In some of those categories I am homo-erotic (i.e., I'm intelligent and eccentric), in others I am hetero-erotic (i.e., I have light skin and dark eyes and hair). To be perfectly frank, I can barely imagine what it's like to be a lesbian or a straight

woman, to be attracted to women because they are female—and that is sexy—or to men because they are male. In that way I feel like both of them share a common perception which I will never know—that I am color blind or tone deaf to a gender-erotic world.

I can relate more easily to people who are not primarily gender-erotic, but who are what is commonly referred to as fetishistic. At a gut level I can imagine what it might be to be erotically attracted to frilly lingerie or leather or the smell of the sea. The clearest way for me to understand lesbians and straight women is to accept them as fetishists. From my viewpoint straight women are malegender-fetishists and lesbians are femalegender-fetishists who are so culturally supported in their sexual attractions that most of the time they hardly understand my different reality.

Of course I live in a world in which gender is a much more powerful concern than leather or the smell of the sea. Gender, along with race, class, ethnicity, and age, is one of the most profound social status determinants in our society. I could choose to only act on my attractions to female persons for political/social concerns. However, I instinctively resist straight-jacketing my sexual feelings for political reasons . . .

I don't define my sexuality so much by what I might or might not like—women, men, orgies, masturbation, romantic music, intimacy, anonymous sex, cunnilingus, etc.—but by honest exploration of my sexual desires. What I am sexually is sovereign.[10]

Yet, responsible scientific investigation into the kinds of issues raised above by Litwoman and Shuster is woefully lacking! Even sociologists such as Philip W. Blumstein and Pepper Schwartz, who have done extensive research on bisexuality, say that "little research has investigated the route bisexuals take to this identity or any of the common qualities of those who identify themselves as bisexual."[11] Still, so that we may better understand from where we start, a brief survey of the bisexuality research that *does* exist is in order.

RESEARCH BASED ON A MONOSEXUAL FRAMEWORK = BIPHOBIA

> *Dividing people for purposes of study into only two groups, "heterosexual" and "homosexual," which is done most of the time, and defining all people at gay dances or all men found in gay bars as "homosexual," has the effect of lumping bisexuals into these groups and makes interpretation of the results extremely difficult.*
> —Dr. F. Klein, *The Bisexual Option*[12]

Bisexuals are continually being studied, mostly by non-bisexuals, who base their research on a monosexual framework and then claim that we don't exist, or are rare, or are perverted, or are really on our way to something else. And, as with homosexuality, many of the studies on bisexuality are done from the heterosexual assumption that we're unnatural or sick to begin with. These researchers seem to forget they're only studying clients who come to them for counseling. What's important is that these studies, therefore, rarely distinguish between healthy and distressed bisexuals. The researchers have no sense for what is really intrinsic to being bisexual. Therefore, biphobia—the irrational fear of bisexuality in oneself or others and the distrust and discrimination practiced against us because of this fear—has permeated almost all existing research up to this point.

In the seventies, with the unfolding of the women's and gay liberation movements, an explosion of articles and studies on bisexuality appeared in the popular press. Most of them sensationalized us according to the myths mentioned earlier. Even the better books, like *The Bisexual Option*[13] and *View from Another Closet*,[14] rely heavily on the case-study method of interviews and surveys and the voice of the expert authority. The only first-person account, *Barry and Alice: Portrait of a Bisexual Marriage*,[15] is out of print.

Another problem with current studies on alternative sexuality is that they focus on married couples almost exclusively, and within these couples usually only one partner is gay, or bisexual.[16] Not only are single bisexual people ignored, no surveys of the many bisexuals leading closeted lives in the gay and lesbian communities are available. Gay people in heterosexual relationships are mentioned only within the research framework that there is no such thing as a bisexual, and that their homosexuality is their only true sexuality.

Klein's *The Bisexual Option* is especially good in pointing out how invisibility perpetuates research errors. He quotes noted sex researchers claiming that true bisexuality doesn't exist, and then catches them in their own errors.[17] On the gay research side of the myopia surrounding bisexuality, books such as John D'Emilio and Estelle Freedman's *Intimate Matters: A History of Sexuality in America*, assign less text and index space to bisexuality than to "bestiality."[18] Bestiality is mentioned three times in their index, bisexuality not once. And their book is not unusual.

What has been written *about* bisexuals is also not grounded in a feminist analysis of sexuality and power. Therefore, this kind of information provides an incomplete, distorted picture, and tends more to perpetuate myths about us than to dispel them.

BUDDING BI-POSITIVISM: SOME SIGNS OF CHANGE

> I do not in the least underestimate bisexuality. . . . I expect it to provide all further enlightenment.
>
> —Sigmund Freud[19]

> "There are not two discrete populations, heterosexual and homosexual. . . . Only the human mind invents categories and tries to force fact into separated pigeon holes. . . . The sooner we learn this . . .

> the sooner we shall reach a sound understanding of the realities of sex."
>
> —Alfred Kinsey[20]

> "What is new is not bisexuality, but rather the widening of our awareness and acceptance of human capacities for sexual love. Today the recognition of bisexuality in oneself and in others is part of the whole mid-20th century movement to accord to each individual, regardless of race, class, nationality, age or sex, the right to be a person who is unique and who has a social identity that is worthy of dignity and respect. . . . Even a superficial look at other societies and some groups in our own society should be enough to convince us that a very large number of human beings, probably a majority—are bisexual in their potential capacity for love. . . . We will fail to evolve in our understanding of human sexuality if we continue to see homosexuals merely as "heterosexuals-in-reverse," ignoring the vast diversity actually represented by society's many varied expressions of love between people.
>
> —Margaret Mead[21]

Even with these few positive attitudes quoted here, the biological and environmental origins of sexual identification are still hotly debated today. Authorities don't agree on what causes what, much less on what part bisexuality plays. And incredible hostility and misunderstanding is still directed toward bisexuals and bisexuality. However, a number of bi-positive writers and researchers are beginning to speak against the phobic tide.

In a 1985 article, "Bisexuality: Reassessing our Paradigms of Sexuality,"[22] Dr. Jay Paul—one of a handful of "out" bisexual psychologists writing professionally on bisexuality—identifies current research errors on bisexuality:

There is far more variability and fluidity in many people's sexual patterns than theoretical notions tend to allow, suggesting that researchers have imparted an artificial consistency to an inchoate sexual universe.

It is not that science has ignored the indisputable fact that the sexual biographies of many include sexual experiences with both men and women, but rather the theoretical meanings given to those experiences. The tendency is to deny the legitimacy of one's erotic responsiveness to either males, or females; thereby, one assumes that all people are either basically heterosexual or homosexual. This refusal to allow for an equivalent basic bisexuality in some portion of the population leads to a variety of explanations for bisexual patterns.

(And, we might add, few of them adequate or good.)

Hansen and Evans, writing in the same journal, cite the common misinterpretation or misuse of the Kinsey scale, stressing that it describes only genital behavior patterns, not identity.[23]

In another article in the same issue, Dr. Gary Zinik[24] points out that in the forties and fifties the country was shocked by Kinsey's discovery of high rates of homosexual behavior among men and women. But what was even *more* overlooked was that "significantly higher percentages of people exhibit bisexual behavior than exclusively homosexual behavior." He explains that this is because a "conflict model" of bisexuality (in research circles, in researchers' minds) assumes that homosexual interests eradicate heterosexual responsiveness—that they can't exist peacefully side by side. But this isn't true for a significant number of people. In fact, the notion that "one drop of homosexuality indicates latent homosexuality in a straight" theory sounds suspiciously like the "one drop of black blood makes you black and you can't go to our schools" racist attitude in U.S. public schools last generation.

Zinik instead proposes a "flexibility model," where "indeed men and women are not considered opposite sexes so much as variations on a theme."

After all, what is the theme? The theme is life, in all its diversity. We are trained from birth to think of ourselves as either/or—female or male—and indoctrinated in sex-role conditioning under what Adrienne Rich calls "compulsory heterosexuality," based on and rooted in male supremacy. But if these things change, would we men and women really be so different, so opposite, so far apart?

Some feminists would have us believe so, saying that men's biology dooms them to violence (and thus women to be their inevitable victims and servants, as well as their prized possessions on pedestals). But other lesbian and feminist writers disagree. For example, French writer Elisabeth Badinter has caused great discussion in Europe with her book, *The Unopposite Sex: The End of the Gender Battle*,[25] where she argues that men and women are growing more and more alike in the modern age and that the basic bisexuality of all of us will be more and more revealed.

From the gay research angle, on the other hand, it is interesting to note that *The Many Faces of Homosexuality*[26]—a 1986 cross-cultural, anthropological study of homosexual behaviors in various times and places—clearly illustrates that much homosexual behavior is *actually* bisexual behavior, and that our modern U.S. Western model of who gay people are does not apply cross-culturally at all. Two modern gay writers who would agree are Warren Blumenfeld and Diane Raymond, whose highly readable book, *Looking at Gay and Lesbian Life*,[27] features a section called "The Homosexual/Bisexual/Heterosexual Continuum." They discuss the many aspects of gay and bisexual behavior versus identity, physical diversity among all sexual minorities, and what part of our behavior is chosen, what part innate.

Some of the best studies on bisexuality come from outside the U.S. The late-seventies publication *Bisexuality: A Study,* by British author Charlotte Wolff,[28] is still unsurpassed in its feminist understanding of all sexuality, though it is somewhat outdated now in the age of AIDS. More recently, a group of bisexuals living in and around London published a small anthology, *Bisexual Lives*,[29] that served as one inspiration for [our work].

The debate and this present polarized state of affairs will go on. However, since AIDS has put sex and sexuality in the public eye more than ever before, we can no longer afford to deny the many issues it exposes, including the current rigid monosexual framework overlying the fluid nature of sex. We need new mediating approaches. Bisexual liberation is one of them. But for a more whole, peaceful way to come into existence, we must face ourselves—name our own bisexual potential—first.

NOTES

1. Rebecca Shuster, "Sexuality as a Continuum: The Bisexual Identity," in *Lesbian Psychologies: Explorations and Challenges,* ed. Boston Lesbian Psychologies Collective, University of Illinois Press, 1987.
2. As quoted in *Bisexual Lives,* London: Off Pink Publishing, 1988. This quote was originally from Millett's book *Flying,* now reprinted by Simon & Schuster, 1990.
3. Noted sex researcher Dr. John Money of Johns Hopkins University estimates that there may be as many as one hermaphrodite born per thousand births, but that we cannot know accurately at this time. Doctors do not report such statistics to any national database, and often perform surgery on such children's "in-between" genitals shortly after birth to make them one sex or the other.
4. *Webster's New Collegiate Dictionary,* Springfield, Mass.: Merriam, 1977, p. 536.
5. *Monosexual* is a term coined by the bisexual movement to mean anyone (gay or heterosexual) who is attracted to just one sex, their own or the opposite one.
6. For more on this, see "Myths/Realities of Bisexuality," following these notes.
7. When society is dominated by one race, sex, or class of people, the groups not in power are seen as Other. White-male-dominated society,

for instance, has portrayed women as more sexually insatiable and unclean than men; people of color as more immoral and sexual; and gays as child molesters. Actually it's mostly straight men who molest, and women and people of color, as groups, certainly do not have the negative characteristics that have been projected upon them as Other.

8. Loraine Hutchins, "Biatribe: Towards a Politic of Feminist Bisexuality," *off our backs,* February 1988.
9. *From Women and Honor: Some Notes on Lying,* Pittsburgh: Motherroot Publications, 1977.
10. From "Some Thoughts on Bisexuality," *Lesbian Contradictions,* Winter 1990.
11. Philip Blumstein and Pepper Schwartz, "Bisexuality: Some Social Psychological Issues," *Journal of Social Issues* 33 (Spring 1977): 30–45.
12. Dr. Fred Klein, M.D., *The Bisexual Option: A Concept of One Hundred Percent Intimacy,* New York: Berkeley Books, 1980, p. 152.
13. Ibid.
14. Janet Bode, *View from Another Closet,* New York: Hawthorn Books, 1976.
15. Barry Kohn and Alice Matusow, *Barry and Alice: Portrait of a Bisexual Marriage,* Prentice Hall, 1980.
16. See, for instance, *The Bisexual Spouse* by Ivan Hill, McLean, Va.: Barlina Books, 1987; and *Uncommon Affairs: Gay Men and Straight Women,* by Catherine Whitney, New American Library, 1990.
17. Klein, *The Bisexual Option.* See in particular pp. 126–128 and 139.
18. John D'Emilio and Estelle B. Freedman, *Intimate Matters: A History of Sexuality in America,* Harper & Row, 1988. Billed as the "first full-length study of the history of sexuality in this country," this book contains much fascinating information. However, its fourteen-page index lists three references for bestiality, six for cross-dressing, and eleven for sexual revolution (including feminists, gay liberation, singles life, youth rebellions, and sexual vulnerability of women), but not one mention of bisexuality! You would think our experience is rarer than any of the above and that we played no part in the entire sexual revolution they chronicle over the past twenty to two hundred years.

19. Sigmund Freud, "Three Essays on the Theory of Sexuality," in *Readings in Human Sexuality,* ed. Samuel T. Wilson, Richard L. Roe, and Lucy E. Autrey, pp. 71–79, New York: West, 1975. And as discussed by Christine Downing, a lesbian Jungian, in her *Myths and Mysteries of Same Sex Loving,* Continuum, 1989. (*Myths and Mysteries* is also of interest because its Jungian author discusses her own heterosexual marriage, her current long-term partnership with a woman, and her sexual, loving relationships with gay men.)

20. *Bisexual Lives,* op. cit.

21. Margaret Mead, "Bisexuality: What's It All About?" *Redbook,* January 1975, pp. 29–31.

22. F. Klein, M.D., and Timothy J. Wolf, Ph.D., eds., *Bisexualities: Theory and Research: Journal of Homosexuality,* vol. 2, nos. 1/2, Haworth Press, 1985, pp. 21–22.

23. Ibid., p. 3.

24. Ibid., pp. 7–11.

25. Elizabeth Badinter, *The Unopposite Sex: The End of the Gender Battle,* Harper & Row, 1989. (First published in English in Great Britain by Collins Harvill under the title *Man/Woman: The One Is the Other.*)

26. Evelyn Blackwood, ed., *The Many Faces of Homosexuality: Anthropological Approaches to Homosexual Behavior,* New York: Harrington Park Press, 1986.

27. Warren Blumenfeld and Diane Raymond, *Looking at Gay and Lesbian Life,* Boston: Beacon Press, 1988.

28. Dr. Charlotte Wolff, *Bisexuality: A Study,* London: Quartet Books, 1979.

29. *Bisexual Lives,* op, cit. (See note 2.)

READING 39

I Am a Queer Heterosexual

Sharon Kelly

This oxymoronic statement is more than a semantic conundrum, it is an accurate refection of my sexual being. Over the last year the New Queer Politics have taken up many column inches in the lesbian and gay press. Occasionally Queer theory has managed to get a hearing in the mainstream broadsheets. In the main, however, the theory has been ghettoised as a solely lesbian and gay debate.

Yet the definitions of Queer refuse exclusivity. "The word *queer*," says Peter Tatchell, a member of the lesbian and gay rights group OutRage, "has been adopted as a new comprehensive self-definition which embraces all sexual dissidents—lesbians, gay men, bisexuals, transvestites and transsexuals. It is also a term which implies an acceptance of diverse consensual sexual practices, including activities such as sadomasochism and group sex."

The New Queer Politics argues that using the word *queer* is in itself a political act. It reclaims an oppressive homophobic word and redefines it as an expression of pride. As the definition shows, *queer* is a term that goes beyond lesbian and gay men. Those heterosexuals who have had a same-sex partner and those who have had a heterosexual relationship with a lesbian or gay partner can and should use the word *queer.*

I liked to define myself as heterosexual despite having slept with a number of women. I had convinced myself that my sexual desire in relation to women was not important. There have been times when I have actively sought out women but I have always argued, to prove my heterosexuality, that I am unable to fall in love with a woman. Recently I had a

Source: Body Politic, www.body.arc.co.uk/body4/queer.html. Copyright © 1996 Body Politic Ltd. Copyright © 1997 Arc Net Ltd.

three month sexual relationship with Richard, a gay man. Sleeping with Richard has led me to question my own lack of mutability. In having a relationship with me, he has managed a leap of faith. I, by acknowledging his gayness, have leapt too. Both of us are Queer. He is gay identified and I am heterosexual identified, but being Queer means that those labels are no longer exclusive. "When I first came out," says Richard, "it was very important to have a communality of view and share the same identity as other gay men. I saw gay men as beleaguered, embattled, socially marginalised and oppressed by a straight society and there was a sense of being with fellow sufferers. I was part of a minority, part of the same struggle." He believes that over the last four or five years his gayness has become less relevant. He feels that there is a difference between the drive for sex which occasions sexual release and desire, which works in the unconscious. People get themselves into sexual situations for multiple reasons. Desire is not just a mere animalistic function. Sexual attraction is the tip of the iceberg. "Sexuality is a reductive term and it gets parcelled off from the rest of human life," he argues. "There is a tendency in Western medical and psychiatric thought to isolate sexuality. The label 'homosexual' may be a useful term but it is not a complete understanding." For Richard the label "homosexual" may only be half the story, but he feels that his desire is predominantly directed towards men. I have also felt in the past that my inability, in the main, to eroticise the female body is proof of the difficulties in transcending the boundaries of sexuality.

Writer and performer Claire Dowie has addressed the complexities of cross-sexuality desire in her play *Death and Dancing,* which deals with the problematic relationship between a bisexual woman and a gay man. In one part of the play, the androgynous Dowie has a long flirtatious dance with a gay man. He desires her until he realises she is a woman. Dowie questions the notion that desire stems from what is between our legs. Dowie has found that attempts to define her own sexuality have led to constraint. "We desire certain types of people, so why confine ourselves to looking at genitals?" she asks. "If I call myself a lesbian, I am only looking in one direction, rejecting men. We should educate people to know that it doesn't matter who you sleep with. I have tried saying I was bisexual, and I got it in the neck from both sides. I don't know what my sexuality is anymore."

Many bisexuals face a similar reaction. Bisexual men are charged with being closeted gays, while bisexual women stand accused of pretending to be bisexual in order to fulfill the fantasies of heterosexual men. Tatchell argues vehemently that being bisexual is not a cop-out. "People do have a genuine dual attraction to people of both the same and opposite sex."

Dowie believes that desire is a learned response, pointing to the Pavlovian relationship between heterosexual men and stockings and suspenders [garter belts] as an obvious example. "Men have been told that those things are sexy, so they believe it to be true. If a man was to really look at stockings and suspenders he would realise how stupid they look. Gay men and lesbians are such amazing people, because despite the brainwashing, their desires resist those of mainstream society." The trouble with gay politics, she feels, is the wholesale rejection of heterosexuality. For her, the rigidity of many lesbians and gay men leaves them as open to the charge of being almost as prejudiced as many heterosexuals.

"If lesbians and gays were allowed to be who they wanted to be culturally, how many would stick exclusively to same-sex relationships?" she asks. "In a television programme where gay men were asked when they first realised that they were gay, some said that they realised they were sissy boys at the age of five or six. But sissyness has nothing to do with who you want sex with." Dowie feels that people train themselves to desire a certain sex in order to fit in with societal demands.

Tatchell believes sexual desire should be freed from regimentation and oppression. "Desire tends to be quite fluid, ambiguous and diverse," he says. "Sexual orientation may involve some biological factors, however. All the psychological and anthropological evidence suggests that sexuality is primarily culturally conditioned. In other words, a more liberal society would probably result in many more people having both heterosexual and homosexual relationships in their lifetime."

HIV prevention campaigns have dramatically underlined the falsehood and artificiality of rigid distinctions between heterosexual and homosexual. Research statistics now point to a more fluid approach than sexual ideology from either gay or heterosexual camps. Many homosexuals have had heterosexual encounters and vice versa.

A study by a group of researchers in Italy showed that of 343 women in lesbian meeting places in Rome, Milan, Bologna and Florence, more than twenty per cent had had some kind of sexual encounter with men in previous months. A 1991 California study of 141 lesbians showed that eighty-one per cent of these women had had penetrative vaginal sex with men at some time in their lives, eighteen per cent had had anal sex. A study in the USA showed that forty-three per cent of the women who have sex with other women who answered the questionnaire had also had penetrative vaginal sex with men since 1980. Thirty-two per cent of the male sexual partners were identified as gay and bisexual. A City Limits survey showed that forty-seven per cent of self-defined gay men interviewed had had sexual relationships. Bisexual men are charged with being closeted gays, while bisexual women stand accused of pretending to be bisexual in order to fulfill the fantasies of heterosexual men with women. Five per cent said

they had had such an encounter in the preceding year.

The reason for some of this crossover may be linked with the desire to have children. The possibility of having children has been a big part of my relationship with Richard. Often gay men and lesbians who engage with heterosexual partners to have children are accused of sacrificing sexual identity and copying heterosexual conventions. Singer Tom Robinson has shown that it is possible to remain glad to be gay whilst having a relationship with a woman, with whom he has a child.

My relationship with Richard caused much controversy among our friends. "Sleeping with a woman," says Richard, "acts against the fixity of gayness. People don't like other people getting out of their boxes." One friend, Saul, started out on the other side of the fence from Richard. He had a five-year relationship with a woman before finally deciding he was gay. He defends his reasons for wanting people kept in boxes.

> There is nothing inherently wrong in a genitally based act between a gay man and a heterosexual woman. The problem comes in motivation. I don't see it as a liberating act of transgression but rather a regression—being co-opted back into the norm. When I hear heterosexuals say that they would want to sleep with a gay man or lesbian I feel that it is an intrusion that somehow heterosexuals have a pass that says "Access All Areas." The rights of lesbians and gays have yet to be established beyond all doubt. Heterosexuals operate from a large power base and it is very easy, therefore, to dip into diverse sexualities without risk.

Richard argues that when he is convinced that there are just as many heterosexuals ascribing to the notion of queer politics as there are lesbians and gay men, he will consider the idea to be valid. But it seems that it is yet again gays and lesbians bending over backwards to accommodate heterosexuality. "The law already makes sure that we have to consider heterosexuals before ourselves at every turn. Ninety per cent of the world belongs to straight people. What's so wrong in being protective of my ten per cent?"

Of course he is right. Gays and lesbians are consistently at the vanguard of the sexual liberation movement. Many heterosexuals remain ignorant of the laws that control desire, unlike lesbians and gay men. For example it is illegal for heterosexuals to have anal sex or see the depiction of erect penises, and there is a law that makes sex in a public place illegal even when there are no onlookers to offend. The Operation Spanner trial of men involved in sadomasochistic practices has proved that it is not our prerogative to do as we like with our bodies.

"Queer Politics," says Tatchell, "is trying to help create a society where everyone feels free to relate sexually to anyone else, without guilt or discrimination. Queer Politics is escaping from ghettoisation within a narrow lesbian and gay framework. It is high time heterosexuals took the leap into Queerness. Why should a person be proud to be labelled as such? To a great extent sexuality is invisible. In this time of AIDS with its inherent backlash against gay men it is even more important that we stand up and be counted."

Steve, a man married for twelve years, has decided to do just that. "I've been struggling with my desire for men in relation to my attraction to women, or more particularly my wife, for years. I felt I couldn't have both and hated the term *bisexual* because I didn't think it adequately explained my feelings. I was not experiencing an equality of desire for men and women." Although still with his wife, Steve has just finished a six-month relationship with a man. He feels that taking up the label of Queer is a useful as well as more accurate way of describing his feelings. "Calling myself queer makes less demands on my conscience. It adequately encompasses the lack of sureness that I am experiencing with my sexuality at this point in my life. Should I choose not to sleep with a man ever again, I will continue to subscribe to the concepts of queer. It has been a liberation for me."

I agree with Steve. Calling oneself a Queer heterosexual is a liberating experience. It frees one from the straitjacket of assumed sexual identity. A heterosexually identified person using the word *queer* is a powerful weapon in the fight against sexual oppression.

READING 40

Heterosexual Questionnaire

Martin Rochlin

Most lesbians and gay men are put, all too frequently, into situations where they have to defend their sexuality. This places a considerable burden on people who resent feeling they need to justify or explain their sexual lifestyle. To help non-gay people understand how it feels to be placed in such a situation, Martin Rochlin devised a questionnaire, which is based on "heterophobic" premises, rather than homophobic premises, which exist chronically in our society.

1. What do you think caused your heterosexuality?
2. When and how did you first decide you were a heterosexual?
3. Is it possible your heterosexuality is just a phase that you may grow out of?

Source: Changing Men, Copyright © 1982.

4. Is it possible your heterosexuality stems from a neurotic fear of others of the same sex?

5. Isn't it possible that all you need is a good gay lover?

6. Heterosexuals have histories of failures in gay relationships. Do you think you may have turned to heterosexuality out of fear or rejection?

7. If you've never slept with a person of the same sex, how do you know you wouldn't prefer that?

8. If heterosexuality is normal, why are a disproportionate number of mental patients heterosexual?

9. To whom have you disclosed your heterosexual tendencies? How did they react?

10. Your heterosexuality doesn't offend me as long as you don't try to force it on me. Why do people feel compelled to seduce others into your sexual orientation?

11. If you should choose to nurture children, would you want them to be heterosexual, knowing the problems they would face?

12. The great majority of child molesters are heterosexual. Do you really consider it safe to expose your children to heterosexual teachers?

13. Why do you insist on being so obvious, and making a public spectacle of heterosexuality? Can't you just be what you are and keep it quiet?

14. How can you ever hope to become a whole person if you limit yourself to a compulsive, inclusive heterosexual object choice, and remain unwilling to explore and develop your normal, healthy, God-given homosexual potential?

15. Heterosexuals are noted for assigning themselves and each other narrowly restricted, stereotyped sex-roles. Why do you cling to such unhealthy role-playing?

16. How can you enjoy a fully satisfying sexual experience or deep emotional rapport with a person of the opposite sex, when the obvious physical, biological, and temperamental differences between you are so vast? How can a man understand what pleases a woman sexually or vice-versa?

17. Why do heterosexuals place so much emphasis on sex?

18. With all the societal support marriage receives, the divorce rate is spiraling. Why are there so few stable relationships among heterosexuals?

19. Wouldn't you ask the far-out straight types, like Swingers, Hell's Angels, and Jesus Freaks to conform more? Wouldn't that improve your image?

20. How could the human race survive if everyone were heterosexual like you, considering the menace of overpopulation?

21. There seem to be very few happy heterosexuals. Techniques have been developed with which you might be able to change if you really want to. Have you considered trying aversion therapy?

22. A disproportionate number of criminals and other irresponsible or antisocial types are heterosexual. Why would anyone want to hire a heterosexual for a responsible position?

23. Do heterosexuals hate and/or distrust others of their own sex? Is that what makes them heterosexual?

24. Does heterosexual acting-out necessarily make one a heterosexual? Can't a person have loving friends of the opposite sex without being labeled a heterosexual?

25. Why are heterosexuals so promiscuous?

26. Why do you make a point of attributing heterosexuality to famous people: Is it to justify your own heterosexuality?

27. Could you really trust a heterosexual therapist/counselor to be objective and unbiased? Don't you fear he/she might be inclined to influence you in the direction of his/her own leanings?

From Holiness to Wholeness: My Sexual Journey

Josiah Gromley

It was in high school that my sexuality and my spirituality began to clash. I had been involved with a number of Christian denominations in junior high and early high school, leaving each when the guilt I felt became too much for me to bear. I went through a particularly negative time in my senior year; I turned in desperation to Satanism and my depression grew.

A teacher, reputed to be a good Christian, took an interest in me. I began to talk to him and debate religion and philosophy. He finally convinced me to return to Christianity, after which I became involved with the church and with a Christian youth group. I confided to my teacher that I was struggling with homosexuality. He and some other members of the group convince me to start seeing a Christian counselor. The counselor had experience with the groups Exodus International and Homosexuals Anonymous. He assured me that both groups had helped his brother in making the transition to heterosexuality.

He explained to me that the cause of my homosexuality was that my sexual identity was injured because I had failed to bond with my father when I was young. He told me that, like certain cannibalistic tribes who eat their enemies in order to absorb their strength and courage, I was sleeping with men because subconsciously I was trying to absorb their masculinity.

The "cure" involved establishing my own masculinity. I was told to start dressing more maturely, wearing dress shirt and pants, at least on Sundays, and I was to become more involved with masculine activities such as sports. I was also told to establish a support group of heterosexual men that I could bond with and to whom I would be accountable. At the same time, I was told to reject anything considered pro-gay. No more gay books or magazines. No more gay friends. No more of my favorite music. I think the idea was that, much like dealing with alcoholism or drug addiction, I was to avoid the temptation at all cost. I thought of it as the sexual equivalent of quitting cold turkey. I can still remember the reluctance I felt at giving up my music. Culture Club was one of the few positive musical representations of homosexuality that I remember while growing up. I felt isolated and alone, but if that was part of being cured, I was willing to pay that price. I did change my outward actions, but in my heart and mind the feelings remained. I couldn't figure out why there were no inward changes. I prayed every day and I thought that since there was no change it was somehow my fault. Did I not pray enough? Did I not have enough faith? Why was I such a failure? Did the God I loved so much hate me?

Each failure to repress my feelings for the same sex brought me deeper into depression. Finally, I began questioning my faith and myself again. I investigated more liberal versions of Christianity and Gnosticism. When my friends at the youth group heard about my doubts, I was told to leave and not return until I changed my ways. That was the last straw. When I was 18, I left the church, I left my "friends," I left my small town, and I moved to Pittsburgh, Pennsylvania.

In Pittsburgh I joined the Job Corps, a government vocational training program, and I was living in their dorms. The resident advisor and I became friends, and she helped me to come out to my family. I was planning to go home for the Fourth of July holiday, so I wrote a letter home telling them I was gay. The resident advisor gave me some advice on the wording. I also called my sister, who I knew had gay friends, and told her to call and let me know if it went badly. She didn't call back, so I thought it must be safe to go home. That ride home seemed like the longest I had ever taken. When I got home I talked to my parents. My father, as usual, didn't really say anything, but my mother said, "As long as you're happy and as long as you're safe, that's all we care about." Their acceptance of me gave me the confidence to come out to my friends as well.

I was still feeling some guilt, and some of my friends began to play upon that guilt. They convinced me that my homosexuality was caused by demonic possession. I was invited to a deliverance service, which is a service that concentrates on prayer to free people who are possessed or oppressed by demons. The deliverance actually began a few days before I went to the service. I was talking to a friend and we got into an intense discussion about religion and my sexuality. I left him and went to sit near some steps behind the Job Corps building. He came out back and the guilt again got to be too much for me. He started to pray with me. I began to experience what felt like something constricting me around my neck, and my face felt like it was swelling. I looked up at my friend and tried to speak, but I couldn't. He put his hand on me and said, "In the name of Jesus!" Then he ran. The next thing I knew, I was at the bottom of the short flight of steps. I finally got enough strength to say, "Jesus help me," and the sensation of pressure left. I got up and went to find my friend. I hugged him and I kept saying, "I'm going to be all right." That is when he invited me to the deliverance service at his church that weekend. At the end of the emotionally charged service, they invited anyone who wanted prayer to come forward. I struggled to the front and began experiencing the same sensations as I had at the Job Corps center. As they were praying for me, there seemed to be a breakthrough and the sensation left once again. I was baptized that same night, and as I was leaving the church, someone asked me to "tarry for the Holy Spirit." I had only a vague idea of what that meant. I knew it was in reference to the Book of Luke in the Bible when Jesus says, "Tarry in Jerusalem until the Holy Ghost shall come upon you." I said yes, and people surrounded me and began to speak in tongues. I was overcome by a sense of peace and joy greater than I had ever felt before. I also began to speak in tongues and was later told that this is the sign of being filled with the Holy Spirit. Once again I began to struggle against my sexual feelings. This time the struggle was compounded by the fact that each stirring of my feelings was seen as an attack from Satan and his demons.

After I graduated from Job Corps, I rented a room from a lady who was convinced that the power of the Holy Spirit could change me. She prayed with me when temptations came and rejoiced at anything I did that was even remotely heterosexual. I spent another two years struggling with my feelings, especially those I was experiencing for my best friend, a man struggling with his own bisexual identity. I again started to doubt my spiritual path and began to study New Age literature. Only then did I begin to realize that maybe Spirit had created me this way.

One day as I sat on a bus watching a handsome man, I started to quote 1 Corinthians 6:9–11: "Do you not know that the unrighteous shall not inherit the kingdom of God? Do not be deceived: . . . neither effeminate, nor homosexuals . . . shall inherit the kingdom of God. And such were some of you; but you were washed, you were sanctified, you were justified in the name of the Lord Jesus Christ, and by the Spirit of our God." As instructed, I told myself that God had made me straight. Suddenly, I realized how stupid that sounded. There I was telling myself, "I'm not gay. I'm not gay." When, in fact, the whole time I was imagining this guy sitting beside me being naked! It was ridiculous!

At that point, I began to live a double life—my gay life and my church life. I felt schizophrenic and paranoid most of the time. I went from having anonymous sex in the restrooms of porn theaters on Saturday to being a tearful repentant choir member on Sunday. I lived in fear that a church member would be walking down the street as I was exiting the local gay bar or bookstore. After some time, I told my landlady about my new spiritual path and that I was finally able to accept my sexuality. She gave me five days to get out. I was devastated that someone who claimed to be a follower of Christ could do this to me. I didn't know where I could go! I was thankful that my best friend was quickly able to pull some strings and get me into the Y.M.C.A.

After that, I became very promiscuous, and at the same time, my feelings for my best friend grew into love. Unfortunately, he met a woman whom I thought he was in love with, and I just couldn't handle it. I moved back to the small town where I was born and raised.

I began to study more self-affirming spiritual paths. Eventually, I found Wicca, an earth-centered spiritual tradition. Two books in particular that were instrumental in my choosing that path were *Witchcraft and the Gay Counterculture* by Arthur Evans and *Another Mother Tongue* by Judy Grahn. Both books deal with the connection between homosexuality and a special spiritual status in many pagan societies. It was through these two books that I learned to see my homosexuality as a gift from the Goddess. Through my studies and participation in a variety of religious traditions, my spiritual path has broadened. The same sense of joy and peace that I first felt at charismatic Christian meetings, I have since felt during a Buddhist meditation, in Neo-pagan circles, in Native American sweat lodge ceremonies, and while reading Sufi poetry. Although I consider myself Wiccan, I am open to experience the Divine wherever it may manifest.

The eleven years since I left Pittsburgh has been a journey toward healing my soul. I am now out and proud and in the process of trying to make my small town a safe place for anyone to come out. I am a member of a local organization that attempts to educate the community about gay, lesbian, bisexual, and transgender issues. I have been on panel discussions on sexuality at the local college. I am an active member of the local Unitarian-Universalist Church. I think the most important thing any of us can do is just to be authentic and practice what the author Starhawk calls, "The art of remaining who you truly are."

READING 42

The *Straight*jacket of My Homophobia

Benjamin B. Herold

Homo-phobia is my fear of that which is the same as me.

For me, homophobia is a fear of men. It is not a fear of homosexuals, although it does result in me fearing homosexuals and being threatened by them. Homophobia means acting on this fear—most often in avoidance of homosexuals or places where I know there will be homosexuals, but occasionally in silent acceptance of homophobic violence or harassment, and almost always in a lack of sympathy or understanding for homosexuals.

For me, homophobia also means being afraid to be close to men.

Homophobia means being afraid to be close to myself; I am a man.

Homophobia means not being able to be intimate with other men who are like myself—men who have been similar places, done similar things, felt similar emotions, and cared about me in a way similar to how I care about them. I often feel close with them, but I almost always feel we are unable to share our feelings about our shared experiences, no matter how close they have made us. This is often true, despite my wish for it to be otherwise, with my father, my brothers, my best friend from high school, and other men I am close to.

Homophobia means that I am unable to reveal my feelings to other men because I know from experience that they will not understand, will look at me like I don't make sense, will attempt to joke with me rather than ask me questions about how I am feeling, will rarely share a similar experience to make me feel better, will make fun of me, or will ignore me. It means often unthinkingly responding in those ways to men who attempt in their own ways to reveal their feelings to me, especially when other men are around.

Homophobia means that I can never feel comfortable touching other men openly and freely. Usually we shake hands. If we hug, we almost always clasp hands in front of our chests first, and clap each other on the back—this makes it more of an action and less of a sharing moment. It means that I can never feel comfortable touching or being touched by another man in any way that is directly and openly connected to his or my emotions.

Homophobia means that although I sometimes do reveal my feelings to men in spite of these fears, and although I sometimes do hug or hold other men when they are upset, and although this usually makes me feel much better, I have a difficult time taking that sense of sharing outside of that specific situation. I tend to act like talking about my feelings once makes everything O.K. After I am O.K., I can pretend that I was never really having feelings of confusion or fear or hurt in the first place, and I can pretend that I really didn't need to talk about my feelings.

Homophobia means that I pretend to myself and to others that this kind of connection with other men isn't really important to me. I don't let other people, including whoever I have been able to reveal my feelings to, know how much it means to me.

Homophobia means almost never telling men that I love them. It means pretending—acting as if—the intimacy that I do share with men isn't very important to me, and instead emphasizing the closeness that doesn't involve sharing our feelings or touching each other (unless we are playing sports together.)

Homophobia means that, because I am unable to make my intimacy with other men a conscious and active part of my general life, I end up feeling worse soon after sharing my feelings with another man. I end up wondering what happened to my initial feeling of closeness that resulted from sharing my feelings. It usually seems to disappear all of a sudden. Because it was a lie, I forget that I told myself and others that sharing my feelings wasn't important to me. It means, in the end, believing even more that talking about my feelings with another man isn't important to me or helpful to me.

Homophobia means that I feel even further removed from my own experience and my own feelings than when I started out; after I have shared my experience and feelings with a man who I know can relate personally to what I am saying better than anyone else. It doesn't make everything better in the long run, I feel even more confused, hurt, or afraid. I feel very alone.

Homophobia means daily telling myself stories and lies to convince myself that I don't really have those feelings, or that they don't really affect me that much. It means daily telling myself the lie that it wasn't important to me to share my feelings with another man, only now I tell myself this in stronger tones, to make sure that I convince myself.

Homophobia means that I seem to keep getting farther and farther away from knowing the simplest of things, what I am feeling. It means that I feel the need to rely on somebody outside of my life, who I am not particularly close to, to make sense of what I am uncertain about. It means that I put a lot of faith in experts, officials, authority figures, and scientific studies to tell me what I could be telling myself if I was willing to listen as closely to myself as I do to them.

Homophobia means working hard to explain my feelings to myself. It means working hard to make sure that I don't actually feel them, and it means convincing myself that this is right and good because I don't need to feel them, I already "understand" them.

Homophobia means knowing all along in the back of my mind that I have no idea what I am feeling, why I am feeling it, or how I am feeling it. It means knowing in the back of my mind that I am getting mad at people I care about for reasons that don't really have to do with them, but never admitting this. It means telling people close to me that nothing is wrong when something is wrong. It means telling myself that nothing is wrong when something is wrong. It means knowing in the back of my mind that what I am feeling doesn't make any sense to me.

Homophobia means going for long stretches of time without talking about how I feel and without even really noticing that all of these feelings are building up inside of me, and then all of a sudden becoming overwhelmed with those feelings. Homophobia means reaching a point on a regular basis where I feel the overwhelming need to let out all of my feelings at once. It means a persistent longing to be known, to be understood, and to reveal myself.

Homophobia means not knowing how to do anything other than those things.

Homophobia means then turning to the women that I am close to in order to try to deal with these feelings. I have already proven that trying to share these feelings with a man doesn't seem to make them more real to me and thus ends up making me feel worse in the long run. I have already convinced myself that being close with men is more important than being intimate with them, and I have already convinced myself that revealing my feelings to them is counterproductive.

Homophobia means believing that women should fill all of my needs for emotional intimacy—it is their duty, their responsibility, and their area of expertise.

Homophobia means that I begin to think of women only in this way.

Homophobia means expecting the woman that I am close to, and with whom I want to share my feelings, to help me say what I don't know how to say, even though she usually has no idea what I want to say and makes this abundantly clear to me.

Homophobia means getting upset at the woman I am close to when I have trouble saying what I need to say.

Homophobia means finally breaking down and just saying anything and everything that is in my mind and heart—weeks worth of injustices, hurts, insecurities, fears, confusion—all in about 5 minutes. It means looking up only after I'm done and being crushed to find the woman that I care about looking at me with confused eyes. It means not realizing that I couldn't have made much sense, that I was talking more to myself than to her, and that there is no reasonable way I could expect her to piece together everything I said.

Homophobia means resenting her for not understanding.

Homophobia means failing to consider or accept the possibility that the problem is with me.

Homophobia means immediately closing back up, getting defensive almost immediately after sharing my feelings with the woman I am close to, and feeling threatened because I have worked so hard to expose myself and now I feel doubly revealed. This woman I am close to now knows not only that I have many feelings that don't make sense to me, but also that I really put myself out in trying to explain them. She knows that I have failed.

Homophobia means feeling even worse for having tried to share my feelings and feeling even more alone because I can't share my feelings with the men and women I am close to. It means making myself even more resolved to not let these feelings get to me from now on.

Homophobia means still wishing that I could share my experiences, still wishing that there was someone who could know what I went through and could share it with me. It means trying once again to share it with the men in my life by simply spending time together, or doing something together, or making fun of our own stupidity for worrying about our feelings. It means being pretty sure that this strategy is working *this* time, and being glad that I have men who I feel close to. It means reconvincing myself that the woman I am close to must then be somehow at fault for everything that happened, and making sure that the same thing won't happen again. It means cutting her off from my feelings, which are starting to build up again, but which I am resolved to get the better of this time.

Homophobia means knowing in the back of my mind that the woman I am close with was really the one who made the greatest effort to try to understand me, but not being willing or able to admit this to myself.

Homophobia means telling myself that I don't really do any of these things, and it means believing what I would like to be true about myself much more than I believe what is true about myself.

Homophobia, by this point, means being afraid to be close to men, women, and myself.

It does not, however, mean that I don't still yearn strongly for this closeness.

Homophobia means that I seek to fill many of these emotional needs through sex. Since these emotional needs are primarily about becoming reconnected to my own experience and feelings, which I constantly feel like I am losing, sex becomes primarily about wanting to become reconnected to myself.

Homophobia means that sex becomes more about feeling good about myself and for myself than about feeling a shared pleasure through being physically intimate with another person.

Homophobia means that most things that connect to these emotional become sexualized. It means that love and sex become the same thing. It means that touching and physical closeness—which often make me feel better about myself—must lead to sex. Once I begin to become aware of my emotional needs and once they start to be met, I am quickly overcome with realizing all of my feelings of inadequacy and wanting to get rid of these feelings as fully as possible. I think that the way to do this is to have the most fully sexual experience possible.

Homophobia means that sex becomes a central goal and theme in my life, because it is the only way I can think to address these feelings of inadequacy and make myself feel better without having to reveal my feelings, without having to address someone I am asking for help as an equal, and without having to really know myself.

Homophobia means that I only have to know what I feel in my penis during sex. It means that the actual sex act becomes purely physical because I am working hard not to expose the feelings of inadequacy that emotional closeness during sex exposes. It means that sex can often be very physical but less than erotic because I am spending all my time and energy in trying not to confront my feelings and focusing on how I feel, particularly in my penis, and so little time and energy in actually sharing myself physically and paying close physical attention to my partner.

Homophobia means that I often feel horrible and empty after sex. I have been trying to fill a space that I have closed off. I have been using my own body to distance myself from my own feelings. I have been using another person's body to tell me something about myself. I know all this, but I often block it out of my mind during sex, and immediately after sex I have to go to work overtime telling myself stories to convince myself that none of it is really true.

Homophobia means that I feel empty because I know how beautiful and pleasurable sex can be and has been at times when I wasn't seeking solely to fill my own unadmitted emotional needs, and how good it can make me feel. But I can't figure out why it isn't always like that. I don't understand that when I try to use those feelings to *do* something for me, I lose them.

Homophobia means that I increasingly have to treat women as sex objects. Since it is their duty, responsibility, and area of expertise to fill my emotional needs, and since I increasingly find that the only way I can consistently approach these needs is sexually, it thus becomes women's duty, responsibility, and area of expertise to fill my emotional needs sexually.

Homophobia means that I not only increasingly treat women as sex objects to feel better about myself, I also treat them as sex objects that are less than equal with me. If I were to treat women as equal, that would imply that what they thought about me mattered.

Homophobia means being deeply afraid of what women think about me.

Homophobia means, then, being caught in a horrible bind and taking my frustration and anger out on women. It means that I am relying solely on women to reconnect me to my feelings and experiences, but also that I am afraid of what women will tell me. It means a cycle of asking for women's thoughts, sexuality, and talents, and then getting scared at the last minute and doing everything I can to devalue what she has said and is about to say in order to convince myself that I don't have to listen to her.

Homophobia means that I devalue women because I am afraid to find out the truth about myself. In no area is this more true than in sexuality. As much as I want a woman to love me, find me attractive, arousing, and pleasing, I am more scared that these things are not true. I will try to convince myself that I am attractive, arousing, and pleasing by trying to convince her that these are true, but rarely will I ask her if these things are true. Almost never will I provide an open and comfortable space for her to say what she wants to say, in the way she wants to say it, when she wants to say it.

Homophobia means that I only directly seek emotional fulfillment through sex. It also means that under no circumstances can there be any sexual elements to my relationship with another man. Although I am looking, ultimately, to find myself attractive, to be able to feel good in a simple, equal, and healthy way, and to be able to understand my own experiences, including and especially my sexual experiences, I can never ask a man for these things. This despite the fact that the men I am close to share these same general desires, the same male bodies, and the same general experiences.

Homophobia means that I refuse to look where I know I should most easily be able to find an empathetic companion.

Homophobia means that when I masturbate, it almost never makes me feel better about myself. Usually, the best thing masturbating can make me feel is a sense of relief, followed by a kind of escaping tiredness. More often, it also makes me feel empty.

Homophobia means that I cannot seek to pleasure myself sexually, I can only seek to cause myself to ejaculate. It means that I think these are the same thing. This means that usually I think about something (even if it's a person, the person becomes in my mind a thing that I can control as I wish) besides my own body before ejaculation. It means that as pleasurable as the sensation of ejaculation is in my penis, I feel empty all throughout my body almost immediately afterward.

Homophobia means that I never focus my actions or thoughts during masturbation on making my entire body and mind feel good.

Homophobia means not understanding why I can't seem to fill my emotional needs or feel good about myself no matter how many times I ejaculate.

Homophobia, in sum, means that I am afraid of homosexuals because they threaten a part of myself, that I do not know how to know myself, that I cannot admit that I have problems, that I cannot look to share myself with other men, that I treat women extremely unfairly to avoid the truth about myself, and that my sexuality becomes about many things other than sharing erotic expressions of intimacy.

Homophobia is not the only factor that can potentially contribute to my feeling these ways, and homophobia can mean many more or fewer things to me. Not all of these things directly or perfectly characterize me, but there is more than enough truth in them for me to find myself, which is ultimately what I am looking to do.

Homophobia means that as I was writing this paper, I worried despite myself that the men at the computers next to me would see what I was writing about and think that I am gay.

READING 43

Sexualities in Community: Past and Present

SEXUALITY AND RELATIONSHIPS IN THE SHAKER, ONEIDA, AND MORMON COMMUNITIES

Lawrence Foster

Why has sexuality been restructured and expressed so differently in communities that claim a religious or spiritual basis? Do long-lived communities from the past that have struggled with such issues have insights to offer us today?

Source: Reprinted with permission from Communities magazine. Sample issue, $6; subscription, $20. store@ic.org.

These are issues that have continued to fascinate me for more than two decades as I have intensively studied three colorful communal religious experiments from nineteenth-century America—the Shakers, the Oneida Community, and the Mormons.

Each of these groups attempted a radical restructuring of relations between women and men within their communities as part of what they viewed as the immanent coming of the kingdom of heaven on earth. Yet the sexual systems these groups advocated and practiced differed greatly from each other—celibacy among the Shakers, "free love" or group marriage in the Oneida Community, and polygamy among the Mormons.

What were the social and intellectual factors that made possible such divergent experimentation in the early nineteenth-century years of the young United States, especially the 1830s and 1840s before the Civil War? How were religious and sexual impulses fused in each communal experiment?

To appreciate the complex challenges faced by people who organized or joined these three unconventional religious groups, we must first place these movements into their larger social and intellectual context. Our tendency today is to feel that we live in a uniquely turbulent age. We often think that nineteenth-century America, in particular, was somehow more "stable," "traditional," "conservative," or "Victorian."

This impression is highly misleading. Not only have there been other periods of uncertainty and rapid transition in American life, but one of the most disruptive of those periods came in the 1830s and 1840s when Americans were leaving behind earlier, relatively more stable, colonial patterns but had not yet arrived at the newer, Victorian approach. All the earlier social institutions were being called into question on matters ranging from religion to politics to economics to family life.

No region of the country was undergoing more rapid transition than western New York state following the completion of the Erie Canal in 1825. This "burned-over district," as it was called because of the frequency with which the fires of the revival spirit swept through the area, was a hotbed of new religious and social movements, much like California is today. Every conceivable mainstream or unorthodox group seemed to be able to find a following in the burned-over district.

Many people were at loose ends, seeking for answers to pressing religious questions and for a more satisfying lifestyle, but none more insistently than the Shakers, the Oneida Perfectionists, and the Mormons. In New York, the Shakers set up or enlarged their celibate communities, the Oneida Perfectionists established a "free love" colony, and Joseph Smith saw visions, "translated" his golden plates, founded the Mormon church, and may first have considered the idea of plural marriage, which he would later begin to introduce among his followers in Illinois in the early 1840s.

THE SHAKERS AND CELIBACY

Although the Shakers experienced a period of disruptive "spiritual manifestations" and attracted many new members in the 1830s and 1840s, their roots actually went back to England in the mid-1700s. There they were known as "Shaking Quakers," or simply "Shakers," because of their highly emotional religious services in which they literally shook, shouted, danced, and spoke in tongues.

Under the leadership of Ann Lee, a poor but highly intelligent and dynamic Manchester factory worker, the Shakers also developed their distinctive commitment to celibacy. Ann Lee had experienced four traumatic deliveries, losing all of her children either in infancy, or, in one case, at the age of six. Rather than viewing these tragic experiences as her unique problem, she instead came to the remarkable conclusion that her traumas represented a universal human condition. She argued that only by giving up carnal intercourse entirely and devoting all energies to God could humankind ultimately be redeemed.

This message attracted few converts in England, but in America during the disruptive aftermath of the American Revolution the Shakers developed a highly committed following of several thousand people, many of them teenagers. The unusual Shaker worship services, which by their own admission could sometimes be heard from as far away as two miles, created considerable hostility, as did their demand for celibacy, which many saw as an outrageous assault on normal human relationships and indeed the entire social order.

Following the death of Ann Lee and the other English leaders because of the intense persecution they experienced, American Shaker leaders formally set up essentially monastic communities in which women had complete equality with men in religious leadership. Men and women lived together as "brothers" and "sisters" in communal "families" of between 50 and 100 or more individuals under one roof, but strictly separated in all their daily activities. Although men and women had equal roles in the hierarchical religious system of the Shakers, economic roles were very traditional, with Shaker women doing typical women's work—cooking, sewing, cleaning, and washing—while Shaker men did traditional male tasks in the fields, shops, and similar locations.

During the pre-Civil War years, there were some 60 semi-autonomous Shaker communities at 18 geographical locations, and with as many as four thousand members scattered from Maine to Ohio, Indiana, and Kentucky. By the Civil War, when the intensity of their proselyting ardor slackened, the Shakers had become increasingly respected and even admired by many of their neighbors. Today the Shakers, who have dwindled to a handful of members in one village at Sabbathday Lake, near Poland Spring, Maine, are best remembered for the quality of their workmanship, especially their functional furniture, and for their hymns such as "Simple Gifts," which provided the chief theme for Aaron Copland's composition "Appalachian Spring."

THE ONEIDANS AND "FREE LOVE"

At least as complex and remarkable as the Shaker movement was the community founded by John Humphrey Noyes at Oneida, New York, in 1848. This "free love" group, which also was based on deep religious conviction, has fascinated journalists, scholars, and the general public for more than a century. John Humphrey Noyes began as an intense young theology student at Yale, then wandered quixotically around New England and New York trying to convert the world to his highly unorthodox religious beliefs. Failing to

achieve that goal, he turned his sights to establishing a community and spreading his message via the newspapers he printed.

For more than 30 years, first in his hometown of Putney, Vermont, and then at Oneida in central New York State, Noyes successfully presided over a communal system of "complex marriage" that the journalist Charles Nordhoff described as an apparently unprecedented "combination of polygamy and polyandry with certain religious and social restraints." The group members, who numbered more than 200 adults at the community's peak, considered themselves all married to each other in an "enlarged family." Men and women exchanged sexual partners frequently within the community; while breaking up all exclusive romantic attachments, which were described as "special love," antisocial behavior threatening communal order.

Associated with this unorthodox system were a number of complex control mechanisms. All members lived together in one large communal Mansion House, ate together, worked together, had a system of communal child rearing, and shared all but the most basic property in common. Community government was achieved by having daily religious-and-business meetings which all adults attended, as well as by using an informal method of group feedback and control called "mutual criticism," in which smaller groups of 10 to 15 men and women would meet regularly to candidly assess strengths and weaknesses of members of the group. Also important was an informal status hierarchy known as "ascending and descending fellowship," in which those deemed as being of higher "spirituality" (usually older members) would associate, sexually and in other ways, with those deemed as being of lower "spirituality" (usually younger individuals) in order to help bring the "less spiritual" individuals to a higher level.

Among the most complex of the Oneida control mechanisms was its system of birth control by "male continence." Under male continence, a practice technically known as coitus reservatus, a man and woman would join together physically but the man would not ejaculate, either during intercourse or after withdrawal! Noyes argued that male continence allowed for fuller expression of "amative" sexual communication than normal "propagative" sexual intercourse could. The practice also was effective as birth control. During a 21-year period when it was the only sanctioned method of birth control at Oneida, only 12 unplanned births occurred in a community of some 200 adults, equally balanced between the sexes, and exchanging sexual partners as often as twice a week. In the final decade at Oneida, a controversial "stripculture" experiment in selective human breeding was introduced in which certain members volunteered or were chosen by a committee to have children, with the aim of genetically producing the best quality human stock.

At Oneida, sex roles were perhaps more radically revised than in any comparable American communal group. There was far less role stereotyping, men and women worked alongside each other, and women served in positions of authority over men in certain jobs. The system of complex marriage, which was associated with these practices, existed at Oneida from 1848 until 1879, when it was given up because of a combination of internal dissatisfaction and external pressure. In 1881 the group also officially gave up its communistic system of economic organization, reorganized as a joint-stock corporation, and went on to become one of the most successful small businesses in the United States, best known for its silverware, which is marketed today throughout the country. Today descendants of the community are indistinguishable from ordinary Americans; if anything, they are more conservative in their social and political orientation.

THE MORMONS AND PLURAL WIVES

Larger and more successful then either the Shakers or the Oneida Community—at least in numbers—was the Church of Jesus Christ of Latter-day Saints, or Mormon church, as it is popularly known. The roots of Mormonism go back to Joseph Smith, a precocious, sensitive, and ambitious young farm boy living near Palmyra, New York. Deeply disturbed by the cacophony of ideas and causes that surrounded him, young Joseph began having a series of visions in the early 1820s. He concluded that all existing religions were wrong and that God had specially chosen him to set up a new religious and social synthesis.

Smith began by engaging in what he described as a "translation" "by the gift and power of God" of inscriptions on golden plates he claimed to have found buried in a large hill near his home. Published as the Book of Mormon in 1830, the same year that Smith officially founded the Mormon church, both the book and the Mormon movement were a focus of curiosity and controversy from the very beginning. Fierce persecution developed because many individuals viewed Mormon religious claims as an outrageous hoax and their rapidly growing, close-knit church as a threat to American democratic values. During their first 20 years, the Mormons were forced to move repeatedly—from New York, to Ohio, to Missouri, to Illinois, and eventually to Utah.

An important factor that eventually contributed to the hostility faced by the Mormons was Joseph Smith's decision in the early 1840s to introduce the idea and practice of polygamy secretly among his closest followers living at the Mormon headquarters in Nauvoo, Illinois, along the Mississippi River. In 1843 Joseph Smith privately promulgated a new revelation there calling for restoration among the Mormons of polygamous practices similar to those of the biblical patriarchs Abraham, Isaac, and

Jacob. These new standards were set within the larger context of a conception of marriage, growth, and development lasting throughout all eternity. Not surprisingly, many of Joseph's closest followers who were strong supporters of monogamy were outraged by this move. In 1844 Joseph Smith and his brother Hyrum were murdered in a jail in Carthage, Illinois, while awaiting trial on charges arising in part from the dissatisfaction of some of their followers with the new polygamous beliefs and practices.

This tragic denouement might have been expected to cripple the young church and lead it to abandon polygamy. Instead, the reverse occurred. Under Brigham Young's leadership, and following a heroic trek to the Great Basin region, polygamy became fully established among the Mormons. From 1852, when the Mormons in Utah first announced to the world their commitment to plural marriage, until 1890, when intense federal pressure combined with internal Mormon dissatisfaction to force official discontinuance of the practice in the United States, polygamy was accepted as the highest standard of marriage by more than one hundred thousand Mormons in Utah and adjacent areas of the American West. Today, the strong family ideal that undergirded polygamy has been transferred by Mormons to an equally strong commitment to the nuclear family as the core of Mormon religious and social life. As memories of polygamy have receded, Mormonism has developed an increasingly positive public image, becoming one of the fastest growing religious movements in the United States and securing more than nine million members worldwide by 1995.

The unorthodox sexual systems of the 19th-century Shaker, Oneida, and Mormon communities have continued to be a focus of curiosity and misunderstanding. Nonetheless, they have implications for us as we struggle with similar problems today.

SHAKERS: THE APPEAL OF CELIBACY

Shaker sexuality and interpersonal relationships have perhaps been more widely misunderstood than any of the other groups I studied. Americans typically have great difficulty comprehending why individuals would want to renounce all sexual intercourse and devote their full attention to the worship of God. Shakers often have been caricatured as aged bachelors and spinsters without strong sexual impulses, sweet but slightly daft individuals who devoted their time to producing fine furniture and singing "Simple Gifts." In fact, Shaker celibacy appealed to a wide range of individuals from teenagers to families with as many as 10 to 15 children! And while most Shaker communities were located in rural areas, one black Shaker outfamily was located in Philadelphia, and another large Shaker family drew much of its membership from Brooklyn and New York City.

The passion with which the Shakers struggled to overcome their carnal natures and the unorthodox conclusions they reached about lustful sexual intercourse as the root of all evil are conveyed in a powerful statement from the one of the basic Shaker theological works, first published in 1808:

What is there in the universe, within the comprehension of man, that has so sensible, so quick and ravishing an operation, as a corresponding desire of the flesh in the different sexes? As a gushing fountain is more powerful in its operations than an oozing spring; so that desire of carnal enjoyment, that mutually operates between male and female is far more powerful than any other passion in human nature. Surely then, that must be the fountain head, the governing power that shuts the eyes, stops the ears, and stupifies the sense to all other objects of time and eternity, and swallows up the whole man in its own peculiar enjoyment. And such is that feeling and affection, which is formed by the near relation and tie between male and female; and which being corrupted by the subversion of the original law of God, converted that which in the beginning was pure and lovely, into the poison of the serpent; and the noblest of affections of man, into the seat of human depravity.

ONEIDANS: REINVENTING HUMAN SEXUALITY

If the Shakers sought to overcome the raw power of sexuality and devote their full attentions to God by living celibate lives, the Oneida Community attempted to achieve similar goals by universalizing heterosexual contacts among adults in the "enlarged family" at Oneida. Oneida sexuality has been most as misunderstood as Shaker celibacy. For many years, it was fashionable to describe Oneida as part of the vanguard of sexual liberation and women's rights, a prototype for the future with much to say to us today. More recently, many feminists have gone back to Oneida records and concluded that John Humphrey Noyes was really a male chauvinist and his community a disappointment to those seeking true equality.

Neither of those approaches does justice to the extraordinary complexity of the system that emerged at Oneida, with both its repressive and liberating features. John Humphrey Noyes made this remarkable statement in one of his theological articles, suggesting the great openness possible at Oneida in understanding human sexuality:

Most of the difficulties which have arisen in respects to our social [i.e., sexual] theory, have been based on the idea that woman is a perishable article—that after her first experience in love, she is like an old newspaper, good for nothing. A virgin is considered more attractive than a married woman who has had experience. But the reverse of this should be the case, and when things come to their right hearing, it will be seen that the reverse of the common idea is the truth. It is a scandal to God, and man, and

woman, that in the estimation of men, a virgin is better than a married woman. It is so universally preferred, but why? It is because woman has yielded to the worldly idea, and lost her self-respect. She supposes the enigma is solved, and does not carry about with her fresh consciousness of mystery and worth, that a virgin does. The married settle into the feeling that the enigma is solved, and that makes them less attractive. The principle operates, in the same way, in both sexes.

MORMON PLURAL WIVES: EARLY FEMINISTS?

Like the Shaker and Oneida sexual systems, Mormon plural marriage in the nineteenth century has been widely misunderstood. Mormon plural wives were viewed by the outer world as a benighted and oppressed class, the victims of a system of institutionalized lust perpetrated by a wicked and lascivious male Mormon priesthood. In fact, however, despite the very real emotional strains polygamy caused, Mormon women in frontier Utah enjoyed a remarkable degree of real power, influence, and independence. Mormon women, many of them plural wives, voted earlier than women in any other state or territory in the United States, including Wyoming, and they played an important role in the national women's suffrage movement. For more than 40 years, Mormon women put out the *Women's Exponent*, the first major women's newspaper west of the Mississippi River, which fearlessly criticized women's inequalities with men in the social, economic, and political spheres. In the environment of frontier Utah, and with the aid of their powerful women's organization, the Relief Society, Mormon women temporarily adopted a variety of new roles beyond those possible to other Victorian women in the late nineteenth century.

Only in the twentieth century, and especially since World War II as the Mormon church has experienced a ninefold increase in its membership, have Mormon women's roles been so sharply restricted. Visiting Utah today, one feels one has stumbled into another era, into a scene from a mid-Victorian advice manual. Almost everywhere, the ideal that is held up for Mormon women conveys the gush and cloying sentimentality of the "cult of true womanhood." Even though half of all Mormon women in Utah today work outside the home to help make ends meet, they are repeatedly told by the Mormon hierarchy that their role should be limited to the home. As one sensitive Mormon woman put it recently:

> I feel that what we're losing in the Church is diversity. There's such a push for uniformity and conformity that all the beautiful little nuances of differences are being swept aside. That's what God really enjoys. Otherwise, he wouldn't make every leaf and snowflake different. You should have the freedom to have some time to be yourself, and to have people appreciate that you're different. You should try to appreciate this in your children and not try to push them all into a prescribed mold. I think that in an authoritarian church this is one of the dangers. We have to let some pilot projects develop in individual lives, too. Until we do that, how are we going to let a woman make the individual contribution which is particularly her own?

In conclusion, the Shakers, Oneidans, and Mormons all grappled, often in quite different ways, with how human sexuality should be expressed in interpersonal relationships within their communities. While the particular solutions they developed to the social disorder they perceived around them may not always seem appealing, the problems with which they struggled are perennial ones which continue to confront us as we seek to achieve more harmonious and fulfilling relationships between the sexes today.

A SMORGASBORD OF ALTERNATIVES

Ivy Bressen

Not long ago I heard a fascinating tale about the filming of "The Wizard of Oz." You probably remember the grand welcome Dorothy receives from the Munchkins when they learn that her house has landed on the wicked Witch of the East—dancing, prancing, singing, and all sorts of fun.

Now in real life the Munchkins were played by dwarfs, a cast of hundreds. The story is that previously most of the dwarfs lived more or less isolated existences. Suddenly, when they arrived on the set, they had an opportunity to get together with more dwarfs than they had ever dreamed possible. Apparently they had such a good time that the filmmakers had trouble keeping a handle on them. Numerous relationships were formed, and some of these presumably extended long past the time the movie was complete.

Similarly, many people who arrive at an intentional community encounter a group containing more like-minded folks than they have ever been able to associate with. Often the newcomers have spent years toiling away, holed up in some stifling urban or suburban existence, continually afraid of being, at best, laughed at and, at worst, attacked for their views. Suddenly they find themselves in a place where others also believe in stewarding the earth or making less money or eating vegetarian or encouraging women to fix cars or simply speaking from the heart, "Eureka! I am not alone," they cry with elation. They look around them and see a group of 12 to 20 or 100 potential friends, playmates, and lovers.

SPECIAL SUPPORT FOR RELATIONSHIPS

While communitarians in relationships face some unusual difficulties, several unique support structures also exist which are not available to the population at large. (Outside of community; people say one should never become involved with someone you work with, but in community almost everyone you meet is someone you work with. A number of communitarians circumvent this issue by refusing to become lovers with anyone in the community; limiting themselves to outsiders.) In any case, one community support structure is the presence of people there who, either by necessity, experience, or inclination are skilled at conflict mediation. These services are generally accessible with no fee and with a decent level of respect from the wider group for trying it.

A second support, while it may seem odd, is the set-up of the situation itself. If the choice were between leaving the community you were devoted to, remaining there in utter misery, or getting over your emotional buttons and living there happily, which would you choose? The harshness of the first two creates a powerful push toward the third. You may be dragged over the evolutionary precipice kicking and screaming, but you are likely to be dragged nonetheless. Obviously, this is a simplified version of what can happen, for in real life such changes tend to happen in painful fits and starts with only occasional exhilarating breakthroughs. Luckily, along with the conflict mediators there are plenty of co-counselors, support groups, outside therapists, and good old-fashioned shoulders to cry on.

In addition, there is a whole range of intimacy available, so that even if one loses a lover, one can meet many of those needs through other types of relationships. Besides the aforementioned mental health services, there may be groups for personal growth or contact improvisation or free writing or yoga. Sometimes opportunities arise for more casual sexual encounters. And in the community I live in, it is common for friends to sleep together quite companionably with no sex involved at all.

In fact, given the opportunity in a utopian community to theoretically create almost any kind of relationship, it's surprising how few people break out of the usual molds: friends; colleagues; heterosexual serial monogamy with various attendant transgressions; political allies or enemies; or some combination of the above. Presumably this is because we all arrive with the same social conditioning we received on the outside with everyone else. It is equally difficult to cast out that kind of limited thinking along with learning to live without greed, competition, and excessive individualism.

FREEDOM FOR ALTERNATIVES

Another aspect of the culture at Acorn is a noticeable lack of monogamy. Of the dozen or so members of whom I have reliable knowledge concerning their relationship patterns, only one is definitely monogamous. The others range along a continuum. Elissa, for instance, hasn't let the fact that her lover joined, at her request, in a monogamous relationship keep her from participating in at least one group sexual encounter (her lover was invited but declined). Several others are willing to go along with whatever arrangements their lovers want. I locate myself at the other end of the spectrum, the staunch nonmonogamist of the group.

My guess is there are probably a few members not romantically involved with anyone at present who would tend toward monogamy if they were, but we're not discussing a silent majority here. Even if I assumed every person I was unsure of was monogamous (an unlikely proposition), that would still total well under half the community. There's also a lot of bisexuality, especially among women, but I suspect nonmonogamy overlaps more age (older members tending more toward monogamy) than sexual orientation.

These characteristics make Acorn unusual among FEC communities. *(The FEC is a network of egalitarian, income-sharing communities, including Acorn, Twin East Wind—Ed.)* However, both I and East Wind were known earlier in their history for having strong norms toward nonmonogamy. Ten or 20 years from now when Acorn is larger and more established, will we also have settled into relationship orientations which mirror the dominant patterns on the outside? Personally I hope not, but only time will tell.

One difference between nonmonogamy here at Acorn compared with the early days of Twin Oaks or East Wind is that here there is no community ideology supporting it. People seem to be practicing nonmonogamy because that's what they want to do, rather than because the community as an institution has set out to change the American moral code. I am probably the only member likely to launch into a rhetorical condemnation of monogamy, and I don't think anyone here has changed her or his behavior on the basis of my oration.

It is possible that as a young community (Acorn was founded in 1993), we are more likely to attract people who are somehow different or more radical. It makes intuitive sense that people with nontraditional ideas would be drawn to a community still in its formative stages, where they could more likely work their ideas into the fabric of the culture.

Or perhaps chance brought together enough people to form a critical mass, which now continues to grow into the future. For instance, in my own search for an intentional community, I was nervous about leaving behind the less intentional but still important community I had participated in, which supported my relationship choices.

When my partner Bean and I began looking full-time for a community to settle down in, the existence of people who identified openly as bisexual (or my preferred term, polysexual) or had more than one relationship partner at the same time were a few of the factors I would use to rate communities on my internal checklist. At several communities, while my sexual and relationship orientations were deemed theoretically acceptable, I saw very few people actually practicing them. Therefore I figured the chances of finding partners in the adventure were slim.

When I arrived at Acorn, relationship preference was one of many ways in which I felt at home. Several people had more than one lover, various sexual orientations were in evidence, and the atmosphere seemed generally easygoing about the whole topic. This made quite a good impression on me, given that the community had less than a dozen members at the time. This, along with many other positive factors, collectively led me to decide to live here.

Now I have been here since the fall, and we're talking about hosting a polysexual gathering very soon. A conference center was one of the early business ideas for the community, and clearly the events can precede the facilities. I enjoyed doing a lot of polysexual activism before I joined Acorn, and helping to organize this gathering would be a way of continuing that effort in community. Once we put on a public event, we'll become known among polysexuals as a welcoming place, and more of them will visit or tell their friends about us and eventually a few more will move here. Thus, the cycle will continue.

It is hoped, though, that we will never reach a point where a happily married couple would feel out of place. Many of us share a goal of sincerely and institutionally welcoming as much diversity as possible. And no matter what kinds of relationships people form here, they are affected by additional aspects of community life based on the fact that we live, work, play, sleep, and eat together.

Because we spend so much time together, some people think that relationships tend to move through various stages faster than on the outside. In fact, life in general sometimes seems accelerated here, with three months' worth of events taking place in the space of a week.

Most of all, you see everyone at their best and everyone at their worst, and they see you those ways too. Particularly in a smaller community, there's no hiding who you are or at least how you interact. Each person has access to a more holistic picture of everyone else's humanity, and forms relationships accordingly. It seems to me a better basis from which to build functional, caring, creative relationships, but naturally I'm biased. I live in community!

INFILLING WITH THE SPIRIT AT CHRISTIANSBRUNN KLOSTER

Bro. Johannes Renatus Zinzendorf

Sex and religion are usually a volatile mixture, especially in the confines of a monastic community. Western religious thought traditionally views the body as something to be rigorously controlled if not outright condemned, while the intangible soul is approved and lauded. Such is not the case at Christiansbrunn Kloster, 55 miles northeast of Harrisburg. It helps not being Christian.

We are a post-Christian religion of Harmonists, the religion that, we believe, comes *after* Christianity. As Harmonists, we live and act in the oneness of the Holy Spirit, which to us is the creative force incarnated as our Mother Earth. Each of us, as well as all living and non-living things on the planet, is a facet of the jewel that is the Holy Spirit. Given that we are the spirit incarnate, it follows that sex, as a healthy and healing part of the spirit, is not only natural but encouraged here at the cloister. But we push the envelope one step

further because, as single Brothers, it is specifically gay sex that is important and an integral part of our religion.

We call ourselves the Guardian Angels of the Garden, androgynous as Adam in the beginning, no longer children but returning now as adults to take our place as the eyes and hands of the Holy Spirit. It knows and changes itself through us. We are its consciousness and its conscience. In return for using us, it fills us and makes us whole. And that is where sex comes in, for one of our sacraments is to partake of the Holy Spirit by filling and being filled during sex. I doubt if a straight man can truly know what it means to be filled with and by the spirit, except in a theoretical way. That does not mean straights cannot be Harmonists. It means they must approach the spirit in their own way, just as interested single Sisters must approach being Harmonists from their perspective and community.

In practice, this means that gay sex is not just fun but instructive. It does not mean that all sex here is ritualistic or that there are ongoing orgies. A gay brother could live his entire life here, never have sex with others, being for all intents and purposes celibate, and still be filled with the spirit. Understanding the act is as important as the act itself or else it just becomes mindless humping. Potential visitors generally fall into two categories: those excited by the sex aspects but not interested in the religion, and those interested in the religion but unsure of the sex.

The first kind of visitors are bound to be disappointed. There are not 50 hunky priests here ready to offer hot sex. We are smaller in number than the Shakers and only about eight of them are left. Besides, sex is not for outsiders. It's a gift, not a right of visitation. The second kind of visitors can only be relieved. Sex is not required, expected, or demanded. It must be consensual. If it happens, it happens and it happens as an adult decision. Brothers must be 18 years or older.

The brothers are viewed as a family, each taking the same last name of our gay founder, Christian Renatus Zinzendorf, who died in 1752. Within that family may be pairings, triplets, hermits, whatever, and these may shift over time. But our primary relationship is with the Holy Spirit. We are its brides, the Book of Revelation's "Woman of the Wilderness," waiting for the Divine Bridegroom, the Holy Spirit, to fill us in so many different ways. That is our state of grace and we carry it with us every day, as in the words from our favorite hymn.

*We are the Woman of the Wilderness
Waiting for the Bridegroom to come,
Waiting for his healing grace,
Waiting for his loving embrace,
We are the Woman of the Wilderness
Waiting for the Bridegroom to come.*

PART SIX

COMMODIFIED SEX: THE BUYING AND SELLING OF SEX

Any social discourse on sexuality must address the extent to which sexuality is part of the economic system of the culture. In a Marxist sense, it is not a question about sexuality but about exploitation. In what ways is sex bought and sold? Who buys? Who sells? Who benefits? Who loses? That sex is a commodity in a commodity-driven society is no surprise. It is a concern, however, given that the marketplace is controlled by those who hold social and economic power—by men over other men, men over women, adults over children, and wealthy people over the poor.

Prostitution has become a multibillion-dollar international industry operated for and pursued by people (primarily, but not exclusively, males) with money. Commercial child sexual exploitation has become an increasing concern, especially in economically poor countries such as Thailand that rely on North American and European men for infusion of cash into the economy. Yet commercialized use of children for sex is also a problem in the United States, Mexico, and Canada (Estes and Weiner, 2001).

The largest groups affected—runaways, thrownaways, and other homeless children—use "survival sex" to acquire food, shelter, and clothing, to stay alive on America's streets. Street children, solicited for sex repeatedly by men, are exposed to violence, drugs, rape, and even murder at the hands of pimps,

423

"johns," and traffickers. Many of the runaway and thrownaway youth were victims of physical or sexual abuse at home or are sexual minorities whose families have rejected them. Having left abusive homes, they encounter even greater danger on the streets. According to Estes and Weiner, boys may be the most hidden victims. They are often ignored or ill-served by law enforcement and human service systems, in the belief that boys can "take care of themselves." Other groups of commercially sexually exploited children in the United States are girls in gangs, drug users, foreign children brought illegally, and youth trafficked as part of organized sex crime rings.

When prostitution is called "the world's oldest profession," there is a presumption that it has always been with us, and always will be, which is an essentialist notion. It is more useful to see the selling of sex as related to the patriarchal creation of institutionalized heterosexuality in the form of marriage. The role of "good girl" wife and mother became the opposite of the "bad-girl whore." The "professions" of artist and metalworker evolved prior to the institutions of private property and marriage, therefore would be older professions than that of prostitution. In prepatriarchal cultures, temple priestesses had sacred sexual communion with men, in the name of the goddess. The term "sacred prostitutes" has come into use to describe that role, but it is a misnomer in that it employs a current social construction that is very different from the paradigm of sexual relations between males and females that existed at that time.

Using Crane and Crane-Seeber's historical analysis of the "good girl/bad girl" boxes, what are the conditions that could lead to the practice of exchanging sex for money? What are the implications for men's status? For the prostitute? If the whore is the bad girl, then are all "bad girls" whores, whether or not they get cash for a sexual act? Does the analysis change when males are the prostitutes serving men? Serving women?

When disputes arise around prostitution and pornography, they are generally about whether prostitution should be legalized and whether porn should be censored. While interesting questions, they often reduce the focus to a debate, without much critical analysis about the commodification of sexuality and ways that prostitution and pornography contribute to the ways we image gender, sexuality, and sexual relationships. Who owns "sex" anyway? What do prostitution and pornography reflect and reify about the status of women and children in society? Why do men use prostitutes? Porn? Why do women, and men, engage in sex work? What is the implication for the continuing "whore" stereotype on all women and sexual minorities? Are advertisements that use sexualized bodies to sell products another form of pornography? The stories and articles in this section provide information and theory with which to address such questions.

This section begins with voices of sex workers, sharing the perspectives, experiences, and feelings of those who trade sex for money. Donna Marie Niles in "Confessions of a Priestesstute," talks about how the "standard" treatment of young women—for example, being sexualized on the streets and virtually everywhere or having sex be expected in exchange for a dinner date—made her entrée into prostitution at age 19 an easy transition. To her at the time, it was either one man in marriage or many men for cash. As a white, educated, feminist hooker, she made a lot of money. It was the constant threat of arrest, as well as being in an industry based on the sexual objectification of women, that finally led her to leave that business. Other women and men, depending on class, ethnicity, substance use, orientation, and other circumstances, have widely differing experiences in the sex industry.

T. R.'s reflections, in "What It Cost," are much more stark. He describes the effects of having been a male prostitute from age 12 to age 35. The losses he has experienced include his ability to feel and to be open when he is having sex, effects that are shared by many people who were abused sexually as children.

Gloria Lockett talks about "Leaving the Streets." Police had encouraged her and some friends to get off the streets, to open a massage parlor or run ads. So she and a few other women rented an apartment and ran ads in an adult magazine. Then a vice cop posed as a customer, solicited one of the women who worked there, and made arrests. None of the men who had paid for sex was arrested, although they promised to be witnesses. They got only probation on those charges, which as Lockett reports, the police found very frustrating. Three years later, she, her lover, and a good friend—the only blacks in the group—were arrested on federal charges that she suggests were an attempt by the police to follow through on the case they had lost earlier. All the white people were granted immunity in order to get them to testify. Her lover and her friend went to prison, while she was acquitted, leaving her and her children without their father home with them.

As you reflect on these stories, consider your image of sex workers, and the circumstances of their lives. What feelings and reactions come to you as you read their stories? In what ways might race and class be related to differences in their experiences?

In her analysis of the prostitute as the prototype of the stigmatized woman, "The Social Consequences of Unchastity," Gail Pheterson theorizes what Donna Marie Niles said she felt. The constant sexualizing of women that Niles experienced serves as a justification for abuse, according to Pheterson, in that sexual attractiveness is de facto in this culture a symbol of unchastity. Pheterson theorizes the connections between unchaste and impure, generally defined as mixed with foreign matter, dirty, or discolored. The author makes associations to race, ethnicity, class, and sexuality. Whores and blacks, she states, have traditionally been treated as slaves and criminals—unclean and sexual. Jews too have been stigmatized as unclean and defiled, excuses for the long-term discrimination they have experienced, for example, being forced to live in ghettoes in Europe for many centuries and being decimated in the Holocaust. Working-class people have been portrayed as nobodies, Pheterson maintains, expected to dirty themselves in the interest of commerce and production. Formerly all women who worked in a public job were treated as prostitutes by upper-class men. There was no proof of chastity for a self-identified woman, since any "respectable" woman would be home caring for her husband and family. Pheterson extends her analysis to the meaning of defilement, which refers to experience, pollution, or violation, the opposite of female virginity. She relates the stigma attached to the nonvirgin, the victim of child sexual abuse, or the defiled male/homosexual, as a mark of shame or disease on the unchaste. Vulnerability to the whore stigma is a very real aspect of sexual oppression.

What reactions do you have to the connections the author makes between sexuality and images of defilement and impurity? In what ways does the threat of being seen as a whore serve as an instrument of gendered power relations?

Julia O'Connell Davidson, a British sociologist, presents in an excerpt from "The Sex Exploiter: Theme Paper for the Second

World Congress against Commercial Sexual Exploitation of Children,"* the complex mix of economic, political, social, and legal factors associated with commercial sexual exploitation of children internationally. The problem, she maintains, goes far beyond that of pedophilia. She considers the diversity of "sex exploiters" in terms of their identities, attitudes, and motivations and calls attention to the circumstances that shape demand in a range of settings, in both the first and third worlds. Her definition of sex exploiter—those who take unfair advantage of some imbalance of power between themselves and a person under the age of 18 in order to sexually use them for either profit or personal pleasure—includes the perpetrator as well as those who do the marketing and trafficking. Her analysis draws upon a deep consideration of the complexity of the topic. In what way does this author's discussion of the political and economic conditions underlying sex exploitation add to your thinking on this issue?

Similar questions can be asked about pornography, a billion dollar a year business whose sole purpose is to profit from marketing images of sex. Mariana Valverde, in "Pornography: Not for Men Only," addresses what pornography is and the purpose it serves in society. Defining pornography is in itself a challenge because it is not, as Valverde says, a natural object that can be classified. Rather, it is a complex cultural process. It establishes, and is established by, a set of relations between producer and consumer, between consumer and his or her social context, and between the social context and the producer. Valverde focuses on the social context, which relates strongly to the impact of pornography on women. She sees violent porn as less pernicious for women in some ways than the soft porn of unrealistic and unnatural images of the female body, because few women see the anonymous women in the violent scenes as role models. What about the self-inflicted violence many women suffer, she maintains, because of the mainstream media's use of male-oriented images of beauty and desirability? Popular romance novels directed at women are also soft porn, the author asserts, because they eroticize domination—male sexual power and males' social and economic power over women. Patriarchal ideology is even

---

*We encourage you to view the entire report, with discussion of the environment behind exploitation and recommendations for control, prevention, and reintegration, at the website noted as the source of the reading.

woven into the language to describe sexual arousal and satisfaction. For example, Valverde notes that women in these stories do not lust, they tremble, quiver, or shudder. Valverde explicates her reasons for taking an anticensorship position when it comes to pornography, arguing that the real solution is to empower women and other oppressed groups so that they can begin to redefine what is erotic and what is not. What questions does Valverde's analysis raise for you about what is pornographic and what is not?

In "Pornography and the Alienation of Male Sexuality," Harry Brod discusses how pornography shapes our sense of the sexual, particularly for males for whom porn has been a major early influence. He explores ways in which pornography alienates men from their own sexuality and their ability to have emotionally connected relationships with their partners. Brod illustrates the influence of symbols and the meaning we give them, suggesting that males come to think of sex as something that rests outside of themselves, sex as located in "other"—inviting the perception of having sex with an object—restricting sexuality to what he calls "genital performance." In pornography, Brod suggests, there is no need for the consumer of porn to be intimate and no need to communicate or negotiate the sexual experience. Our sexual needs have less to do with orgasm than with touch, intimacy, and closeness. Yet males are raised, Brod suggests, with the notion of being powerful, while at the same time often feeling alienation and a sense of powerlessness. He discusses the influence of what he calls "fratriachy"—the rule of the brothers—wherein males feel they are without a nurturing or even authoritative father as role model and provider of emotional support. While males collectively may dominate most aspects of society, males individually don't feel powerful. Pornography, says Brod, "is both an expression of their public power and an expression of their lack of personal power." Porn provides males a sense of power—easily obtained through a $5 purchase. In what ways, if at all, does Brod's analysis resonate with your thinking about pornography and men? Might the dynamics he presents affect all men and women, even those who do not use pornography, because of the sexualized images of women that dominate commercial media?

Kathy Myers, in "Towards a Feminist Erotica," asserts that the question of whether sexually explicit material is erotica or pornography depends on the context. Who is the intended viewer? What is the representation of the sexual? What are the conditions of its production and consumption? For what purpose is it being presented? What is the difference between erotica and pornography from your perspective? Can erotica that has been produced by women or sexual minorities help to empower them? In what ways do Myers' questions about the context change the impact of the images?

The articles in this section provide more questions than answers, for these are issues of profound complexity. Like many aspects of a world in which money is power and media is the message, the ways that sexuality has been commodified reflect the gendered, sexual cultures we live in today. Your ideas about these issues, and your behaviors, as a response, matter. Think about it.

REFERENCES

Estes R. and Weiner N. A. (2001). The commercial sexual exploitation of children in the U.S., Canada and Mexico, downloaded from http://caster.ssw.upenn.edu/~restes/CSEC.htm May 8, 2002.

READING 44

Voices of Sex Workers

The following stories relate varying experiences, percep-
tions, and feelings of people who have worked in the sex
trade.

CONFESSIONS OF A PRIESTESSTUTE

Donna Marie Niles

When I was nineteen years old, I made what seemed like a conscious decision to become a prostitute. Having experienced sexual harassment on the job, in the streets, and in virtually every area of life, it was not a particularly fantastic leap to take. It was a very easy transition, raised as I was to be a female. I'm always surprised to find that more women don't choose to enter the life, especially those with extensive "dating" herstories. Any woman who has ever been on a date, who knows what it is to exchange affections or sex for dinner, or kindness, or survival, is quite prepared to be a hooker. Learning to serve, please and appease men is something that binds all women together. It's why secretaries, nurses, waitresses, wives, sales clerks, etc. are on the low paying end of the very same stick. To separate our experiences too much, or to believe that the ways we get by in this woman-hating world are so different, is a mistake. Women as either virgin or whore is one of the greatest lies that men ever created about us.

I took up working as profitably as I could within a structure that basically offered me either one man in marriage or many men for cash. As a white, educated, feminist hooker, I made more money than I ever expected to see

Source: Sex Work: Writings by Women in the Sex Industry, ed. Frédérique Delacoste and Priscilla Alexander. Copyright © 1987, 1998 by Frédérique Delacoste and Priscilla Alexander. Published by Cleis Press.

again in life. Because I was an independent contractor, I had a lot of time left over to live my life in. These were two of the reasons why it was quite difficult to leave.

I'll never forget the depression I experienced in my first straight job out of the business. I was a secretary. As a prostitute, I had to keep moving, life was rarely predictable, and many people were interested in who and where I was: police, hotel security, tricks, cab drivers.

As a secretary, I was invisible, treated with either disregard or patronizing contempt. My credibility (i.e., getting heard or listened to) took a skydive as I changed from hooker to radical lesbian feminist. On top of this, I worked a regimented forty-hour work week for ridiculously low pay. I was literally earning in two weeks what I had previously made in an evening, and paying taxes! It was a shocking welcome back to respectability.

But I have endured, and have not returned for many reasons. One of them is the exhaustion of the constant threat of arrest. It wears you out worrying about going to jail all the time. However, the major reason I left was I simply could no longer justify working in an industry that profited from the sexual objectification of women. Since I felt I could no longer be in collusion with the men who make billions from our suffering, I had a lot of good-byes to work on. I said good-bye to the diet, fashion and the industries, and other institutions that tell me I am ugly and smelly and in need of alteration because I was born a woman.

When men sell women's bodies, or images of women's bodies, it is called pornography and it is legal, its right to exist vehemently defended with the first amendment. But when women sell their own bodies, it is called prostitution, and we can see what an imperative it's been to protect the rights of prostitutes in our society.

I began to get a glimmer of the magnitude, the enormity, behind the expression, "It's a man's world." I saw who was profiting from our blood, our loving, our bodies, and for whose profit and convenience every institution on planet earth was set up.

Ironically, I still expected them to give it all up. I can truly grasp the reformist feminist notion that by simply explaining, repeating the litany over and over, by holding enough demonstrations and writing enough letters, men will finally get it and abdicate. I spent years talking to men, trying to educate them as to the injustice of it all, explaining how feminism would save them, too. It was the only angle on feminism I was able to sustain their attention with.

Ultimately, I have come to realize that it is women who deserve that kind of loving, devoted patience, that passion and tenderness. We can't go around begging for their time, or attention, or power any longer. Men have no reason to surrender and no intention of handing over a system designed to nurture only themselves. We need to take back not just the night, but our lives if we are to have them.

WHAT IT COST

T. R.

I was a male prostitute from age 12 to 35. I am now 48. For 23 years I turned tricks of all kinds from $20 blow jobs to $500 for more "exotic" specialties—BD, SM, etc. I made lots of money, had lots of sex—of one kind or another. So *how* could it have cost me?

It has cost me one hell of a lot more than I ever made!

Anyone who gets into the sex trade, as a child or as an adult, faces the following: lack of trust; loss of intimacy; detachment—turning the senses off; problems with boundaries—towards others, themselves, and others actions

to them; loss of self-worth; confusion of sexual identity; relationships flounder; behaviors; hiding behind false bravado–artificial shield; denial—of what you are doing is harmful, that you are actually enjoying this; so much pain—emotionally, psychologically, intelligently—that you have to try and stifle the pain with drugs, booze, more sex, risky behaviors, and anything else we can find. We deal with loathing of self and sex partners, flashbacks of rapes and violence, the need to pretend we are in control, when in fact, we are not!

In the sex trade you fake intimacy, fake involvement, fake interest. So what happens after you leave prostitution? You are so used to faking everything, you can't do the real thing! You question why anyone wants you, you look for the catch, their real reason for wanting you; or worse, you fall into "automatic pilot"! Your body is there having sex, but you are elsewhere, far away—where it is safe, and you feel nothing!

You can have erections, orgasms, and all that; but you are not there! And the longer you hook, the longer it takes to get over that, if you ever can! For me, sex became a job, as mindless, mind numbing, and boring as flipping burgers at Mickey D's! I turned sex on, on demand, whether I wanted to or not. Give me the money, I'll turn it on. Then get the fuck away from me! And in a lot of ways, sex today is still like that. I don't feel any connection with any partner, even though I am retired from hooking. I don't feel the contempt or apathy toward my partners like I did for the johns, but I am not connected. It is very hard for me to stay interested, focused on what is going on without "zoning" out. My mind is away, somewhere safe.

Today, I have to be the one to initiate sex. That is the only way I can stay grounded enough to enjoy it. If someone was to come up behind me and pat my ass or grab me, they had better duck, cause I will slug 'em. And keep on slugging them. I know that is a result of childhood sex abuse.

Source: HOOK Online, a not-for-profit publication: www.hookonline.org/art/art_dl_0007_cost.htm (retrieved 2/5/02).

I have spent the last 10–12 years working on all of these things. It hasn't been easy. In fact, it has been a real uphill battle. I don't regret my past, but I want to get on with my present and my future.

A new issue has come up as I am learning about healthy intimacy. Do I tell someone interested in me about my past? If so, when? Do they need to know? Do I need them to know?

I have quit drinking, drugs, the sex trade, risky behaviors, and hanging out with that crowd altogether. I am in therapy for years of sex abuse. I am light years away from where I was as a hustler and will probably spend the rest of my life working toward feeling better. I will never be "over it," but I will feel better about it.

Don't think it will never happen to you! It's happening right now. I always thought I was in charge, in control, the one with the power! After all, the johns were willing to pay me, weren't they? And they would pay more for me to humiliate and degrade them!

But was I the one with the power? No! Money controlled me! Money for shelter and food, but more control over me was for the drugs, booze, and partying to deaden my senses, so I wouldn't feel the pain, shame, and all of the other things I didn't want to face. I lived with denial for all the years I was a hustler.

LEAVING THE STREETS

Gloria Lockett

In 1978, I was working on the street in San Jose, California. The police kept on telling me and the other women I worked with how intelligent we were, and how we should not be working the street. They told us we should open a massage parlor, or run ads, or something, but that we were just too bright to work on the street.

So I got together with a few women I knew and trusted, and we decided to get an apartment together and run ads in an adult magazine. The telephone rang constantly. We had an idea that the San Jose vice were among our callers, but what we did not know was that from the first week we were under constant surveillance.

The apartment lasted three months. One day everything changed, and my life hasn't been the same since. The vice called, pretending to be a customer. He came to the apartment with a transmitter in his belt buckle, and solicited one of the women who worked there. They arrested her, me, and four other women. There were four men in the apartment, having paid money to engage in sex with us. None of them were arrested. They only had to promise to be witnesses against us.

We were charged with four misdemeanors: 647(a), soliciting or engaging in a lewd act in a public place; 647(b), soliciting or engaging in an act of prostitution; 315, keeping a house of ill fame (i.e., a house of prostitution); and 318, prevailing upon someone to visit a place for the purpose of prostitution. We were also charged with two felonies: living off the earnings of a prostitute (i.e., pimping); and conspiracy.

I was charged with pimping because one of the women had given me money to put away for her, which is a very common practice among women who work together. She asked for it back, because it was money the vice officer had given her, and it was to be used in evidence. The police immediately told me I was under arrest for pimping. I was not at the time, nor have I ever been, a pimp.

The case stayed in court for two years, at a cost to the taxpayers of approximately one million dollars—the estimate of the prosecutor and the police officer in charge.

Source: Sex Work: Writings by Women in the Sex Industry, ed. Frédérique Delacoste and Priscilla Alexander. Copyright © 1987, 1998 by Frédérique Delacoste and Priscilla Alexander. Published by Cleis Press.

We were willing to plead guilty to being in a house of prostitution, but the prosecutor would not allow that. He wanted a felony conviction. Finally, we were found guilty only of being in a house of prostitution. We were put on probation, and charged a fine, but we were not sentenced to do time in jail. Needless to say, the police were very upset. They vowed to get us.

In 1983, my lover of nineteen years, a very good friend of mine, and I—the only Blacks in our group—were arrested on twenty-four counts of violating federal laws, including three counts of tax evasion, nine counts of violating the interstate travel act, ten counts of mail fraud, one count of a known felon having possession of a weapon, two counts of harboring witnesses, and two counts of racketeering. All the white people in our group were granted immunity in an effort to make them testify against us. My lover was found guilty of twelve of those counts, and is now doing twenty years in a federal prison in New York State. My friend pled guilty and got three years in a federal prison in California, and five years probation. I was fortunate enough to be acquitted.

When my lover and I got together, my children were two and three. This wonderful man is the only father my children have ever known, and now he is in prison thirty-five hundred miles from them.

The Social Consequences of Unchastity

Gail Pheterson

The prostitute is the prototype of the stigmatized woman. She is both named and dishonored by the word "whore." The word "whore" does not, however, refer only to prostitutes. It is also a label which can be applied to any woman. As an adjective, "whore" is defined as "unchaste."[1] Significantly, unchastity in a man does not make him a whore although it may determine his status in other ways. The whore stigma is specifically a female gender stigma which can be defined as "a mark of shame or disease on an unchaste woman."[2] This article provides a framework for understanding that

Source: Sex Work: Writings by Women in the Sex Industry, ed. Frédérique Delacoste and Priscilla Alexander. Copyright © 1987, 1998 by Frédérique Delacoste and Priscilla Alexander. Published by Cleis Press.

stigma along two socially critical dimensions of unchastity, namely impurity and defilement. Those dimensions have been chosen because they expose social justifications for racial, ethnic, and class oppression (grounded in notions of impure identity) as well as for physical and sexual violence (grounded in notions of defilement through experience). Each dimension will be explored for both women and men with the help of research and interview citations.[3] Since one function of the whore stigma is to silence and degrade those it targets, this article is self-consciously committed to giving voice and respect to persons traditionally denied such legitimacy.

IMPURITY

One definition of unchaste is impure. Impure is defined as "dirty, mixed with foreign matter, adulterated, mixed with another colour." Unmistakably, such a definition activates associations of racial and ethnic diversity wherein only white, non-foreign people are chaste. People of color, foreigners (people of different origin than the ethnic norm), and Jewish people become the unchaste ones, the dirty ones. Pure is defined as "clean, white, and unadulterated." Often clean is used in the sense of clean hands; clean hands belong not only to white people but particularly to white middle- and upper-class people. Servants, workers, and childrearers "dirty their hands." An analysis of the impurity dimension of unchastity brings us directly to the links between the whore stigma and racism, anti-Semitism, and classism.

Women of color, Jewish women, and working-class women are vulnerable to the whore stigma as women *with a denigrated status.* Men who deviate from the white heterosexual male norm are also vulnerable, not to the whore stigma but to racial, sexual, or class stigmas. In fact, no one is immune to accusations of unchastity; it appears that no one can fit all norms and that "the dynamics of shameful differentness are . . . a general feature of social life."[4]

RACISM AND THE WHORE STIGMA

Whores and blacks have traditionally been treated as slaves and criminals. They are considered the unclean ones. They are considered the sexy ones. Black women are often assumed to be whores. One black woman who is not a prostitute said, "When I stand waiting for a bus, especially in a white neighborhood, men passing assume that I'm working. My color means 'whore' to them." Black men are often assumed to be pimps. A white woman said, "Since I've had a black boyfriend, people look at me suspiciously, as if I was a whore and he was my pimp. One white man actually asked if my boyfriend was my (smirk) boss, although it sure seemed obvious to me that we were a couple. He even had the nerve to ask if I needed help to get away!"

Black women are assumed to be sexually available; they must prove their honor. Black men are assumed to be sexually predatory; they must prove their worthiness. White men traditionally accuse black men of raping white women, an accusation which has historically led to the murder of black men.[5] White men also traditionally rape black women, a transgression which is blamed on the sexual nature of black women. Both sex and race are seen as dark, mysterious, and dirty. Both are judged unchaste and thereby unfit for public life. Accusations of impurity are used to deny visibility, voice, and power to the "sexy ones" and to the "dark ones." Symbolically, sexy and dark have intertwined into one alluring taboo. People of color are considered mistresses (women) and monsters (men) regardless of their sexual behavior. In essence, the whore stigma together with the racial stigma dehumanizes people of color and transforms human sexuality into a beastial force.

Prostitutes are considered shady women regardless of their color. A black street prostitute, when asked about differences between black and white whores, said, "We're all standing on the same corner. We're all sucking on the same dick. Sure, some white men won't take me, a black lady, into a hotel because they're afraid of being conspicuous, but in private or on the street a whore is a whore." It is true that in some countries (such as the United States), a higher percentage of black women than of white women are sent to jail for prostitution.[6] And, in many countries (such as the Netherlands, France, and Germany) third world women are more likely to be exploited in prostitution than native white women. Such racist mechanisms compound the stigmatization of whores of color but they do not minimize the "dark mark" branded on any prostitute.

Racial impurity is put forth as a justification for prohibition and segregation.[7] Prohibition refers to restrictions in particular about what enters the body. Segregation is an attempt to separate the chaste from bodily temptation and contamination. The impurity assigned to race is glued to the shame assigned to sex. Divisions into the pure and the impure, the madonna and the whore, the wife and the prostitute, or the white and the black mirror divisions of conscience from pleasure, belief from act, or segregation from sisterhood. Laws are made, cities are planned, and children are raised to ensure those divisions either officially or unofficially.

Although unchastity stigmatizes only women as whores, it does stigmatize certain groups of men in other ways. Like men who affiliate with prostitutes, homosexual men and men of color are deemed unworthy. Homosexual men are targeted with a gay or faggot stigma because they are regarded in dominant society as female men; men of color are targeted with a pimp stigma because they are regarded in dominant society as violent and irresponsible men. Stigmatization effectively denies heterosexual white male privilege to gays and men of color and, at the same time, absolves heterosexual white men of identification with sexual variations or of responsibility for sexual violations. One prostitute in Italy said, "Lots of married men prefer pre-operative transsexual prostitutes (men in the process of becoming women who have both breasts and a penis); they want gay sex without forfeiting heterosexual identity."

ANTI-SEMITISM AND THE WHORE STIGMA

Jews, too, have been identified as unchaste. However, whereas black unchastity is primarily attached to mythologies about black women's sexual mysteries and black men's physical violence, Jewish unchastity is primarily attached to mythologies about Jewish women's sexual victimization and Jewish men's financial conspiracies. "The 'beautiful Jewess' is she whom the Cossacks under the czars dragged by her hair through the street of her burning village."[8] Or, perhaps closer to modern associations, the Jewess is she who underwent sexual experiments in Nazi concentration camps. One Dutch woman whose parents both survived Nazi camps said, "I don't know if it's because of my thick black hair which stands out in Holland (racial difference) or my parent's camp background (history of abuse), but my Gentile boyfriends always talk about their excitement in being with a Jewish lover and about feeling protective toward me and about my being different from other Dutch women. It sort of makes me feel like an orphan whore." On the male side, the Jewish man is he who wants money and has intelligence, both of which incite him "to do evil, not good."[9] One Jewish man said, "They wanted my ideas but, as soon as *I* profited from them, they accused me of taking over."

Frequently in contemporary societies, stereotypes about Jews are not specified by gender and both Jewish women and Jewish men are seen as victims and connivers. Jewish victimization is stigmatized as unchaste because of supposed racial impurity (used to justify persecution) and defilement (the condition of having been spoiled by abuse). Jewish intelligence is stigmatized as unchaste because it is supposedly deviant, manipulative, and financially self-serving. A portrait of the Jewess as whore and the Jew man as pimp emerges with little reference to sexuality. That portrait is ambiguous. Victimization and intelligence are stereotypes which elicit contradictory feelings of compassion, blame, resentment, guilt, respect, and jealousy. Unchastity in the case of Jews is therefore both enviable and suspect: Jews are, at least, *acknowledged* as sufferers and *validated* as survivors. On the other side, they are *suspected* both for their history of persecution and for their history of survival. "Why were they persecuted?" "How did they survive?" Those questions glare suspiciously at Jews. The historical link of Jewish survival to oppressive interests, be they tax collection in the past or Western imperialism in the present, is used to stain Jewish credibility. Anti-Semitism is essentially the blaming of Jews for society's ills and injustices. Jews are thereby accused of unchastity not only by the ruling class, but also and most painfully by other oppressed peoples.

Jewish oppression and prostitution oppression have many parallels. Like Jews, prostitutes are unchaste both according to conservative ideologies (for their sexual license) and according to radical ideologies (for their transactions with sexist and capitalist men). Both Jews and prostitutes are denigrated and idealized and blamed for basic social problems. Furthermore, the reality of their persecution and daily abuse is frequently doubted or denied. Both Jews and whores are stigmatized for their past experiences, their non-conforming intelligence, their assumed quest for money, and their assumed sexuality. Historically, they have both been legally forced to identify (and isolate) themselves publicly by wearing certain clothes or symbols such as a strange hat or particular color.[10] They both have had to hide or "pass" or migrate in order to survive. And, they both are perceived as simultaneously passive victims and guilty agents (Jews for communism-or-capitalism, whores for disease-or-disorder).

Whether or not particular Jews are stigmatized as whores or as pimps, they are subject as Jews to the paradoxes of the whore stigma. One Jewish prostitute said, "Sex and money stigmas are nothing new for me and I learned about leading a double life from being a Jew in a community of Gentiles. I also learned as a Jew that it's good and necessary to build your own life regardless of what other people think of you. Besides, I know that people will respect exactly the same things in me that they envy or reject, so it's impossible to please. I've got no choice but to live my own life."

CLASSISM AND THE WHORE STIGMA

Whereas a person of color is portrayed as *bad* and a Jew is portrayed as *different*, a working-class person is portrayed as a *nobody*. It follows that dominant societies have set out to tame the colored, expel or exterminate the Jew, and ignore the worker. Chastity for the worker means invisible subserviance. Working-class people include, of course, people of color and Jews; however, in relation to white Gentile co-workers or certainly white Gentile bosses, people of color and Jews are urged to "know their place" and to "pass" as nobodies, or anybodies. Their position may be different from that of white Gentile workers, but in essence class oppression is a dynamic whereby all workers are pressured into conformity and obedience. Women fall under the same requirements as men within the public labor force; in addition, any woman without a maid to clean or a governess to care for children (the large majority, thus) becomes a worker in the private labor force. There, too, her chastity is measured by the invisibility of her labor.

The labor process is associated with dirt, money, feces, noise, muscle, sweat, tears, pain, and repetition. Workers are expected to dirty themselves in the interest of human reproduction and production. They are considered the work horses of society; as such, their own humanity is denied. They are relegated to the back room or the basement or the "bad side of town". They are excluded from opportunities, culture, public debate, and power. Classically, male workers are hired for their brawn not their brains and female workers are hired for their appearance not their performance. Essentially, the male worker's muscle and the female worker's smile are prostituted to middle- and upper-class demands.

The impurity attributed to women workers leads to sexual assumptions and requirements. A man on a beach in Chicago yelled to a woman: "If you weren't so rich, you'd be a whore!" He was crudely expressing the common assumption that poor women are whores and rich women would be whores if they needed money. In other words, women who work for money are called whores. It is true that the more access a woman has to money and privilege, the freer she is likely to be from selling her labor, especially labor sold at the cost of legitimacy. If a woman can separate herself from images of unchastity, then she can hope to gain immunity from the whore stigma. Even then, however, she remains a nobody. At best, the traditional woman can hope to take on the identity of her husband.

In former times, every woman who worked in a public job was "working-class." And, all working women were treated as prostitutes by higher-class men.[11] Women workers in professions of different classes are presently still in a battle against male sexual presumptions and harassments.[12] However, the struggle amongst women workers for rights is usually articulated as a struggle against being treated like whores, rather than as a struggle against the treatment of whores. Prostitutes serve as models of the stigmatized working woman. Women who work, regardless of their class, are vulnerable to the whore stigma. Especially in countries where cultural values weigh against public labor for women, such as the Netherlands, the whore stigma is firmly attached to the work needs and wishes of women.

Race oppression, Jewish oppression, and class oppression are distinct mechanisms of subordination and control. Impurities of blood, history, and status are attributed to the targeted group and used to justify social ostracism, physical mistreatment or persecution, denial of rights, and sexual abuse of women. Oppressed men are assumed to be mean or greedy or inhuman. Oppressed women are assumed to be whores or whorish unless they prove otherwise; there is, however, no proof of chastity for a self-identified or life-experienced woman, Even white skin, Gentile ancestry, and middle-class status are no guarantee of stigma immunity for women.

DEFILEMENT

Whereas unchastity as impurity refers to identity, unchastity as defilement refers to experience. Female virginity is commonly considered the opposite of defilement: the virgin is unspoiled and the defiled girl (or woman) is "spoiled." Non-virginity refers specifically to sexual experience; defilement refers to physical as well as sexual pollution or violation. Boys and men are not stigmatized by (heterosexual) non-virginity or defilement. In fact, the lost innocence which devalues girls is apt to raise the status of boys. Sex and violence dishonor women and honor men. Women are stigmatized with *The Scarlet Letter*; men are rewarded with *The Red Badge of Courage*.[13] Her shame is his honor.

Most traditionally, a girl is supposed to remain a virgin until she marries at which time her husband "takes her." If she should engage in sexual relations before marriage, then she becomes unchaste and, in some cultures, uneligible for a marriage of standing. Whether the sex was voluntary or imposed is irrelevant to the social damage incurred through the loss of virginity. If the sex was imposed then, on the one hand, the girl can at least claim passivity; on the other hand, imposition implies the double damage of sex and abuse. In either case, girls are stigmatized as whores once they have been exposed to sex, by force or by choice. The anxiety with which parents protect their girls from sexual temptation or violation reflects their awareness of the whore stigma. Because the stigma is so devastating for the future of a girl, parents are socialized to protect their daughter's *reputation* even at the expense of her safety, development, or physical integrity. Such a distortion of values has led some fathers to pathologically "protect" their daughters from *other* men by interrogating them, beating them, and/or by sexually claiming them for themselves. One woman told: "I was daddy's little girl. When I hit high school, around age fifteen, I started screwing around a lot . . . As soon as my father found out, he would find an excuse to beat the crap out of me. It happened whenever I had a new boyfriend." Another woman recounted: "My father didn't physically violate me, although I remember I didn't want to wash dishes because then he would slobber all over me with 'affection,' but he held an inquisition every Sunday morning over exactly what I had done the night before. He also competed with my boyfriends, coming into the room where they were and showing off his muscles. He also told me: 1) he would find me a boyfriend when the time came; 2) I would end up walking the streets; 3) no man would marry a non-virgin; and 4) if I got pregnant, I would not have to run away from home."[14] Another woman said, "My father used me sexually since I was five. And then, when I started going on dates with boys, he would accuse me of being a whore. I asked him why I suddenly became a whore once I had a boyfriend of my age when he'd been fucking me for years! He said that with him it was different because he loved me and it was in the family."

Child sexual abuse is the most classic scenario for the shaming of girls. Accusations of girlhood unchastity are then used to justify and pardon male sexual violation. In one striking example, a judge pronounced in a child molestation case: "I am satisfied we have an unusually sexually promiscuous young lady (a 5-year-old child). And he (the defendent) did not know enough to refuse. No way do I believe (the defendent) initiated sexual contact."[15] And, less extreme but essentially identical, a woman recalls telling her boyfriend about having been molested by a man at age eight: "It was like a ghost returning as the familiar grin came to his face and he said, 'You must have been a sexy little girl."[16] In the same vein, a lawyer said of a 14-year-old incest victim, "I can understand her father; she is a beautiful girl." Female beauty, also of a young girl, was thereby offered as a justification for sexual intrusion.

Unlike fathers, mothers rarely abuse their daughters sexually. However, they are socialized to guard their daughter's chastity, be it with warnings, accusations, or denials. Mothers are commonly known to worry if their daughter develops early physically or if she develops a conspicuously female body. One mother said to her daughter when she saw her modelling a new bathing suit: "You can't go out in that! Some man will rape you!" Implicitly, the girl is held responsible for preventing male sexual assault. And, if she should nonetheless fall victim to abuse, she may be blamed for having been provocative or her mother may blame herself for having given her daughter too much freedom. In other cases, the girl is not blamed for the abuse, but she is expected to act "as if nothing happened." One woman recalled complaining to her mother about "Uncle's messy kisses": "I thought she'd tell off my uncle but instead she slapped *me* across the face!" The tendency of mothers to suppress their daughter's sexuality and of fathers to possess their daughter's sexuality is a part of the gender socialization of women and men. Unintentionally, the "protections" of both parents can function more to stigmatize than to safeguard girl children.

Also therapists classically collude in blaming girls for sexual abuse. A male therapist responded in the following way to an incest victim: "From some of the details which she related of her relationship with her father, it was obvious that she was not all that innocent. But she was unable emotionally to accept her own sexual involvement with him."[17] Other therapists, especially of the classical Freudian tradition, are apt to deny the reality of sexual contact between father and daughter altogether.[18] In that case, sexual abuse is not attributed to the girl's seductiveness but to her wishful fantasies. Indeed, the first response to a child's disclosure of incest has often been to accuse the child of lying. Girls are thereby taught to hide their experiences of abuse and to silence their pain.

Once stigmatized as unchaste, girls may become sexually more active and may begin to identify more with harlot than housewife models of femininity. One woman who became a prostitute said, "I was already labelled a whore as a teenager so why not get paid for it?" Another young woman who had been carefully "saving herself" for marriage said, "I was the perfect 'good girl' and then I got raped. It never had been so great saving myself and, once it had happened, I started doing it a lot." And another woman declared, "I was born a whore. My father used to take me around and all his friends would say, 'Hey, who's your pretty date—give me a hug, honey' . . . Since I was young, I identified with harlot images in movies. I liked the glamor." Another woman who was sexually abused by her father said, "My father would call me all sorts of names and would storm around saying, 'You're no goddam good. You're a whore. You're a nothing. You're this and you're that. You're bad through and through.' They [father and mother] would turn even the most innocent relationship [with a man] into a really dirty thing . . . they're constantly calling me a whore—so therefore I am. So therefore I can go to bed with anybody. It's a vicious circle."[19]

The sexualization and vilification and molestation of girls constitute obvious violations of girlhood integrity. It is a cultural shock to realize the pervasive, even normative, occurrence of such adult invasion and abuse of children in society.[20] One woman who never suffered such violations said, "I was aghast to hear my father list the fact that he had never molested me as one of his accomplishments as a father." Apparently, respect for his daughter's sexual integrity did not come naturally. Unlike her father, the girl was not congratulated for her virginity. Only unchastity is significant for women, and then as a stigma rather than as an accomplishment.

The relation between sexual abuse and the whore stigma is especially important now that the incidence and effects of incest are being exposed (see footnote 20). Given the stigmatizing equation of whore with sexual unchastity with abuse with badness, the abused girl is forced to either bury her experience or relinquish legitimacy. Identifying abuse with female unchastity rather than with female oppression maintains the illusions which surround violence against women. One illusion is that female behavior causes male sexual violence. Another illusion is that male sexual violence causes irreparable damage to female personality. Women are thereby not only violated, but also blamed and stigmatized. They are expected to repent rather than to recover. One woman said, "People make all sorts of assumptions about me when they hear about my past. I had an awful childhood of beatings and rapes. Thank God it's over. But the burden goes on in people's judgment of me. It's as if I became a bad person by being treated badly."

For adult women, the criteria of chastity is not virginity, but monogamous marriage (or religious life). And, the keeper of female sexuality is not the father, but the husband (or God). Like children, adult women are shamed and blamed for abuse. It is interesting to note that sexuality and abuse brand girls as (unchaste) women and brand women as (bad) girls.

Within marriage, sexual and physical abuse of wives by husbands is even more acceptable than abuse of daughters by fathers within the nuclear family. One prosecutor in England referred to husband abuse of wives as "reasonable assault" in certain cases, in particular cases of sexual infidelity.[21] Indeed, sexual infidelity is commonly used by husbands as a justification to exercise control, domination, and/or physical abuse. Even close friends and family members are apt to excuse male violence within marriage. One woman repeated a conversation with her mother: "Mom, Chuck (her husband) has beaten me bloody. He has held a gun to my head and . . . he has forced me to have sex with women and other men. He is always threatening to kill me." The mother replied, "But, Linda, he's your *husband."*[22] Certainly not all officials or families are unsupportive, but the stigma attached to the battered or sexually abused woman is socially legitimized. A battered woman said, "I have learned that the doctors, the police, the clergy, and my friends will excuse my husband for distorting my face, but won't forgive me for looking bruised and broken."[23] Conspicuous mistreatment is taken as a sign of the woman's "misconduct," as if battering is a righteous punishment of female unchastity.

Outside of marriage, women are stigmatized as whores for any sexual encounter. Phyllis Schlafly, the most vocal of American antifeminist campaigners said, "Virtuous women are seldom accosted."[24] In other words, being accosted is evidence of a lack of virtue, or unchastity.[25] Furthermore, a woman victim is classically accused of having provoked, invited, or not resisted sexual violation.[26] Prostitutes serve as models of female unchastity. As sexual solicitors, they are assumed to invite male violence. Supposedly, a whore cannot be violated because she already is in violation of chastity norms. In one case of a prostitute being raped, a Dutch officer of justice said in court that "given her profession, the sexual abuse could not have made a deep impression upon her."[27] A Dutch research study revealed that policemen ranked the rape of street prostitutes as the least serious of all possible rapes. Rape by many strange men was ranked as the most serious. Rape by a boyfriend or male acquaintance and rape of a drunk woman were ranked only slightly more seriously than the rape of a prostitute. The researcher asserts that rape is judged according to the risk taken by the woman in her behavior and whereabouts. Significantly, police judgment of the seriousness of a rape is the primary determinant of whether the case is brought to court.[28] Prostitutes know only too well how difficult it is for a whore to prove that she has been raped. Even the presence of a known prostitute in court is thought to jeopardize the credibility of a rape victim.[29] Identification or association with unchastity (be it sexually, racially, or professionally defined) is considered a sign of defilement and availability. That view of the "female as either pure or common to all"[30] works to condone male violence against so-called unchaste women and to blame those women for any abuse they suffer. Of course, those women could be any woman whose virtue is called into question.

Male unchastity is defined more by color, ethnicity, class, or homosexuality than by heterosexual behavior. Fortunately, those indicators are recognized as prejudices rather than proofs, at least in countries with strong traditions of tolerance, such as the Netherlands. For example, the association of rape with black men is a deeply engrained prejudice, but racial identity would not be acceptable as explicit legal evidence of guilt. A woman's sexual history, however, is frequently brought to bear upon the reliability of her testimony.[31] During the last few years, such information is changing status, thanks to feminist struggle, from proof to prejudice. Nonetheless, many courts in North America and West Europe are still likely to hold the rape victim responsible for the rapist's crime.[32]

The ultimate defilement is death by murder or disease. Then, too, unchastity is blamed for fatal corruption or pollution. In particular, the sexual unchastity assumed of prostitute women and homosexual men is perceived as a choice wrought with shame and vulnerability. Violence, illness, and most extremely, death are considered the punitive consequences of self-imposed danger. Revealingly, the murder of a whore or a gay man is considered a "prostitute murder" or a "homosexual murder." Both the whore and the gay man are seen as accomplices to their own demise. One such case was the murder of Pier Paolo Pasolini in Italy. The trial focused as much on the victim as on the murderer. Public scandal centered around Pasolini: Why did he involve himself in a gay scene? Why did he risk murder?[33] Similarly, the murder of a prostitute is as much an incrimination of her reputation as of the murderer's crime. Murder victims of the infamous Jack the Ripper were described in the press as prostitutes; in fact, some were and some were not. The sexual histories of the victims filled newspapers, as if to warn other women of the perils of sexual unchastity.[34] Significantly, concern was expressed only about the danger to non-prostitutes. Also more recently, whore murderers in Leeds, Los Angeles, and Seattle have not been considered a serious social menace until non-prostitutes have been killed. The murder of whores does not worry, grieve, or outrage dominant society. In fact, violence against prostitutes is likely to increase public dissociation from whores.

Disease, like violence, is often blamed on the unchaste. The whore stigma has been defined as *a mark of shame or disease on an unchaste woman*. Historically, even before sexual transmission of disease was understood, prostitution (the symbol of unchastity for women and men) was erroneously associated with epidemics such as the Plague.[35] Also today, the attribution of disease to prostitution is often more based upon assumption than fact.[36] Unchastity is assumed to begin with the whores and spread from them to chaste society via men. The triangle between "dishonorable whore" and "unworthy husband" and "chaste wife" is most clearly drawn by assumptions of sexual disease transmission. "An 'innocent' woman could only get venereal disease from a 'sinful' man. But the man could only get venereal disease from a 'fallen woman.'" That description is offered in an excellent social historical study of venereal disease which goes on to say that such a "uni-directional mode of transmission reflected prevailing attitudes (at the turn of the century) rather than any bacteriologic reality."[37] The same prejudicial attitudes which prevailed at the beginning of the century still justify the blaming of prostitutes for disease.[38]

Like prostitutes, homosexual men have historically been stigmatized as sexually diseased.[39] However, unlike prostitutes, homosexual men are assumed to be insulated from chaste heterosexual society. They are therefore blamed not for contaminating "sinful men" and "innocent women" but rather for causing their own demise through supposed perverse promiscuity. In reality, homosexual men are not insulated (nor truly distinguishable) from chaste society, as evidenced by the fact that male prostitutes cater primarily to publically heterosexual, married men. That fact illustrates the distortion and hypocrisy of privileging supposedly chaste society. On a practical level, it also illustrates the necessity of sexual education and examination for all sexually active persons rather than for only those publicly identified as unchaste.

Sexuality, abuse, and disease are often perceived as both causes and symptoms of unchastity. Whether those socially significant factors lead to pleasure, pain, or death, they are often interpreted as defilement and as justification for permanent stigmatization. Any woman is vulnerable to the whore stigma as a result of life experience, sexist abuse, or ill fortune. Homosexual men occupy a socially parallel position to prostitute women when it comes to violence and disease. Heterosexual men are likely to feel immune to stigmatization only when they publicly distance themselves from "the unchaste ones."

CONCLUSION

Unchastity is used to justify oppression and abuse. Women in general and deviant or subordinate men are especially subject to stigmatization as impure or defiled persons; dominant men may be subject to stigmatization on the basis of the unchastity of their associates (be they, for instance, prostitutes or homosexuals). The task of recognizing unchastity as a normal human reality and not as a peculiar condition of inferior humans calls for a profound transformation of values and attitudes.

NOTES

1. See: *Collins Double Book Encyclopedia and Dictionary.* London: Collins, 1976. See also: Fowler and Fowler, (eds.) *The Concise Oxford Dictionary.* London: Oxford University Press, 1964, fifth edition in 1974, for this definition of "unchaste: indulging in unlawful or immoral sexual intercourse; lacking in purity, virginity, decency (of speech), restraint, and simplicity; defiled (i.e. polluted, corrupted)." The present article focuses upon two of the above definitions: "lacking in purity" and "defiled." All following definitions in the text are drawn from *The Concise Oxford Dictionary.*

2. This definition was derived by combining the definition of "whore" with the following definition of "stigma": "a brand marked on a slave or criminal; a stain on one's character; a mark of shame or discredit; a definite characteristic of some disease."

3. Much of the material for this analysis was drawn from the author's research on attitudes toward prostitutes, published in Dutch and English: Gail Pheterson, *The Whore Stigma: Female Dishonor and Male Unworthiness.* The Hague: Dutch Ministry for Social Affairs and Employment, 1986. All unreferenced citations throughout the present text were direct communications to the author in personal interviews.

4. Erving Goffman, *Stigma: Notes on the Management of Spoiled Identity* (New Jersey: Prentice-Hall, 1963), p. 167.

5. Angela Y. Davis, *Women, Race and Class.* New York: Random House, 1981.

6. Freda Adler and Rita James Simon, *The Criminology of Deviant Women.* Boston: Houghton Mifflin Company, 1979, pp. 88–89.

7. This analysis was heavily influenced by Lillian Smith, *Killers of the Dream.* London: W.W. Norton and Co., 1949.

8. Jean-Paul Sartre (translated by George J. Becker), *Anti-Semite and Jew.* New York: Schocken, 1948, pp. 48–49.

9. *Ibid*, p. 39.

10. See: Sietske Altink, *Huizen van Illusies, Bordelen en Prostitutie van Middeleeuwen tot Heden.* Utrecht: Veen, 1983, pp. 62–63, for a description of legal dress codes for prostitutes throughout history. See Max I. Dimont, *Jews, God and History.* New York: The New American Library, 1962, p. 230, for a description of legal dress codes for Jews between the sixteenth and eighteenth centuries. Among a host of prescriptions, both were required to wear peaked hats and forbidden to wear fine clothes.

11. An Huitzing, *Betaalde Liefde: Prostituees in Nederland, 1850–1900.* Bergen: OCTAVO, 1983, p. 75.

12. Catharine MacKinnon, *Sexual Harrassment of Working Women.* New Haven, Connecticut: Yale University Press, 1979. Also: Elizabeth Stanko, *Intimate Intrusions, Women's Experience of Male Violence.* London: Routledge and Kegan Paul, 1985.

13. Both novels are American classics of the nineteenth century. *The Scarlet Letter,* written by Nathaniel Hawthorne, was first published in 1850; *The Red Badge of Courage,* written by Stephen Crane, was first published in 1895.

14. Judith Lewis Herman, *Father-Daughter Incest.* London: Harvard University Press, 1981, p. 117.

15. Elizabeth A. Stanko, *Intimate Intrusions.* London: Routledge and Kegan Paul, 1985, p. 95.

16. Ellen Bass and Louise Thornton, *I Never Told Anyone.* New York: Harper and Row, 1983, p. 181.

17. Judith Lewis Herman, *Father-Daughter Incest.* London: Harvard University Press, 1981, p. 185.

18. *Ibid;* Also: Florence Rush, *The Best Kept Secret: Sexual Abuse of Children.* Englewood Cliffs, NJ: Prentice-Hall, Inc., especially the chapter "A Freudian Cover-up." Also: Jeffrey Moussaieff Masson, *The Assault of Truth.* New York: Farrar, Straus and Giroux, 1984.

19. Stanko, p. 30.

20. Judith Herman, *Father-Daughter Incest.* Cambridge, Massachusetts: Harvard University Press, 1981; Jennifer James, "Prostitutes and Prostitution." In: E. Sagarin and F. Montanino (eds.), *Deviants: Voluntary Actors in a Hostile World.* General Learning Press, 1977,

pp. 368–428; Diana Russell, "The Incidence and Prevalence of Intrafamilial and Extrafamilial sexual abuse of female children." *Child Abuse and Neglect* (1983) 7, 2, 133–146; Mimi Silbert and Ayala Pines, "Victimization of Street Prostitutes," *Victimology: An International Journal,* vol. 7, no. 1-4, 1982, pp. 122–133.

21. Stanko, p. 130.
22. Stanko, p. 53. Also See: Eileen Evason, *Hidden Violence: A Study of Battered Women in Northern Ireland.* Belfast: Farset Co-operative Press, 1982, for further elaboration on the theme of husband justifications for violence against wives.
23. Stanko, p. 48.
24. *Ibid*, p. 139.
25. It is irresistible to mention that the loss of honor incurred through sexual abuse has governed women's lives for hundreds of years. A study of prostitution in 15th century France gives the following description: "In the end, the consequences of rape were exactly the same as those of questionable or shameful conduct. The victim was almost always disgraced . . . even those who testified in her favor always considered her defiled by what had happened to her. She herself felt ashamed, guilty, and disgraced. In this respect her youthful assailants had attained their objective, for the raped woman realized that in the eyes of those around her, and indeed in her own mind, the distance separating her from the public prostitute had greatly diminished. Reduced to a state of psychological and physical weakness, she had little hope of regaining her honor as long as she stayed in town." Specific examples of such loss of honor through rape are plentiful. In one case, when a servant girl complained to her mistress about having been attacked and insulted by three bachelors, she was given notice, for "if she was accused of such bad things, (the mistress) was not about to keep her, unless she was given convincing proof indicating whether the girl was a respectable person or a nasty hussy." See: Jacques Rossiaud, "Prostitution, Youth, and Society in the Towns of Southeastern France in the 15th Century," *Selections from the Annales: Economies, Societes, Civilizations,* Volume IV (edited by Robert Forster and Orest Ranum).

Baltimore: The John Hopkins University Press, 1978, pp. 17, 41.
26. Nel Drayer, *Seksueel Geweld en Heteroseksualiteit.* The Hague: Ministerie van Sociale Zaken en Werkgelegenheid, 1984; Diana E.H. Russell, *Rape in Marriage.* New York: Macmillan, 1982; Stanko, 1985.
27. See: Leidsch Dagblad, "Buitenlust," "Officier: Verkrachting Doet Prostituee Minder." Diemen: October 9, 1985. (Dutch words of Mr. Franken van Bloemendaal, officier van justitie, Amsterdamse rechtbank: "Door het beroep dat zij uitoefent, zal het seksueel misbruikt worden wel geen diepe indruk op haar hebben gemaakt").
28. See: E. Ter Mors, "Zedenpolitie. Wie de Goede Zede Wil Verdedigen is Met de Wet Gebrekkig Gewapend." Eindscriptie Politie-Academie, 1978 (discussion of research in Nel Drayer, above). For a discouraging vivid description of nearly identical attitudes in the Middle Ages, see: Leah Lydia Otis, *Prostitution in Medieval Society, The History of an Urban Institution in Languedoc.* London: The University of Chicago Press, 1985, p. 68–69.
29. Specifically, the prosecuting attorney of a rape case in California asked a known prostitute not to be present throughout a rape trial because she thought it would reduce her client's credability. The prostitute was a close friend of the client, a non-prostitute, and had initially been asked by her traumatized friend to be present for emotional support.
30. See above: Jacques Rossiaud, p. 12.
31. See above footnote 26 (Nel Drayer; Diana Russell). Also Diana Russell, *The Politics of Rape.* New York: Macmillan, 1982.
32. For an analysis of court attitudes and judgments in 48 rape cases in the Netherlands from 1980–1984, see: Ed. Leuw, "Verkrachtingszaken voor de rechtbank: een kwalitatieve analyse van observatiegegevens." *Tijdschrift Voor Criminologie.* Boom Meppel: 27e jaargang, juli/oktober, 1985, pp. 212–234. According to this study, the victim is assumed to be "purely innocent" (author's quotation marks) in a majority of cases when the rapist is considered "sick" (psychologically irresponsible) or "bad" (immoral). Gang rapes fall under the category "bad." In 25% of the cases, however, the rapist

is considered "normal" (such as a "failed seductor") and co-responsibility is then often sought in the victim. Some Dutch lawyers also claim victim co-responsibility for rapes which are considered "normative" within the subculture in question (2 of the 48 cases). The characteristics of the rapist and the circumstances/cultural context of the rape are shown to affect court decisions. The Dutch author claims that courts in the Netherlands are far less likely than courts in other countries to claim victim co-responsibility for rape, p. 226.

33. See: Guy Hocquenghem, "Niet iedereen kan in zijn bed sterven." *Tegenlicht of Pasolini.* Translated from the French article in *Liberation,* Paris, November, 1975.

34. Wendy Hollway, "I just wanted to kill a woman. Why? The Ripper and Male Sexual-

ity," *Feminist Review,* no. 9, October, 1981, pp. 33–40.

35. See: Leah Lydia Otis, *Prostitution in Medieval Society, The History of an Urban Institution in Languedoc.* London: The University of Chicago Press, 1985, p. 41.

36. Allan M. Brandt, *No Magic Bullet: A Social History of Venereal Disease in the United States Since 1880.* New York: Oxford University Press, 1985.

37. *Ibid,* pp. 31–32.

38. *Ibid.*

39. Jeffrey Weeks, *Sex, Politics and Society: The Regulation of Sexuality Since 1800.* London: Longman, 1981.

READING 46

The Sex Exploiter: Theme Paper for the Second World Congress against Commercial Sexual Exploitation of Children

Julia O'Connell Davidson

1. INTRODUCTION

The Declaration and Agenda for Action of the First World Congress against the Commercial Sexual Exploitation of Children made it clear that CSEC (commercial sexual exploitation of children) is rooted in a complex mix of economic, political, social and legal factors, and needs to be addressed through a wide range of

Source: adapted from www.ecpat.net/eng/ Ecpat_inter/projects/monitoring/wc2/ yokohama_theme_sex_exploiter.pdf (downloaded February 2002). Copyright © 2001 by Julia O'Connell Davidson. Website copyright © 2001 by ECPAT International.

measures at local, national and international levels. This emphasis on the complexity of CSEC may have exerted some influence upon debates concerning the sexually exploited child over the past five years, but it has remained largely absent from public and policy debate regarding those who commercially sexually exploit children. There has been a continued tendency to assume that the demand-side of CSEC consists of 'paedophiles' and the criminals who supply them with children to abuse, and/or to concentrate on legal and criminal justice aspects of demand. This preoccupation with 'paedophilia' is inconsistent with an understanding of CSEC based upon the United Nations' definition of a child as a person under the age of 18, and the emphasis on law and law enforcement obscures the complexity of the questions, issues and challenges presented by the demand-side of CSEC. This paper starts from the premise that the problem of CSEC includes, but extends far beyond, that of 'paedophilia'. It considers the diversity of 'sex exploiters' in terms of their identities, attitudes and motivations, and draws attention to the social, political and economic factors that shape demand for CSEC in a range of settings. It stresses the fact that there is no single, quick or easy solution to the problems posed by those who commercially sexually exploit children. Efforts to strengthen legal controls over individual offenders must be balanced by efforts to devise and set in place a wide-ranging series of short and long-term measures addressing the factors that underpin and reproduce the demand-side of CSEC.

2. KEY CONCEPTS AND TERMS

This paper employs the term 'sex exploiter of children' (or, for the sake of brevity, 'sex exploiter') only as a shorthand way of referring to those who commit acts of child sexual exploitation, and not as a term to describe a particular kind of individual, or a specific group or class of persons. Indeed, one of the paper's aims is to show that it is impossible to speak of *the* sex exploiter in the sense of a single type of person who possesses some particular or unique set of characteristics. Those who sexually exploit children do so in a range of different social contexts, for a variety of reasons and cannot be distinguished by any specific inner quality, personality trait or even sexual proclivity. Their only common characteristic is the fact that they engage in forms of action that constitute child sexual exploitation. Key conceptual and definitional issues that need to be borne in mind throughout any discussion of the demand-side of CSEC are set out below.

Sex Exploiters and Sexual Consent

Children, defined as persons below the age of 18, are not always or necessarily incompetent or entirely lacking rational autonomy with regard to sexual expression. The sex exploiter cannot therefore be simply defined as 'any individual who has sex with a child', as this would deny all rights of sexual self-expression to everyone aged below 18. Such a definition would, by default, universally raise the age of

sexual consent to 18, making it impossible to acknowledge that a 17 year old, for example, may be capable of consenting to a sexual relationship with a 19 year old girl or boyfriend. It would also mean that when two 15 year olds entered into a sexual relationship based on mutual attraction, each would simultaneously become a child sex exploiter and a sexually exploited child.

Any definition of the 'sex exploiter' must be sensitive to the fact that those under the age of 18 are sometimes, and in some circumstances, capable of experiencing sexual desire and giving meaningful sexual consent. At the same time, however, questions as to whether a child consented to, instigated, or even obtained gratification from, sexual interaction with another person cannot be used to determine whether or not that person has committed an act of sexual exploitation. Our understanding of those who sexually exploit children must also recognise that children can be manipulated, induced or otherwise pressured into consenting to relationships, activities and/or contracts that may harm them. Whether aged 7 or 17, they have a right to protection against those who seek such consent, as well as against those who use force to sexually abuse or exploit them.

Sexual Exploitation, Sexual Abuse and Sexual Violence

The Longman English Dictionary defines 'exploit' as 'to use or develop fully, especially for profit or advantage . . . to take unfair advantage of for financial or other gain'. This emphasis on unfair advantage points to the existence of some imbalance of social, political, economic and/or physical, psychological or emotional power between the exploiter and the exploited, and so serves to distinguish 'exploitation' from simple criminality. The burglar who breaks into a house and steals a diamond necklace commits a crime, but we would not define her or him as an 'exploiter' of the rich. Meanwhile, a multinational corporation that aggressively markets tobacco in poor and developing countries takes advantage of, and profits by, the fact that poorer countries are unable to fund extensive and effective anti-smoking education. It could thus be said to exploit the vulnerability of those countries' populations, even though it may act within the confines of national and international law. Applied to questions about the sexual exploitation of children, this suggests that 'sex exploiters' can be defined as *those who take unfair advantage of some imbalance of power between themselves and a person under the age of 18 in order to sexually use them for either profit or personal pleasure.*

Three points about this definition should be noted. First, it clearly excludes consensual sexual acts between children of equal power and status. Second, it includes what is more usually described as 'child sexual abuse', a term which refers to forms of interaction or bodily contact between a child and an adult or older child which take place for the sexual gratification of the adult/older child. Child sexual abuse thus covers a wide range of sexual behaviours (from exhibitionist exposure, through fondling to vaginal or anal penetration), which can take place in a variety of settings and in the context of very different relationships between the perpetrator and the child concerned. Because the perpetrator invariably takes advantage of an imbalance of power between him or herself and the child in order to abuse, the 'sex abuser' can also be described as a 'sex exploiter'. However, the term 'sex exploiter' further extends to cover third parties who have no actual sexual contact with children, but profit from facilitating or orchestrating children's sexual contact with another person or persons. This is important, given that many countries' existing measures to monitor and control sex exploiters focus primarily upon those who have personally committed acts of child sexual abuse.

Third, the term 'sex exploiter' cannot be automatically applied to all those who commit acts of sexual violence, since violence can transcend social, political, economic and even physical inequality, whereas sexual exploitation cannot take place in the absence of such inequalities. A thirteen-year-old boy might be able to rape his thirty-year-old teacher, for example, but he cannot sexually exploit her. This distinction is, however, complicated by the fact that sex attackers often do exploit the social, political and/or physical vulnerability of certain groups, selecting victims who are least able to protect themselves and/or who are afforded least protection by the state. Furthermore, the definition of 'sex exploiter' provided above does not preclude the possibility that sexual exploitation may include extreme forms of sexual violence. The exploiter may, for example, derive sexual pleasure from performing sadistic acts, up to and including torture and murder, or may seek to profit from the production or distribution of pornographic records of such violence. Yet we must also remember that sex exploiters do not always or necessarily use force against, or cause physical damage to the body of, the exploited, and it is therefore necessary to pay close attention to the social, economic, political and legal structures which make it possible for sex exploiters to obtain children's sexual compliance without resort to physical force.

'Commercial' and 'Non-Commercial' Sexual Exploitation

Children can be sexually exploited in the context of a wide range of social relationships. These social relationships can be loosely divided into three broad types:

- those that are commercial and relatively short term;
- those that involve longer term economic dependency;
- and those that have no commercial element and/or are not primarily economic.

The boundaries between these categories are not hard and fast, and one individual sex exploiter may abuse in all three contexts. However, in terms of understanding the motivations and *modus operandi* of sex exploiters and devising effective child protection measures, it is helpful to examine what is peculiar to each type of relationship, and to consider overlaps between the 'commercial' and the 'non-commercial'.

The term 'commercial sex' embraces a diverse range of phenomena (see O'Connell Davidson, 1998). In most countries of the world, it is possible to divide the commercial sex trade (which includes prostitution, trafficking, pornography and sexual 'entertainment') into two key sectors, one formally organised, the other informally arranged. Children are sexually exploited in both sectors, but within the formal sex industry, sex is sold as if it were a commodity like any other. Here, the exploiter enters into narrow and explicit contracts, so, for example, x sum of money is paid in exchange for a specified sexual 'service', or a particular pornographic video. In the informal sector, exploiter and exploited often enter into more loosely specified, diffuse exchanges, within which the exploited may provide a range of services (perform sexual acts, pose for pornographic photos, clean, cook, shop, flatter, converse, counsel, translate, to name but a few) in exchange for a range of benefits (for example, a bed for the night and a hot shower, a meal, gifts of money or clothing, a place to live, help setting up in business, food rations in a refugee camp, assistance in migrating from a poor to a wealthy country or in escaping from persecution in the child's home country).

The informal sector of the commercial sex trade shades off into sexual relationships that have an economic basis and are exploitative according to the definition provided above, yet have none of the characteristics of relationships between two parties to a simple commodity exchange. So, for example, relatively wealthy adults may provide long term financial support to a poor family on the understanding that this entitles them to a sexually abusive relationship with one of the children, or they may marry, cohabit with, date or adopt children, making sexual use of them and providing them with gifts and economic support in return. Children can also be sexually exploited in the context of longer-term relationships that are explicitly economic but ostensibly non-sexual. So, for example, children who are employed as domestic workers, or as tourism, farm, plantation or factory workers may be forced, pressured or manipulated into sexual acts by their employers, their employers' clients or friends, and/or their adult co-workers. The child may not be offered cash or other benefits in exchange for submitting to individual episodes of abuse, and yet may well feel that her or his continued employment rests upon acquiescing to such demands.

The question of when exploitation ceases to be CSEC and becomes a non-commercial form of child sexual abuse is further complicated by the fact that those who sexually abuse children within what would normally be considered non-commercial relationships (e.g., parent/child, teacher/pupil, priest/supplicant, scoutmaster/scout) also often attempt to secure the child's compliance and/or silence by giving them money, gifts or other benefits. To determine whether or not such relationships are *primarily* economic in basis would require us to decipher the significance of the 'payment' for the victim, something that would raise all manner of problems. Finally, we should note that children who are vulnerable to physical attack (for instance, those who live and/or work on the streets, or in refugee camps, or in institutions in which those in authority fail to provide them with adequate protection against abuse and violence by other inmates) sometimes trade sexual access in exchange for protection, rather than any financial benefit.

Taken together, these points suggest that attempts to completely separate commercial and non-commercial forms of sexual exploitation, either analytically or temporally, are bound to be unsatisfactory. It is better to think in terms of a continuum and to recognise that some cases of child sexual exploitation fall into a grey area between that which is clearly 'commercial' and that which is indisputably 'non-commercial'. When these cases involve children who are above the age of sexual consent, but below the age of 18, they are particularly difficult to legislate against.

'Pedophilia' and Beyond

'Pedophilia' is a clinical diagnostic category with a very specific and limited meaning. According to the American Psychiatric Association's 1995 manual, it refers to a person aged over 16, who 'has had repeated, intense, sexually exciting fantasies for a period of at least six months, has had sexual urges or has carried out behaviours involving sexual acts with one or more children (usually under the age of 13)'. Furthermore, 'the fantasies, the sexual urges or behaviours act as considerable impairments in the individual's ability to function socially, professionally or within other important spheres' (cited in Svensson, 2000: 27). Some of those who conform to this definition pose a very serious risk to children, and can be individually responsible for the sexual abuse of large numbers of children. Yet we should also note that to be clinically diagnosed as suffering from 'pedophilia', an individual need not necessarily have committed any act of child sexual abuse, and we cannot therefore claim that *all* 'pedophiles' are sex exploiters. It would be still more emphatically wrong to claim that all sex exploiters are 'pedophiles', and this would remain the case even if the term were more loosely used to refer to adults with a sexual interest in young children (as it is used in popular parlance).

Sex exploiters who are involved as third party beneficiaries of CSEC are rarely motivated by personal sexual desire or obsessive fantasies. They sexually exploit children for profit, not because their acts of exploitation bring them psychic relief or sexual gratification. Next, there are those who sexually exploit children if and when they find themselves in situations where a child is more readily or cheaply available for sexual use than an adult, but whose satisfaction does not hinge on the physical or emotional immaturity of the individual they exploit. There are also adult men who choose young children as sexual partners primarily on the basis of misconceptions about sexual health, or because they uncritically accept myths about virgins being able to restore potency, bring luck to new business ventures, and so on. None of these people are driven by sexual fantasies about children *per se*.

Furthermore, if children are defined as persons under 18, it is necessary to recognise that adult-child sexual contact is rarely completely proscribed. In most countries, it is legal for an adult to marry, co-habit with or date a person below the age of 18. Meanwhile, most societies attach a good deal of aesthetic and erotic value to youthful bodies. Adults who seek out younger and more attractive sexual partners, including persons under the age of 18, are not necessarily transgressing the socially agreed perimeters of acceptable sexual desires and therefore cannot be automatically described as sexually 'deviant' or psychologically 'abnormal'. To use the terms 'pedophile' and 'sex exploiter' interchangeably is thus to grossly over-simplify the phenomenon of child sexual exploitation. Though we must urgently address the existence of, and harm caused by, those who consistently and consciously seek out young children to abuse, questions about why children are sexually exploited and by whom do not end here. We need also to ask why it is that people who are *not* 'pedophiles' sexually exploit children.

One further point. Those who conform to clinical definitions of 'pedophilia' can display a focused sexual interest in either male or female children, or in both. However, 'pedophiles' have sometimes been stereotyped as men with a fixed interest in boys, and homophobic individuals and groups have asserted that there is a relationship between homosexuality and child sexual abuse. In reality, statistical evidence on child sexual exploitation points only to the conclusion that there is a relationship between gender and abuse, in the sense that a) girl children are far more likely to be victims of sexual exploitation than boy children; and b) males are far more likely than females to commit sexually exploitative acts for personal pleasure. Certainly, some men who self-identify as homosexual sexually exploit boys under the age of 18, just as some men who self-identify as heterosexual exploit girls under the age of 18, but it does not follow that all homosexual men are potential sex exploiters any more than it follows that all heterosexual men pose a threat to girl children.

Moreover, Western usage of terms such as 'homosexual', 'heterosexual' and 'pedophile' is not universally meaningful. There are many places in the world where men have sex with other men or boys without necessarily defining themselves, or being defined by others, as 'homosexual'. In South Asia, for example: 'sociocultural frameworks are supremely gendered, and often sexual relationships are framed by gender roles, power relationships, poverty, class, caste, tradition and custom, hierarchies of one sort or another. Here for many men/males, we have gender identities, not sexual identities' (Khan, 2001, 5).

3. RATIONALISING THE SEXUAL EXPLOITATION OF CHILDREN

The sociologist Orlando Patterson (1982, 18) observes that 'Human beings have always found naked force or coercion a rather messy, if not downright ugly business, however necessary'. Most societies have therefore sought ways in which to clothe the 'beastliness' of power, to propound a set of ideas which make coercive power 'immediately palatable to those who exercise it'. Just as the power of dominant groups in society is typically cloaked or justified by discourses which humanise or deny it, so individuals are usually reluctant to view themselves as abusive, dominating, cruel or evil. Whether we are talking about acts of genocide, rape, wife beating, or child sexual abuse, the vast majority of people will only use force or coercive power against another human being if and when they can tell themselves it is natural, right and justifiable to do so, or when they can conceal from themselves the fact that they are exercising such powers. Thus research has consistently found that very few of those who sexually exploit children consider themselves to be abusive or exploitative, but will rather seek to deny, justify or humanise their sexual use of children.

The concept of 'cognitive dissonance' provides one way in which to understand this finding. Psychologists have pointed out that people experience anxiety where there is a lack of congruence between their attitudes, beliefs and behaviour. For example, if a man believes himself to be a good and moral person, and also believes that those who sexually abuse children are bad and immoral, he will experience anxiety if he has sexual contact with a child, since the propositions, 'I am a good person', 'adult-child sexual contact is always wrong', and 'I have sex with children' are incongruent. To bring them into line, and so reduce his anxiety, the man must adjust at least one of them. He can either revise his view of himself as a good person, or change his attitudes towards adult-child sexual contact, or adjust his beliefs about whether or not he has had sex with children. British and US studies of convicted child sex offenders suggest that they are most likely to respond to the cognitive dissonance associated with child sexual abuse by shifting their attitudes towards adult-child sexual contact and/or towards their victims. Thus, they typically exhibit distorted attitudes and beliefs which allow them to construct children as being in some way responsible for their own abuse, and/or to imagine that children are not harmed by sexual contact with adults, and/or that children are able to consent to, or obtain benefits from, sexual encounters with adults (Ward *et al.*, 2000). This may involve minimizing the meaning and consequences of abuse (as when the abuser tells himself that 'fondling' or oral sex does not really 'count' as sex and causes no harm to the child concerned), and/or denying the coercive nature of the abuse (as when the abuser tells himself that the child instigated, invited or deserved the abuse).

The degree of distortion and denial involved can be quite extraordinary. There are even offenders who claim that their sexual contact with a baby was not wrong because the baby invited or consented to the abuse by, for example, smiling and gurgling when the abuser changed its nappy. Clearly, no existing society's framework of beliefs can support such a stupendous level of self-deception. Those who sexually abuse very young children therefore have to massively distort socially agreed ideas about consent and the powers one human being can legitimately exercise over another, as well as about the proper objects of adult sexual interest and the proper relations between adults and children. Such people often have an extremely fragile hold on their sense of self, and experience great psychological stress as they attempt to maintain a view of their own actions as justified or harmless. However, those who abuse very small children are in a minority amongst sex exploiters, and there are other forms of child sexual exploitation which are much easier to accommodate within the framework of socially prescribed or tolerated attitudes towards sexuality, age, consent and the legitimate exercise of power.

All of this implies that in order to protect children from CSEC, we must concern ourselves with the ideas which inform and guide the action of sex exploiters, and find ways to challenge and undermine the beliefs which allow sex exploiters to deny, justify, humanise or naturalize their acts of exploitation. The way in which adults convince themselves that sexual use of a child is warranted and defensible often hinges in part upon the social relationship within which exploitation occurs. Sections 4, 5, and 6 therefore explore how sex exploiters justify and/or deny the coercive powers they exercise over the children within non-commercial relationships, commercial relationships, and longer-term sexual-economic relationships.

4. EXPLOITERS IN NON-COMMERCIAL CONTEXTS

Western research on convicted child sex offenders has found that a) they often use children to meet demands for emotional intimacy and/or sexual contact because children are easier to control and make fewer demands than adults b) they have little empathy for their victims, and c) they employ cognitive distortions to deny or avoid seriously considering the harmful consequences of abuse for their victims (Grubin, 1998, Ward *et al.*, 2000). Some perpetrators imagine their acts of abuse as the harmless pleasuring of a child within the context of an affectionate, caring and/or reciprocal relationship, and insist that they love the children they abuse. Some perpetrators justify their acts of sexual abuse on grounds that the child invited or deserved it (she or he is worthless, deliberately naughty, wicked, possessed by the devil, and so on), and here the sexual contact may be extremely hostile and punitive, taking place within a relationship that is more generally abusive and violent. So, for example, Borje Svensson of Save the Children Sweden's Boys' Clinic states that 'When it comes to boys who have been sexually abused by their biological fathers, physical violence has often occurred in combination with the assaults' (2000, 21).

No matter what form the abuse takes, there are important connections to be made between child sexual abuse and the ways in which childhood is socially constructed and imagined. Research has consistently shown that children who are sexually abused in non-commercial settings are far more likely to be abused by adults they know than by strangers (Grubin, 1998). Within this, children are at greatest risk of sexual abuse by the adults who exercise the most power over them, which is to say by their parents, guardians, relatives, and adults who act in *loco parentis* in a range of settings, including kindergartens, schools, colleges, residential homes for children with or without disabilities, churches, sports clubs, foreign/educational exchange visits, and so on (Kelly and Regan, 2000). In most societies, parents and adults who act in *loco parentis* are both allowed and expected to exercise powers over children of a type and degree that would be unthinkable in relation to any other social group. Such powers are not granted simply or solely on grounds that children's immaturity prevents them from acting autonomously. They also reflect the fact that childhood is widely viewed as a state of immanence. Children are imagined as adults-in-waiting, incompetent, unformed and unable to realise themselves as individuals, and it is thus often considered acceptable for adults to discount their spoken wishes, to attempt to 'mould' their character, interests and opinions, and to punish them for failing to conform to adults' demands and expectations.

This not only makes it very easy for adults to justify treating children as property/objects, but also allows room for much confusion about whether particular powers are being exercised in the interests of the child or the adult. Thus, people who self-identify as 'paedophiles' will often defend activities aimed at sexually stimulating their victims as somehow helping the child to 'discover' and 'realise' his/her nascent sexuality, and argue that 'paedophiles' can help children by gently guiding them through the difficult terrain of puberty. Whether they legitimate sexual abuse by insisting that the child's needs and interests are identical to their own, or by insisting that adults have a right to use and discipline children as they see fit, there is a sense in which abusers often extend, rather than reject, socially tolerated attitudes towards adult-child relations.

The relationship between social values and attitudes and child sexual abuse is also evidenced by research suggesting that children from social groups that are socially stigmatised (for instance, street dwellers, domestic workers, persons with disabilities) are amongst those at particularly high risk of sexual abuse. Though these children may be targeted because it is easier to access them and/or the abuser calculates that the risk of detection is low, it also seems likely that their widespread social devaluation makes it easy for the abuser to dehumanise the victim, thereby reducing guilt or anxiety that might otherwise arise. This suggests that social norms, ideas and codes which prohibit adult-child sexual contact have a greater inhibitory effect in relation to children who are considered to be part of an abusive adult's own society than in relation to socially excluded or marginalised children. The inhibitory potential of socially agreed codes and prohibitions against adult–child sexual contact also appears to be linked to the adult's sense of connection to the wider society. When this is disrupted, for example in situations of civil war or armed conflict, people often find it possible to rationalise and justify behaviours that would formerly have appeared to them as indefensible.

Finally, we should note that anecdotal evidence suggests that those who sexually abuse children in non-commercial contexts often attempt to buy their victims' compliance and/or silence with money or other benefits. This represents another means through which adults can deceive themselves into believing that the abuse was desired or deserved by the child. When sex abusers give their victims money, they can not only tell themselves that the act of abuse has been mutually beneficial, but also that the victim was somehow morally complicit because she or he accepted the money.

5. EXPLOITERS IN COMMERCIAL CONTEXTS

Sex commerce is a stigmatised activity that generally takes place within a shadow and/or illegal economy. It is therefore extremely difficult to obtain accurate data on any aspect of the global sex trade. However, some claims about the demand for prostitution can be advanced with reasonable confidence. To begin with, research suggests that demand comes overwhelmingly (though not exclusively) from men. Surveys also show a good deal of variation between countries as regards how many men admit to prostitute-use: around 9% in the UK, 14% in Hong Kong, 16% in the USA, 38% in Spain, 60–70% in Cambodia, 75% in Thailand, for instance (Wellings, 1993, FPA, HK, 2000, Mansson, 2000, Brown, 2000). Research further shows that certain subsets of the male population of any given country are especially prone to prostitute-use (see below). Reliable data on the number or background characteristics of clients of children in prostitution are even harder to come by. There is, however, a more general body of empirical evidence on prostitution around the world which allows us to state that whilst there is a small, and largely concealed 'market niche' within prostitution in most countries which caters primarily to demand from people with a specific interest in sex with young children or virgins, the vast majority of children in prostitution are integrated into the mainstream prostitution market, and serve demand from all prostitute users. So, for example, all over the world, girls aged between 12 and 18 years are reported to be prostituting alongside those over 18 in mining encampments, brothel districts, tourist areas, ports and truck stops, on the streets and in a variety of off-street forms of prostitution. Boys under 18 are likewise present in mainstream male prostitution.

This has enormous implications for our understanding of sex exploiters. It means that third party beneficiaries of child prostitution do not usually have a specific or dedicated interest in CSEC, but rather an economic interest in prostitution in general (see Section 8). It also means that the clients of children in prostitution are often simply members of those groups that supply a demand for prostitution in general, rather than people with a focused sexual interest in children. In other words, we can state that many individuals come to sexually exploit children through their prostitute use, rather than using prostitution as a means to get access to children. To answer questions about who sexually exploits children in commercial sexual contexts and why, we therefore need to consider the demand for commercial sex in general.

Groups Especially Prone to Prostitute-Use

There is a great deal of historical and contemporary evidence to suggest that groups of men whose work separates them from home for prolonged periods are particularly prone to prostitute-use. This is especially the case where their employment is sex segregated, and where the work culture is informed by an ethos of machismo. Unsurprisingly, then, prostitute-use is common amongst men in the armed forces. Seafarers, truckers and male migrant workers who spend long periods working in poor conditions in isolated regions (for instance, those who work in logging and mining) are three more significant groups in terms of providing demand for prostitution. Meanwhile, though businessmen may not work away from home for prolonged periods, they often travel a good deal, and in most major cities around the world, adults and children in prostitution report that foreign and domestic businessmen are amongst their clients. In most settings, local men also provide demand for prostitution, including child prostitution. In all the categories mentioned here, there may be individuals who have a focused sexual interest in children, and use prostitution as a means to secure access to them. But there are also many 'situational sex exploiters', i.e., people who sexually exploit children because they find themselves in situations wherein the prostitute who is most cheaply or readily available, or most attractive to them happens to be under 18. Finally, research suggests that people are far more likely to enter into various forms of sexual-economic exchange whilst on holiday than they are when at home. One segment of demand for children in prostitution comes from preferential abusers or 'paedophiles' who travel to poor or developing countries with the explicit aim of buying sexual access to young children. Because it is difficult to secure access to young children in any country of the world, such individuals sometimes group together to form small networks and assist each other by exchanging information and contacts, often via the internet (see Section 7). However, tourism is also strongly associated with the sexual exploitation of adolescent prostitutes by 'ordinary' tourists.

Rationalising the Sexual Exploitation of Children in Prostitution

Attitudes towards gender, sexuality and prostitution are remarkably consistent all over the world. Most societies teach their members to believe that there are natural and fundamental differences between male and female sexuality. It is almost universally assumed that men are *by nature* sexually active and subject to strong sexual urges or appetites, whilst women are assumed to be *naturally* sexually passive and receptive and great value has traditionally been placed upon female sexual purity and continence. These traditional beliefs about gender difference form the basis for the 'double standards' that most societies apply to prostitution. Although prostitution is widely viewed as a distasteful or immoral institution, it is also considered as a 'necessary evil'. There has always been prostitution, people say, because men have always been possessed of uncontrollable sexual impulses. Prostitution is imagined to perform an important social function, 'soaking up' excess male sexual urges which might otherwise lead to rape, marital breakdown and all manner of social disorder, thereby protecting the virginity and innocence of 'good' girls and women. And while men who use prostitutes are generally excused on grounds that they have simply given in to a 'natural' impulse, females who work as prostitutes are condemned and penalised as 'unnatural' women.

The idea that men have sexual 'needs' (as opposed to socially constructed 'wants') may be widely accepted, but in practice, there is no biological imperative to orgasm any set number of times a day, week or year. People may on occasion find it unpleasant to go without sexual release, but the absence of another person to bring them to orgasm does not actually threaten their continued survival. Human sexual desire is grounded in emotional and cognitive, as much as physiological, processes, and notions of biologically based sexual 'needs' cannot provide a direct explanation for prostitute-use. Biology is an enabling, not a determining, factor in human sexual behaviour. However, the idea of male sexual 'need', combined with popular beliefs about contractual consent and the social construction of female prostitutes as 'dirty' and 'impure', does make it very easy for clients to rationalise and defend their own use of both adults and children in prostitution. Research with clients all over the world has found that they invoke popular beliefs about male sexual 'needs' to explain why they wish to use prostitutes. They then justify their prostitute-use by referring to widely accepted ideas about economic life. The client normally tells himself that he is entering into a commodity exchange, rather than a human or social *relationship,* with the prostitute.

This allows him to overlook certain facts about the prostitutes he uses, facts that he might well consider important in his non-commercial sexual life. The prostitute may, for instance, be another man's wife or girlfriend, or pregnant by another man. The prostitute may be being coerced into having sex with the client by a third party. She or he may be extremely young, a mere child. However, because the client imagines himself as entering into a commodity exchange, he does not feel morally compelled to interrogate what lies behind the prostitute's sexual 'consent'. He can simply think in terms of an exchange of values—x amount of money for x sexual benefit. Thus the client of a child prostitute need not experience the anxiety he would feel were he to abuse his own child, niece or nephew, or the child of a neighbour, for example. Where prostitution is contractually organised as a commodity exchange like any other, the buyer can tell himself that the powers he exercises over the child are quite legitimate. He is simply behaving as any sovereign consumer in a free market behaves, and if he does not purchase the child's 'services', the man behind him will.

In this sense, many men's use of children in prostitution is better understood as an act of moral indifference than a wilful act of harm, and this kind of moral indifference is actually widely endorsed in free market societies. Buyers are generally expected to act solely on the basis of self-interest, and to feel no connection with, or moral responsibility towards, those who produce the commodities they purchase. Equally we should note that the demand for commercial sex is known to be high amongst groups of men working in extremely dangerous and exploitative conditions, separated from family and friends, with few opportunities for leisure, relaxation or intimacy (such as miners in parts of Africa and Latin America). Such men exercise very little power or control over their own working lives, and their indifference to questions about the circumstances which lead women and children to enter prostitution contracts with them often mirrors the indifference with which they themselves are regarded by the world.

The idea that there is a firm and meaningful line of demarcation between 'good' and 'bad' women ('Madonnas' and 'whores') further equips clients with a justification for CSEC. Because they 'agree' to sell their sexuality as a commodity, female prostitutes are usually considered to have surrendered their right to belong to, or be protected by, the imaginary community of good, respectable, heterosexuals. Thus the rape, even the murder, of a prostitute does not evoke the same degree of popular outrage as the rape or murder of a 'good' woman. Likewise, the sexual use of a child prostitute has not traditionally been viewed in the same light as the sexual abuse of an 'innocent' child. Girls aged below 18 continue to be subject to criminal sanctions for their involvement in prostitution in many countries, and men who are convicted for sexual offences involving children in prostitution are still often treated more leniently than those convicted for offences against non-prostitute children. Though male prostitutes are rarely legally constructed as a separate class of persons in the same way that female prostitutes are, they are generally socially stigmatised. Boy prostitutes are thus considered to be as 'dirty' and 'corrupt' as girl prostitutes. This helps to explain how it is that ordinary men can use children in prostitution. For most clients, a child's status as 'prostitute' overrides her/his status as 'child'. In this again, clients accept and reproduce what is widely socially endorsed.

Finally, we should note that where societies are hierarchically stratified along ethnic, racial or caste lines, and/or are deeply xenophobic, then it is possible for adults from dominant groups to sexually exploit children from inferiorised groups without this interfering with their view of themselves as moral and good. Research shows that historically and cross-culturally, a large percentage of clients seek prostitutes whose racial, ethnic, caste or national identities are different from their own. Thus we find that women and children in prostitution serving local demand are often migrants, and that men's prostitute-use increases when they are abroad. Racism, xenophobia and ideas about 'caste' encourage sex exploiters to view Otherised groups as 'natural' prostitutes. So, for example, white western sex tourists say that the women and children they exploit in Asia, Africa, the Caribbean and Latin America are *naturally* more sexually willing than white women and children, while in parts of India, men from privileged social groups will declare that the 'lower caste' women and children they use are 'sexually promiscuous' and have incited them. Exploiters' abuse of children in prostitution who do not share their own social identity is facilitated by the assumption that these children either do not need, or are unworthy of, the care and protection that would be accorded to children 'of their own kind'.

In short, clients do not have to cognitively distort dominant attitudes towards sexual life very far at all in order to feel comfortable about using a child prostitute. Popular beliefs about gender, sexuality, race/caste and prostitution allow the client to tell himself that the child instigated sex (s/he solicited his custom), consented to sex (s/he accepted money or another benefit in exchange), deserved to be sexually used (s/he is just a 'dirty' prostitute), and/or was not really harmed by the sexual contact (s/he is not 'one of my own kind', and/or has already been sexually used by many others, so what difference can one more violation make?).

6. SEX EXPLOITERS AND MORE DIFFUSE FORMS OF SEXUAL-ECONOMIC EXCHANGE

'Benefactors' and Sugar Daddies

Vast numbers of children in the contemporary world live in poverty and/or especially difficult circumstances. The role of 'benefactor' to young children who are impoverished and/or homeless and/or neglected or unloved has obvious attractions for those adults who might be diagnosed as 'paedophile' and who yearn for relatively long term, stable and 'affectionate' sexual relationships with children. It is much easier to construct and maintain fictions of consent and mutuality with such children, who may genuinely value the non-sexual aspects of their relationship with the abuser as well as need the material benefits associated with it. Moreover, the child's economic dependence on the adult makes it less likely she or he will report the abuse. However, lack of access to effective sexual health education and to adequate medical care can also encourage adults who do not conform to clinical definitions of 'the paedophile' to seek out young children as sexual partners. There are, for example, reports of adult men in parts of Africa severely affected by the AIDS epidemic providing long-term economic support to impoverished families in exchange for regular sexual contact with one of the children, on the assumption that young children pose no threat of sexually transmitted disease. The rising incidence of child rape in sub-Saharan countries that are bearing the brunt of the AIDS tragedy is also thought to be linked to myths about the cleansing properties of sex with children. Meanwhile, the sexual exploitation of female school pupils by male teachers is reported to represent an increasingly widespread problem in sub-Saharan Africa (Kuleana, 1999, Shumba, 2001).

When adults take advantage of a young child's vulnerable and/or marginalised position in order to sexually exploit them, they clearly transgress socially agreed codes and conventions regarding relationships between adults and children. The same cannot always be said of 'Sugar Daddies'. This is the phenomenon whereby older men provide youthful sexual partners, including adolescents, with long term financial support and/or material benefits in the form of gifts, accommodation and/or access to entertainment and a life-style that would otherwise be beyond the youth's reach. Relationships between adolescents and Sugar Daddies or 'Boops' have recently attracted concern in Jamaica, South Africa and Kenya, but the same phenomenon can be found in many other parts of the world, including in affluent Western countries. Wherever they live, poor and socially excluded youth are vulnerable to this form of sexual exploitation for much the same reasons as those identified by the authors of a study on sex and violence among Xhosa Township youth:

> poverty, mind-numbing boredom and the lack of opportunities or prospects for advancement contribute to young people investing substantial personal effort in the few arenas where entertainment and success are achievable, most notably their sexual relationships. These become an important vehicle for gaining (or losing) respect and 'position' among peers, as well as for material benefit (Wood and Jewkes, 2001, 318).

In contexts such as this, the Sugar Daddy does not need to coerce or 'lure' adolescents into sexual relationships. Furthermore, providing the child concerned is above the legal age

of sexual consent, there is not usually anything in national law to prevent adults from taking unfair advantage of their greater economic power in order to date or cohabit with children. Indeed, far from transgressing dominant social conventions in relation to sexual life, the relationship between Sugar Daddy and adolescent girl often mirrors (albeit perhaps in an exaggerated form) inequalities that are quite normal in heterosexual relationships. In most countries of the world, gender inequalities are so great that there is frequently a huge imbalance of economic, social and political power between heterosexual lovers and spouses, yet few people would accept the proposition that this makes most men 'sex exploiters' in relation to their wives or girlfriends. There are thus many situations in which both adults and children are legally and socially considered capable of giving meaningful sexual consent despite being massively disadvantaged in relation to their sexual partner in terms of socio-economic power. It follows, then, that the Sugar Daddy does not usually need to distort socially agreed ideas about childhood or sexual consent in order to rationalise a sexual relationship with a teenage girl. Nor can his motivations necessarily be described as aberrant. In many cultures, youthful female bodies are considered sexually desirable, and men are expected to demonstrate their masculinity through their capacity to command sexual access to 'desirable' female bodies.

Domestic Work, Forced Marriage and Other Slavery-like Practices

Vast numbers of children work as domestics in the contemporary world (5 million in Indonesia alone, ILO, 1996). In both affluent and developing countries, domestics work in a largely unregulated sphere, are frequently required to work long hours in conditions which pose risks to health and safety, and are vulnerable to physical, psychological and sexual abuse (Anderson, 2000, SACCS, 1999). Often, they are powerless to protest against such abuse not only because they are dependent on their employers for food and shelter and because they lack social status relative to their employer, but also because they are denied legal protections accorded to workers in other sectors. Where domestic workers are migrants, and their immigration status depends on their continued employment by a specific employer, it is still more difficult for them to challenge or escape sexual or physical abuse. Domestic work and domestic workers are widely socially devalued (Anderson, 2000, CMR, 2001). This makes it easier for adults to deny or rationalise their abuse of child domestic workers on grounds that they do not merit the care that would be extended to children of higher social status. Ironically then, though domestic work is frequently vaunted as a harmless and appropriate form of employment for women and girls and a 'respectable' economic alternative to prostitution, it is very often a site of sexual exploitation, as well as other forms of abuse. Little research attention has been paid to the demand-side of domestic work, but pioneering work in this field by Bridget Anderson (2000) suggests that it is often linked to the desire to preserve and demonstrate one's position on status hierarchies along lines of gender, class, race, ethnicity and/or caste. Since these status hierarchies are based on the notion that it is possible to rank human beings as being more or less worthy of privilege, care and protection, it is unsurprising to find that those who imagine themselves to be at the top of such hierarchies may be capable of sexually abusing those they consider to be at the bottom.

Sexual abuse can also feature as one of many forms of oppression suffered by children affected by various forms of debt bondage in the contemporary world (Robertson, 1997). Forced marriage and early marriage represent further traditional practices within which children can be sexually exploited. Though it is difficult to obtain reliable statistical data on these phenomena, it is estimated that millions of children in Africa, Asia and Latin America are affected, a significant minority of whom are married before the age of 15, and some of whom are married below the age of 10 (Forum on Marriage, 2000). Here the exploiter also justifies the powers exercised over the child through reference to beliefs about 'proper' hierarchies of gender and age. Forced and early marriage is thus another form of child sexual exploitation that can be implicitly or explicitly sanctioned by the community within which the exploiter lives.

7. SEX EXPLOITERS, NETWORKING AND PORNOGRAPHY

Individuals who self-identify as 'paedophiles' sometimes make contact with others like themselves, forming networks or 'rings' through which to exchange information, advice and child pornography. These networks may be involved in a number of different forms of CSEC, as illustrated by a 1997 French case involving 7 men who had variously collected and circulated child pornography, sexually abused children in Romania, and brought two Romanian children to France to abuse them and sell them to others to sexually abuse (ACPF, 2001). Often, those who conform to the clinical definition of 'paedophilia' are compulsive collectors of images of children and/or child sexual abuse, including photographic, audiotaped and/or videotaped records of children being sexually abused by self and/or others. Computer and internet technology has greatly enhanced such people's ability to record, store, retrieve and share large collections of child pornography, and the case of the Wonderland Club (see Child Pornography Theme Paper) provides some insights into the motivations of 'on-line' abusers.

As well as giving members access to a vast collection of child pornography, the club provided men who self-identified as 'paedophiles' (and so as beings wholly reviled and rejected by wider society) with a sense of group belonging and self esteem. Thus, one of the British men convicted for his involvement in the club said in an interview for a BBC documentary, "I had friends all over the world. I never had so many friends before", and "we were the elite". Close contact with like-minded men helped to reinforce the distorted thinking necessary to minimise and justify abuse. Even though the collection included pictures of infants being violated, this man explained that *"We* didn't see it as abuse" and was adamant that the photographs and videos had been taken by men who were involved in consensual relationships with their victims. Those who collect and exchange records of child sexual abuse through networks such as the Wonderland Club are not normally motivated to do so for commercial gain. However, UK Customs and Excise officers report that in recent years, they are increasingly intercepting commercially produced child pornography, much of which is produced in Eastern Europe or Central America. These materials have typically been advertised over the internet, and ordered by 'paedophiles' with a collector mentality who wish to possess hard copies of videos or CD Roms depicting abuse. Customs' officers observe that whilst there may not be a mass market for this kind of child pornography, the fact that there are over 100,000 people in the UK with convictions for sexual offences against children suggests that the market is not insignificant either. Considered globally, then, there is certainly room for individuals to make substantial profits through the production and sale of child pornography aimed at those with a focused sexual interest in children.

There has been little systematic research on children's exploitation in the commercial production of pornography aimed at either 'paedophile' or mainstream markets. It is known that one segment of the commercial market is explicitly dedicated to those with a sexual interest in adolescents, however. Internet sites named 'Teen Steam', 'Webs Youngest Women' and 'Live Teen' between them received over 10 million visitors in 1999 (Kelly and Regan, 2000, 55). Though the large companies, which produce wide circulation, glossy magazines may take pains to ensure that the models they use are aged over 18 (even those posing for 'teen' pornography), children under 18 are certainly present in other parts of the mainstream pornography industry. Indeed, many countries' legislation against child pornography offers no protection to children above the age of sexual consent, which may be as young as 14. The fact that pornography for the Western European market appears to be increasingly produced in Eastern Europe and the Newly Independent States is especially troubling in this regard.

It is also important to consider ways in which the mainstream pornography market shades into other forms of commercial and non-commercial sexual exploitation. In Japan, for example, there is not only a high level of demand for prostitutes dressed in school uniforms (who may or may not be under 18), and various types of pornography depicting the sexual use of adolescent girls, but also for a range of commercial sexual services that fall somewhere between 'teen' prostitution and 'teen' pornography. There is, for example, a club in Tokyo which charges clients Y2000 for a service called 'Ripping pants off a schoolgirl', and further offers them an opportunity to molest girls as they stand holding onto handles hanging from the ceiling in a room which simulates the environment of a subway train. This latter reflects a reality of women and girls' lives. Last year, 1,854 men were arrested for molesting women and girls on trains, for 'molesters on the subways, or *chikan,* are incredibly common in Tokyo a survey conducted this year found that 72 per cent of teenage girls had been groped on their way to school' (Wood, 2001, 23).

Next we should note possible overlaps between 'paedophile' networks and organisations formed with the spoken intention of lobbying for legal and attitudinal changes towards 'paedophilia'. Such organisations argue that 'paedophiles' are members of an oppressed sexual minority group, and that 'non-violent' paedophilia should be recognised as a legitimate sexual preference. The idea that adult-child sexual contact can be consensual is thus central to their claims for legitimacy, and to this end, such organisations publicly rehearse the cognitive distortions that convicted child sex offenders typically employ to justify and defend their acts of sexual abuse. Members of such organisations claim to be exercising the right to freedom of thought and expression by lobbying for changes to the law, rather than encouraging people to break the law, and they have met with different responses in different countries. In Britain, for example, one of the leading members of the Paedophile Information Exchange (PIE) was imprisoned for corrupting public morals in the late 1970s, and PIE subsequently collapsed. By contrast, the Danish Pedophile Association (DPA) is a legal organisation under the Danish constitution. Despite considerable lobby work by children's rights organisations, the government has chosen not to close the group, and has instead left it to lobby very actively. Indeed, the DPA claims to have received some 341,645 visitors to its website since March 1999, and has dialogue and connections with similar Swedish and Dutch groups.

Articles published on the DPA website explain, among other things, that children enjoy and benefit from sexual relationships with paedophiles, that child pornography depicts children experiencing sexual pleasure, and that if customers were prevented from buying sex from children in prostitution in the 'Third World', then the children and their families would be thrown into even greater poverty and misery than before. Links to other websites are also provided, as are opportunities for self-identified 'paedophiles' to chat with each other. In short, the DPA openly performs many of the functions performed by more clandestine networks, such as the Wonderland Club. It enables 'paedophiles' from around the world to make contact with each other, share and exchange information, and reinforce each other's beliefs about the harmlessness of child sexual exploitation. A recent television documentary produced evidence to show that members of the DPA were involved in organising tours to India to engage in CSEC, and were also involved in abusing children in Denmark. As a direct result of this documentary, the Danish police have, at last, launched their first ever investigation into the group's activities. However, even if this investigation leads to prosecutions of individual DPA members for sexual offences against children, it is by no means certain that the government will respond by making it illegal to operate a website which facilitates networking between 'paedophiles'.

Finally, it should be noted that pornography depicting sex between those over 18 can be linked to the sexual abuse of children in the sense that it is sometimes shown to children by abusers as a way of preparing or 'grooming' them for sexual abuse.

8. TOWARDS A MORE COMPLICATED AND DIFFERENTIATED VISION OF 'THE SEX EXPLOITER'

Questions about childhood, sexuality and commercial sex can be hugely controversial, and those who campaign against CSEC often attempt to sidestep disagreements by focusing on aspects of abuse and exploitation upon which there is most agreement. In practice, this means keeping the focus firmly on the sexual use of younger children. Thus we find that public awareness raising materials produced both before and since the First World Congress have, through the use of particular images (broken rose buds, discarded toys, small children being led away by large, shadowy male figures), and examples of cases involving children aged between 3 and 12, tended to stress the sexual exploitation of young children, rather than adolescents. While the impulse to stick to uncontroversial, common ground is understandable it also carries certain risks. It leads to an emphasis on sexual abuse and CSEC as the violation of childhood 'innocence', and in so doing, suggests that a particular model of childhood (as a state of passivity and dependence) can be universalised and extended to cover both young children and adolescents up to the age of 18. The general dangers of a discourse about child sexual abuse and exploitation as the theft, shattering, rape, or betrayal of 'innocence' have been incisively discussed by Jenny Kitzinger (1997), and readers are referred to her work. This discourse also poses particular problems in relation to our vision of, and response to, 'the sex exploiter'. By constructing CSEC as the simple and unambiguous meeting of innocence and corruption, good and evil, we not only ignore and erase many of its most painful realities, but also risk proposing solutions that are likely to be at best unworkable or ineffective, and that at worse may contribute to a host of new human rights abuses. It is therefore vitally important to develop a more complicated and differentiated vision of those who sexually exploit children.

Children as Sex Exploiters

Although we tend to think of children as the most socially powerless group of all, it is important to remember that all children are not equally unequal. As well as the massive physical, emotional and psychological differentials between, let us say, a child of 3 and a child of 16, children are divided by class, gender, race/caste, disability and sexual orientation. The teenage sons of a wealthy family, for instance, exercise substantial powers over the teenage girl domestic worker employed by their parents; a child without disabilities can be enormously powerful in relation to a child with disabilities. There is increasing evidence to show that children, as well as adults, can take unfair advantage of such imbalances of power for purposes of sexual/psychological gratification. Recent research in North America, the UK and Sweden reveals that adolescent males are amongst those who commit sexual offences against children (Grubin, 1998, Svensson, 2000). Adolescent males are also amongst those providing demand for prostitution (Monto, 2000, FPA HK, 2000). There are no data available on the age of prostitutes used by child clients. However, given the fact that some boys under 18 are known to use prostitutes in settings where children aged under 18 are present in prostitution, we cannot discount the possibility that children in prostitution may sometimes be exploited by child clients.

Boy children are also known to be involved in more diffuse forms of sexual-economic exchange. For example, a report on young people's sexual health in Kafue, Zambia, notes that girls are increasingly trading sex, and most sexual relations among boys and girls involve the exchange of money or goods. Girls are clear about the fact that poverty leads them to enter into such exchanges, while boys explain that 'having sex with girls is a way of proving that one is a man and it is a means of gaining popularity' (Chikwenya et al., 1997, 21). There are also reports that some adolescent male refugees are seeking younger and younger sexual partners amongst other refugee and displaced children in settings where HIV and AIDS are prevalent. Pornography is also used by persons under the age of 18 (see FPA HK, 2000), and in May 2001, a 13 year old British boy was convicted and placed on the Sex Offenders Register for dealing in pornographic images of children, having downloaded materials from the internet. Finally, we should note that adolescent male soldiers are amongst those involved in some of the most brutal forms of sexual violence/exploitation taking place in the contemporary world (see Section 9), and that both boys and girls under the age of 18 are sometimes involved in CSEC as pimps or procurers.

Save the Children Sweden's clinical and research work with young offenders who abuse in non-commercial contexts concludes that: 'A child or young person does not commit such an abnormal act as a sexual offence on another child unless abnormal circumstances exist in the child's own life. These abnormal circumstances may be short lived or chronic. All children have been violated in one way or another' (Svensson, 2000: 35). This insight may also hold good for some of the adolescent males who sexually exploit other children through their consumption of pornography or their prostitute-use, but in most cases, their behaviour is probably better explained through reference to their society's prevailing attitudes towards gender and sexuality. Masculinity is almost universally idealised as involving the exercise of power over self, others, and material objects, and men who are able to command sexual access to female bodies are widely celebrated in film, fiction and popular song. That teenage boys, who are generally both implicitly and explicitly encouraged to demonstrate their masculinity (and frequently taunted and ridiculed for failing to appear sufficiently 'manly'), should often display an interest in sexually objectified female bodies is hardly surprising. And in settings where men's prostitute-use is widely viewed as normal, adolescent boys may be encouraged by older male relatives, as well as by peers, to buy commercial sex.

As with adults, then, there is an important distinction to be made between children whose acts of abuse against other children express some kind of psychic turmoil or emotional dysfunction, and those whose acts of sexual exploitation are the unintended by-product of a wish to conform to social norms regarding masculine sexual expression. And still further differentiation is necessary if we are to understand the children who sexually exploit other children for financial gain, rather than sexual gratification. Poverty and other forms of social exclusion pave the way into this side of the sex trade, just as they are the major routes into prostitution itself, and the complexity of the issues posed by those who become involved in CSEC as third party beneficiaries is considered in more detail below. First, however, it should be noted that girls who themselves work in prostitution sometimes supplement their income by procuring other children for their pimps or regular clients, for this highlights the fact that females can sexually exploit, as well as be sexually exploited.

Female Sex Exploiters

In most societies, women are imagined as naturally both sexually passive and predisposed to nurture and care for children. Such beliefs make it difficult either to conceive of a female 'sex exploiter', or to understand that sexual abuse by women damages children in the same way as sexual abuse by men. However, Swedish, American and British research suggests somewhere between 5 and 20% of all incidents of child sexual abuse are perpetrated by women, and that the consequences for the children are just as severe as the effects of sexual abuse by male perpetrators (Saradjian, 1996, Grubin, 1998). Clinicians who have worked with women who sexually abuse children observe that they usually exhibit the same kind of distorted thinking as that displayed by their male counterparts. Women can also provide a demand for commercial sex. In Japan, Australia, North America and Western Europe, a small but growing number of women are using their greater economic power to indulge in various forms of commercial sexual experience at home or abroad. Amongst them there are women who sexually exploit adolescent boys aged between 13 and 18 in developing countries, and even some who pay to abuse younger children. Women, both local and foreign, also sometimes take on the role of 'Sugar Mummy', using their greater economic and social power to command access to a series of adolescent boyfriends. Cases of boy children being sexually abused by women in the rebel forces in Sierra Leone have also been reported.

We should, however, remember that women are very much in a minority amongst those who exploit for pleasure in either noncommercial or commercial contexts. The same cannot be said in relation to the sexual exploitation of children for profit, for women have a strong presence in the global sex trade as third party beneficiaries of CSEC.

Third Party Beneficiaries

CSEC takes place within a complex and multifaceted 'sex sector' which is linked in a variety of ways to both the formal and informal economy in any given country (see Lim, 1998). Some of those who derive economic benefits from the sex sector are wealthy and powerful. They can include government and police officials and those who own and control businesses in the leisure and entertainment sector, which often enjoys a symbiotic relationship with the sex industry. Given that persons under the age of 18 are present in the mainstream sex trade, such people can be said to benefit indirectly from CSEC. Large and respectable tourism, mining, logging and shipping companies might also be said to be indirectly involved in the sex sector in the sense that a flourishing demand for prostitution, including CSEC, is one of the by-products of their main profit-making activity and/or employment policies (such as providing dormitory accommodation for a migrant male workforce instead of housing for the men and their families). However, those who own and control companies are rarely held personally responsible for the social or environmental costs associated with the sectors within which they operate. Indeed, they are often loudly applauded for taking even the smallest of steps to ameliorate the negative side effects of their firms' profit-making activities.

Other third parties benefit from CSEC in more immediate ways. Economic rewards can be obtained from CSEC through a variety of activities, including: trafficking children for purposes of sexual exploitation; organising and/or controlling children in prostitution; procuring children; producing and distributing child pornography for commercial gain. Individuals can also obtain economic rewards from CSEC without actually becoming directly involved in arranging any child's sexual exploitation (corrupt officials can benefit from bribes; bar owners can 'turn a blind eye' to CSEC on their premises and benefit from the customers it draws to their establishment; retailers can profit by selling pornographic materials involving persons under the age of 18, and so on). Few of these people dedicate themselves simply and solely to promoting CSEC, and most come to exploit children through their involvement with the sex trade more generally.

We should further note that several exploiters, rather than one single exploiter, are usually implicated in any given child's sexual exploitation. So, for example, a trafficked child's journey from her home to the brothel, street or private flat where she ends up being commercially sexually exploited is usually charted by a number of different social actors: those who recruit her (perhaps people who themselves were originally trafficked into prostitution), those who encourage her (perhaps her own friends or relatives), middle agents, corrupt officials, pimps or brothel owners. This 'division of labour' reduces any sense of responsibility on the part of each of the individuals involved. Those at the start of the chain do not necessarily know or see the end consequences of their actions, whilst those at the end of the chain can blame the people who acted further back down the line for the child's situation. The motives of these different actors are not always identical, and they do not have equal interests in the commercial sex trade. While some rely on that trade as a major source of income, others benefit from their involvement on a 'one-off' or irregular basis.

Very often, the action of those who knowingly derive economic benefits from CSEC is informed by the kind of moral indifference that was described in Section 5. In the course of research in a number of countries, the author has interviewed a range of individuals involved in CSEC as third party beneficiaries. None saw themselves as personally implicated in the sexual abuse of a child. They reasoned that they were not morally responsible for the actions of the client, and if they did not sell him the service he wanted, someone else would. Likewise, it was the child's parents, or perhaps the state, but certainly not they, who had a moral obligation to protect and care for the child. This kind of moral indifference is largely consonant with dominant attitudes towards economic life in most countries of the world, but people can 'buy into' such attitudes to different degrees and for different reasons. Some of those who sexually exploit children for profit are affluent and privileged individuals who are willing to cynically take advantage of the misfortunes of others for their own personal advantage. Often the children they exploit are of a different racial, ethnic, caste or national group from their own, and their willingness to tolerate or promote CSEC is partly linked to their racism/ xenophobia. European and North American expatriates who allow children to solicit from bars they own in tourist resorts in developing countries, or procure children for tourists, provide a good example of this type of exploiter (see O'Connell Davidson and Sanchez Taylor, 2001).

But other third party beneficiaries of CSEC are far from privileged and powerful. Women and children, as well as men, are involved, and it is not uncommon for an individual 'career'

in the sex trade to start with selling sex, then progress to organising the prostitution of others, including children. Nor is it unusual for prostitutes, including children in prostitution, to supplement their income by procuring or pimping others. Regardless of their age or gender, a good many people's involvement as third party beneficiaries of the sex trade is precipitated by exactly the same factors which make children vulnerable to commercial sexual exploitation, including: poverty, lack of alternative economic opportunity, absence of educational opportunities, domestic violence, drug addiction, and/or a range of exclusionary social practices and policies based on discriminatory beliefs about gender, race, ethnicity, caste and/or sexuality. Indeed, many thousands of the world's children grow up in brothel districts or other communities that are entirely economically dependent upon the sex industry, including child prostitution. Often, the stigma attached to prostitution is so great that neither prostitutes nor their children are able to freely leave such communities. A recent study in Bangladesh shows that children born in the brothel community have little sense of what life is like in mainstream society, and no hope of leaving the community. Moreover, 'All but the most protected children are routinely caught up in illicit activities from drinking, drug taking and gambling to theft, pimping and extortion' (Uddin *et al.*, 2001, 45).

In these and other similar communities, adults who are yesterday's exploited children are today exploiting the children who will become tomorrow's exploiters. Such cycles of exploitation have virtually nothing to do with individual morality or criminality, but a great deal to do with the legal and social construction of prostitutes as a separate class of persons and the systematic violation of their human rights. The actions of all those involved as third parties to CSEC are neither identical nor morally equivalent, and it is vitally important that this fact is reflected in the range of policy measures designed to address 'the sex exploiter'. In many instances, the environment behind sexual exploitation rather than the individual who exploits must be the primary focus of our concern and interventions.

9. WHAT IS TO BE DONE?

This paper has emphasised the fact that there is no 'sex exploiter' as such. Instead, there are people (adult and child, male and female) who sexually exploit children in many different ways, for many different reasons and in many different social contexts. Strategies to prevent child sexual exploitation, and to deter, control and/or reintegrate sex exploiters must recognise this diversity. We must also address the fact that there is a strong relationship between socially prescribed or tolerated attitudes and practices and the demand for CSEC. There is a need to develop and fund public education campaigns to challenge and undermine the popular and widely endorsed beliefs about sexuality, gender, race, class, caste, childhood, economic life and/or prostitution which exploiters of all types draw upon to rationalise and defend their actions. This means making links (at local, national and international levels) between efforts to tackle CSEC and efforts to combat other forms of discrimination. So, for example, sexual exploitation needs to be placed on the agenda when racism is being discussed, and vice versa. Equally, the violation of children's rights through CSEC is not separable from, or unrelated to, other human rights' issues, and questions about the demand side of CSEC cannot be divorced from more general questions about poverty, gender relations, social exclusion, child labour, welfare policies, structural adjustment programmes, tourist development, racism, migratory pressures, AIDS and sexual health, and prostitutes' civil and human rights.

This points to the need for 'joined up thinking' on the part of national and international policy makers and governmental organisations in order to devise and implement effective longer term measures addressing the economic, social and political conditions which underpin demand. It also suggests that even broader and more inclusive approaches to partnership building are required. In particular, there is an urgent need for dialogue between children's NGOs, on the one hand, and sex workers' rights organisations, migrant workers' organisations, AIDS prevention groups, and gay rights' and anti-racist activists on the other. These latter groups not only have knowledge and experience that is highly relevant to efforts to tackle the demand-side of CSEC, but also are also sometimes negatively affected by unintended consequences of measures designed to combat CSEC. Such groups can potentially make an invaluable contribution to the struggle against CSEC, but for this to happen, children's NGOs need to engage with their concerns more closely.

Efforts to tackle the demand for CSEC also need to take into account the fact that a sizeable number of those who sexually exploit children are themselves members of groups which are vulnerable, marginalized, and exploited, and/or belong to occupational groups which place members under strong subcultural pressures to engage in commercial sex. Punitive and moralistic campaigns will not necessarily be the most effective way of changing their behaviours or sexual practices. Again, there is a need for broader partnership building. Organisations that have the strongest relationships with groups prone to prostitute-use (for example, seafarers unions, and trades unions in logging, mining and tourism industries, NGOs involved in AIDS prevention out-reach work), need to be involved in the design and implementation of awareness raising and prevention strategies. Equally, employers, including the military, need to become more involved in educational and preventative work with their employees.

There is also a role for the private sector in terms of developing meaningful and sustainable economic alternatives to third party involvement in CSEC. In this regard, it is perhaps even more vitally important to encourage international financial institutions, development banks, and economic advisors to consider the impact of development policies and structural adjustment measures on the demand for commercial sex in any given country or region.

Finally, there remains an urgent need for more extensive and detailed research on the root causes of demand for CSEC, since this would feed into more effective measures for prevention and awareness raising. There is also a need for better and more consistent data collection regarding sexual offences involving children, and for research to evaluate the impact of specific measures.

Above all, we need to remember that there is no simple, single policy solution with regard to those who commercially sexually exploit children. Efforts to strengthen and enforce laws against CSEC must be balanced and complimented by long-term measures to transform the environments that produce sex exploiters. Such measures will require a great deal of investment, and adequate resources must be committed to them if we are serious about combating the problem of CSEC.

ACKNOWLEDGEMENTS

The author is particularly indebted to the following people for invaluable information, references and support: Ola Florin, Hélène Sackstein, Jacqueline Sánchez Taylor, Sun Wen Bin, Travis Kong, Zhang Jie, Ann Gray, Brian Su, Geoff Wade, Maia Rusakova, Tatania Pishkina, Bridget Anderson, Lars Loof, Vernon Jones, David Prosser, Liz Kelly, Laura Agustin, Asmita Naik and Helen Vietch. The support of Save the Children Sweden, which funded the researching and writing of this paper, and the Economic and Social Research Council of Great Britain, which funded research in the Caribbean that also contributed to the paper (Award no: ROOO237625) is gratefully acknowledged.

REFERENCES

ACPF (Association Contre la Prostitution Enfantine) 2001: Draguignan: Trial against sexual tourism. Personal communication: ACPF, 14, rue Mondetour, 75001, Paris, France.

Alexander, P., 1997: 'Feminism, sex workers' rights and human rights', in J. Nagle (ed.) *Whores and Other Feminists.* London: Routledge, pp. 83–97.

Anderson, B., 2000: *Doing the Dirty Work? The Global Politics of Domestic Labour.* London: Zed.

ARC, 2001: Action for the Rights of Children Resource Pack: Critical Issues, Abuse and Exploitation. Geneva: UNHCR.

Brown, L., 2000: *Sex Slaves: The Trafficking of Women in Asia.* London: Virago.

Chikwenya, C., Michelo, W., Lubilo, M., and Fuglesang, M., 1997: What's up Kafue? An assessment of the livelihood, sexual health and needs of young people in Kafue District. Lusaka: SIDA

Forum on Marriage, 2000: Early Marriage: Whose Right to Choose? London: Forum on Marriage and the Rights of Women and Girls.

FPA, HK, 2000: *Report on the Youth Sexuality Study, 1996.* Hong Kong: Family Planning Association.

Grubin, D., 1998: Sex offending against children: Understanding the risk. *Police Research Series*, Paper 99. London: Home Office.

Holman, K., 2001: Treatment of Young Perpetrators of Sexual Abuse: Possibilities and Challenges. Save the Children Alliance Europe Group.

HRI (Human Rights Internet) 2001: The Canadian component of the protection project: A socio-legal analysis of international jurisprudence on the commercial sexual exploitation of women and children. Ottawa: HRI.

ILO, 1996: *Child Labour: Targeting the Intolerable.* Geneva: International Labour Office.

Khan, S. 2001: 'Kothis, gays and (other) MSM', *Pukaar*, Issue 32, London: Naz Foundation International.

Kvinna Till Kvinna, 2000: Annual Report. Stockholm: Kvinna Till Kvinna Foundation.

Kitzinger, J., 1997: 'Who are you kidding? Children, power and the struggle against sexual abuse', in A. James and A. Prout (Eds.) *Constructing and Reconstructing Childhood: Contemporary Issues in the Sociological Study of Childhood*. London: Falmer.

Kuleana, 1999: The State of Education in Tanzania: Crisis and Opportunity. Kuleana Center for Children's Rights, Mwanza, Tanzania.

Lim, L., 1998: *The Sex Sector: The Economic and Social Bases of Prostitution in Southeast Asia*. Geneva: ILO.

Månsson, Sven-Axel, 2001: 'Prostitutes' clients and the image of men and masculinity in late modern society', in B. Pease and K. Pringle (Eds.) *Globalising Men*. London: Zed.

O'Connell Davidson, J., 1998: *Prostitution, Power and Freedom*. Cambridge: Polity.

O'Connell Davidson, J. and Sanchez Taylor, J., 2001: CSEC in Jamaica and the Dominican Republic. (Forthcoming)

Paterson, O., 1982: *Slavery and Social Death*. Cambridge, MA: Harvard University Press.

Robertson, A., 1997: 'Nepal: The struggle against the Kamaiya system of bonded labour', in ASI, *Enslaved Peoples in the 1990s*, London: Anti-Slavery International.

SACCS, 1999: Invisible Slaves: An endeavor to combat domestic child labour. New Delhi: South Asian Coalition on Child Servitude.

Sanchez Taylor, J., 2001: 'Dollars are a girl's best friend? Female tourists' sexual behaviour in the Caribbean', *Sociology*, Vol. 35, No. 3.

Saradjian, J., 1996: *Women who Sexually Abuse Children: From Research to Clinical Practice*. London: Wiley.

Save the Children, 1995: Towards a children's agenda: New challenges for social development. London: Save the Children.

Shumba, A., 2001: 'Who guards the guards in schools? A study of reported cases of child abuse by teachers in Zimbabwean secondary schools', *Sex Education* Vol. 1, 1, pp. 77–86.

Svensson, B., 2000: Victims and perpetrators: On sexual abuse and treatment. Stockholm: Save the Children Sweden.

Uddin, F., Sultana, M., Mahmud, S., (revised and edited by M. Black and H. Goodman), 2001: Childhood in the red light zone: Growing up in the Daulatdia and Kandapara brothel communities of Bangladesh. Save the Children Australia.

USAID, 2000: Children on the Brink. Washington: United States Agency for International Development.

UNHCR, 2000: Refugee children and adolescents: a progress report. Executive Committee of the High Commissioner's programme.

Ward, T., Hudson, S. and Keenan, T., 2000: 'The assessment and treatment of sexual offenders against children', in C. Hollin (Ed.) *Handbook of Offender Assessment and Treatment*. London: Wiley, pp. 349–361.

Weitzer, R. (Ed.), 2000: *Sex for Sale*. New York: Routledge.

Wellings, K., Field, J., Johnson, A., Wadworth, J., with Bradshaw, S., 1993: *Sexual Behaviour in Britain: The National Survey of Sexual Attitudes and Lifestyles*. Harmondsworth: Penguin.

Wood, G., 2001: 'Sex and the city', *Observer Magazine*, The Japan Issue, April 1.

Wood, K. and Jewkes, R., 2001: 'Dangerous' love: reflections on violence among Xhosa Township youth. In R. Morrell (Ed.) *Changing Men in Southern Africa*. London: Zed.

Pornography: Not for Men Only

Mariana Valverde

An innovative approach is required in studying women's relation to pornography. We cannot look at porn as a bad thing out there that men buy and then "act out." We have to see pornography as an *element* that runs throughout our whole culture. Rather than try to isolate porn as a particular object, it might be more useful to speak about "the pornographic" as an aspect of many apparently harmless films, books, and magazines. When we stop worrying about defining porn narrowly enough so that only the worst stuff comes under legal scrutiny, and begin to define it broadly enough to encompass those aspects of mass culture that glamourize the subjection of women, then we will have learned something not just about male lust but also about women's own fantasies and desires. These are to a large extent constructed by traditional feminine culture embodying the same power relations that we see expressed in violent porn.

The effect of pornography on women will be the main focus of this article. I put the discussion in the context of a definition of pornography that encompasses not only male-oriented erotic literature but also those mass-produced cultural products that are addressed to women and which glamourize and eroticize their subordination.

DEFINING PORNOGRAPHY

Pornography is a collection of images and texts, representations which have something in common. Defining that "something" is the subject of a great deal of discussion. However, before we can try to define pornographic content we need some idea of how to analyze and classify *representations* in general.

There are many types of representations in our culture, such as avant-garde visual art, soap operas, Western films, romance novels, symphonies, love songs, housewife magazines, and detective novels. These are just a few of the many genres available to us mostly through mass-produced cultural industries. Just as it is sometimes difficult to establish whether a particular popular song is "country and western" or "pop," or whether a particular popular novel is a detective story or a spy thriller, it is difficult to know exactly what is or is not pornography. *Penthouse* is pornography, more or less by definition, but what about D.H. Lawrence's novels? Or gay male magazines containing erotic photos? Or sex manuals? Or novels written by women about women who have sex frequently? Or television commercials featuring scantily clad blondes draped over a household appliance or a car?

The problem is that there are no litmus tests for what is or is not pornography. For pornography is not a natural object that can be classified, like a particular species of butterfly, but rather a complex cultural *process*. It is a process because it necessarily establishes, and is established by, a particular set of relations between producer and consumer, between consumer and his/her social context, and between the social context and the producer. Pornography does not drop from heaven onto our local corner-store shelves. It is first *produced* by certain people who relate to one another via the pornography industry; it is then *consumed* by customers who buy porn in the expectation of being aroused; and finally, porn derives most of its meaning and significance from the *social context* in which it exists.

Elsewhere I have analyzed in more detail the production and consumption dimensions of pornography. I have commented on the inadequacy of measures that seek merely to interfere either with production (e.g. prior censorship) or with consumption (e.g. bylaws regulating sales), without a broader understanding of the process involved in the creation both of porn itself and of the "porn consumer."[1] Here I would like to focus mainly on social context, partly because it has been almost completely neglected in feminist discussions and partly because it is the element most relevant to our question regarding the impact of pornography on women.

When we look at a *Playboy* centrefold we generally see a young white woman with a flawless body; she is either sitting or reclining, her genital area is exposed in a purposeful manner and is usually in the centre of the picture. In itself, the picture does not have very much meaning. We supply most of the meaning ourselves, from our experience of living in a sexist, ageist and racist society, and from our general knowledge of what *Playboy* is and what is expected of the viewer. We know from sources outside the magazine that it is not coincidental that the woman in the picture is young, slim, white, and helpless-looking. We know from our own experience that the photo was created for a male audience and that when a man looks at it he will react in certain specified ways. He will not merely glance at the photo as he would at a landscape or a family photograph; he will gaze intently, stare at, and *possess* that woman with his eyes. We also know, from our knowledge of how capitalism works, that the purpose of the publication is not to celebrate the female body but rather to use female bodies to make profits. Thus, we use our knowledge of both the production and the consumption processes involved in pornography to interpret the picture and ascribe to it a meaning.

Furthermore, we are informed about the usual relations between men and women in our society, and that information is what produces the feelings we experience when looking at the otherwise harmless photo. We feel embarrassed for the model because we know that her apparent naive innocence is a deception designed to heighten the male's pleasure in conquering the pictured body. We feel angry at men, both those who make money from the photo and those who spend money on it. We feel vulnerable and at risk. But it is not the picture itself which creates these feelings. If men never raped women in real life, the same picture would not have the same power to make us feel violated.

A different, negative example. One could imagine writing a radical feminist sci-fi story in which men were portrayed as stupid creatures only good for sex and reproduction. And yet, even if it offended men, such a story could not make them feel violated, threatened, or at risk, since reality would still be firmly in patriarchal hands. Because women do not have the social power to subdue, exploit, or marginalize men, feminist fantasies of a matriarchal world can never have the same social significance and the same impact on men as pornography does on women. Men may dislike matriarchal fantasies, but no fantasy can succeed in making them afraid to walk the streets alone at night for fear of being attacked by a gang of women.

Thus, our experience in a sexist society helps in a very important way to determine how we will interpret representations of sex and gender. The very meaning of representation is largely determined by its social context. For instance, a photo of a woman kneeling down to perform fellatio on a man has a very different social meaning than a picture of a man kneeling to perform cunnilingus on a woman. The first picture implies subordination, while the second merely implies that a man is giving a woman pleasure. The difference in the connotations is not due to anything in the photos themselves, but rather to the "usual" connotations of women's bodies versus men's bodies.

The meaning of a particular representation is further specified by the context in which the representation appears. If we are watching a pornographic film, a close-up shot of a peach cut in half will have sexual connotations, whereas the same shot would not arouse anybody if it were part of a food advertisement. The following example will make this point clearer.

The June 1985 issue of *Forum*, a soft-core porn magazine published by *Penthouse* and containing only articles and textual erotic fantasies, carried a feature enticingly entitled "Sex Lives of Lesbian Nuns." The piece consisted of a series of excerpts from a book of personal stories by nuns and ex-nuns who had either had lesbian love affairs in the convent, usually with little or no genital sex, or who had come out as lesbians after leaving the convent. The book was edited by two lesbian ex-nuns and published by the U.S. lesbian feminist press Naiad. The sale of excerpt rights to *Forum* was widely denounced by lesbian feminists, including some of the ex-nuns who had contributed their personal accounts to the book on the understanding that it was going to be published by a small feminist press and would be sold as a feminist product to a feminist audience. They were horrified to see their lives turned into pornography.[2]

This is not the place to explore the complicated ethical and legal questions regarding the sale of other people's words. We are only concerned with how this sale of feminist texts to a porn outfit sheds light on the problem of defining pornography. The reader of the book approaches it as a lesbian feminist text, which deals specifically with Catholic experiences and asks many questions about spirituality, bonding between women, sexuality and guilt, repression, and the racial and class contradictions between women in convents. The erotic passages are few and far between: even women who were aware of their lesbianism while they were nuns seldom had sex. Either

through ignorance, shame, or because of the vow of chastity, sexual pleasure was generally limited to kissing and mild fondling. Even in the excerpts published in *Forum*, which were culled for their presumed erotic value, there are few explicit descriptions of sexual pleasure. There are, however, a great many descriptions of sexual guilt, and undoubtedly some readers experience pleasure when reading about sexual guilt.

In the context of *Forum* sexual guilt is pornographic. Whereas in the book the descriptions of guilt serve to illuminate how Catholicism works, and so educate the reader about a particular segment of the lesbian community, in *Forum* the same words come across as pornographic clichés. Convents, Mother Superiors, male confessors, novice mistresses, penances, self-mortification and all the other elements of Catholic life have not coincidentally been part of the stock in trade of pornographers since the Marquis de Sade.

This shift in meaning of the autobiographical elements illustrates the importance of context for defining what is or is not pornography. A story which comes across as a moving personal account of a woman discovering her own sexuality in a Catholic environment suddenly turns into a pornographic cliché, merely because it was taken out of a lesbian feminist context and published in a pornographic one.

The example just mentioned shows that one cannot always decide what is or is not pornography merely by looking at the picture or text in question. This decision involves such other factors as context and mode of production and consumption. Because of the difficulties involved in isolating a specific set of representations and labelling them "pornographic" regardless of purpose, use and context, it might be more useful to speak of pornographic elements in our culture. These elements are present together in most mass-produced films and magazines designed explicitly by the producers as "porn." But each element or even several at once are also found in other cultural genres.

Thus far feminist analyses of porn have tended to focus only on male sexual violence against women. Important as this one component is, there are others which are equally essential in the constitution of pornography as a cultural genre. Looking at a representative sample of soft-core porn magazines (which have much larger circulations than hard-core ones, and are bought by significant numbers of women[3]) I was able to distinguish three main elements almost invariably found in the magazine as a whole, though not necessarily in each article or photo spread.

(1) *The portrayal of men's social and physical power over women as sexy.* This includes eroticizing guns, uniforms, and other symbols of male power, most notably wealth. By contrast, women are eroticized in their powerlessness, as indicated by their extreme youth, physical vulnerability, stance and facial expression. For men, power equals sexiness, whereas for women the equation is reversed. A woman millionaire, a woman Prime Minister, a woman athlete—all these women have to prove they are feminine and desirable to men, because the immediate assumption is that their power renders them masculine or sexless. (cf. the endless discussions by sports writers about whether or not this or that woman athlete is truly feminine. East European athletes are especially suspect because in their societies the use of make-up, fancy haircuts, jewelry, etc. is not as encouraged as in consumer capitalist societies.)

(2) *The depiction of aggression, both sexual and non-sexual, as the inevitable result of power imbalances.* That is, the impression is created that those who have power will tend to abuse it and dominate others. This belief is by no means unique to pornography, but it is used by the producers of porn to signal certain things. For instance, given what we know about gender and race relations, when a pornographic magazine shows us a picture of white cowboys standing beside Indian women, we know the next picture will show the rape or at least the seduction of the Indian women. The pornographer does not have to depict the actual rape; we fill in the blanks ourselves.

This conception of power is found in almost all popular culture, from Westerns to war movies, from Gothic romances to spy thrillers. But in pornography it plays the specific role of equating women's sexual availability with an immediate danger of rape and even murder. While business magazines suggest it is men's nature to forsake all for the sake of profits, pornography assumes that men will abuse or at the very least fuck women whenever they can. Once we have learned this belief, it does not have to be spelled out each time it is used. We can be given only a picture of a sexually aroused male, and we will once more fill in the blanks and assume that any woman in his vicinity is in danger.

(3) *The undermining of social barriers and conventions by the relentless power of sex.* Pornography tends to use stereotyped social roles rather than fully developed characters. We are not presented with such fictional individuals as Anna Karenina or Madame Bovary, but only with such cardboard characters as the bored housewife, the sexy milkman, the nymphet, the young male jock, and the innocent co-ed. Many of these roles would, in real life, put a distance between one person and another. For instance, the milkman has a specific job to do, and the housewife presumably has an allegiance to her husband and is not normally available to other men. But pornography sees its role as demolishing all social

barriers by connecting, through sex, people who are generally kept separate by society's rules. We know this about pornography, so when we begin to read a story about a high school girl and her teacher we immediately expect the usual barrier between teacher and young student to be overcome by mutual lust. Similarly, if a woman is presented as unavailable to men (most commonly the nun and the lesbian) we again expect to see this apparent unavailability denied as sex bursts through the boundaries. Hence, the description of a woman as either a lesbian or a nun will function in the pornographic code as a signal indicating that this woman poses a particular challenge to the male subject. So, in the pornographic context the very word "lesbian" acts as a stimulus to male desire.

This undermining of social distinctions by the power of passion is not necessarily sexist. It is the main ingredient of erotic literature of any kind, from highbrow novels to women's romances. Usually however it is expressed within a sexist context. But the idea of sex as the great leveller which eliminates all social conventions is not per se a patriarchal one.

If this third aspect of pornography is also found in erotic representations that few people would call pornographic, the first two aspects, the most objectionable from a feminist perspective, are also found in many other cultural forms. As for the first, the eroticization of men's domination and women's subordination, a look at any mass-market women's magazine will reveal what sort of man is portrayed as most sexually desirable: men who are physically strong, macho-looking, and who hold a good deal of social power. Doctors, lawyers, professional athletes, executives—these are the men that we are taught to fantasize about, to desire.

We have only to listen to sociobiologists talk about "innate" male aggression and the value

of competitiveness and jealousy to see that the second element, the depiction of aggression resulting inevitably from power imbalances, is not unique to pornography. Now, it is true that in our competitive society everyone is put in the position of having to elbow their way to the top. Power is generally used against others rather than with them. However, this is not necessarily inherent in human nature. Those who portray power in this way are invoking the nebulous concept of "human nature" in order to justify present social arrangements. I do not see why we should assume that because women are usually physically weaker than men, we will forever have to live in fear of being assaulted. There are a lot of very strong women on my soccer team, and it would never occur to them to use their collective strength to intimidate or assault weaker human beings. Surely it is society, not nature, which tells men that women are potential victims of their violence.

In summary, there are indeed pernicious messages contained in, but not unique to, pornography. They are ideological elements found in many mass-produced cultural products. Moreover, the messages cannot be summarized by, or limited to, the legitimation of male violence against women. The depiction of power as necessarily based on, and resulting in, competition and aggression does not only legitimize and promote male domination. It also legitimizes class exploitation, racism and war, and makes them seem somehow "natural."

To focus only on sexual domination is a narrow perspective, and one which white middle-class women might tend to take because they are not subject to other forms of domination. But a feminism which is more broadly based and which takes into account the experience of women of colour and women in the Third World will have to take a serious look at the glamourization of racism and capitalism, not just the glamourization of sexual subordination. Pornography often eroticizes several forms of domination at once. Consider, for example, the cliché scenes about white male explorers coming upon a "primitive" society whose women are portrayed as "natural" sex objects free of the inhibitions of white Protestant ladies.

Pornography eroticizes social domination in general. A picture that presents a white British army officer flogging an Indian soldier (cf. the television series *The Jewel and the Crown*) is in my mind pornographic, even though there are no women involved. The picture has a definite sexual overtone which helps to disguise the real nature of British imperialism, in the same way that *Penthouse* photos of women begging to be penetrated help to disguise the real nature of sexism.

The eroticization of social domination is also an element in advertising, women's magazines, and the mainstream media in general. Soap operas, for instance, probably do more than any other medium to teach women to see wealth and power as erotic. Devotees of *Dallas* know that the glamorous women in the show might make a mistake and fall in love with the "wrong" man. But they would never fall in love with a man of the wrong class or race. The invisibility of black people, of the Chicano population, and of the workers who produce the Ewing millions is a statement in itself. Because these people are outside the world of wealth, they are also outside the realm of significant sexual intrigue.

Pornography is not an aberration in an otherwise civilized and egalitarian culture. It is part and parcel of the cultural industry that has given us sexist advertising, racist war movies, and classist soap operas. My contention here is that its specific role in this cultural industry is to eroticize social domination, and most notably gender domination.

SELF-COERCION AND THE DENIAL OF EROTIC POWER

In trying to isolate the pornographic element in our culture, feminist writers and lawyers have tended to separate violent porn from all other sexual representations and all other portrayals of women. This is a disservice to the women's movement. The early critiques of porn begun in the late sixties were undertaken as part of a wider critique that included advertising images and such practices as beauty pageants. The protest was not just against images of violence, but against any images that portrayed women as stupid and only good for fucking. It is very unfortunate that this connection has taken a back seat to the question of violence in the current debates. Even if violent porn is what angers women most, it is not necessarily the cultural form most dangerous to our own emotional and sexual development. No woman sees the anonymous models portrayed as victims of male violence as role models. But who among us is not influenced by the equally pernicious messages that tell us to be thin, to wear tight jeans, to be attractive to men? I am not convinced that porn increases violence against women, but what about the self-inflicted violence many women suffer as a result of male-oriented images of beauty and desirability? Women destroy their tendons by wearing high heels, spoil their eating habits by alternating binging and dieting, and ruin their emotional health by constantly worrying about their looks.

It would indeed be convenient if all the oppression and violence women suffer were located out there in the pornography industry. But it is not. We degrade and coerce ourselves as soon as we internalize the dictates of sexism, and there is no law or censor board in the world that can protect us against that.

THE EROTICIZATION OF DOMINATION IN FORMULA ROMANCE

If we use the distinction that I drew earlier between *power* and *domination*, we would see that it is true indeed that women's popular romances are pornographic, not because they eroticize power, but because they eroticize domination. There are many novels written by women which eroticize the power that one person has over the other. One individual falls in love with, or is sexually obsessed by another, and is therefore under his/her power. But this power does not correspond with, and is not reinforced by socially structured domination. On the other hand, the paperback romances that so many women consume are full of depictions of *domination* as sexy. It is not the accidental sexual power of one individual over another that is the focus of the story, but rather the eroticized domination of those who rule over those who are ruled. This is not just a matter of eroticizing the traditional imbalance between the sexes; class inequality is eroticized as well. The silver-haired boss is often the prime object of the secretary's desire, and his Rolls and luxurious house are always described in loving detail and presented as constituents of the man's sexual appeal. The man usually abuses his power and exercises domination by sexually harassing the heroine, by being physically aggressive, and/or by threatening to fire her. But all these acts of domination are presented as inherently sexy. These incidents always fuel the flames of the younger woman's desire, even though they simultaneously trigger danger signals in her mind.

The women of these romances are no wimps; they want their independence—up to a point. They work outside the home, they never have parents or other authority figures, and they do not necessarily fall for the first man who flatters them. But the men they do fall for are always more socially powerful than they. The male heroes are white and middle-class; they are also older than the heroines, often a lot older.

The only difference between the hero and the villain (there's invariably a villain) is that the villain actually tries to carry out his threats to rape the heroine or bring her to ruin, while the hero always stops at the last minute. The hero falls in love at some point late in the book, and this acts as a check on his otherwise "natural" impulses to abuse women sexually, emotionally and even financially. In a Silhouette romance, the hero meets the heroine when they talk in his office about a possible contract. He bluntly suggests a dinner date, implying the contract depends on her accepting the date. The heroine is angered at his presumption and his overt use of the economic power he has over her, but she is also sexually flattered. The hero's exercise of gender and class domination is both threatening and intriguing to the young heroine. She is trying hard to become an independent businesswoman, but she secretly yearns to give up control to a stronger being. The discouragements inherent in women's economic struggles are mystified by being "translated" into sexual language. The heroine is presented not as the victim of an unjust economic system, but as a trembling female body yearning to be engulfed by the power of the male.

The real-life problems inherent in women's economic inferiority are simultaneously ignored and glamourized. Male economic power and women's lack of economic power are both given a sexual gloss. Sexual attraction is portrayed as being embedded in unequal socioeconomic relations between the sexes, and financial inequality is sexualized. The marriage at the end of every book is presented as the resolution of all contradictions. Yet what the marriage actually does is institutionalize the inequality. Through marriage the woman will have access to her husband's wealth and power, but she will continue to be the inferior partner.

Thus it is not coincidental that the only sexuality the heroines appear to have consists of passive eroticism. Because of the strong links between socio-economic inequality and eroticism, to allow women an active sexuality would involve revolutionizing a lot more than the bedroom. It would be impossible to equalize the sexual roles in formula romances without challenging the social roles.

To further explore this point, let us quote some typical passages:

> Women always looked at Alex Brent like that . . . His lean, hard body held a menacing sexuality, an implicit threat of sexual violence which attracted women like iron filings to a magnet.

and

> He had hated her with a burning intensity only because he had loved her so deeply. His hatred was as strong as his love. And that was what made her mind up for her. When a man loves you as much as that, she reasoned happily, how can you turn him down?

Now, when one reverses the pronouns in these passages, substituting "he" for "she" and "men" for "women," one does not create an image of a powerful, sexually assertive woman to whom men are attracted like iron filings to a magnet. Rather, the effect is to create a ridiculous piece of prose portraying women as evil witches. No woman would be able to identify with those images of female desire and be turned on by them.

Because active sexuality is equated with domination or the abuse of institutionalized power it is impossible to depict women's active sexual desire without turning the women into monstrous super-bitches. There is no room either for a passive eroticism that is not powerless, or for an active eroticism that is not "menacing" or based on the "implicit threat of sexual violence." Both poles of the dynamic of erotic power have been hopelessly mired in gender stereotypes, and in turn these have been affixed to the social structure of patriarchal capitalism. Women's passive eroticism is described in a distorted and partial way when it is made synonymous with social subordination and personal powerlessness. And women's active eroticism cannot be described at all, except as the evil doings of a crazed nymphomaniac.

Patriarchal ideology is woven into the very language used to describe sexual arousal and satisfaction. Women do not lust after a man, they "tremble," "quiver," "shudder," and display other Jello-like behaviour. Men, by contrast, do not want pleasure as much as they want to dominate. Even an ordinary kiss can become a sadistic tool to convey not passion but "punishment," "He crushed her roughly closer, and as she lifted her chin to protest, drove his mouth down on hers in a kiss that explained everything without words. It was a punishment in itself. . . ."

Popular erotic literature written for women fails them at a sexual level precisely because it fails to challenge the social status quo. It takes social relations for granted and portrays sexual power as belonging exclusively to powerful men. It portrays women's desire as purely passive, as the desire to be dominated and subdued and "rescued" from the hassles of trying to become an independent and financially secure woman. No wonder marriage is invariably the resolution of all contradictions and tensions in the plot. Traditional marriage is the only social means of reconciling male domination with women's protection. It is the only institution that allows women to give in to their sexual desire without being cast into the fringes of society. The institution of marriage tames the male "impulse" to dominate women, or rather channels it into a monogamous and publicly accountable relationship. This provides safety for women while allowing men unlimited access to one female.

Of course this is not necessarily true in reality. For a lot of women marriage is neither sexually pleasurable nor physically safe. But we are speaking about the institution and the ideology of marriage, and paperback romances are concerned with the ideology, not the reality. The ideology is that men are dangerous, and so women can only "let go" with their husbands, because only their husbands have a duty to take care of them after they have fucked them. Only in marriage is the male urge to possess somewhat countered by a duty to protect. One could thus convincingly argue that the view of men presented in formula romances is much more pessimistic and bleak, and hence more anti-male, than the images of men presented in feminist fiction.

In several ways, then, women's popular fiction not only resembles pornography but actually is pornographic. There is an eroticization not only of male sexual power but of social and economic power in general. There is a corresponding glamourization of women's social and sexual subordination to men. The tensions in the plot are invariably resolved by, or at least buried in, marriage, and not any marriage, but a rigidly structured one in which the woman gives up her social autonomy with gay abandon in the hope of obtaining the love, i.e. protection, of an essentially dangerous male. Sexual surrender is tied to economic and social surrender. The woman, romantic soul that she is, makes no demands other than marriage itself in the naive belief that her big, strong hero will love as well as fuck her. If pornography is the depiction of women as the willing slaves of men, and in general the eroticization of institutionalized forms of domination, then one can hardly think of anything more pornographic than a lifetime of formula romance.

CONCLUSION

In conclusion, it is becoming increasingly clear that pornography cannot be tackled as an isolated issue. If the main problem with porn is that it eroticizes the male sexual domination of

women and other forms of social domination, then the only real solution is to empower women and other oppressed groups so that we can begin to redefine what is erotic and what is not. This will involve not only boycotting sexist cultural products and denouncing images which glamourize women's subjection, but also helping to create alternative cultural forms. More generally, since we have shown that a great deal of pornography's impact on us is due not to the images and words themselves but to the social context of men's actual domination of women, then anything we do to empower women and increase their sense of dignity and autonomy will help to rob porn of its power to humiliate us.

Some examples of what women can do to simultaneously attack the sexism of mass-produced culture and *empower* the women engaged in the action are as follows:

- boycott businesses that make money on pornography, and inform the management of our decision

- complain to bookstore owners and other storekeepers, not just about the presence of pornographic magazines but also about the absence of feminist periodicals

- use the handy "this degrades women" stickers available in women's bookstores to record our opinion of billboards, ads in the public transit system, and store window displays

- paint creative graffiti over billboards

- refuse to sell offensive magazines or rent offensive videos in stores that we work in, making sure we get support from our union or from local women's groups

- try to educate the public about our concerns, by writing articles and letters to the editor, speaking in classrooms, organizing pickets at appropriate events

- challenge the men we know who use pornography, and the men we work with who put pin-ups up in public areas. Enlist the support of women workers and supportive men in the attempt to have a working environment that is misogyny-free! One can point out that pornography pollutes the emotional environment just like smoke pollutes the physical environment

If pornography is taken out of its total social and cultural context, it can easily become a bandwagon issue for politicians to use in their own vote-getting campaigns. Equal pay would cost a lot of money, but a pornography law is free, and the right-wing moralists would also like it.

However, the issue of pornography can be used more positively and creatively to empower women. In this chapter I have tried to suggest some avenues for doing this. I have indicated that we need to turn our attention to the difficult problem of how our sexuality is shaped by cultural products, and in particular, cultural products which claim to satisfy our sexual desires (e.g. formula romances) while in fact robbing us of autonomous desires. I have also pointed out that the eroticization of gender oppression by pornography is equally present in other cultural forms, and that this is part of a larger problem of the eroticization of social relations of domination, including racism and class domination.

Pornography cannot be adequately dealt with by isolating and attempting to ban it. For one thing, pornography is not just a male product concocted to satisfy natural male desires. As we have seen, it affects both men and women and is deeply embedded in both the cultural and social relations of our society. Furthermore, a thorough analysis of pornography reveals the unpleasant truth that our task as feminists cannot stop with getting men to change their sexist practices and their traditional approach to sex. On the contrary. Even as we try to educate and change male behaviour, we also have to be courageous enough to turn the spotlight on *female* sexuality, and on feminine ideas about sexuality and feminine patterns of sexual behaviour. And if pornography and all the problems it raises cannot be accurately described as purely male, much less can anyone claim that female desire and women's sexual ethics are islands of purity and simplicity in a sea of male corruption.

NOTES

1. See my article in C. Guberman and M. Wolfe, eds., *No Safe Place: Violence Against Women and Children* (Toronto, Women's Press, 1985), which explores in more depth many of the issues raised in this chapter.
2. R. Curb and N. Monahan, *Lesbian Nuns: Breaking Silence* (Naiad, 1985).
3. Reasonably reliable statistics on the consumption of pornography in Canada can be found in the Badgley *Report on Sexual Offences Against Children* (Govt. of Canada, Nov. 1984), vol. II, pp. 1214–1279.

READING 48

Pornography and the Alienation of Male Sexuality

Harry Brod

1. OBJECTIFICATION OF THE BODY

In terms of both its manifest image of and its effects on male sexuality, that is, in both intrinsic and consequentialist terms, pornography restricts male sensuality in favor of a genital, performance oriented male sexuality. Men become sexual acrobats endowed with oversized and overused organs which are, as the chapter title of a fine book on male sexuality describes, "The Fantasy Model of Sex: Two Feet Long, Hard as Steel, and Can Go All Night."[1] To speak non-euphemistically, using penile performance as an index of male strength and potency directly contradicts biological facts. There is no muscle tissue in the penis. Its erection when aroused results simply from increased blood flow to the area. All social mythology aside, the male erection is physiologically nothing more than localized high blood pressure. Yet this particular form of hypertension has attained mythic significance. Not only does this focusing of sexual attention on one organ increase male performance anxieties, but it also desensitizes other areas of the body from becoming what might otherwise be sources of pleasure. A colleague once told me that her favorite line in a lecture on male sexuality I used to give in a course I regularly taught was my declaration that the basic male sex organ is not the penis, but the skin.

The predominant image of women in pornography presents women as always sexually ready, willing, able, and eager. The necessary corollary to pornography's myth of female perpetual availability is its myth of male perpetual readiness. Just as the former fuels male misogyny when real-life women fail to perform to pornographic standards, so do men's failures to similarly perform fuel male insecurities. Furthermore, I would argue that this diminishes pleasure. Relating to one's body as a performance machine produces a split consciousness wherein part of one's attention is watching the machine, looking for flaws in its performance, even while one is supposedly immersed in the midst of sensual pleasure. This produces a self-distancing self-consciousness which mechanizes sex and reduces pleasure. (This is a problem perpetuated by numerous sexual self-help manuals, which treat sex as a matter of individual technique for fine-tuning the machine rather than as human interaction. I would add that men's sexual partners are also affected by this, as they can often intuit when they are being subjected to rote manipulation.)

2. LOSS OF SUBJECTIVITY

In the terms of discourse of what it understands to be "free" sex, pornographic sex comes "free" of the demands of emotional intimacy or commitment. It is commonly said as a generalization that women tend to connect sex with emotional intimacy more than men do. Without romantically blurring female sexuality into soft focus, if what is meant is how each gender consciously thinks or speaks of sex, I think this view is fair enough. But I find it takes what men say about sex, that it doesn't mean as much or the same thing to them, too much at face value. I would argue that men do feel similar needs for intimacy, but are trained to deny them, and are encouraged further to see physical affection and intimacy primarily if not

Source: Rethinking Masculinity: Philosophical Explorations in Light Feminism, ed. Larry May and Robert A. Strikwerda with Patrick D. Hopkins. Copyright © 1992 by Littlefield Adams Quality Paperbacks.

exclusively in sexual terms. This leads to the familiar syndrome wherein, as one man put it: "Although what most men want is physical affection, what they end up thinking they want is to be laid by a Playboy bunny."[2] This puts a strain on male sexuality. Looking to sex to fulfill what are really non-sexual needs, men end up disappointed and frustrated. Sometimes they feel an unfilled void, and blame it on their or their partner's inadequate sexual performance. At other times they feel a discomfitting urgency or neediness to their sexuality, leading in some cases to what are increasingly recognized as sexual addiction disorders (therapists are here not talking about the traditional "perversions," but behaviors such as what is coming to be called a "Don Juan Syndrome," an obsessive pursuit of sexual "conquests"). A confession that sex is vastly overrated often lies beneath male sexual bravado. I would argue that sex seems overrated because men look to sex for the fulfillment of nonsexual emotional needs, a quest doomed to failure. Part of the reason for this failure is the priority of quantity over quality of sex which comes with sexuality's commodification. As human needs become subservient to market desires, the ground is laid for an increasing multiplication of desires to be exploited and filled by marketable commodities.[3]

For the most part the female in pornography is not one the man has yet to "conquer," but one already presented to him for the "taking." The female is primarily there as sex object, not sexual subject. Or, if she is not completely objectified, since men do want to be desired themselves, hers is at least a subjugated subjectivity. But one needs another independent subject, not an object or a captured subjectivity, if one either wants one's own prowess validated, or if one simply desires human interaction. Men functioning in the pornographic mode of male sexuality, in which men dominate women, are denied satisfaction of these human desires.[4] Denied recog-

nition in the sexual interaction itself, they look to gain this recognition in wider social recognition of their "conquest."

To the pornographic mind, then, women become trophies awarded to the victor. For women to serve this purpose of achieving male social validation, a woman "conquered" by one must be a woman deemed desirable by others. Hence pornography both produces and reproduces uniform standards of female beauty. Male desires and tastes must be channeled into a single mode, with allowance for minor variations which obscure the fundamentally monolithic nature of the mold. Men's own subjectivity becomes masked to them, as historically and culturally specific and varying standards of beauty are made to appear natural and given. The ease with which men reach quick agreement on what makes a woman "attractive," evidenced in such things as the "1–10" rating scale or male banter and the reports of a computer program's success in predicting which of the contestants would be crowned "Miss America," demonstrates how deeply such standards have been internalized, and consequently the extent to which men are dominated by desires not authentically their own.

Lest anyone think that the analysis above is simply a philosopher's ruminations, too far removed from the actual experiences of most men, let me just offer one recent instantiation, from among many known to me, and even more, I am sure, I do not know. The following is from the *New York Times Magazine*'s "About Men" weekly column. In an article titled "Couch Dancing," the author describes his reactions to being taken to a place, a sort of cocktail bar, where women "clad only in the skimpiest of bikini underpants" would "dance" for a small group of men for a few minutes for about 25 or 30 dollars, men who "sat immobile, drinks in hand, glassy-eyed, tapping their feet to the disco music that throbbed through the room."

Men are supposed to like this kind of thing, and there is a quite natural part of each of us that does. But there is another part or us—of me, at least—that is not grateful for the traditional male sexual programming, not proud of the results. By a certain age, most modern men have been so surfeited with images of unattainably beautiful women in preposterous contexts that we risk losing the capacity to respond to the ordinarily beautiful women we love in our bedrooms. There have been too many times when I have guiltily resorted to impersonal fantasy because the genuine love I felt for a woman wasn't enough to convert feeling into performance. And in those sorry, secret moments, I have resented deeply my lifelong indoctrination into the esthetic of the centerfold.[5]

3. ALIENATION AND CRISIS

I believe that all of the above can be translated without great difficulty into a conceptual framework paralleling Marx's analysis of the alienation experienced by capitalists. The essential points are captured in two sentences from Marx's manuscripts:

1. *All* the physical and intellectual senses have been replaced by the simple alienation of *all* these senses; the sense of *having*.[6]
2. The wealthy man is at the same time one who *needs* a complex of human manifestations of life, and whose own self-realization exists as an inner necessity, a need.[7]

Both sentences speak to a loss of human interaction and self-realization. The first articulates how desires for conquest and control prevent input from the world. The second presents an alternative conception wherein wealth is measured by abilities for self-expression, rather than possession. Here Marx expresses his conceptualization of the state of alienation as a loss of sensuous fulfillment, poorly replaced by a pride of possession, and a lack of self-consciousness and hence actualization of one's own real desires and abilities. One could recast

the preceding analysis of pornographic male sexuality through these categories. In Marx's own analysis, these are more properly conceived of as the results of alienation, rather than the process of alienation itself. This process is at its basis a process of inversion, a reversal of the subject–object relationship, in which one's active powers become estranged from one, and return to dominate one as an external force. It is this aspect which I believe is most useful in understanding the alienation of male sexuality of which pornography is part and parcel. How is it that men's power turns against them, so that pornography, in and by which men dominate women, comes to dominate men themselves?

To answer this question I shall find it useful to have recourse to two other concepts central to Marxism, the concept of "crisis" in the system and the concept of "imperialism."[8] Marx's conception of the economic crisis of capitalism is often misunderstood as a prophecy of a cataclysmic doomsday scenario for the death of capitalism. Under this interpretation, some look for a single event, perhaps like a stock market crash, to precipitate capitalism's demise. But such events are for Marx at most triggering events, particular crises, which can shake the system, if at all, only because of the far more important underlying structural general crisis of capitalism. This general crisis is increasingly capitalism's ordinary state, not an extraordinary occurrence. It is manifest in the ongoing fiscal crisis of the state as well as recurring crises of legitimacy, and results from basic contradictory tensions within capitalism. One way of expressing these tensions is to see them as a conflict between the classic laissez-faire capitalist market mode, wherein capitalists are free to run their own affairs as individuals, and the increasing inability of the capitalist class to run an increasingly complex system without centralized management. The result of this tension is that the state increasingly becomes a managerial committee for the capitalist class, and is increasingly called upon to perform functions previously left to individuals. As entrepreneurial and laissez-faire capitalism give way to corporate capitalism and the welfare state, the power of capitalism becomes increasingly depersonalized, increasingly reft from the hands of individual capitalists and collectivized, so that capitalists themselves come more and more under the domination of impersonal market forces no longer under their direct control.

To move now to the relevance of the above, there is currently a good deal of talk about a perceived crisis of masculinity, in which men are said to be confused by contradictory imperatives given them in the wake of the women's movement. Though the male ego feels uniquely beleaguered today, in fact such talk regularly surfaces in our culture—the 1890's in the United States, for example, was another period in which the air was full of a "crisis of masculinity" caused by the rise of the "New Woman" and other factors.[9] Now, I wish to put forward the hypothesis that these particular "crises" of masculinity are but surface manifestations of a much deeper and broader phenomenon which I call the "general crisis of patriarchy," paralleling Marx's general crisis of capitalism. Taking a very broad view, this crisis results from the increasing depersonalization of patriarchal power which occurs with the development of patriarchy from its precapitalist phase, where power really was often directly exercised by individual patriarchs, to its late capitalist phase where men collectively exercise power over women, but are themselves as individuals increasingly under the domination of those same patriarchal powers.[10] I would stress that the sense of there being a "crisis" of masculinity arises not from the decrease or increase in patriarchal power as such. Patriarchal imperatives for men to retain power over women remain in force throughout. But there is a shift in the mode of that power's exercise, and the sense of crisis results

from the simultaneous promulgation throughout society of two conflicting modes of patriarchal power, the earlier more personal form and the later more institutional form. The crisis results from the incompatibility of the two conflicting ideals of masculinity embraced by the different forms of patriarchy, the increasing conflicts between behavioral and attitudinal norms in the political/economic and the personal/familial spheres.

4. FROM PATRIARCHY TO FRATRIARCHY

To engage for a moment in even broader speculation than that which I have so far permitted myself, I believe that much of the culture, law, and philosophy of the nineteenth century in particular can be reinterpreted as marking a decisive turn in this transition. I believe the passing of personal patriarchal power and its transformation into institutional patriarchal power in this period of the interrelated consolidation of corporate capitalism is evidenced in such phenomena as the rise of what one scholar has termed "judicial patriarchy," the new social regulation of masculinity through the courts and social welfare agencies, which through new support laws, poor laws, desertion laws and other changes transformed what were previously personal obligations into legal duties, as well as in the "Death of God" phenomenon and its aftermath.[11] That is to say, I believe the loss of the personal exercise of patriarchal power and its diffusion through the institutions of society is strongly implicated in the death of God the Father and the secularization of culture in the nineteenth century, as well as the modern and postmodern problem of grounding authority and values.

I would like to tentatively and preliminarily propose a new concept to reflect this shift in the nature of patriarchy caused by the deindividualization and collectivization of male power. Rather than speak simply of advanced capitalist patriarchy, the rule of the *fathers*, I suggest we speak of fratriarchy, the rule of the *brothers*. For the moment, I propose this concept more as a metaphor than as a sharply defined analytical tool, much as the concept of patriarchy was used when first popularized. I believe this concept better captures what I would argue is one of the key issues in conceptualizing contemporary masculinities, the disjunction between the facts of public male power and the feelings of individual male powerlessness. As opposed to the patriarch, who embodied many levels and kinds of authority in his single person, the brothers stand in uneasy relationships with each other, engaged in sibling rivalry while trying to keep the power of the family of man as a whole intact. I note that one of the consequences of the shift from patriarchy to fratriarchy is that some people become nostalgic for the authority of the benevolent patriarch, who if he was doing his job right at least prevented one of the great dangers of fratriarchy, fratricide, the brothers' killing each other. Furthermore, fratriarchy is an intragenerational concept, whereas patriarchy is intergenerational. Patriarchy, as a father-to-son transmission of authority, more directly inculcates traditional historically grounded authority, whereas the dimension of temporal continuity is rendered more problematic in fratriarchy's brother-to-brother relationships. I believe this helps capture the problematic nature of modern historical consciousness as it emerged from the nineteenth century, what I would argue is the most significant single philosophical theme of that century. If taken in Freudian directions, the concept of fratriarchy also speaks to the brothers' collusion to repress awareness of the violence which lies at the foundations or society.

To return to the present discussion, the debate over whether pornography reflects men's power or powerlessness, as taken up recently by Alan Soble in his book *Pornography: Marxism, Feminism, and the Future of Sexuality*, can be resolved if one makes a distinction such as I have proposed between personal and institutional male power. Soble cites men's use of pornographic fantasy as compensation for their powerlessness in the real world to argue that "pornography is therefore not so much an expression of male power as it is an expression of their lack of power."[12] In contrast, I would argue that by differentiating levels of power one should more accurately say that pornography is both an expression of men's public power and an expression of their lack of personal power. The argument of this paper is that pornography's image of male sexuality works to the detriment of men personally even as its image of female sexuality enhances the powers of patriarchy. It expresses the power of alienated sexuality, or, as one could equally well say, the alienated power of sexuality.

With this understanding, one can reconcile the two dominant but otherwise irreconcilable images of the straight male consumer of pornography: on the one hand the powerful rapist, using pornography to consummate his sexual violence, and on the other hand the shy recluse, using it to consummate his masturbatory fantasies. Both images have their degree of validity, and I believe it is a distinctive virtue of the analysis presented here that one can understand not only the merits of each depiction, but their interconnection.

5. EMBODIMENT AND EROTICA

In the more reductionist and determinist strains of Marxism, pornography as ideology would be relegated to the superstructure of capitalism. I would like to suggest another conceptualization: that pornography is not part of patriarchal capitalism's superstructure, but part of its infrastructure. Its commodification of the body and interpersonal relationships paves the way for the ever more penetrating ingression of capitalist market relations into the deepest reaches of the individual's psychological makeup. The feminist slogan that "The Personal is Political" emerges at a particular historical moment, and should be understood not simply as an imperative declaration that what has previously been seen solely as personal should now be viewed politically, but also as a response to the real increasing politicization of personal life.

This aspect can be illuminated through the Marxist concept of imperialism. The classical Marxist analysis of imperialism argues that it is primarily motivated by two factors: exploitation of natural resources and extension of the market. In this vein, pornography should be understood as imperialism of the body. The greater public proliferation of pornography, from the "soft-core" pornography of much commercial advertising to the greater availability of "hard-core" pornography, proclaims the greater colonization of the body by the market.[13] The increasing use of the male body as a sex symbol in contemporary culture is evidence of advanced capitalism's increasing use of new styles of masculinity to promote images of men as consumers as well as producers.[14] Today's debates over the "real" meaning of masculinity can be understood in large part as a struggle between those espousing the "new man" style of masculinity more suited to advanced corporate, consumerist patriarchal capitalism and those who wish to return to an idealized version of "traditional" masculinity suited to a more production-oriented, entrepreneurial patriarchal capitalism.[15]

In a more theoretical context, one can see that part of the reason the pornography debate has been so divisive, placing on different sides of the question people who usually find themselves allies, is that discussions between civil libertarians and feminists have often been at cross purposes. Here one can begin to relate political theory not to political practice, but to metaphysical theory. The classical civil liberties perspective on the issue remains deeply embedded in a male theoretical discourse on the meaning of sexuality. The connection between the domination of nature and the domination of women has been argued from many Marxist and feminist points of view.[16] The pivot of this connection is the masculine overlay of the mind-body dualism onto the male-female dichotomy. Within this framework, morality par excellence consists in the masculinized mind restraining the feminized body, with sexual desires seen as the crucial test for these powers of restraint. From this point of view, the question of the morality of pornography is primarily the quantitative question of how much sexual display is allowed, with full civil libertarians opting to uphold the extreme end of this continuum, arguing that no sexual expression should be repressed. But the crucial question, for at least the very important strain of feminist theory which rejects these dualisms which frame the debate for the malestream mainstream, is not *how much* sexuality is displayed but rather *how* sexuality is displayed. These theories speak not of mind-body dualism, but of mind/body wholism, where the body is seen not as the limitation or barrier for the expression of the free moral self, but rather as the most immediate and intimate vehicle for the expression of that self. The question of sexual morality here is not that of restraining or releasing sexual desires as they are forced on the spiritual self by the temptations of the body, but that of constructing spirited and liberating sexual relationships with and through one's own and others' bodies. Here sexual freedom is not the classical liberal freedom *from* external restraint, but the more radical freedom *to* construct authentically expressive sexualities.

I have argued throughout this paper that pornography is a vehicle for the imposition of socially constructed sexuality, not a means for the expression of autonomously self-determined sexuality. (I would add that in contrasting imposed and authentic sexualities I am not endorsing a sexual essentialism, but simply carving out a space for more personal freedom.) Pornography is inherently about commercialized sex, about the eroticization of power and the power of eroticization. One can look to the term's etymology for confirmation of this point. It comes from the classical Greek "*pornographos,* meaning 'writing (sketching) of harlots,'" sometimes women captured in war.[17] Any distinction between pornography and erotica remains problematic, and cannot be drawn with absolute precision. Yet I believe some such distinction can and must be made. I would place the two terms not in absolute opposition, but at two ends of a continuum, with gray areas of necessity remaining between them. The gradations along the continuum are marked not by the explicitness of the portrayal of sexuality or the body, nor by the assertiveness vs. passivity of persons, nor by any categorization of sexual acts or activities, but by the extent to which autonomous personhood is attributed to the person or persons portrayed. Erotica portrays sexual subjects, manifesting their personhood in and through their bodies. Pornography depicts sex objects, persons reduced to their bodies. While the erotic nude presents the more pristine sexual body before the social persona is adopted through donning one's clothing, the pornographic nude portrays a body whose clothing has been more or less forcibly removed, where the absence of that clothing remains the most forceful presence in the image. Society's objectification remains present, indeed emphasized, in pornography, in a way in which it does not in erotica. Erotica, as sexual art, expresses a self, whereas pornography, as sexual commodity, markets one. The latter "works" because the operation it performs on women's bodies resonates with the "pornographizing" the male gaze does to women in other areas of society.[18] These distinctions remain problematic, to say the least, in their application, and disagreement in particular cases will no doubt remain. Much more work needs to be done before one would with any reasonable confi-

dence distinguish authentic from imposed, personal from commercial, sexuality. Yet I believe this is the crucial question, and I believe these concepts correctly indicate the proper categories of analysis. Assuming a full definition of freedom as including autonomy and self-determination, pornography is therefore incompatible with real freedom.

6. CONCLUSIONS

It has often been noted that while socialist feminism is currently a major component of the array of feminisms one finds in academic feminism and women's studies, it is far less influential on the playing fields of practical politics.[19] While an analysis of male sexuality may seem an unlikely source to further socialist feminism's practical political agenda, I hope this paper's demonstration of the interconnections between intimate personal experiences and large-scale historical and social structures, especially in what may have initially seemed unlikely places, may serve as a useful methodological model for other investigations.

I would like to conclude with some remarks on the practical import of this analysis. First of all, if the analysis of the relationship between pornography and consumerism and the argument about pornography leading to violence are correct, then a different conceptualization of the debate over the ethics of the feminist anti-pornography movement emerges. If one accepts, as I do, the idea that this movement is not against sex, but against sexual abuse, then the campaign against pornography is essentially not a call for censorship but a consumer campaign for product safety. The proper context for the debate over its practices is then not issues of free speech or civil liberties, but issues of business ethics. Or rather, this is the conclusion I reach remaining focused on pornography and male sexuality. But we should remember the broader context I alluded to at the beginning of this paper, the question of pornography's effects on women. In that context, women are not the consumers of pornography, but the consumed. Rather than invoking the consumer movement, perhaps we should then look to environmental protection as a model.[20] Following this line of reasoning, one could in principle then perhaps develop under the tort law of product liability an argument to accomplish much of the regulation of sexually explicit material some are now trying to achieve through legislative means, perhaps developing a new definition of "safe" sexual material.

Finally, for most of us most of our daily practice as academics consists of teaching rather than writing or reading in our fields. If one accepts the analysis I have presented, a central if not primary concern for us should therefore be how to integrate this analysis into our classrooms. I close by suggesting that we use this analysis and others like it from the emerging field of men's studies to demonstrate to the men in our classes the direct relevance of feminist analysis to their own lives, at the most intimate and personal levels, and that we look for ways to demonstrate to men that feminism can be personally empowering and liberating for them without glossing over, and in fact emphasizing, the corresponding truth that this will also require the surrender of male privilege.[21]

NOTES

1. Bernie Zilbergeld, *Male Sexuality: A Guide to Sexual Fulfillment* (Boston: Little, Brown and Company, 1978).
2. Michael Betzold, "How Pornography Shackles Men and Oppresses Women," in *For Men Against Sexism: A Book of Readings,* ed. Jon Snodgrass (Albion, CA: Times Change Press, 1977), p. 46.
3. I am grateful to Lenore Langsdorf and Paula Rothenberg for independently suggesting to me how this point would fit into my analysis.
4. See Jessica Benjamin, "The Bonds of Love: Rational Violence and Erotic Domination," *Feminist Studies* 6 (1980): 144–74.
5. Keith McWalter, "Couch Dancing," *New York Times Magazine,* December 6, 1987, p. 138.
6. Karl Marx, "Economic and Philosophic Manuscripts: Third Manuscript," in *Early Writings,* ed. and trans. T. B. Bottomore (New York: McGraw-Hill, 1964), pp. 159–60.
7. Marx., pp. 164–65.
8. An earlier version of portions of the following argument appears in my article "Eros Thanatized: Pornography and Male Sexuality" with a "1989 Postscript," forthcoming in Michael Kimmel, ed., *Men Confronting Pornography,* (New York: Crown, 1989). The article originally appeared (without the postscript) in *Humanities in Society* 7 (1984) pp. 47–63.
9. See the essays by myself and Michael Kimmel in Brod, *The Making of Masculinities.*
10. Compare Carol Brown on the shift from private to public patriarchy: "Mothers, Fathers, and Children: From Private to Public Patriarchy" in Lydia Sargent, ed., *Women and Revolution* (Boston: South End Press, 1981).
11. According to Martha May in her paper "'An Obligation on Every Man': Masculine Breadwinning and the Law in Nineteenth Century New York," presented at the American Historical Association, Chicago, Illinois, 1987, from which I learned of these changes, the term "judicial patriarchy" is taken from historian Michael Grossberg *Governing the Hearth: Law and the Family in Nineteenth Century America* (Chapel Hill: University of North Carolina Press, 1985) and "Crossing Boundaries: Nineteenth Century Domestic Relations Law and the Merger of Family and Legal History," *American Bar Foundation Research Journal* (1985): 799–847.
12. Alan Soble, *Pornography: Marxism, Feminism, and the Future of Sexuality* (New Haven: Yale University Press, 1986), p. 82. I agree with much of Soble's analysis of male sexuality in capitalism, and note the similarities between much of what he says about "dismemberment" and consumerism and my analysis here.
13. See John D'Emilio and Estelle B. Freedman, *Intimate Matters: A History of Sexuality in America*

14. See Barbara Ehrenreich, *The Hearts of Men: American Dreams and the Flight from Commitment* (New York: Anchor-Doubleday, 1983); and Wolfgang Fritz Haug, *Critique of Commodity Aesthetics: Appearance, Sexuality, and Advertising in Capitalist Society,* trans. Robert Bock (Minneapolis: University of Minnesota Press, 1986).

15. See my "Work Clothes and Leisure Suits: The Class Basis and Bias of the Men's Movement," originally in *Changing Men* 11 (1983) 10–12 and 38–40, reprint forthcoming in *Men's Lives: Readings in the Sociology of Men and Masculinity,* ed. Michael Kimmel and Michael Messner (New York: Macmillan, 1989).

16. This features prominently in the work of the Frankfurt school as well as contemporary ecofeminist theorists.

17. Rosemarie Tong, "Feminism, Pornography and Censorship," *Social Theory and Practice* 8 (1982): 1–17.

18. I learned to use "pornographize" as a verb in this way from Timothy Beneke's "Introduction" to his *Men on Rape* (New York: St. Martin's Press, 1982).

19. See the series of ten articles on "Socialist-Feminism Today" in *Socialist Review* 73–79 (1984–1985).

20. I am indebted to John Stoltenberg for this point.

21. I attempt to articulate this perspective principally in the following: *The Making of Masculinities,* Introduction and "The Case for Men's Studies"; *A Mensch Among Men: Explorations in Jewish Masculinity* (Freedom, CA: The Crossing Press, 1988), especially the Introduction; and "Why Is This 'Men's Studies' Different from All Other Men's Studies?," *Journal of the National Association for Women Deans, Administrators, and Counselors* 49 (1986): pp. 44–49. See also generally the small men's movement magazines *Changing Men: Issues in Gender, Sex and Politics* (306 North Brooks St., Madison, WI 53715), *brother: The Newsletter of the National Organization for Changing Men* (1402 Greenfield Ave., #1, Los Angeles, CA 90025), and *Men's Studies Review* (Box 32, Harriman, TN 37748).

READING 49

Towards a Feminist Erotica

Kathy Myers

Many feminist critiques of the representation of women hinge on the assumption that it is the act of representation or objectification itself which degrades women, reducing them to the status of objects to be "visually" or "literally" consumed.

I want to argue that this assumption can lead feminism into deep water. On the one hand, it works to deny women the right to represent their own sexuality and on the other it side-steps the whole issue of female sexual pleasure. I want to suggest that questions of representation and of pleasure cannot be separated, and that a feminist erotica could examine the nature of this relationship . . .

. . . This article holds that images themselves cannot be characterized as either pornographic or erotic. The pornographic/erotic distinction can only be applied by looking at how the image is contextualized through its mode of address and the conditions of its production and consumption. . . .

An analysis of pornography which focuses purely on its content is in danger of falling into a kind of "reductive essentialism," e.g., the notion that exploitation resides in the representation of female sexuality *per Se,* rather than in

Source: Gender, Race, and Class in Media, ed. Gail Dines and Jean M. Humes. Copyright © 1995. Sage Publications.

its contextualization: the conditions of its production and consumption; the ways in which meanings are created, etc. Unless we can shift the debate on representation away from the image, there is very little "positive" work which can be done.

Whilst it is true that we designate certain images as pornographic, pornography also refers to a particular mode of productive relations which market and sell sexuality: e.g., the choice of model/subject matter, the photographer-model relationship and the conditions under which they work, the choice of medium and distribution, all affect our reception and interpretation of what constitutes pornography. This economy of pornography works to structure not only to whom the material is made available, but also the kinds of pleasures and responses which are elicited.

. . . We have to understand the ways in which images work to construct our own experience of our sexuality. Rather than running away from the powers of the imagination and fantasy, we have to reappraise the role of representations in structuring our needs and desires as a step towards constructing new meanings for the experience and representation of our sexuality.

I want to illustrate this point with one image taken from a softcore porn magazine and one from a woman's journal. By comparing them, I want to suggest that woman's sexuality is deployed in a variety of ways. This deployment is dependent upon the context in which the image appears, its mode of production as well as consumption.

On first impression, the two images seem remarkably similar: the model's pose and attitude, the seaside setting, etc. The main difference appears to be that the Slix model [in the woman's journal] sports a bikini whilst the porn model is naked. It could be argued that women's exploitation is only a matter of degree along a scantily clad continuum. However, the surface similarities belie fundamental differences in the representation of female sexuality and in the kinds of pleasures offered to audiences.

Many of these differences are hidden from the viewer. For example, the production of pornography differs in most respects from the production of a fashion advert. This affects their economic foundation, the choice of studio, photographer, model, etc. They are specialist discourses which retain their autonomy. For example, the "photographic life" of models is extremely limited. Few nude models ever make the transition to become fashion models, partly because of the stigma which certain forms of nude modeling carry, and partly due to the fact that different selection criteria operate. Fashion models have become increasingly slender, younger and taller. Most nude models are considered too "curvy" for fashion work: different "aesthetics" operate. In turn this visual aesthetic cannot be divorced from the respective audiences for fashion and pornographic imagery. To put it simply, there is an overall tendency to market "fleshier" women to men and thinner, sometimes sexually androgynous, images of women to female audiences. This micro-politics of body style speaks of the aesthetic and pleasurable segregation of sexuality across a range of visual discourses, which cannot be simply explained away in terms of "taste" nor patriarchal oppression but require further examination.

Selling female sexuality to a woman is not the same as selling it to a man. The anticipated gender of the audience is crucial in structuring the image. For example, [consider] the angle of the women's heads in the two images. The pornographic model's face is angled towards the viewer. Her mouth is open, a classic signifier of sexual receptiveness and anticipation. In the small inset photo the same model faces and acknowledges the camera. Behind the camera, we, the audience, are located.

By comparison the Slix model, sweeping back her hair, looks across the scope of the camera. She does not face us, her mouth is closed. Not so much a sulky pout as an expression of relaxed langour. Like the pornographic image, she is aware of being on display. But the tenor of her demeanour is proud and inaccessible. She sweeps back her hair from the heat of the sun, not from passion.

By comparison, her legs are together. The Slix model's mouth and legs offer no point of entrance. The body of the Slix model is a matt sandy tone, she is relaxed. The skin of the nude model is oiled to give the effect of a sheen of perspiration which can signify sexual activity and tension.

The girls in the background of the Slix image look at each other not at the camera. Self-absorbed, they reiterate the confident, self-engrossed narcissism of the foregrounded model. She takes pleasure in her sunbathing, not in the presence of her audience. Only the small inset model in the beach jacket to the right of the image pays the camera a cursory glance.

What differentiates the pornographic image from the fashion shot is the mode of address. The Slix mode of address is characterized by the tension which it establishes between the model's desirability in conventional terms, and her inaccessibility. The advert works to secure a distancing effect between image and audience.

By comparison, the nude model's sexuality is posed as invitational. The pleasure of looking at her merges with the pleasure of being with her. Her sexuality stretches out to embrace the viewer. The nude model "asks" the audience to possess her. It is a form of sexual consumption which implicitly genders the audience as male. The model's apparent expression of pleasure is not for herself. She is not autonomous, her pleasure is always for the consumption of another, and herein lies one of the fundamental alienations of pornographic imagery.

By comparison, the Slix advert positions the audience as spectator, to keep a safe distance and to observe, not to touch. Sexual inaccessibility is conveyed through the structure of the image. For example, the self-absorbed pose of the model, the cropping, editing and retouching of the photograph, work together to reinforce the displayedness of the model, and in doing so, distance the audience.

The impact of the Slix advert is based on the strength of the photograph. Its scale and use of full colour works to dominate the page. The seaside location, the pattern on the bikini, the sense of displayed style are all anchored in the copy line "New Waves." These associations are cemented by reference to the brand name of Slix which is in bold type. Image and copy line work together. "New Waves" links the image to the body of the text.

Whilst the image celebrates the tension between desirability and inaccessibility, the body of the text suggests sexual provocation. Unlike the provocative pose of the pornographic image, the Slix advert suggests sexual power as opposed to sexual availability and perhaps vulnerability. The wearer in the Slix bikini is promised power over others, the power of sexual display: "Slip into Slix and make a few ripples."

The target audience for this advert is women. The advert is designed to appeal to women. One of the pleasures which the advertising system offers women is the promise of a kind of power and self-determination. Images of women marketed to women rarely present female sexuality purely in terms of vulnerability, accessibility or availability. But the power which the advertising of beauty and personal products offers women is always of a limited kind, located in terms of sexual display, appearance and attractiveness. What the advert may offer for consumption is an ideal version of self. It also plays on women's pleasure in looking at attractive women. This kind of visual pleasure is inscribed in the image.

We may find many images of women unacceptable, glamorized, exploitative or whatever;

but we cannot simply interpret women's pleasure in reading them as evidence for the extent to which the female consciousness has been colonized by patriarchy. We have to account for women's pleasure in looking at images of women.

The advertising image and the pornographic image offer different kinds of pleasure to their respective audiences. If audiences did not find them in some way pleasurable they wouldn't work; magazines and products wouldn't sell. It is their pleasurable associations which perpetuate them. But pleasure as a concept cannot be tackled in isolation, we need to understand how pleasure is produced through the structuring of power and sexuality.

TOWARDS A FEMINIST EROTICA

One of the central objections put forward by feminists in their critique of pornography and other modes of representation is that it "objectifies" women. Objectification has become a much abused term. There is a sense in which the process of sight and perception necessarily entail objectification in order to conceptualize and give meaning to the object of our gaze. Within feminism, objectification has a quite specific meaning: through the process of representation, women are reduced to the status of objects. This is partly derived from a common-sense use of the Marxist idea of commodity fetishism; images of women have become commodities from which women are alienated. Their status as commodity works to deny their individuality and humanity. The second sense of objectification which has informed its current usage is derived from Freud's concept of sexual fetishism: the idea that objects or parts of the anatomy are used as symbols for and replacements of the socially valued phallus. Hence, the argument goes, men have difficulty in coping with women's sexuality because of its castrating potential, and because of its lack of a phallus. In order to cope with

this anxiety, men fetishise aspects of female sexuality—for example, the legs or breasts—as symbols of acceptable sexual power.

The use of the term "objectification" is coupled with a tendency to interpret all forms of sexual symbolization as evidence of sexual fetishisation. In the analysis of female imagery two processes of symbolization are brought under closer scrutiny: that of sexual fragmentation and sexual substitution. Frequently these processes of metonym (where the part stands for the whole) and metaphor (where one object or aspect of the anatomy stands for another) operate together. For example, the depiction of female sexuality through the representation of a stiletto-shod foot isolates and fragments the sexual by focusing on a part of the anatomy and fetishises the foot by overvaluing it as a phallic symbol. Psychoanalytic interpretations of this kind of imagery have suggested that the stiletto as phallic symbol serves to "give" the woman her missing phallus, thus circumnavigating the castration threat which she poses for male sexuality and rendering her safe.

Whilst this kind of analysis may provide an adequate interpretation of the dominant associations of stilettos in our culture, can we say that all forms of sexualized imagery can be interpreted in terms of phallic substitution? There exists a repertoire of conventionalized symbols which have become imbued with fetishistic associations of which the stiletto is only one example; but symbolization is not a closed system of limited or fixed meaning. Symbolism is polysemic (has no one, fixed meaning); there always exists the possibility of powerful symbolism which works to activate forms of sexual expression which are not recognized by phallocentric interpretation.

Because fetishisation usually employs a fragmented image, there is a danger of assuming that all fragmentary images are necessarily fetishistic. The process of sexual fetishisation (specific phallic associations) is always complicated by that of commodity fetishisation, whereby the image of a woman's legs, for example, becomes isolated and estranged. They become a commodity, an object of display to be visually consumed by an audience.

What is at issue is not so much the perceptual processes of objectification and fragmentation which are a necessary part of rendering a complex world meaningful but rather the specific forms of objectification entailed in commodity and sexual fetishism. It therefore seems important to create a working distinction between the process of fragmentation, which implies a breaking up or disabling of the physical form, and what could be termed "a pleasure in the part"—the pleasure derived from looking at a picture which depicts the curve of an arm or the sweep of the neckline. Such images could be interpreted not as a butchering of the female form but as a celebration of its constituent elements, giving a sense of the scope and complexity of sensual pleasure which breaks with specific genital sexual associations and with the necessity of overdetermining phallic substitution in the representation of the female form.

It seems that we have to clarify whether it is the process of necessary objectification entailed in perception which we object to (used, for example, whenever we look at the world, at art, at a book, etc.) or the meaning which it carries for women under specific patriarchal formations. These are two separate issues which tend to be collapsed into each other when feminists talk about the representation of women in art, photography, etc. To refuse to differentiate between the two modes of objectification is to endorse a kind of perceptual essentialism—that objectification is inherently exploitative and demeaning.

To see objectification in essentialist terms is to deny the possibility of any alternative practice within the representation of women. Feminists would be denied the possibility of visual communication and new forms of perception. . . .

It is in terms of the pleasure derived from representational systems that we need to reintroduce a notion of the erotic. Within sexual politics we have to find a way of accounting for women's sexual attraction to each other; the visual pleasure of leafing through a glossy women's magazine; the appeal of the heroine star systems, etc. Such pleasure cannot be simply dismissed as more evidence of patriarchal oppression, that women are continually gulled into a search for the ideal type simply to appeal to "their man." We cannot dismiss sexual attraction as further evidence of patriarchal mystification.

. . . Ultimately the distinction between pornography and other modes of sexual representation cannot rest on the characteristics of the image. The differences between pornographic vaginal imagery and medical vaginal imagery are learned through contextualization: they are not innate.

In the reappraisal of our sexuality, there may appear to be an overlap between the kind of images designated as pornographic as opposed to erotic. This means that the exploration of female sexual pleasure through imagery will remain politically controversial.

Some suggestions for the kind of questions which need to be asked when producing or appraising potentially progressive images of women:

- How is the image produced?
- Whose fantasy is being recorded[7]
- What power relationship exists in the photographer-model relationship?
- How are models selected; what is their relationship to the overall production process?

How will the image be distributed and where will it be circulated?

- The politics of distribution cannot be separated from those of production, nor of consumption. Where an image is distributed will affect who will see it, in what context, etc. It is obviously important to sort out whether an image is for private or public consumption, whether it will be seen in a gallery or a magazine, etc. It needs to be asked whether an image's validity or "usefulness" depends on how an audience will use or interpret an image. For example, does the risk of appropriation by men invalidate producing erotic imagery for women? This risk could be countered by showing these images in, for example, *Camerawork*.

Visual conventions of the image.

- How do we classify an image as erotic? What conventions and genres of representation does an image trade on?
- To what extent does an oppositional system need to reuse and question familiar styles in order to go forward and create new meanings?

- What are the signifiers of sexuality?
- How do we recognize the gender of the subject?
- In fact how important is the thwarting of easy gender assignment for erotic pleasure?

The audience and pleasure.

- What kind of pleasures does an image offer its audience?
- How is the sexuality and subject position of the audience constructed—are they sexed as male or female?
- What kind of emotional responses does the image demand? Does it demand any kind of audience interaction to interpret the meaning of the image? To what extent does the image challenge assumptions already held?

PART SEVEN

SEXUAL ABUSE AND RAPE

What would it be like if sexuality was not associated with power imbalances that lead to child sexual abuse, rape, and assault? It is difficult to imagine, because it is so far outside our experience. Children get warnings early on in life about "watching out" for dangerous people who might touch them in wrong ways. Then many children, and women, as well as men in certain situations, find those who would misuse them are already right there, in close relationship or within the walls of their home. The world too quickly becomes unsafe. Sexual assault, especially "date rape," takes place within a societal framework that can condone the behavior. The disempowerment of those affected is both a precursor and an outcome. It relies on adult/child and gendered power relations that encourage and excuse the behaviors.

In a culture in which status equality and mutuality were the norms, a man would not be interested in "taking" a woman who did not invite him in. There would be no "thrill of conquest" if use of another for pleasure were outside his frame of reference, just as the idea of using the body of a young child for one's own gratification would be impossible if children were not in a powerless position in society. What if adults (men or women) could not perceive of being sexual with anyone except those with whom they shared equal power?

491

Some people think that sexual violence is just part of the human condition. Those who see all sexually related behavior as being associated with biological drives, who hold an essentialist perspective, might argue that we should expect sexual violence. They might even toss up their hands and say, "That's just the way things are!" Yet sexual violence is not a given, based on what we know about the matrifocal clans of the Paleolithic era and about cultures that do not have rape, or have much lower rates. The possibility of rape appears to be rooted not so much in our biological drive as the social context of our lives. Humans are biologically capable of sexual violence, but we are also highly capable of reducing the incidence of violence. Anthropologists find there is a higher likelihood of rape and sexual assault in cultures in which males dominate (Sanday, 1981). Rape has less to do with sex than it has to do with the presumption of and desire for power over another person.

At the same time, for some men who rape, rape can be what sex looks like. Since childhood, they have heard that the male sex drive is a desperate one that men cannot control and for which women (the "seductress" in cultural history) are ultimately responsible. Males receive less touch, less physical and emotional intimacy from other males and adults in general, as they grow up. Then the culture gives males a sense of privilege, a sense that they have the right to control situations (and relationships), to compete, to "win." This can contribute to the greater likelihood of males becoming rapists, of forcing sex on another person in order to satisfy what may seem like a desperate need to "have" sex and exert power.

Child abusers, like rapists, tend to go after people they perceive to be vulnerable or over whom they have power. In addition, children and youth are susceptible to sexual abuse for economic and political reasons, as Julia O'Connell Davidson discusses in her paper on commercial sexual exploitation of children in the previous section of this book. In some cases, they are runaways or cast-offs. They may have been sold into prostitution by families desperate for money or deceived about what "labor" will be expected.

Children are generally at lower risk of sexual abuse, and more likely to report it, when they are well informed about sexuality and feel they can talk with adults and be listened to on topics that are important to them. Yet this occurs all too seldom. Many children grow up having confusing, scary experiences for which they have no words and no one safe to turn to for help. They are either being abused by a family member—a father, step-father, mother's partner, brother, or uncle—and think it's just the way things are, or they were molested by a stranger and warned that very dire things will happen if they tell.

The two poems that begin this section, "Teacher" by Scott and "Last Chance" by Mary Reilly, bring the images and realities of the sexual use of children into sharp relief. While very different, they both reflect the feeling of the child trying to make sense of experiences that somehow are not supposed to be happening. Whether at age 12 or age 14, sex should be something we feel in charge of (not victimized by), which is not the case here. What feelings or responses do these poems bring to mind? If confusing and/or abusive experiences have been part of your childhood or youth, do you know where to turn to talk about them? It can be a good idea to call a counseling center or crisis hotline if you find yourself struggling emotionally as you read this section of the book.

In "The Alchemy of Healing: Transforming from Victim to Victor," Regina Rivers shares her personal story of healing from childhood sexual abuse. This narrative is about the process of opening, facing the pain as memories return, finding strength within, as well as support from a therapist, husband, and friends, so that the healing could proceed. Her poem that follows, "Lullaby," relates the questions and thoughts a caring adult might express as s/he talks with the child who has experienced abuse. What do they reveal of the dynamics of abuse? Is this Rivers as an adult, speaking to the child she once was? Why don't children tell?

As you read the poems and the narrative, reflect on how the sexual use of children interrupts so much—the safety that is "supposed" to go with childhood, as well as the gradual coming into sexual awareness on one's own terms, when one's sexual experience is not imposed by an adult. Think as well, about Pheterson's article from the last section of this book, on unchastity and defilement. Once used, the child, as he or she grows up and proceeds into adulthood, must struggle to let go of shame and fear, to begin to feel again, to heal, to reclaim one's own sexual path, and to take good care of oneself. Many people experienced sexual abuse as children. When someone tells you his or her experience, it can be helpful to say, "I'm sorry that ever happened to you. It wasn't your fault." Then listen, as they heal.

In "Men, Women, and Rape," Susan Brownmiller explores the legal history of rape in an article from her classic 1977 book, *Against Our Will: Men, Women, and Rape.* The author sees marriage as having evolved as both a protective arrangement for women and as a way for a male to assure access to a specific female body. The need for such a social structure assumes a fearful, warring state of affairs in which women were booty or bounty that did evolve in at least some parts of the world over the past 10,000 years. Although it is not part of Brownmiller's analysis, it is important to recall from earlier articles in this book on the history of sexuality that such conditions are not "natural." Peaceful, matrifocal cultures for all of prior human history showed no evidence of war, slavery, or rape, which is true as well of many indigenous cultures, as reported by anthropologists.

Brownmiller's history covers approximately the last 4,000 years, beginning with ancient Babylonian and Mosaic legal codes. The current view of rape as a crime against women is relatively new. For much of our patriarchal history, the taking of a girl's virginity was a crime against her father. Sexually assaulting nonvirgins was of little consequence, unless they were married, in which case it was a crime against her husband. This related, in either case, to women of propertied families. Women with no means lacked recourse, as it was not a matter of much legal concern to men. Brownmiller relates that the first reference to a broadened legal concept of criminal rape came in the 13th century, when it included, at least in principle, the rape of "matrons, nuns, widows, concubines and even prostitutes."

Rape and the threat of sexual violence serve to keep women (and marginalized/feminized men who are victimized by other men) in their place. In addition, the "rape culture" keeps men in theirs, as perpetrators—rapists, as well as those who sexually harass, intimidate, and make sexual assaults that stop short of rape. These actions do not represent all men. In fact, men who attempt to interrupt such actions are kept from interrupting the harassment, sexist comments, and language through intimidation, put-downs, and threats of violence, from those same males who harass and rape women.

Does our rape-oriented culture lead women to think they need a male "protector," to somehow reduce the risk of victimization by a male aggressor? Using the analysis of Betsy Crane and Jesse Crane-Seeber in an earlier part of this book, do we tolerate and even encourage male aggressive behaviors as the price we pay in order to assure we raise boys to fulfill their "protector/dominator" role? Is that what having men escort women back to their residence halls at night on college campuses is about? Do such programs to protect women just put some males into the role of protector, while the real issue of male socialization around sex goes unquestioned?

"The Day My Life Changed," relates a woman's story of the aftermath of a gang rape. Her feelings of needing to regain a sense of control and dignity kept her from telling others what happened or facing her feelings. After five years alone with her memories, she saw a therapist whose words, "It wasn't your fault," opened the way for healing. Her story reflects that sense of confusion and helplessness that many of us feel about sexual violence itself and that the survivor experiences in the most deep and profound way. This story does not relate the gang rape itself, but only what it left behind. What do you imagine was the aftermath of the rape for the men involved? Given the idea of masculinity as performance, is a gang rape a staged event? What is the motivation of the leaders? We know that some men "go along" despite feelings of uneasiness or even revulsion. Why?

In the early 1990s, women at Antioch College had had enough, according to Kristine Herman in "Demands from the Women of Antioch." Appalled by rapes on campus, but even more so by administrative handling of the rapes, a group of women determined that a policy and protocol must be established, and they put enormous effort into organizing action to bring that about. To create a protocol for addressing incidents of sexual assault, they first had to define what was and what was not an offense. The final "Antioch College Sexual Offense Policy" contains a verbal consent provision (the consent section of the policy accompanies the article). The Antioch policy asserts that all sexual contact and conduct must be consensual, with consent defined, in part, as obtaining verbal consent with each new level of physical and/or sexual contact. This policy was subsequently lampooned by the national media. As Herman notes, part of the attention given to the policy had to do with its redefinition of rape, and thus, of our conceptualization of sex.

The policy is not gender-specific, so it applies equally to males and females and to sexual behavior between same-sex and other-sex participants. What are the implications of such a policy? In what ways does this redefine how we conceptualize sex? Since it requires both partners to take responsibility for what they want sexually and for communicating that, what challenges might this pose for females who have been taught to "just say no" if they want to be perceived as "good girls"? Some Antioch students (including males) have said they like the policy because it reduces the awkwardness of assuming what your partner wants based on nonverbal cues that can be confusing. What do you think?

Luoluo Hong tells a complex gendered, racialized story of sexual assault in "Breaking the Silence, Making Laughter: Testimony of an Asian-American Sister." Hong describes undergoing a 15-month long experience of nonconsensual, coercive sex during which she felt herself annihilated as both a woman and an Asian-American. As a result, she says, she saw "both identities as weak, worthless, powerless, dirty, undesirable, and most important—somehow responsible for my own victimization." There are elements in the narrative of her shut-down, inert response to this man's behaviors that are reminiscent of the experience of victims of child sexual abuse. What is it about the way that we construct and conceptualize sex—for college-age women as well as for children—that contributes to such responses of denial, acceptance, and shame? To what degree are both children and females set up as powerless receivers of whatever happens to them?

The report "Male Rape Victims in Prison Get Little Empathy," reprinted from *Contemporary Sexuality*, makes it clear that rape of men in prison is common, ranging from estimates of inmates of 1 in 3 prisoners being forced into sex, to an estimate of 1 in 8 by administrators. Few prison administrations take rape seriously, according to this report, in terms of procedures for medical examination or counseling for men who are raped. Other reports indicate that guards may even set men up for rape as a punishment, by assigning them to share cells with known sexual predators. In what way is rape of men in prison a part of the "rape culture" discussed in other articles in this chapter?

In "Men on Rape: What They Have to Say about Sexual Violence," Timothy Beneke remarks that if violence against women is to end, we need a resolution in consciousness among men.

Beneke refers to powerful social constructions of sex—for example, sex as conquest, performance, triumph, and commodity—along with metaphors that treat women as animals, children, or objects. Given the ever-present nature of these messages, the author states, it is an act of courage and an act of love for males to acknowledge and reject the ways they have learned to regard women as less than human. In what ways have the messages Beneke identifies affected not only men but women as well? What does it take to imagine sex outside of the "caveman" pictures that Beneke references, so often used to maintain that "rape has always existed"—which it has not. To what extent are the metaphors Beneke cites still powerful, 20 years after he wrote? Have there been changes? Are there new metaphors for sex outside of rape?

REFERENCES

Sanday, P. R. (1981). The socio-cultural context of rape: A cross-cultural study. *Journal of Social Issues, 37*(4), 5–27.

Two Poems

TEACHER

Scott

At age twelve, I see you
standing next to me in
the school locker room,
giggling nervously, voice
soft in the dark. "Don't
tell anyone." Feel your
hand move down my body,
start stroking. Intake
of breath, then warm
shame on my stomach,
running down my thighs,
wondering if this is
right, knowing you
will be teaching me
algebra in twenty minutes.

Source: Speaking Our Truth: Voices of Courage and Healing for Male Survivors of Childhood Sexual Abuse, ed. Neal King. Copyright © 1995, Harper & Row Publishers.

LAST CHANCE

Mary Reilly

August pulls
Sticky sounds from tires
And slick, black, macadam.
Farm-trucks, Buzz's Super Bee, a Z28
Zip past Mack's appliance shop
Where a dark-faced Magnavox, Motorola,
and Zenith TV wait.
Each wants to be fixed, repaired, and taken
home.
The screens stare blankly
Like mirrored sunglasses reflecting a parade.

Source: Original work. Copyright © 2001. Reprinted with permission from the author.

I sit on the shop's stoop and watch the cars
pass by
One-by-one.
I smoke into the evening hours.
The twelfth Marlboro is snuffed out.
Another inch of fringe now hangs from my
Levi cut-offs
Each strand pulled away between puffs of
smoke.
Night comes and I fling the glowing sticks
onto the street.

There is something comforting yet
exceedingly lonely
It seems the entire world is passing me by.
Not noticing I am fourteen.

I don't know that I remember turning
fourteen.
I already had
My first drunk
My first man
My first taste of rebellion.
My last hug from my father,
My last quarter for playing the piano,
My last chance at being innocent.

I am stuck in the middle
Like the Motorola behind the glass front.
I am stopped at the intersection
Like the farm trucks that circle round and
round
Stopping briefly to obey the word of the law,
The law of man,
      of God,
        of nature.

The law of man states that old men like
young girls
The law of God states that they shall not.
The law of nature wins out.
Only the strong survive.
The strong drive Z28s
Stopping no more than once in a dead-end
town.

THE ALCHEMY OF HEALING:
Transforming from Victim to Victor

Regina Rivers

Many people believe that if they look too deeply into their wounds they will open Pandora's box and never again be able to stop the pain within from pouring forth. I remember once believing that "I just know I will die if I get into the pain of my childhood." The thought of opening that box is sometimes scary to the point of backing away from the healing process altogether.

I have learned that healing comes to me in workable cycles—not all at once in one gigantic ball of unstoppable misery. The alchemy of healing is one of gradually and purposefully changing myself from victim to victor—becoming an empowered person.

Part of this alchemy included challenging my beliefs about my childhood. For most of my life my belief was that my childhood did not include abuse. My protective self sheltered me from the pain I had experienced until I was capable of dealing with it as an adult in an adult manner. I have met so many people who, like me, believed that they enjoyed a pain-free childhood only to later learn that they also had been abused. When I tell my story, many people can't believe that I am the person I am talking about. They see me as a healthy, well-balanced person, and I am. Yet, like many people, I have walked around with unresolved pain. Most of us choose not to acknowledge and deal with our pain at all. However, the outward appearance of a person doesn't always tell the inner story. I was fortunate. I made the decision to check in with my inner self and to deal with what I discovered.

First of all, I learned that it's okay to challenge my beliefs about those whom I thought were my protectors as a child. It's okay to challenge these beliefs because as individuals, each person can only be the person they are according to the tools or knowledge of life they own in any given moment. I tell you this because I want you to know that this article is not about blame and shame. This article is about healing. Blaming others would keep me in my childhood pain instead of putting my efforts into healing. The point of my story is to share how I continue to uncover the truth about my past so that I can continue to heal in the present moment. Looking into my past with authentically opened eyes helps me to determine if there is anything behind me that yet needs to be healed.

In order to make this process clear, I will talk about my discoveries of childhood abuse and, at the same time, share with you my personal healing transformations as they continued to happen in my life. It is with love for and from my spouse, parents, siblings, children, and friends that I continue to walk with confidence on the path of healing. Because I wish no harm to those in my life story, I have chosen to change, as necessary, the names and places of those involved.

IN THE BEGINNING

It is my belief that joy begins when we first discover the wound, for only then can we begin to administer the "medicine" necessary for healing.

Around the age of 40 (1989), I began to see flashes of a mustached man from my childhood who was affectionately known as "Uncle" Jed and of whom I had been especially fond. I didn't understand why I would cringe and feel nauseated over these memories, and I became concerned.

I saw glimpses of us sitting on the couch at his house. I was around 3 years old. It was

Christmas time, and we were watching Perry Como singing carols on TV. The only sources of light came from the black-and-white TV set and a tree in the corner decorated with blue lights and spun angel hair that created strange patterns on the ceiling and walls. I remember the sound of a miniature train slowly circling on its tracks around the bottom of the tree and the strong smell of his cigar and how its smoke spiraled in the air. Later, as an adult, seeing blue lights and the smell of cigars nauseated me.

As these flashes emerged, I recognized them as actual memories that I hadn't thought much about since my childhood, but now they seemed quite odd to me. Both he and I had big families, and I wondered where everybody else was, including "Aunt" Linda, his kids, my siblings, and my parents. Why were he and I alone in that room watching a Christmas show on TV? And above all—why during a very cold snowy northeastern Christmas was I sitting there in only my underpants?

At another time, I began to remember being alone with him in his bathroom where the green fluorescent lighting was dim and eerie looking to me as a child. I was sitting on the toilet and he was standing in the doorway. I believe he was telling me to, "Wipe harder." The image I get is that there is something dark-colored in my panties and he wants me to wipe it away. Now, as an adult, I often find myself holding my breath when I am in the bathroom putting on makeup or fixing my hair. I have to actually tell myself to breathe. In fact, without knowing it, these cues—holding my breath in the bathroom, becoming nauseated when seeing blue lights or smelling the scent of a cigar—were triggering the emotions I had repressed as a child.

Some of the flashes are still fuzzy to me. Because I didn't want to accuse anyone unjustly, for a long time I allowed myself to believe that those flashes were simply products of my imagination. It was easy for me to pass off the

truth as imagination so that I wouldn't have to deal with the pain of those truths. I didn't realize that the pain of denying the truth was much greater than admitting to that truth. I believe that this is one reason why there are so many walking wounded in our society, who continue the cycle by wounding others instead of dealing with their own pain.

Jed died in the mid 1970s, way before I began my healing process. In fact, part of my later healing concerned not having the possibility of confronting him personally, a choice that some people make to deal with past abuse. At that time of my life, however, I must say that I was glad that his death let me off the hook. I don't think that I would have been ready to face him then. Instead, I began to focus on learning the truth of my past in order to help me understand why I had made certain unhealthy life choices that I call self-abuse. Some of these I will talk about later.

ACKNOWLEDGING THE WOUNDS

Many months and many flashbacks later, I began to hear people talking about something called "repressed memories." I came to understand that when traumatic events occur at a time in our lives when we don't have the means of dealing with those traumas, we instead have the ability to repress or hide the memories of those events deep within our psyches. Later, when we are emotionally capable of dealing with those memories, they may begin to surface of their own accord in the form of flashes or dreams. The return of memories is known in the field of psychology as "recalled" or "recovered memory."

With this new information, I finally decided to go see a psychotherapist. I chose not to tell my parents or family about any part of what was happening to me. I believed that they remembered Jed as a wonderful family friend, and I didn't want to destroy that memory for them. Besides, I wasn't sure that they would believe me. So only a couple of my closest, most supportive friends knew that I had begun counseling. As I later realized, it was deciding to see a therapist that caused me to finally be able to acknowledge that I had been wounded as a child.

Since active research of repressed and recovered memories was a fairly new psychological phenomenon at that time, beginning in or around the 1980s, my therapist didn't push the idea. She just let me talk about all that had occurred for me. She seemed more interested in helping me to be okay in the here and now rather than in delving into past memories. I believe that not being pushed into any particular box by a therapist is an important step in therapy. I was already in what I thought was a box and was desperately trying to get out of it.

EVIDENCE—OPENING PANDORA'S BOX

For another four years, the only information I had came from those foggy, disjointed flashbacks that continued to make it easy for me to pass off my memories as imagination. Since 1991 I'd been living in another city and was seeing a second therapist for an entirely different issue. In mid-1993 I was making plans to move across the state to live with my future husband. While packing, I found a child's book that I figured was one from a pile of books left behind when Jed had moved his family to another state in the late 1960s. I didn't remember owning it and hadn't look inside it before that day.

Without much thought, I opened it to a page, and immediately, every hair on my body stood on end and I began to cry. There before me was a child's pencil drawing on a blank page in the book. To me, it depicted a girl who was being led up to the second floor of a house by a man with a mustache. They were on the outside of the house in which all the windows were up high—none were on the first floor that could be seen into. Somehow I knew at

that moment that this book and the drawing had belonged to "Uncle" Jed's daughter, Emily, who was 6 years younger than I was. It was the most horrifying drawing I have ever seen in my life, and the tale it told me was grotesque and alarming. I turned to the inside cover of the book and there, as expected, I found Emily's name written in full.

I can't begin to tell you of all the emotions that were running through my mind and body. I looked through the rest of the book and found several other drawings. Each seemed to be telling something about this young girl's inner life. On another page a house's windows, door, and chimney were drawn with frightening angry faces with sharp jagged teeth, much like those carved into scary jack-o-lanterns at Halloween. Still another was of a female dressed in a frilly gown. Over her chest area were several hearts and the words "I love you." Then overlaying the hearts and words of love was massive scribbling, that to me seemed to be crossing out, or hiding, the earlier loving feelings. One more page was an actual printing in the book in which the crotch area of a mustached man was erased until there was a hole in the page.

It was immediately after seeing that first drawing that I believed that Jed had sexually abused his daughter, and most likely me as well before her. I really hadn't wanted to think that this man, whom I had grown up loving, could have done such horrible things. This was the first real evidence that I had that solidified all those flashes I had experienced. I was both horrified and relieved. I cried and yelled and cursed the father of this child.

I was most thankful that I was in therapy at the time. It seems to me that healing events tend to occur more for me now that I have the necessary life tools, such as therapy, to cope with them. I think that this is true for all of us. True healing comes in layers much like those of an onion. I have found the ability to peel them back slowly, one at a time, in order to give each layer my full attention so that I can heal each particular aspect of myself. Much as the onion, there are many layers of my life and many individual healings that need to take place when the time is right and ripe. Healing is not a one-shot deal. My healing is a process and a commitment I have made to myself in order to be as healthy as I am able to be. When trauma occurs, I do my best to get the help I need as soon as I am able to do so. It is also important for me to realize that, whether or not something has actually happened to me in my past, it is the way in which the belief of an event, real or unreal, formulates my life or creates my personality that may be good cause for therapy. The focus, then, is not on the actual event, but the feelings surrounding my beliefs or emotions.

THE DOOR IS OPENED—MORE EVIDENCE

Not too long after I had found the book, my mother came to visit me. Out of the blue, she began telling me about a time when she had babysat Emily when she was two years old. Mom said that when having her diaper changed, the toddler was lying very still with a strange look on her face. Mom then told me that as she removed the diaper she noticed that the child's genitals were red and swollen and she didn't understand why. Hearing this, I automatically began to cry. It was only then that I told her about my suspicions. Fortunately, she told me that she believed me and held me while I cried. She then offered me other information about Jed that had always caused her to be wary of him. It wasn't until then that she had actually understood her guardedness.

On another separate occasion, I was told that not long after Jed died, Emily came back to visit some of her friends. A mother of one of her friends told Emily that she was sorry that Jed had died, and in reply, Emily said that she was glad he had died. Death of the abuser is a sure way of escaping an abusive situation.

REVICTIMIZATION

As time went by and I continued therapy, I realized that there were other cases of emotional, physical, and sexual abuse in my life. Around the time I was five, my half-brother, who is five years older than I am, began abusing me, as did a woman who came to baby sit at our home for a week while my parents were away. When I was 16, my boyfriend unsuccessfully tried to rape me at knifepoint. My first husband was sexually and psychologically abusive to me. And, over a period of many years, there was a string of unhealthy relationships that occurred after that divorce.

My education over the years has taught me that multiple abuse is often a pattern with childhood abuse victims, and that with sibling abuse, the older child tends to be five or so years older than the sibling who is being abused. I also realize that many of my life patterns and behaviors can be attributed to the abuse I received from all of these people.

For many years I used drugs to numb my senses and relationships to find the love that I couldn't find within myself for myself. Sometimes revictimization occurs in the form of self-abuse. Rather than realizing that my behaviors were symptoms of deep-seated unhealthy self-concepts, I chose to do whatever I could to escape from my feelings of unworthiness and pain. The challenge to trying to escape pain is that I was causing myself even more damage. Because I was so young when abuse first occurred in my life, I was oblivious to the fact that I had even been abused. For me, my life was normal. In my mind, hurt, pain, fear, and dealing with these issues alone was how everyone coped (or didn't).

Now that I am an adult, any hurt, anger, sadness, or hatred that accompanies painful situations is easier for me to express. As a child, I had stuffed these emotions. As a child I was silenced by some and not heard by others. "Oh, he really didn't mean to do that to you!" "It couldn't have hurt that much!" "Stop crying or I'll give you something to cry about!" "Don't be so god-damned dramatic!" I quickly learned that I was on my own and had to deal with abuse and pain in the only means available to me then—forget it, stuff it, in order to live with it.

HEALING

My healing journey has been long and difficult, and yet I know that I still have more work to do. Just within the past several months of writing this article, I was given the opportunity to peel back more layers of the onion. Because of my ability to identify my wounds (albeit with the help of my husband and friends) and use all the tools I now know are available for recovery, I have been able to move forward in my healing process much more quickly than I might have been able to 10 years ago. I am no longer in denial. I no longer turn to drugs. I no longer allow abuse to go on interminably in any aspect of my life.

How do I peel the layers? First and foremost, I come to grips with what has happened to me. It is important for me to acknowledge that physically, emotionally, and sexually hurtful incidents have happened to me. This is still not always an easy first step for me. Sometimes I may be in shock or confused about the situation that occurred and tend to retreat to my childhood reactions of denial and repression. As I gently begin to work on being an adult who chooses to take care of myself, I then begin to focus on where in my body any emotions are occurring. When I am ready to deal with the event, I usually talk to my husband about it first in order to relieve the pressure that may be building inside me. Depending on how great the event is, I either call my therapist or begin to write about what is going on in my life. For me, journaling is extremely important in the healing process. It takes the secret out of the experience and helps me to see choices I can make. Sometimes talking or writing about my experience allows me

the space to cry, yell, or scream in order to release the damaged energy I may be holding inside. What I no longer want to do is to hold on to secrets and pain. Any way that these hurtful emotions can be released, other than harming myself or another person, brings me out of my pain and back to a healthy balanced life. There are many forms of therapy, counseling, and self-care that are available for working through past trauma. Body massage and meditation practice have been especially beneficial for me. Each individual may pick what is most comfortable for him or herself.

My painful past is still not completely healed. Healing is the work of a lifetime. Sometimes I have nightmares that include the essence of sexual abuse, a common occurrence for survivors. Sometimes I still doubt my worth or need to be reassured that I am loved for who I am. I continue to work on myself in the present in order to understand my past so that my future can be healthier. And, through the alchemy of healing, I continue to transform myself from a victim to a victor.

LULLABY

Child, alone, so quiet,
What would you say if you knew you were safe and could tell?
If you knew that I would listen and believe you?

Did he hurt you?
Did he tell you not to tell?
Did he say that you were special—
That the others would be jealous if they knew?

Did he call you his beautiful princess,
And promise to buy you pretty things?

Did he touch you here and there and say,
"Shhh, this is quiet time"?
And was it dark and you were unsure, confused, afraid?

Have you forgotten only to have flashes slip
by and catch you unaware?
Do you awaken at night crying, not really
knowing why?

Are you growing up feeling out of control—
unable to manage your life?
Do you misunderstand your deep longing to
be loved—
The sense of abandonment that haunts you?

I know, Child. I know!
You can tell me all about it.
I am here for you.

I will hold you in my arms like a nurturing
mother,
And rock you till you cry no more and sooth-
ing sleep finally comes.
Let it all out.
The time is here to let go—
Release the silent burden you have carried for
so very long.
I am here.
I am here.
I am here.
I am here.
I am you.

READING 52

Men, Women, and Rape

Susan Brownmiller

THE MASS PSYCHOLOGY OF RAPE

Krafft-Ebing, who pioneered in the study of
sexual disorders, had little to say about rape.
His famous *Psychopathia Sexualis* gives amaz-
ingly short shrift to the act and its doers. He
had it on good authority, he informed his readers, that most rapists were degenerate, im-
becilic men.[1] Having made that sweeping
generalization, Krafft-Ebing washed his hands
of the whole affair and turned with relish to
the frotteurs and fetishists of normal intelligence who tickled his fancy.

Sigmund Freud, whose major works followed Krafft-Ebing's by twenty to forty years,
was also struck dumb by the subject of rape.
We can search his writings in vain for a

quotable quote, an analysis, a perception. The
father of psychoanalysis, who invented the
concept of the primacy of the penis, was never
motivated, as far as we know, to explore the
real-life deployment of the penis as weapon.
What the master ignored, the disciples tended
to ignore as well. Alfred Adler does not mention rape, despite his full awareness of the historic power struggle between men and
women. Jung refers to rape only in the most
obscure manner, a glancing reference in some
of his mythological interpretations. Helene
Deutsch and Karen Horney, each from a differing perspective, grasped at the female fear of
rape, and at the feminine fantasy, but as
women who did not dare to presume, they
turned a blind eye to the male and female
reality.

And the great socialist theoreticians Marx
and Engels and their many confreres and disciples who developed the theory of class oppression and put words like "exploitation"
into the everyday vocabulary, they, too, were
strangely silent about rape, unable to fit it
into their economic constructs. Among them
only August Bebel tried to grasp at its historic
importance, its role in the very formulation
of class, private property and the means of

production. In *Woman Under Socialism* Bebel used his imagination to speculate briefly about the prehistoric tribal fights for land, cattle and labor power within an acceptable Marxist analysis: "There arose the need of labor power to cultivate the ground. The more numerous these powers, all the greater was the wealth in products and herds. These struggles led first to the rape of women, later to the enslaving of conquered men. The women became laborers and objects of pleasure for the conqueror; their males became slaves."[2] He didn't get it quite right, making the rape of Women secondary to man's search for labor, but it was a flash of revelation and one that Engels did not achieve in his *Origin of the Family.* But Bebel was more at ease researching the wages and conditions of working-women in German factories, and that is where his energies went.

It was the half-crazed genius Wilhelm Reich, consumed with rage in equal parts toward Hitler, Marx and Freud, who briefly entertained the vision of a "masculine ideology of rape."[3] The phrase hangs there in the opening chapter of *The Sexual Revolution,* begging for further interpretation. But it was not forthcoming. The anguished mind was in too great a state of disarray. A political analysis of rape would have required more treachery toward his own immutable gender than even Wilhelm Reich could muster.

And so it remained for the latter-day feminists, free at last from the strictures that forbade us to look at male sexuality, to discover the truth and meaning in our own victimization. Critical to our study is the recognition that rape has a history, and that through the tools of historical analysis we may learn what we need to know about our current condition.

No zoologist, as far as I know, has ever observed that animals rape in their natural habitat, the wild. Sex in the animal world, including those species that are our closest relations, the primates, is more properly called "mating," and it is cyclical activity set off by biologic signals the female puts out. Mating is initiated and "controlled," it would seem, by the female estrous cycle. When the female of the species periodically goes into heat, giving off obvious physical signs, she is ready and eager for copulation and the male becomes interested. At other times there is simply no interest, and no mating.

Jane Goodall, studying her wild chimpanzees at the Gombe Stream reserve, noted that the chimps, male and female, were "very promiscuous, but this does not mean that every female will accept every male that courts her." She recorded her observations of one female in heat, who showed the telltale pink swelling of her genital area, who nevertheless displayed an aversion to one particular male who pursued her. "Though he once shook her out of the tree in which she had sought refuge, we never saw him actually 'rape' her," Goodall wrote, adding, however, "Nonetheless, quite often he managed to get his way through dogged persistence."[4] Another student of animal behavior, Leonard Williams, has stated categorically, "The male monkey cannot in fact mate with the female without her invitation and willingness to cooperate. In monkey society there is no such thing as rape, prostitution, or even passive consent."[5]

Zoologists for the most part have been reticent on the subject of rape. It has not been, for them, an important scientific question. But we do know that human beings are different. Copulation in our species can occur 365 days of the year; it is not controlled by the female estrous cycle. We females of the human species do not "go pink." The call of estrus and the telltale signs, both visual and olfactory, are absent from our mating procedures, lost perhaps in revolutionary shuffle. In their place, as a mark of our civilization, we have evolved a complex system of psychological signs and urges, and a complex structure of pleasure. Our call to sex occurs in the head, and the act is not necessarily linked, as it is with animals, to Mother Nature's pattern of procreation. Without a biologically determined mating season, a human male can evince sexual interest in a human female at any time he pleases, and his psychologic urge is not dependent in the slightest on her biologic readiness or receptivity. What it all boils down to is that the human male can rape.

Man's structural capacity to rape and woman's corresponding structural vulnerability are as basic to the physiology of both our sexes as the primal act of sex itself. Had it not been for this accident of biology, an accommodation requiring the locking together of two separate parts, penis and vagina, there would be neither copulation nor rape as we know it. Anatomically one might want to improve on the design of nature, but such speculation appears to my mind as unrealistic. The human sex act accomplishes its historic purpose of generation of the species and it also affords some intimacy and pleasure. I have no basic quarrel with the procedure. But, nevertheless, we cannot work around the fact that in terms of human anatomy the possibility of forcible intercourse incontrovertibly exists. This single factor may have been sufficient to have caused the creation of a male ideology of rape. When men discovered that they could rape, they proceeded to do it. Later, much later, under certain circumstances they even came to consider rape a crime.

In the violent landscape inhabited by primitive woman and man, some woman somewhere had a prescient vision of her right to her own physical integrity, and in my mind's eye I can picture her fighting like hell to preserve it. After a thunderbolt of recognition that this particular incarnation of hairy, two-legged hominid was not the Homo sapiens with whom she would like to freely join parts, it might have been she, and not some man, who picked up the first stone and hurled it. How surprised he must have been, and what an unexpected

battle must have taken place. Fleet of foot and spirited, she would have kicked, bitten, pushed and run, *but she could not retaliate in kind.*

The dim perception that had entered prehistoric woman's consciousness must have had an equal but opposite reaction in the mind of her male assailant. For if the first rape was an unexpected battle founded on the first woman's refusal, the second rape was indubitably planned. Indeed, one of the earliest forms of male bonding must have been the gang rape of one woman by a band of marauding men. This accomplished, rape became not only a male prerogative, but man's basic weapon of force against woman, the principal agent of his will and her fear. His forcible entry into her body, despite her physical protestations and struggle, became the vehicle of his victorious conquest over her being, the ultimate test of his superior strength, the triumph of his manhood.

Man's discovery that his genitalia could serve as a weapon to generate fear must rank as one of the most important discoveries of prehistoric times, along with the use of fire and the first crude stone axe. From prehistoric times to the present, I believe, rape has played a critical function. It is nothing more or less than a conscious process of intimidation by which *all men* keep *all women* in a state of fear.

IN THE BEGINNING WAS THE LAW

From the humblest beginnings of the social order based on a primitive system of retaliatory force—the *lex talionis:* an eye for an eye—woman was unequal before the law. By anatomical fiat—the inescapable construction of their genital organs—the human male was a natural predator and the human female served as his natural prey. Not only might the female be subjected at will to a thoroughly detestable physical conquest from which there could be no retaliation in kind—a rape for a rape—but the consequences of such a brutal struggle might be death or injury, not to mention impregnation and the birth of a dependent child.

One possibility, and one possibility alone, was available to woman. Those of her own sex whom she might call to her aid were more often than not smaller and weaker than her male attackers. More critical, they lacked the basic physical wherewithal for punitive vengeance; at best they could maintain only a limited defensive action. But among those creatures who were her predators, some might serve as her chosen protectors. Perhaps it was thus that the risky bargain was struck. Female fear of an open season of rape, and not a natural inclination toward monogamy, motherhood or love, was probably the single causative factor in the original subjugation of woman by man, the most important key to her historic dependence, her domestication by protective mating.

Once the male took title to a specific female body, and surely for him this was a great sexual convenience as well as a testament to his warring stature, he had to assume the burden of fighting off all other potential attackers, or scare them off by the retaliatory threat of raping *their* women. But the price of woman's protection *by some men* against an abuse *by others* was steep. Disappointed and disillusioned by the inherent female incapacity to protect, she became estranged in a very real sense from other females, a problem that haunts the social organization of women to this very day. And those who did assume the historic burden of her protection—later formalized as husband, father, brother, clan—extracted more than a pound of flesh. They reduced her status to that of chattel. The historic price of woman's protection by man against man was the imposition of chastity and monogamy. A crime committed against her body became a crime against the male estate.

The earliest form of permanent, protective conjugal relationship, the accommodation called mating that we now know as marriage, appears to have been institutionalized by the male's forcible abduction and rape of the female. No quaint formality, bride capture, as it came to be known, was a very real struggle: a male took title to a female, staked a claim to her body, as it were, by an act of violence. Forcible seizure was a perfectly acceptable way—to men—of acquiring women, and it existed in England as late as the fifteenth century.[6] Eleanor of Aquitaine, according to a biographer, lived her early life in terror of being "rapt" by a vassal who might through appropriation of her body gain title to her considerable property.[7] Bride capture exists to this day in the rain forests of the Philippines, where the Tasadays were recently discovered to be plying their Stone Age civilization.[8] Remnants of the philosophy of forcible abduction and marriage still influence the social mores of rural Sicily and parts of Africa.[9] A proverb of the exogamous Bantu-speaking Gusiis of southwest Kenya goes "Those whom we marry are those whom we fight."[10]

It seems eminently sensible to hypothesize that man's violent capture and rape of the female led first to the establishment of a rudimentary mate-protectorate and then sometime later to the full-blown male solidification of power, the patriarchy. As the first permanent acquisition of man, his first piece of real property, woman was, in fact, the original building block, the cornerstone, of the "house of the father." Man's forcible extension of his boundaries to his mate and later to their offspring was the beginning of his concept of ownership. Concepts of hierarchy, slavery and private property flowed from, and could only be predicated upon, the initial subjugation of woman.

A female definition of rape can be contained in a single sentence. If a woman chooses not to have intercourse with a specific man and the man chooses to proceed against her will, that is a criminal act of rape. Through no fault of woman, this is not and never has been the legal definition. The ancient patriarchs who came together to write their early covenants had used the rape of women to forge their own male power—how then could they see rape as a crime of man against woman? Women were wholly owned subsidiaries and not independent beings. Rape could not be envisioned as a matter of female consent or refusal; nor could a definition acceptable to males be based on a male-female understanding of a female's right to her bodily integrity. Rape entered the law through the back door, as it were, as a property crime of man against man. Woman, of course, was viewed as the property.

Ancient Babylonian and Mosaic law was codified on tablets centuries after the rise of formal tribal hierarchies and the permanent settlements known as city-states. Slavery, private property and the subjugation of women were facts of life, and the earliest written law that has come down to us reflects this stratified life. Written law in its origin was a solemn compact among men of property, designed to protect their own male interests by a civilized exchange of goods or silver *in place of force* wherever possible. The capture of females by force remained perfectly acceptable *outside* the tribe or city as one of the ready fruits of warfare, but clearly *within* the social order such a happenstance would lead to chaos. A payment of money to the father of the house was a much more civilized and less dangerous way of acquiring a wife. And so the bride price was codified, at fifty pieces of silver. By this circuitous route the first concept of criminal rape sneaked its tortuous way into man's definition of law. Criminal rape, as a patriarchal father saw it, was a violation of the new way of doing business. It was, in a phrase, the theft of virginity, an embezzlement of his daughter's fair price on the market.

About four thousand years ago the Code of Hammurabi, chipped on a seven-foot column of diorite stone, made plain by its omissions that a female was allowed no independent status under Babylonian law. She was either a betrothed virgin, living in the house of her father, or else she was somebody's lawfully wedded wife and lived in the house of her husband. According to Hammurabi, a man was to be seized and slain if he raped a betrothed virgin, but the victimized girl was considered guiltless. As an interesting indication of the powers and rights of patriarchs over their female dependents, Hammurabi decreed that a man who "knew" his own daughter (i.e., committed incest) was merely banished from the walls of the city. A *married* woman who had the misfortune to get raped in Babylon had to share the blame equally with her attacker. Regardless of how the incident occurred, the crime was labeled adultery and *both participants* were bound and thrown into the river. Appeal from such stern justice is revealing. A husband was permitted to pull his wife from the water if he so desired; the king, if he wished, could let his errant male subject go free.[11]

Influenced by Hammurabi's code but lacking the glorious Tigris and Euphrates, the ancient Hebrews substituted death by stoning for a watery grave. When Moses received his tablets from God on the top of Mount Sinai, "Thou shalt not rape" was conspicuously missing from the Ten Commandments, although Moses received a distinct commandment against adultery and another, for good measure, against the coveting of thy neighbor's wife, bracketed this second time around with thy neighbor's house, his field, his servant, ox and ass. Like her Babylonian sister, a married woman within the Hebrew culture who was victimized by rape was considered culpable, adulterous and irrevocably defiled. She was stoned to death along with her attacker at the gates to the city. But unlike the woman of Babylon, who before her last gasp might be rescued by her grief-stricken husband, for the women of Israel there was no reprieve. Reprieve from adultery, real or imagined, had to wait till the Gospel of St. John, in which appears Jesus' famous statement, "He that is without sin among you, let him first cast a stone at her."[12]

We must cut through the thicket of some minor passages in Deuteronomy, written long after the original Ten Commandments, to arrive at the true Hebraic concept of a criminal act of rape, one in which the violator, and not the violated, bore full responsibility for his unlawful act.

In the Hebrew social order, which differed only in its exquisite precision from the simpler Babylonian codes, virgin maidens were bought and sold in marriage for fifty pieces of silver.[13] To use plain language, what a father sold to a prospective bridegroom or his family was title to his daughter's unruptured hymen, a piece of property he wholly owned and controlled. With a clearly marked price tag attached to her hymen, a daughter of Israel was kept under watch to make sure she remained in a pristine state, for a piece of damaged goods could hardly command an advantageous match and might have to be sold as a concubine.

Like the Hebrew wife who was held responsible for her own defilement, a Hebrew daughter was given the task of guarding her own untouched flesh. If a man raped a virgin within the walls of the city both shared the same fate of death by stoning, for the elders reasoned that if the girl had screamed she would have been rescued. Patriarchal wisdom allowed that if the act of rape took place outside the city or while the girl was laboring in the field, for all her screaming, no one might hear, so a judicious solution was put into effect. The rapist was ordered to pay the girl's father fifty silver shekels in compensation for what would have been her bride price and the pair was simply commanded to wed. But if the maiden who was raped in a field was already betrothed to someone else, and betrothals in infancy were common, Hebraic wrath descended with

unilateral vengeance on the rapist's head. No civil exchange of money and goods could be countenanced, for not only was the original betrothal null and void, but the house of the father had suffered an irreparable blow to its honor. In this singular instance the incautious rapist was stoned to death while the girl went unpunished, to be sold at a markdown to one who might have her.

One authority on the blood-vengeance justice of the early Assyrians has noted that under the *lex talionis* the father of a raped virgin was permitted to seize the wife of the rapist and violate her in turn.[14] Before the codification of Mosaic law, Hebrew retribution for rape was even deadlier than this, particularly if the offender came from outside the tribe. The story of Dinah stands as a warning to any who might violate a Hebrew daughter. It is also a serious warning to young women of what might befall them if they stray too far from their father's house.

As told in Genesis, Dinah was a virgin daughter of Jacob by Leah. She was raped by a gentile when she left the house one day to go to visit some female friends. Dinah's attacker, who was not without his own tribal code, then applied to Jacob's family for permission to marry the woman he had violated. Pretending agreement, Jacob's sons suggested to the eager young man that he and all the male members of his uncivilized tribe undergo the ritual of circumcision. Three days later, the Bible tells us, when the gentile tribe was still sore from the painful operation, Jacob's sons descended on their encampment, slaughtered the weakened men and made captives of their women and oxen. Thus was the house of Jacob vindicated, but what benefit accrued to Dinah is questionable.[15]

Protecting wellborn daughters of Israel from rape by the threat of massive retribution was obviously serious business, but as the story of Dinah shows, men of the Hebrew tribes, like their neighbors, had no compunctions against freely raping women of tribes they had conquered, for in this way they prospered and grew. Captured slave women were lawfully employed as servants, field hands, concubines and breeders of future slaves in much the same manner that the eighteenth-century American slaveholder made use of his black female slaves, and indeed, this Biblical parallel was often cited as religious justification by upholders of American slavery.

The unfortunate lot of women caught in the middle of intertribal warfare *within* the confederated twelve tribes of Israel is demonstrated by a series of swiftly moving events reported in the Book of Judges. A Levite, accompanied by his unfaithful concubine, seeks rest and shelter for the night with an old man in Benjamite territory. Hearing that a stranger has come to town, some men of Benjamin approach the house with the intention of committing homosexual abuse. The Levite's protector offers up his own virgin daughter and the Levite's concubine to deflect the energy of the eager young bloods. They graciously decline the use of the daughter but they rape the concubine through the night. When the Levite discovers her dead on the doorstep in the morning, he calls on the other tribes of Israel to defend his honor. In the ensuing battle most of the Benjamite men and all of the Benjamite women are slaughtered. Now the Hebrew elders become seriously concerned, for without women the tribe of Benjamin will cease to exist. They arrange for the defeated Benjamites to catch and rape four hundred young virgins of neighboring Shiloh, and thus secure for them legal wives.[16]

With all this lawful rape as the order of the day, it comes as no surprise that the Bible's major rape parable is not concerned with the plight of an unfortunate female or even with the efforts of her father and brothers to avenge their house. The famous story of Potiphar's wife is an important morality lesson in Hebrew, Christian and Moslem folklore, and it expresses the true, historic concern and abiding fear of egocentric, rapacious man: what can happen to a fine, upstanding fellow if *a vengeful female lies* and cries that she has been assaulted.

Joseph the Israelite was a highly placed slave in the household of Potiphar the Egyptian. As recorded in Genesis, Potiphar's wife—she is not identified by a first name—cast a lecherous eye upon the Hebrew slave. She was always pestering this unwilling sex object to "lie with me," and the virtuous Joseph was forever reminding her of their master in common. One day Joseph and Potiphar's wife found themselves alone in the house. Seizing her opportunity, Potiphar's wife caught Joseph "by his garment" and commanded, "Lie with me." At this point, supposedly, Joseph fled—and Potiphar's wife began crying rape or its Biblical equivalent.[17]

This is the Hebrew male side of the story, I must stress. When Potiphar came home his wife showed him Joseph's torn cloak and wailed, "The Hebrew . . . came in unto me to mock me!" Potiphar had no choice but to throw his favorite slave into prison. But God, as would be expected, remained on the side of the Israelite. Once in jail Joseph became quite the prison leader, and by correctly interpreting the Pharaoh's dreams he won a full pardon and rose to become prime minister. The moral of the story of Potiphar's wife is that a woman scorned—especially if she is gentile—can get a good man into a hell of a lot of trouble by crying rape.

The legend of Potiphar's wife, in some form or other, is a familiar staple in many ancient cultures.[18] Joseph's misfortune occupies a place of importance in the teachings of the Koran and a similar tale has been traced to Egyptian folklore of 1300 B.C. A variation appears in Celtic myths. One historian of sexual attitudes has noted the frequent recurrence of the theme in romantic histories of the Crusades, where "very often the rapacious maiden is a Saracen who jumps into the bed of a crusader," all the more significant when we remember that the Crusades were marked by Christian rape and pillage of Moslems as the crusaders pursued the Holy Grail. The universal promulgation of a parable of rape that places the full burden of blame squarely on a lascivious female of another race or nation can hardly be accidental. Aggressive warlike peoples must have found it highly expeditious to promote this sort of legend as they went about their routine business of conquering others. What better way, after all, to absolve themselves from guilt as they plucked the fruits of victory?

As the centuries rolled by and Jewish women began to win a measure of independence, the learned men who interpreted the Bible became increasingly concerned about an act that was not quite rape but had some elements of mutual seduction. The emergence of an independent female, one whose father had died or one who did not marry, began to affect the ground rules governing criminal-rape prosecutions for "she herself became a litigant," writes a modern rabbinical authority, and "her consent to the act had great bearing on the payments due."[19] Talmudic theorists of the Middle Ages, the Jewish intellectual elite, manfully sought to cover all the new contingencies. Virginity remained the *sine qua non* of individual rape prosecutions, but maidens who displayed "sexual eagerness" were added to the official list of statutory nonvirgins, along with gentile women, captives and slaves.

Under Talmudic interpretation, a raped virgin was no longer required to marry her rapist.[20] If she had acquired a semi-independent status and her age fell between three and twelve and a half—the rabbis were real sticklers about the age of *bone fide* virgins—she was permitted to receive the fine of fifty coins herself. Allowing a female to keep the money tampered with the hallowed concept of rape as the theft of virginity. In time the award came to be seen as punitive damage for

injury to a female's body, as well as payment for enjoying sexual intercourse with a virgin. This was real progress for women, hard won. The great Jewish theologian Maimonides was forever arguing that in his view a raped virgin had no right to receive monetary compensation.[21] He did not prevail.*

Concepts of rape and punishment in early English law are a wondrous maze of contradictory approaches reflecting a gradual humanization of jurisprudence in general, and in particular, man's eternal confusion, never quite resolved, as to whether the crime was a crime against a woman's body or a crime against his own estate.

Before the Norman Conquest of 1066 the penalty for rape was death and dismemberment, but this stern justice pertained exclusively to the man who raped a highborn, propertied virgin who lived under the protection of a powerful lord.[23] Feudalism took root in the Middle Ages as ownership of land became an inherited right, "the lands passing by immemorial custom from father to son . . . maintained, among ways by the system of wardship and marriage."[24] Since females *were* allowed to inherit property, a matter of necessity if there were no extant male heirs, "trading in marriages," to borrow a telling phrase from G. G. Coulton, was a lucrative enterprise among the nobility, practiced in much the same manner "as men trade in shares and investments today."[25] For obvious economic reasons a landed heiress could not marry without

---

*Maimonides dominated Jewish philosophic thought in the twelfth century and beyond, but on matters pertaining to women this strict constructionist was often overruled by other rabbis. It is a little known fact that in addition to his other accomplishments, the great Maimonides was the author of a slender sex manual that had quite a vogue in its day. Women figure hardly at all in his little book, which is mainly about food. Not to put too fine a point on it, Maimonides' manual is a collection of recipes guaranteed by the author to sustain an erection.[22]

permission of her overlord, under penalty of losing her inherited fortune. Yet once the nuptials had taken place, their legal and churchly sanctity could not be challenged, and so the custom of "stealing an heiress" by forcible abduction and marriage became a routine method of acquiring property by adventurous, upward-mobile knights. As a matter of record, not until a fifteenth-century edict of Henry VII was heiress-stealing ruled a felony unto itself.[26]

Gothic literature has made heiress-stealing a subject of great romance, replete with midnight assignations, loyal maidservants and a great thundering of horses' hooves, but in actuality it was predicated on the desire for land, not love. If a captured virgin managed to escape before her forced marriage, or if an errant knave had merely taken her on the spot, she could attempt to seek redress in the court of her lord's manor. Trial for capital crime in those days was by physical ordeal, and grueling tests by water and hot irons were probably employed to arrive at the "truth."

Henry of Bratton (Bracton), who lived and wrote in the thirteenth century, is our best authority for these ancient Saxon times, accepted by Coke, Hale and Blackstone, the later giants of English jurisprudence. Bracton informs us that during the tenth-century rule of King Athelstan, if a man were to throw a virgin to the ground against her will, "he forfeits the King's grace; if he shamelessly disrobes her and places himself upon her, he incurs the loss of all his possessions; and if he lies with her, he incurs the loss of his life and members." Vengeance did not stop at death, for, Bracton continued, "even his horse shall to his ignomy be put to shame upon its scrotum and tail, which shall be cut off as close as possible to the buttocks." A similar fate awaited the rapist's dog, and if he happened to own a hawk, "Let it lose its beak, its claws and its tail."[27]

After his animals were cropped and his own human life was taken, a rapist's land and money were supposed to be given to the ravished virgin. But one manner of redemption was possible. As a benevolent way of saving him from terrible death, a raped virgin might be permitted by King and Church to accept her ravisher in marriage.[28] Since consolidation of property was uppermost in the minds of men, we may assume that a violated virgin was encouraged or *not* encouraged toward matrimony depending on which arrangement of the land was most beneficial, or least inconvenient, to the domain of Church and King.

Punishment for raping a virgin of property was thoughtfully reduced to castration and the loss of both eyes by William the Conqueror.[29] The mode of trial under William also switched from ordeal to combat, so we may assume that unless the stakes were high, few virgins were actually championed by their chivalrous kin. Speaking to this point, the English legal historians Pollock and Maitland remark, "In one respect a woman's capacity of suing was curtailed by her inability to fight."[30]

Castration and blinding was still the appropriate penalty for raping a virgin in Bracton's day and he explained the law's intent—"member for member"—with these words: "Let him lose his eyes which gave him sight of the virgin's beauty for which he coveted her. And let him lose as well the testicles which excited his hot lust."[31]

King Henry II, the Plantagenet who married Eleanor of Aquitaine, brought the principles of Frankish law to England during his twelfth-century reign. If a raped virgin filed a civil suit or "appeal" and an indictment was obtained, the resulting trial was by jury in the king's assize instead of by combat or duel. This was clearly an advance in procedures. Bracton was most meticulous as to the proper form the suit should take. He entitled his instructions "An appeal concerning the rape of virgins." An appeal concerning the rape of nonvirgins does not appear anywhere in his compendium, for Bracton was describing the king's jurisdiction, which by this time included murder, mayhem and major theft. "Minor" offenses were still being handled by the manorial courts. In fact, Bracton tells us that a raped virgin's appeal and a wife's appeal in the matter of a husband "slain within her arms" were the only suits a woman could bring to the courts of the king.[32] The procedure a raped virgin was to follow went like this:

> She must go at once and while the deed is newly done, with the hue and cry, to the neighboring townships and there show the injury done to her to men of good repute, the blood and her clothing stained with blood, and her torn garments. And in the same way she ought to go to the reeve of the hundred, the king's serjeant, the coroners and the sheriff. And let her make her appeal at the first county court, unless she can at once make her complaint directly to the lord king or his justices, where she will be told to sue at the county court. Let her appeal be enrolled in the coroners' rolls, every word of the appeal, exactly as she makes it, and the year and day on which she makes it. A day will be given her at the coming of the justices, at which let her again put forward her appeal before them, in the same words as she made it in the county court, from which she is not permitted to depart lest the appeal fall because of the variance . . .[33]

If the man whom our raped virgin accused protested his innocence, "Let the truth be ascertained by an examination of her body, made by four law-abiding women sworn to tell the truth as to whether she is a virgin or defiled." If she proved to be defiled, the trial might continue; if she proved a virgin still, the case was dismissed and the false accuser was thrown into custody.

The man accused, Bracton writes, had several possible defenses. He might say

> that he had her as his concubine and *amica* before the day and the year mentioned in the appeal . . . or that he had her and defiled her with her consent and not against her will, and that if she now appeals him it is in hatred of another woman

whom he has as his concubine, or whom he has married, or that it is at the instigation of one of her kinsmen. He may also except that on the year and day the deed was supposed to be done he was elsewhere, outside the realm. . . . Or he may also except on the ground of an omission made in the appeal. . . . Many other matters may constitute exceptions though I do not now call them to mind.[34]

Despite a spirited defense, the male justices who heard the case might sometimes decide they had to convict, and then our victim-prosecutrix* would be given her old option of marrying her rapist as a benevolent way of saving him from gruesome mutilation.

Bracton allowed that this time-honored custom of redeeming a rapist through marriage could cause considerable mischief to the social structure, for "a common person might bring perpetual disgrace upon a woman of nobility and good family by a single act of defilement and take her to wife to the disgrace of her family." On the other hand, "But suppose that the ravisher is a nobleman and the woman raped a common person; will it be for the defiled person to exercise a choice and decide whether she will marry the nobleman or not?"[35]

Apparently this was to be—if the nobleman valued his sight and his testicles—but the chance that a man of nobility might be convicted of raping a commoner would have been slight. "As a rule," Sidney Painter writes in his *History of the Middle Ages*, "the nobleman's crime was blamed on his men." Painter

---

*The term "prosecutrix" stems from this time in English history when a female had the burden of instituting a civil suit in order for a rape trial to take place. Today, of course, it is the state, not the woman, that prosecutes for rape, yet "prosecutrix" continues to appear with regularity in appellate briefs that are written by rapists' defense attorneys, where it is used interchangeably with "complainant" and "alleged victim." Much of legal language is archaic, but in this instance it is hard not to conclude that the word is favored for the harsh, vindictive quality of personal prosecution that it plainly connotes.

reports on one case in which a young girl was abducted on the highway, taken to a knight's house, and raped by the knight and his men: "The court solemnly accepted the statement of the knight that he was horrified to hear that she had not been in his house of her own free will. . . . Even in England," he continues, "if a member of the feudal class committed his crimes against anyone other than the king or a great lord, he was fairly safe from prosecution, or at least from punishment."[36]

("Even in England" is an important qualifying phrase, for while the Middle Ages was a time of savage wife beating, Court prostitution, and general all-around lawlessness and feudal oppression, things seemed to be far worse for women on the Continent.[37] The *jus primae noctis*, right of the first night or *droit du seigneur*, the custom of giving the manorial lord the right to take the virginity of the bride of any one of his vassals or serfs unless the bride and bridegroom paid a specific amount of produce in redemption dues—certainly a form of rape—appears to have been enforced irregularly in certain parts of Germany, France, Italy and Poland but not, however, in England.[38] Still, it cannot be overstressed that "even in England" the law that evolved was feudal class law, designed to protect the nobleman's interest. Although it took place much later, the celebrated eighteenth-century trial and acquittal of Frederick Calvert, the seventh and last Lord Baltimore, for a rape upon the body of Sarah Woodcock, a milliner, is a case in point.[39] Baltimore had the twenty-nine-year-old virgin hat-maker abducted and he kept her a virtual prisoner for more than a week. At the trial he claimed consent and pleaded, "Libertine as I am represented, I am sure I have sufficiently atoned for every indiscretion, which a weak attachment to this unworthy woman may have led me into, by having suffered the disgrace of being exposed as a criminal at the bar." Apparently the judge and jury agreed.

The wonder of Lord Baltimore's case is that it came to trial at all.)

How was justice secured for raped women who were not propertied virgins, that is, as Bracton himself was careful to enumerate, for "matrons, nuns, widows, concubines and even prostitutes?"[40] The legal scholar who so minutely described the procedures and punishments in regard to "an appeal concerning the rape of virgins" hurriedly passed by the rest of womankind's rapists with the comment, "Punishment of this kind does not follow . . ." although he did report that it might be "severe." What precise punishment *did* follow he never records, and probably for good, practical reason. Either he had few convictions to go by, or the penalties were not uniform, or he and his fellow men did not consider the matter of any great legal concern. All three of these possibilities are highly likely in concert. Pollock and Maitland, the law historians, write, "Concerning these matters we find little case-law. Appeals of rape were often brought in the thirteenth century; but they were often quashed, abandoned or compromised."[41] But what is significant is that by Bracton's time, the thirteenth century, the legal concept of criminal rape had clearly, if haphazardly, been broadened by the manorial courts to include at least in principle the rape of "matrons, nuns, widows, concubines and even prostitutes." Bracton's glancing reference may be the first in written history.

The comprehensive Statutes of Westminster put forward by Edward I at the close of the thirteenth century showed a gigantic advance in legal thinking as the Crown, and by "Crown" Americans should read "state," began to take an active interest in all kinds of rape prosecutions, not just those concerning violated virgins.[42] Our modern principle of *statutory* rape—felonious carnal knowledge of a child in which her "consent" is altogether immaterial—dates from this time and these statutes.[43]

Of critical significance, Westminster extended the king's jurisdiction to cover the forcible rape of married women as well as virgins, with no difference in punishment to offending males. To further erase the distinction between the rape of a virgin and the rape of a wife, the old, ignoble custom of redemption through marriage was permanently banned under suits by the king. In concession to the proprietary rights of husbands—for the Crown had ventured into an area it had never ventured into before—Westminster also saw fit to legislate a definition of lesser ravishment, a sort of misdemeanor, applicable in cases where it could be argued that a wife did not object strenuously enough to her own "defilement." The aggrieved party in these cases was the husband, and the wife was peremptorily stripped of her dower. *Within* a marriage, the theory went—and still goes—that there could be no such crime as rape by a husband since a wife's "consent" to her husband was a permanent part of the marriage vows and could not be withdrawn.[44]

To give the new law teeth, Edward I decreed that if a raped woman or her kin failed to institute a private suit within forty days, the right to prosecute automatically passed to the Crown. This bold concept, applicable only to virgins in previous reigns, was a giant step for the law and for women. It meant that rape was no longer just a family misfortune and a threat to land and property, but an issue of public safety and state concern.

The First Statute of Westminster, enacted in 1275, set the Crown's penalty for rape at a paltry two years' imprisonment plus a fine at the king's pleasure, no doubt to ease the effect of a major transition, for what had occurred at the Parliament of Westminster was only tangentially and in retrospect a recognition of women's rights; its inexorable, historic purpose had been to consolidate political power in the hands of the king. But within a decade an emboldened Second Statute of Westminster amended the timorous First. By a new act of Parliament, any man who ravished "a married woman, dame or damsel" without her consent was guilty of a full-blown felony under the law of the Crown, and the penalty was death.*

It read better on parchment than it worked in real life, but the concept of rape as a public wrong had been firmly established.

From the thirteenth to the twentieth century, little changed. The later giants of jurisprudence, Hale, Blackstone, Wigmore and the rest, continued to point a suspicious finger at the female victim and worry about her motivations and "good fame."

"If she be of evil fame and stand unsupported by others," Blackstone commented, "if she concealed the injury for any considerable time after she had the opportunity to complain, if the place where the act was alleged to be committed was where it was possible she might have been heard and she made no outcry, these and the like circumstances carry a strong but not conclusive presumption that her testimony is false or feigned."[45]

NOTES

1. Richard von Krafft-Ebing, *Psychopathia Sexualis* (1886), trans. from the Latin by Harry E. Wedeck, New York: Putnam, 1965, p. 435.
2. August Bebel, *Women Under Socialism* (1883), trans. from the German by Daniel DeLeon, New York: Labor News Press, 1904, p. 27. See also pp. 29, 56–58.
3. Wilhelm Reich, *The Sexual Revolution* (1945), trans. from the German by Theodore P. Wolfe, New York: Farrar, Straus, 1969, p. 27.
4. Jane van Lawick-Goodall, *In the Shadow of Man*, New York: Dell, 1972, pp. 193–94.
5. Leonard Williams, *Man and Monkey*, London: Deutsch, 1967, p. 157. See also pp. 80, 88.

*Under modern English law the maximum penalty for rape is life imprisonment.

6. William Blackstone, *Commentaries on the Laws of England*, 10th ed., London, 1787,Vol. IV, p. 208.

7. Amy Kelly, *Eleanor of Aquitaine and the Four Kings*, New York: Random House Vintage ed., 1959, p. 4.

8. John Noble Wilford, "Stone-Age Tribe in Philippines Is Imperiled," *New York Times*, Oct. 17, 1971.

9. Peter Kayser, "Situationer—Women," Reuter, Rome, Aug. 7, 1973: "In Sicily another sex ritual was recently acted out when a shepherd, Guiseppe Ilardo, 30, kidnapped 18-year-old Anna Puccia, raped her and then fled hoping she would marry him to clear her name. Following the traditional Sicilian scenario, he then asked for the girl's hand through some friends but Anna refused, clearing the way for police to arrest Ilardo and jail him on rape charges. Her action went strongly against all tradition . . ."

10. Robert A. LeVine, "Gusii Sex Offenses: A Study in Social Control," *American Anthropologist*, Vol. 61 (Dec. 1959), p. 966.

11. Chilperic Edwards, *The Hammurabi Code*, London: Watts, 1921, pp. 27–31.

12. John 8:7.

13. Deuteronomy 22:13–29.

14. Louis M. Epstein, *Sex Laws and Customs in Judaism*, New York: Bloch Pub. Co., 1948, p. 180.

15. Genesis 34.

16. Judges 19–21.

17. Genesis 39.

18. H. R. Hays, *The Dangerous Sex* (1964), New York: Pocket Books, 1972, p. 109.

19. Epstein, p. 188.

20. Epstein, pp. 183–91. I am also indebted to Epstein for his interpretation of Biblical legislation, pp. 179–82, and for his brilliant concept of "theft of virginity," which I have shamelessly appropriated.

21. Epstein, p. 188 n.

22. Moses Maimonides, "On Sexual Intercourse," *Medical Historical Studies of Medieval Jewish Medical Works*, Brooklyn: Rambash Pub. Co., 1961, Vol. I.

23. Blackstone, IV, p. 211.

24. G. G. Coulton, *Medieval Panorama*, Cambridge, Eng.: The University Press, 1938, pp. 48–49.

25. *Ibid.*

26. Blackstone, IV, p. 208.

27. Samuel E. Thorne, trans. and ed., *Bracton on the Laws and Customs of England*, Cambridge, Mass.: Belknap Press of Harvard, 1968, vol. II, p. 418.

28. *Ibid.*

29. Blackstone, IV, p. 211.

30. Frederick Pollock and Frederic William Maitland, *The History of English Law Before the Time of Edward I* (1895), Cambridge, Eng.: The University Press, 1968, vol. I, p. 485.

31. *Bracton*, II, pp. 414–15.

32. *Bracton*, II, p. 419.

33. *Bracton*, II, p. 415.

34. *Bracton*, II, pp. 416–17.

35. *Bracton*, II, p. 417.

36. Sidney Painter, *A History of the Middle Ages*, New York: Knopf, 1960, p. 120.

37. *Ibid.*

38. For an interesting discussion, see August Bebel, *Woman Under Socialism* (1883), trans. from the German by Daniel DeLeon, New York: Labor News Press, 1904, pp. 56–58.

39. *The Trial of Frederick Calvert Esq., the baron of Baltimore in the kingdom of Ireland, for a Rape on the Body of Sarah Woodcock*, held at the Kingston Assizes for the County of Surry, taken in shorthand by Joseph Gurney, London: W. Owen, 1768.

40. *Bracton*, II, p. 415.

41. Pollock and Maitland, Vol. II, pp. 490–492.

42. These statutes are recorded in full, with annotations, in Edward Coke, *The Second Part of the Institutes of the Laws of England* (2 vols.), London: W. Clarke, 1809. Westminster I, Cap. 13, enacted in the third year of the reign of Edward I (1275), appears in Vol. I, pp. 179–81. Westminster II, Cap. 34, enacted in the thirteenth year of Edward's reign (1285), appears in Vol. 2, pp. 432–36. The historic importance of the Westminster rape statutes is confirmed by Pollock and Maitland, among others.

43. *American Journal of Legal History*, Vol. 7, 1963, pp. 162–63. See also *South Carolina Law Review*, Vol. 18, 1966, p. 254.

44. Matthew Hale, *History of the Pleas of the Crown*, Philadelphia: R. H. Small, 1847, vol. I, p. 628.

45. Blackstone, IV, p. 213.

The Day My Life Changed

Have you ever had an experience that is of such importance that you now view your life in terms of before it and after it? Mine was being gang raped.

I was doing voluntary work in a foreign country when it happened. I remember thinking at the time that I was going to die afterwards wishing that I had. In the moments afterwards, once I realised that I was alive, I made the decision that this would be my terrible secret. The decision made, I switched to automatic pilot and my actions and decisions from then on were carried out with cold detachment. Like any of the medical model management plans, I mentally went through the checklist of everything that needed to be done. For example, first initial assessment of the damage; next deal with the injuries as best as possible; next get back to base; next check for all the possible complications and then deal with each accordingly, and so it went on.

There were no facilities in the country I was working in, and I was due back in Britain in the next few days so I waited until I could be seen at an accident and emergency department so that nothing could be documented in my official notes. I attended a genitourinary medicine clinic anonymously, although I had an agonising six months' wait until I could be checked for HIV. All this had to be done in a neighbouring town as I had worked in my local genitourinary medicine clinic and all of the staff would have recognised me.

Source: *British Medical Journal*, vol. 321, issue 7268, p. 1089. Copyright © 10/28/2000. Reprinted with permission from British Medical Journal.

I was fortunate. There were no lasting physical complications of my ordeal. As for the psychological ones, what psychological ones? I wouldn't say that I was completely in denial. I was aware of the scary monsters hiding under the stairs threatening to break loose, but I didn't have the time or energy to deal with the havoc that their escape would cause. So I continued with my denial and distraction strategy. From an outsider's point of view, it might have seemed a productive time in my life. I was so terrified of the possibility of thinking about it, that I threw myself into continuous frenzied activity which, if nothing else, certainly had a beneficial effect on my curriculum vitae.

To think was dangerous. To think was to acknowledge that I couldn't cope, and then it would all come out, and then other people would find out, and then they would blame me, and then they would treat me differently, and then my career would be over. No, denial and distraction were the best strategy. But slowly but surely they stopped working. My coping mechanisms were failing me. How could this be?

It took me five long years, but eventually, with a great deal of scepticism, I sought the help of a trained counsellor. Before this, I had always been the counsellor, so what did I need counselling for? That was what other people did. She was fantastic. I still remember her words. It was as if she had suddenly kicked me in the stomach. "It's not your fault." I was stunned as the realisation sank in. It wasn't my fault? But I should have been dressed differently, screamed louder, struggled harder.

No, it wasn't my fault. From that point on, I made progress. The counsellor made me aware of the terrible price I was paying for keeping my shameful secret to myself.

It was as if I had a chronic abscess inside even though I wasn't aware of it, sapping all my strength and energy. Although it was terribly painful at the time, the abscess had to be squeezed to let all the poison out if there was to be any chance of healing. All my poison came out during these counselling sessions, and although there will always be some scarring, I can now say with confidence that the wound is well and truly healed.

My experience is not unique. Many women have been through what I went through, although we may have coped with it differently. Some may have gone to the police straight away, others may have told loved ones and friends or sought the help of counsellors and support groups. Others may still be living in a permanent state of denial or not have the support or opportunity to deal with their experience. I think what unites us all is our fear that other people will blame us for our ordeal or think less of us because of it.

It doesn't bother me now what other people think. I know that I was not to blame and that's what matters. What's more, I no longer see myself as a victim or even a survivor; that would only be letting my assailants win. I am a victor who has got her life back again. At long last my demons have been exorcised.

READING 54

Demands from the Women of Antioch

Kristine Herman

The women of Antioch, in response to the recent rapes on campus, demand that the following become Antioch College policy:

1. That a community member who is accused of rape shall immediately (within twenty-four hours of the report of rape) be removed from campus until guilt is assessed; and that if this person is determined to be guilty, that s/he shall be immediately and permanently removed from the Antioch community (a student must be expelled, an employee must be fired);

2. That the Dean of Students and/or the Advocate shall immediately inform the community that a rape has occurred; and that the rape survivor shall determine whether the name of the rapist and/or the name of the survivor shall be publicized;

3. That the rape survivor be informed of her/his rights; and informed of, supported with, her/his rights to prosecute;

4. That a support network be established for rape survivors that includes a new position, a woman Advocate who could act as the rape survivor's representative, and who would ensure that disciplinary measures against the rapist be carried out. This Advocate shall be given the power to enact the above disciplinary measures against said rapist;

5. That a one-credit PE self-defense course shall be offered each quarter;

6. That orientation shall incorporate rape education, rape awareness, and consent workshops for men and women;

7. That a permanent support group for survivors of rape and sexual assault be established in the counseling center.

If these demands are not met by November 13, 1990, we, the women of Antioch, will (1) inform the Antioch community of this lack of support for rape survivors; (2) distribute a (national) press release detailing Antioch College's lack of support for rape survivors and discussing the recent rapes on campus and the lack of effective

Source: Just Sex: Students Rewrite the Rules on Sex, Violence, Activism, and Equality, ed. Jodi Gold and Susan Villari. Copyright © 2000. Rowman & Littlefield.

disciplinary measures taken, and (3) hold a Day of Action wherein radical physical measures will be taken.

—Created 5 November 1990

THE DEVELOPMENT OF THE ANTIOCH COLLEGE SEXUAL OFFENSE POLICY

This list of demands was formulated by women in the Antioch community after being outraged at administrative handling of two reported rapes on campus. There would be a policy and protocol established specific to sexual offense, even if it meant that some women would sacrifice credits, sleep, sanity, and their degrees.

It took enormous efforts on the part of many women at Antioch to get the Antioch Sexual Offense Policy implemented at last, a policy known nationally as radical, innovative, and, to some, extreme. The policy has been viewed as both paternalistic—for coddling women and treating them as inherent victims —and empowering for both men and women—because of its reliance on verbal consent. But only those of us who were there, saw it come together, understand its history, and lived under it truly know how important and monumental the policy is in the movement to prevent and fight sexual violence.

I entered Antioch College, a small liberal arts college located in Yellow Springs, Ohio, in 1990 at the age of seventeen. Antioch is known for its commitment to social justice and political activism. I began confronting my experience as a rape survivor in the context of the two reported rapes on campus and the early formulations of the Sexual Offense Policy. I nervously attended meetings and participated in the larger protests, but my attitude about the policy was that it was too harsh.

I arrived at college believing that rape was wrong . . . but if a woman was drinking, well, then things became a little ambitious. After I was raped at the age of thirteen, I internalized the messages that tell us we are responsible and that you can't blame a guy for taking advantage of a situation if, after all, you asked for it. Instead of feeling angry, I felt guilt and embarrassment.

That fall of 1990 there were two reported rapes of students by students. In each incident the woman knew her perpetrator and reported the rape to the dean. At that time there existed only an ambiguous written policy addressing sexual harassment. The dean of students spoke with the perpetrators and made her decision as to what disciplinary measures would be taken if any.

One woman's perpetrator was removed from campus but remained enrolled. The other woman's perpetrator was not removed from campus. This lax administrative response to these rapes enraged the women at Antioch and led to the list of demands that ended in the student-initiated Sexual Offense Policy. Emergency meetings at the Women's Center drew nightly crowds of over fifty women to discuss and strategize a response to the inadequate administrative response to rape. The meetings were emotional and volatile, as we found divisions among the women's community at Antioch. Some women thought that we should allow input from the men at Antioch; other women felt strongly that we had waited long enough and that support from men was welcomed but their input was not. In the end, men were not involved in the drafting of the original policy.

Over the course of a few crucial days political actions were staged to get the need for a Sexual Offense Policy on the college's official agenda. Over thirty women stood silently along the walls during a meeting of the Advisory Committee to the President: dressed in black, rape whistles hanging symbolically from their necks. This action successfully pressured the committee into putting The List on the committee agenda. Another action, intended to demonstrate the prevalence of rape and enlist the support of other students, took place at one of our weekly campus community meetings. Every six minutes a woman broke out crying as a piece of duct tape was slapped on her back with the word "RAPED" written across it, reflecting that every six minutes a woman is raped in the United States.

A group of fifteen third- and fourth-year women students, many of them friends of the survivors of the two on-campus rapes, wrote the first draft of the Antioch Sexual Offense Policy. Some were so dedicated that they sacrificed graduation because so much time and energy went into developing the policy.

The policy was intended to outline the protocol for addressing incidents of sexual offense on our campus, but it was obvious that to do so required defining what was and was not a sexual offense. The Antioch Sexual Offense Policy outlined six forms of sexual offense: rape (any nonconsensual penetration of the vagina or anus, nonconsensual fellatio or cunnilingus); sexual assault (nonconsensual sexual conduct exclusive of that included in the definition of rape, but including attempted penetrations, attempted fellatio, or attempted cunnilingus); sexual imposition (nonconsensual sexual contact that includes the touching of thighs, genitals, buttocks, the pubic region, or the breast/chest area); insistent/persistent sexual harassment (insistent/persistent emotional, mental, or verbal intimidation or abuse found to be sexually threatening or offensive); nondisclosure of a known positive HIV status or other known sexually transmitted disease. The Sexual Offense Policy requires that all sexual conduct and contact with an Antioch community member must be consensual.

The policy defines consent as "the act of willingly and verbally agreeing to engage in specific sexual act of conduct." It requires consent by all parties in a sexual encounter and states that "obtaining consent is an ongoing process in any sexual interaction. Verbal con-

sent should be given with each new level of physical and/or sexual contact in any given interaction." The media latched on to this controversial element. Camille Paglia found the policy absurd "as if sex occurs on the verbal realm," a belief that is dangerously reminiscent of outdated notions of what sex should be like in an age that sees AIDS as the number-one killer of people between the ages of twenty-three to forty-four years of age, and when one in four college women are victims of rape or attempted rape.

The bulk of the policy is devoted to the procedures available when a sexual offense has occurred. A gradated list of remedies is included in the policy; for instance, an individual found to have committed rape according to the policy's definition is to be expelled immediately, whereas someone found to have been in violation of the policy's definition of sexual imposition may receive suspension or be required to undergo some sort of educational/counseling program.

Equally important in the policy is the element of antirape education, including mandatory sexual consent workshops for all students, and self-defense courses. The Sexual Offense Prevention and Survivors' Advocacy Program features year-round antirape education, residence advisor training, and group and individual counseling services for survivors of rape and sexual abuse.

The Sexual Offense Prevention and Survivors' Advocacy Program was beginning to develop by my second year at college. I came to know other survivors, hear their stories, and I grew angry. I was seeing patterns of violence, not the sporadic, unrelated occurrences of rape by a stranger in the bushes at knife point. My involvement as an advocate for survivors of rape began and grew; I became a residence advisor for a dorm of first-year women and became active in community politics. My opinion about the policy changed drastically, and my job as a residence advisor convinced me that anything short of verbal and willing consent could result in a harmful "sexual experience." In this role I witnessed several first-year students, many of them seventeen years old, assaulted and raped, often under the influence of alcohol. These women came to me, slept in my room because of nightmares or fear of being alone, and asked for support. They needed to be told of their right not to be victimized, regardless of how much they had to drink or whether or not they were flirting, brought someone back to their room, or made the first move to kiss.

In light of these experiences I became convinced that the important work had to begin with prevention—not the standard "teaching women how not to fall prey to sexual victimization," as if the responsibility once again lies with the victim, but addressing the potential perpetrators and circumstances that lend themselves to sexual violence. The emphasis on consent in the policy attempts to do just that, by requiring people to obtain verbal consent for every level of a sexual interaction, and by trying to eliminate the gray areas that exist when people make silent assumptions about what their partner wants, then act without consulting their partner.

Undoubtedly the Antioch Sexual Offense Policy validated all women's and men's rights not to be sexually victimized. By requiring all persons to seek verbal consent, permission, for each new level of a sexual interaction, responsibility is shifted to the initiator of sexual contact. I felt tremendously empowered living on a campus where I was supposed to be asked before being touched, where my voice was required to be heard. Silence does not equal consent. As a survivor struggling to regain a healthy sense of sexuality, it was much easier for me to say no once I was asked than for me to stop nonconsensual advances once someone

has already violated my boundaries. For many survivors it is extremely difficult to voice an objection when it is apparent that someone is just moving ahead physically. A freezing phenomenon occurs, wherein we shut down and just wait for it to be over because it has proved either futile to protest a sexual offense in our pasts, or too scary a situation. This is particularly true when there is a noticeable difference in size and physical stature between the survivor and the person we are with. Being asked gives us the space as well as the confidence that our opinion will be respected this time, that this person wants to make sure that we want to move forward physically too.

In June of 1992 the final revision of the Antioch Sexual Offense Policy was passed by the Advisory Committee to the President and approved by the University Board of Directors. The next two entering classes attended mandatory workshops designed to educate students about the policy and its definition of "consent," and to address the importance of, and new students' concerns about, living under the policy. As a result of these workshops and ongoing campus dialogue, the idea of verbal consent was no longer so shocking. The controversy around the Sexual Offense Policy had died down.

In late 1993 a reporter for the *San Francisco Examiner* mentioned the Antioch Sexual Offense Policy in a story about a California campus rape. Immediately following the *Examiner* article, Jane Gross of the *New York Times* did an in-depth article about the Antioch policy, which led to the AP newswire running the story worldwide; and so began the media explosion of 1993. During the 1993–94 academic year, Antioch received visits from, and provided interviews for, hundreds of national and international publications and radio and television programs.

By this point I was working in antirape education in several capacities: I facilitated sexual consent workshops; consulted with the police department regarding their sexual assault protocol; served as an advocate for survivors of sexual offense on campus; and worked as liaison to the Sexual Offense Prevention and Survivors' Advocacy Program for the Student Housing Office. As a result I was asked by the college administration to be a media spokesperson. I participated in panels at nearly a dozen universities and appeared on numerous television and radio programs and talk shows.

The policy, as it received global recognition and attention from figures such as Rush Limbaugh, Katie Roiphe, Camille Paglia, and Doctor Ruth, was criticized on a number of levels, many of which were riddled with misinformation about its contents. Instead of the policy's being viewed as an instrument by which we hoped to curtail the incidence of sexual violence on our campus, we were seen as legislating sex.

MEDIA INTERPRETATION AND RESPONSE FROM OUTSIDE

The media, within their own limited scope and understanding of the policy, defined it in terms of its effects on sexual interactions according to gender roles only. This artificial polarization of men's and women's interests was not based in the reality of the Antioch policy but was an oversimplification of the issue of sexual violence on college campuses. Media coverage framed the Antioch policy in a way that divided men and women into groups with conflicting and competing interests, instead of portraying a policy that created a cohesive community devoted to eliminating the frequency with which sexual violence is perpetrated on college campuses.

A widely ignored aspect of the policy was its intentionally non-gender-specific language. The Antioch Policy recognizes, acknowledges, and validates that men and women can be raped, and that both men and women can be perpetrators of sexual violence. The policy strives to be nonheterosexist and is inclusive of all sexual orientations. To describe the policy as "requiring men to ask women at each level of a sexual interaction" excludes a large portion of our campus and society who are gay, lesbian, and bisexual, and does not acknowledge that sexual violence occurs between people of the same sex.

The policy has also been criticized under the notion that it limits the spontaneity of romantic sexual relations and unrealistically burdens students to talk about sex. Anyone who is currently sexually active must be aware of the dangers of STD/HIV/AIDS infection and the necessity to talk about safer sex. This alone makes the idea of nonverbal sex both outdated and dangerous. Communication is a vital component of sexual interaction. When verbal communication is not a central part of a sexual encounter, false assumptions occur that can result in a sexual assault.

The media have contributed to a backlash against women and the antirape movement by misdirecting the issues. Instead of accurately gathering data on the incidence of rape on college campuses, the media have responded with a different slant to the debates about rape, prevention, and sexual relations. An example of the minimization of the problem of rape can be found in Dr. Ruth Westheimer's comments about the Antioch Sexual Offense Policy on *Eye to Eye with Connie Chung*. Dr. Ruth chose to focus not on rape or sexual assault at all, but instead on the way the policy might affect a man's ability to maintain an erection if he is expected to be verbal during a sexual encounter. This clearly demonstrates the priorities of mainstream media when addressing a movement focused on the prevention of sexual violence.

Part of the fascination about the policy was that it actually redefined rape, and in doing so threatened the ways in which we have all been socialized to conceptualize sex. In the context of the Clarence Thomas hearings and the Lorena Bobbitt story, discussions about sexual abuse, harassment, and rape were occurring nationally. The Antioch Sexual Offense Policy contributed to this debate.

The implications of the necessity for verbal consent are vast in that we, culturally, must look at the mechanisms by which people are socialized and the messages that are sent regarding sexual relations. The *Connie Chung* segment showed a clip from the movie classic *Gone with the Wind,* where Rhett Butler whisks Scarlett O'Hara into his arms as she struggles to get away, beating on him as he carries her up the stairs to their bedroom. The next day she is happy and giddy, implying that she really wanted it or at least enjoyed it. We used to view this—the woman saying no when she really means yes—as a romantic scene; many still do. By Antioch definitions, and considering many of the shifting attitudes about rape, this could now be viewed as a rape scene.

The media's focus on the Antioch Sexual Offense Policy diverted a strong movement of antirape education toward addressing issues of old-fashioned notions about spontaneity, what it means to be romantic, and how the burden of verbal consent will affect men. This is not surprising, given that acceptance of Antioch's definitions of sexual violence, and the expectation of consent, forces us all to reexamine our own sexual histories. Many of us find that we have ambiguous and uncomfortable pasts—we may have done something that could now be called sexual assault, or we may have experienced a sexual assault but did not call it so at the time.

Challenging "traditional" beliefs about sex has resulted in societal defensiveness and negative reactions to documents such as the Antioch policy, and other instances whereby the status quo is shaken. Another example of this type of response can be seen in the battle against homophobia. Some major corporations are finally beginning to acknowledge domestic partnerships, while some states are responding by passing discriminatory homophobic legislature. The struggles of all women, people of color, and gay, lesbian, and bisexual people overlap in that they threaten to disrupt the dominant paradigm.

Though the general public missed the urgent need for the policy, Antioch College received an incredible response from other universities, with over two hundred requested copies of the policy during the fall of 1993 alone.

POSTGRADUATION IMPACT

In my own life, as a second-year law student with a master's in social work, my work in the antirape movement continues. The Antioch Sexual Offense Policy affected my views on sex and power dynamics in sexual situations. Women and men are not on completely equal ground sexually; many women have internalized messages that tell us we owe sex if a man has spent a lot of money on us, or if we have allowed a situation to go to a certain point. A first-year man in a sexual consent workshop at Antioch once expressed what many men fear about the policy when he said, "But if I have to ask for what I want, I won't get it."

The Antioch Sexual Offense Policy introduced the importance of consent in sexual interactions. It aims to resocialize students to be verbal with each other in sexual situations in order to eliminate different perceptions of the same experience. The efforts of the original drafters of the policy, as well as all of us who participated, and the resulting document are something to be extremely proud of. For many the Antioch Sexual Offense Policy is the embodiment of the principle that the personal is political.

With the issue of sexual violence introduced into the public arena, we must now look at the directions that need to be explored to further decrease the prevalence of rape and sexual assaults on college campuses. Anthropologists such as Peggy Sanday, and feminist theorists such as bell hooks, have begun writing about a "rape culture." Some people consider this to be the third wave of the antirape movement, one that aggressively addresses rape, domestic violence, and sexual harassment in a new light, armed with social science research, statistics, and personal stories. What we have learned from the Antioch Sexual Offense Policy and from the efforts of students on campuses all over the United States is that we are involved in a process of learning from each other strategies, ideas, and tools to combat sexual violence on an interpersonal, campus, societal, national, and international level.

THE ANTIOCH COLLEGE SEXUAL OFFENSE POLICY

Approved by the Board of Trustees in June 1992

All sexual contact and conduct on the Antioch College campus and/or occurring with an Antioch community member must be consensual.

When a sexual offense, as defined herein, is committed by a community member, such action will not be tolerated.

Antioch College provides and maintains educational programs for all community members, some aspects of which are required. The educational aspects of this policy are intended to prevent sexual offenses and ultimately to heighten community awareness.

In support of this policy and community safety, a support network exists that consists of the Sexual Offense Prevention and Survivor's Advocacy Program and Counseling Services. The Advocate (or other designated adminis-

trator) shall be responsible for the initiation and coordination of measures required by this policy.

The implementation of this policy also utilizes established Antioch governance structures and adheres to contractual obligations.

CONSENT

1. For the purpose of this policy, "consent" shall be defined as follows: the act of willingly and verbally agreeing to engage in specific sexual contact or conduct.
2. If sexual contact and/or conduct is not mutually and simultaneously initiated, then the person who initiates sexual contact/conduct is responsible for getting verbal consent of the other individual(s) involved.
3. Obtaining consent is an ongoing process in any sexual interaction. Verbal consent should be obtained with each new level of physical and/or sexual contact/conduct in any sexual interaction, regardless of who initiates it. Asking "Do you want to have sex with me?" is not enough. The request for consent must be specific to each act.
4. The person with whom sexual contact/conduct is initiated is responsible to express verbally and/or physically her/his willingness or lack of willingness when reasonably possible.
5. If someone has initially consented but then stops consenting during sexual interaction, she/he should communicate withdrawal verbally and/or through physical resistance. The other individual(s) must stop immediately.
6. To knowingly take advantage of someone who is under the influence of alcohol, drugs, and/or prescribed medication is not acceptable behavior at Antioch College.

Excerpted from the actual policy distributed by Antioch College in June of 1992.

7. If someone verbally agrees to engage in specific contact or conduct, but it is not of her/his free will due to any circumstances stated in (a) through (d) below, then the person initiating shall be considered in violation of this policy if:

a) the person submitting is under the influence of alcohol or other substances supplied to her/him by the person initiating;

b) the person submitting is incapacitated by alcohol, drugs, and/or prescribed medication;

c) the person submitting is asleep or unconscious;

d) the person initiating has forced, threatened, coerced, or intimidated the other individual(s) into engaging in sexual contact and/or sexual conduct.

Breaking the Silence, Making Laughter: Testimony of An Asian-American Sister

Luoluo Hong

My sexual assault at age eighteen by a white male was a sexist act in which racial humiliation was wielded as the weapon. My sexual assault at age eighteen by a white male was also a racist act in which sexual degradation cut my soul. That night I experienced a total annihilation of my identity both as a woman and as an Asian American. As a result, I regarded both identities as weak, worthless, powerless, dirty, undesirable, and—most important—somehow responsible for my own victimization. In healing I discovered two contrasting elements embedded within my Asian American culture. The first was a tradition of female passivity that increased my vulnerability to the rape. Simultaneously, though, I

possessed the tools enabling me to cope with and accept the rape.

My perpetrator was twenty years old and heavily consumed pornography, particularly that involving Asian women. His name was Blake, and he was from Dallas, Texas—a state in which he assured me the "men were bigger and better" than anywhere else in the world. At six foot, two inches tall, and over 200 pounds, he was certainly big to me; I, at a petite five foot, five inches, just under 110 pounds, was no match for him. Blake and I were not dating at the time, merely casual acquaintances—he a sophomore and a member of the Men's Glee Club, and I the accompanist for that group, just finishing my first year at Amherst College. After our performance on Saturday, May 2, 1987, he followed me to my residence hall from the postconcert party and knocked at my door on the pretense of "checking up" on me. I drank six or seven beers at the party, and he was purportedly concerned about whether or not I had made it back to my room safely. He raped me three times that night. I cried; I pummeled my fists against his chest; I sobbed out "no" several times. A conqueror who tramples on another's dignity does not listen or pity, and Blake was no exception.

I went back to visit that room sometime during my sophomore year. When I caught a partial glimpse of the inside through a cracked door, memories overtook all of my senses: the scent of cheap bourbon on his breath and on his neck, the recklessness in his eyes as he ripped off my clothing and pinned down my arms and legs on that night of reckoning. The sweat drenched his body as he shoved his penis in and out of me, not caring that he hurt me. All the while he muttered things to me: "You looked so hot tonight in that dress," "Just relax and you'll like it better," and "I know that you've been wanting this, I could see it in your 'chink' eyes"—each statement further sealing my self-blame in the incident. Then he grunted like an animal when he ejaculated. By this time I was floating somewhere above, gazing down in self-pity and mourning at how helpless my body looked crushed beneath his. Even when he rolled over and fell asleep, I had no peace. He raped me two more times.

The next morning he awoke and got dressed. Kissing me on the cheek and rubbing my hair, he smiled and thanked me, saying he had a good time and that he would see me soon. Then he left to go to church, as nonchalantly as if we had gone on a respectable date. I slept for hours, waking up in the late afternoon to take a long, hot shower in a desperate attempt to wash his stench off my body. I changed the sheets on my bed. Frantically wadding up my clothes from the night before, I shoved them into a hamper, then donned white underwear and a white T-shirt. I didn't think I would ever feel clean again. Devoid of all feeling, I fell asleep again.

Blake returned to my room the following Wednesday at two in the morning. Like a zombie, I let him in the room. I wish I could tell you that I was the wiser for having been burned once. I wish I could tell you that I fought him off with kicks and scratches. I cannot tell you these things, for I no longer had anything to protest. I had no will to fight for myself, for I had no more value in my own eyes. The first rape eradicated my personal

and sexual boundaries. I lay there as Blake had his way with me, shell of a person that I was—unfeeling, unresponding, uncaring. I didn't know at the time that my experience is shared by nearly half of all women who survive rape.[1] It would be easy to conclude that having sex again with Blake meant that I wasn't raped in the first place—reflecting the essential irony in rape that the victim is blamed for her victimization. In fact, Catharine MacKinnon argues that until political and social power are redistributed in our society, all sexual intercourse experienced by women can be contextualized as coercive sex.[2] The first rape was forced sex; the incidents that ensued were coerced sex. By succumbing "willingly" on that second night, I could maintain a false sense of normalcy.

When I haltingly told my boyfriend, who was attending school in Washington, D.C., at the time, that somebody "took advantage" of me, he called me a "slut" and insinuated that I was cheating on him; we promptly ended our year-long relationship. When I met with a psychologist at the campus counseling center to get some help in understanding why I was feeling so depressed, she suggested that I refrain from using sex to rebel against my parents' strictness.

I had no vocabulary back then to describe what happened; "acquaintance rape" was a term that would later pervade the media headlines. Having internalized the stigma that society places on rape, I had yet to develop the awareness to label my experience for what it truly was. Rape was supposed to be something to be ashamed of for any woman, and especially for an Asian woman. Purity and virginity are valued even more earnestly in my culture than in the mainstream one. Denial was the easiest method of coping with my sexual assault.

Blake continued to sexually abuse me about two to three times a week for the next year and a half. Blake used any of a number of means to attain my "consent." He would track me down at parties, where, given my intoxicated state, I was unable to resist him. He might show up at my door at three or four o'clock in the morning, when the confusion of disturbed slumber also made me easy prey. Or he would simply cover my mouth with his hand to silence the protests and throw me against the wall or bed. He frequently wanted to "act out" a scene from a pornographic movie he had just watched.

I experienced sexual intercourse only two other times before Blake raped me. I therefore learned about my sexuality and about sex from him. I learned that it was painful, and that it was dirty. He did not hesitate to restrain me or hit me if I resisted, which was rarely. I never had an orgasm; he always did. I was subjected to sexual contact with him in every way imaginable: vaginal, oral, anal. I never cried out. I just didn't feel anything. Afterward, when he rolled over and fell asleep with loud snores, I would stare quietly into the darkness, trying to fight the feeling of nausea as I felt his semen seep out of me—he had marked me, much as a wolf marks his territory. Sometimes, to preserve my sanity, I would pretend that he and I were actually lovers, that he cared for me deeply.

Throughout the entire period of Blake's assaults, I remember very little about school and other events. I do know that I became very adept at predicting when Blake would come for me, and organized my academic demands accordingly. Sometimes I deliberately provoked his visits on a particular night to ensure a good night's sleep before an important exam—a rational response to an insane situation. I abused alcohol heavily, partially to numb the intense self-hatred I felt, and to alleviate the shame and humiliation of Blake's violation. My eating habits became sporadic. Already thin, I continued to lose more weight and experienced a thyroid disorder during my junior year of college. The inheritance of my

mother's mental instability—she battled several bouts of severe depression—stirred within me. At one point in February 1988 I seriously contemplated suicide; a phone call from my sister to inquire about life in general and about mundane details in particular convinced me otherwise.

My victimization did not occur in private. Blake bragged frequently of his sexual conquests among his fraternity brothers and other friends, and many of them approached me to go to bed with them. I usually didn't care whether or not I did; the deciding factor tended to be how intoxicated I was at the time. My emotionless sex with these faceless men, who cared nothing for me, were acts of self-mutilation, of self-deprecation—an attempt to be free of Blake. Blake did not hesitate from "pimping" me, either. He would bet his friends a case of beer that they couldn't get me to go to bed with them; some approached him and offered him a quarter keg for the privilege of "sampling the foreign goods." Incredibly, these men made no qualms about revealing or bragging about these transactions to me.

I sometimes wonder angrily how those who lived around me and with me in the residence halls over the fifteen months that Blake abused me did not realize what was going on; they saw my tearstained face in the early morning. They heard Blake's derogatory accounts; yet they could only conclude that I was a "whore" who didn't know any better. My closest women friends witnessed the struggles that preceded each rape, regarding me with eyes that pitied but showed no mercy; they blamed me in my own plight, my own victimization. Perhaps they were afraid to admit their own vulnerability; perhaps they just didn't know any better. Not until I came out of denial about the abuse did I realize that they, too, were co-opted into the social phenomenon of "rape culture," described by Dianne Herman as a culture in which men's and women's values and beliefs about heterosexual intercourse are molded on a model of forced sexual intercourse.[3] Such a culture renders what happened to me usual and unremarkable.

I wondered often if I had perhaps been aptly nicknamed Jezebel by my abuser—the connotation of that label haunts me still. I doubted my innocence in my own exploitation and wondered if in fact I had consented to those sexual horrors by my very failure to stop them. He would whisper, "Jezebel," with careless ease, wrapping my long black hair around his wrist or neck. I cut off that hair in the spring of 1990—a symbolic rite of passage into my newfound commitment to ardent feminism and female empowerment.

> Chinese-Americans, when you try to understand what things in you are Chinese, how do you separate what is peculiar to childhood, to poverty, insanities, one family, your mother who marked your growing with stories, from what is Chinese? What is Chinese tradition and what is the movies? (Maxine Hong Kingston, *The Woman Warrior*)

The scripted role of a Chinese daughter is the expectation of demure obedience and lackluster femininity. I conformed to the strict, traditional ways because I had a strong desire to please and to receive approval. Yet my inner self knew that what was being asked of me was not who I really was. The most fervent point of contention between my mother and me centered on dating: I was absolutely not allowed to date until I was twenty years old; parties at friends' houses were also banned. My days were filled with piano practice, reviewing lessons, and diligently completing my homework—all in an effort to maximize my chances of fulfilling the dreams my mother spun for me.

Deprived of typical social experiences, such as attending school dances or going to movies, I quickly learned that it was easier to manipulate my books and homework than to raze the insurmountable walls of protective tradition my mother so vehemently erected. I was socially awkward throughout high school, escaping into my studies. I was sweet and pliant, and all of my teachers liked me, but I had very few friends other than those I might study with, and no close friends. My primary companions were my sister and brother, both younger than I. While we occasionally fought, the friendship and kinship we felt were strengthened and unified both by the gaping emotional distance between us and our parents, and by our constant conflict with them. In the fighting between parents and children, battle lines were drawn not only across generational differences, but across cultural ones as well.

I longed for a strong and doting father figure, longed to be "daddy's little girl." I despised my father's seeming coldness and seeming absorption with what I considered the minutiae of life. He worked hard, tended to the maintenance of our house and our lawn with meticulous devotion, and occasionally graced us with his quick and stormy temper. Silently, we watched as mother and father cycled through stages of threatening divorce, only to succumb again to the ultimate Chinese duty of preserving the family, followed by a period of mutual indifference. Then the pattern repeated itself. We witnessed my father hitting my mother and dragging her down the basement stairs. Instead of abusing alcohol to ease his feelings of helplessness, my father emotionally and physically battered us. My mother destroyed entire dinnerware sets, hurling them at my father or at the floor. She often gathered us to her bosom to share her secret desires. She wished that she had never married and that we were never born to partake of this hell. Feeling unwanted, we vowed to disappoint our mother less often and achieve great things so that she might love us after all.

The feelings of helplessness and frustration I developed were bottled and left to simmer unnoticed throughout my teenage years. Preserving the family's honor and maintaining its harmony were of primary importance; we were taught always to "save face," which meant you did not discuss your problems with others. Each of us learned early on to conceal pain from outsiders. Counselors and psychologists especially were not in our repertoire of acceptable family contacts. We were encouraged to seek only each other's support, no matter how unsoothing it was, or to seek no support at all. In retrospect I see that I had no role model of a healthy relationship, and wonder often if my tolerance for abuse and violence was developing even before I was ever violated.

College bound at the tender age of seventeen, I vaguely comprehended the meaning of what it was to be Chinese American but yearned desperately to be free of those invisible chains and to join the outside world I knew as "American culture." I did not realize when I entered the gates of Amherst College—gates laden with decades of patriarchal tradition and academic excellence—into one of the premier liberal arts campuses in the country, that I would exit four years later with my most valuable lessons acquired not inside the classrooms but outside of them. I commenced my career as an undergraduate with the same hopes of any young adult who enters this stage of life, eager to meet the world, and hopeful that it would accept me and deem me worthy. I chose never to look back, at least not if I could help it.

> Asian-Americans are used as pawns in the power games of racism. We are often held up as model minorities to keep other minorities in line. One outcome of this has been to place Asian-Americans at odds with other people of color who question the legitimacy of our minority status. (Jean Kim, "The Limits of Cultural Enlightenment")

As are African American, Hispanic, and Native American women, Asian American women are caught in the double jeopardy of being both women and people of color. We derive our identity and cultural values from both race and gender. As such, we often experience "double jeopardy"—subjected to oppression because of our gender as well as our ethnicity. And, like other women of color, Asian American women for the most part have not participated actively in the U.S. feminist movement, a movement that since its inception has reflected predominantly white, middle-class values.[4] For Asian American and other women of color, participating in such a movement artificially separates gender identity from racial identity—often to the detriment of the latter. As Audre Lorde eloquently stated in her essay "There Is No Hierarchy of Oppressions," "I simply do not believe that one aspect of myself can possibly profit from the oppression of any other part of my identity."

According to Chow, Asian American women must resolve the tension between their Asian ethnic heritage and their adopted American values. This tension falls along four primary dimensions: (1) obedience versus independence; (2) collective (or familial) versus individual interest; (3) fatalism versus change; and (4) self-control versus self-expression or spontaneity. Resolving the dilemma involves creating a bicultural existence that successfully blends elements of both cultural domains.[5] On the one hand, adherence to traditional Asian values fosters submissiveness, passivity, and adaptiveness—characteristics that are not conducive to activism, that may also have increased my vulnerability to rape. On the other hand, acceptance of the American values of mastery of one's environment through change, assertiveness, and emotional expression are consistent with self-empowerment as well as with political activism. At the same time, however, my Chinese upbringing ultimately imbued me with the necessary strength and perseverance for surviving a life event as traumatic as rape—a rape that took place within the context of one of the most rape-prone societies in the modem world by Sanday's definition.[6] There are elements in each culture to keep and to discard

Given my own experience, I believe it is critical for Asian American women to participate in political and social activism that advances the status of women and of minorities in the United States. We need to alter the traditional roles that Asian women are expected to fulfill in the Asian home and redefine the image of Asian American women that is propagated in the U.S. mainstream culture. These battles are one and the same.

In my cultural heritage sons are inherently more valued than daughters. Financial and social power are transmitted through patriarchal lines in the family, and a woman is merely property of her father, her husband, her brother, or her son. In fact, she exists solely to honor them, by being a dutiful daughter, obedient wife, gracious sister, or sacrificing mother.[7] Some unknowing American males may buy into the myth that the ideal home life consists of a Japanese wife, a Chinese cook, and a Korean maid. The notion that Asian women embody the ultimate definition of femininity—fragile, dependent, pliant, childlike, and erotic—is widely propagated in the mass media, including television shows, mainstream movies, and pornography.[8] U.S. veterans of World War II, the Korean War, and the Vietnam War have brought back and disseminated a similar legacy, either with memories of sexual escapades with "geisha girls" and "China dolls," or with physical proof in the form of biracial children. According to the Coalition against Trafficking in Women—Asia, catalogs such as Lotus Blossom are widely distributed both in the United States and in Western Europe, targeting older middle- to upper-class men who are inclined to having a traditional-minded mate.[9]

In my own life I have had many potential dates—white, black, and Hispanic—say to me some variation of "I've always fantasized about being with an Oriental girl; I hear they treat their men really good." If I ever argued with them, some partners even expressed surprise, confessing that they expected Asian women to be more meek and agreeable.

The eroticization of Asian women's passivity creates several dilemmas. First, we are caught between a dual expectation of pleasure giving and self-restraint. Characterized as the purveyors of Oriental "secrets of lovemaking," Asian women are brought up to believe that we have no sexual identity or urges separate from our husbands; our bodies are for their pleasures only. Otherwise, sex is wrong—a shameful secret to be confined to the realm of wifely duties.

Second, insomuch as Asian women symbolize extreme femininity, we incite fear in men, so much so that they must beat us down, tie us down, hold us down. As Dworkin points out, boys and men will engage in violence against women to renounce whatever they have in common with women so as to experience no commonality with them.[10] Ironically, Asian women's passivity and vulnerability almost incite more violence, more silencing. We are battered; we are raped; we are murdered with very little afterthought. In pornography the most violent acts are perpetrated against Asian women; she is hung, cut, mutilated, defiled, and destroyed. For example, the December 1984 cover of *Penthouse* portrayed Asian girls being hung from trees in lynchlike fashion; this act was imitated when eight-year-old Jean Kar Har was left strangled, raped, and hanging in a tree in North Carolina in February of 1985. Portrayed as enduring any type of trespass or degradation, and vested with less value than a stray dog, the Asian female's personhood is blurred. Warshaw described the ways in which college women in general make ideal victims.[11] Asian women's greater silence makes us especially ideal victims, for we will rarely ever speak out or complain; to do so means "losing face" and shaming the family.

Violence and victimization become normalized for the Asian American female. This reality does not touch every Asian woman, but it defined my existence for a very long time.

> Truth is harder to bear than ignorance, and so ignorance is valued more—also because the status quo depends on it; but love depends on self-knowledge, and self-knowledge depends on being able to bear the truth. (Andrea Dworkin, *Intercourse*)

Blake's transgressions ended in October of 1988 when he was expelled from Amherst College for violating academic probation. I do not know when the abuse would have ended if he had not left. I certainly had not yet reached a sufficient stage of empowerment to leave him. I first came out of denial and found a name for what happened to me after reading *I Never Called It Rape* by Robin Warshaw, a book about acquaintance rape on campus. That was one of the most cathartic experiences of my life. Reading the book conferred on me the power of naming, the power that "enables men to define experience, to articulate boundaries and values, to designate each thing its realm and qualities, to determine what can and cannot be expressed, to control perception itself." For the first time in my life, I was able to conceive of the notion that what happened was not entirely my fault or of my asking. I name my experience for what it was: rape—not a mistake I made, not "boys will be boys," not a "night to regret."

I asked the one essential question every rape survivor asks: Why me? Until I realized that there was no meaningful answer for this question, I could move no further with my recovery. It was obviously too late to report the assault to police. I searched for another means to reclaim control. Besides, I doubted that the legal system, bereft of objectivity in matters of sexual violence, had the capacity to accommodate my case. My experience would be with me for the rest of my life affecting the way I

think, respond, and behave. The wound would heal, but the scars would remain forever—an important reminder of the pain I had experienced and the growth I would come to know.

Early in my recovery, flashbacks and nightmares invaded my consciousness. Every glimpse of khaki pants worn with Dock-Siders shoes and no socks, coupled with clean-cut good looks, would vividly remind me of Blake. Momentarily, my breathing would stop, I would get a choking feeling in my throat, and a wave of nausea would hit my stomach. I also began to have a recurrent nightmare in which I chopped Blake up into hundreds of little pieces with an ax, filling the bathtub with his blood and evil. When the police knocked on the door, I desperately stuffed the evidence of my revenge into plastic garbage bags and buried them in the backyard. I woke up time and time again from this horrifying dream with a constricted feeling in my chest. This dream was most vivid in the beginning of my healing. The intensity abated as I came to terms with the plethora of my emotions. Reading the work of Burgess and Holmstrom, I realized that my reactions and feelings were a natural part of healing from rape.[12]

My shame was overwhelming. Why had I let him do those things to me? Of course, it was years before I realized that I did not "let him" do anything; those things were done to me. At age twenty, I needed to develop a viable language for discussing subjects that were taboo in traditional Asian culture—sex, sexuality, rape, and violence. I also felt guilty, as if I had let my parents down by not being more cautious and careful.

I learned how to feel and express anger. Such emotions were not acceptable in my childhood. For Asians, anger constitutes an imbalance in what should be a predominantly intellectual, analytical mind, as opposed to an emotional, irrational one. As such, any such outpourings were punished. Now I certainly had plenty of opportunity to practice anger.

Music became an outlet for my anger, even as it became a source of my pain. I studied and performed as a pianist for over seventeen years. Blake would watch me play during Glee Club rehearsals and concerts; he attributed to me the magnetism of a mythological siren, like one of those who tempted Odysseus. Music became tainted with the seduction perceived by Blake, even as it was also a source of control and escape—an outlet for communicating my pain and hope—throughout much of the sexual abuse. I could not let Blake take my music away; it was mine. At times the poetry of Chopin or Debussy were the only outlets for voicing the agony and reclamation for which I then had no words. I bought a piano in 1995 before I possessed any other real furniture in my apartment. My playing has become less frequent since graduating from college, but I will listen to recordings of my performances, particularly the one of Chopin's Piano Concerto No.2 in F Minor—it captures both the anger the hope that Blake's act engraved on my spirit.

Healing from violence took all of the courage I could muster. To ease the psychological pain that could so suddenly overwhelm me in remembering, I developed an infectious, jaded sense of humor. Humor was sometimes the only way to cope with what I had lost, and laughter was my salvation, for it refurbished the warmth of my inner core. Though I was quiet and reserved as an adolescent, my adult personality began to take shape.

Ironically, being raped conferred upon me a strength and an invaluable insight that I would exchange for nothing. I am no longer ashamed to say, "I am a rape survivor." Having lost so much, I reprioritized my goals, wants, and desires, as well as what I thought was important. I became an activist instead of a reactionist. I sought to reclaim my soul and my existence.

I reevaluated and changed my career goals; turning my back on both medical school and law school, I instead pursued the true calling in my heart: teaching. It was an opportunity to help others and, in so doing, heal myself. I realized that what happened to me wasn't only the fault of one man, but the responsibility of an entire society's cultural norms.

I was hired as a peer health educator two weeks after Blake raped me: Destiny does work in surprising and purposeful ways. This field appealed tremendously to me, even before the full import of why it probably did was revealed. It energized me in a manner that nothing else ever did, including music. It was as if I was desperately trying to reach out to others and help shield them from experiencing the harm that I had experienced. To this day I believe wholeheartedly that I would not have found health education as my chosen profession and lifelong commitment if not for Blake. Through my commitment I take back what he stole. During my senior year of college I publicly revealed my status as a rape survivor and founded a self-help support group for other women on campus who had experienced sexual violence. I lovingly called it H.E.R.S.—Helping and Empowering Rape Survivors. That acronym consumed hours of brain power to generate, I assure you. The response at the first meeting, when it convened in January 1990, was remarkable: Eight women showed up. The group continued to grow over time. Sharing with these other survivors, as well as validating each other's pain and growth, was essential for me in confronting the rape. Our newly forged bond culminated when, bearing a banner that we designed and signed, we marched in Take Back the Night during April 1990.

My recovery was marked by what became almost an obsession with any topic related to sexual assault: culture, media, substance abuse, eating disorders, sex role socialization, and so on. I consumed books, journal articles, movies, news articles, reports, and anything else that addressed rape with a voracious appetite. I wanted to learn everything there was to know about it. I also did things in the hope of reducing rape in our society. I wrote my master's thesis on it. I presented at national conferences. I volunteered and worked at local rape crisis centers both in New Haven, Connecticut, and here in Baton Rouge, Louisiana. I spoke out publicly as a survivor whenever and wherever appropriate. Violence became my area of expertise as a health educator and consultant. I also advise Men against Violence at Louisiana State University, where I now work as a health educator. The first campus organization of its kind, MAV focuses on men's role in fostering cultural change. Working with the group has been immensely healing.

Eminent in my healing was learning to take care of myself again. First, I learned to forgive myself, then accept and love myself again. My self-esteem had to be rebuilt. Being treated badly can become a comfortable habit, and just as difficult to break. After having my will repeatedly thwarted and ignored and trampled on for so long, succumbing to another's will became the default, the path of least resistance—and of least physical harm. My personality exhibits a situational schizophrenia that always fascinates me. Although I am confident and assertive in academic and professional situations, assuming leadership roles with ease and excelling in organizational tasks, I have failed to be so in my relationships with men until very recently. That side of my life was instead beset with crisis after crisis. Setting boundaries, both physical and emotional, is a skill that I must continually and consciously work on.

The reaction of friends and boyfriends when I finally chose to disclose that I was a rape survivor became of importance, as well. I became very adept at picking those whom I could tell. I wanted those close to me to understand that this experience greatly altered my life, but not to perceive me as being somehow vulnerable or weak, "messed up" or unstable, "used" or "dirty." Most were unable to comprehend the sexual abuse in its entirety and found it more comfortable to blithely ignore the subject. Some, of course, blamed me for putting myself in harm's way; a few did not believe me. A key point of contention for many when I share my story is whether or not I had been clear about my nonconsent with Blake. I don't know: I always thought that "no" was pretty clear in every language, even by most "reasonable woman standards." Frankly, the issues were too volatile for most of my friends to handle logically, objectively. Their blaming questions only further implicated me in my own victimization: "Why didn't I go to the police?" "Why didn't I just stop the abuse?"

Only a special few—many of them survivors themselves—regarded my telling as a gift that I bestowed upon them: I shared something of deep magnitude as far as explaining who I was and defining what I wanted to be. My younger sister and brother both know. Someday I hope I will be able to tell my parents, too; the fear of their disownment—maybe unfounded—stops me from doing so thus far.

It was always hardest for me to tell partners. Men seem always to take this sort of thing personally. The white men and the men of color whom I dated exhibited different reactions. White men were generally appalled and disgusted at the horror committed by a fellow male and rushed to separate themselves from those kinds of "pigs." They approached me with the attitude of a carpenter about to repair a broken piece of furniture; they assumed I needed fixing, protecting, and shielding. In other words, the rape was a big deal; they did not like to talk about it or hear the real details, which were too degrading. It was enough to be assured that they were not like my rapist. I have a theory that rape is only too characteristic of white men as a whole, committing innumerable unpunished crimes against women and nonwhites throughout all of history; if I were a white man, I suppose the burden of that guilt would be best left unattended. Black men, however, having survived prejudice and discrimination at the hands of white men since the slavery era, had a more palatable, supportive perspective about sexual violence. Oppression became a bond that we could share. Rape was something that strengthened me; I received their empathy, not pity.

I defied that most basic of Asian tenets that demands "saving face." It is only through the support of those close to me and the help of mental health professionals, as well as through speaking out, that I will be able to continue the lifelong process of healing. Building walls around myself will not shield me from pain or shame; they only confine them within me to fester. As a Chinese proverb cautions, "Dry ground only cracks; nothing will grow there until it has softened."

> Being in this intimate relationship with my young body, I grew to understand and confirm three things: my body belongs exclusively to me, my soul is not at rest when my body is detached, and we (body and soul) must take good care of each other. (Pamela R. Fletcher, "Whose Body Is It Anyway?")

My physical self-image suffered tremendously as a result of such long-term sexual abuse. When I looked at myself in the mirror, what stared back was the face of a woman attached to the body of a child. My dark eyes, olive skin, and sensuous, full bottom lip were maturely provocative, but my flat breasts and narrow hips were prepubescent. I was attractive by most standards, and beautiful to some. Historically for me, though, attractiveness conveyed danger: It invited further victimization. I wanted to be sexually desirable, yet I was

afraid that it would result in unwanted sexual aggression. In recent years, as I have been better able to accept my sexuality, my physical self-image has improved accordingly. I have allowed the passionate and sensual aspects of my personality to emerge, and I have enjoyed the maturation of my body into more womanly curves. This stage of healing was especially difficult to reach but critical. While feminists stress that rape is a crime of power, not of passion, the act of rape has ramifications on the sexual self.

After coming out of denial about my rape, I confronted the uncomfortable fact of how many men I had slept with during the alcohol-drenched mental haze that characterized the period of my sexual abuse. I had yet to take ownership of my sexuality. At nearly twenty-one years old, I had never experienced an orgasm—didn't even know such a thing existed for women. Inevitably, I went through a period for almost two years, spanning my senior year and into my first year of graduate school, during which the very thought of a man touching me was downright revolting. This was a cleansing period, an opportunity to foster my "second virginity," so to speak. As I ended my first year of graduate work toward a master's of public health at Yale University, I was ready to develop a sexual self defined in my own terms.

I participated in sex that I wanted, that I chose to have. I learned to separate sex from humiliation. At first certain sexual positions and certain smells would cause me to have flashbacks about Blake. As I gradually reconditioned myself to associate sex with pleasure instead of humiliation, these flashbacks waned in frequency. With each additional positive sexual encounter, my feelings of vulnerability dissipated and I began to trust men in sexual situations. I entered a stage of sexual abandon and freedom during which I explored the limits of how my partner and I could make our bodies feel good. I consumed my partners with the voracity of someone who had stumbled upon a full bottle of Thirst Quencher after hours of running under a hot sun.

Ultimately, developing a healthy romantic relationship is an important landmark in recovery. This has been perhaps the greatest challenge for me. For a long time I believed that I didn't deserve happiness with a caring partner because of what happened to me—I was "used goods," tainted and soiled by the rape and sexual abuse. I have stayed in some lousy relationships because of this feeling— sometimes repeating the abusive pattern I experienced with Blake.

The advantage of being in so many unhealthy relationships is that you learn what a healthy one looks and feels like. For me a healthy relationship entails finding the appropriate balance between two contrasting states. On the one hand, to share intimacy with another person means rendering yourself vulnerable; I, however, have many secrets, many of which are still somewhat shameful for me. So the pressure of being able to open myself up completely without fear of being rejected for my past or for my periodic insanity is tremendous and scary. At the same time, a relationship also means being able to assert yourself and set boundaries, so that the interdependence does not become codependent but instead fosters mutual growth. With my history of long-term abuse, this aspect of a relationship is unfamiliar and uncomfortable. Because we are rarely taught the appropriate skills and know-how by our parents, mentors, and other adults, healthy relationships are certainly hard work for anybody. They are especially challenging for a rape survivor. Bad habits must first be unlearned with great reluctance and then rescripted with new, healthy ones.

I now live and work in Baton Rouge, Louisiana. I think I left the North in some vain attempt to escape what happened to me in college. I know now that I will never outrun it. I function in a constant state of vulnerability; being raped doesn't confer some sort of immunity on you, like having the chicken pox, because rape isn't about what the victim does. It is all about what the aggressor wants.

I completed a Ph.D. in educational leadership and research in December 1998. I was promoted in June 1998 and now oversee health education, disability services, and the Women's Center at Louisiana State University. In addition, I volunteer at the local rape crisis center. Most recently, I have been traveling to campuses all over the United States as a speaker and consultant with the agency CAMPUSPEAK. Eventually, I hope to write and lecture on a full-time basis.

After nearly two years of court proceedings, my parents divorced in 1994; both reside in Connecticut. My sister, also a health educator, lives in Chicago, while my brother is about to complete his senior year at the University of Pennsylvania. My sister and I have raised him to respect women, and to respect himself. I live with Toby, a cocker spaniel with a wonderfully affectionate and malleable temperament, and six cats named Mozart, Whitney, Aiwa, Bacchus, Athena, and Puck. I'm entering that decade in life when my closest women friends (whom I treasure) are starting to get married and have babies. I myself have settled comfortably into a tender, stable, and healthy relationship with a Nordic from Wisconsin. Through his acceptance and understanding, he has been a part of my healing. Most important, he has taught me that I am worthy of being loved, and he has allowed my sexuality to be my own. We eloped in February 1998. Married life suits me; I found my soulmate.

I am very compulsive; I hate messy rooms, kitchens, or bathrooms. Sometimes I check whether I've locked the door at night three or four times before I go to bed. I obsess about it when I go out of town. I suppose these are efforts at maintaining control in a world that I know can be so uncontrollable. I love to cook.

I love John Grisham novels. I love to dance; there is nothing as freeing as dancing for hours to music with a driving bass beat and then leaving the club drenched with perspiration. These are my hobbies, my home, my family, and friends—you see, I was raped, but I'm still me.

Recovery is forever. In Mandarin Chinese my given name means "happiness"—combined with my family name ("Hong" means "great" or "abundant"), my name means "great joy," or "music." The blessing that my mother gave me has been slow to coalesce. These days I am happy most of the time. I deliberately live life to its fullest because I know how tenuous one's hold on it can be. There are days, sometimes weeks, when I am engulfed by self-pity and mourning for the innocence and health that were stolen from me, for the mistakes that I made but could never change, for the pain that the sexual abuse has caused in my life and in those around me. These periods occur less frequently as the years wane. Usually, though, I am very much in touch with living. Each day that I learn and give and think and plan and look ahead, I am striving to repair all the damage that my rapist wreaked— to take back the control he not only took away but almost destroyed. By breaking the silence, I am reclaiming that which was stolen, and reframing that which was horrible and unspeakable. I will never give Blake the satisfaction that I succumbed to the ugliness and darkness he brought into my life. In fact, I am laughing. I just wonder if Blake would ever get the joke.

NOTES

1. Mary P. Koss, Christine A. Gidycz, and N. Wisniewski, "The Scope of Rape: Incidence and Prevalence of Sexual Aggression and Victimization in a National Sample of Higher Education Students," *Journal of Consulting and Clinical Psychology* 55 (1987): 162–70.
2. Catharine MacKinnon, *Feminism Unmodified* (Cambridge, Mass.: Harvard University Press, 1987).
3. Dianne Herman, "Rape Culture," in *Women: A Feminist Perspective*, 4th ed., ed. Jo Freeman (Mountain View, Calif.: Mayfield, 1989).
4. Esther Ngan-Ling Chow, "The Feminist Movement: Where Are All the Asian American Women?" In *Making Waves: An Anthology of Writings by and about Asian American Women*, ed. Asian Women United of California (Boston: Beacon Press, 1989).
5. Esther Ngan-Ling Chow, *Acculturation of Asian American Professional Women* (Research Monograph) (Washington, D.C.: National Institute of Mental Health, Department of Health and Human Services, 1982).
6. Peggy Sanday, "The Sociocultural Context of Rape: A Cross-Cultural Study," *Journal of Social Issues* 37 (1981): 5–27.
7. Chow, 1989.
8. Renee E. Tajima, "Lotus Blossoms Don't Bleed: Images of Asian Women," in *Making Waves: An Anthology of Writings by and about Asian American Women*, ed. Asian Women United of California (Boston: Beacon Press, 1989).
9. Anne Mi Ok Bruining, "Speak Out: Working with Asian Women," in *Reclaiming Our Lives: A Training Manual for Those Working with Victims/Survivors of Sexual Assault*, ed. Elba Crespo and Candace Waldron (Boston: Massachusetts Department of Public Health, Women's Health Unit, 1987).
10. Andrea Dworkin, *Pornography: Men Possessing Women* (New York: E. P. Dutton, 1979), 53.
11. Robin Warshaw, *I Never Called It Rape* (New York: Harper and Row, 1988). Dworkin, *Pornography*, 17.
12. Ann W. Burgess and Lynda L. Holmstrom, *Rape: Crisis and Recovery* (Bowie, Md.: Robert J. Brady, 1979).

Male Rape Victims in Prison Get Little Empathy

Rape is a little documented but well known fact of life for the incarcerated, and it comes with few legal remedies.

A recent Human Rights Watch study on the prevalence of rape in male prisons revealed scarce definitive numbers. One anonymous southern state reported that inmates estimated that 1 in 3 prisoners were forced into sex, but prison guards put the number at 1 in 5. Meanwhile, administrators said only 1 in 8 prisoners were victims of sexual abuse.

Truth is, penal and legal officials may never know how many inmates are subjected

to forced sex, instead assuming acts to be consensual.

"Many inmates find that when they try to report a rape, the guards don't want to hear it," says Joanne Mariner, a Human Right Watch attorney. "They tell them to act like a man, to deal with the problem themselves. There are very few prisons that follow good procedures for counseling, or sending inmates for a medical examination."

Nearly one-half of states do not collect data on the topic. Some only do it haphazardly. A 1996 Nebraska survey found that 21 percent of inmates that that they had been coerced into sexual contact, and about 7 percent said they had been raped. One year later, the state told Human Rights Watch such incidents were "minimal."

About two million American men are in prison. Only four states and the Federal Bureau of Prison reported more than 50 cases of sexual assaults to Human Rights Watch. (*New York Times*, April 15)

Men On Rape: What They Have to Say about Sexual Violence

Timothy Beneke

Rape may be America's fastest growing violent crime; no one can be certain because it is not clear whether more rapes are being committed or reported. It *is* clear that violence against women is widespread and fundamentally alters the meaning of life for women; that sexual violence is encouraged in a variety of ways in American culture; and that women are often blamed for rape.

What is often missed when people contemplate rape is the effect of the *threat* of sexual violence on women. I have asked women repeatedly, "How would your life be different if rape were suddenly to end?" (Men may learn a lot by asking this question of women to whom they are close.) The threat of rape is an assault upon the meaning of the world; it alters the feel of the human condition. Surely any attempt to comprehend the lives of women that fails to take issues of violence against women into account is misguided.

Through talking to women, I learned: *The threat of rape alters the meaning and feel of the night.* Observe how your body feels, how the night feels, when you're in fear. The constriction in your chest, the vigilance in your eyes, the rubber in your legs. What do the stars look like? How does the moon present itself? What is the difference between walking late at night in the dangerous part of a city and walking late at night in the country, or safe suburbs? When I try to imagine what the threat of rape must do to the night, I think of the stalked, adrenalated feeling I get walking late at night in parts of certain American cities. Only, I remind myself, it is a fear different from any I have known, a fear of being raped.

It is night half the time. If the threat of rape alters the meaning of the night, it must alter the meaning and pace of the day, one's relation to the passing and organization of time itself. For some women, the threat of rape at night turns their car into armored tanks, their solitude into isolation. And what must the space inside a car or an apartment feel like if the space outside is menacing?

I was running late one night with a close woman friend through a path in the woods on the outskirts of a small university town. We had run several miles and were feeling a warm, energized serenity.

"How would you feel if you were alone?" I asked.

"Terrified!" she said instantly.

"Terrified that there might be a man out there?" I asked, pointing to the surrounding moonlit forest, which had suddenly been transformed into a source of terror.

"Yes."

Another woman said, "I know what I can't do and I've completely internalized what I can't do. I've built a viable life that basically involves never leaving my apartment at night unless I'm directly going some place to meet somebody. It's unconsciously built into what it occurs to women to do." When one is raised without freedom, one may not recognize its absence.

The threat of rape alters the meaning and feel of nature. Everyone has felt the psychic nurturance of nature. Many women are being deprived of that nurturance, especially in wooded areas near cities. They are deprived either because they cannot experience nature in solitude because of threat, or because, when they do choose solitude in nature, they must cope with a certain subtle but nettlesome fear.

Women need more money because of rape and the threat of rape makes it harder for women to earn money. It's simple: if you don't feel safe walking at night, or riding public transportation, you need a car. And it is less practicable to live in cheaper, less secure, and thus more dangerous neighborhoods if the ordinary threat of violence that men experience, being mugged, say, is compounded by the threat of rape. By limiting mobility at night, the threat of rape limits where and when one is able to work, thus making it more difficult to earn money. An obvious bind: women need more money because of rape, and have fewer job opportunities because of it.

The threat of rape makes women more dependent on men (or other women). One woman said: "If there were no rape I wouldn't have to play games with men for their protection." The threat of rape falsifies, mystifies, and confuses relations between men and women. If there were no rape, women would simply not need men as much, wouldn't need them to go places with at night, to feel safe in their homes, for protection in nature.

The threat of rape makes solitude less possible for women. Solitude, drawing strength from being alone, is difficult if being alone means being afraid. To be afraid is to be in need, to experience a lack; the threat of rape creates a lack. Solitude requires relaxation; if you're afraid, you can't relax.

The threat of rape inhibits a woman's expressiveness. "If there were no rape," said one woman, "I could dress the way I wanted and walk the way I wanted and not feel self-conscious about the responses of men. I could be friendly to people. I wouldn't have to wish I was ugly. I wouldn't have to make myself small when I go on the bus. I wouldn't have to respond to verbal abuse from men by remaining silent. I could respond in kind."

If a woman's basic expressiveness is inhibited, her sexuality, creativity, and delight in life must surely be diminished.

The threat of rape inhibits the freedom of the eye. I know a married couple who live in Manhattan. They are both artists, both acutely sensitive and responsive to the visual world. When they walk separately in the city, he has more freedom to look than she does. She must control her eye movements lest they inadvertently meet the glare of some importunate man. What, who and how she sees are restricted by the threat of rape.

The following exercise is recommended for men.

> Walk down a city street. Pay a lot of attention to your clothing; make sure your pants are zipped, shirt tucked in, buttons done. Look straight ahead. Every time a man walks past you, avert your eyes and make your face expressionless. Most women learn to go through this act each time we leave our houses. It's a way to avoid at least some of the encounters we've all had with strange men who decided we looked available.[1]

To relate aesthetically to the visual world involves a certain playfulness, a spirit of spontaneous exploration. The tense vigilance that accompanies fear inhibits that spontaneity. The world is no longer yours to look at when you're afraid.

I am aware that all culture is, in part, restriction, that there are places in America where hardly anyone is safe (though men are safer than women virtually everywhere), that there are many ways to enjoy life, that some women may not be so restricted, that there exist havens, whether psychic, geographical, economic, or class. But they are *havens,* and as such, defined by threat.

Above all, I trust my experience: no woman could have lived the life I've lived the past few years. If suddenly I were restricted by the threat of rape, I would feel a deep, inexorable depression. And it's not just rape; it's harassment, battery, Peeping Toms, anonymous phone calls, exhibitionism, intrusive stares, fondlings—all contributing to an atmosphere of intimidation in women's lives. And I have only scratched the surface; it would take many carefully crafted short stories to begin to express what I have only hinted at in the last few pages. I have not even touched upon what it might mean for a woman to be sexually assaulted. Only women can speak to that. Nor have I suggested how the threat of rape affects marriage.

Rape and the threat of rape pervade the lives of women, as reflected in some popular images of our culture.

RAPE SIGNS

Close your eyes and imagine a caveman. What is he doing and to whom?

Most people see him clubbing a cavewoman (usually walking by herself) over the head and dragging her off by the hair. Most people *don't* see blood gushing from the cavewoman's head, scrapes and bruises accumulating on her legs as she's dragged over uncleared ground, her look of dazed horror when she's hit. And the scene in the cave? What happens there? Presumably he rapes her while she's un- (or semi-) conscious.

This scene, which lives in most of our minds, which has evoked wry laughter in most of us at one time or another (I remember its winsome presentation in cartoons), is a *rape sign.* A rape sign is a way of expressing ideas and feelings about rape without acknowledging them to ourselves. As we shall see, the caveman scene expresses many ideas and feelings related to rape, yet we ordinarily fail to notice that the scene is *about* rape. Rape signs are manifest in jokes, images, verbal expressions, songs, stories, etc. Rape can be humorized, eroticized, aestheticized, athleticized, and (usually) trivialized, without anyone realizing that rape has been referred to. Rape is made safe because we are allowed to express possibly dangerous feelings and thoughts while simultaneously discounting them. Rape signs mask a tenuous, anxiety-ridden relationship to rape.

We *need* rape signs. We *demand* them. The evidence is their ubiquity. Rape signs stand between us and the reality of rape, obfuscating and numbing our vision and sensitivity. They paralyze thought much in the way habit paralyzes spontaneity. They tell us false stories about rape, men, and women without our consciously hearing the stories.

Why is it, *how* is it that I say the caveman scene for years and never connected it to rape? How is it that many of us have been laughing at rape for years without knowing it?

We can relate to the caveman scene in at least three ways. (1) We can contemplate what, in the very simplest sense, the scene expresses. (2) We can examine and analyze the ideas about men, women, our sexual selves, etc., which are expressed by the scene. Or, (3) we can experience the scene in the ambiguous half-conscious way most of us experience such phenomena; perhaps as droll, or trivial, or distracting—but nonetheless as something that insidiously teaches us about the world.[2]

Let us contemplate the scene in the simplest sense. A cavewoman is walking along. Is she thinking? Does she think in a way similar to the way we do? Is she afraid? Is she attuned to her senses in a way wholly different from the way we are? Is her universe full of friendly and unfriendly spirits? How does one begin to relate to her?

And the caveman. What is his mood? Why does he commit this vicious assault? It is painful to ponder the blood and bruises as he drags her away. Taken simply, this scene is quite horrible. Yet many of us miss the horror and half-consciously "receive" a familiar set of ideas about men, women, sexuality, power, and our "natural" selves.

Let us look at some of the ideas suggested by the caveman scene. First, that rape is natural, that in some natural state, unfettered by civilization and its discontents, men would rape women, especially if women are walking by themselves. Since rape is natural, men are not ultimately responsible.

Second, that rape isn't rape. We see the image repeatedly and never connect it with rape. We laugh at it, we are overfamiliar with it. *Somehow* we deny that it's rape. Just as words like "passed away" or "powder room" serve to hide the realities of death and excretion, the caveman scene hides the reality of rape while simultaneously legitimizing it.

Third, that physical strength is a legitimate source of power in a man/woman and other types of interaction. We see a *big* caveman and a *little* cavewoman. This idea of the legitimacy of physical strength as a source of power in relations between men and women is much more with us than is generally acknowledged. Superior male strength and the threat of violence provides a kind of background to relations between men and women. Its exploitation can be seen in men's raised voices in arguments, their catcalls, their body language, to say nothing of their actual physical violence against women.

Fourth, that women don't really suffer when they're attacked and raped. We don't see or hear her cry out; we don't see her struggle or resist; we don't see her blood. The reality of her experience is denied; we don't identify with her.

Fifth, that women are somehow supposed to be attracted to brute strength. Her lack of resistance, her lack of visible suffering suggest that she secretly wishes to be ravished by the (big, strong) man.

Sixth, the caveman's experience is legitimized. We are encouraged to identify with and admire him. He experiences a kind of triumph, what one might call the thrill of conquest.

Seventh, the scene implies that uncontrolled violent emotion and desire is "primitive" and rational control and decency are "civilized," something the "advanced" civilizations of the twentieth century scarcely confirm.

And we are in the habit of seeing the caveman scene without recognizing or examining these ideas, and without objecting to their destructive consequences as beliefs about men and women.

The notion that rape is "just human nature" and therefore cannot be stopped pervades our thought about rape. As one district attorney said, "You're not going to stop rape. Social rapes are always going to happen. I don't care if it's Adam and Eve, or Luke Skywalker and Princess Leah, it's always going to happen. That's just human nature."

But rape is not just "human nature"; rape is *not* "natural." In her study of rape in tribal societies, anthropologist Peggy Reeves Sanday found that out of ninety-five tribal societies, 47 percent were rape free, 18 percent rape prone, and 35 percent somewhere in between. According to Sanday:

> Rape in tribal societies is part of a cultural configuration which includes interpersonal violence, male dominance, and sexual separation. In such societies, as the Murphys say about the Mundurucu: "men . . . use the penis to dominate their women." The question remains as to what motivates the rape prone cultural configuration. Considerable evidence suggests that this configuration evolves in societies faced with depleting food resources, migration or other factors contributing to a dependence on male distribution capacities as opposed to female fertility.[3]

According to Sanday, when men are in harmony with their environment, rape is usually absent.

> It's important to understand that violence is socially and not biologically programmed. Rape is not an integral part of male nature, but the means by which men programmed for violence express their social selves. Men who are conditioned to respect the female virtues of growth and the sacredness of life do not violate women. It is significant that in societies where nature is held sacred, rape occurs only rarely.[4]

Once we acknowledge that rape is not natural, we are forced to acknowledge that something has gone wrong in a culture such as ours where rape is common. Thinking of rape as natural can no longer be used to evade responsibility for it.

Cartoons in men's magazines provide another occasional source of rape signs. Such cartoons often portray a man chasing a woman, usually around a room. It may be a judge chasing a woman accused of a crime, a boss chasing a secretary, a patient chasing a nurse. Such cartoon clearly portray a man trying to force sex on a woman; they clearly suggest that such situations are funny. They exploit the widely held belief that if a man and a woman know each other, or if the man has no weapon, it's not really rape if the man forces sex upon the woman. Yet we seldom connect such cartoons to rape.

Rape signs pervade American culture. One can find them in pornography, advertising, song lyrics, album covers, novels, etc. And there is an important sense in which the rape fantasies of men (and probably women) constitute a kind of rape sign. In all of the sexual fantasies of rape that I have heard men recount, the experience as described by women, with its terror and fear of death, is denied. Just as rape signs make it difficult to think clearly about rape, men's fantasies of rape may make it difficult for men to think about the reality of rape.

RAPE LANGUAGE[5]

> *fuck (taboo) vt. To cheat, trick, take advantage of, deceive or treat someone unfairly. Very common. The relationship between sex and fraud is best illustrated by this usage . . .*
> Dictionary of American Slang, compiled by Harold Wentworth and Stuart Berg Flexner.

Two apparently conflicting statements are often made about rape. First, that rape is a crime of violence that has little to do with sex. And second, that rape is merely an extension of the sex roles and sexual behavior regularly played out between men and women. In discussing this, we must distinguish the experience of the victim from that of the rapist.

It is clear that the experience of being raped for a woman has plenty to do with violence and terror, and little to do with sex. And it is important to get people to understand rape not in terms of sex, but as brutal physical and psychic violence. And it appears to be true that rapists (at least the ones who end up incarcerated and studied) are seldom trying to meet "sexual needs" when they rape.

But what exactly is a sexual need? And what distinguishes sexual from nonsexual needs? Are "ordinary men" when they seek to have sex with women trying to meet sexual needs? Are there any similarities between "ordinary men" and rapists when they have sex?

One way to answer such a question is by analyzing the way men talk about sex and women. George Lakoff and Mark Johnson, in a remarkable book, *Metaphors We Live By*,[6] acutely discern many fundamental metaphorical concepts by which we conceive of, live in, and experience the world. In a metaphor, we understand and experience one kind of thing in terms of another. According to Lakoff and Johnson, most of the way we understand and structure our experience is metaphorical. A *metaphorical concept* is a way in which we *repeatedly* understand and structure our experience that is manifested in the way we speak. To illustrate:

TIME IS MONEY: You've got to learn to *budget* your time. That *cost* me a lot of time. He's living on *borrowed* time. This gadget will *save* you hours. That's a stupid way to *spend* your time.

"Time is Money" functions as a metaphorical concept structuring our experience of and relationship to time. According to Lakoff and Johnson:

Metaphors may create realities for us, especially social realities. A metaphor may thus be a guide for future action. Such actions will, of course, fit the metaphor. This will in turn reinforce the power of the metaphor to make experience coherent. In this sense metaphors can be self-fulfilling prophecies.[7]

How do men metaphorically structure their experience when they wish to have sex consensually with a woman, or when they have just had sex consensually with a woman? How do they understand what they have done, would like to do, or are going to do? One them, particularly common to younger men who are seeking an initial sexual encounter with a woman, goes like this: having sex is an achievement; the achievement is gaining the possession of a valued commodity; the valued commodity is a woman. Men who are relating to women in this way will tend, when they speak, to focus either on sex as achievement or the woman as a commodity.

Sex as achievement is often expressed in simple, straightforward ways.

SEX IS ACHIEVEMENT: I'd like to *make it* with her. Maybe I'll *get her into bed*. You didn't have to *work very hard to get into her pants*.

The achievement can also be expressed as a successful hunt or conquest, as doing well in a game, as wining a gambling game, as winning a war, or as getting a woman to provide sexual servicing:

SEX IS A HUNT, A CONQUEST: I'm going *to go out and get a piece of ass* tonight.

SEX IS A GAME: I hope I *score* tonight. I *struck out* with her.

SEX IS A GAMBLING GAME: If you *play your cards right*, you'll score. Your *best bet* is not to come on too strong.

SEX IS A WAR: I tried to get her into bed but *got shot down*. If I can *wear down her resistance*, I'll score. He's always *hitting on* women.

SEX IS BEING SERVICED BY A WOMAN: She wouldn't *put out for me*. She *did it for him* but she wouldn't *do it for me*.

After the man has succeeded in gaining the woman's consent, sex is still achievement. Only now the achievement is performing well sexually.

SEX IS PERFORMANCE: You were *great last night*. I wasn't able to *fill the bill* sexually with her. I got *rave reviews* in bed. He's *good in bed*.

And one's performance may be understood as instruction, triumph, or triumph through inflicting pleasure.

SEX IS INSTRUCTION: I *know how to show a woman a good time*. A man needs to be in good shape when he *takes a woman to bed*. You could *learn a lot* from me, baby. I could *teach her a thing or two*.

SEX IS TRIUMPH: I really *put it to her!* I really *stuck it to her!*

SEX IS TRIUMPH THROUGH INFLICTING PLEASURE: Boy did I *make her moan!* I *got her so hot* she could hardly stand it!

When the emphasis is on the woman as a valued commodity, she is taken to be an object, sometimes food, that can be possessed or stolen.

SEX IS A COMMODITY: I've never had to *pay for pussy*. Why should a man rape if he can *get it for free*? She wouldn't *give me any*. I've been *getting it regularly* lately. Do you know any *available* women?

SEX IS POSSESSION: I'd like to *have her* for a night. I bet I could *get her* if I tried. You're *gonna lose* that girl.

SEX IS THEFT: She's good *snatch*. If she won't give it, I'm going to *take it*. He's *robbing the cradle*. I'd like to *cop some ass*.

SEX IS FOOD: She was the *best piece of ass* I ever had. What a *dish!*

WOMEN ARE OBJECTS: She's a cute *thing*. Take off your clothes and show me your *stuff*. Check *that* out. How would you like a *little bit of that?* She likes to *flaunt it*.

Men may think of women as animals, children, or their genitals.

WOMEN ARE ANIMALS: She's a nice *chick*. Wow, check out the *pet* of the month. She works as a Playboy *bunny*. She's real *foxy*. Let's

see if we can shoot some *squirrel* (or *beaver*). She's really a *dog*. What a *bitch!*

WOMEN ARE CHLDREN: Do you like the *girls* at the office? Janice is our *playmate* of the month. Hey, *baby!*

WOMEN ARE THEIR GENITALS: She's a *cunt*.

Sexual feelings may be seen as being out of one's control. This notion pervades much of our talk about sex.

SEX IS MADNESS: I'm *wild* with desire. Every time I look at a woman *I go crazy*.

SEXUAL FEELING IS ELECTRICITY/FLUIDS CONTROLLED BY A WOMAN: She *turns me on*. She really *got my juices flowing*. One look at her and I'm all *stirred up*.

If sexual feeling is out of one's control, it is not surprising that sex itself may be understood as violence.

SEX IS HITTING A WOMAN'S GENITALS: I'd like to *bang* her *box*.

MASTURBATION IS HITTING ONE'S OWN GENITALS: I *beat my meat* last night. I like to *whack off*.

IMPREGNATION IS AN ACT OF VIOLENCE: He *knocked her up*.

A PENIS IS A GUN; SPERM IS AMMUNITION: He *shot his load* into her.

The above examples partially illustrate how a significant number of heterosexual men structure their experience of themselves, women, and sex. Most heterosexual men have used some of the above phrases at one time or another, and some men regularly talk this way. What characterizes men's activity when they regard sex as an achievement, and the achievement as gaining possession of a valued commodity, and the valued commodity is a woman? I will address four basic aspects: *status, hostility, control,* and *dominance*.

Status. Clearly, achievement has much to do with status. Performing, triumphing, instruction, winning wars, conquering, and being serviced are all activities that confer superior status. And gaining possession of a valued commodity also gives one status in two ways:

one has status over the woman because one possesses her, and one is given status in the eyes of other men.

Hostility. To regard women as commodities to possess is an act of hostility. To regard women as objects, animals, food, or children is also, as is thinking of sex as war, triumph, theft, hitting a woman's genitals, a hunt, or possession.

Control. In achieving possession of a commodity, one is trying to maintain control, to control the woman's behavior and control one's own performance.

Dominance. To possess a commodity is to dominate it; to triumph, win a war, succeed in a hunt, win a game, or be serviced by a woman all express dominance.

It would appear that for many seeking sex with a woman, sex has more to do with the above than with sensual pleasure or sexual satisfaction. Is there a similarity between what such men are concerned with when they have sex with a woman and what rapists are concerned with?

Status, hostility, control, and dominance. I first found these features mentioned in clinical psychologist Nicholas Groth's discussion of rapists. Based upon careful clinical study of over five hundred sex offenders, Groth concluded:

> Rape, then, is a pseudosexual act, a pattern of sexual behavior that is concerned much more with *status, hostility, control,* and *dominance* than with sensual pleasure or sexual satisfaction. It is sexual behavior in the primary service of nonsexual needs.[8] (Italics mine).

Not every man is a rapist, but every man who grows up in America and learns American English learns all too much too think like a rapist, to structure his experience of women and sex in terms of status, hostility, control, and dominance. If we are going to say that, for a man, rape has little to do with sex, we may as well add that sex itself often has little to do with sex, or, if you like, that rape has plenty to do with sex as it is often understood and spoken about by men.

Contrary to the impression one might get from reading newspapers, much rape appears to be between acquaintances, often on dates. If men go out on dates with the idea that sex is achievement of possession of a valued commodity, the woman's consent is likely to be of peripheral concern.

I am unaware of any felicitous way of talking about sex in American English. One can speak of wanting to go to bed with, sleep with, or make love with a woman. It is as if to speak in a somewhat human, sharing way about sexual desire requires that the funky, lusty side of sex be denied. *I am not aware of any common English phrases that allow one to express sexual desire in a way that acknowledges both lust and humanity.* And at any rate, men speak the way they do regarding sex in part because of the way they feel and because of what their language and culture provide. And being repulsed by most of the language available to talk about sex and learning to speak a different language doesn't mean that one's gut feelings about sex or women change.

Consider five more or less familiar statements:

> Fuck you!
> I got screwed by the I.R.S.
> Get fucked!
> He's a real mind fuck!
> Fuck it!

These statements reflect a common folk theory of sex.[9] A folk theory is a commonsense model of some aspect of reality. In a metaphor we understand one thing in terms of another; in a folk theory two normally separate things may be collapsed together that it is difficult to separate them. We are able to make sense of the above statements because we not only understand sex in terms of aggression and degradation, but because we actually take sex to *be* that.

SEX IS AGGREESIVE DEGREDATION: I'd like to *screw* her. I want to *fuck* her.

And if sex is aggression or degradation, a penis is a weapon.

"Fuck you!" and "Get fucked!" are both rape insults. In an insult one often verbally wishes on someone what one would like to see happen physically. "I got screwed," expresses a feeling of violation; "Fuck it" a desire to dominate and abuse (through sexual means). Someone mind-fucking you is abusing your mind and treating it disrespectfully.

Try saying "Fuck you!" aloud several times. What thoughts, feelings, or images arise? Is there anyone you wish to say this to? In wishing to say this, are you wishing violation and rape upon them? A rapist who uses his penis as a weapon is acting out a value that we express regularly. A man may never relate to women in a sexually abusive way, but if he uses this language he is reflecting a view of sex as an aggressive, degrading act.

"Fuck" (in its narrowly sexual sense) doesn't always signify aggressive degradation of one person by another. "Let's fuck" expresses both lust and mutuality (of a sort). Tone of voice and context can give "fuck" many different connotations, but there is usually a sense of dirt and degradation attached to it.

When we say "Fuck you!" etc., we are expressing anger and frustration. But in calmer moments we agree that it is wrong and undesirable to fuck someone over, or to "screw" someone. We don't, for the most part, say with pride: "I really fucked him over!"

But there does exist a set of phrases men use where forced aggression, a kind of symbolic rape, is considered desirable and where men express pride and triumph in it.

WINNING IS FORCED AGGRESSION: Go out there and *stick it to them!* We really *put it to the Acme Corporation! Sock it* to them! Any time a situation exists which is sufficiently competitive to be thought of as a war (athletic events, competition in business, intellectually competing schools in academia) the sentiment may arise that we must stick it (put it, sock it) to them before they stick it to us.[10]

This language may well have the unconscious effect of intimidating women. If the fear of rape (or avoiding situations that may evoke the fear of rape) is a significant part of a woman's life, then what is the effect of hearing all this rape language? Suppose a woman has been sexually assaulted. What is the effect, however unconscious, of hearing expressions that imply a cultural view of sex as aggression or degradation? (That some women themselves use this language is no indication that it doesn't intimidate. One can be intimidated by one's own language).

This language probably will not change till our conception of sex changes. For the present, it is important to know what we're saying and why we're saying it.

We have analyzed some of the ways men conceive of sex: now we will look at some of the ways they view rape.

First, when men speak sympathetically about women's experiences of being raped, they conceived of it as a violent intrusion; the violent intrusion can be either a cut or an invasion of sacred space. (Women often conceive of rape in this way as well.)

RAPE IS A PHYSICAL WOUND, PROBABLY A CUT: One speaks of a *sexual trauma*. Rape is often referred to as a *wound* that takes time *to heal* and leaves a *scar.* This is not generally thought of as a metaphor, since the idea of a psychic trauma is itself not thought of as a metaphor. This metaphor appears to cohere with many of the processes women go through after they've been raped.

RAPE IS INVASION OF SACRED SPACE: Many people speak of rape as the violation of the most private, sacred part of a person. This suggests that the vagina is a private, sacred space and, perhaps, that sex is a religious experience.

When men identify with the rapist they often speak of rape as theft, instruction, defilement, revenge, and "natural."

RAPE IS THEFT OF A VALUED COMMODITY: Men often speak of rape as "going out and taking it." "Why should a man rape if he can *get it* for free?" suggests one man. If a man understands sex as a commodity, then rape may be seen as theft of the commodity. This view is reflected in the absence of marital rape laws in all but a few states: a man can't steal what he already owns.

RAPE IS INSTRUCTION: Rapists sometimes say to their victims, "I'll show you what life is about." And men who think sex is instruciton have been known to say things like: "Rape isn't so bad. He's only trying to show her a good time."

RAPE IS DEFILEMENT OF PROPERTY: This view is reflected in the notion that one can't rape a prostitute because one can't defile already de-filed goods. And some relationships between men and women break up because the man no longer regards the woman as "pure"; he sees her as dirtied or spoiled or cheapened. It is as if her vagina is clean, valued property and rape dirties it.

RAPE IS REVENGE: When they examine their own rape fantasies some men find their origin in revenge. Some men feel that women have enormous power in their appearance and that rape is getting even. And Chuck speaks of rape as getting back at women who'd hurt him in the past.

RAPE IS NATURAL, BOYS BEING BOYS: As has al-ready been elaborated, there is nothing "nat-ural" about rape.

What is taken by men to be the woman's weapon? Consider a few more expressions.

> She's a *knockout*!
> What a *bombshell*!
> She's *strikingly* beautiful!
> That woman is *ravishing*!
> She's really *stunning*!
> She's a *femme fatale*!
> She's *dressed to kill*!

Clearly, *to men, a woman's appearance is a weapon.*[11] It can knock a man out, explode and kill him, strike him, it can ravish him (notice the reversal—*she* rapes *him* with her appear-ance), it can stun, i.e., hit him on the head and again (twice) it can kill him. Everyone, man or woman, who learns American English and can understand the seven sentences above at least unconsciously understands a woman's ap-pearance as a powerful physical force.

Most heterosexual men have felt this. This power is due not so much to anything physio-logical (though that must play a role) but more to the ways men understand sex. If sex is achievement, then the presence of an attractive woman may result in one's feeling like a fail-ure. One's self worth, or "manhood" may be-come subtly (or not so subtly) at issue in her presence. And how does one feel toward someone who "makes one feel like a failure"? Like degrading them in return. As long as sex is achievement ("I want to *make it* with her"), it will probably also be aggressive degradation ("I want to *fuck* her"). Explains "Jay":

> Let's say I see a woman and she looks really pretty and really clean and sexy, and she's giving off very feminine, sexy vibes. I think, "Wow, I would love to make love to her," but I know she's not really interested. It's a tease. A lot of times a woman knows that she's looking really good and she'll use that and flaunt it, and it makes me feel like she's laughing at me and I feel *degraded*. I also feel dehumanized, because when I'm being teased I just turn off, I cease to be human. Because if I go with my human emo-tions I'm going to want to put my arms around her and kiss her, and to do that would be unac-ceptable. I don't like the feeling that I'm sup-posed to stand there and take it, and not be able to hug her or kiss her; so I just turn off my emo-tions. It's a feeling of humiliation, because the woman has forced me to turn off my feelings and react in a way that I really don't want to. If I were actually desperate enough to rape some-body, it would be from wanting the person, but also it would be a very spiteful thing, just being able to say, "I have power over you and I can do anything I want with you," because really I feel that *they* have power over *me* just by their pres-ence. Just the fact that they can come up to me

and just melt me and make me feel like a dummy makes me want revenge. They have power over me so I want power over them.

He feels degraded, he experiences humiliation in the presence of an attractive woman. So he wants to humiliate and degrade in return. Since sex is achievement, he feels like a failure around attractive women; he feels humiliated and degraded and wants to aggressively degrade back.

Notice the effect of women's appearances on him. Women are "giving off very feminine, sexy vibes"; he has "to stand there and take it"; he says that "the woman has forced me to turn off my feelings and react"; he claims that they have power over him "just by their presence"; they can come up to him and just "melt" him. A woman's appearance forces him to have sexual feelings he can't act upon; since he finds it unpleasant not to be able to act upon his sexual feelings, he must turn them off. It is, in part, an issue of potency. Women as he experiences them force him to feel sexually excited and then force him to turn off his excitement. They arouse and castrate him. His desire to get even constitutes a desire to reclaim potency.

Concepts like sexual *attraction*, which blur the distinction between sexual feeling and sexual action, are potentially dangerous. The notion of sexual attraction is a metaphor derived from the natural sciences where two bodies are attracted to each other through magnetic, gravitational, or some other force. If having sexual feeling also means moving toward someone then at times when such movement is inappropriate, one must either repress sexual feelings or behave inappropriately. Neither solution works. If men can enjoy sexual feeling without needing to act upon it or be moved by it, they will feel less anger toward women and will be less likely to act out their anger.

Most heterosexual men have probably felt some of Jay's anger and frustration at one time

or another. For many men, the predominant mood of adolescence is humiliation (or at least flight from humiliation through achievement); some it is sexual humiliation, feeling inundated and barraged by images of women, whether from images in their own experience, the media, or their own psyches. Many men come to resent the power of these images and their own sexuality as well. One understanding of the penis as weapon: a means of getting even by inflicting pleasure (sex is triumph) and at least momentarily silencing the power of women's appearance, the power of women as images.

Growing up, I was thrown willy-nilly into a virtual manic-depressive oscillation between triumph and humiliation. The point of competition was to win, to triumph at someone else's expense. In sports, the ideas was to humiliate one's opponent, to beat him (winning is battery), to stick it to him (winning is forced aggression). The situation was no different in the classroom; intellectual argument was war ("I *demolished* his argument") and one was supposed to win the war and demonstrate the stupidity of one's opponent. Feeling humiliated by women must be seen as a part of this larger humiliation; it must also be seen that this humiliation has little to do with women and much to do with absurd conceptions of masculinity.

Conceptions of sexual interaction that picture men as active and women as passive may ring false for many men, in part because they experience the woman's appearance as acting upon them. Looking at a man and a woman on a date from a third-person perspective, one may think that the man appears aggressive and the woman passive; the man and woman may experience themselves as equally acted upon, equally passive.

The idea that a woman's appearance is a weapon is inseparable from the notion that sexual pleasure makes one helpless. This idea pervades American culture, from the familiar

Hollywood scene in which the heroine resists the kisses of the hero till, at a crucial moment, her resistance turns to the heavy breathing of sexual arousal and pleasure, to the stereotypical (and largely nonexistent) rapist who is said to have lost control at the sight of an attractive woman.

The appearance-as-weapon theme is used to justify rape and to justify insensitivity to women who have been raped. Part of the mentality goes: I cannot be sympathetic to people who have power over me and abuse that power; women have power over me and abuse that power in the way they dress, therefore I will not be sympathetic to women who are raped while they're abusing their power, i.e., who dress to look attractive.

George Lakoff (in conversation) has pointed out that the appearance-as-weapon theme is part of a more general passive theory of perception. Perception is understood in terms of external stimuli bombarding the senses— something that happens to me, over which I have no choice. We know that this is not true, that human beings actively perceive and make choices, whether conscious or unconscious, about what they perceive. Men often choose to perceive women's bodies in hidden, stolen ways, which brings us to our next section— pornographizing.

PORNOGRAPHIZING

Much has been written about pornography and rape. I would like to discuss *pornographizing* and rape. Pornographizing is important if we are to understand: (1) a bit more of most heterosexual men's consciousness of women; (2) pornography as an extension of that consciousness; and (3) how policemen, lawyers, doctors, and other men sometimes "re-rape" rape victims.

Pornographizing: the process by which men relate to women, images of women, the visual presence of women, stories about women,

women in any ways as *pornea*, which is Greek for "low whore."[12] How does one relate to a low whore? As property one uses for "sexual" pleasure. In pornographizing, one anonymizes the woman and fails to acknowledge her moral, spiritual, or emotional being. One relates to her as a thing without soul. The woman as a locus of experience is denied. And often, one relates to her body as a fetish. A fetish: the new pair of shoes you stare and stare at that won't quite give you what you want. The new watch that shines in the dark but somehow leaves you empty. The thighs, breasts, calves, rears of women searched for throughout your adolescence. Images savored and extorted for lust. Pornographizing is the perceptual counterpart to sex as achievement of possession of a commodity and sex as aggressive degradation.

A connection exists between (1) men's repression of sexual (and other) feelings; (2) men's obsession with images of women as a kind of substitute for sexual feeling (the more one loses touch with sexual feeling, the more one needs images as a substitute) and (3) the brutalization of women. If sexual feeling is repressed and therefore sex is regarded as dirtying and evil, men may need to become obsessed with images of women's bodies to feel sexual. Those images may be regarded as evil and dirty. Women who are sexual may be so regarded. And since sexual women are dirty and evil (so goes the mentality), they deserve to be brutalized.

To the extent that one is obsessed with images, one relates to women as visual surfaces from which one can extort lust. Sexual feeling somehow begins to inhere in images of women, and women are given a strange, mystifying power. The intensity of one's orgasm may become connected to the intensity of the images one can evoke. The humanity of women can get lost in this process. Attractive women may come to signify undifferentiated lust. The woman's desire and the man's desire may become inseparable in the man's consciousness.

Sociologist Erving Goffman (in conversation) distinguishes two socially defined views of women's bodies: a stolen and an authorized view. An example of a stolen view would be a man stealing glances of women's breasts, thighs, etc., in a social situation. An example of an authorized view would be the Venus de Milo or any nude statue of a woman. And if a man stares lustfully at the crotch of the Venus de Milo? Then it becomes a stolen view.

I believe that there also exist authorized stolen views, stolen hearings, askings, touchings, and that stolen glances can at times be seen as *stealing visual property*. Let us look more closely at these distinctions.

AUTHORIZED VIEWS   That a view is authorized confers no moral legitimacy upon it, though one reason views are unauthorized is because they're dehumanizing. Consider several authorized views of women's bodies.

A male art student in an art class drawing a nude woman model. He is authorized to look at her body in an attempt to faithfully render visual detail. If he looks out of a desire to excite lust in himself, his view is stolen. It is not *what* but *how* he sees that makes his view stolen.

Judges judging a bathing beauty contest are objectifying but not pornographizing women, at least in their capacity as judges. Their presumed concern is with proportion, grace of movement, etc. They are grading women's bodies. Again, if they see in a lustful way, their view becomes stolen.

A loving, nonsexist man looking lustfully at his wife. He experiences lust for her body while at the same time recognizing it as *her* body. It is simultaneously lust for her body or lust for her. He does not anonymize her.

One woman said to me: "I don't care how my lover looks at me as long as he knows that it's me. I broke up with a guy once because I didn't like the way he looked at me." If a man looks at his wife and blanks out her personality and just relates to her sexually as an anonymous body, then his view is stolen and pornographized. (Views can be stolen yet not pornographized, as we shall see.) He is relating to her as sexual property. This can be done in a spirit of play or sexual exploration (a form of authorized stealing) and be desirable. When done without clarity or honesty, it tends to be alienating.

STOLEN VIEWS   The prototypical stolen view is a man in a social situation stealing glances of women's bodies. This process is so fundamental a visual reflex in many men that they don't know they are doing it. If a man steals and retains an image of a woman and later uses it to enhance his orgasm, he is in a sense stealing visual property. The image becomes his to use to give himself pleasure.

Consider a scene in a bar where a man is with his wife, whom he regards more or less as his property. Suppose another man looks lustfully at her. "What are you looking at?" says the husband. He regards his wife as his property; the man staring at her is stealing visual property that belongs to him. Only *he* is allowed to relate visually to her body in a sexual way. An unspoken element in his objection may have to do with his awareness that the man may steal her image.

Consider the notion of a Peeping Tom—he is essentially regarded as guilty of stealing visual property. And look at this entry from the *Dictionary of American Slang*.

> *Free show*—a look or glance, usually at a girl's or woman's thighs or breasts, or occasionally at a nude woman, most often without the female's knowledge or consent, as when a girl or woman crosses her legs, or inadvertently forgets to close a door while disrobing. Mainly boy or young teenager use.[13]

Cleary, boys and young teenagers learn to regard a woman's body as valued visual property, which they can at times get to enjoy for free. In the conception of sex as a commodity, sex is something a man can buy, sell, get for free, or steal (rape). Similarly, a woman as visual property can be treated as a commodity to be bought, sold, gotten for free, or stolen.

No one should feel guilty about any sexual thoughts or feelings or fantasies they may have (though it is important to understand the meaning of such phenomena). Ideally, sexual feeling should make life delightful. Lust may intrude its ambivalent presence in many situations. Stealing glances of women's bodies need not be pornographizing. One can peripherally notice a woman's attractiveness without denying her humanity. A young boy may seek out glimpses of women's bodies with a certain wondrous sexual curiosity; it is only when he is properly socialized that he may learn to relate to women as less than human.

When stealing glances becomes disrespectful and intrusive, when it makes women uncomfortable, it becomes one end of a continuum that includes (among other things) catcalls, street and office harassment, battery, and rape.

The activity of relating to women as property in any form is oppressive; relating to women as visual property is significant because it is so seldom clearly acknowledged. Visual property has a kind of psychic primacy in men's relation to women as property. It is, I think, the first way that a boy learns to speak of a woman as property. And there exists an unpleasant psychic parallel between a man scanning his environment for visual property to steal and a rapist scanning his for women to rape.

AUTHORIZED STOLEN VIEWS   In American culture, authorized stealing is taken to be a source of pleasure. Forbidden fruit that one is authorized to eat tastes best. Look at a *Playboy* centerfold. Everything in the framing of the image and the image itself authorizes one to blank

out the woman as a locus of experience and steal her image and appropriate it for pleasure.

Or a group of men harassing a woman as she walks by. They authorize each other to pornographize her, to relate to her as visual property, which they are unabashedly stealing.

Or a strip show. Men pay to enjoy visual property. A man deciding whether to hire a woman for a strip show is evaluating her as visual property.

Or the idea of a peep show. One pays to "peep," to steal an ostensibly illicit view.

SEMI-AUTHORIZED STOLEN VIEWS   In singles' bars, where men and women dress with the understanding that they will "check each other out," apparently a certain semi-authorized stealing is allowed.

We can begin to relate these distinctions to what happens to a woman who's been raped.

If she goes to a doctor for an examination, he is authorized to view and touch her body. It is not what but how he sees and touches that determines whether he pornographizes her. He is technically authorized to make medical discriminations regarding the state of her body. If he pornographizes her and his body language, tone of voice, or comments reveal this, then he will have, in effect, re-raped the victim.

Just as there are authorized and stolen views, there are authorized and stolen askings and hearings. A policeman may be authorized to ask a rape victim questions he would otherwise never be authorized to ask a stranger—intimate, sexual (or pseudosexual) questions. If he and his fellow policemen are unethical or sexist, he may be authorized to pornographize in his questions and hearings. He may ask inappropriate questions, in effect treating the woman and her account of the rape as pornographic property. He may engage in no stolen asking but the way in which he hears may be stolen. No *what*, but *how* he hears and how he relates to what he hears may constitute pornographizing. His comments or behavior may reveal his pornographizing. After reporting her rape to the police, one woman was told by the officer, "I don't want to be crude or nothing but your rapist sure knows how to pick 'em."

The same principle applies to the treatment of rape survivors by defense attorneys, prosecuting attorneys, and judges. A Denver judge, John Kane, was quoted as saying: "I just love to have a garden variety rape case. It keeps you awake in the afternoon and provides a little vicarious pleasure."[14] That he could even say this within earshot of the press and keep his job suggests that he feels (and is) authorized to pornographize rape survivors. Women sometimes speak of the "little rapes" that occur when they report the crime; the phrase strikes me as appropriate.

The ultimate pornographizing, the ultimate "stealing" is, of course, rape. Men are currently authorized to rape their wives in forty states. In many jurisdictions there exists a de facto authorization for men to rape women if they're on a date, if the woman is close friends with the man, if they have had sex before, or if they have consumed alcohol together. Anyone who pornographizes or mistreats a woman who's been raped is authorizing rape by making it harder for women to report the crime.

Stolen touchings is another category on a continuum with rape. There are plenty of jokes about "copping a feel—you can do a lot in a crowd." On subways, buses, and in other crowds, people are authorized to touch in inadvertent ways, but not to caress, poke, paw, etc. Most women who regularly spend time in crowds have stories to tell of stolen touchings.

Authorized touchings may be no better. Uncle Charlie may be socially authorized to hold his niece in his lap, but the way he holds her may constitute child molestation. His stolen touchings are another form of pornographizing.

What is it women often say about men stealing glances, hearings, touches from them?

That they feel humiliated, cheapened, degraded, dehumanized. In short, they feel treated like *pornea*, low whores, and that is exactly what some men are doing to them. Other men, "good" men who tolerate this, collude in this brutalization.

I have discussed a number of ways we think about rape, sex, men, and women. Many of these ways result, as we shall see, in a further brutalization of women that is both cruel and insidious—blaming the rape victim.

"SHE ASKED FOR IT"—BLAMING THE VICTIM[15]

Many things may be happening when a man blames a woman for rape. We can now make a few points about what goes on when men (and some women) say, "She asked for it," (or are otherwise insensitive or dismissive) after a woman has been raped. (These points apply repeatedly to many of the interviews that follow.)

First, in all cases where a woman is said to have asked for it, her appearance and behavior are taken as a form of speech. "Actions speak louder than words" is a widely held belief; the woman's actions—her appearance may be taken as action—are given greater emphasis than her words; an interpretation alien to the woman's intentions is given to her actions. A logical extension of "she asked for it" is the idea that she wanted what happened to happen; if she wanted it to happen, she *deserved* for it to happen. Therefore, the man is not to be blamed. "She asked for it" can mean either that she was consenting to have sex and was not really raped, or that she was in fact raped but somehow she really deserved it. "If you ask for it, you deserve it," is a widely held notion. If I ask you to beat me up and you beat me up, I still don't deserve to be beaten up. So even if the notion that women asked to be raped had some basis in reality, which it doesn't, on its own terms it makes no sense.

Second, a mentality exists that says: a woman who assumes freedoms normally restricted to a man (like going out alone at night) and is raped is doing the same thing as a woman who goes out in the rain without an umbrella and catches a cold. Both are considered responsible for what happens to them. That men will rape is taken to be legitimized given, part of nature, like rain or snow. The view reflects a massive abdication of responsibility for rape on the part of men. It is so much easier to think of rape as natural than to acknowledge one's part in it. So long as rape is regarded as natural, women will be blamed for rape.

A third point. The view that it is natural for men to rape is closely connected to the view of women as commodities. If a woman's body is regarded as a valued commodity by men, then of course, if you leave a valued commodity where it can be taken, it's just human nature for men to take it. If you left your stereo out on the sidewalk, you'd be asking for it to get stolen. Someone will just take it. (And how often men speak of rape as "going out and *taking it*.") If a woman walks the streets at night, she's leaving a valued commodity, her body, where it can be taken. So long as women are regarded as commodities, they will be blamed for rape.

Which brings us to a fourth point. "She asked for it" is inseparable from a more general "psychology of the dupe." If I use bad judgment and fail to read the small print in a contract and later get taken advantage of ("screwed" or "fucked over") then I deserve what I get; bad judgment makes me liable. Analogously, if a woman trusts a man and goes to his apartment, or accepts a ride hitchhiking, or goes out on a date and is raped, she's a dupe and deserves what she gets. "He didn't *really* rape her" goes the mentality—"he merely took advantage of her." And in America it's okay for people to take advantage of each other, even expected and praised. In fact, you're considered dumb and foolish if you

don't take advantage of other people's bad judgment. And so, again, by treating them as dupes, rape will be blamed on women.

Fifth, if a woman who is raped is judged attractive by men, and particularly if she dresses to look attractive, then the mentality exists that she attacked him with her weapon so, of course, he counter-attacked with his. The preview to a popular movie state: "She was the victim of her own *provocative beauty*." Provocation: "There is a line which, if crossed, will *set me off* and I will lose control and no longer be responsible for my behavior. If you punch me in the nose then, of course, I will not be responsible for what happens: you will have provoked a fight. If you dress, talk, move, or act a certain way, you will have provoked me to rape. If your appearance *stuns* me, *strikes* me, *ravishes* me, *knocks me out*, etc., then I will not be held responsible for what happens; you will have asked for it." The notion that sexual feeling makes one helpless is part of a cultural abdication of responsibility for sexuality. So long as a woman's appearance is viewed as a weapon and sexual feeling is believed to make one helpless, women will be blamed for rape.

Sixth, I have suggested that men sometimes become obsessed with images of women, that images become a substitute for sexual feeling, that sexual feeling becomes externalized and out of control and is given undifferentiated identity in the appearance of women's bodies. It is a process of projection in which one blurs one's own desire with her imagined, projected desire. If a woman's attractiveness is taken to signify one's own lust and a woman's lust, then when an "attractive" woman is raped, some men may think she wanted sex. Since they perceive their own lust in part projected onto the woman, they disbelieve women who've been raped. So long as men project their own sexual desires onto women, they will blame women for rape.

And seventh, what are we to make of the contention that women in dating situations say "no" initially to sexual overtures from men as a kind of pose, only to give in later, thus revealing their true intentions? And that men are thus confused and incredulous when women are raped because in their sexual experience women can't be believed? I doubt that this has much to do with men's perceptions of rape. I don't know to what extent women actually "say no and mean yes"; certainly it is a common theme in male folklore. I have spoken to a couple of women who went through periods when they wanted to be sexual but were afraid to be, and often rebuffed initial sexual advances only to give in later. One point is clear: the ambivalence women may feel about having sex is closely tied to the inability of men to fully accept them as sexual beings. Women have been traditionally punished for being openly and freely sexual; men are praised for it. And if many men think of sex as achievement of possession of a valued commodity, or aggressive degradation, then women have every reason to feel and act ambivalent.

CONCLUSION

A man can grow up in the finest family, get educated at the best schools, call himself literate, humanitarian, and cultured and not once contemplate something fundamental in his experience: women live in social environments far more menacing than men. He can even become a successful psychiatrist and never perceive that the threat of rape constitutes a major mental health issue for all women in American culture.

We cannot count upon the criminal justice system to end rape. If its efficiency were suddenly doubled (an unlikely prospect), not two or three, but four or six of every hundred rapists would find themselves in prison.

For a man to acknowledge and reject all the different ways he has learned to regard women as less than human is an act of courage and an act of love. If violence against women is to end, we will need nothing less than a revolution in consciousness among men. We must create a consciousness that relates to women as people instead of property, that acknowledges and refuses to accept as normal lives of constraint for women, a consciousness that ceases to blame women for rape, and finally a consciousness that is able to acknowledge with clarity its anger at women and put that anger aside.

NOTES

1. From "Willamette Bridge" in *Body Politics* by Nancy Henley, Prentice Hall, 1977, p. 144.
2. This method of analysis is derived from Roland Barthes. See "Myth Today" in *Mythologies*, Hill and Wang, 1979, for a remarkable lucid and subtle exposition.
3. *Journal of Social Issues,* forthcoming.
4. Ibid.
5. I wish to thank George Lakoff for many enlightening discussions on the material in this section.
6. *Metaphors We Live By* by George Lakoff and Mark Johnson, University of Chicago Press, 1980.
7. Ibid., p. 156.
8. *Men Who Rape*, Nicholas Groth, Plenum, 1980, p. 13.
9. Some other sexual assault insults: "Eat me!" "Go fuck yourself!" "Take this job and shove it!" "Up yours!"
10. A tennis star, after winning the tournament at Wimbledon, had difficulties getting along with the English. When they rescinded his invitation to the championship dinner upon his request to arrive late, he said, "The only reason they said it was a big deal was because I won their tournament. That's the only way you can *beat* them . . . that's the only way you could *stick it to them. I stuck it to them real good.*" (Italics mine.) (*San Francisco Chronicle,* July 7, 1981, p. 43.)
    Notice: He invokes "winning is battery"—*he beat them* and "winning is forced aggression"— he *stuck it to them real good.*

11. Women sometimes speak of makeup as "war paint."

12. In using this phrase I don't mean to legitimize oppressive images of prostitution; I only seek to describe a process in men's consciousness.

13. *Dictionary of American Slang,* Harold Wentworth & Stuart B. Flexner, T. Y. Crowell, 1980.

14. *Ms.,* December 1980.

15. Again, I would like to thank George Lakoff.

PART EIGHT

SEX, POLITICS, AND POLICIES

Sex is political. Consider the controversies about whether sexuality education should be taught in the schools (and what information should be taught) or the debate about whether gays or lesbians can serve in the military. Until the last part of the twentieth century, many states had laws making interracial marriage illegal. Engaging in oral or anal sex (regardless of the gender of the couple) is still illegal in many states due to sodomy laws.

The politics of sex can influence our thinking and behaviors in ways that we wouldn't necessarily anticipate. Few people question the right of straight people to vote on whether same-sex marriages should be legal. But consider the effects of power imbalance. Gays and lesbians, being a minority, cannot influence whether straight people can marry. Political institutions at every level are involved daily in making decisions about sex. These include decisions about prostitution, pornography, abortion, teenage sexuality, sexual abuse, assault, marriage, access to birth control, or decisions about public nudity that may vary in context—women being topless at strip clubs but not at public beaches (a right men have but that is denied to women).

It is easier to get rules and laws passed that restrict sexuality than it is to promote policies that permit or inform sexual expression. People are often unaware of laws regulating sexuality, or may feel that restrictive or oppressive laws are necessary, without considering facts. For instance, many people believe abstinence-only based sexuality education is needed in order to reduce sexual activity by young people. The federal government currently subsidizes sex education in schools only when classes teach an abstinence-only curriculum, expecting that students hearing this message will be less likely to have sex prior to marriage. Studies show this is not the case. Teens exposed to the abstinence-only curriculum are just as likely to become sexually involved as those not exposed to this curriculum, though they have less information and are potentially at greater risk for disease or unintended pregnancies. Yet for teachers or principals to advocate for more effective sexuality education—one that informs young people about sex, sexual options, and resources—could cost them their job in many communities.

Passions about sex run deep and can lead to ignorance about the ways policies in one area of human sexuality influence practices in other arenas. Consider how state and federal governments prevented access to birth control for women until the mid to late 1900s. Government and religious leaders (nearly all male) feared that women would become promiscuous if they had access to birth control and that such practices would prevent the "natural" process of pregnancy from occurring. The belief of these institutions was that sex was intended for procreation, particularly where women were concerned. Many people believed that a divine force would determine whether a pregnancy should occur, and any interruption of that divine determination was wrong. Thus, religious belief became public law.

There were unintended consequences to this policy. One was to legitimize men's use of prostitutes. Wives often resisted having intercourse because they feared pregnancy (as well as being perceived as "bad girls" if they enjoyed sex too much). Men's use of prostitutes went unpunished, even though prostitutes themselves were vulnerable to arrest.

At the same time, advocates for changes in laws governing access to birth control were seen as a threat to the status quo. Margaret Sanger, a public health nurse who founded Planned Parenthood, was jailed in the early part of the 20th century for distributing birth control devices. Debates today about the "morning-after" pill or the abortifacent RU 486—which has been available in Europe for a number of years, but only recently in the United States—reflect a similar conflict over sexuality and social policy, as does the ongoing national debate over women's access to abortion services. Abortion is still legal at the time this book is being written, which may change if a Supreme Court judge is appointed by the current administration and Roe v. Wade is overturned. Yet women who seek abortions are often left with few choices of providers, because medical schools are not training physicians in performing abortions because of the stigma attached to this procedure and the harassment of providers. This relates back to the politics of sex, since women have been held to second-class status because of their sexuality—that they menstruate and give birth. Women's reproductive capacity has historically been seen as a weakness that would prevent them from active participation in the workplace, politics, or positions of authority in religious organizations.

The regulation of sex can be a vector of oppression. Gayle Rubin (1984), theorized in "Thinking Sex: Notes on a Radical Theory of the Politics of Sexuality" how the soiled identities of sexually stigmatized groups have been used to limit people's access to status and legitimacy. Such identities include those of women who have had an abortion or used birth control, single women who are not virgins, someone with a sexually transmitted disease, a prostitute, or someone who is lesbian, gay, bisexual or transgender. Society creates sexual castes, according to Rubin. Sexual hierarchies reflect idealized notions of sexuality, with sexual "perverts" placed in descending order based on the stigma attached to particular sexual behavior or identity. Perversion can refer to any sexually stigmatized quality exhibited in socio-historical context. Why does sex within marriage go virtually unregulated, while sex outside of marriage, by teens for instance, or people of the same sex, is subject to extensive regulation? Is sex different within marriage? More moral and free of problems?

While much of the regulation of sexuality is situated in religious and legal codes of conduct, reflecting the varying cultural biases of these institutions, the medical and psychiatric communities have played a role in codifying stigmatization as well. The medical profession has used a disease model to identify "healthy" compared to "sick" sexuality—classifications which at various times have medicalized and problematized women's sexual urges (as we know from Rachel Maines's article on vibrators earlier in this book). Children's sexual development (including childhood and teen masturbation), teen sexual relationships, and of course, same sex attractions, have all been subject to pathologizing (being seen as a problem of the individual) by the medical community.

Perhaps sex is taken all too seriously in Western culture, and as a result, regulated beyond that which is necessary. Do we need, as Rubin suggested, a "radical theory" of the politics of sex? The term "radical" in a sociological sense refers to proposals that seek not just minor changes or adjustments to the status quo. Rather, the term suggests a complete re-thinking of the very foundation, including assumptions, values, and beliefs upon which social norms are based. Radical proposals imply a need for systems change—change in the embedded relationships of members of society, and changes in social institutions themselves.

As you read this section of the book, think about the regulation of sex. Who should decide? What is the effect of stigmatization? Of power imbalances? Under what conditions are regulations necessary or desirable? Can laws be reasonably enforced? Can they be enforced without costing all people some degree of sexual freedom? Are we born sexually out of control with a "dangerous biologically driven libido," as some who impose strict laws governing sexual expression would argue? If we are not out of control, then do we need to enact any laws governing sexuality?

In "Contraceptive Policy and Ethics: Illustrations from American History," Kathleen Powderly provides a historical perspective on the birth control movement in the United States. This movement, from the late 1800s to the present, has been the result of differences in perception about women's access to resources for controlling their reproductive lives. Powderly outlines the central ethical issue that informs the debate over birth control— whether or not women should have control over their own reproductive capacity. She also suggests that much of the struggle has been a class struggle. Wealthier women have been more likely to access birth control—smuggled in from Europe prior to its legalization in the United States—while poorer women, with less access and fewer resources to purchase birth control, have been accused of having "too many babies." Powderly notes that in the late 1800s, prior to having virtually any legal access to birth control and long before abortion was decriminalized, women's deaths from self-induced abortions were fifteen times higher than deaths from women giving birth.

Efforts to legalize access to birth control, as well as to legal abortions, have been fraught with questions about who decides whether or not a woman has a baby. Some early advocates for birth control saw it as a means to discourage poor women from having children, a class-based argument grounded in a eugenics notion that only the better-off should reproduce. Others in the movement argued it was a right of women, and not the state, to determine whether they would have children. The actions by the state have at times resulted in promoting birth control for some women, such as the very poor and mentally retarded, while at other times, actively opposing it for others. Until the 1960s, says Powderly, sterilization was performed on poorer women as well as the mentally retarded, in many cases without the woman being fully informed about the procedure. As you read this article, consider the role of government in determining the reproductive decisions of women. Does restricting women's access to reproductive services serve a purpose? For whom? Who should decide? What reasons justify the use of birth control, sterilization, or abortion? Again, who should decide?

"Rights: Treatment of Sexual Minorities a Global Shame," by Marwaan Macan-Markar draws on a report by Amnesty International to describe the extent to which sexual minorities, including people who are transgender, lesbian, or gay, experience discrimination, abuse, torture, and death at the hands of intolerant, or at minimum, insensitive governments. Amnesty International is a public nonprofit organization that investigates human rights abusers and advocates for an end to such practices. Amnesty International's study found a "conspiracy of silence" among nations for abuses based on sexuality. Countries that criminalize same-sex relationships and transgender people often impose further abuse on sexual minorities by the way they are treated by police, prison guards, and administrators. These additional abuses often are supported in subtle and sometimes overt ways by government and religious leaders.

In those countries where same-sex relationships or transgender identity can result in threat of violence, prison, or death, the risks to those who do speak out can be substantial. The result is a "catch-22" effect—those countries with the most restrictive policies are least likely to hear the voices of those whose lives are threatened. At the same time, Amnesty International is concerned that there is little being done by any elected government or international group to address the issues. Even NGOs (non-governmental organizations) advocating for changes around sexually oppressive policies have difficulty gaining access to government meetings and international forums to advocate for change. Voices advocating for the sexually oppressed are not ones most politicians want to hear.

Considering that voices of sexual minorities can be squelched by those in positions of power, what approaches can be used to change policies? Should outside groups advocate for changes in countries where organizing by sexual minorities is forbidden? Do sexual minorities have a right to exist without fear of arrest, harassment, or abuse? How have sexual minorities been treated in your own country, community, school, or family?

When Sally Armstrong describes female genital mutilation (FGM) in her article, "Not My Daughter," she is talking about a practice that is rooted in the customs and cultures of 28 countries. Over 126 million women around the globe, says Armstrong, have experienced FGM—a practice that involves cutting the genitalia of young girls, varying from reduction or removal of the clitoris to infibulation, sewing tight the entrance to the vagina. It is a practice rooted in culture, in ritual, and in perceptions of female sexuality. Boys and men come to believe the practice is necessary for women if they are to be good wives. Women are fearful that if their daughters are not cut, they will not be desirable to men, believing they have no viable alternatives. Armstrong reports that in Sierra Leone and other countries, through efforts by women and men who challenge the custom, and through advocacy at the international level, these practices are being contested and new beliefs are beginning to replace old ones.

Armstrong's article, like ones earlier in this chapter, raises questions about the influence of power and its effect on the least powerful. It raises questions about what is done in the name of traditions that receive institutional legitimacy, and about the role of people outside a culture influencing change. Armstrong's report also calls on us to question the oppressive traditions related to sexuality that we were raised with in our own culture. To what extent should practices based on religious beliefs be challenged? In what way does Armstrong's article suggest that not only women, but men as well, are socialized into accepting traditions without fully understanding the implications and without questioning that status quo? How does this article relate to others you've read in this book? Consider issues of body image and female beauty, the practice of male circumcision, the taboos against various sexual practices and orientations. What it will take to bring about change?

Like Sierra Leone, the Netherlands, Germany, and France have undergone change in how they approach social issues related to sexuality. During the past 50 years, these countries, like others in Europe, and more recently South Africa, have made changes in laws and social policies that are intended to reduce oppression of sexual minorities, increase information and support for young people who are sexually active, and reduce the incidence of unintended pregnancies, disease, and other negative outcomes of sexual relationships. Maureen Kelly and Michael McGee, in their article, "Report from a Study Tour: Teen Sexuality Education in the Netherlands, France, and Germany," describe the effects of a sex-positive approach to information, education, and access to resources for young people. These countries now experience a substantially lower incidence of sexuality-related problems when compared to more conservative countries such as the United States. As the authors note, teen birthrate per 1,000 girls in the United States (between 15 and 19 years of age) is 64, while in Germany it is 13, in France, 19, and in the Netherlands, 7.

The experience of these countries tells us that with greater access to information and support, teens experience fewer negative outcomes from being sexually active. As we note earlier in this book, teenagers in the United States have sexual intercourse at about the same age and as frequently as teens in these countries, but the incidence of problems related to disease, pregnancy, and even rape and sexual assault, are higher in the United States. Kelly and McGee describe how the information and support for young people is woven into the culture. There is not just one institution involved in supporting teens around sexuality. Rather, this support is a joint effort of families, schools, religious organizations, and government. Both the authors are sexuality educators in the United States. What they learned from their "tour" of sexuality education in Europe helped them understand how important government policies can be to reducing the incidence of sexuality related problems.

As you read this article, consider what it would be like for you to have the job of sexuality education director in your community. What would you want to do? What outcomes could you anticipate? Given the comparison of sexual practices by U.S. teens and those in the countries Kelly and McGee describe, what prevents the United States from being as successful?

When David Satcher, the former U.S. Surgeon General, issued his report "The Surgeon General's Call to Action to Promote Sexual Health and Responsible Sexual Behavior, 2001," the reception by politicians was mixed. Many conservatives attacked the report as being too liberal, while liberals accepted the report as evidence of the need for extended sexuality education and support services. Dr. Satcher's report lacked support within the Bush administration, and in fact, he resigned the year after the report came out. Reactions to Dr. Satcher's report make it clear that sex is a political act. We've included his letter introducing the report as well as the report's vision for the future, as the final reading in this section because of its focus on sexual practices, policies, and problems in the United States. We encourage to view the full report at http://www.surgeongeneral.gov/library/sexualhealth/call.htm.

The Surgeon General discourages the use of sexual scare tactics and "abstinence-only" education, calling on schools to provide young people with information about how to prevent the spread of disease and reduce the risk of unintended pregnancy. He also acknowledges the role of parents and family members and other community supports for helping young people in the decision-making process. But it isn't just young people Dr. Satcher is concerned about; he calls for a better-informed and better-resourced nation when it comes to understanding sexuality and being sexually active.

As you read the Surgeon General's letter and vision, consider why his report has been controversial. What portions of it would most likely be points of contention by political and religious advocates? What might prevent, or enhance, the chances that his recommendations will be followed? What would be the likely response of your local community if his policies were implemented? Why?

Rubin, G.S. (1984) Thinking Sex: Notes for a radical theory of the politics of sexuality, in G.S. Vance (ed), *Pleasure and Danger: Exploring Female Sexuality*, Boston: Routledge & K. Paul.

Contraceptive Policy and Ethics: Illustrations from American History

Kathleen E. Powderly

While the technology of long-term contraceptives is relatively new, many of the ethical and policy dilemmas surrounding their use are not. The history of the birth control movement in this country over the past 125 years provides clear examples of the tensions that have always existed between empowering women to control their fertility and promoting limitations on fertility for the disadvantaged. While this is not an exhaustive survey, several important developments in the history of the American birth control movement have been chosen to illustrate these tensions.

In the late nineteenth century, Victorian opinion tolerated promiscuity among men and promoted sexual self-control among women. Prostitutes were a common and accepted solution to this dichotomy. Despite the view that female sexuality was to serve the end of reproduction rather than the woman's pleasure, contraception was widely practiced among all social classes. The methods employed varied by class, however, due to cost and availability. The upper classes were more likely to use relatively expensive methods of contraception such as condoms, spermicides, and douches. They might also have had access to diaphragms and cervical caps, which were smuggled in from Europe at a high cost. Withdrawal and rhythm were often the only methods available to the poor. In an era when menstrual cycles were poorly understood, pregnancies often resulted. Abortion, often self-induced and always dangerous, was re-

Source: Hastings Center Report, special supplement, vol. 25, issue 1. Copyright © 1995.

sorted to frequently. It is estimated that by the 1850s one out of every five to six pregnancies in America ended with an abortion.[1] Mortality from septic abortions was extremely high. In 1888, death from abortion was estimated to be fifteen times greater than maternal mortality.[2]

During this era, American feminists supported the concept of "voluntary motherhood."[3] Far from empowering women and providing them with sexual freedom, however, voluntary motherhood sustained traditional family roles for women. According to this concept, limiting family size enhanced women's ability to fulfill their societal roles as wives and mothers. Feminists were joined by moral reformers, who were concerned about excessive breeding among the lower classes, particularly immigrants. Targeting the lower class and members of minority groups in the effort to reduce fertility has strong historical roots in the late nineteenth century.

Although contraception was widely practiced in private, many were not willing to risk public expressions of support for it or admit to its use. This reluctance influenced public policy. Abortion was declared illegal for the first time in the United States in 1830. A majority of states had declared it so by 1870.[4] A great legal blow was dealt to contraception in 1873 with the passage of what came to be known as the Comstock laws—a federal statute that made it illegal to transport obscene materials through the mail. Contraceptive devices such as condoms and diaphragms, as well as sexually explicit literature, were confiscated under this law. It took the work of one of birth control's leading proponents, Margaret Sanger, to weaken its effects.

MARGARET SANGER AND THE MOVEMENT FOR PLANNED PARENTHOOD

Perhaps no name is more closely associated with birth control, family planning, and reproductive freedom for women than Margaret

Sanger. The daughter of Irish immigrants, Sanger was born in 1879 and played a strong role in the birth control movement in the United States and abroad until her death in 1966. While she promoted access to birth control for all women, she focused particularly on the poor, as upper-class women had some access to contraception from their private physicians. Poor women did not. Sanger believed that uncontrolled fertility and large families were inextricably linked to poverty. Her efforts to empower poor women, however, had affinities with the eugenics movement. Many eugenicists supported the idea of limiting population growth, particularly among those they viewed as undesirable. They were greatly troubled by the idea that the upper classes would use birth control and the lower classes would continue to breed. The tension between empowering poor women to control their fertility for their own best interest and limiting fertility among the poor and the underclass persists to this day in the debate about long-acting contraceptives.

Margaret Sanger brought birth control directly to the poor women of Brooklyn on 16 October 1916 when she opened a freestanding clinic in Brownsville. Immigrant women from many cultures lined up with their baby carriages to learn how to prevent future pregnancies. In the few weeks of the clinic's existence, 464 women were provided with sex education and contraceptive information. The clinic was raided by the New York City Vice Squad and Sanger and her sister, Ethel Byrne, the clinic's nurse, were jailed. The trial produced an important legal victory for birth control. The New York State Court of Appeals interpreted the law to allow for prescription of contraceptives by physicians, not only to prevent or cure venereal disease—an interpretation largely applied to men—but also for any health reason. This opened the door for physicians to prescribe contraceptives for women. Sanger's victory, however, was bought at a price. Birth control from that point on was a physician-dominated enterprise. Nurses, and to a large extent, women, were not to control the provision of contraceptives.[5]

STERILIZATION

The first reported tubal sterilization was performed by Samuel Lungren, an Ohio physician, in 1880.[6] The procedure was proposed in the early nineteenth century as a means of long-term contraception in women undergoing Caesarean sections. It was not until the latter part of the century, when asepsis and safer anesthesia were available, that Caesareans were attempted with any frequency, and even then they were still quite risky. The mortality rate for the sixty-eight Caesarean sections that had been performed in the U.S. from 1882 to 1891 was 40 percent.[7] Surely, if a woman survived one section, avoidance of another might be desirable. Many of the early tubal ligations were recommended for "protective" indications, i.e., to protect the life and health of the woman.[8]

After the turn of the century, however, eugenics was a dominant reason for tubal sterilization, particularly involuntary sterilization. Compulsory sterilization began to be recommended for individuals with hereditary disease, the "feeble-minded" (e.g., the insane and demented), and the mentally retarded. There were also racial overtones, as undesirable characteristics were perceived to occur more often in people of Asian and African origin and in the foreign-born. In addition, there were some moves to sterilize habitual criminals. While recommendations for habitual criminals dealt largely with men, efforts to control hereditary and mental illnesses were often directed at women.[9] Efforts to train women living in mental institutions gave way to a program to keep them from reproducing.

The view that deviance was hereditary was supported, in large part, by studies of two families: the Jukes and the Kallikaks. Richard Dugdale, a social reformer, studied 709 people over five generations in a family he called the Jukes. Although Dugdale believed both heredity and environment were to blame for the Jukes' propensity to crime, intemperance, and prostitution, he laid special emphasis on heredity, estimating that the family had cost society $1,308,000.[10] In 1912 Henry Goddard contributed significantly to the belief that deviance was hereditary when he published *The Kallikak Family*. Goddard had been studying feeble-mindedness when he discovered the family, which he traced back over six generations. The progenitor had produced both a legitimate line, consisting of upstanding citizens, and an illegitimate line, consisting of large families with a disproportionate number of feeble-minded individuals.[11]

Already concerned with the effects of immigration on population demographics, eugenicists were given superb ammunition with these two studies. The eugenics movement also received financial support from some of the country's most prominent philanthropists, including Mrs. E. H. Harriman, John D. Rockefeller, Dr. John Harvey Kellogg, and Samuel Fels.[12] Even Theodore Roosevelt supported the movement, urging Americans to avoid "racial suicide." The upper classes must not be outnumbered in their progeny by immigrants and the lower class.

The nation's first involuntary sterilization law was passed in 1907 in Indiana. California followed suit in 1909 and by 1913, fourteen states had laws allowing involuntary sterilization. The effect of the laws varied. From 1907 to 1921 there were 3,233 documented sterilizations performed under state laws. These sterilizations were seen by many within the mental hygiene movement as beneficial to society and, at the very least, as not harmful to the individual. On the other hand, seven of the laws were declared unconstitutional. While there was much popular and professional support,

eugenic sterilization was still controversial. Additional statutes, drafted with greater concern for constitutional constraints and greater care about guardians' consent, were more successful. Ultimately, the Supreme Court provided a boost for involuntary sterilization in Buck v. Bell. In that 1927 decision, Oliver Wendell Holmes wrote: "It is better for all the world, if instead of waiting to execute degenerate offspring for crime, or to let them starve for their imbecility, society can prevent those who are manifestly unfit from continuing their kind." The number of states with sterilization laws increased to thirty and the number of involuntary sterilizations increased to more than 60,000 persons. Sterilization programs were active through the 1940s and 1950s, uninfluenced by reactions to Nazi sterilizations, indeed, there was a dramatic increase in the percentage of women who were sterilized in the U.S. after 1930.[13] Eugenic sterilization virtually disappeared after the 1960s as the nation entered an era of awareness of patients' rights and, most especially, of the need for society to protect the vulnerable.

The major ethical conflict regarding sterilization today is balancing the rights of a mentally retarded or mentally disabled person to sexual freedom with a protection of her best interests regarding childbearing. Even in cases where it is clear that the individual has no ability to comprehend childbearing and may be harmed by the experience, it is difficult to obtain a court order for sterilization because of the history of the abuses.

Ethical issues have also come up in voluntary sterilization of mentally competent individuals. Some women, particularly poor women, have not had access to desired sterilization. Married women were sometimes required to have their husband's consent or were denied sterilizations until they had produced a certain number of children. Young women who had never given birth were also denied tubal ligations on the grounds that they cannot always be successfully reversed, should the woman later want children. Previous pregnancies, marital status, and age, while important considerations, should not be used to deny a woman a tubal sterilization if she really desires one.

Sterilizations have sometimes been advocated for women with serious medical conditions such as tuberculosis, diabetes, or cardiovascular disease. While these illnesses may make pregnancy medically undesirable, it is important to recognize that they are conditions more common among the poor and women of color.[14] Thus, although sterilization under these circumstances may be offered with the best of medical intentions, it is apt to be perceived as racist or promoting eugenics. Counseling regarding sterilization as a contraceptive option must be done with sensitivity to the historical context.

BIRTH CONTROL AND THE MODERN ERA

The 1960s and 1970s saw great technological advances in contraception. The development and approval of oral contraceptives finally provided a highly effective form of contraception that was not associated with individual sexual acts. Intrauterine devices also became popular choices for women and couples who wanted to control fertility. Although IUDs would later become less available because of legal challenges related to side effects of the Dalkon Shield, they were a method of choice for many women during this time.

In addition to technological advances, there were legal and policy gains for birth control. A significant victory in this regard occurred in New York City in 1957, when Dr. Louis M. Hellman, in violation of the policies of the Commissioner of Hospitals, fitted with a diaphragm a severely diabetic woman who had just given birth. The media had been notified and the resulting coverage precipitated a policy change that allowed women to receive contraceptive counseling and devices in municipal hospitals in New York City.[15]

In 1965 the Supreme Court declared contraception a constitutional right for married couples, in Griswold v. Connecticut. The Comstock laws were finally repealed in 1971 and the Supreme Court guaranteed a woman's right to abortion in Roe v. Wade in 1973. This, however, did not ensure that women would have access to contraceptives and abortion services. Some women could not afford contraceptives. For others, partners or spouses prohibited the use of desired contraceptives. In addition, the fight against legalized abortion rages on, and has escalated to violent outbursts that threaten the providers and users of abortion services. There is also the danger that women who do not desire contraceptives will be coerced into using them by partners or social pressures.

The current ethical and policy issues with long-acting contraceptives have an important historical context. Well-intentioned efforts to empower all women, including poor women of color, must be balanced with a keen sense of the abuses evident in the history of the birth control movement. Racism and eugenic concerns have been consistent issues in debates about controlling fertility, and our targeted educational programs and initiatives must be sensitive to community concerns. Empowering women to make their own reproductive choices is a praiseworthy goal. It can only be achieved if we maintain an awareness of the successes and failures in the history of the birth control movement.

NOTES

1. Ellen Chesler, *Women of Valor: Margaret Sanger and the Birth Control Movement in America* (New York: Simon and Schuster, 1992), p. 63.
2. M. A. La Sorte, "Nineteenth Century Family Planning Practices," *Journal of Psychohistory* 4 (1976):163–83.

3. Linda Gordon, *Woman's Body, Woman's Right: Birth Control in America* (New York: Penguin, 1981), pp. 95–115.

4. La Sorte, "Family Planning," pp. 163–83.

5. Chesler, "Women of Valor," pp. 150–60.

6. S. S. Lungren, "A Case of Cesarean Section Twice Successfully Performed on the Same Patient," *American Journal of Obstetrics* 14 (1881):78.

7. *Brooklyn Gynecological Society Minutes,* vol. 1, 1890–1899. Medical Research Library of Brooklyn, Archives, SUNY Health Science Center at Brooklyn.

8. Per E. Bordahl, "Tubal Sterilization: A Historical Review," *Journal of Reproductive Medicine* 30, no. 1 (1985):19.

9. Philip R. Reilly, *The Surgical Solution* (Baltimore: Johns Hopkins University Press, 1991).

10. Richard L. Dugdale, *The Jukes: A Study in Crime, Pauperism, Disease and Heredity* (New York: G. P. Putnam & Sons, 1877).

11. Henry H. Goddard, *The Kallikak Family* (New York: Macmillan, 1912).

12. Philip R. Reilly, "Involuntary Sterilization in the United States: A Surgical Solution," *Quarterly Review of Biology* 62, no. 2 (1987):153–70.

13. Reilly, "Involuntary Sterilization," pp. 154–60.

14. Barron Lerner, "Constructing Medical Indications: The Sterilization of Women with Heart Disease or Tuberculosis, 1905–1935," *Journal of the History of Medicine and Allied Sciences* 49 (1994):362–79.

15. Louis M. Hellman, "Family Planning Comes of Age," *American Journal of Obstetrics and Gynecology* 109, no. 2 (1971):214–24.

READING 59

Rights: Treatment of Sexual Minorities a Global Shame

Marwaan Macan-Markar

Mexico City, Jun 24 (IPS World Desk)—Governments and societies in all parts of the world continue to violate the human rights of sexual minorities in pervasive, pernicious, and often violent ways, investigators say.

The discrimination faced by gay men, lesbians, bisexuals and transgender people is so extensive and profound—ranging from social censure to torture and death—that the human rights group Amnesty International has termed it "an unacknowledged global shame."

A panel of independent UN experts is appealing to communities around the world to submit information to help it investigate sexual minority issues.

"The right to sexual preference should not be violated," says Hina Jilani, the UN secretary-general's special representative on human rights defenders. "We are concerned about the level of discrimination and persecution."

Jilani's colleagues on the panel include Nigel Rodley, the UN's special rapporteur on torture, and Radhika Coomaraswamy, the special rapporteur on violence against women.

Rodley plans to include information on "individual cases of torture and general allegations" against homosexuals and transsexuals in his next annual report to the UN Commission on Human Rights.

Similar patterns of abuse and discrimination on the basis of sexual identity are enshrined in social mores—and legitimised by law, policy and government practice—in countries as apparently unlike as Brazil, Syria and the United States, human rights monitors say.

Abuses range from torture, ill treatment, and sexual assault to forced medical or psychiatric treatment, according to Amnesty.

Source: IPS World Desk Online. Copyright © 2001 Inter-Press Service. Reprinted with permission from IPS World Desk.

"The world over, lesbians, gay men, bisexual and transgender people are at particular risk of human rights violations because of their sexual identity," the London-based human rights watchdog says in a report, "Torture based on sexual identity—an unacknowledged global shame."

Police and prison officials are among the perpetrators of such abuses in the 30 countries Amnesty studied for its report. In Brazil, for instance, three transvestites were arrested in one town and taken to the police station where they were "brutally beaten with rubber sandals studded with nails and forced to clean filthy lavatories."

Amnesty also highlights "physical and psychological violence—often amounting to torture—in the community and even in the family." In Syria, it reports, a gay student was held back after school and raped by a teacher who told him he was a "sin to this world."

"The prevalence of sexism and homophobia in society means that lesbians are at particular risk of abuse, including being forced into marriage or sexual relationships with men," Amnesty adds.

Although such abuse is pervasive across continents and cultures, it is surrounded by "a conspiracy of silence" stemming from "generalised tolerance" of abuse against these victims and "fear of retaliation and reluctance by the victims to gain exposure," the group says.

Equally disturbing, notes Amnesty, are laws that condemn same-sex acts. "In over 70 countries same-sex relations are considered a crime, and in some instances they incur the death penalty."

According to another, US-based rights group, these "sodomy laws" have led to violence against homosexuals and transsexuals in Romania, India, Saudi Arabia, Egypt and elsewhere.

Laws "regulating sexual behaviour, social norms, or gender give a pretext for detention and for police brutality and inhuman treatment," according to the San Francisco-based International Gay and Lesbian Human Rights Commission (IGLHRC).

The group blames governments for legitimising violence against sexual minorities.

"In many countries, governments either directly or indirectly permit violence against those who belong to a sexual minority," says Sydney Levy, IGLHRC's communications director. "Being a member of a sexual minority comes at a heavy price."

Many states, Levy adds, "hold the view that gays and lesbians do not need protection even if they are persecuted."

Even where laws appear less overtly hostile to sexual minorities, the group says, policies that contain discriminatory treatment based on sexual orientation or gender identity contribute to creating "a class of people whose existence may not be criminalised, but whose, citizenship is clearly second-class."

Such discriminatory practices include the banishment of gays from organisations such as the Boy Scouts of America and the refusal to recognise same-sex marriages, resulting in the denial of health insurance and other benefits customarily offered to heterosexual couples.

Jilani, the UN special representative, says, "Human rights cannot be separated into different boxes, and the marginalisation of a people is a violation of minority groups. They have a right to be part of the mainstream."

T. Kumar, of Amnesty's U.S. section, says governments cannot claim to uphold human rights if the rights of sexual minorities are denied. "As a first step, they should change the laws in the books that declare same-sex acts as a crime," he says.

Thereafter, governments should create an atmosphere for "public acceptance" of gay and lesbian rights, he argues, adding, "The rights of NGOs (non-governmental organisations) working on these issues have to be protected."

Kumar's appeal on behalf of NGOs is particularly timely. On Monday, the UN General

Assembly begins a three-day special session on HIV-AIDS. Many grassroots groups— including those having nothing to do with sexual minorities—have complained of being marginalised or excluded from the event as well as the series of prior negotiations to hammer out a declaration for governments to adopt at the formal session. Reportedly, this has been done at the behest of delegates from the United States, Sudan, Syria, Pakistan, Malaysia, Egypt and the Philippines, among others.

Sexual minorities are at particularly high risk of contracting HIV-AIDS, according to UNAIDS, the joint agency spearheading the world body's response to the deadly epidemic. Yet, the IGLHRC is among groups that have been barred from the UN session's human rights roundtable.

Not My Daughter

Sally Armstrong

The contrasts are stunning: the beauty and serenity of the women sitting in the circle: the hideous brutality of the stories they share. It was in this little meeting room that they learned that the ancient ritual of excision (female circumcision) performed on them as little girls was the cause of the horrific health problems they suffer as adults. It was here they learned that cutting off a girl's external genitals had nothing whatsoever to do with religion. And it was here they made a public declaration to forever ban an ethnic tradition that has been going on for 1,000 years.

The women of Malicounda, a village in the West African country of Senegal, are as far away from the cosmopolitan offices of worldly bureaucrats as you can get. But here, amidst the clusters of thatched roof huts, herds of bleating goats and towering Baobab trees, they have succeeded where diplomats, politicians and scores of western women had failed. They made history as the first village to stop what's known to most of the world as female genital mutilation (FGM). Today, the movement they started is spreading like a grass fire.

More than 126 million women in 28 countries have been sexually mutilated in the name of tradition. Every day, 6,000 little girls are subjected to the old woman known as the cutter, or excisist, who slices off their genitalia with a razor. There's no anesthetic, no sterilization. There's only agony, sometimes death and always a future of pain. And in the time-tested tradition of keeping a stranglehold on the status quo, there is a taboo about speaking of the procedure to anyone.

Given the power of the taboo, it was with some trepidation that Dr. Winnie Tay, the country director of Plan International in Sierra Leone (known as Foster Parents Plan International in Canada), organized the country's first-ever conference on FGM in May, 1996. Today, in his new office in Dakar, the Senegalese capital, Tay recalls that the vice-president of Sierra Leone was supposed to give the opening address but cancelled at the last minute. "Later, he said to me, 'As a medical doctor I support you. As a politician, I can't touch this.'"

Tay's gamble paid off. The conference hall was packed. The secret was at last at the debating table. The truth was about to be told.

The attendees, including sociologists, aid workers, religious leaders, teenagers and their fathers and mothers, sat in stunned silence as they watched the horror of FGM on a video-tape recorded in Ethiopia.

The child in the video is only eight years old. Today is her birthday. Her mother takes her by the hand and leads her to a hut at the edge of the village. Inside the hut she is tied to a chair, her legs splayed apart. An old woman clutching a rusty razor tells her to be brave and not to make a noise. Then she grasps the skin above the child's clitoris and begins cutting. The child screams in agony while the woman slices off piece after piece; the hood of the clitoris, the clitoris itself, the labia minora, the labia majora. She closes the gaping bloody wound with three thorns and slathers it with what looks like herbs and raw eggs. The child is removed to a mat, her legs are tied together and she's told that now she is a woman.

If she doesn't bleed to death, if she doesn't die from shock or pelvic infection or tetanus, she faces a lifetime of pain. The opening she's left with is the size of the tip of the little finger. Passing urine is so painful, she'll try to retain it, which causes urinary tract infection and sometimes septicemia. When she's old enough to menstruate, she'll suffer again as the menstrual flow pools inside the scarred wall simply because it can't exit through the tiny opening. And when she marries and is re-cut with a razor to make intercourse possible, she faces the added burden of becoming pregnant with a birth canal that has been mutilated. She'll adopt the expression so many women before her have learned, "The first one always dies. It is making a passage for the other children." Because the labia minora that stretches and aids in a baby's birth has been cut off, the labor is prolonged and the baby is often starved of oxygen.

The participants at the symposium were thunderstruck. The men claimed they had no idea that's what was being done to their wives and daughters. In fact the women themselves didn't know the details as it was not a subject they could discuss with anyone. Apart from prompting shock, the disturbing images of the procedure served to forever exorcise the taboo. People, at least here in the conference hall in Sierra Leone, wanted to talk.

The roots of this brutal rite of passage are as confounding as the business of stopping it. Some say it is a religious requirement but although it is practised by both Muslims and Christians and some Jewish sects, it is not mentioned in either the Koran or the Bible. Some say it is to improve the health and child-bearing capabilities of the women, despite irrefutable medical evidence to the contrary. Others claim it is to make a woman more attractive, a better and more sexually satisfied wife. In fact, it can hobble a woman with scarring, pain and trauma. Others claim that like foot binding in China and other misogynist practices, it is an obsession with purity, sanctioned by tradition, and has an inherent tendency to catch on and spread, using women as scapegoats.

The United Nations has tried for more than a decade to stop FGM. World courts have made it a criminal offence. So have many of the countries where it is practised. Western women have descended on the villages with accusations of barbarism. But until Malicounda set an example in July, 1997, the village women ignored the UN, refused to obey a law that threatened their ancient customs and basically told western women to go home and mind their own business.

A few months after the declaration by the women of Malicounda, 12 more villages took the same oath. Then, in June of this year, 18 villages in the southern region of Kolda, people of the Fulani and Mandinka ethnic groups, also declared a ban on FGM. In October, women in the neighboring country, Mali, invited the women of Malicounda to come to discuss the business of declaring an end to FGM. And in the St. Louis region in the north of the country, another 70 villages are moving toward making a public declaration.

This is one of those overnight success stories that was seven years in the making. And by all accounts the story begins with Molly Melching, a woman from smalltown U.S.A. (Danville, Ill.) who came to Dakar 24 years ago as an exchange student and never went home. She learned the language, adopted the styles of the people, moved into a village and in the process experienced an epiphany: change isn't an external event, it's an internal event. In other words, if someone tells you to stop doing something that you think to be right, you'll reject the advice out of hand. A simple analogy: "if someone tells you that putting braces on your child's teeth is bad because it causes brain damage, you'd think they were crazy."

"Given the opportunity to gather the information needed for change, you'll make the best decision yourself," says Melching, a six foot tall charismatic woman who fills a room with her presence. And if it's your idea, it will work." That realization inspired Melching and her Senegalese team to create a program that would help women to make their own decisions. "By the way," she says, when she learns that I'm Canadian, "Canada was the only country in the world willing to fund our idea."

In 1991, Melching started a nongovernmental organization called Tostan, which means "breakthrough" in the native Wolof language. She developed a six-part program for women which included basic hygiene, literacy and problem-solving. Melching knew the dropout rate in literacy classes was very high and felt that if she could make the classroom a nurturing place where women wanted to be, where they could talk about issues important to them, they would stay. She uses storytelling, songs and theatre as her teaching tools. Soon enough the women told her they wanted to learn about their own health, their bodies. "I realized they didn't know about menstruation, about menopause. I also realized that they didn't know what their rights were. When I told them about human rights and that they

have the right to health, we began to have incredible conversations. They discussed wife assault for the first time. They talked about child labor and discovered that the children had the right to education, to being with their parents and shouldn't be sent off at the age of 10 to work as maids in the towns. Then I asked them what problems they had with excision [FGM]. They, said, 'None.' So I asked if we shouldn't talk about it. 'Yes, talk about it,' they said. 'But you'll never ever change it.'"

Up until then, when health workers asked women who'd been circumcised if they had problems with, for example, urinating or delivering babies they would say no. They presumed it was normal to take 15 minutes to urinate and three to five days of hard labor to deliver a baby. When women in Melching's classes began to realize that other women didn't have the health problems they had, the floodgates opened. Women shared their stories and began to draw an inevitable conclusion: they needed to make change.

But change, particularly one that dismantles a thousand-year-old ritual, comes with cost. Soon after the women banished FGM, a backlash whipped up like a tropical storm. They had agreed to allow reporters from Dakar to come to the village and ask them questions. On July 31, 1997, their story was splashed across the front page of every newspaper in the country. The month of August bore witness to the perilous path of pioneers. Some newspapers portrayed them as revolutionaries. Some religious leaders scorned the women. Their husbands accused them of having no *sutura* (discretion) by speaking publicly about such a private and culturally sensitive issue. And some militant defenders of cultural identity wished a pox on their houses.

And so the women called a meeting, a return to the circle in the little yellow room where they had met weekly for two years. When Melching arrived and talked with the women, she was truly worried about what was going on. "You have already suffered enough," she told them. "You could go back. Or stop talking to others about the decision you've made. This backlash could get worse."

The silence was deafening. Then Tene Cissoko, a 31-year-old mother of four, stood up. The tension in the room was palpable. All eyes turned to the attractive woman who, like her ancestors, had never before questioned FGM. "No," she said. "We'll never go back. We made this decision based on what we know to be true. We are Amazon women. We'll continue the struggle even if it means problems."

Every woman in the room stood with her. Their collective vow in the face of a swirling controversy: "Never again. Not my daughter."

Like apostles of their newly discovered human rights, they started spreading the word. When the village of Kër Simbara was preparing for its annual circumcision rites, the Malicounda women traveled the 60-kilometre distance to that village to tell them why they had decided to stop the tradition.

They knew that sharing their knowledge with the women wasn't enough. They needed to talk to the men, the elders and the Imam (the Muslim leader of the area).

Initially the people of Kër Simbara were furious. But the Imam, an old man called Demba Diawara, was upset by the stories he heard that day. Could it be true, he wondered. He told the women, "We are a family of 11 villages. We could never do this without talking to the rest of our family."

Speaking in the epigrammatic style he favors, Diawara explains to me, "Your brain always has two voices. One will give you advice. One will stop you from changing. I thought I had to listen to this new information. But I also thought our traditions need to be respected. I felt it was my obligation at that point to put on my shoes and go and talk to the rest of our family about this."

He and his nephew Cheikh Traore trekked from village to village. They met with the chief, the leader of the women's group and the young people. "We didn't just go once. We went back three or four times. These things had never been discussed publicly." Traore adds, "I went and talked to a medical doctor about what the women were saying. He said, 'This is something you practise but it is very detrimental to the health of women and girls.' He gave me examples and it all began to make sense to me. We'd heard stories we couldn't believe. If we'd known this before, we would have stopped excision a long time ago."

On November 20, 1997, the president of Senegal, Abdou Diduf, made a declaration of his own. "I want all the villages of Senegal to follow the example set by the women of Malicounda." On February 3 of this year he began the process of writing the ban into the law of the land.

While social anthropologists have always believed it would take hundreds of years to end FGM, research fellows like Gerry Mackie of the University of Oxford in England, who has written extensively about foot binding in China, say that this no longer holds true. In fact, says Mackie, Melching's approach indicates that FGM "will end suddenly and universally."

Although foot binding persisted in China for 1,000 years, once reform began, it ended in about 10. "The work of anti-foot binding reformers had three aspects," says Mackie. "First, they carried out a modern education campaign which explained that the rest of the world did not bind women's feet. Second, they explained the advantages of natural feet and the disadvantages of bound feet. Third, they formed natural foot societies whose members publicly pledged not to bind their daughters' feet nor to let their sons marry women with bound feet. The women of Malicounda reinvented the techniques of the anti-foot binding reformers when they took part in the Tostan program." The key, he says, is the public pledge and the fact that Tostan provides the education but never tells people what to do.

Molly Melching is delighted, if somewhat overwhelmed, by the rapid-fire success of her program. Plan International director Winnie Tay calls her a "tour de force." And UNICEF manager Teresa Pinilla says, "None of this would have happened without Molly." But Pinella admits funding has become a problem. The program is spreading all across the country and six neighboring countries have asked for Tostan's assistance. Although it was the Canadian International Development Agency (CIDA) that funded her through UNICEF to begin with, she didn't make CIDA's list for continued funding and presently relies on UNICEF and the American Jewish World Service to continue the program. Watching her making phone calls, faxing proposals for funding and trying to find time to tend to her devoted flock of teachers and villagers makes this observer think the funding matter is more of a crisis than a problem.

On the road to eliminating a practice that has been a scourge to African women, Melching has also experienced her share of the backlash. One man spit on her in Dakar. Another shrieked obscenities at "the woman who is destroying our traditions." But mostly Melching is received like family by an ever increasing number of Senegalese people who see her as their hero.

One is Ibrahima Ndiaye, office manager at a large European airline in Dakar, who got snared in the web of ritual and rites of passage.

When I got married my wife and I couldn't have intercourse because she was closed. I knew this was done to women but I'd never given any thought to the consequences. Then her aunt came and opened her up with a razor. I couldn't believe what was happening. My wife was in terrible pain. I vowed that such a thing would never be done to my daughters. We have six daughters and one son. When the first two girls were little my wife's aunt kept telling me they had to be cut or they'd never be accepted at the village. I said, "Too bad. They'll never be cut."

Then one day I came home from work and I knew the moment I opened the door that something was wrong. The aunt was there. My wife's face was a mask of fear. Usually my little girls—they were two and four at the time—came running to the door to greet me. They weren't there. I asked my wife what was going on. She said, "They're in the bedroom." I rushed in and there were my little daughters lying on the bed, their legs bound by bloody robes. I was furious. I wanted to call the police but the aunt said, "Go ahead, they won't do anything. This is our tradition." She had come with the excisist while I was at work and said to my wife, "We're here to do the girls." We didn't have a phone. There was nothing my wife could do. The aunt said, "Maybe you're angry now but you'll thank me when it's time for them to marry, because no man will have a girl who is not excised." I told her that any man who wanted to marry my daughter because she was excised would never have my permission. He can marry her for love, never for excision. Then I made it clear that she hadn't better touch any of my children again.

Back in Malicounda, we sit in the meeting room and this time the tropical storm raging outside is for real. It's the rainy season in Senegal, the first rainy season that didn't mark the completion of circumcision rites of girls. Everybody wants to talk about the pride, courage and confidence they have gathered since their decision. But first they share the indignation and pain they felt when they were accused of hurting their daughters. They explain, "This was our tradition. If a girl was not circumcised she would be an outcast in the village. She could not wash with the others, prepare food with the others. She could not marry. The other children would see her as unclean."

The lessons with Melching changed all that. For Tacko Cissoko, a midwife who attends births in her own ethnic group that practises FGM as well as those ethnic groups that do not, the penny dropped when they discussed childbirth. "I saw the women during delivery. The women who weren't excised didn't tear. The women who were tore terribly. I always suspected excision was the cause." The women speak as one when they say, "This is a chance for our daughters. They won't have to suffer. They won't lose their health. They won't spend all their money on health problems when they're adults."

They know it's about power. The power to decide for yourself; a paradigm shift for women. By taking a stand, the women of Malicounda have fired a shot at gender apartheid a shot that's being heard throughout Africa—and around the world.

Report From a Study Tour: Teen Sexuality Education in The Netherlands, France, and Germany

Maureen A. Kelly and Michael McGee

You would think a two-week trip to Europe would yield stories of picturesque walks through ancient towns and beautiful churches and conversations over a glass of wine or a great cup of coffee. Our stories do involve such things, but the real story behind our trip is not simply tourism.

In 1985, the Alan Guttmacher Institute published the findings from their "Euroteen" study highlighting the different rates of teen pregnancy, births, and abortion in 37 developed countries.

To learn how some European countries yield their low rates of negative outcomes and high rates of positive outcomes from adolescent sexual behavior, Advocates for Youth and the University of North Carolina at Charlotte organized a six-city study tour of three countries in July and August of 1998.

On July 25, 40 professionals and graduate students from the United States set out to learn about adolescent sexual behavior and responsibility from some of the people and places that report the greatest success—the residents of The Netherlands, France, and Germany.

From site visits and lectures, to panel discussions with health educators, youth workers, policy makers, AIDS activists and general practitioners, we have returned to the United States with a new view of the positive impact of access to sexuality education, public information, and medical services targeted to young people.

WHAT DID WE FIND?

In The Netherlands, France, and Germany, adolescent sexuality is regarded as a health issue, rather than a political or religious one. An overwhelming majority of the people and institutions in these countries support sexual health. In all three countries, but most notably in The Netherlands, teens are educated about safer sex and have access to both birth control pills and condoms if they have sexual intercourse.

In a lecture given by Jany Rademakers, one of the premiere researchers on adolescent sexuality at The Netherlands Institute of Social Sexological Research (NISSO), we learned that the efforts toward education and access are

Source: Siecus Reports, vol. 27, no. 2 (December 1998/January 1999). Copyright © 1998 *Siecus Reports.* Reprinted with permission from *Siecus Reports* and the authors.

working: 85 percent of Dutch teens use contraceptives at first intercourse; 46 percent report using condoms only, and 24 percent report using both a condom and birth control pills, known in The Netherlands as "Double Dutch." Birth control pills and condoms used together not only work to prevent pregnancy and sexually transmitted infections, but they also encourage both partners to take an active role in preventing infection and pregnancy.

In the countries studied, adolescents are valued, respected, and expected to act responsibly. Equally important, most adults trust adolescents to make responsible choices because they see young people as assets, rather than problems. That message is conveyed in the media, in school texts, and in health care settings.

Consider these simple comparative facts. According to 1990–95 data from the United Nations Population Division, the teen birth rate per 1,000 girls 15 to 19 years old is 64 in the United States, 13 in Germany, 9 in France, and 7 in The Netherlands.[1]

Teen abortion rates are also profoundly lower in Europe than in the United States. Comparative data compiled by Advocates for Youth shows that the abortion rate per 1,000 women 15 to 19 years old is 17 in the United States, 7.9 in France, and 5.2 in The Netherlands. (For Germany, the abortion rate is 8.7 for women ages 15 to 49.)[2] Additionally, in the countries studied, teens begin having sexual relations more than one year later than American teens and have fewer sexual partners during their teen years than their American peers.[3]

The reality is that teens in The Netherlands, France, and Germany have intercourse without as many negative consequences as teens in the United States. But European teens get something that American teens don't. They get inundated with positive messages aimed at helping them avoid unplanned pregnancy and sexually transmitted infections.

Most important, the messages sent to Dutch, German, and French teens are not designed to ask them to abstain from intercourse until marriage. In our visit to the Mouvement Francais pour le Planning Familial (MFPF), we asked the speaker, Monique Bellanger, director of the MFPF Documentation Center, if her organization promoted abstinence until marriage. Her response was to laugh and say, "We don't give such a message. It's bad for your health!"

The impetus to provide access to contraception, condoms, and comprehensive sexuality education is based on the desire to further reduce abortions and sexually transmitted diseases. Sexuality education is not necessarily one "course," but is integrated throughout many subjects and grade levels. The focus of sexuality education is on normalizing sexuality in the context of adolescent development, assuring medical accuracy, promoting values of respect and responsibility, and encouraging communication in relationships.

In reviewing curricula at a site visit to the Catholic Pedagogical Center (a teacher training center in The Netherlands), we were struck by how much sexuality was taken for granted. At first glance, the curricula stumped us. We wondered where the sexuality education was. On closer inspection, and with the help of a translator, we found that nearly all the curricula included sexuality information within the context of life skills.

One chapter would explain how to do laundry. The next would explain contraception. School teachers also reported taking this comprehensive approach to heart by leading discussions and lessons on relationships and sexuality in literature classes while reading classics such as *Romeo and Juliet*.

In Germany, there is a national sexuality education policy, but individual states can determine which curricula to use. In France, sexual health is promoted through national campaigns that encourage students to participate in safer sex and AIDS prevention poster contests. The winning posters then become an integral part of national media campaigns. In The Netherlands, schools distribute safer sex pamphlets just before the school holidays because officials know that many students will have sexual relationships while on vacation. Students in The Netherlands are also tested on national school exams for proficiency in sexuality education.

One of the key findings from our review of educational materials in all three countries about the various teaching approaches to sexuality was that professionals and educational materials honored the fact that sexuality exists for more than one week during one year in high school.

All three countries also have massive public education campaigns targeting safer sex behaviors and condom use. Media are engaged in helping young people make healthy sexual choices, not simply titillating audiences with sexual content for the sake of advertisers' money. Television, radio, billboards, tour buses, discos, pharmacies, post offices, and medical clinics are all enlisted in the public education efforts. In The Netherlands, parents can pick up informational booklets on tips for talking to their children about sexuality from their local post office. One of France's safer sex media campaigns targeting young people during school breaks exclaims, "On Holiday I forget everything . . . except condoms!"

These countries also appear to have little concern that sexually explicit media messages will encourage young people to have intercourse. In fact, most of the school curricula for adolescents include some nudity, as do most television and print media campaigns. Humor also plays a big role in conveying messages of safer sex and responsibility. The bottom line for the European media approaches to sexuality is that accurate and factual information is used in accessible, realistic, and humorous ways to reach their audiences.

The mass media sexuality education campaigns are supported and encouraged by a broad array of people with an equally broad array of beliefs and values, ranging from AIDS educators and parents to religious leaders and policy makers. We in the United States can learn from this non-adversarial relationship between religious communities and advocates for sexuality education, and, as a result, should encourage all groups to make strides toward a place where young people and families are supported to be sexually healthy.

Religion and politics have little influence on policies related to adolescent sexuality in the European countries we visited. For example, the church in France doesn't involve itself in school sexuality education, contraceptive services, or safer sex messages in the media. And with multiple political parties in The Netherlands, no single candidate or party can polarize the electorate around adolescent sexual issues.

National health insurance in all three countries gives youth convenient access to sexual health care, including contraception and emergency contraception. In The Netherlands, a teen girl who wants to use a birth control pill does not need to have a medical exam, to complete any forms, or to give her real name at the clinic. A health professional interviews the young woman, conducts a health history screening, and barring any contraindications, the young woman will leave with free birth control pills.

All three countries provide youth-friendly access to sexual health care by having free or low-cost services, numerous locations with generous hours of operations, and social support for making responsible sexual choices. Most young people get contraceptives through their family physicians, and clinics run by MFPF in France, the Rutgers Stichting in The Netherlands, and Pro-Familia in Germany provide services as well.

The tour yielded little new information about working with parents on family communication about sexuality. European studies about family sexuality education revealed dynamics similar to American families. In a study presented by Janita Ravesloot, a professor from Leiden University in The Netherlands, Dutch parents and teens expressed different impressions of the communication and education that happens at home regarding sexuality. This finding is similar to studies of parent-child communication in the United States.

Although European young people report receiving very little sexuality education at home, when asked specific questions about sexuality and sexual health, it becomes clear that young people are still successful in getting information about responsibility in relationships, where and how to get safer sex protection, and their family's values about sexuality.

Parents in The Netherlands may not directly teach their children everything they want to know about sex—a third of parents in the study view their adolescents' sexual lives as private.[4] Dutch parents consider themselves "supportive from a distance" around their teens' sexual behaviors. They don't forbid sexual intercourse because they don't want their teens' experience to be like the parents'. They fear it may push their children to rebellion and risk. One parent we interviewed said, "I don't want my kids to be sneaky." Most parents don't set rigid rules—but they do want children to have serious, responsible, healthy relations. As in the United States, mothers do most of the communication with their children about sexual and relationship issues. Mothers negotiate with teens about their sex lives. Also, as in the States, parents say they've talked with their children about sex, while their children say they have not. Parents say they are "liberal" while their adolescents say they (their children) are restricted. Parents consider themselves liberal in comparison to their own upbringing. Only 1 percent of Dutch parents in the study insisted on abstinence for their adolescents.

In a German study, the findings were similar to the Dutch. Some of the specifics include the fact that 80 percent of the family communication about sexuality is introduced by the moth-

ers, and that 40 percent of German young men report that they get no sexuality education from their parents.[5] Findings from the same German study indicate that almost 60 percent of parents regard human sexual behavior as a natural part of their life and, as a result, German families are taking sexuality education far more seriously than earlier generations. The role of the family in sexuality education is profound, not simply as a prevention method, but as a model for building healthy relationship and communication skills.

All three countries that we visited during the European Study Tour have one major thing in common. The positive and inclusive nationally funded sexuality education initiatives have all come about in the past 40 years. The Dutch, French, and Germans have made significant strides within the last two decades toward implementing national harm-reduction programs at their best. They saw the negative outcomes of HIV infection and too-early pregnancy, and worked collaboratively to create educational materials and provide access to services to address the negative outcomes, not by attempting to prevent sexual behaviors.

A portion of an interview journalist Bill Beckley had with artist Louise Bourgeois appeared in the September 1998 *Harper's Magazine*. The exchange that follows best sums up the contrasting social norms between European countries and the United States. The interview read:

Bill Beckley: You were born in France, but you lived a long time in the United States. What is the difference between the aesthetics of the two countries?

Louise Bourgeois: I'll tell you a story about my mother. When I was a little girl growing up in France, my mother worked sewing tapestries. Some of the tapestries were exported to America. The only problem was that many of the images of the tapestries were of naked people. My mother's job was to cut out the—what do you call it?

Beckley: The genitals?

Bourgeois: Yes, the genitals of the men and women, and replace these parts with pictures of flowers so they could be sold to Americans. My mother saved all the pictures of the genitals over the years, and one day she sewed them together as a quilt, and then she gave me the quilt. That's the difference between French and American aesthetics.[6]

CLOSING THOUGHTS

Reframing our society and culture while affecting beliefs and practices about adolescent sexual behavior in the United States will not be easy, but we have seen that it can be done.

We cannot ignore the fact that poverty, lack of hope for the future, and an inadequate public education are strong predictors for sexual risk taking. But we can help adolescents make responsible choices about sexuality.

Adolescents can make healthy decisions. We need to help build a context in which they are supported to feel good about themselves and their bodies, remain healthy, and build positive, equitable, loving relationships. Our European neighbors reminded us that sexuality can be a normal, healthy, and pleasurable aspect of being human—even for adolescents.

REFERENCES

1. *How Does the U.S. Compare to Europe?* (Advocates for Youth, Washington, DC, May 1998).
2. Ibid.
3. *Major Data Comparisons* (Advocates for Youth, Washington, DC, October 1998).
4. J. Raveslot, *Parents and Children: Dutch Families and Communication About Sexuality* (Leiden University, the Netherlands, July 1998).
5. N. Kluge. *Is Sex Education in the Family Better Than Its Reputation?* (A published proceeding froth the Federal Center for Health Education's First European Conference "Sex Education and Adolescents," Cologne, Germany, November 1994.)
6. B. Beckley, "An Interview with Louise Bourgeois," *Harper's Magazine,* September 1998, p. 34

READING 62

The Surgeon General's Call to Action to Promote Sexual Health and Responsible Sexual Behavior

A LETTER FROM THE SURGEON GENERAL, U.S. DEPARTMENT OF HEALTH AND HUMAN SERVICES

I am introducing the *Surgeon General's Call to Action to Promote Sexual Health and Responsible Sexual Behavior* because we, as a nation, must address the significant public health challenges regarding the sexual health of our citizens. In recognition of these challenges, promoting responsible sexual behavior is included among the Surgeon General's Public Health Priorities and is also one of the *Healthy People 2010* Ten Leading Health Indicators for the Nation. While it is important to acknowledge the many positive aspects of sexuality, we also need to understand that there are undesirable consequences as well—alarmingly high levels of sexually transmitted disease (STD) and HIV/AIDS infection, unintended pregnancy, abortion, sexual dysfunction, and sexual violence. In the United States:

- STDs infect approximately 12 million persons each year;

- 774,467 AIDS cases, nearly two-thirds of which were sexually transmitted, have been reported since 1981;
- an estimated 800,000 to 900,000 persons are living with HIV;
- an estimated one-third of those living with HIV are aware of their status and are in treatment, one-third are aware but not in treatment, and one-third have not been tested and are not aware;
- an estimated 40,000 new HIV infections occur each year;
- an estimated 1,366,000 induced abortions occurred in 1996;
- nearly one-half of pregnancies are unintended;
- an estimated 22 percent of women and two percent of men have been victims of a forced sexual act; and
- an estimated 104,000 children are victims of sexual abuse each year.

Each of these problems carries with it the potential for lifelong consequences—for individuals, families, communities, and the nation as a whole. As is the case with so many public health problems, there are serious disparities among the populations affected. The economically disadvantaged, racial and ethnic minorities, persons with different sexual identities, disabled persons, and adolescents often bear the heaviest burden. Yet it is important to recognize that persons of all ages and backgrounds are at risk and should have access to the knowledge and services necessary for optimal sexual health.

These challenges can be met but first we must find common ground and reach consensus on some important problems and their possible solutions. It is necessary to appreciate what sexual health is, that it is connected with both physical and mental health, and that it is important throughout the entire lifespan, not just the reproductive years. It is also important to recognize the responsibilities that individuals and communities have in protecting sexual health. The responsibility of well-informed adults as educators and role models for their children cannot be overstated. Issues around sexuality can be difficult to discuss—because they are personal and because there is great diversity in how they are perceived and approached. Yet, they greatly impact public health and, thus, it is time to begin that discussion and, to that end, this *Surgeon General's Call to Action* is offered as a framework.

It is, however, only a first step—a call to begin a mature and thoughtful discussion about sexuality. We must understand that sexuality encompasses more than sexual behavior, that the many aspects of sexuality include not only the physical, but the mental and spiritual as well, and that sexuality is a core component of personality. Sexuality is a fundamental part of human life. While the problems usually associated with sexual behavior are real and need to be addressed, human sexuality also has significant meaning and value in each individual's life. This call, and the discussion it is meant to generate, is not just intended for health care professionals or policy makers. It is intended for parents, teachers, clergy, social service professionals—all of us.

I would like to add a few words for the many thousands of persons living with HIV/AIDS in this country. We realize that you are not the enemy; that the enemy in this epidemic is the virus, not those who are infected with it. You need our support and encouragement. At the same time, it is also important that you realize you have an opportunity to partner with us in stemming the spread of this illness; to be responsible in your own behavior and to help others become aware of the need for responsible behavior in their sexual lives. Working together, we can make a difference.

This *Call to Action* has been developed through a collaborative process. It is based on a series of scientific review papers contributed by experts in relevant fields, on recommendations developed at two national conferences, and on extensive review and comment as the document was being prepared—all of which sought the broadest possible input and brought together a wide range of experience, expertise and perspective with representation from the academic, medical and religious communities, policy makers, advocates, teachers, parents and youth. The strategies presented here provide a point of reference for advancing a national dialogue on issues of sexuality, sexual health, and responsible sexual behavior. It can begin among individuals, but must also involve communities, the media, government and non-government agencies, institutions, and foundations.

In developing this *Call to Action,* we have received a wide range of input, and have identified several areas of common ground. A major responsibility of the Surgeon General is to provide the best available science based information to the American people to assist in protecting and advancing the health and safety of our Nation. This report represents another effort to meet that responsibility.

Finding common ground might not be easy, but it is possible. The process leading to this *Call to Action* has already shown that persons with very different views can come together and discuss difficult issues and find broad areas of agreement. Approaches and solutions might be complex, but we do have evidence of success. We need to appreciate the diversity of our culture, engage in mature, thoughtful and respectful discussion, be informed by the science that is available to us, and invest in continued research. This is a call to action. We cannot remain complacent. Doing nothing is unacceptable. Our efforts not only will have an impact on the current health status of our citizens, but will lay a foundation for a healthier society in the future.

David Satcher, M.D., Ph.D.
Surgeon General
July 9, 2001

VISION FOR THE FUTURE

Strategies that cover three fundamental areas—increasing awareness, implementing and strengthening interventions, and expanding the research base—could help provide a foundation for promoting sexual health and responsible sexual behavior in a manner that is consistent with the best available science.

1. Increasing Public Awareness of Issues Relating to Sexual Health and Responsible Sexual Behavior

- Begin a national dialogue on sexual health and responsible sexual behavior that is honest, mature and respectful, and has the ultimate goal of developing a national strategy that recognizes the need for common ground.

- Encourage opinion leaders to address issues related to sexual health and responsible sexual behavior in ways that are informed by the best available science and that respect diversity.

- Provide access to education about sexual health and responsible sexual behavior that is thorough, wide-ranging, begins early, and continues throughout the lifespan. Such education should:
  - recognize the special place that sexuality has in our lives;
  - stress the value and benefits of remaining abstinent until involved in a committed, enduring, and mutually monogamous relationship; but
  - assure awareness of optimal protection from sexually transmitted diseases and unintended pregnancy, for those who are sexually active, while also stressing that there are no infallible methods of protection, except abstinence, and that condoms cannot protect against some forms of STDs.

- Recognize that sexuality education can be provided in a number of venues—

homes, schools, churches, other community settings—but must always be developmentally and culturally appropriate.

- Recognize that parents are the child's first educators and should help guide other sexuality education efforts so that they are consistent with their values and beliefs.

- Recognize, also, that families differ in their level of knowledge, as well as their emotional capability to discuss sexuality issues. In moving toward equity of access to information for promoting sexual health and responsible sexual behavior, school sexuality education is a vital component of community responsibility.

2. Providing the Health and Social Interventions Necessary to Promote and Enhance Sexual Health and Responsible Sexual Behavior

- Eliminate disparities in sexual health status that arise from social and economic disadvantage, diminished access to information and health care services, and stereotyping and discrimination.

- Target interventions to the most socioeconomically vulnerable communities where community members have less access to health education and services and are, thus, likely to suffer most from sexual health problems.

- Improve access to sexual health and reproductive health care services for all persons in all communities.

- Provide adequate training in sexual health to all professionals who deal with sexual issues in their work, encourage them to use this training, and ensure that they are reflective of the populations they serve.

- Encourage the implementation of health and social interventions to improve sex-

ual health that have been adequately evaluated and shown to be effective.

- Ensure the availability of programs that promote both awareness and prevention of sexual abuse and coercion.

- Strengthen families, whatever their structure, by encouraging stable, committed, and enduring adult relationships, particularly marriage. Recognize, though, that there are times when the health interests of adults and children can be hurt within relationships with sexual health problems, and that sexual health problems within a family can be a concern in and of themselves.

3. Investing in Research Related to Sexual Health and Disseminating Findings Widely

- Promote basic research in human sexual development, sexual health, and reproductive health, as well as social and behavioral research on risk and protective factors for sexual health.

- Expand the research base to cover the entire human life span—children, adolescents, young adults, middle-age adults, and the elderly.

- Research, develop, disseminate, and evaluate educational materials and guidelines for sexuality education, covering the full continuum of human sexual development, for use by parents, clergy, teachers, and other community leaders.

- Expand evaluation efforts for community, school and clinic based interventions that address sexual health and responsibility.

REFERENCES

American Psychiatric Association. (2000). *Position statement on therapies focused on attempts to change sexual orientation (reparative or conversion therapies).* Washington, DC: American Psychiatric Association.

Brewster KL et al. (1993). Social context and adolescent behavior: the impact of community on the transition to sexual activity. *Social Forces,* 71:713–740.

Centers for Disease Control and Prevention. (1999a). *Prevention of Genital HPV Infection and Sequelae: Report of an External Consultant's Meeting.* Atlanta: Centers for Disease Control and Prevention.

Centers for Disease Control and Prevention. (1999b). CDC surveillance summaries. *MMWR,* 48(No. SS-4).

Centers for Disease Control and Prevention. (1999c). *CDC HIV/AIDS prevention research project compendium of HIV prevention interventions with evidence of effectiveness.* Atlanta: Centers for Disease Control and Prevention.

Centers for Disease Control and Prevention. (2000a). *A glance at the HIV epidemic.* Atlanta: Centers for Disease Control and Prevention.

Centers for Disease Control and Prevention. (2000b). *HIV/AIDS surveillance report, mid-year edition,* 12 (No. 1).

Centers for Disease Control and Prevention. (2001a). *Surveillance supplemental report,* 7(No. 1).

Centers for Disease Control and Prevention. (2001b). HIV/AIDS—United States, 1981–2000. *MMWR,* 50(No. RR-9).

Centers for Disease Control and Prevention. (2001c). HIV incidence among young men who have sex with men: Baltimore, Dallas, Los Angeles, Miami, New York City, San Francisco, and Seattle, 1994–2000. *MMWR,* 50(No. RR-9).

Christopher FS, Roosa MW. (1990) An evaluation of an adolescent pregnancy prevention program: is "just say no" enough? *Family Relations,* 39:68–72.

Croft CA, Asmussen L. (1993) A developmental approach to sexuality education: implications for medical practice. *Journal of Adolescent Health,* 14:109–114.

Fleming DT et al. (1997) Herpes simplex virus type 2 in the United States 1979 to 1994. *New England Journal of Medicine,* 337:1105–1111.

Haldeman, DC. (1994) The practice and ethics of sexual orientation conversion therapy. *Journal of Consulting and Clinical Psychology,* 62:221–227.

Institute of Medicine. (1995) *The best intentions: unintended pregnancy and the well-being of children and families.* Brown SS and Eisenberg L, editors. Washington, DC: National Academy Press.

Institute of Medicine. (1997) *The hidden epidemic: confronting sexually transmitted diseases.* Eng TR, Butler WT, editors. Washington, DC: National Academy Press.

Institute of Medicine (2000) *No time to lose: getting more from HIV prevention.* Ruiz, MS et al. editors. Washington, DC: National Academy Press.

Jemmott JB et al. (1992) Reductions in HIV risk-associated sexual behaviors among black male adolescents: effects of an AIDS prevention intervention. *American Journal of Public Health,* 82(3):372–377.

Kirby D et al. (1997) The impact of the postponing sexual involvement curriculum among youths in California. *Family Planning Perspectives,* 29(3):100–108.

Levesque RJR. (1998) Emotional maltreatment in adolescents' everyday lives: furthering sociolegal reforms and social service provisions. *Behavior Sciences and the Law,* 16:237–263.

Melchior A. (1998) *National evaluation of Learn and Serve American School and Community-Based Programs.* Waltham, MA: Center for Human Resources, Brandeis University.

St. Pierre TL et al. (1995) A 27-month evaluation of a sexual activity prevention program in Boys & Girls Clubs across the nation. *Family Relations,* 44:69–77.

Sutton MJ et al. (in press) Shaking the tree of knowledge for forbidden fruit: where adolescents learn about sexuality and contraception. In: Brown JD et al., editors. *Sexual teens, sexual media.* Mahwah, NJ: Lawrence Erlbaum.

Thomas SB, Quinn SC. (1991) The Tuskegee Syphilis Study, 1932 to 1972: implications for HIV education and AIDS risk education programs in the Black community. *American Journal of Public Health,* 81:1498–1505.

U.S. Department of Health and Human Services. (2000a) *Child maltreatment 1998: Reports from the States to the National Child Abuse and Neglect Data System.* Washington, DC: US Government Printing Office.

U.S. Department of Health and Human Services. (2000b) *Tracking Healthy People 2010.* Washington, DC: US Government Printing Office.

Wyatt GE. (1997) *Stolen women: reclaiming our sexuality, taking back our lives.* New York: Wiley.

PART NINE

POSSIBLE SEXUALITIES: IMAGES OF SEXUALITY BEYOND OPPRESSION

What are the possibilities for sexuality? Given what you know about the social, historical construction of sexuality, can you now step outside, at least in your imagination, to wonder how sexuality could be experienced differently? As stated in the introduction to this book, sex can be seen as a tool of oppression when we realize that the beauty of our bodies, our ability to experience pleasure, and our capacity for reproduction, has historically been used as a form of social control. Resulting societal norms and expectations, including rigid gender roles and narrow assumptions about sexual orientation, present us with an alienated and distorted sense of sexuality.

While it is helpful to be aware of the problems, having a vision of how it could be different enhances the possibility for change. What would it take to change, to heal from past hurts imposed on us, to pass along a healthier, richer experience of our individual and collective sexuality? Such an undertaking would mean identifying ways to avoid being weighed down with the oppression of sexual power imbalance, lack of knowledge, abuse, fear, shame, and guilt.

Are people making changes? Is change possible? For this final section of the book, we selected pieces that illustrate an intentional effort to create a new construction of sexuality, that hold out a vision, or at least provide an image of changes to come.

585

In "Cuntist Mystique," Inga Muscio argues for reclaiming the word *cunt.* Having found a positive reference to this word in ancient writings, Muscio reflects on ways that formerly women-centered words and beliefs came to be used against women by patriarchal systems. *Cunt,* she says, has been in the triumvirate of deprecatory words for women—*cunt, bitch,* and *whore.* Muscio maintains that since this word cannot be used against women any more than it already has, it can now be re-owned as "an all new woman-centered, cuntlovin' noun, adjective, or verb."

As you think about words used for sex and sexual body parts, ask what kind of words they are. Are they male or female centered? How would it be if women adopted new words, or resurrected words like *cunt,* to use them in a sexually empowering way? Can you change your sense of the meaning of *cunt* to one that is woman-positive? What does this say about symbolic representation and power? If women and men change the way "old" words have been used, in order to create new meaning based on a different power relation, does this create a new social reality?

In "My Sexual Odyssey: A Father's Reflections," H. J. Randolph talks about his own sexual journey and what he wants to pass on to his son, or not. Parents are agents of socialization for the next generation through the messages they give their children, either directly or indirectly, based on their own behavior. Thus, parents can play an important role in creating new sexual possibilities. Randolph talks honestly about his enjoyment of sex, especially cunnilingus, as well as things he wishes had gone differently in relationships. As he thinks about future conversations with his son, Zack, he commits to addressing the emotional side of relationships, the interplay between sex and love. He speaks about his use of pornography and the problems it has caused for him, the images of women that he carries with him from pornography, saying, "I don't want Zack's impressions of women to be influenced to the degree mine have been by pornographic images." Randolph, who co-parents with his ex-wife, hopes that the role modeling Zack gets from the way his parents handle relationships will serve him well. He says, "I will remind him that sex—whether passionate and intense or tender and languorous—can be a joyful and enriching part of being alive."

As you reflect on Randolph's story, what thoughts and feelings do you have about parents' role in sexuality education?

Thinking about yourself as a parent, will you be open with your children about your ideas and values around sexuality? What will help you do this, and what will hold you back? What social institutions in your life will support your intentions and visions? What institutional influences might challenge your intentions and constrain your parenting behaviors?

Laurie Essig, in "Heteroflexibility," playfully introduces a way to rethink sexual orientation. Hearing her students refer to heteroflexibility in the first person, as in, "I'm heteroflexible," led Essig to think about a world where rigidity of any variety becomes as taboo as homosexuality used to be. Think about it, she says. The opposite of heteroflexible is heterorigid! She credits her students and their generation with introducing new imaginings of sexual desires; where sexual identity is less mired in the unimaginative binary of hetero and homo. What reaction do you have to this idea and word choice? Is use of *heteroflexible* a way to leave the hetero-homo-bi labels behind? What are the implications? How might changes in our language and perceptions influence the experience of those who have sexual interests in members of either the same or the other sex?

British writers Mick Cooper and Peter Baker discuss ways that men can overcome limiting and negative messages about sex in "Sex: The Sensual Man." Cooper and Baker discuss concerns about sexual performance, frequency of sex, penis size, premature ejaculation, and impotence, regarding them as "phallacies" of a phallocentric approach to sex. They suggest that male-centered sex is a cultural legacy related, in part at least, to fear of intimacy. Is it easier to penetrate than be physically or emotionally penetrated? Is it easier to see one's penis as having sex, rather than our emotions or spirit? The authors' suggestion to men who want to release sexual anxieties is to let go of the struggle to be "real men." Moreover, they say, talk with women about what they want sexually, instead of assuming you are supposed to know. And talk with other men about their experience of sex—real honest talk, without boasting, that leads to finding out you are not alone.

What do you think about the authors' connection between sexual difficulties and the social construction of masculinity? Are men fearful of penetration and emotional openness? How does this relate to the "nice guy/tough guy" dialectic in the article by Crane & Crane-Seeber? What makes it hard for men to talk about sex with men, or men and women talking openly and honestly? What's fun about it?

Thomas Moore, in "Sex: American Style," takes sex into the public sphere, calling for a greater integration of the sensual into our daily lives. Disenchanted with the sharp delineation between private sexuality and our public lives, Moore imagines a world in which public life carries more of the qualities associated with sex. Why not have comfortable chairs and benches in public places, he asks, as well as delightful colors, flowers, and trees as a central part of urban spaces? Let's have rivers and streams in the foreground rather than hidden behind old industrial buildings. The mind–body split in Western philosophy, according to Moore, has led us to see what is human and natural as being contrary to what is spiritual and divine. Are we embarrassed with our bodies and what we do with them? Is modern pornography all that lingers of the public eroticism still evident on walls of Indian temples and Greek pottery, or the writings of Sappho? Moore suggests we overcome the obsession/repression pattern of societal norms around sexuality with an alignment of sex with intelligence, civility, spiritual values, and other aspects of our daily lives. We can embrace our desires, he asserts, and make wise decisions about their expression. We can chose intimacy rather than distance, and seek deep pleasures over superficial entertainment.

What do you think about Moore's suggestions? In earlier chapters, we have discussed sexual oppression as including the commodification of the sexual, negating and making it lurid and bad, then selling it back to us in the form of unrealistic body images and pornography. How would it be if public life were more sensual? How might you apply Moore's vision in your own life?

Margo Anand, in "Tantric Vision," brings ancient wisdom about wholeness to our vision of possible sexuality. In much earlier times—at least since Tantra recorded tantric practices in India in 5,000 BCE—sex was seen as united with spirit, energy, and ecstasy. "The more energy you have," Anand asserts, "the more blissful you can be, and the better sex becomes." To Anand, this means that orgasm is an energy event that can be learned—learning to contain the energy of arousal and relaxing into it. Resulting feelings of ecstasy can be experienced with or without a partner, for long periods. It can be empowering, she says, to take responsibility for one's own well-being in sex. Because the

Tantric vision is one of wholeness, Anand reports, each human being is seen as having both masculine and feminine qualities that can be explored playfully in sex.

Anand emphasizes that in other cultures, and other times, sexual energy is seen as a physical expression of spiritual power. She states, "The desire to unite sexuality with another human being is a reflection of an underlying spiritual need to experience wholeness and complete intimacy, transcending the individual's sense of separateness and isolation." Anand connects the cultural deprivation of sex's sacred dimension with repression of sexual energy, leading to abuse of power, disrespect, rape, and other forms of sexual violence.

How does Anand's conceptualization of sex as sacred relate to your experience of sexuality? Could sex have been the earliest form of humans having a sense of communion with the divine? How might current assumptions around gender and sex be changed if the Tantric vision was integrated into mainstream spiritual teachings? Are there ways you can use these teachings to bring greater integration into your own life experience?

We conclude the book as we started, with student voices. Summer Killian, an undergraduate student, heralds women's sexual agency in her erotic poem, "Something New: Let's Talk about Dirty." The genuine ease and joy in her explicit reporting of her experience of sex evokes a shift of paradigm for women and sexuality. When Killian says, "Don't use words like *intense*/or *beautiful*/or *nice*./Tonight/it's dirty and that's the way/I like it," she dismisses any interest in being the "good girl." Some might label a woman who expresses such feelings as a slut, while if she was male, he might be admired for the beauty of the images. Is Killian's poem startling? Is its explicit owning of sexual pleasure closer to what we expect of males? If you are male, would you like it if your female partner wrote about sex in this way? If you are female? What's fun and whole about it?

Dave Justice's "I Have a Dream," also written while he was an undergraduate, draws from Martin Luther King's civil rights movement speech to write about his own vision of a world that honors the plurality of sexuality and gender. Justice's dream includes the end of sexual violence as well as open communication between men and women about sexual experiences, needs, and desires. He ends saying, "I have a dream . . . Here is where it starts."

Coming full circle, out to societal influences and back to self, also ends this book, bringing us back to ourselves. Social and historical influences exhibit themselves daily in our own feelings and behaviors. What is your dream, your vision, for sexual possibilities?

READING 63

Cuntist Mystique

Inga Muscio

I came across the power of "cunt" quite accidentally. After writing an article for a newspaper, I typed in "word count," but left out the "o." My editor laughingly pointed out the mistake. I looked at the two words together and decided "Word Cunt" seemed like a nice title for a woman writer. As a kind of intraoffice byline, I started typing "Word Cunt" instead of "word count" on all my articles. The handful of people who saw hard copies of my work reacted strongly and asked why I chose to put these two words on my articles. After explaining my reasoning to editorial assistants, production magis, proofreaders and receptionists, I started wondering about the actual, decontextualized power of "cunt."

I looked up "cunt" in Barbara G. Walker's twenty-five-year research opus, *the Woman's Encyclopedia of Myths and Secrets,* and found it was indeed a title, back in the day. "Cunt" is related to words from India, China, Ireland, Rome and Egypt. Such words were either titles of respect for women, priestesses and witches, or derivatives of the names of various goddesses:

> In ancient writings, the word for "cunt" was synonymous with "woman," though not in the insulting modern sense. An Egyptologist was shocked to find the maxims of Pah-Hotep "used for 'woman' a term that was more than blunt," though its indelicacy was not in the eye of the ancient beholder, only in that of the modern scholar. (Walker, 1983, 197)

The words "bitch" and "whore" have also shared a similar fate in our language. This seemed rather fishy to me. Three words which convey negative meanings about women, specifically, all happen to have once had totally positive associations about women, specifically.

Of the three, "cunt" garners the most powerful negative reaction.

How come?

This was obviously a loaded question to be asking myself, 'cause the answer evolved into quite the life-consuming project.

According to every woman-centered historical reference I have read—from M. Esther Harding to bell hooks—the containment of woman's sexuality was a huge priority to emerging patrifocal religious and economic systems.

Cunts were anathema to forefather types. Literally and metaphorically, the word and anatomical jewel presided at the very nexus of many earlier religions which impeded phallic power worship. In Western civilization, forefather types practiced savior-centered religions, such as Catholicism. Springing forth from a very real, very fiscal fear of women and our power, eventually evolving into sexual retardation and womb envy, a philosophy and social system based on destruction was culled to thriving life. One of the more well-documented instances of this destruction-oriented consciousness is something called the Inquisition. It lasted for over *five hundred years.* That is how long it took the Inquisition to rend serious damage to the collective spirit of non-savior-centered religious worshippers.

The Inquisition justified the—usually sadistic—murder, enslavement or rape of every woman, child and man who practiced any form of spiritual belief which did not honor savior-centered phallic power worship.

Since the beginning of time, most cultures honored forces which were tangible, such as the moon, earth, sun, water, birth, death and life. A spirituality which was undetectable to any of the human senses was considered incomprehensible.

One imagines victims of the Inquisition were not hard to come by. Women who owned anything more than the clothes on their backs and a few pots to piss in were religiously targeted by the Inquisition because all of women's resources and possessions became property of the famously cuntfearing Catholic Church. Out of this, the practice of sending "missionaries" into societies bereft of savior-centered spiritualities evolved.

Negative reactions to "cunt" resonate from a learned fear of ancient yet contemporary, inherent yet lost, reviled yet redemptive cuntpower.

Eradicating a tried and true, stentorian-assed word from a language is like rendering null the Goddess Herself.

It's impossible.

Ancient, woman-centered words and beliefs never, like, *fall off the planet.* Having long done taken on a life of their own, they—like womankind–evolve, and survive.

Chameleon style.

For women this has involved making many, many concessions, such as allowing our selves, goddesses, priestesses and words to be defined and presented by men.

Many words found in woman-centered religions, such as cunt, bitch, whore, dog, ass, puta, skag and hag, along with the names of just about all goddessess—over time—assimilated bad connotations. As matrifocal lifestyles became less and less acceptable, "cunt" survived, *necessarily* carrying a negative meaning on into the next millennium.

Words outlive people, institutions, civilizations. Words spur images, associations, memories, inspirations and synapse pulsations. Words send off physical resonations of thought into the nethersphere. Words hurt, soothe, inspire, demean, demand, incite, pacify, teach, romance, pervert, unite, divide.

Words be powerful.

Grown-ups and children are not readily encouraged to unearth the power of words. Adults are repeatedly assured a picture is worth a thousand of them, while the playground response to almost any verbal taunt is "Sticks and stones may break my bones, but words will never hurt me."

I don't beg so much as command to differ.

For young girls in this society, coming into the power we are born with is no easy task. As children, our power is not culled out of us as it is for boys. Still, culling power is—above and beyond all social conditioning—a very surmountable *task* to which womankind collectively rises higher each day.

But we need a language.

A means of communication demands and precedes change.

I posit that we're free to seize a word that was kidnapped and co-opted in a pain-filled, distant past, with a ransom that cost our grandmothers' freedom, children, traditions, pride and land. I figure we've paid the ransom, but now, everybody long done forgot "cunt" was ours in the first place.

I have lived the past couple years of my life writing a book called *Cunt.* When people ask me what I do, sometimes I bypass the whole conversation and say I'm a taxidermist. Reactions to a book called *Cunt* always lead to an intense grilling. Ain't never encountered ambivalence. At this juncture, I am still absolutely unable to gauge reactions to this word.

Living with the title of this book as such a huge fixture in my day-to-day life has been a very weird anthropological study unto itself. "Cunt" is a bad, bad word, but *damn* if it don't *intrigue* people when it's the title of a book instead of a meanspirited expletive.

Since everybody already knows that the diabolization of "cunt" is an absolute reality of our language, nobody has to waste time and energy defending its honor.

A cunt by any other name is still a cunt.

"Cunt" is a highly satisfying word to utter on a regular basis.

Every girl and lady who is strong and fighting and powerful, who thrives in this world in a way that serves her, is a rockin', cuntlovin' babe doing her part to goad the post-patriarchal age into fruition.

"Cunt" is the crusty, disgusting bottle in the city dump pile that is bejewelled underneath and has a beautiful genie inside.

Here is a nice story about the transformation of destructive negative, crap-ola into constructive, positive brilliantiana.

Once upon a time, civil rights activist Dick Gregory went into a restaurant and ordered some chicken. Three or four men who wore pointy white hoods for their nighttime fashion statement presently came into the restaurant and said, (I'm paraphrasing here) "Yo, boy. Anything y'do tah dat chicken, we're gone do tah yoo."

Mr. Gregory looked at the chicken on the plate before him and was silent.

The men repeated, "Anything y'do tah dat chicken, boy, we're gone do tah yoo."

Everybody in the restaurant stopped what they were doing and stared.

Mr. Gregory sighed, picked up the chicken and gave it a big ol', sweet ol' kiss.

Perhaps, as some "historians" may have it, I fabricated the historic considerations in reassessing the way we presently perceive "cunt."

Even if "cunt" were simply four spontaneous letters someone strung together one day 'cause his wife didn't have dinner on the table when he got home from a hard day's labor offing witches or indigenous peoples, it is still *our word.* Demographically, the women who have *no chance* of negatively being called "cunts" throughout life can be found in totally cloistered nunneries and maybe Amish communities.

Based on the criteria that "cunt" can be neither co-opted nor spin-doctored into having a negative meaning, venerable history or not, it's ours to do with what we want. And thanks to the versatility and user-friendliness of the English language, "cunt" can be used as an all new woman-centered, cuntlovin' noun, adjective, or verb.

I, personally, am in love with the idea.

REFERENCES

Walker, B. G. (1983). *The woman's encyclopedia of myths and secrets.* San Francisco: HarperSan Francisco.

My Sexual Odyssey: A Father's Reflections

H. J. Randolph

It was the summer of 1973. On the living room rug of my lover's house, at age 23, I lost my virginity in the community I called home for most of my life. I was ecstatic, joyful, relieved. It's embarrassing for a man in this culture to admit to late sexual blooming! Seven years after that summer I married a hometown girl. In

Source: Men and Intimacy: Personal Accounts. Exploring the Dilemmas of Modern Male Sexuality, ed. Franklin Abbott. Copyright © 1990 Crossing Press.

1982, my son Zachary was born. At 37 I was divorced and became a joint custody father.

Since that time, with unbounded delight and periodic apprehension, I have watched Zack grow into a beautiful, bright, rollicking child. Luckily, he shares his father's quick wit, indelicate sense of humor, and modesty. Once when he asserted, "Daddy, you are in another dimension," I felt constrained to retort, "You could be right." On another occasion Zack claimed I was in need of "sensibility." The pedestrian "Alvin Show" theme song we hear on television is transformed into the rousing "Bullshit Show" when Zachary belts it out in my car. During a conversation about food one day I asked, "Zack, do you like curry?" The impish reply: "Who's he?"

Then there's the metaphysical Zack, who, upon removing a candy bar wrapper, muses about having "ripped open a dimensional window." I can only gaze in wonderment at a son who tells me, "My memory goes on and on and when it ends, I shall die." The tender Zack worries that my leg is a "little bit broken" when I experience some pain there, or pleads during my nightly lie-down, "Oh, my sensitive daddy, won't you stay in bed two more minutes?"

Whether hurling a football, eating dim sum, playing Nintendo (he always crushes me), or concocting a shaving cream and spices "potion" together, there is a closeness between us that deeply enriches my life.

Like all parents, I want my child to benefit from what I have learned along the way, to impart whatever wisdom I can, to advise him as he makes choices in life. My own sexual history has featured its share of frustration and disappointment amid its pleasures. Now, at 39, I ponder that history in an effort to make Zack's sexual odyssey smoother than mine has been. What was I taught about sex, what were my sexual experiences, and what lessons about a healthy sexuality can I teach my son?

I grew up in a small town in southeast Iowa. Like most children of my generation, I received no useful sex education from my parents. I remember telling a story at the supper table one night that I had heard at school about some boy being busy "on Cherry Hill." Cherry Hill, as it turns out, was a girl in his class. Relating this tale led to a brief after-dinner lecture from my father about "being careful" with girls, whatever that was supposed to mean. Regrettably, that is the only memory I have of any discussion of sexuality with my parents.

They never told me about masturbation, "how babies were made," or contraception. They never explained what it took to create a caring, loving relationship between two people. I wasn't encouraged to ask questions about such things or referred to a book that would enlighten me. A product of their time, my parents were not alone in their discomfort. Feeling ill-equipped or awkward about discussing sex with children was common, and is still a challenge today. Nevertheless, I believe the lack of information I received from my parents retarded my sexual development.

Even if my father never breathes a word to me about sex, he still subscribed to *Playboy*. I remember pulling the issues down from the closet shelf in my parents' bedroom and furtively flipping through the pages with a high school friend. It was exciting to look at the naked bodies, wondering what mysteries of the flesh awaited me in the future. Although I may have pored over issues of *Playboy*, I don't recall talking to friends about sex and I had no older brother who might pique my interest about sexual matters or to whom I could turn for guidance.

As a boy, I was shy around girls, and I'm still somewhat uneasy when approaching women as an adult. I either lacked curiosity as a young man or repressed most sexual feelings. When I was about 12, I did "play doctor" with a neighbor girl in the bushes. Once I was caught playing strip poker in a car with a male pal, but I don't remember either experience as being overtly sexual. I had occasional wet dreams as a teenager and recall times when I lay in bed for hours at night, alone with fantasies of female classmates. Still, I only dated a few times in high school and was never sexually intimate. Moreover, I have no memory of ever masturbating during those years.

Tentative and unsure of myself in the sexual arena, I missed out on potential sexual activity because I wasn't aggressive enough. Susan, Laura, and Bernice remain part of my fantasy life, and I still sometimes wonder where they are now and if they would be surprised by my memories of desire and fleeting pleasure. When, at 16, I sang the Rolling Stones' lyrics "So don't play with me cause you're playin' with fire," my mother thought it was a joke. Who could argue with her? As a teenager, I wasn't a hot sexual property. Not until my freshman year of college did I passionately kiss a woman for the first time. I still vividly recall us thrashing about on a dusty fraternity couch in the darkness.

I was on a Greyhound bus en route to Chicago for a Rolling Stones concert in the early '70s the first time I remember masturbating. In the back of the bus I started touching myself in this marvelous way and was a little embarrassed yet thrilled by the electric feelings that surged through my penis—and whole body—when I climaxed. I immediately concluded that this wonderful event merited further deliberation. I guess the Stones and I have some sort of history.

A passion for cunnilingus was kindled in the summer of 1971, when I would linger for hours beneath my girlfriend's billowing dresses on her porch in sultry summer evenings. I am intoxicated by its wonderful, heady, sensual delights. An inherently tender, loving act, I think cunnilingus is as sexually intimate as one can be with a woman. I've always known that "real sex" in our culture is not simply intercourse. Though that can be deeply fulfilling, I'm a man who has never

equated sexual pleasure with just "getting laid." I believe I've satisfied most of my lovers—perhaps more with my tongue than with my penis, cunning linguist that I am.

My first experience of intercourse catapulted me into an intense period of fascination about everything sexual. I composed "Awakening," my dewy-eyed poem to lost innocence. I became conversant with Johnny Wadd, Marc Stevens, and Marilyn Chambers—marquee names of leading porn stars. I bought a vibrator and a dildo (and once even an outrageous rubber "vagina"). When my first two-year romance ended, I began a period of sexual experimentation that was more feasible in pre-AIDS America. This included several lovers, as well as group sex dalliances with both women and men. Though I had the desire, I never attended a full-fledged orgy. I did, however, have an unusual encounter with a man on a bus once (I guess I had a thing about buses, too).

Although to this day I enjoy sexually explicit magazines and movies, I have often felt that it was wrong to be attracted to them, that it was politically indefensible. Though I am repulsed by images of women or men being hurt or humiliated, certain pornographic materials do arouse me. Even when I'm involved in a sexual relationship, I still masturbate on occasion to pornographic stimuli. And I've enjoyed situations where I could observe the sexual frolics of others. I just wish more high-quality sexually explicit images were available. David Steinberg's *Erotic by Nature* is one place to start.

I'm no Tom Selleck, so I don't hold women to impossibly high standards of physical attractiveness. Nevertheless, I remain unduly influenced by pornographic images of what women's bodies are "supposed" to look like. I sometimes feel I'm an unwilling prisoner of these images, which prevent me from beginning liaisons with women with "imperfect" bodies or cause my sexual interest to disappear if their ability to arouse me cannot match my fantasies. Am I always in tune with my real-life lover or do I measure her against an unrealistic ideal?

The end of my first serious romantic relationship in my 20s and of my marriage two and a half years ago can be attributed in part to waning sexual desire. This has caused me considerable pain and regret, because I feel I am a sensitive and imaginative lover. Eventually dissatisfaction with my first lover's boyish body was one factor in our break-up, however, and I suppose I never fully appreciated her sensuality. Similarly, my former wife and I never found a way to bridge the sexual gulf that developed between us. We did a miserable job of communicating about our sexual problems and, even when we did, we were unable to resolve them. Those problems were ultimately symptomatic of other troubles that eventually led to our divorce.

Though the notion of a "normal" sex life is illusive, it seems that too much of my adulthood has been characterized by relationships with either little or unsatisfying sex, punctuated by dispiriting interludes of celibacy. I have contemplated the sexual relationships in my life that have been gratifying in an attempt to understand what too often has been lacking. My hope is that in future relationships I can confront sexual issues directly when they arise and remove the shroud of silence that has often concealed them.

I have been single for over two and a half years. The age of AIDS and other sexually transmitted diseases has altered the nature of sex. Although I am willing to use them, my penis has never met a condom it really liked (or could stand up to) particularly well. After an unexpected exchange of "bodily fluids" a year and a half ago with my last lover, I insisted that we undergo AIDS tests despite our being at extremely low risk. Though the results were negative, it was a scary experience that reaffirms the prudence of my current search for one special lover.

My life as a joint custody father has also changed the context of romance. I have the impression that some—maybe most—women are reluctant to date a single father, are hesitant to become involved in the life of a child even if, as in my case, the father is not acrimoniously entangled with his former spouse. Though my son is accustomed to the notion of his mom or dad being in bed with another person, a lover may understandably not wish to sleep overnight when your child is with you. Remember that embarrassing moment in the movie *Kramer vs. Kramer* when the child and his father's lover meet unexpectedly on the way to the bathroom in the middle of the night?

And is one's lover receiving enough attention or instead feeling neglected when we focus so much energy on our children? Ministering to our children's needs—as it has been historically for single mothers—is paramount for single and joint custody fathers. Though we need the freedom to create satisfying sexual relationships separate from our lives as parents, potential lovers must understand how important our children are to us.

My last lover and I dealt with all of these issues. Though we were never "in love," our fourteen months together featured a stimulating, sometimes rapturous sex life. She always respected the amount of time I needed to dedicate to my son and enjoyed his company on the infrequent occasions we all shared together. Yet she never stayed overnight with me when Zack was in the bedroom down the hall. In retrospect, this simply reflected her awareness that the uncertainty of our relationship didn't merit creating unrealistic expectations in my son that I was involved with a potential stepmom.

Living in a society more supportive of parents providing sexual information to their children than in my parents' generation, I wonder how I can do a better job teaching Zachary about sex. I want to be able to talk to him in an informed and intelligent way. I have tried to answer his questions about sex directly (there haven't been many yet) without foisting too much on him before he's ready. Although I am open to his questions, and will try to help him make wise choices, I realize that I'm not going to be perfect in my efforts, just as my parents weren't. Informative books on explaining sex to children can be invaluable. Peter Mayle's *Where Did I Come From?*, which explains the facts of life in a way that children can understand and parents can enjoy, has been informative. Zack chose it for his bedtime story just the other night. Wardell Pomeroy's *Boys and Sex* is another excellent resource for boys and their parents.

I haven't sent negative messages to Zack about touching his genitals or being curious about other children's. A fascination with penises seems perfectly natural for boys. Zack's penchant for backrubs from Dad at bedtime shows his appreciation of the importance of touch. Massage has been a satisfying part of my sensual experiences and I hope Zack is similarly blessed.

My son already exhibits his father's erotic curiosity. Not long ago he asked me if I liked movies that had sex in them. "Sometimes," I replied. "Then you ought to see *My Stepmother Is an Alien*," he suggested. He's also asked me why I have so many books about sex in my apartment (actually, he had simply stumbled upon that particular section of my library). Just recently he informed me of the little-known anatomical fact that "the penis bone is connected to the bladder bone."

A couple months ago I discovered that a late '80s version of the "Cherry Hill" joke of my youth still retains its vitality. A generation later, the girl's name is "Blackberry Hill." I hope my response was more meaningful than the one I was offered in my youth. Occasionally, to be provocative, Zack feigns revulsion at the notion of a penis and vagina uniting. I resist the provocation and submit that some day he'll love the idea. Though uncertain about how to respond in all of these situations, I feel quite comfortable broaching sexual matters, speaking as I am from the heart to my son.

At some point we will need to discuss intercourse and other forms of sexual intimacy in detail, as well as pregnancy and contraception. There's so much ahead to talk about! How do I bring up the subject of masturbation and orgasms? We have to deal with the bodily changes of puberty (we shared a few words about pubic hair not long ago), wet dreams, preadolescent sexual exploration, and the challenges of the dating world. We've already addressed the issue of homosexuality once already. And when is the right time to consider these topics?

I want Zack to feel comfortable with his sexuality and to understand the changes his body will be undergoing. At an appropriate time, I would hope that sharing my sexual growth (or lack thereof) as a boy would prove instructive for my son. In learning how to bring pleasure to sexual partners, I want him to remember that he has a right to be assertive about his desires, too. Though he will surely come to appreciate how enjoyable sex can be, I also want him to understand the responsibilities of being a sexually active person.

Though unfettered sexual exploration may never again be possible in our society, I will encourage Zack to act intelligently whatever the form of his sexual encounters. I want to teach him not to feel pressured into sex—in the name of masculinity—before he is ready. I will caution him to love carefully in the age of AIDS. As for his inevitable exposure to pornography, I will explain its impact on my life and try to help him sort out what it all means. I don't want Zack's impressions of women to be influenced to the degree mine have been by pornographic images.

Though as adults we continue to ponder this, I will have to address the emotional side of relationships with Zachary—the interplay between sex and love—and what I have learned and am still learning. One thing I'll be sure to discuss is the importance of direct and honest communication, a lesson I unfortunately failed to learn in my marriage.

As a child of divorce, he has lived through the deterioration of a loving relationship. Still, I don't think he will grow up cynical about marriage or the permanence of relationships. *Dinosaur's Divorce: A Guide for Changing Families*, by Laurene Krasny Brown and Marc Brown, has been a valuable resource in helping my son better understand why parents divorce, what kinds of feelings children expe-rience after divorce, what it's like to live in two homes, with a single parent, or with a stepparent (Zack's life the past two and a half years), and other pertinent issues about divorce and its aftermath.

Zack knows his parents still love him dearly. He has seen his mother become romantically committed to another man, quite fond of Zack, whom she will soon marry. I hope my involvement with women since the divorce can provide a positive role model for Zack to emulate in his future romantic life. Bearing in mind Dorothy Sayers' observation that "the only sin passion can commit is to be joyless," I will remind him that sex—whether passionate and intense or tender and languorous—can be a joyful and enriching part of being alive. That is the finest legacy I could leave my son.

READING 65

Heteroflexibility

Laurie Essig

There is nothing like teaching college students to make a person feel hopelessly out-of-date. This fact first hit me at the tender age of 30. I was teaching what I thought was the hippest version of sociology imaginable. As part of my haute hipness, I had included readings on Elvis Presley. None of the students, however, had the faintest idea who Elvis Presley was. One thought that he might have been an actor. Another said she thought he had invented a diet because he had always been fat.

The generation gap between the students and me was bad enough, but then my teaching assistant, a nice man who was neither as young as they nor as old as I, decided to help me communicate more effectively the King's cultural significance. "Elvis Presley," he explained to the students, "was someone our parents used to listen to. He sang this stuff called rock 'n' roll. It came before rap music."

The students nodded their heads, as if they had just remembered that rap music did not always exist. I shook mine, having realized for the first time that Elvis really was dead. And in Elvis's death, I felt my own mortality.

Faced with the eternal youth of college students, my own aging can only become more obvious with each passing semester. I vowed to accept this fact gracefully and never again try to wow them with my knowledge of popular culture.

But now it's not just popular culture that divides us. It's sexuality as well. Oh I don't mean straight, gay or bi. I don't even mean queer. What I'm talking about here is "heteroflexibility."

If you don't know what that is, it's time to admit that you're as out of it as I am. Heteroflexibility is the newest permutation of sexual identity. According to my students, a person uses heteroflexibility in the first person, as in "I'm heteroflexible." This means that the person has or intends to have a primarily heterosexual lifestyle, with a primary sexual and emotional attachment to someone of the opposite sex. But that person remains open to sexual encounters and even relationships with persons of the same sex. It is a rejection of bisexuality since the inevitable question that comes up in bisexuality is one of preference, and the preference of the heteroflexible is quite clear.

Heteroflexible, I am told, is a lighthearted attempt to stick with heterosexual identification while still "getting in on the fun of homosexual pleasures." One student, Lisa, explained it like this: "Heteroflexibility is Ally McBeal kissing Ling." I pretended I knew what she was talking about, but of course I didn't (and not just because I don't watch television).

My reaction was predictable. I was ashamed of my own inability to stay current, and I was also deeply pissed. How could these kids go and invent yet another identity when "we" solved that problem for them in the 1980s and '90s? The word they were looking for was "queer" or even "bisexual," dammit. I was angry that they would throw out the politics and the struggles of naming that had come before them. And what did they throw it out for? A monstrosity of a word, a mix of sexology and yoga practices.

My anger wasn't just the anger of the middle-aged toward disrespectful youth (even if it was primarily that). I resented the fact that they would root their marginal sexual practices in the safety of heterosexuality. I resented that they would be so committed to *not* having primary relationships with someone of the

same sex that they would preclude such possibilities with that abominable prefix. I resented that feminism had died so that women now felt free to name their primary commitment to men while proclaiming their sexual availability to other women.

And then my middle-aged rage mellowed enough to see the true genius behind this new term. Heteroflexibility—not homosexuality or bisexuality—would bring about an end to the hegemony of heterosexuality. Think about it. The opposite of heteroflexible is heterorigid. Imagine saying to anyone that you're heterorigid. Sounds awful, right? Like some very stiff politician in a suit and tie who is so busy being heterorigid that he can't relax his sphincter muscles enough to look natural. Heterorigidity has none of the promises of pleasure that heterosexuality has. There is no sexual potential in an identity rooted in denial of possibility.

Of course, it's not just heterosexuality that will wither away with the advent of heteroflexibility, but homosexuality as well. Being homorigid doesn't sound as appealing as homoflexible. Homorigidity brings to mind the lesbian who won't even have penetrative sex because she's afraid it might be too much like heterosexuality, a person so bent on identity that her sexual desires get bent into knots.

I can imagine a world where rigidity of any variety becomes as taboo as homosexuality used to be. In the post-rigid age, we will all identify as flexible (even if we're not). And sexual identity will become much less mired in the unimaginative binary of hetero and homo. The world will in fact start to look a lot more like that queer nation "we" envisioned when we were in school—just like the queer nation we envisioned turns out to be not that different from the one envisioned by the gay liberationists before us, and the homophiles before them and so on and so forth.

And so my students will replace me and others like me with new imaginings of sexual desires. And I will become increasingly entrenched in my own generation's way of seeing the world and sexual desires and ourselves until one day it will not be my sexual rigidity that makes me old and them young, but my generational rigidity. Or more accurately, it is my generation's superiority that will make me old and them young, since anyone born before 1970 surely knows a lot more about sex than these heteroflexible punks ever will.

The Sensual Man

Mick Cooper and Peter Baker

PERFORMING ZEAL

It's been a passionate night of lovemaking. You reach for a cigarette, a mug of herbal tea or whatever takes your fancy. 'Darling,' you say, 'how was that for you?'

'To be honest,' she replies, 'boring, unadventurous and irritating. You didn't go down on me, you half squashed me to death, and you didn't even bother finding out whether I'd come or not!'

How would that make you feel? The answer is probably something like 'terrible.' 'gut-wrenched' or 'humiliated.' It's not as if someone's just told you you've got a lousy golf swing or your car needs a paint job. Criticism of our sexual virility hits us right where it hurts—our identity as a man. Real men, so we've been told, are maestros between the sheets. They can unclip a woman's bra straps without spending 20 minutes trying to work out whether the catch is on the front or the back; they can find her clitoris without fumbling; and they can bring her to a moaning, shuddering orgasm just by unzipping their trousers.

Of course, the real man is not only technically perfect, he also makes love like a Martini—any time, any place, anywhere. Whether he's in the middle of the park or on the back seat of a bus, he doesn't say, 'Look, this is really embarrassing, can we stop it.' Instead he's ever-prepared with an everlasting erection, a 'stiffy' that refuses to wilt even after the seventh time that night. 'Yes honey,' he says, 'of course I want more. Let's keep doing it.'

As well as being the ultimate sex machine, a lot of us feel we should be walking copies of *The Good Sex Guide.* We can easily believe good sex is largely a matter of technique and that, to be a great lover, we must know about everything from position 209 of the *Kama Sutra* to the mysteries of the G-spot. After all, isn't that what women expect?

The problem is, while real men might be super-studs with PhDs in sexology, most of us don't actually come close. And if we feel we're sexual failures unless we live up to the image of the sex god, then we're putting ourselves under an inordinate amount of pressure. Instead of sex being an opportunity for us to experience intimacy with another person, or just the chance to have fun, it can become a deeply anxiety-ridden affair, where the worry of "Am I Mr. Perfect-in-bed?' detracts from the physical and emotional pleasures of making love. When we're striving hard to be good between the sheets, it's almost impossible to let go and

Source: The MANual: The complete Guide to Life. Copyright © 1996 Thorsons. Reprinted with permission of Thorsons.

fully immerse ourselves in the act of sex. To give our 'best' performance, we feel we must stay in control throughout.

So the irony is that performance-anxiety, if anything, makes for poorer lovemaking. Apart from the fact that our tension may well be obvious and prevent our lover from relaxing, a mind focused on performance isn't going to be very aware of the fact that there's another person in the bed. This can make a woman feel we're distant and disconnected. Moreover, even if we could become technically perfect, sex is about two people being together, not about one person and a sex machine. If our partner wanted purely physical stimulation, she'd probably go for a vibrator.

It's also worth remembering that sexual knowledge is something we learn, not something we're born with and, if we expect to know it all straight away, we're going to be in for a nasty shock and a lot of humiliation. In fact, claiming to know it all actually stops us from finding out more, because we're either too afraid to ask or too freaked out to listen when someone comments on our sexual behaviour. Flying off into fits of suicidal despair when a woman informs us that we're trying to stick our penis up her anus not her vagina (when it's her vagina we're aiming for) does not actually help us do it right the next time. Listening to what she has to say and learning from her, however, provides a much better chance of developing our sexual awareness.

THE CASANOVA COMPLEX

. . . Sleeping around undoubtedly makes many of us feel good—we enjoy the conquest of new flesh in much the same way as an explorer loves to conquer new lands. We may enjoy the sex, we may even like our partner, but if we can make a woman succumb, it makes us feel powerful, virile, attractive and desirable. The next day, we walk out of the bedroom with a proud, taut body, bursting at the seams with manhood.

For some men, sex can become a virtual addiction, just like nicotine or alcohol. Sex addiction has many possible causes, but often what it comes down to is that men feel unloved and uncared for and use sex as a way of trying to get close to people. Strangely, it's often easier to have sex than it is to talk and share openly, honestly and intimately. And this can be just as true for the man who feels a compulsive need to have sex with one partner as the man who has sex with hundreds. Men whose sexual behaviour is motivated in this way often eventually realize that they never really feel satisfied or fulfilled, no matter how many women they sleep with or how often they have sex. They find they have to discover other, longer-lasting ways of meeting their needs.

Although many men still aspire to be Casanova, the harsh reality is that most of us come nowhere near. The British National Survey of Sexual Attitudes and Lifestyles, which, in the early 90s, looked in detail at the behaviour of over 8,000 men aged 16–59, found that 21 per cent have had only one heterosexual partner and 29 per cent between two and four partners, 24 per cent have had ten or more partners, but under 2 percent have had five or more partners in the last year. The same survey found that about one in five men aged 16–24 are still virgins, as are almost 2 percent of all 16–59-year-olds. However, the study did find one man who claimed to have had 4,500 partners, so there may be at least one real man around after all.

The same survey suggests that we're not at it all the time either. Although it's easy to believe everyone else is shagging like bunnies, the average heterosexual of any age doesn't make love more than five times a month. The study also found that only a small number of people have sex up to 130 times a month, perhaps not surprisingly since bonking four or five times a day wouldn't leave very much time for anything else!

But for those men who are not copulating at all, even these statistics may make depressing reading. Unwanted celibacy when you're between relationships can seem bad enough, but virginity can seem an almost intolerable burden, especially as a man gets older. Virginity simply doesn't seem a desirable condition for any aspiring real man. It suggests that we're unattractive, we can't control women and we certainly can't get them into bed. The image we have of the male virgin—a wimpy, soft, mummy's boy, probably more interested in trainspotting than girls—isn't one that many men would happily aspire to.

Embarrassment about sexual inexperience can actually make it more difficult for a man to lose his virginity. Although he may be desperate to sleep with someone, he may also be afraid that he'll be humiliated when his partner discovers he doesn't know what he's doing—especially if he's at an age where he feels his virginity should be long gone. So he either avoids any opportunities for sexual contact altogether, or else he's so nervous when the possibility comes up that he's more in a state of panic than one of sexual arousal.

The concept of virginity also puts a lot of emphasis on penetration as opposed to other sexual practices. It's as if we're only a 'proper' adult once we've 'gone all the way'—nothing else counts, even if we have a steady partner. This can make it difficult for any of us to value anything short of intercourse. The focus, especially for younger men, is on 'making fourth base' rather than enjoying what we're doing and taking it slowly and sensually.

SMALL IS BEAUTIFUL?

Most of us reckon we've come to terms with the size of our penis—by our late teens we probably know it's not going to grow any more, although we may still have strong feelings about it. As men, the size of our 'pole' can be more than just the dimension of an or-gan which dangles between our legs—it's a symbol of virility, manliness and self-worth. So if we consider ourselves a 'big boy', we're liable to feel proud of our penis, showing it off in the school showers or carefully manoeuvring our body to ensure that our lovers get a good eyeful. If we could, we'd probably even consider snipping it off for display on the mantelpiece.

On the other hand, a man who thinks his penis is too small may have strong feelings of shame and self-doubt. He might dart into the changing rooms after swimming so no-one can see the non-existent bulge, or always get undressed in the dark to prevent lovers from commenting on his minor member. Penis-size anxiety can, in some cases, disrupt a man's enjoyment of a sexual experience. If he's so worried that his lover's going to burst into laughter the moment she sees his penis and shout, 'Make love with that, I couldn't even pick my teeth with it!', the chances are he won't be very relaxed. For many of us, being told our penis is too small could be a profoundly humiliating experience.

As men, we compete with each other over numerous things, but the battle of the trouser bulges differs from a lot of other competition in one very dramatic way: we can go on a body-building course to strengthen our muscles, we can buy a bigger car, we can search around for a more beautiful wife, but—short of plastic surgery—it's impossible for us to get a bigger penis. It's an unchanging symbol of our masculinity. So it's no wonder that young boys watch their penises growing as anxiously as a cook watching his soufflé rising. Once it stops, we're stuck.

What adds to penis-size anxiety is the fact that many of us assume that other men's penises are bigger than they actually are. Straight men have few opportunities to observe other men's penises (especially erect ones). Since the only ones we tend to know about are the 10-inch monsters depicted in pornography, it's hardly surprising that we can end up feeling inadequate. After all, compared to King Dong's 'stonker', most of us are still playing hunt the acorn. In fact, the average penis is a much more modest 6 inches long when erect, and 90 per cent of penises fall 1 inch either side of this. To get a better idea of the actual size of your organ, try looking at it sideways on in a mirror; peering down can give a highly misleading perspective.

Although it's clearly a nonsense to value ourselves by the length of our penis, before we rejoice and proclaim, 'Size doesn't count', it's important to listen to what women have to say. A large survey of British and German women for the sex magazine *Women Only* found that while 90 per cent felt that penis size didn't affect their orgasm, about the same proportion considered penis length and width to be 'sometimes' or 'always' important while making love. Of those women with experience of a larger than average penis (8–9 inches), 56 per cent found it more satisfying than normal. An *Arena/New Woman* survey also found that almost four in ten women thought penis size was 'vital' or 'quite important' for a fulfilling sex life.

But before digging out the ruler from the bedside cabinet, it's important to remember that when women say that size does matter, they almost certainly are not saying they only admire or respect a man if he's got a big penis. To men, penis size is a matter or pride. To women, it's much more a matter of sexual pleasure. So it's not that they don't respect or enjoy sex with a lightly-hung man, it's just that a bigger penis might feel nicer inside them—in the same way that some men find a tighter vagina provides a snugger fit.

BEFORE IT'S TIME

Exactly when an ejaculation is premature is a topic of some debate among sex therapists. Indeed, one therapist discovered a man who thought he suffered from premature ejaculation because he couldn't hang on for more than 45 minutes of vigorous thrusting! But ejaculation is obviously premature if the man comes before he's walked through the front door, and it's probably premature if he starts spurting before or at the moment of penetration. Apart from that, however, it's difficult to say what's too fast. It probably makes most sense to say that an ejaculation is premature when its early appearance causes a problem in a sexual relationship.

Premature ejaculation is in fact the most common male sexual problem. Shere Hite's survey of over 7,000 American men found three-quarters were concerned that they came 'too soon'. Premature ejaculation can be caused by a variety of factors: anxiety, stress, not having learned to control ejaculation or sexual trauma. Having sex again after a long period of abstinence can also be a factor. There are no known physical causes.

Of course, real men can keep going for hours, so a man who can't hold on until his partner's had her third multiple orgasm may well feel pretty useless. Moreover, premature ejaculation can leave men's partners frustrated, hurt or even angry—high, but not exactly dry. The problem, however, is that knowing this doesn't make it any easier for men not to come too soon. Anxiety about premature ejaculation can, in fact, lead to a vicious circle where the problem seems just to get worse and worse.

The good news is that the syndrome is not inevitable. Men can learn to control their orgasms. Traditional methods of ejaculation control tend to involve bizarre mind-games—some sex manuals suggest concentrating on football scores, train timetables or even Einstein's theory of relativity. In one of his nightclub routines, Woody Allen describes how he used to think about baseball games to stem the flow. He jokes that he once became so preoccupied with a match that he didn't realize he'd finished having sex until he discovered that his partner had been in the shower for ten minutes.

The mind-game strategy, however, while sometimes effective, is no longer recommended by most sex therapists as it reduces men's involvement in the sex act, as well as their pleasure, without really tackling the root of the problem. So what can you do if you suffer from premature ejaculation? Your best bet is simply to try not to rush straight towards penetration. The more your partner is turned on before you enter her, the more quickly she could come, leaving you less time to hold on. Wearing a condom can also reduce sensitivity and hence the speed of orgasm. Another possibility is that your partner can help you with the so-called 'squeeze technique'—she squeezes the head of your penis for four seconds every few minutes during sex. Over time, this can help you to learn to control your ejaculations. Many sex therapists also use so-called 'sensate focus' exercises to treat premature ejaculations.

It also helps to remember that it's actually quite difficult for most women to orgasm while we're inside them. As any woman will tell you, when it comes to coming, the clitoris is much more important than the vagina, and it's not necessarily directly stimulated by your penis. So don't assume you simply have to hump away until something happens to her. You can always try taking your penis out and using your tongue or fingers instead.

SOFTWARE PROBLEMS

Keith reflects on an experience he had when he was 18:

Soon after I was inside her, I realized something wasn't right. My friends at school had told me to expect a mountain of orgasmic pleasure but I couldn't feel a foothill. I was worried and then my fear hit me like a bolt of lightening—I realized my erection had wilted. My throat became dry and my bowels felt like they were turning to water. For the first time, I understood what it meant to

want the earth to open. I pulled out my willy and watched with horror as it tried to hide itself away between my legs. I felt like being sick and ran, shaking and pale, into the bathroom.

Keith was prepared to try anything:

Standing naked and cold on the tiles, I desperately tried to revive my previous virility. I tried to focus on memories of images that had aroused me when masturbating earlier that evening. I even tried applying a tub of my friend's hair gel, but to no avail. Each semi-erection I managed to coax was soon ruined by the overpowering fear of failure that was consuming me. Both physically and mentally, I was completely impotent.

Impotence—the inability to maintain an erection during sexual intercourse—is the second most common male sexual problem. Technically, the occasional erectile problem isn't impotence—that could be due to too much booze, stress or exhaustion. To be truly impotent, a man's erectile dysfunction has to last for at least several weeks. The Erectile Dysfunction Information Bureau believes that one quarter of men aged over 16 have experienced impotence and that 5 per cent of men are permanently impotent. And it gets bigger with age—the problem, that is. A major US study found that while under 10 per cent of 20–39-year-olds suffered from impotence, almost 60 per cent of 70-plus-year-olds were affected.

There are a number of causes of impotence. Some of these are physiological, including alcohol abuse, diabetes, high blood pressure, hardened arteries, the side effects of some drugs (such as beta-blockers, prescribed for high blood pressure) and low testosterone levels. However many cases of impotence (perhaps 50–60 per cent) have psychological causes, such as feelings of resentment or anger towards a partner, fears about the possible consequences of intercourse (pregnancy or acquiring a sexually transmitted disease, for example) or childhood traumas such as sexual abuse. Often, the cause of impotence can also be traced back to the pressures men feel around performance. If a man is over-anxious to impress, it's possible he'll find it harder to get hard.

Whatever the causes, an inability to sustain an erection represents the ultimate sexual failure for many men. It can lead to devastating feelings of embarrassment, shame and humiliation. And if this happens, a man may be terrified that he'll go through the whole nightmare scenario again the next time he tries to make love—indeed, like premature ejaculation, impotence can easily become a vicious cycle. The harder a man tries to will his penis up, the only thing likely to rise is his anxiety level, and that means his penis will stay firmly (or not so firmly) down.

If you can't get an erection with a partner but can get one when you masturbate, when you have non-penetrative sex or during the night or on waking, the chances are that your impotence is psychologically rooted rather than physiological (although it's always a good idea for any sufferer to see a doctor for a check-up). If this is the case, trying to force an erection is the worst thing you can do. Focusing less on the penis, or its erection, can help you to let go of self-perpetuating fears, and spending more time on foreplay is one good way of doing this.

If the cause of impotence is physiological, there are several different and effective treatments that can improve the condition. Depending on the exact cause, these can include injections into the penis, using vacuum pumps or vascular surgery. In recent years, 'penile implants' have also been developed, particularly for cases that can't be treated in any other way. There are two types. The first is a semi-rigid silicone rod that keeps the penis erect permanently but allows it to be bent out of the way when not needed. The second type consists of two inflatable silicone cylinders inserted in the penis and connected to a small fluid-containing balloon in the abdomen with a pump in the scrotum. When the pump is squeezed, fluid

flows into the cylinders and an erection results. A valve on the pump can later be used to deflate the penis. Fortunately the mechanism is not electronic, so the Sunday newspaper story about a man with a penile implant who had an erection every time his neighbour opened her electronic garage door is about as probable as finding a World War II bomber on the moon.

PHALLACIES

In-out, in-out, shake it all about, fall asleep—unfortunately for many of us that's about the sum total of our sex lives. Despite the anxieties some of us can have about pleasing our partners, the other side of the coin is that we can also be pretty selfish in the bedroom. Sex is centred almost exclusively on *our* genitals and *our* orgasm; while areas such as foreplay, communication, caressing and romance becomes relegated to the sexual dustbin. Men often rush sex, eager to get inside their partner as quickly as possible. And that's a shame, because a long, lingering build-up can be really exciting. Good sex is like a fine meal: it's possible to enjoy all the different delicacies and luxuriate in the sensual experience. We might like fast food now and again but, as we all know, one good belch and we're hungry again.

Such a penis-oriented—'phallocentric'—approach to sex can frequently leave a female partner feeling disappointed and frustrated. If things go too quickly, by the time we're into our first snore, she may be just getting turned on. Moreover, as we've seen, women's main centre of sexual pleasure—the clitoris—is usually not directly stimulated through vaginal intercourse. So just plugging it in and hoping for the best probably won't work—at least not for her.

Part of the reason why many men have a phallocentric approach to sex may be a fear of intimacy—a perennial issue for us. Sex is, after all, an extremely personal thing to do—when we penetrate someone we're right inside them, both literally and metaphorically. And because many of us are scared of the closeness this brings, we may distance ourselves from the emotional intimacy by locating our sexual desire purely in our penis. It's as if we're saying, 'I'm not having sex, my penis is.' The penis is given a life of its own, like the Wicked Willie cartoon character. It's divorced from the rest of the body and from our feelings. Through reducing sex between two people from 'making live' to 'shagging', 'bonking' or 'fucking', the sex act is depersonalized. There's no fear of being hurt or of being out of control. It's a purely physical affair.

THE BEST SEX EVER

Whether we're worried about our sexual performance, our sexual knowledge, our virginity, our penis size, our premature ejaculation or our impotence, the way to overcome these problems may well be essentially the same— letting go of our struggle to be real men. The bottom line is that it's OK for us to not be conquistadors in bed and, the sooner we realize this, the sooner we can begin to overcome any sexual anxieties we might have.

One of the best ways men can change their point of view is by talking to women. Most of us carry a series of false assumptions about the way women want us to be. We think that unless we can come five times a night and have a penis the size of the Eiffel Tower they won't respect us. However, because women haven't been brought up with the same attitudes towards sex, often what they really think is very different. Most women, like most men, want to be sexually satisfied, but this doesn't mean that they'll necessarily think any less of a man who has some problems under the duvet. What's important is for us to find out what our partners really want, not what we think they want. That way, we're more likely to satisfy them, and also more likely to take unrealistic pressures off ourselves.

It's also invaluable to talk to other men about sex, although this has to be done openly and honestly, otherwise it can do more damage than good. So choose who you talk to carefully—after all, typical male sexual boasting just heightens everyone's anxiety. The first guy says he's slept with ten women in the last year and the second one says 20 and the third says 50. So when they all go home to their bachelor pads which haven't seen a woman for the last two years, they're all thinking, 'God, have those other two really slept with so many women? I must be doing something wrong!'

Talking about sex honestly, on the other hand, can help us to realize that we're not alone with our problems, or inadequate freaks just because we don't know 35 variations of the missionary position. Once we see that others have the same fears, concerns and experiences, sex stops being such a frightening, 'unspoken' activity and becomes something we can feel much more comfortable around. We can also have a lot of fun talking about the things we love and hate about sex, and discovering that other men may feel the same way. Talking about sex can also help us to improve our sex lives by learning from one another.

Sex (American Style)

Thomas Moore

If we spiced our lives with more sensuality, we might make public life more sensuous and the gutters classier.

As I've been writing a book about sex in recent months, I've had the *Kama Sutra*, the Indian guide to personal sexual culture, on my desk, and occasionally I've consulted the Internet to track down relevant books and articles. On the Internet, I've noticed, as soon as you venture in the direction of sex you quickly come upon crude, unadorned images of stark sexual union. Apparently we have finally found a public place where we can show our private parts and secret fantasies, free of the repressive eyes of the government agencies that serve our culture's dominant Puritan philosophies. But here there is no love, little sentimentality, and almost nothing that could be called foreplay in any innocent sense of the word.

In contrast, the *Kama Sutra* discusses a wide range of sexual matters, from the general comportment of one's life (*dharma*) to the establishment of personal economic security (*artha*) and the cultivation of the arts of love (*kama*). The *Kama Sutra*, graphic and open-minded in its own way, places sex within the context of a refined, humane life, while the Internet focuses on organs and acts. I'm reminded of the beautiful erotic figures carved into the Indian temples of Kharujaho and Konarak more than 1,000 years ago, images that depict every imaginable sex act within a context of worship and prayer, and I wonder why the Indians put their sexual fantasies on temples while we give ours over to pornography. This is one of

those questions that I believe, if we could answer it, would pinpoint exactly what's wrong with our culture.

Although I'm convinced we're all moralists at heart, I'm not interested in making any judgments here about the ethics or appropriateness of the *Kama Sutra*, the temple sex couples, or the Internet, but I am interested in the sexual life of the community in which I live. We seem to be obsessed with sex and embarrassed by it. Sex sells, I'm told by almost everyone who hears I'm writing about the theme. Some insinuate that I must be writing about sex for the royalties alone, cashing in on our mass compulsion, but I wonder if I'll lose readers, because you aren't supposed to be interested in both spirituality and sex—unless you're writing about sacred sex (whatever that is), or offering suitably cantankerous health or moral cautions.

Medieval monks spend hours copying the Bible, while in the margins, called gutters, they would occasionally doodle obscene images and phrases. We do something similar when we create an efficient, clean world of speedy highways and no-nonsense office buildings, while our extravagant sexual images—our dirty thoughts—are funneled into red-light districts, a 42nd Street or a Hollywood and Vine, or into an unregulated highway called the Internet. We divide sex from ordinary life and then wonder why it enjoys emotional autonomy in our lives.

History shows that sex has always had its selected areas of tolerance—usually far from the center of daily commerce, except perhaps in ancient Pompeii, Greece, Rome, or Sodom and Gomorrah. I'm not arguing for a democratization of sexual images; it is appropriate to be as careful about sex in public as a parent might be about it at home. But I do question the sharpness of the line drawn between public life and the gutter. I wonder why we demand that our political leaders be without sexual fault—I discovered while practicing

Elizabeth Amanacer, Winter Trees, 2001 (*Source:* Elizabeth Amanacer)

psychotherapy that everyone, including our most upright fellow citizens, has skeletons in the closet or lurid dreams and fantasies.

Maybe if we spiced our daily lives with qualities associated with sex, we might make public life more sensuous and the gutters classier. People used to build beautiful, sexy bridges, for instance, but now we build them for cost-efficiency. People used to build roads that you'd want to drive on for a Sunday outing, but today we just want to get from one place to another as quickly as possible—no foreplay. In some parts of the world they still make life itself sexy with their sensuous movies, their extravagant cuisines, and their seductive streets. In, say, a piazza in Rome or a plaza in Mexico, cafés fill the square with chairs and tables decked out with food that makes you salivate as you pass by. We have our oases of public sensuality (Bourbon Street in New Orleans and maybe the casinos in Las Vegas) but usually they are so removed from the culture at large that they quickly become outrageous and tinged with unsavory—a telling word—associations.

When I'm out in public spaces, I look in vain for a good chair. Most have no place to sit down, or if they do, the seats appear to be designed for something other than the human body. Sitting on a concrete slab doesn't do much for my sexuality. My body would also like to see some nourishing color in place of the ubiquitous metallic glass; an abundance of flowers and trees instead of an architect's skimpy afterthought—the token juniper and the de rigueur marigolds; and sensuous flowing water that isn't hidden behind warehouses and bridge supports. I hope it's obvious that food, flowers, seats, colors, and water have something to do with sex.

Office buildings are the most sexless places in public life. Our vision of work translates into hard marble, cold granite, pale walls, authorless art, green-only vegetation, scarce windows, white light, modular desks, thin carpets, and disembodied background music. No wonder Eros ignites the office affair as often as possible; it's his only refuge. Here I find a rule that has broad application: Take sex out of the world we live in daily, and it will become a giant, unsettling force in our personal lives.

Religion has a powerful influence on sex in America, but the religious institutions merely reflect an attitude deep in the American psyche. Spiritually we are virtually all believers in transcendence, imagining our values, inspiration, and faith all coming from above the clouds, off the earth, out of our bodies, far from sex. We believe in the mind, and we don't trust the body. We are profoundly unsettled when we hear about a priest, preacher, or guru caught in some sexual scandal—our outrage comes from the old theological idea that humanity is contrary to divinity. We are working up a fever making new laws against touching, and we're more scandalized by a photograph or painting showing a nipple or a penis than by the image of a starving child on a dry, dusty road.

The body is our central embarrassment—merely having one, making love with one, or indulging in the human fascination for the sexual body. To all appearances, we'd like to be bodiless, and most of our recent inventions point toward that goal; they encourage us to sit in front of a screen and work, play, shop, and meet with old friends electronically. But after a lifetime of avoiding the body, we meet it face to face in illness, where, not coincidentally, we also discover our souls. Illness teaches us lessons our high-tech education has overlooked: We are mortal, we have a body, to be human is to have sensation, and we could discover what is really important by paying attention to the body's reactions. I suspect we could learn all these lessons more pleasurably by living every day less mentally and more sexually.

The repression of the body and its main work, sex, wounds the soul immeasurably and deprives us of our humanity. Often we refer to sex as "physical love," the work of a soulless body, and then we try to justify this biological act morally by making sure that it's in the service of affection. But the bifurcation of body and soul can't be healed so easily. We have yet to discover that sex is not physical love but the love of souls. You don't have to spiritualize sex to make it valuable, because by its very nature sex is a deep act of the interior life and always brings with it a wealth of emotional and spiritual meaning.

Mircea Eliade, the religion scholar, remarked that the sacred sometimes lies camouflaged in the mundane. As a student of world religions myself, I notice that the positions and organs on the Web's erotic pages are identical to those on Indian temples, on Greek pottery, in ancient ritual, and in religious legend and lore. Oddly, pornography may, at its root, be an unconscious attempt to preserve the sacredness of sex. Where do you find graphic sexual imagery today? In pornography, in religious ritual and statuary, and in dreams. If we assume that dreams portray the soul's interests in pure form, untainted by conscious manipulation, then they tell of the psyche's necessities and of what role erotic feeling and fantasies play in the economy of the heart. Religious erotic art shows us how profound sex is in the nature of things, and how much like religious ecstasy is the pleasing oblivion it grants. Pornography plays the role of providing a symptomatic presentation of the erotic realities that we've excluded from our canons of propriety.

We have lost religion, not as an institution or as a set of beliefs, but as a way of living in touch with the raw roots of desire and meaning. With religion absent, sex, historically wedded to religious practice, falls into the gutter, as much outside of life as religion. Now shaded in darkness, potent sexual imagery, removed from public life, appears only in graffiti and in taboo magazines and movies. Artists, always intimate with religion, intuitively perceive the relation between sex and religion and try to give Eros

a prominent place in their work, but since art, too, has become marginalized, we misjudge sexual imagery in art as irreligious and pornographic.

Sex is trying to break through and out of our secularism, but we misread the signs, thinking we're beholding the work of the devil instead of the angels. Pornography is the return of the repressed, the religious nature of sex presenting itself in dark instead of bright colors. Every time we think of sex as biological, every time we teach sex education as a secular study, we are setting ourselves up for more pornography. But mercifully, for all its stupidity, lack of taste, and outrageousness, pornography keeps sex from becoming the heartless preserve of the medical establishment and the social scientist.

Sex is the ritual recovery of vitality and life. It makes marriages, creates families, and sustains love. It takes us momentarily out of our minds and into our souls. In sex we "come"— come back to ourselves in unmediated sensation, come back into our world from our mental outposts. It's no wonder we're obsessed with sex, since it is the very epitome of vitality, and yet, because it is full of vibrancy, we're also deathly afraid of it. Unlike many other cultures, we don't appreciate orgy, even within strict ritual limits. We leave it to pornography, where it is either indulged compulsively in the way of a spectator or moralized against, or both simultaneously.

The most common story I heard from people in psychotherapy dealt with a happy marriage in which one or both partners felt compelled to engage in an extramarital affair. The parties involved couldn't understand the reason for the overwhelming allure of another carnal liaison. They assumed something must be wrong in the marriage or in their own past. They never considered that there might be some deep need for orgy, for sex without the weight of moralism, or for enough and varied sex to offset the bodiless, passionless life that modern work and family values insist upon.

In many cases, the affair looks to me like the office flirtation and the pornographic photo—it's symptomatic of a failure to give sex enough prominence in daily life and in the privacy of a marriage. I don't advocate affairs, but I can understand their allure in an age of incessant labor, anxious leisure, compulsive entertainment, uprooted ethics, and a public life built on efficiency and machinery. In this cool, gray world, we're starved for friendship, excitement, and intimate conversation. One sought-after reward of an affair might be a forgetting of responsibilities, as the participants risk their reputations, marriages, and, in some cases, their livelihoods for a few wicked hours of carnal delight.

Some, of course, would say that affairs are the result of a breakdown in traditional morality. Whatever the merits of this analysis, it is generally presented in a self-righteous, paternalistic, and uncompassionate tone—indicating discomfort with sex and with the moral complexity it may bring into the lives of ordinary people. It's difficult to trust an approach to life's most fascinating and challenging mystery that demonizes sex or deals with sexual problems without showing heart.

One solution to our obsession/repression pattern would be to align sex with intelligence, civility, spiritual values, and all the other aspects of our daily lives. In the realm of the psyche, it seems that the segregation of any element leads to trouble. If the only thing in life is your depression, then you may have little chance of being liberated from it. If money is the aim of your life, they it will probably reveal its emptiness in due time. Sex makes important demands for privacy and secrecy, but if we cut it off from the fabric of life's totality, it may begin to show itself as odd and even monstrous.

It isn't enough to make easy intellectual deals—"I'm willing to understand that sexual feelings are basically good and normal, if you, Sex, are willing to leave me alone and let me live my life according to my plans." A more substantive weaving of sex into life may be accomplished by softening the barriers between ordinary living and sexuality.

We might temper our moralistic approaches to food. If you want to feel guilty these days, eat a sumptuous dinner with friends or boldly buy some food that someone in a lab coat has determined is bad for you. Few things in life are closer to sex than food, and yet we have gone too far in surrendering this ordinary pleasure to the medicine-haunted guardians of kitchen virtue.

Or, in a culture that frowns on idleness, give yourself some completely unproductive time. Excessive productivity is incompatible with an erotically interesting life because the senses get distracted by busyness. Not spending your time profitably might be the best thing you can do for your sex life.

We might give serious attention to qualities associated with sex, such as pleasure, desire, intimacy, and sensuality, and give these very qualities a place in all aspects of daily life. We might take the body's needs into consideration as we build and arrange our world. Sex finds its way by means of desire, and it follows that if we were to live in tune with our sexuality, we would give desire its proper place. Some would object that responding to our appetites is narcissistic and irresponsible, but taking desire into account is not the same as doing whatever we feel like. We are not sophisticated about desire, and so tend to reduce discussion of it to absurd, simplistic, and obviously objectionable terms.

Every day desires spring up from the pool that is the human soul and source of life. Some are strong, some weak. Some often contradict others. Some are impossible to satisfy, some we can deal with in a few minutes. The point is, desire serves vitality and ushers in life. We can't act on all desires. If that were possible, at this moment I'd be living in several states and countries. Some desires stay with us for years—late in life we may find a desire fulfilled after many years of containment. Being loyal to desire, giving certain desires time to show themselves more fully and reveal how they might make their way into life, is a form of sexual living. Broadly speaking, it is an erotic way of life.

We could learn from sex to live all of life more intimately. There's something sexual, again in a broad sense of the word, in a warm neighborhood community. I will never forget the afternoon, shortly before we moved from Massachusetts, when our family gathered our neighbors together for a goodbye ritual. We created a small, spontaneous ceremony in which we all said something from the heart about our history in the neighborhood and about the loss we were all feeling. This moment reflected an intimate way of living there. We could have kept our thoughts and feelings to ourselves, but the closeness of that moment represent the Eros, the sexuality, of living among good friends.

In the area of sex, our society can hardly be called compassionate. We quickly judge celebrities whose private sexual difficulties become public. We dispose of politicians and military personnel who miss the mark of our anxiously protected norms. Because sex is so full of life, it is rarely neatly arranged or easy to deal with. In general, if we want to live a soulful life we have to allow some latitude for the unexpected in ourselves and others, but this is especially true of sex. It is the nature of sex, maybe its purpose, to blast some holes in our thinking, our planning, and our moralisms—sex is life in all its boldness.

Read the biographies of the men and women who have made extraordinary contributions to humanity. List their achievements in one column and their sexual idiosyncrasies in another. Notice the direct proportion between sexual individuality and creative output, between desire heeded and compassion acted upon. Then reflect long on your moral attitudes: Are they suitably deep, humane, compassionate, and complex?

Every day we could choose to be intimate rather than distant, acting bodily rather than mentally, responding thoughtfully from desire instead of from discipline, seeking deep pleasures rather than superficial entertainments, getting in touch with the world rather than analyzing it at a distance, making a culture that gives us pleasure rather than one that merely works, allowing plenty of room in our own and in others' lives for the eccentricities of sexual desire—generally taking the role of lovers rather than doers and judges.

The Tantric Vision

Margo Anand

Sex is first of all a matter of energy. The more energy you have, the more blissful you can be, and the better sex becomes. If you mobilize your energy and express it more fully, you can experience orgasm as an *energy event* that can be learned and duplicated independent of the sexual context. Once you have learned how to experience orgasm as an energy event outside the sexual context, you feel empowered to take responsibility for your own well-being in sex. You know that the true source of your pleasure lies not in your partner but within yourself.

You can then learn to contain the energy, relax into it, and expand it. Ecstasy happens to you when you stay relaxed and aware in high states of sexual or nonsexual arousal. You can experience this state with or without a partner, for long periods of time.

Source: David Steinberg, ed., *The Erotic Impulse: Honoring the Sensual Self.* Copyright © 1992. Jeremy P. Tarcher/Perigee Books. Reprinted with permission of Penguin Putnam, Inc.

This is not, as one may experience in ordinary sex, an alternation between arousal and relaxation, but a simultaneous *resonance* between them. You allow the energy to rise to higher and higher levels while at the same time relaxing into the excitement, letting it spread through the body and containing it for longer and longer periods. You generate high levels of sexual arousal that are followed, just before the point of orgasmic release, by complete stillness of mind. At the same time, you relax certain muscles, breathe deeply and slowly, and apply other simple techniques that transform the nature of your orgasm. This prepares you for a full-body orgasm, which depends on the body's ability to vibrate beyond conscious control. Instead of a localized genital release, you experience a prolonged series of subtle, continuous, wavelike pulsations that spread through the body, resulting in the impression that you are melting into your partner.

In this state, the orgasmic sensations are no longer exclusively dependent on genital interaction but are often perceived as an altered state of consciousness. Unlike the short peak of genital orgasm, what you feel is not a reflex act that leads to a sudden and uncontrolled release of energy, but a deep letting-go that is reached through a consciously controlled practice. As the energy between your bodies melts and merges, sexual communion becomes an experience of deep intimacy.

Most lovemaking is very dynamic. You move vigorously, and you breathe hard, building up sexual passion until you explode the energy outward in a final release. In contrast, the orgasm of the brain resembles the smooth, endless gliding of a kite in the wind. This orgasm greatly stimulates the brain cells and creates a bridge between the right and left hemispheres, fusing the intellect of the left hemisphere with the intuitive faculties of the right. It is this fusion that creates the experience of ecstasy, in which body, mind, heart, and spirit all participate.

Our culture has lost the understanding that sexual energy is a physical expression of spiritual power. In truth, the desire to unite sexually with another human being is a reflection of an underlying spiritual need to experience wholeness and complete intimacy, transcending the individual's sense of separateness and isolation. It is a need to return to the original source of creation, to the oneness we experienced in our mother's womb and, beyond that, to a oneness within the self. Sexual union without this sacred element, carried out only for the sake of pleasure, is commonly thought to be enough to satisfy our needs. But it rarely does, and then only fleetingly. With the sacred element added, it is possible for us to experience a connection with the life force itself, with our deepest creative impulses.

When the sexual force is considered to be a purely physical, instinctual drive, it is often misused and becomes associated with personal power—the dominance of one gender over another—and conquest. Deprived of its sacred dimension, sexual energy is repressed and eventually directed against life itself. This, in turn, results in disrespect, disease, abuse, rape, and other forms of sexual violence.

Negative social conditioning about sex inevitably creates fear, and this fear is passed from generation to generation by well-intentioned agents such as parents, teachers, and religion. In early childhood most of us absorb condemnatory attitudes about sex without even becoming aware of the process. This conditioning cripples our spontaneity, our expression of sexual vitality, our pleasure, and our ability to love and honor one another.

When people think of Tantra, they often think of celibate monks and yogis and, therefore, the suppression of orgasm. This is a misconception, implying that the attainment of ecstasy is based on the denial of one of life's most enjoyable activities. Indeed, it is out of the seed of lovemaking that the flower of ecstasy grows. Another popular view is that

Tantra resembles a sexual orgy and promotes hedonistic indulgences.

In fact, Tantra is a middle path. It is neither indulgence nor repression. It teaches you to look directly into your sexuality so that you can understand, experience, and transform it rather than being either antagonistic to or enslaved by sex.

Tantra was born in India around 5000 B.C., through the cult of the Hindu god Shiva and his consort, the goddess Shakti. Shiva was worshipped as the embodiment of pure consciousness in its most ecstatic state, and Shakti as the embodiment of pure energy. The Hindus believed that through uniting spiritually and sexually with Shiva, Shakti gave form to his spirit and created the universe. Tantra, therefore, views the creation of the world as an erotic act of love. The joyful dance between Shiva and Shakti is reflected in all living beings and manifests itself as pleasure, beauty, and happiness. This, in Tantra, is the nature of the divine, the root of all that exists.

Tantra originally developed as a rebellion against the repressive, moralistic codes of organized religions and the ascetic practices of the Brahmins—the Hindu priesthood—particularly against the widespread belief that sexuality had to be denied in order to attain enlightenment. *Tantra* means "weaving," in the sense of unifying the many and often contradictory aspects of the self into one harmonious whole. *Tantra* also means "expansion," in the sense that once our own energies are understood and unified, we grow and expand into joy. Always a rebellious and nonconformist approach that challenged taboos and belief systems, Tantra branched out and influenced not only the Hindu but also the Taoist and Buddhist traditions. Tantra influenced Western religious history through the ecstatic cult of the Greek god Dionysus around 2000 B.C.

The great mystics of the Tantric tradition scandalized mainstream society and were often condemned and persecuted. The style of their teaching is characterized by what the Tibetan Tantric tradition calls *crazy wisdom,* a process in which the teacher uses paradoxical stories, seemingly absurd questions, and unexpected behavior to tease, jolt, startle, and provoke people to drop conventional attitudes and embrace the whole spectrum of life, with no contradiction between the sacred and the profane, the spiritual and the sexual.

One of the most extraordinary Tantric mystics was Saraha, who lived in India around the ninth century. Respected in his day as a great scholar and philosopher, he shocked everybody, so the legend goes, by becoming the consort of an enlightened Tantric woman teacher. They lived together in a cemetery, dancing and singing with such contagious ecstasy that everybody who arrived to bury the dead lost their sadness and became enraptured and enlightened. Through him, it is said, the king and queen of the land became enlightened, and eventually the whole kingdom entered a period of great joy and peace.

The Tantric vision *accepts everything.* There is nothing forbidden in Tantra. Everything that a person experiences, regardless of whether it is usually judged as good or bad, is an opportunity for learning. For instance, a situation in which you feel sexually frustrated is not viewed negatively in Tantra, but as a teaching.

In Tantra there is no division between what is good and what is bad, what is acceptable and what is unacceptable. For instance, Tantra, as I understand it, places no moral judgment on your sexual preferences. In Tantra the focus is not so much on with whom you do it but rather on how you do it. Hence, Tantra can be practiced by anyone who is attracted to this path.

The Tantric vision is one of wholeness, of embracing everything, because every situation, whether pleasant or unpleasant, is an opportunity to become more aware about who you are and how you can expand your capacities. And this provides a great opportunity for integrating all aspects of yourself, including those parts that you may normally reject or hide. This vision also recognizes that within each adult human being there is a natural, unspoiled, childlike spirit who can openly and innocently explore unfamiliar territory. The innocence of this spirit remains intact and represents our natural capacity to enjoy life, to love, to play, and to be ecstatic.

Because Tantra believes in wholeness, it embraces opposites, seeing them not as contradictions but as complements. The concepts of male and female therefore are not set apart, forever divided by a gender gap, but are viewed as two polarities that meet and merge in every human being. Tantra recognizes that each human being, whether man or woman, has both masculine and feminine qualities.

What this means is that by discarding our gender stereotypes, we can expand our sexual identities tremendously, honoring the polarity in ourselves that until now has been largely ignored. In Tantra the man can be encouraged to explore his soft, receptive, vulnerable, feminine aspects. He can slip out from beneath the weight of his male responsibilities, stop performing, and relax, taking his time in sex, making love without a specific goal, allowing himself to receive while his partner initiates. For her part, the woman can explore her masculine dimension, recognizing that she is capable of dynamic leadership in lovemaking, taking the initiative, creating new ways of guiding, teaching, and giving herself and her partner pleasure. The man does not give up his masculinity, nor does the woman abandon her femininity. They simply expand their potential to include the other polarity.

In Tantra, when the male and female polarities merge, a new dimension becomes available—the sense of the sacred. When the sacredness of sexual union is felt, it is possible to experience your connection to the life force itself, the source of creation. This connection lifts your consciousness beyond the physical plane into a field of power and energy much greater than your own. Then you feel linked, through your partner, to everything that lives and loves. You feel that you are a part of the great dance of existence; you feel one with it.

Tantra views sexual union not only as sacred, but as an art. Interestingly, the Sanskrit root of the word *art* means "suitably united." To become Tantrikas, practitioners of Tantra, lovers were required to be versed in a multiplicity of skills, such as conversation, dance, ceremony, massage, flower arrangement, costumes and makeup, music, hygiene, breathing, and meditation, among others.

When we learn the erotic arts in this way, a deep healing of our sexuality takes place. The sex act is not a hurried and tense affair, fraught with the dangers of disease (transmitted by partners who do not take time for thorough preparations), but a safe and healthy exchange between partners who respect and know each other intellectually, emotionally, and sensually before they enter into sexual union. This is what is urgently needed today: a playful, loving, and comprehensive perspective on sex that makes it safe and ecstatic at the same time.

According to Tantra, sex is first a matter of energy, and Tantra views energy as the movement of life. Within the human body, energy is continuously in motion. For example, the nucleus and electrons of an atom have characteristic vibratory movements and rhythms. The same goes for the molecules, cells, and organs of the human body. Each cell in the body pulsates rhythmically, and so do the heart, diaphragm, intestines, lungs, brain, and many other physiological components. The vibrations from these rhythmic movements generate bioelectrical currents that stream continuously through the whole body. They also generate energy fields that surround the body, and our moods and emotions generate specific vibrations that alter these energy fields as well.

One of the deepest insights of Tantra is that the human body is a single energy phenomenon. At one end of the spectrum, at the physical level, this energy is expressed as the sex drive. At the other end of the spectrum, at the level of the nervous system and the brain, energy is experienced as ecstasy. The sexual drive is instinctual, raw, unrefined energy. This same sexual drive can be transformed and refined into ecstasy. It is one energy manifesting itself in different ways. Sexual energy is therefore to be accepted and respected as the raw material, the crude oil, from which the high-octane fuel of ecstasy is produced.

It is said that the earliest Eastern mystics obtained their first glimpses of spiritual enlightenment at the moment of orgasm. Indeed, many people know that orgasm can temporarily transport them to a state of rapture. For a few seconds the mind becomes devoid of thought, the egocentric view of life disappears, and we step outside of time into the timeless *now* of bliss. So sex, to the early mystics, was the very source of the religious experience, as it can still be today, given the right attitude and conditions. Some aspects of the Tantric attitude are these:

Learn self-love. Love begins at home, with loving yourself—not self-centered indulgence, but the ability to trust yourself and listen to your inner voice, the intuitive guidance of your own heart. Loving yourself means that you realize that you deserve the experience of ecstasy. Loving yourself also means that you are not willing to compromise or settle for less than you really want, especially in sex. Trying to love another when you do not love yourself does not work. You end up feeling possessive, jealous, and dependent. By contrast, when you really begin to love yourself, you become a magnet, attracting the love of others.

Yet you don't need others to feel whole. Love becomes a state of being. Out of your own sense of abundance, you want to share and celebrate—you are grateful to receive and to give. This is freedom, the basis of true partnership.

Drop guilt. Guilt goes very deep, below our conscious thoughts. For centuries organized religions have used guilt about sex as a subtle way of manipulating and exploiting people, and the recent liberalization of sexuality has not yet succeeded in erasing this cruel legacy.

Enjoy spontaneity. We have a tendency to trust experts, methods, and techniques while denying our own spontaneous feelings. Life is a great mystery. Give yourself the freedom to respond to the new and unfamiliar. Trust your own originality. Explore your own natural, original, unique ways of making love.

Cultivate pleasure. Our culture has trained us to believe that we don't really deserve pleasure, that cultivating leisure is selfish, that giving pleasure is more honorable than receiving it, that having fun is wasting time—a distraction from more important matters. When we do allow ourselves to receive pleasure, we give ourselves conditions such as, "I should give him something in return for all this pleasure I am experiencing"; "I am taking too much of her time"; or "I shouldn't show how much I enjoy this, or he'll think I'm a whore!"

Discover meditation. By sitting in a position of relaxation and stillness, focusing your attention inside and deepening the rhythm of your breathing, the busy chatter of your thought gradually settles. As your mind quiets down, you are able to direct more attention to your feelings and sensations, expanding your ability to experience pleasure. Heightened awareness of body, heart, and mind allows higher, more intense levels of pleasurable experience. By quieting the mind, meditation also allows freshness and innocence to return to the act of lovemaking.

Give up goal orientation. You cannot *will* ecstasy. You can simply prepare the right conditions for ecstasy to happen to you. This is why so many Western lovers are frustrated in their attempts to experience ecstatic sex. They strive to achieve it through willpower and control, whereas it is actually a question of creating very intense experiences that are immediately followed by relaxing and letting go.

Allow surrender. Surrender is an essential aspect of Tantra. There is, however, a lot of confusion about what surrender means. People are suspicious of this term, which they equate with loss of free will and personal power. In fact they are confusing surrender with submission, which is a passive attitude that implies giving up responsibility for one's behavior. True surrender is a conscious choice made from free will. It means opening your heart and trusting the person you are with.

READING 69

Student Voices

SOMETHING NEW: LET'S TALK ABOUT DIRTY

Summer Killian

Let's talk about dirty:

Making it with you is dirty and
I don't feel like being clean!

Everywhere is
dripping and
we couldn't stop it if we tried
sweat tears semen
droplets stream
from between my legs
you say
I can feel you
feel it trickle down my thighs
part this river of me
and I know you will
dream tonight of
sliding into all of it
at once

Inside this shell
there are ruby walls
stubborn and tough
made of pastry and clay
I bring you in
and the stops give
way

to
go
further down
forward in

This love smells sweet like syrup
the floor unyielding
We are roaring burning inside
and out
bleeding lust and fury

And

There's nothing clean—
there's nothing neat about it
we can't find our socks when we're done
your cheeks turn crimson
my pink cunt throbs
And
Don't use words like intense
or beautiful
or nice
Tonight
it's dirty and that's the way
I like it

I HAVE A DREAM

Dave Justice

I have a dream . . . that somewhere more
parents will talk to their children about sex,
sexuality,
and being positive and responsible sexual
people
No longer will children be punished or
silenced for expressing interest or curiosity in

"this thing called sex"
Parents and middle school teachers will no
longer explain sex
simply as unwanted pregnancy and deadly
disease
Adolescent girls will learn more about sex
than what their period is
Adolescent boys will learn more about sex
than what a "wet dream" is
Girls and boys will learn more about their
own and each other's bodies
Adolescent girls and boys will learn about the
joys of sex
and the pleasures sex can bring coupled with
the responsibilities of being a sexual person
Masturbation will not be looked down upon
as a selfish, dirty act
More women will be inclined to masturbate
and explore their bodies
Women as sexual beings will be accepted
Women and men will feel comfort in celebrating their sexuality

I have a dream . . . that somewhere parents
will no longer
subject their children to stereotypical gender
roles
Blue will just be the color blue and
pink will just be the color pink
Being called a girl will reflect one's strengths
rather than
condemn one's weakness
Baby girls will be tossed and played with as
much as baby boys
Baby boys will be held and hugged as much
as baby girls
Girls will no longer be labeled sluts, nor boys
labeled studs for being sexually active
Adolescent boys will no longer be rewarded
by their peers
for making it to "home base"
Girls will no longer be criticized or ridiculed
for showing their vulnerability
Girls will no longer be personally judged by
their physical appearance and beauty

Boys will no longer be personally judged by
their physical strength and athletic ability

Rather, girls will be encourage to act on their
assertiveness
and voice their opinions
Boys will be encouraged to express their emotion and feelings,
even if it means being vulnerable in front of
others
Both girls and boys will be acknowledged
and rewarded for
their strength of character
I have a dream . . . that somewhere the traditional values of
women as homemakers and men as bread-
winners
will be broken
Women who work and provide for their families will no longer
be seen as abandoning their children
Men who stay home to raise their children,
cook, and clean
will no longer be seen as incapable of supporting one's family
It will be a joint responsibility for both
women and men

I have a dream . . . that somewhere the concept of beauty will be redefined
Attractiveness will no longer be determined
by how slender one is
Celebrities and other public figures will
resemble body images of the average
person
Female models will no longer have to endure
liposuction,
enlarge their breasts or remove their ribs
Women will not be constantly critiqued or
criticized
by men and other women for their
appearance
Diets and weight loss programs will be
motivated
by health reasons rather than feelings of low
self-esteem,

unacceptance insecurity, and disgust in one's
body

I have a dream . . . that somewhere, sexual
diversity will be celebrated
All women and men whether homosexual,
heterosexual, or bisexual
will be equally acknowledged and honored
for their differences
Women and men will no longer be judged
solely by
their sexual orientation
Those in same-sex relationships will be accepted by
all religious institutions and politicians
Gays and lesbians will have the same opportunities for marriage as heterosexuals
Transgender and transsexual persons will be
admired for
their courage and determination in fulfilling
their sexual identity

I have a dream . . . that somewhere one's apti-
tude of maleness will be based on affection
rather than toughness
Men will comfortably greet and depart each
other with
warm hugs instead of high-fives
Men will not feel threatened to walk down
the streets together,
arm in arm or hand in hand
Males will no longer express destructive feelings of homophobia
through violent language or action
Men will be allowed to cry openly in public
Groups of men will choose to stop and listen
to a rally protesting
sexual violence, rather than laugh and move
on to happy hour
Men will bond with one another in ways
other than drinking beer
and watching the Super Bowl

I have a dream . . . that somewhere a safe
environment

will be provided for women to roam freely
and independently
Blue lights on university and college campuses will no longer be necessary
Women will be able to walk alone down the
streets
without fear of being sexually violated
Women will no longer need to travel in
groups
or take self-defense classes to feel safe
Women will no longer need to check in on
each other every time they meet a man, in
fear of his potential to manipulate or violate
Women will no longer fear going unconscious
because
some stranger, or friend, slipped a drug into
their drink
when she stepped out of the room

I have a dream . . . somewhere women and
men
will efficiently communicate about sexual
experiences
with one another
Men will learn to listen
Women and men will adapt to the needs and
desires of others
in their relationships without forfeiting what
is valuable to themselves
Women will no longer have to verbally say
"NO!"
during an unwanted sexual encounter
because
it will already be felt whether there is
pleasure or fear
Men will bear more responsibility for the
problems
of sexual violence in their community and
will take the initiative to do something
about it

I have a dream . . . Here is where it starts

INTERNET RESOURCES

PART ONE: SEXUALITY IN HISTORICAL, RELIGIOUS, AND CULTURAL PERSPECTIVE
Cornell Human Sexuality Collection: http://rmc.library.cornell.edu/HSC/faq/hscfaq.htm
Kinsey Institute: www.indiana.edu/~kinsey
Magnus Hirshfeld Archive for Sexology: www2.hu-berlin.de/sexology
SIECUS links page: www.siecus.org/links/links.html
SexQuest: www.SexQuest.com
Sexuality Research Council: www.ssrc.org/fellowships/sexuality
World Association for Sexology: www.worldsexology.org/English

PART TWO: BECOMING SEXUAL
College Sex Talk: www.CollegeSexTalk.com: Offers discussions by college students about the realities of college life, specifically in the areas of sex, love, dating and relationship issues.
Coming of Age: From Facts to Action for Adolescent Sexual and Reproductive Health: www.sexplained.com/
Planned Parenthood resources for teens: www.plannedparenthood.org/teens/

Sexuality Information and Education Council of the United States: www.siecus.org/

PART THREE: GENDERED SEXUALITY
European Profeminist Men's Network: www.europrofem.org/
Gender Education and Advocacy (GEA): www.gender.org/
International Foundation for Gender Education: www.ifge.org
National Association for Women (NOW): www.now.org
Renaissance Transgender Association: www.ren.org
University of Amsterdam sociology department's website, Feminism and Women's Issues: www.pscw.uva.nl/sociosite/Topics/Women.html

PART FOUR: SEX AND THE BODY
American Boyz:ftm www.amboyz.org
Female-to-Male International: www.ftmi.org
Intersex Society of North America: www.isna.org
Men's health and sexual concerns: www.health-library.com/men/index.html

Q Web Sweden, Women's health issues in cross-cultural perspective: www.qweb.kvinnoforum.se/main.html
Sexual Health Network: www.sexualhealth.com/
Women and health concerns: www.womenshealth.org

PART FIVE: SEXUALITIES

Campaign to End Homophobia: www.endhomophobia.org/
Gay and lesbian organizations and publications: faculty.washington.edu/alvin/gayorg.htm
Hetrick-Martin Institute, which seeks to create safe environments for lesbian, gay, bisexual, and transgender teens and their families: www.hmi.org/
Loving More: New Models for Relationships: www.lovemore.com/
OutProud, The National Coalition for Gay, Lesbian, Bisexual, and Transgender Youth: www.outproud.org/

PART SIX: COMMODIFIED SEX

Child Sexual Exploitation (National Center for Missing and Exploited Children): www.missingkids.com/html/ncmec_default_ec_cse.htm
Prostitutes' Education Network: www.bayswan.org/penet.html

PART SEVEN: SEXUAL ABUSE AND RAPE

National Clearinghouse on Family Violence, Canada, links to resources on child sexual abuse: www.hc-sc.gc.ca/hppb/familyviolence/
Rape 101: resources and education for stopping rape: www.rape101.com/
Sexual Abuse of Children, Child Pornography, and Paedophilia on the Internet: www.unesco.org/webworld/child_screen/conf_index_2.html

PART EIGHT: SEX, POLITICS, AND POLICIES

Alan Guttmacher Institute: www.guttmacher.org
American Civil Liberties Union: www.aclu.org
Gay and Lesbian Alliance Against Defamation (GLAAD): www.glaad.org/glaad
Planned Parenthood Federation of America: www.ppfa.org

PART NINE: POSSIBLE SEXUALITIES

Coalition for Positive Sexuality: www.positive.org/

BIO-SKETCHES OF AUTHORS: Sexual Lives: A Reader

Sharon A. Abbot is a professor of sociology at Fairfield University in Fairfield, Connecticut. She shares equally with Liahna E. Gordon in the authorship of their paper, "The Social Constructionist's 'Essential' Guide to Sex."

Elizabeth Amanacer is a retired teacher and a budding photographer. She lives in Indiana, Pennsylvania and travels extensively throughout the United States and abroad.

Margo Anand has studied with many Tantric masters and conducts sexual ecstasy workshops in Europe and the United States. She is the author of *The Art of Sexual Ecstasy*.

Sally Armstrong is a journalist and human rights activist. Her book on the lives of women in Afghanistan, entitled *Veiled Threat* is to be published by Penguin Books.

Peter Baker, coauthor of *The Manual: The Complete Man's Guide to Life*, along with Mick Cooper, has been involved in men's studies and activities since the early seventies. Baker and Cooper are both past editors for *Achilles Heel*, the radical men's magazine in England.

Judith Barker is a professor in the Sociology Department at Ithaca College in Ithaca, New York, where she teaches a course entitled "Sexual Oppression."

Sandra Lipsitz Bem is professor of psychology and women's studies at Cornell University in Ithaca, New York, and has written extensively on gender and women's studies, including *The Lenses of Gender: Transforming the Debate on Sexual Inequality* (1994).

Timothy Beneke is a freelance writer and author of *Men on Rape* (1983) and *Proving Manhood: Reflections on Men and Sexism* (1997). He lives in Oakland, California.

Laurel Black, an associate professor of English at Indiana University of Pennsylvania, is interested in sociolinguistics, gender, class, and the everyday.

Ivy Bressen settled at the Acorn community in the fall of 1994 after a year on the road visiting communities. When she's not networking as "Visitor Czar," she can be found playing piano or walking with her canine primary, Kashi.

Harry Brod is professor of philosophy and humanities, and head of the honors program at the University of Northern Iowa. He is also an author and lecturer on fatherhood and male identity issues.

"Josh" was a senior student majoring in sociology when he wrote the reflection assignment included herein.

Susan Brownmiller has been a television news-writer, an antiwar activist, and a researcher/writer at *Newsweek*. She has written on the history of the women's movement and is the author of *Against Our Will* and *Femininity*.

Jamie Buki was an undergraduate student at Indiana University of Pennsylvania majoring in sociology when she wrote the essay about her sister. She is currently a graduate student in Sussex, England.

Mick Cooper, coauthor of *The Manual: The Complete Man's Guide to Life*, along with Peter Baker, has been involved in men's studies and activities since the early seventies. Cooper and Baker were both past editors for *Achilles Heel*, the radical men's magazine in England.

Betsy Crane is associate professor of sociology at Indiana University of Pennsylvania and co-editor of this book.

Jesse Crane-Seeber is a recent graduate of Ithaca College where he created his own course of study in "Resisting Hegemony." He currently lives in Germany and is looking forward to continuing his education in a graduate program in international relations.

Sophia Demasi is a professor in the Department of Social Sciences at Montgomery County College in Blue Bell, Pennsylvania.

Diane di Mauro is Director of the Sexuality Research Fellowship Program at the Social Science Research Council.

Oliva M. Espin is a professor in the Department of Women's Studies at San Diego University and parttime core faculty at the California School of Professional Psychology in San Diego, specializing in the psychology of Latinas, immigrant and refugee women, and women's sexuality across cultures.

Laurie Essig is a professor of sociology at Yale University and the author of *Queer in Russia* (Duke University Press, 1999).

Anne Fausto-Sterling is professor of biology and women's studies at Brown University. Portions of this article were adapted from her recent book *Sexing the Body* (Basic Books, 2000).

Leslie Feinberg is a social activist and writer whose most recent book is *Transgender Warriors: Making History from Joan of Arc to Dennis Rodman.*

Lawrence Foster is a professor of American history at Georgia Tech in Atlanta He drew from his books *Religion and Sexuality* and *Women, Family, and Utopia* for this article.

Loren Frankel is a PhD candidate in the Human Development Department at Cornell University. His research focuses on the development of masculine identity in adolescence and early adulthood.

Carla Golden is professor of psychology at Ithaca College. She has written widely on women's sexuality, gender development, and psychoanalytic theory.

Liahna E. Gordon is a professor of sociology at California State University at Chico. She shares equally with Sharon A. Abbot in the authorship of their paper, "The Social Constructionist's 'Essential' Guide to Sex."

Avery Grauer worked as a mental health worker at several inpatient pediatric psychiatry units in the Boston area while attending medical school.

Josiah Gromley is an eclectic Wiccan Mystic who works to increase the visibility and understanding of spiritual and sexual minorities.

Helen Gurley Brown is the former editor of *Cosmopolitan*. Her latest book is titled *I'm Wild Again.*

Rachel-Storm Heasley sprung into life in Anchorage, Alaska. She has been working in the human services field since her graduation from Ithaca College in 1998. She is a creative soul, a writer, and a sociologist.

Kristine Herman graduated from Antioch College in 1994 and completed her MSW at Tulane University and her law degree at Northeastern University. She works on advocacy and policy issues related to domestic violence and sexual assault.

Benjamin B. Herold was an undergraduate student when he wrote his reflection on the effects of homophobia in his life.

Luoluo Hong is Assistant Vice President of Student Affairs and Dean of Students at Shepherd College, in Shepherd, West Virginia. She has developed a national reputation for her innovative work with the campus peer leadership organization and Men against Violence.

bell hooks, author of many books, including *Ain't I A Woman: Black Women and Feminism*, is devoted to critical consciousness and awareness of oneself and society. At present Dr. hooks teaches at the City College of New York.

Allan Hunter is a social theory hobbyist and a male person whose politics are those delineated by radical feminist theory (which may or may not make him a "radical feminist," that being a subject of ongoing debate). A doctoral candidate at the time this article was written, Allan Hunter went on to flunk out of graduate school and now designs Filemaker Pro databases for a living.

Loraine Hutchins is coeditor of *Bi Any Other Name: Bisexual People Speak Out*. She helped put the "B" in LGBT. She addresses sexual diversity and spirituality issues and offers lectures and workshops on bisexual politics and identity and sexual healing.

Susannah Indigo is editor in chief of *Clean Sheets Magazine* and editor of *Slow Trains* literary journal. She is a writer, editor, and consultant whose work, widely published in magazines, books, and CDs, has won several awards.

Chrys Ingraham is professor of sociology at Russell Sage College, where she is co-director of women's studies and cofounder of Allies Center for the Study of Difference and Conflict. Her book, *White Weddings*, provides an in-depth look at ritualized heterosexuality.

David Justice was an undergraduate student at Ithaca College when he wrote his reflection for a class on sexuality and gender.

Lani Kaahumanu is the founder of the Bay Area Safer Sex Sluts, a "live-action" safer-sex education troupe. As a writer and organizer, Kaahumanu focuses on bisexual activism. She is coeditor of *Bi Any Other Name: Bisexual People Speak Out*.

Maureen Kelly is the Director of Education and Training with Planned Parenthood of Tompkins County in Ithaca, New York. She is currently serving on the board of directors for the Sexuality Education and Information Council of the United States.

Sharon Kelly is the author of "I Am a Queer Heterosexual," which first appeared in the publication *Body Politic*, published in London, England.

Summer Killian was an undergraduate student at Ithaca College when she wrote the poem included in this book.

Michael Kimmel is professor of sociology at SUNY at Stony Brook. He is author of several books on men and masculinity, including *Manhood in America: A Cultural History* (1997). He is a spokesperson for the National Organization for Men against Sexism (NOMAS).

Eric Leadbetter is a community health specialist and works with HIV/AIDS Surveillance and Reporting. Eric dedicates his article to Eppy for this journey, and to his family for their incredible support.

Gloria Lockett, a prostitute for 18 years, is the former co-director of the prostitutes' rights organization COYOTE (Call Off Your Old Tired Ethics) and Executive Director of the California Prostitute Education Project (CAL-PEP), an Oakland-based, nonprofit AIDS and HIV prevention organization that works with street prostitutes. She has been published in several anthologies.

Michael McGee is Vice President of Education for the Planned Parenthood Federation of America located in New York, New York.

Rachel Maines is the author of *The Technology of Orgasm: "Hysteria," the Vibrator, and Women's Sexual Satisfaction* (Johns Hopkins, 1998) and articles on material culture and technological history.

Marwaan Macan-Markar is a correspondent for Inter Press Service, a third world news agency. He is currently based in Bangkok and is a freelance photographer.

L. Maurer is the Coordinator of the Center for LGBT Education, Outreach, and Services at Ithaca College in Ithaca, New York. Maurer set out on a gender journey years ago, with little more than a compass and a box of crayons. Today, as a sexuality educator, consultant, activist, and author, that journey is still unfolding.

Michael Messner is associate professor of sociology and gender studies at the University of Southern California. He has authored several books with a focus on gender and sports, and children, gender and media.

Melinda S. Miceli is assistant professor of sociology at the University of Wisconsin–Eau Claire. Her interests are in the political framing processes used by social movement organizations that support, and those that oppose, the rights of gay, lesbian, and bisexual students.

Thomas Moore is the author of the best-selling *Care of the Soul* and, more recently, *The Re-Enchantment of Everyday Life* and *The Soul of Sex*.

Igna Muscio is a writer and lecturer on women's lives and sexuality. Her articles have appeared in *Bust* and *Curve* and she has given talks at a range of colleges in the United States.

Kathy Myers is the author of "Towards a Feminist Erotica," which also appeared in *Gender, Race, and*

Class in Media, edited by Gail Dines and Jean Humez for Sage Publications.

Jerome Ng is a graduate student in organizational communications, learning, and design at Ithaca College, New York. He wrote his essay as an undergraduate student. He aspires to earn a PhD.

Donna Marie Niles was previously a sex worker.

Julia O'Connell Davidson is professor of sociology at the University of Nottingham in the United Kingdom with a focus on gender, race, class and global inequalities, and contract, employment relations, selfhood, and human rights. She conducted studies of entrepreneurial prostitution, sex tourism, and children's involvement in the global sex trade.

"Patricia" was an undergraduate student when she wrote her essay.

Gail Pheterson is an associate professor of psychology at the University of Picardie Jules Verne, Amiens, France. She is a social psychologist and co-director of the International Committee for Prostitutes' Rights and consults European governments on prostitution.

Kathleen E. Powderly is acting director in the Division of Humanities in Medicine and is clinical assistant professor of nursing and obstetrics & gynecology at the SUNY Downstate Medical Center in Brooklyn, New York.

H. J. Randolph, a Seattle-area resident, is an editor, freelance writer, and teacher. His older son is a sophomore in college and his younger son is an eighth-grader. He married for the second time in 1995.

Mary Reilly completed her undergraduate and master's degrees in sociology at Indiana University of Pennsylvania. Her interests include sociolinguistic analysis of addiction and recovery in women's narratives.

Harriet Reiss is coauthor, with Ira Reiss, of *Solving America's Sexual Crises* (Prometheus Books, 1997).

Ira L. Reiss is professor emeritus of sociology at the University of Minnesota and former president of the International Academy of Sex Research, the Society for the Scientific Study of Sexuality, and the National Council on Family Relations.

Diane Richardson is professor and head of the Department of Sociology and Social Policy and Director of the Centre for Gender and Women's Studies at the University of Newcastle in the United Kingdom. Her focus is in the sociology of sexuality, heterosexual transmission of HIV, and queer theories.

Regina Rivers is a sociology graduate from Indiana University of Pennsylvania. Her main focus is on childhood abuse. A freelance writer, she is the editorial assistant for *Sexual Lives: A Reader* and is co-editing a book of readings on recovery from childhood sexual abuse. She dedicates her article to her husband and best friend, Philip Rivers.

Martin Rochlin lives in West Hollywood, California.

Fred Rothbaum is a professor in the Eliot-Pearson Department of Child Development at Tufts University in Medford, Massachusetts. He has written numerous articles on parent-child relationships and children's emotional problems.

David J. Rubin is a freelance writer with a special interest in child development.

Harilyn Rousso is Executive Director of Disabilities Unlimited Consulting Services in New York City.

Virginia Rutter teaches in the Department of Sociology at the University of Washington in Seattle. Her interests are in the areas of family, relationships, gender, and sexuality.

Kent L. Sandstrom is an associate professor of sociology at the University of Northern Iowa, Cedar Falls, Iowa.

David Satcher was United States Surgeon General from 1998–2001.

Pepper Schwartz is professor of sociology at the University of Washington in Seattle. Her areas of study include marriage, family, and sexuality.

Sonia Shah is a freelance writer and former editor at South End Press. Her most recent edited book in entitled *Dragon Ladies* from South End Press.

Linda Smogor is a photographer, dancer, mother, and outdoor enthusiast currently living in Eugene, Oregon. Her photographs have been exhibited throughout Alaska and across the lower 48 states. Publication credits include *Life, American Photo,* the *New York Times, Mothering, Alaska Magazine, Illinois Times, Shots,* and the *Sun.*

Ron Stodghill II is the Detroit bureau chief for *Time* magazine. This article first appeared in the June 1998 issue of *Time* magazine.

Leonore Tiefer is a psychologist at Albert Einstein College of Medicine in New York City and a sex therapist in private practice. She is the author of

Sex Is Not a Natural Act and Other Essays (1995) and coeditor, with Ellyn Kaschak, of *A New View of Women's Sexual Problems* (2002).

Mariana Valverde is a professor of criminology at the University of Toronto and writes extensively in the areas of theory, gender, and sexuality.

Del LaGrace Volcano is a photographer whose work has been exhibited and published widely across the United Kingdom and the United States.

Jeffrey Weeks is a professor and Dean of Faculty of Humanities and Social Science at South Bank University in London. He has authored *Coming Out* (1977) and *Same Sex Intimacies* (2001).

Kai Wright is a freelance writer based in Washington, D.C. His work focuses largely on health and sexuality in the African American community.

Johannes Renatus Zinzendorf co-reestablished Christiansbrunn Brotherhood in 1987, after a lapse of 191 years. Since then he has helped to construct many buildings in preparation for other brothers to join them.